Publishing, Books & Reading in Sub-Saharan Africa

A Critical Bibliography

Hans M. Zell

*With an introductory essay
by Henry Chakava*

Access to the electronic edition:
Online access is bundled with print. Purchasers of the print edition are entitled to access the electronic version at no extra charge. This requires registration at www.hanszell.co.uk/pbrssa/index.shtml. If access via IP address recognition is required, please indicate the applicable IP address ranges in the field provided on the online registration form (see also p. xxvi).

Hans Zell Publishing
Lochcarron ◆ Ross-shire ◆ Scotland

First edition 1984, published as *Publishing and Book Development in Africa: A Bibliography/ L'édition et le développement du livre en Afrique: une bibliographie* (Paris: UNESCO, "Studies on Books and Reading", no. 15)

Second edition 1996, published as *Publishing and Book Development in Sub-Saharan Africa: An Annotated Bibliography*

Third edition 2008, published as *Publishing, Books & Reading in Sub-Saharan Africa: A Critical Bibliography*

British Library Cataloguing in Publication Data

Zell, Hans M.
 Publishing, books and reading in Sub-Saharan Africa : a critical bibliography. – New ed.
 1. Publishers and publishing – Africa, Sub-Saharan – Bibliography
 2. Book industries and trade – Africa, Sub-Saharan – Bibliography
 I. Title II. Zell, Hans M. Publishing and book development in Sub-Saharan Africa
 016'.0705'0967

 ISBN-13 : 9780954102951

10067936 66

ISBN-13: 978-0-9541029-5-1
Published by Hans Zell Publishing (T/A Hans Zell Publishing Consultants)
Glais Bheinn ✦ Lochcarron ✦ Ross-shire IV54 8YB ✦ Scotland ✦ UK
Telephone: +44-(0)1520-722951 Fax: +44-(0)1520-722953
Email: hanszell@hanszell.co.uk or hzell@btopenworld.com
Web: www.hanszell.co.uk

Online access is bundled with print. Purchase of this print edition of *Publishing, Books & Reading in Sub-Saharan Africa: A Critical Bibliography* entitles purchasers to free access to the electronic version. To access the online version please see the instructions on page xxvi. Registration, access and delivery is at www.hanszell.co.uk/pbrssa/index.shtml.

Cover design by Michael Stuart Green, Lochcarron, Scotland.

Printed on acid-free paper.

Printed and bound in the United Kingdom by Antony Rowe Ltd., Chippenham, Wiltshire.

Contents

Preface to the new edition   xi

Introduction   xvii
    Access to the electronic edition   xxvi
    Periodicals cited in the bibliography   xxix

Introductory essay   xxxvii
    African Publishing: From Ile-Ife, Nigeria, to the Present
    by Henry Chakava

Organizations and associations   1
    International and Africa-based organizations   1
    Foundations, donors, networks, and other organizations
       supporting the book and information sector in Africa   9

1   Serials and reference   47
Serials   47
    African book trade and book professional journals   47
    Other journals, newsletters, and book review media covering   53
       African book publishing output
Bibliographies and continuing sources, and special collections   63
Collective online catalogue databases   68
Directories and book trade reference tools (Continent-wide)   70
    Books in print   70
    Directories of publishers and the book trade   71

2   General, comparative, and regional studies   77
Comparative studies (General/comparative studies on publishing
    in developing countries)   77
Africa: General studies   90
Regional studies: Africa, East   119
Regional studies: Africa, Southern   121
Regional studies: Africa, West   123
Regional studies: Africa, Francophone   124

3   Country studies   138

Angola   139
    Associations and book-related organizations   139
    Books, articles, reports, and interviews   140
Benin   141
    Associations and book-related organizations   141
    National bibliography, books in print, and book trade directories   141
    Books, articles, reports, and interviews   141
Botswana   142
    Associations and book-related organizations   142
    National bibliography, books in print, and book trade directories   143
    Books, articles, reports, and interviews   143
Burkina Faso   145
    Associations and book-related organizations   145
    National bibliography, books in print, and book trade directories   146
    Books, articles, reports, and interviews   146
Burundi   147
    Books, articles, reports, and interviews   147
Cameroon   147
    Associations and book-related organizations   147
    National bibliography, books in print, and book trade directories   147
    Books, articles, reports, and interviews   148
Cape Verde   152
    Associations and book-related organizations   152
    Books, articles, reports, and interviews   152
Central African Republic   152
    Associations and book-related organizations   152
    Books, articles, reports, and interviews   152
Congo (Brazzaville)   153
    Associations and book-related organizations   153
    Books, articles, reports, and interviews   153
Congo Democratic Republic   153
    Associations and book-related organizations   153
    National bibliography, books in print, and book trade directories   154
    Books, articles, reports, and interviews   154
Côte d'Ivoire   156
    Associations and book-related organizations   156
    National bibliography, books in print, and book trade directories   157
    Books, articles, reports, and interviews   157
Eritrea   159
    Associations and book-related organizations   159
    Books, articles, reports, and interviews   159

Ethiopia 160
    Associations and book-related organizations 160
    National bibliography, books in print, and book trade directories 161
    Books, articles, reports, and interviews 161
Gabon 164
    Associations and book-related organizations 164
    National bibliography, books in print, and book trade directories 164
    Books, articles, reports, and interviews 165
The Gambia 165
    Associations and book-related organizations 165
    National bibliography, books in print, and book trade directories 166
    Books, articles, reports, and interviews 166
Ghana 167
    Associations and book-related organizations 167
    National bibliography, books in print, and book trade directories 169
    Books, articles, reports, and interviews 169
Guinea 174
    Associations and book-related organizations 174
    National bibliography, books in print, and book trade directories 174
    Books, articles, reports, and interviews 175
Guinea-Bissau 176
    Books, articles, reports, and interviews 176
Kenya 176
    Associations and book-related organizations 176
    National bibliography, books in print, and book trade directories 179
    Books, articles, reports, and interviews 180
Lesotho 191
    Associations and book-related organizations 191
    National bibliography, books in print, and book trade directories 191
    Books, articles, reports, and interviews 192
Liberia 193
    Books, articles, reports, and interviews 193
Madagascar 194
    Associations and book-related organizations 194
    National bibliography, books in print, and book trade directories 195
    Books, articles, reports, and interviews 195
Malawi 196
    Associations and book-related organizations 196
    National bibliography, books in print, and book trade directories 197
    Books, articles, reports, and interviews 198
Mali 200
    Associations and book-related organizations 200
    National bibliography, books in print, and book trade directories 201
    Books, articles, reports, and interviews 201

Mauritania   202
   National bibliography, books in print, and book trade directories   202
Mauritius   202
   Associations and book-related organizations   202
   National bibliography, books in print, and book trade directories   203
   Books, articles, reports, and interviews   204
Mozambique   205
   Associations and book-related organizations   205
   National bibliography, books in print, and book trade directories   205
   Books, articles, reports, and interviews   206
Namibia   208
   Associations and book-related organizations   208
   National bibliography, books in print, and book trade directories   209
   Books, articles, reports, and interviews   210
Niger   212
   Associations and book-related organizations   212
Nigeria   212
   Associations and book-related organizations   212
   National bibliography, books in print, and book trade directories   216
   Books, articles, reports, and interviews   219
Réunion   245
   National bibliography, books in print, and book trade directories   245
   Books, articles, reports, and interviews   245
Rwanda   245
   Associations and book-related organizations   245
   Books, articles, reports, and interviews   246
São Tomé and Principe   246
   Books, articles, reports, and interviews   246
Senegal   246
   Associations and book-related organizations   246
   National bibliography, books in print, and book trade directories   248
   Books, articles, reports, and interviews   248
Seychelles   254
   National bibliography, books in print, and book trade directories   254
   Books, articles, reports, and interviews   254
Sierra Leone   255
   Associations and book-related organizations   255
   National bibliography, books in print, and book trade directories   256
   Books, articles, reports, and interviews   256
South Africa   259
   Associations and book-related organizations   259
   National bibliography, books in print, and book trade directories   267
   Books, articles, reports, and interviews   271

Sudan 305
    Associations and book-related organizations 305
    National bibliography, books in print, and book trade directories 305
    Books, articles, reports, and interviews 305
Swaziland 306
    Associations and book-related organizations 306
    National bibliography, books in print, and book trade directories 306
    Books, articles, reports, and interviews 307
Tanzania 308
    Associations and book-related organizations 308
    National bibliography, books in print, and book trade directories 310
    Books, articles, reports, and interviews 310
Togo 314
    Associations and book-related organizations 314
    National bibliography, books in print, and book trade directories 315
    Books, articles, reports, and interviews 315
Uganda 316
    Associations and book-related organizations 316
    National bibliography, books in print, and book trade directories 318
    Books, articles, reports, and interviews 318
Zambia 322
    Associations and book-related organizations 322
    National bibliography, books in print, and book trade directories 322
    Books, articles, reports, and interviews 323
Zimbabwe 328
    Associations and book-related organizations 328
    National bibliography, books in print, and book trade directories 331
    Books, articles, reports, and interviews 332

4   Studies by topic 337
The acquisition of African-published material 337
African Books Collective Ltd. (ABC) 346
African books in the international market place 348
African Publishers Network (APNET) 356
Authors and publishers/Publishing of African writers and African
    literature (in Africa and elsewhere) 360
Book and journals assistance and donation programmes 376
Book fairs 389
Book marketing and promotion 396
Bookselling and book distribution 404
Book trade and book development organizations 411
Children's book publishing 415
Christian publishing and mission presses 450

Community and rural publishing   454
Copyright and legal deposit/Authors' rights   456
Digital media and electronic publishing/New printing technology   479
Educational and school book publishing   492
Intra-African book trade   500
Journals and magazine publishing   504
Libraries and publishing   526
Mass market and popular literature publishing   528
Multinational publishers in Africa   532
National book policies   536
The Noma Award for Publishing in Africa   539
Open access publishing   545
Publishing in African languages   552
Reading culture and reading promotion   571
Rights sales, licensing and publishing partnerships   592
Scholarly publishing (General)   599
Scientific, technical and medical publishing   621
Women in African publishing/Publishing by and for women   630

5   Book industry training/Self-publishing   646
Articles and reports   646
Training manuals and resources   653
Handbooks for authors and self-publishing   664

Author index (and selected titles)   671

Subject and geographical index   689

Index of organizations and associations   707

Preface to the new edition

The content and focus of this reference resource, the previous edition of which was published in 1996 under the title *Publishing and Book Development in Sub-Saharan Africa: An Annotated Bibliography*, has been very substantially recast in several ways. The new edition has a new title and sub-title and, as the sub-title suggests, annotations and abstracts, particularly of recent literature, are now more evaluative on the whole. Much greater emphasis is placed on the relative significance of the material included, thus offering a more critical dimension in reviewing the available literature on the topic.

The new edition contains 2,517 for the most part extensively annotated entries, of which 1,612 are entirely new entries.

The change in title reflects the fact that the bibliography includes a very large number of citations on complementary aspects of publishing and the "book chain" in Africa. While not every related aspect has been covered in great depth – for example that of reading and the promotion of a reading culture – an attempt has been made to cite the key literature on each topic. Some other areas relating to books and information provision in Africa, for example the vital role of library services, continue to be excluded as the literature on these topics is already covered in other bibliographic sources.

In order to free up space this new edition covers primarily material published over the last two and a half decades, although some literature published earlier has been retained because of its historical importance. The previous edition included over 2,200 entries, but quite a large proportion of the literature cited was perhaps of a more peripheral nature, and/or is now very dated, and has been dropped for this edition. In many sections this amounted to more than half of the entries in the previous edition. However, a number of these earlier citations may still be of value to researchers, and they can continue be consulted in libraries holding a copy of the 1996 edition.

The previous edition also listed a sizeable number of unpublished papers from conferences and workshops. These were originally meant to become available through the ➜ **African Publishers' Network/APNET (5)** as part of a document delivery service, but unfortunately this never materialized, and they have now been omitted from this edition.

In this new edition annotations offer more qualitative judgements and attention is drawn to particularly important contributions to the literature for a range of entries which, arguably, might be considered to be among the most significant – and in some cases seminal – contributions to the literature on publishing and book development in Africa. They therefore merit the special attention of students and scholars undertaking research on publishing and the book sector in Africa.

Annotations are often quite extensive (some up to 300 words or more), particularly those for recent literature. Annotations of such length might be considered somewhat excessive but, together, they are intended to provide a critical narrative, or a kind of synthesis, of past and current thinking on the growth and development of indigenous publishing, and the promotion of books and reading on the continent. Quoted passages from the articles are frequently included to provide extra insights.

Several of the annotations of book titles and edited collections are based on critical reviews that have appeared in the "Professional reading" columns of the ➜ **African Book Publishing Record (168)** over the last two decades.

Contents and arrangement of the bibliography has also been reorganized to some extent; a few topic-specific sections have been dropped (e.g. those on manufacturing, and on the pulp and paper industries) or merged with others, while a number of entirely new topic headings have been added, for example African books in the international market place, Open access publishing, and Women in African publishing/Publishing by and for women. New and expanded sections on digital media and electronic publishing reflect the recent dramatic changes in the scholarly communications environment, the growth of the Internet in Africa, and new printing technologies that are now available to the African book professions.

Listings for each country in Section 3 are now part directory and part bibliography. The directories of African book professional and allied associations that precede each country section have been fully updated, as have been the listings of organizations and agencies elsewhere supporting publishing and the book and information sector in Africa. They include full address details, telephone and fax numbers, contact information, email addresses, and Web sites for most of them. All directory-type entries will be kept current, as far as is possible, by regular updates in the online edition.

Each country section in this new edition now also includes listings of national bibliographies and full details are provided for all those sub-Saharan African countries that produce national bibliographies at this time. However, in many countries where national bibliographies exist they are currently dormant or seriously in arrear in their publication schedule, some by several years, or even decades. On the other hand, one welcome development is the fact that a small number of African national bibliographies are now available online.

Online resources
When the previous edition was published in 1996, barely a handful of articles were available in electronic formats, but the picture has now changed dramatically. Almost 500 articles, reports, presentations, surveys, e-theses, and other documents cited in this new edition are now available online (the majority of them freely accessible), which has merited publication of this new edition both in print format and as a searchable electronic version. Access to the online version is bundled with purchase of the print edition. Providing the online resource as an integral part of the print version of the bibliography allows multiple users to access its contents concurrently, and from a place of their own choosing.

Several articles originally published in print format only have, through the initiative of the authors of these articles, now become available online, while ➔ **UNESCO (118)** has recently digitized some of their early mission reports and other documents on publishing and book development in Africa, now offering them freely available in electronic formats.

Two particularly valuable online archives containing a wide range of articles, reports, views and perspectives on publishing and the book in Africa are the ➔ **Bellagio Publishing Network Newsletter (155)**, and the papers and reports of seminar presentations hosted by the ➔ **Southern African Book Development Education Trust/SABDET (113)**, and offered freely accessible on its Web site.

Another welcome new development is that all back issues of the journal **Logos. Forum for the World Book Community (160)** (formerly *Logos. The Journal of the World Book Community*) are now accessible online (access to the archives requires a subscription, or articles can be purchased for a modest document delivery fee). The *Logos* archive currently consists of almost 700 articles, including over thirty on publishing and the book trade in Africa, and it is an enormously rich resource.

A number of documents, reports, and major surveys now available online consist of pdf files of some size, up to 7-8MB, and which could be time-consuming to download for those without access to broadband connections, especially those in Africa. Accordingly, file sizes are indicated for online documents that are larger than 2.5MB.

References to book reviews
As another new feature in this edition, references to select reviews of some of the book titles and edited collections are now included, some of them accessible online.

Expanded index
In addition to an author index, this new edition contains an improved and much expanded subject and geographical index, as well as an index of organizations and associations.

Access to the literature
This new edition cites literature from a total of 256 serial publications, as well as many books and monographs, edited collections, book sector studies and reports, presentations, theses, and training guides and manuals. Much of the material should be accessible in major academic libraries, especially those with substantial Africana collections.

However, access to articles that have appeared in a number of African book trade journals may be more problematic, as few of them are held in academic libraries in the countries of the North. Complete or near-complete runs of many African books trade serials are held by the ➔ **African Publishers Network/APNET (5)**, as part of an archival collection of journals, articles, books, reports and other material, covering 35 years of African publishing and book development (1960-1995), donated by this writer to APNET's Research & Documentation Centre in 1996. It should be noted however that, as at May 2008, APNET's Research & Documentation Centre is not currently operational, and the collection is still held in storage following APNET's relocation to Accra. The collection's future status is uncertain at this time, but it may be moved to a new home at an African university institution, where it will be fully catalogued and will then become accessible again. It is also possible that some of the material held may then become available in digitized format.

Introductory essay
Thirty-five years ago, in December 1973, the University of Ife in Nigeria (now Obafemi Awolowo University) hosted a major conference on publishing and book development in Africa, and subsequently published the proceedings of that conference, in which

> conference participants reconfirmed their belief that books are an indispensable cornerstone in education and that a nation's book industry must be considered an essential industry in terms of national development planning.

In his wide-ranging introductory essay, "African Publishing: From Ile-Ife to the Present", Henry Chakava, Chairman of East African Educational

Publishers in Nairobi, provides a succinct state of the art analysis of the African book industry today, exploring most of the key issues from a historical perspective. He reviews progress since the historic Ife conference, and offers a candid assessment of the present state of publishing, books, and writing and reading in the countries of Africa south of the Sahara, highlighting the most significant problems and constraints that remain, and identifying the challenges that lie ahead.

It is entirely fitting that Henry Chakava should contribute this introductory retrospective, as he is widely recognized as one of the continent's most innovative and enterprising publisher, and has amassed a wealth of experience during a lifetime devoted to strengthening the indigenous book industries in Africa. He is one of the most prolific authors of articles and studies on many aspects of the state of the book in Africa, and has been the recipient of several awards and honours. In 2000 he received the inaugural Zimbabwe International Book Fair Award for his "life-long contribution to the African book industry". In 2005 Oxford Brookes University conferred him with an honorary doctorate of literature, and in 2007 the → **Prince Claus Fund for Culture and Development (104)** in the Netherlands awarded him the Prince Claus Award to honour his lifetime's work in developing African publishing, for nurturing and promoting writers in a difficult context, and "for his major contribution to intellectual and cultural development in East Africa."

Future editions of the bibliography
This ongoing bibliographic project to record and analyze the literature on publishing and book development in sub-Saharan Africa started with the publication of the earliest version of the bibliography, published as part of UNESCO's "Studies on Books and Reading Series" in 1984. It was followed by the predecessor of the current volume, published in 1996.

Following publication of this latest and now substantially recast version, I should perhaps signal that it is not my intention to produce further editions of the bibliography on my own. However, it is vital that research and documentation on the African book industries, and on all aspects of the "book chain" in Africa, will continue. It is my hope that an African book development organization, or a library at an academic institution in Africa, will be able to take over the work, and will systematically seek to collect and analyze new material, eventually leading to a new, revised and fully updated edition of the bibliography sometime in the years ahead.

Acknowledgements
There are a number of book professionals and academics that have written prolifically on many aspects of publishing and book development in Africa,

and all these were approached individually requesting up-to-date lists of their publications, published in print or online formats. Not all of them responded, but I am grateful to those who did:
Sulaiman Adebowale, Bodunde Bankole, Paul Brickhill, Henry Chakava, Chris Chirwa, Richard Crabbe, Woeli Dekutsey, Eve Gray, Jay Heale, Colleen Higgs, Jacob Jaygbay, Jane Katjavivi, Ruth Makotsi, Viviana Quinones, Ian Montagnes, Francis Nymanjoh, Akoss Ofori-Mensah, Ayo Ojeniyi, Peter Reiner, Diana Rosenberg, Monica Seeber, Irene Staunton, Christine Stilwell, and Damtew Teferra.

I am also indebted to African book trade associations who updated and verified their entries in the directory sections of this bibliography and, in particular, to the Nigerian Book Fair Trust, the Nigerian Publishers Association, the Publishers Association of South Africa, and the South African Booksellers Association, who provided copies of back issues of their trade journals or other publications.

For assistance in the development of the electronic version of the bibliography I wish to acknowledge the help and expertise provided by Sue Martin of Smart Internet Services, Helston, Cornwall.

Hans M. Zell
Lochcarron, Wester Ross, Scotland
May 2008

Introduction

This is a new, substantially recast and fully updated edition of a reference resource first published in 1996 under the title *Publishing and Book Development in Sub-Saharan Africa: An Annotated Bibliography* (co-edited with Cécile Lomer), and which in turn was based on the earlier *Publishing and Book Development in Africa: A Bibliography/L'édition et le développement du livre en Afrique: une bibliographie*, published in UNESCO'S "Studies on Books and Reading Series" in 1984. It charts the growth of publishing and book development in the countries of Africa south of the Sahara, covering all segments of publishing and the book trade, as well as including a large number of entries on many other topics as they relate to books and reading in Africa.

This edition contains over 2,500 entries, of which more than 60% are new entries, the majority of them published during the period from 1996 through to the end of 2007. Most of the material listed is in English, but there are also a considerable number of citations in French and on publishing and the book sector in the francophone nations of Africa.

Material is arranged under five main sections, and is extensively cross-referenced throughout. It is indexed by author and now includes an improved and expanded subject index, and an index of organizations and associations, to further enhance the bibliography's utility.

As well as including a very large number of articles, books, and other material published since publication of the previous edition, this new edition now also contains a substantial number of entries covering articles, reports and other documents that are available online, most of them freely accessible.

Sources used
In addition to listing over 1,600 entirely new citations, the new edition of the bibliography brings together and cumulates material previously included in these sources, although many items listed in the 1996 bibliography have now been dropped, for the reasons set out in the Preface.

(i) *Publishing and Book Development in Sub-Saharan Africa: An Annotated Bibliography* (with Cécile Lomer), London: Hans Zell Publishers, an imprint of Bowker-Saur, 1996. (ii) *A Bibliography of Publishing and the Book Chain in Sub-Saharan Africa-1996*, London: Association for the Development of Education in Africa, Working Group on Books and Learning Materials (Perspectives on African Book Development, 3), 1997. (iii) *A Bibliography of Publishing and the Book Chain in Sub-Saharan Africa-1997*, London: Association for the Development of Education in Africa, Working Group on Books and Learning Materials (Perspectives on African Book Development, 6), 1998; as well as (iv) material listed in the select bibliography in chapter 18 of *The African Publishing Companion: A Resource Guide*, Lochcarron: Hans Zell Publishing, 2002. (This resource did not include country-specific studies or articles, and no further editions have been published.)

New material, most of which the compiler has personally acquired for examination and abstracting purposes, has been tracked down by a wide scan of bibliographies, indexing services, databases, and online library catalogues. This has included, for example, the annual *Africa Bibliography, The African Book Publishing Record, African Studies Abstracts/African Studies Abstracts Online, International African Bibliography*, the *Quarterly Index to African Periodical Literature* published by the Library of Congress Office in Nairobi, as well as the OCLC's massive WorldCat database. Extensive searches on Google, using a combination of search strategies, have also been conducted and have helped to locate quite a significant number of reports and documents (many of them available online) not picked up by any of the major bibliographic or indexing databases.

Scope and type of material included
This new edition covers primarily material published over the last 28 years, from 1980 through to the end of 2007, although some key literature published before 1980 has been retained because of its historical importance. This includes a number of seminal studies on particular aspects of publishing and book development in Africa, for example in the area of scholarly publishing, or publishing for children. Also retained are some early studies that have appeared in the University of Toronto Press journal *Scholarly Publishing*, later ➔ **Journal of Scholarly Publishing (161)**, as well as all articles published in the quarterly ➔ **African Book Publishing Record/ABPR (168)** since it started publication in 1975. Complete runs of back issues of both journals are readily available in many academic libraries. (ABPR is published in print format only to vol. 26, 2000; print and online as from vol. 27, 2001.)

As mentioned in the Preface, a substantial number of entries in the previous edition (a total of 1,362) have been dropped – for example short reports and profiles, unpublished conference and workshop papers, or articles which are now very dated – and much greater emphasis is now placed on the relative significance of the material included.

The bibliography aims to cover all aspects of book publishing and the book chain in Africa, book marketing and distribution, and the retail book trade on the continent. Additionally, there are numerous citations on more specialist areas of publishing, such as publishing for children, journal and magazine publishing, scholarly publishing, publishing in African languages, women in African publishing and publishing by and for women, as well as digital media and electronic publishing; and there are many sections on complementary aspects of book development, for example authors and publishing, copyright (primarily as it relates to books, and rights of authors), national book policies, training for book industry personnel, and there are select references to reading in Africa and the promotion of a culture of reading. The bibliography also includes many citations on a number of other related topics, such as book assistance and donation programmes, the acquisition of African-published material, African books in the international market place, and publishing (in Africa and elsewhere) of African writers and African literature. There are separate sections devoted to two of Africa's major book trade organizations, the ➔ **African Publishers Network/APNET (5)**, and the Oxford-based ➔ **African Books Collective Ltd/ABC (3)**. A further separate section is devoted to articles and other material about Africa's premier book prize, the ➔ **Noma Award for Publishing in Africa (98)**.

The bibliography includes books, reports and surveys, papers in edited collections, periodical articles, book sector studies and similar documents, government and official publications, as well as a number of theses and dissertations, some of which are now freely accessible online as full-text documents or e-theses.

African book trade journals
In addition to the (currently dormant) ➔ **African Publishing Review (129)** published by the ➔ **African Publishers Network (5)**, there are a number of other African book trade journals and magazines, or newsletters published by book professional associations. However, most of them are published very irregularly and it has been difficult to verify their current availability status, and acquiring new issues published over the last ten years or more. Some of them may contain important contributions on particular aspects of the book sector in specific African countries, or carrying articles on related issues such as national book policies, copyright, book piracy, etc., but unfortunately they are rarely available as part of serial holdings at major academic libraries or as part of African studies library collections in the

countries of the North. In view of this there may well be some gaps in the literature covered.

Arrangement and classification
Arrangement of entries is in alphabetical order by author (or editor/compiler, or title for serials). Books or articles by the same person are arranged *chronologically* by date of publication. Capitalization for entries in English follows humanities (or headline) style. Author headings have been standardized as far as possible.

Entries are grouped under five major sections: (1) Serials and reference; (2) General, comparative and regional studies; (3) Country studies; (4) Studies by topic, listing material under 30 subject headings, and (5) Book industry training/Self-publishing, which also includes handbooks for authors.

Listings for each country in Section 3 are part directory and part bibliography, and are subdivided by (i) Associations and book-related organizations in each country, where they exist; (ii) National bibliography, books in print, and book trade directories, where available, and (iii) country-specific books, articles, reports, and interviews. However, for several African countries there is very little published literature, and for some (Chad, Mauritania, and Niger) there would appear to be no literature of any kind on publishing and the book sector.

Books and articles that primarily offer overviews of publishing and the state of the book in a particular country or region (e.g. book sector studies, articles on national book policies, biographical accounts or interviews with prominent members of the book professions), are classified under country or region.

It is important to note that, as a general rule, most articles on particular topics or areas of the book trade, e.g. bookselling, publishing for children, publishing in African languages, copyright, marketing, scholarly publishing, etc. are classified under *topic*, but are indexed both by topic and by country (or region). For example, an article on publishing and marketing of African language materials in Cameroon will appear in the section 'Publishing in African languages'; a study on publishing for children in Uganda will appear under 'Children's book publishing'; or an examination of young people's reading habits in South Africa will appear under 'Reading culture and reading promotion'.

Section 2 includes a number of entries on general or comparative studies on publishing in developing countries or the 'Third World', but it should be noted that this is merely a small selection of the relevant literature.

In Section 4, Studies by topic, a number of the topic headings include explanatory notes on scope, limitations and exclusions for each section and a series of cross references guide the user to related topics.

A complete list of periodicals cited in the new edition of the bibliography appears on pp. xxix-xxxvi.

Material excluded

Short articles, reports, and news items of a page or two (or less than 1,500 words) – such as reports about conferences, workshops, seminars, book fairs, book prizes and awards, or general book trade news – that have appeared in e.g. *The African Book Publishing Record, African Publishing Review* the *Bellagio Publishing Network Newsletter, BookLinks, Publishers Weekly,* or the UK trade journal *The Bookseller,* are not included for the most part. The exceptions are items that are of continuing and/or special interest, and short articles or overviews of publishing and the state of the book in some of the smaller countries in Africa, for which very little literature on the book sector currently exists.

While newspaper articles are also excluded, an excellent source for newspaper reports and stories on the book industries in Africa is the Washington-based news service ➜ **AllAfrica.com (154)**. It also offers links to news stories about book launches, book promotional or literary events, and news items about book awards and prizes that have appeared in online African newspapers.

Literature on the following topics is *excluded*: authorship (except as it relates to African authors and their relationship with publishers); censorship; newspaper publishing, mass media and communication; literature on library services and information provision in Africa, or more special topics such as that of the South-North flow of information, or preserving and protecting indigenous knowledge systems. Also excluded are articles and studies on writing generally, e.g. writing learning materials, or writing for specific audiences, such as writing for children. While there is a section on reading and reading promotion, books and articles devoted to literacy, teaching reading, or developing reading skills, are not included.

General articles on good practice in publishing (including editing, marketing, production, etc.), for example those that have appeared in the ➜ **African Publishing Review (129)** and in the magazines of some African book trade associations, are not included. However, articles on training for the African book professions, and training manuals and resources, are listed in Section 5.

Open access publishing

The topic of open access publishing for or in developing countries has generated a great deal of debate and a very substantial number of papers and studies have been published in recent years. While this new edition includes a section on open access publishing, it is restricted to articles and papers about open access initiatives and projects that deal, in whole or in part, with open access, or open access models, for African scholarly publishing.

More general articles about open content, open access movements, open source software, or open access for e-learning are not included, nor are those that deal with open access publishing in the developing world generally.

Annotations and abstracts

Annotations, or in many cases full abstracts, are included for most of the literature, except for a small number of entries for which it was not possible to obtain and/or examine a copy of the document. This includes documents or mission reports with limited or restricted circulation, for example a series of book sector studies on individual African countries commissioned by donors, the ➔ **World Bank (124)**, the UK Overseas Development Administration, or private consulting firms.

Where author-prepared abstracts were available these have been used in preference, although usually edited or cut in length.

While some of the annotations are of a more descriptive nature, many of them aim to provide critical analysis – especially for the more recent literature – and attention is drawn to particularly important contributions to the literature on publishing and the book in Africa.

Citation of reviews

As a new feature in this edition, references to reviews of some of the book titles and edited collections are now included, notably those which have appeared in journals such as the quarterly ➔ **African Book Publishing Record (168)** (in its "Professional reading" review columns), ➔ **African Publishing Review (129)**, ➔ **African Research & Documentation (150)**, ➔ **Africana Libraries Newsletter (149)**, the ➔ **Bellagio Publishing Network Newsletter (155)**, ➔ **Logos. Forum for the World Book Community (160)**, and occasional reviews in other journals, such as *Publishing Research Quarterly*. Additionally, there are a small number or reviews that have appeared in African studies and professional library journals, and online reviews published in the H-Net H-Africa reviews discussion forums. Usefully, many of the reviews in the *Bellagio Publishing Network Newsletter* are also available online, although in view of the uncertain future status of this currently dormant network organization, this may not continue indefinitely.

Material available online

This new edition now includes a substantial number of articles, reports, and other documents and resources that are available online. A total of almost 500 online resources are cited, the majority of them freely accessible. This includes a number of presentations available online in PowerPoint formats. All URLs for freely accessible resources have been checked up to March 2008, and the date last accessed/verified is indicated for each entry, in square brackets. Changes in URLs which come to our attention will be updated in the electronic version of the bibliography. To report any dead links please email hanszell@hanszell.co.uk.

All journals indicated in *bold italics* type face in the list of periodicals cited on p. xxix are available online, or back issues are partially available online covering the most recent volumes. For many journals published by commercial publishers that are available online a subscription is usually required. However, in most cases online access is possible by authorized users at academic institutions whose libraries subscribe to the journal, and this also applies for back issue articles which are available via JSTOR http://www.jstor.org/ (and see also JSTOR African Access Initiative below). Alternatively, articles can usually be purchased for a modest document delivery fee and paid by credit card.

Online access to the full text of the *current* issues of many scholarly print/online journals is available to subscribers to Project Muse http://muse.jhu.edu/.

URLs for articles available online are only indicated for freely accessible documents, for ➔ **Logos. Forum for the World Book Community (160)**, and for a number of commercially published journals, e.g. *Learned Publishing*, which offer free access to a select number of back issues. (*Note:* from January 2008 articles in *Learning Publishing* will be made freely available 12 months after their first publication.)

JSTOR African Access Initiative

As part of JSTOR's (Journal STORage) mission to create an archive of scholarly literature and extend access to the archive as broadly as possible, it has recently adopted a plan to waive participation fees for any academic or not-for-profit institution on the continent of Africa.

For more details, and instructions for initiating participation, visit http://www.jstor.org/about/africa/index.html.

Associations and organizations

A directory of African-based, continent-wide and regional book trade and allied associations is included on pp. 1-8. This is followed by a separate directory (pp. 9-45) listing the principal agencies, donors, foundations, and other organizations that have supported (and/or are currently supporting) the book sector and library development in Africa, in one form or another. This includes those supporting textbook development and provision, book industry training, those providing support for African writers or writers' groups, as well as book charities and the major book assistance and donation programmes. It also covers some agencies that have provided assistance in the area of scholarly communication, and a number of organizations that have been supportive of publishing and book development in Africa by means other than financial assistance, for example networks of librarians and Africanist library groups.

National African book trade associations and book-related organizations, where they exist, are listed under country headings in Section 3, giving full address details, email addresses, Web sites where available, and contact information. This includes publishers' and booksellers' associations, book development councils, and other book promotional bodies, as well as reproduction and literary rights organizations, and authors' and writers' groups of various kinds.

As far as has been possible all information has been verified, although several associations and organizations failed to respond to requests to verify information for currency and accuracy. In view of this a proportion of entries may be dated, or the organizations may be currently dormant.

Book trade directories, books in print, and national bibliographies

Entries for national book trade directories and books in print, where they exist, are also listed under country headings in Section 3, as are national bibliographies. However, the present state of national bibliographies in sub-Saharan Africa presents a dismal picture, and a large number of them are very irregularly published, are currently dormant, or have ceased publication altogether. Usually published by the national libraries or public library boards in each African country – sadly, many of them shamefully underfunded by their governments – they are published on a regular basis in less than ten countries at this time.

Cross-referencing and indexes

There is extensive cross-referencing between entries (or cross-references to organizations and associations) by means of boldface type marked with an → arrow symbol. In the electronic version the cross-references lead directly to the entry as a hyperlink.

Three indexes are included: (i) an author index, also including selected titles, such as serial titles listed as main entries, e.g. African book trade journals and national bibliographies, and titles of reference works such as books in print; (ii) a combined subject/geographical index, together with (iii) an index of organizations and associations.

Although the main arrangement of the bibliography, together with its system of cross-references, already provides access to countries, regions, or topics, the subject index is intended to provide a variety of additional means of access. References are to item numbers.

Access to the electronic edition

Online access to the electronic edition of *Publishing, Books & Reading in Sub-Saharan Africa: A Critical Bibliography* is bundled with print. Purchase of the print edition entitles purchasers access to the searchable electronic version at no extra charge. Online access requires registration.

Registration, access and delivery is at

www.hanszell.co.uk/pbrssa/index.shtml

The terms and conditions for online access (copied below), are set out as part of the registration pages, and in registering for electronic access the customer agrees to be bound by the terms and conditions by clicking the "I accept" button at the foot of the Web page. No paperwork is required, and there is no need for a formal exchange of a hard copy licensing agreement.

As part of the registration process customers will be asked to indicate an approximate date of purchase of the print edition, and whether the book was purchased direct from the publisher, through a vendor (vendor name is required), or acquired through other means (e.g. donation).

The terms and conditions of online access are as follows:

Period of online access/Expiry date
Purchasers of the print edition of *Publishing, Books & Reading in Sub-Saharan Africa: A Critical Bibliography* are entitled to free access to the online version. Access to the electronic version will continue to be available while the print edition remains in print, and/or for a period of at least four years from date of first publication of the print edition. There are no plans at this time for publication of a subsequent edition.

Access methods and server availability
Access to the online version of *Publishing, Books & Reading in Sub-Saharan Africa: A Critical Bibliography* is either by user ID/password or via IP address recognition for libraries requiring their own authentication methods. Applicable IP ranges can be indicated when registering for online access, in a field provided on the registration form.

Access is permitted at any time, but the publisher will not be liable for any delay, down time, or other failure of performance. However, the publisher will make all reasonable efforts to correct any performance problems brought to its attention.

Authorized users

For libraries and other institutional purchasers who have arranged online access using their own authentication methods via IP address recognition, access is restricted to authorized users of these institutions' secure library networks, on campus connected to the network directly, or off campus using the institution's proxy or Virtual Private Network (VPN) servers and dial-in services.

Authorized users at academic institutions shall be identified by authorized Internet Protocol (IP) addresses. Client shall limit on-site access to current students, faculty, and staff who are primarily affiliated with the licensed campus, as well as walk-in users who are permitted access to the secure network from computer terminals within the library premises and who are making inconsequential use of the resources for their scholarly, research, educational, or personal use only. Remote access is limited to current students, faculty, and staff.

Permitted and prohibited uses

Material contained in *Publishing, Books & Reading in Sub-Saharan Africa: A Critical Bibliography* is subject to copyright and database protection. Authorized users may search, view, retrieve and display all content. Making one or more copies in hard copy form of the output of any search is permitted, but such copies may not be sold. Downloading search results to hard disk or diskette is permitted provided that such data are not made available to anyone who is not an authorized user. Scholarly sharing of selective portions of the resources with researchers not affiliated with the purchaser of *Publishing, Books & Reading in Sub-Saharan Africa: A Critical Bibliography* is permitted within the bounds of "fair use".

Systematic downloading of entire sections of the database is prohibited, as is electronically transmitting online content to mailing lists or electronic bulletin boards, exploitation of the database for monetary reward by means of sale or resale of content, systematically making print or electronic copies of multiple extracts (other than providing printed copies of sections of content for individual authorized users), or bulk reproduction and distribution of materials in any form.

Downloading select content for use in course packs, or print or electronic course reserves, is acceptable, provided due acknowledgement is made of the original source. Downloading or republication of substantial parts of the book, or entire sections (and beyond "fair use"), is not allowed without prior permission in writing from Hans Zell Publishing. Stable links to full-text content in the database may be generated for syllabi or other course materials. Interlibrary loan is only permitted for the print version of the product.

Recompiling, copying, publication or republication of data beyond "fair use", in any form or medium whatsoever, may be done only with specific written permission from Hans Zell Publishing.

Infringement of the above terms and conditions may result in termination of online access, but the publisher agrees to give prior written notice to users of such withdrawal.

Limited warranty
Information contained in the database of *Publishing, Books & Reading in Sub-Saharan Africa: A Critical Bibliography* is provided to end-users without warranty of any kind. While the compilers have taken great care to ensure accuracy, the Publisher cannot assume, and hereby disclaims, any liability to any party for any loss or damage caused by omissions or inaccuracies in *Publishing, Books & Reading in Sub-Saharan Africa: A Critical Bibliography*, whether such errors or omissions result from negligence, accident, or any other cause.

If you encounter any problems in accessing the electronic version please get in touch with the publisher at hanszell@hanszell.co.uk.

Periodicals cited in the bibliography

Journals in **bold italics** are available in both print and online formats, although back issues may not be available electronically for articles published before 2000, or may only be partially available. Access to full text is either available free, subject to a subscription, or articles can be obtained via document delivery on a pay-per-article basis. Many journal back issues are also accessible via JSTOR through participating university libraries.

Place of first publication is indicated, but many journals have moved publishers over the years, and as indicated by [etc.] following place of publication. Several of the periodicals listed here have ceased publication.

African national bibliographies listed under countries in Section 3 are not included here.

Accessions List of the Library of Congress Office Nairobi
Acquisitions Librarian Binghamton, NY
Africa Bibliography Edinburgh
Africa Book Centre Book Review London
Africa Media Review Nairobi
Africa Now London
Africa Report New York
Africa Review of Books Dakar
Africa Rome
Africa Today Denver [etc.]
Africa, an international business ...monthly London
African Affairs London
African Association of Science Editors Newsbrief-Ethiopian Chapter Addis
   Ababa
Africana Libraries Newsletter Boston [etc.] (online only as from 2006)
Africana Research Bulletin Freetown
Africscope Lagos
African Book Publishing Record (The) Oxford [etc.] (online, subscription-based, as from vol. 27, 2001-)
African Crop Science Journal Nairobi
African Environment Dakar
African Journal of Library, Archives and Information Science Gaborone
African Languages and Cultures London

African Literature Association Bulletin Edmonton, Canada [etc.]
African Publishing Review Harare [etc.] (some available online)
African Research & Documentation London
African Review of Books Salisbury, UK (online only)
African Studies Johannesburg
African Studies Outreach Bloomington, IN
African Studies Review Atlanta, GA [etc.]
Africultures Nyon, France
Afrique Contemporaine Paris
AfriquEducation Montrouge, France
Afriscope Lagos
Agenda Bishopsgate, South Africa
AllAfrica.com-Book Reviews Washington, DC (online only)
Alternation Durban, South Africa
American Libraries Chicago
American Presbyterians Philadelphia, PA
ANA Review Lagos
Annales Aequatoria Kinshasa
Annals AAPSS Philadelphia
Artes Natales Durban
ASA News Atlanta, GA [etc.] (online only as from 2007)
Asian/Pacific Book Development Tokyo

BBC Arts and Africa London
Bellagio Publishing Network Newsletter Buffalo, NY [etc.] (full-text online
    as from no. 20, 1997-)
Bendel Library Journal Benin-City, Nigeria
Bibliothèques Paris
Bookbird Basle [etc.]
Book History Baltimore, MD
Book Industry (The) Kumasi, Ghana
Book Nigeria (The) Lagos
Book Power Harare
Book Research Quarterly see *Publishing Research Quarterly*
Bookchat Grabouw, South Africa
BookLinks London
Bookmark Bellville, South Africa (select material available online)
Books Abroad see *World Literature Today*
Books Ikeja, Nigeria
Bookseller (The) London
Botswana Library Association Journal Gaborone
British Medical Journal London
British Overseas Development London
Bukku Conakry

Bulletin des Etudes Africaines de l'INALCO Paris
Bulletin on Islam and Christian-Muslim Relations in Africa Ibadan

Cahiers de l'Economie du Livre Paris
Canadian Journal of Communication Montreal
Cape Librarian Cape Town
Catholic Media Council Information Bulletin see *Mediaforum*
Choice Chicago
Communication et Langages Paris
Comparative Education Review Chicago, IL
Congo Afrique Kinshasa
Copyright Bulletin/e-Copyright Bulletin Paris
Copyright News Lagos
Courier ACP-EU (The) Paris
CREPLA Bulletin of Information Yaoundé, Cameroon
Cultures Sud Paris (formerly *Notre Librairie*; select material available online)
Current Bibliography on African Affairs (A) Washington, DC [etc.]

D&C. Développement et Coopération Bonn [etc.]
Development Dialogue Uppsala, Sweden
Development in Practice Oxford
Discovery and Innovation Nairobi
D-Lib Magazine Reston, VA (online only)

East African Bookseller Nairobi (formerly *The Kenya Bookseller*)
Education Libraries Journal Leicester, UK
Educator Eldoret, Kenya
English in Africa Johannesburg
Ethiopia Observer Addis Ababa
Ethiopian Journal of Languages and Literature Addis Ababa
Ethiopiques Dakar

FID Bulletin The Hague (superseded by *FID Review*)
Finance and Development Washington, DC
First Monday Chicago, IL (online only)
Focus on International & Comparative Librarianship London
Fréquence Sud Yaoundé

Géopolitique Africaine Paris
Ghana Book World Accra
Ghana Library Journal Accra
Glendora Books Supplement Lagos
Glendora Review Lagos
Government Publications Review London

Guardian Review Lagos
History in Africa Madison, WI

IASP Newsletter Oslo
Ife Psychologia Ile-Ife, Nigeria
IFLA Journal The Hague
INASP Newsletter Oxford
Index on Censorship London
Information Development London
Information Technologist Minna, Nigeria
Innovation Pietermaritzburg (select material available online)
Interlending & Document Supply Bingley, UK
International Information and Library Review London (formerly
  International Library Review)
International Information, Communication and Education Lucknow, India
International Journal of Educational Development Oxford [etc.]
International Library Review see *International Information and Library Review*
International Publishers Bulletin Geneva
International Review of Education Paris [etc.]
International Review of Children's Literature and Librarianship (superseded by
  The New Review of Children's Literature and Librarianship)
ISBN Review Berlin
Issue: A Journal of Opinion Atlanta, GA [etc.]

Journal of Academic Librarianship Ann Arbor, MI [etc.]
Journal of African Children's and Youth Literature Atlanta, GA [etc.] (formerly
  Journal of African Children's Literature)
Journal of Asian and African Studies Willowdale, Canada [etc.]
Journal of Commonwealth Literature Oxford [etc.]
Journal of Cultural Studies Agw-Iwoye, Nigeria
Journal of Humanities Zomba, Malawi
Journal of Modern African Studies Cambridge
Journal of Multicultural Librarianship London
Journal of Popular Culture Bowling Green, OH
Journal of Religion in Africa Leiden, Netherlands
Journal of Scholarly Publishing Toronto (formerly *Scholarly Publishing*)
Journal of Southern African Studies London
Journal of the Royal Society London
Journal on the Teaching of English (A) Pretoria

Kalabash Windhoek
Kenya Bookseller see *East African Bookseller*
Kunapipi Aarhus, Denmark

Lagos Journal of Library and Information Science Lagos
Learned Publishing Beckenham, UK
Le Monde Diplomatique Paris
Lesotho Books and Libraries Maseru
Lesotho Law Journal Maseru
Liberal Education Washington, DC
Library Acquisitions: Practice and Theory see *Library Collections, Acquisitions Technical Services*
Library & Information Science Research Oxford
Library Collections, Acquisitions & Technical Services Elmsford, NY [etc.] (formerly *Library Acquisitions: Practice and Theory*)
Library Management Bingley, UK
Library Review Glasgow [etc.]
Library Trends Urbana, IL
Libraries and Culture see *Libraries & the Cultural Record*
Libraries & the Cultural Record Austin, TX (formerly *Libraries and Culture*)
Libri Copenhagen
Link-up London
Literature and Society in South Africa Johannesburg
Litereratur Nachrichten Frankfurt (articles in English only)
Livre Africain Cotonou
Livres de France Paris
Livres Hebdo Paris
Logos. Forum of the World Book Community London [etc.] (formerly *Logos. The Professional Journal of the Book World*, thereafter *Logos. Journal of the World Book Community*)
Luso-Brazilian Review Madison, WI

Maktaba Nairobi
Mala Bulletin Zomba, Malawi
Matatu Amsterdam [etc.]
Media Development London
Mediaforum Aachen, Germany (formerly *Catholic Media Council Information Bulletin*)
Médiafriq Yaoundé
Médianes Grenoble, France
Mitteilungen/Newsletter. Namibia Scientific Society Windhoek
Modern Africa London
Mondes et Cultures Paris
Moto Gweru, Zimbabwe
Mots Pluriels et Grandes Themes de Notre Temps Crawley, Australia (online only)

NIWA-Info Windhoek
Namibia Review Windhoek
New African London
New Gong Magazine Lagos (online only)
New Review of Information and Library Research London
Newswatch Lagos
Ngoma Ottawa
Nigerbiblios Lagos
Nigeria Magazine Lagos
Nigerian Bookseller Lagos
Nigerian Journal of Economic and Social Studies Ibadan
Nigerian Libraries Ibadan
Nordic Journal of African Studies Uppsala, Sweden
Notes Africaines Dakar
Notre Librairie see *Cultures Sud*

Okike Nsukka, Nigeria
Optima Marshalltown, South Africa
Orbit Lusaka

PABA Newsletter Lagos [etc.]
Pan African Journal New York [etc.]
Pan African Book World Enugu, Nigeria
Partners in African Publishing Oxford [etc.]
Pegboard Emmarentia, South Africa (select material available online)
Penant Paris
Politique Africaine Paris
Prospects Paris
Public Library Journal London
Publisher (The) Ibadan
Publishers Weekly New York
Publishing Research Quarterly New Brunswick, NJ [etc.] (formerly *Book Research Quarterly*)

Quarterly Bulletin of the South African Library Cape Town
Quarterly Index to African Periodical Literature Nairobi

Radical History Review New York
Reading Teacher Newark, NJ
Research in African Literatures Austin, TX [etc.]
Review of English and Literary Studies Ibadan
Revue de Littérature Comparée Paris
Revue des Livres pour Enfants (La) Paris
Revue de l'Océan Indien Madagascar Antananarivo

Rights Paris

SA BookNews Online Strand, South Africa (online only)
Sankofa Baltimore, MD
Saudi Medical Journal Riyadh
Scientific American New York
Serials Newbury, UK
Serials Librarian London [etc.]
Serials Review Amsterdam
Scholarly Publishing see *Journal of Scholarly Publishing*
School Libraries Worldwide Zillmere, Australia
Scientometrics Budapest [etc.]
Scrutiny Pretoria (formerly *Unisa English Studies*)
SHARP News Baltimore, MD
Sierra Leone Library Journal Freetown
Society of Malawi Journal Blantyre
South London
South African Historical Journal Pretoria
South African Journal of Libraries and Information Science Pretoria
South African Journal on Human Rights Cape Town
South African Law Journal Cape Town
South African Medical Journal Cape Town
South African Panorama Pretoria
Southern Africa Political and Economic Monthly Harare
Southern African Review of Books Cape Town [etc.]
Spore Wageningen, Netherlands
Staffrider Johannesburg
Sudanow Khartoum

Takam Tikou Paris
Tanzania S & T News Dar es Salaam
Third World Libraries see *World Libraries*
This Week Ibadan
Times Literary Supplement London
Toguna Athens, OH
Transition Kampala (later *Ch'indaba*, Accra; now *Transition*, New York)

Uganda Book News Kampala
UNESCO-Africa, Paris
UNESCO Courier Paris
Unisa English Studies see *Scrutiny*
University of Dar es Salaam Library Journal Dar es Salaam
USA/Africa Dialogue Austin, TX (online only)
Usawa Kinshasa

Wajibu Nairobi
Wasafiri London
West Africa London [etc.] (superseded by *Africa Week*)
Whydah Nairobi
Wilson Library Bulletin New York
Wiplash London
World Libraries River Forest, IL (formerly *Third World Libraries*)
World Literature Today Norman, OK (formerly *Books Abroad*)
Writers World Somerset West, South Africa

Zaire-Afrique Kinshasa
Zambia Library Association Journal Lusaka
Zeitschrift für Kulturaustausch Stuttgart (articles in English only; superseded
  by *Kulturaustausch. Zeitschrift für internationale Perspektiven*)
Zimbabwe Libarian Bulawayo
Zimbabwean Review Harare

Introductory essay

African Publishing: From Ile-Ife, Nigeria to the Present

by
Henry Chakava [1]

INTRODUCTION

The first major conference on African publishing was held in Ile-Ife, Nigeria, in December 1973. It was hosted by the University of Ife (now Obafemi Awolowo University), and attracted participants ranging from publishers, booksellers, and librarians, to writers (a host of them, with Chinua Achebe giving the opening address), literary critics, and academicians. The conference resulted in the publication of a book, *Publishing in Africa in the Seventies* edited by Edwina Oluwasanmi, Eva Mclean and Hans Zell [2] which, for the most part, was a catalogue of the litany of problems facing the African book industry.

In this essay I will attempt a state of the art analysis of the (sub-Saharan) African book industry today, exploring most of the key issues from a historical perspective. Achievements, failures and the challenges that lie ahead will be highlighted, and a way forward suggested. My approach will be that of an insider, having been at Ife, and having continued both as a participant and a witness to the industry all these 35 years. A fair question to ask is: Has African publishing come of age? As we shall see, some progress has been made, but the general picture is one of mixed fortunes.

Overall, the industry recorded considerable growth in the 1970s, declined in the 1980s, and has been growing in leaps and bounds since. True, there have

---

[1] Dr. Henry Chakava is Chairman of East African Educational Publishers, Nairobi, Kenya.

[2] Ile-Ife, Nigeria: University of Ife Press, 1975. *See* entry ➔ **301**.

Cross-references have been added to organizations and associations mentioned in the text, full address and contact details of which can be found in the section ➔ **Organizations and associations**.

been many other conferences since Ife, in and out of Africa, addressing the industry in whole or in part. Books and monographs have been published analyzing and providing solutions to challenges encountered. Support has come from foreign governments, international lending institutions such as the World Bank (➔ 124), UNESCO (➔ 118), and donors such as the Bellagio Group, led by SIDA (➔ 115).

As a result of these interventions, new book fairs have emerged in Ghana, Kenya, Senegal, South Africa, and Zimbabwe. Indeed, one can say that every African country now has an annual book event of some magnitude. Continental organizations such as the African Publishers Network/APNET (➔ 5), the Pan African Writers Association/PAWA (➔ 22), and the Pan African Booksellers Association/PABA (➔ 21) have emerged. Regional associations such as the East African Book Development Association/ EABDA (➔ 13), national bodies such as book development councils, and stakeholder associations of publishers, printers, writers, booksellers, librarians, etc. can be found in most countries. They offer training, facilitate trade, and network among themselves, along with other activities. On the flip side, these associations are still very weak in structure and management, and the majority cannot survive without donor support.

In spite of this support and local initiatives in some countries, Africa has not achieved its potential, and remains at the bottom of the world book production chart. An analysis of book production statistics from the UNESCO Institute of Statistics (UNIS) shows that the United Kingdom, the world's leading book producer in 2005, published a lot more books than the whole of Africa combined. In order to appreciate fully the level of achievement of African book publishing, I offer below a quick survey of the book chain. Problems such as lack of capital, training, equipment and raw materials, an underdeveloped market, and competition from multinationals – all identified at the Ife conference – may have subsided, but they have not gone away, as we shall see.

WRITING

There has been steady growth in all categories of African writers since the 1970s. The highest increase has been in those authoring textbooks, which have increased substantially, and where expatriate writers have given way to local ones. Also gone up has the number of children's books writers who, although they made a late start, have been very prolific since the 1980s. Drawing their inspiration mostly from traditional folklore, they have now produced a rich repertoire of African children's books. Currently, the tertiary and scholarly areas are still dominated by foreigners, with local authors only beginning to gain confidence to venture into them through university presses, some of the larger commercial houses, and, increasingly, through the publishing activities of the Dakar-based Council for the Development of Social Science Research in Africa/ CODESRIA (http://www.codesria.org/Publications.htm), the independent Pan-African research organization.

African publishing houses are swamped with works of fiction for which they do not have capacity to handle. The majority are rejected, either because they do not meet the required standards, but mostly because editors do not have the time and patience to advise authors on how to revise and rewrite to an acceptable level. In other words, Africa's fictional output, and its quality, could rise significantly if African writers were nurtured and guided in the art of writing and script presentation.

It is fair to say African writers lack publishing capacity within the continent. Some set their sights abroad because they feel they will get better services, will be more effectively distributed, earn bigger royalties, and gain international recognition. The fact that more and more African writers publish abroad is evidence of the intellectual wealth that abounds in Africa, and which should be a challenge to its publishing industry. At its peak, the Heinemann African Writers Series (AWS) was an attraction and an incentive to African creative writers. Its demise has given rise to local imprints, especially in Kenya, Nigeria, South Africa and Zimbabwe, but all of which are struggling to generate an Africa-wide appeal, and international recognition, such as the AWS enjoyed.

In addition to lack of publishing outlets and international exposure mentioned above, Africa is yet to develop an environment conducive to writers and writing. Below, I take a random look at some of the constraints:

Training: There are few opportunities for professional or full-time training for African writers. Some of the writers' workshops which used to be held in Kenya, Nigeria and Zimbabwe, no longer take place. A few writers have had the opportunity to attend writers' workshops outside the continent, in particular, the Iowa Writers' Workshop, a two-year residency programme at the University of Iowa in the USA (www.uiowa.edu/~iww/). A welcome development is that the winners of the Caine Prize for African Writing (www.caineprize.com/) have normally been assisted to further their careers through training and publishing opportunities in journals, magazines, and books.

Freedom to create: African writers do not have the freedom to create freely. They are not given the space to critically analyze the ills in their societies. African governments are particularly sensitive to criticism, and some still retain censorship boards. Books are frequently banned, and writers imprisoned. For this reason, many writers have fled their countries and now live abroad. Indeed, at one time, most of Malawi's writers were living in exile in fear of Banda's regime.

Incentives: There are many ways in which writers can be given incentives or can be recognized for their work. Writers like Achebe, Soyinka and Ngugi have won numerous international prizes and have been honoured in their own countries. But they are the exception; a majority of African writers could do with a bit more recognition, promotion in the workplace, a sponsored trip to some destination, a little prize money, or even just a certificate. The Noma Award for Publishing in Africa (➔ 98), the Caine Prize already referred to above, and the Commonwealth Writers' Prize (www.commonwealthfoundation.com/culturediversity/writersprize/) are the only continental prizes to date. There should also be more national prizes such as the Jomo Kenyatta and Wahome Mutahi prizes in Kenya. Africa needs to reward its writers more, and in every possible way, with home made prizes, well before they attract international attention.

Writers' unions: African writers have not effectively networked among themselves; they are not properly organized, and are constantly squabbling. Here in Kenya, there are no less than ten writers' associations, all working at cross purposes. Attempts to unite them under one union have not been successful, as gains made have normally been short-term. I know of no regional writers' association, and the Pan-African Writers Association would appear to be very low key in their current activities. Attempts by the Norwegian reproduction rights organization Kopinor (➔ 89) to organize African writers' groups have borne fruits in the area of copyright protection, and copyright licensing agencies, sometimes referred to as collective management organizations, now exist in several countries.

PUBLISHING
The African publishing industry has grown substantially since Ile-Ife, with books published increasing both in number and quality. Many new publishing houses have sprung up over the period, although quite a number have disappeared or gone moribund. The growth has been particularly noticeable in the textbook area, both at primary and secondary level. Children's books have increased significantly since the early 1990s, as World Bank textbook funded projects have included a component of them. Fiction and general books have been steady with output increasing during times of reduced economic hardship. Production quality has improved progressively although it has not yet achieved international standards. For example, most of the children's books could benefit from better editing, design, layout and illustrations if they are to appeal to international markets. Moreover, as mentioned earlier, the output is far lower than what one might expect for

each country, and for the continent as a whole. Little progress has been made in general, academic, scholarly and journal publishing, despite the mushrooming of university presses. The issues raised at Ile-Ife, and echoed at subsequent conferences, have not been fully addressed as the following brief commentary on each will show.

Issues from Ife

Policies: Many African governments still lack policies to guide publishing development, although a few are currently involved in the process of formulating book policies, and a number now have textbook policies following pressure from the World Bank. The relationships between public and private sector publishing is not clearly defined, and several countries still engage in state publishing, or seek to control the private sector in one way or the other. Clear policies would address important issues such as textbook development, language of instruction, distribution, early childhood and adult education, and book use, as well as other areas where clear policies are required.

Multinational publishers: These were perceived as a threat to indigenous publishing development as they were more established, better capitalized, staffed, and supported by their parent companies. However, over the years, and in spite of globalization, the influence of multinationals in Africa is waning or taking on a different form, as in South Africa. The multinationals have enough struggles of their own at home, and they have tended to come and go according to the economic weather in Africa. They have pulled out of some countries and have been bought out in others. The time has come for these multinationals to enter into partnerships with local publishers for mutual benefit, as they are doing in South Africa.

Training: The issue of training permeates the entire African publishing industry. Much progress has been made, thanks to the initiative of some governments, APNET, and national publishers' associations. Currently, publishing training is available in a number of African universities in Cameroon, Ghana, Kenya, Nigeria, South Africa, and Zimbabwe. In the first ten years of its existence, APNET was able to devise a curriculum and to offer intensive training in all aspects of the publishing process. The East African Book Development Association/EABDA has also been active in this area, offering training across the industry in the last ten years. The bigger national publishers' associations offer training to their members and, indeed, the larger houses provide in-house training for their new employees. In my view this issue has been adequately addressed. What is required now is a mechanism to sustain the training opportunities available.

Scholarly and journal publishing: This area of publishing has recorded the least improvement even as enrolments in African universities have increased dramatically, and almost every university has set up its own press in some form or another. However many university presses have been are started without adequate planning, lack of proper equipment and skilled personnel, and they are ill-prepared to operate in a commercial environment, being controlled, in large measure, by the university administration. It is lamentable that even with new technologies that make journal publishing affordable, fewer and fewer journals are being published each year. It also says something about the academic malaise that has afflicted African universities. The World Bank has plans to install digital Print-on-Demand (POD) machines at strategic locations in Africa. If these plans come to fruition, we hope periodicals, monographs, and academic titles will increase their presence in the African book and journals marketplace. However, there is a need for African universities to give much more attention to publications, and consciously work to develop and maintain vibrant presses that take advantage of modern technology. At the same time, commercial publishers are encouraged to look at this area, as it provides an opportunity that could be utilized for product diversification and profitability.

Emerging issues

In the meantime, a number of new publishing issues have emerged since the 1970s, inviting a response from the African publisher. These include, among others, harnessing the new technologies, NGO publishing, the role of the World Bank, and the value of translations.

New technologies: The production of books by means of desk-top publishing, digital print-on-demand, or even through photocopying, has been made faster, cheaper and more efficient. Africa is only slowly beginning to benefit from these innovations, especially the pre-press end. These technologies make it possible to publish viably even in small runs. The continent stands to gain from these technologies as soon as they become available and affordable.

NGO involvement: NGO involvement in African publishing has developed at a scale higher than anticipated. Some NGO's have set up publishing units of their own, while others have sponsored their publications through local or overseas commercial houses. Some international agencies such as USAID (➔ **121**), or UN agencies such as UNICEF and UNESCO (➔ **118**), have developed or sponsored full publishing programmes, sometimes in unexplored areas such as children's books and scholarly publications. It can be assumed, therefore, that their efforts were responding to the many gaps in Africa's publishing development.

The World Bank: The World Bank (➜ **124**) has become a major player in African publishing, especially during the last 20 years. It has encouraged private sector publishing, and established funding mechanisms that can help Africa achieve education for all. Because of this, the last few years have witnessed substantial growth in African publishing for schools, especially at the primary and secondary level. So dominant has been the Bank's influence that fears are growing that some countries may not be in charge. A look at the situation in some countries of East and Central Africa shows that World Bank consultants have tended to prescribe the same medicine for every publishing ailment without full understanding of the realities on the ground. For example, they have driven up book prices by insisting on unrealistic technical specifications, in the process forcing publishers to print in Asia and the Far East, at the expense of local printers.

The other World Bank policy of limiting the number of textbooks approved for each class, ostensibly intended to reduce costs, is ill-advised and can lead to knowledge stagnation. A dynamic curriculum environment where new textbooks are continuously being published must be encouraged, as is the case in the developed world.

On the positive side, the technical specifications policy has improved the physical appearance of African textbooks, although the trickle down effect of this funding on the local printing industry is lost. Additionally, the practice of placing textbook money in schools and directing them to procure through bookshops is good for the retail book trade, if carefully monitored.

As can be seen, the entry of the World Bank on the African publishing scene is both a blessing and a curse. It is a blessing because it provides funding for textbook purchases, and a curse when African governments and their publishing industries are pushed off the driving seat.

PRODUCTION

Printing capacity has existed in Africa since colonial times when governments, missionaries, and resistance groups acquired printing presses for their propaganda wars. Newspaper companies, whether controlled by the state or private enterprise, have also been used to print books. Strewn all over Africa are old Heidelberg machines of varying shapes and sizes, which continue to churn out books and other related materials. However, some printing firms have continued to use such machines while also investing in state-of-the-art technology that can undertake both pre-press activities such as filming and plate-making, as well as printing. I believe such outfits provide a prototype from which a thriving African printing industry can emerge. Kenya, South Africa and Zimbabwe can be said to be self sufficient in printing, as all three countries have paper manufacturing plants producing certain types of paper.

It has been claimed that printing prices in Africa are higher than anywhere else. This is not true. Given that the machinery and raw materials such as paper, film, inks, etc., are all imported and substantial duties levied, and considering that printing prices are not much higher than India, a real opportunity to produce books at very low cost exists. If African governments can come forward with incentives such as those relating to tax, African printers can take advantage of the cheap labour and the existent nascent skills that need harnessing. However, I have already referred to the World Bank technical specifications on the manufacturing side, which are driving lucrative textbook printing contracts out of Africa.

African printing has been blamed for poor quality. This is true only when one imposes Western standards on African books. It must be appreciated that we cannot develop printing ahead of everything else; rather it has to be in tandem with the rest of African development. In the 1970s, books coming out of India were of very poor quality. The eventual improvement in the quality of Indian books was not as a result of externally imposed specifications, but rather in response to an internal competitive dynamic.

Printing is labour intensive, and there is no shortage of cheap labour in Africa. School enrolment is on the rise and the demand for books, at all levels, is growing. African governments should encourage local investment in paper manufacturing plants, assembly of printing machines, complete with the more recent technological innovations in this area. An invigorated printing industry will positively impact on publishing and hence the entire book chain.

DISTRIBUTION & MARKETING

In spite of the many distribution bottlenecks that have been widely documented about publishing in Africa, the situation is slowly improving. African publishers are gradually waking up to the need to market and distribute their books more effectively. Obstacles exist within each country of course, and it is still not possible for books to travel across the continent, from East to West and vice versa, but this may be for reasons beyond the industry itself. For a long time, lack of foreign exchange was blamed as the culprit, but it is now possible to buy the US dollar in any African country, using local currencies, although these have been severely devalued since the advent of structural adjustment programmes and globalization.

African publishers are gradually getting into the habit of preparing catalogues, price lists and other promotional materials, although there is as yet no evidence of provision of new title advance information with forward publication dates. Mailings to schools have become fairly routine among the big educational publishers, even as the numbers of these schools have continued to rise. Standard practices such as employing representatives to visit schools, use of inspection copies, and direct mail, are all being employed. Some countries still engage in centralized buying of books for free distribution to schools, or via district education boards, but this is being phased out, thanks to World Bank intervention. General books are less well distributed, although book reviews in newspapers and radio, author visits, and launch parties are nowadays not uncommon.

While the number of bookshops and libraries (both community and public) has increased over the last 30 years, many more are needed in the rural areas. The major challenges have been reaching them, as road transport remains difficult and expensive, and postage and freight costs continue to be high, slow and unreliable. As the cost of distribution has continued to rise, booksellers have put pressure on publishers, who have had to increase trade discounts from an average of 20% in the 1970s to 40% at present.

Trade promotion is one of the anchor aims of APNET and PABA, the two continental book development associations set up in the 1990s. These associations have been active in promoting regional trade, and have been represented at the African "international" book fairs mentioned above. APNET has been invited to most world book fairs, and has exhibited a range of African-published books. The fact that African books now feature on international databases such as Nielsen BookData, and appear in the search results of major Web search engines such a Google, would seem to indicate that we are beginning to come out of the woods.

The African Books Collective/ABC (➔ 3) has done commendable work in promoting and selling African books outside the continent. Based in Oxford in the UK, and with US distribution arrangements through Michigan State University Press, the Collective stocks a diverse range of academic, general and children's books, which it sells to bookshops, libraries and individual book buyers around the world. It has negotiated wholesale arrangements with Gardners in the UK who carry some of its stock. It has recently entered into an arrangement with Lightning Source Ltd. to digitize, print-on-demand, and provide online sales services, both retail and wholesale. These moves have enabled ABC to leap into the 21st century as far as electronic publishing is concerned, and to steer in a direction which will free it from donor dependency and achieve self sustainability.

It is clear from the foregoing that book distribution and marketing has made some progress in the last twenty years. However, a great deal more remains to be done in order to increase visibility, and revenues both from the home and export markets. National bibliographies, books in print, and other book trade reference resources need to be prepared, and regularly updated.

Emphasis needs to be placed on regional trade, as is currently the case in East Africa, before moving to other parts of the continent. Most African publishing firms are small, with tiny marketing and publicity budgets that, if spread out thinly across the vast African continent, will make little impact.

READING
There was a lot of talk in Ile-Ife about fostering the reading habit in African peoples, almost as if this condition is innate. Since then, this topic has attracted many conference papers, and a host of theories has been propounded. In the meantime much has changed: cultural and missionary influences have receded into the background, the children of the 1970s are now adults, and the African publishing environment has improved. This writer's view is that all people are the same, and it no longer makes sense to talk about creating a reading culture in Africa. It is true that Africans read less than other people, and the reasons for this are as much cultural as they are economic, sociological, and even environmental.

It is true that colonial and missionary education did not present the book positively as a source of knowledge and pleasure. Indeed, people were forced to school and made to read books they could not relate to on promises of employment and a good life thereafter. It is also true that Africans derive more pleasure from the oral and performing arts: talking, singing, dancing and socializing. But some of the arguments about reading habits can no longer hold, for example with Ghana celebrating 50 years of independence, and a majority of the population having been born after independence.

There is paucity of reading material at all levels and those available are, in some cases, badly written, lack variety, or are unattractively produced. Some imported books are culturally inappropriate and normally unavailable, or unaffordable. The last 40 years have shown that the pace of reading has developed side by side with the continent's publishing output. Reading campaigns in the countries where they have been conducted, through book weeks, reading tents, library development and book donations (and as demonstrated by EABDA activities), have produced excellent results, especially in primary schools, and even among communities at large.

In addition to the issues discussed above, the African reader is particularly disadvantaged as far as leisure reading opportunities are concerned. At school, there are few books and no library, and the rigid timetable cannot allow quiet reading. If the child is permitted to take a book home, and this is not always the case, more obstacles get in the way of reading. Many children are used for household chores, running errands, mundane tasks such as fetching water or firewood, or looking after animals. The same problems apply to adult learners who may gain literacy through literacy programmes available in some countries, but fail to sustain it through lack of engagement and follow-up reading materials. Few public and community libraries exist and much of what they stock is elitist and irrelevant to the new literates.

Socio-economic and environmental factors also need to be put into consideration. Statistics show that nearly half of Africa is illiterate. Such people have no use for books. Also, just over 40% of African peoples survive on the equivalent of US$1 per day. For such people, buying a book would be an unnecessary luxury as they struggle for the essential commodities of health, food and shelter. Environmental factors include crowded housing in the urban areas and lack of electricity in most rural areas.

UNESCO (➜ 118), the International Reading Association (➜ 83), and other external agencies have provided significant logistical support in the promotion of reading in Africa, while Book Aid International (➜ 38) and CODE (➜ 48) have assisted with book donations as well as library training and development. National reading associations are slowly taking root in Africa, and it is hoped they will sustain the reading campaigns currently underway, especially in East Africa. It has been suggested that the new media such as television, video, CDs, iPods, and so on, pose a threat to the future of reading. This threat exists only on a very small scale in the urban centres of Africa, but the reading campaigns in hand should be able to harness and exploit its power in the promotion of books and reading.

CHALLENGES
This paper would be incomplete if I did not point out some of the key issues plaguing the African book industry and which, to date, remain largely unresolved. A majority of these have been highlighted elsewhere in this paper, and can be attributed to Africa's general state of underdevelopment. They are issues that can only be addressed by governments themselves with assistance, perhaps, from the international community. The rest are industry based, and result from a lack of government policies or weaknesses within the industry, which have led to the present unsatisfactory state of affairs.

External Factors
Policies: To what extent should African states involve themselves in publishing? If African governments came up with comprehensive publishing and book policies, this question would be answered. Africa remains a net importer of books and there should be rules to guide this

process. Currently legislation governing importation of books is varied and even contradictory. For example, book imports may be zero-rated for tax, while importation of paper and machinery attracts tax. A streamlined tax regime covering the entire publishing process, with built-in incentives, could make the industry more competitive.

Language: Language remains both a major challenge and a dilemma for African publishing. Currently the majority of books published are in foreign languages: English, French and Portuguese. The need to publish in African languages is widely acknowledged, yet it is not possible to do this in the more than 1,000 languages that exist on the continent, half of them currently without orthographies. Most African countries have adopted policies which provide that learning in the first three years of primary education be in mother tongue; a meaningless gesture that peters off with time. Countries like Eritrea, Uganda and South Africa have singled out certain languages for development and use in education, and it remains to be seen how this experiment will fare.

Illiteracy: Illiteracy is a major problem in Africa, and although serious attempts have been made at universal primary education and adult literacy programmes, half of Africa is still illiterate. There are many children of school going age who do not go to school, and adult literacy programmes are not sustained with life-long reading materials. While we appreciate the enormity of the problem, it must be said that African governments, assisted by their international partners, have not done enough to speed up the eradication of illiteracy. In some countries, progress has been painfully slow, and some learners have lapsed into illiteracy. Illiteracy and poverty go together, and one explains the other. It takes on a socio-economic dimension if we realize that tackling illiteracy is one way of fighting poverty.

Poverty: Poverty is to blame for the lack of the infrastructural facilities that militate against reading development, as set out above. Schools are poorly equipped with books: with a pupil ratio averaging 1:10, and have a record of poor book use. School libraries are still a rarity. Elsewhere in the community, libraries are few, and home libraries are unheard of. I believe that until Africa develops a middle class with access to disposable incomes, its publishing industries will continue to lag behind.

Internal Factors

Investment capital: The African publishing industry lacks access to investment capital that can enable it to grow and be strong. It lacks favour with national governments and banking institutions, and has been slow to attract international partners. It is heavily tilted towards curriculum publishing, perceived to be less risky, at the expense of general publishing.

Consequently, key areas such as scholarly publishing, or early childhood and adult education, are mostly ignored. The sometimes poor quality of products is the result of a combination of lack of skills and insufficient investment funds.

Trade and book marketing: African publishers have yet to realize that books are commodities that need to be vigorously promoted in a competitive marketplace. Consequently, they do not put aside sufficient funds for advertising, catalogues, leaflets, and other promotional material. Most do not have publicity departments, and do not mail out information about their new and forthcoming books. As a result their output is not known for the most part, even in their own countries, much less in neighbouring and export markets. The emerging African book fairs, referred to above, will not have much impact until the African publisher learns to approach them with a business mind frame. The same applies to international book fairs, and the increasing number of international bibliographic databases that offer free publicity.

Copyright and piracy: The growth in publishing activity in countries like Kenya, Nigeria, South Africa, Tanzania, and Uganda, has brought with it the spectre of piracy. Fast-selling locally published or imported books are indiscriminately and illegally printed, and offloaded to unsuspecting schools, in a swift and carefully orchestrated racket that is difficult to beat. A majority of African countries have enacted copyright laws and are signatories to international copyright conventions and the WTO. Their enforcement agencies are slowly beginning to appreciate this threat, and are working with publishers and international agencies such as World Intellectual Property Organization/WIPO (➔ **126**) to end this menace. Piracy is a major disincentive to business and, if allowed to continue, can destroy creativity.

THE WAY FORWARD
At this point one might ask, where does the future of African publishing lie? I am convinced the answer lies in partnerships, among the local publishers themselves, and with foreign publishers as well. Partnerships will unlock the resources, the skills, and the market penetration required to reach the vast African market with books in sufficient quantities. Foreign partnerships should come hand in hand with liberalization of the copyright regime to enable the licensing and reprinting, or adapting of key titles published in the North, for Africa. In other words, the buying and selling of rights should be easier in the new dispensation. This approach will increase the quantity and quality of products available in the market in a very short time, and economies of scale will bring prices down. One example is the kind of

partnership James Currey Publishers in the UK has with a number of African publishers in the field of African studies.

Secondly, I believe the future of African publishing lies in translations. This genre has the greatest potential for African publishing, but currently remains largely unutilized. Traditional knowledge, contained in the more than 1,000 African languages needs to be transcribed, translated and the content shared among the African peoples themselves, as well as with outsiders. Likewise, existing materials in foreign languages (and not just English, French and Portuguese) should be translated into African languages as this will enrich and broaden our knowledge base. In this we should borrow a leaf from the mission presses and their translation programmes in Africa.

CONCLUSION

African book development is part and parcel of African development itself, and cannot be seen in isolation. The book does not reside where there is extensive poverty, where people have no access to medical care; where there is inadequate shelter and poor roads, where there is no food. The book thrives where there is a responsive government that provides security, good governance, shies away from graft, and constructively engages its citizenry in nation building—in such an environment it will be possible to develop strategies that can enable government and industry to marshal the resources and manpower needed to take African book development to the next stage.

The African publishing industry still has a long way to realize its potential. Poor leadership has turned the continent into a pawn of the West (and now the East) and it continues to squander its resources on externally driven projects that carry little benefit to its people. Since the publishing technology and all its recent developments come from the North, Africa needs to engage with Northern governments and institutions to create partnerships and agreements that can facilitate the transfer of this technology to the South. Above all, it must take charge of its own destiny, get over its colonial warp, and put its house in order. But, at this point, it is not possible to say that African publishing has come of age.

30 April 2008

Organizations and associations

International and Africa-based organizations

The organizations listed in this section cover international, primarily African-based, regional and pan-African book trade associations, book promotional bodies, writers' and editors' associations, and a number of other book-related organizations.

For *national* organizations and associations see the directory sections preceding each country in ➜ **Section 3, Country studies.** For agencies, foundations, donors, networks, book charities and other organizations supporting the book and information sector in Africa (outside Africa) *see* ➜ **Foundations, donors, networks and other organizations supporting the book sector in Africa** on page 9.

For a complete alphabetical list of all organizations and associations consult the ➜ **Index of organizations and associations**.

1   Africa Book Development (ABD)
BP 727
Yaoundé
Cameroun
Tel: +237-756 3268 (Mobile) Fax: +237-230768
Email: b.kor@iccnet.cm
Secretary General: Buma Kor
President: The Hon. Amougou Noma Nicolas
Note: not verified, organization dormant?

2   African Association of Science Editors (AASE)
c/o Addis Ababa University Research and Publications Office
PO Box 1176
Addis Ababa
Ethiopia
Tel: +251-1-114323/111514 Fax: +251-1-552350
Email: sue@padis.gn.apc.org
Note: not verified, organization dormant?

3   African Books Collective Ltd (ABC)
PO Box 721
Oxford OX1 9EN
UK
Tel/Fax: +44-(0)1869-349110
Email: abc@africanbookscollective.com or
orders@africanbookscollective.com
Web: http://www.africanbookscollective.com
Chair, Council of Management: Walter Bgoya (Tanzania)
Chief Executive Officer: Mary Jay mary.jay@africanbookscollective.com
Directors: Akwe Amosu, David Brooks

4   African Network for Book Development
41 Idimu Road Egbeda
Lagos
Postal address:
PO Box 13168
Ikeja
Lagos
Nigeria
Tel/Fax: +234-1-492 5620
Email: pememe@nova.net.ng
Chair/Executive: Abiodun Ayodele
Secretary: David Audu
Note: not verified, organization dormant?

5   African Publishers Network (APNET)
Plot No. G Block 612
Jonkobiri Street
Laterbiokoshie
Accra
Ghana
Postal address:
PO Box CT 1176
Cantonments
Accra
Ghana
Tel: +233-21-325471 Fax: +233-21-320087
Email: apnettrade@yahoo.com Web: http://www.apnet.org/
Chair: Brian Wafawarowa (South Africa) brian@newafricabooks.co.za/or
bwafa@mweb.co.za
Executive Director: Tainie Mundondo

African Intellectual Property Organisation *see* ➔ **Organisation Africaine de la Propriété Intellectuelle (19)**

6   African Regional Intellectual Property Organisation (ARIPO)
PO Box 4228
Harare
Zimbabwe
Tel: +263-4 -794054/ 794068 Fax: +263-4-794066
Email: mail@aripo.org or aripo@ecoweb.co.zw
Web: http://www.aripo.org/
Director: Gift Sibanda gsibanda@aripo.org
See also ➔ **Organisation Africaine de la Propriété Intellectuelle (OAPI)/ African Intellectual Property Organisation (19)**

7   Afro-Asian Book Council (AABC)
4835/24 Ansari Road
Darya Ganji
New Delhi 110002
India
Tel: +91-11-2325 8865, 23276802 Fax: +91-11-2326 7437
Email: afro@aabcouncil.org
Web: http://www.aabcouncil.org/servlet/acHome
Director: Saumya Gupta sgupta@aabcouncil.org
Secretary General: Sukumar Das sdas@ubspd.com
Executive Secretary: M.L.Ahuja

8   Association d'Éditeurs Francophones d'Afrique Sub-saharienne/ Afrilivres
04 BP 1154
Cotonou
Benin
Tel: + 229-50 30 31 86
Email: afrilivresieg@yahoo.fr
Web: http://www.afrilivres.com (Web site based in France)
Président: Béatrice Lalinon Gbado
See also ➔ **Afrilivres** (France) **(29)**

9   Association Internationale des Libraires Francophones
27 rue Bourgon
75013 Paris
France
Tel: +33-1-44 41 13 24
Email: contact@librairesfrancophones.org
Président: Philippe Goffe

Coordinatrice: Anne Lise Schmitt
Afrique de l'Ouest :
Agnès Adjaho (Immediate past President)
Tel: +229-21 31 40 94 avognes@intnet.bj
Marie-Reine Amouzou
Tel: +228-221 3628 amareine@yahoo.fr
Afrique Centrale:
Chiel Lidjsman
Tel: +250-570298/13-14 ikirezi@rwanda1.com

10   Association Livres d'Afrique/Salon Livres d'Afrique
20 boulevard Beaumarchais
75011 Paris
France
Tel/Fax: n/a
Email: livresdafrique@yahoo.com Web: http://www.livresdafrique.com/
Président: Jean-Paul Mvogo
Chef de projet: Gilles-Aimé Harerimana
Responsable des partenariats: Astrid Lioret

11   Association of Catholic Publishers in Africa
c/o Paulines Publications
PO Box 49026
Nairobi
Kenya
Tel: +254-20-442202 Fax: +254-2-442097
Email: paulines@paulinesafrica.org Web: http://www.paulinesafrica.org/
Secretary: n/a
Note: not verified, organization dormant?

**12   Centre Africain de Formation à l'Edition et à la Diffusion
       (CAFED)**
9 rue Hooker Doolittle
1002 Tunis – Belvedéré
Tunisia
Tel.: +216-71-794955 Fax: +216-11-781 221
Email: cafed@email.ati.tn or capjc@email.ati.tn
Web: http://www.capjc.nat.tn/fr/cafed.asp
Technical Director: Ridha Najar capjc@email.ati.tn

13   East African Book Development Association (EABDA)
Regional Secretariat:
PO Box 6618
Kampala
Uganda
Email: info@eabda.com or ruth@eabda.com Web: http://www.eabda.com/
Office of the Executive Secretary:
East African Book Development Association
c/o PO Box 13422
00800 Nairobi
Kenya
Tel:/Fax: +254-20-444 7815
Email: ruth@nbnet.co.ke
Chair: Henry Chakava
Executive Secretary: Ruth Makotsi

**14   Espace Afrique. Diffusion et Promotion du Livre Africain
         Francophone**
ICC Route de Pré-Bois 20
CP 1801
1215 Geneva 15
Switzerland
Tel: +41-22723 2660 Fax: +41-22 723 2662
Email : info@espace-afrique.ch Web: http://www.espace-afrique.ch/
Bureau Afrique :
Bureau Afrique de l'Espace Afrique Diffusion & Promotion
02 BP 239 Porto-Novo
Benin
Tel : 229-93 80 51 14
Email: fngandu@espace-afrique.ch
Directrice Général: Awa N'Diaye andiaye@espace-afrique.ch
Gestionnaire de projets: Dalila El Mansour del@espace-afrique.ch
Directeur pour l'Afrique: Freddy Ngandu fngandu@espace-afrique.ch

15   Forum of African Medical Editors (FAME)
Communications Unit
Special Programme for Research & Training in Tropical Diseases (TDR)
World Health Organization
1211 Geneva 27
Switzerland
Tel: +41-22-791 3251 Fax: +41-22-791 4854
Email: tdr@who.int
Web: http://www.who.int/tdr/networking/fame/default.htm
Information Officer: Edith Certain certaine@who.int

FAME Secretariat:
Kenya Medical Research Institute (KEMRI)
PO Box 54840
00200 Nairobi
Kenya
Tel +254-20-2722541 Fax +254-20-2720030
Email: director@kemri.org
Web: http://www.kemri.org/
Director: Davy Kiprotich Koech

16   Foundation for the Promotion of Children's Science Publishing in Africa (CHISCI)
PO Box 61301
Nairobi
Kenya
Tel: +254-20-442341/573029 Fax: +254-20-564376/217244
Email: chisci2@excite.com
Head: Mary Bugembe
Note: not verified, organization dormant?

17   Illusafrica. Association Panafricaine d'Illustrateurs
Rue des Fripiers
17 Bloc II/231 Galerie du Centre
1000 Bruxelles
Belgium
Tel. +32-478 938 918 Fax: +32-478 709 128
Email: illusafrica@yahoo.com
President: Dominique Mwankumi

18   Network of Technical Publications in Africa (TEPUSA)
Plot no. 28/186016
Morogoro Road
Dar es Salaam
Postal address:
PO Box 22638
Dar es Salaam
Tanzania
Tel: +255-51-114876 Fax: +255-51-112434
Email: tepusa@intafrica.com
Secretary: Thomas A.D. Massawe [?]
Note: not verified, organization dormant?

19   Organisation Africaine de la Propriété Intellectuelle (OAPI)/ African Intellectual Property Organisation
BP 887
Yaoundé
Cameroon
Tel +237-22 20 57 00/22 20 39 11 Fax: +237-22 20 57 27/22 20 57 21
Email: oapi.oa@oapi.oa.wipo.net
Web: http://www.oapi.wipo.net or http://www.oapi.int
Directeur Général/Director General: Paulin Edou Edou
See also ➔ **African Regional Intellectual Property Organisation (6)**

20   Organization of Women Writers of Africa, Inc.
PO Box 652 Village Station
New York NY 10014
USA
Tel: +1-212-998 2130 Fax: +1-212-995 4109
Email: info@owwa.org Web: http://www.owwa.org/index.html
Board of Directors: Ama Ata Aidoo, Margaret Busby, Jayne Cortez, Alexis
DeVeaux, J.e. Franklin, Paula Giddings, Lorna Goodison, Cheryll Greene,
Rashidah Ismaili, Renee Larrier, Louise Meriwether, Tess Onwueme

21   Pan African Booksellers Association (PABA)
c/o University Bookshop Makerere Ltd
PO Box 488
Kampala
Uganda
Tel: +256-41-543442/3 Fax: +256-41-534973
Email: ctugaineyo@muucsf.org
or:
Pan African Booksellers Association
c/o Moi University Bookshop
PO Box 3900
Eldoret
Kenya
Tel: +254-53-43122 /+254-53-43259 Fax: +254 53 43259
Email: lnyariki@yahoo.com or lnyariki@multitechweb.com
Web: http://www.panafricanbooksellersassociation.org/default.htm
Chair: Lily Nyariki
Honorary Secretary: Catherine Tuganeiyo

22   Pan African Writers' Association (PAWA)/Association Pan Africaine des Écrivains/Jumuia Ya Waandishi Wa Afrika

PAWA House
Roman Road Roman Ridge
Accra
Postal address:
PO Box CT 546 Cantonments
Accra
Ghana
Tel: +233-21-773062/762355 Fax: +233-21-773042
Email: pawa@gmail.com or info@panafricanwritersassociation.org
Web: http://panafricanwritersassociation.org
Secretary General: Atukwei Okai

23   Per Ankh African Publishing Cooperative

Per Ankh Building
Popenguine Village
Postal address:
BP 2
Popenguine
Senegal
Tel: +221-957 7113 Fax: +221-957 7114
Email: perankheditions@arc.sn
Web: http://www.perankh.info/ [site not accessible 30/03/08]
Contacts: Ayi Kwei Armah, Ama Gueye

Foundations, donors, networks, and other organizations supporting the book and information sector in Africa

This is a directory of agencies, foundations, donor organizations, government bodies, NGOs and other organizations, mostly outside Africa, that have supported (and/or are currently supporting) the book and information sector and library development in Africa. This covers areas such as capacity building, textbook development and provision, training for the book professions, support for African writers or writers' groups, as well as agencies that have provided assistance in the field of ICT and scholarly communication, and those that promote public access to information for equitable and sustainable development.

Additionally, there are listings of the major book charities, book and journal assistance or donation programmes, as well as a number of organizations that have been supportive of publishing and book development in Africa by means other than financial assistance (for example through sponsorship of workshops), such as networks of librarians and Africanist library groups, or those that have supported reproduction rights organizations in Africa.

All information, contact details, etc. is current as at February/March 2008.

It should be noted that most of the major donor agencies listed here are *not* grant-making bodies, and do not provide support, grants, etc. outside bilateral programmes either with individual African countries or through NGOs.

Note: for regional and pan-African book promotional bodies and other book-related organizations *see* ➜ **International and Africa-based organizations** on page 1. For national book promotional organizations and associations see the directory sections preceding each country in ➜ **Section 3, Country studies**.

24   Access to Knowledge (A2K) Southern Africa
Open Society Initiative for Southern Africa/OSISA
PO Box 678
Wits, 2050
Johannesburg
South Africa
Tel: +27-11-403 6131 Fax: +27-11-403 1130
Email: Tsakani@cepd.org.za Web: http://www.access.org.za/ [pages not accessible 07/02/08] or http://www.osisa.org/

Contact: Tsakani Chaka
Note: the **"African Access to Knowledge Alliance" (AAKA)** was set up as a result of the African Copyright Forum was held in Kampala, Uganda, from 28-30 November 2005 (ACAIA). In January 2007 the pan-African body of this Alliance was registered as a Trust in Botswana. An Interim Board has been elected, with Thulaganyo Thutoetsile as Interim President.
Interim address:
Southern African Regional Distance Education Centre (SARDEC)
Botswana College of Distance and Open Learning (BOCODOL)
Garamothose Road
Plot number 39972/1
Gaborone
Botswana
Tel: +267-318 1470 Fax +267-319 1089
Email: tmogotsi@bocodol.ac.bw or tthutoetsile@bocodol.ac.bw
Interim President: Thulaganyo Thutoetsile

ACP Secretariat *see* ➔ **The Secretariat of the African, Caribbean and Pacific Group of States/Secrétariat du Groupe des Etats d'Afrique, des Caraïbes et du Pacifique (111)**

25   African Academy of Sciences (AAS)
Miotoni Lane Karen
PO Box 14798
00502 Nairobi
Kenya
(or PO Box 24916, 00502 Nairobi)
Tel: +254-20-884401/884620 Fax: 254-20-884406
Email: aas@aasciences.org Web: http://www.aasciences.org/
President: Mohamed H. A. Hassan
Secretary General: Shem Arungu Olende
Acting Executive Director: I. Kone i.kone@afornet.org

26   Africana Librarians Council (ALC)
c/o Miriam Conteh-Morgan, Secretary, ALC
African Studies Librarian
Ohio State University Libraries
1858 Neil Avenue Mall
Columbus OH 43210-1286
USA
Tel: +1-614-688 8776 Fax: +1-614-292 7859
Email: conteh-morgan.2@osu.edu
Web: http://www.loc.gov/rr/amed/afs/alc/
Chair (2007-2008): Peter Limb, Africana Bibliographer & Adjunct Associate

Professor, History Dept., Michigan State University, 100 Library (Room E224B), Michigan State University Libraries, East Lansing MI 48824-1048 USA, limb@msu.edu
Secretary (2007-2008): Miriam Conteh-Morgan (address as above)

27   African Council for Communication Education (ACCE)
University of Nairobi
Education Building 3rd Floor
PO Box 47495
Nairobi
Kenya
Tel: +254-20-215270/227043 Fax: +254-20-216135
Email: acce@wananchi.com Web: http://www.africancouncilcomed.org/
President: Ikechukwu Nwosu
Executive Secretary: Wilson Ugangu

28   African Journals Online (AJOL)
19 Worcester Street
PO Box 377
Grahamstown 6140
South Africa
Tel: +27-46-622 9698 Fax: +27-46-622 9550
Email: info@ajol.info Web: http://www.ajol.info/
Contact: Margaret Crampton

African Publishing Initiative *see* ➜ **The World Bank. Office of the Publisher (125)**

29   Afrilivres. Association d'Éditeurs Francophones d'Afrique Sub-saharienne
c/o Africultures
Les Pilles
26110 Nyon
France
Tel: +33-4 -75 27 74 80
Email: redac@africultures.com Web: http://www.afrilivres.com/
Head, Coordination North: Olivier Barlet olivier-barlet@africultures.com
Coordination Africa:
c/o Editions Ruisseaux d'Afrique
04 BP 1154
Cotonou
Benin
Tel: +229-383186/947925
Email: ruisseau@mail.leland.bj

Agence Canadienne de Développement International *see* → Canadian International Development Agency (46)

Agence de Coopération Culturelle et Technique (ACCT) superseded by → Organisation Internationale de la Francophonie (101)

30   Agence de Médiation Culturelle des Pays du Sahel
5 Centre Pierre Mendès France
33165 Saint Médard en Jalles
France
Tel/Fax: +33-5-56 95 74 09
Email: mediation.culturelle@wanadoo.fr
Web: http://www.mediation-culturelle.net/
Directrice Général: (Mme) Safiatou Faure

Agence Intergouvernementale de la Francophonie/AIF
see → Organisation Internationale de la Francophonie (101)

**31   Alliance des Éditeurs Independents pour une Autre
       Mondalisation/Alliance of Independent Publishers for Another
       Globalization**
38 rue Saint Sabin
75011 Paris
France
Tel: +33-1-43 14 73 66 Fax: +33-1-43 14 73 63
Email: egalliand@alliance-editeurs.org
Web: http://www.alliance-editeurs.org/
Director: Etienne Galliand
Co-publications and Communication Manager: Alexandre Tiphagne

32   Alliance Française
101 boulevard Raspail
75270 Paris Cedex
France
Tel: +33-1-42 84 90 00 Fax: +33-1-42 84 91 00
Email: info@alliancefr.org
Web: http://www.alliancefr.org/sommaire.php3?lang=fr (French version)
Web: http://www.alliancefr.org (English version)
Sécrétaire Général: Jean-Claude Jacq
Note: for Alliance Française offices and contact details in Africa *see*
http://www.alliancefr.org/rubrique.php3?id_rubrique=231

Les Amis de la Joie par les Livres *see* ➔ La Joie par les Livres. Centre National du Livre pour Enfants (86)

Association d'Éditeurs Francophones d'Afrique Sub-saharienne *see* ➔ Afrilivres (29) (and entry ➔ 7)

33   Association for Progressive Communications (APC)
PO Box 29755
Melville 2109
South Africa
Tel: +27-11-726 1692 Fax: +27-11-726 1692
Email: info@apc.org Web: http://www.apc.org/en/home (English)
http://www.apc.org/fr (French)
Executive Director: Anriette Esterhuysen
Communications & Information Policy Programme Manager: Willie Currie

34   Association for the Development of African Education/
        L'association pour le Développement de l'Éducation en Afrique
        (ADEA)
7-9 rue Eugène-Delacroix
75116 Paris
France
Tel: +33-1-45 03 77 57 Fax: +33-1-45 03 39 65
Email: adea@iiep.unesco.org Web: http://www.ADEAnet.org
Executive Secretary: Mamadou Ndoye
Note: for contacts of various Working Groups *see*
http://www.adeanet.org/workgroups/en_workgroups.html
See also entry ➔ 35 below

35   Association for the Development of Education in Africa.
        ADEA Working Group on Books and Learning Materials
Carew Treffgarne, ADEA Working Group Leader
Department for International Development (DFID)
1 Palace Street
London SW1E 5HE
UK
Tel: +44-(0)20-7023 0658 Fax: + 44-(0)20-7023 0287
Email: c-treffgarne@dfid.gov.uk
Web: http://www.adeanet.org/workgroups/en_wgblm.html
Working Group Leader: Carew Treffgarne

36   Association pour la Diffusion de la Pensée Française (ADPF)
Ministère des Affaires Etrangères
6 rue Ferrus
75683 Paris Cedex 14
France
Tel: +33-1-43 13 11 00 Fax: +33-1-43 13 11 25
Email: ecrire@adpf.asso.fr Web: http://www.adpf.asso.fr/ (Main home
page) or http://www.adpf.asso.fr/afrique-en-creation/afrique-en-creations-
par-disciplines/po16.html (Afrique en création pages, Livre et écrit)
Président: François Neuville
Secrétaire-Général: Nicole Lamarque

Baobab Children's Book Fund *see* ➜ **Kinderbuch Fonds Baobab (88)**

37   Bellagio Publishing Network Secretariat
PO Box 1369
Oxford OX4 4ZR
UK
Tel/Fax: +44-(0)1865-250024
Email: bellagio@bellagiopublishingnetwork.com
Web: http://www.bellagiopublishingnetwork.com/ (previously at
http://www.bellagiopublishingnetwork.org)
Coordinator: Katherine Salahi ks@bellagiopublishingnetwork.com
Note: this Network is currently dormant, although the Web site and the
archives of the ➜ **Bellagio Publishing Network Newsletter (155)** is still
accessible.

38   Book Aid International (BAI)
39-41 Coldharbour Lane
Camberwell
London SE5 9NR
UK
Tel: +44-(0)20-7733 3577 Fax: +44-(0)20-7978 8006
Email: info@bookaid.org Web: http://www.bookaid.org
Director: Clive Nettleton
Head of Operations: Rob Sarjant

39   Book Link
64 Elgin Crescent
London W11 2JJ
UK
Tel: +44-(0)20-7727 3129 Fax: +44-(0)20-7727 1416
Email: booklink@irbeard.net Web: http://www.booklinkweb.co.uk/
Director: Irene Beard

40   BookPower
120 Pentonville Road
London
N1 9JN
Tel: +44-(0)20-7843 1938 Fax: +44-(0)20-7837 6348
Email: BookPower@mistral.co.uk Web: http://www.bookpower.org/
Chair, Board of Trustees: Seymour Fortescue
Head of Administration: Valerie Teague

41   Books Abroad
Unit 1
Richmond Avenue Industrial Estate
Rhynie
Huntly AB54 4HJ
Scotland
UK
Tel/Fax: +44-(0)1464-861446
Email: booksabroad@aol.com Web: http://www.booksabroad.org.uk/
Founder: Keith Brunskill
Chair: Steve Read

42   Books for Africa
253 East 4th Street Suite 200
Saint Paul, MN 55101
USA
Tel: +1-651-602 9844 Fax: +1-651-602 9848
Email: bfa@booksforafrica.org Web: http://www.booksforafrica.org/
Founder: Thomas Warth
Board President: Michael Henley
Executive Director: Patrick Plonski

43   The British Council
Headquarters:
10 Spring Gardens
London SW1A 2BN
UK
Tel: +44-(0)20-7930 8466 Fax +44-(0)20-7839 6347
British Council Information Centre: Tel: +44-(0)161-957 7755
Fax: +44 (0)161-957 7762
Development Services Headquarters:
The British Council
Bridgewater House
58 Whitworth Street
Manchester M1 6BB

UK
Tel: +44-(0)161-957 7000 Fax: +44-(0)161-957 7111
Email: general.enquiries@britishcouncil.org (General enquiries, in UK)
developmentservices@britishcouncil.org (Development Services)
Web: http://www.britishcouncil.org (Main home page)
http://www.britishcouncil.org/development.htm (Development Services pages)
Chief Executive: Martin Davidson
Director, Africa and Asia: Cathy Stephens
Director Development Services: Mike Hardy
Regional Information Co-ordinator, Sub-Saharan Africa (Manchester-based): Chaudhry Javed Iqbal
Note: for British Council offices in Africa and worldwide, including full contact information, *see* http://www.britishcouncil.org/home-contact-worldwide.htm

44   Brother's Brother Foundation
1200 Galveston Avenue
Pittsburgh PA 15233
USA
Tel: +1-412-321 3160 Fax: +1-412-321 3325
Email: mail@brothersbrother.org Web: http://www.brothersbrother.org/
President: Luke Hingson
Vice President Development/Administration: Karen Dempsey

45   Bureau International de l'Édition Française (BIEF)
        (formerly France Edition)
Office de Promotion Internationale
115 boulevard Saint Germain
75006 Paris
France
Tel: +33-1-44 41 13 13 Fax: +33-1-46 34 63 83
Email: accueil_bief@bief.org Web: http://franceedition.org
Directeur Général: Jean-Guy Boin
Formation et échanges professionnels: Pierre Myszkowski
Communication, publications: Catherine Fel
Etudes: Karen Politis k.politis@bief.org

46   Canadian International Development Agency (CIDA)/Agence
        Canadienne de Développement International (ACDI)
200 Promenade du Portag
Hull QC K1A 0G4
Canada
Tel: +1-819-997 5006 Toll free (US and Canada only) 800-230 6349

Fax: +1-819-953 6088
Email: info@acdi-cida.gc.ca Web: http://www.acdi-cida.gc.ca/home (Main
home page, English)
http://www.acdi-cida.gc.ca/cidaweb/acdicida.nsf/Fr/Accueil (Home
page, French)
http://www.acdi-cida.gc.ca/cidaweb/acdicida.nsf/En/NIC-5595719-JDD
(Sub-Saharan Africa pages/index)
Vice President, Africa Branch: Paul Hunt
Director General, West and Central Africa: Barbara Brown
Director General, East, the Horn and Southern Africa: Diane Jacovella
Director, Pan African Program: Louise Clément
Senior Development Officer: Diana Chaplin

47   Carnegie Corporation of New York
437 Madison Avenue
New York NY 10022
USA
Tel: +1-212-371 3200 Fax: +1-212-754 4073
Email: n/a (Telephone and mail communications accepted only)
Web: http://www.carnegie.org (Main home page)
http://www.carnegie.org/sub/program/intl_development.html
(International Development Program)
Program Chair, African Higher Education: Claudia Frittelli
Program Officer, International Development (and Manager African Libraries
Project): Rookaya Bawa

Centre Technique de Coopération Agricole et Rurale ACP-UE (CTA)
→ *see* **Technical Centre for Agricultural and Rural Cooperation ACP-EU
(116)**

48   CODE (Canadian Organization for Development through
        Education)
321 Chapel Street
Ottawa ON K1N 7Z2
Canada
Tel: +1-613-232 3569 Toll free (USA and Canada only) 800-661 2633
Fax: +1-613-232 7435
Email: codehq@codecan.org
Web: http://www.codecan.org/english/index.html (English)
http://www.codecan.org/francais/index.html (French)
Chair: Christopher Bredt
Executive Director: Scott Walter
See also → **International Book Bank (70)**

49   The Commonwealth Foundation
Marlborough House
Pall Mall
London SW1Y 5HY
UK
Tel: +44-(0)20-7930 3783 Fax: +44-(0)20-7839 8157
Email: geninfo@commonwealth.int
Web: http://www.commonwealthfoundation.com/
Director: Mark Collins
Programme Manager, Culture and Diversity: Andrew Firmin

50   Commonwealth of Learning (COL)
1055 West Hastings Street   Suite 1200
Vancouver BC V6E 2E9
Canada
Tel: +1-604-775 8200 Fax: +1-604-775.8210
Email: info@col.org Web: http://www.col.org
President and Chief Executive Officer: Sir John Daniel
Director, Knowledge Management & Information Technology: Paul G. West
Learning Manager, International Organizations: Angela Kwan

51   Commonwealth Secretariat
Governance and Institutional Development Division-Africa Section
Marlborough House
Pall Mall
London SW1Y 5HX
UK
Tel: +44-(0)20-7747 6500
Fax: +44-(0)20-7930 0827
Email: info@commonwealth.int (Media and Public Affairs Enquiries)
Web: http://www.thecommonwealth.org/
Secretary General: Rt Hon Donald C McKinnon
Director of Governance and Institutional Affairs Division: Jacqueline Wilson
j.wilson@commonwealth.int
Media & Public Affairs Enquiries, Africa: J. Mucunguzi
j.mucunguzi@commonwealth.int

52   Coopération par l'Éducation et la Culture (CEC)
18 rue Joseph II
1000 Brussels
Belgium
Tel: +32-2-217 9071 Fax: +32-2-217 8402
Email: info@cec-ong.org or cec-ong@yucom.be

Web: http://www.cec-ong.org/
Administratrice Déléguée/Chief Executive: Ann Gerrard
Coordination générale: Dominique Gillerot

53   Copy South Research Group
[no physical address available at this time]
Email: contact@copysouth.org
Web: http://www.copysouth.org/

54   Culture et Développment (C&D)
9 rue de la Poste
38000 Grenoble
France
Tel: +33-4-76 46 80 29 Fax: +33-4 76 46 06 05
Email: nord.sud@culture-developpement.asso.fr
Web: http://www.culture-developpement.asso.fr/site/index.php
Président: Etienne Féau
Chargée de mission Livre/Lecture: Céline Ducroux

55   Dag Hammarskjöld Foundation
Övre Slottsgatan 2
75310 Uppsala
Sweden
Tel: +46-18-102772 Fax: +46-18-122072
Email: secretariat@dhf.uu.se Web: http://www.dhf.uu.se
Executive Director: Henning Melber
Associate Director: Niclas Hällström

56   Danish International Development Assistance (DANIDA)
Ministry of Foreign Affairs
Asiatisk Plads 2
1448 Copenhagen K
Denmark
Tel: +45-33-920000 Fax: +45-33-540533
Email: um@um.dk Web: http://www.um.dk/da/menu/Udviklingspolitik/
(Main home page) http://www.um.dk/en (Home page, English version)
http://www.um.dk/en/menu/DevelopmentPolicy/DanishDevelopmentP
olicy/DanishDevelopmentPolicy (Danish Development Policy)
Head of Communications & Information: Eva Egesborg Hansen
Head of Secretariat/Information Officer: Lisbeth Rubinstein

57   Department for International Development (DIFD)
1 Palace Street
London SW1E 5HE
UK
Tel: +44-(0)20-7023 0000 (Main switchboard) Fax: +44 (0)20-7023 0019
Tel: +44-(0)-1355-843132 (Public enquiry points from outside the UK)
Fax: +44-(0)-1355-843632
Email: enquiry@dfid.gov.uk Web: http://www.dfid.gov.uk
Director, East & Central Africa Division: Dave Fish
Director, West & Southern Africa: Beverley Warmington
Senior Education Advisor: Carew Treffgarne (*see also* entry ➔ 35)
Note: for Country Profiles-Africa, and full contact information for DFID
offices in Africa, *see* http://www.dfid.gov.uk/countries/africa/

**Deutsche Stiftung für Internationale Entwicklung/German Foundation for
International Development** *see* ➔ **InWEnt – Internationale Weiterbildung
und Entwicklung gGmbH. Capacity Building International (85)**

58   Electronic Information for Libraries/eIFL.net
c/o ADN Kronos
Piazza Mastai 9
00153 Rome
Italy
Tel: +39-6-5807216/17 Fax: + 39-6-5807246
Email: info@eifl.net Web: http://www.eifl.net/cps/sections/home
Chair, Advisory Board: Johanna Sander
Director: Rima Kupryte

59   Electronic Publishing Trust for Development
Wilmots
Elmton
Worksop S80 4LS
UK
Tel: +44-(0)1909-724184 Fax: +44-(0)1909-724190
Email: ept@biostrat.demon.co.uk Web: http://www.epublishingtrust.org
Chair, Board of Trustees: Judy Ugonna
Secretary: Barbara Kirsop

**60   Electronic Supply of Academic Publications to and from
         Developing Regions (ESAP)**
c/o International Federation of Catholic Universities (IFCU/FIUC)
21 Rue d'Assas
75270 Paris
France

Tel. +33-1-44 39 52 26 Fax +33-1-44 39 52 28
Email: e.simons@icarin.fiuc.org
Web: http://www.fiuc.org/esap/index2.php?page=esaphome
General Manager: Ed J. Simons

Finnish Ministry of Foreign Affairs *see* ➜ **Utrikesministeriet/Finnish Ministry of Foreign Affairs (122)**

61   Fondation Charles Léopold Mayer
Executive Office:
38 rue Saint Sabin
75011 Paris
France
Tel: +33-1-43 14 75 75 Fax: +33-1-43 14 75 99
Email: paris@fph.fr
Headquarters and Swiss office:
Chemin de Longeraie 9
1006 Lausanne
Switzerland
Tel: +41-21-342 5010 Fax: +41-21-342 5011
Email: lausanne@fph.ch Web: http://www.fph.ch/
Directeur général: Pierre Calame

62   The Ford Foundation
320 East 43rd Street
New York NY 10017
USA
Tel: +1-212-573 5000 Fax: +1-212-351 3677
Email: office-communications@fordfound.org
Web: http://www.fordfound.org (Main home page)
http://www.fordfound.org/program/education.cfm (Knowledge, Creativity and Freedom program; includes Media, Arts and Culture)
Director, Community and Resource Development unit: Suzanne Siskel
Director, Education, Sexuality, Religion unit: Janice Petrovich
Director, Media, Arts and Culture unit: Margaret B. Wilkerson
(for Directors of other units see Web site)
Ford Foundation Offices in Sub-Saharan Africa:
Ford Foundation, Southern Africa
PO Box 30953
Braamfontein 2017
Johannesburg
South Africa
Tel: +27-11-276 1200 Fax +27-11-276-1248
Email: ford-johannesburg@fordfound.org

Web:
http://www.fordfound.org/global/office/index.cfm?office=Johannesburg
Representative: Alice L. Brown
Ford Foundation, East Africa
PO Box 41081
00100 Nairobi
Kenya
Tel: +254-20-271 0444 Fax: +254-20-271 2203
Email: ford-nairobi@fordfound.org
http://www.fordfound.org/global/office/index.cfm?office=Nairobi
Representative: Omotade Aina
Ford Foundation, West Africa
PO Box 2368
Lagos
Nigeria
Tel. +234-1-773 8926 Fax: +234-1-262 3973
Email: ford-lagos@fordfound.org
Web: http://www.fordfound.org/global/office/index.cfm?office=Lagos
Representative: Adhiambo P. Odaga
See also **Trust Africa** ➔ **117**

France Edition *see* ➔ **Bureau International de l'Édition Française/BIEF (45)**

Frankfurt Book Fair *see* ➔ **Gesellschaft zur Förderung der Literatur aus Afrika, Asien, und Latinamerika e.V./Society for the Promotion of African, Asian and Latin American Literatures (64)**

63   Bill & Melinda Gates Foundation
PO Box 23350
Seattle WA 98102
USA
Tel: +1-206-709 3100 Fax: +1-206-709 3280
Email: info@gatesfoundation.org (General or grant enquiries)
libraryinfo@gatesfoundation.org (Library programs)
Web: http://www.gatesfoundation.org/
Co-founders: William (Bill) H. Gates III; Melinda French Gates
Chief Executive Officer: Patty Stonesifer
Chief Operating Officer: Cheryl Scott
President, Global Development Program (including Global Libraries Program): Sylvia Mathews Burwell
Director, Global Libraries Program: Martha Choe

64   Gesellschaft zur Förderung der Literatur aus Afrika, Asien, und Latinamerika e.V./Society for the Promotion of African, Asian and Latin American Literatures
Reineckstrasse 3
PO Box 10 01 16
60001 Frankfurt am Main
Germany
Tel: +49-69-210 2247 Fax: +49-69-210 2227
Email: litprom@book-fair.com or www.litprom.de
Web: http://www.litprom.de
Chair: Peter Weidhaas
Contact for Africa: Corry von Mayenburg mayenburg@book-fair.com

65   Goethe Institut
Dachauer Strasse 122
Postfach 19 04 19
80604 Munich
Germany
Tel: +49-89-159210 Fax: +49-89-1592 1450
Email: info@goethe.de Web: http://www.goethe.de (German version)
http://www.goethe.de/enindex.htm (English version)
Generalsekretär/Secretary General: Hans-Georg Knopp
For departmental and sectional contacts *see*
http://www.goethe.de/uun/adr/zen/prt/deindex.htm;
Note: for Goethe Institutes worldwide, including those in Africa, with full contact information, *see* http://www.goethe.de/ins/wwt/sta/enindex.htm

66   Heinrich Böll Stiftung/Heinrich Böll Foundation
Rosenthaler Strasse 40/41
10178 Berlin
Germany
Tel: +49-30-285340 Fax: +49-+30-285 34109
Email: info@boell.de Web: http://www.boell.de
Leitung Afrika-Referat/Africa Desk: Kirsten Maas-Albert
Note: For names of African regional offices and project coordinators *see*
http://www.boell.de/de/05_world/221.html

67   Humanistisch Instituut voor Ontwikkelingssamenwerking (HIVOS)
Raamweg 16
PO Box 85565
2508 CG The Hague
Netherlands
Tel: +31-70-376 5500 Fax: +31-70-362 4600

Email: info@hivos.nl Web: http://www.hivos.nl/english/index.html
(Home page, English version)
http://www.hivos.nl/english/partners/search?country=afrika (Partner
pages, Africa)
Executive Director: Manuela Monteiro
Head of Bureau — ICT, Culture and Media: Loe Schout

68   International African Institute/Institut Africain International
c/o School of Oriental and African Studies
Thornhaugh Street
Russell Square
London WC1H 0XG
UK
Tel: +44-(0)20-7898 4420 Fax: +44-(0)20-7898 4419
Email: iai@soas.ac.uk (General enquiries) sk111@soas.ac.uk (Publications)
Web: http://www.internationalafricaninstitute.org/
Chair: Prof .Y. Mudimbe
Hon. Director: Prof. Philip Burnham
Chair, Publications Committee: Stephanie Kitchen

69   International Association for Digital Publications (IADP).
       IADP - South Africa
South African Institute for Distance Education
PO Box 31822
Braamfontein 2017
South Africa
Tel: +27-11-403 2813
Email: katek@saide.org.za Web: http://www.iadpnet.org/
President: Angus Scrimgeour
Executive Officer: Tazeen Hasan-Granier
Head, IADP South Africa: Jenny Louw jennyl@saide.org.za

70   International Book Bank
PO Box 1662
Baltimore MD 21203
USA
Tel: +1-410-685 2665 Fax: +1-410-362 0336
Email: info@internationalbookbank.org
Web: http://www.internationalbookbank.org
Executive Director: Valerie Staats
Note: affiliated with ➜ **Code** *see* entry **48**

71   International Board on Books for Young People (IBBY)
Nonnenweg 12
Postfach
4003 Basle
Switzerland
Tel: +4-61-272 2917 Fax +41-61-272 2757
Email: ibby@ibby.org
Web: http://www.ibby.org/ (Home page)
http://www.ibby.org/index.php?id=552&L=0 (Books for Africa/Books
from Africa pages)
President: Patricia Aldana paldana@groundwoodbooks.com
Director Member Services, Communications and New Projects: Liz Page
liz.page@ibby.org
Note: for address details and contacts for IBBY African sections (Ghana,
South Africa, and Uganda), see the directories preceding country sections in
→ **Section 3, Country studies.**

72   International Development Research Center (IDRC)
150 Kent Street
PO Box 8500
Ottawa ON K1G 3H9
Canada
Tel: +1-613-236 6163 Fax: +1-613-238 7230
Email: info@idrc.ca Web: http://www.idrc.ca/
President: Maureen O'Neill
(for names of Directors of Regional Offices in Africa see below)
IDRC offices in Sub-Saharan Africa:
IDRC Regional Office for Eastern and Southern Africa
PO Box 62084
00200 Nairobi
Kenya
Tel: +254-20-271 3160/61 Fax: +254+20-271 1063
Email: vngugi@idrc.or.ke Web: www.idrc.ca/esaro
Director, Regional Office for Eastern and Southern Africa:
Constance Freeman
IDRC Regional Office for West and Central Africa
BP 11007
Peytavin
Dakar
Senegal
Tel: +221-864 0000, ext. 2074 Fax: +221-825 3255
Email: jgerard@idrc.org.sn Web: www.idrc.ca/braco
Director, Regional Office for West and Central Africa (Dakar): Gilles Forget

73   International Education Partners
Barley Mow Centre
10 Barley Mow Passage
London W4 4PH
UK
Tel: +44-(0)20-8996 1766
Email: enquiries@iepartners.co.uk Web: http://www.iepartners.co.uk/
Executive Director: Andy Smart

**74   International Federation of Library Associations and Institutions
        (IFLA)**
PO Box 95312
2509 CH The Hague
Netherlands
Tel. +31-70-314 0884 Fax +31-70-383 4827
Email: IFLA@ifla.org Web: http://www.ifla.org/index.htm
President (2007-2009): Claudia Lux
President-Elect (President 2009-2011): Ellen Tise
Secretary General: Peter J. Lor
See also entries ➜ **75** and ➜ **76** below

**75   International Federation of Library Associations and Institutions.
        Action for Development through Libraries Programme Core
        Activity (ALP)** (formerly IFLA Core Programme for the
        Advancement of Librarianship in the Third World)
c/o Uppsala University Library
Box 510
75120 Uppsala
Sweden
Tel: +46-18-471 3990 Fax: +48-18-471 3994
Email: IFLA.ALP@ub.uu.se or gunilla.natvig@ub.uu.se
Web: http://www.ifla.org/VI/1/alp.htm
Programme Director: Birgitta Sandell
Administrative Officer: Gunilla Natvig

**76   International Federation of Library Associations and Institutions.
        Africa Regional Section**
Chair/Treasurer:
Helena R. Asamoah-Hassan, University Librarian
Kwame Nkrumah University of Science and Technology
KNUST Library
Kumasi
Ghana

Tel: +233-51-60133 Fax +233-51-60358
Email: maadwoa2000@yahoo.com
Secretary:
Buhle Mbambo, Executive Director
UNISA Library Services
PO Box 392
Pretoria 0003
South Africa
Tel: +27-12-429 3131/429 3844
Fax +27-12-429 2925
Email: mbambtb@unisa.ac.za
Web: http://www.ifla.org/VII/s25/index.htm#Newsletter
Note: the above Web pages include Africa Regional Section details, strategic
plan, projects, conferences and workshops, and access to the Africa Regional
Section online Newsletter.

**77   International Federation of Reproduction Rights Organisations
(IFRRO)**
Rue du Prince Royal 87
1050 Brussels
Belgium
Tel: +32-2-551 0899 Fax: +32-2-551 0895
Email: secretariat@ifrro.org Web: http://www.ifrro.org/ (Main home page)
http://www.ifrro.org/show.aspx?pageid=activities/regionaldev/africa&cu
lture=en (IFRRO Development Committee for Africa and the Middle East
pages)
Chief Executive and Secretary General: Olav Stokkmo
olav.stokkmo@ifrro.org
Communications and Information Officer: (Ms) Wiebke Dalhoff
wiebke.dalhoff@ifrro.org
Office Administrator: Céline Rafalowicz
See also ➜ **Kopinor 89**

78   International Institute for Educational Planning (IIEP)
7-9 rue Eugène-Delacroix
75116 Paris
France
Tel: +33-1-45 03 77 00 Fax: +33-1-40 72 83 66
Email: info@iiep.unesco.org Web: http://www.unesco.org/iiep/
Director: Mark Bray
IIEP Administrator: Papa Malick Gaye pm.gaye@iiep.unesco.org
Head of Field Activities: Khalil Mahshi k.mahshi@iiep.unesco.org
Head of Higher Education Programmes: N.V. Varghese
nv.varghese@iiep.unesco.org

Head of Training: David Atchoarena d.atchoarena@iiep.unesco.org
Head of Documentation Centre: Asunción Valderrama
a.valderrama@iiep.unesco.org
See also ➔ **Association for the Development of African Education/**
L'association pour le Développement de l'Éducation en Afrique
/ADEA (34)

79   International Law Book Facility
DX 149121 Canary Wharf 3
10 Upper Bank Street
London E14 5JJ
UK
Tel: n/a
Email: info@ILBF.org.uk
Web: http://www.ilbf.org.uk/
Chair, Board of Trustees: Rt. Hon. Lord Justice John Thomas
Chair, Operating Committee: Paul Lowenstein

80   International Library and Information Group of the Chartered
        Institute of Library and Information Professionals
CILIP
7 Ridgmount Street
London WC1E 7AE
UK
Email: see ILIG Secretary below
Web:
http://www.cilip.org.uk/specialinterestgroups/bysubject/international
Chair: Hazel Dakers
ILIG Secretary: Diana Rosenberg ilig@cilip.org.uk
Membership Secretary & ILIG Treasurer: Kathleen Ladizesky
ladizesky@yahoo.com (Postal address: Glantrisant, Trisant, Aberystwyth,
Ceredigion SY23 4RL, Wales, UK)

81   International Network for the Availability of Scientific
        Publications (INASP)
60 St. Aldates
Oxford OX1 1WG
UK
Tel: +44-(0)1865-249909 Fax: +44-(0)1865-251060
Email: inasp@inasp.info Web: http://www.inasp.info
Executive Director: Tag McEntegart tmcentegart@inasp.info
Director, Programmes: Sara Gwynn sgwynn@inasp.info
Head of Information Delivery: Lucy Browse lbrowse@inasp.info
Head of Library Development: Peter Burnett pburnett@inasp.info

Head of Publishing Support: Julie Walker jwalker@inasp.info
Head of Training: Martin Belcher mbelcher@inasp.info

82   International Publishers Association (IPA)

3 avenue de Miremont
1206 Geneva
Switzerland
Tel : +41-22-346 3018 Fax : +41-22-347 5717
Email : secretariat@internationalpublishers.org
Web: http://www.internationalpublishers.org/
President: (Ms)Ana Maria Cabanellas
cabanellas@internationalpublishers.org
Secretary General: Jens Bammel bammel@internationalpublishers.org
Director, Freedom to Publish: Alexis Krikorian
krikorian@internationalpublishers.org

83   International Reading Association

800 Barksdale Road
PO Box 8139
Newark DE 19714-8139
USA
Tel. 1-800-336-READ/1-800-336-7323 (US & Canada only),
+1-+302-731 1600 elsewhere Fax: +302-731-1057
Email: pubinfo@reading.org (Public Information Office)
customerservice@reading.org (Member and Customer Service Department)
Web: http://www.reading.org/
President: (from June 2008) Barbara J. Walker (Oklahoma State University)
bwalker@reading.org
Executive Director: Alan E. Farstrup afarstrup@reading.org
Chair, International Reading Association-International Development in Africa
Committee:
Samuel Andema
Kyambogo University
Languages and Literature Department
PO Box 1
Kyambogo
Kampala
Uganda
Tel: +256-77-251 165 Email: andemasam@yahoo.co.uk

84   International Trade Centre (UNCTAD/WTO)

54-56 rue de Montbrillant
Palais des Nations
1211 Geneva 10

Switzerland
Tel: +41-22-730 0111 Fax: +41-22-733 4439
Email: itcreg@intracen.org Web: http://www.intracen.org/
Executive Director: Patricia Fisher
Director of Technical Cooperation Coordination: Siphana Sok
Director of Trade Support Services: (Ms) Aichatou Pouye
Director of Programme Support: Eva K. Murray
Chief, Office for Africa, Division of Technical Cooperation: Magdi Farahat

85   **InWEnt – Internationale Weiterbildung und Entwicklung gGmbH. Capacity Building International** (formerly Deutsche Stiftung für Internationale Entwicklung/German Foundation for International Development)
Friedrich-Ebert-Allee 40
53113 Bonn
Germany
Tel: +49-228-4460 0 Fax: +49-228-4460 1766
Email: info@inwent.org or use email enquiry form on Web site
Web: http://www.inwent.org/
Chief Executive: Ulrich Popp
Soziale Entwicklung, Beauftragte für Afrika: Carola Donner-Reichle
Bildung/Education: Ingrid Jung
Note: for other contacts see the Organigram pdf file on the Web site.

86   **La Joie par les Livres. Centre National du Livre pour Enfants**
25 boulevard de Strasbourg
75010 Paris
France
Tel: +33-1-55 33 44 44 Fax: +33-1-55 33 44 55
Email: contact@lajoieparleslivres.com or
interculturels@lajoieparleslivres.com
Web: http://www.lajoieparleslivres.com
Directeur: Jacques Vidal-Naquet
Directeur Adjoint: Olivier Piffault
Other contacts (Editors, *Takam Tikou*): Viviana Quiñones
viviana.quinones@lajoieparleslivres.com, Hasmig Chahinian
hasmig.chahinian@lajoieparleslivres.com

87   **Journal Donation Project**
The New School for Social Research
65 Fifth Avenue
New York NY 10003
USA

Tel: +212-229-5789 Fax: 212.229.5476
Email: jdp@newschool.edu
Web: http://www.newschool.edu/centers/jdp/
Founder & Director: Arien Mack
Program Managers: Tracey McPeake, Beatrice Wainaina

88   Kinderbuch Fonds Baobab/Baobab Children's Book Fund
Dornacherstrasse 192
4053 Basle
Switzerland
Tel: +41-61-333 2727 Fax: +41-61-333 2726
Email: info@baobabbooks.ch
Web: http://www.baobabbooks.ch/
Director: Sonja Matheson

89   Kopinor. The Reproduction Rights Organisation of Norway
Stenersgata 1A
0050 Oslo
Norway
Tel: +47-22-179417 Fax: +47-22-179422
Email: kopinor@kopinor.no Web: http://www.kopinor.no/
Chair: Helge Rønning
Executive Director: Yngve Slettholm

90   Librarians Without Borders (LWB)
PO Box 47015 UCC Postal Outlet
1151 Richmond Street North
London ON N6G 6G6
Canada
Fax: +1-519-6613506 (mark for attn. LWB)
Email: info@lwb-online.org
Web: http://www.lwb-online.org/index.html
Co-Executive Directors: Rebecca Jansen, Catherine Baird
Secretary: Sandra Hodgson secretary@lwb-online.org

91   Link. A Network for North-South Library Development
64 Ennersdale Road
London SE13 6JD
UK
Tel: +44-(0)20-8318 5186
Email: gillianharris@btinternet.com Web: n/a
Contact: Gillian Harris

92   The Andrew W. Mellon Foundation
140 East 62nd Street
New York NY 10021
USA
Tel: +1-212-838 8400 Fax: +1-212-500 2302
Email: inquiries@mellon.org Web: http://www.mellon.org/
President: Don Michael Randel
General Counsel and Secretary: Michele S. Warman
Program Officer, Scholarly Communications: Donald J. Waters
djw@mellon.org
Vice President for Research in Information Technology: Ira H. Fuchs
ihf@mellon.org
Note: for other programme areas see Web site.

**93   Ministère de la Culture et de la Communication. Direction du
         Livre et de la Lecture. Mission Européenne et Internationale**
182 rue Saint-Honoré
75033 Paris Cedex 01
France
Tel: +33-1-40 15 73 32/40 15 73 44 Fax: +33-1-40 15 74 04
Email: info.dll@culture.gouv.fr Web:
http://www.culture.gouv.fr/culture/dll/misinter.htm
Directeur adjoint: Marc-André Wagner
Mission européenne et internationale, Chargé de mission:
Corinne de Munain corinne.de-munain@culture.gouv.fr

**94   Ministère des Affaires Étrangères. Direction Générale de la
         Coopération Internationale et du Développement**
244 boulevard Saint-Germain
75007 Paris
France
Tel: +33-1-43 17 90 00
Email: cooperation.dgcid@diplomatie.gouv.fr
Web: http://www.diplomatie.gouv.fr/fr/ or
http://www.diplomatie.gouv.fr/fr/ministere_817/missions-
organisations_823/structure-administration-centrale_808/direction-
generale-cooperation-internationale-du-developpement_3146/dgcid-au-
coeur-du-dispositif-francais-cooperation_7424.html
Directeur Général: Bruno Delaye
Directeur, Direction de la coopération culturelle et du français: Xavier North

95   Ministère des Affaires Étrangères. Direction Générale de la
      Coopération Internationale et du Développement. Direction de la
      Coopération Culturelle et du Français. Division de l'Écrit et des
      Médiathèques, Affaires Étrangères
244 boulevard Saint-Germain
75303 Paris 07
France
Tel: +33-1-43 17 80 38 Fax: +33-1-43 17 88 83
Email: ccf.cem@diplomatie.gouv.fr Web: www.diplomatie.gouv.fr
Direction de la coopération et du français, Ministère des Division de l'écrit et
des médiathèques: Yves Mabin
Other contact: Régine Fontaine regine.fontaine@diplomatie.fr

96   Netherlands Ministry of Foreign Affairs. Directorate-General for
      International Cooperation, Sub-Saharan Africa Department
Bezuidenhoutseweg 67
PO Box 20061
2500 EB The Hague
Netherlands
Tel: +31-70-348 6486 Fax: +31-70-348 4848
Email: daf@minbuza.nl (Sub-Saharan Africa Department)
Web: http://www.minbuza.nl/en/developmentcooperation
Contact: use email form on Web site, or telephone Information Desk +31-70-
348 6789

97   Network for Information and Digital Access (NIDA)
37/39 Ludlow Road
London W5 1 NX
UK
Tel: +44-(0)20-8997 3274
Email: carol.priestley@nida-net.org
Web: http://www.nida-net.org/Home.html
Director: Carol Priestley

98   The Noma Award for Publishing in Africa
Secretariat:
PO Box 128
Witney OX8 5XU
UK
Tel: +44-(0)1993-775235 Fax: +44-(0)1993-709265
Email: maryljay@aol.com Web: http://www.nomaaward.org
Founder: Shoichi Noma (deceased), Kodansha Ltd., Japan
Chair, Noma Award Jury: Walter Bgoya
Contact, and Secretary to the Noma Award Managing Committee: Mary Jay

99   Norwegian Agency for Development Co-operation (NORAD)
Ruseløkkveien 26
Postboks 8034 Dep
0030 Oslo
Norway
Tel: +47-22-242030 Fax: +47-22-242031
Email: postmottak@norad.no
Web:
http://www.norad.no/default.asp?V_ITEM_ID=1139&V_LANG_ID=0
(English version)
Director General: Poul Engberg-Pedersen
Head of Civil Society Department: Bernt Ivar Gulbrandsen
Head of Education and Research Department: Ragnhild Dybdahl
Head of Information Department: Eva Bratholm
Senior Project Leader, Information Department: Thore G. Hem
For other heads of departments *see*
http://www.norad.no/default.asp?V_ITEM_ID=1167

100   The Open Society Institute/The Soros Foundation
400 West 59th Street
New York NY 10019
USA
Tel: +1-212-548-0600 Fax: +1-212-548-4600
Washington Office:
OSI-Washington DC
1120 19th Street NW 8th Floor
Washington DC 20036
USA
Tel: +1-202-721 5600 Fax: +1-202-530 0128
Email: use email form on Web site
Web: http://www.soros.org/ (Open Society Institute)
http://www.soros.org/initiatives/regions/africa (Africa region pages)
Founder and Chair: George Soros
Executive Vice President: Stewart J. Paperin
Director of International Operations: Robert Kushen
Regional Director, Office of Africa: Julie Hayes (New York-based)
Chair, OSIWA Board of Directors: Abdul Tejan-Cole (Freetown-based)
Senior Policy Analyst for Africa: Akwe Amosu (Washington-based)

101   Organisation Internationale de la Francophonie (OIF)
(formerly Agence Intergouvernementale de la Francophonie/AIF)
13, quai André Citroën
75015 Paris
France
Tel: +33-1-44 37 33 00 Fax: +33-1-45 79 14 98
Email: agence@francophonie.org (General enquiries)
Web: http://www.francophonie.org/ (Main home page)
http://www.francophonie.org/actions/arts/ini-livre.cfm (Le livre et la
lecture publique pages)
http://www.francophonie.org/actions/arts/fin-cafed.cfm (CAFED pages)
Secrétaire general: Abdou Diouf
Administrateur: Clément Duhaime
Direction éducation et de formation: Soungalo Ouédraogo
Responsable de projets Edition scolaire: Amadou Waziri
Direction de la langue française, de la diversité culturelle et linguistique:
Frédéric Bouilleux
Chef de division Diversité culturelle et linguistique: Rémi Sagna
Directeur, Bureau régional pour l'Afrique de l'ouest (BRAO):
Etienne Merseu Alingué
Directeur, Bureau régional pour l'Afrique centrale et l'océan Indien (BRAC):
Valentin Loemba-Bayonne
For regional Bureaux in Africa address details *see*
http://www.francophonie.org/oif/adresses.cfm#brao

102   Partnership for Higher Education in Africa
IGEMS, NYU Steinhardt School of Education
726 Broadway Room 532
New York NY 10003
USA
Tel: +1-212-998 5514 Fax: +1-212-995 4510
Email: Sue.Grant.Lewis@nyu.edu
Web: http://www.foundation-partnership.org
Coordinator: Suzanne Grant Lewis

103   Partnerships in Health Information
Library and Learning Centre
Bournemouth University
Talbot Campus
Fern Barrow
Poole BH12 5BB
UK
Tel: +44-(0)1202-965208 Fax: +44-(0)1202-965475
Email: estanley@bournemouth.ac.uk

Web: http://www.intute.ac.uk/healthandlifesciences/hosted/phi/
Programmes Officer: Emma Stanley

104   Prince Claus Fund for Culture and Development
Hoge Nieuwstraat 30
2514 EL The Hague
Netherlands
Tel: +31-70-427 4303 Fax: +31-70-427 4277
Email: info@princeclausfund.nl
Web: http://www.princeclausfund.org/en/index.html (English version)
Director: Els van der Plas

105   Ptolemy Project
The Office of International Surgery
The Hospital for Sick Children
555 University Avenue, Room S-107 Elm Wing
Toronto ON M5G 1X8
Canada
Tel: +1-416-813-6430 Fax: +1-416-813-6414
Email: ptolemy.info@utoronto.ca
Web: http://www.ptolemy.ca/index.htm
Principal Investigators: *see* http://www.ptolemy.ca/investigators.htm
Ptolemy in Africa:
Mrs. Hadija Kweka
c/o COSECSA
PO Box 1009
Arusha
Tanzania
Fax: +255-27-250 4142
Email: ptolemy_cosecsa@crhcs.or

106   Public Knowledge Project (PKP)
Department of Language and Literacy Education
University of British Columbia
Vancouver BC V6T 1Z4
Canada
Tel: +1-604-822 3950 Fax: +1-604 822 3154
Email: use email form on Web site
Web: http://pkp.sfu.ca/ (Main home page) http://pkp.sfu.ca/node/634
(Strengthening African Research Culture and Capacities)
Director/Principal Investigator: John Willinsky john.willinsky@ubc.ca
or john.willinsky@stanford.edu

107   The Publishing Training Centre at Book House
45 East Hill
Wandsworth
London SW18 2QZ
UK
Tel: +44-(0)20-8874 2718   Fax: +44-(0)-20-8870 8985
Email: publishing-training@bookhouse.co.uk
Web: http://www.train4publishing.co.uk/
Chief Executive: John Whitley
Head of Courses: Orna O'Brien

108   The Rockefeller Foundation
420 Fifth Avenue
New York NY 10018
USA
Tel: +1-212-869 8500 (General enquiries) Toll free (US/Canada only) (800) 645-1133 Fax: (212) 764-3468
Email: media@rockfound.org (Media enquiries only)
Web: http://www.rockfound.org (Main home page)
http://www.rockfound.org/efforts/afr_u/afr_u.shtml (Partnership for Higher Education in Africa; *see also* http://www.foundation-partnership.org/)
President: Judith Rodin
Associate Vice President and Managing Director: Maria Blair
Chief Operating Officer: Peter Madonia
Associate Vice President, Office of Strategy and Learning: Joyce L. Moock
Director, Communications: Peter Costiglio
Director, Creativity & Culture: Morris Vogel
For other contacts *see* http://www.rockfound.org/about_us/roster.shtml (and annual report)
Regional Office in Sub-Saharan Africa:
The Rockefeller Foundation Eastern & Southern Africa Program
Eden Square, 5th Floor, Block1
Chiromo Road, Westlands
PO Box 66773 (GPO)
Nairobi 00800
Kenya
Tel: +254-20-3750 627 Fax: +254-20-3750 653
Email: info@rockfound.or.ke
Director, Africa Regional Program (Nairobi): Peter Matlon

109   Room to Read
87 Grahma Street Suite 250
PO Box 29127
San Francisco CA 94129
USA
Tel: +1-415-561 3331 Fax: +1-415-561 4428
Email: info@roomtoread.org or media@roomtoread.org (Press Office)
Web: http://www.roomtoread.org/index.html (Home page)
http://www.roomtoread.org/countries/south_africa.html (South Africa pages)
http://www.roomtoread.org/countries/zambia.html (Zambia pages)
Founder and CEO: John Wood
Chief Operating Officer: Erin Ganju
Country Director, South Africa: vacant
Country Director, Zambia: Lovemore Nkhoma

110   Sabre Foundation, Inc.
872 Massachusetts Avenue Suite 2-1
Cambridge MA 02139
USA
Tel: +1-617-868 3510 Fax: +1-617-868 7916
Email: inquiries@sabre.org Web: http://www.sabre.org/index.php
Executive Director: Tania Vitvitsky tania@sabre.org
Book Donation Program Manager: Colin McCullough colin@sabre.org

SCOLMA *see* → **Standing Conference on Library Materials on Africa (114)**

111   The Secretariat of the African, Caribbean and Pacific Group of States (ACP Secretariat). Support Programme to Cultural Industries in ACP countries/Secrétariat du Groupe des Etats d'Afrique, des Caraïbes et du Pacifique (Secrétariat ACP). Programme d'appui aux Industries Culturelles des Pays ACP
Programme Management Unit (PMU)
Chaussée de la Hulpe 150
1170 Brussels
Belgium
Tel: +32-2-743 0600 Fax: +32-2-735 55 73
Email: info@acp.int (General enquiries) Web: http://www.acpsec.org/
Coordination in ECO: Nina Hoffmann nina.hoffmann@eco3.be
Senior Expert for the Fund: Marta Carrascosa marta.carrascosa@eco3.be
Senior Expert for the Observatory: Burama Sagnia burama.sagnia@eco3.be

112   Shuttleworth Foundation
PO Box 4163
Durbanville 7551
South Africa
Tel: +27-21-970 1200 Fax: +27-21-970 1201
Email: use email form on Web site
Web: http://www.shuttleworthfoundation.org/home
Principal Advisor: Helen King
Intellectual Property Fellow: Andrew Rens
Office Manager: Wendy Stoffels

Sida *see* ➔ **Swedish International Development Co-Operation Agency/Sida (115)**

Society for the Promotion of African, Asian and Latin American Literature *see* ➔ **Gesellschaft zur Förderung der Literatur aus Afrika, Asien, und Latinamerika (64)**

Soros Foundation *see* ➔**The Open Society Institute/The Soros Foundation** ➔**(100)**

113   Southern African Book Development Education Trust (SABDET)
25 Endymion Road
London N4 1EE
UK
Tel: +44-(0)20-8348 8463 Fax: +44-(0)28-8348 4403
Email: margaret.ling@geo2.poptel.org.uk
Web: http://www.sabdet.com/index.htm
Chair of Trustees: Kelvin Smith
Hon. Secretary: Margaret Ling

114   Standing Conference on Library Materials on Africa (SCOLMA)
c/o Ian Cooke, Secretary, SCOLMA
The Library
Institute of Commonwealth Studies
28 Russell Square
London WC1B 5DS
UK
Tel: +44-(0)20-7580 5876
Email: Ian.Cooke@sas.ac.uk Web: http://www.lse.ac.uk/library/scolma/
Chair: David Blake, Librarian, Commonwealth Secretariat, Marlborough House, Pall Mall, London SW1Y 5HX UK Email: scolma@hotmail.com
Secretary: Ian Cooke (at address above)

115   Swedish International Development Co-Operation Agency/Sida
Valhallavägen 199
10525 Stockholm
Sweden
Tel: +46-8-698 5000 Fax: +46-8-208864
Email: sida@sida.se
Web: http://www.sida.se/sida/jsp/sida.jsp?d=121&language=en_US
(Home page, English version)
http://www.sida.se/sida/jsp/sida.jsp?d=223&language=en_US and
http://www.sida.se/sida/jsp/sida.jsp?d=101&a=3760&language=en_US
(Department of Africa pages)
Chairperson and Director General of Sida: Anders Nordström
Head (Acting), Department for Africa (AFRA): Kristina Kühnel
Head (Acting), Department for Democracy and Social Development (DESO):
Annika Magnusson
Head, Department for Research Cooperation (SAREC): Berit Olsson
Note: for other departmental heads *see*
http://www.sida.se/sida/jsp/sida.jsp?d=130&language=en_US

**116   Technical Centre for Agricultural and Rural Cooperation ACP-EU
        (CTA)/Centre Technique de Coopération Agricole et Rurale ACP-
        UE**
Agro Business Park 2
Postbus 380
6700 AJ Wageningen
Netherlands
Tel: +31-317-467100 Fax: +31-317-460067
Email: cta@cta.nl Web: http://www.cta.nl/
Director: Hansjörg Neun
Executive Secretary: Helen Oguli
Manager, Communication Channels and Services Department:
Oumy Ndiaye
Manager, Information and Communication Management Skills and Systems
Department: Thierry Doudet
Manager, Information Products and Services Department: Joseph Mugah
Programme Coordinator, Co-publications: Chantal Guiot

117   TrustAfrica
Mermoz Pyrotechnie
Route de la Stèle Lot No. SR 12
BP 45435
Dakar–Fann
Senegal
Tel.: +221-869 4686 Fax: +221-824 1567

Email: info@trustafrica.org Web: http://www.trustafrica.org/index.php
Executive Director: Akwasi Aidoo
Note: set up in June 2006 with the financial support of the →**Ford Foundation (62),** TrustAfrica is a new African foundation that promotes peace, economic prosperity, and social justice throughout the continent. It hosts dialogues and workshops, makes grants for collaborative projects and capacity building, and provides technical assistance. While it has not thus far supported publishing or library development, it has recently established the *African Writers Fund,* a special fund to support the work of independent creative writers living on the continent. (Do not submit requests for funding, TrustAfrica does not accept unsolicited proposals.)

118   United Nations Educational, Scientific and Cultural Organization (UNESCO)/ Organisation des Nations Unies pour l'Education, la Science et la Culture
7 Place de Fontenoy
75352 Paris 07 SP
France
and at:
1 rue Miollis
75732 Paris Cedex 15
Tel: +33-1-45 68 10 00 Fax: +33-1-45 67 16 90
Email: bpiweb@unesco.org or use email form on Web site Web:
http://www.unesco.org (Main home page)
http://portal.unesco.org/en/ev.php-
URL_ID=19521&URL_DO=DO_TOPIC&URL_SECTION=201.html (Africa Department home page)
http://www.unesco.org/culture/industries/book/html_eng/index_en.sht ml (Books and Reading pages, last updated February 2003)
Director General: Koïchiro Matsuura
Head, Office of the Director General: Françoise Rivière
Head, Africa Department (AFR/ ADG): Noureni Tidjani-Serpos
Assistant Director-General for Communication and Information: Abdul Waheed Khan
Director, Communication Development Division (CI/ COM): Wijayanand Jayaweera
Director (Acting), Division of Cultural Expression and Creative Industries (CLT/ CEI): Indraseen Vencatachellum
Director: Division of Cultural Policies and Interculture Dialogue (CLT/ CPD): Katerina Stenon
Director, Division of Higher Education (ED/ HED): Georges Haddad
Director for Promotion of Basic Education (ED/ BAS):
(Ms) Ann Therèse N'dong Jatta
Director, International Fund for the Promotion of Culture:

(Ms) Milagros del Corral
Advisor for Communication and Information in Eastern Africa, Nairobi
Office: Alonso Aznar
Adviser for Communication and Information in Southern Africa, Harare
Cluster Office: Gervasio Kaliwo
Adviser for Communication and Information, Dakar Cluster Office:
Jeanne Seck
Note: for other Service and Sector contacts *see* interactive organizational chart
at
http://www.unesco.org/orgchart/en/ORG_vis_EN.htm
For contact details of UNESCO National Commissions in Africa, and
Permanent Delegations to UNESCO for African countries *see*
http://portal.unesco.org/en/ev.php-
URL_ID=11151&URL_DO=DO_TOPIC&URL_SECTION=201.html and then
select Africa from the Regions/Country menu
Note: see also http://portal.unesco.org/ci/en/ev.php-
URL_ID=1300&URL_DO=DO_TOPIC&URL_SECTION=201.html (UNESCO
activities in Communication and Information pages and contacts);
http://portal.unesco.org/ci/en/ev.php-
URL_ID=1645&URL_DO=DO_TOPIC&URL_SECTION=201.html
(UNESCO's activities in communication and information by themes);
http://www.unesco.org/cgi-
bin/webworld/portal_bib2/cgi/search.cgi?query=Africa (UNESCO
Libraries Portal)
UNESCO Nairobi Office
UN Complex Gigiri Block C   United Nations Avenue
PO Box 30592
00100 GPO Nairobi
Kenya
Tel: +254-20-621234 Fax: +254-20-622750
Email: nairobi@unesco.org Web: http://www.unesco-nairobi.org/
Director: Joseph M.G. Massaquoi
See also entries ➔ **119** and ➔ **120** below

**119   UNESCO/DANIDA--Basic Learning Materials Initiative (BML).
         UNESCO Division of Basic Education**
7 Place du Fontenoy
75352 Paris
France
Tel: +33-1-45 68 10 37 Fax: +33-1-45 68 56 26/7
Email: w.Gordon@unesco.org
Web: http://www.unesco.org/education/blm/
Contact: Winsome Gordon, Director, Primary Education Section
BLM Programme Coordinator: (Mrs) Janne Kjaersgaard

**120   UNESCO Regional Office for Education in Africa/ Bureau
Régional de l'Unesco pour l'Éducation en Afrique (BREDA)**
12 avenue L.S. Senghor
BP 3318
Dakar
Senegal
Tel: +221-849 2323 Fax: +221-823 8393
Email: dakar@unesco.org
Web: http://www.dakar.unesco.org/bureau_reg_en/breda.shtml
Director: (Mrs) Lalla Aïcha Ben Barka

**United Nations Conference on Trade and Development (UNCTAD).
International Trade Centre** *see* **➔ International Trade Centre
(UNCTAD/WTO) (84)**

**121   United States Agency for International Development (USAID).
Bureau for Africa**
Ronald Reagan Building
Washington DC 20523-1000
USA
Tel: +1-202-712 4810 (General enquiries) Fax: +1-202-216 3524
Email: see under contacts below
Web: http://www.usaid.gov/ (Main home page)
http://www.usaid.gov/locations/sub-saharan_africa/ (Sub-Saharan Africa
pages)
Assistant Administrator, Bureau for Africa, US Agency for International
Development: Katherine J. Almquist
Director, Office of Sustainable Development: Jeffrey M. Borns
Email: borns@usaid.gov
Director, Office of West African Affairs: Natalie Freeman
Email: nfreeman@usaid.gov
Director, Office of Eastern Africa Affairs: Jeffrey M. Borns
Email: jborns@usaid.gov
Director, Office of Southern Africa Affairs: Eric Loken
Email: eloken@usaid.gov
Note: for Country Desk Officers contacts see
http://www.usaid.gov/locations/sub-
saharan_africa/utility/directory.html

122   Utrikesministeriet/ Finnish Ministry of Foreign Affairs
Department for Africa and the Middle East
PO Box 176
00161 Helsinki
Finland

Tel: +358-9-16005 Fax: +358-9-1629840
Email: kirjaamo.um@formin.fi Web: http://global.finland.fi
Director General, Department for Africa and the Middle East: Teemu Tanner
Education Adviser: Heikki Kokkala

123   Voluntary Service Overseas (VSO)
317 Putney Bridge Road
London SW15 2PN
UK
Tel: +44-(0)20-8780 7200 Fax: +44-(0)20-8780 7300
Email: enquiry@vso.org.uk Web: http://www.vso.org.uk (VSO UK)
Chief Executive: Mark Goldring
Director, International Programmes Group: Richard Hawkes

124   The World Bank
1818 H Street NW
Washington DC 20433
USA
Tel: +1-202-473 1000 (General enquiries) 1-202-473 4467 (Africa region)
Fax: +1-202-477 6391
Email: use feedback email form on Web site for general enquiries
Email for Africa region: africainfo@worldbank.org
Web: http://www.worldbank.org/ (Main home page)
http://www.worldbank.org/afr (Sub-Saharan Africa pages)
President of the World Bank Group: Robert B. Zoellick
Vice President and Corporate Secretary for the World Bank Group:
W. Paatii Ofosu-Amaah
Vice President, Africa region: (Ms) Obiageli Ezekwesili
Note: for country office information and Country Directors in Africa *see*
http://go.worldbank.org/3MYYOPUTF0
See also entry ➜ **125** below

125   The World Bank-Office of the Publisher
1818 H Street NW
Mailstop U11-1104
Washington DC 20433
USA
Tel: + 1-202-458 7717 Fax: +1-202-522 2422
Email: books@worldbank.org (for orders, for other email address contacts
see below)
Web: http://publications.worldbank.org/ecommerce/ (Publications)
Office of the Publisher (EXTOP), Publisher: H. Dirk Koehler
Email: dkoehler@worldbank.org
Office of the Publisher, Head of Client Relations: Richard Crabbe

Email: rcrabbe@worldbank.org
Office of the Publisher, Rights Manager: Valentina Kalk
Email: pubrights@worldbank.org
Note: details about the World Bank's **African Publishing Initiative** can be
found at http://go.worldbank.org/MPLH6G3200

126   World Intellectual Property Organization (WIPO)
34 chemin des Colombettes
PO Box 18
1211 Geneva 20
Switzerland
Telephone: +41-22-338 9111 Fax: +41-22-733 54 28
Email: use email enquiry form on Web site
Web: http://www.wipo.int/portal/index.html.en
Director General: Kamil Idris
Executive Director, Office of Controller: (Ms) Carlotta Graffigna
Executive Director, Office of Strategic Use of Intellectual Property for
Development: Sherif Saadallah
Executive Director, Office of Strategic Planning and Policy Development,
and the WIPO Worldwide Academy: Yoshiyuki Takagi
For the complete list of WIPO principal officers for different divisions see
http://www.wipo.int/about-wipo/en/intburo.htm
See also ➜ **Organisation Africaine de la Propriété Intellectuelle (OAPI)/
African Intellectual Property Organisation (19)**

1
Serials and reference

Serials

African book trade and book professional journals

Note: for a more comprehensive listing of African book trade journals and magazines – most of which unfortunately have ceased a long time ago – see entries 1-48 in the first (1996) edition of this bibliography.

Although many African book trade serials have ceased, back issues of a number of them are still available in several North American libraries with major African studies collections, as well as in a number of major Africana collections in Europe. Where ascertained through the OCLC's *WorldCat* searches, approximate holdings in North America are indicated with the entries. To identify location details of these and other journals enter the journals' names into the "Title" search field at this web site: http://www.worldcatlibraries.org/advancedsearch. However, it should be noted that whereas *WorldCat* presents a fairly accurate picture of book and serials holdings of libraries in North America, this is, at this time at least, much less the case for Europe, Africa and the rest of the world, as coverage is limited to academic or other libraries that are members of OCLC. For sub-Saharan Africa coverage is largely confined to libraries in South Africa at the present time.

Unless otherwise indicated, all journals are published in print format only.

127   African Association of Science Editors Newsbrief. (Ethiopian Chapter). 1993-? Irregular, ceased? Addis Ababa: African Association of Science Editors.
Reports about the activities of the ➜ **African Association of Science Editors (2),** and provides a variety of tips and suggestions for good practice in scientific publishing.

128   African Journal of Library, Archives and Information Science. 1990- Twice yearly. ISSN 0795-4778
Edited by L.O. Aina ainalo2000@yahoo.com Ibadan: Department of Library and Information Science, PO Box 20492, University of Ibadan, and

Gaborone: Department of Library and Information Sciences, University of Botswana,
Online: (Table of contents and abstracts only; full-text articles available via document delivery)
http://www.ajol.info/journal_index.php?jid=158&tran=0&ab=0 [09/02/08]
Provides a forum for librarians, archivists, documentalists, information scientists and other information professionals in Africa to report their research findings, and as such primarily includes articles on the library and information sciences in Africa. Although not a book trade journal, it also publishes occasional papers on publishing aspects, legal deposit, and reading promotion.

129   African Publishing Review/Revista da da Edições Africana/Revue de l'Edition Africaine. 1992- Quarterly, currently irregular/dormant (last issue examined/published vol. 13, no.3, 2004)]. Print and (partially) online
ISSN 1019-5823
Edited by Tainie Mundondo tp@apnet.org, and an editorial collective.
Harare, later Abidjan, now Accra: African Publishers Network. [Some issues also published as separate French editions
Online: (partially online from vol. 12, but only vol. 12, nos. 4-6, 2003, and vol. 13, no. 2, 2004 are currently available)
http://www.apnet.org/news/newsletters.htm [09/02/08]
The journal of the →**African Publishers Network (5)**, a Pan-African network of national publishers' associations and publishing communities founded in 1992, with the objectives to strengthen and promote indigenous publishing in Africa. It aims to provide a forum for discussion of common problems as well as keeping people informed of activities in African publishing. Includes news, analysis, and in-depth perspectives on African publishing. It also contains reports on APNET activities, and a wide variety of short articles on publishing in Africa, together with profiles of people in publishing, reports about training courses, country reports, listings of rights on offer and business opportunities, announcements of newly published titles from African publishers, and occasional book reviews. The *African Publishing Review* is indexed in the Library of Congress Nairobi Office's **Quarterly Index to African Periodical Literature (180)**. Enter search terms, or authors, etc.; or, for browsing purposes, select broad subject in the pull down menu, and thereafter click on Publishing and Book Trade. According to WorldCat, about 20 libraries in North America have fairly complete runs of this serial.

130   Bookchat. 1976-1997. Quarterly, print version ceased with issue no. 132.
Online: http://www.bookchat.co.za/ [30/03/08]
Edited by Jay Heale. Grabouw, South Africa: Bookchat. Email:
jayheale@telkomsa.net
Bookchat began as a newsletter for a children's book group and was the only magazine in South Africa dealing solely with books for children, including articles, news, and reviews. After 21 years of publication, producing 132 issues, the print version ceased in 1997. However, in early 2008 *Bookchat* was re-launched as an

attractive Web site devoted to news and reviews of South African children's books. It also provides access to the fully searchable online version of ➜ **SCABIP/South African Children's Books in Print (963)**, as well as a database of book reviews published between 2000 and 2007. Additionally, the Web site includes links to South African publishers producing children's books, children's book organizations and book-related Web sites, South African children's book awards with details of the most recent winner(s) of each award, listings of recommended books by age groups, notable overseas children's books, and pages giving details of book world events with relevance to South African children's literature. This is an extremely rich resource on South African children's books.

131   The Book Industry. 1990- Irregular.
Kumasi, Ghana: Kwame Nkrumah University of Science and Technology, Design and General Studies Department, College of Art.
Contains short articles on publishing in Ghana, especially educational publishing, books for children and scholarly texts. Also contains practical articles on writing and editing. Sponsored by the Kumasi Book Industry Programme. [No recent issues examined.]

132   Bookmark. 2005- Irregular; quarterly as from 2008-. Print and (partially) online [No ISSN]
Edited by Jessica Hadley Grave bookmark@sabooksellers.com Bellville, South Africa: South African Booksellers Association.
Web/Online: (select articles only)
http://www.sabooksellers.com/general/bookmark.asp [09/02/08]
The informative news magazine of the ➜ **South African Booksellers Association (951)**, distributed free to all SABA members (and partially freely accessible to others in its online version). It contains book industry news and advertisements; reports and news about SABA activities and events; pre-publication announcements and a "Buyer's Guide"; reports about conferences, meetings and book fairs; international news, as well as a variety of short articles of interest to the book professions.

133   Bukku. Publier en langues nationales. Bulletin de liaison des professionnels du livre en Afrique. 1996- Irregular, ceased?
Edited by Mamadou Aliou Sow. Conakry: Editions Ganndal [BP 542, Conakry].
Bukku (which means "book" in several African languages) is a newsletter for book professionals in Africa who are involved in the publication, promotion, and distribution of African language publications in various parts of the continent. Contains news about African language publishing activities, and reports about various new initiatives. [No recent issues examined.]

134   CREPLA Bulletin of Information/CREPLA bulletin d'Information. 1978-1989? Twice yearly, ceased.
Edited by William Moutchia. Yaoundé: Centre Régional de Promotion du Livre en Afrique, CREPLA.

Contained news, reports and articles on publishing in Africa, and news about the Centre's activities, seminars and courses held, etc. The UNESCO regional book promotion centre in Africa, CREPLA, has been dormant for many years now, but back issues of the *Bulletin* may still be accessible in a number of African studies libraries, although a WorldCat search comes up with no holdings.

135   The East African Bookseller. (formerly *The Kenya Bookseller*) 1988-Irregular, ceased?
Edited by Stanley Irura. Nairobi: Bookman Consultants [Garden Chambers, Mokhtar Daddah Street, PO Box 31191, Nairobi].
Became the *East African Bookseller* in 1993 and acts as a forum for matters concerning education and publishing in Uganda, Kenya and Tanzania, with articles from all sectors of the publishing industry in the region. Also contains notes and news about book promotion events, company profiles, and book reviews. [No recent issues examined; no WorldCat holdings.]

136   Ghana Book World. 1978-1991? Irregular, ceased?
Accra: Ghana Book Development Council.
The official publication of the ➜ **Ghana Book Development Council (536).** Includes articles and reports about publishing and book development activities, book promotional events, etc. in Ghana, as well as papers on children's writing, copyright issues, training for book industry personnel, and more. WorldCat shows back issue holdings by 6 US libraries.

137   Journal of African Children's and Youth Literature. (formerly *Journal of African Children's Literature*). 1989- Annual, ceased? ISSN 0795-4506
Edited by Osayimwense Osa. Benin City: Paramount Publishers [PO Box 54843, Benin City].
Aims to provide a forum for scholars working in the field of children's literature, also including occasional articles on publishing aspects of children's literature. Latest issue examined was vol. 6 (1994/95) Northwestern University Library has "v.15/16 (2004/2006)", but current status not verified. WorldCat shows 6 holding libraries.

138   KPA News 2005- Quarterly [irregular, latest issue is vol. 2, no. 1, February 2006)]. Print and online [No ISSN]
Edited by Janet Njoroge *et al*
Editorial address: Kenya Publishers Association, 2nd floor Occidental Plaza PO Box 42767, Nairobi 00100, Kenya info@kenyapublishers.org or kenyapublishers@wananchi.com
Online: http://www.kenyapublishers.org/newsletter.html
The newsletter of the ➜ **Kenya Publishers Association/KPA (581),** which carries news about KPA activities and book-related events, reports about the Nairobi Book Fair, together with short items about developments in the educational sector, textbook projects, and copyright issues. The KPA plans to transform the current newsletter into a fully-fledged trade magazine, to include articles and feature stories

on publishing and the book trade, new printing technology, libraries, literary awards, and more.

139   Le Livre Africain. Le Journal de la Culture, de l'Education & du Développement. 1995-? Quarterly, ceased?
Edited by Bertin Fondjo. Cotonou: Intermonde SARL [01 BP 327, Recette Principale].
Quarterly journal that aims to promote the book industries in Africa, as well as promoting educational and cultural development. Contains news items, short feature articles, poetry, book reviews, etc. [No recent issues examined.]

140   The Nigerian Bookseller. 2006- Twice yearly?
Edited by Kolade Mosuro info@mosuro.com Lagos: Nigerian Booksellers Association.
Editorial address: Kolade Mosuro, Mosuro The Booksellers Ltd, 52 Magazine Road, POB 30301, Jericho, Ibadan, Nigeria
This recently launched new magazine aims to provide a resource that will enhance professionalism among Nigerian booksellers, and contains news about the book trade, events, awards, profiles of Nigerian writers, as well as articles on the retail book trade in Nigeria. [Not examined]

141   PABA Newsletter. 2000- Irregular [1-2- issues annually]. Print and online [No ISSN]
Edited by Lily Nyariki lnyariki@yahoo.com and Catherine Tuganeiyo ctugaineyo@muucsf.org Lagos, later Nairobi: Pan African Booksellers Association.
Online: (sign up page for Newsletter)
http://www.panafricanbooksellersassociation.org/default.htm [24/01/08]
An informative newsletter of the ➜ **Pan African Booksellers Association (21)**. Its aim is "to gather together information concerning the bookselling business in Africa and to keep members informed of the activities of PABA." PABA promotes the rights and welfare of booksellers, and the newsletter includes a variety of news on bookselling-related activities and initiatives, as well as reports about workshops and training programmes, book fairs, and other book promotional events in Africa.

142   Pan African Book World. 1981-1982 ceased. Quarterly. Enugu, Nigeria: Fourth Dimension Publishing Company.
A pioneering pan-African book trade journal, but which unfortunately did not survive beyond publication of just three issues. WorldCat reports holdings of back issues by 10 US libraries.

143   PEGboard. Professional Editors' Group Newsletter. 1995- Quarterly. Print and (partially) online ISSN 1815-3607
Edited by André Snyders peg@editors.org.za Craighall, South Africa: Professional Editors' Group.

Online (select contributions only): http://www.editors.org.za/ [09/02/08]
A lively newsletter and bulletin of the ➜ **Professional Editors' Group (944),**
primarily intended for professional editors and freelancers working in South Africa,
but also of interest to a wider audience. Includes short news items about
developments within the South African book industries; company news, reports
about book fairs and other book promotional events, announcements and reports
about conferences, meetings, and training courses, as well as articles about good
practice in professional editing and occasional book reviews of professional
literature.

144   The Publisher. 1985- Twice yearly, but currently irregular [1 issue
annually] ISSN 0331-7714
Edited by G. Ayodeji Fatehinse c/o nigpa@skannet.com Ibadan: Nigerian
Publishers Association.
The magazine of the ➜ **Nigerian Publishers Association/NPA (739),** which aims to
provide a platform for publishers in Nigeria and "serve to educate, entertain and
inform the public on what publishing is all about, who publishers are and what
contributions they make to national development". Contains articles on many topics,
including copyright and piracy, scholarly publishing, children's book publishing,
book industry training, bookselling and the retail trade, as well as papers and guides
to good practice in book publishing. Additionally, it carries reports about the
Association's annual meeting, book training programmes and workshops, reports
about book fairs and book promotional events, articles about bibliographic standards
for the book industry, and more. The most recent number, vol. 14, no. 1, November
2007, is a special issue on rebuilding the publishing industry and rebranding the
NPA. According to WorldCat, 12 US libraries hold back issues of this journal.

SA BookNews Online Newsletter *see* ➜ **SA BookNews Online SA
/BookNews Online Newsletter (145)**

145   SA BookNews Online/ SA BookNews Online Newsletter. 2006-
Online only
Edited by Delani Webb Spies delani@booknews.co.za Strand, South Africa:
SA BookNews Online, Publications Network (Pty)/SAPnet.
Editorial address: Unit 4368, Greenways, Strand 7140, South Africa
http://www.booknews.co.za/general/index.asp [09/02/08]
Hosted by the South African branch of Nielsen BookData (SAPnet), *SA BookNews
Online* was launched at the Cape Town Book Fair in June 2006, and is an initiative
that at aims to provide an online news and information service for both the South
African book industry and the book-buying public, as well as for the international
book community. It is a rich resource and contains a wealth of information about
book and publishing-related activities in South Africa, including new release
highlights, authors in the news, links to online book reviews, listings of forthcoming
titles, a calendar of book-related events, news about book fairs and book promotional
events, book awards and literary prizes, job vacancies and appointments in the book
industry, resources and book trade reference tools, bookselling news, library
developments, advice for authors about getting published, and more. Also offers the

(free) *SA BookNews Online Newsletter* that is sent to subscribers each Friday and highlights the previous week's news, new releases, job opportunities and events.

146   Uganda Book News. 1996- Quarterly, irregular
Edited by Martin Okia? Kampala: Uganda Booksellers Association.
The official publication of the ➔ **Uganda Booksellers Association (1153)**. Contains notes and news about the activities of the Association, and short articles about publishing and library development in Uganda. [No recent issues examined.]

147   Writers' World. The South African Word Crafter's Journal. 1991-1999? Quarterly, print version ceased. Now online only.
Edited by Monica Cromhout monica@optionsunlimited.co.za Somerset West, South Africa: Options Publishing [PO Box 1588, Somerset West 7215].
Superseded by the online **Writers World. An Information Resource for South African Writers**, and **Trilogy**, a free email newsletter
http://www.optionsafrica.co.za/ [09/02/08]]
Originally published as a networking tool that aimed to keep writers apprised of developments in the literary market-place, and opportunities for publishing their work. Included articles by South African authors writing about their work, and articles by editors writing about their experience in working with authors. Now available as a Web resource and an email newsletter. The Web pages Include "news snippets" of interest to writers, and also offer an excellent links collection of writers' groups, journals, competitions, services, and other Web sites and resources of interest to writers.

Other journals, newsletters, and book review media covering African book publishing output

This section covers journals, most of them published outside Africa, that are not primarily book trade journals or bibliographic tools, but which include regular reports, articles, and news about African publishing and the book trade. Book review media covering African publishing output are also included.

148   The Africa Book Centre Book Review. 1995- Three times yearly. Print and online ISSN 1363-2477
Edited by Adrian Howe & Saara Marchadour London: The Africa Book Centre.
Online: (issues 27 and 28, 2004/2005 only; no further issues available online)
http://www.africabookcentre.com/abc/Review27.pdf [10/02/08]
http://www.africabookcentre.com/abc/review28.pdf [10/02/08]
The *Africa Book Centre Book Review* "aims to be the best source of timely and current information on the African book industry." Contains occasional book reviews or review essays, together with news items, but the most substantive part of the journal

consists of two separate listings 'New Books from Africa' and 'New Books on Africa', many of them published in Africa. These are arranged under broad subject groups with a brief annotation on each title, together with prices and full bibliographic and ordering data. All books listed can be ordered from the Africa Book Centre and entries are marked indicating availability status. No further issues published since 2005.

149   Africana Libraries Newsletter. 1975- Irregular, twice yearly as from 2008- Print [to 2006] and online ISSN 0148-7868
Edited by Bassey Irele and Timothy Johnson. Boston [etc.]: Africana Librarians Council, African Studies Association.
Editorial address: Bassey Irele, Assistant Librarian for Sub-Saharan Africa, Widener Library, Harvard University, Collection Development Department Cambridge, MA 02138, USA birele@fas.harvard.edu; or Timothy Johnson Librarian (Africana Studies, Anthropology, and Food Studies), New York University Bobst Library, Mezzanine, 70 Washington Square South, New York NY 10012, USA timothy.johnson@nyu.edu
Online: http://www.indiana.edu/~libsalc/african/aln/alnindex.html [10/02/08] (archives of issues 90, April 1997 through no. 121, October 2007 are accessible online; print edition no longer available as from 2006.)
The newsletter of the (US) African Studies Association's ➔ **Africana Librarians Council (26)** with reports on meetings and conferences and other items of interest to Africana librarians and those concerned about information resources about or in Africa. Also publishes book reviews of new African studies reference resources, news about serials, and notices about vendors of African studies materials, including those supplying books and journals, government documents, etc. published in Africa.

The African Book Publishing Record *see* ➔ **Bibliographies and continuing sources (168)**

150   African Research & Documentation. 1962- Three times yearly. ISSN 0305-826X
Edited by Terry Barringer. London: Standing Conference on Library Materials on Africa/SCOLMA.
Editorial address: Terry Barringer, 70 Mortlock Avenue Cambridge CB4 1TE tabarringe@aol.com
Online (tables of contents only of recent issues):
http://www.lse.ac.uk/library/scolma/ardcontents.htm [10/02/08]
The official publication of the ➔ **Standing Conference on Library Materials on Africa (114)**, *African Research & Documentation* has for long been supportive of African publishing and librarianship. In addition to articles, book reviews, and news items on aspects of Africana bibliography, and about library and archive collections relating to Africa, it includes frequent articles on publishing and book development in Africa.

151   The African Review of Books (AroB). 2003- Online only.
Edited by Richard Bartlett and Raks Seakhoa
mail@africanreviewofbooks.com
Salisbury, UK: African Review of Books, [Kelsey Cottage, 2 The Green,
Laverstock SP1 1QS, UK] and Johannesburg: African Review of Books [PO
Box 10024, Johannesburg 2000, South Africa].
http://www.africanreviewofbooks.com [10/02/08]
The online, freely accessible, *African Review of Books* (easily confused with the ➔
Africa Review of Books, *see* entry **152** below) aims to provide "a space in which the
books, literature and scholarship of Africa can be discussed and debated", and "a
step towards bringing together, in one place, news, reviews and information relating
to Africa's publishing industry and African scholarship." Features reviews of books
published both within and outside Africa, together with essays, news, and
announcements about new books, book fairs and book promotional events, book
prizes, and obituaries. The emphasis is primarily on fiction, drama and poetry, and
biography rather than academic titles. Also offers a free email newsletter. This is a
very useful resource, although updates of pages have been rather sparse in recent
months (in 2007).

152   The Africa Review of Books (ARB). 2004- Twice yearly (in English
and French). Print and online. ISSN 0851–7592 Dakar: Council for the
Development of Social Science Research in Africa (CODESRIA).
Editors: Bahru Zewde & Hassan Remaoun (French Editor)
Managing Editor: Taye Assefa
Editorial address: Forum for Social Studies, PO Box 25864 Code 1000, Addis
Ababa, Ethiopia, Email: arb.fss@telecom.net.et
Editorial address for contributions in French: CRASC, Cité Bahi Ammar,
Bloc A, N° 01 Es Sénia, Oran, Algeria, Email: crasc@crasc.org or ral@crasc.dz
Online:
http://www.codesria.org/Links/Publications/review_books/current_issue
.htm [04/02/08]
Note: this URL changes for each issue; the last issue published in print
format is vol. 3, no. 2, September 2007, but online versions are currently
[04/02/08] only available up to Volume 2, Number 1, March 2006.
ARB covers works on Africa in the social sciences, humanities, and the creative arts
(published in Africa and elsewhere), and the journal also aims to serve as forum for
critical analysis, reflections, and debates about Africa. According to an inaugural
mission statement in the first issue, the new review journal will seek to "bring
interesting work published in Africa, but which are not sufficiently well
disseminated, to the attention of a wider reading audience both within and outside
the continent." Reviews are published in English and French, about a dozen in each
issue; most are in-depth critical reviews or review essays, and there are also general
articles. In addition to the print version – which is published in a large size A3 format
– all reviews and articles are also freely accessible online.
Reviews:
African Research & Documentation no. 98 (2005)

Africana Libraries Newsletter no. 115 (April 2005)
Online: http://www.indiana.edu/~libsalc/african/aln/no116.pdf [04/02/08]

153   Africultures. La revue des cultures africaines. 1998- Quarterly (print version). Print and online ISSN 1276-2458
Edited by Ayoko Mensah. Managing Editors: Virginia Andriamirado and Olivier Barlet
Editorial address: Les Pilles, 26110 Nyon, France redaction@africultures.com
Paris: L'Harmattan Edition Diffusion [5-7 rue de l'Ecole Polytechnique, 75005 Paris, France] harmattanl@wanadoo.fr
Online (select articles from recent issues freely accessible online; others available by purchase of individual issues or as individual articles):
http://www.africultures.com/index.asp (Main home page, French) [10/02/08]
http://www.africultures.com/index.asp?menu=revue_sommaires (Summaries of contents only) [10/02/08]
An informative monthly magazine (quarterly in print format) with each issue focusing on a particular aspect of the African arts and cultures, including literature, theatre, art, music, photography, cinema, etc. together with a calendar of African cultural events, reports about exhibitions, reviews, interviews, and more. *Africultures* no. 57, published in December 2003, was a special issue devoted to "Où va le livre en Afrique?" ("Books in Africa: What future?" *see* entry ➔ **369**). The Africultures Web site provides a forum of information and debate about African cultural expression, and a offers wide variety of information about the arts and cultures in Africa and elsewhere. At this time (February 2008) it offers access to over 6,000 articles, 71 "Dossiers", almost 13,000 reviews and notices of books, films, and CDs, Videos and DVDs. A weekly online newsletter, *La Lettre d'Information d'Africultures* is available free on request, and includes a diary of forthcoming events and the latest news provided by a network of 19 cultural associations throughout Africa. *See also* ➔ **Afrilivres (185).**

154   AllAfrica.com – Book reviews.
Online http://allafrica.com/books/ (Book related news stories, book launches, book promotional events, etc.) [10/02/08]
http://allafrica.com/bookreviews/ (Book reviews) [10/02/08]
AllAfrica.com, the major African news provider, started publication of online book reviews in 2003, drawing on their own commissioned reviews, as well as providing access to book reviews published in many African newspapers. This is an excellent source to quickly retrieve the latest reviews published in online African newspapers. It also includes book industry news, and links to news stories about book launches, book promotional or literary events, and book awards and prizes.

155   Bellagio Publishing Network Newsletter. 1992-2002. Twice yearly, later quarterly, currently dormant.
Edited by Philip G. Altbach. Buffalo, NY, later Chestnut Hill, MA: Bellagio Publishing Network, School of Education, Boston College. As from 1998-

Oxford: Bellagio Publishing Network Secretariat, edited by Katherine Salahi ks@bellagiopublishingnetwork.com. As from no. 28, November 2001, edited by Katherine Salahi and Sulaiman Adebowale. Print and online (online from issue 20, 1997) [No ISSN]
Back issues no. 20, November 1997 to no. 31-2002 are freely available as full-text documents (either in HTML or PDF format) online at http://www.bellagiopublishingnetwork.com/newslett_index2.htm [10/02/08] while table of contents are accessible for issues 11-19.
Last issue published was no. 31, November 2002
http://www.bellagiopublishingnetwork.com/newsletter31/toc.htm [10/02/08]
Important note: the domain name for the Bellagio Publishing Network was previously www.bellagiopublishingnetwork.org whereas it has now migrated to www.bellagiopublishingnetwork.com, but this change in domain may *not* be permanent.
The newsletter of the ➔ **Bellagio Publishing Network (37),** the (now apparently defunct) informal association of donors and other organizations dedicated to the strengthening of indigenous publishing in the Third World. The newsletter contains reports, news items, short articles, perspectives and commentary on various aspects of publishing and the book trade in Africa, and elsewhere in the developing world. This includes reports about new initiatives, conferences, book fairs, training for book industry personnel, reports about the activities of organizations supported by the Bellagio Group, as well as reviews of new professional books and reference resources. The online archive of this newsletter offers an enormously rich resource on many aspects of publishing and the promotion of books in the countries of the South. WorldCat lists 9 libraries in the US that hold complete or near-complete runs of this newsletter.

156 Bibliodiversité. La lettre mensuelle de l'Alliance des éditeurs independents/Bibliodiversity. The Newsletter of the Alliance of Independent Publishers. 2006- Monthly [latest is issue no. 7, December 2006] Print and online ISSN 1778-4018
Edited by Etienne Galliand egalliand@alliance-editeurs.org
Editorial address 38 rue Saint Sabin, 75011 Paris France
Online: http://www.alliance-editeurs.org/download-images/logos/bibliodiversity%207.pdf [URL changes for each issue]
This newletter of the ➔**Alliance des Éditeurs Independents pour une Autre Mondalisation/Alliance of Independent Publishers for Another Globalization (31)** includes short news items about the activities of the Alliance's African members, and profiles of some African publishers. It also contains book reviews and reports about Alliance activities worldwide.

157 BookLinks. The Networking Forum for the Book Chain. 2002- Irregular [latest is issue no. 7, 2007] Print and online [No ISSN]

Edited by Karen Edwards booklinks@bookaid.org London: Bookaid International.
Online: (each issue has an individual URL), select issue from the download page at http://www.bookaid.org/cms.cgi/site/whatwedo/booklinks.htm [20/11/08]
Latest issue:
http://www.bookaid.org/resources/downloads/booklinks/BookLinks_7.pdf [20/01/08]
Replacing ➔ **Partners in African Publishing (164)** which ceased in December 2000, BookLinks aims "to help strengthen links between librarians, publishers and booksellers: to help understand each other's perspectives and activities, to develop a common platform, and to work more closely together in the interests of sustainable development." Recognising the essential role that libraries have to play in development and the alleviation of poverty, BookLinks in particular "aims to highlight and encourage the positive work being done by libraries to provide access to information for people who would otherwise have none." Includes a wide variety of short articles on libraries, publishing, bookselling, reading promotion, ICT issues, together with reports about workshops and training programmes, and a section devoted to useful new information sources for the African book professions.

158 Cultures Sud. (as from issue no. 167, 2007-; formerly *Notre Librairie: Revue des littératures du Sud*) 1969- Quarterly. Print and online ISSN 0755-3854
Edited by Nathalie Philippe cultures-sud@culturesfrance.com Paris: CulturesFrance, Ministère des Etrangères Affaires.
Editorial address: 1 avenue de Villars, 75007 Paris, France
Online: (articles, news items, and book reviews, etc. are freely downloadable in pdf format, text only without illustrations) at
http://www.culturesfrance.com/librairie/presentation/index.html [10/02/08]
Search facility for back issues is at
http://www.culturesfrance.com/publications-et-ecrit/revues/po25_2.html [10/02/08]
A very attractively produced journal that covers various aspects of African literature, sometimes reviewing literary output by country and sometimes choosing special subject areas such as theatre, poetry, lusophone and Hispanic literature. Other recent numbers have included issues focussing on the African cinema, African music, bookselling in Africa, literature and development, emerging new African writers, and language and linguistics. Includes articles, interviews, profiles of African writers, and an extensive number of book reviews in each issue, covering titles on Africa or African literature published in France as well as in francophone Africa, and providing full bibliographic and acquisitions data. The site includes a search facility for searching for articles (authors, countries/regions, or keyword) from issue no. 72, 1985 through 132, 1999, containing a database of almost 2,500 items.

159   Glendora Books Supplement. 1997-2001? Quarterly, ceased? Print and online [supplement to *Glendora Review. African Quarterly on the Arts*]. Edited by Olakunle Tejuoso (Publisher).
Managing Editor: Ololade Bamidele glendora@glendorabooks.net
Lagos: Glendora Review [Shop C4 Falomolo Shopping Centre, 168 Awolowo Road, PO Box 50914, Ikoyi, Lagos,].
Web: http://www.glendorabooks.net/GBS/default.htm [25/01/08; some pages not accessible]
Online: Available online as part of the African e-journals project at http://digital.lib.msu.edu/projects/africanjournals/html/browse.cfm?colid =309 [25/01/08]
including the complete archive from vol. 1, no. 1, 1997 to vol. 1, no. 6, 2001
Note: all issues published are erroneously cited as "volume 1", but a total of six issues only have been published.
A well-produced book review journal published as a supplement to the (now defunct?) *Glendora Review*. It contains reviews and review essays of some 1,000-2,000 words in length, of books published both within Africa and elsewhere, mostly in the arts, literature and social sciences, but also reference resources. It has also published occasional articles on African publishing and book development. Although billed as a quarterly publication is has been published irregularly (the last issue examined was no. 6, 2001, and no information about more current issues is available from the publisher's Web site.)

160   Logos. Forum of the World Book Community. 1990- (formerly *Logos: The Professional Journal of the Book World*, 1990-1995; *Logos: The Journal of the World Book Community*, to vol. 17, no. 2, 2006) Quarterly. Print and online
ISSN 0957-9656
Edited by Gordon Graham logos-marlow@dial.pipex.com (to 2005, now Editor Emeritus). Currently (2006-) edited by Charles M. Levine logos-marlow@dial.pipex.com or logo-editor@att.net London: Whurr Publishers Ltd., to vol. 16 no. 4, 2005 ; 2006- Marlow: Logos International Publishing Education Foundation
Sales and business correspondence to: Gordon Graham, 5 Beechwood Drive, Marlow, Bucks SL7 2DH, UK
Web: http://www.logos-journal.org
http://www.logos-journal.org/topic-portfolio.htm (topic portfolios) [10/02/08]
Online: access via Atyponlink at http://www.atypon-link.com/LOG/loi/logo (requires subscription; or purchase individual articles on a document delivery basis at a fee of $12.00/£6.00 per article)
Logos offers to the world book community "a forum in which it can debate the issues which concern it and which both unite and divide it." It seeks to publish experiences and ideas which are not ephemeral and which are capable and worthy of travel, "paying equal respect to passionate beliefs and detached analysis." Since it first started publication in 1990 this fine journal has carried a substantial number of

contributions on publishing in Africa and the developing world (all of which are listed and abstracted in this bibliography). The complete archive is now freely accessible online to subscribers of the journal; or, for non-subscribers, on a pay-per-view and document delivery basis, at a modest charge of £6.00 per article. The *Logos* archive is a marvellously rich resource.

161   Journal of Scholarly Publishing. 1969- (formerly *Scholarly Publishing*, to vol. 25, no. 2, January 1994) Quarterly. Print and (partially) online ISSN 1198-9742
Founding Editor: Elenanor Harman, later edited by Ian Montagnes.
Currently edited by Tom Radko tradko@wesleyan.edu   Toronto: University of Toronto Press.
Subscription orders to University of Toronto Press, Journals Division, 5201 Dufferin Street, Toronto, ON M3H 5T8, Canada.
journals@utpress.utoronto.ca
Editorial address: Tom Radko, 3 Orange Road, Middletown, CT 06457, USA
Web: http://www.utpjournals.com/jsp/jsp.html
Online: as from volume 33, no. 1, October 2001 (requires subscription; or purchase articles on a document delivery basis at a fee of $12.00 per article); or access back issues via Project Muse
http://muse.jhu.edu/journals/journal_of_scholarly_publishing/
This high-quality journal has, for almost 40 years now, covered a very broad range of the diverse aspects of editing and scholarly publishing in North America and other parts of the world. It aims "to combine philosophical analysis with practical advance and aspires to explain, argue, discuss and question the large collection of new topics that continuously arise in the publishing field." It has also examined the future of scholarly publishing, scholarship on the Web, digitalization, copyrights, editorial policies, computer applications, marketing and pricing models. Over the years it has published many contributions on scholarly publishing in Africa and in other parts of the developing world.

162   Médianes. Revue des partenaires du développement culturel en Afrique et revue des partenaires du développement du livre et de la lecture en Afrique. 1995- Irregular [1 or 2 issues annually; 25 issues published to 2006] Print and online [No ISSN] Grenoble: Culture et Développement
Editorial address: Association Culture et Développement, 9 rue de la Poste 38000 Grenoble, France, nord.sud@culture-developpement.asso.fr
Online: http://www.culture-developpement.asso.fr/site/rubrique.php3?id_rubrique=5 (requires subscription or purchase articles on a document delivery basis at a fee of €3.00 per article) [11/02/08]
Published by Grenoble-based Association ➜ **Culture et Développement (54)** this cultural development journal has published several issues devoted to topics on different aspects of the book and reading in francophone Africa, the promotion of

books and libraries, book donation programmes, as well as short articles and stories on publishing, book distribution and the retail book trade in different African countries, and children's book publishing. The following issues will be of particular interest:

No. 5: **Libraires et librairies en Afrique** (primarily on Benin)
1997, 8 pp.
No. 7: **Des livres pour l'Afrique: le don et la raison** (primarily on Cameroun)
October 1997, 12 pp.
No. 9: **Les Comores inaugurent la route du livre**
July 1998 12 pp.
No. 11: **Librairies par terre. Le livre-débrouille** (focusing on street booksellers in Cameroun and in Niger)
November 1998, 16 pp.
No. 20: **Le don de livres en question(s)**
January 2001, 12 pp.
No. 21: **Agir pour le livre en Afrique (Ivry-sur-Seine, 18 janvier 2002)**
Spring 2001, 8 pp.
No. 22: **Savoir pour tous en Mauritanie**
May 2002, 16 pp.
No. 24: **Numéro spécial Sénégal** (focusing on books, publishing and reading in Senegal)
January 2003, 20 pp.

163   Ngoma. Talking Drum. 1986- Twice yearly. Print and (partially) online [No ISSN]
Edited by Tony Richards codehq@codecan.org Ottawa: CODE. (also available in a French version)
Editorial address: Ngoma, CODE, 321 Chapel Street, Ottawa, ON K1N 7Z2 Canada
Online (from vol. 21, no. 2, Summer 1998-)
http://www.codecan.org/english/pub_ngoma.html [30/03/08]
Note: URL changes for each issue, latest is vol. 29, no. 2, Winter 2007, http://www.codecan.org/english/documents/ngoma_winter2007.pdf.
The official newsletter of ➔ **CODE (48)**, a Canadian non-governmental organization committed to support a sustainable literate environment in the developing world by helping create national publishing industries, supporting the professional development of teachers, librarians, authors and publishers, as well as building library collections through local and donated North American books. *Ngoma* contains frequent short articles on publishing, library and book development, and literacy programmes, as well as reports about CODE-supported projects in Africa.

Notre Librairie *see* ➔ **Cultures Sud (158)**

164   Partners in African Publishing. Information Source for African-European Publishing Cooperation. 1995-2000 ceased.
Edited by Kelvin Smith. (Text in English and French) Oxford: CODE Europe; as from issue 12/13, 1998-2000. London: Book Aid International
The last issue of this useful newsletter from the Partners in African Publishing Programme was issue 20, December 2000. Its aim was to encourage and facilitate cooperation between publishers and development organizations in Africa and

Europe. It was replaced by a new publication from ➔ **Book Aid International (38),** entitled ➔ **BookLinks. The Networking Forum for the Book Chain (157).**

165   Sankofa: A Journal of African Children's and Young Adult Literature. 2002- Annually ISSN 0034-5210
Edited by Meena Khorana meenakh@aol.com or english@morgan.edu
Baltimore, MD: Department of English, and Language Arts, Morgan State University. Editorial address: 202-E Holmes Hall, Morgan State University, 1700 E. Cold Spring Road, Baltimore, MD 21251, USA,
Online (table of contents only):
http://jewel.morgan.edu/~english/english.htm [11/02/08]
Sankofa's primary objective is "to disseminate information on African children's and young adult literature; recognize common inaccuracies, stereotypes, and biases in books set in Africa; provide readers with in-depth book reviews and scholarly articles on emerging trends in African and African diaspora literatures; and stimulate a global conversation on the comparative patterns in the representation of children in literature." Articles primarily focus on writing for children of different age groups – frequently by prominent African children's writers – and on overviews of the status of children's literature in different African countries. The journal also covers aspects such as illustrating and translating of children's books, and there are occasional articles on the challenges of publishing for children in Africa. The full table of contents of the six volumes published to date can be accessed at the above Web site.

Scholarly Publishing *see* ➔ **Journal of Scholarly Publishing (161)**

166   Takam Tikou. Le bulletin de la joie par les livres. 1991- Twice yearly. ISSN 1271-6103 Paris: Centre national du livre pour enfants.
Editors: Marie Laurentin marie.laurentin@lajoieparleslivres.com
Viviana Quiñones viviana.quinones@lajoieparleslivres.com
Hasmig Chahinian hasmig.chahinian@lajoieparleslivres.com
Editorial address: 25 boulevard de Strasbourg, 75010 Paris
Web/Online (tables of contents only):
http://www.lajoieparleslivres.com/Default.asp?INSTANCE=JOIE [11/02/08]
Established in 1965 and published by ➔ **La Joie par les Livres (86)** (formerly Les Amis de la Joie par les Livres) promotes quality children's literature, aims to support initiatives that encourage children to read, and facilitates access to books by children in Africa. Attractively illustrated, *Takam Tikou* includes a diverse range of articles on children's books from and about Africa, African creative writing, and development of authorship, together with news and reports, interviews, bibliographic listings, and extensive reviews of new books (published in both Africa and in France), all with full acquisitions data.

Bibliographies and continuing sources, and special collections

Note: for a fuller listing of earlier bibliographies on the topic of publishing in Africa see entries in the previous (1996) edition of the bibliography.

167 Accessions List of the Library of Congress Office, Nairobi, Kenya. (formerly *Accessions List: East and Southern Africa*) 1968- ISSN 1527-5396 Six times yearly? Nairobi: Library of Congress Office, (In the US use the following ordering address: Field Director-LOC, Unit 64110, APO AE 09831-4110, Email: nairobi@libcon-kenya.org]
The Library of Congress Office in Nairobi is one of six overseas offices administered by the African/Asian Acquisitions and Overseas Operations Division of the Library of Congress. The office acquires and catalogues publications from 25 countries primarily in eastern and southern Africa, but as from 1998 it also started acquiring material from West Africa. Acquisitions include publications from many sources: commercial publishers, international, governmental and non-governmental organizations, and also includes a great deal of ephemera and grey literature. As a record of the publications it acquires the office publishes this bi-monthly accessions list, with a biennial Serials Supplement (available on CD-ROM only) and a useful *Annual Publishers Directory*. Additionally the office publishes the → **Quarterly Index to African Periodical Literature (180)**. All these publications are freely available to libraries and other institutions on request.

168 The African Book Publishing Record. 1975- Oxford: Hans Zell Publishers 1975-1979; Munich & London: Hans Zell Publishers, an imprint of K.G. Saur Ltd 1980-1988.; Sevenoaks, later East Grinstead: Hans Zell Publishers, an imprint of Bowker-Saur Ltd., 1988-2000; K.G. Saur, 2001- Munich. Quarterly Print and (partially) online ISSN 0306-0322
Edited by Hans M. Zell & Cécile Lomer; from vol. 28, no. 3, 2002- edited by Cécile Lomer africanbookpublishingrecord@gmail.com or CecileLomer@cs.com
Online: (as from vol. 27, 2001-) http://www.atypon-link.com/WDG/loi/abpr (requires subscription; or purchase articles on a document delivery basis at a fee of $32.00 per article/sections)
Editorial address: Cécile Lomer, Editor, The African Book Publishing Record, Petit Bersac, 24600 Ribérac, France
Currently (2008) in its 34th year of publication, the quarterly *African Book Publishing Record* (ABPR) is probably the single most comprehensive source of current African book publishing output. Since ABPR first started publication in 1975 it has listed over 60,000 new African-published books, from some 1,600 African publishers, research institutions with publishing programmes, as well as NGOs, professional associations and learned societies, and others. Moreover, it has published close to 4,000 book reviews, contributed by reviewers from all over the world, including many in Africa. ABPR provides bibliographic coverage of new and forthcoming titles in English and

French, as well as those in African languages. Its bibliographic sections provide triple access to new books: by subject, by author, and by country of publication, and in each issue there is directory of publishers whose titles are listed in that issue. Complete bibliographic and acquisitions data is provided for each title. ABPR also includes news items, and occasional articles, relating to various aspects of publishing and book development in Africa, as well as news and reports about book promotional activities and events. All titles published in ABPR are cumulated in ➔ **African Books in Print/Livres africains disponibles (188)**.

169 Alemna, A. Anaba **"Publishing and the Book Trade in Ghana."** *Scholarly Publishing* 21, no. 2 (January 1990): 99-107.
An annotated bibliography of 41 items on publishing and the book trade in Ghana, including books, reports and articles.

170 Altbach, Philip G., and Eva-Maria Rathgeber **Publishing in the Third World. Trend Report and Bibliography.** New York: Praeger, 1980. 187 pp.
Presents an overview of the problems and prospects of publishing in the Third World and includes a fairly comprehensive bibliography. In two parts, the first discusses major trends in the literature on publishing in the Third World and the second is the bibliography, listing books and journal articles in French, English, Spanish and German arranged by country, region and by subject, with cross-referencing. Cites 969 references.

171 Altbach, Philip G., and Hyaeweol Choi **Bibliography on Publishing and Book Development in the Third World, 1980-1993**. Norwood, NJ: Ablex Publishing Corp. (Bellagio Studies in Publishing, 3) 1993. 152 pp.
Partially annotated, this bibliography lists some 200 references relating to publishing and book development in Africa (largely, but not exclusively, published between 1980 and 1993), together with another 650 items on publishing in other Third World countries. Intended as a supplement to the preceding entry ➔ **170**. Also includes an introductory essay by Philip Altbach, "What We Know about Third World Publishing: Issues and Debates".

172 Alman, M., and Carole Travis **Periodicals from Africa: A Bibliography and Union List of Periodicals Published in Africa.** Boston: G.K. Hall, 1977. 619 pp.
Lists over 17,000 serials, including those which have ceased publication.

173 Anyakoha, Maduha W. **"Publishing in Africa: A Bibliography."** *Current Bibliography on African Affairs*, no. 8 (1975): 296-319.
255 citations covering literature published up to 1974, using a geographical arrangement.

Bessière, Audrey, ed. **Livres d'images d'Afrique noire: auteurs-illustrateurs Africains: catalogue des collections des bibliothèques pour enfants de la Ville de Paris** *see* ➔ **Section 4, Studies by topic: Children's book publishing** entry **1552**

174   Ecole de Bibliothécaires, Archivistes et Documentalistes, Université de Dakar **Le livre et la presse en Afrique au Sud du Sahara.** Dakar: EBAD, 1980. 155 pp.
Analytical bibliography in seven sections: general, historical, legal, economics, conservation and funding documents, publishing and printing, cultural promotion and public reading habits. A descriptive bibliography (records 396-454) – with indexes by author, geographical location and subject – cites a total of 454 references.

175   Koenig, Mary *et al* **Issues and Trends in Government Publishing in the Third World and their Implications for Collection Development.** *Government Publications Review* 19 no. (January-February1992): 1-59.
Contains three contributions that discuss government publishing in developing countries and its effects on library collection development. Reviews issues such as national information policies, user expectations, cultural influences, bibliographic control, and acquisition and access to publications from Africa and Asia. Also includes "Government Publishing in the Third World - A Bibliography of Works about Official Publishing in Developing Countries." by L. Hallewell (pp. 23-59), which cites 236 works about publishing in developing countries.

176   Lindfors, Bernth **Black African Literature in English.**
Six volumes published to date:
Black African Literature in English. A Guide to Information Sources. Detroit: Gale Research Company (American Literature, English Literature, and World Literatures in English Information Guides Series, 23), 1979. 512 pp.
Black African Literature in English, 1977-1981 Supplement. New York: Africana Publishing Company, 1986. 412 pp.
Black African Literature in English, 1982-1986. London: Hans Zell Publishers, 1989. 472 pp.
Black African Literature in English, 1987-1991. London: Hans Zell Publishers (Bibliographical Research in African Literatures, 3), 1995. 718 pp.
Black African Literature in English, 1992-1996. Oxford: Hans Zell Publishers, an imprint of James Currey, 2000. 697 pp.
Black African Literature in English, 1997-1999. Oxford: Hans Zell Publishers, an imprint of James Currey, 2003. 490 pp.
This series of bibliographies compiled by Bernth Lindfors provide remarkably comprehensive coverage of critical writing (and bibliographical material, interviews, etc.) on anglophone black African literature. Among its 26 topic headings the volumes include sections on 'Censorship', 'Children's Literature', 'Publishing', 'The Role of the Writer', 'Craft of Writing', and 'Periodicals'. They are particularly strong for coverage of articles and short pieces published in African newspapers and "little magazines", which are frequently difficult to track down bibliographically. All volumes are meticulously indexed. An outstanding resource.

177   Montagnes, Ian **The Literature of the Book: Publishing Development.** *Logos. The Journal of the World Book Community* 15, no. 2 (2005): 92-94.
Online: http://www.atypon-link.com/LOG/doi/pdf/10.2959/logo.2004.15.2.92
A short, critically annotated listing of significant literature in two categories: (i) books that examine the environment of publishing in developing countries, and (ii) books and training manuals that have been written specifically to assist publishers in those countries.

178   Oxford Brookes University Library **Publishing in Africa Collection.**
http://www.brookes.ac.uk/library/speccoll/africa.html [23/02/08]
The Paul Hamlyn Foundation/CODE Europe Special Collection on Publishing in Africa is a joint initiative between Oxford Brookes University Library and the Oxford Centre for Publishing Consultancy and Research, and was set up with a generous donation from the Paul Hamlyn Foundation, as well as funding received from Macmillan and Heinemann Publishers. The subject coverage of the collection is much broader than just publishing, and all areas of the book trade in Africa are covered, as well as libraries, information provision, literacy and education, where they relate to the industry. Examples of the output of the publishing industry in Africa are also included. Recent acquisitions include novels that were included in promotions such as *Africa's 100 Best Books*. Notable groups of material in the collection include press releases and other items from the records of the Zimbabwe International Book Fair (UK); a large number of titles from the Heinemann 'African Writers Series'; a selection of books from African literacy projects; and journals covering publishing in Africa and related fields. The collection is housed in the Headington Library and is accessible to publishers, researchers, students of publishing and all those with an interest in publishing in and for Africa. The online catalogue of the collection can be searched by linking to the catalogue of Oxford Brookes University Library, but to gain admission to the Library visitors from other higher education institutions in the UK will need to show the ID card from their home institution. Other visitors will need to provide ID, plus evidence of their home address.

179   Priestley, Carol **"Bibliography of African Book Sector Studies."**
Bellagio Publishing Network Newsletter, no. 9 (March 1994): 17-19.
Lists 48 major African book sector and similar studies commissioned by the World Bank, ODA, SIDA, UNESCO, CODE, and a number of similar organizations.

180   **Quarterly Index to African Periodical Literature.** [formerly *Quarterly Index to Periodical Literature, Eastern and Southern Africa*] 1991- Print and online Quarterly ISSN 1527-5388 Nairobi: Library of Congress Office [PO Box 30598, Nairobi]
(US ordering address: Library of Congress Office, Unit 64110, APO AE 09831-4110, Email: nairobi@libcon-kenya.org)
Online: http://lcweb2.loc.gov/misc/qsihtml/ [12/02/08]
This is another outstanding resource from the Library of Congress Office in Nairobi

(*see also* ➔ **167**), which provides an index to over 300 selected periodicals that are acquired regularly from 29 African countries, most of them of a scholarly nature. Each issue includes a register of citations listing articles under some 30 broad subject groups, and, additionally, each number also contains an author index, geographical index, subject term index, and a title of article and title of journal index. The freely accessible online database is supported by excellent search facilities: search by title, author, subject, date, country or journal; or browse by index term, article title, author, journal, broad subject area, or geographic area. Headings for broad subject areas include Publishing and Book Trade, Library and Information Science, and Communication.

181   Zell, Hans M. **Publishing and Book Development in Africa: A Bibliography/ L'édition et le développement du livre en Afrique: une bibliographie.** Paris: UNESCO (Studies on Books and Reading, 15), 1984. 143 pp.
Online: http://unesdoc.unesco.org/images/0006/000609/060911mb.pdf [12/02/08]
The earliest version of the bibliography, superseded by the 1996 volume below (*see* ➔ **182** below), lists titles by topic and region, and includes author, subject, geographical indexes. Cites 685 references, and includes an introductory essay in English and French. It is now also available online, and contains a number of citations of early literature no longer included in the present work.

182   Zell, Hans M., and Cécile Lomer **Publishing and Book Development in Sub-Saharan Africa: An Annotated Bibliography.** London: Hans Zell Publishers, an imprint of Bowker-Saur/Reed Reference Publishing, 1996. 424 pp.
Supplementary volumes:
Zell, Hans M. **A Bibliography of Publishing and the Book Chain in Sub-Saharan Africa - 1996.** London: Association for the Development of Education in Africa (ADEA), Working Group on Books and Learning Materials (Perspectives on African Book Development, 3), 1997. 90 pp.
Zell, Hans M. **A Bibliography of Publishing and the Book Chain in Sub-Saharan Africa - 1997.** London: Association for the Development of Education in Africa (ADEA), Working Group on Books and Learning Materials (Perspectives on African Book Development, 6), 1997. 82 pp.
The first edition of, and superseded by, the present work, together with its two supplementary volumes. The main bibliography contains 2,267 entries covering books, serials, reference sources, reports, papers in edited collections, book sector studies and similar documents, periodical articles drawn from literature published in over 360 journals and magazines, and well as a substantial number of unpublished documents and ephemera. It contains a large number of citations of early literature, and short papers, reports, etc. no longer included in the present work.

Collective online catalogue databases

183   The Africa Book Centre Ltd.

http://www.africabookcentre.com [12/02/08]
This specialist UK dealer and library supplier of books on Africa, maintains a
database of about 35,000 titles and stocks of some 5,000 books are carried, including
an extensive range of African-published material. The company does not, at this
time, maintain a complete integrated online catalogue as such, but you can access the
complete archive of weekly listings going back for a few months, plus an archive of
select backlist titles. There are special sections devoted to new titles, book of the
month, African languages and linguistics, award winners, signed copies, African
music and CDs, children's books, African food and drink, or browse by
country/region or by subject.

184   African Books Collective Ltd.

http://www.africanbookscollective.com [12/02/08]
The Oxford-based ➜ **African Books Collective/ABC (3)** provides a single source of
supply for the books from over a hundred African publishers, from 19 African
countries, currently offering over 1,000 titles — scholarly, literature, and children's
books. The complete stock list can be accessed at the ABC Web site, which provides
a secure ordering environment. Browse by new titles, by broad subject groups, or
search for specific titles. Under subject groups titles can be viewed by title,
publication date (most recent titles on top), country or publisher. The site also
includes author profiles, news about ABC exhibits, and information about award-
winning books. Most of the titles have recently been digitized and are now available
on a print-on-demand (POD) basis, or through POD wholesale channels. A large
number of titles held in physical stock are available through the UK wholesaler
Gardners. The online catalogue of ABC's North American distributor, Michigan State
University Press, is at http://msupress.msu.edu/series.php?seriesID=22 [12/02/08]
while an attractive showcase for ABC-distributed titles, entitled "The African Books
Collective   Reading   Room",   can   be   found   at
http://www.msupress.msu.edu/Reading%20Room_abc_page.php   [12/02/08]
which provides an opportunity to preview books, browse catalogues, view sample
chapters, illustrations, or other extracts from a very wide range of ABC-distributed
African titles. From this page you can also download the *Kitabu, Iwe, Buku* catalogue
of select titles stocked by MSUP – including many titles that will be of interest to
public and school libraries – or download sections of it. North American customers
can view the full list at http://msupress.msu.edu/abc_order_form.pdf. [12/02/08]

185   Afrilivres. Livres d'Afrique et des Disasporas.

http://www.afrilivres.com/ [12/02/08]
An important new initiative launched in November 2002 by the journal ➜
Africultures (153) and the ➜ **Association d'Éditeurs Francophones d'Afrique Sub-
saharienne (8)**, in partnership with the organization, **Culture et Développement
(54)**, the ➜ **French Foreign Ministry (95)**, and financially supported by the ➜
Fondation Charles Lépold Mayer (61). It is a collaborative Web portal for a group of
francophone African publishers, currently comprising 55 publishers from 15 African

nations, and offering over 1,300 titles online. The full publisher list can be found at http://www.afrilivres.com/spip.php?rubrique2. [12/02/08] The site offers access to new books and select backlist titles – some with cover images, and including full bibliographic data and ordering information – together with profiles about participating publishers, and details of their various book series. It incorporates the electronic versions of a series of catalogues of select backlist titles, and which also includes children's books. The site offers a facility to search by title, key words, or by name of author, publisher, ISBN, and country.

Note: until recently a large proportion of the books could be ordered online in a secure environment via the distributor Servédit. However, this facility now [February 2008] seems to have been withdrawn, and orders (from outside Africa) can now be placed with the ➜ **Agence de Médiation Culturelle des Pays du Sahel (30)**, 5 Centre Pierre Mendes France, 33165 Saint Medard en Jallees, France mediation.culturelle@wanadoo.fr.

186   L'Alliance des éditeurs indépendents pour une autre mondalisation. Catalogue 2005 of French-speaking Publishers.

http://www.alliance-editeurs.org/catalogues/accueil.php?l=1 [12/02/08]
Set up in 2002 and supported by the ➜ **Fondation Charles Lépold Mayer (61)** and the ➜ **Ford Foundation (62)**, ➜ **L'Alliance des éditeurs independents pour une autre mondalisation (31)** is a not-for-profit alliance and network of independent, progressive publishers, at this time primarily those in the French-speaking areas of the world, including many in Africa. Members of the group meet regularly, develop and facilitate co-publishing projects and, as part of collaborative marketing schemes, this also includes joint exhibits at major international book fairs. On the occasion of the Salon du livre de Genève in 2005, it published a collective catalogue of select titles from 28 of its member publishers, with full ordering and contact information. It is published both in print format and available online. Access is by publisher and for each title complete bibliographic and price information is provided, together with a short description of content and a small cover image. It includes both scholarly and general publishers (and those publishing children's books) from Benin, Burkina Faso, Cameroon, Côte d'Ivoire, Gabon, Guinea, Madagascar, Mali, Morocco, and Tunisia. For each publisher the Web site also offers informative company profiles.

187   SAPnet/BookData.

http://www.bookdatasapnet.co.za/include/index.asp [12/02/08]
The South African office of BookData is an affiliate of the London-based Nielsen BookData Ltd., which creates and maintains databases of publishers' title records (including a description, synopsis of contents, and a subject classification), and then makes them available to booksellers, wholesalers, library suppliers, and librarians. BookData also offers *BookFind-Online*, a Web-based subscription service for library professionals. In 1999 Book Data joined forces with the South African information agency SAPnet and its sister company First Edition to build and maintain a comprehensive database, SA BookSearch, of titles published and/or distributed in South Africa, and which includes extended book information. Searches can be conducted over a range of criteria including title, author, publisher, and ISBN. The South African branch of BookData also sends title records to Book Data in the UK where the information is merged with their global database.

Directories and book trade reference tools (Continent-wide)

Books in print

Note: for *national* books in print compilations see under individual countries in ➔ **Section 3, Country studies.**

188   African Books in Print/Livres africains disponibles. 6th ed. Edited by Cécile Lomer. Munich: K. G. Saur, 2006. 2 vols. 1,684 pp.
A major source of reference and selection tool for African publishing output, *African Books in Print* (ABIP) cumulates and updates titles listed in ➔ **The African Book Publishing Record/ABPR (168).** Volume 1 includes the introductory and prelim matter, the directory of publishers, the subject index, and the A-J author index – listing titles under some 7,500 subject headings/sub-headings, country and regional headings, language headings, etc., and extensively cross-referenced – with the K-Z author and the title index making up volume 2. ABIP aims to provide a systematic, reliable and functional reference tool and buying guide to African-published material currently in print. The latest (6th) edition provides full bibliographic details of 33,261 titles in print as at the end of 2005, from 893 publishers and research institutions with publishing programmes, in 45 African countries. This includes a cumulation of all titles listed in volume XXVI, no. 1, 2000 through volume XXXII, no. 1, 2006, of the quarterly ABPR; plus approximately 1,550 additional records not previously listed in either ABIP or ABPR. The directory of publishers in each edition of ABIP provides full name and address details of all publishers included, with telephone and fax numbers, email addresses, Web sites where available, and the names and addresses of European and US distributors (where applicable).
Earlier editions:
1st edition: **African Books in Print. Part 1, 1975, English and African Languages.** Edited by Hans M. Zell. London: Mansell Information/ Publishing Ltd., 1975. 491 pp.
6,300 titles (in English and African languages) from 188 publishers in 19 African countries.
2nd edition: **African Books in Print. An Index by Author, Subject and Title/Livres africains disponibles. Index par auteurs, matières et titres.** Edited by Hans M. Zell. 2 vols. London: Mansell Information/Publishing Ltd., 1978. 969 pp. (Westport, Conn: Meckler Books; Paris: France Expansion; Ile-Ife: University of Ife Bookshop Ltd.)
12,240 titles from 396 publishers (including research institutions with publishing programmes) in 37 African countries.
3rd edition: **African Books in Print/Livres africains disponibles. An Index by Author, Title and Subject.** Edited by Hans M. Zell. 2 vols. London: Mansell Publishing Ltd., 1984, 1,396 pp.
18,700 titles from 604 publishers in 43 African countries.
4th edition: **African Books in Print/Livres africains disponibles. An Index by Author, Title and Subject.** Edited by Hans M. Zell. 2 vols. London: Hans Zell Publishers, an imprint of Bowker-Saur Ltd., 1993, 1,520 pp.
23,186 titles from 745 publishers in 45 African countries.
5th edition: **African Books in Print/Livres africains disponibles. An Index by Subject, Author, and Title.** Edited by Hans M. Zell, with Cécile Lomer. 2 vols. London: Bowker-Saur/Reed Business Information, 2000. 2,314pp
31,664 titles from 921 publishers in 45 African countries.

189   L'Afrique en livres. Paris: France Edition [115 boulevard Saint Germain, 75006 Paris, France], 1998. 333 pp.
Something of a mini books-in-print for African material in French, this useful catalogue lists some 4,000 books in French on Africa, from 600 publishers, including many published in francophone Africa. Titles (with full bibliographic details and prices) are arranged under six major headings and a range of sub-headings. Part 1 provides an extensive listing of African literature titles, part 2 is devoted to books for children, part 3 covers the humanities and social sciences under a number of subject groups, and which is followed by sections on the sciences, 'Vie Pratique' (cookery, travel, etc.), and a final section devoted to the arts, cinema, music and photography. No further editions have been published to date.

SACBIP: South African Children's Books in Print *see* ➜ **Country studies: South Africa (963)** and *see also* ➜ **Bookchat (130)**

Directories of publishers and the book trade

Note: for *national* book trade directories see under individual countries in ➜ **Section 3, Country studies**.

190   Accessions List of the Library of Congress Office, Nairobi, Kenya . Annual Publishers Directory. 1968- Annual ISSN 1527-540X. Nairobi: Library of Congress Office [PO Box 30598 Nairobi]
This annual directory published as a supplement to the ➜ **Accessions List of the Library of Congress Office, Nairobi, Kenya (167)** contains full address details (and fax numbers and email addresses where available) of all the publishers whose titles appeared in the catalogue records for the *Accessions List* in the preceding year. Arranged in country order, this is an excellent source for tracking down publishers' addresses, particularly small and obscure publishers, research institutions with publishing activities, government ministries, NGOs, professional associations, and learned societies.

191   African Books Collective Ltd. Research & Dissemination Unit, comps. Women in Publishing and the Book Trade in Africa. An Annotated Directory. 2nd rev. and expanded ed. Oxford: African Books Collective Ltd., 1997. 34 pp.
Supersedes a provisional listing prepared by ABC in June 1995 now revised and expanded and containing 145 entries, each with a short annotation covering areas of publishing and/or providing a short company profile. The directory is arranged in five sections (i) Women publishers in Africa (i.e. owners or directors of publishing companies or their chief executives); (ii) women in senior management positions in African publishing; (iii) women in the retail book trade and in book distribution; (iv) women in other sectors of the African book world; and (v) some African women's organizations with publishing programmes. Each entry provides contact details and

full address, telephone and fax numbers, and email addresses for some (some of which will now be very dated). No further editions published.

192   The African Book World and Press: A Directory/Répertoire du livre et de la presse en Afrique. 4th edition. Edited by Hans M. Zell. London: Hans Zell Publishers, an imprint of Bowker-Saur/Reed Business Information, 1989. 336 pp.

Comprehensive fully annotated listings of over 4,600 libraries, publishers, booksellers, magazines and periodicals, and major newspapers throughout Africa. Now very dated and no further editions have been published.

Earlier editions:

1st edition: **The African Book World and Press: A Directory/ Répertoire du livre et de la presse en Afrique.** Edited by Hans M. Zell. Oxford: Hans Zell Publishers Ltd., 1977. 299 pp. (Detroit: Gale Research Co.; Paris: France Expansion; Munich: Verlag Dokumentation)

2nd edition: **The African Book World and Press: A Directory/ Répertoire du livre et de la presse en Afrique.** Edited by Hans M. Zell. Oxford: Hans Zell Publishers Ltd., 1980, 253 pp. (Detroit: Gale Research Co.; Paris: France Expansion; Munich: K.G. Saur).

3rd edition: **The African Book World and Press: A Directory/Répertoire du livre et de la presse en Afrique.** Edited by Hans M. Zell and Caroline Bundy. Oxford: Hans Zell Publishers, 1983. 313 pp.

193   The African Publishers' Networking Directory 1999/2000. 3rd edition. Oxford: African Books Collective Ltd, 1999. 72 pp.

A reference guide and networking tool for all those interested in the book industries and book development in Africa. The directory provides detailed information on some 300 major and/or most active publishers operating in Africa [at at 1999], giving very full information for each entry, including name and address, telephone/fax numbers, email addresses, Web sites (where available), names of chief executives, number of titles in print and average number of new books published each year, and the nature of each publisher's list and areas of specialization. Now very dated and no new editions have appeared.

194   The African Publishing Companion. A Resource Guide. Compiled and edited by Hans M. Zell. Lochcarron, Scotland: Hans Zell Publishing, 2002. 356 pp. (originally published in print and online editions, but online version no longer available and the print edition is out-of-print)

Containing over 1,600 entries and extensively cross-referenced, this is a comprehensive albeit now dated documentation and information resource on African publishing and the book trade. Content includes (1) a directory of almost 700 African publishers' email addresses and Web sites (where available), including those of NGOs and research institutions with publishing activities. (2) Over 500 annotated directory listings of organizations, associations, book development councils, networks and donors supporting African publishing, bibliographic tools, journals and magazines, book review outlets, dealers and distributors of African books, booksellers and library suppliers in Africa, African book fairs and book promotional events, book and literary awards, book industry training courses, and more; full address and contact information is provided for each entry, including email addresses and Web sites, where available. (3) A separate section describing schemes, book series, and other projects promoting African book and journal publishing. (4) Information and resources on African publishing statistics and publishing capacity, and a chronology of key dates in the development of indigenous African publishing. (5) The final section is a bibliographic guide to select literature about African publishing and book development (excluding country studies). No further editions are planned.

Reviews:

The African Book Publishing Record vol. 29, no. 4, 2003

Bellagio Publishing Network Newsletter no. 31, November 2002

Online: http://www.bellagiopublishingnetwork.com/newsletter31/diabate.htm [13/02/08]

Booklinks no. 3, Summer 2003

Online:

http://www.bookaid.org/resources/downloads/booklinks/BookLinks_3.pdf [13/02/08]

Logos. Journal of the World Book Community vol. 13, no. 3, 2002

Online: http://www.atypon-link.com/LOG/doi/pdf/10.2959/logo.2002.13.3.177

Choice vol. 40, no. 3, November 2002

H-Africa H-Net Reviews June, 2003

http://www.h-net.org/reviews/showrev.cgi?path=247181058802294 [13/02/08]

195   L'association internationale des libraires francophones: Nos libraires.

Afrique Centrale: Burundi, Cameroun, Congo Brazza (RC), Congo Kinshasa (RDC), Rwanda, Tchad

http://www.librairesfrancophones.org/rubrique.php3?id_rubrique=19 [13/02/08]

Afrique de l'Ouest:

Benin, Burkina Faso, Côte d'Ivoire, Ghana, Guinée, Mali, Niger, Nigeria, Senegal, Togo (includes booksellers in English speaking West African countries which specialize in French books)

http://www.librairesfrancophones.org/rubrique.php3?id_rubrique=20 [13/02/08]

Océan indien

Comores, Djibouti, Madagascar

http://www.librairesfrancophones.org/rubrique.php3?id_rubrique=25 [13/02/08]

(Also *Maghreb*: Algérie, Maroc, Mauritanie, Tunisie

http://www.librairesfrancophones.org/rubrique.php3?id_rubrique=24)

Hosted by the Association internationale des libraires francophones – the international association of booksellers in the francophone countries of the North and the South, including a large number in Africa – this is an excellent online directory of the leading booksellers in most countries in French-speaking Africa. Each entry provides full name and address, telephone and fax numbers, email address, and the name of the owner or Managing Director of each bookshop. For a number of countries, for example Madagascar and Senegal, the directory-type information is supplemented by informative profiles about the bookshops, their history, range of stocks and/or areas of specialization, book promotional activities, etc., together with colour photographs of their premises.

196   The Book Chain in Anglophone Africa. A Survey and Directory.
Edited by Roger Stringer. Oxford: International Network for the Availability of Scientific Publications (INASP), 2002. 274 pp. Print and online
Online: http://www.inasp.info/file/57/the-book-chain-in-anglophone-africa-a-survey-and-directory.html
[13/02/08]
http://www.inasp.info/uploaded/documents/Book_Chain_rev.pdf
[13/02/08] (download page for complete text)
A valuable information resource that provides a country-by-country analysis of the "book chain" in 18 English-speaking Africa countries, together with an annotated directory of the major players that make up the book chain within those countries. Four introductory essays provide overviews of book and library development in anglophone Africa from different perspectives. These are followed by country surveys, each prepared by a book professional from the country concerned, most of them librarians. The final section, a 170-page Directory of Selected Organizations in the Book Chain in Anglophone Africa, provides listings of the major players in the book chain in each of the countries covered, including professional associations, major publishers, printers, booksellers and libraries; regional and international bodies supporting book development, and training institutions for librarianship and the book industries. Each entry gives full address, telephone and fax numbers, email addresses (and Web sites for some), and many entries include a short description. *Note:* some of the papers in this volume are individually abstracted elsewhere in this bibliography.
Reviews:
The African Book Publishing Record vol. 29, no. 4, 2003

197   Bookman Consultants Ltd. "East African Book Trade Directory-Supplement. A Guide to Publishers, Printers, Booksellers, Libraries and the Book Trade in East Africa: Kenya, Uganda & Tanzania, 1995-1996."
The East African Bookseller, no. 12 (1995?): 1-48.
Provides detailed information about publishers, booksellers and the printing industries in three East African countries, together with listings of libraries, magazines and periodicals in two of these countries. Now very dated.

198   Cape Town Book Fair. Exhibitor Catalogue.
http://www.capetownbookfair.com/home (Main home page)
http://www.capetownbookfair.com/exhibitors/catalogue
(2007 Catalogue search) [26/11/07]
http://www.capetownbookfair.com/exhibitors/whos-who-search
(2007 Who's Who Search) [26/11/07]
Note: the above URLs for the 2007 catalogue search and the Who's Who will shortly be replaced by their 2008 versions, but URLs are not available at

press time. Click on the main home page for links to the latest version of the exhibitor catalogue.

The Cape Town Book fair online exhibitor catalogue offers a useful, freely accessible search tool. Significantly, it includes both publishers who had individual exhibits at the Fair, as well as those represented at collective exhibits, e.g. those who exhibited at the stand of the ➜ **African Publishers Network (5)**, or publishers represented by agents and distributors. Search or browse by country, key words relating to areas of publishing, branch of business (e.g. publishers, booksellers, literary agents, printing and manufacture sector, multimedia, wholesalers/distributors, service providers, etc.), and nature of products sold (e.g. books, magazines, audio, video, film, CD-ROM, electronic, print-on-demand, software, etc.) Each entry provides full name and address, telephone and fax numbers, email, Web site (where available), information about areas of publishing, together with a brief company profile. The data currently [November 2007] displayed in the catalogue are those of the Cape Town Book Fair held in June 2007 (URLs change for each year's fair). A companion tool is an online **Who's Who Search** (covering *registered* visitors only; search or browse by country, profession/trade, main interests, areas of responsibility, etc.), which is helpful for tracking down individuals in particular book professions.

199   Humphrey, Lesley **Overview of Book Trade Journals, Newsletters, Handbooks, and other Reference Material Published in Five African Countries: Ghana, Kenya, Namibia, South Africa, and Zimbabwe."** In *Development Directory of Indigenous Publishing 1995*, compiled by Carol Priestley. Harare: African Publishers' Network, 1995, 98-107.

A useful (albeit now significantly dated) annotated directory of tools of the trade available for five African countries, including book trade magazines, directories of publishers, books-in-print, and other reference resources.

La Joie par les livres **L'édition africaine pour la jeunesse** *see* ➜ **Section 4, Studies by topic: Children's book publishing** entry **1613**

200   Priestley, Carol, comp. **Development Directory of Indigenous Publishing, 1995.** Harare: African Publishers' Network (APNET Reference Handbooks), 1995. 201 pp.

Contains essays on aspects of indigenous publishing in various African countries (see also individual entries), overviews on the state of publishing in specific regions, a directory of book trade publications and reference sources published in five African countries, plus two inventories of (i) African book development organizations, and (ii) international organizations promoting indigenous publishing.

201   **Trade Directory/Répertoire Commercial/O Directório Commercial, 2000/2001.** Harare, later Abidjan/Accra: African Publishers' Network, 2000. 97 pp. [latest ed. published is for 2002/2003?]

A directory of publishers throughout Africa, arranged alphabetically by country. Each entry gives full address details, telephone and fax numbers, and email addresses and Web sites for some. Many entries give a contact person – usually the company or organization's chief executive, or marketing personnel – and an indication of the nature of the publisher's list and/or areas of specialization. Preceding each country section there is a brief country profile giving population size and literacy rates, a small map, and an indication of each country's national book trade association, their aims and objectives, and their activities. New and updated editions of this directory were promised for every two years, but have not appeared in recent years.

Zimbabwe International Book Fair Trust/Southern African Book Development Education Trust **African Periodicals Exhibit Catalogue 1999** *see* ➔ **Section 4, Studies by topic: Journals and magazine publishing** entry **1991**

2
General, comparative, and regional studies

Comparative studies (General/comparative studies on publishing in developing countries)

This section offers select references to a number of general articles on publishing in developing countries that include discussions on the state of the book industry in Africa.

202   Agenau, Robert **"A Comparative Approach to the Publishing Chains in Africa and Europe."** In *Promoting Technical Publishing in Africa. Seminar Proceedings. Arnhem, Netherlands, 3-6 November.* Wageningen, Netherlands: Technical Centre for Agricultural and Rural Cooperation of ACP-EU (CTA), 1994, 29-32.
The Managing Director of Editions Karthala, Paris, whose list focuses primarily on books on Sub-Saharan Africa and the Maghreb, compares the publishing chains of Europe and Africa.

203   Akinleye, Michael **"Publishing Personnel & Management in Developing Countries: A Nigerian View."** *The African Book Publishing Record* 6, no. 3/4 (1980): 215-217.
A revised and expanded version of a paper presented to the 21st International Publishers Association Congress, Stockholm, Sweden, in 1980. It addresses the question of what, in a free market situation, the strategy of a publishing house should be in order to ensure its survival, bearing in mind the particular problems of a developing environment.

204   Altbach, Philip G. **"Publishing and the Intellectual System."** *Annals AAPSS* (September 1975): 1-13.
Considers factors such as levels of literacy, book buying habits, libraries, copyright and bookshops in the light of the effect they have on the nature of the publishing and book industry. Asserts that the education system is an integral part of the publishing industry, and argues that "it is impossible to ignore the broader elements of the modern intellectual community in discussing publishing."

205   Altbach, Philip G. **"Literary Colonialism: Books in the Third World."** In *Perspectives on Publishing.* Lexington: D.C.Heath and Company, 1976, 83-101.
Also published in *Harvard Educational Review* 45, no. 2 (May 1975): 226-236.

An overview of the special problems of books in the Third World, with a discussion of the heritage of colonialism, the current [1976] situation, the orientation of intellectuals, the economics of the book trade, and scholarly publishing, offering possible strategies for the development of this sector of the book industries.

Altbach, Philip G. **"The Role and Nurturing of Journals in the Third World."** *see* ➜ **Section 4, Studies by topic: Journals and magazine publishing** entry **1916**

206 Altbach, Philip G.; Amadio A. Arboleda, and S. Gopinathan, eds. **Publishing in the Third World.** London: Mansell Publishing Ltd., 1985. 225 pp.
This was the first study of "Third World" publishing on an international scale, with chapters on countries in Asia, Africa, Latin America and the Middle East. Provides an analysis of the key issues relating to publishing in developing nations, and stresses the need to promote increased awareness of publishing as a crucial part of education, scholarship, intellectual life and research. Contains articles on general topics such as textbook publishing, copyright and distribution, followed by sections on specific countries and regions, including Ghana and Kenya.

207 Altbach, Philip G.; Amadio A. Arboleda, and S. Gopinathan, eds. **"Publishing in the Third World: Some Reflections."** In *Publishing in the Third World*, edited by Philip G. Altbach, Amadio A. Arboleda, and S. Gopinathan. London: Mansell Publishing Ltd., 1985, 1-10.
This introductory essay to *Publishing in the Third World* (*see* entry ➜ **206** above) endeavours to provide an "understanding of the realities and issues of publishing in the Third World", and discusses some of the major problems which beset publishing in developing countries [in the 1980s].

208 Altbach, Philip G., and S. Gopinathan **"Textbooks in the Third World: Challenge and Response."** In *Publishing in the Third World*, edited by Philip G. Altbach, Amadio A. Arboleda, and S. Gopinathan. London: Mansell Publishing Ltd., 1985, 13-24.
Also reprinted in *Readings on Publishing in Africa and the Third World*, by Philip G. Altbach. Buffalo, NY: Bellagio Publishing Network, Research and Information Center (Bellagio Studies in Publishing 1), 1993, 201-212.
Reviews the state of textbook publishing in the developing world, examining the multiple roles of textbooks, the historical context, the international context, and the issue of language.

209 Altbach, Philip G.; and Gail P. Kelly, eds. **Textbooks in the Third World: Policy, Content and Context.** New York: Garland Publishing, 1988. 277 pp.
A volume of essays on government and international agency policies regarding the provision of textbooks in developing countries, analysing problems and constraints, and examining the economic, social, and pedagogic questions involved in textbook

writing for both primary and secondary schools and for tertiary education. The second part of the book considers the content of textbooks and the influence of textbooks in classroom practice, with examples from texts to show how they relate to the life of the audiences for whom they are written, and the relationship between textbook content and state policies or ideology. Individual papers include "Textbooks in Developing Countries: Economic and Pedagogical Choices" (Joseph P. Farrell, Stephen P. Heyneman); "Textbooks in Third World Higher Education" (Philip G. Altbach; S. Gopinathan); "The Politics of Textbook Selection and Control: The Case of Interwar Indochina and West Africa" (Gail P. Kelly); "Gender and Textbooks: An African Case Study" (Karen L. Biraimah); "Language and Texts in Africa" (Dennis Mbuyi); "Language and the Content of School Texts: The Nigerian Experience" (Chuka Eze Okonkwo).

Reviews:
Comparative Education vol. 26, no. 1, 1990
World Libraries vol. 1, no. 1, Summer 1990
Online: http://www.worlib.org/vol01no1/print/priestley_print.html [21/02/08]

210 Altbach, Philip G. **"Third World Publishers and the International Knowledge System."** *Logos. The Journal of the World Book Community* 2, no. 3 (1991): 122-126.
Online:
http://www.atypon-link.com/LOG/doi/pdf/10.2959/logo.1991.2.3.122
Also reprinted in *Readings on Publishing in Africa and the Third World,* by Philip G. Altbach. Buffalo, NY: Bellagio Publishing Network, Research and Information Center (Bellagio Studies in Publishing 1), 1993, 87-91.
Reviews the access for Third World countries to international knowledge systems, and comments on the need for governments to be reminded that "free and flourishing publishing industries" should be both encouraged and assisted.

211 Altbach, Philip G., ed. **Publishing and Development in the Third World.** London: Hans Zell Publishers; New Delhi: Vistaar Publications; Nairobi: Heinemann Kenya, 1992. 441 pp.
This benchmark volume (widely reviewed, see below) stems from the papers commissioned for a major international seminar on Publishing in the Third World, held at Bellagio, Italy, in February 1991. It presents the first full scale discussion of publishing in Asia and Africa, and features perspectives from 25 prominent publishers and recognized leaders in the field. It aims to provide a better understanding of the problems and the accomplishments of book publishing in Africa and Asia. Includes discussions of innovative ideas in Third World publishing, loan guarantee programmes, joint marketing and distribution, translation programmes and co-publication. Other papers analyse a number of programmes and initiatives sponsored by Western agencies, the World Bank, and multilateral programmes. *Note:* several of the papers in this collection are individually abstracted elsewhere in this bibliography.

Reviews:
Africa Today vol. 39, no. 4, 1992
African Publishing Review vol. 2, no. 2, March/April, 1996

African Studies Review vol. 37, no. 3, 1994
Against the Grain February, 1993
Australian Library Review vol. 9, no. 4, 1992
Focus on International & Comparative Librarianship vol. 23, no. 2, 1992
International Journal of Information & Library Research vol. 5, no. 1, 1993
Journal of Academic Librarianship July 1993
The Library Quarterly April 1993
Logos. The Journal of the World Book Community vol. 3, no. 3, 1992
Online: http://www.atypon-link.com/LOG/doi/pdf/10.2959/logo.1992.3.3.134
Publishing Research Quarterly vol. 9, no. 2, Fall 1993
Online:
http://www.vanderbilt.edu/peabody/heyneman/PUBLICATIONS/199304.pdf
[21/02/08]
Scholarly Publishing vol. 23, no. 4, July 1992, pp. 231-241 [this is an extensive review essay by Ian Montagnes, "Sustainable Development in Book Publishing"]
Third World Libraries vol. 2, Spring, 1992, p. 67

212   Altbach, Philip G. **"Publishing in the Third World: Issues and Trends for the 21st Century."** In *Publishing and Development in the Third World*, edited by Philip G. Altbach. London: Hans Zell Publishers, 1992, 1-27. Also published In *The Political Economy of the Media*, edited by Peter Golding and Graham Murdock. London: Edward Elgar Publishing Ltd., 1997, 324-350.

Presents the state of publishing in the Third World [in the early 1990s], examining the successes and failures of publishing in the post-colonial period. Considers the stresses placed on the publishing industry by economic crises, technological change, and the extraordinary rate of expansion of knowledge in industrialized nations. Analyzes the importance of indigenous publishing, the vexed question of copyright, as well as other issues particular to the Third World, and discusses regional variations affecting the publishing industry.

213   Altbach, Philip G. **"The Unchanging Variable: Textbooks in Comparative Perspective."** In *Afro-Asian Publishing. Contemporary Trends*, edited by Narendra Kumar, and S.K. Ghai. New Delhi: Institute of Book Publishing, 1992, 11-30.

A comprehensive review of all aspects of textbook publishing including such issues as internationalization, the nature of textbooks as a defining component in education, whether textbooks should be published by state or private companies, the problems at the level of publishing infrastructure, and the future of the textbook in a complex world.

214   Altbach, Philip G., ed. **Readings on Publishing in Africa and the Third World.** Buffalo, NY: Bellagio Publishing Network, Research and Information Center, in association with the Comparative Education Center and School of Information and Library Studies, State University of New York at Buffalo (Bellagio Studies on Publishing, 1), 1993. 226 pp.

A selection of some of the best analytical writings on African and Third World publishing and book development. Contains 12 contributions on publishing in Africa, most reprinted from ➔ **The African Book Publishing Record (168)**, including some individual country studies.

215 Altbach, Philip G., and Damtew Teffera, eds. **Publishing and Development: A Book of Readings.** Chestnut Hill, MA: Bellagio Publishing Network Research and Information Center, (Bellagio Studies in Publishing, 9), 1998. 191 pp.
Co-published with the Obor Foundation this is a collection of nine articles/reprints (previously published elsewhere) on key issues affecting the book industries in the developing world. They covers topics such as multinationals and Third World publishing, the economics of publishing, copyright, distribution, educational publishing and book provision, the transition from state to private sector publishing, and electronic publishing and new technologies that have transformed the book publishing process.
Reviews:
Publishing Research Quarterly vol. 15, no. 1, Spring 1999

216 Altbach, Philip G. **"Issues and Trends: Book Publishing."** In *UNESCO. World Information Report*, 1997/98. Paris, UNESCO, 2000, 338-348.
Also published in French as **"Débats et tendances: l'édition."**
Online (English version):
http://unesdoc.unesco.org/images/0010/001062/106215e.pdf [30/11/07]
A general overview on book publishing worldwide and the nature of the publishing enterprise and the current challenges facing publishing worldwide, but with some coverage of the state of the book industries in Africa and other parts of the developing world.

217 Askerud, Pernille **A Guide to Sustainable Book Provision. From Plan to Print**. Paris: UNESCO (Document ED-97/WS/24), 1997. 116 pp.
Online: http://www.unesco.org/education/blm/guidecontent_en.php [30/01/08]
French online version [no title indicated]
http://www.unesco.org/education/blm/blmintro_fr.php#1 [30/01/08]
[Also available in Spanish]
Shorter version also published in *Publishing and Development: A Book of Readings*, edited by Philip G. Altbach and Damtew Teffera. Chestnut Hill, MA: Bellagio Publishing Network Research and Information Center (Bellagio Studies in Publishing, 9), 1998, 91-110;
as **"Textbooks for Developing Countries: Why Projects Fail"** in *Logos. The Journal of the World Book Community* 9, no. 2 (1998): 109-112.
http://www.atypon-link.com/LOG/doi/pdf/10.2959/logo.1998.9.2.109

and, as an adaptation from the *Logos* article, also freely accessible at http://www.osi.hu/cpd/policyresources/AskerudENG.html [30/01/08]
Although not specifically dealing with the African situation, and primarily intended for educational planners and policy makers in developing countries – and their counterparts in development, and donor agencies – this is an excellent guide that aims to assist governments to establish technically and economically sound and sustainable planning and management systems for the development and provision of good quality learning materials. The author identifies the most acute problems in book provision, describes the different publishing processes, and the professional skills required in the publishing industry. Other chapters set out the differences between general publishing and the development, production and distribution of educational materials, and how to deal efficiently with the issues and problems that are raised in this book, together with suggestions for the development of an effective national book policy. (*See also* ➜ UNESCO/DANIDA Basic Learning Materials Initiative **Guidelines for the Conduct and Organization of National Book Sector Consultations,** entry **244**)
Reviews:
The African Book Publishing Record vol. 24, no. 2, 1998

218 Barker, R.E., and R. Escarpit, eds. **The Book Hunger.** Paris: UNESCO; London: Harrap, 1973. 155 pp.
Also published in French as **La faim du livre**.
One of the earliest studies providing an overview of publishing in developing countries, covering book production, likely future trends, distribution, copyright, and the reading habit.

219 Behrstock, Julian **"Books For All? UNESCO's Long Love Affair with the Book."** *Logos. The Journal of the Book Community* 2, no. 1 (1991): 29-36.
Online:
http://www.atypon-link.com/LOG/doi/pdf/10.2959/logo.1991.2.1.29
Describes the history of ➜ **UNESCO's (118)** long-standing commitment to promoting the cause of the book, including its *Charter of the Book*, which defines the principles that should govern national and international policies relating to books and the book sector.

Butalia, Urvashi, and Rita Menon **Making a Difference: Feminist Publishing in the South** *see* ➜ **Section 4, Studies by topic: Women in African publishing/Publishing by and for women** entry **2373**

220 Durand, Rosamaria **"UNESCO's Section for Books and Reading: A Holistic View of Book Development."** *African Publishing Review* 4, no. 5 (September/October 1995): 16-17.

Also in *International Publishers Bulletin* 11, no. 3 (1995): 11-13; shorter version also published in *Bellagio Publishing Network Newsletter*, no. 14 (August 1995): 9-10

Looks at past support by ➜ **UNESCO (118)** of book development and book promotional activities. It reviews the various initiatives and campaigns with which it has been associated since 1950, including UNESCO's role as a catalyst to effect positive changes in the book world, and its collaboration with other organizations that promote books and reading.

221 Escarpit, Robert **The Book Revolution.** London: Harrap; Paris: UNESCO, 1966. 160 pp.

A classic study on the state of the book, published in 1966, which devoted some attention to book publishing in developing countries.

222 Farrell, Joseph P., and Stephen P. Heyneman, eds. **Textbooks in the Developing World: Economic and Educational Choices.** Washington, DC: The World Bank (EDI Seminar series), 1989. 286 pp.

Summary article also published in: Altbach, Philip G. and Gail P. Kelly, *Textbooks in the Third World: Policy, Content and Context.* New York and London: Garland Publishing Inc., 1988, pp. 19-45.

Online:

http://www.vanderbilt.edu/peabody/heyneman/PUBLICATIONS/19890 4.pdf (3.6MB) [30/01/08]

A collection of 16 papers that focus on what has been learned in two decades of developing and implementing large-scale national textbook programmes, and the ➜ **World Bank's (124)** role in assisting textbook development. Organized into four parts it covers (1) The Design and Implementation of Textbook Programs: An Overview; (2) Policy Issues in Textbook Program Development; (3) Provision of Textbooks: Developed Systems and Infant Industries; and (4) The Future: Will New Electronic Media Make the Textbook Obsolete? Includes a case study on Lesotho.

223 Heyneman, Stephen P. **"Producing Textbooks in Developing Countries."** *Finance and Development* (March 1990): 28-29.

Online:

http://www.vanderbilt.edu/peabody/heyneman/PUBLICATIONS/19900 1.pdf [30/01/08]

Urges Ministries of Education and educational policy makers in developing countries to rethink their views and heavy involvement in publishing of textbooks and calls for more competition. The author argues that the yawning gap between the demand and supply of quality textbooks makes it imperative for governments to alter their approaches.

224 Heyneman, Stephen P. **"Protection of the Textbook Industry in Developing Countries: In the Public Interest?"** *Book Research Quarterly* 5, no. 4 (Winter 1990): 3-11.

Online:
http://www.vanderbilt.edu/peabody/heyneman/PUBLICATIONS/19900
5.pdf [30/01/08]
Takes a deliberately provocative stance on the question of protecting the book industries in developing nations, discussing under what circumstances, how, and who among governmental or non-governmental bodies should be in the business of producing educational materials. The author argues that governments should get out of the business of textbook production—and adds "publishers who are not employed by governments may find this a very welcome piece of advice, but my arguments may shock those who are."

225   Johnston, Laurie, ed. **Printed Educational Materials Development in the Third World. An International Workshop, 1989, England.** London: The Harold Macmillan Trust, 1989. 112 pp.
The proceedings of a workshop organized by the Harold Macmillan Trust in conjunction with the **→ CODE/Canadian Organization for Development through Education (48)**. The framework for discussions included questioning whether developing countries have succeeded in providing school systems with the educational printed materials essential for supporting the curriculum. Discusses the constraints which impede progress in this area, what measures should be taken to overcome these constraints, and how to use existing educational materials more effectively in the classroom.

226   Kumar, Arvind **"The Publisher's Place in the 21st Century."** *African Publishing Review* 6, no. 6 (November/December 1997): 5-9.
States that any effort for the development of human resources cannot succeed in the absence of a sustained programme of producing appropriate and affordable learning materials for different segments of the population. Examines some of the issues of publishing in developing countries, including language, content and cost of books, public involvement in publishing, foreign funding, and publishing as a business, including marketing strategies: "the objective of a publisher's marketing strategy should go beyond taking a bigger share of the book market; it should enlarge the market share of books."

227   International Book Development Ltd./International Federation of Library Associations. **Key Policy Issues in International Book, Library and Information Development. An IBD/IFLA Seminar on Policy Development for Aid Agencies, Policy Planners, Librarians, Publishers and Information Suppliers, Imperial Hotel, Harrogate, 12-13 July 1995.** London, IBD Ltd. & Boston Spa: IFLA Offices for UAP and International Lending, c/o The British Library [Boston Spa, Wetherby, LS23 7BQ], 1995. var. pp.
A collection of 11 papers presented at a meeting which brought together a number book and information specialists with a particular interest in the developing world, and which examined the fundamental problems and issues of sustainable and adequate book and information provision.

228 McCartney, Murray **Books for Millions. A Seminar on Low-cost and Affordable Book Production and Distribution, Harare, 30 July 1995**. New Delhi: Afro-Asian Book Council, 1996. 16 pp.
Summary report about a one-day seminar jointly organized by the ➔**African Publishers Network (5)** and the ➔ **Afro-Asian Book Council (7),** with summaries of the papers, and the seminar conclusions and recommendations.

229 Macpherson, John, and Douglas Pearce **Publishing Educational Materials in Developing Countries. A Guide to Policy and Practice.** London: Harold Macmillan Trust and CODE, 1990. 48 pp.
Seeks to present the themes which emerged from discussions held during an international workshop on Printed Educational Materials Development in the Third World held in the UK in 1989. It also includes background papers that aim to be helpful to Third World decision makers who are struggling to overcome the problems that impede the preparation, production and distribution of educational materials.

230 Minowa, Shigeo **"The Mythology of Publishing Development."** In *Publishing and Development in the Third World,* edited by Philip G. Altbach. London: Hans Zell Publishers, 1992, 55-62.
Presents the author's perceived hypocrisy of publishing development aid, which has been massively supported by multilateral organizations, under bilateral aid programmes, or aid support by foundations, "but the fruits of all these endeavours have by no means lived up to expectations" and there have been many failures. Minowa argues that what is required, first of all, is "theoretical work elucidating how societal, economic, and cultural aspects relate to the issue of publishing development." He then sets out his perspective on what is publishing development, examining the mechanisms of modern publishing, the impact of population size and income levels on publishing, and stresses the need for publishing economics, and publishing stratagems. He concludes that publishing is predominantly a product of endogenous cultural development, and that it can not be created artificially by interventions from the outside: "publishing development can be realized only by the passionate endeavours of those within."

231 Montagnes, Ian **EFA 2000 Assessment. Thematic Study on Teaching/Learning Environments. Textbooks & Learning Materials 1990–1999: A Global Survey.** Paris: UNESCO, Education for All, Division of Basic Education, 2000. 101 pp.
Online: http://www2.unesco.org/wef/en-leadup/findings_textbooks.shtm (Summary) [30/01/08]
http://www2.unesco.org/wef/en-docs/findings/bookfinal.pdf (Full text) [30/01/08]
This survey is one of a series prepared for the UNESCO Education for All (EFA) Assessment, under the auspices of the ➔ **UNESCO Division of Basic Education (119)** and the United Kingdom ➔ **Department of International Development (57)** for the International Consultative Forum on Education for All. The EFA objectives

are concerned with broad policy goals and targets in the provision of school books and other learning materials, including distribution mechanisms. While this survey also covers the situation in South and Central Asia, the Pacific Islands, the Anglophone Caribbean, and some parts of Central and Eastern Europe, special attention is paid to Africa, "where the book shortage has attracted more external support and generated more documentation over the past decade than any other region." Part of the synthesis is based on a range of classroom studies commissioned by the → UNESCO/ Danida Basic Learning Materials Initiative (119), covering Egypt, Guinea, India, Jamaica, Kazakhstan, Samoa, Senegal, and Tanzania. The survey first examines the basic issues and constraints relating to textbook availability and provision, and the role of funding agencies and donors. Thereafter it looks at global trends – in terms of decentralization, liberalization, funding, quality and use, etc. – followed by a survey of regional developments in the areas covered.

232 Montagnes, Ian **"Sustainable Development in Book Publishing."** *Scholarly Publishing* 23, no. 4 (July 1992): 231-241.
Shorter version also published in *African Publishing Review* 2, no. 3 (May/June 1993): 6-7.
This is an extensive review essay of → **Publishing and Development in the Third World**, edited by Philip G. Altbach **(211)**.

233 Neumann, Peter H. **Publishing for Schools. Textbooks and the Less Developed Countries.** Washington, DC: The World Bank (World Bank Staff Working Paper, 398), 1980. 79 pp.
Concentrating on the complexities of large scale primary and secondary school textbook production, this paper aims to provide guidelines and information for creating viable publishing industries in developing countries. Statistical analysis, personal experience, case studies, and responses to a questionnaire on the publishing roles of the public and private sectors in developing countries form the basis from which the author constructs his blueprint for publishing of textbooks in the countries of the South. Neumann concludes that textbooks, teacher editions, and related materials are cost effective, efficient tools and vital factors in upgrading academic achievement, especially where teachers are less qualified.

234 Nwafor, B.U. **"Problems of the Book Trade Infrastructure in Developing Countries in Relation to University Library Objectives."** *IFLA Journal* 10, no. 4 (1984): 357-369.
Explores the magnitude and variety of the problems which beset the book industry in developing countries by examining various aspects of the book trade infrastructure, and the role of libraries in the book industry chain.

235 Olden, Anthony **Information, Publishing and Libraries in the Developing World.** Ealing, UK: Centre for Information Management, Thames Valley University [St Mary's Road, Ealing, London W5 5RF], 1994. 59 pp.
Although now somewhat dated, this is a useful collection of extracts from key texts and other relevant material to illustrate the main issues and problems in the

literature on library and book development in developing countries. It is intended for students taking the Information, Publishing and Libraries in the Developing World modules offered within the BA/BSc and Postgraduate Diploma/MA/MSc Information Management programmes.

236   Pearce, Douglas **Textbook Production in Developing Countries. Some Problems of Preparation, Production and Distribution.** Paris: UNESCO, 1982. 51 pp.
One of a series of background materials prepared for the World Congress on Books held in London in 1982. Deals with the various stages of textbook publishing, which is the mainstay of the book industry in most less developed countries. Discusses the difficulties faced by both government and private sector textbook publishing organizations, and examines methods of overcoming these difficulties.

237   Pearce, Douglas **A Guide to Planning and Administering Government School Textbook Projects. With Special Emphasis on Cost-reduction Factors** 2nd ed. Paris: UNESCO (Document reference ED-88/ws-35), 1990. 105 pp.
Online: http://unesdoc.unesco.org/images/0008/000805/080509e.pdf [30/01/08]
Supplements the author's earlier UNESCO publication **Textbook Production in Developing Countries** (*see* entry ➔ **236** above), and at the same time aims at synthesizing the main findings of the numerous seminars and reports and papers which have been published by UNESCO in this subject area. It examines, in a non-technical manner, the problems and issues associated with government sponsored textbook provision programmes in developing countries, placing special emphasis on cost reduction factors in such textbook programmes. The main aim of the Guide is "to take account of present problems of government textbook schemes, and their needs for better resources and more trained personnel, and to assist them by posing questions which may lead to a greater understanding of problems, and more adequate planning and improved administration of projects, with consequent reduced costs and the production of better textbooks."

238   Read, Anthony **"Textbook Availability in the Third World."** In *Nothing to Read? The Crisis of Document Provision in the Third World*, edited by D.J. Membrey. Birmingham: International and Comparative Librarianship Group of the Library Association, 1990, 27-33.
Reports on research undertaken by the (UK) Book Development Council in preparation for a major World Bank review of policy options for improving the quality of primary education in developing countries.

239   Read, Anthony **"International Experiences in Third World Publishing Development with Particular Reference to World Bank Intervention."** In *Publishing and Development in the Third World*, edited by Philip G. Altbach. London: Hans Zell Publishers, 1992, 307-324.

Examines the involvement of the ➔ **World Bank (124)** and other aid agencies in funding textbook publishing in Africa and other parts of the developing world. The author notes that the fundamental role of books in education was not, however, widely recognized at first, and relatively few early education projects had book-provision or book-development elements; specific assistance to book publishing was a later development. He reviews some of the pre-1985 activities of the World Bank in the sphere of textbooks and discusses common problems in their implementation. The history of aid agency involvement in book provision is still relatively short. It started only in the 1970s and it was inevitable that mistakes would be made initially; but recognition of the mistakes and the development of a more catholic approach came very rapidly, and within ten years there were clear signs by the aid agencies of much deeper thinking in this complex sector. The latest [1990s] generation of aid agencies is approaching book provision from a much wider basis, and many projects are extremely complex. "The World Bank recognizes this and sees it both as an important development but also an increased risk. In many countries there is a much more conscious attempt to involve local commercial organizations in developmental work and the benefits of bank investment."

240   Prakash, O., and Clifford M. Fyle **Books for Developing Countries.** Paris: UNESCO (Reports and Papers on Mass Communication, 47), 1965. 37 pp.
Online: http://unesdoc.unesco.org/images/0005/000595/059546eo.pdf [30/01/08]
One of the earliest investigations into the book industries in developing countries. Contains two contributions: "The Production and Flow of Books in South East Asia", and "The Production and Flow of Books in Africa". Still available online at the above UNESCO Web site.

241   Smith, Datus C. jr. **"The Bright Promise of Publishing in Developing Countries."** *Annals of the American Academy of Political and Social Science* 421, (September, 1975), 130-139.
Also in *Perspectives on Publishing*, edited by Philip G. Altbach and Sheila McVey. Lexington, MA: D.C. Heath, 1976, 117-128.
The late Datus C. Smith jr., Director of Princeton University Press between 1942 and 1953 – and later President for 15 years of Franklin Book Programs, which had offices in many developing countries, exchanging books and personnel with publishers in the United States – believed publishing in Asia and Africa had a bright future. Writing in 1975 he forecast, correctly it now turns out, that the future promised significant improvements in manufacturing methods, and that one of the most useful developments, in both educational and business terms, might be the integration of publishing with electronic media. However, he felt that the most critical publishing need was development of nationwide distribution systems for mass marketing of books at low prices. He also suggested that, in the scholarly publishing field, Asia and Africa, were not yet immovably locked into a pattern and thus might be able to provide "a serviceable kind" of scholarly publishing; that they would do well to avoid some wasteful American practices, and might use on-demand publishing as an economical method for some specialized materials with low sales potential.

242 Smith, Datus C. jr. **The Economics of Book Publishing in Developing Countries.** Paris: UNESCO (Reports and Papers on Mass Communication, 79), 1977. 44 pp.
Also reprinted in *Readings on Publishing in Africa and the Third World,* by Philip G. Altbach. Buffalo, NY: Bellagio Publishing Network, Research and Information Center (Bellagio Studies in Publishing 1), 1993, 92-123.
Based on the findings of a detailed survey of publishers in various parts of the developing world, this classic study identifies the key problems for the book industries in the countries of the South. Offers a general picture of the state of publishing in each of the regions, including Africa, and proposes a range of strategies to help strengthen the book sector.

243 Smith, Datus C. jr. **"Scholarly Publishing in the Third World."**
Scholarly Publishing 12, no. 3 (April 1981): 195-218.
A survey of scholarly publishing in developing countries that draws on Datus Smith's twenty-two years of experience in the field. The author finds that its growth – particularly among university presses – has been impeded by problems of marketing and distribution, and by administrative misunderstandings of its functions.

244 UNESCO/DANIDA Basic Learning Materials Initiative **Guidelines for the Conduct and Organization of National Book Sector Consultations.** Paris: UNESCO/DANIDA Basic Learning Materials Initiative,[n.d.] 44 pp. (Request print copy by sending an email to J.kjaersgaard@unesco.org)
Online: http://www.unesco.org/education/blm/opmItoc_en.php [22/03/08]
Also published in French as **Principes directeurs pour l'organisation et la conduite des concertations nationales sur le livre.**
Online: http://www.unesco.org/education/blm/blmintro_fr.php [22/03/08]
The ➜ **UNESCO/DANIDA Basic Learning Materials Initiative (119)** originated in the International Consultative Forum on Education for All. The first phase of the programme began in 1993, with a survey of the book sector in selected countries, and culminated in the publication of a manual entitled **A Guide to Sustainable Book Provision. From Plan to Print** (*see* entry ➜ **217**). This further manual is designed to assist UNESCO National Commissions and Ministries of Education, in the organization of the various logistical aspects of national book sector consultations. Since its first conception in 1997, it has been revised several times, after the experiences gained in several African countries. It includes suggested guidelines for the organization of national book sector consultations, recommended agenda, and a range of notes to assist chairpersons, facilitators, and presenters.

Africa: General studies

245   Akporji, Chii P. **"Opportunities for African Publishers to Work with the World Bank."** *African Publishing Review* 9, no. 4 (2000): 1-3.
Describes the broad objectives of the World Bank's African Publishing Initiative (API) that originated in the ➔ **World Bank Office of the Publisher (125)**. API seeks to develop sustainable partnerships with the various players in the book industry in Africa to support efforts to building publishing capacity in Africa, and at the same time provides for co-publication, licensing, or reprints of African editions of select World Bank developmental publications. Other components of the initiative include a publication grants and translation programme, organization of World Bank workshops at book events in Africa, and a print-on-demand (POD) pilot project to be set up in six sub-Saharan African countries.

246   Altbach, Philip G. **"Perspectives on Publishing in Africa."** *Publishing Research Quarterly* 9, no. 1 (March 1993): 44-62.
Also reprinted in *Readings on Publishing in Africa and the Third World*, by Philip G. Altbach. Buffalo, NY: Bellagio Publishing Network, Research and Information Center (Bellagio Studies in Publishing 1), 1993, 1-19.
Probes into the needs, role, and status of publishing in Africa [at at 1992], and discusses such issues as the nature of the African reading public, the politics of language, the role of multinationals, problems of distribution, and technology. The author describes the challenges faced in developing an African book industry and suggests some possible approaches to providing assistance.

Altbach, Philip G., ed. **Readings on Publishing in Africa and the Third World** *see* ➔ **Comparative studies** entry **214**

247   Altbach, Philip G., ed. **The Challenge of the Market: Privatization and Publishing in Africa**. Chestnut Hill, MA: Bellagio Publishing Network Research and Information Center, (Bellagio Studies in Publishing, 7), 1996. 114 pp. (Distributed by African Books Collective Ltd., Oxford)
This collection of papers focuses on the transition from state to private sector publishing in Africa. Two overview evaluations draw attention to the fact that the road to privatization is not necessarily an easy one, and that there are costs as well as benefits involved. Four cases studies, from Ghana, Ethiopia, Zambia and the Côte d'Ivoire provide accounts of specific experiences. *Note:* papers in this collection are individually abstracted elsewhere in this bibliography.
Reviews:
The African Book Publishing Record vol. 23, no. 2, 1997
Information Development vol. 13, no. 2, June 1997
The Library Association Record vol. 99, no. 6, 1997

248   Altbach, Philip G. **"Perspectives on Privatization in African Publishing."** In *The Challenge of the Market: Privatization and Publishing in Africa*, edited by Philip G. Altbach. Chestnut Hill, MA: Bellagio Publishing

Network, Research and Information Center (Bellagio Studies in Publishing, 7), 1996, 3-8.

Also published in *Bellagio Publishing Network Newsletter*, no. 17 (July 1996): 16-18; also in *The Bookseller* as **"A Fair Climate in Africa"**, no. 4726 (1996): 26-27; and in *West Africa* as **"Publishing in Africa"**, no. 4123 (1996): 1711-1712.

State publishing in Africa, a powerful ideological force in the 1960s, has by and large failed to deliver, and state-run publishers have exhibited a combination of negative characteristics. Indigenous publishing does not have deep roots in Africa, and circumstances during the colonial era and its aftermath did not favour it. However, indigenous private sector publishing is now seeking to prove itself as a desirable alternative to state publishing, although it faces some daunting challenges and problems. The article reviews some of these elements – public policy, freedom to publish, access to credit, market size, competition with the multinationals, the ➔ **World Bank (124)** and the Bank's textbook programmes, and intra-African book trade – which the author believes are central to providing a context, and to understanding the potential for successful private-sector publishing in Africa.

249   Badisang, Bobana **"Factors Influencing Indigenous Publishing in Africa."** *African Research & Documentation*, no. 66 (1994): 6-17.

Assesses the development of the indigenous publishing industry in sub-Saharan Africa by examining economic, infrastructural, marketing and distribution problems, and makes a number of recommendations on the possible way forward.

250   Bgoya, Walter **"Autonomous Publishing in Africa: The Present Situation."** *Development Dialogue*, nos. 1-2 (1984): 83-97.

Now rather dated, but this article remains a useful overview of publishing in Africa, by one of its leading practitioners. Contains a wide-ranging discussion of the ideological, practical, and technical issues involved in book publishing. The author argues that transnational publishing houses cannot serve as acceptable alternatives to autonomous, indigenous publishing firms, regardless of how well they may perform, or how appropriate their books may be.

251   Bgoya, Walter **"Publishing in Africa: Culture and Development."** In *The Muse of Modernity: Essays on Culture as Development in Africa*, edited by Philip G. Altbach and Salah M. Hassan. Trenton, NJ: Africa World Press, 1996, 151-179.

Also published in *The African Writers' Handbook*, edited by James Gibbs and Jack Mapanje. Oxford: African Books Collective Ltd., 1999, 59-84.

A wide-ranging essay examining the state of the African publishing industry "which is cast in a special position of privilege and disadvantage." Starts off with a broad overview of publishing in Africa, and then analyzes textbook publishing as a tool for the promotion of culture, liberation history as a special publishing project, and the factors influencing the growth of the indigenous book industries, such as curricula, market size, the colonial legacy, and language issues. It also examines the role played by recent collaborative initiatives such as ➔ **African Books Collective (3)** and the ➔

African Publishers' Network (5), book fairs, copyright issues and, in a final section, the author discusses the prospects for publishing of African creative writing, and journals publishing. In his conclusion the author argues that "cultural publishing deserves just as much attention as educational publishing", and that "publishing in African languages should be given first priority, so that as many people as possible may encounter the adventures of living that are found in fiction, poetry, and drama."

252 Bgoya, Walter **"The Development and Future of Publishing in Africa. 12 Years After Arusha I."** *Development Dialogue*, nos. 1-2 (1997): 15-38.

An update of an earlier article published by Bgoya in *Development Dialogue*, nos. 1-2, 1984 (*see* ➔ entry 250), providing an extensive overview of indigenous publishing in Africa [as at 1997], reviewing progress, developments, and achievements since the first ➔ **Dag Hammarskjöld Foundation (55)** conference on indigenous publishing held in Arusha in April 1984 - 'Arusha I'. It also examines the essential requirements for the future of the book industry in Africa, and the possible scenarios that might lead to success. The author argues that only if there are clear policies in the areas of education, books and language, backed up by practical implementation, will be the conditions created in which indigenous publishing can grow and flourish. He suggests a number of practical self-help options that publishers might wish to consider, including joint ventures with overseas publishers, and South-South co-operation. The article includes a useful Appendix: "Frame work for establishing equitable and mutually beneficial joint ventures in publishing in Africa."

253 Bgoya, Walter **"How Can Independent African Publishers Survive Against National Monopolies and Transnational Corporations?"** In *Academic Book Production and Distribution in Africa. Support from Nordic Countries. Report from a conference at Chr. Michelsen Institute, Bergen, 10-11 April 1997,* edited by Kirsti Hagen Andersen. Fantoft, Norway: Ch. Michelsen Institute 1997, 8-16.

Examines how small independent African publishers struggling to survive might successfully compete in the area of textbook publishing in the face of state monopolies in some countries, when they have to compete against transnational corporations who still maintain a stronghold on textbook publishing in many African countries, and where the transnationals "are almost in conspiracy with the governments of countries where they go to marginalize independent publishing." Bgoya believes that one impediment is the generally poor though gradually improving quality of books from many autonomous African publishers, and he examines ways to improve the quality of African publishing in order to gain a competitive edge, one area being more training programmes for the African book professions. On the question of state participation in publishing the author says that "state companies still have a place as long as governments do not legislate other publishers out of the market." He also suggests that "in the final analysis, independent African publishers will have only one way to go in the future. They must leap-frog into electronic publishing."

254 Bgoya, Walter "**The Effect of Globalisation in Africa and the Choice of Language in Publishing.**" *International Review of Education* 47, nos. 3-4 (2001): 283-292.

Discusses the problems of the domination of the ex-colonial languages for intellectual life in Africa, including its effect as a choice of language in publishing. Bgoya states that English fundamentally serves the interests of those for whom it is both an export commodity and a language of conquest and domination. He argues that there is no compelling reason for adopting a foreign language as a national one. On the contrary, there is ample evidence, he asserts, that such linguistic imposition does more harm than good. When a language is artificially imposed, students are rarely able to master it sufficiently to work comfortably in it. Not only do they fail to acquire proficiency in the foreign language; they also lose proficiency in their own languages, thus becoming twice disadvantaged. The author sees dependency on a foreign language, like other forms of dependency, as a liability that a nation can ill afford.

255 Bgoya, Walter "**Africa and Publishing: Reflections.**" *Pambazuka News*, no. 215 (15 July 2005)

http://www.pambazuka.org/en/category/comment/28874 [21/02/08]

There is a general opinion that publishing in Africa is developing. This view is based on evidence that more books are being published today than two decades ago, and on the proliferation of indigenous publishing houses. This is indeed the case, but the author believes that the development has been more quantitative than qualitative and this is not a good enough method to measure development of a publishing industry. "Behind the backwardness of the publishing industry is a history of inappropriate educational and cultural policies, absence of national book policies including ineffective copyright laws, high duties and taxes on paper and other printing inputs, no or underfunding of libraries. Book production and distribution cannot prosper in societies where reading is limited to functionality — passing school and professional examinations." Bgoya contends that publishing in Africa remains an enclave industry serving foreign multinationals and their joint ventures, "which are actually comprador companies, established to legitimise the former's presence and exploitation." More of the same textbooks covering the same core school subjects are published annually. The author also declares that "there is little or no publishing of books of interest and relevance to the majority of the people." Not even do-it-yourself type of books, for example covering aspects of agriculture and animal husbandry, health promotion and disease prevention, building construction, carpentry, brick laying, and similar material that people need to improve their surroundings and their incomes. And the few that are published are invariably in foreign rather than African languages. He concludes that any measures designed to improve the publishing environment in Africa can only be successfully accomplished "by governments that recognise the strategic importance of the publishing industry; that realise education, in addition to classrooms, teachers and textbooks, is also libraries, bookshops, journals, magazines, newspapers, the Internet and other forms in which knowledge is packaged."

256 Bischof, Phyllis B. **"Publishing and the Book Trade in Sub-Saharan Africa: Trends and Issues and their Implications for American Libraries."** *Journal of Academic Librarianship* 16, no. 6 (January 1991): 340-347.
Examines developments in publishing since independence, important scholarly and fictional themes, writing in African languages, the role of state-supported publishing, and religious publishing houses. It also describes the cooperative methods developed by American librarians to collect, access and preserve African publications. Now rather dated, but still a useful round up.

257 Book Aid International **Books for Development. A Workshop to Bring Key Stakeholders in the Book Chain Together. 27th-30th September 2002, Kampala, Uganda. Draft Report.** London: Book Aid International, 2002. 42 pp.
Online:
http://www.bookaid.org/resources/downloads/ugandaworkshop-2002.pdf [page not available 21/02/08]
Report of a participatory workshop facilitated by the ➔ **African Publishers Network (5)**, ➔ **Book Aid International (38)**, and the ➔ **Pan African Booksellers Association (21)**. The goal of the workshop was to increase mutual understanding and more effective collaboration between librarians, booksellers and publishers in order to develop the book chain, and to give books and access to information greater prominence on the policy agenda at national level.

258 Book Aid International **Submission to the Africa Commission.**
http://www.bookaid.org/resources/downloads/BookAid_Submission_to_Africa_Commission.PDF [page not available 21/02/08]
A two page statement submitted by ➔ **Book Aid International (38)** to the Commission for Africa, an initiative launched by [former] British Prime Minister Tony Blair in February 2004. The aim of the Commission was to take a fresh look at Africa's past and present and the international community's role in its development path. This document sets out the case for support for libraries and books in sub-Saharan Africa, identified as "the basic tools for literacy and learning". Among its conclusions and recommendations are: (i) Policymakers should recognise that libraries have a key role to play in the delivery of education goals and in maintaining people's literacy skills for life. (ii) Policymakers should work to create a supportive environment in which local authors, publishers, booksellers and libraries can flourish, and work together, so local language publications and culture can be promoted.

259 Brickhill, Paul **"Regional and Collaborative Approaches in African Publishing."** In *Publishing in Africa: The Crisis and the Challenge. An ASA Roundtable. The African Book Publishing Record* 20, no. 1 (1994): 19-21.
Stresses the need for regional approaches and collaborative strategies, to tackle the many problems faced by African publishers, for example in the area of training for book industry personnel. Also reviews the work and activities of a number African collaborative ventures in the book sector.

260 Brickhill, Paul **"The Transition from State to Commercial Publishing Systems in African Countries."** In *The Challenge of the Market: Privatization and Publishing in Africa,* edited by Philip G. Altbach. Chestnut Hill, MA: Bellagio Publishing Network Research and Information Center (Bellagio Studies in Publishing, 7), 1996, 9-28.
Also published in *Publishing and Development: A Book of Readings,* edited by Philip G. Altbach and Damtew Teffera. Chestnut Hill, MA: Bellagio Publishing Network Research and Information Center (Bellagio Studies in Publishing, 9), 1998, 111-130.
Offers some insights into the problems and issues in the transition from state to private sector publishing now underway in several African countries. Based on studies undertaken in Tanzania, Zambia and Malawi, and based on observations and discussions with publishers from elsewhere, the author sets out the background to state intervention in the book sector and analyzes some of the effects of state control in publishing, its advantages and its critical weaknesses. While welcoming the transition to commercialization, the author identifies some flaws in some approaches to textbook provision by the private sector and states that there is "the apparent failure to recognize that the commercial sector must provide the impetus for change and demonstrate the technical proficiency required for textbook provision"; and that the commercial systems requires genuine competition among publishers, rather than being dominated by one or two, and without which it is likely to suffer many of the shortcomings of the previous state monopolies. The author also argues forcefully that a liberalized system of textbook supply must include all those who are part of the "book chain", including booksellers and the retail book trade, and that Ministry of Education officials should not assume the role of booksellers, or attempting to manage book distribution systems.

261 Brickhill, Paul **"How Can Publishers, Booksellers and Librarians Co-operate to Stimulate Book Production and Distribution in Africa?"** In *Academic Book Production and Distribution in Africa. Support from Nordic Countries. Report from a conference at Chr. Michelsen Institute, Bergen, 10-11 April 1997,* edited by Kirsti Hagen Andersen. Fantoft, Norway: Ch. Michelsen Institute 1997, 71-82.
Brickhill argues that the only chance for survival of the African book industries is in the development of a sustainable, commercially viable book chain, and that this means publishers and booksellers must work closer together. He then sets out the essential components of a functioning book chain and makes some proposals which he believes would work to mutual benefit for both publishers and booksellers, and, at the same time, would bring them closer together.

262 Brickhill, Paul; Chris Chirwa, and Bengt Lindahl, eds. **Changing Public/Private Partnerships in the African Book Sector.** Paris and London: Association for the Development of Education in Africa (ADEA), Working Group on Books and Learning Materials (Perspectives on African Book Development, 15), 2005. 264 pp. (distributed by African Books Collective Ltd, Oxford)

Until recently most African countries controlled publishing of textbooks for schools through state-owned monopolies, thus excluding the private publishing sector from the school book markets; and, with central purchasing authorities and through free textbook provision, also effectively bypassed booksellers. However, since the 1990s there has been a decisive shift towards greater liberalization of textbook provision, and interaction, and partnerships, between the state and the commercial book sector is growing rapidly, leading to more decentralized procurement of books for Africa's schools. This ADEA study charts the trend toward the increasing liberalization in textbook provision, and identifies some of the key challenges in public-private partnerships. It is based on field research undertaken in 13 African countries, the findings of which are presented here as a series of country studies. They are preceded by an excellent eight-chapter introductory section and overview, which sets out the background to textbook provision in Africa, its gradual liberalization, and the emergence of the indigenous commercial sector. In their conclusions the authors of the study advocate diversity, as opposed to monopoly approaches, as the cornerstone of national and textbook policies, and as "a positive development path on which to strengthen bookselling, publishing, readership and access to books generally." The study finds that the key challenge in emerging public-private sector partnerships in textbook provision is how to increase the capacity, resources and diversity of the private sector in such a way that schools are the direct and long term beneficiary; and that policy approaches and triangular relationships in textbook provision – involving government, funding agencies, and the private sector – must always be considered against one performance indicator, "the quality, volume and scope of learning materials in the classroom, leading directly to improved education levels and equity." This is a highly informed and penetrative analysis of textbook procurement in Africa, and the policy shifts and fundamental changes that have recently taken place in this area of the African book sector.
Reviews:
The African Book Publishing Record vol. 32, no. 2, 2006

263   Chakava, Henry **"An Autonomous African Publishing House: A Model."** *Development Dialogue*, nos. 1-2 (1984): 123-131.
Also published in *The African Writers' Handbook*, edited by James Gibbs and Jack Mapanje. Oxford: African Books Collective Ltd., 1999, 85-93.
One of the most experienced publishers in Africa presents a model of a "viable, autonomous, indigenous African publishing house, where viability is also seen to entail longevity and permanence." Examines in some detail the various aspects of the publishing business, covering both overall policy questions and the economic, technical and practical issues that confront publishers in Africa.

264   Chakava, Henry "An Indigenous African Book Publishing Industry: In Search of a New Beginning." *African Publishing Review* 2, no. 5 (September/October 1993): 9-11.
Examines questions of ownership, manpower and capital needs for an autonomous African book industry, and reviews aspects of manufacturing, distribution problems, the size of the market, and government policies. Calls for "a new beginning with more aggressive policies born out of our experiences and past failures."

265   Chakava, Henry M. **"State Publishing: In Search of a Model for the African Publishing Industry."** In *Proceedings of the Info Africa Nova Conference 1993,* volume 1, edited by A.G. Coetzer. Pretoria: Info Africa Nova CC, 1993, 181-185.
Examines the role and experience of state participation in publishing. The author is critical of government monopolies in the book sector, which stifle competition, authorship and writing, and lead to falling standards. Argues that "African book publishing thrives best when left in the hands of the local publishers themselves."

266   Chakava, Henry **"The Missing Links in the African Book Publishing Chains."** In *Promoting Technical Publishing in Africa. Seminar Proceedings. Arnhem, Netherlands, 3-6 November 1992.* Wageningen, Netherlands: Technical Centre for Agricultural and Rural Cooperation of ACP-EU (CTA), 1994, 33-38.
African publishers, the author states, do not want to perpetuate colonial links, "which would forever make them recipients rather than creators of technical publications." Instead, they want to be assisted in becoming independent, autonomous and viable commercial enterprises, seeking joint-ventures, co-publication agreements, sub-licence deals, and agency and translation agreements with partners in the North, to mutual benefit. Chakava argues that there are in fact no missing links in the African book publishing chain. "The chain is there, but it is a weak one", and that is is up to African publishers, with the support of governments, donor agencies, and partners in the North to strengthen the chain, and thus help bring about an environment that will enhance self-sustainability and growth.

267   Chakava, Henry **"Publishing in Africa: Kenyan Publisher Spells out the Problems."** *NIWA-Info* 5, nos. 2/3 (July/September 1994): 4-9.
[Not examined]

268   Chakava, Henry **"The World Bank and African Publishing."** *African Publishing Review* 3, no. 5 (September/October 1994): 14-15.
Reviews the ➜ **World Bank's (124)** textbook provision schemes, its tendering procedures, and the Bank's African book sector studies. Also reports about an APNET delegation to the World Bank, and about the discussions held with World Bank officials concerning the future relationship between the Bank, African governments, and the African publishing industry.

269   Chakava, Henry **Publishing in Africa: One Man's Perspective.**
Chestnut Hill, MA: Bellagio Publishing Network Research and Information Centre (Bellagio Studies in Publishing, 6); and Nairobi: East African Educational Publishers, 1996. 197 pp.
Online: complete e-book, freely downloadable as a pdf file,
http://www.bc.edu/bc_org/avp/soe/cihe/publications/pub_pdf/chakava.pdf [22/02/08]
A collection of essays and articles by one of Africa's most prolific commentators on the African publishing scene, bringing together his writings on many diverse topics,

such as autonomous publishing, book marketing and distribution, author-publisher relations, regional cooperation, the ➔ **World Bank (124)** and African publishing, reading promotion, the inequalities of international copyright, and the problems of censorship and government repression. Also contains one entirely new paper ➔ **"Book Marketing and Distribution: The Achilles Heel of African Publishing"**, *see* entry ➔ **1467.**
Reviews:
The African Book Publishing Record vol. 22, no. 2, 1996
Africana Libraries Newsletter no. 90, April 1997
Online: http://www.lib.msu.edu/lauer/aln/aln90.html [22/02/08]
Bellagio Publishing Network Newsletter, no. 18, November 1996, (same review as in *The African Book Publishing Record*)
IASP [International Association of Scholarly Publishers] Newsletter no. 6, 1996
The Library Association Record vol. 99, no. 6, 1997
Logos.The Journal of the World Book Community vol. 8, no. 2, 1997
Online: http://www.atypon-link.com/LOG/doi/pdf/10.2959/logo.1997.8.2.105

270 Chakava, Henry **"Wind of Change at the World Bank."** *African Publishing Review* 6, no. 5 (September/October 1997): 1-3.
Slightly different version also published, as **"World Bank to Change Course on Book Development?"** *Logos. The Journal of the World Book Community* 8, no. 4 (1997): 220-222.
Online:
http://www.atypon-link.com/LOG/doi/pdf/10.2959/logo.1997.8.4.220
Henry Chakava – who attended a meeting held between African publishers and officials of the ➔ **World Bank (124)** in September 1997 – detected a wind of change at the Bank and reports that "it became clear that the bank is ready to change and to adopt new policies that could strengthen the role of local publishers and, in the process, drastically reduce the dominance of the multinational publishers in the developing world." If the recommendations that emerged for the meeting are adopted as Bank policy, and a programme of action is put in place for their implementation, "local publishing in the developing world will undergo a sea-change and the World Bank will emerge as a strategic partner in a new deal."

271 Chakava, Henry **Production and Distribution of Cultural Publications in Africa: In Search of Lasting Partners.**
http://www.hivos.nl/index.php/content/download/6529/36717/file/d80
501c1862159369294f063fc1e3453 [22/02/08], or
http://www.hivos.nl/index.php/nederlands/english/arterial/presentation
s_conference [22/02/08]
A paper presented to the arterial conference on Vitalising Africa's Cultural Assets, held at Gorée Island, Senegal, in March 2007. Chakava states that publishing general books in Africa is a risky business, and publishing cultural books – such a fiction, drama and poetry, children's books, or books on arts and crafts, music, dance and the oral tradition, etc. – even more so. "The market is small and hard to capture because of poverty and underdevelopment." He briefly describes the challenges faced by the book industries, and how these challenges are being met, although many near

insurmountable obstacles and constraints remain, and there has been little positive support by African governments. Draws attention to the two organizations that have had the greatest impact in putting African publishing on the map, the ➔ **African Publishers Network/APNET (5)** and the ➔ **African Books Collective/ABC (3)**, whose thrust has primarily been the advancement of cultural publishing at home and abroad. Both are organizations that, because of their nature, cannot be financially self-sustainable, but which have been supported, until very recently, by several donors. However, funding has now dried up for the most part and the author notes that, as a result of changes of donor policies, it is governments once more who are the preferred partners of the international donor community. Chakava argues "for cultural publishing to take off and thrive, it is imperative for stakeholders in the book industry to lobby their governments to formulate book policies and cultural policies that would serve as a guide to the exercise." He urges donors to revert to supporting private sector initiatives in the African book industry, and that organizations such as the African Books Collective deserve continuing donor support.

272   Crabbe, Richard **"Market Trends in the African Book Industry."** *African Publishing Review* 9, no. 4 (2000): 4-5.
The [then] Chairman of the ➔ **African Publishers Network (5)** sums ups the major market trends in the African book publishing industry, and the changing needs of readers in Africa at the beginning of the new millennium.

273   Crabbe, Richard **"Equipping to Compete."** *BookLinks*, no. 7 (August 2007): 6-7.
Online:
http://www.bookaid.org/resources/downloads/booklinks/BookLinks_7.pdf [22/02/08]
Extracts from a keynote address presented at an international conference held during the 2007 Nigeria International Book Fair. The author – a former Chair of the ➔African Publishers Network (5) and current Head of Client Relations at ➔ **The World Bank. Office of the Publisher (125)** – puts forward a range of suggestions for building capacity in the African book publishing industry: identifying the key areas and essential components, and the roles and responsibilities in terms of human resource development, organizational development, and policy issues.

274   Dag Hammarskjöld Foundation Seminar Participants **"Towards Autonomous Publishing Capacity in Africa."** *The African Book Publishing Record* 11, no. 2 (1985): 89.
A statement by the participants at the historic 1984 ➔ **Dag Hammarskjöld Foundation (55)** Seminar on the Development of Autonomous Capacity in Publishing in Africa, Arusha, April 1984. The statement gives the broad consensus of the participants.

275   Darko-Ampem, K.O. **"Indigenous Publishing in Africa: An Overview of Accelerated Training and Research, and African Self-help Efforts."** *Mots Pluriels*, no. 13 (April 2000): 10 pp.
http://www.arts.uwa.edu.au/MotsPluriels/MP1300koda.html [22/02/08]

A broad overview of current [2000] developments in the African publishing industry, including the establishment of national book development councils, national book trade associations, national book policies, the provision of resources for training and research, the activities of donors and other organizations supporting African publishing, and the role played by ➔ **African Books Collective Ltd. (3)** and the ➔ **African Publishers' Network (5)**.

276 Davies, Wendy **The Future of Indigenous Publishing in Africa. A Seminar Organized by the Dag Hammarskjöld Foundation in Arusha, Tanzania, March 25-28, 1996. Seminar Report.** Uppsala: Dag Hammarskjöld Foundation, 1996. 32 pp.
Also published as **"The Future of Indigenous Publishing in Africa. A Seminar Report."** *Development Dialogue*, nos. 1-2 (1997): 68-96.
A report about a seminar, sponsored by the ➔ **Dag Hammarskjöld Foundation/DHF (55),** which brought together 30 participants from eight countries, including publishers, writers, librarians, academics, and bankers. The report summarizes developments in indigenous African publishing since 1984 (when the DHF organized an earlier seminar on 'The Development of Autonomous Publishing Capacity in Africa'), and thereafter identifies the key issues that emerged from the papers presented and from the discussions: publishing as a strategic industry, reading and cultural environment, national book policy, communication and networking, the electronic revolution, marketing and distribution, and finance. Also includes a summary of the conclusions, and a list of participants.

277 Dekutsey, Woeli A. **"The Indigenous Publisher in Africa Today."** In *Development Directory of Indigenous Publishing* 1995, compiled by Carol Priestley. Harare: African Publishers' Network, 1995, 2-15.
Woeli Dekutsey, a small independent Ghanaian publisher, examines the hazardous life and precarious existence of the indigenous publisher in Africa today, provides an "anatomy of an African publisher", and reviews aspects such as problems of finance, competitiveness with the multinationals, marketing and distribution.

278 Domatob, Jerry **"Communication Research for Textbook Writing in Sub-Saharan Africa: Challenges and Options."** In *Communication Industry in Nigeria. The Crisis of Publications*, edited by A. Tom Adaba, Ololeka Ajia and Ikechukwu Nwosu. Nairobi, African Council for Communication Education, 1988, 96-117.
Examines the challenges involved in providing suitable textbooks in the field of communication and provides some guidelines for their production.

279 Enahoro, Peter **"Publishing in Africa."** *Africa, an international business ... monthly*, no. 15 (November 1972): 67-70.
An interesting early perspective on the publishing situation in Africa, by a prominent Nigerian journalist. Discusses the 1972 Frankfurt Book Fair and the contributions of African publishers who "still have to realize the business opportunities in publishing", especially considering the reduction in import allocation budgets for

books in may African countries. Stresses that there is a proven market for "literature that is truly native" while noting that "generally African writers of good standing prefer to have their books published abroad." Contends that publishing in Africa must build itself a strong reputation to serve as a basis when the industry begins to boom.

280   Gedin, Per I. **"Publishing in Africa - Autonomous and Transnational: A View from Outside."** *Development Dialogue*, nos. 1-2 (1984): 98-112.
Swedish publisher Per Gedin views the building up of an autonomous publishing industry in Africa as the most central issue in creating a vital African literature. He argues that it is vital that financial organizations, in conjunction with educational institutions, should guarantee loans for autonomous publishing. Concludes that "a strong autonomous publishing industry is a prerequisite for a great, varied and vital indigenous literature and that it is something that can be achieved at a comparatively very low cost. And with the establishment of a publishing industry, development of the infrastructure of distribution centres, bookshops, book clubs, etc. will naturally follow."

281   Gedin, Per I. **"Cultural Pride: The Necessity of Indigenous Publishing."** In *Publishing and Development in the Third World*, edited by Philip G. Altbach. London: Hans Zell Publishers, 1992, 43-53.
Draws attention to the key role which publishers play in influencing book development. Gedin argues that everything needed to create a literary marketplace already exists in Africa, but that an indigenous publishing industry needs proper commercial support. Concludes by stating "the indigenous publisher, and no one else, will invest in the writing of his country, which will eventually result in a national literature as important for his country as for the rest of the world."

282   Gedin, Per I. **"Private Enterprise Publishing in Africa: Why and How it Should be Fostered."** *Logos. The Journal of the World Book Community* 2, no. 3 (1991): 133-139.
Online:
http://www.atypon-link.com/LOG/doi/pdf/10.2959/logo.1991.2.3.133
Focuses on the importance of encouraging indigenous national publishers, who can identify strongly with their own culture and are prepared to invest in the future of both their companies and culture, as opposed to "transnational" publishers who have a different outlook on cultures other than their own, and are primarily concerned with profitability. Contends that the prevalence of transnational publishers can impede the construction of an infrastructure for local publishing and that, paradoxically, the creation of government institutions for the publishing of textbooks can have the same effect. Concludes that the only way to foster a national literature is to establish a viable private sector publishing industry.

283   Hofmeyr, Isabel **"From Book Development to Book History. Some Observations on the History of the Book in Africa."** *SHARP News* 13, no. 3 (Summer 2004): 3-4.

A brief survey of the literature on the history of the book in Africa and the different genres of publishing: missionary, colonialist, nationalist, popular literature, etc.

284   Irele, Abiola **"The Problems of African Publishing."** *Revue de Littérature Comparée* 67, no. 265 (January-March 1993): 115-119.
This article (in English, although published in a French language periodical) draws a direct correlation between the current crisis of development in Africa and the book famine in Africa, and is critical of African governments' failures to actively support their indigenous book industries. The focus of the article is on the Nigerian experience, particularly on marketing and distribution problems.

285   Isoun, T.T. **"Publishing in Africa."** *Discovery and Innovation* 6, no. 4 (December 1994): 336-339.
Reviews some of the current obstacles that create an unfavourable publishing environment in Africa, particularly for scholarly and scientific publishing. Suggests that one of the major challenges for publishers in Africa "is to ensure the establishment of a viable and functioning African book and journal marketing network so that the huge potential market for books and journals is actualised."

286   Kirkpatrick, Roger **"A Scramble from Africa? Publishing in the Global Economy."** *Publishing Research Quarterly* 20, no. 3 (Fall 2004): 34-39.
Reflects on "A Scramble from Africa", the title of a seminar held within the framework of the London Book Fair in 2004. It consisted of a series of presentations aimed to raise the levels of consciousness about the need to support indigenous African publishing and to help them develop markets for their books; to strengthen library services, and information and communication development in an effort to bridge the current digital divide, and thus provide equitable access to information on the Web.

287   Jamal, Amir H. **"The Cultural Dimensions of Development: National Cultural Values Versus Transnational Cultural Domination."** *Development Dialogue*, nos. 1-2 (1984): 76-82.
The opening address delivered at the Dag Hammarskjöld Seminar on "The Development of Autonomous Capacity in Publishing in Africa" (*see* entry ➔ **274**) It is concerned with the broad processes of cultural evolution, and hypothesizes that technology turns time and space into a rapidly alternating flow "threatening to transform the entire human society into a mindless amalgam in the form of a global market place." Urges that it is important to recognize "that unrestricted market forces sustain cultural aggression as much as economic disenfranchisement of Third World societies."

288   Kalenga, E.M. **"A Cursory Comment on Research, Publishing and Book Distribution in Africa."** In *Proceedings of the Info Africa Nova Conference 1993*, volume 1, edited by A.G. Coetzer. Pretoria: Info Africa Nova CC, 1993, 205-215.

Laments the apparent "inability to create and sustain an aggressive research culture among the academic community" at African institutions of higher learning, and the inability to develop viable and efficient publishing and distribution infrastructures and networks, which is seen as a direct manifestation of the absence of such a research culture. Argues that the development of a research culture "should be at the core of knowledge-creation because unless knowledge is created there is nothing of African scholarship to disseminate other than ignorance."

289   Kotei, S.I.A. **"Some Cultural and Social Factors of Book Reading and Publishing in Africa."** In *Publishing in Africa in the Seventies* edited by Edwina Oluwasanmi, Eva McLean, and Hans M. Zell. Ile-Ife, Nigeria: University of Ife Press, 1975, 174-205.
A wide-ranging examination of the state of the book and reading in Africa, within the "three-dimensional framework of writer-reader-publisher." The author attempts to isolate the major social and cultural factors affecting book publishing and reading in West Africa, and identifies the role of the publisher in society, using the lessons of history from the advent of Islam to the present. Discusses utilitarianism, reading comprehension and the second language barrier, and provides a lengthy discussion of culture and recreational reading, and writing in African languages. Although written and published over 30 years ago, this paper remains a significant contribution on the issue of the social and cultural factors that have influenced, and are continuing to influence, books and reading in Africa.

290   Kotei, S.I.A. **The Book Today in Africa.** Paris: UNESCO, 1981 (Books about Books series). 210 pp.
Also published in French as **Le livre en Afrique aujourd'hui.**
Sam Kotei's book was one of the first major in-depth studies on the state of the book and publishing in Africa, in which the author looked back on a decade of special efforts to alleviate the "acute shortage of books" identified at the UNESCO meeting on books in Accra in 1968. The author notes that progress was uneven and that many of the problems identified in 1968 still remained, although African publishing had generally made "impressive strides". The author surveyed the available literature, questioned writers, publishers, printers, libraries, bookshops, national book development councils, and interviewed book industry professional in several African countries in order to produce this overview of the situation in the 1970s and 1980s. Concludes with an examination of the future prospects of the book industry in Africa. Kotei's book remains a seminal study, not least for purposes of comparison as it relates to the growth of the African book industries since the 1980s.

291   Krynauw, Paula **"Problems and Implications of Western Dominance in the Production and Distribution of Books in Africa."** *Innovation. Journal of Appropriate Librarianship and Information Work in Southern Africa*, no. 8 (June 1994): 4-10.
Online:
http://www.library.unp.ac.za/Innovation/InnovationPdfs/No8pp4-10Krynauw.pdf [22/02/08]

Publishing in Africa is traced back to its colonial origins, which created a dependency perpetuated after independence; and the dominance of foreign and imported material was found to contradict development priorities and aspirations. The power of the multinational companies, a still weak indigenous publishing industry, and repressive government policies in some African countries, have all helped to reinforce this situation. In her conclusion, the author says that "on political, economic and cultural grounds one can criticise the overwhelming export of Western media to Africa", but that a conflict has arisen "because on the one hand there is universal appreciation of traditional, ethnic ways and a trend towards them, but on the other hand there is a need for development including a local media production industry. Some part of every traditional culture must be sacrificed as it develops and unfortunately we do not always understand what these sacrifices will be. The problem for the future will be to guarantee this development and minimise cultural disruption."

292   Lema, Elieshi **"The Future of the African Indigenous Publisher: Report of the Arusha Seminar."** *Bellagio Publishing Network Newsletter*, no. 17 (July 1996): 4-6.
A report about the presentations made at the ➜ **Dag Hammarskjöld Foundation's** (**55**) 'Arusha II' seminar (and *see also* entry ➜ **276** above).

293   MacLam, Helen **"Reading Africa."** *Choice* (February 1994): 895-897.
Reflections on a trip by a group of American librarians to visit libraries and publishers in the Côte d'Ivoire and in Ghana.

294   Made, S.M. **"African Economics and Book Requirements."** *Zimbabwe Librarian* 14, nos. 3 & 4 (July-December 1982): 43-49.
Also published in *African Research and Documentation*, no. 32 (1983): 1-7.
Contrasts the common issues relating to publishing in all countries with the special problems that affect developing countries, and African countries in particular. Examines questions of copyright, book distribution, and production problems.

295   Newton, Diana **"Bridging the Anglophone-Francophone Divide."** *Bellagio Publishing Network Newsletter*, no. 15 (August 1995): 11-12.
Argues that, when it comes to book publishing in Africa, "the English-French linguistic divide has created two distinct communities, with severely limited interaction between the two", and that "both sides will need to establish and maintain mechanisms for effective and timely information sharing that reach beyond isolated actions and token bilingualism." Recommends a number of activities that could be undertaken on the anglophone side to improve the situation.

296   Nigerian Book Fair Trust **Capacity Building in the African Publishing Industry. Papers Presented at the Sixth Nigeria International Book Fair, 7-13 May, 2007.** Lagos: Nigerian Book Fair Trust [c/o Literamed Publications Ltd., PMB 21068, Ikeja, Lagos, Nigeria], forthcoming 2008.
[Not examined]

297 Nottingham, John **"Establishing an African Publishing Industry. A Study in Decolonization."** *African Affairs* 68, no. 272 (April 1969): 139-144. Also published in *Education in Africa*, edited by Richard Jolly, Nairobi: East African Publishing House, 1969, 301-307.
This was one of the earliest articles on autonomous African publishing, by the former director of the (now long defunct) East African Publishing House in Nairobi. Nottingham argued that Africa needs a strong indigenous publishing industry, with ownership, production, personnel, and profits controlled by Africans, and proposed that local branches of British publishing houses should become indigenous companies, with majority shareholding held by Africans.

298 Nyamnjoh, Francis B. **"From Publish or Perish to Publish and Perish: What 'Africa's 100 Best Books' Tell Us About Publishing in Africa."** *Journal of Asian and African Studies* 39, no. 4 (October 2004): 331-355. Online: http://www.sabdet.com/Nyamnjoh%20ASAUK%20%20doc.pdf [22/02/08]
also at http://www.nyamnjoh.com/files/publish_or_perish.pdf [22/02/08]
Draws on the African publishing industry's initiative to determine 'Africa's 100 Best Books of the 20th Century', to discuss writing, scholarship and publishing in and on Africa. It highlights the challenge of promoting commitment to African humanity and creativity "without producing a simplistic reductionism or the inflation of belonging in Africa." The author also argues for the need "to problematize" what is published and read on Africa, and to determine how sympathetic to Africa culturally, morally, and scientifically authors and publications are. The article concludes with suggestions on how to reverse the process of writing and publishing on Africa and Africans as the 'heart of darkness' dreamt up by Joseph Conrad "and perfected by social science at the service of ambitions of dominance."

299 Nyamnjoh, Francis B. **"Globalization and the Cultural Economy: Africa."** In *Cultures and Globalization. Cultures and Tensions*, edited by Helmut Anheier and Yudhishthir Raj Isar. Thousand Oaks, CA and London: Sage Publications, forthcoming 2008.
The author uses publishing and filmmaking to illustrate the impact of global hierarchies and local repression on the cultural economy in Africa, and states that publishing and film-making demonstrate "how the logic of profitability impinges on the cultural economy in and on Africa." Nyamnjoh argues that African cultural production does not attract sufficient attention from cultural entrepreneurs, who are mostly white and located in the global North, unwilling to risk profitability through investing in cultures that are largely perceived to be socially inferior, economically uncompetitive and located in 'hearts of darkness' difficult to penetrate. Nor are African investors, intellectuals and political elites – "well schooled in negative representations and debasement of Africa" – all that keen to develop these sectors in ways that capture their creative encounters with cultural others. Nyamnjoh contends that "there is little or no publishing of books of interest and relevance to the African majority, and of those that are published, most are by multinational publishers who target the elite few who can read and write European languages and who – for economic, cultural or political reasons – reproduce work informed by a global

hierarchy of creativity in which Africans are perceived to be at the very bottom." In his conclusions and policy recommendations the author states "the African is, because of his race and place in society or geography, allowed to excel in consumption of cultural products and its vehicles of transmission, but not to harness the technological processes and political economy of the cultural economy." The author further argues that although African publishing is heavily reliant on school textbooks, the lion's share of subventions for and business in such projects goes directly to multinational publishers or their local affiliates. "Yet these multinational publishers are less keen on investing some of the profit made into developing the local publishing industry, local content and/or promoting publishing in local languages. The disadvantaged African publishers who are interested do not make enough from textbooks to venture into other aspects of publishing. This calls for policies that protect African publishers against uneven competition with established giants driven primarily by profitability."

300   Ofeimun, Odia **"A Cultural Economy of the Book in Africa."**
Glendora Books Supplement 1, no. 5 (2000): 8-14.
Online:
http://archive.lib.msu.edu/DMC/African%20Journals/pdfs/glendora%20s
upplement/issue5/
[23/02/08]
This is primarily an extensive book review essay of ➔ **The African Writers'**
Handbook (2507), which is described as "the harvest of two decades of matching diverse views and impressions, ambitions and tactics, from across Africa in the light of global trends." However, it also offers some astute observations on the development of an autonomous publishing industry in Africa, the relations between African writers and indigenous publishers, and the confrontations and recriminations between publishers and authors, which "lie in too narrow an appreciation of the difficulties that the other must contend with." Odia Ofeimun is a well known Nigerian poet and journalist, and is the former General Secretary and President of the ➔ **Association of Nigerian Authors (732)**.

301   Oluwasanmi, Edwina; Eva McLean, and Hans M. Zell, eds.
**Publishing in Africa in the Seventies. Proceedings of an International
Conference on Publishing and Book Development, held at the University
of Ife, Ile-Ife, Nigeria, 16-20 December, 1973.** Ile-Ife, Nigeria: University of
Ife Press, 1975. 377 pp.
An important historical document, these are the proceedings of the International Conference on Publishing and Book Development held at the University of Ife, Ile-Ife, Nigeria (now Obafemi Awolowo University) in December of 1973. Contributions came from many prominent figures in the field of African publishing active in the 1970s, as well as from writers (Chinua Achebe among them), editors, booksellers, and librarians. The volume includes some of the contributed papers, summaries of all papers, and the recommendations that were put forward at that time. Conference participants concluded "there is no doubt that a lively and flourishing publishing industry is vital for the development of the reading habit, to foster and preserve a country's culture, and to produce inexpensive books which meet local needs." Long

out-of-print, but copies should be available in major academic libraries. A small number of the papers in the collection, although now dated, merit inclusion for their historical significance, and are listed as separate entries elsewhere in this bibliography.

302 Onibonoje, Gabriel O. **"Wanted! A Cultural Revolution, Not a Dialogue on Publishing in Africa in the Seventies and After."** In *Publishing in Africa in the Seventies,* edited by Edwina Oluwasanmi, Eva McLean, and Hans M. Zell. Ile-Ife, Nigeria: University of Ife Press, 1975, 262-272.
A provocative paper contributed to the Ife conference (*see* entry ➜ **301** above) by the pioneering Nigerian publisher Gabriel Onibonoje. It begins by addressing "the futility of grandiose conference aims and pious resolutions", tracing the aims, resolutions and sponsorship of previous conferences on publishing, in an attempt to demonstrate that they are "invariably barren of any worthwhile and lasting results." Concludes "the African author must speak the language, fulfil the expectations and satisfy the needs of the ordinary African reader. The social richness of African literature, that is, the number, the intensity and quality of the 'earth' connections, must be determined by the African reading public. Our literature must find its inspiration from the hard life of the people and focus on our reality, know it better and thus create the necessary critical consciousness among the people and ultimately lead them to true development and freedom."

303 Owens, Cora, ed. **From Papyrus to Print-out: The Book in Africa Yesterday, Today and Tomorrow. Bibliophilia Africana 8 Conference Proceedings. Centre of the Book Cape Town, 11-14 May 2005.** Pretoria and Cape Town: National Library of South Africa/Centre of the Book, 2005. 297 pp.
Loosely divided into three sections that focus on the past, the present, and the future, the papers in the proceedings of the 2005 Bibliophilia Africana conference offer a wide variety of contributions on the state of the book in Africa, and on topics such as promoting a reading culture, book and newspaper publishing, collecting books and archival materials, preservation of books and oral literature, public libraries, and accessibility of literature. There also some papers on the impact of new technology and the Internet on book development and publishing. The volume includes book related experiences from South and Southern Africa, as well as contributions from Argentina, the USA, and the UK. *Note:* some of the papers in this collection are individually abstracted elsewhere in this bibliography.
Reviews:
The African Book Publishing Record vol. 32, no. 2, 2006

Oxford Brookes University Library **Publishing in Africa Collection** ➜ *see* **Section 1, Serials and reference: Bibliographies and continuing sources, and special collections** entry **178**

304 Oyeoku, Kalu K. **"Publishing in Africa: Breaking the Development Barrier."** In *Publishing in Africa in the Seventies,* edited by Edwina

Oluwasanmi, Eva McLean, and Hans M. Zell. Ile-Ife, Nigeria: University of Ife Press, 1975, 277-288.

Oyeoku argues that the most serious barrier to effective publishing in Africa is not finance or technical know-how, but the lack of interest in the development of the book. He also describes his innovative plans for an experiment to develop a community library of sound on tapes, for a rural community of about 5,000 inhabitants (who have shared language and have the same history and traditions) the hypothesis of the experiment being "that the vast majority of Africans can be interested enough to buy and read books if the book is introduced to them from the grassroots in a more acceptable fashion."

305   Oyeoku, Kalu K. **"The Library and the Third World Publisher: An Inquiry into a Lop-sided Development."** *Library Trends* 26, no. 4 (Spring 1978): 505-514.

The former acquisitions librarian at the University of Nigeria in Nsukka attempts to demonstrate that Third World countries have "basic handicaps which retard the growth of book production and dissemination." Suggests steps which can be taken to stimulate book production and states that "the best results will be achieved by means of experimentation, trying and failing and trying again." Concludes that a national book council representing all sectors of the book professions is an essential requirement to promote book development.

306   Perera, Santosh **"A Strong Case for Books."** *Modern Africa* 10, no. 2 (March/April 1986): 5-7.

Describes the great need for books in Africa and contends that this [in the mid-1980s] is an opportune time for indigenous African publishers to make a significant breakthrough, but that in order to do so they will need support.

307   Perry-Widstrand, Rede **Publishing in Africa.** Uppsala: Scandinavian Institute of African Studies [restricted circulation], 1974. 361 pp.

Also published, in a condensed version, in *Pan African Journal*, no. 8 (1975): 403-424.

Investigates the background and development of publishing in Africa by examining the reading public, the illiteracy factor, and the question of language.

308   Rathgeber, Eva-Maria **"The Book Industry in Africa, 1973-1983: A Decade of Development."** In *Publishing in the Third World*, edited by Philip G. Altbach, Amadio A. Arboleda, and S. Gopinathan. London: Mansell Publishing Ltd., 1985, 57-75.

Reviews the recommendations of the Ile-Ife conference proceedings contained in ➔ **Publishing in Africa in the Seventies (301),** discusses the efforts that have been made to implement some of the recommendations, and examines the obstacles remaining to the establishment of strong indigenous publishing industries in African countries.

309 Rathgeber, Eva-Maria **"African Book Publishing: Lessons from the 1980s."** In *Publishing and Development in the Third World*, edited by Philip G. Altbach. London: Hans Zell Publishers, 1992, 77-99.
Provides an overview of the status of the book industry in Africa in the 1980s and examines and evaluates the efforts made by African publishers to improve their working environments, and to build new markets for their books. Special attention is given to the book industry in Zimbabwe, which has developed a small, yet vibrant publishing industry since independence in 1980. The author concludes that the optimism of the publishing scene in Zimbabwe belies the overall decline of book publishing in Africa, and shows that there is still scope for innovation and optimism.

310 Rea, Julian **"Aspects of African Publishing 1945-74."** *The African Book Publishing Record* 1, no. 2 (April 1974): 145-149.
Also published in *African Studies Since 1945*, edited by Christopher Fyfe, Harlow: Longman, 1976.
An overview of publishing in Africa up to the mid-1970s, including a historical perspective and account of the early days between 1945 and the late 1950s when African publishing for schools and universities was controlled and directed from outside. The author (who was Director of the Africa Division of the Longman Group), thereafter describes the catalysts of educational expansion, the major publishing influences, problems facing publishers, and other constraints hindering book development on the continent, offering some suggestions how developing nations in Africa might solve these problems.

311 Rønning, Helge **"Perspectives on Support from the Nordic Countries to Publishing and Book Production in Africa."** In *Academic Book Production and Distribution in Africa. Support from Nordic Countries. Report from a conference at Chr. Michelsen Institute, Bergen, 10-11 April 1997*, edited by Kirsti Hagen Andersen. Fantoft, Norway: Ch. Michelsen Institute 1997, 105-112.
Looks at issues of support for the African book industries by donors and other agencies in the Nordic countries, and analyzes some of the reasons why it can be difficult for aid agencies to provide support for books and other media. Also identifies some areas for which requests for support might be sympathetically considered, for example projects which cut across all the individual elements in the book chain, and would benefit all the different players in the writing, publishing, and distribution of African books. Buy-back and monograph subsidy schemes, or incentives for writers to break into print, might be among other schemes that deserved consideration.

312 Salzano, Carmela **Making Book Coordination Work!** London: Association for the Development of Education in Africa (ADEA), Working Group on Books and Learning Materials; Paris: UNESCO/DANIDA Basic Learning Materials Initiative (Perspectives on African Book Development, 13), 2002. 81 pp. (distributed by African Books Collective Ltd, Oxford).
Based on contributions to a round table meeting, 'Structures for Book Sector Coordination' held during the 1999 Zimbabwe International Book Fair, this book

describes the changing role and functions of book sector coordination bodies in Africa. It identifies the key issues and the practical considerations that need to be addressed in the establishment of national coordination mechanisms, and the lessons learned regarding the financing, functions, structure, organization, composition, and membership of national book development councils, drawing on the experience from stakeholders in the public, private and NGO sector in 13 African countries. An appendix provides an example of a constitution for a book development council, using the model of the ➔ **National Book Development Council of Tanzania (1119)**.
Reviews:
The African Book Publishing Record vol. 29, no. 3, 2003
Logos. The Journal of the World Book Community vol. 15, no. 1, 2004
Online:
http://www.atypon-link.com/LOG/doi/pdf/10.2959/logo.2004.15.1.49

313   Schmidt, Nancy J. **"The Future of the Book in Sub-Saharan Africa."**
Liberal Education 79, no. 1 (Winter 1993): 36-41.
The former African studies librarian at Indiana University Libraries analyzes the factors that have contributed to the crisis in African publishing and the widespread book famine in the region. Also examines some of the problems faced by African university libraries, and reviews a number of book donation programmes.

314   Smith, Keith **"Books and Development in Africa -- Access and Role."**
Library Trends 26, no. 4 (Spring 1978): 469-487.
Probes into the role of books in development, and asks who has access to books in Africa. Discusses the function of school books as tools of education, and examines the opportunities that are available to African academics for publishing in Africa, or overseas. Also examines some cultural attitudes towards books in Africa, for example that reading is usually seen merely a tool to advancement and that the contents of books are often considered indisputable. Also deals with literacy, books in African languages, literary output, light fiction and popular non-fiction.

Smith, Keith **"Who Controls Book Publishing in Anglophone Middle Africa?"** *see* ➔ **Section 4, Studies by topic: Multinational publishers in Africa** entry **2026**

315   Southern African Book Development Education Trust (SABDET)
Changing Times – Changing Africa. Seminar held during the 2002 London Book Fair. Seminar Reports.
Seminar One: **Marketing Africa's Best**.
http://www.sabdet.com/LBF02sem1rep.htm [23/02/08]
Seminar Two: **The Book Supply Chain in Africa**.
http://www.sabdet.com/LBF02sem2rep.htm [23/02/08]
The reports of two seminars held during the 2002 London Book Fair, organized by the ➔ **Southern African Book Development Education Trust (113)** in association with the Zimbabwe International Book Fair. The first seminar was devoted to 'Marketing Africa's Best' and speakers included Kasahun Checole, President and Publisher of Africa World Press; a literary agent, Isobel Dixon; and writer Wangui

wa Goro. The topic of the second seminar was 'The Book Supply Chain in Africa', with presentations by Justus Mugaju, editor at Fountain Publishers in Uganda; James Ng'ombe, Managing Director of Jhango Heinemann in Malawi; and Barnard Bagenda, Senior Principal Librarian at the Uganda Public Libraries Board. The material offered here includes summaries of papers presented and transcripts of the discussion that ensued after each presentation.

316 Sow, Mamadou Aliou **"Anglophone Publishing in Africa As Seen By a Francophone Book Professional."** In *The Book Chain in Anglophone Africa. A Survey and Directory*, edited by Roger Stringer. Oxford: International Network for the Availability of Scientific Publications (INASP), 2002, 8-9.
Online:
http://www.inasp.info/file/57/the-book-chain-in-anglophone-africa-a-survey-and-directory.html [23/02/08]
Compares the growth and development of publishing, and mechanisms for book and reading promotion, in the anglophone and francophone regions in Africa. Notes an increase in partnerships between publishers from the two regions, working on co-publication projects and bilingual co-productions, and which is expected to lead to better knowledge, and easier availability of, anglophone titles among the francophone reading public.

317 Sturges, Paul, and Richard Neill **The Quiet Struggle. Libraries and Information for Africa.** 2nd ed. London: Mansell Publishing, 1998. 244 pp.
Online: http://www.lboro.ac.uk/departments/dils/people/psturges.html [23/02/08] or
http://www-staff.lboro.ac.uk/%7Elsrps/Quiet%20Struggle%20E-Book/The%20Quiet%20Struggle%20Small%20Version/The%20Quiet%20Str uggle%20PDF/The%20Quiet%20Struggle%20Electronic%20Edition%202.pdf
(full text file) [23/02/08]
A benchmark volume (now freely accessible as a full-text e-book) that examines information needs, and access to information in Africa, in all its dimensions. The authors analyze the successes and failures of information provision and literacy programmes in various part of the continent, and convincingly argue that there is a need for new approaches to librarianship in Africa. Includes a discussion (pp. 24-40) of the African publishing industries, and publishing for children.
Reviews: (of 1st ed.)
African Affairs vol. 91, no. 362, January 1992
African Studies Review vol. 34, no. 1, April 1991
Journal of Librarianship and Information Science vol. 23, no. 1, 1991
Journal of Modern African Studies vol. 37, no. 2, 1999

318 Taubert, Sigfred, and Peter Weidhaas, eds. **The Book Trade of the World, vol. 4: Africa.** Munich: K.G. Saur, 1984. 391 pp.
The fourth and final volume of the *Book Trade of the World*, a series of books that aimed to provide a convenient reference tool to the world's publishing and

bookselling industries, and to the institutions, organizations, and journals which are associated with them. The information on each country is contributed by a leading authority in the field and is presented under 35 thematic headings. The African volume contains an extensive introductory essay by Hans Zell, and an index to all four volumes in the series, compiled by Caroline Bundy. While now inevitably very dated, the books is still useful as source showing the historical development of the book trade in African countries, from the earliest times up to the period of the early 1980s.

319 Tumusiime, James **"Book Procurement: Will the World Bank Change Strategy?"** *Bellagio Publishing Network Newsletter,* no. 21 (December 1997): 2-3.
Online:
http://www.bellagiopublishingnetwork.com/newsletter21/tumusiime.htm [23/02/08]
Examines the ➔ **World Bank (124)** procurement policies for textbook policies, and the Bank's International Competitive Bidding procedures for textbook production, which have been the subject of intense criticism by publishers in developing countries because they tended to favour multinational publishers. Also reports about a meeting convened by the World Bank in 1997, during which publishers from different backgrounds were given an opportunity to voice their criticism of the policies in an open and frank exchange of views, and to discuss the major problems facing indigenous publishing industries.

320 Tumusiime, James **"World Bank Changes Textbook Provision Policy."** *Bellagio Publishing Network Newsletter,* no. 25 (July 1999): 2-3.
Online:
http://www.bellagiopublishingnetwork.com/newsletter25/tumusiime.htm [23/02/08]
Reports about a visit to the ➔ **World Bank (124)** in March 1999 by the [then] Vice-Chair of the ➔**African Publishers' Network (5)** to represent APNET as a panellist in a discussion about a new draft policy on World Bank textbook provision. The policy addressed a number of the key issues that represented a considerable shift from previous polices.

321 United Nations Educational, Scientific, and Cultural Organisation **Book Development in Africa. Problems and Perspectives.** Paris: UNESCO, (Reports and Papers on Mass Communication, 56), 1969. 37 pp.
Also published in French as **La Promotion du livre en Afrique: problèmes et perspectives**.
Online: http://unesdoc.unesco.org/images/0005/000595/059548eo.pdf [23/02/08]
A historically important document (and still available online at the UNESCO Web site above), this was one of the earliest studies on publishing and book development in Africa. It consists of a report of a meeting of experts on book development in Africa, convened by ➔ **UNESCO (118)** and held in Accra in February 1968.

Delegates to the conference examined in detail the problems facing book development in Africa, looking at the role of books in economic and social development, suggesting measures to promote book production in the general and educational publishing sectors, as well as considering aspects such as the distribution, promotion, and the international flow of books.

322 United Nations Educational, Scientific, and Cultural Organisation **Regional Meeting of Experts on National Book Strategies in Africa. Report.** Paris: UNESCO (Doc. CC.81/WS/37), 1982. 102 pp.
Also available in French **Réunion regionale d'experts sur les strategies nationals du livre en Africa. Rapport de la Réunion**.
Online: http://unesdoc.unesco.org/images/0004/000475/047510eb.pdf (English) [23/02/08]
http://unesdoc.unesco.org/images/0004/000475/047510fb.pdf (French) [23/02/08]
Contains the working papers, contributions submitted by participants, and the final report of the Regional Meeting of Experts on National Book Strategies in Africa, which was held in Dakar in February 1982. It opens with a working paper submitted by the UNESCO Secretariat on National Book Strategies in Africa, followed by general overviews of the state of the book and publishing in Africa, and studies on book development and book policies in Benin, Congo (Brazzaville), Ghana, Kenya, Nigeria, Sierra Leone, and Tanzania. Now inevitably very dated, but still useful for historical background on the development of the book industries in several African countries.

Wafawarowa, Brian **Intellectual Property Rights and Knowledge Production in Africa** *see* **Section 4, Studies by topic: Copyright and legal deposit/Authors' rights** entry ➜ **1827**

323 Wafawarowa, Brian **Publishing for Africa. Working Creatively Around the Challenges.** *Bookmark. News Magazine of the South African Booksellers' Association* 11, (July-September 2007): 8-9
Online:
http://www.sabooksellers.com/pdf/Publishing%20for%20Africa.pdf [23/02/08]
The current Chairman of the ➜ **African Publishers Network (5)** believes the way forward for African publishing is through publishing partnerships, exploiting economies of scale, and making more effective use of recent advances in production technology. "In scholarly publishing, especially where the economies of scale are too small to warrant conventional publishing, it is high time that African publishers embraced the open access agenda and look at how best to network the activities of scholarly publishers on the continent and outside the continent." Publishing for Africa is a tough challenge "that takes a publisher who can think around all the barriers and challenges by working creatively with other book practitioners on the continent and take appropriate advantage of existing technology."

324 Wafawarowa, Brian **The Business of Book Publishing in Africa**.
(Document ref. WIPO/IP/IND/GE/07/14)
http://www.wipo.int/edocs/mdocs/mdocs/en/wipo_ip_ind_ge_07/wipo
_ip_ind_ge_07_14.doc [08/02/08]
A paper presented to the ➔ **World Intellectual Property Organization/WIPO (126)**
International Conference on Intellectual Property and the Creative Industries,
Geneva, October 29-30, 2007. The author finds that, compared to the developed
world, the African and the developing world's book publishing industry is too
dependent on textbook publishing and procurement by the state, the World Bank,
and donor agencies. This presentation looks at the challenges facing general book
publishing in Africa as a whole and South Africa in particular and offers a number of
recommendations on how best to go about publishing for Africa and the developing
world. Wafawarowa contends that general publishing is a better indicator of the level
of development of any publishing sector, and highlights some of the problems that
inhibit publishing and distribution of general books across the continent. Through a
series of case studies he attempts to demonstrate how some of these challenges can
be overcome through the creation of better economies of scale, and how collaboration
and simple production technology can be utilized to achieve this.

325 Wallace, M.S. **"Africa's War of Words."** *South*, no. 7 (15 April-May
1981): 33-37.
Discusses the anti-colonial movement in Africa and its aims to decolonialize Africa's
cultural and intellectual life, and examines how this has affected publishers and
authors. Maintains that "Africa's publishers have placed themselves in the front-line
of the struggle to end Western domination of the continent's intellectual and cultural
life."

326 Walsh, Gretchen **Publishing in Africa: A Neglected Component of
Development.** Boston: African Studies Center, Boston University (Working
Papers, 56), 1991. 33 pp.
Examines the complex factors that affect publishing in Africa, using a three-part
model involving the reader, the writer and the publisher. Among the topics the
author covers are the importance of textbooks in any discussion of African
publishing, the need for children's books, the dynamic between writer and reader,
the relationship between writer and publisher, and the myriad problems African
publishers face, especially in the area of marketing and distribution. Walsh suggests
that to approach publishing rationally, it is essential that there is interaction between
writer, reader and publisher, making it possible for real change to be effected in
Africa both in and through the book trade.

327 Westra, Pieter E., and Leonie Twentyman Jones, eds. **The Love of
Books. Proceedings of the Seventh South African Conference of
Bibliophiles held at The South African Library, Cape Town, 8-10 May
1996**. Cape Town: South African Library (Bibliophilia Africana VII, South
African Library General Series, 26), 1997. 219 pp.
The main themes of Bibliophilia Africana VII – a series of conferences that began in
Cape Town thirty years ago – were publishing today and in earlier times, the

development of book collections in South African libraries, bibliography, and some other book-related topics. This book brings together the wide-ranging papers that were presented at the conference, containing a total of 22 contributions. Of particular interest are three overview papers "Current State of Publishing & Bibliography of African Materials" by John McIlwaine, "Current Publishing Trends in South Africa" by Eve Horwitz, and "Current Publishing Trends in Southern African Countries" by Sally Schramm; and there are also two historical accounts, "History of the South African Publishing and Book Trade" by A.S.C. Hooper, and "Mission Presses in Natal" by B.M. Spencer. An article by Monica Cromhout, "Entrepreneurial Publishing: The Exciting Trend towards Publishing in Short Runs", examines the mathematics of publishing, attitudes to self-publishing, and provides some tips for the entrepreneurial short-run author-publisher. Other contributions deal with CD-ROM publishing, collecting offprints, rare books collections, book design, book auctions, books vs. electronic media, and the depiction of the Zulu wars in South African children's books. *Note:* some of the papers in this collection are individually abstracted elsewhere in this bibliography.
Reviews:
The African Book Publishing Record vol. 24, no. 1, 1998

328   Zaher, Celia R. **"Directions for the Future: UNESCO's Role in Supporting Future Book Production and Distribution in Africa."** In *African Studies. Papers Presented at a Colloquium at the British Library 7-9 January 1985.* London: The British Library, 1985, 309-313.
The [then] Director of UNESCO's book promotion division, reports about ➜ **UNESCO (118)** programmes and activities for book promotion in Africa, describing its primary objectives. The author observes that the programmes have gradually shifted from general promotion of the book to more specific action and initiatives, thus making a significant contribution in the establishment and strengthening of book industry infrastructures.

329   Zegeye, Abebe **"Knowledge Production and Publishing Africa."** Paper presented at the Africa-Europe Group for Interdisciplinary Studies (AEGIS) conference SABDET panel at SOAS on the 2 July 2005 under the title "Getting Published, Getting Heard: Debate and Democracy in Africa". http://www.sabdet.com/aegis2005zegeye.htm [23/02/08]
The author, who is a former Director of UNISA Press in South Africa, examines the issues in the "slippery" relationship between knowledge production and publishing in Africa. He asks: "What is African knowledge? Are we talking of European knowledge in Africa, or African knowledge in Europe? What are the other forms of knowledge economies existing in Africa that have been marginalised by powerful multi-national publishing houses working with their local agents? How and where can these knowledge forms on the edge be mainstreamed into the public domain as valid African knowledge through publishing in Africa? Lastly, what are the links created between knowledge production and publishing in Africa in the context of the equally daunting task of democratising the knowledge production infrastructure and the African societies themselves?" He thereafter offers tentative answers to some of

these questions and proposes what he believes could be "democratising perspectives in producing and publishing knowledge in Africa."

330   Zeleza, Paul **"A Social Contract for Books."** *The African Book Publishing Record* 22, no. 4 (1996): 251-255.
Also published in *National Book Policies for Africa. The Key to Long-term Development. Proceedings of the Zimbabwe International Book Fair Indaba 96, Harare, Zimbabwe, 26-27 July 1996*, edited by Murray McCartney. Harare: Zimbabwe International Book Fair Trust, 1996, 12-20; and in *The African Writers' Handbook*, edited by James Gibbs and Jack Mapanje. Oxford: African Books Collective Ltd., 1999, 3-14.
A slightly edited version of an eloquent keynote speech delivered by Paul Zeleza – winner of the 1994 ➔ **Noma Award for Publishing in Africa (98)** – at an 'Indaba' on national book policies held during the 1996 Zimbabwe International Book Fair. It focuses, first, on the political and cultural economies of the African book industry and, secondly, the social contract which the author believes needs to be forged between the six stakeholders he identifies, namely African governments, publishers, writers, educational institutions, libraries, and the general reading public. The author contends that a social contract for books, for the development of a vigorous reading culture and a flourishing indigenous book industry, requires specific commitments and tangible contributions from each of the stakeholders. He sets out what these requirements are, and concludes, "Culture and books are too serious to be left to sympathetic foreigners or governments. All of us have a stake in them, for they embody our values, practices and possibilities, dreams and destiny, pasts and futures, our investment in a reflective, critical, and tolerant humanity."

Zeleza, Paul Tiyambe **"Manufacturing and Consuming Knowledge. African Libraries and Publishing"** *see* ➔ **Section 4, Studies by topic: Libraries and publishing** entry **1997**

331   Zeleza, Paul Tiyambe **"The Dynamics of Book and Library Development in Anglophone Africa."** In *The Book Chain in Anglophone Africa. A Survey and Directory*, edited by Roger Stringer. Oxford: International Network for the Availability of Scientific Publications (INASP), 2002, 3-7.
Online: http://www.inasp.info/file/57/the-book-chain-in-anglophone-africa-a-survey-and-directory.html [23/02/08]
Discusses, first, general trends in book and library development in anglophone Africa and, secondly, focuses on two key challenges: the questions of literacy and language. In a concluding section the author assesses the challenges and opportunities offered by the new information and communication technologies for the development of African publishing and reading cultures, and, at the same time, analyzes some of the problems of ICTs and electronic publishing in terms of access, Internet connectivity, cost, archiving, and issues relating to technical competence. Zeleza argues that it is easy to dismiss the need for e-publishing, to stress that there are more pressing needs in other areas. "But we must resist giving in to despair or to

the populist dismissal of new technologies on the grounds that they are patronized by a minority or the elite. The same can be said about print publishing and libraries themselves: the vast masses of African peoples do not buy books or go to libraries, but few would regard that as sufficient reason to shut the libraries and publishers down. The challenge is to expand their usage and utility for more people."

332   Zell, Hans M. **"Africa - The Neglected Continent."** *Logos. The Journal of the World Book Community* 1, no. 2 (1990): 19-27.
Online:
http://www.atypon-link.com/LOG/doi/pdf/10.2959/logo.1990.1.2.19
Also published in *Publishing and Book Development in the Third World*, edited by Philip G. Altbach, London: Hans Zell Publishers, 1992, 65-76;
Afro-Asian Publishing. Contemporary Trends, New Delhi: Institute of Book Publishing, 1992, 33-47; and in *Zeitschrift für Kulturaustausch* 41, no. 3 (1991): 333-340.
A critical examination of the state of the book and the African book industries in the late 1980s, which is described as a publishing industry in severe crisis, heavily affected by a weak infrastructure in most African countries, as well as by "past corrupt regimes, capital flight, devastating years of drought and famine, political unrest, and the consequences of the major hikes in the price of oil." The author states that "the picture of Africa at the end of the 1980s is largely of a *bookless* society" and examines the book famine, that is inflicting long-lasting damage across a whole generation going through primary, secondary and university education in Africa. While the author states that a viable indigenous publishing industry is "still a dream in most parts of the continent", and despite the overall gloomy picture, the very difficult economic conditions and lack of government encouragement, new imprints, nonetheless, continue to mushroom all over Africa and "some privately-owned firms have shown imaginative entrepreneurial skill in the midst of adversity."

333   Zell, Hans M. **"Publishing in Africa: The Crisis and the Challenge."**
In *A History of Twentieth-Century African Literatures*, edited by Oyekan Owomoyela. Lincoln & London: University of Nebraska Press, 1993, 369-87.
Examines the crisis in the African book industry and the challenges facing indigenous publishers. Also provides an overview of literary publishing in Africa south of the Sahara, including literary periodicals and magazines, which tend to live a somewhat precarious existence.

334   Zell, Hans M. **"The Growth of Publishing in Sub-Saharan Africa. A Chronology and Some Landmarks."** *The African Book Publishing Record* 20, no. 3 (1994): 175-179.
Also published in *African Publishing Review* 3, no. 5 (September/October 1994): 6-8.
Another version (updated, but listing key dates, landmarks and initiatives only) published as **"Key Dates in the Development of Indigenous African Publishing"** In *The African Publishing Companion: A Resource Guide and Directory.* Lochcarron, Scotland: Hans Zell Publishing, 2002, 150-154.

A chronology providing the founding dates of a number of the more important publishers in sub-Saharan Africa, including some of the early mission presses, government sponsored literature bureaux, and the major UK multinationals who established a presence in Africa. Additionally, the chronology gives details of what might be considered landmark events (conferences, meetings, book fairs, initiatives, etc.) in the growth and development of the autonomous publishing industries in Africa. The original version of the chronology covered the period to 1975 and post-1975 to 1985, while the updated version covers the period 1947 through to 2001.

335 Zell, Hans M. **"Publishing in Africa."** In *International Book Publishing. An Encyclopedia*, edited by Philip G. Altbach and Edith S. Hoshino. New York: Garland Publishing, 1995, 366-73.

A broad sweep of the development of publishing in Africa, from the first mission printing presses in Nigeria in the nineteenth century to indigenous publishing in Africa today [in the mid 1990s]. Provides some historical background, examines the role of the multinational publishers which dominated the publishing scene in the 1960s and 1970s, and charts the establishment and growth of autonomous, African-owned publishing enterprises. Also analyzes some of the key issues that have effected the development of the book industries in Africa.

336 Zell, Hans M. **"The Fifth Edition of** *African Books in Print.* **New Features and Old Problems."** *African Research & Documentation* no. 82 (2000): 31-38.

Describes the difficulties encountered in the data gathering and verification process for the 5th edition of ➜ **African Books in Print/Livres Africaines Disponibles (188)**, and the various new features introduced for that edition, which was published in 2000.

337 Zimbabwe International Book Fair Trust **Access to Information. Proceedings of the ZIBF Indaba 97. Harare 2-3 August 1997.** Harare: Zimbabwe International Book Fair Trust 1997. 232 pp (distributed outside Africa by African Books Collective Ltd., Oxford)

Contains the papers that were presented at the Zimbabwe International Book Fair 'Indaba 97', whose topic was 'Access to Information'. The workshop split into four groups: 'National Book Policy', 'Information Technology and Rights', 'Scholarship and Research', and 'Community Access to Information', and the papers are presented in this order. *Note:* some of the papers in this collection are individually abstracted elsewhere in this bibliography.

Regional studies

Regional studies: Africa, East

Note: country- or topic-specific studies on publishing and book development in East Africa can be found under the appropriate headings in → **Section 3, Country studies** or → **Section 4, Studies by topic**.

338 E.A.E.P. 40th Anniversary. Our Life Has Just Begun. Edited by Peter Kimani, *et al.* Nairobi: East African Educational Publishers, n.d. [2005]. 32 pp.
An informative special edition of the newsletter of East African Educational Publisher (EAEP) commemorating 40 years of publishing. The glossy brochure includes tributes to Henry Chakava, the driving force behind the company, together with short pieces by members of staff and a historical account charting the growth of the company over the years, first as Heinemann Educational Books (East Africa) Ltd, thereafter Heinemann Kenya, until it became the present-day East African Educational Publishers. There are also contributions and tributes by prominent EAEP authors.

339 Ellerman, Evelyn **"The Literature Bureau: African Influence in Papua New Guinea."** *Research in African Literatures* 26, no. 4 (Winter 1995): 206-214.
A study of literature bureaux as agencies designed to serve the literary and educational needs of the newly literate. It traces the history and development of the East African Literature Bureau, which had served as a model for the establishment of the Papua New Guinea Literature Bureau, and compares the role, activities and success of the two organizations.

340 Fontaine, Régine; and François-G. Barbier Wiesser, eds. **Livres et réseaux documentaries/Publishing and Libraries' Cooperation. Nouvelles perspectives de partenariat: Afrique anglophone-Afrique francophone-France/Towards Partnership between English-speaking Africa, French-speaking Africa, and France. Documents de travail/Working Papers.** Paris: Ministère des Affaires étrangères DCCID/CCF/CE. Sous-direction de la cooperation culturelle et artistique. Division de l'écrit et des médiathèques [244 blvd. Saint Germain, 75303 Paris 07 SP], 2002. 172 pp.
The text of 14 papers presented to a three day conference sponsored by the French Foreign Ministry held in Nairobi 2002. The title of the collection could be somewhat misleading, as it contains very little about collaboration between libraries and publishers in Africa on the one hand, nor about collaboration between publishers in Francophone and Anglophone Africa on the other. Apart from one short paper on publishing in Kenya, most of the papers focus on the current [2002] state of library and information services in a number of African countries, primarily in East Africa, together with papers on African studies in France, cooperation in the area of children's book publishing, the role of French cultural centres in Africa, and on other topics such as library networking in anglophone Africa.

341 Kitinya, Ishmael O. **The Book and Newspaper Trade for Africa.**
Nairobi: Africa Book Services Ltd., 1981. 91 pp.
Examines publishing, writing, printing, bookselling, and the newspaper trade, primarily in East Africa.

342 Lema, Elieshi **"Book Publishing in East Africa: A Neglected Strategic Industry."** *African Publishing Review* 11, no. 6 (2002): 3-4.
A paper presented at a ➔ **Publishers Association of Tanzania (1120)**/APNET seminar on strategic marketing of East African literature, which examines the prerequisites of a dynamic publishing industry in East Africa, and the need of a national book policy to become a springboard for strategic action.

343 Makotsi, Ruth **"Organising the Publishing Industry at the Regional Level."** Paper presented at the International Conference on the Book, Oxford Brookes University, September 2005.
http://www.sabdet.com/ICB2005makotsi.htm [23/02/08]
Examines the recent growth of the book sector in East Africa, private sector initiatives, the role of the ➔ **East African Book Development Association (13)** launched at the end of 2000, the strategies and activities of this regional forum, and the benefits it has brought to the book industries.

344 Mwangi, David M., and John Nottingham **"Problems and Policies in the East Africa Region Book Trade."** *Maktaba* 6, no. 2 (1981): 24-29.
[Not examined]

345 Olden, Anthony **"Reading Matter and Libraries for East Africans."**
In *Libraries in Africa. Pioneers, Policies, Problems*, by Anthony Olden. Lanham, MD: Scarecrow Press, 1995, 76-97.
An extensive discussion of the (now defunct) East African Literature Bureau under its former director Charles Richards, and its role in the development of publishing and library services. *See also* entry ➔ **346** below.

346 Olden, Anthony **"No Carpet on the Floor: Extracts from the Memoirs of Charles Granston Richards, Founding Director, East African Literature Bureau."** *African Research and Documentation*, no. 71 (1996): 1-32.
Extracts from the Richards papers (on deposit at the School of Oriental and African Studies, University of London), which form an important historical record of the development of publishing, bookselling, and library services in East Africa. *No Carpet on the Floor* was written at the request of the University of Oxford Development Records Project, Rhodes House Library, and writing and revisions took place between 1977 and 1995. The extracts are a slightly abbreviated narrative of the years 1935 to 1965, and include accounts of Charles Richard's time with the CMS Bookshop in Nairobi (1935-1948); the East African Literature Bureau (1948-1963), and at Oxford University Press Eastern Africa (1963-1965). It also includes a section on the magazine *Tazama/Tunuulira* by David McD. Wilson, and an article on the establishment of public library services in East Africa by Sydney Hockey.

347 Smith, Keith **"Interview: Charles Richards."** *The African Book Publishing Record* 2, no. 3 (July 1976): 161-164.
An interview with Charles Richards, who played a pivotal role in East African bookselling and publishing for thirty years, from 1935 until 1965. He was the founding director of both the Ndia Kuu Press and of the East African Literature Bureau, and later established the Eastern Africa branch of Oxford University Press. *See also* entries ➔ **345** and ➔ **346** above.

348 Sweetman, David **"Interview with Bernth Lindfors"** [about publishing and the literary atmosphere in Kenya.]" *BBC Arts and Africa*, no. 345 (1980): 1-4.
Transcript of an interview between David Sweetman and Bernth Lindfors about the fate of the small East African publishing houses which were created in the late 1970s.

Regional studies: Africa, Southern

Note: country- or topic-specific studies on publishing and book development in Southern Africa can be found under the appropriate headings in ➔ **Section, 3 Country studies** or ➔ **Section 4, Studies by topic**.

349 Bolton, Patricia, ed. **Textbook Provision and Feasibility of Co-operation Among SADC Countries: Botswana, Malawi, Namibia, Zambia, Zimbabwe.** Paris: UNESCO (Doc. ED.96/WS/17), 1996. 106 pp.
Online: http://unesdoc.unesco.org/images/0010/001037/103772e.pdf [23/02/08]
It has become increasingly clear to those involved in textbook projects that textbook publishing should not be isolated from book publishing in general, but should be an integral part of it. A major Conference on Textbook Provision and Library Development in Africa, which took place in Manchester in October 1991 made an attempt to contribute to that end. As a follow-up to the Manchester conference, ➔ **UNESCO (118)**, with UNDP funding, undertook a study on Textbook Provision and the Feasibility of Cooperation among SADC countries, where national specialists and task forces conducted a systematic analysis of the strengths and difficulties within their country's textbook provision system. The process of carrying out national case studies for five SADC countries contributed to the development and institutionalization of comprehensive and integrated policies for textbook provision, and helped in particular to identify constraints which have prevented effective textbook provision. The exercise itself was intended as a capacity building strategy. Each case study examined the mode of book provision and identified strengths and weaknesses, and brought together basic information and statistics. The exercise clearly indicated that the interaction between book industries and textbook publishing still are still inadequate in many countries.

350   Brickhill, Paul **"Co-operation and Conflict in SADCC Publishing - Reflections on the Problems of Publishing in the SADCC countries."** *Zeitschrift für Kulturaustausch* 41, no. 3 (1991-3): 368-371.
Excerpts of a paper presented at a Seminar on Communication, Cultures and Development, held in Zimbabwe in May 1990, describing the publishing situation, and publishing constraints, in the countries of the Southern African Development Coordination Conference (SADCC).

351   Evans, Julie **"The Southern African Book Scene: Current Issues for Librarians, Booksellers and Publishers: Some Personal Comments."** *African Research and Documentation*, no. 71 (1996): 41-44.
A summary of the papers presented at a seminar hosted by the ➜ **Southern African Book Development Trust (113)** held during the 1996 London International Book Fair. *Note:* some of the papers from this seminar (available online) are individually abstracted elsewhere in this bibliography.

352   Hofmeyr, Isabel, and Lize Kriel **"Book History in Southern Africa : What is it and Why Should it Interest Historians?"** *South African Historical Journal*, no. 55 (2006): 1-19.
[Not examined]

353   International ISBN Agency **"Seminar on the Development of the Book Sector in Southern African Countries."** *ISBN Review* 17 (1996): 161-372.
The papers from a seminar held at the ISBN agency in Berlin, May 19-25, 1995, to which participants from eleven Southern African countries were invited. The 23 papers included follow a standard format, each of them describing the current state of the book sector in various countries of Southern Africa, and reporting about the state of libraries, publishing and the retail book trade; current book and copyright legislation, national book policies, programmes to promote the reading habit, laws and legislation covering the book sector and copyright, activities of library and book trade professional bodies, book trade organization, training for the book industries, the use of ISBNs, and more. *Note:* some of the papers from this issue of *ISBN Review* are individually abstracted elsewhere in this bibliography.

354   Meldrum, Andrew **"Banking on Books."** *Africa Report* (January/February 1992): 65-66.
Discusses the sixth Zimbabwe International Book Fair and looks at the prospects of regional cooperation within the publishing industry in Southern Africa.

355   Reece, Jane **"The Southern African Book Scene: Current Issues for Librarians, Booksellers and Publishers."** *Focus on International & Comparative Librarianship* 27, no. 2 (10 September 1996): 82-86.
A resumé of the papers and discussions held at the 1996 ➜ **SABDET (113)** London International Book Fair seminar.

356 Nyangulu, J. N. **Report of a Meeting on Textbook Provision and the Feasibility of Cooperation among SADC Countries held on the 5th and 6th August, 1993 at the UNESCO Sub-regional Office for Southern Africa, Harare.** Lilongwe: Ministry of Education, Science and Technology, 1994. 35 pp.
[Not examined]

357 Taylor, Sally **"Critical Challenges for Educational Publishers in Africa."** *Bellagio Publishing Network Newsletter*, no. 19 (March 1997): 21-24.
Earlier version published as **"South Africa Today: An Eye on the Future",** *Publishers Weekly* (September 9, 1996): 43-59.
An adaptation of the *Publishers Weekly* article above about the major challenges facing educational publishers in Southern Africa today [late 90s], including the provision of educational, children's and general books in the major languages of the region.

Regional studies: Africa, West

Note: country- or topic-specific studies on publishing and book development in West Africa can be found under the appropriate headings in ➔ **Section 3, Country studies** or ➔ **Section 4, Studies by topic.** Regional studies on the book industries in francophone West Africa are listed, in this section, under ➔ **Regional studies: Africa, Francophone.**

358 Elaturoti, Folorunso **"Data Generation and Utilization in Book Publishing within the West African Sub-Region."** *The Publisher* 4, no. 1 (September 1996): 15-19.
Examines the need for a data bank on all aspects of publishing, to aid the planning and successful execution of book production programmes, and to facilitate resource sharing among publishers in the West African sub-region. Sets out a proposed modus operandi for data gathering and for building up databases on pupil/student enrolment, infrastructural facilities for book production, sales outlets, authorship skills and resources, training and manpower development, shared mother-tongue languages, as well as bibliographic databases.

Hasan, Abul **Developing Human Resources of the Book Industry in West Africa** see ➔ **Section 5, Book industry training/Self-publishing: Articles and reports** entry **2433**

359 Ike, V. Chukwuemeka **"The Book Crisis in the ECOWAS Subregion: An African Writer's Appraisal."** In *International Seminar on Book Development and Reading in Ecowas Sub-Region.* Lagos: Book Development Centre, Nigerian Educational and Research Council, 1990, 39-41.
A condensed version of a paper presented by the author, Director of the ➔ **Nigerian Book Foundation (738)** at a seminar on evaluation of book development and reading

in the ECOWAS Subregion, organized by ➔ **UNESCO (118)** in association with ECOWAS and the Nigerian Educational Research and Development Council, Ibadan in January 1990. Addresses the calamitous problem of the book crisis in the ECOWAS region "which threatens ... the future of education and literacy in Nigeria." The author presents an "African writer's views on the grave crisis in which the book has found itself" and summarizes what he sees as the causes for the crisis: insufficient in publishing capacity, decline in foreign publishing, inadequacy of indigenous publishing, lopsidedness in book development, poor promotion and book marketing, the high cost of books, piracy, and hit and miss planning in book development.

360 Zell, Hans M. "**Publishing in West Africa: Producing Books Against the Odds.**" *West Africa* (27 August 1979): 1550-1553.
Focuses on Nigeria, Ghana, Liberia, Sierra Leone, francophone West Africa and also discusses the formation of book development councils, and other book promotional bodies in the region.

Regional studies: Africa, Francophone

Note: country- or topic-specific studies on publishing and book development in francophone African countries are listed under the appropriate headings in section ➔ **3 Country studies**, or section ➔ **4 Studies by topic**.

361 Agence de Coopération Culturelle et Technique **Table ronde des editeurs, des desponables de l'education et des bailleurs de fonds, Tunis du 28 au 30 novembre, 1994, Rapport général.** Paris: ACCT, Direction Générale de l'Education et de la Formation Ecole Internationale de Bordeaux (DGEF-EIB), 1994.
Report of an ACCT-sponsored conference on educational book publishing and textbook writing in francophone Africa, which examined the problems faced by the struggling book industries.

362 Agence de la Francophonie (ACCT). Direction Générale de l'Education et de la Formation. Ecole International de la Francophonie **Les métiers du livre en Afrique francophone. Situation et besoins de formation.** Edited by Ridha Najar. Bordeaux: Agence de la Francophonie (ACCT)/Ecole Internationale de la Francophonie (EIF) [15-16 Quai Louis XVIII, 3300 Bordeaux], 1996. 217 pp.
A comprehensive overview and situation report of the state of the book and the book industries in six francophone African countries, two in West Africa: Côte d'Ivoire (Marie Agathe Amoikon & Omar Sylla) and Senegal (Madieyna Ndiaye); two in Central Africa: Cameroun (David N'dachi Tagne) and Zaire (Ntita Nyembwe); and in two countries of the Maghreb: Morocco (Abdelkader Manaa) and Tunisia (Abdelkader Ben Cheikh). Part I of the book consists of country studies, and each

country study starts off with a brief historical background, and then surveys the different components of the book professions: publishers (government, commercial, educational, academic, religious, etc.), the printing industries, libraries and library development, and the retail book trade and book distribution, identifying common problems and concluding with an assessment of future prospects. Part II of the book provides a synthesis of the country studies, supported by graphs and charts, and a wide variety of statistical data; and Part III provides a general conclusion and an analysis of a questionnaire survey that was used as part of the study. *Note:* the former Agence de Coopération Culturelle et Technique (ACCT) is now part of the ➜ **Organisation Internationale de la Francophonie (101).**
Reviews:
The African Book Publishing Record vol. 24, no. 2, 1998

363   Akindes, Simon Adetona **The African Publisher: The Cultural Politics of Indigenous Publishing in Benin and Côte d'Ivoire.** Athens, OH: Ohio University, 1996. PhD thesis. 260 pp. (Available from UMI Proquest Dissertation Abstracts, Publication number AAT 9639762)
This PhD thesis, "theoretically informed by Giroux's concepts of border and critical pedagogy", examines how indigenous publishers manage to give a voice to cultures in an environment characterized by conflicting interests mediated by the State. It aims to provide an understanding of "the intersection of social structure and human agency in the process." To shed light on publishers' cultural practices, the author investigated their publishing output and their interaction with the wider cultural environment. He conducted interviews with editors and private sector publishers, sought the publishers' views on state intervention (and domination) in publishing, as well as interviewing government officials and writers. The author found that indigenous publishers are conscious of their cultural role, but that they need more professionalism, that there is a need for both national and regional cooperation, and a sharper understanding of indigenous publisher's role "of giving a voice to the voiceless majority – and their various identities – through the written word." The author argues that the exclusive use of French in education and publishing complicates their task, and partially explains how indigenous knowledge is neglected, and how the cultures of the underprivileged are marginalized.

364   Anon. Special issue **Les métiers du livre**, *Ethiopiques* 5, nos. 1-2, 1988. 282 pp.
A collection of articles to salute Léopold Senghor on the subject of publishing, illustration, printing, bookshops, books and society.

365   Association Culture et Développement **Actes assises nationales: des livres pour le développement: de la dotation en ouvrages à l'appui à l'édition, Lille, 11 et 12 décembre 1998**. Grenoble, France: Culture et developpement, 1998. 204 pp.
On libraries, book development, reading promotion, and book donation programmes. [Not examined]

L'association internationale des libraires francophones: Nos libraires *see* → Section 1, Serials and reference: Directories and book trade reference tools entry 195

366   Baï, Vréza Christian **L'édition littéraire dans deux pays d'Afrique francophone sub-saharienne: le Cameroun et le Sénégal**. Sherbrooke, Canada: Université de Sherbrooke, 1994. MA thesis. 144 pp.
[Not examined]

367   Baillargeon, Jean-Paul. **La francophonie et la diffusion du livre: un cas type de relations entre langues, scolarité et développement**. In *Les mutations du livre et de l'édition dans le monde du XVIII ème siècle à l'an 2000*, edited by Jacques Michon and Jean-Yves Mollier. Laval, Canada: Les Presses de l'Université de Laval, 2001, 555-565.
[Not examined]

368   Bessat, Colette, and Jose Bessat **Trouve l'appui dans le domaine du livre et de écrict: evaluation de l'aid publique française (1980-1992).** Paris: Ministère de la Coopération, Ministère des Afffaires étrangères, Centre d'Information et de Documentation [57 boulevard. des Invalides, 75007 Paris]. 1994. 242 pp.
An evaluation of French government aid in the book sector, and support for writing and reading promotion, in sub-Saharan Africa. Examines some of the different schemes and approaches, the needs they serve, their efficiency, their success (or otherwise), and makes a number of suggestions how future aid schemes might be improved.

369   Bourgueil, Isabelle, ed. and co-ordinator **Où va le livre en Afrique ?** *Africultures* no. 57 (December 2003). Paris: L'Harmattan, 2003. 239 pp. Online:
http://www.africultures.com/index.asp?menu=revue_sommaire&no_dossi er=57 [23/02/08]
A rich special issue of the journal → **Africultures (153)**, devoted to "Où va le livre en Afrique?" ("Books in Africa: What future?"), containing many contributions on various aspects of publishing, the book trade, and the state of the book and readership in (primarily francophone) Africa. It also includes articles on special aspects of publishing in Africa, e.g. scholarly publishing, children's book publishing, publishing in African languages, literary publishing, as well as interviews with writers and prominent members of the African book professions. *Note:* some of the articles in this special issue are individually abstracted elsewhere in this bibliography.

370   Bourgueil, Isabelle **"Afrilivres: miroir des livres disponibles édités en Afrique francophone."** *Africultures* no. 57 (December 2003): 19-30.

Online:
http://www.africultures.com/index.asp?menu=revue_affiche_article&no=3
170&dispo=fr [23/02/08]
Describes the background that led to the establishment of the ➔ **Afrilivres (185)**
initiative, a collaborative Web portal for a group of francophone African publishers,
comprising over 50 publishers from 15 African nations, and offering more than 1,300
titles online. The author also presents a general overview of the publishing situation
in francophone Africa today: she provides some employment figures of those
working in the book sector, reviews publishing in African languages, and looks at
problems and obstacles of the book industries, which include high costs of
production, shortage of skilled personnel, and lack of long-term training
programmes for book professionals. The article includes some useful charts showing
number of publishers by country, number of titles in print by country, book
publishing output for adults and children by category, number of writers and
illustrators by country, book trade infrastructure by country, and number of book
professionals by country.

371   Bourgueil, Isabelle **"Aide publique française: de la coopération au
commerce. Le livre édité en Afrique dans l'aide publique au
développement française."** *Africultures* no. 57 (December 2003): 57-68.
Online:
http://www.africultures.com/index.asp?no=3175&menu=revue_affiche_art
icle [23/02/08]
Takes a critical view of French development assistance in the book sector, which
includes purchases/donations of French books through bilateral, multilateral or
other assistance schemes, grants and awards, as well as support for public libraries in
the francophone nations of Africa. The author examines the activities of various
French aid agencies and government ministries. While it is argued that some of these
projects have helped to create an environment conducive to books and promotion of
the reading habit, there is a lack of direct core support to help strengthen the
indigenous book industries, and the various book donation and assistance schemes
include very little African-published material.

372   Bourgueil, Isabelle **"Politiques du livre en instance, les éditeurs et la
lecture en souffrance…"** *Africultures* no. 57 (December 2003): 38-44.
Online:
http://www.africultures.com/index.asp?menu=revue_affiche_article&no=3
173&dispo=fr [23/02/08]
Reports about a survey conducted among francophone African publishers as it
relates to national book policies, or the lack of it. The need for national book policies
has been discussed at many seminars and conferences, and at government level, but
most countries still lack clear policies as it relates to the book sector. Some countries
still levy VAT (TVA) on books, and/or import duty on paper required for local
manufacturing. In most countries this is between 5-10%, except in Burkina Faso
where it reportedly is a staggering 56.6%. The net result is that the only beneficiaries
are publishers in the countries of the North, whose books can be imported duty-free.

373 Chabert, Laurence, and Fabrice Piault **"La profession. Editer pour l'Afrique."** *Livres de France,* no. 69 (November 1985): 99-105.
Reviews what has been achieved in school book publishing in francophone Africa, examining the situation in a number of individual African countries. Also sets out a step-by-step procedure of how a school book is produced from start to finish, and suggests guidelines for producing books that are relevant for an African reading public.

374 Cévaér, Françoise **Littérature d'Afrique noire les conditions de production et de circulation du livre de 1960 à nos jours.** Paris: Université Paris-Nord, 1992. PhD thesis. 619 l.
[Not examined]

375 Dogbé, Yves-Emmanuel **Réflexions sur la promotion du livre Africain.** Lomé: Editions Akpagnon, 1984, 118 pp.
Reflects on the status of the book in Africa, and analyzes the many difficulties encountered when writing, publishing, and distributing books in Africa. The author, who is a prominent Togolese publisher, argues forcefully that the production of books is a vital cultural endeavour, and urges those in power to strengthen the book industry in Africa.

376 Estivals, Robert **"Le livre en Afrique noire francophone."** *Communication et Langages* 46, no. 2 (1980): 60-84.
Discusses problems of printing and publishing in African countries that are undergoing the "decolonization" process. Suggests that these countries are unusual in that the State and the private sector are both involved in this process. Explores several possible models for successful decolonization.

377 Fofana, Souleymane **"Il faut sortir de la gratuit."** *AfriquEducation* no. 13 (September 1995): 28.
An interview with Régine Fontaine, the official in charge of books at the Ministry of Cooperation in France, in which she defines French policy towards African educational books, and explains what action was taken after the devaluation of the CFA to avoid doubling of prices of school books.

Fontaine, Régine, and François-G. Barbier Wiesser, eds. **Livres et réseaux documentaries/Publishing and Libraries' Cooperation. Nouvelles perspectives de partenariat: Afrique anglophone-Afrique francophone-France/Towards Partnership between English-speaking Africa, French-speaking Africa, and France. Documents de travail/Working Papers** *see*
➜ **Regional studies: Africa, East** entry **340**

378 Haut Conseil de la Francophonie **La production et la diffusion des biens culturels et médiatiques de l'Afrique francophone sub-saharienne.** Paris: Haut Conseil de la Francophonie (Les cahiers de la francophonie, 4), 1996. 182 pp.

Examines the production and distribution of cultural and multimedia materials (including books) in sub-Saharan francophone Africa, and the impact of new technologies on communication networks.

379 Heisslier, Nina; P. Lavy, and A. Candela **Diffusion du livre - développement de la lecture en Afrique (Tchad-Sénégal).** Paris: Editions L'Harmattan, 1979. 300 pp.
Uses interviews with the public, local publishers and book distributors in order to find ways to improve the development of reading in Africa on the one hand, and more effective distribution of appropriate reading materials on the other. With a focus on Tchad and Senegal.

380 Hutchison, John P., and Michael K. Nguessan, eds. **The Language Question in Francophone Africa**. West Newbury, MA: Mother Tongue Editions, 1995. 86 pp.

A collection of papers on the issues surrounding language policy in francophone Africa. It includes two papers on publishing aspects: "Indigenous Publishing in Francophone West Africa: The Necessity of Independent Publishers", by Simon Adetona Akindes, and "The Politics of Educational Publishing in Francophone Africa: 1944-94 " by John Hutchison. [Not examined]

381 Jacquemin, Jean-Pierre, and Monkasa-Bitumba, eds. **Forces littéraires d'Afrique. Points de répères et témoignages.** Bruxelles: De Boeck-Wesmael, 1987. 235 pp.
A collection that celebrates the lively state of creative writing in Africa, with a selection to show the diversity of production from 20 African writers, alongside some creative writing by African and European researchers. Includes three papers on publishing in francophone Africa.

382 Janssens, Jean-Claude, and Jacques Lafarge, eds. **L'édition scolaire dans les pays du Sud. Enjeux et perspectives.** Bordeaux: Agence de la Francophonie (ACCT)/Ecole Internationale de la Francophonie (EIF) [15-16 Quai Louis XVIII, 33000 Bordeaux], 1996. 62 pp.
As part of the multilateral activities undertaken by the Agence de Coopération Culturelle et Technique (ACCT) – now integrated with the ➔ **Organisation Internationale de la Francophonie (101)** – it provided support for the development of national book policies, and the production and delivery of educational tools in the countries of the South, with a priority focus on textbooks for basic education. As a component of this strategy it published two important studies analyzing the book sector in developing countries in general, and the book industry in francophone Africa in particular. The first title (for the other *see* entry ➔ **362**) looks at the current [1996] state and prospects of educational publishing in the countries of the South. It examines the basic issues as they relate to infrastructural and social factors, surveys the different players involved in the writing and publishing of educational materials, and the common problems they face. The study also probes into the financial and training aspects of book development, and makes a number of suggestions that might lead to a healthy environment for the development of effective national book

policies, and the publication of high-quality schoolbooks and other educational materials.
Reviews:
The African Book Publishing Record vol. 24, no. 2, 1998

Jaygbay, Jacob **"Scholarly Publishing in Francophone Africa."** *see* ➔
Section 4, Studies by topic: Scholarly publishing entry **2300**

383   Kloeckner, Hélène **"À quand une édition scolaire africaine?"**
Africultures no. 57 (December 2003): 71-85.
Online:
http://www.africultures.com/index.asp?menu=revue_affiche_article&no=3
180&dispo=fr [24/02/08]
Educational textbooks represent 75-90% of the total book market in francophone Africa. Yet, the author asserts, barely 1% of these requirements are manufactured in Africa, and the rest are book imports from French publishing multinationals. She examines the historical, economic and political background to the presence by Northern publishers, and their continuing dominance in the African markets. Today the major players in educational publishing are African governments, donor agencies, and publishing conglomerates. This includes a number of African publishing houses established with the support African governments together with French publishing interests, and some of which have enjoyed monopolies in primary school publishing. Other publishers have produced co-editions with French partners. Most of the business in educational publishing is done on the basis of tenders invited by the World Bank or the African Development Bank. Those bidding for the contracts must meet a certain number of stringent conditions (e.g. filing of tender bonds) which, in practice, rules out most private sector African publishers from competing. However, one area in which indigenous publishers are now making their presence felt is that of publishing of material in national languages, which could well lead to more opportunities for them to enter the more lucrative textbook markets in due course, and might eventually lead to a levelling of the playing field.

384   Konaté, Sié, *et al* **Les produits culturels dans la francophonie: cadre politique et juridique: étude du livre en Afrique noire francophone: le livre en Afrique de l'ouest francophone, production et structures de distribution.** Montréal: Institutut Québécois de la recherche sur la culture/IQRC, 1992. 47 l.
[Not examined]

385   Konaté, Sié; Florian Sauvageau, and Pierre Trudel **Le livre en Afrique de l'Ouest francophone production et structures de distribution.** Ste-Foy, Canada: Les Presses de l'Université Laval, 1991.
[Not examined]

386   Laroussinie, Claude **Études de faisabilité pour l'établissement d'un consortium international de diffusion de livres africains: Régional Afrique - (mission).** Paris: UNESCO (Doc. FMR/CLT/BCR/92/105; RP/1990-1991/III.2.2/Rapport de mission) [Restricted circulation, available on request]. 1992. 26 pp.
A feasibility study that examined the setting up of an international consortium for the joint distribution of books from publishers French-speaking Africa, in Burkina Faso, Côte d'Ivoire, Mali, and Senegal .

387   Leguéré, Jean-Pierre **Approvisionnement en livres scolaires: vers plus the tranparence Afrique francophone.** Paris: Institut International de Planification de l'Education/UNESCO, 2003. 99 pp.
Online: http://unesdoc.unesco.org/images/0013/001362/136266f.pdf [24/02/08]
Over the last decade expenditures devoted to the textbook provision and teaching equipment for basic education, in the whole of French-speaking Africa, amounted to more than CFA500bn. Yet, even such a massive investment has failed to achieve the goal "Un livre un enfant en l'an 2000" ("A book a child in the year 2000"), nor has there been significant development of an indigenous book industry. This study attempts to identify the principal opportunities and causes of corrupt practises that exist throughout the textbook financing, production and publishing chain, and the distribution of schoolbooks and other the educational materials in French-speaking Africa. Additionally, it endeavours to define the conditions that would favour more transparency and good practice in textbook provision, and – using projects in Tunisia, the Côte d'Ivoire and in the Congo Democratic Republic as case studies – makes a number of proposals how this might be achieved.

388   Maack, Mary Niles **"Books and Libraries as Instruments of Cultural Diplomacy in Francophone Africa During the Cold War."** *Libraries & Culture* 36, no. 1 (Winter 2001): 58-86.
During the period of the Cold War, Britain, France, and the United States employed similar strategies in the cultural efforts they directed toward francophone Africa. All three countries sponsored language instruction, and set up cultural centres with libraries reflecting their national heritage, but the priority that each nation gave to these activities was a result of underlying ideologies that provided the foundation for its cultural diplomacy. Although this essay analyzes and compares British, French, and American book-related programmes throughout the region, particular attention is given to Senegal, whose capital city, Dakar, had formerly served as the federal capital for all of French West Africa.

389   Mateso, Emmanuel Locha **"ACCT Support to Textbook Publishing in the South."** *Bellagio Publishing Network Newsletter*, no. 17 (July 1996): 9-10.
An account of the work of the Agence de Coopération Culturelle et Technique (ACCT) – now part of the ➜ **Organisation Internationale de la Francophonie (101)** – its programme 'Edition scolaire du Sud' (Educational publishing in the South), and the agency's textbook support fund, which assists the production and distribution of

educational tools in francophone Africa, with a priority focus on textbooks for basic education.

390 Michelman, Frederic **"New Life for Francophone Publishing in Africa."** *The African Book Publishing Record* 4, no. 3 (July 1978): 163-167.
Examines the contrast between francophone publishing in Africa pre-1975, when African writers were published in Paris if at all, with the situation in the late 1970s. Focuses on the contribution of Editions CLE, Nouvelles Editions Africaines, and a number of small presses.

391 Newton, Diana C. **"ACCT Roundtable on Textbooks."** *Bellagio Publishing Network Newsletter*, no. 13 (April 1995): 5-6.
Reports about a roundtable organized by the Agence de Coopération Culturelle et Technique (ACCT) – now part of the **→ Organisation Internationale de la Francophonie (101)** – to define the main elements of ACCT's future support to textbook publishing in the South; to consider strategies to provide students and teachers in the South with the most appropriate and most accessible textbooks; and how to create an enabling business environment for a flourishing private-sector book industry.

392 Newton, Diana C. **L'édition au service de l'alphabétisation durable en Afrique francophone.** Ottawa: International Publishing Partnership, 1994. 100 pp.
Condensed English version also published as **"Publishing for Sustainable Literacy in Francophone West Africa."** *The African Book Publishing Record* 20, no. 2 (1994): 107-11.
The potential contribution of private sector publishers to the long-term retention of sustainable literacy in francophone West Africa is the focus of this paper. Information is drawn from a four month research project undertaken in Côte d'Ivoire, Mali and Benin in 1993/94. The author argues that one of the best ways for the international community to contribute to more solid achievements in literacy than those registered since the 1960s is to encourage local private sector publishers, working alone or within north-south or south-south partnerships, to create and disseminate appropriate printed materials for literacy and post-literacy.

393 Newton, Diana C. **"Devaluation of CFA Franc in Francophone Africa May Offer Hope to a Beleaguered Publishing Industry."** *Bellagio Publishing Network Newsletter*, no. 9 (March 1994): 6-7.
The author believes that the (1993) 50% devaluation of the CFA Franc against the French franc might well be a blessing in disguise. Locally published and produced books have become vastly more competitive and, as a result, indigenous publishers in francophone Africa could finally break free from the domination of powerful French publishing houses who thus far have effectively controlled the lucrative textbook market.

394 Newton, Diana C. **L'impact de la dévaluation du Franc CFA sur le manuel scolaire. Document d'orientation et de réflexion préparé pour la Direction régionale de l'Afrique de l'Ouest ... Genève, 21-24 février 1995.** Paris: UNESCO; Geneva: WHO (WHO/UNESCO/ICO/RT/ education/95, restricted circulation), 1995. 27 pp.

A paper presented to a UNESCO/WHO-sponsored conference which was convened to determine the impact of the devaluation of the CFA Franc on the education and health sectors of the affected countries and to map out a plan of action for the future. For textbooks the main potential benefit of the devaluation is seen in the impetus it could give to local publishing by import substitution. The author examines educational and school book publishing capacities in francophone Africa before and after devaluation, the effects of the devaluation, and government measures taken in some countries to support their indigenous book industries and make them more competitive. The paper also recommends essential strategies that should be pursued to allow for the development, on a national or regional basis, of sustainable publishing capacity.

395 Newton, Diana C. **"Francophone Africa."** In *International Book Publishing. An Encyclopedia*, edited by Philip G. Altbach and Edith S. Hoshino. New York: Garland Publishing, 1995, 373-84.

Seeks to provide an overview of the current status [1995] of the book publishing industry in ten francophone African countries. The author analyzes the factors that have encouraged, and those that have prevented, the development in francophone Africa of a profitable private-sector industry under majority African control, and predicts some future trends likely to affect publishing activities in the region.

396 Nnana-Rejasef, Marie-Claire **"Livres scolaires. Vers une guerre nord-sud?"** *AfriquEducation* no. 13 (September 1995): 17-18.

Debates the necessity for Africa to produce its own educational books, and asks how this might be achieved. States that progress could be improved if the education sector was not seen as merely as a machine for spending money and suggests the integration of the education sector in a national book development strategy. Reiterates the need for cooperation and imaginative initiatives in the educational book production sector.

397 Piault, Fabrice **"Cinq semaines en Afrique."** *Livres Hebdo,* nos. 354-358 (1999): [20 pp. total]

A series of five short articles describing the current [late 1990s] state of the book and the publishing industries in francophone African countries, including overviews of educational and school book publishing.

398 Pinhas, Luc **Editer dans l'espace francophone. Législation, diffusion, distribution et commercialisation du livre**: Paris: Alliance des éditeurs independents (Collection "Etat des lieux de l'édition"), 2005. 288 pp.

An comprehensive inventory on all aspects of the state of the book in the francophone world, including production, legislation affecting books, copyright and taxation, national book policies, as well as marketing and distribution. Includes sections on the book chain in the francophone countries of sub-Saharan Africa and those in North Africa.

399   Pinhas, Luc **"L'édition africaine à la croisée des chemins."** *Africultures,* no 69, (December 2006)
An overview of the publishing situation in French-speaking sub-Saharan Africa. [Not examined]

400   Poussou, Vincent **"Le livre Français en Afrique francophone."** *Cahiers de l'Economie du Livre,* no. 4 (1990): 20-36.
Analyzes the results of a study to pinpoint relevant markets for French books in developing countries, and suggests viable marketing strategies. Emphasizes that the overseas book market is very important for French publishers, and concludes that publishers must adapt themselves to the market as it is, rather than seeking to change the market.

401   Prillaman, Jerry **"Books in Francophone Africa."** In *Publishing and Development in the Third World,* edited by Philip G. Altbach. London: Hans Zell Publishers, 1992, 199-210.
Examines the predominantly French language book industry in francophone Africa, taking into consideration school textbooks, general literature, bookshops, and censorship. Analyzes the market in global terms and presents a discussion of French government book programmes and the help given to indigenous publishers. Now very dated, but this study remains a useful overview.

402   Rocher, Annie **"Le livre en Afrique Noire."** *Livres Hebdo* 2, no. 33 (23 September 1980): 112-130.
Discusses the roots and problems of publishing in the francophone regions of Africa [in the 1980s], and suggests measures that might alleviate the lack of books being published by indigenous publishers. Also raises the question of what effect audio-visual media will have in Africa, and whether once writers and publishers of the "old school" are gone, the need for books will be overlooked, or even forgotten.

403   Rudiak, Michael D. **"Publishing in Sub-Saharan Francophone Africa: Do All Roads Still Lead to Paris?"** *Logos. The Journal of the World BookCommunity* 4, no. 3 (1993): 152-58.
Online:
http://www.atypon-link.com/LOG/doi/pdf/10.2959/logo.1993.4.3.152
A critical appraisal of the growth, development, and control of publishing and book distribution in francophone Africa. Looks at the forces that dominate these markets, as small independent publishers find it difficult to compete with the quasi monopolies of the parastatal partnerships, who have maintained strong links with French publishing interests.

404   Schieffer, Jean Pierre, and Ridha Najar **La role des médias dans la promotion du livre en Afrique.** Bordeaux: Agence de la Francophonie (ACCT)/Ecole Internationale de la Francophonie (EIF), 1992. 98 pp.
The papers from a meeting held in Tunis in Mary 1992, which analyzed the role of the media in the promotion of books and writing, and the relations between book professionals with those in the media, including radio and TV.

405   Simon, Günter **"The Book in Francophone Black Africa: A Critical Perspective."** *The African Book Publishing Record* 10, no. 4 (1984): 209-215.
Originally written in German and published by the Frankfurt Book Fair, this is a penetrating analysis of the state of the book and the book industries in francophone Africa in the early 1980s. Gives a brief historical overview of the history of publishing in francophone Africa and thereafter analyzes the structure of publishing, covering state participation in publishing, religious publishers, small publishing houses, and those cooperating with overseas publishers. Also includes some discussion about the activities of African publishers in France, African writing in translation, and the different kinds of bookshops operating in francophone Africa. The author offers a number of suggestions on the way forward.

406   Sow, Mamadou Aliou **"Défis et perspectives de l'édition africaine francophone d'aujourd'hui."** *Africultures* no. 57 (December 2003): 9-12.
Online:
http://www.africultures.com/index.asp?menu=revue_affiche_article&no=3
168&dispo=fr [24/02/08]
Presents a review the current state of publishing in francophone Africa, and the significant achievements of the private sector book industries over the last decade. Examines issues relating to government support for indigenous publishing, emerging book trade associations and organizations such as the → **African Publishers Network (5)**, and notes a marked increase in publishing partnerships and production of co-editions. Also describes recurrent problems and constraints, the absence of national book policies, taxation on book imports in some countries, and other remaining obstacles.

407   Sylla, Ibrahima, and Fory Bah **"Venance Kacou et Comlan Prosper Deh: nous voulons notre part du gâteau."** *AfriquEducation* no. 13 (September 1995): 24, 26.
Also published in *Le Livre Africain* no. 6, (September-October 1996): 11-13.
Interview with the chief executives of Editions CEDA in Côte d'Ivoire and Editions CLE in Cameroon, during which both stress that policy makers and donors should work more close together to help the school book industry in Africa. Discusses the problems of funding, progress to date, and a plan of action for future development.

408   Tambwe Kitenge Bin Kitoko, Eddie **La chaîne du livre en Afrique noire francophone. Qui est éditeur, aujourd'hui?** [Avec] Contributions de Achille Penou Somé et Marc Ngwanza Kasong'Abor. Paris: L'Harmattan ("Recherches en Bibliologie"), 2006. 178 pp.

An overview of the book trade, and the players that comprise the "book chain", in 14 countries in francophone Africa today. The author seeks to shed light on the current state of the book industries in these countries and, for each country, provides some historical and educational background, book import figures (books imported from France), an assessment of the "environnement du livre" with brief details of major public and academic libraries, major bookshops, followed by descriptions and profiles of publishers and the nature of their list, notable authors, areas of specialization, etc., albeit without publisher address details. Apparently information gathered for this book was based on a series of questionnaires mailed to publishers, and not all of them responded. Somewhat surprisingly, no details of book trade associations are mentioned for any of the countries, nor the role played by pan-African organizations such as ➜ **African Publishers Network (5).** The book also lacks a documentary apparatus of any kind.

409 van de Werk, Jan Kees **"Challenges and Reality in West African Publishing."** In *Publishing and Development in the Third World*, edited by Philip G. Altbach. London: Hans Zell Publishers, 1992, 191-198.
A review of the activities of the establishment and sponsorship by the Dutch development organization Interchurch Coordination Committee for Development Projects (ICCO) of Editions HaHo, Lomé, Togo, together with an account of a colloquium on publishing in Africa which took place in Bamako, Mali in 1988.

410 Vilasco, Gilles, and Dominique Hado Zidouemba **"Le livre et l'édition en Afrique francophone."** *Afrique Contemporaine*, no. 151 (March 1989): 41-54.
Explores the many roles played by the book in contemporary society: cultural, economic and social. Analyzes the particular problems experienced in francophone Africa, identifying the obstacles that impede the development of the book industry, and proposes some strategies for the future. Compares the situation in the late 1980s with that of the period since 1960, the composition of readership and access to books, the infrastructure of publishing, and the constraints faced by the book industries amidst difficult economic conditions.

411 Vilasco, Gilles, and Dominique Hado Zidouemba **"Books and Publishing in Francophone Africa."** *UNESCO-Africa*, no. 2 (July 1991): 26-41.
Essentially an update (in English) of the previous entry (*see* ➜ **410**). Describes the economic difficulties faced by African publishers and expresses the hope that micro-publishing techniques will make it possible in the future to produce the low-cost reading materials that are much needed to promote literacy and expand potential readership.

Vilasco, Gilles, and Dominique Hado Zidouemba, eds. **L'édition scientifique en Afrique francophone. Actes de la table ronde** *see* ➜ **Section 4, Studies by topic: Scientific, technical and medical publishing** entry 2363

412 Vinck, Honoré **"Livres scolaires coloniaux: methodes d'analyse — approache herméneutique."** *History in Africa* 26 (1999): 379-408.
Online:
http://www.abbol.com/commonfiles/docs_projecten/colschoolbks/manu els_sc_met.php [24/02/08]
An analysis of the nature of colonial school books in the former Belgian Congo, including those published in numerous vernacular languages. It is based primarily on the extensive archives and holdings at the Centre Aequatoria in Mbandaka [BP 276, Mbandaka, Congo Democratic Republic]. Taking a hermeneutic approach in terms of interpretation, the author examines the different genres of school texts, and the authors, publishers, printers, of distributors of these books.

413 Zidouemba, Dominique Hado **La bibliologie en Afrique noire francophone**. Dakar: Université Cheikh Anta Diop, 1984. PhD thesis.
[Not examined]

414 Zidouemba, Dominique Hado **"Stratégies pour la promotion du livre en Afrique."** *Africa* (Rome), no. 56, no 3 (2001): 414-428.
The author notes that various conferences that have taken place on promotion of the book in Africa have stressed the need for African countries to become self-sufficient in book production, and that this could only be accomplished through an integrated national book policy. This article reviews what has been achieved thus far in this direction, and Zidouemba offers a number of recommendations as they relate to possible strategies to achieve these goals, including more effective development of libraries and readership, and co-publishing and joint distribution agreements between publishers on the continent.

3
Country studies

This section is devoted to books and articles that are primarily country-specific, and cover general overviews and perspectives of the book industries – and book development generally – in particular African countries. This includes national book sector studies, articles and documents on national book policies, biographical and autobiographical accounts of members of the book professions, interviews with publishers, profiles of individual companies and imprints, and obituaries or tributes to personalities in publishing in different African countries. However, personal accounts of *women* in the book industry in various parts of Africa appear under ➜ **Section 4, Studies by topic: Women in African publishing/Publishing by and for women**.

It is important to note that most articles on special topics or areas of the book trade, e.g. bookselling, publishing for children, publishing in African languages, copyright, journal publishing, legal deposit, marketing, scholarly publishing, etc. are classified under *topic*, rather than under this section on country studies. For example, an article on publishing and marketing of African language materials in Cameroon will appear in ➜ **Section 4, Studies by topic: Publishing in African languages**; a study on publishing for children in Uganda will appear under ➜ **Section 4, Studies by topic: Children's book publishing**; or a paper on promoting reading and a reading culture in Nigeria will appear under ➜ **Section 4, Studies by topic: Reading culture and reading promotion**. However, all such entries are indexed both by topic and by country or region.

In this new edition listings for each country in Section 3 are part directory and part bibliography, and are subdivided as follows:

1. Book professional and writers' associations (where they exist), also including reproduction rights organizations.
2. National bibliography, books in print, and book trade directories (where available).
3. Country-specific books/studies, articles, reports, and interviews.

The inclusion of national bibliographies is a new feature in this edition, and details are provided for all those countries that produce national bibliographies. However, more than 20 countries in Africa still have no national bibliography, and many others in countries where national bibliographies exist they are currently dormant or seriously in arrear in their publication schedule, some by several years, or even decades. However, one welcome development is the fact that for a small number of sub-Saharan African countries – Ethiopia, Mauritius, Namibia, Senegal, and South Africa – (and also Algeria in North Africa) recent issues of national bibliographies can now be freely downloaded online.

For each national bibliography the name and address of the issuing body or publisher is provided, together with email address and Web site (where available), year first published, an indication of the latest issue or volume, and notes on cumulative volumes published.

For a small number of national book trade associations contact details are currently incomplete (e.g. lack of email addresses), and if they become available at a later time the entries will be updated in the online version.

For listings of *regional* or *pan-African* book trade associations, book promotional bodies, and writers' associations *see* ➔ **Organizations and associations: International and Africa-based organizations** entries 1-23.

Angola

Associations and book-related organizations

415   Associação dos Editores e Livreiros Angolanos (AELA)
c/o Instituto Industrial Cultural
Rua Cirilo da Conceicao Silva, No. 7 2 andar
Postal address:
CP 1248
Luanda
Angola
Tel: +244-2-331371 Fax: +244-2-895 5162/332714
Email: isna@ebonet.net or inald@ebonet.net
Web: n/a
Chair/Executive: Antonio de Brito
Secretary General: Gabriel Cabuco

416   União dos Escritores Angolanos
CP 1248
Luanda
Angola

Tel: 244-323205/322421 Fax: +244-323205
Email: uea@uea-angola.org
Web: http://www.uea-angola.org/
President: n/a

Books, articles, reports, and interviews (in English only)

417 Aparaicio, Alexandra **"Status of the Library and the Publishing Sector in Angola."** *ISBN Review* 17 (1996): 169-174.
Slightly shorter version also published in *African Publishing Review* 6, no. 2 (March/April 1997): 8-9.
One in a series of overview articles in a special issue of *ISBN Review* focusing on the book sector in various countries of Southern Africa, and which report (for the most part) about the state of libraries, publishing and the retail book trade; current book and copyright legislation, national book policies, programmes to promote the reading habit, laws and legislation cover the book sector and copyright, activities of library and book trade professional bodies, book trade organization, training for the book industries, the use of ISBNs, and more.

418 Cabuço, Gabriel **"The Book Market in Angola. The Prospects for its Development."** In *Indaba 2000. Millennium Marketplace,* edited by the Zimbabwe International Book Fair Trust. Harare: Zimbabwe International Book Fair Trust, 2001, 65-69.
Another version also published in *African Publishing Review* 9, no. 5 (2000): 11-12. [In same issue, Portuguese version of article **"Estado actual do Mercado do livre em Angola: Perspectives do seu desenvolvimento"** 1-2, 8; also in French]
A brief overview of the current constraints and challenges of book publishing in Angola [as at 2000], a country in which the government subsidises the production of educational books, where school books are still produced outside the country, leaving only the high risk area of general publishing in the hands of the private sector.

419 Read, Anthony, *et al.* **Angola Book Sector Study. Interim Report.** London: International Book Development, 1990. 112 pp.
Describes the current [1990] situation regarding the state of book provision in Angola, examining key issues in book supply, predicting future needs, and reviewing curriculum development, local authorship and local publishing capacity.

420 Read, Anthony, *et al.* **Angola Book Sector Study.** Washington, DC: The World Bank, 1992.
[Not examined]

421 Van-Dunem, Domingos **"People's Republic of Angola."** In *The Book Trade of the World, vol. IV: Africa,* edited by Sigfred Taubert and Peter Weidhaas. Munich: K.G. Saur, 1984, 67-70.
Overview of publishing and the book trade in Angola. Now very dated.

Benin

Associations and book-related organizations

422 **Association des Editeurs du Benin (ASEDIB)**
c/o Les Editions du Flamboyant
C92 OHEE
Cotonou
Postal address:
08 BP 271
Cotonou
Benin
Tel: +229-310220/350472 Fax: +229-946628
Email: mregomez@yahoo.fr
President: Michael Robert-Gomez

National bibliography, books in print, and book trade directories

423 **Bibliographie du Benin.**
Porto Novo: Bibliothèque Nationale [BP 401, Porto Novo] 1978-
Irregular, latest is no. 6 (2003-2004), published 2005 (print and CD-ROM).
Email: bn.benin@bj.refer.org
Web: http://www.bj.refer.org/benin_ct/tur/bnb/bibliogr2.htm [page under construction, 25/02/08]

Books, articles, reports, and interviews

424 Association des Editeurs du Bénin (ASEDIB) **Pour relever le défi de l'édition au Bénin**. Cotonou: Les Editions du Flamboyant, 1994. 93 pp.
Brings together the debates and speeches made during the 1994 general assembly of the members of the Benin Publishers Association, addressing a variety of issues as they relate to publishing, writing, and book development in Benin.

425 Barra, Yacoubou **"People's Republic of Benin."** In *The Book Trade of the World, vol. IV: Africa,* edited by Sigfred Taubert and Peter Weidhaas. Munich: K.G. Saur, 1984, 71-74.
Overview of publishing and the book trade in Benin. Now very dated.

426 de Souza, Oscar **"The Challenge of Publishing in Benin."** *African Publishing Review* 6, no. 3 (May/June 1997): 8-9.
An analysis of private sector publishing in Benin and its present strengths and weaknesses. Calls for more South-South co-operation between indigenous African publishers.

427 Gomez, Michel Robert E. **Le livre Béninois à la 40ème Foire du Livre.** Cotonou: Bureau d'Etude pour l'Education en Afrique - Nouvelles Messageries du Bénin, 1988. 34 pp.
Describes the state of literature in Benin, the promotion of writing in national languages, the development of school books, rebirth of the newspaper industry, and noting the increase in the number of bookshops. The second part of the book contains a bibliography of Beninois books exhibited at the 40th Frankfurt Book Fair, which comprise literary items, school texts and texts in national languages. The final part is a directory of bookshops in Benin.

428 Médéhouégnon, Pierre, and Michel-Robert Gomez **"L'édition et la politique du livre au Bénin: un défi à relever."** *Notre Librairie* no. 124 (October/December 1995): 40-43.
A short overview of the state of the publishing industry in Benin. Analyzes the history of publishing since independence, and reviews the current [1995] production capacity and distribution outlets. Discusses the effect which the devaluation of the CFA had on the industry, and suggests co-publishing as a remedy to overcome chronic problems of funding and distribution.

429 Tervonen, Taina **"Sur le chemin de l'indépendance. Entretien avec Béatrice Lalinon Gbado, directrice des Editions Ruisseaux d'Afrique (Bénin)."** *Africultures* no. 57 (December 2003): 101-103.
Online:
http://www.africultures.com/index.asp?no=3194&menu=revue_affiche_art icle [24/02/08]
Interview with founder and director of Editions Ruisseaux d'Afrique in Benin, Béatrice Lalinon Gbado, a firm that specializes in publishing African children's literature, with over 50 titles currently in print. She talks about the nature of the books they publish, their print runs, pricing, and the difficulties they face in competing with French multinationals in the crucial school book markets.

Botswana

Associations and book-related organizations

430 **Botswana Publishing Industry Association (BOPIA)**
c/o Mmegi Publishing Trust
Private Bag BR 298

Gaborone
Botswana
Tel: +267-372305 Fax: +267-371832
Email: mpt@mmegi.bw or ntebela@mmegi.bw
Web: n/a
President: Motlhaleemang Ntebela

431   Botswana Writers' Group
Department of English
University of Botswana
Private Bag 00703
Gaborone
Botswana
Tel: +267-355 2651 Fax: +267-318 5098
Email: n/a
Secretary: n/a
Note: not verified, organization dormant?

National bibliography, books in print, and book trade directories

432   National Bibliography of Botswana.
Gaborone: Botswana National Library Service [Private Bag 0036, Gaborone],
1969-
Twice yearly, latest is vol. 29, no. 2, 1997.
Email: bnls@info.bw or rmotlhabane@gov.bw
Web: n/a

Books, articles, reports, and interviews

433   Ahmad, Mahmoud "Republic of Botswana." In *The Book Trade of the World, vol. IV: Africa*, edited by Sigfred Taubert and Peter Weidhaas. Munich:
K.G. Saur, 1984, 75-80.
Overview of publishing and the book trade in Botswana. Now very dated.

434   Badisang, Bobana "Indigenous Book Publishing and Public Libraries-with Special Reference to Botswana." *Link-up* 6, no. 1 (March
1994): 10-12.
Focuses on Botswana public libraries' collections and how they are affected by the local publishing industry. Includes a brief overview of the structure of book publishing and distribution outlets in Botswana; also addresses the role played by libraries in the promotion of indigenous literature.

435 Bahta, Samuel Ghile, and Stephen M. Mutula **"Indigenous Publishing in Botswana: The Current Situation and the Way Forward."** *Information Development* 18, no. 4 (December 2002): 231-235.
Examines the challenges of publishing in local languages in Botswana, discussing aspects such as readership and the limited market for books, the prospects for developing local language publishing, and the important role indigenous language publishing has in eliminating illiteracy and creating a reading and writing culture.

436 Botswana. Ministry of Education, and Association for Development of Education in Africa (ADEA) **Report on the National Consultation Forum on the Development of Botswana's National Book Policy. Boipuso Conference and Exhibition Centre, Gaborone, Botswana, 6th-8th October, 1997.** Gaborone: Ministry of Education, and London: Association for Development of Education in Africa, Working Group on Books and Learning Materials, 1997. 81 pp.
The report of a consultation forum which brought together 58 participants from book-related organizations and institutions in Botswana, and which was convened to identify the key issues in book development, the problems facing the book industries in Botswana, and the way forward to lead to the establishment of a national book policy for the country. Individual sessions looked at procurement and distribution of textbooks, publishing of reading materials for new literates, providing suitable reading materials for the general public in Botswana, and the challenges of publishing in local languages. The report includes the papers that were presented (or summaries thereof), a summary of the group discussions, and the recommendations that were generated by the consultation exercise.

437 Kgosidintsi, Thandiwe, and Neil Parsons **"Publishing in Botswana."** *The African Book Publishing Record* 15, no. 3 (1989): 171-174.
A fairly comprehensive review of the history and development of the publishing industry in Botswana. Addresses issues such as publishing laws and legislation, book professional associations, literacy, writers and illustrators, publishers, bookshops and libraries.

438 Kotei, S.I.A., and D.B.T. Milazi **National Book Policy for Botswana. Investigation of Reading Habits and Book Needs Among Literates and Semi-Literates.** Gaborone: University of Botswana, 1984. 102 pp.
[Not examined]

439 Phikani, Chris **"Publishing for Botswana: A Symposium on Problems and Issues."** *Botswana Library Association Journal* 5, no. 1 (August 1983): 23-25.
Reports on a symposium organized by the Department of Library Studies, University of Botswana in April, 1982, which reviewed the state of publishing in the country.

440 Motlhabane, Ratanang **"The Book Chain in Botswana."** In *The Book Chain in Anglophone Africa. A Survey and Directory*, edited by Roger Stringer. Oxford: International Network for the Availability of Scientific Publications (INASP), 2002, 23-26.
Online: http://www.inasp.info/file/57/the-book-chain-in-anglophone-africa-a-survey-and-directory.html
[04/02/08]
Part of a series of useful country surveys and overviews – each prepared by a book professional from the country concerned – that review the state of the book, and the major players in the "book chain", in English-speaking African countries. Each country survey covers printing, book publishing, bookselling and distribution, library services, professional associations, book promotional bodies and book promotional events, training for the book professions, as well as examining some of the major issues as they relate to book development, such as languages, literacy, writers and writing, the reading habit, and national book policies. For each country this is supported by an annotated directory of government ministries, professional associations, book publishers, booksellers and distributors, printers, major libraries, and training institutions, with full address and contact details.

441 Mulindwa, Gertrude Kayaga **"The Book Trade in Botswana."** *ISBN Review* 17 (1996): 175-184.
One in a series of overview articles in a special issue of *ISBN Review* focusing on the book sector in various countries of Southern Africa, and which report (for the most part) about the state of libraries, publishing and the retail book trade; current book and copyright legislation, national book policies, programmes to promote the reading habit, laws and legislation cover the book sector and copyright, activities of library and book trade professional bodies, book trade organization, training for the book industries, the use of ISBNs, and more.

Burkina Faso

Associations and book-related organizations

442 **Association des Editeurs du Burkina Faso (ASSEDIF)**
c/o Editions Sankofa
BP 7027
Ouagadougou
Burkina Faso
Tel: +226-50 36 43 44
Email: jean.naba@univ-ouaga.bf or sankogur@yahoo.fr
Chairman: Ignace Hien
Secretary: Jean Claude Naba

National bibliography, books in print, and book trade directories

443   Bibliographie du Burkina Faso.
Ouagadougou: Bibliothèque Nationale, Ministère de la Culture, des Arts et du Tourisme [03 BP 7007, Ouagadougou 03], 2007?-
Annual, in preparation; cumulative volume for 1967–1990 also currently in preparation
Email: culture-arts@liptinfor.bf
Web: http://www.culture.gov.bf/textes/ministere_sr_bn.htm

Books, articles, reports, and interviews

444   Bakouan, Bali Augustin; Elie Yougbare, and J. Bernardin Sanon "Une vie littéraire en devenir." *Notre Librairie. Revue du Livre Afrique Noire, Maghreb, Caraïbes, Océan Indien. Littérature du Burkina Faso,* no. 101 (April-June 1990): 96-112.
This report combines several articles on the book trade in Burkina Faso, describing the difficulties and complexities involved in book production and distribution in the country. Also included are interviews, descriptions of the role of the media in promoting books, reports about the activities of writers' organizations and the University of Burkina Faso, and a bibliography of works by Burkinabe authors.

445   Kaboré, Armand Joseph L'édition du livre au Burkina Faso. Paris: L'Harmattan, 2007. 78 pp. (also available as an e-book)
Offers a socio-economic approach of publishing and the book markets in Burkina Faso. Probes into the infrastructural aspects and the organizational framework of the book trade and discusses issues such as distribution methods, and the emergence of unconventional pavement booksellers in Ouagadougou, known as "librairies par terre".

446   Sanon, Bernardin "Les problèmes de l'édition littéraire au Burkina."
In *Recommandation sur l'édition littéraire. Annales, special number, séries A: sciences humaines et sociales.* Ougadougou: University of Ougadougou, 1988, 57-74.
On the problems of literary publishing in Burkina Faso. [Not examined]

Yonli, Emile D. **"L'édition scientifique au Burkina Faso"** *see* ➔ **Section 4, Studies by topic: Scientific, technical and medical publishing** entry **2364**

Burundi

Books, articles, reports, and interviews

Burafuta, Jean-Paul **"L'Edition scientifique au Burundi"** *see* ➔ **Section 4, Studies by topic: Scientific, technical and medical publishing** entry 2337

447 Mwroroha, Emile **"Republic of Burundi."** In *The Book Trade of the World, vol. IV: Africa,* edited by Sigfred Taubert and Peter Weidhaas. Munich: K.G. Saur, 1984, 81-83.
Overview of publishing and the book trade in Burundi. Now very dated.

Cameroon

Associations and book-related organizations

448 **Association des Editeurs du Cameroun (AEC)/ Cameroon Publishers Association**
BP 13 807
Yaoundé
Cameroun
Tel: +237-9591 1373/+237-9808516 Fax: +237-231-8896
Email: japhetbidjek@yahoo.fr
President: (Acting) Serge Kouam
Secretary: Japhet Bidjek [?]

449 **National Book Development Council of Cameroon (NBDC)**
NBDC House
Campaign Street
Great Soppo
Buea
South West Province
Cameroon
Tel/Fax: +237-322106
Email: gngwane@yahoo.com
Web: n/a
Chair: George Ngwane

National bibliography, books in print, and book trade directories

450 **Bibliographie nationale du Cameroun.**
Yaoundé: Bibliothèque Nationale du Cameroun [BP 1053, Yaoundé], 1990? -

Irregular, latest is cumulative volume *Bibliographie nationale du Cameroun: des origines à 1996.*
Email: n/a
Web: n/a

451 Ndachi-Tagne, David **"Who's Who. L'édition au Cameroun de A à Z."** *Notre Librairie. Revue du Livre de l'Afrique Noire, Maghreb, Caraïbes, Océan Indien. Littérature Camerounaise*: 2. Le livre dans tous ses états, no. 100 (January-March 1990): 60-61.
A directory of book trade organizations and publishing companies active in Cameroon.

Books, articles, reports, and interviews

452 Anon. **"De toutes nouvelles maison d'édition en Afrique: 'une aventure exaltante.' Entretien avec Pierre-Yves Njeng, président de l'association AILE-Cameroun."** *Takam Tikou*, no. 6 (January 1997): 22-26.
An interview with Pierre-Yves Njeng, President of the AILE-Cameroun Association which recounts the history of AILE-Cameroun, founded in 1993 by author-illustrator Marie Wabbes. The Association started as a permanent creative workshop which met once a week with a group of about 15 young people to illustrate children's stories. It has become a creative business endeavour that includes the Akoma Mba publishing house, which publishes and promotes African literature for young people.

453 Bjornson, Richard **The African Quest for Freedom and Identity. Cameroonian Writing and the National Experience.** Bloomington: Indiana University Press, 1991. 507 pp.
Primarily on Cameroonian writing and literature, but also contains some discussion about the activities of Editions CLE in Yaoundé, the wider role of the church in publishing, and textbook publishing.

Dayeko, Paul **"Publier, diffuser, rayonner ... l'expérience de Silex"** *see* ➔ Section 4, Studies by topic: Authors and publishers/Publishing of African writers and African literature entry **1332**

454 Dihang, Jean **"United Republic of Cameroon."** In *The Book Trade of the World, vol. IV: Africa*, edited by Sigfred Taubert and Peter Weidhaas. Munich: K.G. Saur, 1984, 84-89.
Overview of publishing and the book trade in Cameroon. Now very dated.

Dogbé, Yves-Emmanuel **"Publier, rayonner, diffuser ... l'expérience d'Akpagnon"** *see* ➔ Section 4, Studies by topic: Authors and publishers/Publishing of African writers and African literature entry **1334**

455 Doo Bell, Jacques **"Problématique d'une politique du livre au Cameroun."** *CREPLA Bulletin d'Informations,* no. 9 (August 1984): 23-25.
Discusses and rejects the preconception that Africans in general, and Cameroonians in particular, do not read, and at the same time makes suggestions for a viable national book policy.

456 Dunton, Chris **"25 Years on the Shelf."** *West Africa* (May 9 1988): 835.
Reflects on the "mid-life crisis" facing the Cameroonian publishing house Editions CLE of Yaoundé.

457 Joachim, Paulin **"Un poète Camerounais dans la jungle de l'édition: Paul Dayeko et les Editions SILEX. "** *Géopolitique africaine,* no. 3 (1986): 131-141. Also in published in *Ethiopiques* 5, nos. 1-2 (1982): 56-63.
Interview with Paul Dayeko, editor and publisher of Editions SILEX, who is also a distinguished poet.

Keim, Karen R. **"Popular Fiction Publishing in Cameroon"** *see* ➜ **Section 4, Studies by topic: Mass market and popular fiction publishing** entry **2006**

458 Kloeckner, Hélène **"Réformer pour faire fonctionner le marché du livre scolaire. Entretien avec Serge Kouam, directeur de l'Africaine d'édition et de services (AES, Cameroun)."** *Africultures* no. 57 (December 2003): 89-91.
Online:
http://www.africultures.com/index.asp?no=3187&menu=revue_affiche_article [25/02/08]
Interview with Cameroonian publisher Serge Kouam, head of L'Africaine d'édition et de services (AES), about recent reforms in the educational textbook publishing sector in the country, and the difficulties and business risks local publishers face in the process of getting their books adopted for classroom use.

459 Lambert, Fernando **"The Emergence of Local Publishing: Cameroon."** In *European-Language Writing in Sub-Saharan Africa,* vol. 1, edited by Albert S. Gérard. Budapest: Akadémiai Kiado, 1986, 557-572.
Concentrates on the role of the Centre de Littérature Evangélique (Editions CLE) in the development of Cameroonian literature in French in the 1960s. Offers a detailed analysis of CLE's publications and activities, combined with a précis of the most common plot themes for prose fiction.

460 Newton, Diana C. **Autonomous Publishing in Francophone Africa. Case Study Cameroon.** Ottawa, ON: Carleton University, 1989. MA thesis.
[Not examined]

461 Newton, Diana C. **"Autonomous Publishing in Cameroon."** *The African Book Publishing Record* 17, no. 2 (1991): 95-99.

Also reprinted in *Readings on Publishing in Africa and the Third World*, by Philip G. Altbach. Buffalo, NY: Bellagio Publishing Network, Research and Information Center (Bellagio Studies in Publishing 1), 1993, 46-52.
Based on the above MA thesis (*see* entry ➔ **460**). Sets out to provide a rationale for the promotion of an autonomous publishing industry in Cameroon by trying to identify the interests of the key participants in the industry. Examines some policy alternatives that might lead to true autonomy for the publishing industry.

462   Ngandu Tshimanga, Freddie, and Julius Che Tita **"Cameroon Publishers Against Monopoly."** *African Publishing Review* 8, no. 1 (1999): 1-3.
A statement by the ➔ **Cameroon Publishers Association/L'Association des Editeurs du Cameroun (448)** arguing that a state monopoly in publishing and book distribution by the government-owned company CEPER, is unfair to the struggling private sector book industry, detrimental to authorship, has a damaging effect on local bookshops, and is unhealthy for book development in the country.

463   Ngwane, Mwalimu George **"The Cameroon Book Industry: Challenges and Changes."** *The African Book Publishing Record* 31, no. 2 (2005): 91-93.
Online: http://www.gngwane.com/2005/04/strongthe_camer.html [25/02/08]
A "diagnosis" of the book sector in Cameroon, covering professional initiatives, public partnerships, and the government's involvement and responsibilities, which the author hopes will stimulate discussion "to provide a remedy to the dearth of the book culture in Cameroon", and a revamped indigenous book industry.

464   Ntonfo, André **"Book Production and Consumption in Cameroon."** *African Publishing Review* 3, no. 3 (May/June 1994): 16-17. (same, in French, pp. 16-17)
A brief historical overview of writing and publishing in Cameroon.

465   Philombe, René **Le livre Camerounais et ses auteurs: une contribution à l'histoire littéraire de la République Unie du Cameroun de 1985 à nos jours, avec une notice bio-bibliographique des auteurs**.
Yaoundé: Editions Semences Africaines, 1984. 302 pp.
The late René Philombe (who died in 2001) was one of Cameroon's most prolific writers, as well as a journalist and political activist, and heading his own publishing house, Editions Semences Africaines. Although primarily focusing on writing – and presenting a literary history of Cameroon – this extensive study also includes the author's thoughts on publishing and the state of the book in general. The first part deals with the question of oral literature and examines the situation in colonial times. The second part studies the socio-cultural climate between 1940 and 1949, the "golden age of anti-colonial literature", while part three examines the moving factors in the "new awakening of literature" and the development of new talent.

466 Philombe, René **"Le métier d'editeur."** *Notre Librairie. Revue du Livre Afrique Noire, Maghreb, Caraïbes, Océan Indien. Littérature Camerounaise: 2. Le livre dans tous ses étâts,* no. 100 (January-March 1990): 52-53.
An interview with René Philombe, the well-known Cameroonian writer who founded his own publishing company, Editions Semences Africaines.

467 Publishers Association of Cameroon **"Move Towards a National Book Policy in Cameroon."** *African Publishing Review* 10, no. 1 (2001): 9-11.
A paper presented by the ➜ **Cameroon Publishers Association/L'Association des Editeurs du Cameroun (448)** to a national book forum held in November 2000. It sets out what the Association views as essential requirements for a sound national book policy, and deals with aspects such as book conception and editorial development, policy making, financing textbook provision, the publishing process, distribution, and the structure and governance of a national book commission.

468 Shafack, Rosemary M., and Kiven Charles **"The Book Chain in Cameroon."** In *The Book Chain in Anglophone Africa. A Survey and Directory,* edited by Roger Stringer. Oxford: International Network for the Availability of Scientific Publications (INASP), 2002, 27-30.
Online: http://www.inasp.info/file/57/the-book-chain-in-anglophone-africa-a-survey-and-directory.html [25/02/08]
One in a series of useful country surveys and overviews – each prepared by a book professional from the country concerned – that review the state of the book, and the major players in the "book chain", in English-speaking African countries. Each country survey covers printing, book publishing, bookselling and distribution, library services, professional associations, book promotional bodies and book promotional events, training for the book professions, as well as examining some of the major issues as they relate to book development, such as languages, literacy, writers and writing, the reading habit, and national book policies. For each country this is supported by an annotated directory of government ministries, professional associations, book publishers, booksellers and distributors, printers, major libraries, and training institutions, with full address and contact details.

469 Tewafo, Ferdinand **"Heurs et malheurs de l'édition."** *Notre Librairie. Revue du Livre de l'Afrique Noire, Maghreb, Caraïbes, Océan Indien. Littérature Camerounaise: 2. Le livre dans tous ses états,* no. 100 (January-March 1990): 44-51.
Examines the successes and setbacks encountered by Editions CLE in the context of publishing in Cameroon, and reviews some of the most acute problems and constraints. Also reflects on the difficulty experienced by Cameroonian authors in getting their works published in their own country.

470 Zogo, F. **"Les déterminants fiscalo-douaniers du marché éditorial au Cameroun: essai sur la problématique de l'incidence des politiques fiscales sur l'économie du livre."** *Fréquence Sud,* no. 14, (1998): 137-154.
[Not examined]

Cape Verde

Associations and book-related organizations

471 **Instituto da Biblioteca Nacional e do Livro** (formerly Instituto Cabo-verdeano do Livro)
Praia
Cape Verde
Tel: n/a
Email: bibnac@cvtelecom.cv
Web: http://www.bn.cv/
President: Joaquim Morais

Books, articles, reports, and interviews

472 Instituto Caboverdeano do Livro **"Republic of Cape Verde."** In *The Book Trade of the World, vol. IV: Africa,* edited by Sigfred Taubert and Peter Weidhaas. Munich: K.G. Saur, 1984, 90-93.
Overview of publishing and the book trade in Cape Verde. Now very dated.

Central African Republic

Associations and book-related organizations

473 **Collectif de Distribution du Livre en Centrafrique (CODILCA)**
BP 2965
Bangui
Central African Republic
Tel: +236-503207 Fax: +236-613561
Email: rayms_mbadjire@yahoo.com
Director: Raymond Mbadjiré

Books, articles, reports, and interviews

474 Saint-Dizier, Jacqueline **"Vendre, acheter, lire."** *Notre Librairie. Revue du Livre de l'Afrique Noire, Maghreb, Caraïbes, Océan Indien. Littérature Centrafricaine,* no. 97 (April-May 1989): 96-99.
The librarian of the Centre Culturel Français (CFF) presents a brief overview of the status of books and publishing in the Central African Republic, including the retail book trade, and the role of the CCF library.

475 Zidouemba, Dominique **"Le livre en République Centrafricaine."** *Notes Africaines,* no 196 (1999): 19-25. [Not examined]

Congo (Brazzaville)

Associations and book-related organizations

476   Association Nationale des Editeurs et des Imprimeurs
c/o Editions Lemba
20 avenue des Emeteurs Sangolo-OMS
Brazzaville
Postal address:
BP 2351
Brazzaville
Congo
Tel: +242-667 6558
Email: editions_lemba@yahoo.fr or asbasseha@yahoo.fr
Executive Secretary: Appolinaire Singou-Besseha

Books, articles, reports, and interviews

477   Badijo, Auguy **"L'édition."** *Notre Librairie. Revue du Livre de l'Afrique Noire, Maghreb, Caraïbes, Océan Indien. Littérature Congolaise*, no. 92-92 (March-May 1988): 205.
Contrasts the high quality of writing with the poor state of the publishing industry in the Congo, and the alleged failure of the indigenous publisher Les Editions Littéraires Congolaises.

478   Cardorelle, David **"Congo People's Republic."** In *The Book Trade of the World, vol. IV: Africa*, edited by Sigfred Taubert and Peter Weidhaas. Munich: K.G. Saur, 1984, 97-101.
Overview of publishing and the book trade in the Congo. Now very dated.

Congo Democratic Republic

Associations and book-related organizations

479   Association Nationale des Editeurs et Diffuseurs du Livre (ANEDIL)
c/o Editions Universitaires Africaines
Avennue de l'Université
Kinshasa
Postal address:
BP 146
Kishasa XI
Democratic Republic of the Congo

Tel/Fax: +243-815-108667
Email: anedil2003@yahoo.fr or editions_eua@hayoo.fr
President: Bertin Makolo Muswaswa

National bibliography, books in print, and book trade directories

480 **Bibliographie Nationale** [de la République démocratique du Congo].
Kinshasa-Gombe: Bibliothèque nationale [BP 13897], 1977-
Irregular, latest is 1999/2000.
Email: n/a

Books, articles, reports, and interviews

481 Cassiau-Haurie, Christophe **"Publishing in Hard Times: DR Congo
1990–2000."** *Bellagio Publishing Network Newsletter*, no. 31 (November 2002):
16-19.
http://www.bellagiopublishingnetwork.com/newsletter31/cassiau-
haurie.htm [25/02/08]
Also re-published in its original French version in *Africultures*, 6 September
2007 as **"Publier loin de l'Occident: l'édition au Congo-Zaïre durant l'arrêt
de la coopération de 1990 à 2000."**
http://www.africultures.com/index.asp?menu=affiche_article&no=6883
[25/02/08]
A survey of publishing activities in the Democratic Republic of the Congo for the
period 1990 to 2000, which witnessed a marked increase in new published works,
albeit heavily dominated by publishing in the area of "religious knowledge." The
authors analyzes this publishing output, the nature of books published, and the
different publishing companies. He reports that "of the nearly 1,500 published
works, 195 are from publishers with just one title and 351 titles are from publishers
with a maximum of five titles in their list, often by the same author. In fact, these
'occasional publishers' publish on behalf of an author, who often writes the preface,
publishes, distributes and disseminates the book. Inevitably the result, in spite of
their efforts, demonstrates a level of amateurishness."

482 Cassiau-Haurie, Christophe **"L'état contre le livre, le cas du Congo
démocratique."** *Africultures* no. 57 (December 2003): 45-56.
Online:
http://www.africultures.com/index.asp?menu=revue_affiche_article&no=3
174&dispo=fr [25/02/08]
Another version also published in *Congo-Afrique* 44, no. 382 (2004): 104-115.
Deplores the lack of a coherent government policy in the Democratic Republic of the
Congo as it relates to publishing, books and reading, and general support for the
book sector and library development. Many libraries are in a state of disrepair and
have to operate on pitiful budgets even those at the country's major universities.
While, under the patronage of the Ministry of Culture, Kinshasa, the country's

capital, holds the "world record for the number of literary and book fairs" there is no collaboration of any kind between the organizers of these events. Taxation on books and book imports – with all booksellers required to pay an additional 5% tax of their "cultural activities" to a cultural advancement fund – has led to very high book prices. There is neither promotion nor implementation of international book standards; legal deposit of publications is subject to a charge; and confusion surrounds copyright protection for locally published books, performance rights, and other creative output. Meantime state participation in publishing, through the government owned SONECA company, has been a failure; and the government has also failed to develop a national book policy. All this has created a hostile environment for book and cultural development, which is a great shame for a country that has so much to offer in terms of literature, music, and the dramatic and visual arts.

483   Himwiinga, Paulsen A. **"Republic of Zaïre."** In *The Book Trade of the World, vol. IV: Africa*, edited by Sigfred Taubert and Peter Weidhaas. Munich: K.G. Saur, 1984, 324-334.
Overview of publishing and the book trade in [then] Zaïre. Now very dated, but contains some useful historical background.

484   Kadima-Nzur, Mukala **"The Emergence of Local Publishing: Congo/Zaïre."** In *European-Language Writing in Sub-Saharan Africa*, vol. 1, edited by Albert S. Gérard. Budapest: Akadémiai Kiado, 1986, 541-557.
Describes the emergence of writing in Zaïre in the 1950s in the light of post-colonial cultural awakening, and the rapid intellectual growth that found expression in creative writing. Examines the evolution of Zaïrian poetry and drama during the 1960s and 70s, in contrast to the static nature of prose writing during the same time. Discusses the publishing venture Les Belles Lettres, started by Emile Witahnkenge, which published almost anything submitted and which may have encouraged the official government sponsorship of publishing of creative writing. Also discusses the activities of several [then] Zaïrian publishing houses including Les Editions du Mont Noir and Editions Pléaide du Congo, among others.

485   Kangafu, Gudumbagana **"L'édition Zaïroise."** *Notre Librairie. Revue du Livre Afrique Noire, Maghreb, Caraïbes, Océan Indien. Littérature zaïroise*, no. 63 (reissued 1989): 83-86.
A brief account of the state of publishing in the former Zaïre, now Congo Democratic Republic

486   Lukomo, Bivuatu Nsundi **Le financement de la culture et de l'industrie du livre au Zaïre.** Kinshasa: Société d'Etudes et d'Editions, 2nd ed. 1990, 150 pp. 2 vols.
Presents an overview of publishing activities in [then] Zaïre, the problems and constraints facing the book industries, and examines the particular problem of "financing culture" in relation to book publishing.

487   Mukuama, L. **"Les conditions de promotion de l'édition du livre au Zaïre."** *Usawa*, nos. 9-16, (1991-1994): 337-341.
[Not examined]

488   Sivry, Jean Michel **Examen des besoins et analyse des possibilités de formation et de développement des ressources humaines de l'Industrie du livre au Zaïre - (mission).** Paris: UNESCO (FMR/CC/BAE/86/165), 1986. 29 pp.
A UNESCO mission report on the training of professionals for the book industries.

489   Vinck, Honoré **"Anciens imprimés en Lingala."** *Annales Aequatoria*, no. 13 (1992): 491-497.
Examines early printed materials published in Lingala and describes the activities of the presses that produced them.

Vinck, Honoré **"Livres scolaires coloniaux: methodes d'analyse — approache herméneutique"** *see* ➔ **Section 2, General, comparative, and regional studies, Regional studies: Africa, Francophone** entry **412**

490   Yates, Barbara A. **Knowledge Brokers: Books and Publishers in Early Colonial Zaire.** *History in Africa*, 14 (1987): 311-340.
Deals with the processes, problems, and politics of knowledge transfer in King Leopold's Congo, during which time availability of printed materials in local African languages served as the primary means of achieving literacy and subsequently knowledge. Between 1879 and 1908, when the Congo was under the rule of Leopold II, nineteen Congolese languages were represented in written form and more than 400 titles in these languages were published. The paper describes the pioneer publishers, their presses and the volume and nature of the material they produced. It analyzes the social factors affecting the demand for and supply of this printed material, discusses the content and quality of this literature; and examines early efforts to consolidate book publishing and to standardize language usage.

Côte d'Ivoire

Associations and book-related organizations

491   **Association des Editeurs Ivoiriens (ASSEDI)**
09 BP 682
Abidjan 01
Côte d'Ivoire
Tel: +225-07 68 76 31 Fax: +225-20 21 01 53
Email: edition@nei-ci.com
President: Akattia Famie
Secretary: Anges N'dakpri ange_fn@caramail.com

National bibliography, books in print, and book trade directories

492 Bibliographie de la Côte d'Ivoire
Abidjan: Bibliothèque Nationale [BB V-180, Abidjan], 1970-
Annual, latest is 1975.
Email: n/a
Web: n/a

Books, articles, reports, and interviews

493 Amoikon-Fauquembergue, Marie-Agathe **Enjeux économiques et financiers du secteur du livre en Côte d'Ivoire. Rapport.**
http://www.espace-economique-
francophone.com/e/SituationsecteurLivreCoteIvoire_Amoikon.doc
[05/01/08]
A report commissioned in 2003 by the Agence Intergouvernementale de la Francophonie, now part of the ➜ **Organisation Internationale de la Francophonie (101)**. It examines the situation and prospects of educational book supplies in the light of the recent liberalization of this part of the book sector by the Ivoirian government; its intention to gradually provide up to two million school pupils with free books as part of its 'Education for All' goals, and to develop a coherent strategy for the production and distribution of such didactic materials. The author looks at the principal players involved in this ambitious plan, analyzing the feasibility of the proposal and how it is going to be financed, its likely impact on the book industries, and possible problems and constraints in its implementation.

494 Association des Editeurs Ivoiriens **Réflexions relatives à la problématique de la circulation et de la diffusion du livre en Afrique francophone (cas de la Côte d'Ivoire), Etude APNET-ADEA, août-septembre 2006.** Abidjan: Association des éditeurs ivoiriens [09 BP 68, Abidjan 01], 2006.
[Not examined]

495 Carlos, Jérôme **"Autour du Livre: des questions que nous nous posons."** *Notre Librairie. Revue du Livre Afrique Noire, Maghreb, Caraïbes, Océan Indien. Littérature de Côte d'Ivoire: 2. Ecrire aujourd'hui,* no. 87 (April-June 1987): 110-112.
Asks how literature and publishing in Côte d'Ivoire can progress, bearing in mind the legacy of colonial culture and considering the added problem of multiple national languages.

496 Cévaër, Françoise **"Interviews d'auteurs Africains et d'éditeurs."**
Revue de Littérature Comparée 67, no. 1 (1993): 161-176.

Interviews with authors Calixthe Beyala and Tierno Monénembo, and publishers Paul Dayéko of Editions Silex, and Caroline Ogou of the Centre d'Edition et de Diffusion Africaines in Abidjan.

497 Côte d'Ivoire. Ministère de la Culture **Le Livre en Côte d'Ivoire: actes du 1er séminaire national pour le développement de l'édition, de la promotion et de la lecture en Côte d'Ivoire 26-30 October 1987.** Abidjan: Ministère de la Culture, 1987? 149 pp.
Proceedings of the first national seminar on publishing development, distribution and reading in Côte d'Ivoire. [Not examined]

Déazon, André, and Gilles Vilasco **"L'édition scientifique à l'Université Nationale de Côte d'Ivoire"** *see* ➜ **Section 4, Studies by topic: Scientific, technical and medical publishing** entry **2342**

498 Escudier, Denis **"Republic of the Ivory Coast."** In *The Book Trade of the World, vol. IV: Africa,* edited by Sigfred Taubert and Peter Weidhaas. Munich: K.G. Saur, 1984, 143-153.
Overview of publishing and the book trade in Côte d'Ivoire. Now very dated.

499 Kloeckner, Hélène **"Le libraire, un maillon essentiel de la chaîne du livre. Entretien avec M. Soro, directeur de la Librairie de France à Abidjan."** *Africultures* no. 57 (December 2003): 92-94.
Online:
http://www.africultures.com/index.asp?menu=revue_affiche_article&no=3188&dispo=fr [26/02/08]
Interview with the Director of Librairie de France in Abidjan (now the largest bookshop chain in the country with 26 retail outlets) discussing educational school book supplies, competition between publishers and booksellers – and competition from the seasonal "librairies par terre" (pavement booksellers) – and the constantly dwindling purchasing power of the general public.

500 Mamari, K. **"Les Librairies."** *Notre Librairie. Revue du Livre Afrique Noire, Maghreb, Caraïbes, Océan Indien. Littérature de Côte d'Ivoire: 2. Ecrire aujourd'hui.* no. 87 (April-June 1987): 133-138.
Takes a look at the main bookshops in Abidjan, radio, television, and the major newspapers, as well as giving a brief guide to bookshops in other parts of the country.

501 Palmeri, Robert J. **"Privatization of Publishing in the Côte d'Ivoire."** In *The Challenge of the Market: Privatization and Publishing in Africa,* edited by Philip G. Altbach. Chestnut Hill, MA: Bellagio Publishing Network, Research and Information Center (Bellagio Studies in Publishing, 7), 1996, 79-93.
Provides a historical background to publishing and the book market in French-speaking Africa in general, and the Côte d'Ivoire in particular. Examines the

educational and trade publishing markets; the activities and shareholding, etc. of the two major publishing companies in the country, the Centre d'Edition et Distribution Africaine (CEDA) and Nouvelles Editions Ivoiriennes (NEI), their links with French publishing interests, and the emergence of several new independent presses. The dominance of one foreign publisher – Hachette, who now owns 40% of CEDA and 55% of NEI, together with Hachette's associated distribution company EDIPRESS which enjoys a virtual monopoly on newspaper and magazine publishing – is not seen as creating a favourable climate for the emergence of more private sector indigenous publishers, unless they are allowed to compete on an equitable basis and will get a fair share of the textbook markets, with adoption of some of their titles by the Ministry of Education. The author also argues that meantime francophone African publishers must become more export-oriented, as they still export very little of their production even to adjacent francophone countries.

Eritrea

Associations and book-related organizations

502   Eritrea Publishers Association (ERIPA)
c/o Hidri Publishers P.F.D.J.
PO Box 1081
Asmara
Eritrea
Tel: +291-1-126177 Fax: +291-1-120048
Email: hidrip@pfdj.org.er
Web: n/a
Executive Secretary: Solomon Dirar

Books, articles, reports, and interviews

503   Abraha, Assefaw "The Book Chain in Eritrea." In *The Book Chain in Anglophone Africa. A Survey and Directory,* edited by Roger Stringer. Oxford: International Network for the Availability of Scientific Publications (INASP), 2002, 31-34.
Online: http://www.inasp.info/file/57/the-book-chain-in-anglophone-africa-a-survey-and-directory.html [26/02/08]
One in a series of useful country surveys and overviews – each prepared by a book professional from the country concerned – that review the state of the book, and the major players in the "book chain", in English-speaking African countries. Each country survey covers printing, book publishing, bookselling and distribution, library services, professional associations, book promotional bodies and book promotional events, training for the book professions, as well as examining some of the major issues as they relate to book development, such as languages, literacy, writers and writing, the reading habit, and national book policies. For each country this is supported by an annotated directory of government ministries, professional

associations, book publishers, booksellers and distributors, printers, major libraries, and training institutions, with full address and contact details.

Ethiopia

Associations and book-related organizations

504   Ethiopian Booksellers Association (EBA)
PO Box 9144
Addis Ababa
Ehiopia
Tel: +251-1-551688 Fax: +251-1-115249
Email: mde@telecom.net.et
Chair: Kahsay Abraha

505   Ethiopian Publishers Association (EPA)
c/o Mega Publishing Enterprises
PO Box 22284
Addis Ababa
Ethiopia
Tel: n/a
Email: omegapub@telecom.net.et or mde@telecom.net.et
Web: n/a
Chair: Solomon Ayalew

506   Ethiopia Reads
PO Box 2677
Addis Ababa
Ethiopia
Tel: +251-670643 or +251-670644
Email: ebcefethiopia@yahoo.com
In the US:
Ethiopia Reads
50 South Steele Street Suite 325
Denver CO 80209
Tel: +1-303-468 8422 Fax: +303-355 7190
Email: laura@ethiopiareads.org
Web: http://www.ethiopiareads.org/index.html
Executive Director: Yohannes Gebregeorgis
Director of US Operations: Laura Bond

National bibliography, books in print, and book trade directories

507   Ethiopian Publications. Books, Pamphlets, Annuals and Periodical Articles Published in Ethiopia in Ethiopian and Foreign Languages.
Addis Ababa: Institute of Ethiopian Studies, Addis Ababa University [PO Box 1176, Addis Ababa], 1965-?
Annual, (cumulative volume for 1963-1964), latest is 1978?
Note: an earlier cumulation, *Ethiopian Publications, 1941-1963*, was published in 1974.
Email: ies.aau@Telecom.net.et
Web: http://www.ies-ethiopia.org/

508   National Bibliography of Ethiopia. (in Amharic and English, consists of several parts, see Web site)
Addis Ababa: National Archives and Library of Ethiopia [PO Box 717], 1982?-
Annually, latest is *National Bibliography of Ethiopia 1998 E.C.* [i.e. 2005/2006], published June 2006.
Online: English versions
Volume 24, No. 1, 2005-2006
http://www.nale.gov.et/National%20Bibliography/BIBLIO.%20OF%20BOOKS%20ON%20ETHIOPIA%20(ENGLISH).pdf [26/02/08]
Volume 24, No. 2, 2005-2006
http://www.nale.gov.et/National%20Bibliography/BIBLIO.%20OF%20ETHIOPIAN%20WRITERS%20.pdf [26/02/08]
Volume 24, No. 3, 2005-2006
http://www.nale.gov.et/National%20Bibliography/BIBLIOGRAPHY%20OF%20BOOKS%20(ENGLISH)1998.pdf [26/02/08]
Web: http://www.nale.gov.et/national_bibliography_of_ethiopia.htm
Email: nale@telecom.net.et or amtatawar@yahoo.com
Web: http://www.nale.gov.et/

Books, articles, reports, and interviews

509   Anon. "Socialist Ethiopia." In *The Book Trade of the World, vol. IV: Africa*, edited by Sigfred Taubert and Peter Weidhaas. Munich: K.G. Saur, 1984, 113-120.
Overview of publishing and the book trade in Ethiopia. Now very dated.

510   Ayalew, Solomon "Focus on the Ethiopian Publishing Industry." *African Publishing Review* 10, no. 4 (2001): 3-4.
Looks back on Ethiopia's long history of literature, printing and book publishing, profiling the major publishers active today, and providing some statistical analysis of book production by categories of books published from 1997 to 2001.

511   Ayalew, Solomon **"What Ethiopian Publishers Have Done Since 1995."** In: *Changing Lives. Promoting a Reading Culture in Africa. Indaba 2001. Harare, Zimbabwe 4-5 August, 2001*, edited by the Zimbabwe International Book Fair Trust. Harare: Zimbabwe International Book Fair Trust, n.d. [2002], 82-86.
Another version also published in *African Publishing Review* 11, no. 1 (2002): 6-8.
A brief history of printing and publishing in Ethiopia, together with an account of developments in the book trade since 1995.

512   Denning, Carmelle **Ethiopia Book Sector Study: Educational Books in the English Medium.** London: Overseas Development Administration/ODA, 1992. 64 pp.
[Not examined]

513   Ficquet, Eloi and Shiferaw Bekele **Le marché du livre éthiopien à l'épreuve de la diversité**. *Politique Africaine* no. 99 (2005): 83-96
Examines the state of the book and the book industries in Ethiopia following the period of political liberalization in the country as from 1991, and, in particular, the nature of publishing in the national language of Amharic.

514   Gupta, S. **"The Development of Education, Printing and Publishing in Ethiopia."** *International Information and Library Review* 26, no. 3 (September 1994): 169-180.
Provides an overview of literacy, education, printing, publishing, and library provision in Ethiopia. Discusses the role of the church, the development of education, including higher education, and reviews printing presses and publishing houses in the country.

515   Hameso, Seyoum Y. **"Language and Access to Books and Education in Ethiopia."** *Focus on International & Comparative Librarianship* 28, no. 2 (September 1997): 74-75.
Summary of a talk given at an IGLA seminar during the London International Book Fair in 1997 about the current situation [1997] of the book and the book industries in Ethiopia.

516   Leka, Wanna **"Publishing in Ethiopia: A Brief Overview."** In *Development Directory of Indigenous Publishing 1995*, compiled by Carol Priestley. Harare: African Publishers' Network, 1995, 64-65.
A short account of the development of publishing in Ethiopia.

517   Ourgay, M. **"Printing, Publishing and Book Development in Ethiopia up to the Year of Menelik II."** *International Information and Library Review* 24, no. 3 (September 1992), 221-227.

Printing, publishing and book development may be considered as the prerequisites for the development of any library and information system in any society. This paper attempts to cover publishing in Ethiopia from 1500-1900. During this period numerous ecclesiastical and a few original works by Ethiopians and foreigners had appeared in Ge'ez and in other dialects. The role of the missionary societies in book development was also significant. Most of the products of the printing presses were kept either in church archives or in Royal Libraries. The establishment of any modern type libraries was entirely neglected. Consequently, most of the literate population of that time had no opportunity to find out what was being published in their own country.

518 Pankhurst, Richard **"The Foundations of Education, Printing, Newspapers, Book Production, Libraries and Literacy in Ethiopia."** *Ethiopia Observer* 7, no. 3 (1962), 241-290.
[Not examined]

519 Rouaud, Alain **"Contribution à l'histoire des impressions Ethiopiennes à l'Imprimerie Nationale de Paris."** *Bulletin des Etudes Africaines de l'INALCO* 2, no. 4 (1982): 119-129.
A history of early printing in Ethiopia. [Not examined]

520 Rouaud, Alain **"Quelques précisions sur les impressions et Imprimeries Ethiopiennes."** *Bulletin des Etudes Africaines de l'INALCO* 6, no. 11 (1986): 131-145.
Describes early printing in Ethiopia. [Not examined]

521 Wassie, Atnafu **"Ethiopia: A New Beginning in Publishing."** *Bellagio Publishing Network Newsletter*, no. 16 (Spring 1996): 9-11.
An overview of book publishing in Ethiopia [as at 1996]. Examines the changing environment for publishing, problems faced by the book industries, and the challenges that lie ahead.

522 Wassie, Atnafu **"Privatization and the Challenges for Publishing in Ethiopia."** In *The Challenge of the Market: Privatization and Publishing in Africa*, edited by Philip G. Altbach. Chestnut Hill, MA: Bellagio Publishing Network, Research and Information Center (Bellagio Studies in Publishing, 7), 1996, 47-61.
The state's dominant role in the past in book development and publishing in Ethiopia has had a very negative effect, but the current government has now disengaged from its monopoly role in textbook publishing and has established clear policies on privatization. The author presents an overview of the publishing industry in the context of past developments and current [1996] problems, and examines factors such as the new language policy, the need for a national book policy, the challenges facing local writers, the deterioration of library services, and other pertinent issues. The author concludes that recent events have opened up a more favourable environment for book publishing, but that "its future is not dependent on privatization alone. The

strategic involvement of the state and aid agencies is essential...to accelerate present activities toward the sustainable development of the publishing industry."

523 Wassie, Antafu **"The Book Chain in Ethiopia."** In *The Book Chain in Anglophone Africa. A Survey and Directory*, edited by Roger Stringer. Oxford: International Network for the Availability of Scientific Publications (INASP), 2002. [Not included in print version]
Online: http://www.inasp.info/pubs/bookchain/profiles/Ethiopia.html [now at http://www.inasp.info/file/57/the-book-chain-in-anglophone-africa-a-survey-and-directory.html, but Ethiopian chapter not currently available]
One in a series of useful country surveys and overviews – each prepared by a book professional from the country concerned – that review the state of the book, and the major players in the "book chain", in English-speaking African countries. Each country survey covers printing, book publishing, bookselling and distribution, library services, professional associations, book promotional bodies and book promotional events, training for the book professions, as well as examining some of the major issues as they relate to book development, such as languages, literacy, writers and writing, the reading habit, and national book policies. For each country this is supported by an annotated directory of government ministries, professional associations, book publishers, booksellers and distributors, printers, major libraries, and training institutions, with full address and contact details.

Gabon

Associations and book-related organizations

524 **Union des Editeurs Gabonais (UEG)**
c/o Editions Raponda – Walker
BP 7969
Libreville
Gabon
Tel: +241 742023/774825
Email: izolwe@internetgabon.com
Web: n/a
President: Guy Rossatanga–Rignault

National bibliography, books in print, and book trade directories

525 **Bibliographie nationale du Gabon.**
Libreville: Direction générale des Archives Nationales, de la Bibliothèque Nationale et de la Documentation Gabonaise [BP 1188, Libreville], 1994-?

Annually, latest is 2000?, earlier cumulation *Bibliographie du Gabon 1978 –
1993*, published 1999.
Email: ayimambe@tiggabon
Web: n/a

Books, articles, reports, and interviews

526   Mba-Zue, Nicolas **"La creation littéraire et les difficultés d'édition
au Gabon."** *Notre Librairie. Revue du Livre de l'Afrique Noire, Maghreb,
Caraïbes, Océan Indien. Littérature Gabonaise*, no. 105 (April-June 1991): 134-
136.
An interview, held in June 1988, broadcast on Radiodiffusion Télévision Gabonaise
with a group of young poets, in which they discuss problems of production,
publication, and distribution of literary works in Gabon.

527   Ngou, Honorine **"Le livre et la lecture au Gabon."** *Notre Librairie.
Revue du Livre de l'Afrique Noire, Maghreb, Caraïbes, Océan Indien. Littérature
Gabonaise*, no. 105 (April-June 1991): 126-129.
Reviews the role of books and publishing in Gabon, including a brief study of the
infrastructure of book distribution. Questions the low level of interest in reading in a
country where 95% of children attend school and suggests reform in methods of
offering books to the reading public.

528   Ondo, Rose **"Etre libraire à Libreville."** *Notre Librairie. Revue du Livre
Afrique Noire, Maghreb, Caraïbes, Océan Indien. Littérature Gabonaise*, no. 105
(April-June 1991): 130-133.
Rose Ondo interviews the managing directors of two bookshops in Libreville.

The Gambia

Associations and book-related organizations

529   Association of Gambian Writers
c/o Hassum Ceesay
National Council for Arts and Culture
PO Box 151
Banjul
The Gambia
Tel.: +220-229730
Email: hassum.ceesay@yahoo.com
Web: n/a
Secretary: Hassum Ceesay

National bibliography, books in print, and book trade directories

530 **The Gambia National Bibliography.**
Banjul: The Gambia National Library [Reg Pye Lane, Banjul], 1979-
Annual, latest is cumulative volume 1996-2000, published in 2001.
Email: national.library@qanet.gm
Email: n/a
Web: n/a

Books, articles, reports, and interviews

531 Kamm, Anthony **Book Development. The Gambia**. Paris: UNESCO
(FMR/CC/DBA/77/102; RP/1975-76/4.141.3/End-of-assignment report),
1977. 15 pp.
An early ➔ **UNESCO (118)** mission report about book development, reading
promotion, textbook production, use of vernacular languages, and curriculum
development in the Gambia [in the late 1970s].

532 Mbye, Abdou **"The Book Chain in The Gambia."** In *The Book Chain in
Anglophone Africa. A Survey and Directory*, edited by Roger Stringer. Oxford:
International Network for the Availability of Scientific Publications (INASP),
2002, 35-40.
Online: http://www.inasp.info/file/57/the-book-chain-in-anglophone-
africa-a-survey-and-directory.html [26/02/08]
One in a series of useful country surveys and overviews – each prepared by a book
professional from the country concerned – that review the state of the book, and the
major players in the "book chain", in English-speaking African countries. Each
country survey covers printing, book publishing, bookselling and distribution,
library services, professional associations, book promotional bodies and book
promotional events, training for the book professions, as well as examining some of
the major issues as they relate to book development, such as languages, literacy,
writers and writing, the reading habit, and national book policies. For each country
this is supported by an annotated directory of government ministries, professional
associations, book publishers, booksellers and distributors, printers, major libraries,
and training institutions, with full address and contact details.

533 N'Jie, S.P.C. **"Republic of The Gambia."** In *The Book Trade of the
World, vol. IV: Africa*, edited by Sigfred Taubert and Peter Weidhaas. Munich:
K.G. Saur, 1984, 122-124.
Overview of publishing and the book trade in The Gambia. Now very dated.

Ghana

Associations and book-related organizations

534   CopyGhana
Copyright Society of Ghana (COSGA)
Copyright Office
Private Mail Bag
Ministries Post Office
Accra
Ghana
Tel: +233-21-2122 4282
Fax: +233-21-2122 4282
Email: Copyghana_2004@hotmail.com
Web:
http://www.ifrro.org/show.aspx?pageid=members/rrodetails&memberid
=18
Chair: Kwami Segbawu
Managing Director: Ben Nyadzi

535   Ghana Association of Writers
PO Box 4414
Accra
Ghana
Tel.: +223-21-776586
Email: n/a
Web: http://www.geocities.com/ghana_association_of_writers [pages not
accessible 26/02/08]
Acting Administrator: Rex Quartey

536   Ghana Book Development Council (GBDC)
PO Box M430
Ministry Branch Post Office
Accra
Ghana
Tel: +233-21-229178 Fax: +233-21-300567
Email: use email form on Web site
Web: http://www.edughana.net/bookdevelopment.htm
Executive Director: Agnes van Dyck

537   Ghana Booksellers Association (GBA)
c/o University Bookshop
P.O. Box LG, 1 Legon, Ghana

Tel: +233 21 500398
Fax: +233 21 500774
Email: bookshop@ug.edu.gh
President: Emmanuel Tonyigah

538   Ghana Book Publishers Association (GBPA)
PO Box LT 471
Lartebiokorshie
Accra
Ghana
Tel: +233-21-220107 Fax: +233-21-220271
Email: stevebrob@yahoo.co.uk
Web: n/a
President: Elliot Agyare elliotagyare@yahoo.co.uk
Executive Secretary: Stephen Brobbey

539   Ghana Book Trust (GBT)
PO Box LG 536
Legon
Accra
Ghana
Tel: + 233-21-502495/+233-244-38829 Fax: + 233-21-502495
Email: gbt@africaonline.com.gh
Web: http://www.ghana-book-trust.org/
Executive Director: Robert K. Amoako rkamoako@netscape.net

540   Ghana Section of IBBY
c/o Ghana Library Board
PO Box 663
Accra
Fax: +233-21-247768
Liaison Officer: Susannah Minyilla

541   The Writers Fund
[no postal address provided on Web site]
Accra
Ghana
Tel: n/a
Email: info@thewritersfund.org
Web: http://www.thewritersfund.org/
Secretary: Nii Ayikwei Parkes

National bibliography, books in print, and book trade directories

542 Appiah-Padi, Stephen K. **"Who is Who in the Ghana Book Industry."**
Ghana Book World, no. 5 (1991): 60-70.
A who's who of people involved [as at 1991] in the book professions in Ghana, including those at the Ghana Book Development Council, the Ghana Association of Writers, Ghana Printers and Paper Converters Association, Ghana Association of Book Designers and Illustrators, Ghana Book Publishers Association, Ghana Booksellers Association, and the Children's Literature Foundation.

543 Crabbe, Richard, ed. **Ghana Book Publishers Association Catalogue.**
Volume 1, no. 1, 1993/94- Biennial [no further eds. published?] Accra:
Ghana Book Publishers Association, 1994.
Was promised for publication every other year, but no further editions have apparently been published since this initial volume for 1993/94, which listed over 300 titles from 20 Ghanaian publishers, arranged alphabetically by publisher, and indexed by author and title.

544 **Ghana National Bibliography.**
Accra: Ghana Library Board, George Padmore Research Library on African Affairs [PO Box 2970, Accra], 1965-
Annual, latest is 1992.
Email: Padmoresl@yahoo.com.uk
Web: http://www.ghana.com.gh/padmore [pages not accessible 26/02/08]

Books, articles, reports, and interviews

545 Alemna, Anaba A. **"The Ghana National Book Congress."** *The*
African Book Publishing Record 17, no. 3 (1991): 205-206.
Reports on a National Book Congress held in Accra in March 1991 organized by the Ghana Ministry of Information and other government departments, with the theme "Books are vital to national development" and attracting participants from all sections of the "book chain". Includes summaries of the papers presented, and a set of recommendations put forward for consideration by the government.

546 Alemna, Anaba A. **"The Book Chain in Ghana."** In *The Book Chain in*
Anglophone Africa. A Survey and Directory, edited by Roger Stringer. Oxford:
International Network for the Availability of Scientific Publications (INASP),
2002, 41-44.
Online: http://www.inasp.info/file/57/the-book-chain-in-anglophone-
africa-a-survey-and-directory.html [26/02/08]
One in a series of useful country surveys and overviews – each prepared by a book professional from the country concerned – that review the state of the book, and the major players in the "book chain", in English-speaking African countries. Each country survey covers printing, book publishing, bookselling and distribution, library services, professional associations, book promotional bodies and book

promotional events, training for the book professions, as well as examining some of the major issues as they relate to book development, such as languages, literacy, writers and writing, the reading habit, and national book policies. For each country this is supported by an annotated directory of government ministries, professional associations, book publishers, booksellers and distributors, printers, major libraries, and training institutions, with full address and contact details.

547 Andrew, Jeff **Ghana Publishing Market Profile 2002.** London: The Publishers Association and The British Council, 2002. 36 pp. (accessible by purchase only for non-PA members/GPI subscribers, cost £50) http://www.publishers.org.uk/en/home/market_reports_and_statistics/g pi/reports/html_reports/ghana_publishing_market_profile_2002/ (table of contents only)
An analysis of the book markets in Ghana, providing general background, details of the education system, together with overviews of the general, academic and professional, and school book markets, and supported by a range of appendices and tables. [Not examined]

548 Anon. **Ghanaian Private Sector Case Story: Ms. Akoss Ofori-Mensah – Sub Saharan Publishers**
http://www.ambaccra.um.dk/NR/rdonlyres/B4A20215-5C90-420B-9791-48CBC04C1ECE/0/GhanaianPrivateSectorcasestorySubSaharanPublishers.p df [26/02/08]
A profile of Akoss Ofori-Mensah, founder of Sub-Saharan Publishers in Accra, which she established in 1998. The company – which has benefited from the ➔ **Danida (56)** Business Sector Programme Support sponsored BUSAC fund – specializes in publishing high-quality children's books, primarily picture-story books and textbooks.

549 Bortey, Emmanuel **"The Future of Publishing in Ghana."** *Ghana Book World*, no. 4 (1988): 8-12.
Reflects on the future of publishing in Ghana from the perspective of a publisher and identifies the need for policy makers to liberalize the textbook market in order to encourage entrepreneurs to enter into the publishing arena.

550 Bureau of Ghana Languages **The Bureau of Ghana Languages at a Glance.** Accra: Bureau of Ghana Languages [PO Box 1851], 1996. 26 pp.
A short history of the Bureau of Ghana Languages and its role in publishing books in 11 Ghanaian languages. Includes some photographs of current and past members of staff.

551 Cabutey-Adodoadji, E. **"Book Development and Publishing in Ghana: An Appraisal."** *Libri* 34, no. 2 (1984): 48-53.
Reviews the situation in the book trade and provides a history of the development of publishing in Ghana. Examines the constraints which affect the publishing industry in Ghana and makes suggestions for strengthening the book industries.

552 Crabbe, Richard A.B. **"The Transition to Privatization in Publishing: Ghana's Experience."** In *The Challenge of the Market: Privatization and Publishing in Africa,* edited by Philip G. Altbach. Chestnut Hill, MA: Bellagio Publishing Network, Research and Information Center (Bellagio Studies in Publishing, 7), 1996, 29-46.
Another version in In *Educational Publishing in Global Perspective. Capacity Building and Trends,* edited by Shobhana Sosale. Washington, DC: The World Bank, 1998, 71-85.
Sets out some of the issues involved in the transition from state-controlled to private sector publishing, drawing on the experience in Ghana. The author examines how publishers have adapted to these changes, and looks at factors such as financing and profitability of publishing, the development of a national book policy, publishing capacity, training of book industry personnel, the role of book trade associations, distribution, library services in the country, publishing in local languages, and the question of donor agency support. Concludes with a range of guidelines and "a checklist for privatizing the book industry", setting out the components that the author believes are essential integral parts in the growth of a thriving indigenous publishing industry.

553 Darko-Ampem, Kwasi **"Publishing for Secondary Education in Ghana: A Policy Review."** *Bellagio Publishing Network Newsletter,* no. 31 (November 2002): 19-23.
Online:
http://www.bellagiopublishingnetwork.com/newsletter31/darko-ampem.htm [27/02/08]
A condensed version of a paper presented to International Standing Conference for the History of Education ISCHE XXIV Paris, July 10-13, 2002. The author stresses the link between publishing and education, especially in developing societies like Africa, and the book as the traditional medium for the distribution of information, ideas, education and culture. The main theme of the paper is the new Ghana government policy aimed at private sector participation in the growth and development of the country; and in particular, the recent government announcement that the Ministry of Education has ceased to be its own publisher and distributor. Since its establishment in 1976, the → **Ghana Book Publishers Association (538)** has expressed serious concerns about the continued involvement of the Curriculum Research and Development Division of the Ministry of Education in the writing of school textbooks. The context of this new policy framework, in the overall development of the school textbook market, is reviewed, and its implications for both the local publishing industry and the entire educational system, especially at the secondary school level. The author recommends the implementation of a comprehensive national book policy to address this vital but often neglected sector of development, and emphasizes the need for a holistic approach to the development of the local book industries, beyond the provision of school books alone.

554 Dekutsey, Woeli **"Ghana: a Case Study in Publishing Development."** *Logos. The Journal of the World Book Community* 4, no. 2 (1993): 66-72.

Online: http://www.atypon-
link.com/LOG/doi/pdf/10.2959/logo.1993.4.2.66
A critical analysis of the growth and development of the Ghanaian book industries,
examining, production, training, marketing and the role of book trade associations.
Describes the posture of publishing in Ghana today [as at 1993] as "Becketian. They
are waiting. For what? Some kind of miracle which will rouse them from the passive
and tame state to which their fruitless struggles against political, social and economic
obstacles have reduced them?" The author believes the future lies in the hands of the
private sector. The three big government-sponsored publishing houses – the Ghana
Publishing Corporation, the Ghana Universities Press, and the Bureau of Ghanaian
Languages – have been around for years. But owing to financial constraints,
unwittingly imposed on them by government, their impact on the public psyche has
not been greatly felt. Meantime younger private houses are carving market niches for
themselves.

555 Dekutsey, Woeli **"Publishing in Ghana."** In *Development Directory of
Indigenous Publishing 1995*, compiled by Carol Priestley. Harare: African
Publishers Network, 1995, 66-67.
A brief overview of the book industries in Ghana [as at 1995], and the major
constraints they face.

556 Djoleto, Amu **"Publishing in Ghana: Aspects of Knowledge and
Development."** In *Publishing in the Third World*, edited by Philip G. Altbach,
Amadio A. Arboleda, and S. Gopinathan. London: Mansell Publishing Ltd.,
1985, 76-86.
The former Director of the ➜ **Ghana Book Development Council (536)** narrates the
development of publishing in Ghana, commencing with a historical overview,
thereafter providing a statistical, quantitative and qualitative picture, and concluding
with a look at the future prospects for publishing in Ghana.

557 Djoleto, Amu **"State of the Ghana Book Industry."** *Ghana Book
World*, no. 4 (1988): 1-6.
A critical assessment of the Ghanaian book industries in the 1980s.

Hasan, Abul **Developing Human Resources of the Book Industry in West
Africa** see ➜ **Section 5, Book industry training/Self-publishing: Articles
and reports** entry **2433**

558 Jenkins, Ray **"Intellectuals, Publications Outlets and 'Past-
Relationships'. Some Observations on the Emergence of Early Gold
Coast/Ghanaian Historiography in the Cape Coast, Accra and Akropong
'Triangle': c. 1880-1917."** In *Self-Assertion and Brokerage: Early Cultural
Nationalism in West Africa*, edited by P.F. de Moraes Farias and Karin Barber.
Birmingham: Centre of West African Studies, 1990, 68-77.
[Not examined]

559 Nimako, Annor **"Republic of Ghana."** In *The Book Trade of the World, vol. IV: Africa*, edited by Sigfred Taubert and Peter Weidhaas. Munich: K.G. Saur, 1984, 125-138.
Overview of publishing and the book trade in Ghana. Now very dated.

560 Nimako, Annor **"The State of the Book Industry in Ghana."** *Ghana Book World*, no. 5 (1991):1-8.
Highlights the difficulties of establishing and successfully managing indigenous book publishing houses, whilst asserting that this very industry "remains the backbone of the nation's literacy, educational and literary programmes."

561 Nyarko, Kwame **"Some Aspects of the Book Trade in Ghana."** *The African Book Publishing Record* 6, no.3/4 (1980): 241-246.
While very dated, this remains a useful survey of the foundations of the book trade in Ghana, "the sporadic nature of its growth", the activities of some Ghanaian publishing houses in the 1980s, the problems facing the industry, and the author's assessment of the prospects for the future.

562 Nyarko, Kwame **"The Book Industry in Ghana."** *Ghana Library Journal* 6, no.1 (1988): 9-19.
To some extent an update of the previous entry (*see* ➜ **561**). Discusses printing, publishing and bookselling in Ghana, and offers some suggestions for the future development of the industry.

563 Ofei, Eric **"The State of Publishing in Ghana Today."** *Bellagio Publishing Network Newsletter*, no. 20 (Autumn 1997): 14-17.
Online:
http://www.bellagiopublishingnetwork.com/newsletter20/ofei.htm
[27/02/08]
Presents a synopsis of the current [1997] state of publishing in Ghana, reviewing the country's national book policy, its educational structures, the government's involvement in book publishing, financing for publishing ventures, publishing capacity, piracy, and the role of the ➜ **Ghana Book Publishers Association (538)**.

564 Ofori-Mensah, Akoss **"Book Scheme for Basic Schools in Ghana."** Bellagio Publishing Network Newsletter, no. 26-27 (November 2000): 19-21. Online: http://www.bellagiopublishingnetwork.com/newsletter2627/ofori-mensah.htm [27/02/08]
Faced with rapidly declining standards of education at the basic level, in 1998 the British government provided a grant of £53 million to the Ghana Ministry of Education to rehabilitate the basic education system, and the Ministry decided to use £8.5 million to buy supplementary readers for the primary schools to revamp reading habits among children. Both local and foreign publishers submitted titles for consideration, and some four million books were subsequently purchased including one million local language books. Sixty per cent of the books came from British publishers and 40 per cent from local publishers. Payment was prompt. The author

provides an account of the implementation of the scheme, which was rated as a very considerable success for all parties involved. However, the distribution aspect, getting the books into the hands of teachers and pupils in 11,000 public primary schools, proved to be a tough assignment.

Guinea

Associations and book-related organizations

565   Association des Editeurs du Guinée
BP 542
Conakry
Guinea
Tel: +224-60 21 23 50 Fax: +224-30 46 35 07
Email: ganndal@mirinet.net.gn
Web: n/a
Chair: Mamadou Aliou Sow

566   Club des Amis du Livre (CAL)
Maison des Jeunes et de la Culture de Gbessia Centre
5943 Conakry
Guinea
Tel: +224-60 54 19 97/60 26 08 94
Email: clubdesamisdulivre@yahoo.fr
Director: Elisée Fassou Kolié fassouseny@yahoo.fr

567   Division Livre et Lecture publique
Ministère de la Jeunesse, des Sports et de la Culture
BP 5122
Conakry
Guinea
Tel: +224-452232 Fax: + 224-452931/411926
Email: 3p-plus@mirinet.net.gn
Directeur national adjoint de la Culture: Muhamed Salifou Keita

National bibliography, books in print, and book trade directories

568   Bibliographie nationale de Guinée.
Conakry: Bibliothèque nationale [BP 139, Conakry], 1985-
Annual, latest is 1988?
Email: n/a
Web: n/a

Books, articles, reports, and interviews

569   Anon. **"Mamadou Aliou Sow, un editeur Guinéen à la tête de l'APNET."**
Takam Tikou. Le Bulletin de la Joie par les Livres, no. 10 (Février 2003): 17-20.
An interview with the former Chair of the ➔ **African Publishers Network (5),** who is also Managing Director of Editions Ganndal in Guinea. Some of the issues discussed include children's book publishing, and publishing in African languages.

570   Marsaud, Olivia **L'édition africaine, entre déboires et espoirs Le secteur peine encore à s'organiser.** *Afrikcom* 16 January 2004.
http://www.afrik.com/article6950.html [28/02/08]
An interview with Guinean publisher Aliou Sow on the problems and challenges facing the African book industries.

Seck, Camara Sarang, and Nabé Mohamed **"L'édition scientifique en Guinée"** *see* ➔ **Section 4, Studies by topic: Scientific, technical and medical publishing** entry **2358**

571   Sow, Mamadou Aliou **"Book Publishing in Guinea."** In *Development Directory of Indigenous Publishing 1995,* compiled by Carol Priestley. Harare: African Publishers Network, 1995, 68-69.
A brief account of the still limited publishing activities in Guinea, a country which thus far has only a small number private sector publishing houses.

572   Sow, Mamadou Aliou **"A Guinean Perspective - Book Publishing and Distribution."** *Bellagio Publishing Network Newsletter,* no. 23 (October 1998): 11-12
http://www.bellagiopublishingnetwork.com/newsletter23/sow.htm [28/02/08]
Offers a short history of publishing in Guinea, and describes the birth of a national book sector brought about by the liberalization of the economy, the current socio-economic environment for publishing, and the launching, in May 1998, of a national professional network comprising all the partners involved in book publishing and distribution.

573   Sow, Mamadou Aliou **Guinée: édition et diffusion du livre**
Médiafriq'. Le Magazine des médias et de la Communication en Afrique, no. 1 (October-December 1997): 28-29.
Also published online in *Mots Pluriels,* no. 5 (1998)
http://motspluriels.arts.uwa.edu.au/MP598mas.html [28/02/08]
Essentially the same article (in French) of the preceding entry (*see* ➔ **572**).

Guinea Bissau

Books, articles, reports, and interviews

574   Lopes, Carlos **"Publishing and Visibility in Guinea-Bissau (2002-2005)."** *Africa Review of Books* 1, no. 2 (December 2005): 3-5.
Online: http://www.codesria.org/Links/Publications/arb_dec05/lopes.pdf [14/01/08]
An account of the development of (primarily) academic and institutional publishing in Guinea Bissau, and the attempts made by Portuguese-speaking African academics to achieve more visibility for their work in the Portuguese-speaking world and elsewhere.

Miranda, Maria Filomena Ribeiro **"L'édition scientifique en Guinée-Bissau"** *see* ➜ **Section 4, Studies by topic: Scientific, technical and medical publishing** entry **2350**

Kenya

Associations and book-related organizations

575   **Children's Literature Association of Kenya (CLAK)**
c/o Lake Publishers and Enterprises
PO Box 1743
Kisumu
Kenya
Tel: +254-35-22291 Fax: +254-35-22291/22707
Email: gadod@swiftkisumu.com
Web: http://www.aboleodaga.com/
Contact: Asenath Bole Odaga

576   **Christian Booksellers and Publishers of Kenya**
c/o Evangel Publishing House
Private Bag 28963
00200 Nairobi
Kenya
Tel: +254-20 -8560839 Fax: +254-20-8562050
Email: publisher@evangelpublishing.org or info@evangelpublishing.org
Chair: Barine Karimi [?]
Note: not verified, organization dormant?

577   Femart-K - Kenya Women Writers' Foundation
c/o Gender and Development Centre
Impala Walk Aga Khan Road
Nairobi
Postal address:
PO Box 1588
Kisumu
Kenya
Tel/Fax: +254-35-22791
Email: gadod@arcc.or.ke
Web: n/a
Chair: n/a
Note: not verified, organization dormant?

578   Friends-of-the-Book Foundation (FBF)
PO Box 39624
Nairobi
Kenya
Tel: +254-2-251490/812413 Fax: +254-2-448753
Email: friendsb@insightkenya.com
Web: n/a
Director: (Prof) James Otiende
Note: not verified, organization dormant?

579   Kenya Booksellers and Stationers Association
PO Box 32413
Nairobi
Kenya
Tel: +254-20-580557 Fax: 254-20-8562050
Email: n/a
Chair: J.N. Mwendah
Note: not verified, organization dormant?

580   Kenya Non-Fiction Authors Association (KENFAA)
c/o Professor Chris Wanjala
Department of Literature
University of Nairobi
Education Building
Nairobi
Postal address:
PO Box 30197-00100
Nairobi 00100
Kenya

Tel: 254-020-318262 Fax: 254-020-245566
Email: dept-literature@uonbi.ac.ke or literature@uonbi.ac.ke
Web: n/a
Chair: (Prof) Christopher Wanjala cwanjala@zeinet.co.ke
Secretary: Evan Mwangi [?]

581   Kenya Publishers Association (KPA)
2nd floor Occidental Plaza
Muthithi Road Westlands
Nairobi
Postal address:
PO Box 42767
Nairobi 00100
Kenya
Tel: +254-20-375 2344/+254-20-375 4076
Email: info@kenyapublishers.org or kenyapublishers@wananchi.com
Web: http://www.kenyapublishers.org/index.html
Chair: Nancy Karimi
Executive Officer: Lillian Inziani

582   Kwani Trust
Suite 1S, 1st Floor Madonna House
Westlands Road off Mpaka Road Westlands
Nairobi
Postal address:
PO Box 2895
Nairobi
Kenya 00100
Tel: +254-20-445 1383 Fax: +254-20-4450490
Email: info@kwani.org
Web: http://www.kwani.org
Founder/Director: Binyavanga Wainaina

583   National Book Development Council of Kenya (NBDCK)
PO Box 45314
Nairobi
Kenya
Tel. 254-20-444700/442539
Email: hchakava@africaonline.co.ke
Web: http://www.nationalbookcouncil-kenya.org/ [pages not
accessible/site under construction as at 28/02/08]
Chair: Henry Chakava
Executive Officer: Attienna Okundu

584 The Reproduction Rights Society of Kenya (KOPIKEN)
PO Box 44265 GPO
00100 Nairobi
Kenya
Tel: +254-20-374 0822 Fax: +254-20-374 0836
Email: kopiken@wananchi.com
Web: http://www.kopiken.org/
Chair: Ezekiel Mutua
General Manager: Lynnette Kariuki

585 Writers Association of Kenya
Department of Literature
University of Nairobi
PO Box 30197
Nairobi 00100
Kenya
Email: dept-literature@uonbi.ac.ke
Tel.: +254-20-318262 or +254-20-318262 ext. 28070 Fax: 254-20-245566
Chair: (Prof) Henry Indangasi

National bibliography, books in print, and book trade directories

586 Kenya Books in Print 1997. Compiled and edited by the Kenya
Publishers Association. Nairobi: Kenya Publishers Association, 1997. 380 pp.
Lists almost 3,000 titles from 38 publishers, in print as at May 1997. Listings are
grouped under three principal indexes: author index, title index, and subject index.
The latter is further sub-divided into 'Pre-School Books' arranged under four sub-
sections, 'Primary Textbooks', arranged under 20 broad subject groups, 'Secondary
Textbooks' arranged under 27 subject groups, and finally 'General Books', which are
listed under some 60 subject headings, with a number of subject groupings further
sub-divided by language category. Full bibliographic data - including local prices,
and overseas prices where established - is provided in the author and title indexes,
but not in the subject index, where listings are confined to author, title and publisher.
Many publishers are indicated in abbreviated form, but a directory of publishers in
the front matter includes details of acronyms used. The publisher's directory gives
not only full name and addresses, but also telephone and fax numbers. No further
editions would appear to have been published to date.

587 Kenya National Bibliography.
Nairobi: Kenya National Library Servi
1980-
Annual, latest is 2002.
Email: knls@nbnet.co.ke
Web: http://www.knls.or.ke/publ

588   Kenya Publishers Association – Members
http://www.kenyapublishers.org/members.html [28/02/08]
A very useful set of profiles of 34 members of the ➔ **Kenya Publishers Association
(581)**, each giving full address and contact details, email address and Web site (where
available), together with images of company logos, a short description about the
history and background of each company, their core publishing activities and nature
of their list, and areas of specialization.

Books, articles, reports, and interviews

589   Andrew, Jeff Kenya Publishing Market Profile 2004. London: The
Publishers Association and The British Council, 2004. 66 pp. (accessible by
purchase only for non-PA members/GPI subscribers, cost £249)
http://www.publishers.org.uk/en/home/market_reports_and_statistics/g
pi/reports/html_reports/kenya_publishing_market_profile_2004/
(table of contents only)
An analysis of the book markets in Kenya, providing general background, details of
the education system, together with overviews of the general, academic and
professional, and school book markets, and supported by a wide range of appendices
and tables. [Not examined]

**590   Chakava, Henry "Publishing in a Multilingual Situation: The Kenya
Case."** *The African Book Publishing Record* 3, no. 2 (April 1977): 83-90.
A modified and expanded version of a paper originally presented at a ➔ **UNESCO
(118)** sponsored symposium on the publication of books in the various languages of
multilingual countries, Moscow-Alma Ata, September 1976. Discusses the problems
of a publishing industry which has to face the prospect of publishing in English,
Kiswahili and in a multitude of other African languages across the entire range of
books: educational books and those for children, religious books, mass paperbacks,
novels, reference books, and more.

591   Chakava, Henry Books and Reading in Kenya. Paris: UNESCO
(Studies on Books and Reading, 13), n.d. [1983]. 55 pp.
One of a series of national monographs on the state of books and reading in a
number of countries, in order to provide book professionals and the interested public
with detailed surveys of matters relating to authorship, publishing, material
production and distribution of books and reading. This monograph by the Managing
Director of [then] Heinemann Educational Books (East Africa) Ltd. [now East African
Educational Publishers] sets out the position of the book in Kenya: language policies,
authorship, publishing and printing, distribution, training and the legal and
institutional framework for publishing. Now inevitably rather dated, but still useful
as an overview of the emergence of indigenous publishing in Kenya.

592   Chakava, Henry **"A Decade of Publishing in Kenya: 1977-1987. One Man's Involvement."** *The African Book Publishing Record* 14, no. 4 (1988): 235-241.
Also published in *Das Recht auf den eigenen Verlag. Zeitschrift für Kulturaustausch* 41, no. 3 (1991-3): 341-354; and also reprinted in *Readings on Publishing in Africa and the Third World*, by Philip G. Altbach. Buffalo, NY: Bellagio Publishing Network, Research and Information Center (Bellagio Studies in Publishing 1), 1993, 67-73.
Henry Chakava describes his role in the development of Heinemann Educational Books (East Africa) Ltd., later to become Heinemann Kenya between 1977-1987 [and now East African Educational Publishers], discusses his personal publishing style and strategies in detail and gives a brief survey of publishing in Kenya. Relates his own involvement in publishing popular fiction and describes his experimentation (supported by statistics) with publishing creative writing, and in the translation of books into African languages.

593   Chakava, Henry **"The Role of Publishing in National Development."** *The Kenya Bookseller* 1, no. 4 (October/December 1988): 28-30.
Examines the role of the publisher in Kenya, the problem of illiteracy and how this affects national culture, reading habits in Kenya, and book distribution. Also addresses issues relating to book donations, local authorship and training. Stresses the need for a national debate on books and publishing.

594   Chakava, Henry **"Publishing in Kenya."** In *Africa Bibliography 1988*, compiled by Hector Blackhurst. Manchester: Manchester University Press, 1989, vi-xiv.
Begins with a survey of the available literature on publishing in Kenya and follows with a historical overview of the printed word in Kenya. Describes the objectives of the East African Literature Bureau when it was set up in 1948 and the arrival of multinational publishers OUP and Longman. Examines the changes which took place in publishing after independence in 1963 and the proliferation of multinational publishing houses in Kenya at that time. Gives a detailed analysis of titles which were in demand during the 1970s and 1980s. Notes the subsequent drop in publishing output by indigenous Kenyan publishers, and asks why the industry has not grown in any sustainable fashion since the mid-1970s. Examines the climate for Kenyan publishers in the late 1980s, and issues such as the status of children's books, language policy, and libraries. The author concludes that the future prospects are good as "the level of literacy is growing gradually and Kenyans are slowly being inculcated into book-reading and book buying."

595   Chakava, Henry **"Kenyan Publishing: Independence and Dependence."** In *Publishing and Development in the Third World*, edited by Philip G. Altbach. London: Hans Zell Publishers, 1992, 119-150.
A comprehensive discussion of the origins and development, successes and failures, and opportunities and challenges of the Kenyan book industry, which spans from the

time of Kenya's independence to the present day [1992]. Begins by discussing the state of the industry at independence, the coming of foreign publishers, the creation of new institutions and the advent of local publishers. Continues with an analysis of the present state of affairs [early 1990s] of all areas of the book sector, concluding that the percentage of books imported is still too high, and recommending strategies for reversing this trend.

596   Chakava, Henry **"Private Enterprise Publishing in Kenya: A Long Struggle for Emancipation."** *Logos. The Journal of the World Book Community* 4, no. 3 (1993): 130-135.
Online:
http://www.atypon-link.com/LOG/doi/pdf/10.2959/logo.1993.4.3.130
Presents a picture of the Kenyan publishing scene [in the mid 1990s]: the long battle of Kenyan indigenous publishers trying to get a fair share of the textbook markets, the prospects for the future for private enterprise publishing, and the transition of a former multinational company, Heinemann Kenya, into an independent, wholly African-owned firm, East African Educational Publishers.

597   Chakava, Henry **"Kenya."** In *International Book Publishing: An Encyclopedia*, edited by Philip G. Altbach and Edith S. Hoshino. New York: Garland Publishing, 1995, 384-96.
Analyzes the key issues that have changed, shaped, or influenced publishing in Kenya, in particular the period of the last decade. Provides some historical background, discusses government policies and the government's monopoly of the school book market, ownership and control, publishing output, taxation, distribution, and other factors such as illiteracy, the reading habit, and external aid.

598   Chakava, Henry **"The Laws of Literacy."** *Index on Censorship* 25, no. 2 (March/April 1996): 124-127.
Also published, in slightly revised form, as **"Publishing and State Censorship in Kenya"**, *Bellagio Publishing Network Newsletter*, no. 16 (Spring 1996): 12-14.
Examines manifestations of state censorship in Kenya, the banning of a number of publications, detention and harassment of writers, and systematic attempts to stifle creativity through curtailment of literary seminars, journals and writers' workshops; and a general lack of facilities or incentives to promote and reward academic excellence or creative talent. Chakava also argues that the creation of state publishing institutions, which are largely controlling the textbook markets, represents another subtle form of censorship.

599   Chege, John Waruingi **Copyright Law and Publishing in Kenya.** Nairobi: Kenya Literature Bureau, 1978. 160 pp.
A somewhat contentious study in which the author argues that Kenya's adherence to international copyright conventions "has made it possible for foreign publishers to have easy access to Kenya as a market for their publications", to the detriment of local publishers, and advocates that Kenya should abrogate these laws.

600 Durrani, Shiraz **Never be Silent. Publishing and Imperialism in Kenya, 1884-1963.** London & Nairobi: Vita Books [PO Box 2908, London N17 6YY], 2006. 271 pp.
A narrative of publishing in Kenya from the time of the Berlin Conference of 1884 through to the Lancaster House Conference in 1963, spanning the entire colonial period of Kenyan history. It documents publishing activities during the period, from the earliest information bulletins of the colonial settler state to the Mau Mau liberation movement publications in the 1950s and 1960s during the struggle for independence, and examines how this struggle was reflected in the communications field. Durrani offers a fresh interpretation on an important aspect of Kenyan colonial history from a working class point of view, and aims to provide a new perspective on how communications can be a powerful weapon for social justice in the hand of liberation forces. In terms of its coverage of publishing, the book is primarily concerned with newspaper publishing and magazines, the activities of small printing presses, and those of a wide variety of associations, organizations, trade unions, and nationalist movements that were part of the liberation struggle. It charts the history of these publications chronologically, and gives the full political context of each period. The book, which contains an introduction by Ngugi wa Thiong'o, is a well-documented history of the struggle of Kenyan people against British colonialism and the battle for press freedom and free expression.
Reviews:
African Studies Review vol. 50, no. 1, April 2007
Focus on International and Comparative Librarianship vol. 38, no. 1, 2007
Online: http://www.cilip.org.uk/NR/rdonlyres/F5494F41-760F-4BE5-86A7-A2CCD69B59FC/0/focus3812007.pdf [10/03/08]

E.A.E.P. 40th Anniversary. Our Life Has Just Begun *see* ➜ **Section 2, General, comparative, and regional studies, Regional studies: Africa, East** entry **338**

601 Gundu, George S. **"Publishing Problems in Kenya."** *Information Development* 6, no. 3 (July 1990): 154-157.
Reviews the historical background of publishing in Kenya before reviewing the present [1990s] situation, including the role of both indigenous and foreign firms. Discusses the major problems of a high rate of illiteracy, lack of reading habit, and insufficient number of local writers, language problems, finance, high production costs, marketing and distribution problems, as well as lack of publishing expertise and inadequate publicity. Concludes that despite this multiplicity of problems, Kenyan publishing has a bright future.

602 Hamrell, Sven, and Olle Nordberg **"Loan-Guarantee Programs for the Development of Autonomous Publishing Capacity in Kenya."** In *Publishing and Development in the Third World*, edited by Philip G. Altbach. London: Hans Zell Publishers, 1992, 421-423.
A short review of the implementation and administration of a loan-guarantee scheme for publishers in Kenya funded by the ➜ **Dag Hammarskjöld Foundation** (55).

603   Kobia, J.M. **"Publishing Educational Materials for Institutions of Higher Education in Kenya: Challenges and Prospects."** *Educator* 1, no. 1: (2006): 93-101.
[Not examined]

604   Lindfors, Bernth **"Interview: David Maillu."** *The African Book Publishing Record* 5, no. 2 (April 1979): 85-88.
Also published in *Mazungumzo: Interviews with East African Writers, Publishers, Editors and Scholars*, Athens: Ohio University, Center for International Studies, 1980, 64-73.
Interview with David Maillu, a popular writer in East Africa who also worked in television as an actor and as a graphic artist before setting up the publishing house Comb Books. Maillu tells how he began writing and how he got involved in publishing.

605   Lindfors, Bernth **"Interview: John Nottingham."** *The African Book Publishing Record* 5, no. 2 (April 1979): 81-85.
Also published in *Mazungumzo: Interviews with East African Writers, Publishers, Editors and Scholars* Athens: Ohio University, Center for International Studies, 1980, 111-122.
John Nottingham was the founder and Managing Director of the (now long defunct) East African Publishing House (EAPH) and, upon leaving EAPH, established Transafrica Book Distributors based in Nairobi. The interview addresses the history of EAPH, the markets for books in East Africa, and the growth in other areas of publishing.

606   Lindfors, Bernth **"Interview with Henry Chakava."** In *Mazungumzo: Interviews with East African Writers, Publishers, Editors and Scholars.* Athens: Ohio University, Center for International Studies, 1980, 3-11
Interview with the Managing Director of [then] Heinemann Educational Books based in Kenya. Investigates the impact of Heinemann on publishing and writing in East Africa, the African Writes Series, publishing in Swahili, and the future for Heinemann.

607   Makotsi, Ruth and Lily Nyariki **Publishing and Book Trade in Kenya.** Nairobi: East African Educational Publishers, 1997. 172 pp. (distributed by African Books Collective Ltd., Oxford)
Financed by the ➜ **Dag Hammarskjöld Foundation (55),** this is a major and in-depth study of the problems and obstacles encountered by the Kenyan publishing industry in the manufacture, distribution, and marketing of their books. The first four of seven chapters provide the historical background and present an overview of publishing in Kenya. Subsequent chapters deal with education, culture and publishing, the special problems of the book industries, and a concluding chapter contains a number of recommendations how some of the problems of the industry might be tackled, and which will need to be addressed by the government, NGOs and donor agencies, book industry professionals, and the general public. The volume also contains a

substantial amount of statistical and other data collected during the preparation of the study, and a series of appendixes list major publishers and active booksellers in Kenya.

Reviews:
The African Book Publishing Record vol. 27, no. 2, 1998

608   McCall, James "**Textbook Evaluation in East Africa: Some Practical Experiences**" In *Caught in the Web or Lost in the Textbook? Eighth International Conference on Learning and Educational Media,* edited by Éric Bruillard *et al.* Caen, France: IUFM de Basse-Normandie/STEF/IARTEM [186 rue de la Délivrande, 14053 Caen Cedex 04] 2006, 394-398.
Online: http://www.caen.iufm.fr/colloque_iartem/pdf/mccall.pdf [28/02/08]
An examination of the methodology used in the evaluation of textbook submissions by publishers for the Kenya Textbook Project, and the various components of evaluation criteria as they relate to content and conformity to the curriculum, writing and editorial quality, design and presentation, illustrations, suitability of the language for the intended reader, whether and how they encourage active learning, whether they promote positive social and cultural values and/or diversity, their gender responsiveness in both text and illustrations, and other significant issues. The author concludes that "the Kenyan project was judged to be a success not only because it gave teachers a choice of quality textbooks and effectively liberalised the book trade, which had previously been dominated by a state centralist publishing system. It was also judged successful because the evaluation and selection of the textbooks was based on a fair and objective system which gave no publisher or textbook a significant advantage over any other. The Kenyan project was in that respect, and in others also, a model for other publishing industries to follow."

609   McGregor, C., K. Mortimer, and T. Lisher **Study on Book Provision in Kenyan Education.** London: Overseas Development Administration/ODA, 1990. 77 pp.
[Not examined]

610   Muita, David "**Kenya Introduces National Textbook Policy.**" *Bellagio Publishing Network Newsletter,* no. 23 (October 1998): 2-3.
Online:
http://www.bellagiopublishingnetwork.com/newsletter23/muita.htm [28/02/08)
September 1998 saw the launch by the Kenyan government of a new National Policy on Textbook Publication, Procurement and Supply (*see also* entry ➜ **624**). In order to examine how far the policy will be helpful to the book industry in Kenya, the author looks back at the struggle that preceded the launch of the new policy in both colonial times and textbook policies since independence, examines the gradual move to privatization, and reviews the many benefits to be accrued by the policy shift, not only by publishers but also by the Ministry of Education and the end users.

611 Munyiri, Wilfred **"100 Years of Printing and Publishing in Kenya."**
The East African Bookseller, no. 13 (1996): 10-14.
An overview of the development of Kenya's publishing industry.

612 Nabwera, Alice **"Towards a National Book Policy: Kenya."** In
*Formulating the National Book Policy. Needs and Guidelines. Report of the
UNESCO/APPREB Sub-Regional Consultation on National Book Policy and
National Book Development Councils in South Asia.* New Delhi: Afro-Asian
Book Council, 1994, 46-51.
Calls for more active cooperation between the government and among all the
different elements that make up the book industry in Kenya; and for the
establishment of a pro-active book development council to provide direction for the
formation of a national book policy.

613 Ndegwa, John **Printing and Publishing in Kenya: An Outline of
Development.** London: Standing Conference on Library Materials on
Africa, n.d. [1974]. 28 pp.
An essay prepared as part of an MA dissertation in librarianship at University
College London, by the [then] Librarian of the University of Nairobi. Outlines the
history of printing and publishing in Kenya from the missionary and early
newspaper printing period, the beginning of commercial publishing and the
situation of commercial publishing, through to the situation in Kenya in the 1970s.
Although published over thirty years ago, this study remains a useful resource on
the history of publishing and the press in Kenya.

614 Nyariki, Lily, and R. A. Hadao, eds. **UNESCO/CREPLA Seminar on
National Book Distribution Strategies in Rural Kenya : 22nd-26th
September, 1986, Kisumu-Kenya, Final Report.** Nairobi: UNESCO Nairobi
Office, 1986. 147 pp.
[Not examined]

615 Nyariki, Lily **"Publishing in Kenya."** In *Livres et résaux
documentaries/Publishing and Libraries' Cooperation*…edited by Régine
Fontaine and François-G. Barbier Wiesser. Paris: Ministère des Affaires
étrangères DCCID/CCF/CE. Sous-direction de la cooperation culturelle et
artistique. Division de l'écrit et des médiathèques, 2002, 43-46.
A short overview of the publishing scene in Kenya [as at 2002], with some
discussions about possible areas of co-operation between different players in the
book sector, and stressing the need for more research needed to study reading habits
in Kenya.

616 Odini, Cephas **"The Book Chain in Kenya."** In *The Book Chain in
Anglophone Africa. A Survey and Directory*, edited by Roger Stringer. Oxford:
International Network for the Availability of Scientific Publications (INASP),
2002, 45-49.

Online: http://www.inasp.info/pubs/bookchain/profiles/Kenya.html
[28/02/08]
One in a series of useful country surveys and overviews – each prepared by a book professional from the country concerned – that review the state of the book, and the major players in the "book chain", in English-speaking African countries. Each country survey covers printing, book publishing, bookselling and distribution, library services, professional associations, book promotional bodies and book promotional events, training for the book professions, as well as examining some of the major issues as they relate to book development, such as languages, literacy, writers and writing, the reading habit, and national book policies. For each country this is supported by an annotated directory of government ministries, professional associations, book publishers, booksellers and distributors, printers, major libraries, and training institutions, with full address and contact details.

617 Okwanya, Fred Ojienda **"Publishing in Kenya."** In *Publishing in the Third World*, edited by Philip G. Altbach, Amadio A. Arboleda, and S. Gopinathan. London: Mansell Publishing Ltd., 1985, 87-95.
A short review of publishing in Kenya, by one of the country's small indigenous publishers in the mid-1980s, focusing on education, and Kenya's relationships with regional and international publishers.

618 Otike, J.N. **"Bibliographical Control in Kenya."** *Information Development*, no. 5 (January 1989): 23-28.
Includes an examination of the current state of publishing in Kenya, and comments on the need for a national coordinating body in publishing.

619 Pala, Francis Otieno **"Republic of Kenya."** In *The Book Trade of the World, vol. IV: Africa*, edited by Sigfred Taubert and Peter Weidhaas. Munich: K.G. Saur, 1984, 154-161.
Overview of publishing and the book trade in Kenya. Now very dated.

620 Pontefract, Caroline and Nereah Were **"Towards a Unified Textbook System in Kenya."** *Bellagio Publishing Network Newsletter*, no. 26-27 (November 2000): 21-23.
Online: http://www.bellagiopublishingnetwork.com/newsletter26-27/pontefract.htm [28/02/08]
The supply of textbooks to Kenyan schools over the last 20 years has been affected by many national policy changes and the social and economic situation. Now, with the support of donor partners, the country is moving towards a unified system of textbook provision that involve key stakeholders at all levels. The authors review the new national system of textbook procurement (launched by the government in 1998), which is underpinned by key principles of book trade liberalization, school selection, accountability, equity and participation. With the ongoing support of all the key stakeholders, "Kenya will be well on the way to achieving a unified approach to the provision of textbooks in its primary schools."

621   Pugliese, Cristiana **Author, Publisher and Gikuyu Nationalist.**
The Life and Writings of Gakaara wa Wanjau. London: University of
London, 1993. PhD thesis.
Available in published form in the Bayreuth African Studies Series no. 37, *see* entry
➜ **622** below.

622   Pugliese, Cristiana **Author, Publisher and Gikuyu Nationalist: The**
Life and Writings of Gakaara wa Wanjau. Bayreuth, Germany: Universität
Bayreuth (Bayreuth African Studies Series, 37), 1995. 240 pp.
Earlier edition, Nairobi: IFRA, 1995.
The prominent Kenyan writer Ngugi wa Thiong'o drew international critical
attention to the importance for African writers to write in African languages. Gakaara
wa Wanjau proceeded Ngugi as a writer, a political activist and detainee for the cause
of Gikuyu language, literature, and culture. As a writer, educationist, editor, and
publisher Gakaara wa Wanjau – who was the joint winner, in 1984, of the ➜ **Noma**
Award for Publishing in Africa (98) – advocated a language policy that made him
politically suspect before and after independence. His work is presented here in the
wider political context of colonialism and neo-colonialism in Kenya. Based on the
thesis in the preceding entry, *see* ➜ **621**.

623   Rotich, Daniel Chebutuk **Publishing and Distribution of Educational**
Books in Kenya: A Study of Market Liberalisation and Book
Consumption. London, Reading, Slough: Thames Valley University, 2000.
PhD thesis.
[Not examined]

624   Rotich, Daniel Chebutuk **"Textbook Publishing in Kenya Under a**
New Policy on School Textbook Procurement." *Publishing Research*
Quarterly 16, no. 2 (June 2000): 60-72.
Addresses the implications for textbook publishing in Kenya under a new policy on
textbook procurement launched by the government in September 1998. The main aim
of the policy was to transform a largely government run publishing system by
liberalizing the textbook market through private sector participation, and thus to give
schools and parents the freedom to choose the books to be used in their schools.
However, with the continuing reduction in government textbook expenditure, the
author questions whether parents will have enough purchasing power to buy books.
He argues that the intensity of marketing to schools and parents will have to be
stepped up by publishers if they are to succeed in the now more competitive market
place.

625   Rotich, Daniel Chebutuk **"The Affordability of School Textbooks in**
Kenya. Consumer Experiences in the Transformation to a Liberalising
Economy."
Nordic Journal of African Studies 13, no. 2 (2004): 175–187.
Online: http://www.njas.helsinki.fi/ [29/02/08]

The growth of educational publishing in Kenya depends heavily on the disposable income of its customers. This article looks at the incomes of both actual and potential customers, and how they prioritize their spending. The findings are based on extensive research carried out by the author between 1997 and 2000 (*see also* entry **624** above), revised and updated in 2003. In selecting the areas to conduct the research, socio-economic factors, geographical conditions and level of development were considered. It was found that most textbook purchasers think that textbooks are very expensive in comparison with their income levels. The study also demonstrated that the rate at which textbook prices increase is higher than the increase in income levels, and, as a result, there will always be a shortage of textbooks in schools, and in the homes of consumers as they will always choose their own priorities: "Textbooks will always be the last of the priorities of most Kenyans, as they will search for the essential commodities of life first. Although the government is planning to purchase textbooks for primary schools, the problem will still persist as the books bought for use in schools will be only the recommended textbooks, while parents will still be buying supplementary textbooks."

626   Rotich, Daniel Chebutuk, and Joseph Musakali "**Evaluation and Selection of School Textbooks in Kenya: The Role of the Ministerial Textbook Vetting Committee."** In *Caught in the Web or Lost in the Textbook? Eighth International Conference on Learning and Educational Media,* edited by Éric Bruillard *et al.* Caen, France: IUFM de Basse Normandie/STEF/IARTEM [186 rue de la Délivrande, 14053 Caen Cedex 04] 2006, 349-360.
Online:
http://www.caen.iufm.fr/colloque_iartem/pdf/chebutukrotich_musakali. pdf [29/02/08]
Examines the processes of evaluation and approval of suitable textbooks submitted by publishers in Kenya in accordance with the requirements and timetable established for the procedures by the Ministry of Education and the Kenya Institute of Education (KIE). Various documents were analyzed in the preparation of this study, including the issues of approved lists of textbooks for primary and secondary schools (2003 to 2005), the guidelines on production of textbooks, the actual textbooks, and other related documents. "The justification for analyzing these materials was three-fold, first, to understand what publishers are required to produce and submit to KIE; secondly to evaluate what publishers produced after the evaluation exercise, and finally to compare the number of textbooks that are recommended from the categories of publishers: the local private sector publishers, the state owned companies, and the multinationals."

627   Salahi, Katherine "**Talking Books. Henry Chakava in Conversation with the Editor."** *Bellagio Publishing Network Newsletter*, no. 21 (December 1997): 14-16.
Online:
http://www.bellagiopublishingnetwork.com/newsletter21/salahi2.htm [29/02/08]

An interview with Henry Chakava, one of Africa's foremost indigenous publishers and Chairman of East African Educational Publishers Ltd., which was formerly Heinemann Kenya, and before that Heinemann Educational Books East Africa Ltd. Chakava talks about his training for publishing and his professional career, the transition from being a subsidiary of Heinemann UK to being an independent; what he sees as the pre-requisites for a successful African publisher, the role of international agencies in Africa, and the role of the multinationals, of which he says: "I'm a product of the multinationals. Many of the people who have had a good impact on publishing in Africa have also had that background, so it's really the kind of relationship one has with the multinationals that counts. If it's purely exploitative, then it doesn't work. But if there is some kind of partnership which involves transfer of skills, than that is something I would encourage. Unfortunately some multinationals don't think like that. But some do."

628   Salahi, Katherine "**Serah Mwangi Interviewed by the Editor.**"
Bellagio Publishing Network Newsletter, no. 22 (July 1998): 15-17.
Online:
http://www.bellagiopublishingnetwork.com/newsletter22/salahi2.htm
[29/02/08]
An interview with Serah Mwangi, founder and Managing Director of Focus Publications Ltd., Nairobi.

629   Shibanda, G. "**The Structure of the Publishing Industry in Kenya.**"
African Journal of Library, Archives and Information Science 4, no. 1 (April 1994): 69-72.
Examines the factors which influence the development of publishing industry in Kenya; discusses the pattern of publishing focusing on five different categories of organizations involved, and analyzes the ratio of indigenous Kenyan to foreign imprints.

630   Waruingi, Gachege "**The Indigenous African Publisher: The Kenya Perspective.**" In *Development Directory of Indigenous Publishing 1995*, compiled by Carol Priestley. Harare: African Publishers Network, 1995, 70-73.
Traces the development of indigenous publishing houses in Kenya, a "road marked more by tombstones than milestones", and examines some of the factors which have contributed to the demise or poor performance of a number of Kenyan publishers.

Lesotho

Associations and book-related organizations

631   Leshotho Booksellers Association
c/o Morija Sesuto Book Depot
PO Box 4
Morija 190
Lesotho
Tel.: +266-360810 Fax: +266-360204
Email: n/a
Chair: E. T. Lengoasa

632   Lesotho Publishers Association (LPA)
c/o Morija Museum & Archives
PO Box 4
Morija 190
Lesotho
Tel.: +266-22-360204
Email: mam.letsie@nul.ls
Web: n/a
President: Paul Motlatsi Morolong
Secretary: (Mrs) Maitumeleng Mochochoko

633   Lesotho Writers Association
National University of Lesotho
PO Roma 180
Roma
Lesotho
Tel: +266 340601 Fax: +266 340000
Email: I.ranko@nul.ls
Web: n/a
Chair: (Professor) Z. A. Mats'ela

National bibliography, books in print, and book trade directories

634   Lesothana: An Annotated Bibliography of New and Newly Located Lesotho Materials.
Roma: National University of Lesotho, Institute of Southern African Studies [PO Box 180, Roma], 1982-
Irregular, latest is no. 8, 1986.
Email: t.khalanyane@nul.ls
Web: http://www.nul.ls/institutes/isas.htm
Note: this is not national bibliography, but serves as a substitute.

Books, articles, reports, and interviews

635   Aime, Albert, and John Overton **"The Textbook Project in Lesotho."** In *Textbooks in the Developing World: Economic and Educational choices,* edited by J.Farrell and S. Heyneman. Washington, DC: The World Bank, 1989, 173-184.
[Not examined]

636   Djoleto, S.A. Amu **Establishhment of the Lesotho Book Development Council.** Paris: UNESCO (Restricted Technical Report RP/1984-1985/111.3.1), 1985. 36 pp.
Online: http://unesdoc.unesco.org/images/0006/000695/069523eo.pdf [11/03/08]
A ➔ **UNESCO (118)** mission report to assist the Government of Lesotho in the establishment of a National Council for Book Development; to advise the government on the objectives and functioning of such a Council, to assist in the drafting of the Council's constitution and advise on its staff and budget; and to assist in the preparation of a detailed work plan of the Council as well as its administrative and management plan.

637   Mairot, F. **"The Economics of Publishing in Lesotho."** In *Book Promotion and the Sharing of Resources in Africa,* edited by K. Bonde *et al.* Maseru: Lesotho Library Association, 1980, 8-16.
Discusses the steps involved in the production of a book, describing a group of potential authors in Lesotho, the readers, publishers, printer and booksellers. Also gives a detailed analysis of the publishing activities of the Mazenod Institute, and its policies for costings, book pricing, and relations with its authors.

638   Morija Press Board **"Kingdom of Lesotho."** In *The Book Trade of the World, vol. IV: Africa,* edited by Sigfred Taubert and Peter Weidhaas. Munich: K.G. Saur, 1984, 162-164.
Overview of publishing and the book trade in Lesotho. Now very dated.

639   Morolong, Paul Motlatsi **"Indigenous and Modern Book Sector Development and the Economics of Publishing in Lesotho."** *ISBN Review* 17 (1996): 175-184.
One in a series of overview articles in a special issue of *ISBN Review* focusing on the book sector in various countries of Southern Africa, and which report (for the most part) about the state of libraries, publishing and the retail book trade; current book and copyright legislation, national book policies, programmes to promote the reading habit, laws and legislation covering the book sector and copyright, activities of library and book trade professional bodies, book trade organization, training for the book industries, the use of ISBNs, and more. This particular article also provides an interesting account of the historical development of publishing in Lesotho, which started as early as 1833 with the arrival of the first missionaries from France.

640 Moshoeshoe-Chadzingwa, M.M. **"Publishing in Lesotho."** *African Publishing Review* 4, no. 4 (July/August 1995): 10-11.
A brief account of Lesotho's publishing history and recent developments. Surveys the activities of church-owned printers and publishers, multinational companies, academic publishers, government agencies, and the activities of the ➔ **Lesotho Publishers Association (632).** Concludes that "the indigenous publishing industry is still feeble."

641 Read, Anthony, *et al.* **Lesotho: Report on Institutional Reforms and Policy Development in the Provision of Textbooks, Supplementary Materials and Journals/Periodicals, Vol. 1: Institutional Development; Vol. 2, Lesotho School Survey.** Washington, DC: The World Bank, 1991.
[Not examined]

642 Sgwane, Pontso **"Lesotho Country Report on ISBN."** *ISBN Review* 17 (1996): 199-201.
A brief look at the work of the Lesotho ISBN agency and its relations with local publishers.

643 Taole, Nthabiseng **"The Book Chain in Lesotho."** In *The Book Chain in Anglophone Africa. A Survey and Directory*, edited by Roger Stringer. Oxford: International Network for the Availability of Scientific Publications (INASP), 2002, 50-52.
Online: http://www.inasp.info/file/57/the-book-chain-in-anglophone-africa-a-survey-and-directory.html [01/03/08]
One in a series of useful country surveys and overviews – each prepared by a book professional from the country concerned – that review the state of the book, and the major players in the "book chain", in English-speaking African countries. Each country survey covers printing, book publishing, bookselling and distribution, library services, professional associations, book promotional bodies and book promotional events, training for the book professions, as well as examining some of the major issues as they relate to book development, such as languages, literacy, writers and writing, the reading habit, and national book policies. For each country this is supported by an annotated directory of government ministries, professional associations, book publishers, booksellers and distributors, printers, major libraries, and training institutions, with full address and contact details.

Liberia

Books, articles, reports, and interviews

644 Cordor, Henry S. **"The Stages of Publication of Liberian Writings."** In *Towards the Study of Liberian Literature*, edited by H. Cordor. Monrovia: Liberian Literature Studies Programme, 1972, 123-136.

Includes some observations on the publishing industry and author-publisher relations.

645 Henries, Doris Banks **"Republic of Liberia."** In *The Book Trade of the World, vol. IV: Africa*, edited by Sigfred Taubert and Peter Weidhaas. Munich: K.G. Saur, 1984, 165-168.
Overview of publishing and the book trade in Liberia. Now very dated.

Note: the above two now very dated articles would appear to be the only literature on book publishing and the book trade in (until recently) war-torn Liberia. However, an excellent resource on creative activity and Liberian arts and letters, with contributions by Liberians in the diaspora and elsewhere, is the online journal *Sea Breeze. Journal of Contemporary Liberian Writings* http://www.liberiaseabreeze.com/ [01/03/08], devoted to publishing art, creative non-fiction, short fiction narratives, cultural stories, poetry, interviews, book reviews, criticism, theory, and social and political commentary by Liberians arising out of Liberian life wherever they are. The journal, founded in 2004, is published from Castro Valley, California and the complete archive of back issues is freely accessible.

Madagascar

Associations and book-related organizations

646   Centre Malgache de Promotion du Livre et de l'Art (CMPL)
9 rue Docteur Villette
Antananarivo 101
Madagascar
Tel: +261-20-222 4462 Fax: +261-20-222 4086
Email: cmpl@wanadoo.mg or cmpl@dts.mg
Web: n/a
Note: not verified, organization dormant?

647   Syndicat National des Auteurs, Éditeurs et Libraires de Madagascar (SYNAEL)
c/o Librairie Mixte
37 bis avenue du 26 juin Analakely
Antananarivo
Tel: +261-20-223 7616
Fax: +261-20-222 5130
Email: librairiemixte@wanadoo.mg or tahinar@club-internet.fr
Web: n/a
President: Aina Jean Razakasoa

648   L'Union des Poètes et Ecrivains Malgache (HAVATSA-UPEM)
45-47 Avenue de l'Indépendance Analakely
Antananarivo 0101
Madagascar
Email: n/a
http://www.havatsa.upem.frantsa.org/ (French section of HAVATSA-
UPEM)
President: Henri Rahaingoson

National bibliography, books in print, and book trade directories

649   Bibliographie nationale de Madagascar. (formerly *Bibliographie annuelle de Madagascar*)
Antananarivo: Bibliothèque universitaire d'Antananarivo / Bibliothèque nationale [BP 257, Antananarivo], 1966-
Annual, latest is 2000? Earlier cumulation, *Bibliographie nationale de Madagascar (1956-1963)*, published in 1971.
Email: bu@univ-antananarivo.mg or bu@refer.mg
Web: http://www.bu.univ.antananarivo.mg/ [page not accessible 01/03/08]

650   Bibliothèque nationale Répertoire des organismes de documentation, des maisons d'éditions, des imprimeries et des librairies de Madagascar.
Antananarivo, Bibliothèque nationale, 1985. n.p.
A directory of 772 entries, covering libraries and documention centres, publishers, printers, and booksellers.

651   Syndicat national des auteurs, éditeurs et libraires de Madagascar (SYNAEL) Annuaire du livre malgache 2007: Les livres édités à Madagascar (Ny boky rehetra nantonta teto Madagasikara). Antananarivo: SYNAEL, 2007. 150 pp.
The first edition of a national books in print for Madagascar, listing over 1,100 titles available from local publishers, published both in French and in Malagasy, covering all types of books, including those for children. Will be published annually in future.

Books, articles, reports, and interviews

652   Andriamalala, E.D. "Democratic Republic of Madagascar." In *The Book Trade of the World, vol. IV: Africa*, edited by Sigfred Taubert and Peter Weidhaas. Munich: K.G. Saur, 1984, 175-179.
Overview of publishing and the book trade in Madagascar. Now very dated.

653   Andrianombana, Alice **"Une politique à encourager."** *Revue de l'Océan Indien Madagascar*, no. 196 (October 1999): 48-50
A short account of publishing in Madagascar.

654   Rakotobe, Mamy Emmanuel **"L'écrivain et son public."** *Notre Librairie. Revue du Livre Afrique Noire, Maghreb, Caraïbes, Océan Indien. Madagascar: 2. La littérature d'expression française*, no.110 (July-September 1992): 108-110.
Reports on a programme begun in 1988 to generate interest in books and reading in people of all ages. Asks do the public read? And if so, what do they read? What do they prefer to read about? Do authors satisfy their audience? How can a reader acquire books? Concludes with a brief examination of bookselling in Madagascar and the role of libraries in book dissemination.

655   Rakotomalala, Voahangy **"Imprimer, éditer, diffuser."** *Notre Librairie. Revue du Livre Afrique Noire, Maghreb, Caraïbes, Océan Indien. Madagascar: 2. La littérature d'expression française*, no.110 (July-September 1992): 111-115.
Probes into the lack of locally produced books in Madagascar, the small number of authors, problems encountered by printers, and the absence of indigenous publishers. A brief outline of libraries and literary institutions is also provided. The author concludes that books are still just "another product" in Madagascar.

Malawi

Associations and book-related organizations

656   **Book Publishers Association of Malawi (BPAM)**
Cheshire Homes Campus (Nyambadwe)
PO Box 32653
Chichiri
Blantyre 3
Malawi
Tel: +265-1-620 810/644387
Email: bypam@africa-online.net
Web: n/a
President: James Ng'ombe
Secretary/Administrator: (Ms) Chance Mkandawire

657   **Copyright Society of Malawi (COSOMA)**
Johnstone Road
Lilongwe
Postal address:
PO Box 30784
Lilongwe 3

Malawi
Tel: +265-1-751148 Fax: +265-1-753018
Email: cosoma@sdnp.org.mw
Web: http://www.cosoma.org/
Copyright Administrator/Executive Director: Serman W. Chavula

658   Malawi Booksellers Association
PO Box 503
Blantyre
Malawi
Tel: +265 624894 Fax: +265 624894
Email: n/a
Note: not verified, organization dormant?

659   Malawi National Book Development Council
National Library Service
PO Box 30314
Lilongwe
Malawi
Tel: +265-783700 Fax: +265-781616
Email: nls@malawi.net
Web: n/a
Chair: M. Ngaunje

660   Malawi Writers' Union
PO Box 31780
Chichiri
Blantyre
Malawi
Tel: +265-650523; +265-871969
Fax: +265-650523
Email: n/a
President: n/a
Note: not verified, organization dormant?

National bibliography, books in print, and b   ~tories

661   Malawi National Bibliography.
Zomba: National Archives of Malawi [PO
Annual, latest is 2001.
Email: archives@sdnp.org.mw
Web: http://chambo.sdnp.org.mw/rule

662 National Archives of Malawi **Directory of Publishers in Malawi.**
http://www.sdnp.org.mw/ruleoflaw/archives/Publishers-Directory.htm
[01/03/08]
A comprehensive directory of publishers in Malawi, based on legal deposit of
publications at the National Archives of Malawi. Each entry gives full address,
telephone and fax numbers, and ISBN identifier. (Lacks email addresses).

Books, articles, reports, and interviews

663 Gurnah, Abdulrazak **"A New Dawn in Malawi."** *The Bookseller,*
no. 4739, (18 October 1996): 26-27.
Following 30 years of repression under the regime of Hastings Kamusu Banda,
Malawi's writers, intellectuals, and publishers, are looking forward to a new
cultural environment. Here the distinguished Tanzanian writer Abdulrazak
Gurnah reports on the poet's Frank Chipasula's vision of returning home from
exile in the United States to organize the first Malawi literary festival and book
exhibit.

664 Mchazime, Hartford, Esme Kadzamira, and Juliet Nyangulu **A Study
on Textbook Provision in Malawi and Feasibility of Cooperation Among
SADC Countries.** Lilongwe: Malawi National Commission for UNESCO.
1993 [PO Box 30278, Lilongwe 3] 60 pp.
[Not examined]

665 Mchazime, Hartford; Esme Kadzamira, and Juliet Nyangulu
Provision of Textbooks and Other Reading Materials in Malawi. Blantyre:
Malawi National Commission for UNESCO, 1993. 59 pp.
Provides a detailed analysis of the state of textbook provision in Malawi at all levels
of education. Discusses the development of curriculum and textbooks, the
management of publishing and textbooks, marketing, sales and distribution, the
finance of textbooks, and ends with recommendations for improving the provision of
textbooks in Malawi.

666 Mpanga, Egidio H. **"Publishing in Malawi. Current Situation and
Problems."** *ISBN Review* 17 (1996): 221-234.
Slighly different "updated" version also published in *African Publishing
Review* 6, no. 6 (November/December 1997): 10-11.
One in a series of overview articles in a special issue of *ISBN Review* focusing on the
book sector in various countries of Southern Africa. This short article
(complementing entry ➔ **668** below) assesses state of publishing in Malawi [as at
1996], and the problems and prospects of the local book industries and the retail
book trade.

667 Msiska, Augustine W.C. **"The Publishing Industry in Southern
Africa, with Special Reference to Malawi: Problems and Prospects."** In

Proceedings of the Info Africa Nova Conference 1993, volume 1, edited by A.G. Coetzer. Pretoria: Info Africa Nova CC, 1993, 154-173.
Examines the factors that have hindered the development of a viable indigenous publishing industry; it highlights some of the problems faced by publishers in Southern Africa in general, and in Malawi in particular, and offers a number of possible solutions to these problems.

668   Msiska, Augustine W.C. **"The Book Trade in Malawi: A Country Report."** *ISBN Review* 17 (1996): 203-219.
One in a series of overview articles in a special issue of *ISBN Review* focusing on the book sector in various countries of Southern Africa. This paper concentrates on bookselling and the retail book trade in Malawi, but also includes a fairly full historical account of the development of book trade in the country, and reviews the major factors which hinder the growth of indigenous publishing and bookselling enterprises.

669   Mwiyeriwa, Steve S. **"Printing Presses and Publishing in Malawi."** *The African Book Publishing Record* 4, no. 2 (April 1978): 87-97.
Also published in *Society of Malawi Journal* 31, no. 2 (1978): 31-53.
Reviews the establishment of printing presses in Malawi and examines the policies of some of the country's publishing houses and book distribution agencies. Offers hope that the pattern of cultural evolution since independence will encourage a healthy future for the printing and publishing industry in Malawi. Now dated, but remains useful for a detailed historical account of the development of printing and publishing in the country.

670   Mwiyeriwa, Steve S. **"Republic of Malawi."** In *The Book Trade of the World, vol. IV: Africa,* edited by Sigfred Taubert and Peter Weidhaas. Munich: K.G. Saur, 1984, 180-186.
Overview of publishing and the book trade in Malawi. Now very dated.

671   Mwiyeriwa, Steve S. **"The Book Chain in Malawi."** In *The Book Chain in Anglophone Africa. A Survey and Directory,* edited by Roger Stringer.
Oxford: International Network for the Availability of Scientific Publications (INASP), 2002, 53-55.
Online: http://www.inasp.info/file/57/the-book-chain-in-anglophone-africa-a-survey-and-directory.html [01/03/08]
One in a series of useful country surveys and overviews – each prepared by a book professional from the country concerned – that review the state of the book, and the major players in the "book chain", in English-speaking African countries. Each country survey covers printing, book publishing, bookselling and distribution, library services, professional associations, book promotional bodies and book promotional events, training for the book professions, as well as examining some of the major issues as they relate to book development, such as languages, literacy, writers and writing, the reading habit, and national book policies. For each country this is supported by an annotated directory of government ministries, professional

associations, book publishers, booksellers and distributors, printers, major libraries, and training institutions, with full address and contact details.

672 Namponya, C.R. **"History and Development of Printing and Publishing in Malawi."** *Libri* 28, no. 3 (September 1978): 169-181.
Considers the historic place of mission presses in Malawi and the role of the government in printing and publishing. Analyzes the history of commercial printing and general publishing, academic publishing, newspaper publishing, as well as magazines and periodicals.

673 Ulanda, A.E. **"Activities of Popular Publications in Malawi."** *MALA Bulletin*, no. 2 (March 1981): 41-44.
Describes the publishing programme of Popular Publications; by one of its former editors.

Mali

Associations and book-related organizations

674 **Association Malienne des Libraries Professionelles**
603 Avenue Modibo Keita
Bamako
Postal address:
BP 2539
Bamako
Mali
Tel/Fax: +223-2219706
Email: ahtoure2002@yahoo.fr
President: Amadou Toure

675 **Comité Provisoire sur le Livre** [Mali National Book Development Council]
Responsable de l'Unité Manuels Scolaires
c/o Institut Pédagogique National
Ministère de l'Education de Base
BP 119
Bamako
Mali
Tel: + 223-224262Fax: + 223 22 35 08
Email: n/a
Contact: Mamadou Sissima

676   Organization Maliene des Editeurs (OMEL)
c/o Editions Asselar
Rue 126 Porte A, AC300 Logement
Ex Garantiguibougou
Bamako
Postal address:
BP 490
Bamako
Mali
Tel: +223-229 6289 Fax: +223-229 7639
Email: mairasow@yahoo.fr
Web: n/a
President: Hamidou Konate [?]
Secretary General: Alain Kone

National bibliography, books in print, and book trade directories

677   Bibliographie nationale du Mali.
Bamako: Direction Nationale des Bibliothèques et la Documentation du Mali
[BB E 4473, or BP 159], 1964-
Annual, latest is cumulative volume for 1995-1999, published in 2002?
Email: dnbd@afribone.net.ml or lisidibekaye@yahoo.fr
Web: n/a

Books, articles, reports, and interviews

**678   Coulibaly, N'Golo "The Role of the Education Sector in National
Book Policy: Management or Facilitation?"** In *National Book Policies for
Africa*, edited by Murray McCartney. Harare: Zimbabwe International Book
Fair Trust, 1996, 27-29.
Describes the emergence of a national book policy in Mali and asserts that "education
for all cannot be realized without a national book development policy for books
written in both national and foreign languages."

679   Deffontaines, Marie Therèse "Jeunes Maliens en quête d'identité." *Le
Monde Diplomatique* (March 2007): 31.
Online :
http://www.monde-diplomatique.fr/2007/03/DEFFONTAINES/14554
[02/03/08]
Weak local publishing and the prohibitive cost of imported titles, deprives Malian
readers access to the writing of their own homeland authors, although efforts are
now being made to address the situation through book festivals and other book
promotional events. This includes local writers giving talks about their work in
schools and colleges, thus promoting interaction and dialogue with their potential
readers.

Doumbia, A.T., and R. Ba Touré **"L'édition scientifique au Mali"** *see* ➔ **Section 4, Studies by topic: Scientific, technical and medical publishing** entry **2344**

680   Fofana, Chérif Moctar **"Republic of Mali."** In *The Book Trade of the World, vol. IV: Africa,* edited by Sigfred Taubert and Peter Weidhaas. Munich: K.G. Saur, 1984, 187-189.
Overview of publishing and the book trade in Mali. Now very dated.

681   Jacquey, Marie-Clotilde **"Editer et imprimer. Entretien avec Ibrahim Berthe, Directeur des EDIM."** *Notre Librairie. Revue du Livre Afrique Noire, Maghreb, Caraïbes, Océan Indien. Littérature Malienne,* no. 75-76 (reissued 1989): 160-165.
An insightful interview with Ibrahim Berthe, director of Edition-Imprimeries du Mali.

682   Marsaud, Olivia **Le Figuier: arbre de connaissance et de communication**.
http://www.afrik.com/article1462.html [02/03/08]
An short interview, conducted in November 2000, with Malian writer, editor and publisher Moussa Konate of Editions Le Figuier (founded in 1997), in which he talks about the activities of his publishing company, his publishing vision, and the problems and constraints they face.

Mauritania

National bibliography, books in print, and book trade directories

683   **Bibliographie nationale de Mauritanie.**
Nouakchott: Bibliothèque Nationale de Mauritanie [BP 20, Nouakchott], 200.?-
Irregular, latest is ? (not known)
Email: bibliothequenationale@yahoo.fr or yahmedou@netcourrier.com
Web: n/a

Mauritius

Associations and book-related organizations

684   **Association des Editeurs Mauricien (AEM)/Association of Mauritian Publishers**
c/o Editions Vizavi
29 rue St. Georges

Port Louis
Mauritius
Tel: +230-211 2435 Fax: +230-211 3047
Email: vizavi@intnet.mu
Web: n/a
Chair: Pascale Siew
Secretary: Clifford Colimalay

685   Mauritius Society of Authors (MASA)
3rd Floor NPF Building
Douglas Sholte Street
0230 Beau Bassin
Mauritius
Tel: +230-467 2219 Fax: +230-454 0578
Email: copyrightsoc@intnet.mu
Web: http://www.gov.mu/portal/sites/ncb/masa/index.htm
Chair: Marcel Poinen
Director: Gerald Louise

National bibliography, books in print, and book trade directories

**686   Directory of Libraries, Documentation Centres and Bookshops in
Mauritius**, comp. by Yves Chan Kam Lon. Port Louis: National Library of
Mauritius, 2000. 153 pp.
[Not examined]

687   National Bibliography of Mauritius. (*supersedes Bibliography of
Mauritius: Supplement* 1955?-)
Port Louis: National Library of Mauritius [2nd Floor, Fon Sing Building, 12
Edith Cavell Street],
Cumulative volumes published every 3 years, latest is 2001-2003, published
in 2005.
Email: natlib@intnet.mu
Web: http://www.gov.mu/portal/sites/ncb/mac/nlibrary/bib.html
Online: (1996-2000 volume, in two parts):
http://www.gov.mu/portal/sites/ncb/mac/nlibrary/nbm/nbm1.pdf
[03/03/08]
http://www.gov.mu/portal/sites/ncb/mac/nlibrary/nbm/nbm2.pdf
[03/03/08]

Books, articles, reports, and interviews

688   Benoit, Marie, and Gaëtan Benoit **"Libraries and Publishing in Mauritius."** *The African Book Publishing Record* 6, no. 3/4 (1980): 225-228.
This comprehensive overview of libraries and publishing in Mauritius [in the 1980s] covers the National Library, public, academic, special and school libraries and gives a brief history of printing and publishing from 1773 onwards. The problems caused by an abundance of imported books are discussed, with an appraisal of the achievements of Editions de l'Océan Indien. Concludes that Mauritius suffered from the same publishing constraints as other developing nations.

689   Benoit, Gaëtan and Marie Benoit **"Mauritius."** In *The Book Trade of the World, vol. IV: Africa*, edited by Sigfred Taubert and Peter Weidhaas. Munich: K.G. Saur, 1984, 192-208.
Overview of publishing and the book trade in Mauritius. Now very dated.

690   Bissoondoyal, Surendra **"Publishing in Mauritius."** In *Afro-Asian Publishing. Contemporary trends*, edited by Narendra Kumar, and S.K. Ghai. New Delhi: Institute of Book Publishing,1992, 101-102.
A brief review of the hazards of publishing in Mauritius, from the perspective of an editor at Editions de l'Océan Indien.

691   Bissoondoyal, Surendra **"Mauritius: A Bridge Between Africa and Asia."** *African Publishing Review* 2, no. 6 (November/December 1993): 7-8.
A broad overview of the history and development of publishing in Mauritius – especially of Editions de l'Océan Indien – and the links which Mauritian publishers have with publishers in Asia and the Far East.

692   Colimalay, Clifford **"Report on the ISBN System in Mauritius from the Publisher's Point of View."** *ISBN Review* 17 (1996): 243-247.
Assesses the benefits, from the point of view of publishers, of using the ISBN system, and current attitudes and practice of the system by Mauritian publishers.

693   Colimalay, Clifford **"Use of ISBN in Mauritian Bookshops."** *ISBN Review* 17 (1996): 249-250.
A brief report about the use of ISBNs by Mauritian booksellers.

694   Masson, Brigitte **"Editer à Maurice: plaidoyer pour une action."** *Notre Librairie. Revue du Livre Afrique Noire, Maghreb, Caraïbes, Océan Indien. Littérature Mauricienne*, no. 114 (July-September 1993): 157-159.
The managing director of Maison des Mécènes describes the publishing situation in Mauritius and urges a positive attitude for future publishing endeavours.

Mozambique

Associations and book-related organizations

695   Associação dos Escritores Moçambicanos (AEMO)
Av 24 de Jahlo 1420
Maputo
Mozambique
Postal address:
PO Box 4187
Maputo
Mozambique
Fax: +258-1304438
Email: aemo@zebra.uem.mz or aemo@tvcabo.co.mz
Web: n/a
Secretary-General: Juvenal Bucuana

696   Instituto Nacional do Livro et do Disco (INLD)
24 Avda de Julho
1921 CP 4030
Maputo
Mozambique
Tel: +258-1-314397 Fax: +258-429700
Email: inst.nacdisco@teledata.mz
Web: n/a
Chair: Boaventura Afonso
Note: not verified, organization dormant?

697   Sociedade Moçambicana de Autores (SOMAS)
Av 25 de Setembro 1521 5°-56
Maputo
Mozambique
Email: avarro@zebra.uem.mz
Secretary: n/a
Note: not verified, organization dormant?

National bibliography, books in print, and book trade directories

698   Moçambique a Través dos Livros. Subídios para uma Bibliografia Nacional (Junho 1975 - Agosto 1998). Compiled by by Júlio Navarro and António Sopa. Maputo: Instituto Camões, Centro Cultural, 1999. 103 pp.
Provides, in lieu of a national bibliography, a bibliography of books – including government and official publications – published in Mozambique between June 1995 and August 1998. Titles are arranged by broad Universal Decimal Classification

headings and sub-divisions; there are approximately 1,200 entries, most in Portuguese, but also a few in English. Lacks directory of publishers, and there is no index. No further editions would appear to have been published to date.

Books, articles, reports, and interviews (in English only)

699 Abrahamsson, Hans, and Anders Nilsson **Education and Society. The Role of Education and Textbook Policy in a Society under Transition. Swedish School Book Support - The Case of Mozambique.** Stockholm: SIDA, 1990?. 58 pp.
Discusses how Mozambican textbook policies have changed in order to allow the integration of the private sector into the processes of editing, printing and distribution of books.

700 Akesson, Gunilla **School-Books and Buying Power. A Study of Schools and Prescribed Books in the Rural Areas of Mozambique.** Stockholm: SIDA, 1992. 108 pp.
An investigation into the numbers of school books owned by primary school pupils in rural areas of Mozambique. Identifies the crucial factors which determine whether parents are able to buy books. Also examines the distribution of school books.

701 Darch, Colin M. **"The Book Trade and Publishing in Mozambique."** *The African Book Publishing Record* 19, no. 1 (1993): 9-12.
Examines the Mozambican publishing and literary scene, which is small and operates under very difficult conditions. Reviews the history of publishing in Mozambique, legal publications and the literary scene, academic publishing, trade publishing, political and specialized publications, newspaper and, finally, looks at likely publishing trends for the future.

702 Denning, Carmelle **Mozambique. Book Sector and a Primary School Textbook Policy.** London: International Book Development Ltd., 1990. 48 pp.
An overview of plans, strategies, policies and recommendations for textbook provision in Mozambique, especially for primary school texts.

703 Huppert, Rémi **Developing Human Resources of the Book Industry: The People's Republic of Mozambique - (Mission).** Paris: UNESCO (FMR/CC/BAE/87/104; PP/1984-1985/III.3.3/technical report; restricted circulation), 1987. 35 pp.
Mission report. [Not examined]

704 Hyltenstam, Kenneth and Christopher Stroud **The Evaluation of Teaching Materials for Lower Primary Education in Mozambique. Vol. 2, Language issues.** Stockholm: SIDA, 1993. 146 pp.
The final report of an investigation in linguistic studies initiated by the Mozambican Ministry of Education. Provides an interpretation of how school materials,

curriculum design, and teaching methodologies incorporate and adapt to the multilingual reality in Mozambique.

705   Liljeson, Lars; Peter Stoye, and Gunalla Akesson **Textbooks in Mozambique. Organisation, Publishing, Distribution and Financing. Part 1: Editora Escolar.** Stockholm: SIDA, 1990. 23 pp. + annexes
An overview of the state of textbook publishing in Mozambique, including recommendations as they relate to policies of the government-owned publishing house Editora Escolar.

706   Liljeson, Lars; Peter Stoye, and Gunilla Akesson **Textbooks in Mozambique. Organisation, Publishing, Distribution and Financing. Part 2: Textbook Distribution.** Stockholm: SIDA, 1990. 38 pp. + annexes
Reviews the unsatisfactory state of book distribution services to schools from the warehouses of the state distribution company, DINAME, throughout Mozambique.

707   Matola, Samuel **"The Book in Lusophone Africa: An Unreal Reality."** In *Development Directory of African Publishing 1995*, compiled by Carol Priestley. Harare: African Publishers Network, 1995, 74-76.
A brief account of publishing in lusophone Africa, particularly Mozambique, and the prospects for the book industries in the years ahead.

708   Muhate, Zephanias **"Interministerial Collaboration. More Effective Book Distribution: The Mozambique Experience."** In *Millennium Marketplace.* [Proceedings of the ZIBF] *Indaba 2000, Harare, Zimbabwe, 31 July – 1 August 2000.* Harare: Zimbabwe International Book Fair Trust, n.d. [2001], 248-251.
Also published in *African Publishing Review* 10, no. 2 (2001): 5-6
An overview of policies, structures and government regulations affecting textbook provision and distribution in Mozambique, and makes some suggestions how better coordination of policies could lead to more effective distribution.

709   Navorro, Júlio **"The Book World in Mozambique - A Brief Survey."** *ISBN Review* 17 (1996): 251-257.
Slightly shorter version also published in *African Publishing Review* 6, no. 2 (March/April 1997): 10-11.
One in a series of overview articles in a special issue of *ISBN Review* focusing on the book sector in various countries of Southern Africa, and which report (for the most part) about the state of libraries, publishing and the retail book trade; current book and copyright legislation, national book policies, programmes to promote the reading habit, laws and legislation covering the book sector and copyright, activities of library and book trade professional bodies, book trade organization, training for the book industries, the use of ISBNs, and more.

710 Oliveira, Ruy **"People's Republic of Mozambique."** In *The Book Trade of the World, vol. IV: Africa*, edited by Sigfred Taubert and Peter Weidhaas. Munich: K.G. Saur, 1984, 214-219.
Overview of publishing and the book trade in Mozambique. Now very dated.

Namibia

Associations and book-related organizations

711   Association of Namibian Publishers (ANP)
c/o Gamsberg Macmillan
19 Faraday Street   Southern Industria
Windhoek
Postal address:
PO Box 5934
Windhoek
Namibia
Tel: +264-61-232165 Fax: +264-61-233538
Email: gmpubl@iafrica.com.na
Web: n/a
Chair: Peter Reiner

712   Namibia Book Development Council (NBDC)
PO Box 25601
Windhoek
Namibia
Tel: + 264-61-230303 Fax: + 264-61-230303
Email: nepetrob@iafrica.com.na
Web: n/a
Chair: Petrus Hakskeen [?]
Training Co-ordinator: (Ms) Nepeti Nicanor

713   Namibian Children's Book Forum
PO Box 22657
Windhoek
Namibia
Tel: +264-61-307 2194 Fax: +264-61-307 2444
Email: n /a
Chair: (Prof) *Andree-Jeanne Tötemeyer*

714   Namibia National Writers Union (NANAWU)
PO Box 22592
Windhoek
Namibia
Tel: +264 61 271015 Fax: +264 61 233538
Email: n/a
President: Shiimi Ya-Shiimi

National bibliography, books in print, and book trade directories

715   Directory of Namibian Libraries, Publishers and Booksellers 1992,
comp. by Johan Loubser, *et al*. Windhoek: Ministry of Education and
Culture, 1992. 53 pp.
[Not examined]

**716   Namibian Books in Print, 1999/2000. A Catalogue of Books from
Namibia Available Through the Book Trade. Including the Namibian
Book World Directory.** 3rd edition. Compiled by Werner Hillebrecht.
Windhoek: Association of Namibian Publishers, in cooperation with the
National Library of Namibia, 1999. 114 pp.
Note: 4th edition published for 2004/2005, but no further volumes published
thereafter.
Divided into two principal sections: (i) general books – but which in fact also
includes many specialized scholarly monographs and reports – and (ii), school
books, including textbooks, teacher's guides and teaching aids. Complete
bibliographic data is provided for each entry except prices. For all entries in African
languages the language is identified. Also contains a listing of Namibian serials
publications, a directory of ISBN publisher prefixes for Namibian publishers, a
Namibian Publishers Directory with full address details, telephone and fax numbers,
and email addresses where available (and Web sites for a small number of entries),
plus a Namibian Book Trade Directory that provides equally full details on the retail
book trade and book distributors.

717   Namibia National Bibliography. (supersedes *Namibische National-
Bibliographie/Namibian National Bibliography.* Basle, Switzerland: Basler Afrika
Bibliographien, 1978-1981, 3 cumulative volumes published)
Windhoek: National Library of Namiba [Private Bag 13349, Windhoek],
1996-
Annually, in print format latest is 1996-19
Online: 2007-
1990 to 1998 records now available online
included shortly.
Searchable database at http://209.88.21.3
NAMLIT records are used as a basis for 1
(NNB) which is a separate database.

Annual, vol. 1 (1990-1992)-
Email: natlib@mec.gov.na
Web: http://www.nln.gov.na/
For more information *see also*
Zulu, Paul **Namibia National Bibliography: Strides and Challenges**
http://www.ifla.org/IV/ifla73/papers/136-Zulu-en.pdf [03/03/08]
(Paper presented to the 73rd IFLA General Conference and Council in 2007.)

Books, articles, reports, and interviews

718   Gebhardt, L. **"Namibia."** In *The Book Trade of the World, vol. IV: Africa*,
edited by Sigfred Taubert and Peter Weidhaas. Munich: K.G. Saur, 1984, 220-
222.
Overview of publishing and the book trade in Namibia. Now very dated.

719   Hillebrecht, Werner **"ISBN in Namibia: Experiences in
Administering the National Agency, and in Daily Library Practice."** *ISBN
Review* 17 (1996): 259-268.
Looks at the current use, practice and promotion of the ISBN system from the
perspective of the National Library of Namibia, and some of the problems associated
with ISBN use.

720   Humery, Marie-Eve, and Katia Clavea **The Book Sector in Namibia.**
Windhoek: Gamsberg Macmillan, 1998. 28 pp.
[Not examined]

721   Katjavivi, Jane **"Perils, Problems and Passions of Publishing in
Namibia."** *Mitteilungen/Newsletter. Namibia Scientific Society* 35, no. 7-8
(1994): 98-101.
Narrates the difficulties of publishing in the small market of Namibia [in the 1990s],
with a 40% illiteracy rate, many different languages and the recent introduction of
English as the official language, plus a poor inherited education system. Yet there are
also publishing possibilities in an environment of change and financial inputs into
education. The author talks about the leap of faith needed to publish in this
environment, and the excitement of following a passion for books, "rather like the
Bumblebee, which flies even though aerodynamically it apparently shouldn't be able
to."

722   Katjavivi, Jane **"Publishing and Book Development in Namibia."**
African Publishing Review 3, no. 5 (September/October 1994): 11-13.
A brief account of the current [1994] state of the book industries in Namibia; also
reports about the activities, and a detailed programme of action, of the ➔ **Namibia
Book Development Council (712),** established late in 1992.

723   Katjavivi, Jane **"Book Publishing in Namibia."** In *Development Directory of Indigenous Publishing 1995*, compiled by Carol Priestley. Harare: African Publishers Network, 1995, 77-82.
An overview of publishing and the retail book trade in Namibia; includes some historical background, an outline of the post-independence reform of the country's educational system, and reports about the activities of the →**Association of Namibian Publishers (711)** and the →**Namibia Book Development Council (712)**.

724   Maasdorp, Eben **"Use of ISBNs Among Namibian Publishers."** *ISBN Review* 17 (1996): 269-271.
A brief examination of the use and trends of ISBNs by commercial publishers in Namibia.

725   Namhila, Ellen, and Werner Hillebrecht **"The Book Chain in Namibia."** In *The Book Chain in Anglophone Africa. A Survey and Directory*, edited by Roger Stringer. Oxford: International Network for the Availability of Scientific Publications (INASP), 2002, 56-61.
Online: http://www.inasp.info/file/57/the-book-chain-in-anglophone-africa-a-survey-and-directory.html [03/03/08]
One in a series of useful country surveys and overviews – each prepared by a book professional from the country concerned – that review the state of the book, and the major players in the "book chain", in English-speaking African countries. Each country survey covers printing, book publishing, bookselling and distribution, library services, professional associations, book promotional bodies and book promotional events, training for the book professions, as well as examining some of the major issues as they relate to book development, such as languages, literacy, writers and writing, the reading habit, and national book policies. For each country this is supported by an annotated directory of government ministries, professional associations, book publishers, booksellers and distributors, printers, major libraries, and training institutions, with full address and contact details.

726   Reiner, Peter; Werner Hillebrecht, and Jane Katjavivi **Books in Namibia. Past Trends and Future Prospects.** Windhoek: Association of Namibian Publishers, 1994. 37 pp.
An informative history of books and publishing in Namibia; also examines the present situation [mid-1990s] and assesses the future prospects for the book industries.

Reiner, Peter **"Promise and Pitfalls. A Commercial View of Publishing in African Languages"** *see* → Section 4, Studies by topic: Publishing in African languages

727   Strauss, A. **"Guidelines and Recommendations for a Book Policy in Namibia."** *Kalabash* (December 1994): 3-5.
[Not examined]

728 Weidhaas, Peter **"Promoting Namibian Books Outside Namibia."**
Mitteilungen/Newsletter. Namibia Scientific Society 35, no. 7-8 (1994): 105-107.
The [former] Director of the Frankfurt Book Fair offers some suggestions how to
promote Namibian books in the international market place.

729 West, R.C., and E. Maasdorp **Study on Textbook Provision and the
Feasibility of Cooperation among SADCC Countries: Namibia Case
Study**. Paris: UNESCO (Docs/textbook/UNESCO AAA draft 1; UNESCO
report 940531), 1994. 48 pp.
A detailed study and analysis of textbook provision in Namibia investigated by a
private sector consultant and a public sector consultant, who conclude that the
general state of the industry is healthy with scope for development, and propose the
initiation of inter-country discussions on curriculum content.

Niger

Associations and book-related organizations

730 **Association Nigerienne des Professionnels du Livre (ANPL)**
c/o Etablissment Daouda
BP 11 380
Niamey
Niger
Tel: +227-20 73 46 16
Email: etdaouda@intnet.ne
President: Daouda Issoufou

Nigeria

Associations and book-related organizations

731 **Academic and Non-Fiction Authors' Association of Nigeria
(ANFAAN)**
c/o Dr. Olalere Oladitan
Obafemi Awolowo University
Department of Foreign Languages
PO Box 1016
Ile-Ife Oyo State
Nigeria
Tel/Fax: +234-36-230214
Email: ooladita@oauife.edu.ng or ooladita@yahoo.co.uk
Executive Secretary: (Dr) Olalere Oladitan

732   Association of Nigerian Authors (ANA)
26 Oladipo Olabinjo Crescent, Off Bode Thomas
Surulere
Lagos
Nigeria
Tel: +234-1-835233/258057 Mobile: 080 3301 2574/080 3334 1157
Email: ananational@yahoo.com or info@ana-ng.org
Web: http://www.ana-ng.org/home.htm [these pages not available
30/03/08] or
http://web.archive.org/web/20050403105217/www.ana-ng.org/home.htm
[30/03/08, archival pages, some pages not accessible]
Blog: http://www.lagosana.blogspot.com/ [30/03/08]
Chair: Chike Ofili
President: (Dr) Wale Okediran president@ana-ng.org
Vice President: (Dr) Jerry Agada
General Secretary: Raph Tathagata secretary@ana-ng.org

733   Book Development Centre
Nigerian Educational Research and Development Council (NERDC)
Lokoja-Kaduna Road, Sheda
PMB 91, Garki
Abuja
Nigeria
Lagos Annex Office:
3 Jibowu Street
Yaba
Lagos
Tel: +234-1-470 5638
Email: n/a
Web: http://www.nerdcnigeria.org/book.html
Contacts: (Dr) Eric Adeche Apeji, Director, Library and Informatics Centre;
Angela Chinyere Nwagbara, Deputy Director & Head of Book Development
Centre

**734   Children's Literature Documentation and Research Centre
(CLIDORC)**
18 Soleh Boneh Way
Ikolaba New Bodija
Ibadan
Postal address:
UI PO Box 20744
Ibadan
Nigeria

Tel: +234-22-711254
Email: info@mabelsegun.com
Web: http://www.mabelsegun.com/
Director: Mabel Segun
Note: not verified, organization dormant?

735   Christian Booksellers Association of Nigeria (CBA-Nigeria)
Doxology House May Hospital 24/26
Sadiku Street Ilasha
Mushin
Lagos
Nigeria
Tel: +234-1-892 9267
Email: cbanigeria@yahoo.com or lasebooks@hotmail.com
President: Esther Aworinde
Administrative Secretary: Jonathan Efe Okunbor

736   National Book League of Nigeria (NBLN)
PO Box 14019
University of Ibadan Post Office
Ibadan
Nigeria
Tel: +234-2-231 3411 Fax: +234-1-492 2681
Email: n/a
Director: Tosin Awolalu
Note: not verified, organization dormant?

737   Nigerian Book Fair Trust
Literamed Building
Plot 45
Oregun Industrial Estate
Alausa Bus-Stop
Ikeja
Postal address:
PMB 21068
Ikeja
Lagos State
Nigeria
Tel: +234-1-482 3402/496 2512/778 0316 Fax: 234-1-493 5258/778 0340
Email: info@nibf.org
Web: http://www.nibf.org/
Chair: Yinka Lawal-Solarin
Executive Secretary: Bose Adetunji

738   Nigerian Book Foundation (NBF)
4 Ezi-Ajana Lane Umukwa
PO Box 1132
Awka
Anambra State
Nigeria
Tel/Fax: +234-48-552615
Email: nbkfound@infoweb.abs.net
Web: n/a
President: Chukwuemeka Ike

739   Nigerian Publishers Association (NPA)
Book House
Quarter 673 Jericho GRA
GPO Box 2541
Ibadan
Nigeria
Tel: +234-2-7515352/7507618
Email: nigpa@skannet.com or nigpa_apd@yahoo.com
Web: n/a
President: Gbenro Adegbola
Executive Secretary: Olakunle Sogbein

740   Poets Palace
Ikorodu Road Onipanu
Lagos
Postal address:
PO Box 1785
Shomolu
Lagos State
Nigeria
Tel: +234-8034978359
Email: poetsnigeria@yahoo.com
Founder/President: Wale Ajakaye

741   The Reproduction Rights Society of Nigeria (REPRONIG)
Quarter 673 Idishin
GRA Jericho
GPO Box 12324
Dugbe Ibadan
Oyo State
Nigeria
Tel: +234-803-355 1544/+234-803-385 9062
Email: repronig2004@yahoo.com

Web:
http://www.ifrro.org/show.aspx?pageid=members/rrodetails&memberid
=39
Executive Director: Inyang Anietimfon Ekanem

742   Synergy Educational Nigeria
Synergy Educational
12 Olanrewaju Street
Oregun
Lagos
Postal address:
PO Box 7763
Ikeja
Lagos
Nigeria
Tel/Fax: +234-1-891 8083
Email: synergyeducational@yahoo.com
Web: http://www.synergyed.org [pages not accessible 04/03/08]
Chair: Chuma Nwokolo
Executive Director: Richard Mammah
Note: not verified, organization dormant?

National bibliography, books in print, and book trade directories (and other
reference works)

743   Directory of Nigerian Book Development (Maiden Edition 1998).
Edited by Chukmuemeka Ike. Awka, Nigeria: Nigerian Book Foundation
and Enugu: Fourth Dimension Publishing Co., 1998. 228 pp.
This is a remarkable and pioneering publication and is probably the first reference
work published anywhere in Africa which provides a wide range of information
about the *entire* book community in a single country, and in a single source.
Published jointly by the ➔ **Nigerian Book Foundation/NBF (738)** and Fourth
Dimension Publishing Company, the project forms part of the NBF's mission to
establish a comprehensive database on all aspects of book development in Nigeria.
The directory brings together a massive amount of information, which is grouped
under five distinct parts, each preceded by a short introductory essay. Part 1 is a
Directory of Published Nigerian Authors, a total of 749 entries covering both creative
writers as well as academic authors. Entries include full name and address, telephone
number, date of birth, details of published books, awards and honours received, and
other information. Part 2 is a Directory of Book Publishing Houses, 74 entries giving
a wide array of specifics on each publisher, e.g. date founded, number of books in
print, number of new titles published annually, types of books published and
primary markets, in addition to financial information, number of employees, name of
chief executive, and full name and address, telephone/fax numbers. Part Three is a
Directory of Book Printing Presses, listing 66 companies and providing similar

information as for publishers, but also including more printing-specific information such as typesetting and origination services offered, printing and binding equipment available, and more. Part Four covers the retail trade and bookshops/distribution organizations (70 entries), again with very full information on each organization, including nature of business, name of chief executive, type of sales outlets and principal promotion channels, annual turnover figures (where disclosed), and specialized services offered. Part Five, finally, is a directory of libraries throughout Nigeria, grouped by States, but unlike parts 1-4 listings are confined to just name and address and an indication of the type of library.

Reviews:
The African Book Publishing Record, vol. 25, no. 1, 1999
Same review also in *Bellagio Publishing Network Newsletter,* no. 24, December 1998, p. 17
Online:
http://www.bellagiopublishingnetwork.com/newsletter24/review_zell2.htm [04/03/08]
Glendora Books Supplement, vol. 1, no. 3 & 4, 1998
Online:
http://digital.lib.msu.edu/projects/africanjournals/html/itemdetail.cfm?recordID= 2861 [04/03/08]
Journal of Modern African Studies, vol. 38, no. 4, 2000

744 Maiyanga, Alex A., and Burbur J. Medugu, eds. **Journals Catalogue of Nigeria.**
Abuja, Nigeria: National Commission for Colleges of Education, 2005. 342 pp.
[Not examined]

745 Mammah, Richard, ed. **The Nigerian Books Directory and Guide 2003-2004.** Lagos: Mace Books for Synergy Educational, 2003. 223 pp.
[Not examined]

746 National Bibliography of Nigeria. (supersedes *Nigerian Publications: Current National Bibliography,* 1958-1972)
Lagos: National Library of Nigeria [PMB 12626, Lagos], 1973-
Monthly, with bi-annual and annual cumulations; later annually, latest is 2004. Computerized since 2001, and now available in both print and online formats.
Email: natbcdnlnig@yahoo.com
Web: http://www.nlbn.org/
For more information *see also*
Laisi, J. **"National Bibliographic Control and National Bibliography of Nigeria"** In *National Book Policy, HIV/AIDS and Sustainable Development. Papers Presented at the Fifth Nigeria International Book Fair, 8-13 May, 2006.* Lagos: Nigerian Book Fair Trust [c/o Literamed Publications Ltd., PMB 21068, Ikeja, Lagos, Nigeria], 2007, 186-197.

747 Nigerian Publishers Association **Nigerian Books in Print 1996.**
Compiled and edited by the Nigerian Publishers Association. Ibadan:
Nigerian Publishers Association, 1996. 488 pp.
Published under the auspices of the ➜ **Nigerian Publishers Association (739)**, this
volume contains some 5,000 entries from 65 Nigerian publishers, in print at as the
end of 1995. Titles are listed in four different sequences (Pre-Primary/Primary,
Secondary, Tertiary, and General Publications) each with their separate author index.
Some entries/listings are incomplete, lacking either author, authors' surnames or
initials, and/or sometimes even lacks name of publisher, and frequently do not
provide full bibliographic data. Many publishers' names are indicated as acronyms
but not all are identified in the Directory of Publishers. There are a substantial
number titles from publishers for which addresses cannot be found in the Directory
of Publishers. Sadly, this is a seriously flawed reference work.
Reviews:
The African Book Publishing Record vol. 24, no. 3, 1998
Glendora Books Supplement vol. 1, no. 1, 1997
Online:
http://digital.lib.msu.edu/projects/africanjournals/html/itemdetail.cfm?recordID=
2823 [04/03/08]

748 Nigerian Publishers Association **Nigerian Books in Print, volume 2,
1996-2002.** Ibadan: Nigerian Publishers Association, 2002. 189 pp.
The title of this book is a misnomer, it is *not* a books in print, but simply a selective
catalogue of Nigerian book publishing output for the years 1996 to 2002 (published
as "volume 2" of the preceding entry ➜ **747**) and containing some 2,000 entries,
principally books published by NPA members. The arrangement is cumbersome,
listing titles under four different categories (Pre-Primary/Primary School
Publications, Secondary School Publications, Tertiary and Research Publications, and
General Publications), each with a small number of broad subject (and some
language) headings, and with three separate indexes by author. This makes it rather
awkward to use as a reference tool. A two page introductory section sets out style
and arrangement, but provides no details about the data gathering process, and how
the information was collected and verified. Bibliographic data given includes author,
author surname or initials (although surnames or initials are lacking for many
entries), title and sub-title, publisher, ISBN, year of publication, size in mm, and page
extent. The names of publishers are indicated in abbreviated form, and a key to
abbreviations appears as part of the Directory of Publishers, which is split into two
separate sections, NPA member firms, and non-members. Headings and topics
descriptors are inadequate, and many include an odd mixture of titles. To make
matters worse, titles are listed under a mixture of authors' first and last names. Style
and other inconsistencies abound. Like its predecessor, this is a carelessly compiled
reference resource.
Reviews:
The African Book Publishing Record vol. 31, no. 1, 2005

Books, articles, reports, and interviews

749   Adaba, Tom A.; Olalekan Ajia, and Ikechukwu E. Nwosu
Communication Industry in Nigeria: The Crisis of Publications. Nairobi:
African Council on Communication Education (Africa media monograph
series, 6), 1988. 286 pp.
The paucity of textbooks on mass communications in Nigeria, the economic
restrictions on the importation of books [in 1988], the continued increase of mass
communications training institutions together with the concomitant increase in the
number of trainees and practitioners of this profession, inform the theme of this
publication. The sixteen contributions, by experts drawn from both the
communications and publishing industry in Nigeria, are divided into four parts:
general overview of the publishing industry in Nigeria (4 papers), research needed
for communications book production (4), the contents of mass communications
books (6) and distribution and production costs (2).

750   Adesanoye, Festus A. **"Professionalism in Nigerian Publishing:
Myth or Reality."** *Books* 1, no. 2 (January 1988): 5-14.
Examines the major components of publishing and makes a series of suggestions for
achieving improved professionalism in book publishing in Nigeria. Calls for a
greater involvement of the ➔ **Nigerian Publishers Association (739)** in organizing
in-service training courses for book industry personnel, and suggests the formation
of a Nigerian Publishing Institute to train or re-train publishers.

751   Adesanoye, Festus A. **"The Book and the Nigerian Environment."**
Review of English and Literary Studies 5, no. 2 (1988): 170-182.
[Not examined]

752   Adesanoye, Festus A. **"Publishing: Catalyst for Political and Socio-
Economic Development in Nigeria."** *The Publisher* 1, no. 2 (March 1989): 33-
39.
Seeks to establish a link between a "virile book publishing industry" and purposeful
national development.

753   Adesanoye, Festus A. **The Book in Nigeria Today. Some Current
Issues.** Ibadan: Sam Bookman Educational and Communication Services,
1995 [published 1997]. 175 pp. (distributed by African Books Collective Ltd.,
Oxford)
A collection of essays, by the [then] Director of Publishing at Ibadan University
Press, on various aspects of the book situation in Nigeria, which have previously
been published in various journals and magazines or as chapters in books. The
essays cover topics such as books in national development, nurturing a book culture,
professionalism in Nigerian publishing, book editing, scholarly publishing, and a
somewhat tongue-in-cheek "Editing the Nigerian Editor". A final chapter provides
an overview of book publishing in Nigeria today [1994]. The books also contains a

useful bibliography of about 80 items, most on Nigerian publishing, including some unpublished reports and articles in Nigerian newspapers.

754   Adesanoye, Festus A. **"Towards a More Constructive Printer-Publisher Relationship in Nigeria."** *The Publisher* 5, no. 1 (October 1997): 10-14.
Tackles some of the main issues in the publisher-printer relationship in general, and the sometimes thorny publisher-printer relationship in Nigeria in particular. Argues that especially in view of the severe economic constraints prevailing in the country, the current infrastructural inadequacies (erratic power supplies, constant fuel shortages, etc.) and a generally hostile publishing environment, communication between the groups must be improved. The author cites instances of unprofessional conduct by some publishers, which has led to strained relationships with their colleagues in the printing sector. Calls for a more harmonious relationship and more dialogue between publishers and printers, and makes some suggestions as to how this might be achieved.

755   Adesanoye, Festus A., and Ayo Ojeniyi, eds. **Issues in Book Publishing in Nigeria. Essays in Honour of Aigboje Higo at 70.** Ibadan: Heinemann Educational Books (Nigeria) plc, 2005. 291 pp. (distributed by African Books Collective Ltd, Oxford)
This collection of essays was published to honour Chief Aigboje Higo on his 70th birthday. Higo, by many considered to be the doyen of Nigerian book publishing, was a founding father and two-time president of the ➜ **Nigerian Publishers Association (739),** and for many years Managing Director and later Chairman of Heinemann Educational Publishers (Nigeria) plc. The 15 contributions that are brought together in this *Festschrift* include essays by many prominent members of the African book professions, including Bodunde Bankole, Henry Chakava, Ayo Odeniyi, the late Victor Nwankwo, as well as Keith Sambrook, a former director of Heinemann's in the UK, whose chapter recounts the story of his visit to Nigeria in 1964 when he and the late Alan Hill (then Chair of Heinemann's) met up with Aig Higo and asked him to join HEB and take charge of their business in Nigeria and West Africa. There are also papers on the economics of publishing, training for book industry personnel, and Bodunde Bankole presents an interesting account of the history and development of the Nigerian Publishers Association and its collaboration with international book trade organizations to provide more visibility for Nigerian book publishing output. A flawed index apart, this is a valuable source of information on the development of publishing and the book trade in Nigeria, and also provides useful overviews of current publishing practise in the country.
Reviews:
The African Book Publishing Record vol. 32, no.2, 2006

756   Adesanoye, Festus A. **"Rebuilding the Publishing Industry. Rebraning the NPA."** *The Publisher* 14, no. 1 (November 2007): 3-13.
Offers some thoughts on the rebuilding and strengthening of the Nigerian publishing industry, an industry that has been hard hit by a rapid decline in the Nigerian economy that started in the 1990s. Laments the fact that the government has never

positively supported the indigenous book industries, and that most pronouncements by the government regarding the importance of books are hardly ever matched by concrete action; and that the government is yet to promulgate a national book policy, which thus far has not gone beyond several draft versions. As a consequence of the massive devaluation of the Naira, and because of the foreign exchange requirements to purchase modern equipment from abroad, is that very few Nigerian printers have been able to replace obsolete printing equipment, and which has led to some very poorly produced books. Other factors compound the problems, for example unstable electricity supplies. The author, who is a former Director of Ibadan University Press, also addresses the need for the rebranding and repositioning of the ➔ **Nigerian Publishers Association (739),** and makes a number of suggestions how this might be achieved by, for example, more assertive action, more visibility and a higher profile for the Association, and improved book industry training programmes.

757 Adichie, Chimamanda Ngozi **"Blinded by God's Business."** *Guardian Review*, (19 February 2005): 7.
Online: reproduced as *USA/Africa Dialogue* no. 432, at this University of Texas site
http://www.utexas.edu/conferences/africa/ads/432.html [04/03/08]
Chimamanda Ngozi Adichie, celebrated author of *The Purple Hibiscus*, writes on why no one reads fiction in Nigeria, and why, if her celebrated novel had been first published in Nigeria, it could only have been self-published, and thus unable to gain the wide international attention it has received; and would not have been entered for the prestigious Orange Prize, for which it was short-listed in 2004, and was also awarded the Commonwealth Writers' Prize for the Africa Region 'Best First Book' category for 2005.

758 Adimorah, E.N.O. **"Data Collection, Monitoring and Management: Implications for Book Development."** In *Creating a Conducive Environment for Book Publishing*, edited by Chukwuemeka Ike. Awka, Nigeria: Nigerian Book Foundation, 1996, 49-59.
The Director of Nigeria's National Information and Documentation Centre (NIDOC) argues that data collection plays a key part in book development. He sets out the opportunities offered by different databases, provides a short overview of data organization, data processing operations and database management, and assesses the likely benefits for Nigeria's book industries.

759 *African Publishing Review* Special issue: **Tribute to Chief Victor Uzoma Nwankwo/Hommage au très respecté Chief Victor Uzoma Nwankwo.**
African Publishing Review 11, no. 5 (2002), 39 pp.
The late Victor Nwankwo, who was brutally killed by political assassins near his home in Enugu, Nigeria on the night of August 29, 2000, was the founding Chairperson of the ➔ **African Publishers Network (5),** and this special issue of APNET's *African Publishing Review* pays homage to his wisdom, vision, and leadership, and his enormous contribution to African publishing over the years. It contains many tributes by his former colleagues in the African publishing world, by African book trade associations, as well as members of the international book

community. It also reprints one of Victor Nwankwo's last articles on African publishing "Print-on-Demand: An African Publisher's Experience" (*see* entry ➔ **1850**).

760 Agbebi, E.A. **"A Conceptual Framework for a Cost-Effective Book Distribution Network in Nigeria."** In *Making Books Available and Affordable*, edited by Ezenwa-Ohaeto. Awka, Nigeria: Nigerian Book Foundation, 1995, 93-100.
Contends that existing book distribution systems are not responsive to the needs of Nigerian consumers. Examines a number of conventional book distribution systems and marketing channels, and proposes the establishment of a central distribution organization and book wholesale agency.

761 Akinfolarin, O. **"Economic Reform and the Dearth of Books in Nigeria."** *Book Research Quarterly*, no. 5 (Winter 1989-90): 30-36.
Discusses how the economic reforms in Nigeria have affected the price of books and the importing of books from overseas. Examines the effects the reforms have had on the publishing industry as a whole and on the education system, and makes a number of suggestions how to tackle the book crisis.

762 Alimole, Nat B. **"Financial Management in the Nigerian Book Publishing Industry."** *The Publisher* 3, no. 1 (January 1995): 28-30.
Looks at the intricacies of financial management in the Nigerian book publishing industry, an industry which has been hard hit by the vicissitudes of the Nigerian economic, political and educational systems—an unprecedented high level of inflation and unpredictable educational policies, with many publishers facing severe cash flow problems because of non-payment, or very late payment, of books supplied to state governments.

763 Anon. **"Citation: Read on the Occasion of the Presentation of a Farewell Memento by the Nigerian Publishers' Association to Mark the Retirement of Chief Felix Arimoku Iwerebon."** *The Publisher* 2, no. 2 (October 1993): 49.
An address given on the retirement of Chief Felix Arimoku Iwerebon, former Chief Executive of Longman Nigeria plc.

764 Anon. **"Citation: the Right Reverend Dr. T. Tanimowo Solaru. Papa Solaru: A Legendary Publisher."** *The Publisher* 2, no. 2 (October 1993): 50-51.
An address given on the conferring of the first Fellowship Award of the ➔ **Nigerian Publishers Association (739)** on Chief T.T. Solaru, first chairman of Oxford University Press Nigeria (now University Press Ltd.).

765 Apeji, E. Adeche **"Developments in Education, Libraries and Book Publishing in Nigeria."** *The Publisher* 4, no. 1 (September 1996): 19-24.
Asserts that a flourishing book industry requires a harmonious relationship between the educational sector, libraries, and publishers. The contributions the multinational

and other publishers have made in the provision of books in Nigeria depended to a large extent on developments in education and libraries. Conscious of these mutual relationships, the government should ensure, through deliberate policies, that "increase in enrolment is necessarily backed up by improved library and publishing facilities to meet new and increasing demand."

766   Apeji, E. Adeche **"Book Production in Nigeria: An Historical Survey."** *Information Development* 12, no. 4 (December 1996): 210-214.
Reviews the historical background to the development of the Nigerian printing and book industries, and sees the early efforts of Christian missionaries as laying the foundation for "today's thriving book industries in Nigeria". Examines the government's involvement in publishing, the role of the multinationals, university press publishing, the activities of Franklin Book Programs in the 1960s, together with a brief note about indigenous initiatives.

767   Apeji, E. Adeche **"Book Publishing in Nigeria: A Discursus."** *Libri* 48, no. 2 (1998): 88-95.
Based on data collected by means of a questionnaire, the author reviews the activities of indigenous, non-indigenous, and multinational publishing companies in Nigeria, and assesses the part they have played, and the impact they have made, over the years. Also explores the role of publishing in the education of Nigeria's citizens and probes into the challenges of the book industries in the years ahead.

768   Apeji, E. Adeche **"Readers without Books. A Nigerian Case Study."** *Logos. The Journal of the World Book Community* 11, no. 2 (2000): 69-72.
Online: http://www.atypon-link.com/LOG/doi/pdf/10.2959/logo.2000.11.2.69
Based on a survey of Nigerian publishing output undertaken during 1998, the author (who is head of the Library and Informatics Centre at the Nigerian Educational Research and Development Council/NERDC) alleges that the Nigerian publishing industry, notably six multinational companies, concentrate almost entirely on the safe textbook markets, and that they fail to cater for the general interest market. He states "Nigeria is not the only country where publishing is dominated by the textbook, but it is unique in the size of its literate population and the timidity of its publishers." The authors calls for a national book policy "which would require that all publishers in Nigeria devote no less than 30% of their resources to general interest titles, both in English and in the local languages." He is also critical of the Nigerian government's lack of commitment to the issue of book provision, leaving "a yawning gap between public goals and private endeavours." (For a response to this article, by Victor Nwankwo, *see* ➔ **824**.)

769   Apeji, E. Adeche **"Problems of Writing and Publishing for Life-Long Learning in Nigeria."** *The Publisher*, 11, no. 1 (November 2004): 11-13.
Examines the extent to which the publishing sector can address the challenges of providing adequate learning materials in aid of life-long education programmes in Nigeria. The article surveys the needs in these areas: books for literacy, books for

primary school learners, and literacy through non-formal education programmes, such as books to acquire vocational skills and books for recreation. The author asks how far can the Nigerian publishing industry contribute towards meeting the book requirements in this area, which he estimates to be in excess of 44 million books, yet the publishers "produced only 750,000 and this translates to only 1.65% of need." He argues "to bridge the yawning gaps between supply and demand, there must be a deliberate government intervention policy."

770   Awoniyi, Adedeji **"Publishing in Nigeria in the 21st Century: Prospects and Challenges."** *The Publisher* 5, no. 1 (October 1997): 18-21.
Declares that if publishing in Nigeria is to survive and prosper and face the challenges and prospects of the 21st century, "then numerous reappraisals and hard decisions have to be taken by each of the publishing houses." The author then goes on highlight the areas which require reappraisal, namely the legal status of publishing houses, their management style, financing of publishing ventures, readership coverage, interpersonal relationships amongst publishers, publisher-author relations, and publishing and the new information technology. In assessing the prospects of the latter, and the advent of the Internet, the author pronounces, somewhat optimistically, that "anyone who is hooked on the line [the Web] will have the whole world on his finger tips and can discard of any publisher"!

771   Badejo, Rotimi **"Towards Local Communication Textbook Production: the Language Issue."** In *Communication Industry in Nigeria. The Crisis of Publications,* edited by A. Tom Adaba, Ololeka Ajia and Ikechukwu Nwosu. Nairobi, African Council for Communication Education, 1988, 53-65.
Gives a brief overview of textbook publishing in Nigeria and asks "in what language should our communications textbooks be written?" Advocates caution in the publishing of academic books in indigenous languages--"academic publishing is an international affair, and so its medium of expression cannot but be international."

772   Bakare, Muhtar **Publishing Literature in Nigeria – Challenges and Opportunities.**
http://www.sabdet.com/ASAUK2006Bakare.htm [04/03/08]
A paper presented during a ➔ **SABDET (113)** panel titled 'Writing in the Diaspora, Writing for the Diaspora' at the African Studies Association of the UK (ASAUK) biennial conference in September 2006. Muhtar Bakare Publisher of *Farafina Magazine* http://www.kachifo.com/farafina.cfm and head of the privately owned Kachifo Ltd. in Lagos http://www.kachifo.com/index.cfm, describes the publishing activities of his company and looks at the challenges of publishing in Nigeria from the perspective of an entrepreneur with a mission to make culturally useful as well as commercially viable books available to the general reading public. In analyzing the current [2006] publishing situation in the country, he considers the low level of investments in their business by existing publishers as one of the main impediments for growth of the local publishing industry in Nigeria. Other factors are the dearth of an adequate commercial infrastructure to support the industry, with limited and fragmented distribution and retail networks, significant collection problems of sales proceeds, as well as the collapse of basic social services such as electricity supply, a

good road network, reliable postal services, and affordable telecommunications. All these factors contribute "to make the cost of doing business prohibitive, discourage investments and lead to the easy option of sacrificing quality for cost." In his conclusion, the author asserts that "in terms of sheer ambition, chutzpah and achievement" Nigerian publishers have the most to learn from its banking sector.

773 Banjo, Ayo **"Publishers as Members of the Academic Community."** *African Publishing Review* 8, no. 5 (1999): 7-8.
Also published in *The Publisher* 6, no. 1 (May 1999).
Some reflections, and questions, about the responsibility of publishers promoting a healthy intellectual life in Nigerian society.

774 Bankole, Chris, ed. **Spectrum at Ten. A Decade of Dynamic Publishing.** Ibadan: Spectrum Books Limited, 1989. 42 pp.
A special anniversary publication to celebrate 10 years of publishing activities of Spectrum Books Limited, Nigeria, from 1978-1988. Provides an overview of the history of publishing in Nigeria, examines likely trends for the future, and lists ten significant books in the literary history of Nigeria.

775 Bankole, E. Bejide **"Federal Republic of Nigeria."** In *The Book Trade of the World, vol. IV: Africa,* edited by Sigfred Taubert and Peter Weidhaas. Munich: K.G. Saur, 1984, 225-233.
Overview of publishing and the book trade in Nigeria. Now very dated.

776 Bankole, S. Bodunde **"Indigenous Publishing of Tertiary Level Books in Nigeria: Issues and Problems."** *The African Book Publishing Record* 11, no. 4 (1985): 197-200.
A study by the former director of Lagos University Press of indigenous publishing of tertiary level books, discussing policy dilemmas and the problems of under-capitalization. Also addresses the issues of the market, as well as editorial and production problems.

777 Bankole, S. Bodunde **"Publishing in Nigeria."** In *Afro-Asian Publishing. Contemporary trends,* edited by Narendra Kumar, and S.K. Ghai. New Delhi: Institute of Book Publishing, 1992, 51-72.
Traces the growth of publishing in Nigeria, including the different types of publishing companies and highlights the problems and issues affecting the book industry.

778 Bankole, S. Bodunde **"Books in Nigeria: the Problems of Scarcity."** *African Publishing Review* 3, no. 3 (May/June 1994): 5-8.
Another version also published in *Nigerian Literary Index,* edited by Afolabi Adesanya. Lagos: A-Productions Nigeria Ltd., 1995, 92-101.
Looks at the root causes of the dearth of books in Nigeria and its consequences — with a book industry in crisis, and the buying power of the Nigerian reading public, parents, and students now greatly reduced. Offers a number of recommendations,

and includes a plea to government to create an environment for a competitive free market for books, to encourage small tertiary publishers through a systematic subsidy scheme for book purchases, and the need for a determined effort by government to improve library services.

779   Bankole, S. Bodunde **"The Need for a Nigerian Book Policy."** *The Publisher* 5, no. 1 (October 1997): 14-18.
Argues that although Nigeria has no book policy in place at the present time "the ingredients for such a policy are all around us and only need to be co-ordinated and coalesced for a viable book policy to evolve in Nigeria for the 21st century." Discusses the current recessionary situation of the Nigerian book industry, how this might be reversed by positive government intervention, and puts forward a number of proposals how a viable book policy for Nigeria might be evolved.

780   Bello, Sule, and Abdullahi Augi, eds. **Culture and the Book Industry in Nigeria.** Lagos: National Council for Arts and Culture [PMB 12534, Inagmu, Lagos], 1993. 298 pp.
The papers from a 1983 symposium on 'Culture and the Book Industry in Nigeria', although not published until ten years later. Arranged in three parts, it contains 16 papers on various aspects of the state of the book in Nigeria in all its dimensions: writing and authorship, orality, literacy, readership, library development, academic publishing, and book distribution. It is preceded by an introduction, and an eloquent keynote address delivered at the symposium by Jibril Aminu, entitled "Books into Peoples." The collection also contains some papers on author-publisher relations, publishing in Nigerian languages, and production and distribution of scholarly journals.

781   Berkhout, Joop **"Publishing and HIV/AIDS in Nigeria."** In *National Book Policy, HIV/AIDS and Sustainable Development. Papers Presented at the Fifth Nigeria International Book Fair, 8-13 May, 2006.* Lagos: Nigerian Book Fair Trust [c/o Literamed Publications Ltd., PMB 21068, Ikeja, Lagos, Nigeria], 2007, 114-119.
Chief Joop Berkhout of Spectrum Books, one of Nigeria's most dynamic publishers, suggests how publishers can respond to the AIDS problem through education and information and by publishing appropriate books for children, so that they can learn about HIV/AIDS, and how it affects them, their families, their school and teachers. He believes publishers ought to be at the vanguard of any movement to create books "that deliver the HIV/AIDS prevention message in a strong, unequivocal, convincing and effective manner."

782   Bgoya, Walter, and Mary Jay **"A Giant of African Publishing."** *West Africa,* 4-10 November (2002), 23.
A tribute to the late Victor Nwankwo, former Managing Director of Fourth Dimension Publishing Company, and former Chair of the ➔ **African Publishers' Network (5),** who was gunned down by assassins outside his home in Enugu on August 29, 2002.

783 Bolodeoku, B.O. **"Innovative Strategies for Cost Reduction in Book Publishing for Enhancement of Increased Sales and Better Profitability."** *The Publisher* 3, no. 1 (January 1995): 34-37.
Looks at the peculiar nature of publishing as a business – in particular for those operating in the difficult economic terrain of Nigeria – and how its uniqueness calls for a special effort of cost reduction, increasing sales, and achieving better profit margins.

784 Carew, F.C. **Educational Materials Distribution Study: Borno and Kano.** Washington, DC: The World Bank & London: ODA, 1989. 11 pp.
[Not examined]

785 Christopher, Nkechi M. **"Book Publishing in Nigeria: The Journey so Far and the Way Forward."** *The Publisher*, 11, no. 1 (November 2004): 25-35.
This is an excellent in-depth study of the current [2004] state of the book industries in Nigeria. The author believes that a thriving book and reading culture is central to, and an indicator of, development in any country. However, "the inadequacy of the Nigerian publishing industry as a supplier of knowledge, personal development and leisure products is evident, if not coterminous with, poor educational performance, as well as retrogression and retardation in various aspects of development in the country." With the support of some statistical analysis (based on data collected as part of a questionnaire mailing sent to over 300 publishers in 1993/94), he charts the growth of the Nigerian book industry from its beginnings in the early 1950s, "the good old days" of the 1970s, through to the mid-1990s, examining various issues of performance and the many problems facing Nigerian publishers, of which the unpredictable and unstable nature of the Nigerian economic climate, the high cost of distribution, and cash collection problems for books supplied to state governments, are among the most significant constraints. The author sets out a number of recommendations on a possible way forward, and suggests a range of practical ways book practitioners, as well as the government, "can ensure that the book industry is made responsive to the book needs of the individual and the nation", including the establishment of a national book policy, and more active collaboration between the different players in the book chain.

786 Diala, Isidore **"Conditions of Production for Writing, Publishing and Studying Literature in Africa: The Nigerian Situation."** *African Research &Documentation,* no. 100 (2006): 11-19.
Sets out the background and current [2006] conditions for the publication of creative writing in Nigeria, describing the difficulties budding writers face in getting their work considered and published, shortages of books, the frequently poor quality of library resources, and the absence of an enabling intellectual environment essential for a thriving book culture. It also examines the activities of the ➜ **Association of Nigerian Authors (732),** the state of literary studies as a teaching discipline at Nigerian universities. Despite the gloomy conditions which compelled many of Nigeria's finest scholars and writers to flee the country and seek work elsewhere, the author is inspired to note "how Nigerian students and lecturers continue to strive to

distinction in spite of limited resources, much like their compatriot writers devoted against all odds to the heroic revival of the book."

787   Dingome, Jeanne N. **"The Ibadan Cluster: Mbari."** In *European-Language Writing in Sub-Saharan Africa*, vol. 2, edited by Albert S. Gérard. Budapest: Akadémia Kiado, 1986, 679-688.
Describes the background which led to the setting up of Mbari Publications in Ibadan in December 1991, the brainchild of the German scholar Ulli Beier, working with prominent Nigerian writers such as Wole Soyinka, Christopher Okigbo, and John Pepper Clark. Mbari actively supported Nigerian and other African writers who showed confident daring in their creative ideas, as well as a diversity of views. It gave several gifted writers a launch pad and paved the way towards fame for talented artists. The article gives a detailed history of Mbari and provides a chronological list of Mbari titles published.

788   Diso, Lukman Ibraheem **"Publishing, Distribution and Control in Nigeria."** In *Workshop on Access to Third World Journals and Conference Proceedings* edited by Michael Wise. Boston Spa: British Library/IFLA, 1993, 55-65.
Examines the problems of journal publishing, distribution and control in Nigeria. Argues that the publishing industry is an essential part of the political, socio-economic and cultural context and suggests that other structural problems within Nigeria must be addressed in order to find lasting solutions. Identifies a concern that Nigerians are becoming isolated from the mainstream of intellectual development as a direct result of the crisis in the publishing industry.

789   Enyia, Christian O. **"The Role of the Nigerian Publisher in National Development."** *International Library Review* 23, no. 3 (September 1991): 201-214.
Traces the role of publishers in the national development of Nigeria and looks at some of the problems and handicaps faced by them.

790   Ethiope Publishing Corporation, ed. **Publishing in Nigeria.** Benin City: Ethiope Publishing Corporation, 1972. 71 pp.
Now very dated, but remains a useful collection of essays. It contains articles on the Nigerian and African publishing scene in the 1970s, including articles on the function of university presses, the role of the non-indigenous publisher, publishing for children, and general perspectives on publishing and book development in Africa.

791   Ezenwa-Ohaeto **Making Books Available and Affordable. Proceedings of the First Annual National Conference on Book Development, Held at the National Theatre, Iganmu, Lagos, April 25-29, 1994.** Awka, Nigeria: Nigerian Book Foundation, 1995. 136 pp.
The papers from a conference organized by the ➜ **Nigerian Book Foundation (738),** which examined four possible solutions to overcome some of the formidable problems faced by the Nigerian book industries: (i) book subsidy schemes, (ii) self-

sufficiency in materials for book production, (iii) exploitation of new technologies in book production, and (iv) establishing cost effective distribution and marketing networks. Also includes the recommendations which emerged from the conference and which will influence the programme of action of the Foundation in the years ahead. *Note:* some of the papers in this collection are individually abstracted elsewhere in this bibliography.

792   Fanoiki, M.F.I. **"Publishing for Schools in Nigeria."** *Nigerbiblios* 9, no. 1 (January 1984): 19-20.
Paper presented by the Chief Librarian of Lagos State Library Board at the Symposium held during National Library Week of the Lagos Division of the Nigeria Library Association in October 1983. Suggests that authors and teachers ought to be more imaginative, and that publishers be "more enterprising and daring in their investment. They should also invest money in organizing writing workshops for budding authors."

793   Fayose, Osazee **"Data Collection: The Foundation for Effective Book Development."** In *Creating a Conducive Environment for Book Publishing,* edited by Chukwuemeka Ike. Awka, Nigeria: Nigerian Book Foundation, 1996, 31-48.
The keynote address, by a Nigerian librarian, to the ➜ **Nigerian Book Foundation's (738)** second national conference on book development, which focussed on the importance of data collection, the establishment of databases, the availability of data to aid the book industries, and the need to provide adequate bibliographic control.

Furniss, Graham **"Documenting Kano 'Market' Literature"** *see* ➜ **Section 4, Studies by topic: Mass market and popular literature publishing** entry **2004**

794   Hayatu, Husaini, ed. **50 Years of Truth: The Story of Gaskiya Corporation Zaria 1939-1991**. Zaria: Gaskiya Corporation, 1991. 205 pp.
Founded in 1945, the history of Gaskiya Corporation has always been closely associated with the development of book and newspaper publishing in Northern Nigeria, including the establishment of the oldest surviving Hausa-language newspaper, *Gaskiya ta fi kwabo*. In the 1940s and 1950s the Corporation published a total of sixteen weeklies in Hausa and in other Nigerian languages. In 1948 it began the publication of the national daily *The Nigerian Citizen*. The first part of the book contains historical articles on the Gaskiya Corporation and on publishing in Zaria and Northern Nigeria, by contributors including R.M. East, Husaini Hayatu, Neil Skinner, and Lindsay Barrett. Part two offers biographical information on 26 past and present personalities in the Gaskiya Corporation. Subsequent chapters describe the present [1991] structure and planned future development of the Corporation.

795   Higo, Aigboje **"The Problems of Publishing to Meet the Demands of an Expanding Educational Programme."** *The Book - Nigeria* 1, no. 1 (December 1980):19-26.

The text of a paper delivered at a seminar at the Ife Book fair, Ile Ife, March 1977, describing the problems of publishing to meet the demands of an expanding educational programme and providing statistics to illustrate the size of the problem. Offers possible solutions to some of the problems and briefly examines publishing for other markets.

Higo, Aigboje *see also* ➜ Adesanoye, Festus A., and Ayo Ojeniyi, eds. **Issues in Book Publishing in Nigeria. Essays in Honour of Aigboje Higo at 70** entry **755**

796 Ifidon, B.I. **"Book Scarcity in Nigeria: Causes and Solutions."**
African Journal of Library, Archives and Information Science 4, no. 1 (April 1994): 55-62.
A Nigerian librarian examines the causes of the book famine in Nigeria and offers some possible solutions.

797 Ike, V. Chukwuemeka **"Book Development in Nigeria, 1972-1982: Problems and Prospects."** In *Report of the First Nigerian National Congress on Books, 21-25 March, 1983.* Lagos: Nigerian Book Development Commission, 1983, 55-66.
[Not examined]

798 Ike, Chukwuemeka **Creating a Conducive Environment for Book Publishing. Proceedings of the Second Annual Conference on Book Development, 27 April 1995; and the Third National Conference on Book Development, 14 May 1996, held at the Conference Centre, University of Lagos, Nigeria.** Awka, Nigeria: Nigerian Book Foundation 1996. 249 pp.
Brings together the various presentations made at these two ➜ **Nigerian Book Foundation/NBF (738)** conferences, as well as including the recommendations put forward at the meetings, and the text of the addresses presented during the formal opening ceremonies. The NBF's second conference concentrated on the need for data collection for the Nigerian book industries, while the third conference examined the ideal environment for nurturing authors, and author-publisher relations. The book also includes a study, by its Director, Chukwuemeka Ike, of the role of the NBF as a national book development organization with a review of its activities to date. *Note:* most of the papers in this collection are individually abstracted elsewhere in this bibliography.

799 Ike, Chukwuemeka **Book Publishing in Nigeria.** [September 2004]
http://www.sabre.org/publications/publishing-in-nigeria.pdf [04/03/08]
A short but succinct four page overview of the book publishing industry in Nigeria, which has been in steady decline since the 1980s: "At one stage, prospects for the book industry in Nigeria appeared rosy. The Federal Government established paper and pulp making industries, and an elaborate plan was drawn up for achieving self-sufficiency in the production of books for the nursery/primary, secondary, and tertiary tiers of education. Unfortunately all that, or most of it, collapsed following

the nation's economic downturn of the 1980s. Book famine descended on Nigeria." The author examines various initiatives to improve the state of the book sector to make it meet the needs of the educational system, government decrees regarding indigenous publishing, national book policies (or the lack of it rather at the present time), a national book development council (which has been dormant for years), and other interventions.

800 Irele, Abiola **"Ethiope Publishing Corporation."** *The African Book Publishing Record* 1, no. 1 (January 1975): 27-33.
A revised and expanded version of a paper presented by Abiola Irele during the international conference on publishing and book development in Africa, held at the University of Ife, Nigeria in 1973. Professor Irele was executive chairman of Ethiope Publishing Corporation in Benin City, Nigeria and he outlines the problems encountered in setting up this company. Contends [in 1975] that the future of publishing in Nigeria has great prospects. Pinpoints the inadequacy of production facilities, the haphazard nature of organization in the retail trade, and the necessity for a more dynamic approach to bookselling.

801 Irele, Abiola **"The Book Publishing Industry in Nigeria. Problems and Prospects."** In *Africa Bibliography 1987*, compiled by Hector Blackhurst. Manchester: Manchester University Press, 1988, vi-xvi.
Examines the crisis in the book trade in Nigeria today [as at 1987] caused by a severe shortage of books and reading materials and constant increases in book prices. Discusses the situation in the industry prior to the economic crisis and the irony implicit in the situation where Nigerian authors published overseas cannot be read by Nigerians in Nigeria. Provides an overall picture of the book publishing industry in Nigeria, including printing, distribution, and the activities of both multinational publishers and indigenous publishers. Examines some of the major problems and constraints, and sets out a range of proposals intended "to foster the growth of a viable publishing industry in Nigeria through local production of books on a scale that will match present and future needs."

802 Iroh, Eddie **"The Role of Publishing in Sustainable Human Development."** *The Publisher* 12, no. 1 (November 2005): 3-7.
A keynote speech delivered at the 2004 annual conference of the ➔ **Nigerian Publishers Association (739),** on the significance of books and publishing in national development, the role of writers in social transformation, and the role and benefits of publishing for both social and cultural development as well as for financial empowerment, poverty alleviation and economic emancipation. Iroh also addresses the issue of piracy as a serious threat to authorship and publishing, and offers a number of recommendations for transforming the Nigerian publishing industry.

803 Iwe, J.I. **"Book Production and Publishing in Nigeria."** *Aslib Proceedings* 42, no. 6 (June 1990): 189-197.
[Not examined]

804 Iwerebon, F.A."**The Supply of Educational Books in the 1990s - Quo Vadis?**" *The Publisher* 2, no. 1 (March 1991): 21-26.
A paper delivered at the opening ceremony of the 14th Ife Book Fair in February 1990. Provides some background by looking at the preceding twenty years of publishing of educational books in Nigeria and predicts growth through hard work.

805 Iwerebon, Felix "**Academic Book Development in Nigeria.**" In *National Book Policy, HIV/AIDS and Sustainable Development. Papers Presented at the Fifth Nigeria International Book Fair, 8-13 May, 2006.* Lagos: Nigerian Book Fair Trust [c/o Literamed Publications Ltd., PMB 21068, Ikeja, Lagos, Nigeria], 2007, 80-89.
Veteran Nigerian publisher Chief Felix Iwerebon offers a historical overview of the development of tertiary level education in Nigeria and academic book provision for this market. Unfortunately, the current situation, as a consequence "of the dismal socio-political and economic climate for tertiary education in Nigeria" is not a happy one. Iwerebon identifies some of the reasons which have lead to this situation, and some of the factors that have militated against the development and production of academic books by indigenous publishers in the country.

806 Jegede, Oluremi "**Book Scarcity, Law Libraries and the Legal Profession in Nigeria.**" *International Information and Library Review* 25, no. 2 (1993): 141-164.
Book scarcity is an ongoing problem plaguing both the educational programmes and professional practices in Nigeria. The author – a former Librarian at the Nigerian Institute of Advanced Legal Studies – discusses the genesis of the book scarcity, and makes some suggestions to ameliorate the problems. She however advocates that a lasting solution is to publish books for the legal professions locally. In this regard the government needs to provide funding for publishing textbooks and professional books; and encourage government departments to purchase the books. The author pleads for more cooperation and resource sharing among libraries in order to achieve greater coverage in the acquisition of legal materials.

Jegede, Oluremi "**Publications Laws of Nigeria: Need for a Review**" *see* → Section 4, Studies by topic: Copyright and legal deposit/Author's rights entry **1774**

807 Keartland, E. **Distribution Study: Primary Education Subsector Study, Nigeria.** Washington, DC: The World Bank & London: Overseas Development Administration/ODA, 1989.
[Not examined]

808 Lawal-Solarin, O.M. "**Publishing in Nigeria.**" *African Publishing Review* 6, no. 2 (May/June 1997): 10-12.
Presents a short account of the Nigerian publishing industry [in 1997], discussing the role of government as it affects publishing, publication of professional journals, marketing, training for book professionals, piracy, and some other issues.

809   Longe, H.O.D. **"Developing a Database for Effective User Access in the Book Industry."** In *Creating a Conducive Environment for Book Publishing*, edited by Chukwuemeka Ike. Awka, Nigeria: Nigerian Book Foundation, 1996, 58-65.
Argues that effective database systems are an essential requirement for the Nigerian book industries. Discusses the relevance of a distributed database approach in relation to data management, and analyzes the different components required.

810   Mammah, Richard **The History and Prospects of the Nigerian Book.** Lagos: Mace Books for Synergy Educational and French Cultural Centre, 2002. 94 pp.
Charts the history of the Nigerian book and from its earliest days through to the 1980s and 90s - when the publishing industries went into a period of marked decline – and through to the present day. Examines various aspects of the contemporary publishing scene including issues such as copyright and piracy, and presents the author's views on the history, merits, and future of Nigerian book fairs. The author is Executive Director of the Nigerian NGO ➜ **Synergy Educational (742).**
Review:
The African Book Publishing Record vol. 30, no. 4, 2004

811   Mountain, Penny **"Nigeria: The End of an Era?"** *The Bookseller* (March 12 1983): 956-959.
Discusses the economic pressures that transformed Nigeria from one of the most important export markets for British books in the developing world, to a situation where the Nigerian government owed huge sums to Nigerian publishers and through them to their UK associates. Concludes that caution will be necessary in future relations.

812   Mosuro, Kolade **"Book Development, Production, and Distribution."** In *National Book Policy, HIV/AIDS and Sustainable Development. Papers Presented at the Fifth Nigeria International Book Fair, 8-13 May, 2006.* Lagos: Nigerian Book Fair Trust [c/o Literamed Publications Ltd., PMB 21068, Ikeja, Lagos, Nigeria], 2007, 70-79.
Kolade Mosuro is well-known Nigerian bookseller. In this provocative paper he examines some of the reasons for the acute shortage of books in the country and why book prices are so high, at least partly due to incongruous government policies as they relate to the book sector and paper and printing supplies: for example the fact that educational textbooks can be imported for free, while import duty on paper was recently increased to 20%. Mosuro is also critical of the government because – unlike the highly successful Educational Low-Priced Books Scheme/ELBS that operated three or more decades ago (funded by the UK government Overseas Development Administration as part of the British government's overseas aid programme) – Nigerian government agencies, whenever they have intervened to provide books under similar schemes, "they circumvent the book chain and operate only between the publishers and the end users", thus excluding booksellers and the retail sector. Meantime new books "are launched without any consideration or use of the

distributive arm. No wonder the books are launched and die the same day because you will rarely find them in any bookshop."

Mosuro, Kolade **"Publishing and Bookselling: A Bookseller's Observations"** *see* ➔ **Section 4, Studies by topic: Bookselling and book distribution** entry **1507**

813 Mwoltu, P.P. **Educational Material Distribution Study: Gongola and Plateau.** Washington, DC: The World Bank & London: Overseas Development Administration/ODA, 1989.
[Not examined]

814 Nigerian Book Fair Trust **Publishing for Peace. Papers Presented at the First Nigeria International Book Fair, 14-19 May, 2002.** Lagos: Nigerian Book Fair Trust [c/o Literamed Publications Ltd., PMB 21068, Ikeja, Lagos, Nigeria], 2002. 85 pp.
One in a series of collections from the ➔ **Nigerian Book Fair Trust (737)** containing the opening addresses, keynote speeches, and papers presented at the Nigeria International Book Fair, held annually since 2002, each fair focusing on a special topic or topics. Nobel Laureate Wole Soyinka was the keynote speaker at the first book fair held in 2002, which had "Publishing for Peace" as its theme, and his address, "Between the Open Book and the Closed Text" is reproduced in this volume. It also includes the speeches made during the presentation of the 2001 ➔ **Noma Award for Publishing in Africa (98)**, held at a special ceremony during the 2002 Nigeria International Book Fair, among them the acceptance speech by Abosede Emanuel, who was the winner of the 2001 award for his book *Odun Ifa/Ifa Festival*.
Reviews:
The African Book Publishing Record vol. 34, no. 1, 2008

815 Nigerian Book Fair Trust **National Book Policy, HIV/AIDS and Sustainable Development. Papers Presented at the Fifth Nigeria International Book Fair, 8-13 May, 2006.** Lagos: Nigerian Book Fair Trust [c/o Literamed Publications Ltd., PMB 21068, Ikeja, Lagos, Nigeria], 2007. 270 pp.
One in a series of collections from the ➔ **Nigerian Book Fair Trust (737)** containing the opening addresses, keynote speeches, and papers presented at the Nigeria International Book Fair, held annually since 2002, each fair focusing on a special topic or topics. The theme of the 2006 book fair focused on two topics: "National Book Policy and Sustainable Development" and "HIV/AIDS and Sustainable Development". *Note:* some of the papers in this collection are individually abstracted elsewhere in this bibliography.
Reviews:
The African Book Publishing Record vol. 34, no. 1, 2008

Nigerian Book Fair Trust **Capacity Building in the African Publishing Industry. Papers Presented at the Sixth Nigeria International Book Fair, 7-13 May, 2007** *see* ➜ **Section 2, General, comparative and regional studies: Africa: General studies** entry **296**

816 Nwakanma , Chukwuemeka Dean **"Research Publications in Library and Information Science (LIS) in Nigeria: Publishing to the Wrong Audience?"** *African Journal of Library, Archives and Information Science* 13, no. 2 (2003): 93-106.
A comparative study of Nigerian library and information science (LIS) researched articles published in foreign and local LIS journals, and an analysis of LIS articles, as contained in the online versions of *Library and Information Science Abstracts* (LISA), *Library Literature* (LL) and *Information Science Abstracts* (ISA), from 1968 to June 2002. The results show that a majority of the authors published in foreign LIS journals from the early 1980s and continue to do so today. The author argues that due to difficulties encountered in accessing foreign journals in Nigeria, publishing Nigerian LIS research in foreign journals deprives the nation of the benefits of utilizing these research results to enhance library and information science research in Nigeria.

817 Nwali, L.O. **"Book Publishing in Nigeria. Problems and Prospects."** *Publishing Research Quarterly* 7 (Winter 1991-92): 65-71.
An overview of indigenous book publishing in Nigeria, examining some of the major problems such as lack of capital resources, unskilled authors and publishers, poor production quality, and inadequate distribution networks. The author offers some recommendations and suggestions for establishing and maintaining a lively and prosperous book industry.

818 Nwankwo, Arthur **Thoughts on Nigeria**. Enugu, Nigeria: Fourth Dimension Publishing House (Issues in Nigerian Development series, 1), 1986. 220 pp.
This is a collection of speeches by Arthur Nwankwo, founder of Fourth Dimension Publishing House (and elder brother of the late Victor Nwankwo), on the topics of publishing, the media and nation-building, economic development, and social change.

819 Nwankwo, B.C. **Educational Material Distribution Study: Imo and Rivers.** Washington, DC: The World Bank & London: Overseas Development Administration/ODA, 1989.
[Not examined]

820 Nwankwo, Victor **"Publishing in Nigeria Today."** In *Publishing and Development in the Third World*, edited by Philip G. Altbach. London: Hans Zell Publishers, 1992, 151-168.
Presents a general picture of publishing in Nigeria, beginning with a description of the historical background of publishing in the country and followed by an examination of book needs and the current [1991] publishing situation in Nigeria.

Thereafter reviews issues such as authorship, production, marketing and distribution, fiscal and monetary measures, international trade, training and copyright. Recommends measures with which to solve the problems of publishing in Nigeria, and concludes that the way to combat book shortages in Nigeria is to find adequate investment finance for the publishing industry.

821   Nwankwo, Victor **"Nigeria: Publishing in a Situation of Crisis."** *Bellagio Publishing Network Newsletter*, no. 8 (December 1993): 4-5. Also published in *The Publisher* 3, no. 1 (January 1995): 19-21.
Sets out the problems faced by Nigerian publishers in a situation of crisis: an unstable political climate, a traumatized economic environment, a rapidly declining currency, scarcity of essential materials for the printing industry, procurement and production problems, reluctant transporters, and uncertain markets.

822   Nwankwo, Victor **"Nigeria."** In *International Book Publishing. An Encyclopedia*, edited by Philip G. Altbach and Edith S. Hoshino. New York: Garland Publishing, 1995, 396-415.
A comprehensive insight into the Nigerian publishing scene. Sets out the historical background, reviews the country's book needs, and then goes on to examine some of the crucial issues such as authorship, investment finance, cost of raw materials, import tariffs, marketing and distribution, interaction with government, international book aid to the country, and the effects of monetary, fiscal and other dispositions. Also looks at the role of professional trade bodies, the Nigerian Copyright Council, and author-publisher relations.

823   Nwankwo, Victor **"Inter-sectoral Co-ordination in the Book Industry: The Publishing Sub-sector."** In *National Book Policies for Africa*, edited by Murray McCartney. Harare: Zimbabwe International Book Fair Trust, 1996, 58-61.
States that the need for a national book policy is now well recognized and no longer an issue for debate, but that "translating this recognition into an effective policy is a burning concern." Examines various initiatives towards a coherent national book policy in Nigeria and the roles played by the Nigerian Book Development Council and, more recently, by the ➔ **Nigerian Book Foundation (738)**. Concludes that Nigeria's national book policy still lacks the enabling book legislation "necessary to bring it to practical usefulness, but it has come a long way."

824   Nwankwo, Victor **"Readers without Books: A Nigerian Publisher's Response."** *Logos. The Journal of the World Book Community* 12, no. 2 (2001): 99-102..
Online: http://www.atypon-link.com/LOG/doi/pdf/10.2959/logo.2001.12.2.99
A sharp rebuke to Apeji's **"Readers without Books. A Nigerian Case Study"** (*see* entry ➔ **768**), by the [then] Managing Director of Fourth Dimension Publishing Company, one of Nigeria's major private and indigenously-owned publishing firms Nwankwo says "the trouble with the piece lies in the things the author failed to say",

that the result is a distorted picture of the publishing industry in Nigeria, and that the article is seriously flawed because its analysis is based on the publishing activities of six former British multinationals, but ignores the publishing activities of numerous medium-sized publishers or general book publishing companies which hardly publish any textbooks at all. Nwankwo asserts that Apeji also failed to address "the crucial role of the conditions in which Nigerian publishers valiantly operate, to properly locate the reasons for the paucity of general reading material"; and that an attempt should perhaps be made to find the reasons for the book shortages and the government's role in this unfortunate state of affairs.

Note: a further rejoinder to this debate, by Dr. Apeji, appeared in the 'Letters to the Editor' column in *Logos* 13, no. 1 (2002): 58-59, online at http://www.atypon-link.com/LOG/doi/pdf/10.2959/logo.2002.13.1.58, in which he concludes "the point which I hope I have made sufficiently clear is that publishers who are too timid to develop and conquer the vast Nigerian book market must not be allowed to use blackmail and subterfuge to frustrate the government's intervention in policies. The government, I insist, has a responsibility towards its citizens."

825   Nwoga, Chinyere **"The Book Chain in Nigeria."** In *The Book Chain in Anglophone Africa. A Survey and Directory*, edited by Roger Stringer. Oxford: International Network for the Availability of Scientific Publications (INASP), 2002, 62-67.

Online: http://www.inasp.info/file/57/the-book-chain-in-anglophone-africa-a-survey-and-directory.html [04/03/08]

One in a series of useful country surveys and overviews – each prepared by a book professional from the country concerned – that review the state of the book, and the major players in the "book chain", in English-speaking African countries. Each country survey covers printing, book publishing, bookselling and distribution, library services, professional associations, book promotional bodies and book promotional events, training for the book professions, as well as examining some of the major issues as they relate to book development, such as languages, literacy, writers and writing, the reading habit, and national book policies. For each country this is supported by an annotated directory of government ministries, professional associations, book publishers, booksellers and distributors, printers, major libraries, and training institutions, with full address and contact details.

826   Nwosu, C.B. **"International Standards for Book Publishing."** In *National Book Policy, HIV/AIDS and Sustainable Development. Papers Presented at the Fifth Nigeria International Book Fair, 8-13 May, 2006.* Lagos: Nigerian Book Fair Trust [c/o Literamed Publications Ltd., PMB 21068, Ikeja, Lagos, Nigeria], 2007, 144-163.

The Deputy Director of the National Library of Nigeria Readers and User Services Department discusses the nature, development and application of bibliographic standards for book and serials publishing in Nigeria, and effectively sets out the benefits associated with their adoption and implementation.

827   Obidiegwu, Dan **"Indigenous Publishing and National Development."** In *Publishing in Indigenous Languages. Papers Presented at the*

Fourth Nigeria International Book Fair, 10-14 May, 2005. Lagos: Nigerian Book Fair Trust [c/o Literamed Publications Ltd., PMB 21068, Ikeja, Lagos, Nigeria], 2006, 113-118.

Dan Obidiegwu asks what, in the face of declining standards of education in Nigeria and rapidly deteriorating quality of graduates from Nigeria's tertiary institutions, indigenous publishers can do to address this alarming trend. He identifies a number of tasks that should be accomplished in order to bring about change, and as publishers' contribution towards enhancing educational development in the country.

828   Obidiegwu, Dan **"Enhancing Productivity in the Publishing Industry."** *The Publisher* 13, no. 1 (November 2006): 3-10, 26.

The keynote address presented at the annual conference of the ➔ **Nigerian Publishers Association (739)** in 2005. It starts off with a roundup of the current [2005] status of the Nigerian book publishing industry, and thereafter looks at the major impediments that have contributed to stunted growth and productivity, the reasons for the high costs of books, and other current problems such as inadequate printing capacity and poor quality printing and finishing due to obsolete printing equipment. Other reasons cited include frequent changes in recommended textbooks, inadequate funding for libraries in the country, poor bookseller-publisher relationships, and erratic government policies. The author then presents a number of possible remedies and strategies that might inject new vigour into the publishing industries. These include strategic mergers and the benefits this would bring, shared services, more visibility for Nigerian books abroad, better training facilities, and the need to make effective use now offered by new information and communication technologies.

829   Obioma, Godswell **"National Book Policy in the Context of Globalization."** In *National Book Policy, HIV/AIDS and Sustainable Development. Papers Presented at the Fifth Nigeria International Book Fair, 8-13 May, 2006.* Lagos: Nigerian Book Fair Trust [c/o Literamed Publications Ltd., PMB 21068, Ikeja, Lagos, Nigeria], 2007, 48-57.

The author argues that while globalization is transforming educational systems, that change may not actually show up at classroom level in Nigeria; and that in the context of globalization, a Nigerian national book policy should not only cover printed books, but should also embrace e-learning and e-resources as part of the country's educational system, and that provision should be made for making such e-based resources accessible to those in other parts of the world.

830   Ogunleye, Bisi **"Establishing a Cost-Effective National Book Distribution Network in Nigeria."** In *Making Books Available and Affordable*, edited by Ezenwa-Ohaeto. Awka, Nigeria: Nigerian Book Foundation, 1995, 86-92.

Sets out a possible strategy for more effective distribution and marketing of Nigerian-published material, and proposes the establishment of a National Book Distribution Company that would handle promotion and distribution both domestically and for markets elsewhere in Africa.

831 Okojie, Victoria, and Abraham A. Azubuike **"Local Initiatives in the Nigerian Book Industry."** *Information Development* 4, no. 1 (January 1988): 28-32.
Despite severe economic constraints there have been a number of notable initiatives in Nigeria to develop the book industries, which are described in this article.

832 Okoli, Enukora Joe **"Afrocentric Publishing."** *West Africa*, no. 3329 (18 May 1981): 1098-1103.
Profile of Arthur Nwankwo, founder and Chair of Fourth Dimension Publishing Company in Enugu, one of Nigeria's most prominent indigenous publishers, established in 1977.

833 Okoro, Innocent **"From Onitsha Market Literature to General Trade Book Publishing in Nigeria."** Paper presented during the biennial conference of the African Studies Association of the UK, September 9-11, 2002
http://www.sabdet.com/ASAUK2002_Okoro_paper.htm [04/03/08]
Traces the rise and fall of popular Onitsha market literature in Nigeria from its heydays in the late 1950s and early 1960s through to their decline and near extinction, primarily as a result of the Nigerian civil war. Also offers some comments and observations on the current situation of Nigerian trade book publishing.

834 Okwilagwe, Andrew Oshiotse **Book Publishing in the Social Change (Value System Re-orientation) Process in Nigeria: A Theoretical Perspective.** Stirling, Scotland: University of Stirling, 1984. M.Litt. dissertation.
[Not examined]

835 Okwilagwe, Andrew Oshiotse **"The Book Industries and Cultural Development in Nigeria: Problems and Prospects."** In *Cultural Development and Nation Building,* edited by S.O.Unoh. Ibadan: Spectrum Books, 1986, 89-109.
[Not examined]

836 Okwilagwe, Andrew Oshiotse **Information Input as a Factor in Organizational Effectiveness of the Publishing Industry in Nigeria.** Ibadan: University of Ibadan, 1993. PhD thesis. 202 pp.
[Not examined]

837 Okwilagwe, Andrew Oshiotse **Book Publishing in Nigeria.** Ibadan : Stirling-Horden Publishers, 2001. 245 pp.
[Not examined]
Reviews:
African Journal of Library, Archives and Information Science vol. 12, no. 2, October 2002

838   Okwilagwe, Andrew Oshiotse **"The Relevance of the International Standard Bibliographic Description (ISBD) to Book Publishing in Nigeria."** *The Publisher* 12, no. 1 (November 2005): 34-35.
Describes the characteristics of International Standard Bibliographic Description (ISBD), its relevance to book publishing in Nigeria, and the benefits accruing to publishers from its use, particularly in terms of marketing opportunities and national and international visibility.

839   Okwilagwe, Andrew Oshiotse **"Book Piracy. Robbery of Intellectual Property."** *The Publisher* 14, no. 1 (November 2007): 17-23.
Examines the nature of book piracy in Nigeria, the different types of piracy activities and copyright violations, the methods employed by the pirates, and the destructive impact illegal reproduction of books has had on authorship and the Nigerian book industries. Also offers some observations on the nature of the reading culture in Nigeria.

840   Olajide, Akin **"The Impact of African Publishing on World Literature."** *African Publishing Review* 12, no. 3 (2003): 1-4.
Primarily an account of the development of publishing in Nigeria, and the publishing activities of some of the Nigerian branches of major international companies, notably Oxford University Press (now University Press plc), including the publication of linguistic and literary works in Nigeria's major languages.

841   Olude, O.O. **"The National Book Distribution Network: Suggestion for Textbook Distribution to Schools."** In *Making Books Available and Affordable,* edited by Ezenwa-Ohaeto. Awka, Nigeria: Nigerian Book Foundation, 1995, 101-107.
Reviews some of the problems which affect book distribution of educational materials in Nigeria, and describes the rationale and working methods of the government-initiated Book Depot and Distribution Outlet (BDDO).

Orimalade, Oluronke **"Problems Facing Bookselling in Nigeria."** *see* ➜ **Section 4, Studies by topic: Bookselling and book distribution** entry **1512**

842   Otokunefor, H.C., and C.O. Nwodo **The Coming of Age of Book Publishing and Indexing in Nigeria.** *Library Review* 39, no. 4 (1990): 33-40.
Provides a short history of book publishing in Nigeria and reviews the activities of the different kinds of publishing houses. The author evaluates the quality of book indexing by these publishers and examines the indexing practices of the publishers in relation to internationally accepted criteria. The author found that indexing was generally of a high standard.

843   Osakwe, G.C. **"Government and Book Publishing in Nigeria."** *The Publisher* 1, no. 1 (December 1985): 30-34.
Looks at government involvement in publishing in Nigeria, and discusses the role of the [now defunct] Nigerian Book Development Council.

844 Popoola, Dimeji **"The Spectrum Story. Ten Years of Dynamic Publishing."** *Books* 1, no. 2 (April 1988): 23-24.
A profile of the Nigerian publishing house Spectrum Books Limited, Ibadan, founded in 1978 by Dutchman Joop Berkhout.

845 Read, Anthony **Nigeria: Textbook Provision.** London: Overseas Development Administration/ODA, 1988. 69 pp.
[Not examined]

846 Read, Anthony **Nigeria Books Sector Study: Summary Report.** Washington, DC: The World Bank & London: Overseas Development Administration/ODA, 1990. 38 pp.
A report on the state of the book sector commissioned by the Nigerian Federal Ministry of Education, funded by the ➜ **World Bank (124)** and Overseas Development Administration, and carried out by the ➜ **British Council (43)** and the Book Development Council.

847 Ricard, Alain **Livre et communication au Nigéria.** Paris: Présence Africaine, 1975. 136 pp.
Examines the institutions and the different players concerned with the media and communication in Nigeria, books and book production, writers and the printed word, and Nigerian culture. Now of course very dated, but still useful for the historical background the book provides.

848 Ricard, Alain **"Faim de livres au Nigeria."** *Politique Africaine*, no. 23 (September 1986): 119-122.
Online: http://www.politique-africaine.com/numeros/pdf/023119.pdf [04/03/08]
Laments the book famine in Nigeria [in the mid-1980s] and asks whether the Nigerian printing and publishing industries are in fact capable of supplying the huge numbers of books that are needed.

849 Roberts, Kern, and Chris Nott **Nigeria Publishing Market Profile 2006.** London: The Publishers Association and The British Council, 2006. 56 pp. (accessible by purchase only for non-PA members/GPI subscribers, cost £249)
http://www.publishers.org.uk/en/home/market_reports_and_statistics/gpi/reports/html_reports/nigeria_publishing_market_profile_2006/ (table of contents only)
An analysis of the book markets in Nigeria, providing general background, details of the education system, together with overviews of the general, academic and professional, and school book markets, and supported by a wide range of appendices and tables. [Not examined]

850 Roukbah, B.F. **In Search of Solutions to the Present Publishing Problems in Nigeria.** Zaria, Nigeria: Albah Publishers, 1990. 92 pp.
[Not examined]

851 Russell, N. **Nigeria: Print and Production Survey.** Washington, DC: The World Bank & London: Overseas Development Agency/ODA, 1989.
[Not examined]

852 Salahi, Katherine **"Chief Victor Nwankwo in Conversation with Katherine Salahi."** *Bellagio Publishing Network Newsletter,* no. 23 (October 1998): 15-16.
Online:
http://www.bellagiopublishingnetwork.com/newsletter23/salahi.htm
[27/08/07]
An interview with the late Chief Victor Nwankwo, former Managing Director of Fourth Dimension Publishing Company, Enugu, Nigeria, and former Chair of the ➔ **African Publishers' Network (5).**

853 Sani, Abba Aliyu; Jibrin Ibrahim, and Emmanuel Babatunde Omobowale **Creative Writing, Writers, and Publishing in Northern Nigeria.** Ibadan: IFRA (IFRA Occasional Publications, 11), 1997. 52 pp.
Addresses various aspects of creative writing in northern Nigeria, with short profiles of male and female writers writing both in Nigerian languages and in English since the 1980s. This is followed by a survey of publishing activities, a chapter on strategies for enhancing literary production, a list of new Hausa 'soyya' romantic novels (or also referred to as 'Kano market literature') together with a historical overview of creative writing in northern Nigeria.

854 Saro-Wiwa, Ken **"Notes of a Reluctant Publisher."** *The African Book Publishing Record* 22, no. 4 (1996): 257-259.
Also published in *The African Writers' Handbook,* edited by James Gibbs and Jack Mapanje. Oxford: African Books Collective Ltd., 1999, 105-110.
The late Ken Saro-Wiwa was an enterprising and innovative African publisher. On 10 November 1995, he was summarily and callously executed on the orders of the [then] Nigerian junta despite pleas from world leaders to save his life. This article was submitted to ➔ **The African Book Publishing Record (168)** as a provisional version in 1992, but he never managed to expand it, as had been his wish. It was published posthumously by ABPR with only minor editorial changes, and as a tribute to Ken Saro-Wiwa. It provides an account of his school days as the scribe of school magazines, his first steps on "the painful path of self-publishing", and the setting up a "do-it-yourself operation" that became known as Saros International Publishers.

855 Tahir, Gidado **"Eradication of Poor Quality Books in Schools."** *The Publisher* 12, no. 1 (November 2005): 28-32.

The Executive Secretary of the Universal Basic Education Commission (UBEC) addresses the serious issue of the poor quality of books submitted for use in a major Supplementary Reader's Project – part of the Federal Government's Universal Basic Education (UBE) programme – a project that served as a good reference point for comparing the quality of Nigerian books with those from other parts of the world, including African countries. About half of the books printed in Nigeria for evaluation failed to meet the required criteria, with the books scoring badly, particularly in the areas of binding, cover artwork, and illustrations. The author sees a need for a national benchmark, and an effective national book policy, to guide the future quality of books produced in the country.

856   Taiwo, Oladele **Reading and Writing for National Development: The Nigerian Experience.** Lagos: University of Lagos Press, 1990. 24 pp.
An inaugural lecture delivered at the University of Lagos in January 1990 that discusses in some detail the factors which have influenced Nigerian book production including piracy and the loss of confidence between writers and publishers, with special emphasis on the school textbook market. Taiwo also expresses some acerbic views on the book launch practice in Nigeria.

857   Tamuno, O.G. **"Printing and Publishing in Nigeria: A Historical Survey."** *Nigerian Libraries* 9, no. 1/2 (April/August 1973): 1-12.
Published in 1973, but this survey remains valuable as a detailed account the history of printing and publishing in Nigeria, focusing on the rapid development in the 1960s of writing by Nigerians and the growth of indigenous publishing houses. The author concluded (at that time) that "the revolution begun in the early 1960s to Nigerianise the Nigerian book industry seems to be yielding good dividends today."

858   Thomas, Akin **"A Book Subsidy Scheme for Nigeria: The Way Forward."** In *Making Books Available and Affordable*, edited by Ezenwa-Ohaeto. Awka, Nigeria: Nigerian Book Foundation, 1995, 25-38.
Provides some historical background to educational publishing in Nigeria and assesses the potential market for books on the basis of enrolment of school pupils and students at institutions of higher learning. Thomas is critical of the lack of government support for the educational book industry, and states that despite pious pronouncements by various government officials over the past two decades little progress has been made, and the government is still to implement most of the recommendations and resolutions passed at numerous conferences. Defines the author's own concept of 'subsidy' – which he sees in a broader sense of support for authorship – book design and illustrations, editing, printing and binding, marketing and distribution, libraries, as well as other areas of support such as fellowship awards, sponsorship of literary awards, or (citing the Norwegian model) support by way of purchase of bulk quantities of books from Nigerian publishers for distribution to libraries throughout the country.

859   Uwalaka, M.N. **Book Publishing Performance in the Nigerian Economic Environment.** Ibadan: University of Ibadan, Department of Communication and Language Arts, 2000. PhD thesis. [Not examined]

860   Waddington, Jenny **"Nigeria: Education and Books in Crisis."**
African Publishing Review 3, no. 5 (September/October 1994): 18-19.
A compilation of reports from the Nigerian press concerning the state of education and the crisis of the national book industries [in the mid-1990s].

861   Wolters, Stephanie **African Books for All.** ZA@Play June 15, 2007
http://www.chico.mweb.co.za/art/2007/2007june/070615-books.html
[05/03/08]
An interview with Adewale Maja-Pearce, co-founder of the Lagos-based New Gong Publishing House, about the challenges of African publishing for small independent imprints, and selling books to overseas markets. Maja-Pearce is a former Editor of the Heinemann "African Writers Series".

862   Yesufu, Abdul R. **"Mbari Publications: A Pioneer Anglophone African Publishing House."** *The African Book Publishing Record* 8, no. 2 (1982): 53-57.
A detailed history of the pioneering, Ibadan-based Mbari Publications, examining how a consortium of writers and artists promoted creative writing, African art and culture, set up their own publishing house and published a wide range of exciting titles – and the influential journal *Black Orpheus* - some of which now have become collectors' items.

863   Zell, Hans M. **"Ken Saro-Wiwa."** *The African Book Publishing Record* 21, no. 4 (1995): 243.
A tribute to Ken Saro-Wiwa, the Nigerian author, publisher, environmental activist and Ogoni minority rights crusader, who was sentenced to death by a Nigerian military government-appointed tribunal following a sham trial. He was denied the right of appeal, and was summarily and callously executed on the orders of the junta on 10 November 1995, despite pleas from world leaders to save his life. Ken Saro-Wiwa was an enterprising and innovative indigenous African publisher and his firm, Saros International Publishers, became a member of the Oxford-based ➔ **African Books Collective (3)** in 1992.

864   Zell, Hans M. **"In Memoriam: Chief Victor Nwankwo."** *The Guardian* Tuesday October 22, 2002, 22.
Online: http://www.guardian.co.uk/obituaries/story/0,,816501,00.html
[05/02/08]
Also in *The African Book Publishing Record* 28, no. 3, (2002): 195-196, and in *Bellagio Publishing Network Newsletter* no 31 (November 2002): 23.
Online:
http://www.bellagiopublishingnetwork.com/newsletter31/zell.htm
[05/03/08]
Obituary of one of Africa's leading publishers, Chief Victor Nwankwo, who was brutally murdered on 29 August 2002 outside his home in Enugu, the victim of a political assassination.

Réunion

National bibliography, books in print, and book trade directories

865   Bibliothèque Universitaire de la Réunion. **Lire et se documenter à la Réunion et à Mayotte, 2005; répertoire des bibliothèques, centres de documentation, librairies, espaces presse, points de vente multimédia, éditeurs et associations, périodiques.** 3rd ed. St. Denis: Bibliothèque universitaire de la Réunion. 2005. 158 pp.
A directory of the book world in Réunion and Mayotte, covering libraries, documentation centres, publishers, bookshops and multimedia outlets, associations, and periodicals.

Books, articles, reports, and interviews

866   Jack, Belinda **"Publishing on Réunion."** *The African Book Publishing Record* 10, no. 1 (1984): 139-141.
Recounts the long and remarkable history of publishing in Réunion (still a département of France) and finds that literary publishing in the country [in the 1980s] is flourishing.

867   Roda, J.C. **"Overseas French Department of Réunion."** In *The Book Trade of the World, vol. IV: Africa,* edited by Sigfred Taubert and Peter Weidhaas. Munich: K.G. Saur, 1984, 234-235.
A brief account of publishing and the book trade in Réunion. Now very dated.

Rwanda

Associations and book-related organizations

868   **Association des Editeurs Rwandaise**
No. 9775 Remera II
Boulevard de Umuganda
Kigali
Postal address:
BP 3404
Kigali
Rwanda
Tel: +250-587268
Email: macwra@rwanda1.com
Chair: Twagira Azzy

Books, articles, reports, and interviews

869 Hategekimana, Grégoire **Edition et distribution du livre au Rwanda: problèmes actuels et perspectives d'avenir.** Butare: Université National du Rwanda, Bibliothèque universitaire, 1979. 7 pp.
Paper presented to the first congress of Rwandan artists, writers, printers and publishers, that focussed on the problems of publishing and book distribution in Rwanda. Comments on the lack of creative writing and ascribes this to [trans.] "the Belgian colonial mentality, little versed in the literary and artistic", and the education system prevalent under the colonial administration. Describes organization of publishing in Rwanda (in the late Seventies) and details the problems in book distribution.

870 Hategekimana, Grégoire **"Republic of Rwanda."** In *The Book Trade of the World, vol. IV: Africa*, edited by Sigfred Taubert and Peter Weidhaas. Munich: K.G. Saur, 1984, 236-244.
Overview of publishing and the book trade in Rwanda. Now very dated.

Sao Tomé and Principe

Books, articles, reports, and interviews (in English only)

871 da Costa, Juliao José **"Democratic Republic of Sao Tomé and Principe."** In *The Book Trade of the World, vol. IV: Africa*, edited by Sigfred Taubert and Peter Weidhaas. Munich: K.G. Saur, 1984, 245-246.
A brief account of publishing and the book trade in Sao Tomé and Principe. Now very dated

Senegal

Associations and book-related organizations

872 Afrique Livres
Association d'aide à la publication et à la diffusion
Cité Universitaire
BP 22464
Dakar
Senegal
Tel: n /a
Email: aflivres@le-senegal.com
Web: http://www.le-senegal.com/afriquelivres/ [pages not accessible 05/03/08]
President: Aminata Soumaré

Secretary-General: Laurent Badji
Note: not verified, organization dormant?

873   Associates in Research & Education for Development (ARED)/ Groupe d'Initiative pour la Promotion du Livre en Langues Nationales (GIPLLN)
Sacré Coeur I
Villa 8253
Dakar
Postal address:
BP 10737
Dakar Liberté
Senegal
Tel: +221-8-257119 Fax: +221-8-247097
Email: ared@enda.sn
Note: not verified, organization dormant?

874   Association des Ecrivains du Sénégal (AES)
127 Avenue Lamine Gueye
Dakar
Postal address:
BP 4213
Dakar
Senegal
Tel: +221-869 1400 or +221-630 6132/825 8009
Email: alibeye@fesman.org
President: Alioune Badara Bèye

875   Association Senegalaise des Editeurs (ASE)
c/o Nouvelles Editions Africaines
BP 260
Dakar
Senegal
Tel: +221-821 1381/822 1580 Fax: +221-822 3604
Email: amisyneas@yahoo.fr **or** jeynandiaye@yahoo.fr
Web: n/a
Chair: Madieyna Ndiaye

876   Direction du livre et de la lecture
Ministère de la Culture et du Patrimoine historique classé
Avenue Hassane II
Dakar
Postal address:
BP 3393

Dakar
Senegal
Tel: +221-889 6300 Fax: +221-842 3409
Email: use email form on Web site
Web: http://www.culture.gouv.sn/article.php3?id_article=19
Director: Sahite Sarr Samb
Other contact: Mariétou Diongue Diop

National bibliography, books in print, and book trade directories

877 **Bibliographie du Sénégal.** (supersedes *Eléments de bibliographie du Sénégal*, and thereafter *Bulletin bibliographique des Archives du Sénégal*, published to 1964)
Dakar: Bibliothèque des Archives du Sénégal [Immeuble administratif, Avenue Léopold Sédar Senghor, Dakar], 1972-
Annually, with periodic cumulations in print format; latest cumulation covered the period 1990-1993, published in 1994; cumulative volume for the period 1994-1997 to be published in 2007.
Online: (period 1984-1986-)
Currently accessible is the cumulative volume for the period 1994-1997 at http://www.archivesdusenegal.gouv.sn/bibliographie.html [05/03/08]
Email: Bdas@telecomplus.sn or ssissoko@hotmail.com
Web: http://www.archivesdusenegal.gouv.sn/index.html

878 Direction du Livre et de la Lecture, Senegal **Liste des éditeurs au Sénégal.**
http://www.culture.gouv.sn/article.php3?id_article=187 [05/03/08]
An online directory of publishers in Senegal, giving full address details, contact, telephone and fax numbers, and email addresses (where available). Lists 14 publishers at this time.

879 Direction du Livre et de la Lecture, Senegal **Liste des librairies au Sénégal.**
http://www.culture.gouv.sn/article.php3?id_article=188 [05/03/08]
An online directory of the major bookshops in Senegal, giving full address details, and telephone/fax numbers. Lists 10 bookshops at this time.
Note: also available online, and offering a rather more complete listing than that for publishers and booksellers, is a directory of libraries throughout Senegal, **Réseau des bibliothèques du Sénégal,** http://www.culture.gouv.sn/article.php3?id_article=324 [05/03/08], giving full address details, contacts, and telephone and fax numbers.

Books, articles, reports, and interviews

880 African Publishers Network **"Djibril Faye Remembered."** *African Publishing Review* 7, no. 5 (September/October 1998): 14-15.

Tributes by his former colleagues to the late Djibril Faye (1950-1998), who was Marketing Director of Nouvelles Editions Africaines in Dakar, and who played a very active role in the development of the ➔ **African Publishers Network (5)** in the francphone regions of the continent.

881 Anon. **"Entretien avec Monsieur Ali Meroueh, Libraire à Dakar."** *Ethiopiques* 5 nos. 1-2, (1988):132-133.
Interview with the owner of the well known Dakar bookshop, Librairie aux Quatre-Vents.

882 Bourdin, Florence **Etat des lieux du secteur marchand du livre au Sénégal: rapport de stage effectué à la Direction du Livre et de la Lecture du Sénégal du 1er juin au 1er août 2002.** Toulouse: Université Méditerranée, Dept. IUT Information-communication, 2002. 53 pp.
An inventory of the current [2002] commercial sector book in Senegal, together with a report about a training course for booksellers that took place in Dakar in August 2002.

883 Bullock, Adrian, and Tom French **Higher Education Book Sector Study Report, Senegal, November 1990.** London: International Book Development, 1990. 46 pp.
Report based on a study mission to Senegal that aims to provide a descriptive and statistical survey of the current level of textbook and library provision at tertiary level in Senegal.

884 Correa, Antoinette **"Book Hunger in Schools."** *Focus on International & Comparative Librarianship* 28, no. 2 (September 1997): 90-92
Summary of a talk given at an IGLA seminar during the London International Book Fair in 1997 by a librarian from Dakar University. Examines the demand for books in schools and libraries in Senegal "which is not being met by book production within the country or through its library services."

885 Diallo, Abdou Karim **Le livre de langue française au Sénégal (1960-1980) modernes.** Lyon, France: Université Jean Moulin, 1989. MA thesis (Thèse de Lettres). 310 pp.
[Not examined]

886 Diallo, Mariam **"Les 'librairies par-terre'."** *Notre Librairie. Revue du Livre Afrique Noire, Maghreb, Caraïbes, Océan Indien. Littérature de Côte d'Ivoire:* 2. Ecrire aujourd'hui, no. 87 (April-June 1987): 138-141.
Reflects on the prevalence of pavement second-hand book stalls that can be found in every area of Dakar.

887 Dieye, Adama Sow **"Etre libraire à Dakar."** *Notre Librairie. Revue du Livre Afrique Noire, Maghreb, Caraïbes, Océan Indien. Littérature sénégalaise,* no.81 (reissued 1989): 162-163.

An interview with Ali Meroueh, owner of Librairie Aux Quatre Vents, one of the oldest and largest bookshops in Dakar.

888   Dieye, Adama Sow, and B. Baritaud **"La vie de l'édition."** *Notre Librairie. Revue du Livre Afrique Noire, Maghreb, Caraïbes, Océan Indien. Littérature sénégalaise*, no. 81 (reissued 1989): 161-162.
A brief description of the main publishing house in Senegal, Les Nouvelles Editions Africaines.

889   Diongue Diop, Mariétou **"Les politique nationales du livre – le cas du Sénégal."**
http://www.ifla.org/IV/ifla68/papers/171-082f.pdf [05/03/08]
A paper presented to the 68th IFLA Council and General Conference, August 18-24, 2002. The author, who is head of Bibliothèque Centrale at Cheikh Anta Diop University in Dakar, reaffirms UNESCO's declaration that (i) education is an indispensable investment for development, and (ii) books are an essential instrument for education, but finds that access to books and information is still not available to large parts of the population in Senegal. Reviews the essential ingredients for an effective national book policy and thereafter examines the politics of books and reading in the country, the creation of literary works, the state of the publishing and printing industries, book distribution, libraries, promotion of books and reading, and copyright legislation and protection. The author also notes new government initiatives in the book sector, including the establishment of a ➔ **Direction du Livre et de la Lecture (876)** and a Conseil Supérieur du Livre, which she considers as encouraging signs that the government is providing positive support for the "book chain" and the promotion of a reading culture in the country.

Diop, Bara, *et al.* **"L'édition scientifique au Sénégal"** *see* ➔ **Section 4, Studies by topic: Scientific, technical and medical publishing** entry **2343**

890   Dorsinville, Roger **"L'édition en Afrique. Problèmes et perspectives."** *Notre Librairie. Revue du Livre Afrique Noire, Maghreb, Caraïbes, Océan Indien. Littérature sénégalaise*, no. 81 (reissued 1989): 162-163.
A short analysis of the publishing industry in Senegal and the challenges of the future.

891   Fall, Anne-Marie **Les problèmes du livre au Sénégal: grande enquête de fin d'études**. Dakar: Cesti, 1987. 48 pp.
[Not examined]

892   Faye, Djibril **"Publishing in Senegal."** In *Development Directory of Indigenous Publishing 1995*, compiled by Carol Priestley. Harare: African Publishers Network, 1995, 83-84.
A brief description of publishing in Senegal, which thus far has been largely dominated by Les Nouvelles Editions Africaines (NEA).

893   Faye, Djibril **"Publishing in Senegal. Current Developments."**
Bellagio Publishing Network Newsletter, no. 10 (June 1994): 11.
An update of the previous entry (*see* ➜ 892), surveying publishing developments in Senegal.

894   Fofana, Ramatoulaye **L'édition au Sénégal: bilan et perspectives de développement.** Villeurbanne, France: Ecole nationale supérieure des sciences de l'information et des bibliothèques [17-21, boulevard du 11 Novembre 1918, 69623 Villeurbanne Cedex] (Mémoire d.étude, Diplôme de conservateur de bibliothèque, DCB 12), 2003. 107 pp.
Online: http://www.enssib.fr/bibliotheque/documents/dcb/fofana.pdf [24/02/08]
or http://www.enssib.fr/bibliotheque-numerique/document-727
Senegal is one of the few sub-Saharan African countries which, since the 1970s, has enjoyed a deliberate government policy to promote books and reading. The government has been keenly aware of the role of books in economic development and, from the period of French colonization, the country has also inherited a publishing tradition. Senegal now has a generally good infrastructure to publish and distribute French-language books, with many publishing houses, research institutes with publishing activities, bookshops, and libraries. However, the author believes that the model adopted since independence, designed to develop the indigenous publishing sector, is not entirely appropriate for the socio-economic realities, and the cultural and linguistic environment of the country. Part 1 of the study provides some historical background and an overview of the book sector and the book professions in Senegal. This is followed, in part 2, by an analysis of current problems and constraints facing the book industries. Part 3 includes an examination of language policies, probes into the current national book policy in Senegal, and offers a range of alternative proposals for the development of the book sector. In her conclusions Fofana calls for a reassessment of the role of the different players in the book chain, and that they ought to seek alternative and innovative methods to promote and distribute books throughout the country. She also calls for more effective development of libraries and distribution mechanisms for books in rural areas, and stresses the need to revitalize publishing in African languages, where Senegal could well benefit from the experiences of African language publishing in other francophone countries in Africa, for example in Mali, Guinea, or Burkina Faso. The book includes an extensive bibliography.

895   Gassama, Makhily **"Republic of Senegal."** In *The Book Trade of the World, vol. IV: Africa*, edited by Sigfred Taubert and Peter Weidhaas. Munich: K.G. Saur, 1984, 248-257.
Overview of publishing and the book trade in Senegal. Now very dated.

896   Gérard, Albert S. **"The Nouvelles Editions Africaines."** In *European-Language Writing in Sub-Saharan Africa*, vol. 1, edited by Albert S. Gérard. Budapest: Akadémiai Kiado, 1986, 574-580.

Describes the founding, in 1972, of Les Nouvelles Editions Africaines by the Senegalese government and French publishing interests, joined soon thereafter by Côte d'Ivoire, developing a joint venture with independent branches in Dakar, Abidjan, and Lomé. NEA has not only published books by authors from other West African countries but also from Mauritius, Djibouti and Haiti. Titles included novels, drama, poetry and the documentary narrative "Vie Africaines" series.

897   Jaygbay, Jacob **"A Glimpse at Publishing in Senegal."** *Bellagio Publishing Network Newsletter,* no. 19 (March 1997): 19-21.
Offers a short overview of educational and commercial publishing in Senegal, the printing sector, and book distribution and the retail trade in the country. The author makes a number of recommendations that would aid the growth of the book industries.

898   Kloeckner, Hélène **"Les grands groupes manquent de vision, d'envie, de stratégie. Entretien avec François Boirot, directeur général des Nouvelles éditions africaines du Sénégal (NEAS)."** *Africultures* no. 57 (December 2003): 86-88.
Online:
http://www.africultures.com/index.asp?menu=revue_affiche_article&no=3 186&dispo=fr [05/03/08]
An insightful interview with the Director General of Nouvelles Editions Africaines du Sénégal [in 2003], covering topics such as textbook development, competitive bidding for World Bank textbook contracts, and issues as they relate to the stringent conditions attached to these contracts, which makes it difficult for African publishers to compete with French multinationals.

899   Ly, Oumou Khairy **L'édition et la distribution commerciale du livre au Sénégal**. Dakar: Ecole de Bibliothécaires, Archivistes et Documentalistes, Université Cheikh Anta Diop [BP 3252, Dakar, Senegal] (Mémoire de fin d'études), 1985. 98 pp.
Shorter version also published in *Ethiopiques* 5, nos.1-2 (1988): 120-128.
Analyzes the picture [in the mid 1980s] of commercial book distribution in Senegal and suggests the creation of a legal framework to protect intellectual rights, and a structure for book promotion and library development.

900   Nancasse, Dillia **Les librairies par terre: approche d'une nouvelle source de lecture à Dakar et leurs incidences dans le circuit de la distribution traditionnel du livre.** Dakar: Ecole de Bibliothécaires, Archivistes et Documentalistes, Université Cheikh Anta Diop [BP 3252, Dakar, Senegal] (Mémoire de fin d'études), 1985. 76 pp.
A study of pavement booksellers in Dakar, their methods of selling and reaching out to customers, and their not insignificant contribution to book distribution in the country.

901   Osségué, Nelly **L'analyse du marché de l'édition du livre au Sénégal.**. Dakar: Institut Supérieur de Management (Mémoire de fin d.études), 2002. 62 pp.
[Not examined]

902   Sadji, Youssoupha **Etude de cinq maisons d'édition: les Editions Khoudia, les Editions Maguilen, les Editions Djamra, les Editions Juridiques Africaines et l'INEADE.** Dakar : Ecole de Archivistes et Documentalistes, Université Cheikh Anta Diop [BP 3252, Dakar, Senegal] (Mémoire de fin d'études), 1984. 58 pp.
A series of profiles of five publishers in Dakar, describing their activities, and the nature of their publishing lists.

903   Sankale, Eva **"BREDA: A Regional Publishing Relay."** *UNESCO-Africa* 7 (1993): 27-31.
Describes the scholarly publishing activities of the Dakar-based Bureau Régional de l'UNESCO pour l'éducation en Afrique/UNESCO Regional Office for Education in Africa (BRREDA).

904   Sarr, Charles Malick **Sahite Sarr Samb, directeur du livre et de la lecture: Sans la famille, il sera difficile de faire revenir les jeunes à une culture du livre.**
http://www.xalima.com/SAHITE-SARR-SAMB-DIRECTEUR-DU [05/03/08]
An interview, conducted in April 2007, with Sahite Sarr Samb, the head of the ➜ **Direction du livre et de la lecture (876)** in the Senegalese Ministry of Culture. He talks about the status of reading and the book in the country, the development of public and school libraries, copyright, and the challenges of ICT for the book sector; and how the reading habit and a culture of reading can be inculcated despite the "threat" of new technologies and new forms of communication.

905   Sene, Henri **Le livre et l'écrit de langue arabe dans la société sénégalaise des origines au début du XXème siècle.** Bordeaux: Université de Bordeaux, 1982. MA thesis (Thèse de Lettres Modernes). 353 pp.
[Not examined]

906   Sene, Henri **"Le commerce du livre de langue arabe au Sénégal Jusqu'au début du 20e siècle."** *Libri* 36, no. 2 (1986): 146-159.
Charts the trade in books in Senegal written in Arabic until the beginning of the twentieth century. Based on the above thesis *(see* ➜ **905**).

907   Sene, Mamadou **Les Nouvelles Editions Africaines de Dakar: 1972-1987.** Dakar: Ecole de Archivistes et Documentalistes, Université Cheikh Anta Diop [BP 3252, Dakar, Senegal] (Mémoire de fin d'études), 1988. 276 pp.
[Not examined]

908   Touzard, Philippe **"Panorama de l'édition au Sénégal."** *The African Book Publishing Record* 1, no. 4 (October 1975): 301-305.
An overview of publishing in Senegal [in the 1970s] by the [then] Marketing Manager of Les Nouvelles Editions Africaines in Dakar. Explains the differences in the book markets between African and industrialized countries and gives a detailed run-down of the structure, activities and future of NEA.

909   Turquety, Sarah **"L'universel est là, pas là-bas. Entretien avec Aminata Sow Fall."** *Africultures* no. 57 (December 2003): 113-115.
http://www.africultures.com/index.asp?no=3205&menu=revue_affiche_art icle [05/03/08]
A short interview with Aminata Sow Fall, founder and director of Editions Khoudia in Dakar, in which she talks about her motivation in establishing this small publishing enterprise.

910   Wade, Assane **L'édition au Sénégal.** Paris: Université Paris XIII/Villeneuve d'Asq, France: Presses universitaires du Septentrion, 2002. PhD thesis. 355 pp.
[Not examined]

Seychelles

National bibliography, books in print, and book trade directories

911   **National Bibliography of the Seychelles.**
Victoria, Mahé Seychelles National Library [PO Box 45, Victoria, Mahé], 199?-
Irregular, no information available; earlier cumulation *Bibliography of the Seychelles National Archives, 1974-1978*, published by the National Archives of Seychelles, BP 720, La Bastille, Mahé, Email: seymus@seychelles.net).
Email: natlib@seychelles.net
Web: http://www.national-library.edu.sc/

Books, articles, reports, and interviews

912   Lionnet, Guy **"Republic of Seychelles."** In *The Book Trade of the World, vol. IV: Africa*, edited by Sigfred Taubert and Peter Weidhaas. Munich: K.G. Saur, 1984, 258-260.
A short account of publishing and the book trade in Seychelles. Now very dated.

Sierra Leone

Associations and book-related organizations

913   Sierra Leone Book Development Council
Ministry of Education
Freetown
Sierra Leone
Tel: +232-22-240881
Email: n/a
Note: not verified, organization dormant?

914   Sierra Leone Booksellers Association
c/o 23 Garrison Street
Freetown
Sierra Leone
Tel: n/a
Email: n/a
President: Alfred Kagbo
Secretary: Alie Mansaray
Note: not verified, organization dormant?

915   The Sierra Leone Book Trust
c/o Sierra Leone Library Board
Rokel Street
PO Box 326
Freetown
Sierra Leone
Tel: +232-22-223848
Email: sierrabookt@yahoo.com
Director: Sallieu Turay

916   Sierra Leone Publishers Association
14a Wallace Johnson Street
Freetown
Sierra Leone
Tel: +232-22-220495 Fax: +232-22-224439 or 228430
Email: sierraleonepen@yahoo.co.uk
Web: n/a
Chair: Ansu E. Momoh
Note: not verified, organization dormant?

National bibliography, books in print, and book trade directories

917 **Sierra Leone Publications**
Freetown: Sierra Leone Library Board [PO Box 326, Freetown], 1964-
Annual, latest is 1987.
Email: sielib2002@yahoo.com
Web: n/a

Books, articles, reports, and interviews

918 Dillsworth, Gloria **"Paper submitted ... at the Unesco Regional Meeting of Experts on National Book Strategies in Africa ... 1981."** *Sierra Leone Library Journal* 7, no. 1 (1981): 2-29.
A comprehensive overview of the publishing situation in Sierra Leone [in the 1980s] by the former Chief Librarian of the Sierra Leone Library Board. Discusses the problems of national languages, the production of orthographies and primers in various languages with the attendant need for translators and authors. Describes the activities of the United Christian Council Provincial Literature Bureau and the Bunumbu Press in the spheres of literacy, and incentives available for various organizations in this area. Examines text book production, library markets and some more unconventional distribution channels. The author also reviews the financing of the publishing industry in Sierra Leone, the urgent necessity for training for the book professions, and outlines the major constraints and pitfalls in publishing and book production.

919 Djoleto, S.A. Amu **Sierra Leone: Developing the Textbook Industry and the National Book Development Council**. Paris: UNESCO (Restricted Technical Report RP/1981-1983/4/3.5/07), 1982. 43 pp.
Online: http://unesdoc.unesco.org/images/0005/000513/051320eo.pdf [07/03/08]
A UNESCO mission report whose purpose was to assist the Sierra Leone Ministry of Education in the review of existing facilities for the preparation, production, printing and distribution of textbooks in Sierra Leone (particularly those for primary schools); identify any inherent weaknesses and recommend appropriate solutions; and to assist the setting up of a National Book Development Council, and preparing its administrative and management plan in order for it to become operational.

920 Fallon, Helen **"A Literature of Our Own: Publishing in Post-War Sierra Leone."** *Focus on International Library and Information Work* 36, no. 3 (2005): 109-110.
Online: http://www.cilip.org.uk/NR/rdonlyres/FAB7FD78-3027-4146-AFBE-23CFE7FFFA73/0/focus3632005.pdf [07/03/08]
Focuses on the activities of PEN Sierra Leone, its recently-launched imprint PenPoint Publishers, its writers' centre and the work is it is undertaking, despite the lack of government support, to encourage reading and writing in post-war Sierra Leone.

921   Harding, Oliver **"The Book Chain in Sierra Leone."** In *The Book Chain in Anglophone Africa. A Survey and Directory*, edited by Roger Stringer. Oxford: International Network for the Availability of Scientific Publications (INASP), 2002, 68-71.
Online: Online: http://www.inasp.info/file/57/the-book-chain-in-anglophone-africa-a-survey-and-directory.html [07/03/08]
One in a series of useful country surveys and overviews – each prepared by a book professional from the country concerned – that review the state of the book, and the major players in the "book chain", in English-speaking African countries. Each country survey covers printing, book publishing, bookselling and distribution, library services, professional associations, book promotional bodies and book promotional events, training for the book professions, as well as examining some of the major issues as they relate to book development, such as languages, literacy, writers and writing, the reading habit, and national book policies. For each country this is supported by an annotated directory of government ministries, professional associations, book publishers, booksellers and distributors, printers, major libraries, and training institutions, with full address and contact details.

922   Jones, Eldred **"Sierra Leone: Publishing Needs and Problems."** In *Publishing in Africa in the Seventies*, edited by Edwina Oluwasanmi, Eva McLean, and Hans M. Zell. Ile-Ife: University of Ife Press, 1975, 166-173.
An account of the publishing situation in Sierra Leone in the mid-1970s. Contends that "in ideal circumstances, the majority of the books used at all stages in education in Africa should be produced in Africa", but laments the fact that such an ideal scenario is unfortunately still a long way off. Identifies the major problems and constraints of the book industries, and offers a set of recommendations on the way forward, and the kind of initiatives that are needed.

923   Kargbo, John Abdul **"Book Publishing in Sierra Leone."** *International Information & Library Review* 36, no. 2 (June 2004): 87-93
Books remain a vital necessity for the socio-economic advancement of society, but the fact that Sierra Leone continues to import over 90% of its book needs is a matter of grave concern. Most academic, technical and reference books continue to be imported, as local publishers do not have the capability to publish them. This article is an attempt to offer fresh insights on the challenges and constraints of book publishing in a small African country.

924   Lucan, Taban Aisie **"Republic of Sierra Leone."** In *The Book Trade of the World, vol. IV: Africa*, edited by Sigfred Taubert and Peter Weidhaas. Munich: K.G. Saur, 1984, 261-267.
An overview of publishing and the book trade in Sierra Leone. Now very dated.

925   Momoh, Ansu **"Publishing in Sierra Leone."** In *Development Directory of Indigenous Publishing 1995*, compiled by Carol Priestley. Harare: African Publishers' Network, 1995, 85-87.

A brief account of the development of publishing in Sierra Leone and an examination of the current [1995] problems and constraints faced by the book industries.

926   Momoh, Ansu **"Problems of Book Publishing in Sierra Leone."** *Bellagio Publishing Network Newsletter*, no. 19, (March 1997): 15-19.
Sierra Leone has been a book-importing country for a long time, book needs have largely been met by publishers in the North, and this factor has contributed significantly to the slow growth of indigenous publishing companies. The author provides some background about the development of publishing in the country and the significant role played by a number of bookselling organizations in a once flourishing retail trade some years ago. The author points out that at the present time little publishing goes on outside the government or public-sector publishing unit, which is concentrating mainly on school textbooks and supplementary readers. This is done to the virtual exclusion of private-sector publishers, and whose activities are in any event severely restricted by market size. The author calls for a national book policy with a strong mandate for private-sector publishing, increased support for local private-sector publishing, commercial publishing partnerships (North-South or South-South), and with an emphasis on private/public sector partnerships.

927   Read, Anthony; M. Bailor, R. Parry Jones, T. Simkins, and P. Cohen
Sierra Leone Education: Primary, Secondary, Tertiary, Technical and Library Sectors. London: Overseas Development Administration/ODA, 1985. 112 pp.
[Not examined]

928   Smith, Arthur **"The Struggle for the Book in Sierra Leone."** *Focus on International Library and Information Work* 37, no. 1 (2006): 28-31.
Online: http://www.cilip.org.uk/NR/rdonlyres/3EE68BC6-858C-4DD1-A020-5D32A466B9F7/0/focus3712006.pdf [07/03/08]
An informative overview of the state of the book in Sierra Leone today, which presents a sad picture of neglect. As the author rightly points out, in the 1960s and 70s Sierra Leone had many flourishing bookshops and well stocked libraries – at Fourah Bay College and elsewhere – and there were also some indigenous publishing activities. Today the shelves of once burgeoning bookshops are empty, or the bookshops have closed a long time ago. Fourah Bay College Library presents a picture of abandonment, facing almost perennial power failures, its reading halls are deserted, and book and journals acquisitions stopped after 1987, with this library, and public library services in the country, now depending mostly on book donations from abroad.

929   Smith, Arthur **"Problems Hindering the Development of Sierra Leone Literature."** *EzineArticles* 11 October 2007.
http://ezinearticles.com/?Problems-Hindering-The-Development-Of-Sierra-Leone-Literature&id=770687 [07/03/08]
There are numerous problems hindering the growth of Sierra Leonean literature, most notably the lack of a publishing house that caters for creative writing, and the

lack of alternative outlets such as literary journals or magazines. Another problem facing literary output in the country is the total lack of support thus far from the government for literary activities of any kind; and once flourishing bookshops in Freetown have closed their doors a long time ago. However, the author sees some promise in the publishing programme of the Adult Education Association, who have published a range folktales and some plays; the recent launch of the Sierra Leone Writers Series by Osman Mallam Sankoh, the online journal *Mabayla Review* http://www.mabaylareview.org/home/ [07/03/08] and the activities of Sierra Leone Pen.

930   Turay, Sallieu **The Sierra Leone Book Trust Book Programme Report: 2002-2004.**
http://www.sabre.org/publications/SLSalbot.pdf [07/03/08]
A report, by its Director, about the activities of the ➔ **Sierra Leone Book Trust (915)**, set up by the government of Sierra Leone as an NGO in 2002, and the programmes that have been initiated with the support of the ➔ **Sabre Foundation (110)**.

931   Turay, Sallieu **State of Publishing in Sierra Leone.**
http://www.sabre.org/publications/SLstate.pdf [10/12/07]
A paper presented to the ➔ **Sabre Foundation's (110)** 'Dialogue of Partners-II' meeting held in Dar es Salaam in September 2004. Presents a brief review of publishing in anglophone Sub-Saharan Africa, and thereafter examines the nature of publishing in Sierra Leone, and the challenges that face the book industry in that country. The current state is described as a worrying situation, as "writing, publishing, book distribution and the reading environment has reached an alarming state" — induced by poverty, chaos, coups and countercoups, and ten years of a barbarous civil war. Other reasons are lack of access to capital, the very high cost of printing, frequent power cuts, and a dearth of bookshops and other retail outlets. While the present situation is gloomy, there have been two promising new initiatives – the Sierra Leone PEN and the ➔ **Sierra Leone Book Trust (915)** – that are working together to try to reverse the negative trend.

South Africa

Associations and book-related organizations

932   **Academic and Non-Fiction Authors' Association of South Africa (ANFASA)**
PO Box 31134 Braamfontein
Johannesburg 2017
South Africa
Tel: +27-11-489 5193
Email: info@anfasa.org
Web: http://www.anfasa.org.za/
Director: Monica Seeber

Associated Booksellers of Southern Africa (ABSA) superseded by
South African Booksellers Association (SABA) *see* entry ➔ **951**

933   Biblionef South Africa
4 Central Square
Pinelands 7405
Cape Town
South Africa
Tel: +27-21-5310447 Fax: +27-21-5310455
Email: bibsa@iafrica.com
Web: http://www.biblionefsa.org.za/
Executive Director: Jean Williams

934   Centre for the Book
62 Queen Victoria Street
Cape Town
Postal address:
PO Box 15254
Vlaeberg 8018
South Africa
Tel: +27-21-423 2669 Fax: +27-21-424 1484
Email: cbreception@nlsa.ac.za
Web: http://www.nlsa.ac.za/NLSA/centreforthebook
Executive Head: Mandla Matyumza mandla.matyumza@nlsa.ac.za
Secretary, and PA to the Executive Head: Bukelwa Baba
bukelwa.baba@nlsa.ac.za

935   Children's Literature Research Unit
Department of Information Science
University of South Africa
PO Box 392
Pretoria 0003
South Africa
Tel: +27-12-4296520 Fax: +27-12-4293221
Email: vdwaltb@unisa.ac.za
Web: http://www.childlit.org.za/index.html
Chair: (Prof) Thomas van der Walt

936   Christian Booksellers Association of Southern Africa
6 Windsor House Main Road
Fish Hoek 7975
South Africa
Tel: +27-21-782 0628 Fax: +27-21-782-0629
Email: admin@cbsa.org.za or grant@hatfield.co.za

Web: http://www.cbsa.org.za/home/
President: Grant Neuper
Note: association dissolved March 2007

937   Congress of South African Writers
1 President Street
New Town 2001
Postal address:
PO Box 421007
Fordburg 2003
Johannesburg
South Africa
Tel: +27-11-833 2530 Fax: 27-11-833 2532
Email: cosaw@wn.apc.org
President: Mzwakhe Mbuli
Note: not verified, organization dormant?

938   Dramatic Artistic and Literary Rights Organisation (Pty) Limited (DALRO)
73 Juta Street (corner De Beer)
Braamfontein
2001 Johannesburg
Postal address:
PO Box 31627
2017 Braamfontein
South Africa
Tel: +27-11-489 5000 Fax: +27-11-403 9094
Email: dalro@dalro.co.za
Web: http://www.dalro.co.za/
Contacts: Gérard Robinson; Monica Seeber

939   IBBY SA. The International Board on Books for Young People South Africa
PO Box 847
Howard Place 7450
South Africa
Tel: +27-21-532 05 55
Email: info@ibbysa.org.za
Web: http://www.ibbysa.org.za
Chair: Robin Malan robinmal@iafrica.com
Secretary: Yvette Couperthwaite

940   Illustrators' Portfolio/ Sparx Media
11 Firdale Mansions
Firdale Avenue
Gardens
Cape Town 7925
South Africa
Tel: +27-21-422 0283
Email: sparxmedia@iafrica.com
Web: http://www.illustrators.co.za/
Contact: Michael Thorne

941   LitNet
Louwstraat 8
Stellenbosch 7600
South Africa
Tel: +27-21-886 5169 Fax: +27-86-512 6782
Email: use email form on Web site
Web: http://www.oulitnet.co.za/
Contacts/Management Committee: Etienne van Heerden, Russell Hanley

942   Online Publishers Association – South Africa
[No postal address available]
Tel: +27-11-715 6849 Fax: +27-11-715 6850
Email: info@opa.org.za
Web: http://www.online-publishers.org.za
Secretary: Theresa Vitale tvitale@opa.org.za

943   Print Industries Cluster Council (PICC)
W.J. Louw Builing 1st floor
7 Old Paarl Road
Bellville 7530
Postal address:
PO Box 583
Sanlamhof 7532
South Africa
Tel: +27-21-945 3300 Fax: +27-21-945 3325
Email: n/a
Web: http://www.picc.org.za/ [Web site currently (March 2008) in the
process of being changed to that of the recently launched South African
Book Development Council]
Chair: n/a
Note: The Print Industries Cluster Council (PICC) was formed in 1999 to
represent the book value chain. Members include the Paper Manufacturer's
Association of South Africa (PAMSA), Printing Industries Federation of

South Africa (PIFSA), Publisher's Association of South Africa (PASA) and the South African Bookseller's Association (SABA).
See also ➜ **South African Book Development Council (950)**

944   Professional Editors' Group
PO Box 411684
Craighall 2024
South Africa
Tel: +27-11-955 3059 (Membership Secretary)
Email: peg@ananzi.co.za Web: http://www.editors.org.za/
Chair: Marion Boers
Membership Secretary: Lulu van Molendorff

945   Publishers' Association of South Africa (PASA)
Unit 305 2nd Floor
The Foundry
Prestwich Street
Green Point 8005
South Africa
Postal address:
PO Box 106
Green Point 8051
South Africa
Email: pasa@publishsa.co.za
Web: http://www.publishsa.co.za/
Chair Executive Committee (2006/07): Nhlanhla Ngubane
Executive Director: Dudley Schroeder dudley@publishsa.co.za
National Manager: Samantha Faure samantha@publishsa.co.za
Member Support Officer: Marion Boltman pasa@publishsa.co.za

946   READ Educational Trust
4 Handel Road
Ormonde 2091
South Africa
Tel: +27-11-496 3322
Email: cynthiah@read.co.za or readmat@read.co.za
Web: http://read.org.za
Chair: C. Gawe
National Director: Cynthia Hugo cynthiah@read.co.za

947   Reading Association of South Africa
[No postal address available]
Fax: +27-21-680 1504

Web: http://www.rasa.uct.ac.za/
Email: jcondy@mweb.co.za
Chairperson and IRA representative: Janet Condy
Treasurer and Director of Research: Mastin Prinsloo
mp@humanities.uct.ac.za
Secretary and Director of Projects: Shelley O'Carroll
shelleyoc@worldonline.co.za

948   Society of Children's Books Writers and Illustrators, South African Chapter (SCBWI-SA)
153 Beach Road
Gordon's Bay
Cape Town 7140
South Africa
Tel: +27-21-856 0432 Fax: +27-21-856 0432
Email: marjorie@grafikon.co.za
Web: http://www.scbwi.org/
Regional Advisors: Marjorie van Heerden, Paddy Bouma

949   South African Association of Industrial Editors (SAAIE)
PO Box 4808
Midrand 1685
South Africa
Tel: +27-11-315 0724 Fax: +27-11-315 0888
Email: n/a
Secretary: Marselle Ralph
Note: not verified, organization dormant?

950   South African Book Development Council
Tijger Park III
2nd Floor Room 202
Willie van Schoor Drive
Bellville 7530
South Africa
Postal address:
PO Box 583
Sanlamhof 7532
South Africa
Tel: + 27-21-914 8626/7 Fax: +27-21-914 8615
Email: admin@picc.org.za
Web: http://www.picc.org.za/index.q [This is the Web site of the ➔ **Print Industries Cluster Council (943)**, currently (March 2008) in the process of being changed to the recently launched South African Book Development Council*]

Executive Director: Elitha Van der Sandt
See also
http://www.sabooksellers.com/pdf/Launch%20of%20the%20SABDC.pdf
[08/03/08] and
http://www.info.gov.za/speeches/2007/07062610151001.htm [08/03/08]

951   South African Booksellers Association (SABA)
PO Box 870
Belville 7535
South Africa
Tel: +27-21-945 1572 Fax: +27-21-945 2169
Email: saba@sabooksellers.com
Web: http://www.sabooksellers.com/general/home.asp
President and Chairman, Central Region: Guru Redhi
Vice President and Chairman, Southern Region: Hentie Gericke
Secretary and Chairman, General Trade: Peter Adams
For details of other members of the Executive Committee see
http://www.sabooksellers.com/general/exccomm.asp
National Manager: Frikkie Nel
Note: the complete list of SABA members can be found at
http://www.sabooksellers.com/members/member_list.asp

952   South African Children's Book Forum
Huis der Nederlanden
4 Central Square
Pinelands
Cape Town
Postal address:
PO Box 872
Howard Place 7450
South Africa
Email: sacbf@worldonline.co.za
Web: http://www.sacbf.org.za/sacbfhome.html
Chair: Carina Diedericks-Hugo
Secretary: Yvette Couperthwaite

953   South African Writers' Circle (SAWC)
Postnet Suite 522
Private Bag X4
Kloof 3640
South Africa
Tel: +27-82-928 8391 Fax: +27-866-534132
Email: sawriters@webmail.co.za Web: http://www.sawc.sos.co.za/

Chair: Helen Osborne info@third-rock.co.za
Secretary: Irene Aarons peaceangel@ionet.co.za

954   South African Writers' Network
PO Box 2720
Port Alfred 6170
Eastern Cape
South Africa
Tel: + 27-46-624 2793 Fax: + 27-46-624 2793
Email: see below
Web: http://www.sawn.co.za/
Co-editors: Theresa Lütge-Smith theresa@imaginet.co.za or
ecottage@gmail.com
Gary Bruce Smith gary@imaginet.co.za or gary@internext.co.za
Note: for additional Writers Groups in South Africa *see also*
http://www.sawn.co.za/writinggroups.htm

955   Southern African Writers' Council (SAWCO)
2nd floor Accacia Grove
Grove City
196 Louis Botha Avenue
Postal address:
PO Box 10024
Johannesburg 2000
South Africa
Tel: +27-11-483 3866 Fax: +27-11-483 1562
Email: sawfed@icon.co.za or sawco@sn.apc.org
Web: n/a
Chair: Raks Morakabe Seakhoa
Note: not verified, organization dormant?

956   The Write Company
Suite D, Block D
Coachman's Crossing Office Park
Brian Road, Off Peter Place
Bryanston
Sandton
Postal address:
Postnet Suite 278
Private Bag X9
Benmore 2010
South Africa
Cape Town office:

20 Dunkley Mews
Dunkley Square
Gardens 8001
Tel: + 27 11 706-4021 Fax: + 27 11 252-8890 (Johannesburg office)
Tel: +27-21-462 7580 Fax: +27-86-617 3046 (Cape Town office)
Email: info@thewriteco.co.za or capetown@thewriteco.co.za
Web: http://www.itsallwrite.net/aspbite/categories/index.asp
Founder and Chief executive: Amanda Patterson
Managing Director: Susan Greenhalgh
General Manager & Course Coordinator: Wida Hamman
Cape Town Director: Sarah Bullen

957   Writers World
PO Box 284
Somerset Mall 7137
South Africa
Tel: +27-21-852 4728 Fax +27-21-851 2592
Email: network@optionsunlimited.co.za or options@optionsafrica.co.za
Web: http://www.optionsunlimited.co.za/
Contact: Monica Cromhout

National bibliography, books in print, and book trade directories (and other
reference works)

958   Christian Booksellers Association Southern Africa **Members
[Directory].**
http://www.cbsa.org.za/members/ [08/03/08]
Includes details of 88 members of the Association, both wholesalers and retailers.
Each entry includes full address, telephone/fax numbers, email (form), and Web
sites where available.

959   Fisher, Maire, and Colleen Higgs, eds. **South African Small
Publishers' Catalogue.** Cape Town: Centre for the Book, 2006. 142 pp.
(distributed by Stuart-Clark & Associates cc /Publishing Print Matters, PO
Box 640, Noordhoek 7979, South Africa info@printmatters.co.za
http://www.printmatters.co.za/saspc.html)
Online: http://thesouthafricansmallpublishersblog.wordpress.com/
or http://bdg.org.za/blogs/saspb (these pages not available as at March
2008; a new online version may become available when a new second
edition of the print version is published)
This is a publishers' directory with a difference. Attractively produced, it provides a
showcase of the diversity, vitality, and enterprise of small-scale publishing in South
Africa today, and at the same time offers a forum for lively, and sometimes quirky
and controversial debate about small publishing. It includes detailed information

about the activities of over 60 small independent presses, covering presses that publish fiction, children's books, literary magazines, community publishers, as well as those publishing on the Web via blogs. For each publisher, in addition to full contact and address details (with email addresses for most and Web sites for some), there is an informative profile setting out areas of publishing, average print runs, select publications – many with cover images, photographs, or extracts from books and reviews – submission guidelines/requirements, and details of distribution or retail outlets. The listings are interspersed with a variety of short pieces contributed by the publishers themselves, recounting their experience as struggling small-scale publishers, providing insights into their distribution and marketing methods, their rewards and frustrations, as well offering useful tips and advice how to avoid the pitfalls. *Note:* the online version of this excellent resource is unfortunately no longer accessible, but may become available again upon publication of a new second edition of the directory in due course.

Reviews:
The African Book Publishing Record vol. 32, no. 3, 2006

960   The PASA Freelancer's Directory
http://www.publishsa.co.za/index.php?cmd=freelancerdir
[31/01/08]
The complete list (browse all names) is at
http://www.publishsa.co.za/index.php?cmd=freelancerdir&scmd=list&cat
Id=0 [31/01/08]
An online directory of book professionals and book industry professional services in South Africa, providing full address details, telephone and fax numbers, email addresses, Web site where available, together with details of services undertaken, qualifications and experience, and areas of specialization. Covers designers, typesetting/data capture and DTP services, editors, illustrators, indexers, proofreaders, translators and cartoonists. Fully searchable online. Currently (January 2008) the database contains 47 entries.

961   The PASA Member's Directory. Greenpoint, South Africa: Publishers' Association of South Africa. Print and online, latest print version is 2008 edition.
Online: http://www.publishsa.co.za/index.php?cmd=publisherdir
[31/01/08]
The complete directory (browse list of all members) is at
http://www.publishsa.co.za/index.php?cmd=publisherdir&scmd=list&catI
d=0 [31/01/08]
Contains very full information on all current member publishers and associate members of the ➔ **Publishers' Association of South Africa (945)** Arranged alphabetically each entry gives name and address, telephone and fax numbers, email addresses, and Web sites were available, together with information on executive and senior personnel (and their positions), nature of list, and areas of specialization. The online version is fully searchable, and currently (January 2008) the database contains 163 entries.

962 Publishers' Association of South Africa **Writings in Nine Tongues. A Catalogue of Literature and Readers in Nine African Languages for South Africa.** Green Point, South Africa: Publishers' Association of South Africa, 2007. 631 pp. + CD
Online: http://www.publishsa.co.za/index.php?cmd=nineLang [04/01/08]
(Select from 9 different pdf files, by language)
An initiative of the ➔ **Publishers' Association of South Africa (945)** – and produced with the support of the South African Department of Arts and Culture and the collaboration of National Library of South Africa – this a comprehensive and very attractively produced catalogue that showcases over 4,000 titles in nine African languages — IsiNdebele, IsiXhosa, IsiZulu, Sesotho, Sesotho sa Leboa/Sepedi, Setswana, SiSwati, Tshivenda, and Xitsonga. For each language titles are grouped under these genres: Novels, Traditional literature, Short stories, Drama, Poetry, Essays and prose, Multi-genres, and Non-fiction. Each entry (many accompanied by cover images in colour) gives author, title and description in the original language, publisher, ISBN, age level, together with an English translation of the title description. A directory of publishers, with full contact details including email addresses, Web sites and publisher logos, completes the volume. This is a marvellous resource.
Reviews:
Africana Libraries Newsletter no. 122, March 2008
Online: http://www.indiana.edu/~libsalc/african/ALN122/122bookreviews.html [30/03/08]
African Research & Documentation no. 104, 2007

963 SACBIP. **South African Children's Books in Print,** compiled by Jay Heale. Grabouw: South Africa, Jay Heale, 1995. [ceased] 104 pp.
http://www.bookchat.co.za/index.asp [30/3/08]
The last print version of the above was published in 1995, but an online version of the database was launched in early 2008 at the new ➔ **Bookchat. South African Children's Books (130)** Web site of Jay Heale. The freely accessible database is searchable by author, title, illustrator, by geographical setting, or by literary flavour or main theme. Search results generate full author, title, and publisher details, ISBN, year first published, editions (i.e. in languages other than English), and, for most, provide other details such as illustrator, reading age level, genre, main themes, geographical setting, literary flavour, and awards won (where applicable). An excellent resource.

964 SANB: **South African National Bibliography/Suid-Afrikaanse Nasionale Bibliografie.**
Pretoria: The State Library; later Pretoria: The National Library of South Africa [PO Box X990, Pretoria 0001], 1933-
1933-1958 published as mimeographed monthly lists; 1959-1999 as printed national bibliography; from 1960 three quarterly issues – with the final quarter included in the annual cumulated edition – replaced the monthly lists (and also available as a weekly card service up to 1995). A cumulation

for the period 1968-1971 was also published, but not for subsequent years. Database computerized from 1972-1982-
Online: (limited free access to the database of all recorded documents in the National Library of South Africa collections, including the *South African National Bibliography*)
http://natlib1.sabinet.co.za/search~S7 [08/03/08]
Email: Info.ofNLSA@nlsa.ac.za
Web: http://www.nlsa.ac.za/NLSA/
For more details *see also*
Battison, Susan **The South African National Bibliography: 1933-to Date. From Isolation to Co-operation**
http://www.ifla.org/IV/ifla73/papers/136-Battison-en.pdf [08/03/08]
(Paper presented to the 73rd IFLA General Conference and Council in 2007.)
Note: The SANB is also available, by subscription, on the *Africa-Wide: NiPAD* database published by NISC and coverage includes 1989 to date. Baltimore & Grahamstown, South Africa: National Information Services Corporation/NISC, 1994- http://www.nisc.co.za/databases?id=1

965   South African Book Development Council **Development Initiatives.**
http://www.picc.org.za/initiatives.q [08/03/08]
A useful directory of publishing and book promotional initiatives, projects, and networks, including those devoted to reading campaigns and literacy development, and organizations providing mobile library units. Information provided includes a brief description of each organization's mission and objectives, together with full contact details.

966   **South African Booksellers Association-Member List**
http://www.sabooksellers.com/members/member_list.asp [08/03/08]
This is the complete online list of 265 members of the ➜ **South African Booksellers' Association (951),** organized by regions. Each listing gives name, city, and telephone and fax numbers. By clicking on the entry it provides access to a members profile with additional information. (However, this facility was not operational as yet when last accessed as at 30/03/08.)

South African Children's Books in Print *see* ➜ **SACBIP: South African Children's Books in Print** entry **963**

967   **Southern African Books in Print: A Tool for Librarians and Booksellers, 1998.** Cape Town: Books in Print Information Services [PO Box 15129, Vlaeberg, Cape Town 8018, South Africa], 1998.
Published since 1994, this publication aims to provide a comprehensive list of all books published and sold in South Africa. The latest (1998) edition included 34,300 titles in 31 languages, ranging from Afrikaans to Zulu, as well as 17,512 titles in English. Complete bibliographic and acquisitions data is provided for each title. The publisher list contains 1,146 records, which consist of the publisher name, address,

telephone and fax number. Available in printed format (annually), on microfiche (semi-annually) and also on CD-ROM (quarterly). *Note:* unable to verify availability of further editions published since 1998.

968   State Library, Pretoria/National Library of South Africa. **Directory of South African Publishers/Adresboek van Suid Afrikaanse Uitgewers**, Pretoria, National Library of South Africa 1991-1999[?] ISSN 1018-7626
Available in electronic format 1999?-
Contains full address details, contact numbers, subjects of speciality and ISBN numbers of South African publishers. Available in book format (to 1999?) or electronic format (ASCII text) thereafter. *Note:* unable to verify the current availability status of the online version of this directory.

969   Taitz, Laurie **Directory of Book Publishing in South Africa, 1995**. Braamfontein: British Council & Publishers' Association of South Africa, 1995. 158 pp.
Provides fully annotated listings of individuals and organizations in the South African book world, including publishers and publisher's agents, freelance editors and proof-readers, designers, illustrators, etc. and also includes a directory of book training institutions, as well as listing of book-related and writers' organizations. Now inevitably very dated, but still useful for authors looking for publishers to whom they can submit their work.

Books, articles, reports, and interviews

970   Academy of Science of South Africa **Report on a Strategic Approach to Research Publishing in South Africa**. Pretoria: Academy of Science of South Africa [PO Box 72135, Lynnwood Ridge, 0040 South Africa], 2006. 168 pp.
Online: http://www.assaf.co.za/strat_report.html (download individual chapters of the report) [08/03/08]
http://blues.sabinet.co.za/images/ejour/assaf/assaf_strategic_research_pu blishing.pdf (full report download) [08/03/08]
Commissioned by the Department of Science and Technology of the government of South Africa, this is a major study of the present state of research publishing policy and practice in South Africa. The goal of the six-chapter report is to help to "develop and maintain a robust national system of innovation that contributes materially to the sustainable prosperity of all South Africa's people." Individual chapters cover a bibliometric assessment of South African research publications; a comprehensive analysis of South African research journals; a survey of journal editors' opinions; and an analysis of global e-research trends and their implications for South African research publishing, both in print and online formats. The final chapter sets out conclusions and recommendations for a strategically enhanced role of research publishing in South Africa. It recommends that all stakeholders in the South African research enterprise should each in their own way support local/national research journals that actively seek to be of international quality and are indexed in an

internationally recognised, bibliometrically accessible database, through following best-practice in editorial judgment and peer review. Among other main recommendations of the report are: that funds should be allocated from the grants made by the Department of Education for research publication to support scholarly publishing in South Africa; that the Department of Science and Technology should take responsibility for ensuring that Open Access initiatives are promoted to enhance the visibility of all South African research articles and to make them accessible to the entire international research community, including the development of research repositories; and that the Academy of Science of South Africa be mandated to carry out external peer review and associated quality audit of all South African research journals in five-year cycles, and act as a support and quality control body for scholarly publishing. *Note*: some of the papers in this study are individually abstracted elsewhere in this bibliography.

Anderson, Elisabeth **"Women in Publishing and the Wider Book Chain in South Africa, 2001"** *see* ➔ **Section 4, Studies by topic: Women in African publishing/Publishing by and for women** entry **2363**

971 Andrew, Jeff **South Africa Publishing Market Profile 2004**. London: The Publishers Association and The British Council, 2004. 124 pp. (accessible by purchase only for non-PA members/GPI subscribers, cost £249) http://www.publishers.org.uk/en/home/market_reports_and_statistics/g pi/reports/html_reports/south_africa_publishing_market_profile_2004/ (table of contents only)
A comprehensive analysis of the South African book markets, providing general background, details of the education system, together with overviews of the general, academic and professional, and school book markets, and supported by a wide range of appendices and tables. [Not examined]

972 Anon. **"Opposition Publishing in South Africa - The Case of Ravan Press."** *Media Development* 32, no. 2 (1985): 22-24.
Describes how Ravan Press, through its magazine *Staffrider* became a channel for the florescence of creative writing in English, mainly by black writers, and which followed the Soweto uprising of 1976. Gives details of the reorganization and "democratization" of Ravan and examines how this has changed the [now defunct] press and its relationship with the reading community.

973 Arnold, Anna-Marie **A Review of the State of the Publishing Industry in South Africa and National Influences.**
http://www.liasa.org.za/interest_groups/lacig/LACIG_Conference_May2 004_Arnold.pdf [08/03/08]
A paper presented to the Third Southern African Library Acquisitions Conference held in May 2004, which reviews the state of the publishing industry in South Africa and its link to the library sector in the country. The first part of the paper provides a brief explanation of some of the main influences on the information sector in South Africa during the past decade, while the second part looks at current trends in the publishing industry in South Africa. The trends analyzed are based on statistics of

the publishing industry provided by the National Library of South Africa. These statistics make it possible to discern distinct publication patterns in the publishing industry for the period 1994 to 2001, and the trends in the publishing industry are explained in the light of the national socio-economic, political and cultural influences during this period.

974 Bailey, Barbara **An Eccentric Marriage: Living with Jim**. Cape Town: Tafelberg, 2005. 276 pp.
The late Jim Bailey, son of mining magnate Abe Bailey, author, journalist, and founder and publisher of the legendary *Drum* magazine – a family magazine aimed at black readers in South Africa – was something of a South African icon, as well as a bit of an eccentric. Here his wife Barbara charts the life they created together, in diary entries and narratives, spanning fifty years.
Note: Bailey's African History Archives at http://www.baha.co.za/ [20/01/08] holds 40 years of material from all the editions of *Drum* magazine and it's various sister publications. The archives contain a wealth of information from politics to culture.

975 Balkema, A. A. **Liber amicorum pro A.A. Balkema**. Cape Town/Kaapstad: Friends of the South African Library/Vriende van die S.A. Biblioteek, 1984. 85 pp.
A festschrift in honour of South African publisher August Aimé Balkema. Published in a limited edition, with contributions in Afrikaans and English.

976 Berger, Guy **"Publishing for the People: The Alternative Press 1980-1999."** In *The Politics of Publishing in South Africa,* edited by Nicholas Evans and Monica Seeber. London: Holger Ehling Publishing and Scotsville, South Africa: University of Natal Press, 2000, 73-103.
An excellent study of the alternative press in South Africa and the challenges faced by various publications that were pitted against apartheid, including grassroots community newspapers, progressive alternative weeklies, and other oppositional publications. The author also examines some of the reasons why many alternative weeklies, and other publications linked to social movements, did not survive democracy: "the rise and fall of the country's alternative press from 1980 to 1999 shows the difficulty of the challenge, but reminds us that the goal of publishing for the people remains relevant."

977 Breytenbach, Kerneels **"Book Publishing in a Multicultural South Africa. "** In *Book Publishing in South Africa for the 1990s.* Cape Town: South African Library, 1991, 25-28.
Probes into the publishing situation in South Africa (in the early 1990s), asks who buys books, and describes an ideal situation vs. the harsh reality. Concludes by calling for a clear definition of the term "multicultural", and demands that all literate South Africans are taken into consideration.

978   Broady, Marie **The State of Book Publishing in Post-apartheid South Africa.** New York: Pace University, 2005. MS thesis. 370 l.
[Not examined]

979   Bundy, Caroline **"The Voice of the Voiceless. An Interview with Jaki Seroke."** *The African Book Publishing Record* 10, no. 4 (1984): 201-204.
[followed by "A reply from Ravan Press", pp. 205-206.]
Also published in *Index on Censorship* 14, no. 3 (1985): 38-39.
The South African writer Jaki Seroke was one of the founding members of Skotaville Publishers, established in 1982. This insightful interview (conducted in 1984) sheds light on how Skotaville was founded and financed, how it is run, how it perceives its role as a publisher in South Africa, its authors, and how it distributes and markets books. The interview also touches on issues of censorship laws and banning orders, and publication of the journal *The Classic*. Before setting up Skotaville Publishers Seroke worked for Ravan Press, and in this interview makes a number of critical comments and statements about Ravan Press, especially as it relates to ownership, decision-making, salaries, and communication at Ravan Press. The editor of the *African Book Publishing Record* felt it was right, in the interests of free speech and debate, to give Ravan Press their right of reply in the same issue, and their full text, "A reply from Ravan Press" appears on pp. 205-206.

980   Cachalia, Coco **"Affirmative Action and Training in the Publishing Industry."** In *Publishing for Democratic Education*, edited by Steve Kromberg *et al.* Johannesburg: The Sached Trust, 1993, 155-161.
Addresses the problem of affirmative action by redressing or correcting imbalances caused by historical, racial, and sexual inequalities.

981   Cheh, M.M. **"Systems and Slogans: The American Clear and Present Danger Doctrine and South African Publications Control."** *South African Journal on Human Rights*, no. 2 (1986): 29-48.
[Not examined]

982   Cloete, Dick **"Alternative Publishing in South Africa in the 1970s and 1980s."** In *The Politics of Publishing in South Africa,* edited by Nicholas Evans and Monica Seeber. London: Holger Ehling Publishing and Scotsville, South Africa: University of Natal Press, 2000, 43-72.
An interesting account of oppositional publishing houses and alternative publications that played a significant role in building the awareness, ideas, and committed action that put an end to apartheid. The article focuses on book and magazine publishing (for a study of alternative newspapers in South Africa *see* the article by Guy Berger, entry ➜ **976**) and the activities of publishers such as Ravan Press, Skotaville Publishers, SACHED Books, Buchu Books, and journals and magazines such as *Work in Progress*, the *South African Labour Bulletin, LINK, Speak, Learn and Teach,* and *Staffrider.* The author also examines distribution methods used by these publishers and magazines, and the formidable challenges they faced in this task. A concluding section looks at the collapse of the alternative media in the late

1990s, and a number of new initiatives which have emerged since then, and asks "should would-be alternative publishers return to garage publishing, or seek new possibilities which technologies such as the Internet offer?"

983   Combrinck, Nicholas, and Maggie Davey **"We Will Publish What You Deem to be Great. A Dialogue about Trade Publishing and its Readers in South Africa."** In *The Politics of Publishing in South Africa*, edited by Nicholas Evans and Monica Seeber. London: Holger Ehling Publishing and Scotsville, South Africa: University of Natal Press, 2000, 219-232.

A dialogue about trade publishing in South Africa, discussing topics such as pricing, publishers' returns, readership, "untapped" markets, the nature of the retail trade, new forms of publishing, and the challenges of the new economy and how publishers can respond to this. It presents a strong argument in favour of publishing diversity in the context of books becoming fast-moving consumer items.

984   Corder, Hugh **"Censorship: A Model for a New South Africa."** In *Book Publishing in South Africa for the 1990s.* Cape Town: South African Library, 1991, 29-39.

Postulates that there will be some measure of censorship in the 'new' South Africa. and that the form of the censorship will depend on social tolerance and material welfare.

985   Coussy, Denise **"Hond Publishing, une jeune maison d'édition."** *Notre Librairie*, no. 123 (July-September 1995): 51-57.

Interview with Timothy Duplessis and Rick Hatting, of Hond (and Taurus) Publishing in which they talk about publishing in a climate of censorship and repression during the apartheid days, and the challenges and risks of publishing in the 'new' South Africa for the small independent publisher.

986   Cromhout, Monica **"Entrepreneurial Publishing: The Exciting Trend Towards Publishing in Short Runs."** In *The Love of Books. Proceedings of the Seventh South African Conference of Bibliophiles held at The South African Library, Cape Town, 8-10 May 1996*, edited by Pieter E. Westra and Leonie Twentyman Jones. Cape Town: South African Library (Bibliophilia Africana VII, South African Library General Series, 26), 1997, 40-49.

Examines the strategic factors which can serve as indicators for the growth of entrepreneurial publishing, primarily in South Africa, and in this context mainly the 'micro-publisher' or the self-publisher. Also looks at publishing costs and the mathematics of publishing, attitudes to self-publishing, and provides some tips for the entrepreneurial short-run author-publisher.

987   Cruise, Wilma, Michael Stevenson, Philippa Hobbs, and David Krut. **"Of Deep Throat and Strange Breeds: Art Publishing in South Africa."** *Arte*. 70, (September 2004): 42-49.
[Not examined]

988   Czerniewicz, Laura **"South African Publishing: The Transition Edition."** *Book Power*, no. 2 (1994): 11-16.
Also published in *African Publishing Review* 3, no. 6 (November/December 1994): 11-12.
Takes stock of the current [1994] South African book industries as they are going through a period of change, and as publishers jostle for position to gain a slice of the lucrative textbook market in post-apartheid South Africa.

989   Czerniewicz, Laura **"Curriculum Transformation in South Africa: What it Means to Educational Publishers."** *African Publishing Review* 6, no. 1 (January/February 1997): 12-14.
Reviews the major changes in the curriculum – its backbone being the fairly complex new National Qualifications Framework (NQF) – due to be implemented in South Africa in 1998, and the resultant changes and implications as they will affect educational publishers. Looks at the practicalities of curriculum transformation, and the strategic decisions publishers will have to make in both the short term and the long term.

990   Davey, Maggie **"Yesterday, Today … and Tomorrow?"** *Bookmark. News Magazine of the South African Booksellers' Association* 10 (April-July 2006): 7-9.
Maggie Davey provides a context for the state of the book in South Africa and, drawing on global practice and experience, explores some of the possibilities for its future. She calls for new innovative approaches to bookselling and book distribution, and a "new deal for books", one of its most essential requirements of which ought to be the removal of VAT on books.

991   Davis, Geoffrey V., and Holger G. Ehling **"Levelling the Playing Fields: An Interview with David and Marie Philip."** *Matatu*, no. 11 (1994): 133-42.
David and Marie Philip were the owners and founders of David Philip Publisher, a socially committed publishing firm which, together with Ravan Press and others, was in the forefront of oppositional publishing in South Africa during the repressive apartheid years.

992   Diamond, Denise **"Educational Publishing."** In *Book Publishing in South Africa for the 1990s*. Cape Town: South African Library, 1991, 60-69.
Outlines the picture of educational publishing in South Africa in the 1990s, discussing the role of publishers, the future of the industry, and addressing the problems that remain to be solved.

993   de Kock, Leon **"The State of Publishing in South Africa: Two Publishers Speak Out."** *Scrutiny 2. Issues in English Studies in Southern Africa* 4, no. 1 (1999): 32-38.
Some views and perspectives on the South African publishing scene [in the late 1990s] through interviews with Gus Ferguson and Alison Lowry.

994 de Villiers, G.E., ed. **Ravan, Twenty-five Years 1972-1997. A Commemorative Volume of New Writing.** Randburg, South Africa: Ravan Press. 1997. 176 pp.

Primarily a collection of short stories and poems, but also presents the story of Ravan Press's first twenty-five years of existence in apartheid South Africa, when it was consistently and courageously in the vanguard of oppositional publishing (it later became a subsidiary of the British publisher Hodder & Stoughton, but is now defunct). Lionel Abrahams appropriately describes it as a press that has had a "unique and tremendously significant history." The collection includes contributions by two former managers of the press, one by Peter Randall, one Ravan's founding trustees, "The Beginning of Ravan Press: A Memoir" (pp. 1-12), and the other by Glenn Moss who took over the reigns in 1998, "Ringing the Changes: Twenty-five Years of Ravan Press" (pp. 13-23), together with one by historian Albert Grundlingh "Publishing in the Past: Ravan Press and Historical Writing" (pp. 24-34.).

995 Donker, Ad [i.e. Adriaan] **"English-Language Publishing in South Africa."** *English in Africa* 10, 1 (May 1983): 29-36.

Also published in *Publisher/Writer/Reader: Sociology of South African Literature: Proceedings of a Colloquium 1982, Johannesburg,* Witwatersrand University Press, 1986.

A paper presented at a 1982 conference of the Association of University English Teachers of Southern Africa. It contains an overview of the development of book publishing in the English language, while raising some issues that are particular to publishing in South Africa in the 1970s and 1980s.

996 Drew, Lisa, and Robert Wedgeworth **"The Starvation of Young Black Minds."** *The Bookseller* (12 January 1990): 108-111.

Reports on an American fact-finding mission to South Africa which took place in 1989, to determine the [then] effects of American book boycotts.

997 Dupper, Marion **"Conference Report: Publishing for Democratic Education."** *Innovation. Journal of Appropriate Librarianship and Information Work in Southern Africa,* no. 8 (June 1994): 30-36.

Online:

http://www.library.unp.ac.za/Innovation/InnovationPdfs/No8pp30-36Dupper.pdf [08/03/08]

Report of a conference held in Johannesburg in 1993, hosted by the South African Council of Higher Education and the National Education Coordinating Committee, on the topic "Publishing for Democratic Education". Includes summaries of the papers presented by educators, writers, and publishers. The conference papers were subsequently published by the Sached Trust, *see* ➜ entry **1036**.

998 Eisenberg, Brenda **"Educational Publishing in a New South Africa."** *The Bookseller* (7 August 1992): 412-416.

Considers the implications of the political realignment in South Africa for educational publishing.

999 Essery, Isabel **The Impact of Politics on Indigenous Independent Publishers in South Africa from 1970-2004. Illustrated by a Case Study of David Philip Publishers.** Oxford: Oxford Brookes University, 2004. MA thesis.

An analysis of how publishing changes and develops in response to a changing political situation, with a case study on the independent South African publisher David Philip Publishers, who were in the forefront of oppositional publishing during the apartheid days. Includes a range interviews that informed the author's conclusions. In her conclusions, the author attributes the decline of a number of other indigenous South African publishers after the ending of apartheid not only due to political factors, but to a lack of timely appreciation on the part of their owners of the importance of running a publishing company as a profit-making business.

1000 Essery, Isabel **"Politics and Publishing in South Africa. Interviews with Two Pioneers."** *Logos. Forum of the World Book Community* 17, no. 3 (2006): 151-156.

Online:
http://www.atypon-link.com/LOG/doi/pdf/10.2959/logo.2006.17.3.151

Two interviews – about the past, present, and future of South African publishing – with (i) Marie Philip, of David Philip Publishers, who were in the forefront of oppositional publishing during the repressive Apartheid days, and who are now part of New Africa Educational Publishing/New Africa Investments Ltd; and (ii) South-African born publisher James Currey, who heads the UK's leading African studies imprint James Currey Publishers. His firm actively collaborated with David Philip Publishers and published a series of co-editions with them.

1001 Evans, Nicholas **"National Book Policy in South Africa: Catching up with other Countries."** In *National Book Policies for Africa*, edited by Murray McCartney. Harare: Zimbabwe International Book Fair Trust, 1996, 38-40.

Identifies some of the fundamental questions that will need to be addressed before a viable book awareness campaign, and an effective national book policy, can take off in South Africa.

1002 Evans, Nicholas, and Monica Seeber **The Politics of Publishing in South Africa**. London: Holger Ehling Publishing [4FH Leroy House, 436 Essex Road, London N1 3QP], and Scotsville, South Africa: University of Natal Press, 2000. 300 pp.

This is a major study on publishing in South Africa, providing an in-depth analysis of the book industry, reviewing its social and historical context, and examining its role as a strategic industry in South Africa's future development. With contributions by some of the country's leading book professionals and practitioners, the book examines fields such as policies of literacy and development of African languages, academic publishing, writers and publishing, reading promotion, new digital technologies and their impact on publishing, and issues relating copyright and reproduction rights. There are also some interesting papers on alternative publishing, and the alternative press, under the former repressive apartheid regime. *Note:*

several of the papers in this collection are individually abstracted elsewhere in this bibliography.

Reviews:

The African Book Publishing Record vol. 27, no. 3, 2001

Bellagio Publishing Network Newsletter no. 28, November 2001

Online:

http://www.bellagiopublishingnetwork.com/newsletter28/review_adebowale1.ht m [09/03/08]

Logos. The Journal of the World Book Community vol. 13, no. 1, 2002

Online: http://www.atypon-link.com/LOG/doi/pdf/10.2959/logo.2002.13.1.49

1003   Evans, Nicholas **"A Textbook as Cheap as a Can of Beer. Schoolbooks and Public Education in South Africa."** In *The Politics of Publishing in South Africa,* edited by Nicholas Evans and Monica Seeber. London: Holger Ehling Publishing and Scotsville, South Africa: University of Natal Press, 2000, 189-218.

An analysis of the policy background within which school book publishers in South Africa must operate. It examines the challenges of schoolbook provision in post-apartheid South Africa, tracing some "peculiarly South African debates about the nature and usefulness of school books, and of textbooks in particular", including aspects such as policies, literacy, curriculum, and the nature of the demand for educational materials. It also looks at the relative roles of government, donors, and the private sector in providing materials for classroom use. The author believes that a multiple and coordinated approach is required to fostering differing literacies, which should include a commitment to books as affordable and strategic teaching and learning tools; that this is not an unreasonable challenge and "is largely a matter of political will." The paper includes an extensive bibliography.

1004   French, Edward **"Publishing for Adult Education in a Democratic Future."** In *Publishing for Democratic Education,* edited by Steve Kromberg *et al.* Johannesburg: The Sached Trust, 1993, 115-129.

Describes different facets of the national system of adult education and the tasks and values associated with publishing for adult education. Sets out the challenges faced by publishers: to make books affordable, responsive to curriculum development, inventive, innovative, and expressive.

1005   Galloway, Francis **"Trends in the South African Book Publishing Industry Since the 1990s."** In *From Papyrus to Print-out: The Book in Africa Yesterday, Today and Tomorrow. Bibliophilia Africana 8 Conference Proceedings. Centre of the Book Cape Town, 11-14 May 2005,* edited by Cora Owens. Pretoria and Cape Town: National Library of South Africa/Centre of the Book, 2005, 214-226.

An earlier version also published as **"Statistical Trends in South African Book Publishing During the 1990s."** *Alternation* 9, no. 1, (2002): 204-225.

An investigative account which looks back over the past ten years of the South African book publishing industry, when it had to make the transition from functioning in a colonial and apartheid context to operating in the arena of the unfolding post-apartheid democracy. It investigates whether the industry has grown, and whether it diversified, and then offers the results of an empirical analysis into the shape and size of the industry, based on research undertaken, and publishing statistics assembled, in the Publishing Studies Programme at the University of Pretoria.

1006 Galloway, Francis, and Rudi M.R. Venter **"A Research Framework to Map the Transition of the South African Book Publishing Industry."** *Publishing Research Quarterly* 20, no. 4 (2005): 52-70.
[Not examined]

1007 Gordon-Brown, Alfred **The Settlers' Press: Seventy Years of Printing in Grahamstown Covering the Publication of Books, Pamphlets, Directories, Almanacs, Newspapers, with Historical Notes and Anecdotes and Contemporary Illustrations**. Cape Town and Rotterdam: A.A. Balkema, 1979. 160 pp.
A bibliography devoted to material printed in the City of Grahamstown between 1830 and 1900. Following some historical background – with anecdotes of strong personalities and the events that were the subject of the local literature – it provides an annotated list of books and pamphlets published during the period, together with lists of periodicals, newspapers, directories, almanacs and official publications.

1008 Gray, Eve **Achieving Research Impact for Development. A Critique of Research Dissemination Policy in South Africa, with Recommendations for Policy Reform.** Budapest: Open Society Institute [Nador Utca 9, Budapest 1051, Hungary], n.d. [2007]. 68 pp.
Online: http://www.policy.hu/gray/IPF_Policy_paper_final.pdf
[09/03/08]
This paper reviews the policy context for research publication in South Africa, using South Africa's relatively privileged status as an African country and its elaborated research policy environment as a testing ground for what might be achieved – or what needs to be avoided - in other African countries. The policy review takes place against the background of a global scholarly publishing system in which African knowledge is seriously marginalized and is poorly represented in global scholarly output. Scholarly publishing policies that drive the dissemination of African research into international journals that are not accessible in developing countries because of their high cost effectively inhibit the ability of relevant research to impact on the overwhelming development challenges that face the continent. In this study, South African research policy is tracked against the changing context provided by digital communication technologies and new dissemination models, particularly Open Access. These impact not only on publication but also on the way that research is carried out and they bring with them a growing recognition of the value, particularly for developing countries, of non-market and non-proprietary production in delivering research impact. The paper thus pays particular attention to the potential for new technologies and new publishing models in helping to overcome the global knowledge divide and in offering solutions for what might at first sight appear to be

intractable problems of under-resourcing and a lack of sustainability for African research publications. Eve Gray's main argument is that there is, in the formulation of research policy, a largely uncharted clash between South African national research and innovation policies focused on development and access on the one side, and the traditionally-accepted model of academic publishing on the other. The paper concludes with recommendations at international, national and institutional levels for addressing this situation, arguing that Open Access and collaborative approaches could bring substantially increased impact for African research, with marked cost-benefit advantages.

Gray, Eve, and Monica Seeber, eds. **PICC Report on Intellectual Property Rights in the Print Industries Sector** *see* ➜ **Section 4: Studies by topic: Copyright and legal deposit/Authors' rights** entry **1768**

Gray, Eve *see also* Horwitz Gray, Eve

1009 Haricombe, Lorraine J., and Wilfrid F. Lancaster **"Anatomy of a Book Boycott."** *American Libraries* 26, (July/August 1995): 685-688.
Describes the book boycott of South Africa during the apartheid days, and measures taken by US libraries and institutions to prevent the importation and exportation of books and journals from/to South Africa.

1010 Haron, Muhammed **"The Production of the South African Muslim Book: As a Means of Empowerment and a Source of Identity."** In *From Papyrus to Print-out: The Book in Africa Yesterday, Today and Tomorrow. Bibliophilia Africana 8 Conference Proceedings. Centre of the Book Cape Town, 11-14 May 2005*, edited by Cora Owens. Pretoria and Cape Town: National Library of South Africa/Centre of the Book, 2005, 18-47.
South Africa's Muslim community like all its other religious minority communities has been proactive in preserving its religious identity through the formation of a number of institutions. Over the past three centuries the community has occupied itself in not only erecting mosques and building colleges for Islamic instruction as a way of publicly reflecting the community's religious and cultural identity, but it has also been involved in the preparation of religious texts that assisted in providing more detailed information about its identity. The production of religious literature has however been largely the preserve of a few talented and inspired individuals in the community, over more than two centuries. This paper concerns itself with the production of the 'Muslim book' in South Africa during the 20th century, focussing on the contribution of a number of specific individuals. It thus provides a background sketch of the development of the production of the 'Muslim book,' and demonstrates how these theologians have made a substantial input to South African literature in general.

1011 Hechter, Rhodé **"Publishing as a Representational System for Indigenous Knowledge: With Specific Reference to the South African Environment."**

In SCECSAL 2002. From Africa to the World — the Globalisation of Indigenous Knowledge Systems, edited by Retha Snyman. Pretoria: Library and Information Association of South Africa (LIASA), 2002, 299-310.
Online:
http://www.dissanet.com/jsp/modules/repository/index.jsp?repository=Library&action=view_file&id=Library.1025548558 [14/01/08]
Argues that the South African publishing industry has done a great deal in terms of expressing the rich indigenous knowledge in South Africa, and has been a creator of social awareness as well as a player in the indigenous knowledge support team. The author describes how the industry represents local ideas, how the publishing process itself is uniquely indigenous in providing for indigenous markets, and the way in which publishing supports and sustains indigenous knowledge system programmes.

1012 Hendriksz, Colleen **"Going, Going ... Why is Academic Library Business not Coming Back to SA?"**
Bookmark. News Magazine of the South African Booksellers' Association 9 (July-September 2005): 15-16.
Probes into some of the reasons why many academic libraries in South Africa spend a large proportion of their acquisitions budgets with overseas vendors, rather than placing orders through local library suppliers.

1013 Hendrikz, Francois **"The Book Chain in South Africa."** In *The Book Chain in Anglophone Africa. A Survey and Directory,* edited by Roger Stringer. Oxford: International Network for the Availability of Scientific Publications (INASP), 2002, 72-82.
Online: http://www.inasp.info/file/57/the-book-chain-in-anglophone-africa-a-survey-and-directory.html [09/03/08]
One in a series of useful country surveys and overviews – each prepared by a book professional from the country concerned – that review the state of the book, and the major players in the "book chain", in English-speaking African countries. Each country survey covers printing, book publishing, bookselling and distribution, library services, professional associations, book promotional bodies and book promotional events, training for the book professions, as well as examining some of the major issues as they relate to book development, such as languages, literacy, writers and writing, the reading habit, and national book policies. For each country this is supported by an annotated directory of government ministries, professional associations, book publishers, booksellers and distributors, printers, major libraries, and training institutions, with full address and contact details.

1014 Higgs, Colleen **"A New Wave in South African Publishing?"** *Cape Librarian* 48, no. 5 (September/October 2004): 16-17
Online: http://www.oulitnet.co.za/indaba/colleen_higgs.asp [09/03/08]
Colleen Higgs (formerly of the Centre of the Book in Cape Town) believes there is a new flowering of South African writing, and that is that there is a new energy, a new attractiveness in South African books. She talked to some of the publishers "who are putting out the kind of gritty, realist, expressive fiction, memoir, and creative non-

fiction (in English) that appeals to me", to see if they also felt that there was some kind of new wave happening, and to discover if they could account for it. They all agreed that there is an unprecedented energy in publishing; but they all had different ways of accounting for it.

1015   Higgs, Colleen **"Supporting Small and Micro-Publishing Enterprises."** In *From Papyrus to Print-out: The Book in Africa Yesterday, Today and Tomorrow. Bibliophilia Africana 8 Conference Proceedings. Centre of the Book Cape Town, 11-14 May 2005*, edited by Cora Owens. Pretoria and Cape Town: National Library of South Africa/Centre of the Book, 2005, 204-213. Another version, **"Supporting Small-Scale Publishing"** available online at http://www.nlsa.ac.za/NLSA/News/publications/supporting-small-scale-publishing/ [09/03/08]
The author is the former Manager of the ➔ **Centre of the Book's (934)** Community Publishing Project, and here describes the activities of this innovative new project. The Centre provides funding and technical support for new small publishers, individual writers, and writers' groups in South Africa and helps them to develop publishing skills.

Higgs, Colleen, ed. **A Rough Guide to Small-Scale and Self-Publishing** *see* ➔ **Section 5, Book industry training/Self-publishing: Guides for authors and self-publishing** entry **2509**

1016   Hofmeyr, Isabel **"Putting Together Two Halves: Book Development and Book History in Africa."** In *From Papyrus to Print-out: The Book in Africa Yesterday, Today and Tomorrow. Bibliophilia Africana 8 Conference Proceedings. Centre of the Book Cape Town, 11-14 May 2005*, edited by Cora Owens. Pretoria and Cape Town: National Library of South Africa/Centre of the Book, 2005, 1-6.
Hofmeyr believes that one needs to combine the fields of book history and book development in order to generate a rich and subtle understanding of the past and present of print culture in South Africa. She argues that at present there is little detailed grasp of the history of print culture, while policy ideas tend to draw on presentistic understandings. The paper considers three examples where a historical perspective opens up new issues and avenues that could foreshadow thinking about print culture in the present.

1017   Holland, Mel **"General Publishing in a Textbook-Dominated Market."** In *Publishing for Democratic Education*, edited by Steve Kromberg *et al.* Johannesburg: The Sached Trust, 1993, 107-113.
Contends that the relationship between general and educational publishers is one of mutual interdependence.

1018   Hooper, A.S.C. **"History of the South African Publishing and Book Trade."** In *The Love of Books. Proceedings of the Seventh South African Conference of Bibliophiles held at The South African Library, Cape Town, 8-10 May 1996,* edited by Pieter E. Westra and Leonie Twentyman Jones. Cape Town: South African Library (Bibliophilia Africana VII, South African Library General Series, 26), 1997, 67-76.

A historical account of the development of the South African book trade: from its origins and the establishment of the first printing press in Cape Town by Johan Christian Ritter in 1784, up to the colonial period to 1910 when South Africa became an independent Union within the British empire; the post-colonial period of 1910 to 1960, and through to the period of political isolation from 1960 to 1990 and publishing under apartheid.

1019 Hooper, Tony **"The Case Against the South African Book Boycott."** *Logos. The Journal of the World Book Community* 1, no. 3 (1990): 16-13. Online: http://www.atypon-link.com/LOG/doi/pdf/10.2959/logo.1990.1.3.6

Argues that sanctions against books violate the principles which publishers and library associations have always upheld. Maintains that the free flow of information can act as a positive and constructive force and will eventually help towards the construction of a more just and humane society in South Africa.

1020 Horn, Caroline **"South Africa's New Age."** *The Bookseller*, no. 4730 (16 August 1996): 20-23.

Meeting the educational needs of a South Africa in transition is creating huge headaches for publishers, not least among them the prospect of having to implement in three years the long-awaited new national curricula. However, as the author reports, the pain, and "the crisis management of the transition process", is mitigated by the excitement of participating in something new.

1021 Horowitz, Irving Louis **"Between South African Rocks and Publishing Hard Places."** *The Bookseller*, no. 4203 (26 June 1987): 2403-2404.

A view on the boycott of South Africa, during apartheid days, by McGraw-Hill and other American publishers.

1022 Horwitz Gray, Eve **"The Sad Ironies of South African Publishing Today."** *Logos. The Journal of the World Book Community* 7, no. 4 (1996): 262-267. Online: http://www.atypon-link.com/LOG/doi/pdf/10.2959/logo.1996.7.4.262

This is a sharp dissection of the South African publishing scene [as at 1996]. It paints a rather gloomy picture, and the author sums up the state of South African publishing today as being similar to the state of the nation: "There is panic and compliance; euphoria and despair; experimentation and stagnation; innovation and conservatism. The only certainty is transition. We can also report that transition is not a very comfortable state." The author deplores the fact that those South African publishers who were in the forefront of oppositional publishing during the apartheid years, are now the losers (or have been taken over by some large publishing conglomerate), and are not now enjoying a share of the more lucrative educational markets from which they were for so long politically excluded. The author states that the contents of textbooks now being published haven't thus far substantially changed, and self-serving systems in textbook supply which blighted the old regime remain. Publishing and the book trade remains predominantly in white hands; creative literary lists – apart from the output of a few small presses – are still thin on the ground, and "the literary logjam will be broken only when the book industry more accurately represents the aspirations and needs of our diverse population."

1023 Horwitz Gray, Eve **"Current Publishing Trends in South Africa."** *In The Love of Books. Proceedings of the Seventh South African Conference of Bibliophiles held at The South African Library, Cape Town, 8-10 May 1996*, edited by Pieter E. Westra and Leonie Twentyman Jones. Cape Town: South African Library (Bibliophilia Africana VII, South African Library General Series, 26), 1997, 15-21.
Presents an overview of the state, and current patterns and trends, of publishing in South Africa today [mid-1990s], and the principal players involved. Horwitz Gray finds that "the old apartheid textbooks are still providing the mainstay of the South African publishing industry, not because anybody wants it that way, but simply because it takes time to go through the bureaucratic mill of changing syllabuses and then identifying books to fit these syllabuses", and that this means that "the main bulk of the industry is in a state of uneasy suspension caught half in the past and half-expectantly waiting for a future that ought to be substantially different, but nobody knows quite how." The author asserts that "our Rainbow Nation, for all its diversity, creativity and capacity for forgiveness, is a bookless society", and goes on to say that "the problem is essentially that the publishing industry and the bookselling industry remain predominantly pale, [and] if to decreasing extent, male."

1024 Horwitz Gray, Eve **"The Devil and the Deep Blue Sea: Local and International Perspectives on the South African Book Market."** *Focus on International & Comparative Librarianship* 28, no. 2 (September 1997): 75-81
Summary of a talk given at an IGLA seminar during the London International Book Fair in 1997. Presents a perspective of the library markets in the 'new' South Africa, and assesses the market place for scholarly books and the current state of library provision in the face of inadequate higher education budgets.

1025 Horwitz Gray, Eve **"Dateline Cape Town"** *Logos. The Journal of the World Book Community* 10, no. 2 (1999): 106-110.
Online:
http://www.atypon-link.com/LOG/doi/pdf/10.2959/logo.1999.10.2.106
Some reflections on the parlous state of the South African book publishing industry at the turn of the century by the [then] Publishing Director of the University of Cape Town Press. Educational publishing companies in the country are currently [1999] in crisis and are finding themselves with significantly reduced markets and dramatically increased overheads as a result of the ANC government's decision to unite the previously fragmented apartheid education structure. The dramatic fall in expenditure on textbooks has had a devastating effect on the publishing industry and on the education system. Textbooks have been developed, but have not been bought

in adequate numbers to serve the needs of school children and teachers. Meantime there have also been continuous changes in the dynamics of the industry in response to the new environment, particularly in relation to the involvement of international companies in the market. Moreover, "at exactly the time that one would expect a growth in African literature publishing and the revival of African languages, both these markets are in the doldrums. The publishing and bookselling industry is still a long way from reflecting the profile of South African society. Until it does, and even after it does, there will continue to be incongruities. Caught between a past which is over and a future not yet realized, South African publishers heading for the new millennium need not only strong nerves, but deep reserves of patience."

1026 Horwitz Gray, Eve **Wesgro Background Report on the Publishing Industry in the Western Cape.** Cape Town: Wesgro, 2000. 43 pp.
[Not examined]

Horwitz Gray, Eve *see also* Gray, Eve

1027 Hugo, Nadine **Bringing the Story Home. A Guide for Developing and Selecting Materials for Early Childhood Education: The South African Perspective.** London & Paris: Association for the Development of Education ADEA Working Group on Books and Learning Materials (Perspectives on African Book Development, 17), 2006. 61 pp.
A study carried out by the ➜ **READ Educational Trust** (946), one of the leading education NGO's in South Africa. It focuses on the South African ECD (Early Child Development) book sector as a case study for what is available, or should be available, elsewhere on the continent. The book is designed to guide writers, publishers, booksellers and anyone buying books or creating reading materials for African children to ensure material is relevant to their contexts, is interesting, and level-appropriate. The first phase of the study was a survey undertaken by READ to ascertain what is available for children in the birth to 9 years of age group in order to review the gaps in the market. To this end, READ invited publishers to submit samples of what they have available for this age group, especially materials in South Africa's indigenous languages. The author examines some of the materials for the different age groups, reviews a number of special series of picture-story books, and assesses the quality of their illustrations, including the work of some well known South African children's writers such as Niki Daly and Mari Grobler. She also makes suggestions how children can create their own materials, and concludes with a helpful "Summing it all up" section as it relates to the needs of different age groups in terms of layout, textual and print features. A valuable resource.
Reviews:
The African Book Publishing Record vol. 33, no. 3, 2007

1028 Human, Koos **'n Lewe met boeke.** [in Afrikaans, 'A Life with Books']. Cape Town: Human & Rousseau, 2006. 176 pp.
Koos Human's visionary contribution to South African book publishing has been widely recognised. He was the founder, in 1959, of Human & Rousseau, one of South Africa's leading general and educational publishers. Many regard him as the first

professional publisher of Afrikaans books for the general trade in South Africa, although Human & Rousseau now also have an extensive list of titles in English. In this autobiography he shares his 40 years of experience with books against the background of the literary, political, cultural and social climate over the years, including the repressive apartheid period when publishers faced draconian censorship laws in the 1960s and 1970s.

1029 Joubert, Susan Ruth **Publishing in Another South Africa.** Stirling, Scotland: University of Stirling, 1990. MPhil dissertation.
Also published as a summary version in *The African Book Publishing Record* 17, no. 1 (1991): 9-15; and also reprinted in *Readings on Publishing in Africa and the Third World*, by Philip G. Altbach. Buffalo, NY: Bellagio Publishing Network, Research and Information Center (Bellagio Studies in Publishing 1), 1993, 60-66.
Proposes an alternative approach to publishing in, or for another or 'new' South Africa, assessed in two dimensions: the first ideological, and the second market visibility, as an alternative model that emphasizes the existence of a market that is currently [in 1990s] ignored. Having sketched a broad conceptual framework, the article than addresses specific problem areas in publishing in South Africa, including educational publishing, books for literacy and the newly-literate, distribution and production, and reviews the activities of alternative and oppositional publishers. The author forecasts that "publishing in another South Africa" will disappear in a different political climate, to be published by a single publishing model "that takes cognisance of the true cultural composition of the South African market."

1030 Kantey, Mike **"Publishing in South Africa."** In *Africa Bibliography 1989, Works Published on Africa in 1989.* Manchester: Manchester University Press, 1989, vi-xx.
An extensive account of publishing in South Africa [in the late 1980s] which argues that "the havoc of the past has made reconstruction essential and part of that reconstruction must involve publishing in all its aspects." Begins with a short history of publishing in South Africa, describing the mission presses, the settler presses and the situation after 1948. Explores the make-up of readership and writers in South Africa and describes the organization of the publishing industry, textbook publishing for primary and secondary schools, academic publishing, the book market for children, the role of booksellers and libraries, the printing infrastructure, and marketing and distribution.

1031 Kantey, Mike **"New Approaches to Marketing and Distribution"**, in *Book Publishing in South Africa for the 1990's: Proceedings of a Symposium Held at the South African Library, Cape Town, South African Library, 22-25 November 1989.* Cape Town: South African Library, 1991, 10-17.
[Not examined]

1032 Kantey, Mike **"The Provision of Schoolbooks."** In *Working Papers of the Research Group Language Instruction.* Johannesburg: National Education

Policy Investigation, 1992.
[Not examined]

1033 Kantey, Mike **"Distribution of Educational Materials in South Africa."** In *Publishing for Democratic Education*, edited by Steve Kromberg *et al.* Johannesburg: The Sached Trust, 1993, 139-154.
Discusses the different types of book distribution methods among large and small publishing houses, traditional methods of distribution, methods of distribution by libraries and education departments, as well as alternative methods of distribution. Concludes with the author's recommendations for improved distribution networks and mechanisms.

1034 Kellerman, Barbara C. **"Looking at the Library and Information Sector and the Publishing Sector in South Africa: Country Report."** *ISBN Review* 17 (1996): 273-88.
One in a series of overview articles in a special issue of *ISBN Review* focusing on the book sector in various countries of Southern Africa, and which report (for the most part) about the state of libraries, publishing and the retail book trade; current book and copyright legislation, national book policies, programmes to promote the reading habit, laws and legislation covering the book sector and copyright, activities of library and book trade professional bodies, book trade organization, training for the book industries, the use of ISBNs, and more. This contribution is by the Programme manager, Bibliographic Control, at the State Library in Pretoria, and includes a number of charts providing book production statistics for South Africa for the period 1985-1995.

1035 Kotzé, Arend **"Logistics. More than Walls and Wheels."** *Bookmark. News Magazine of the South African Booksellers' Association* 11 (October 2006-March 2007): 7-9.
In order to achieve cost savings, the South African book industry has been showing an increasing trend towards outsourcing various services such as warehousing and distribution. The author examines the different areas of the book supply chain – educational book supply, the requirements of the academic sector, libraries, and the trade sector – and suggests for which areas outsourcing might be an appropriate solution.

1036 Kromberg, Steve; Meneesha Govender, Natalie Birrell, and Mxolisi Sibanyoni, eds. **Publishing for Democratic Education.** Johannesburg: The Sached Trust, 1993. 182 pp.
Published shortly after the ending of apartheid, this was an important collection containing 17 papers by educationists and publishers. It offered fresh insights, and a comprehensive analysis of how South African textbooks are produced, and suggests ways in which the industry could transform itself in order to provide more, better, and cheaper books for South Africa's post-apartheid education system. The book concludes with a list of twelve recommendations "A Vision for Educational Publishing in South Africa", setting out a framework and a range of guidelines that

might govern the practices of educational publishing in South Africa, and it would be interesting to compare this vision with the reality today, almost ten years later.
Reviews:
The African Book Publishing Record vol. 20, no. 2, 1994

1037 Kromberg, Steve **"Developing a Book Policy for South Africa."** In *National Book Policies for Africa*, edited by Murray McCartney. Harare: Zimbabwe International Book Fair Trust, 1996, 37-38.
Describes some of the prerequisites for a successful book development policy for South Africa.

1038 Krut, Orenna **"The Politics of Publishing in South Africa and What it Means for Writers."** *Staffrider* 10, no. 4 (1992): 65-68.
[Not examined]

1039 Machet, Myrna **"Authorship and Book Publication in South Africa."** In *The Information Society*, edited by Noel Shillinglaw and Wanda Thomas. Johannesburg: Ad Donker, 1988, 77-100.
[Not examined]

1040 Machet, Myrna **"Publishing and Book Selling in South Africa with Specific Reference to the Black Market."** *South African Journal of Library and Information Science* 61, no. 4 (1993): 166-176.
An in-depth examination of the South African publishing industry as it relates to the domination of the industry by the white population. Machet identifies the reasons for this, including the lack of distribution channels to reach the black market. She contends that the lack of reading culture among black people in South Africa is due partly to the fact that the library system is still largely inaccessible to black users and the school library system is inadequate. Examines the effect of colonial interests, and the influence of access to capital on the development of an indigenous publishing industry. Also discusses the consequences of censorship, the emergency regulations, and Eurocentrism on the industry.

1041 Martin, Lianda **"Republican Press – the Picture-Story as Africana?"** In *From Papyrus to Print-out: The Book in Africa Yesterday, Today and Tomorrow. Bibliophilia Africana 8 Conference Proceedings. Centre of the Book Cape Town, 11-14 May 2005*, edited by Cora Owens. Pretoria and Cape Town: National Library of South Africa/Centre of the Book, 2005, 48-54.
The great popularity of "photo-stories" in the 1960's, 70's and 80's seems to be a particular South African phenomenon and is linked to the founding and expansion of Republican Press, who also published, amongst other titles, *Bona* and other popular magazines. This presentation looks at the growth of the "photo-story" industry, the rationale informing the writing of the plots and the unprecedented success of the genre across South Africa's hard cultural boundaries of those decades.

1042   Masokoane, Glenn Ujabe **"Tackling Racism in Textbooks."** In *Publishing for Democratic Education,* edited by Steve Kromberg *et al.* Johannesburg: The Sached Trust, 1993, 61-66.

Illustrates some of the "myriad cultural, historical and ideological considerations" which are still present in South African society [in the 1990s], and as reflected in the content of textbooks.

1043   Mbobo, Themeka C.; Jane Katjavivi, and Yolisa Madolo **"Alternative Initiatives in Publishing/Literatures and Publishing in Africa."** In *From Papyrus to Print-out: The Book in Africa Yesterday, Today and Tomorrow. Bibliophilia Africana 8 Conference Proceedings. Centre of the Book Cape Town, 11-14 May 2005,* edited by Cora Owens. Pretoria and Cape Town: National Library of South Africa/Centre of the Book, 2005, 189-195.

There is a generalization in South Africa about the lack of a reading culture amongst the people. This generalization is usually presented by publishers and booksellers alike and to some extent by librarians, based on the sales (or the lack of sales) of their books, or the number of visitors to the libraries' reading sections. It is also based on a misconception that if people do not read publications written in English (and Afrikaans, perhaps), they therefore do not read at all. This paper aims to demonstrate that South Africans do read books published in indigenous languages, but not enough of such material is published and made available in public libraries. The authors also stress the need to allow emerging as well as established writers to self-publish, thus leading to the production of more, and a wider variety of writing, in a variety of languages, than what is currently being produced by commercial publishers. While the authors recognize that reading is a problem, especially for women, they argue that this does not mean people do not read. Self-publishing is, to some extent at least, seen as a possible solution to the problem, encouraging more writers to engage in the publishing business, and thus generating more readers.

1044   McCallum, Kate **"A New Threat Looms in South Africa — State Publishing."** *African Publishing Review* 6, no. 1 (January/February 1997): 18-19.

The chairperson of the Educational Publishers' Group of the ➔ **Publishers' Association of South Africa (945)** sets out the reasons why, in PASA's view, the possibility of state or parastatal publishing would be a serious threat not only to the indigenous book publishing industries, but also to the provision of quality education, and to the interest of society as a whole.

1045   Merrett, Christopher **"State Versus Documentation: Access to Anti-Apartheid Viewpoints from within South Africa."** *African Research and Documentation,* no. 50 (1989): 1-11.

Includes some discussion of publishing under apartheid, and the role of oppositional publishers.

1046 Moshoeshoe, June **"South Africa: A New and Developing Market."** *Focus on International & Comparative Librarianship* 28, no. 2 (September 1997): 81-82.
Summary of a talk given at an IGLA seminar during the London International Book Fair in 1997, on the prospects of book and library development in South Africa.

1047 Moss, Glenn **"A Critical Overview of Educational Publishing."** In *Publishing for Democratic Education,* edited by Steve Kromberg *et al.* Johannesburg: The Sached Trust, 1993, 21-30.
Offers a general and reflective view of educational publishing in South Africa [in the 1990s]. Argues that the definition of 'educational publishing' is too narrow and is mainly concerned with textbook publishing for primary and secondary schools. Emphasizes that this sector of publishing in fact embraces publishing material for libraries and reference, for supplementary and voluntary reading, for adult education and literacy, and for the general public.

1048 Moss, Glenn **"Educational Publishing in South Africa."** *African Publishing Review* 2, no. 5 (September/October 1993): 5-6.
An edited version of a paper first presented at a Sached/NECC conference on 'Publishing for Democratic Education' held in Johannesburg in May 1993 (*see* preceding entry ➜ **1047**), on the hotly contested terrain of educational publishing in post-apartheid South Africa, and the relationship between publishing, education and democracy.

1049 Moss, Glenn **"Crisis in South African Publishing."** *Bellagio Publishing Network Newsletter*, no. 7 (September 1993): 1-3.
A critical examination of the crisis in South African publishing [in 1993], caused by attempts by a number of publishers to position themselves favourably to facilitate privileged relations with the African National Congress – and hence South Africa's future government – in particular the Macmillan-Thebe agreement.

1050 Moss, Glenn **"Publishing in Post-Apartheid South Africa."** *Logos. The Journal of the World Book Community* 4, no. 3 (1993): 140-43.
Online:
http://www.atypon-link.com/LOG/doi/pdf/10.2959/logo.1993.4.3.140
Reviews the challenges of publishing in post-apartheid society and the forces and counter-forces which exist among publishers as they reposition themselves to secure privileged access to the state educational structures in the 'new' South Africa, the lucrative textbook business, and "the holy grail of the approved list."

1051 Moss, Glenn **"The Life and Times of Ravan Press. Challenges Facing Independent Publishing in South Africa."** In *Proceedings of the Info Africa Nova Conference 1993,* vol. 1, edited by A.G. Coetzer. Pretoria: Info Africa Nova CC, 1993, 186-197.
Recounts the twenty-one year history of Ravan Press, arguably the bravest and most prominent anti-apartheid publisher, who somehow managed to survive despite

various moves against it by the government; whose authors, directors, staff members and books were banned at various times, its offices firebombed, and who probably did the most to actively encourage Black expression—and who went on to scoop up just about every prize or award of substance, not only in South Africa but also elsewhere. The article concludes with an assessment of the challenges that lie ahead in the 'new' South Africa, to secure Ravan's future, and the future of critical and independent publishing. The author was for several years Ravan's General Manager.

1052 Moss, Glenn **"The Life and Changing Times of an Independent Publisher in South Africa."** *Logos. The Journal of the World Book Community* 4, no. 3 (1993): 144-145.
Online:
http://www.atypon-link.com/LOG/doi/pdf/10.2959/logo.1993.4.3.144
Also published in *African Publishing Review* 3, no. 3 (May/June 1994): 10-14.
A shorter version of the preceding entry (*see* ➔ **1051**). Traces the history and growth of Ravan Press of Johannesburg, a socially committed publisher that was in the forefront of oppositional publishing in South Africa until the ending of apartheid in that country.

1053 Mpe, Phaswane **"Language Policy and African Language Publishing in South Africa."** *Bellagio Publishing Network Newsletter*, no. 25 (July 1999): 12-13.
Online:
http://www.bellagiopublishingnetwork.com/newsletter25/mpe.htm
[09/03/08]
South African language policy has become much more democratic since the end of apartheid, which recognized only English and Afrikaans as official languages of the country. The new language policy recognizes in addition nine indigenous African languages, and education policies allow these languages as mediums of instruction in schools. However, as the author reports here, the task of translating policy into practice is fraught with many obstacles. While the new policies, in theory, are good for the publishing industry, especially for those publishing in the historically disadvantaged African languages, practice is stifled by a number of factors: for example, surveys have shown that many parents still prefer their children to be instructed in English as they see this as a language that gives access to economic and other privileges. The new publishing dispensation and book promotion strategies "therefore carry with them the hangover from the previous political and educational conditions, hence the wholesale preference for English at the expense of all other languages in the country" Another seriously limiting factor is that in seven provinces provincial departments still have a school prescription committee. "As long as education departments are happy to remain prescriptive, publishers and their readers are too scared to take [on] unconventional titles, and book promoters are prepared to continue with discriminatory practices based on languages, writers will also remain complacent"—all this to the detriment of healthy publishing practice.

1054 Mpe, Phaswane, and Monica Seeber **"The Politics of Book Publishing in South Africa: A Critical Overview."** In *The Politics of*

Publishing in South Africa, edited by Nicholas Evans and Monica Seeber. London: Holger Ehling Publishing and Scotsville, South Africa: University of Natal Press, 2000, 14-42.
Chronicles the highly politicized story of book publishing in South Africa, starting with an account of the activities of missionary presses and African language publishing, and thereafter examines wholly Afrikaner-owned publishing houses during the apartheid days, "which were ready to publish schoolbooks whose uncritical approach to apartheid ideology posed no problems for the State", through to the emergence of local publishing houses challenging censorship, such as David Philip Publishers, Ravan Press, Ad Donker and Skotaville Publishers. It also looks at recent [2000] plethora of mergers and acquisitions in the publishing industry, surveys literary awards and publishing of African literature, and discusses the crucial aspect of publishing and the new curriculum in post-apartheid South Africa.

1055 Munoo, Rajeen **"Reflecting on Current Trends in South African Higher Education: Contextualizing the Book Market Potential."** *Focus on International & Comparative Librarianship* 28, no. 2 (September 1997): 82-88.
Summary of a talk given at an IGLA seminar during the London International Book Fair in 1997 by the Librarian of Fort Hare University. Reviews the South African government's Green Paper on Higher Education Transformation, the submissions made to the National Commission on Higher Education (NCHE) by the Working Group on Libraries and Information Technology (WGILIT), and the implications these have both for overseas and local publishers. Argues that publishers "need to re-engineer their services and products for the emerging new South African market."

1056 Mutlaotse, Mothobi **"Indigenous Publishing in South Africa: The Case of Skotaville Publishers."** In *Publishing and Development in the Third World,* edited by Philip G. Altbach. London: Hans Zell Publishers, 1992, 211-222.
Reflects on the need for black African writers to break free from imposed European literary traditions. Reviews the history of Skotaville Publishers giving special attention to their literature series. Provides a general view of the situation in South Africa concerning publishing development, state involvement in publishing, book development, censorship, and enrichment programmes. Sets out the future vision for Skotaville Publishers.

1057 Nassimbeni, Mary **"Libraries and Publishers: What will Libraries Need to Serve the Future South Africa?"** In *Book Publishing in South Africa for the 1990s.* Cape Town: South African Library, 1991, 40-59.
Discusses the relationship between libraries and publishing using an examination of the black experience and comments on material available in African languages. The author examines reading motives, preferences, and gaps in the provision of material.

1058 Oliphant, Andries Walter **"Arguments for a Strong, Indigenous Publishing Industry."** In *Publishing for Democratic Education,* edited by Steve Kromberg *et al.* Johannesburg: The Sached Trust, 1993, 97-106.

In two parts, the first centres on a synthesis of facts and offers critical reflections on the publishing industry and the education system, followed by practical suggestions for creating a strong indigenous publishing industry.

1059 Oliphant, Andries Walter **"COSAW and Publishing for All."** *Matatu,* no. 15/16 (1996): 173-182.

COSAW Publishing was set up in 1987 as a semi-autonomous, income-generating operation owned by the Congress of South African Writers. This article provides some perspectives on the work of the organization and its publishing activities [as at 1996]. It looks at the challenges in the years ahead for the small publishing house, including the publication of material in African languages, producing "barefoot" low cost publications aimed to provide outlets for beginners who participate in COSAW workshops in various regions, and the journal *Staffrider*. However, distribution networks are still dominated by the Anglo-American subsidiary Central News Agency (CNA), which has shown little interest in stocking and promoting the COSAW publishing output. The author concludes that "the growth of a viable indigenous publishing industry, capable of serving the needs of the majority of South Africans depends on the extent to which the broader social, economic and political changes break the monopolies and controls acquired by a racially inspired political economy in South Africa."

1060 Oliphant, Andries Walter **"From Colonialism to Democracy: Writers and Publishing in South Africa."** In *The Politics of Publishing in South Africa,* edited by Nicholas Evans and Monica Seeber. London: Holger Ehling Publishing and Scotsville, South Africa: University of Natal Press, 2000, 107-126.

Aims to assess how the colonial legacy that has shaped literary publishing for more than two centuries can be redressed in post-apartheid South Africa. This is dealt with in three sections: first, by providing an overview of literary publishing in South Africa; secondly, by identifying problems, issues, and constraints in this area; and thirdly, by examining the changed publishing environment in a democratic society and the post-apartheid implications for transformation in the field of publishing. The author asserts that "the net result of the period of transition has been that South African publishing has regressed, in terms of diversity in ownership, as well as in the variety of its output, and perhaps also in its social importance"; and that the new publishing environment calls for deep-seated changes and "a reorientation in the cultural and linguistic values which informs the various sectors of the publishing industry."

PASA Snapshot Survey Reports *see* ➜ Print Industries Cluster Council **Annual Industry Profile Studies (AIPS)** entries **1067-1073**

1061 Perold, Helene; Shanoo Chupty, Amanda Jordaan, *et al.* **Research Report on Book Development in South Africa.** Johannesburg: Book Development Council of South Africa, 1997. var. pp.
[Not examined]

1062 Philip, David **"Oppositional Publishing in South Africa from 1945 to 2000."** *Logos. Journal of the World Book Community* 2, no. 1 (1991): 41-48. Online:
http://www.atypon-link.com/LOG/doi/pdf/10.2959/logo.1991.2.1.41
Also published in *Afro-Asian Publishing. Contemporary Trends*, New Delhi: Institute of Book Publishing,1992, 85-98; and another version in *Book Publishing in South Africa for the 1990s.* Cape Town: South African Library, 1991, 9-21.
The founder of David Philip Publishers and first Chairman of the Independent Publishers Association of South Africa – now amalgamated with the ➜ **Publishers Association of South Africa (945)** – gives an overview of the state of oppositional publishing in South Africa from 1948 up until 1992. Includes a brief account of David Philip's own long career in publishing in Southern Africa and recounts the beginnings of his anti-apartheid company, which was started in 1971, with the slogan "Books that Matter for Southern Africa". Discusses the activities of other oppositional publishers such as Ravan Press, Skotaville, SPRO-CAS, Seriti sa Sechaba, the South African Institute of Race Relations, and Bateleur Press. Suggests a continuing role for oppositional publishing even in a post-apartheid society in South Africa.

1063 Philip, David, and Mike Kantey **"South Africa."** In *International Book Publishing. An Encyclopedia*, edited by Philip G. Altbach and Edith S. Hoshino. New York: Garland Publishing, 1995, 414-23.
A comprehensive historical overview of the development of publishing in South Africa, from the earliest period until the 1990s and beyond. The authors examine the role and activities of the leading Afrikaner and other educational publishers, the UK multinationals with offices in South Africa, the effects of censorship and other forms of suppression in the period from 1948 to 1970, and the emergence of anti-apartheid and oppositional publishers since the early 1970s, some of whom suffered constant harassment from the government. Concludes with an assessment of book publishing in post-apartheid South Africa.

1064 Phillips, Howard **"Van Rieebeeck's Journey: the Origins and Destination of the Van Riebeek Society for the Publication of SA Historical Documents 1918-2004."** In *From Papyrus to Print-out: The Book in Africa Yesterday, Today and Tomorrow. Bibliophilia Africana 8 Conference Proceedings. Centre of the Book Cape Town, 11-14 May 2005*, edited by Cora Owens. Pretoria and Cape Town: National Library of South Africa/Centre of the Book, 2005, 64-76.
Recognizing that the 86-year old Van Riebeeck Society for the Publication of South African Historical Documents is unique in South Africa as a long-existing cultural NGO dedicated solely to the publication of primary historical documents, this paper investigates its origins, output, and strategy for continued existence. The author analyzes the nature of the 88 volumes the Society has published to date and concludes that they represent a narrow conception of South African history,

topically, chronologically, linguistically, and in terms of authorship. How this conception is nowadays being broadened is the focus of a final section of the paper.

1065   Politis, Karen **L'édition en Afrique du Sud ou les complexités de la nation "arc-en-ciel".** *La Lettre* (Bureau International de l'édition française) 5 September 2006
http://www.bief.org/?fuseaction=lettre.article&A=308 [summary only, 10/01/08]
Full-text version of the complete study is available from the ➔ **Bureau international de l'Édition française (45)** Email: k.politis@bief.org (Subscription based)
On the complexities of publishing in the "rainbow nation" of South Africa. The author provides an overview of the South African book industries, the major players involved, the nature of publishing activities, prices and print runs, distribution channels, readership and reading habits, and examines the extent of local publishing output vs. imported books. She also notes an increase in interest in French language teaching and French language materials. This is the summary of a much fuller study.

1066   Potenza, Emilia **"It Doesn't Make Sense: Educational Standards in Textbooks."** In *Publishing for Democratic Education*, edited by Steve Kromberg *et al.* Johannesburg: The Sached Trust, 1993, 47-60.
A critical analysis of textbook publishing output by the major educational publishers in South Africa since 1990.

1067   Print Industries Cluster Council **Annual Industry Profile Studies (AIPS).** Bellville, South Africa: Print Industries Cluster Council/South African Book Development Council, 2002 -
Initiated by the ➔ **Publishers Association of South Africa/PASA (945)** and the ➔ **South African Booksellers Association/SABA (951)**, this series of book industry profile studies form part of a systematic data collection exercise, and database developed and housed at the University of Pretoria's Department of Information Science and Publishing Studies. The reports and surveys aim to provide a mechanism to track changes in the "South African book value chain", and which can also be used as a tool to monitor the impact of the country's national book policy. All reports contain detailed information on the methodology of the data gathering process, analysis of response rates, and data analysis supported by tables and charts. Data analysis for publishers includes turnover profiles (for the larger publishers), production profiles (with data on total number of titles in print, new title output annually, etc.), author profiles and analysis of royalty payments to authors, employment profiles (race and gender, job categories and gender), staff (management, editorial, production, marketing, finance and administration, IT, etc.). The following reports and surveys are currently [February 2008] available:

1068   **South African Pulp and Paper Industry. Statistical Data – Quarterly Report, January to December 2004.** Bellville, South Africa: Print Industries Cluster Council/South African Book Development Council, 2004. 32 pp.
Online: http://www.picc.org.za/pdf/pamsaindustrydata2004.pdf [14/02/08]

1069   PASA/SABA Snaphot Survey 2002 Report. Compiled by Francis Galloway, Theo Bothma, and Lise-Marie Greyling. Bellville, South Africa: Print Industries Cluster Council/South African Book Development Council, 2004. 33 pp.
Online: http://www.picc.org.za/pdf/snapshot_survey_2002.pdf [14/02/08]
1070   PASA Snaphot Survey 2003 Report. Compiled by Francis Galloway, Theo Bothma, Colette du Plessis, and Rudi M.R. Venter. Bellville, South Africa: Print Industries Cluster Council/South African Book Development Council, 2005. 48 pp.
Online: http://www.picc.org.za/pdf/2003.pdf [14/02/08]
1071   PASA Annual Industry Survey 2004 Report. Compiled by Francis Galloway, Rudi M.R. Venter, and Theo Bothma. Bellville, South Africa: Print Industries Cluster Council/South African Book Development Council, 2006. 35 pp.
Online: http://www.picc.org.za/pdf/2004.pdf [14/02/08]
1072   PASA Annual Industry Survey 2005 Report. Compiled by Francis Galloway, Rudi M.R. Venter, and Theo Bothma. Bellville, South Africa: Print Industries Cluster Council/ South African Book Development Council, 2006. 35 pp.
Online: http://www.picc.org.za/pdf/2005.pdf [14/02/08]
1073   PASA Industry Surveys. Executive Summary: Broad Trends over Four Years (2002-2005). Compiled by Francis Galloway, Rudi M.R. Venter, and Theo Bothma. Bellville, South Africa: Print Industries Cluster Council/ South African Book Development Council, 2006. 34 pp.
Online: http://www.picc.org.za/pdf/2002-2005.pdf [14/02/08]

1074   Print Industries Cluster Council **Book Retail Industry Survey 2006 Report.** Bellville, South Africa: Print Industries Cluster Council/South African Booksellers Association, 2007. 27 pp.
Online:
http://www.sabooksellers.com/pdf/Book%20Retail%20Industry%20Survey%202006.pdf [14/02/08]
A survey commissioned by the ➜ **South African Booksellers Association (951)** that aimed to provide a broad overview of the shape and the size of the local book retail industry for the calendar year 2006. Data was collected and analyzed for the three sub-sectors of the retail book sector: trade books, academic books, and educational books. Each participant in the survey was asked to provide annual net book turnover values for a range of customer categories, which included direct consumer sales and institutional sales. Additionally, employment statistics collected included employment numbers, total staff remuneration, demographic profiles, and data on expenditure on training was also collected.

1075   Print Industries Cluster Council **Draft Framework for the National Book Policy to be Submitted to the National Department of Arts and Culture in October 2005.**
http://www.liasa.org.za/conferences/conference2005/Draft-framework_NBP_100805.pdf [14/02/08]
The draft version of a national book policy framework for South Africa that, before submission to the government, sought to incorporate the insights of the writing, paper, printing, book publishing, bookselling sectors, as well as that of the libraries and development initiative communities of South Africa. It sets out the objectives and guiding policies of a national book policy, and what its policy priorities ought to be.

1076 Print Industries Cluster Council **Factors Influencing the Cost of Books in South Africa**. Bellville, South Africa: Print Industries Cluster Council/ South African Book Development Council, 2006. 83 pp.
Online:
http://www.picc.org.za/pdf/PICC_Cost%20of%20books%20studyFinal.pdf [14/02/08]
A study commissioned and funded by the South African Department of Arts and Culture. It comprises an investigation of the factors that affect the cost of books in South Africa, conducted in order to identify possible ways in which government, industry members and other stakeholders can work together to reduce the cost of books and make books more accessible. The factors that affect the cost of books are dealt with by examining each of the five principal segments of the book value chain separately, namely paper, printing, publishing, distribution, and bookselling, and by furthermore investigating the sector-specific drivers of cost in the following three book market segments: (1) Educational books, comprising books used in primary and secondary education, i.e. books for [South African] Grades 1 – 12; (2) Academic books aimed at the tertiary education sector; and, (3) Trade books, which include both fiction and non-fiction books aimed at the general market.

1077 Print Industries Cluster Council **National Survey into the Reading Book Reading Behaviour of Adult South Africans.** Bellville, South Africa: Print Industries Cluster Council/ South African Book Development Council, 2007. 74 pp.
Online: http://www.picc.org.za/pdf/NRSDOCopt.pdf (7.81MB) [09/03/08]
Presents the baseline data of quantitative research undertaken into the reading, book reading, and book buying habits of South Africans from the age of 16. The survey was commissioned by the South African Department of Arts and Culture through the Print Industries Cluster Council (PICC), now part of the ➜ **South African Book Development Council (950)**. The survey, supported by a massive amount of statistical analysis in the form of charts and tables, is presented under five sectors: Reading and the research in context; South African leisure life; Reading in South Africa; Book reading in South Africa-segmenting the market, and Strategic interpretations and the way forward. For the management summary and final report *see* entry ➜ **1078** below.

1078 Print Industries Cluster Council **Project Book Worm – Final Report. National Survey into the Reading and Book Reading Behaviour of Adult South Africa.** Bellville, South Africa: Print Industries Cluster Council/ South African Book Development Council, 2007. 37 pp.
Online:
http://www.picc.org.za/pdf/ManagementSummaryNationalReadingSurve y2007.pdf (2.63MB) [09/03/08]
This is the management summary (including the executive summary and the conclusions) of the results from the country's first baseline survey (*see* entry ➜ **1077**) above into the reading and book reading behaviour of adult South Africans. Is a

culture of reading and book reading prevalent in South Africa? Are there any demographic differences in terms of how readers and book readers are differentiated in the population? Similarly, are behavioural and psychological variations identifiable? It is these and many more pertinent questions that are summarized in this report. The focus of the survey was on reading in the context of other leisure activities, and book reading in regard to fiction and non-fiction books, exclusive of school and work-related books. The study was an important milestone for South Africa as it provides, for the first time in South Africa, quantifiable measures on the state of reading and book reading in the country, as well as a profiling of the population in terms of demographic and psychographic analysis.

1079 Proctor, André, and Mary Monteith **"Textbooks, Corruption and Curricula."** In *Publishing for Democratic Education*, edited by Steve Kromberg *et al.* Johannesburg: The Sached Trust, 1993, 31-46.
Sub-titled 'Urgent ethical policy considerations for transition and the transformation of South African education', this paper focuses on various aspects of textbook provision and curriculum development: systems of textbook production, approval and supply; plans for a transition period to address current problems; and enabling the small indigenous publisher to enter the market on reasonably even terms with the multinational publishing companies.

1080 Randall, Peter **"'Minority' Publishing in South Africa."** *The African Book Publishing Record* 1, no. 3 (July 1975): 219-222.
Discusses the "remarkable upsurge of publishing activity in South Africa" against a background of the [then] situation in South Africa, "a repressive society in which power, both economic and political, is firmly concentrated in the hands of the white minority". Describes the whole range of minority and oppositional publishing activities from the political far right to the far left.

1081 Randall, Peter **"Publishing in South Africa: Challenges and Constraints."** *The African Book Publishing Record* 9, nos. 2/3 (1983): 105-108.
Provides a historical overview of publishing in Africa, including the repressive actions of the [then apartheid] government in the sphere of publishing and the eventual liberalization of censorship. Peter Randall was joint founder and General Manager of the oppositional Ravan Press for many years.

1082 Ridge, Stanley G.M. **"The African Bookman: A Progressive South African Publisher before 1948."** In *From Papyrus to Print-out: The Book in Africa Yesterday, Today and Tomorrow. Bibliophilia Africana 8 Conference Proceedings. Centre of the Book Cape Town, 11-14 May 2005*, edited by Cora Owens. Pretoria and Cape Town: National Library of South Africa/Centre of the Book, 2005, 96-109.
Another version in *Constructing South African Literary History*, edited by Elmar Lehmann, Erhard Reckwitz and Lucia Vennarini. Essen, Germany: Die Blaue Eule, 2000, 99-112.

In the 1940s The African Bookman, an 'alternative' or oppositional publisher established by Julian Rollnick, was active in Cape Town, providing reading matter for the often newly literate urban African until it closed in 1948 because of financial difficulties, and problems over marketing and distribution. Among its authors were Es'kia Mphahlele, today one South Africa's best known writer and critic, whose first collection of short stories, *Man Must Live* was published by The African Bookman in 1947 because Mphahlele was unable to find another publisher in the South Africa of that time. The African Bookman offered an outlet for progressive writers and scholars, black and white, despite operating in a repressive racist society, and also pioneered popular publishing in African languages. This interesting article sets the history of this courageous and enterprising small firm in context, and gives a critical account of its achievements.

1083 Rall, Pieter, and Hendri Warricker **Trends in Book Publishing in South Africa for the Period 1990 to 1998.** Pretoria: University of Pretoria, Department of Information Science 2000. M.Bibl. thesis [?].
[Not examined]

1084 Redhi, Guru **Address by Mr. Guru Redhi, President of the South African Booksellers Association (SABA), at the 1st Southern African Library Acquisitions Conference in the Technikon SA Conference Centre, Ormonde Extension One, Gauteng, on Tuesday 15 August 2000.**
http://home.imaginet.co.za/liasa/SABA%20InfoSession.htm [04/01/08]
An address given by the President of the ➜ **South African Booksellers Association (951)** setting out the principal mission, policies and activities of the association, his thoughts on the relationship between booksellers and librarians in the country, and how vendors and librarians might work more closely together to promote a reading culture. *Note:* for a short report about this conference *see also* entry ➜ **1100.**

1085 Roussow, Fransie **South African Printers and Publishers, 1795-1925: from *A South African Bibliography to the Year 1925.*** Cape Town: South African Library, 1987. 262 pp.
[Not examined]

1086 Sached Trust and the National Education Co-ordinating Committee (NECC) **"A Vision for Educational Publishing in South Africa."** In *Publishing for Democratic Education,* edited by Steve Kromberg *et al.* Johannesburg: The Sached Trust, 1993, 177-180.
Sets out the framework of a vision for educational publishing in the 'new' South Africa, highlighting twelve important areas.

1087 Samuel, John **"Educational Publishing for a Democratic South Africa. An African National Congress Perspective."** In *Publishing for Democratic Education,* edited by Steve Kromberg *et al.* Johannesburg: The Sached Trust, 1993, 9-20.

Describes the role of the African National Congress (ANC) in the development of the publishing industry after apartheid, and their educational objectives.

1088 Schur, Michael **Sectors, Clusters and Regions: Printing and Publishing in the Witwatersrand.** Cape Town: University of Cape Town, Development Policy Research Unit, (Working papers, 96/10) 1996. 36 pp. [Not examined]

Sisulu, Elinor **"The Culture of Reading and the Book Chain: How do we Achieve a Quantum Leap?"** *see* ➔ **Section 4, Studies by topics: Reading culture and reading promotion** entry **2219**

1089 Skinner, Douglas Reid **"Book Publishing in a Multicultural South Africa."** In *Book Publishing in South Africa for the 1990s.* Cape Town: South African Library, 1991, 22-24.
Presents a pessimistic view of the past and the future of publishing in South Africa, and predicts a rise in the price of books, with an accompanying decrease in the number of people who can afford to buy them.

1090 South Africa. Department of the Arts, Culture, Science and Technology **The Cultural Industries Growth Strategy (CIGS). The South African Publishing Industry Report . Report to the Department of Arts, Culture, Science and Technology. Final Report, November 1998.** Pretoria: Department of the Arts, Culture, Science and Technology [now Ministry of Arts, Culture, Science and Technology], 1998. 77 pp. Online: http://www.info.gov.za/otherdocs/1998/publishingreport.pdf [09/03/08]
A report commissioned by the South African government's Department (now Ministry) of Arts, Culture, Science and Technology to research South Africa's cultural industries and propose strategies for their growth and development. The term "cultural industries" is used here to describe a wide variety of cultural activities, most of which have commercial objectives as their prime motivating force, with activities taking a number of different forms, from the manufacture or creation of products to the marketing and distribution thereof. The cultural industries on which the report concentrated are the music industry, the craft industry, the publishing industry and the film and television industries. The methodology followed for the study is in the nature of an industry strategy analysis. Each sector report is principally an economic analysis, providing baseline data for each of the four sectors, and focusing on the current economic and social contribution of each sector; the impediments to growth, and the opportunities for employment creation and competitive development. Each sector report concludes with strategic policy recommendations for interventions by both the public and private sector. The book publishing industry is covered in sector 4, electronic publishing in sector 5, and other sectors are devoted to an overall evaluation of the four segments of the industry, a SWOT analysis, and a final section devoted to an analysis of global trends in the publishing industry.

1091   South African Library **Book Publishing in South Africa for the 1990s.**
Cape Town: South African Library, 1991. 117 pp.
The proceedings of a symposium held at the South African Library, Cape Town, in
November 1990. Subjects covered include censorship, publishing in a multicultural
South Africa, educational publishing, children's book publishing, literacy and
development, and marketing and distribution. The papers were given by a wide
selection of professionals including publishers, academics, librarians and
educationalists. *Note:* some of the papers in this collection are individually
abstracted elsewhere in this bibliography.

1092   Struik, Willem **"What's Up with SA Books? A Quest for the Facts."**
Bookmark. News Magazine of the South African Booksellers' Association 9 (July-
September 2005): 7-10, 16.
Takes a closer look at some of the statistics and book trade surveys now available to
the South African book industry. What is the market share, who are the customers,
where do they buy the books, and what books do South African consumers buy?

1093   Struik, Willem **"Room for Growth."** *Bookmark. News Magazine of the
South African Booksellers' Association* 11 (April-July 2007): 7-8.
Nielsen BookScan analyst Willem Struik looks at some statistics of South African
trade book sales in 2006. He notes an encouraging increase in market share, but also
observes that because "of the massive increase in consumer spending, largely due to
the emerging middle class amongst previously disadvantaged communities, very
little has gone to books."

1094   Struik, Willem **"How Big is the Book Trade?"** *Bookmark. News
Magazine of the South African Booksellers' Association* 11 (April-July 2007): 12-
14.
Compares the PASA Annual Industry surveys (*see* ➔ entries **1067-1073**) for 2004 and
2005 with the Nielsen BookScan sales statistics for the same period. While there are
both similarities and differences between the two sets of figures, and the
methodology in data gathering, taken together they can provide a fairly reliable
estimation of the size book trade in South Africa.

1095   Switzer, Les, and Donna Switzer **The Black Press in South Africa and
Lesotho: A Descriptive Bibliographic Guide to African, Coloured and
Indian Newspapers, Newsletters and Magazines 1836-1976**. Boston: G.K.
Hall, 1979. 307 pp.
Online: http://icon.crl.edu/guides/Switzer.pdf (4.19MB) [15/01/08]
A classic reference work, originally published in 1979 but long out-of-print, for which
the full text has recently become available in digitized format (as a large 4MB pdf
file), freely accessible online. The authors' primary aim was to compile a
bibliographical guide to source material which had hitherto received little attention
from researchers writing about the black experience in South Africa and Lesotho.
Fully annotated, entries cover serial newspapers, newsletters and magazines directed

primarily at, or intended for, an African, Indian and "Coloured" (Mixed race) audience.

1096 Taylor, Sally **"South Africa Today: An Eye on the Future."** *Publishers Weekly*, (September 9, 1996): 43-59.
A general overview of publishing and the book trade in South Africa in the mid 1990s, with some coverage of book trade activities elsewhere in the region. Reports about the challenges faced by educational publishers, and also looks at academic and trade publishing, and the retail trade, including attempts to set up more book retail outlets in the black communities.

1097 van der Sandt, Elitha **"Collective Thinking Develops Book Policy."** *Bookmark. News Magazine of the South African Booksellers' Association* 10 (October 2005-March 2006): 8.
Provides a synopsis of progress thus far in developing a national book policy for South Africa.

1098 van Gend, Cecily **"The Independent Presses in South Africa."** *Cape Librarian* 36, no. 7 (1992): 28-31.
[Not examined]

1099 van Schaik, J.J. **"Republic of South Africa."** In *The Book Trade of the World, vol. IV: Africa*, edited by Sigfred Taubert and Peter Weidhaas. Munich: K.G. Saur, 1984, 270-289.
Overview of publishing and the book trade in South Africa. Now very dated.

1100 van Zijl, Carole, and Jean Maree **Libraries, Vendors, Publishers: Strategic Partners in the 21st Century – A Report on the 1st Southern African Library Acquisitions Conference.**
http://home.imaginet.co.za/liasa/background.html [15/01/08]
A short report about this conference, the presentations that were made, and the issues that were discussed.

1101 Wafawarowa, Brian **"Ten Years of Freedom – Wither the South African Publishing Industry."** *African Publishing Review* 13, no. 2 (2004): 1-4.
Online: http://www.apnet.org/documents/vol_13_2.doc [28/01/08]
Takes a critical and candid look at the progress made by the South African publishing industry since the ending of apartheid in 1994, in terms of broader participation, linguistic diversity, ownership, and other indicators. The author finds that the multinational companies still heavily dominate educational book publishing, and that out of the more than ten new publishers that were established since 1994, only one has managed to penetrate mainstream education publishing. "Ownership and economic participation of black people in the industry is dismal and continues to dwindle, even ten years after freedom. Local participation is dismal too. Black people remain confined to selling and publishing African languages." Wafawarowa asserts that the picture in general and trade publishing is even worse and that racial

participation in the industry is still almost exclusively white. As a result, black people are not in any meaningful way involved in deciding what is published in the industry, and even among the little that is published locally "there is virtually no African languages publishing that takes place for adult reading in the trade-publishing sector." The author offers a number of suggestions on the way forward, to bring about a situation in which people of all races and cultural persuasion should have the space to participate in the various aspects of the book sector. He also argues that the same laws that regulate the broader media sector, and the objectives of these laws, need to be applied to the publishing industry; and that the state and the relevant departments need to recognise the centrality of the publishing industry to national development and play a more proactive role. This should include the targeting of the industry for transformation and development and curbing developments that militate against national strategic interests in the sector. To enhance more diverse professional participation, education training authorities should spearhead training programmes aimed at placing more black professionals in the industry through internships, while at the same time creating opportunities for these interns to be absorbed by the industry through the creation of publishing programmes.

1102 Wafawarowa, Brian **"The African Publishing Context and its Relationship with South Africa."** *Bookmark. News Magazine of the South African Booksellers' Association* 10 (July-September 2006): 7-10.
Examines some of the reasons and obstacles why African countries with weak currencies are not exporting their books to South Africa, with its relatively strong Rand; and why, vice-versa, top-end South African books cannot be sold competitively in other parts of the continent. These include trade barriers, quality and content issues, and high transportation and distribution costs. While the author is concerned about market consolidation programmes by the multinationals, regarded as harmful to the emergence and development of indigenous publishing, he believes African publishers need to work together against practices such as irregularities in the bidding process in book procurement programmes. "Local indigenous publishers need to stop mourning and begin to make themselves more competitive on the African market." Meantime South Africa has the potential to be the gateway to the African publishing scene, but is needs to improve its relevance: it "needs to start with a more conscious effort to affirm the majority of the black population in South Africa. This will include both the diversification and transformation of both product and practice."

1103 Westra, Pieter E., ed. **Freedom to Read. The Future of Publications Control and the Free Flow of Information in South Africa.** Cape Town: South African Library, 1994. 78 pp.
The proceedings of a seminar held in South Africa in 1993, which reviewed existing South African legislation affecting censorship of publications and information, discussed possible future trends, and put forward proposals regarding the free flow of information in a 'new' South Africa.

1104 Wright, Claire **"Racism and Sexism: Legal Considerations."** In *Publishing for Democratic Education*, edited by Steve Kromberg *et al.* Johannesburg: The Sached Trust, 1993, 67-79.
Explores the possible ways of putting into effect the elimination of racist or sexist ideas in (primarily South African) publications.

Sudan

Associations and book-related organizations

1105 Sudan Publishers Association
c/o Al Dar Asodania for Books, Printing, Publishing and Distribution
PO Box 2473
Khartoum
Sudan
Tel: n/a
Email: makkawi@sudanmail.net
Web: n/a
Chair: Abdulrahim Makkawi

National bibliography, books in print, and book trade directories

1106 Sudan [national bibliography].
No national bibliography exists at this time. There are a number of substitute publications, notably the "Sudan Bibliography" sections published in *Sudan Notes and Records* 1918-1965; new series, issue 1, 1997- , published by the Philosophical Society of the Sudan, POB 555, Khartoum (US enquiries to Ismail H Abdalla, Department of History, The College of William and Mary, Email: ixabda@factaff.wm.edu)
Other agencies documenting and recording national publishing output:
National Library of Sudan, PO Box 6279, Khartoum
Email: natlib10@hotmail.com
The National Records Office (serves as the National Archives), PO Box 1914, Khartoum
Email: n/a (Fax: +249-11-778603)

Books, articles, reports, and interviews

1107 Ahmed, Medani **"In the Sudan. Characteristics and Challenges of its Book Sector."** *African Publishing Review* 7, no. 3 (May/June 1998): 3-4, 6.
The book sector in the Sudan has suffered, and continues to suffer, from some formidable obstacles and problems, particularly in the areas of production, marketing, and distribution. This is a summary report of the findings of two field

studies carried out in 1996 and 1997 that aimed to investigate and study the main characteristics of the book sector in the Sudan, its structure, the laws governing its performance, and the constraints inhibiting the growth of the book industry. The author also makes a series of recommendations as regards to fiscal, monetary, and economic and trade policies that would enhance the development of the book sector in the country in the years ahead.

1108   Al-Mubarak, Khalid **"Democratic Republic of the Sudan."** In *The Book Trade of the World, vol. IV: Africa*, edited by Sigfred Taubert and Peter Weidhaas. Munich: K.G. Saur, 1984, 290-293.
Overview of publishing and the book trade in Sudan. Now very dated.

Swaziland

Associations and book-related organizations

1109   Swaziland Book Traders Association
PO Box 292
Mbabane H100
Swaziland
Tel: +268-404 2560 Fax: +268-404 4897
Email: webstersbooks@africaonline.co.sz
Chair: n/a

1110   Umdlandla Swaziland Writers and Authors Association
PO Box 1152
Manzini M200
Swaziland
Tel: +268-605 3090
Email: n/a
General Secretary: n/a
Note: not verified, organization dormant?

National bibliography, books in print, and book trade directories

1111   Swaziland National Bibliography.
Kwaluseni: University of Swaziland Libraries [Private Bag 4, Kwaluseni M201], 1976-
Irregular, latest is 1977; cumulative volumes covering 3-4 years, latest is 1986-1987 volume published in 1989.
Email: tndziman@uniswacc.uniswa.sz
Web: http://www.library.uniswa.sz

Books, articles, reports, and interviews

1112 Waal, Pieter **"Booksellers Market in Swaziland."** *ISBN Review* 17
(1996): 309-315.
The Group Managing Director of Websters Ltd. in Mbane provides a brief
background of the retail book trade in Swaziland and current book distribution
channels in the country.

1113 Mavuso, Makana **"The Book Chain in Swaziland."** In *The Book Chain
in Anglophone Africa. A Survey and Directory*, edited by Roger Stringer.
Oxford: International Network for the Availability of Scientific Publications
(INASP), 2002, 83-86.
Online: http://www.inasp.info/file/57/the-book-chain-in-anglophone-
africa-a-survey-and-directory.html [10/03/08]
One in a series of useful country surveys and overviews – each prepared by a book
professional from the country concerned – that review the state of the book, and the
major players in the "book chain", in English-speaking African countries. Each
country survey covers printing, book publishing, bookselling and distribution,
library services, professional associations, book promotional bodies and book
promotional events, training for the book professions, as well as examining some of
the major issues as they relate to book development, such as languages, literacy,
writers and writing, the reading habit, and national book policies. For each country
this is supported by an annotated directory of government ministries, professional
associations, book publishers, booksellers and distributors, printers, major libraries,
and training institutions, with full address and contact details.

1114 Ndwandwe, Elias **"The Publishing Industry in Swaziland."** *ISBN
Review* 17 (1996): 289-296
One in a series of overview articles in a special issue of *ISBN Review* focusing on the
book sector in various countries of Southern Africa. This article concentrates mainly
on the activities of the Macmillan Swaziland National Publishing Company (which is
part-owned by the government) and its partnership with the Swaziland Ministry of
Education.

1115 Steinhauer, D.R. **"Kingdom of Swaziland."** In *The Book Trade of the
World, vol. IV: Africa*, edited by Sigfred Taubert and Peter Weidhaas.
Munich: K.G. Saur, 1984, 294-296.
Overview of publishing and the book trade in Swaziland. Now very dated.

Tanzania

Associations and book-related organizations

1116 Booksellers Association of Tanzania
PO Box 7552
Dar es Salaam
Tanzania
Tel: +255-22-2861281
Email: ipyana@yahoo.com
Executive Secretary: A. Mwaipiyana

1117 Children's Book Project of Tanzania (CBP)
Ali Hassan Mwinyi Road
39B Ursino South near Victoria Bus Stop
Postal address:
PO Box 78245
Dar es Salaam
Tanzania
Tel: +255-51-760750 Fax: +255-51-761562
Email: cbp@raha.com
Web: http://www.cbp.or.tz/
Chair: Ali Mcharazo
Secretary: (Ms) P. Dumea

1118 Kagera Writers and Publishers Co-operative Society
PO Box 1222
Bukoba
Tanzania
Tel: n/a
Email: n/a
Note: not verified, organization dormant?

**1119 National Book Development Council of Tanzania/
    Baraza la Maendeleo ya Vitabu Tanzania (BAMVITA)**
PO Box 14213
Dar es Salaam
Tanzania
Tel.: +255-22-218 2185 or +255-784 302620 (Mobile)
Email: bamvita@hotmail.com or bamvita@gmail.com
Web: http://www.bamvita.or.tz/default.asp
Chair: Adam Shafi
Executive Secretary: Frida Lyaruu

1120   Publishers Association of Tanzania (PATA)
3nd Floor Muscat/NK Building
Misimbazi/Sikukuu Street
Kariakoo Area
Dar es Salaam
Tanzania
Postal address:
PO Box 1408
Dar es Salaam
Tanzania
Tel: +255-22-218 4077 Fax: +255-22-218 1077
Email: pata@raha.com
Web: n/a
Chair: Khalaf Rashid
Secretary: Abel K. Mwanga

1121   Tanzania Book Support Trust
79 Lugalo Road
PO Box 1430
Upanga
Dar es Salaam
Tanzania
Tel: +255-22-212 6980 Fax: -255-22-212 1960
Email: kajia@cats-net.com
Web: n/a
Note: not verified, organization dormant?

1122   Tanzania Writers' Association
PO Box 32740
Dar es Salaam
Tanzania
Tel: +255-22-2184077
Email: uwavita@hotmail.com
Secretary: Willian Mkufya
Note: not verified, organization dormant?

1123   Umoja wa Waandishi wa Vitabu Tanzania (UWAVITA)
c/o Institute of Kiswahili Research
Dar es Salaam University
Dar es Salaam
Postal address:
PO Box 35110
Dar es Salaam
Tanzania

Tel: +255-22-241 0757
Email: mulokozi@tuki.udsm.ac.tz
Web: n/a
Chair: (Prof) M.M. Mulokozi

National bibliography, books in print, and book trade directories

1124 Tanzania National Bibliography.
Dar es Salaam: Tanzania Library Service Board [PO Box 9283, Dar es Salaam], 1974-
Monthly, with annual cumulation, latest is 1988.
Email: tlsb@africaonline.co.tz
Web: n/a

1125 Vitabu vya Tanzania 1997/1998. Compiled and edited by the Network of Technical Publications in Africa (TEPUSA). Dar es Salaam: Network of Technical Publications in Africa, n.d. [1997]. 63 pp.
Translates roughly as 'Tanzanian Books in Print'. Although text is principally in Kiswahili, it contains some English explanatory text, and it lists 1,240 English and Kiswahili titles from 60 Tanzanian publishers. Awkward arrangement of titles, with entries arranged under eight columns, one of which gives the subject in abbreviated form (the other columns providing details of author, title, publisher, page extent, price, ISBN and publication date). Key to abbreviations used is incomplete. Includes a listing of publishers with their abbreviations/acronyms, but lacks publishers' addresses. No further editions published to date.

Books, articles, reports, and interviews

1126 Bgoya, Walter Books and Reading in Tanzania. Paris: UNESCO (Studies on Books and Reading, 25), n.d. [1986?]. 76 pp.
One of a series of national monographs on the state of books and reading in a number of countries, published in order to provide book professionals and the interested public, with detailed surveys of matters relating to authorship, publishing, material production and distribution of books and reading. This monograph was prepared by the [then] General Manager of Tanzania Publishing House, Dar es Salaam, and focuses on the difficulty experienced in obtaining accurate data for the publishing industry. Also discusses the need for professional training in publishing, and examines the legal and institutional framework, with special emphasis on the need for a Book Development Council that could assist in developing a flourishing book industry.

1127 Bgoya, Walter "The Challenge of Publishing in Tanzania." In *Publishing and Development in the Third World,* edited by Philip G. Altbach. London: Hans Zell Publishers, 1992, 169-189.
Looks at the publishing industry in Tanzania and explains the sluggish development despite state commitment to universal adult and primary education. The author links

the underdevelopment of the printing and publishing industries with East Africa's colonial history when the main market place for East Africa was in Kenya. He examines the roles of multilateral agencies and international donor organizations in supporting Tanzania's education and the impact which this had on publishing. Demonstrates why friendly donor organizations have tended to create and nurture a dependency on aid and how this has hindered the development of indigenous publishing. Also discusses the issue of language, and the activities of multinational publishing companies.

1128 Bo Sedin Consultants AB/ASG Transport Development **A Study of the Distribution of Educational Materials in Tanzania. Final report 1993.** [Report by Bertil Dahlin] Stockholm: Bo Sedin Consultants AB [Ästmannagatan 81 ÖG 3tr, 113 26 Stockholm], 1993. var. pp. [restricted circulation]
A distribution study that aimed to assist the Ministry of Education and Culture in Tanzania to overcome problems of distribution of educational materials in the country during a period of transition, i.e. whereby the previously state controlled production and distribution system is gradually making way for the private sector to take over the supply of educational materials. The study finds that the problems faced are not in fact distribution problems but are caused by problems of a financial and managerial/organizational nature, and puts forward a series of short and long term recommendations how the situation might be improved.

1129 Carpenter, Julia, and Ivor Kemp **Tanzania Books and Subsector Study: Libraries and Information Section.** Washington, DC: The World Bank & London: Overseas Development Administration/ODA, 1989. 49 pp. [Not examined]

1130 Chachage, C.S.L. **"Publishing in Tanzania."** In *Africa Bibliography 1990*, compiled by Hector Blackhurst. Edinburgh: Edinburgh University Press, 1991, vi-xviii.
An overview of publishing in Tanzania beginning with a historical review, discussing the question of indigenous languages, and the problems created by the former rule of two separate colonial powers. Reviews the pioneering efforts of mission presses, the activities of the British colonial presses and the newspaper press, and thereafter examines the history and development of indigenous publishing in Tanzania against the backdrop of social, economic and political struggles towards independence and self-determination. Also examines the role of libraries, distribution, printing capacity in the country, and the advent of popular publishing. The author concludes that "the publishing industry needs to free itself from the shackles of short-term profits and become the spokesman for the ordinary member of the public."

1131 Chachage, C.S.L. **The Tanzanian Publishing Industry**. Hull: Department of Sociology and Social Anthropology, University of Hull, 1994. 82 pp.
[Not examined]

1132 Denning, Carmelle, D. Dixon, and K. Lillie **Tanzania: ODA Book Sector Consultancy.** London: Overseas Development Administration/ODA, 1990. 39 pp.
[Not examined]

1133 Grahm, Leif, and Kajsa Pereson, with L.T.D. Minzi **Textbooks for all PPP. The First Step on a Long Journey. Evaluation of the Pilot Project in Tanzania.** (Sida Evaluation 04/08) 2004. 96 pp.
Online: http://www.sida.se/shared/jsp/download.jsp?f=Utv04-08_SIDA3807enWEB.pdf&a=3167 [10/03/08]
A study commissioned by the Education Division of the Swedish donor organization → **Sida (115)** to evaluate a pilot project for publishing (PPP) in Tanzania that run from 1993-2000, following the country's abolition of its state monopoly in textbook production and the launch of a new curriculum for primary schools. The PPP was started as an instrument for implementing the new policy and helping to strengthen the textbook sub-sector. Its main aim was to ensure a smooth transition from a state monopoly to a market system in textbook publishing and distribution by local commercial publishers and booksellers. Market forces and consumer preferences were seen as more efficient in stimulating the development of new and better textbooks. The new textbook policy was complemented by adding new qualitative goals. There should be variation in the supply of textbooks, rather than the supply of standardized materials to the schools. The evaluators studied the conceptual model of PPP, its impact, cost efficiencies achieved, and sustainability; and concluded that textbook publishing in Tanzania today is a sustainable activity, much strengthened by the PPP.

1134 Gulbraar, Kari, and Jorunn Moen **Books and Libraries in Tanzania 1986.** Oslo: Departementet for Utviklingshjelp, 1986. 59 pp.
Reports on a mission to examine the book and library sector of Tanzania and to gather the views of Tanzanian book professionals on existing problems and constraints.

1135 Itatiro, Mello; C. Kaligula, P. Medcalfe, and Anthony Read **Tanzania: Book Subsector Study, Textbook Section.** Washington, DC: The World Bank & London: Overseas Development Administration/ODA, 1988. [not paginated]
The final report of a study of textbook provision in Tanzania, which was part of a wider book sub-sector study financed by ODA and the World Bank. Includes a review of the existing literature, interviews, and reports on field visits to schools. Concludes with an examination of the major issues facing textbook production in the country, including aspects of printing, paper supply, distribution, and finance.

1136 Kalugula, Charles, and Walter Bgoya **"Towards the Creation of a National Book Policy in Tanzania."** In *Access to Information. Indaba 97.* Harare: Zimbabwe International Book Fair Trust, 1997, 38-50.
Presents an overview of the factors and issues involved leading to the creation of an

effective national book policy for Tanzania. Provides essential background information about textbook provision in the country, and sets out developments since December 1991, when the government launched a new textbook policy whose main objective was to liberalize, privatize and commercialize the production and distribution of textbooks. Examines the rationale of the new textbook policy, how it will be operated and what it should try to achieve, and the need for the creation of a favourable environment that will enable commercialized textbook provision to function effectively. Thereafter looks at the present situation [1997], the need for a national book policy, the appropriate institutions required to oversee and implement that policy, and what should be the essential components in a national book policy.

1137 Kaungamno, E.E., and C.S. Ilomo **Books Build Nations**. 2 vols., **vol. 1: Library Services in West and East Africa; vol. 2: Library Services in Tanzania**. Dar es Salaam: Tanzania Library Services/Transafrica Book Distributors, 1979, 169 pp., 272 pp.
Largely on library services and information provision, but includes brief sections on the book industries and the retail book trade in East Africa.

1138 Kaungamno, E.E. **The Book Industry in Tanzania.** Paris: UNESCO (CC-80/CONF.804/COL), 1980. 140 pp.
Also published as **The Book Industry in the United Republic of Tanzania.** In *Cultural Industries: A Challenge for the Future of Culture.* Paris: UNESCO, 1982. 175-192.
Prefaced by a brief study on the situation in Kenya, thereafter provides an overview of the book industries in Africa generally, and then focuses on the situation in Tanzania, including a detailed history of Tanzanian publishing and the major players up to the period ending 1979.

1139 Mbonde, J.P. **"United Republic of Tanzania."** In *The Book Trade of the World, vol. IV: Africa,* edited by Sigfred Taubert and Peter Weidhaas. Munich: K.G. Saur, 1984, 297-306.
Overview of publishing and the book trade in Tanzania. Now very dated.

1140 Mcharazo, Alli A.S. **"The Book Chain in Tanzania."** In *The Book Chain in Anglophone Africa. A Survey and Directory,* edited by Roger Stringer. Oxford: International Network for the Availability of Scientific Publications (INASP), 2002, 87-89.
Online: http://www.inasp.info/file/57/the-book-chain-in-anglophone-africa-a-survey-and-directory.html [10/03/08]
One in a series of useful country surveys and overviews – each prepared by a book professional from the country concerned – that review the state of the book, and the major players in the "book chain", in English-speaking African countries. Each country survey covers printing, book publishing, bookselling and distribution, library services, professional associations, book promotional bodies and book promotional events, training for the book professions, as well as examining some of the major issues as they relate to book development, such as languages, literacy,

writers and writing, the reading habit, and national book policies. For each country this is supported by an annotated directory of government ministries, professional associations, book publishers, booksellers and distributors, printers, major libraries, and training institutions, with full address and contact details.

1141 Publishers' Association of Tanzania **The Text Book Financing Study. Financing options available to PATA. Final Report, November 1994.** Dar es Salaam: Publishers Association of Tanzania/Coopers & Lybrand, 1994. 54 pp.
A study commissioned by the ➔ **Publishers Association of Tanzania (1120)** designed to assess the financing needs (and recommending appropriate funding schemes) for the private sector's participation in the textbook publishing industry. The report considers the administrative set up and operational modalities of two types funding options, namely (i) a loan guarantee scheme, and (ii) a revolving fund.

1142 Shetler, Jan Bender **"The Politics of Publishing Oral Sources from the Mara Region, Tanzania."** *History in Africa* 29, (2002): 413-426.
An interesting contribution on the debate relating to the shift from orality to literacy, and the publication of oral history. While developing a series of locally-written histories from the Mara Region of Tanzania, the author discovered that transforming oral tradition into written form is ultimately political. The change from an oral to a written knowledge base diminishes the power of community elders and puts it into the public domain, where literate people are at an advantage, and where community security may be vulnerable at the same time. The author describes how he found out that the oral traditions that he was collecting were not some antiquated and benign relics of the past to be preserved in dusty archives, but could in fact serve as powerful political tools for negotiating present-day relationships and authority. He also describes how he proceeds in publishing this collection of politically-charged written histories.

Togo

Associations and book-related organizations

1143 Bureau Togolais du Droit d'Auteur (BUTODRA)
161 E rue des Echis
Lomé
Postal address:
BP 14053
Lomé
Togo
Tel: +228-222 18 43/222 1839 Fax: +228-222 6900
Email: butodra@caramail.com
Web: http://www.butodra.org/
Director General: Traoré Aziz Idrissou

1144 Association Togolaise des Auteurs et Illustrateurs de Livres pour Enfants (ATAILE)
c/o Centre Culturel Français
BP 2090
Lomé
Togo
Tel: +228-930-5579/+228-221 0332 Fax: +228-221 3442
Email: ataile.tg@caramail.com
Web: http://www.hogodo.afrikart.net
Contact: Assem Koffivi

1145 Association Togolaise des Editeurs (ATEL)
c/o Les Editions Graines de Penses
BP 7097
Lomé
Tel: +228-222 3243
Email: ateltogo@yahoo.fr or ctekue@yahoo.fr
Web: n/a
President: Christiane T. Ekue
Secretary-General: Yves-Emmanuel Dogbé

National bibliography, books in print, and book trade directories

1146 Bibliographie nationale du Togo.
Lomé: Bibliothèque nationale du Togo [BP 1002, Lomé], 1994–
Irregular, latest is 1995?; cumulative volume, *Bibliographie nationale rétrospective du Togo, 1961-1991*, published in 1995.
Email: dban@tg.refer.org
Web: n/a

Books, articles, reports, and interviews

1147 Akakpo, Claudine Assiba "Togo: édition et diffusion du livre." *Notre Librairie*, no. 131 (July-September 1997): 172-176.
Online: http://www.arts.uwa.edu.au/MotsPluriels/MP598nl.html [10/03/08]
A roundtable discussion with publishers from Togo debating the problems and prospects of the book industries in their country. Participants included Christiane Tchotcho Ekue (NEA-Togo), Yves-Emmanuel Dogbé (Editions Akpagnon), and Victor Aladji (APNET representative for Togo).

1148 Anon. **"Togolese Republic."** In *The Book Trade of the World, vol. IV: Africa*, edited by Sigfred Taubert and Peter Weidhaas. Munich: K.G. Saur, 1984, 307-312.
Overview of publishing and the book trade in Togo. Now very dated.

Nomenyo, Adzowavi Dzigbodi **"L'édition scientifique au Togo"** *see* → **Section 4, Studies by topic: Scientific, technical and medical publishing** entry **2353**

1149 van de Werk, Jan Kees **"Publishing and Literature in Togo."** *The African Book Publishing Record* 11, no. 4 (1985): 201-204.
Jan Kees van de Werk, one of the three co-founders of Editions HaHo, reports on the activities of this Togolese publishing house in the context of publishing and writing in Togo today. Editions HaHo is an autonomous project of the Eglise Evangélique du Togo and is financially backed by the Interchurch Coordination Committee for Development Projects in Holland and the Protestant church in Germany.

Uganda

Associations and book-related organizations

1150   Book Development Council of Uganda (BODECU)
c/o Public Libraries Board
PO Box 4262
Kampala
Tel: +256-41-233633 Fax: +256-41-348625
Email: library@imul.com
Chair: Phenny Birungi

1151   FEMRITE - Uganda Women Writers' Association
Plot 147 Kira Road
Kampala
Postal address:
PO Box 705
Kampala
Uganda
Tel: +256 -41-543943/+256-77-2743943
Email: femrite@infocom.co.ug **or** info@femriteug.org
Web: http://www.wougnet.org/Profiles/femrite.html
President: Hon. Mary Karooro Okurut
Chair: Susan Kiguli
Coordinator: Goretti Kyomuhendo

1152   National Book Trust of Uganda (NABOTU)
Fountain House
55 Nkrumah Road Suite 14
Kampala
Uganda
Tel: +256-41-251121/259163 Fax: +256-41-251160
Email: fountain@starcom.co.ug
Note: not verified, organization dormant?

1153   Uganda Booksellers Association
Plot 16/4 Jinja Road
Kampala
Uganda
Postal address:
PO Box 9997
Kampala
Uganda
Tel: +256 41 236907 Fax: +256 41 251468
Email: gus@swiftuganda.com or mbd@infocom.co.ug
Chair: Martin Okia [?]

**1154   Uganda Children's Illustrators and Writers Association (UCIWA)/
         Ugandan Section of IBBY**
Kampala Children's Library
Kampala
Postal address:
PO Box 31631
Nakivubo
Kampala
Tel: +256-41-510721 Fax: +256-41-51 07 22
Email: barongo@africaonline.co.ug
Liaison Officers: Evangeline Ledi Barongo, Joseph Ndawula

1155   Uganda Publishers Association
Plot M 20 Ntinda Industrial Area
Jinja Road
Kampala
Postal address:
PO Box 24745
Kampala
Uganda
Tel: +256-41-259163 Fax: +256-41-251160
Email: fountain@starcom.co.ug or longhorn@infocomco.ug
Web: n/a

Chair: Fred Matovu
Administrative Officer: Jackie Kateera

National bibliography, books in print, and book trade directories

1156 **National Bibliography of Uganda.** (formerly *Uganda National Bibliography*, 1987-1990, 4 volumes only published)
Kampala: National Library of Uganda [PO Box 4262, Kampala], 2004-
Annually, the first volume of the *National Bibliography of Uganda* was published in 2004 and listed publications received by the National Library of Uganda in 2003 and 2004, as well those received and catalogued by Makerere University Library since 1987.
Email: admin@nlu.go.ug or info@nlu.go.ug
Web: http://www.nlu.go.ug/bibiliography.htm [sic] (site working with this misspelt name, but may eventually be changed to http://www/nlu.go.ug/bibliography.htm)

Books, articles, reports, and interviews

1157 Birungi, Phenny **"The Current Situation Regarding National Book Policy in Uganda."** In *Access to Information. Indaba 97.* Harare: Zimbabwe International Book Fair Trust, 1997, 51-56.
Intermittent efforts have been made in Uganda to formulate a national book policy, and a number of consultations and policy reviews relating to textbook provision have been undertaken, but a comprehensive national book policy is still lacking at this time [1997].

1158 Galiwango, M.L.C. **"Republic of Uganda."** In *The Book Trade of the World, vol. IV: Africa,* edited by Sigfred Taubert and Peter Weidhaas. Munich: K.G. Saur, 1984, 313-314.
A brief account of publishing and the book trade in Uganda. Now very dated.

1159 Gray, Stephen **"Interview: Goretti Kyomuhendo."** *Research in African Literatures* 32, no. 1 (Spring 2001): 123-125.
Goretti Kyomuhendo, interviewed here by South African writer Stephen Gray, is founder of Femrite Publications Ltd. in Uganda, the publishing arm of the ➔ **FEMRITE - Uganda Women Writers' Association (1151)**

1160 Heyneman, Stephen P., and Dean T. Jamison, **"Student Learning in Uganda: Textbook Availability and Other Determinants."** *Comparative Education Review,* vol. 24, no. 2, June 1980, pp. 108-118.
Online:
http://www.vanderbilt.edu/peabody/heyneman/PUBLICATIONS/19800 4.pdf [10/03/08]

Data collected (in 1972) on behalf of the Ugandan government and the National Institute of Education at Makerere University as part of a ➔ **World Bank (124)** research project on "Textbook Availability and Educational Quality." Describes how the basic variables were measured, and then reports on the impact of school resources on student learning, taking the school as the unit of analysis. Thereafter, on the basis of the pupil as the unit of analysis, the study attempts to assess the impact both of pupil characteristics and of school characteristics on student learning.

1161 Ikoja-Odongo, J.R. **"History of Books and Book Publishing in Uganda: 1876–1962."** *Focus on International and Comparative Librarianship* 26, no. 2 (May 1995): 32-43.
A history of the book and publishing in Uganda up to the period of the country's independence. Provides a historical background, describes early publishing activities by Christian missionaries, educational and school book publishing by British multinational publishers, and publishing in African languages by the East African Literature Bureau. Also examines the role of local churches in the evolution of books in Uganda. Concludes with a look at book marketing and distribution at that time. (*See also* entries ➔ **1162** and ➔ **1163**)

1162 Ikoja-Odongo, J.R. **"The Book Industry in Uganda During the Post-Independence Period (1962–1988)."** *Focus on International and Comparative Librarianship* 26, no. 2 (September 1995): 94-108.
The continuation of the preceding entry (*see* entry ➔ **1161**). An account "on that aspect of development in which Uganda has been a cripple, i.e. the book industry during the post-independence period." Reviews the founding of the state-supported Uganda Publishing House in a (short-lived) partnership with Macmillan and the emergence of small independent publishers. Examines the reasons why some indigenous publishing initiatives failed. Also looks at the development of creative writing and readership, book distribution and the retail trade, and finds that indigenous publishers' promotion and book marketing leaves a great deal to be desired.

1163 Ikoja-Odongo, J.R. **"Publishing in Uganda: Trends and Development 1989–2004."** *University of Dar es Salaam Library Journal* 6, no.2 (2004): 80-107.
A further continuation of the previous two entries (*see* entries ➔ **1161** and ➔ **1162**). Analyzes current [2004] trends and developments in publishing in Uganda, including an examination of the role of government in publishing, manuscript development, issues as they relate to publishing in local languages, marketing and the distribution of Ugandan publishing output, the role of book trade associations, and the constraints and challenges of publishing in the country.

1164 Katama, Agnes **"Book Development in Uganda. Unesco/Danida Basic Learning Materials Initiative Workshop."** *Bellagio Publishing Network Newsletter*, no. 20 (Autumn 1997): 4-5.
Reports about one in a series of ➔ **Unesco/Danida (119)** co-sponsored workshops convened to identify key issues in educational book supply in the countries of Africa – in this particular case Uganda – assessing institutional support structures for book

development, the need to make plans for enhancing their capacity, and the book-related training programmes that will be required.

1165 Kigongo-Bukenya, Isaac **"The Book Chain in Uganda."** In *The Book Chain in Anglophone Africa. A Survey and Directory*, edited by Roger Stringer. Oxford: International Network for the Availability of Scientific Publications (INASP), 2002, 90-93.
Online: http://www.inasp.info/file/57/the-book-chain-in-anglophone-africa-a-survey-and-directory.html [10/03/08]
One in a series of useful country surveys and overviews – each prepared by a book professional from the country concerned – that review the state of the book, and the major players in the "book chain", in English-speaking African countries. Each country survey covers printing, book publishing, bookselling and distribution, library services, professional associations, book promotional bodies and book promotional events, training for the book professions, as well as examining some of the major issues as they relate to book development, such as languages, literacy, writers and writing, the reading habit, and national book policies. For each country this is supported by an annotated directory of government ministries, professional associations, book publishers, booksellers and distributors, printers, major libraries, and training institutions, with full address and contact details.

1166 Mutula, Stephen M., and Mabel M.T. Nakitto **"Book Publishing Patterns in Uganda: Challenges and Prospects."** *African Journal of Library, Archives and Information Science* 12, no. 2 (2002): 177-188.
Analyzes the development of Uganda's book industry, assessing the factors that have impeded its growth, and reviewing some of the new opportunities that have now opened for indigenous book publishers. The paper also reviews the activities of regional and national book trade associations active in the country.

1167 Salahi, Katherine **"James Tumusiime in Conversation with Katherine Salahi."** *Bellagio Publishing Network Newsletter*, no. 24 (December 1998): 12-14
Online:
http://www.bellagiopublishingnetwork.com/newsletter24/salahi4.htm
[10/03/08]
An interview with James Tumusiime, who is Managing Director of Fountain Publishers Ltd. in Kampala, Uganda's leading indigenous publisher.

1168 Tumusiime, James **"The State of Publishing in Uganda."** In *Development Directory of Indigenous Publishing 1995*, compiled by Carol Priestley. Harare: African Publishers' Network, 1995, 88-89.
A brief description of the state of publishing in Uganda [in the mid-1990s].

1169 Tumusiime, James **"Uganda's Book Industry on the Way Back."** *Uganda Book News* 1, no. 1 (January/March 1996): 4-7.

Also published in *Uganda. The Cultural Landscape,* edited Eckhard Breitinger. Bayreuth: Eckhard Breitinger (Bayreuth African Studies Series, 39, 1999, 37-45.

The state of publishing and the book industries in Uganda is presently [1996] at the cross-roads. Here the Founder Chairman of the Uganda Publishers and Booksellers Association charts the industry's chequered past, and the growing opportunities that are now opening up for its recovery.

1170 Tumusiime, James **"Uganda's Book Industry: Flourishing Without Roots."** *Bellagio Publishing Network Newsletter,* no. 22 (July 1998): 12-13. Online: http://www.bellagiopublishingnetwork.com/newsletter22/tumusiime.htm [10/03/08]

In stark contrast with the situation in many African countries where the book industry is in disarray, Uganda's book industry would give the appearance that it is flourishing, and the quality of books has markedly improved. In the education sector suppliers of books have grown from two publishers who previously dominated the textbook markets, to over ten companies doing it now, including a number of indigenous publishers. However, most of the publishers have concentrated almost exclusively on publishing primary school books by virtue of an ongoing donor-supported programme. The author laments the fact that "over 90 per cent of all the books distributed in Uganda schools are published by British-based multinational houses whose presence in the country is merely symbolic. Although each of the multinational companies has a local counterpart the partnership is lopsided. The whole editorial process and the printing take place abroad. The local companies are only used for marketing." As a result, hardly any book editors, illustrators, or graphic artists exist in the country, and the output for general and trade publishing, or books for children, has been negligible. And a chicken-egg situation has inevitably developed where printers cannot invest in modern book printing machinery because publishers do not use their services; and where publishers cannot use local printers because they are not adequately equipped to handle large print runs. The author believes that ultimately the local printing industry will have benefited nothing by the time the donor projects wind up, nor have local bookshops that are being bypassed because the Ministry of Education buys books from publishers, consolidates them and delivers them free to schools. He concludes "Uganda's is a stereotype model of donor-supported book industries in Third World countries, which model is now discredited because it does not ensure sustainability of book supplies to schools when donor programmes are over. It is inconceivable how a country without a local publishing industry, where publishing skills are not developed; with no viable book printing industry; and no bookshop network can hope to provide books to its schools without perpetually depending on donors. Such mentality creates a sense of dependency in an industry that is strategic to the country's development."

Zambia

Associations and book-related organizations

1171 Book Publishers Association of Zambia (BPAZ)
PO Box 51109
Lusaka
Zambia
Tel/Fax: +260-1-255166
Email: chrischirwa@yahoo.co.uk or bpaz@zamtel.zm
Web: n/a
Chairperson: Chris Chirwa
Secretary/Administrative officer: Belinda Mwale

1172 Booksellers Association of Zambia
c/o University of Zambia Bookshop
PO Box 46
University of Zambia
Lusaka
Zambia
Tel: +260-1-290032
Email: hudsonunene@yahoo.com
President: Hudson Unene

1173 Zambia Women Writers Association (ZAWWA)
PO Box 38388
Lusaka
Zambia
Tel: +260-97-848 134
Email: hhmusunsa81@hotmail.com **or** medardochalata@yahoo.com
Web: n/a
President: Hilda H. Musunsa
Secretary/Treasurer: Medardo K. Chalata

National bibliography, books in print, and book trade directories

1174 National Bibliography of Zaml
Lusaka: National Archives of Zambia
Annual, latest is cumulation for 1987-?
Email: naz@zamnet.zm
Web: http://www.zambiarchives.org

1175 Zambian Books in Print and ISBN Publishers' Directory.
Edited by Hudwell Mwacalimba and Christine Kanyengo. Lusaka:
Booksellers and Publishers Association of Zambia [now Book Publishers
Association of Zambia], 1995. 282 pp
Provides details of 750 Zambian-published titles. Material is listed under three
sections: by author, title and publisher (with ISBN index) but lacks an index by
subject. Includes full bibliographic and acquisitions data for each title. Detailed
directory of publishers, giving full name and address, telephone and fax numbers.
No further editions would appear to have been published to date.

Books, articles, reports, and interviews

1176 Canadian Organisation for Development through Education (CODE)
Zambia Book Sector Study. Zambia: Booksellers and Publishers
Association of Zambia [now Book Publishers Association of Zambia], 1993.
25 pp.
Provides an insight into the changing book situation in Zambia [in the early 1990s]
and highlights the shortage of books in general and books for children in particular.
Asserts that the industry has a solid base upon which to build.

1177 Chali, Katongo A., and Chris H. Chirwa **A Study on Textbook
Provision in Zambia and Feasibility of Cooperation Among SADC
Countries.** Lusaka: Zambia National Commission for UNESCO, [n.d.] 64
pp.
A national textbook study that aims to identify textbook needs and requirements for
both primary and secondary school population, and to identify areas of possible
cooperation among SADAC member states of the sub-region. The authors are critical
of the lack of legislation and government policies to support the book industries in
general and textbook provision in particular.

1178 Chifwepa, Vitalicy **"The Book Chain in Zambia."** In *The Book Chain in
Anglophone Africa. A Survey and Directory*, edited by Roger Stringer. Oxford:
International Network for the Availability of Scientific Publications (INASP),
2002, 94-97.
Online: http://www.inasp.info/file/57/the-book-chain-in-anglophone-
africa-a-survey-and-directory.html [10/03/08]
One in a series of useful country surveys and overviews – each prepared by a book
professional from the country concerned – that review the state of the book, and the
major players in the "book chain", in English-speaking African countries. Each
country survey covers printing, book publishing, bookselling and distribution,
library services, professional associations, book promotional bodies and book
promotional events, training for the book professions, as well as examining some of
the major issues as they relate to book development, such as languages, literacy,
writers and writing, the reading habit, and national book policies. For each country
this is supported by an annotated directory of government ministries, professional

associations, book publishers, booksellers and distributors, printers, major libraries, and training institutions, with full address and contact details.

1179 Chirwa, Christopher H. **"Publishing in Zambia: The Work of NECZAM."** *Zambia Library Association Journal* 12, no. 2 (December 1980): 56-63.
A paper originally presented at a meeting of the Zambia Library Association by the [then] General Manager of the National Educational Company of Zambia (NECZAM), narrating the history of publishing in Zambia and the emergence of NECZAM. Covers the state of publishing in Zambia in the 1980s, identifies problem areas of publishing in the country, and describes the special role of NECZAM [later to become the parastatal Kenneth Kaunda Foundation].

1180 Chirwa, Christopher H. **"Book Publishing Liberalisation in Zambia."** Bellagio Publishing Network Newsletter no, 26-27 (November 2000): 27-29.
Online: http://www.bellagiopublishingnetwork.com/newsletter26-27/chirwa.htm [11/03/08]
In 1991 the newly-elected government of the Movement for Multiparty Democracy (MMD) proclaimed the liberalization of the production and supply of educational materials in Zambia, thus opening the gates for other educational publishers and suppliers to enter an arena which hitherto had been the exclusive preserve of the Zambia Educational Publishing House (ZEPH). During the years following liberalization Zambia subsequently witnessed the emergence of a number of privately-owned book publishers, as well as booksellers. The government, in its declared commitment to placing all business in the hands of the private sector, made two failed attempts, in 1996 and 1997, to privatise ZEPH, and it later retracted its plans for privatising ZEPH. This was seen to go against the original spirit and principle of true liberalization and ensuring an even playing field as ZEPH may well continue to have an edge over other educational book publishers and suppliers. Nonetheless, the author believes that "the future of book publishing in Zambia appears set for a major leap forward."

1181 Date, Lara **"Volunteers Kick-start Zambia's Book Industry."** *British Overseas Development*, no. 50 (January/February 1997): unpaged [p. 2]
When state controls on publishing were lifted in Zambia, the industry needed help to find its feet. In a pilot programme, the organization ➔ **Voluntary Service Overseas (123)** sent five multi-skilled publishing people from Britain to see whether they could lend a helping hand.

1182 Dean, Elizabeth **"Publishing in Zambia."** *Zambia Library Association Journal* 12, no. 2 (1980): 47-55.
Presents the findings of an investigation into the economic and social factors that affect publishing Zambia, and compares the situation in the country with that in Kenya, Tanzania, Nigeria and Ghana. The author concludes that the "somewhat gloomy picture of publishing in Zambia" is influenced by a number of factors, notably high production costs, a limited market for books, poor distribution

mechanisms, monopolistic structures of the book trade, a small number of private sector publishers, and a largely ineffective state publishing company. She suggests a number of moves towards the resolution of these problems.

1183 Denning, Carmelle; Julia Carpenter, E. Keartland, R.S. Zulu, S. Hakalima and M. Sifuniso **Zambia: Book Sector Study.** 2 vols. London: Overseas Development Administration/ODA, 1990, vol.1, 60 pp.; vol. 2, 130 pp.
[Not examined]

1184 Djoleto, S.A. Amu **Zambia National Council for Book Development.** Paris: UNESCO (Restricted Technical Report RP/1981-1983/4/3.5/07), 1982. 43 pp.
Online: http://unesdoc.unesco.org/images/0005/000525/052588eo.pdf [11/03/08]
A ➔ UNESCO (118) mission report to assist the Government of Zambia in the establishment of a National Council for Book Development; to advise the government on the objectives and functioning of such a Council, to assist in the drafting of the Council's constitution and advise on its staff and budget; and to assist in the preparation of a detailed work plan of the Council as well as its administrative and management plan.

1185 Ferns, Martin **Primary Textbook Publishing in Zambia.** Stockholm: SIDA, 1993. 16 pp.
A report on the national seminar on primary textbook publishing organized by the Educational Materials Unit, Ministry of Education, Zambia.

1186 Kasonde, Christine **"Publishing in Zambia."** In *Development Directory of Indigenous Publishing 1995*, compiled by Carol Priestley. Harare: African Publishers Network, 1995, 90-93.
Describes the growth and development of publishing in Zambia since the 1970s and examines aspects of manuscript development, marketing, and distribution.

1187 Munamwimbu, Ray **"Book Trade in Zambia"** *ISBN Review* 17 (1996): 317-321.
A short account of the development of the book trade in Zambia - which "has entered a new era which is full of challenges" - and an assessment of its current strength and weaknesses.

1188 Munamwimbu, Ray **"Privatization in Publishing: The Zambian Experience."** In *The Challenge of the Market: Privatization and Publishing in Africa*, edited by Philip G. Altbach. Chestnut Hill, MA: Bellagio Publishing Network, Research and Information Center (Bellagio Studies in Publishing, 7), 1996, 63-77.
Provides a historical background to publishing in Zambia and reviews past state participation in publishing and international development assistance. Lack of

competition from private sector companies contributed greatly to the decline of the book industry in the period up to 1991. However, a move by the government to embark on a policy of liberalization for the production and supply of educational materials as from 1992 has now created an enabling environment for the emergence of several new private sector publishing initiatives. Reviews aspects of competition, tendering and procurement systems, the market potential, the performance of private firms compared with parastatals, and the moves towards the establishment of a national book policy and a national book development council. Whereas privatization in publishing has now levelled the playing field, some problems remain however, particularly aspects of textbook development, bookselling, an equitable procurement system, together with other impediments such as lack of capital in an economy suffering from high inflation, and a lack of publishing expertise.

1189 Munamwimbu, Ray **"State of the National Book Policy in Zambia."** In *Access to Information. Indaba 97*. Harare: Zimbabwe International Book Fair Trust, 1997, 35-37.
Reports about progress being made in the formulation of a national book policy for Zambia, and for which a policy document is now in place. A book development council will be established, and will assume responsibility for co-ordinating, overseeing, and monitoring the implementation of the national book policy.

1190 Mwacalimba, Hudwell **"Libraries and Book Sector Development in Zambia: A Country Report."** *ISBN Review* 17 (1996): 323-329.
One in a series of overview articles in a special issue of *ISBN Review* focusing on the book sector in various countries of Southern Africa, and which report (for the most part) about the state of libraries, publishing and the retail book trade; current book and copyright legislation, national book policies, programmes to promote the reading habit, laws and legislation covering the book sector and copyright, activities of library and book trade professional bodies, book trade organization, training for the book industries, the use of ISBNs, and more.

1191 Nalumango, Mbuyu **"Book Publishing in Zambia."** *ISBN Review* 17 (1996): 331-336.
An overview of current problems and prospects of the Zambian book industry which, "though over sixty years old is still in its infancy, almost handicapped, continuously learning to walk."

1192 Sarvi, Jouko **'Quality' of Textbooks - A Holistic Approach: Conclusions on the Basis of the Zambia Educational Materials Project Field Study 1990-1992.** Tampere, Finland: University of Tampere, Nordic Association for the Study of Education in Developing Countries, 1994. 16 pp.
A paper presented at the conference on quality of education in the Context of Culture in Developing Countries held in January 1994 in Tampere, Finland. There were three phases in the project: the first was to rehabilitate existing educational materials for primary schools, phase two focused on the development of new materials for basic and secondary schools, while phase three was to support the development of production and publishing of educational materials in Zambia.

1193   Simwinga, Gideon **"Publish or be Damned."** *Orbit*, no. 60 (1st quarter 1996): 23-24.
The publishing director of Multimedia Zambia argues that indigenous publishing is essential for a country's development, and examines Zambia's attempts to move away from donated books to its own home-grown industry. The author also calls for positive government action to establish a comprehensive national book policy to map out a strategy and set the pace for the development of the book industry.

1194   Williams, Geoffrey J. **"The Zambian Publishing Scene: A Commentary."** *The African Book Publishing Record* 3, no. 1 (January 1977): 15-22
Reviews the dismal of state publishing in Zambia in the late 1970s: bookshops with almost empty shelves, a dearth of commercial magazines and scholarly periodicals, and an ineffective government-owned publishing house. Comments on the high costs and low quality of printing, and expresses the hope that the situation will show improvement with the expected upturn of the Zambian economy and the planned establishment of a national book development council. (*See also* ➔ **1195**)

1195   Williams, Geoffrey J. **"Books in Zambia: The Developing Hunger."** *The African Book Publishing Record* 12, no. 4 (1986): 205-209. Also published in *Readings on Publishing in Africa and the Third World*, by Philip G. Altbach. Buffalo, NY: Bellagio Publishing Network, Research and Information Center (Bellagio Studies in Publishing 1), 1993, 78-82.
An update to the previous entry (*see* ➔ **1194**), by the former Head of the Geography department at the University of Zambia, which finds that the expected upturn in the Zambian economy did not materialize, a national book development council failed to take off, and that consequently the state of publishing and the book trade continues to be in decline. Analyzes book publishing output over a period of years and compares this with that of other countries in the region. Examines the activities of the state-owned publishing house, commercial publishers, scholarly publishing, magazines and serials, and looks at issues such as book distribution, book prices, and the state of libraries in the country. The author recommends the establishment of an effective trade association and applauds the achievement and vitality of Multimedia Zambia and a number of small private sector publishers, whilst encouraging more collaboration within the Southern African region and strengthening of an intra-African book trade.

1196   Zambia. Ministry of Education/Educational Materials Unit **Zambia Educational Materials Project. Distribution Review,** by Arto Rissanen. Lusaka: Ministry of Education, Educational Materials Unit, 1993. 112 pp. [restricted circulation]
Examines the distribution problems of educational materials in the light of modern approaches in the areas of marketing, logistics and management, and the particular complexities of distribution of such materials in Zambia. Finds that there are several deficiencies in management action in terms of planning, implementation and control. Presents models for different parts of the distribution system and, through them, assesses the present and future roles of the government and private sector

enterprises including printers, publishers, distributors and transporters. Concludes with a series of recommendations pin-pointing areas where potential and opportunities for improved performance exist.

1197   Zambia. Ministry of Education **Study on the Educational Materials Provision and Utilisation. Final Report March 1995.** [Report prepared by NCG Sweden AB, in cooperation with the Vantaa Institute for Continuing Education, University of Helsinki]. Stockholm: SIDA/FINNIDA, 1995. var. pp. [restricted circulation]
Final report about the Zambia Educational Materials Project (ZEMP), an educational materials project which has enjoyed Nordic support since the mid 1980s but which is now being phased out. This study aims to determine the potential for development in the educational materials sector after the completion of ZEMP. Reviews the provision and financing of educational materials in Zambia, the state of the market, institutional structures, production capacity, utilization of educational materials, aspects of decentralization and external assistance, and concludes with a development scenario and a set of recommendations towards a sustainable system of supply of educational materials.

Zimbabwe

Associations and book-related organizations

1198   Africa Community Publishing & Development Trust
3rd floor Exploration House
145 Robert Mugabe Road
Harare
Postal address:
PO Box 7250
Harare
Zimbabwe
Tel: +263-4-253608/9 Fax: +263-4-253608
Email: management@bookteam.co.zw or admin@bookteam.co.zw
Web: http://www.bookteam.co.zw [pages not accessible 11/03/08]
Contact: (Mrs) Alien Phiri

1199   Booksellers Association of Zimbabwe
New Book House
78 Kaguvi Street
Harare
Postal address:
PO Box 3916
Harare

Zimbabwe
Tel: +263-4-781772 Fax: +263-4-750282
Email: bazim@mweb.co.zw
President: Albert M. Ndlovu

1200 Budding Writers Association of Zimbabwe (BWAZ)
New Book House
78 Kaguvi Street
Harare
Postal address:
PO Box 4209
Harare
Zimbabwe
Tel: +263-4-774261/750282 Fax: +263-4-751202
Email: bwaz@mweb.co.zw
Secretary: n/a
Note: not verified, organization dormant?

1201 The Reproduction Rights Organization of Zimbabwe (ZimCopy)
123 The Chase
Mount Pleasant
Harare
Postal address:
PO Box BE 579
Belvedere
Harare
Zimbabwe
Tel: +263-4-744339 Fax: +263-4-745123
Email: zimcopy@africaonline.co.zw
Web: n/a
Contacts: Nda L. Dlodlo; Greenfield K. Chilongo

1202 Zimbabwe Academic and Non-Fiction Writers Association (ZANA)
c/o Economic History Department
University of Zimbabwe
PO Box MP 167
Mount Pleasant
Harare
Zimbabwe
Tel: +263-4-303211, ext. 1239 Fax: +263-4-, 333407/3352249
Email: mlambo@ecohist.uz.zw
Web: n/a
Chair: (Prof) Alois Mlambo

1203   Zimbabwe Book Development Council (ZBDC)
2 Durban Road
Avondale
Harare
Postal address:
PO Box A 247
Avondale
Harare
Zimbabwe
Tel/Fax: +263-4-333424/30348
Email: zbdc@samara.co.zw or zbdc@mweb.co.za
Web: http://www.bookcouncil.co.zw/ [pages not accessible 11/03/08]
Executive Director: Miriam Bamhare

1204   Zimbabwe Book Publishers Association (ZBPA)
no. 2 Harvey Brown
Milton Park
Postal address:
PO Box CY 1179
Causeway
Harare
Zimbabwe
Tel: +263- 4-754145 Fax: +263-4-754256
Email: tendaiv@longman.co.zw
Web: n/a
Chair: (Mrs) Ndaizienyi Nyamakura
Secretary: (Ms) Tsitsi Dhliwayo

1205   Zimbabwe International Book Fair Trust
Harare Gardens
Julius Nyerere Way
Harare
Zimbabwe
Postal address:
PO Box CY 1179
Causeway
Harare
Zimbabwe
Tel: +263-4-702104-8, 704112, 707352 Fax: +263-4-702129
Email: information@zibf.org.zw or admins@zibf.org.zw
Web: http://www.zibf.org.zw [pages not accessible 11/03/08]
Executive Director: Greenfield Chilongo

1206   Zimbabwe Women Writers
2 Harvey Brown Road
Milton Park
Postal address:
Private Bag 256A
Harare
Zimbabwe
Tel: 263-4-796374 Fax: 263-4-751202
Email: zww@telco.co.zw
Web: n/a
Director: Chiedza Musengezi
National Co-ordinator: Virginia Phiri

1207   Zimbabwe Writers' Union
206 Rothbart Building
6th Street
Gweru
Postal address:
PO Box 6170
Gweru
Zimbabwe
Tel: +263-54-23284/50041 Fax: +263-54-26147/50020
Email: ziwu@hotmail.co.zw
Web: n/a
Secretary: Kenneth Ruchaka

National bibliography, books in print, and book trade directories

1208   The Directory of Zimbabwe Publishers, 1995. 2nd edition. Harare:
Zimbabwe Book Publishers Association, 1994. 27 pp.
The second edition of a useful reference resource that gives very full details of some
60 Zimbabwean publishers including information on the nature of each publisher's
list, areas of specialization, number of staff, number of new book titles published
during the past three years, journals and magazines published, and more. There is
also an index/directory of periodicals, giving more information on all serials listed
under publishers' entries in the main section. No further editions have appeared after
the second edition was published in 1994.

1209   Zimbabwe Books in Print. 3rd edition. Compiled and edited by the
Zimbabwe Book Publishers Association. Harare: Zimbabwe Book Publishers
Association, 1998. 194 pp.
Lists titles in print as at the end of 1997 and comprises two alphabetical listings, by
author and by title, together with a subject index. Each entry provides full
bibliographic and acquisitions data. The subject index (giving author/title details
only) is divided into three sections: Primary Textbooks, Secondary Textbooks (both

arranged under broad subject categories and further sub-divided by language where appropriate, i.e. English, Ndebele, Shona), and General Books, which are grouped under 34 subject headings, and again with sub-divisions by language. The style and arrangement is clearly set out in the introductory apparatus. A list of publishers and distributors together with their full postal addresses (also including telephone and fax numbers and Email addresses where available) appears as part of the front matter, and replaces and updates the **Directory of Zimbabwe Publishers** (*see* ➜ **1208** above) previously published as a separate publication. No further editions have appeared after the third edition was published in 1998.

1210 Zimbabwe National Bibliography. (supersedes *Rhodesia National Bibliography,* and thereafter *List of Publications Deposited in the Library of the National Archives,* 1961-1978)
Harare: National Archives [Private Bag 7729, Harare], 1979-
Annual, latest is 1995?
Email: archives@gta.gov.zw
Web: n/a

Books, articles, reports, and interviews

1211 Bamhare, Miriam, and Simon Q. Mphisa **A Study of the Zimbabwe Book Sector for the Canadian Organization for Development through Education.** Harare: Zimbabwe Book Development Council, 1993. 44 pp.
Considers some of the issues relating to the state of the book sector in Zimbabwe [in 1993] and puts forward some suggestions and recommendations for the future.

1212 Bamhare, Miriam **"Strategies for Book Development: The Marriage of Structure and Policy."** *ISBN Review* 17 (1996): 337-349.
The Executive Director of the ➜ **Zimbabwe Book Development Council/ZIBDC (1203)** in this paper "seeks to explore strategies for translating the theory of book development into quantitative and qualitative change in all the various aspects of the book provision and consumption systems" and asks how genuine book development can be brought about in the Southern Africa region. Bamhare also examines the structure, and activities thus far, of the ZIBDC, and the difficulties that have been encountered in attracting donor funding for its work, having been "tossed from donor to donor" for four years. The author also claims that the book business in Zimbabwe continues to be controlled and owned by a white minority group "who resist working with the new political order and show no sign of community responsibility" and that the "subversive and undermining activities of a few influential white members of the book trade" are "totally opposed to indigenization of the publishing sector." The author is equally critical of the Zimbabwean government whose "monumental lack of vision [is] shown by the meagre claim books have on national resources."

1213 Bamhare, Miriam **"[National Book Policy] Progress Reviews: Zimbabwe."** In *Access to Information. Indaba 97.* Harare: Zimbabwe

International Book Fair Trust, 1997, 23-27.
Looks back at progress achieved in Zimbabwe toward the establishment of a national policy. Believes that a national book policy *is* emerging and that progress has been made "in answering the most fundamental question", namely "who are the beneficiaries of a national book policy?", which the author considers to be the starting point of any formulation of a national book policy.

1214 Bolze, Louis W. **"The Book Publishing Scene in Zimbabwe."** *The African Book Publishing Record* 6, no. 3/4 (1980): 229-236.
Charts the history of book publishing in Zimbabwe from the first book to be published in colonial days in 1897, through to the emergence of commercial book publishing in the 1960s. Includes information on commercial and independent publishers [as at 1980], book imports, book clubs, literary societies, the retail book trade, and library services, and assesses the prospects for publishing in Zimbabwe in the future.

1215 Bourgueil, Isabelle **"Economie et politique de l'édition au Zimbabwe Entretien avec Chenjerai Hove."** *Africultures* no. 57 (December 2003): 69-70. Online:
http://www.africultures.com/index.asp?menu=revue_affiche_article&no=3
179&dispo=fr [11/03/08]
A short interview with Chenjerai Hove on the parlous state of the publishing industry in the currently very difficult economic conditions in Zimbabwe. Hove is a distinguished Zimbabwean poet, novelist and essayist; a vociferous critic of the Mugabe government, he currently lives in exile in Norway.

Brickhill, Paul **"APNET and the Zimbabwe Book Industry"** *see* **Section 4, Studies by topics: African Publishers Network (APNET) entry 1304**

1216 Chitsike, B.C. **"Publishing in Zimbabwe with Special Reference to Local Languages."** In *Afro-Asian Publishing. Contemporary Trends*, edited by Narendra Kumar, and S.K. Ghai. New Delhi: Institute of Book Publishing, 1992, 75-81.
Reviews the history and difficulties in publishing in Shona and Ndebele and focuses on the work of the [now defunct] Literature Bureau in encouraging the writing and publishing of books in Shona and Ndebele. Looks at the involvement of other publishing houses in this area and concludes that the situation is not encouraging for those writing creative works in English, Shona or Ndebele.

1217 Czerniewicz, Laura **"Publishing in Zimbabwe."** *The African Book Publishing Record* 16, no. 4 (1990): 235-238.
Describes publishing in Zimbabwe since independence in 1980 [to 1990], focusing on literary publishing in English. Part one provides an overview of publishing in the country, examining issues such as ownership of publishing houses, book distribution, the activities of book trade associations, as well as analyzing the major constraints faced by the book industries. Part two is a survey of publishing of

creative writing since the 1980s. Concludes that Zimbabwean publishing "is exciting, problematic, fraught and stimulating."

1218 Galler, Anne M. **Indigenous Publishing, 1981-1992: An IFLA Pilot Project.** *IFLA Journal* 20, no. 4 (1994): 419-427.
Reports about an IFLA pilot project to assist the development of libraries in developing countries by encouraging indigenous publishing, concentrating first on Africa with a project in Zimbabwe to compile a ➜ **Directory of Zimbabwe Publishers (1208)** and a ➜ **Zimbabwe Books in Print (1209)**, which included the mailing of a survey questionnaire to identify the type of publishing activities carried out in the country and to elicit comments on problems faced by the publishing industry. The report examines some of the difficulties faced in the data gathering process and input of data into a database, as well as some other IFLA-related factors that meant that an idea first proposed in the early 1980s only came to fruition in 1993, and the lessons that can be learnt from this experience.

1219 Klother, Annelie **"If not Published – It is Lost. Interview with Publisher Irene Staunton on the Relevance of Books and Literature in Zimbabwe."** *Mediaforum*, no. 2 (2006): 6-9.
Online: http://www.cameco.org/mediaforum_pdf/2-2006.pdf [30/03/08]
An insightful interview with Irene Staunton, currently Managing Director of Weaver Press in Zimbabwe, and formerly publishing director at Baobab Books in Harare, where she developed an award-winning African fiction and non-fiction list, as well as publishing children's books (and *see also* entries ➜ **2225** and ➜ **2413**). Here she talks about the challenges of publishing from Zimbabwe, by Zimbabweans, in the current [2006] difficult conditions, and the development of a reading culture. Staunton states: "It is hugely important for a society and for the development of that society to have access to its fiction. If it is not published, it is lost. Even if it does not sell, a good book provides a singular record. If it is good enough, it will last. It will be there for posterity to show us what people lived through and how they felt about it at the time."

1220 Martin, David **"Zimbabwe Publishing House - The First Two Years."** *The African Book Publishing Record* 9, no. 4 (1983): 181-185.
An interesting account of the establishment of the Zimbabwe Publishing House (ZPH) and its first two and a half years of existence, breaking "many rules of publishing". The article describes the development of the initial list, the difficulties that had to be overcome, and the lessons learned during the process. The late David Martin, together with Phyllis Johnson, were the co-founders of ZPH, which was one of Zimbabwe's most dynamic publishers in the 1980s.

1221 Mphisa, Simon Q., and Miriam Bamhare **A Study on Textbook Provision in Zimbabwe and the Feasibility of Cooperation among SADCC Countries.** Paris: UNESCO, 1993, 64 pp.
Provides the background and details on curriculum and textbook development, publishing and textbook production, marketing, sales and distribution, and the financing of textbook production.

1222 Nyamfukudza, Stanley **"The Book Chain in Zimbabwe."** In *The Book Chain in Anglophone Africa. A Survey and Directory,* edited by Roger Stringer. Oxford: International Network for the Availability of Scientific Publications (INASP), 2002, 98-101.
Online: http://www.inasp.info/file/57/the-book-chain-in-anglophone-africa-a-survey-and-directory.html [11/03/08]
One in a series of useful country surveys and overviews – each prepared by a book professional from the country concerned – that review the state of the book, and the major players in the "book chain", in English-speaking African countries. Each country survey covers printing, book publishing, bookselling and distribution, library services, professional associations, book promotional bodies and book promotional events, training for the book professions, as well as examining some of the major issues as they relate to book development, such as languages, literacy, writers and writing, the reading habit, and national book policies. For each country this is supported by an annotated directory of government ministries, professional associations, book publishers, booksellers and distributors, printers, major libraries, and training institutions, with full address and contact details.

1223 Plangger, A.B. **"Some Observations on Publishing in Zimbabwe."** *Zimbabwe Librarian* 11, no.3/4 (1979): 41-44.
Offers a quantitative survey of publishing output in Zimbabwe between 1962 and 1979.

1224 Plangger, A.B. **"Mambo Press - The First 25 Years: A Brief Look at Ourselves."** *The African Book Publishing Record* 11, no. 1 (1985): 9-10.
Gives an overview of the establishment and development of Mambo Press, founded by Swiss missionaries in 1958 and originally started under the name the Catholic Mission Press. During pre-independence days Mambo Press had a long and honourable record of opposition to the regimes of the time. In 1985 it had over 300 titles in print and is still today one of Zimbabwe's largest publishers, with a strong list of titles in English, Shona and Ndebele.
Note: for a fuller account, published in German, *see* Plangger, A.B. "20 Jahre Mambo Press: 1958-1978." *Neue Zeitschrift für Missionswissenschaft* 34, no. 3 (1978): 207-218; and 34, no. 4 (1978): 264-290.

1225 Poulsen, A.K. **"Book Hunger and Book Sources in Zimbabwe."** *Book Power,* no. 2 (1994):18-21.
[Not examined]

1226 Sithole, Cynthia **"The Publishing Industry in Zimbabwe."** *ISBN Review* 17 (1996): 353-372
One in a series of overview articles in a special issue of *ISBN Review* focusing on the book sector in various countries of Southern Africa, and which report (for the most part) about the state of libraries, publishing and the retail book trade; current book and copyright legislation, national book policies, programmes to promote the reading habit, laws and legislation covering the book sector and copyright, activities of library and book trade professional bodies, book trade organization, training for

the book industries, the use of ISBNs, and more. This substantial paper, by the Publishing Manager of Longman Zimbabwe, applies a SWOT analysis to assess the potential strengths and weaknesses of the Zimbabwean book and printing industries, the potential opportunities and industry prospects, and the potential threats.

1227 Stringer, Roger **A National Book Development Policy for Zimbabwe**. Harare: University of Zimbabwe, 1989. MBA dissertation.
[Not examined]

1228 Stringer, Roger **"Publishing in Zimbabwe."** In *Africa Bibliography 1986*, compiled by Hector Blackhurst. Manchester: Manchester University Press, 1986, xvi-xxv.
Examines the state of publishing in Zimbabwe [in the mid-1980s], particularly developments since independence in 1980. Includes a statistical analysis of book publishing output based on listings in the [then] *Rhodesia National Bibliography*. Identifies particular areas of publishing and the trends which characterize them. Covers the period of transition prior to independence, creative writing, educational publishing, together with a discussion of environment in which publishers operate in Zimbabwe, and the major problems and constraints.

1229 van de Werk, Jan Kees **"Poverty, Affluence and Books: Voices from Zimbabwe."** *Logos. The Journal of the World Book Community* 3, no. 1 (1992): 54-56.
Online:
http://www.atypon-link.com/LOG/doi/pdf/10.2959/logo.1992.3.1.54
Examines differing views on writing, the price of books, and reading habits, gleaned from interviews with Zimbabweans during the 6th Zimbabwe International Book Fair.

1230 Ziduche, S. **"Racial Biases in the Publishing Industry in Zimbabwe."** *Southern Africa Political & Economic Monthly* 7, no. 10 (July 1994): 28-29
[Not examined]

4

Studies by topic

Extensively cross-referenced, this section lists books, articles, reports, presentations, and other documents on particular areas of publishing and the book in Africa, grouped under 30 different topics. For studies that are primarily country-specific, and cover general overviews and perspectives of the book industries and book development in particular African countries – for example national book sector studies, articles and documents on national book policies, etc. – *see* ➔ **Section 3, Country studies**.

The Acquisition of African-published material

See also ➔ **African books in the international market place**

1231 Ajidahun, C.O. "**The Acquisition, Management and Bibliographic Control of Government Publications in Nigerian University Libraries.**" *World Libraries* 14, no. 2 (Fall 2004).
Online [only]: http://www.worlib.org/vol14no2/ajidahun_v14n2.shtml [18/01/08]
Scrutinizes the availability of government publications in Nigerian university libraries. The author examines the problems encountered in the acquisition and classification of these publications, their frequent inaccessibility in academic libraries, inadequate production of the *National Bibliography of Nigeria*, lack of funds, and lack of bibliographic control. A number of suggestions are offered that might enhance the acquisition and processing of government publications in Nigerian university libraries.

1232 Armstrong, James C. **Acquisitions Reports [African countries]** *LC Acquisitions Trends* [1977-1982]
Thirty-eight acquisition reports by James C. Armstrong, former Field Director of the Library of Congress Office in Nairobi, that were published in *LC Acquisitions Trends* from 1977-82. Details are as follows:
Eastern Africa (Nov. 1977) 4-8. Somalia (Feb. 1978) 22-25.
Ethiopia, Djibouti, Seychelles (Aug. 1978) 13-18. Maputo (Aug. 1978) 18-22. Ife Bookfair (Aug. 1978) 22.
Bujumbura (Feb. 1979) 10-13. Malawi (Feb. 1979) 13-16. Lusaka (Feb. 1979) 16-17. Kenya (Feb. 1979) 20-22.
Sound Recordings - Eastern Africa (Feb. 1979) 23-27.
Khartoum (Aug. 1979) 8-10. Mogadishu (Aug. 1979) 10-14. Seychelles (Aug. 1979) 11-16.
Mauritius & Réunion (Feb. 1980) 15-23.

Djibouti (Aug. 1980) 12. Malawi (Aug. 1980) 12-15. Maputo (Aug. 1980)15-20. Lusaka (Aug. 1980) 20-24.
Bujumbura (Feb. 1981) 10-15. Seychelles (Feb. 1981) 15-16. Dar es Salaam (Feb. 1981) 16-19. Zanzibar (Feb. 1981) 19-21.
Lusaka (Sep. 1981) 12-15. Malawi (Sep. 1981) 15-18. Khartoum & Wad Medani (Sep. 1981) 18-20. Réunion (Sep. 1981) 20-23. Mauritius (Sep. 1981) 23-27. Antananarivo (Sep. 1981) 27-32.
Djibouti (Apr. 1982) 12-17. Ethiopia (Apr. 1982) 17-22. Mauritius (Apr. 1982) 22-24.
Mayotte (Apr. 1982) 24-25. Réunion (Apr. 1982) 25-27. Somalia (Apr. 1982) 27-30. Comoros (Apr. 1982) 49-50.

1233   Armstrong, James C. **"Progress in African Bibliography. Current American Acquisition Policies for African materials."** In *Progress in African Bibliography SCOLMA Conference 1977 Proceedings. London: SCOLMA, 1977, section 3, 1-4* [not consecutively numbered].
Discusses the changing policies in the acquisition of African-published material by Africana libraries in the United States [in the late 1970s].

1234   Badisang, B.E., and M.N. Dintwe **"Support Local Industry? Book Buying Patterns in the University of Botswana Library (UBL)."** *African Research & Documentation,* no. 86 (2001): 11-19.
Reviews book buying policies at the University of Botswana through local and overseas suppliers, and also notes the dearth of scholarly publishing in Botswana. Concludes that "local bookshops need to use a more aggressive marketing strategy to sell their services and make more contact with libraries to ensure that their materials are known."

1235   **Book and Serial Vendors for Africa and the Middle East. Results of a Survey of ARL Libraries.** Chicago: ALCTS, division of the American Library Association [50 East Huron Street, Chicago, IL 60611-2795] (Foreign Book and Serial Vendors Directories, 2), 1997. 138 pp.
Designed for acquisitions librarians who are contemplating placing orders with vendors from Africa or the Middle East, information for this directory was gathered with the assistance of Association of Research Libraries member libraries, most of them large research libraries with active overseas acquisitions programmes. Responding libraries that collect from countries in Africa and the Middle East (and indicated for each country by OCLC symbols) were asked to identify vendors/dealers and the kinds of orders sent to them, covering five groups: firm orders, approval/blanket order plans, standing orders and continuations, periodicals, and out-of-print searching. The directory is divided into three sections, plus an appendix: Vendors by Country, Master Vendor List, Libraries Responding to the Questionnaire, and followed by the Appendix, General Vendors for Africa and the Middle East. The analysis that emerges provides a picture of current [1997] acquisitions patterns and collection holdings of African-published material by North American libraries and the major vendors they use, and which includes a number of booksellers in Africa. Now very dated however, and no further editions have been published to date.

1236 Boyd, Allen R. **"African Imprint Library Services - Bringing Together the Requirements of Research Libraries."** *The African Book Publishing Record* 6, nos. 3/4 (1980): 237-239.
African Imprint Library Services are a major dealer in the US for African-published materials. This is a (now somewhat dated) description of their services and activities.

1237 Coelho, Jill Young **"Once, Present (and Always?) Africana Acquisitions Policies."** In *Africanist Librarianship in an Era of Change*, edited by Victoria K. Evalds and David Henige. Lanham, MD: Scarecrow Press, 2005, 13-30.
Reviews the methods and strategies by which Africana librarians have acquired materials during the last decades of the 20th century, and the manifold problems, obstacles, and pitfalls that are associated with the acquisition of sub-Saharan African imprints. The author – who is Librarian for sub-Saharan Africa at Harvard's Widener Library – notes that purchasing African-published material continues to be a major topic of meetings and conversations among Africana librarians; that there are no easy solutions, but by "learning about and using the available tools makes it possible to create a good basic collection; persistence, luck and curiosity will do the rest."

Dilevko, Juris, and Lisa Gottlieb **"Book Titles Published in Africa Held by North American University Research Libraries and Review Sources for African-published Books"** *see* ➔ **African books in the international market place** entry **1276**

1238 Easterbrook, David L. **"North-South Information Links."** In *Access to Information. Indaba 97*. Harare: Zimbabwe International Book Fair Trust, 1997, 179-186.
The Curator of Africana at Northwestern University Library describes the work and activities of the ➔ **Africana Librarians Council/ALC (26)** of the (US) African Studies Association and sets out the information and institutional links between North America and Africa that exist today [late 1990s]. Also reports about a number of projects that aim to strengthen links between the ALC and librarians in Africa; and describes the links that exist that bring books published in Africa on to the shelves of North American libraries, and "those that bring information about Africa's expanding publishing industries to those who build our library collections."

1239 Easterbrook, David L. **"Building Area Studies Collections in African Studies"** In *Building Area Studies Collections*, edited by Dan Hazen and James Henry Spohrer. Wiesbaden, Germany: Harrassowitz (Beiträge zum Buch- und Bibliothekswesen, 52), 2007, 13-29.
Examines African studies collections in terms of research and curricular programmes that focus on sub-Saharan Africa, and includes a discussion of selection materials, with an emphasis on publications from Africa itself. Following some historical background about African studies collection development in the USA, this essay reviews specialized organizations in Africana librarianship, and their publications and Web sites. In discussing African bibliographical resources – and acquisitions

channels and methods – the author stresses that specialist bibliographers need to understand the African book world in terms of its publishing and distribution.

Easterbrook, David L. **"American Libraries, American Markets, African Books"** *see* ➔ **African books in the international market place**, entry **1277**

1240 Hall, Jolyon D.S. **"Directions for the Future: The Standing Conference on Library Material on Africa."** In *African Studies. Papers Presented at a Colloquium at the British Library 7-9 January 1985.* London: The British Library, 1986, 304-308.
Provides an overview of the activities of the ➔ **Standing Conference on Library Materials on Africa/SCOLMA** (**114**) since its founding in 1962 [to 1986], describing the aims of the organization in encouraging libraries to specialize in certain fields for the acquisition of material from Africa and about Africa.

1241 Hogarth, David **"Publishing and Distribution Problems for African Studies in the United Kingdom: An Individual Distributor."** In *African Studies. Papers Presented at a Colloquium at the British Library 7-9 January 1985.* London: The British Library, 1986, 73-76.
Reveals the difficulties faced by a leading UK distributor of books and other materials published in Nigeria, and in other parts of Africa.

1242 Howard-Reguindin, Pamela **Out of Africa...Into International Libraries: The Role of the Library of Congress Nairobi Office in Building Africana Library Collections.**
http://www.ifla.org/IV/ifla73/papers/136-Howard-Reguindin-en.pdf [12/03/08]
A presentation made at the 73rd IFLA General Conference and Council in 2007 that aims to demonstrate the multifaceted role of the Library of Congress Office in Nairobi, Kenya in building stronger research collections dedicated to African studies both in the US and around the globe. The author reports that, through the LC Nairobi acquisitions programme, 43 million African-published items had been sent to participating libraries over the years (and as at 2006), principally 35 academic libraries in North America, but also a number of major national or academic libraries in Germany, South Africa, Switzerland, and the UK. The materials are purchased by 25 part-time acquisitions agents employed in African countries, and then assembled at the LC offices in Nairobi and shipped to participating libraries. The author claims, somewhat contentiously, that "because of small press runs, on-the-spot collecting of African publications has been crucial to the successful assembling of unparalleled resources in contemporary African imprints."

1243 Kagan, Alfred **"Sources for African Language Materials from the Countries of Anglophone Africa."** *IFLA Journal* 22, no. 1 (1996): 42-45.
Online at http://www.ifla.org/IV/ifla61/61-kaga.htm [12/03/08]
Also published in *Library Review* 15, no. 2 (1996): 17-21.

Provides helpful guidance on how to acquire materials in African languages outside their countries of origin, and sets out the mechanisms in collecting this material. Notes the standard current reference sources, blanket and approval plan dealers, bookshops and publishers, printed and online catalogues, and two microform collections.

1244 Kistler, John M. **"Special Acquisitions: Collecting African Materials."** *The Acquisitions Librarian* 15, no. 29 (2003): 31-50.
A new project to begin a depository of Benin resources at West Virginia State College (as part of a partnership with the National University of Benin) may offer ideas for other libraries wishing to do special acquisitions in Africana materials. The article addresses language and cultural barriers, the need for early planning, methods of acquisition, and collection maintenance concerns. The author, Acquisitions Librarian at Utah State University, has worked in acquisitions for special, public, and academic libraries, but has only recently begun to learn the complex issues in Africana acquisitions.

Koenig, Mary *et al* **"Issues and Trends in Government Publishing in the Third World and their Implications for Collection Development"** *see* ➜ Section 1, Serials & reference: Bibliographies and continuing sources entry **175**

1245 Lawal, L.D. **"Acquisition of Locally Published Materials for Libraries in Nigeria: Problems and Solutions."** *The Publisher* 1, no. 2 (March 1989): 42-44.
The [former] Acquisitions Librarian of the University of Ilorin discusses problems encountered in the acquisition of locally published materials in Nigeria, including the unavailability of a comprehensive publishers/booksellers directory, inadequate bibliographic information in review articles, ineffectiveness of local bookshops in coping with orders, lack of bibliographic control, and unavailability of trade journals.

1246 Limb, Peter **"Africana Periodicals: Problems and Progress of Collection and Publication."** In *Africanist Librarianship in an Era of Change,* edited by Victoria K. Evalds and David Henige. Lanham, MD: Scarecrow Press, 2005, 125-140.
Examines the problems associated with Africana journals and their collection, giving particular attention to journals published in Africa. Starts off with a review of current trends in periodical publishing and usage, the profound changes created by the impact of digital technology and the new scholarly communications environment, the proliferation of e-journals, and escalating journal prices. Thereafter the author turns his attention to the problems of identifying and acquiring African-published serials – most still only published in print format at this time – and the perennial problems usually associated with the process, including regularity (or the lack of it) and viability of Africa-based journals, inadequate marketing and distribution, sometimes poor production quality, breakdowns in communications, and other logistical problems. He also describes some recent digital initiatives designed to improve the visibility and accessibility of African journals, but which, while useful

and beneficial in the short run, "have not greatly succeeded in helping African journals achieve greater viability." Limb states that "improving the acquisition of African serials relates closely to their own fate, which in turn rests on the wider African political economy." He calls for more international collaboration, and solid, mutually beneficial partnerships bringing together all stake holders in the journal chain; and argues that Western libraries could do more to serve their primary users and help African journals survive "by organizing and coordinating their acquisition of African journals better, and by doing this in closer conjunction with publishers; but this must be a two-way process."

1247 Malanchuk, Peter **"Africana Acquisitions: Strategies to Locate and Acquire Current and Retrospective Africana."** *Library Acquisitions: Practice & Theory*, no. 15 (1991): 453-461.
Describes the challenge facing librarians who wish to develop Africana collections, and suggests appropriate strategies, selection tools, and resources needed for the successful acquisition of Africana materials. Gives details of bibliographies and selection tools from various sources and institutions, together with a description of the acquisitions process, and recommended suppliers.

Matovelo, Doris S., and Inese A. Smith **"A Study on Africana Collections in UK Libraries: Present State and Future Scenarios"** *see* ➔**African books in the international market place** entry **1285**

1248 McIlwaine, John **"Current State of Publishing and Bibliography of African Materials."** In *The Love of Books.Proceedings of the Seventh South African Conference of Bibliophiles held at The South African Library, Cape Town, 8-10 May 1996*, edited by Pieter E. Westra and Leonie Twentyman Jones. Cape Town: South African Library (Bibliophilia Africana VII, South African Library General Series, 26), 1997, 3-14.
An overview of the issues relating to publishing and bibliographic control of and in Africa, considering both materials published in Africa itself, and also the wider field of Africa-related materials published outside Africa. Reviews the major current bibliographies and continuing sources, national bibliographies, books-in-print, indexes and abstracting services, and some other materials. Also looks at the need and prospects of bibliographic tools in electronic formats.

1249 McIlwaine, John **"*Plus ça change:* Four Decades of African Studies Bibliography."** In *Africa Bibliography. Works on Africa Published During 1999*, edited by T.A. Barringer. Edinburgh: Edinburgh University Press; London: International African Institute, 2001, vii-xix.
An informative article in which the author reviews progress in Africana bibliography, and the various attempts that have been made to improve bibliographic control of sources emanating from and relating to Africa, over a period of some forty years. Taking the International Conference on African Bibliography held at University College, Nairobi, in December 1967 as a starting point, he examines projects, bibliographies and bibliographic services, other reference tools

and publication of archival resources, publishers and publishing activities in the field of African studies bibliography, the development of databases, Pan-African documentation activities, current awareness services, bibliographic serial publications, and electronic sources. He also provides information about the activities of organizations and groups of librarians devoted to Africana libraries and African studies collection development. The author describes the article as "a largely personal tour of aspects of African bibliography that have particularly struck or influenced me over the years." He concludes that "much valuable work has been done, but failures have been at least as numerous as successes", citing lack of resources, both human and financial, as one of the main reasons for failed initiatives.

1250 McKee, Malcolm D. **"Co-operation in African Acquisitions: SCOLMA Looks to the Future."** *African Research and Documentation*, no. 38 (1985): 20-25.
Discusses the achievements [up to the mid 1980s] of the ➔ **Standing Conference on Library Materials on Africa/SCOLMA (114)**, and reports about a series of acquisitions tours to Africa undertaken by librarians.

1251 Obasi, John U. **"The Need for a Planned Acquisitions Policy for Social Science Primary Materials in Nigeria."** *The African Book Publishing Record* 8, no. 3 (1982): 111-119.
A Nigerian librarian discusses the needs for and problems in acquiring African materials for the social sciences in Nigeria. Examines the role of legal deposit and other libraries, exchange and gifts arrangements, conferences and exhibitions, and acquisitions trips.

1252 Obasi, John U. **"The Acquisition of African Ephemera."** In *Research Priorities in African Literatures*, edited by Bernth Lindfors. Oxford: Hans Zell Publishers, 1984, 203-213.
A case study of ephemeral literature in Nigeria that attempts to evaluate how important this material is, its bibliographic control, and the problems of Nigerian scholars and librarians. Affirms the need for cooperative efforts in the acquisition of contemporary African-published materials.

1253 Pinfold, John **"Acquiring Books from Southern Africa: A Librarian's View."** *Focus on International & Comparative Librarianship* 27, no. 2 (10 September 1996): 100-106. Also in *African Research & Documentation*, no. 72 (1996): 54-59
The Head of the Rhodes House Library in Oxford provides a librarian's perspective how librarians find out what has been published in southern Africa, how they go about acquiring such material, the kind of budgetary constraints they are working under, and how they are coping with it. Reviews the various selection tools available and describes policies governing the acquisitions process.

1254   Raseroka, H.K. **"Acquisition of African-published Materials by Libraries in Botswana - and Elsewhere in Africa."** *Focus on International & Comparative Librarianship* 27, no. 2 (10 September) 1996: 86-95.
Also published in *African Research & Documentation*, no. 72 (1996): 45-53.
The Librarian at the University of Botswana examines the problems facing acquisitions librarians in Africa in obtaining regular information of new African-published books, and the purchase of this material. Reviews collection development policies at the University of Botswana and then provides a detailed analysis of sources for selection of African-published material. The author is critical of African publishers' marketing strategies and the failure by some publishers to provide regular advance information and other promotional material, which are essential selection tools for librarians. The absence of effective distribution outlets, and bookselling methods which are not responsive to public needs, further aggravates the problem. The author also argues that "relationships among publishers, booksellers and librarians needs to be better understood by each group and be mutually supportive."

1255   Rathgeber, Eva-Maria **"African Acquisitions Problems: The View from Both Sides."** *Library Acquisitions: Practice and Theory* 6, no. 2 (1982): 137-148.
[Not examined]

1256   Schramm, Sally **"Current Publishing Trends in Southern Africa."** In *The Love of Books. Proceedings of the Seventh South African Conference of Bibliophiles held at The South African Library, Cape Town, 8-10 May 1996*, edited by Pieter E. Westra and Leonie Twentyman Jones. Cape Town: South African Library (Bibliophilia Africana VII, South African Library General Series, 26), 1997, 22-39
A review of the acquisition patterns of Southern African material at the South African Library in Cape Town from 1993-1995, discussing the main sources and selection tools used for acquisitions, legal deposit, acquisitions policies and procedures, vendor reliability, together with an evaluation of the collection built up to date.

1257   Sternberg, Ilse, and Patricia M. Larby, eds. **African Studies. Papers Presented at a Colloquium at the British Library, 7-9 January 1985.**
London: The British Library in association with SCOLMA (British Library Occasional papers, 6), 1986. 351 pp.
An overview of the state of African studies and Africana library services in the UK and (to some extent) in Africa in the mid 1980s. The papers describe the resources available to researchers, the currency of guides and indexes to those resources, publishing and distribution problems for African studies in the UK, collection development including the acquisition of African-published material, and international library and archival collaboration in the African studies field.

1258 Wallace, Marion **"The African Collections in the British Library."** In *From Papyrus to Print-out: The Book in Africa Yesterday, Today and Tomorrow. Bibliophilia Africana 8 Conference Proceedings. Centre of the Book Cape Town, 11-14 May 2005*, edited by Cora Owens. Pretoria and Cape Town: National Library of South Africa/Centre of the Book, 2005, 136-145. Online: http://www.nlsa.ac.za/docs/bibliophilia8_2005/edwallace.doc [page not available 18/01/08]
The Curator of the British Library's African collections provides an overview of the development of the collections, and thereafter describes how publications from Africa are acquired today, how institutional structures and other factors influence acquisitions policies, and how researchers can gain access to the collections.

1259 Walsh, Gretchen **"African Language Materials: Challenges and Responsibilities in Collection Management."** In *Africana Resources and Collections: Three Decades of Development and Achievement. A Festschrift in Honor of Hans Panofsky*, edited by Julian W. Witherell. Metuchen, N.J.: Scarecrow Press, 1989, 89-91.
Sets out the responsibilities of bibliographers in the collection of Africana and discusses what is needed and why. Explains how to discover what is available, gives strategies for the acquisition of materials, and policy guidelines for ensuring that the materials remain accessible once acquired. Concludes by noting that African language material may well, in the near future, be one of the few "remaining opportunities for total involvement in the living matter of knowledge."

1260 Walsh, Gretchen **"Information Dynamics for African Studies: Resources in Libraries and Beyond."** In *African Studies and the Undergraduate Curriculum*, edited by Patricia Alden, David Lloyd, and Ahmed I. Samatar. Boulder, CO; and London: Lynne Rienner Publishers, 1994, 213-228.
Reviews the major reference and information sources for libraries developing African studies collections. Stresses that even modest collections should not be limited to US imprints on Africa, and should incorporate a significant component of African-published material "to give students a substantial taste of information published in Africa by Africans."

1261 Wilson, Paul **"Out-of-Print and Secondhand: A View of the Antiquarian Book Trade."** In *Africa Bibliography. Works on Africa Published During 2001*, edited by T.A. Barringer. Edinburgh: Edinburgh University Press; London: International African Institute, 2002, vii-xiii.
The proprietor of Oriental and African Books in Shrewsbury describes some of the workings of the second-hand and antiquarian book trade relating to Africa and the development of his firm, which specializes in putting together collections on a particular area or theme.

1262 Wolcke-Renk, Irmtraud D. **"Acquisition of African Literature - Problem and Challenge for Bookdealer and Librarian."** *IFLA Journal* 10, no. 4 (1984): 377-384.
Discusses the perennial problems which libraries face in the field of Africana acquisition in general and African literature in particular; by the former head of the Frankfurt University library's African collections.

African Books Collective Ltd. (ABC)

Note: for articles on book marketing and distribution by ABC
see also
→ **African books in the international market place**
→ **Book marketing and promotion**

1263 Courtney, Dana **African Books Collective, an Interview.**
http://www.ybp.com/acad/features/0208_african_books.html [10/02/08]
An interview with Justin Cox, Marketing Manager for the →**African Books Collective Ltd./ABC (3)**, by Dana Courtney, a senior buyer at one of the leading library suppliers, Yankee Book Peddler (YBP). The interview sheds light on recent changes at ABC as it was forced to reconfigure its business model following reductions in funding at the end of a five year donor-funded strategic plan at the end of 2006. A key component in its restructuring is that almost the entire list of over 1,000 titles distributed by ABC have now been digitized and are available on a print-on-demand (POD) basis, and through POD wholesale channels. A large number of other titles still held in physical stock are available through the UK wholesaler Gardners.

1264 Foster, Michael **"Africa in a Jam Factory and in an Abattoir."** *Journal of Multicultural Librarianship* 4, no. 3 (July 1990): 117-120.
A librarian argues the need for, and describes the activities of the Oxford-based →**African Books Collective Ltd./ABC (3)**. The references to a jam factory and an abattoir refer to ABC's office location in a former jam and marmalade factory and its [then] warehouse facilities in a former lairage pen in Burford.

1265 Graham, Gordon **"Africa Comes to Oxford."** *The Bookseller* (20 September 1991): 780-781.
Reviews the ethos and activities of →**African Books Collective Ltd. /ABC (3)**, and states that "in a significant reversal of historical trading directions, Oxford has recently become the world distribution centre for books from the African continent."

1266 Jay, Mary **"African Books Collective - An Innovative Publishing Venture."** In *Yearbook of Co-operative Enterprise 1993.* Long Hanborough, Oxfordshire: The Plunkett Foundation, 1993, 119-123.

Sets out the background which led to the setting-up of ➜ **African Books Collective Ltd. /ABC (3)**, its activities and achievements to date [to 1993], and the prospects for its future growth and expansion.

1267 Jay, Mary **"African Books Collective. Its Contribution to African Publishing."** In *Africa Bibliography 1992*, compiled by Christopher H. Allen. Edinburgh: Edinburgh University Press, 1994, vii-xvii.
Outlines the structure, membership, objectives, and services of ➜ **African Books Collective Ltd. /ABC (3),** and reviews ABC's progress and success to date [to 1993]. Describes some of ABC's special activities such as its Intra-African Book Support Scheme, operated in collaboration with ➜ **Book Aid International (38).**

1268 Jay, Mary "**African Books Collective Limited: An Account of its Evolution**." *Innovation. Journal of Appropriate Librarianship and Information Work in Southern Africa*, no. 8 (June 1994): 11-15.
Online:
http://www.library.unp.ac.za/Innovation/InnovationPdfs/No8pp11-15Jay.pdf [13/03/08]
Charts the evolution of ➜ **African Books Collective Ltd./ABC (3),** and describes its structure, funding, services, staffing, and outlines its promotion and marketing strategies and special activities. Also assesses ABC's main achievements to date [to 1994] and its prospects for the future.

1269 Jay, Mary **"African Books Collective and African Literature."** *The Courier. Africa-Caribbean-Pacific-European Union*, no. 174 (March-April 1999): 64-66.
An update about the activities of ➜ **African Books Collective Ltd./ABC (3)** focusing, in particular, on the challenges of promoting and marketing its wide range of African literature titles. Mary Jay has been the CEO and Senior Consultant to ABC since 1996.

1270 Jay, Mary **"African Books Collective Strategic Plan 2002-2006."** *African Publishing Review* 11, no. 4 (2002): 8-9. *African Publishing Review* 11, no. 4 (2002): 8-9.
Describes African Books Collective's reformulated mission as it relates to its aims and strategies, the cultural context, the challenges of new opportunities, and the focus of activities in the years ahead.

1271 Sida. Department for Democracy and Social Development **Evaluation of the African Books Collective. Final Report. February 2000**. (Sida Evaluation 00/6). By Cecilia Magnusson Ljungman and Tejeshwar Singh. Stockholm: Sida, Department for Democracy and Social Development (SIDA article no. 1303en), 2000. 80 pp.
Online:
http://www.sida.se/sida/jsp/sida.jsp?d=118&a=2215&language=en_US&searchWords=African%20Books%20Collective [13/02/08]

Since 1990 the Swedish donor agency ➔ **Sida (115)** has provided generous core support for ➔**African Books Collective Ltd./ABC (3)**. This is the report of an evaluation of ABC's operations through to 1999, reviewing its mission, strategies, structure, financial management, and its achievements. A final chapter provides an analysis of future prospects, including sustainability, opportunities, and the donors' roles.

1272 Sida. Department for Democracy and Social Development **African Books Collective. Mid-term Review 2006.** (Sida Evaluation 06/10). By Nigel Billany, Jane Katjavivi, and Ruth Makotsi. Stockholm: Sida, Department for Democracy and Social Development (SIDA article no. 28706en), 2006. 98 pp. Online:
http://www.sida.se/sida/jsp/sida.jsp?d=118&a=23706&language=en_US&searchWords=African%20Books%20Collective [13/03/08]
ABC's Strategic Plan 2002-2006 was supported by donor agencies ➔ **Hivos (67)**, ➔ **Norad (99)**, and ➔ **Sida (115)**. The purpose of this further evaluation (commissioned by Sida as the lead agency) was to evaluate ABC's achievements so far and compared to its Strategic Plan 2002–2006, and to evaluate to what extent ABC is reaching sustainability without external grant funding.

1273 Zell, Hans M. **"African Publishing: Constraints and Challenges and the Experience of African Books Collective."** In *Publishing and Development in the Third World*, edited by Philip G. Altbach. London: Hans Zell Publishers, 1992, 102-118.
Examines the main constraints, challenges, and failings of indigenous African publishing and sets out the objectives and structure of ➔ **African Books Collective Ltd./ABC (3)**. This is followed by review of the achievements of the organization to date [to 1991]. Concludes with a projection of the likely future roles and work of ABC. Hans Zell was Senior Consultant to ABC up to 1996.

African books in the international market place

See also
➔ **The Acquisition of African-published material**
➔ **African Books Collective Ltd.**
➔ **Book marketing and promotion**

1274 Agada, Jerry **"Developing African Publishing for the World Market."** *The Publisher* 14, no. 1 (November 2007): 24-32.
Examines how African book publishing output can be developed for the world market, and the role of authors, publishers, universities, governments, and other stake holders, in this endeavour. Agada contends that many African publishers lack ambition to "to achieve any development meaningful enough to be worthy of attention to the world level." He finds that "publishing houses have stopped being venues where authors are discovered; they have become arenas where established

authors are displayed." African writers would do well to place their work with small, fledgling but enterprising presses thus contributing to the development of indigenous publishing. He also laments the demise of many once vibrant African university presses, particularly those in Nigeria, but praises the → **Noma Award for Publishing in Africa (98)** for bringing African writing and scholarship, and African publishing output, to the attention of the world: "I doubt if publishing on the African continent can be encouraged better than the Noma did." The author is the current Vice-President of the → **Association of Nigerian Authors (732).**

1275 Bohm, Fredric **"The North American Distribution and Selling of Books."** In *African Scholarly Publishing Essays*, edited by Alois Mlambo. Oxford: African Books Collective Ltd.; Uppsala: Dag Hammarskjöld Foundation; and Oxford: International Network for the Availability of Scientific Publications (INASP), 2006, 184-189.
Fredric Bohm, until recently Director of Michigan State University Press (which markets and distributes the books from → **African Books Collective (3)** in North America) describes the formidable challenges of selling to the library and retail markets in North America, and the opportunities that exist for co-publication, rights, and distribution partnerships. He provides some helpful tips and advice how small or mid-sized publishers outside the US might penetrate the North American book markets, in the face of constantly dwindling library budgets, and a complex retail market infrastructure now dominated by a few very big players.

1276 Dilevko, Juris, and Lisa Gottlieb **"Book Titles Published in Africa Held by North American University Research Libraries and Review Sources for African-published Books."** *Library & Information Science Research* 25 (2003): 177-206.
A well-documented article that offers some interesting analysis about the presence of African books on the shelves of major North America research libraries (especially institutions that are members of the Association of Research Libraries/ARL http://www.arl.org/), as well as gauging the percentage of African-published non-fiction titles that are reviewed by scholarly journals and major library reviewing tools such as *Choice*, to ascertain whether the presence of such reviews is related to the number of African-published non-fiction titles owned by North American libraries. It finds that although ARL university libraries at institutions with well-established African studies programmes in stand-alone academic units typically have strong collections of sub-Saharan African-published titles, ARL university libraries at institutions not meeting such criteria have relatively weak collections of such material. The authors also urge *Choice* to revisit some of their current practices and policies that unintentionally exclude African-published titles from their review pages, thus assuring wider visibility of African publishing output.

1277 Easterbrook, David L. **"American Libraries, American Markets, African Books."** In *Indaba 2000. Millennium Marketplace*, edited by the Zimbabwe International Book Fair Trust. Harare: Zimbabwe International Book Fair Trust, 2001, 164-169.

The curator of the Melville J. Herskovits Library of African Studies at Northwestern University (the largest Africana collection in the world), looks at the acquisition methods for African books by American libraries, discusses some of the selection tools and resources they use, and offers some suggestions what publishers might do to make their books more easily available in North America, in particular in the use of the Internet and postings to online mailing lists and discussion groups.

1278 Jay, Mary **"The Book Chain: African Books Collective and UK Book Buyers."** *Focus on International and Comparative Librarianship* 26, no. 2 (September 1995): 90-94.
Also published in *African Research & Documentation*, no. 69 (1995): 30-33.
Outlines the services offered by the Oxford-based ➔ **African Books Collective Ltd. (3)** and describes the wide range of its promotional activities. Laments the current paucity of funding for book acquisitions for African studies and multicultural materials by UK public and academic libraries.

1279 Jay, Mary **"How Can Publishers Effectively Distribute Books in and out of Africa?"** In *Academic Book Production and Distribution in Africa. Support from Nordic Countries. Report from a conference at Chr. Michelsen Institute, Bergen, 10-11 April 1997*, edited by Kirsti Hagen Andersen. Fantoft, Norway: Ch. Michelsen Institute 1997, 77-82.
Examines the role and contribution of the ➔ **African Books Collective Ltd. (3)** in the promotion and marketing of African books, and providing visibility for African creative writing, culture, and African scholarship. Also offers some suggestions how African publishers could more effectively distribute their books both within Africa and reaching markets overseas.

1280 Jay, Mary **"African Books Collective and Creative Writing and Publishing in Africa."** In *The African Writers' Handbook*, edited by James Gibbs and Jack Mapanje. Oxford: African Books Collective Ltd., 1999, 119-127.
Examines the needs of African writers to have their work read and widely disseminated outside Africa, and the ➔ **African Books Collective /ABC's (3)** role in effective overseas distribution of the publishing output of its member publishers. It describes ABC's aims and objectives, its structure, finance, and activities, as well as its achievements to date [to 1999]. It also looks at the wider issues of African literature and its importance and place within the culture and development of the continent; and the multiplicity of factors and constraints that still hinder the publication and sales of English-language African literature both within Africa and overseas. "Selling African literature overseas is, in ABC's experience, an uphill task" primarily because African literature is not in the mainstream in the same way as literatures of, e.g. from Latin America, India or Japan. "ABC is not merely trying to tap the markets: it is having to stimulate creation of the markets." However, despite the many obstacles, African literary publishing remains alive. "African publishers have been foresighted in founding ABC, and the task now is for a greater number of creative writers to publish with African publishers, and contribute, to their mutual

benefit, to the wide recognition outside Africa of the richness of Africa's literary talent, and indeed to the cultural renaissance of the continent."

1281 Jay, Mary, and Ros Sherwin **"Marketing African Books Worldwide: The ABC Experience"** In *Book Marketing and Promotion: A Handbook of Good Practice*, by Hans M. Zell. Oxford: International Network for the Availability of Scientific Publications (distributed by African Books Collective Ltd), 2001, 225-243.
A detailed account of the marketing methods and strategies employed by the Oxford-based → **African Books Collective (3),** to promote and sell a very wide range of African-published books in the countries of the North. It describes the type of promotional materials produced, mailing lists and other marketing tools used, exhibits, Web site marketing, selling to particular markets (retail book trade, academic markets, children's books, African literature, etc.), together with an assessment of current [2000] trends and constraints, and an evaluation of future markets prospects for African-published material.

1282 Jay, Mary **"The Northern Marketplace."** In *Indaba 2000. Millennium Marketplace,* edited by the Zimbabwe International Book Fair Trust. Harare: Zimbabwe International Book Fair Trust, 2001, 170-174
Describes the experience of → **African Books Collective/ABC (3)** over a period of ten years of trading and promoting books to the major markets in the countries of the North. It summarizes the principal methods and techniques used in marketing the more than 1,400 titles ABC distributes. Also reports about current difficult market conditions and constantly declining library acquisitions budgets, as well as a decline of interest in African studies. "There are opportunities for African publishers in the dawn of the digital age, but at the moment the negative implications for their competitive position are more evident."

1283 Leishman, A.D.H. **"Tell Me Another."** *African Publishing Review* 3, no. 3 (May/June 1994): 14-15.
Reports about the operations and experiences of Leishman & Taussig, a [former] UK bookseller and importer and distributor of African books.

1284 Ling, Margaret **"Reading Africa."** *Focus on International Library and Information Work* 35, no. 1 (2004): 9-13.
http://www.cilip.org.uk/NR/rdonlyres/E20E7664-1C18-448B-B1B1-114CF7EBBFDF/0/focus3512004.pdf [13/02/08]
A report about the → **Southern African Book Development Education Trust's (113)** 'Reading Africa' campaign, designed to convince readers and librarians in the UK and in Europe to explore African literature. The campaign was inspired by the Zimbabwe International Book Fairs' list of *Africa's Best Books of the 20th Century,* and included a series of book festivals in the UK, and participation and exhibits at major international book fairs in Europe.

1285 Matovelo, Doris S., and Inese A. Smith **"A Study on Africana Collections in UK Libraries: Present State and Future Scenarios."** *Library Collections, Acquisitions & Technical Services* 25 (2001): 21-36.
Based on a questionnaire survey and interviews with librarians and suppliers of Africana materials in the UK, the authors attempt to shed some light on the current situation relating to the demand, acquisitions policies, extent and adequacy of Africana acquisitions, and the tools and sources used by libraries in the selection process. The study found that 41% of academic libraries surveyed acquired African-published material, but many were affected by budgetary constraints. It also found that, surprisingly, well-established bibliographic services covering African book publishing output, such as the quarterly ➜ **African Book Publishing Record (168)**, were only used as a buying and acquisitions tool by 21% of the libraries surveyed.

1286 Ngandu, Freddie "**Espace Afrique International Pour la Diffusion du Livre Africain Francophone.**" Geneva: Espace Afrique International [ICC, Route de Pré-Bois 20, 1215 Genève 15, Switzerland] 2007. 20 pp. (+ appendixes)
Presents an overview of the various collaborative initiatives relating to online marketing and promotion, sales and distribution of francophone African books overseas. Also describes the structure and objectives of the Geneva-based ➜ **Espace Afrique International (14)** a new coalition of publishers from the francophone regions of Africa, founded in June 2006, which aims to reach a global audience for their books and conquer the world markets.

1287 Ripken, Peter **"African Literature in the Literary Market Place Outside Africa."** *The African Book Publishing Record* 17, no. 4 (1991): 289-291.
Addresses the problems facing the promotion and dissemination of African literature outside Africa, considering the disparity in perception by readers, the difficulties of translation, and the overriding problem of a minority readership for African literature outside Africa.

1288 Ripken, Peter **"Marketing African Books Through the Frankfurt Book Fair (and other Book Fairs.)"** *African Publishing Review* 10, no. 2 (2001): 7-8.
The director of the ➜ **Society for the Promotion of African, Asian and Latin American Literature (64)** offers some sound advice for African publishers about participation at foreign book fairs, what to expect, and what to offer, and at the same time he refutes a number of common erroneous assumptions about the Frankfurt Book Fair. He stresses the need for a coherent strategy: "participation in a foreign book fairs needs careful planning, and a sober assessment of what to expect and how to prepare for it." And that it cannot be a hit-and-run-affair, but will require perseverance and stamina to achieve any success, and that this can only be achieved over a period of several years of attending a major book fair such as Frankfurt.

1289 Salon Livres d'Afrique 2006. Dossier de presse. Deuxième edition Paris: L'association Livres d'Afrique, 2006. 26 pp.

Online:
http://www.livresdafrique.com/files/pdf/2006/Dossier%20de%20presse%20LA%202006.pdf [30/03/08]
The press pack for the annual Salon Livres d'Afrique in Paris organized by the → **L'association Livres d'Afrique (10)**, with details of the 2006 fair programme and associated events, and short profiles of some of the exhibitors. *Note:* 2007 programme not available at press time.

1290   Schär, Helene **"Children's Books from South to North."** In *Books and Children. Proceedings of the ZIBF Indaba 1998, Harare, Zimbabwe, 1-2 August 1998*, edited by the Zimbabwe International Book Fair Trust. Harare: Zimbabwe International Book Fair Trust, 1998, 143-146.
Helene Schär, former Director of the → **Baobab Children's Book Fund (88)** in Basle, Switzerland – which encourages and supports publication of children's books by authors from Africa, Asia and Latin America in German translation – reports about their experience, and issues such as trying to overcome fixed images of European readers, commercial relations with publishing companies, competitive books, and the expectations of readers and critics.

1291   Schulz, Hermann **"Bringing African Literature to Germany."** *Logos. The Journal of the Book Community* 3, no. 2 (1992): 94-97.
Online:
http://www.atypon-link.com/LOG/doi/pdf/10.2959/logo.1992.3.2.94
Recounts fifteen years of promoting African books and writing in Germany. Pinpoints two main impediments to the acceptance of African literature in Europe: the economic and cultural gap between the "third" and "first" worlds, and the fragmented nature of the publishing scene in Africa. Calls for the formation of "a partnership among those in the developed world who are deeply concerned about the state of the Third World. African authors and publishers should seek out their counterparts in the developed world. Their books will pave the way."

1292   Scull-Carvalho, Susan **"How to Tackle the US Market.** *"African Publishing Review* 7, no. 6 (November/December 1998): 7-8
A short but informative account of the attempts by a Kenyan publisher, Jacaranda Design Ltd., to sell their range of high-quality children's books into the North American trade and educational markets.

1293   Scull-Carvalho, Susan **"The Jacaranda Experience. Kenyan Children's Books in America."** In *Books and Children. Proceedings of the ZIBF Indaba 1998, Harare, Zimbabwe, 1-2 August 1998*. Harare: Zimbabwe International Book Fair Trust, 1998, 160-166.
Recounts the experience of the Kenyan publisher Jacaranda Designs Ltd in selling a range of high-quality African children's books to the American educational markets. It describes the company's marketing and sales strategies, and the obstacles and prejudices it faced on several fronts in trying to penetrate these markets, and the lessons that were learned from the experience. It found that the US is a demanding

and expensive market place, requiring a very considerable investment and high profile strategies — "to make sales happen in the US requires more and constant promotion and special efforts."

1294 Smith, Kelvin **"African Publishing from the Outside."** In *From Papyrus to Print-out: The Book in Africa Yesterday, Today and Tomorrow. Bibliophilia Africana 8 Conference Proceedings. Centre of the Book Cape Town, 11-14 May 2005*, edited by Cora Owens. Pretoria and Cape Town: National Library of South Africa/Centre of the Book, 2005, 272-285.
Also published in *African Research & Documentation*, no. 100 (2006): 3-10.
Slightly different and shorter online version also available as the text of a paper presented at the African Publishing and Writing Conference panel, British Library, 17 October 2005, online at http://www.sabdet.com/afrpubwritconf.htm [13/02/08]
A thought-provoking paper – drawing inspiration from an acceptance speech made by Henry Chakava as the recipient of the first "ZIBF Award for the Life-Long Contribution to the African Book Industry", made during the Zimbabwe Book Fair in August 2004 – in which the author addresses the issue of "democratising the book" in Africa: not only the perennial obstacles of making books available, accessible, and affordable to all of Africa's peoples, but also bringing more equality to the world of the book, and correcting the imbalances in the relationships between publishers in Africa and those in the countries of the North. Kelvin Smith points out that in the area of academic and scholarly publishing in Africa, for example, "there are few African sources of information that make their presence felt in the global reaches of the Internet....Those who do not know where to look will not find African information on the Internet, visibility remains low and the opportunity to build a market at a global level is lost." He also draws attention to the fact that much of the information about the book in Africa comes to the world either from or via non-African sources, and that a search on Google for the term 'African book' will display top ten results from Web sites and resources outside Africa. "If African publishing is to get on the world map, it might do well to focus energy on the creative and energetic use of information and communications technology, to make sure that more information on the Internet is from African sources", and that "more of the messages need to originate in Africa, rather than rely on the intercession of organizations in other continents."

1295 Southern African Book Development Education **Trust Africa at the Fair. How Can Literary Festivals and Book Fairs Promote African Books and Reading?**
http://www.sabdet.com/seminars04.htm#sam [13/02/08]
A report about a seminar hosted by the ➜ **Southern African Book Development Education Trust (113)** during the London Book Fair in March 2004, whose aim it was to explore how the quality and diversity of African books and writing can enrich the programmes of book fairs and literary festivals. It includes summaries of the presentations and a record of the discussions that took place. Between them, the speakers had a wide range of experience of bringing Africa to popular audiences at book fairs and festivals in the UK, Europe and Africa. They shared a common

interest in achieving more exposure for African books and writers amongst the general reading public, more awareness and interest, and growing readership and sales.

1296 Stein, Claudia **"Selling African Children's Literature. Some Practical Experiences in Europe."** In *Books and Children. Proceedings of the ZIBF Indaba 1998, Harare, Zimbabwe, 1-2 August 1998*, edited by the Zimbabwe International Book Fair Trust. Harare: Zimbabwe International Book Fair Trust, 1998, 147-151.
Claudia Stein of the ➔ **Society for the Promotion of African, Asian and Latin American Literatures (64)** describes some of her practical experiences in trying to place children's books by African authors with German publishers at the Frankfurt Book Fair, for possible translation. Sets out some of the editorial conventions and pre-conceptions, the high expectations (for example in terms of quality of artwork and illustrations), and other hurdles that have to be overcome. Concludes with a helpful number of recommendations and suggestions as to what African publishers should do, and what they should avoid.

1297 Violet, Jean-Marie **"A 'Good' Children's Book is One Which Arises from the Child's Own Culture."** *Mots Pluriels*, no. 22 (September 2002). http://www.arts.uwa.edu.au/MotsPluriels/MP2202mlj.html
An interview with Mary Jay, current head of ➔ **African Books Collective Ltd (3)**, in which she discusses the rising demand for children's books published in Africa, the problems associated with children's book publishing, sales of African children's book in the UK and the US, and the most popular books. She also examines interpretations of what constitutes a "good" children's book in Africa, which she defines "as one which arises from the child's own culture, which is aesthetically attractive, and which is available in the child's mother tongue."

1298 Zell, Hans M. **"Effective Promotion and Marketing, and the Size of the Export Market for African Books."** *African Publishing Review* 4, no. 2 (March/April 1995): 16-18.
Outlines the basic needs and requirements for effective promotion and marketing, and developing mailing lists. Assesses the sales potential, and the size of the export market for African books, in the principal English-language markets outside Africa, and urges African publishers to become more export-minded.

1299 Zurbrugg, Tony **"A Perspective on the Trade in Books from and About Africa in Anglophone Europe."** In *Africa Bibliography. Works on Africa Published During 2002*, edited by T.A. Barringer. Edinburgh: Edinburgh University Press; London International African Institute, 2003. vii-xvii.
A useful survey of bookshops in "Anglophone Europe" (a term the author identifies as "broadly non-Latin western Europe"), who hold some kind of stocks of books on Africa, principally in the UK but also covering the Netherlands, Belgium, and Denmark. There is especially good coverage of bookshops in London, which includes full addresses, telephone numbers, and a short description of stocks held and/or

areas of specialization. Also covers some "off the High Street" distributors, library suppliers and online booksellers.

African Publishers Network (APNET)

See also ➔ **Book trade and book development organizations**

1300   African Publishers Network **Register of African Publishing Consultants/Register des consultants de l'édition Africaine. 2001.** Harare: African Publishers Network, 2001. 117 pp. (supersedes *APNET Consultants Register, 1998/1999*)
The purpose of this register is to provide more visibility of the work and expertise of African publishing consultants, and to provide a handy reference source to the range of services provided by them. The register, now in its second edition, is arranged alphabetically by country giving very full information on each consultant listed, including (and in addition to complete contact details) educational background and qualifications, professional experience, and specialist areas of expertise. A name index as well as an index by areas of specialization is also included. No further editions would appear to have been published to date.
Reviews:
African Research & Documentation no. 81, 1999 (review of first edition)

1301   Anon. **"Change and Continuity."** *African Publishing Review* 6, no. 4 (July/August 1997): 4-6.
Interviews with the outgoing and incoming Chairpersons of APNET – the late Victor Nwankwo and Richard Crabbe respectively – discussing their work and their visions for the future development of the network, and the challenges ahead for APNET.

1302   Anon. **"Five Years of APNET."** *African Publishing Review* 6, no. 2 (March/April 1997): 1-4.
The ➔ **African Publishers Network (5)** was established in 1992. Five years on, the Secretariat looks at how the network has grown and changed, and what has been achieved in different areas such as training and trade promotion.

1303   Brickhill, Paul **"Breaking the Barriers: APNET's First Year: March 1992-March 1993."** *African Publishing Review* 2, no. 2 (March/April 1993): 1-3.
APNET's [then] Executive Secretary looks back on the first year of activities of the Harare-based ➔ **African Publishers Network (5)**. Published in English, French and Portuguese.

1304   Brickhill, Paul **"APNET and the Zimbabwe Book Industry."** *Book Power*, no. 3 (1994): 4-9.
Reports about the aims and objectives of the ➔ **African Publishers Network (5)** and its activities to date [to 1994]; assesses to which extent the Zimbabwe book industry

can benefit from APNET, and the opportunities now open to Zimbabwean publishers to find partners in other African countries.

1305 Brickhill, Paul **"Report on the APNET Mission to the World Bank."** *African Publishing Review* 3, no. 2 (March/April 1994): 2-3. (same, in French, pp. 1-2).
A delegation from the ➔ **African Publishers Network (5)** visited the ➔ **World Bank (124)** in Washington DC in December 1993, to explore ways in which African publishers could benefit from World Bank book provision schemes within their educational support programmes. Here APNET's [then] Executive Secretary reports about this visit and evaluates the prospects for African publishers to profit from World Bank projects.

1306 Brickhill, Paul **"APNET: The African Publishers Network Report on Projects and Activities, 1st October 1993 to 30 September 1994."** *Focus on International and Comparative Librarianship* 26, no. 2 (September 1995): 78-90.
Also published in *African Research & Documentation*, no. 69 (1995): 34-46.
Describes the principal objectives of the [then] Harare-based African Publishers Network, and provides a chronology of its varied activities between 1993 and 1994.

1307 Chakava, Henry **"The African Publishers Network (APNET): An Overview."** In *Development Directory of Indigenous Publishing 1995*, compiled by Carol Priestley. Harare: African Publishers Network, 1995, 57-61.
A brief account charting the growth of ➔ the **African Publishers Network (5)**, its mission, and its achievements during the first two years of its existence.

1308 Dekutsey, Woeli **The Story of APNET. A Study of the Origins, Structure, Activities and Policy of the African Publishers Network**.
Harare: African Publishers Network, 1995. 18 pp.
Also published in French as **L'historique de l'APNET. Une étude des origines, de la structure, des activités et des principes directeurs du Réseau des éditeurs africains**.
A ➔ **UNESCO (118)**-commissioned study that sets out the background that led to the establishment of the ➔ **African Publishers Network/APNET (5)**, its constitution, policies, programmes and activities, publications, and its achievements to date [to 1995.] Also examines APNET's relations with the ➔ **World Bank (124)** and with donor agencies.

1309 Diabate, Dafina Blacksher **Empowering Indigenous Publishers Through Collective Action: The African Publishers Network (APNET)**.
Ithaca, NY: Cornell University, 2003. MA thesis. 154 l.
This thesis examines the mission, strategies and activities of the ➔ **African Publishers Network/APNET (5)** in its quest to empower indigenous publishers. The author probes the nature of publishing development in African countries, utilizing selected cases of anglophone countries as illustrations. Her analysis of the primary and secondary textbook market, as a microcosm of the larger publishing context,

demonstrates the numerous obstacles still confronting indigenous publishing houses in their endeavour to provide quality, affordable, and relevant book for African readers. Based on a qualitative research method, the author used in-depth interview data collected at the Zimbabwe International Book Fair 2002 to inform her work. She believes that the collective nature of the organization enhances its ability to effect positive change and that, in its mission to promote publishing development, APNET operates as an agent of decolonization by decreasing Africa's dependence on the North for its book needs.

1310   Global Knowledge Partnership **Global Knowledge 1997 Conference GK 97 Working Sessions. Working Session 5.15: African Publishers Network. Partnerships for Knowledge (APNET).**
http://www.globalknowledge.org/gkps_portal/GK97/working%20session s/Wednesday%20Session%205.15.pdf [13/02/08]
Abstracts of presentations made at one of the workings sessions at the GK 97 conference. This particular session sought explore how local private publishers, large international publishers, and government can work together to increase access to knowledge and information while building local capacity and encouraging new partnerships. One of the panellists was the late Chief Victor Nwankwo, former Chairman of APNET.

1311   Humphrey, Lesley **"Paul Brickhill Bids APNET Farewell."** *African Publishing Review* 4, no. 5 (September/October 1995): 5-8.
Paul Brickhill, who was the first Executive Secretary of the ➜ **African Publishers Network/APNET (5)** since it was founded in February 1992, stepped down as Secretary at the end of November 1995. In this interview he examines and evaluates these formative years, reviews APNET's achievements to date, and looks at possible directions for the future.

1312   Mafela, Lily **Networks: A Potent Vehicle for Going to Scale**. Paris: Association for the Development of Education in Africa (ADEA), 2001. 27 pp.
Online: http://www.adeanet.org/biennial/papers/en_arusha_mafela.doc [18/01/08]
This study was one in a series of papers commissioned by the ➜ **Association for the Development of Education (34)** for its biennial meeting held in Arusha in October 2001 with the theme "Reaching Out, Reaching All –Sustaining Effective Policy and Practice for Education in Africa". It aims to provide background information on a variety of educational ADEA partner networks, with a view to determining what kind of status could be extended to these new partners in order to promote synergy between the activities of the partners and those of ADEA. The networks covered as case studies are the ➜ **African Publishers Network (5),** the Forum for African Women Educationalists (FAWE), and the African Economic Research Consortium (AERC). The three networks deal with a diverse range of issues, and have diverse functions and activities. The study sought to determine how and why networks succeed in taking educational policies to scale.

1313 Nwankwo, Victor **"International Networking: APNET and the IPA."** *African Publishing Review* 6, no. 2 (March/April 1997): 13-14.
The ➔ **African Publishers Network/APNET (5)** was formally admitted to the ➔ **International Publishers Association (82)** as a regional group during the 25th IPA Congress. Here, its former Chairperson, the late Victor Nwankwo, reports on the growing relationship between the two organizations, and the benefits this will bring to APNET and, in turn, to individual African publishers.

1314 Nyambura, Gillian **"A Time to Reflect."** *African Publishing Review* 6, no. 4 (July/August 1997): 11-15.
Another version also published in *Bellagio Publishing Network Newsletter*, no. 20 (Autumn 1997): 2.
Online:
http://www.bellagiopublishingnetwork.com/newsletter20/nyambura.htm [13/03/08]
In August 1996 the Board of the ➔African Publishers Network (5), in anticipation of the end of the 1995-97 programme and funding cycle, took the decision to undertake a review of its work and to plan the next phase. This decision took further shape in the form of a meeting to reflect on APNET's vision, programme and future strategies, held in Nyeri, Kenya in March 1997. This report sets out the key elements and core values that were examined at this reflection meeting. The key outcomes of the meeting were a new vision and mission statement; a revised constitution; clearer objectives, roles and responsibilities; and a crystallization of the core elements of the next programme cycle. The various recommendations were reformulated into a draft programme of activities and a funding proposal that was later submitted to the General Council meeting in Bamako.

1315 Sida. Department for Democracy and Social Development. **Strengthening Publishing in Africa. An Evaluation of APNET.**
(Sida Evaluation 99/2). By Lars P. Christensen, *et al.* Stockholm: Sida, Department for Democracy and Social Development (SIDA article no 1340en), 1999. 98 pp.
Online:
http://www.sida.se/sida/jsp/sida.jsp?d=118&a=2249&language=en_US&searchWords=APNET (4.9MB) [13/03/08]
The Swedish donor agency ➔ **Sida (115)** has been one of the core donors of the ➔ **African Publishers Network/APNET (5)** since its inception in 1992. This evaluation, undertaken by the international consulting group COWI, was designed to assess the achievements of APNET with a view to promote learning within APNET and make recommendations for the future. In addition, the effectiveness of the donor support for APNET was reviewed. The evaluation was undertaken from August to December 1998. The evaluation report includes five country case studies, the purpose of which was to gather and analyze information that provides a more complete picture of the environment that APNET works within, how APNET is making an impact and whether it is meeting the needs. In addition to an evaluation of APNET the report also includes a useful chapter on "African Publishing: Past and Present", providing a

historical perspective, together with an overview of recent developments of, and the challenges facing, African publishing in the 1980s and 1990s.

Authors and publishers/Publishing of African writers and African literature (in Africa and elsewhere)

See also
→ **Copyright and legal deposit/Authors' rights**
→ **Reading culture and reading promotion**
→ **Section 5, Book industry training/Self-publishing: Handbooks for authors and self-publishing**

Note: this section is primarily devoted to the – sometimes rather strained – relationship between African writers and African publishers, and the difficulties African writers face in breaking into print. It also includes articles about publishing of African writers and African literature, and perspectives on the publishing experience of African writers with both African as well as UK publishers, such as Heinemann's and its renowned African Writers Series (AWS).

Articles on authors' rights – including the rights of academic and non-fiction authors – can be found in the sub-section → **Copyright and legal deposit/Authors' rights**.

1316 Achebe, Chinua **"Power of Print-2. What do African Intellectuals Read?"** *Times Literary Supplement* (12 May 1972): 547.
This much-quoted and somewhat controversial article by the distinguished Nigerian novelist endeavours to answer the question what do African intellectuals read, and identifies certain constraints on the intellectual such as lack of time and undeveloped reading habits. Achebe contends that since African intellectuals view reading as a means to an end rather than merely as a pastime, fiction does not figure prominently amongst their reading materials. He states that "present-day school children are much more aware of literature" and links this improvement to the greater availability of books and the actual existence of books "with a familiar ring and background." Draws some interesting conclusions about how the lack of reading is likely to affect the African intellectual's view of the West.

1317 Achebe, Chinua **"Publishing in Africa: A Writer's View."** In *Publishing in Africa in the Seventies,* edited by Edwina Oluwasanmi, Eva McLean, and Hans M. Zell. Ile-Ife: University of Ife Press, 1975, 41-46.
Chinua Achebe's paper presented to the historic 1973 Ife international conference on publishing and book development in Africa. Sets out the intermediaries who intervene between the writer and his audience: booksellers, printers, editors, publishers. Achebe argues that "writers, especially established writers, have a

responsibility to support an indigenous publisher who displays the necessary qualities of intellect, creativity and organization", while at the same time acknowledging the important role which some foreign publishers have played in bringing important African authors to light.

1318   Adeniyi, Dapo **"Before your Text Goes into a State of Permanence."** In *The African Writers' Handbook*, edited by James Gibbs and Jack Mapanje. Oxford: African Books Collective Ltd., 1999, 99-104.
Dapo Adeniyi, [then] editor of the Nigerian literary and cultural magazine the *Glendora Review* and its ➜ **Glendora Books Supplement (159)**, offers some advice to "suspicious, angst-ridden authors-in-waiting" – many of whom have been going through the painful experience of rejection – in their dealings with editors at publishing houses. Adeniyi believes most writers are in too much of a rush to get into print, and he reminds them that many great works in the canon of modern African writing "existed in different versions for years before they were eventually published."

1319   Armah, Ayi Kwei **"Negatives-The Colonial Publisher as Pirate."** In *The Eloquence of the Scribes. A Memoir on the Sources and Resources of African Literature* by Ayi Kwei Armah. Popenguine, Senegal: Per Ankh. The African Publishing Cooperative [BP 2, Popenguine, Senegal] , 2006, 307-338.
The celebrated Ghanaian writer Ayi Kwei Armah is the author of, among others, *The Beautyful Ones Are Not Yet Born, Fragments, Why Are We So Blest, The Healers* and *Two Thousand Seasons*, most of them first published by Heinemann in the UK in their African Writers Series/AWS (and some in separate US editions), and subsequently reprinted on several occasions, or sub-licensed for reprints by Heinemann branches and affiliates in Africa. Armah has reportedly had a long-standing feud with Heinemann, but it is not until recently, as a chapter in this new essay collection, that he has set out the reasons for the dispute and provides some documentary evidence. He is highly critical of the African Writers Series, and blatantly accuses Heinemann of fraud—"Heinemann stole my royalties." Armah reproduces extensive correspondence he has had with Heinemann and their agents, and from which it looks as though much of the dispute centres on the issue of royalties payable on the basis of published price, as opposed to royalties based on net receipts, a frequently contentious issue in author-publisher relations. It does seem clear from the evidence and correspondence presented here that Heinemann, at the very least, acted rather unprofessionally. However, Armah's accusations also raise a lot of questions, which are not answered here. For example, if Armah had such a low opinion of the "slyly named" African Writers Series – and that the series, and its publisher, "did its worst to stunt the growth of African talent" – why then did he agree for his books to be published in the series in the first place? And if he was so aggrieved with Heinemann, why then did he not take up his grievances with fellow writer and AWS Series Editor, Chinua Achebe? This account tells only one side of the story, but whatever the truth of the matter, it is a very sad tale and it is unfortunate to say the least that an African writer of such distinction should have such a low esteem of his publishers—or indeed, judging by other passages about "foreign publishers" elsewhere in this collection, of publishers anywhere.

Reviews:
The African Book Publ.ishing Record vol. 33, no. 2, 2007

1320 Armah, Ayi Kwei **"PER ANKH-A Home for Life."** In *The Eloquence of the Scribes. A Memoir on the Sources and Resources of African Literature* by Ayi Kwei Armah. Popenguine, Senegal: Per Ankh. The African Publishing Cooperative [BP 2, Popenguine, Senegal] , 2006, 295-306.
PER ANKH (the ancient Egyptian name for intellectual institutions at the time, meaning 'the house of life') is an African publishing cooperative set up by the distinguished Ghanaian writer Ayi Kwei Armah in the seaside village of Popenguine in Senegal in collaboration with a worldwide association of friends and partners. Here he sets out the raison d'être that led to the founding of the cooperative and how it works, its business and accounting model, and some of the difficulties it faced, e.g. crippling postage charges to mail its publications to customers outside Senegal. In addition to its book publishing acitivities, PER ANKH, through its workgroup SESH (described elswhere in this elsewhere in this collection as chapter 20 "PER SESH-Freeing Social Oxygen", pp. 275-294), also runs writers' workshops, training programmes, and hands-on seminars on the use of current technology for literary productivity.

1321 Awolalu, Tosin **"Beyond Patronage and the Spilt Ink."** In *Creating a Conducive Environment for Book Publishing*, edited by Chukwuemeka Ike. Awka, Nigeria: Nigerian Book Foundation, 1996, 184-207.
Questions whether the current environment in Nigeria can support primary authorship. The author finds that "the environment that produced the first generation of Nigerian authors had greater consideration for literary merit than other factors in arriving at publishing decisions", that "there is a great literary inertia in Nigeria" at the present time [1996], and that it has become very difficult for the new generation of Nigerian authors to get publishers to accept manuscripts of creative writing. The author is sympathetic with the enormous problems faced by the Nigerian book industries, but also critical of Nigerian publishers' lack of encouragement and active support of authorship, and especially of those publishers "who do not rank high in integrity when it comes to matters of royalties or other earnings due to authors."

1322 Bahah, S.T. **"Understanding the Nigerian Publishing Industry: Hopes and Aspirations of the Nigerian Author in the 21st Century."** *The Publisher* 6, no. 1 (1999): 38-39.
[Not examined]

1323 Cévaër, Françoise **"African Literatures Take the Offensive."** *Research in African Literatures* 22, no. 1 (Spring 1991): 100-106.
An interview with Cameroonian poet Paul Dayeko, the founder and editor of the successful small publishing house Editions Silex. Explains some of the risks and challenges facing publishers attempting to keep African literature alive in the marketplace

1324   Chakava, Henry **"Publishing Ngugi: The Challenge, the Risk and the Reward."** *African Publishing Review* 3, no. 4 (July/August 1994): 10-14. Also published in *Matatu* 15/16, (1996): 183-200; and in *The African Writers' Handbook*, edited by James Gibbs and Jack Mapanje. Oxford: African Books Collective Ltd., 1999, 111-118.
Shorter version published in *Bellagio Publishing Network Newsletter* no. 10, (June 1994), 3-5; and extracts also in *Logos. The Journal of the World Book Community 5*, no. 4 (1994): 176.
Online:
http://www.atypon-link.com/LOG/doi/pdf/10.2959/logo.1994.5.4.176
Henry Chakava, the Kenyan publisher of Ngugi wa Thiong'o, describes the "pleasurable and enriching experience" of working with, and publishing the writing of, one of Africa's most distinguished writers--an experience which was "very rewarding both intellectually and commercially." Recounts, for example, the discussions and debates they had concerning Ngugi's strong commitment to writing and publishing in Gikuyu rather than in English, and the challenges of promoting and distributing Ngugi's books internationally. Also tells the story of the difficult years of Ngugi's detention by the Kenyan government, and the period immediately following his release, when the author and Ngugi spent much time together. Henry Chakava, who took personal risks in publishing Ngugi – and whose company (Heinemann Educational Books East Africa Ltd., later Heinemann Kenya, now East African Educational Publishers) suffered because of its association with Ngugi's books – describes Ngugi as "one of the few writers who believe that publishers are honest and decent people."

1325   Chinweizu **"An Interview with Chinua Achebe."** *Pan African Book World* 1, no. 1 (August 1981): 1-7.
Also published in *Okike*, no. 20 (1981): 19-32.
An interview with one of the pioneers of modern African literature, Chinua Achebe, who urges indigenous publishers to produce more easily accessible books about politics and current affairs. He comments on the role of multinational publishers in bringing African literature into the public eye, outlines the necessity for a strong indigenous publishing industry, and expounds on the importance of local literary magazines. Achebe also discusses the particular problems of publishing in Nigeria, while at the same time expressing faith in the prospects for the future, pointing to Fourth Dimension Publishers as an example for other indigenous publishers to follow.

1326   Clarke, Becky **"The African Writers Series—Celebrating Forty Years of Publishing Distinction."** *Research in African Literatures* 34, no. 2 (Summer 2003): 161-174.
Looks back at the achievements of the now defunct Heinemann African Writers Series (AWS), widely considered to be a canonical and influential series of African literature, which developed into the single most important avenue for literary creativity on the continent. The author is a former Series Submissions Editor at Heinemann. She sets out some of the background to the establishment of the series by the late Alan Hill and its growth over the years, and the different genres of

writing that were published in the series. She also examines some of the wider issues of cultural and literary production, and some of the criticism the series has been subjected to. The author states that "work produced in an African cultural context and published in European publishing houses means that decisions about the control and the most acceptable forms of representation of Africans is fraught with tension."

1327 Clarke, Becky **The African Writers Series: History, Development and Effect of the Series on African Culture and Publishing.**
http://www.brookes.ac.uk/schools/apm/publishing/culture/colonial/aw s.html!#bc [13/02/08]
Online version of a talk given in 1998 at the Oxford International Centre for Publishing studies at Oxford Brookes University's in 1998, about the history and cultural impact of the (now defunct) Heinemann African Writers Series (AWS), by one of its former literature submissions editor. It looks at the dominant themes in the books that were published in the series over the years, and how some prominent African writers "perceive their position within the wider market of mainstream publishing in the international context."

1328 Currey, James **"African Writers Series - 21 Years On."** *The African Book Publishing Record* 11, no. 1 (1985): 11.
James Currey was in charge of the African Writers Series (AWS) from 1967-1984 while he was editorial director at Heinemann Educational Books. He then became a consultant on African and Caribbean writing and started his own imprint, in 1985, James Currey Ltd., based in Oxford, publishing books on African studies. Here he looks back on the achievements of the series.

1329 Currey, James **"Chinua Achebe, the African Writers Series and the Establishment of African Literature."** *African Affairs* 102, no. 409, (2003): 575-585.
In the list of 'Africa's 100 Best Books' publicized by the Zimbabwe International Fair Fair in 2002, over a quarter of the books listed were published in the (now defunct) Heinemann African Writers Series (AWS). Chinua Achebe, the distinguished Nigerian writer, was for many years Editorial Adviser to the series. This is an account of his creative role in developing the series, encouraging new writers from Africa, and thus offering an international market for African writers in Europe, North America and the rest of the world. The author of the article, James Currey, was editorial director of the African Writers Series from 1967 to 1984.

1330 Currey, James **"The African Writers Series: A Chronology with Notes."** *African Research & Documentation,* no. 101 (2006): 47-51.
James Currey, former editorial director at Heinemann's, provides a chronology of the famous Heinemann African Writers Series (AWS) from its inception in 1962 through to its 40th anniversary in 2002. Includes some insights about the involvement in the development of the series by (then) Heinemann branches in Africa.

1331 Currey, James **Africa Writes Back. The African Writers Series and the Launch of African Literature.** Oxford: James Currey Publishers, forthcoming 2008. ca. 288 pp.
James Currey was the Editorial Director at Heinemann Educational Books in charge of the African Writers Series (AWS) from 1967 to 1984, and this book tells the story of a publishing enterprise of considerable significance. Includes chapters on publishing, in the AWS Series, of writers such as Chinua Achebe, Ngugi wa Thiong'o, Nuruddin Farah, Alex la Guma, Dennis Brutus, Bessie Head, and Dambudzo Marechera, among others. [Not examined, forthcoming]

1332 Dayeko, Paul **"Publier, Diffuser, Rayonner ... l'Expérience de Silex."** In *Forces Littéraires d'Afrique. Points de répères et témoignages*, edited by Jean-Pierre Jacquemine and Monkasa-Bitumba. Bruxelles: De Boeck-Wesmael, 1987, 143-145.
The Cameroonian director of Editions Silex narrates the story of his publishing house, which consists of a collective of writers and critics devoted to creating and publishing African literatures.

1333 Dekutsey, Woeli **"Stimulating Writing in Africa."** In *Academic Book Production and Distribution in Africa. Support from Nordic Countries. Report from a Conference at Chr. Michelsen Institute, Bergen, 10-11 April 1997*, edited by Kirsti Hagen Andersen. Fantoft, Norway: Ch. Michelsen Institute 1997, 40-48.
A Ghanaian publisher looks at the factors which stimulate writing in Africa and which create a conducive environment for authorship as well laying the foundations for a flourishing book industry. Also calls on African publishers to improve their relations with authors.

Diala, Isidore **"Conditions of Production for Writing, Publishing and Studying Literature in Africa: The Nigerian Situation"** *see* ➜ **Section 2, Country studies: Nigeria** entry **786**

1334 Dogbé, Yves-Emmanuel **"Publier, Rayonner, Diffuser ... l'Expérience d'Akpagnon."** In *Forces Littéraires d'Afrique. Points de répères et témoignages*, edited by Jean-Pierre Jacquemine and Monkasa-Bitumba. Bruxelles: De Boeck-Wesmael, 1987, 147-150.
Describes how the author came to create his own publishing house in Togo, Editions Akpagnon.

1335 Egejuru, Phanuel Akubeze **Towards African Literary Independence. A Dialogue with Contemporary African Writers.** Westport, CT: Greenwood Press, 1980, 173 pp.
Chapter 3, "Publication and Distribution", contains interviews with African writers expressing their views about publishing their books at home and abroad.

1336 Ehmeir, Walter **"Publishing South African Literature in English in the 1960s."** *Research in African Literatures* 26, no. 1 (Spring 1995): 111-131.
A detailed account of publishing of South African literature in English in South Africa and elsewhere in the 1960s, a period marked by censorship and repressive publication laws imposed by the then apartheid government. Also charts the history of several South African literary magazines - for example *The Purple Renoster, Fighting Talk, New Coin, Contrast,* and *The Classic* - which provided outlets and publishing opportunities for many for South African writers, both black and white.

1337 Ekwensi, Cyprian D. **"Creative a Conducive Environment for Authorship."** In *Creating a Conducive Environment for Book Publishing,* edited by Chukwuemeka Ike. Awka, Nigeria: Nigerian Book Foundation, 1996, 160-173.
A contribution to the debate on a conducive environment for authorship by the distinguished Nigerian writer Cyprian Ekwensi, who states that "Nigeria has a world bank of ideas and remedies until it comes to implementation" and that an awareness of professional authorship doesn't exist, much less an enabling atmosphere. He is also critical of cavalier attitudes to copyright and the rights of authors in Nigeria, both by individuals and by the government; and examines author-publisher relations and urges publishers to become more export-oriented. Concludes that "a conducive atmosphere is a product of several factors working together or at times independently" and that "above all else, political stability remains the most conducive atmosphere of all."

1338 Fawcett, Graham **"The Unheard Voices of Africa."** *Logos. The Journal of the World Book Community* 5, no. 4 (1994): 172-171.
Online:
http://www.atypon-link.com/LOG/doi/pdf/10.2959/logo.1994.5.4.172
"African literature today is locked away in African languages and few people care to find the key and use it." This is the conclusion of a survey made by the author as part of an overall review of the present state of literary translation into English. As part of this survey he interviewed a number of scholars and publishers concerned with African literature. Publishers in the UK are found to be sceptical of the market prospects of African language material in English translation: "It's hard enough to sell African authors who have written in English, let alone in translation", says one.

Gibbs, James, and Jack Mapanje, eds. **The African Writers' Handbook** *see* ➔
Section 5, Book Industry training/Self-publishing: Handbook for authors and self-publishing, entry **2507**

1339 Griswold, Wendy **Bearing Witness. Readers, Writers, and the Novel in Nigeria.** Princeton, NJ: Princeton University Press (Princeton Studies in Cultural Sociology), 2000. 340 pp.
This is an impressive and innovative study, and perhaps one of the most comprehensive sociological analyses of a literary system ever written. While the book is primarily devoted to an analysis and understanding of the novel in Nigeria,

chapter 2: "The Nigerian Fiction Complex" (pp. 26-119), offers some interesting and fresh insights of the publishing business, author-publisher relations, the publishing careers of Nigerian writers, aspects of distribution and promotion of books, together with an extensive analysis of readership and reading culture: Who reads? How do they read? What do they read? What do they make of what they read? It draws on interviews with Nigerian writers, publishers, booksellers, readers, surveys, and a reading of almost 500 Nigerian novels, from lightweight popular fiction to acclaimed literary masterpieces.

1340 Habila, Helon **"The African Writer: Facing the New."** Paper presented at the Africa-Europe Group for Interdisciplinary Studies (AEGIS) conference SABDET panel at SOAS on the 2 July 2005 under the title "Getting Published, Getting Heard: Debate and Democracy in Africa". http://www.sabdet.com/aegis2005habila.htm [13/03/08]
Helon Habila reflects on some the issues facing African writers today, and "what are the things that stand between the writer and his desire to express himself", especially political issues. He also recounts his experience when in 2000 he published his first book with a Nigerian printing firm, and which was eventually to become the winner of the 2001 Caine Prize for African Writing http://www.caineprize.com/ [13/03/08].

1341 Hamilton-Jones, Ruth **The African Writers Series.**
http://www.brookes.ac.uk/schools/apm/publishing/culture/colonial/aw s.html!#rhj [13/03/08]
Online version of a talk given at the Oxford International Centre for Publishing studies at Oxford Brookes University's in 1998, about the history and cultural impact of the (now defunct) Heinemann African Writers Series (AWS), by one of its former editors. It look backs at [then] 36 years of the AWS and provides some interesting insights into the series's history, its list development under different series editors, and how the series was "repackaged" several times to make it appeal to a wider market.

1342 Hill, Alan **"British Publishers' Constructive Contribution to African Literature."** *Logos. The Journal of the World Book Community* 3, no. 1 (1992): 45-52.
Online:
http://www.atypon-link.com/LOG/doi/pdf/10.2959/logo.1992.3.1.45
The late Alan Hill was the founder of Heinemann Educational Books. He describes the beginning of the African Writers Series which followed on the huge success of the publication of Chinua Achebe's *Things Fall Apart*. Refutes a charge of "cultural imperialism" and gives a brief history of the role of multinational companies in Africa over the previous thirty years. *See also* Alan Hill's autobiography *In Pursuit of Publishing*, entry ➔ **2021**.

1343 Hill, Alan **"Thirty Years of a New World Literature."** *The Bookseller* (15 January 1993): 58-59.

Alan Hill was managing director of Heinemann Educational Books when the African Writers Series was started. In this article he describes how and why the series came into being.

1344 Ike, Chukwuemeka **"Creating a Conducive Environment for Authorship."** In *Creating a Conducive Environment for Book Publishing*, edited by Chukwuemeka Ike. Awka, Nigeria: Nigerian Book Foundation, 1996, 78-137.

The President of the ➜ **Nigerian Book Foundation (738)**, and also a prolific and widely published Nigerian writer, sets out his concept of authorship and puts forward a wide range of recommendations covering areas in which positive action is required by the Nigerian government to help create a conducive environment for authorship in the country. He reviews the role of the formal education sector, the role of family and society, the role of publishers and bookseller, libraries and information services, as well as the role of authors' and writers' associations. He also critically examines author-publisher relations, and argues that Nigerian publishers must become more aggressive in their marketing methods, both at home and overseas.

1345 Kibble, Matt **"The Digitisation of the African Writers Series."** *Africana Libraries Newsletter*, no. 120 (May 2007).
http://www.indiana.edu/~libsalc/african/ALN%20120/aln120vendor.html [13/03/08]

The well-known Heinemann African Writers Series was launched in 1962 and, until it ceased in 2003, published a total 359 volumes. Although discontinued in print format, the series is now available in digital format published by Chadwyck-Healey, http://www.proquest.com/products_pq/descriptions/african_writers_ser.shtml [13/03/08] the specialist humanities imprint of Pro-Quest CSA. The digitization of the AWS texts as part of an extensive searchable database allows new kinds of research and enquiry to be pursued, allowing researchers to run searches across a whole corpus of texts. Here the Development Manager of the AWS in digital format describes the project, which is now offering full-text access to a body of work with a unique cultural and historic significance. To ensure wide access by libraries and institutions within Africa, Pro Quest is offering subscriptions at either heavily discounted rates or entirely free-of-charge.

1346 Kimenye, Barbara **"Kenyan Writers Versus Publishers."** *The Bookseller* (20 July 1990): 167-169.

A well-known children's author describes in detail the problems which face creative writers in Kenya, including allegedly poor treatment from indigenous publishers, and contrasts this with the performance of Heinemann Kenya and Macmillan. States that these two publishing houses alone are "insufficient to cope with the sudden upsurge of fine creative writing in Kenya." Applauds the initiative of Kenyan authors in forming themselves into "a protective society."

1347 Korley, Nii Laryea **"Ayi Kwei Armah Speaks."** *West Africa*, no. 4128 (9-15 December 1996): 1923-1924

An interview with the distinguished Ghanaian writer Ayi Kwei Armah, now resident in Senegal, and who established his own publishing company called Per Ankh, which stands for 'The House of Life' in ancient Egyptian.

1348 Ku-Mesu, Katalin Egri **"African Literature Survival Outside the Real of Large World Publishers: Illusion or Reality."** *Mots Pluriels,* no. 5 (1998) http://www.arts.uwa.edu.au/MotsPluriels/MP598ke.html [13/03/08]
Looks at the different types of African literature (oral, popular, African language literatures, and modern African writing), the African reading public, the African writer's choice of where to work and publish, and "the publishing factor", i.e. the state of indigenous book industries, which largely determines whether authors can get published, and outside Africa, where "the second generation of African writers hardly seems to be published by large publishers."

1349 Larson, Charles R. **The Ordeal of the African Writer.** London: Zed Books, 2001. 192 pp.
This book is about the problems and obstacles that African writers still encounter in their attempt to get published. It is an interesting, informed, and well-documented study that combines writers' own testimony (based on responses to questionnaires) and factual investigation in order to explore the problem of the "ordeal" of the African writer. The author deals with some of the issues which confront African writers today, including issues of readership and which language to employ, the question of literacy and audience, and the inadequate number of publishing houses on the continent — as well as other obstacles such as censorship, imprisonment, exile, and worse. Several of the chapters shed new light on the publishing history, and author-publisher relations, of some African writers, both with publishers in the countries in the North as well as with African publishers, and the book includes a chapter on "African Writers and the Quest for Publication", examining the careers of a number of African writers. An overview of "African Publishers, African Publishing" is provided in chapter four. It includes a discussion of the sometimes not very happy relations between African writers and African publishers, and also looks at the obstacles African publishing houses face, and how they treat their authors. The book concludes with a set of recommendations setting out what Charles Larson believes can be done to improve the plight of the African writer, and particularly the next generation of African writers. He also proposes the establishment of a pan-African publishing house, funded by people and institutions both from Africa and the West, with an unpaid advisory board predominantly from the African continent: "crucial to the entire proposal is the belief that Africans should be in control of the publication of their own writers and that the degree of dependence on the West (both financial and editorial) be determined by Africans themselves."
Reviews:
African Arts Summer 2004
Online: http://www.findarticles.com/p/articles/mi_m0438/is_2_37/ai_n7580175 [13/03/08]
The African Book Publishing Record vol. 27, no. 4, 2001
African Studies Review September 2003
Online: http://findarticles.com/p/articles/mi_qa4106/is_200309/ai_n9241345 [13/03/08]

Bellagio Publishing Network Newsletter, no. 28, November 2001 (extracts from the book, on Cyprian Ekwensi's publishing experience)
Online:
http://bellagiopublishingnetwork.com/newsletter29/larson.htm [13/03/08]
Interventions: International Journal of Postcolonial Studies vol. 5, no. 3, August 2003
Journal of Cultural Studies vol. 5, no. 1, 2003
Mail & Guardian (South Africa) February 13, 2002
Online: http://www.chico.mweb.co.za/art/2002/2002feb/020213-great.html
[13/03/08]
Le Monde Diplomatique April 2002
Online: http://www.monde-diplomatique.fr/2002/04/WABERI/16397
[13/03/08]
Times Literary Supplement February 7, 2003

1350 Lawal-Solarin, O.M. **"Creating a Conducive Environment for Authorship: Contribution by a Publisher."** In *Creating a Conducive Environment for Book Publishing*, edited by Chukwuemeka Ike. Awka, Nigeria: Nigerian Book Foundation, 1996, 174-183.
Also published in *The Publisher* 4, no. 1 (September 1996): 6-8.
A publisher's perspective on the debate, and a response to Ike (*see* entry ➜ **1344** above), by the [then] President of the ➜ **Nigerian Publishers' Association (739)**. Examines the concept of authorship and what constitutes "a conducive environment", and cautions against a tendency to compare the Nigerian situation with that prevailing in countries in the North, where disposable income is much higher. Also looks at the role of government and at author-publisher relations and says publishers "must now protest cruelty to Nigerian publishers by authors who have nothing good to say about publishers." Reports about the Nigerian Publishers' Association Code of Conduct and refutes the charges of non-payment of royalties. Argues that the economic crisis in the country has had a detrimental effect on every aspect of the book industry: authorship, publishing, printing and distribution, and that it is up to the government to create an enabling environment for the book industries.

1351 Lawal-Solarin, O.M. **"Author-Publisher Relationship: A Publisher's Perspective."** In *Women Empowerment Through Publishing. Papers Presented at the Second Nigeria International Book Fair, 8-12 May, 2003.* Lagos: Nigerian Book Fair Trust [c/o Literamed Publications Ltd., PMB 21068, Ikeja, Lagos, Nigeria], 2003, 94-102.
A Nigerian publisher's view – and to some extent an update to the previous entry, *see* ➜ **1350** above – on the often acrimonious relationship between authors and their publishers. Lawal-Solarin states that publishing is a business, and authors will need to recognize that publishing in Africa, and particularly in Nigeria, where all materials required for printing need to be imported, is both a highly capital-intensive and risky business, which calls for great caution by publishers in selecting manuscripts for publication; and that non-fiction authors inevitably will always have an advantage over those producing creative writing, as there is likely to be an assured market for educational books. As a publisher,

Lawal-Solarin believes that authors frequently lack a proper understanding of the book business, and will need to become better informed, and which in turn might lead to better author-publisher relations.

1352 Lindfors, Bernth **"Amos Tutuola's Search for a Publisher."** *Journal of Commonwealth Literature* 17, no. 1 (1982): 90-106.
A fascinating account of Nigerian writer Amos Tutuola's quest for a publisher and his subsequent rise to literary fame, first for his story "The Wild Hunter in the Bush of Ghost", and thereafter for *The Palm-Wine Drinkard and His Dead Palm-Wine Tapster in Deads Town.* This was originally submitted to Lutterworth Press of the United Society for Christian Literature, who felt they were unable to publish it themselves but passed on the manuscript to Thomas Nelson & Sons (who rejected it outright), and eventually to Richard de la Mare of Faber and Faber. Faber published it in 1952, and a US edition was published by Grove Press in 1953. Drawing on archives held by Faber and Faber, the article reproduces extracts from the extensive correspondence between Tutuola and his publisher, relating both to the publication of *The Palm-Wine Drinkard* as well as other titles that followed and were published by Faber. There is also correspondence between Faber and Faber and their external readers who were asked to assess the manuscripts. It is evident from all this correspondence that Faber – contrary to some unsubstantiated allegations which appeared in the Nigerian press in 1978 which claimed that Tutuola was cheated by his publishers – always acted with justness and generosity in all their dealings with Tutuola.

1353 Low, Gail **"The Natural Artist: Publishing Amos Tutuola's *The Palm-Wine Drinkard* in Postwar Britain."** *Research in African Literatures* 37, no. 4 (Winter 2006): 15-33.
Explores the interesting correspondence between Amos Tutola and his publisher in the UK (Faber and Faber), in order to assess the value Faber placed on the manuscript, and to explore the part they played in the shaping and presentation of Tutuola's book. In particular, the paper seeks to investigate the interface between the manuscript's alleged importance as an anthropological artifice and/or as a literary product. The author examines aspects of Faber's decisions in terms of manuscript editing and their attempts to preserve Tutuola's original style and prose, the book's cover design, how they handled publicity for the book, and its critical reception. (Dylan Thomas, writing in *The Observer,* gave it a highly laudatory review, calling it a "brief, thronged, grisly and bewitching story". English and American critics alike hailed it as a remarkable success.) The article also includes some discussion of the publishing situation of Anglophone African writing in the late 1950's and early 1960s, when publishing outlets for African writers were largely confined to a small number of independent British publishers, who had begun to show an interest in African writing, aiming to bring it to a wider metropolitan public. *Note:* for a fuller account of the publishing history of Tutuola's *Palm-Wine Drinkard,* and his rise to literary fame, *see also* Bernth Lindfors's account **"Amos Tutuola in Search of a Publisher"**, entry ➔ **1352**.

1354 Maja-Pearce, Adewale **"Starting Out."** In *A Handbook for African Writers*, edited by James Gibbs. Oxford: Hans Zell Publishers, 1988, 209-212.
A Nigerian writer and journalist describes a young writer's first steps towards becoming a professional writer, the various crises he went through as he developed his career as a writer and sought publishing outlets for his work, and how he set about making a living out of writing.

1355 Maja-Pearce, Adewale **"In Pursuit of Excellence: Thirty Years of the Heinemann African Writers Series."** *Research in African Literatures* 23, no. 4 (Winter 1992): 126-132.
A detailed description of the history and success of the African Writers Series published by Heinemann and begun by Alan Hill. The series (now discontinued) began with four titles in 1962 and eventually published over two hundred titles. Examines the kind of books published and the evolution of African writing, which can clearly be seen through these books. Adewale Maja-Pearce was for a time series editor of the AWS in the early 1990s.

1356 Ndiaye, Ndéné **"The Author and his Problems: The Case of Publishing in French-speaking Africa."** In *International Publishing Today. Problems and prospects.* Delhi: The Bookman's Club, 1984, 204-207.
Explores the problems of publishing from the perspective of the author, with particular reference to the copyright agreement established in Senegal with Nouvelles Editions Africaines.

1357 Nyamnjoh, Francis B. **"Pipers, Tunes and Global Hierarchies in African Publishing."** *Bookmark. News Magazine of the South African Booksellers' Association* 10, (July- September 2006): 29-30.
Also published separately online:
http://www.nyamnjoh.com/2006/08/pipers_tunes_an.html#more
[14/03/08]
Drawing on his own personal experience as a novelist and his dealings with two South African publishers and their manuscript reviewers, the author contends that "most sub-Saharan African publishers north of the Limpopo might have the will to promote alternative pipers and tunes, but they simply do not have the means to do so – or to survive doing so. As for the leading publishers, who are mostly South African and white, the tunes they call are preponderantly Western even when the stories and scholarship are geographically located in South Africa. Almost systematically, South African publishers reject pipers and tunes from north of the Limpopo."

Ofeimun, Odia **"A Cultural Economy of the Book in Africa"** *see* ➔ Section **2, General, comparative, and regional studies: Africa: General studies** entry **300**

1358 Onwueme, Tess **"To the Would-be African Female Writer: Husband Yourself First!"** In *The African Writers' Handbook*, edited by

James Gibbs and Jack Mapanje. Oxford: African Books Collective Ltd., 1999, 38-42.
The Nigerian playwright offers some advice to women writers who hope to break into print, and recounts some of her experiences in her dealings with publishers, which included both small Nigerian imprints and major international companies.

1359 Osofisan, Femi **"An Experience of Publishing in Africa."** In *The African Writers' Handbook*, edited by James Gibbs and Jack Mapanje. Oxford: African Books Collective Ltd., 1999, 32-37.
The distinguished Nigerian playwright, scholar, and actor Femi Osofisan has published extensively in Nigeria, with no fewer than 13 Nigerian publishers. Here he explains, with good humour, "this wayward and erratic shift" of allegiances, and why it was that virtually every year he had to turn to a different publisher for his work, besieged as he was by aspiring publishers looking for new work "and promising the whole heaven in remuneration." Promises, as time passed, that would collapse—and "I would turn away, ready to be plucked by the next sweet-tongued adventurer." It was not a happy experience for the most part, royalties were laughably meagre and infrequent – "with the annual money from all the books together I could not replace one of the tyres for my car!" – production standards very poor, there was virtually no marketing or promotion, and, worst, the books could not be found on the shelves of either bookshops or other retail outlets. An attempt at distributing the books himself was something less than successful in business terms, as most of the time he ended up giving out the books for free. However, despite these frustrating times, Osofisan feels compelled to continue to publish at home (although now also publishing elsewhere). And there is a glimmer of hope, the experience thus far with publisher no. 13 (Mosuro Publishers, Ibadan) looks promising, and who, Osofisan reports, has already paid him his royalty entitlements for the entire print run, before even the first copy was sold.

1360 Osundare, Niyi **"The Publisher and the Poet."** In *The African Writers' Handbook*, edited by James Gibbs and Jack Mapanje. Oxford: African Books Collective Ltd., 1999, 17-21.
The Award-winning Nigerian poet recounts his experiences with placing poetry with various publishers, a genre that "provokes goose pimples in publishing circles", and for which the standard initial reaction from publishers is "poetry doesn't sell". Osundare published his poetry with no less than eight publishers, both UK-based and Nigerian publishers. While some Nigerian publishers and editors were very supportive, when it came to royalty accounting the experience was not a happy one. Four of them never submitted statements or paid any royalties, and "not one of all my Nigerian publishers has declared how many copies of my books they have been selling outside Nigeria, and how much has accrued from sales."

1361 Osundare, Niyi **"The Missing Link: Views on the Nigerian International Book Fair held in Abuja, May 2002."** *Bellagio Publishing Network Newsletter*, no. 31 (November 2002): 6-8.
Online:
http://www.bellagiopublishingnetwork.com/newsletter31/osundare.htm

[14/03/08]
Originally published in *Newswatch* 29 July 2002.
Offers some views about the first Nigerian International Book Fair held in Abuja in May 2002. The author is scathingly critical about the lack of active support for the Fair by the Nigerian government, despite the fact that the top brass of Nigeria's political leadership had earlier pledged to attend, and provide moral and financial support for the book fair. He also bemoans the fact that so few writers attended the Fair and that, unlike book fairs elsewhere, the organizers failed to show much interest in involving writers in the Fair and the various associated events, which were largely dominated by publishers and booksellers "in the fervent belief that the books which formed the centre of their business must have dropped from heaven in effortless circumstances....publishers [came] with a retinue of salesmen and women but not a single author." Osundare, one of Africa's best-known contemporary authors, is also highly critical of Nigerian publishers in terms of author-publisher relations and poor royalty accounting practices, and states that the recently published ➔ **African Writers' Handbook (2507)** has comprehensively grappled with these issues, "but even many of the Nigerian publishers who participated in the making of that historic document have flouted every letter of it."

1362   Petersen, Kirsten Holst **"Working with Chinua Achebe: The African Writers Series."** *Kunapipi* 12, no. 2 (1990): 149-159.
Contains the substance of two interviews, one with James Currey and Keith Sambrook and one with Alan Hill recorded in London in August 1990. Alan Hill was director of Heinemann Educational Books, and he reviews his life in publishing in Africa from 1959 when he went to West Africa. Keith Sambrook joined Alan Hill at Heinemann in 1963 and remembers the great African writers of the 1960s. James Currey describes his particular involvement with Chinua Achebe as a part of his role with the Heinemann African Writers Series.

1363   Ripken, Peter **"Creating a Conducive Environment for Authorship."**
In *Creating a Conducive Environment for Book Publishing*, edited by
Chukwuemeka Ike. Awka, Nigeria: Nigerian Book Foundation, 1996, 138-145.
A keynote address delivered to a ➔ **Nigerian Book Foundation (738)** conference in 1996 by the director of the Frankfurt-based ➔ **Society for the Promotion of African, Asian and Latin American Literatures (64).** Regrets the fact that much of the debate about African writing takes place outside Africa, and "does not reach those in Africa who want to write, and want to write better than those who have written before them."

1364   Ruppert, Sophie **"L'Harmattan: Publishing on the Third World."**
Research in African Literatures 22, no. 4 (Winter 1991): 156-159.
Gives a brief history of the Paris-based publishing house L'Harmattan which was founded by Denis Pryen who had been a missionary in Africa. Discusses the commitment of the company to "an unequivocal support for the self-determination and ideological independence of third-world peoples." Provides details of the list

published by L'Harmattan and applauds the courage shown by the firm in publishing works considered too controversial by other publishers.

1365 Schifano, Elsa **L'édition africaine en France: portraits.** Paris: L'Harmattan, 2003. 238 pp.
Describes the changing landscape of African literature publishing in France over the years, the difficulties African writers have faced in getting published, the reception of African literature in France, and the dissemination of that publishing output both in France and in Africa. Also includes some discussion about the problems and challenges of literary publishing within Africa, and the distribution of African writing by both traditional and unconventional methods.

1366 Tlali, Miriam **"The Story of my First Book:** *Between Two Worlds.***"** In *Proceedings of the First Annual National Conference on Women in Writing – Beyond 2000,* edited by Tembeka Mbobo, Joyce Siwani, and Charlotte Witbooi. Kwa-Zuma, South Africa: Centre for Cultural and Artistic Expression [PO Box 908, Kwa-Zuma 1868], 2000, 31-34.
A moving account of the publishing history of Miriam Tlali's (largely autobiographical) first novel, originally entitled *Between Two Worlds,* which examines the life of a black woman working in a white-owned business in Johannesburg. Although completed in 1969 – and after being turned down by several major South African publishers – it was only finally published by Ravan Press in 1975. It appeared with the title *Muriel at Metropolitan* and it had to be published in expurgated form in order to circumvent the draconian censorship laws at the time. Miriam Tlali was the first black woman writer to publish a novel in English inside [then apartheid] South Africa. A second novel, *Amandla,* followed in 1980 and enjoyed considerable success before being banned by the government.

1367 Umomadu, N.O. **"A Response to Creating a Conducive Environment for Authorship."** In *Creating a Conducive Environment for Book Publishing,* edited by Chukwuemeka Ike. Awka, Nigeria: Nigerian Book Foundation, 1996, 146-159
A response to Ike (➔ *see* entry **1344** above) sounding a few caveats, especially about calls for action on the part of the government, which "given our well known Nigerian attitude... will sound like the indistinguishable cacophony of animal and reptilian voices on a starless night." The author is scathing about ostentatious book launches in Nigeria, and equally critical about Nigerian publishers. He claims "the books Nigerian publishers publish never get promoted", royalties are not "correct", and royalty advances non-existent; the retail book trade is in a sorry state, book prices have sky-rocketed and piracy is rife. Public libraries are unable to assume an active role in book development because they are grossly underfunded and their shelves are mostly empty.

1368 Unwin, Vicky **"The African Writers Series Celebrates 30 Years."** *Southern African Review of Books* (March/April 1993): 3-4.
Assesses the impact of the Heinemann African Writers Series and predicts a bright future for African literature.

1369 Vera, Yvonne **"Revelations and Reversals."** In *The African Writers'*
Handbook, edited by James Gibbs and Jack Mapanje. Oxford: African
Books Collective Ltd., 1999, 28-31.

The late Yvonne Vera, the renowned Zimbabwean novelist, narrates her career as a
writer, and the happy and productive relationship with her [then] editor and
publisher at Baobab Books, Irene Staunton—an ideal writer-publisher bonding, rarely
experienced by African writers.

1370 Zell, Hans M. **"The African Writer and his Publisher."** In *Jaw-Bones*
and Umbilical Cords. A Selection of Papers Presented at the 3rd Janheinz Jahn
Symposium 1979 and the 4th Janheinz Jahn Symposium 1982, edited by Ulla
Schild. Berlin: Reimer, 1985, 35-51.

An overview of African literature focusing on publishing in Africa together with a
brief review of publishing of African writing in Europe and the United States.
Concentrates on three major topics: the role and activities of multinational
publishers, the publication of creative writing in African languages, and the question
of audience and readership.

1371 Zell, Hans M. **"African Publishers: Mostly 'Liars and Cheats'?"**
African Publishing Review 4, no. 3 (May/June 1995): 14-16.

Also published in *The African Writers' Handbook*, edited by James Gibbs
and Jack Mapanje. Oxford: African Books Collective Ltd., 1999, 94-97;
and also published in German: "Afrika: Verleger - 'zumeist Lüger und
Betrüger'?" *Literatur Nachrichten*, no. 45 (April-Juni 1995): 9-10.

Finds that many African writers are distrustful and have a low opinion of their
publishers, who are often accused of lacking transparency, being exploitative, and
not being open enough in their relations with authors. Argues that although authors'
pronouncements of this nature must be taken with a good dose of scepticism, some
African publishers have a case to answer; and that publishers should learn that
protecting authors' interests, and openness with authors, will pay dividends in the
long term and will lead to much improved relationships and author loyalty.

Book and journals assistance and donation programmes

Note: this section also includes a number of articles on what has been
termed "the African book famine".

1372 Balarabe, Ahmed Abdu **"Nigerian University Libraries and the**
World Bank Loan." *Third World Libraries* 5, no. 2 (Spring 1995): 31-45.

A critical examination of the ➔ **World Bank (124)** Federal Universities Adjustment
Loan Project, for the provision of books and journals, information technology
facilities and equipment, and staff development in Nigerian libraries. Reviews how
the project has benefited Nigerian university libraries, but also reports about
problems of journals supply and book procurement, caused by lack of current

selection tools and inaccessibility to major international bibliographic databases, and problems with, and disagreements among, suppliers.

1373 Barnett, Stanley A. **"American Book Aid: A Critical Assessment of Two Major Programs of the 1950s-1970s."** In *Publishing and Development in the Third World*, edited by Philip G. Altbach London: Hans Zell Publishers, 1992, 325-348.
Examines the major characteristics, strengths, weaknesses and impacts of two American-sponsored programmes that had a considerable impact on book and library development in the Third World between 1950 and 1970; one organized by Franklin Book Programs Inc. and the other by the Central Book Activities Unit of the Agency for International Development.

1374 Blue, Sophie "**Book Aid International – Relieving the Book Crisis in Developing Countries.**" *Library Review* 43, no. 2 (March 2004): 37-45
Describes the activities of ➔ **Book Aid International/BAI (38)**, the UK book charity, with particular emphasis on their supplying books to meet the specific requirements of recipient libraries in developing countries. Gives a number of specific examples of aid projects providing books to meet different needs within developing countries, and discusses the importance of book aid to those countries.

1375 Book Aid International **Annual Review.** [published annually, latest is *Annual Review 2006*]. London: Book Aid International, var. pp. print and online
Online: (latest report only)
http://www.bookaid.org/resources/downloads/annual_reviews/Annual_Review_2006.pdf [14/03/08]
Annual report of the major UK book charity ➔ **Book Aid International/BAI (38)**, which provides an overview of its work each year, supporting libraries and literate environments in the countries of the South. During the course of 2006 it sent over half a million high-quality books and journal to developing countries, including a large number in sub-Saharan Africa, supporting learning for thousands of people of all ages, both within and outside formal education. BAI is also providing advocacy and support for the book chain in Africa, and has supported indigenous African publishing and the book trade through various schemes and initiatives.
Note: BAI's latest set of annual reports and accounts can be found at
http://www.bookaid.org/resources/downloads/annual_accounts/Accounts_2006.pdf [14/03/08]; its *BookMark* newsletter is at
http://www.bookaid.org/resources/downloads/bookmark/BookMark0207.pdf [14/03/08], while the archive of its ➔ **BookLinks (157)** networking newsletter is at http://www.bookaid.org/cms.cgi/site/whatwedo/booklinks.htm. [14/03/08]

1376 Books for Africa **Literacy in Africa. A Partnership Model. Books for Africa Operations Handbook.** St. Paul, MN: Books for Africa, n.d.16 pp.
Online: http://www.booksforafrica.org/pubs/Literacy_in_Africa.doc [15/03/08]

→ **Books for Africa /BFA (42)** recycles books from the American schools and book distribution systems to African schools, libraries and non-governmental organizations. The books are donated, the labour is largely voluntary, and the only major costs are those of transportation. The other major necessity is a distribution network on the receiving end that ensures the books get into the hands of the readers. This handbook was developed in response to requests from other organizations interested in participating with BFA in ending the book famine in Africa. It outlines the history and organizational structure of the BFA model, and the different partnership options.

1377   Buchan, Amanda **"Book Development in the Third World: The British Experience."** In *Publishing and Development in the Third World*, edited by Philip G. Altbach.   London: Hans Zell Publishers, 1992, 349-363.
Traces the history, influences and experiences within the historical and socio-economic framework of British book development activities, and the evolution of its policy.

1378   Childs, William M. **American Donated Books Abroad. A Guide to Distributing Organizations.** Washington: American International Book Development Council, 1989. 56 pp.
Surveys the programmes and activities of 36 private voluntary organizations engaged in collecting and distributing American donated books abroad.

1379   Crowder, Michael **"The Book Crisis: Africa's Other Famine."** In *Africa Bibliography 1985*, compiled by Hector Blackhurst.   Manchester: Manchester University Press, 1986, xvi-xxi.
Contrasts the book famine in Africa with the well publicized food and technology famine and states that this "insidious famine...may mortgage Africa's future for several generations to come." Discusses the reasons why education has not been the "cure-all" expected, partly due to the brain-drain of intellectuals but also due to the intellectual starvation of those who stayed behind.

1380   Curry, Ann; Tanya Thiessen, and Lorraine Kelley **"Library Aid to Developing Countries in Times of Globalization: A Literature Review."** *World Libraries* 12, no. 2 (Fall 2002): 15-36.
Online: http://www.worlib.org/vol12no2/curry_v12n2.shtml [14/03/08]
A useful review of the literature pertaining to library aid and globalization, including book donation/distribution programmes, and support for local publishers. The study focuses on two questions: what are the major needs of libraries in the developing countries? And whether some of those needs are, or are not, being met. Despite anecdotal evidence gathered by the authors during visits to developing countries, that globalization has affected the type of library aid now needed, no research could be found to substantiate this. It is the contention of the authors, however, that lessons learned from the existing research about more traditional "book aid" remain very relevant to library aid relationships affected by globalization, and that these lessons should be used as the basis for further research that incorporates this new phenomenon of internationalization. "Clearly, in order to

develop effective programs that make a difference within the new global economy and information world, further research on the challenges and opportunities of library aid is needed."

1381   Directory of Book Donation Programs.
http://www.albany.edu/~dlafonde/Global/bookdonation.htm [14/03/08]
Based on a directory originally published in 1992 and prepared for the (US) ➔ **Africana Librarians Council's (26)** Book Donation Committee, this is an annotated listing of book donation programmes active in Africa, primarily those in the US. It provides a brief description of each organization's range of activities, full address details including Web site, and contact personnel. An introductory section sets out guidelines for good practice in book donation projects and offers some suggestions for both recipients and donors. The directory, currently maintained by Deborah M. LaFond, Social Sciences Bibliographer at the University of Albany, was last updated in February 2006. (*See also* entry ➔ **1420**)

1382   Doyle, Robert P. "Donation Programs." In *International Leads.*
[International Relations Round Table, American Library Association]
Chicago: American Library Association, 1994. 8 pp.
Describes some of the issues involved in donation programs and lists some of the major North American organizations involved in donation programmes, with short profiles of their activities.

1383   Durand, Rosamaria "Book by Book...the Making of an International Development Agency." *Bellagio Publishing Network Newsletter*, no. 5 (March 1993): 3-4.
Traces the history and establishment of the ➔ **International Book Bank/IBB (70)**, the Baltimore-based book donation organization, and reports about the IBB's 'Dialogue of Partners Workshop' held in September 1992.

1384   Dyck, Robert "Canadian Experiences with Encouraging Book Supply and Publishing in the Third World." In *Publishing and Development in the Third World*, edited by Philip G. Altbach. London: Hans Zell Publishers, 1992, 381-401.
Quantifies the extent of Canadian assistance that has been given to support and encourage book supply in the Third World, and reviews the experiences of three different approaches in order to focus on the lessons that have been learned.

1385   Friends-of-the Book Foundation Friends-of-the Book Foundation.
Nairobi: Friends-of-the Book Foundation n.d. [1996?]. 25 pp.
A profile of the Nairobi-based ➔ **Friends-of-the-Book Foundation (578)**, a non-profit organization established to help alleviate the book famine in East Africa and to promote functional literacy. The organization facilitates the publication/translation (both in Kiswahili and in English) of key books for the reading public, and makes them available at affordable prices. This booklet sets out the background to the

establishment of the organization, its principal objectives, details of books published to date and those in the pipeline.

1386   Ghana Book Trust **Ghana Book Trust Annual Report 2005-2006.** Accra: Ghana Book Trust, 2006. 51 pp.
http://www.ghana-book-trust.org/Documents/GBT%20ANNUAL%20REPORT%202005-2006-FINAL.pdf [14/03/08]
The ➔ **Ghana Book Trust (539)** is an NGO and book donation organization that promotes literacy, library development, and the supply of locally published and imported books to rural schools and libraries in the urban areas. Its works in partnership with ➔ **CODE (48)** and the ➔ **Sabre Foundation (110)**. This is its latest report and covers activities for the 2005-2006 periods, and also includes an overview of various CODE projects in Ghana.

1387   Groves, T. **"Information Sharing: Getting Journals and Books to Developing Countries."** *British Medical Journal* 307, no. 6919 (18-25 December 1993): 1614-1617.
Describes the work and projects of the ➔ **International Network for the Availability of Scientific Publications (81)**, originally set up to assist individuals and organizations who wish to donate and ships books and journals to recipients in developing countries. Also reviews the activities other organizations involved in similar book and journal donation programmes.

1388   Harrity, Sara **"Extracting the Gold' from Book Surpluses."** *Logos. The Journal of the World Book Community* 5, no. 3 (1994): 153-57.
Online:
http://www.atypon-link.com/LOG/doi/pdf/10.2959/logo.1994.5.3.153
The [former] Director of ➔ **Book Aid International (38)** sets out the history and background of this UK book charity, its policies for a variety of book donation programmes, how they are evaluated, how recipients are selected, and how it collaborates with other organizations such as the ➔ **African Books Collective Ltd. (3)**, BAI's partner in the 'Intra-African Book Support Scheme'. This scheme aims to support African publishers by buying African-published books through ABC to provide much-needed culturally relevant books to schools, libraries, and community groups in selected countries in Africa.

1389   Harrity, Sara, and Maggie Gardiner **"Book Aid International - Bridging the Gap."** *Public Library Journal* 9, no. 1 (January/February 1994): 23-24.
Interview with two senior members of staff of ➔ **Book Aid International (38)** in which they describe the work of BAI in channelling donated books to Africa and other developing countries, and describe some new initiatives being embarked upon by the organization.

1390 Harrity, Sara **"Book Aid International's Role in Community Access to Information."** In *Access to Information. Indaba 97.* Harare: Zimbabwe International Book Fair Trust, 1997, 155-158.
Describes the development of ➔ **Book Aid International (38)** as an organization, its aims, objectives and activities, and its role and contribution in promoting community access to information.

1391 International Book Bank/Dialogue of Partners **Donated Book Programs. A Dialogue of Partners Handbook. A Book Based on the Proceedings of the Dialogue of Partners Workshop, September 14-16, 1992**. Washington, DC: The Center for the Book, Library of Congress, 1993. 104 pp.
A handbook for all those involved in donated book programmes. Aims to eliminate the practice of book "dumping", thus ensuring that all donated book programmes are demand-led and that they take into consideration the expressed needs and interests of those who will be using these resources. Includes profiles of the organizations that participated in the Dialogue of Partners Workshop.
Reviews:
The African Book Publishing Record vol. 20, no.1, 1994

1392 International Network for the Availability of Scientific Publications (INASP) comp. **INASP Directory 2002/2003.** Oxford: International Network for the Availability of Scientific Publications, 2002. 350 pp.
Online: http://www.inasp.info/file/202/directory.html [14/03/08]
While not specifically focusing on Africa, this directory from the ➔**International Network for the Availability of Scientific Publications (81)** is a useful resource as it provides detailed information on almost 400 agencies, organizations, institutions, learned societies, professional associations, donors, and foundations involved in activities that support the production, access and/or dissemination of information and knowledge in or between developing countries. It covers both subject-specific organizations in particular areas of the sciences, the humanities and social sciences, as well as organizations that specialize in library and book development, and for both groups this includes details of book and journal assistance schemes operated, or other type of support provided. Information is very full, and for most entries includes name and address, telephone/fax numbers, email address and Web site, contact personnel, aims and objectives and/or a mission statement, target audience, countries of operation, current activities, publications (if applicable), and future plans.
Note: no further print editions have been published following the 2002/2003 edition, but entries are now continuously updated in the online version. The electronic version can be browsed by the sector each organization works in, and each database entry offers organizational and contact details, profile details, and information about activities. Organizations can also be viewed by country, or searches can be conducted covering the entire database.

1393 Kats, Ivan **"The Story of Obor, or, Assisting Autonomous Publishing."** In *Publishing and Development in the Third World*, edited by Philip G. Altbach. London: Hans Zell Publishers, 1992, 365-380.

Traces the history, publishing activities, and experience of the Obor Foundation – a book and publishing assistance organization largely active in Indonesia – and suggests its might serve as a model for other organizations, and that its successful formula might be replicated, or adapted, in other parts of the developing world.

1394 Levey, Lisbeth **Sub-Saharan Africa Journal Distribution Program. A Profile of Recipient Institutions.** Washington, DC: American Association for the Advancement of Science, 1989. 9 pp.
Also published in *ASA News* (July/September 1989): 24-27.
Explores ways in which access to essential scientific and engineering journals can be made easier for African libraries and scholars, and provides profiles of recipient institutions.

1395 Lindfors, Bernth **"Desert Gold: Irrigation Schemes for Ending the Book Drought."** *Matatu*, no. 10 (1993): 27-39.
Also published in *Long Drums and Canons. Teaching and Researching African Literatures*, by Bernth Lindfors, Trenton, NJ: Africa World Press, 1995, 123-135.
A detailed examination of the causes of the book famine in Africa, and the effect of this on writers as well as on indigenous publishing, libraries, and on the education systems from primary to university level. The author suggests some solutions that might help towards relieving the book famine, including the active participation of academics both in the West and in Africa. Concludes "anyone who writes or edits a book on African literature ought to see to it that a copy of that book is given to every African university or at the very least to every university library in parts of Africa that are discussed in the book. In a sense ... it is an intellectual debt owed to Africa by the Africanist scholar."

Loric, Laurent **"Donor Support for Book Imports"** *see* ➜ **Rights sales, licensing, and publishing partnerships** entry **2245**

1396 Macpherson, John **"The Commonwealth Book Development Programme."** *Journal of the Royal Society* (July 1979): 481-489.
Discusses the practical contributions made by the [now discontinued] Commonwealth Book Development Programme, and describes problems experienced over the funding of training. The author believes that the assistance offered by the programme will continue to be of significant help in assisting Commonwealth developing countries to acquire more books.

1397 Mcharazo, Alli A.S., and Anthony Olden **"The Intra-African Book Support Scheme and Publishing and Library Supply in Kenya and Tanzania."** *The New Review of Information and Library Research*, no. 2 (1996): 179-194.
The Intra-African Book Support Scheme (IABS) was set up in 1991 to support African readers and publishers through improving the distribution of African-published materials to libraries in Africa. The recipient-request led scheme was launched by ➜

African Books Collective Ltd. (3) and → Book Aid International (38), and enjoyed donor support. This study looks at its impact in Kenya and Tanzania, two neighbouring countries in East Africa who have different language policies and publishing backgrounds. A number of publishers and librarians in the two countries were interviewed, as were ABC and BAI staff in the UK. Records and files were consulted were possible. The study concludes that an expansion of the scheme is desirable as the demand for books supplied under the scheme is enormous, but the quantities shipped are still small. Calls on librarians to take the initiative and make a much stronger case for the importance of books and libraries, and to acquire local and African-published material more systematically. The authors also suggest that the possibility of establishing a Kiswahili Books Collective should be investigated.

1398 Membrey, David J., ed. **Nothing to Read? The Crisis of Document Provision in the Third World.** Birmingham: International and Comparative Librarianship Group Library Association, 1990. 107 pp.
The papers from the seventh conference of the International and Comparative Librarianship Group of the UK Library Association, held in Birmingham in September 1989, which examined the book crisis, shortage of reading materials, and the funding of library services in the countries of the South, with many parts of the less developed world turning into virtually bookless societies.

1399 Nwankwo, Victor **"Book Famine in Africa: A Nigerian Case Study."** In *Communication Industry in Nigeria. The Crisis of Publications*, edited by A. Tom Adaba, Ololeka Ajia, and Ikechukwu Nwosu. Nairobi: African Council on Communication Education, 1988, 2-21.
Contends that "as serious as the food famine is, it is less devastating than the pervasive absence of books" and presents a Nigerian perspective within a wider West African view of the book famine problem. Examines where the key areas of need for books are, the impact of the famine both educationally and socially, and offers possible solutions both for the long and short term.

1400 Newton, Diana **"A New Canadian Program: The International Publishing Partnership."** *Bellagio Publishing Network Newsletter*, no. 15 (November 1995): 13-14.
Reports about a new not-for-profit initiative, the International Publishing Partnership (IPP), funded by the Canadian International Development Agency (CIDA) and the Canadian publishing industry, which "seeks to offer an alternative to the status quo of past projects designed by non-publishers, often unfamiliar with the nature and fundamental principles of publishing."

1401 Orimalade, Oluronke **"Book Subsidy Schemes: An International Perspective."** In *Making Books Available and Affordable*, edited by Ezenwa-Ohaeto. Awka, Nigeria: Nigerian Book Foundation, 1995, 8-17.
Also published in *African Publishing Review* 3, no. 6 (November/December 1994): 1-2; and in *The Publisher* 3, no. 1 (January 1995): 22-23.

Examines the nature of book subsidy schemes in Europe, North America, Australia, India, and in Africa.

1402 Otiende, James E. **"Friends-of-the Book Foundation Achieves Autonomy."** *Bellagio Publishing Network Newsletter*, no. 12 (December 1994): 12-14.
Reports about the work of the Obor Foundation in Kenya and its ➔ **Friends-of-the Book Foundation (578).** The Foundation makes available or subsidizes the manufacturing costs of low-cost reprints, translations or adaptations of urgently needed foreign titles, as well as assisting with the publication of booklets and readers in Kenyan languages.

1403 Priestley, Carol **Higher Education Learning Resource Material, Books and Journals: The Needs of Universities in Africa.** London: International African Institute, 1989. [not paginated]
Assesses some of the trends in library and book development [as at the late 1980s], analyzing some problem areas and describing some activities which have a potential for donor involvement. In two parts, the first on libraries and the second on book development. Stresses the importance that support for libraries and book development should be considered in the light of the overall education and the particular needs of the book sector for each country.

1404 Priestley, Carol **"University Book Famine Initiative: The International Campus Book Link."** *African Affairs* 88, no. 353 (1989): 583-584.
Discusses the aims of the International Campus Book Link (ICBL) in providing a clearing house to coordinate and facilitate matching of requests to relevant donors, as well as providing efficient collection, shipment and distribution mechanisms.

1405 Priestley, Carol, comp. **"The Book Famine: A Selective Directory for Book and Journal Assistance to Universities in Africa."** *Africa* 60, no. 1 (1990): 135-148.
Describes some of the major book and journal donation schemes in existence [as at 1990]. Provides profiles of agencies that respond on a request-led basis in the tertiary education sector, and thereafter lists bilateral schemes by country, multilateral programmes in alphabetical order, and offers some suggestions how to make use of the schemes.

1406 Priestley, Carol **Commonwealth Higher Education Support Scheme. Study on a Commonwealth Journal Distribution Programme**. London: Commonwealth Secretariat, 1992. 38 pp.
The final report on the Commonwealth Higher Education Support Scheme (CHESS) reviewing arrangements for journal supply to developing countries, an analysis of needs in this area, supply of Australian, British and Canadian journal subscriptions, provision of indigenous journals, and suggestions for the future.

1407 Priestley, Carol **"Focus on INASP. International Network for the Availability of Scientific Publications."** *Information Development* 9, no. 1/2 (March/June 1993): 87-89.
Profiles the work of the ➜ **International Network for the Availability of Scientific Publications/INASP (81)**, a cooperative network of donors and partners which aims to strengthen and expand programmes that distribute scientific books and journals to institutions, primarily in the developing world. Carol Priestley was Director of INASP since its founding in 1992 until 2006.

1408 Priestley, Carol **"The Difficult Art of Book Aid: An African Survey."** *Logos. The Journal of the World Book Community* 4, no. 4 (1993): 215-21.
Online:
http://www.atypon-link.com/LOG/doi/pdf/10.2959/logo.1993.4.4.215
A résumé of the author's **Book and Publishing Assistance Programs: A Review and Inventory** [of 1993 ed., *see* ➜ **1413** for 2000 ed.]. Examines the book needs of Africa, and evaluates the impact of donor-supported publishing and book development programmes in Africa. Contends "if donor support is to lead to long-term sustainable publishing, it has to assist the selling of books as well as the making of them."

1409 Priestley, Carol **"Availability of Publications in Africa: Exchange of Experience and Future Prospects."** *FID Bulletin* 44, nos. 4/5 (1994): 67-71.
Surveys current [mid-1990s] assistance programmes for book and library development in Africa, reviewing the activities of individual organizations and their experiences to date. Argues that the challenge is to harness donor funding and support in a way that will encourage new national and regional initiatives, reduce dependency, and thus help to promote long term sustainability of autonomous publishing in Africa.

1410 Priestley, Carol **"Donors to African Education (DAE) Working Group on Textbooks and Libraries: Notes from the London Sessions."** *Bellagio Publishing Network Newsletter*, no. 9 (March 1994): 4-5.
Reports about a meeting of the Donors to African Education group [now ➜ **Association for the Development of Education in Africa/ADEA (34)**] its research agenda, and its growing involvement with the private sector in African publishing.

1411 Priestley, Carol **"Publishing and Library Support for Africa: An Update."** In *Africa Bibliography 1993*, compiled by Christopher H. Allen. Edinburgh: Edinburgh University Press, 1994, vi-xvi.
A survey of past and current assistance programmes for book and library development in Africa [as at 1994], describing the objectives and activities of the various schemes. Also provides an update of a number of new initiatives that have been started since 1992.

1412 Priestley, Carol **"Publishing Economics Top DAE Working Group Agenda."** *Bellagio Publishing Network Newsletter*, no. 14 (August 1995): 3-5.

Reports about a meeting of the Working Group on Textbooks and Libraries of the Donors to African Education (DAE) [now ➜ **Association for the Development of Education in Africa/ADEA (34)**] held in Paris in January 1995. Topics discussed included support to publishing in national languages, and the possibility of undertaking a major research study on the economics of textbook publishing to assist donors, African governments and African publishers in developing appropriate strategies for the sustainable provision of textbooks.

1413 Priestley, Carol **Book and Publishing Assistance Programmes. A Review and Inventory.** Chestnut Hill, MA: Bellagio Publishing Network, Research and Information Centre (Bellagio Studies in Publishing, 11), 2000. New [2nd] ed. 168 pp. (distributed by African Collective Ltd., Oxford)
First published in 1993, and with a new introductory essay providing an overview of significant developments since publication of the first edition, this is a survey of the various agencies and assistance programmes that are involved with publishing and book development in Africa and in other parts of the developing world. Profiling over 50 organizations, it provides extensive information about each organization's activities, together with full contact information. In addition to the inventory section, a general review of book assistance programmes (reprinted from the first edition) looks at the context of support, the donor response, the factors affecting donor assistance, and priorities for donor support for long-term, sustainable indigenous publishing.
Reviews:
The African Book Publishing Record vol. 23, no.1, 1997

1414 Read, Anthony **"Book Hunger."** *The Bookseller* (10 June 1988): 2260-2264.
The [then] director of market development at the UK Publishers Association surveys the increasing problem of book hunger throughout the world, and explores possible ways to reduce it.

1415 Rosenberg, Diana **"African Journals Distribution Programme: Report on its Co-ordination by the International African Institute, with an Update to 1995."** *Focus on International and Comparative Librarianship* 27, no. 2 (September 1996): 115-120.
Sets out the needs, objectives and *modus operandi* of the African Journals Distribution Programme (AJDP), a scheme through which scholarly journals published in African countries are made available to scholars and academics in other African countries. To do this the Programme purchases subscriptions on behalf of university libraries in Africa. Also includes an evaluation of the pilot year (1994), when 18 scholarly journals published in 9 African countries were purchased and distributed in 8 anglophone African countries.

1416 Rosi, Mauro **Book Donations for Development**, edited by Gwynneth Evans. Paris: UNESCO (Document ref. CLT/ACE/CEC-05/1); and Ottawa: CODE Canada, 2005. 72 pp.
Online: http://www.codecan.org/english/documents/Book_Donations.pdf

[15/03/08]

Also available in French (published in 2004 by Culture et développement, Grenoble, France) as **La donation du livre pour le développement.**

As part of the education and training for a policy of "correct giving", a 'Donated Books Programs: A Dialogue of Partners' conference was jointly organized by ➔ **UNESCO (118),** ➔ **CODE (48)** and the ➔ **International Book Bank (70)** in Baltimore in September 1992. The meeting led to a series of concrete programmes set up over the last 10 years, and this handbook is one of the outcomes and takes up the Baltimore recommendations as part of a more educational approach. It provides both policy and practical information for donors and recipients of book donation projects, and gives special attention to those in the developing world. All the policy aspects of donation programmes are illustrated in a methodical way, while the practical sections of the donation projects are presented in all their detail and complexity.

1417 Samuelson, Jeff **"South Africa Books Aid Projects."** *Focus on International & Comparative Librarianship* 28, no. 2 (September 1997): 92-95.

Outlines the objectives of the South Africa Books Aid Project (SABAP), a three year project funded by the ➔ **Department for International Development (57)** and managed, at the UK end, by ➔ **Book Aid International (38).** The goal of SABAP is to support local initiatives to improve the quality of basic and adult education in three provinces, and to facilitate and improve access to books in primary schools, educational resource centres and community libraries in these provinces.

1418 Sharples, Carolyn **"Journals for African Universities."** *Focus on International & Comparative Librarianship* 25, no. 3 (31 December 1994): 133-137.

Reports about the work of International Campus Book Link (ICBL), which aims to help fill a small part of the need for tertiary materials by supplying academic journals and books to its partners and recipient libraries in sub-Saharan Africa.

1419 Sharples, Carolyn **"Meeting the Information Need in Developing Countries."** *IASP Newsletter,* no. 2 (1995): 1-4.

Also published in *Learned Publishing* 8, no. 2 (April 1995): 93-98.

Reviews the work and activities of ➔ **Book Aid International (38)** in its three major areas: book and journal donation programmes (including the International Campus Book Link project), book buying projects, and local publishing support through the Intra-African Book Support Scheme.

O'Connor, Brigid **"Donor Support for Textbooks in Africa"** *see* ➔ **Educational and school book publishing** entry **1882**

1420 Walsh, Gretchen **"Book Donation Projects for Africa: A Handbook and Directory."** *ASA News* 25, no. 2 (April/June 1992): 13-20.

Reports on the findings of the book famine Task Force of the ASA which identifies several components in book projects: recipients, donor, books, transportation and communication. Includes a directory of book donation programmes and describes some successful book projects. *Note:* The directory was superseded by an electronic version first published in 2000, *see* entry ➜ **1381**.

1421 Walsh, Gretchen **"The African Book Famine: The Role of U.S. Academic Libraries."** In *The Role of the American Library in International Programs*, edited by Bruce D. Bonta and James G. Neal. Greenwich, CT: JAI Press, 1992, 261-279.
A detailed discussion of the causes and consequences of the book famine in Africa, proposing a combination of approaches to solve the problem. Mentions several initiatives which have tried to do this, and reviews the problem of choosing which books to donate. The author also discusses the dilemmas inherent in any responses to the book famine.

1422 Walter, Scott **"International Donor Review."** In *Development Directory of Indigenous Publishing 1995*, compiled by Carol Priestley. Harare, African Publishers Network, 1995, 94-97.
A critical review of book aid programmes in Africa by international donor organizations. Provides a number of guiding principles that ought to be considered in any book support programmes. The author urges donors to provide more support for smaller projects, and advocates lead funding.

1423 Watkins, Christine **"Changing the World Through Books."** *American Libraries* 28, no. 9 (October 1997): 52-54
Describes the activities of ➜ **Books for Africa (42)**, a US book aid organization which ships nearly 750,000 books to Africa each year in an effort to fill empty shelves in Africa's libraries. The largest proportion of books come from and go to schools and school libraries. Includes a short directory of other book donation organizations.

1424 Williams, Jean **"Biblionef. Bringing Books to the Bookless."** *Cape Librarian* 48, no. 3 (May/June 2004): 14-16.
Online: http://www.capegateway.gov.za/Text/2004/8/may2004_14-16.pdf [15/03/08]
Also published in *Innovation. Journal of Appropriate Librarianship and Information Work in Southern Africa*, no. 26 (June 2003): 43-47.
Many communities in South Africa still lack access to reading materials, and there are many homes without books and schools without libraries, particularly in the rural areas. Although people may have the ability to read, having no access to books puts them at a great advantage. It is this need that ➜ **Biblionef SA (933)** – the South African branch of an international book assistance organization for children's books – seeks to address. The author describes the background of the organization, its principal aims, the methods of distribution of its book donations, and some of its other activities, which includes publishing and reprinting of select titles, and promotion of children's literature in indigenous languages. While Biblionef SA receives book donations, most of its stock is purchased from South African publishers, at reduced prices. An important principle of Biblionef is that it exclusively distributes new children's books.

1425 Williams, Nelly Temu, and Sandrine Coll **"Book Aid International: 50 Years of Sharing Information (1953-2004)."** *African Research & Documentation,* no. 95 (1004): 35-44.
2004 marked the 50th anniversary of the major UK book charity ➜ **Book Aid International/BAI (38)**, which is active in many countries in sub-Saharan Africa, and is involved in strengthening the book chain, building capacity, and leadership skills, supporting advocacy and resource mobilization, hosting training workshops, and working with both African partners and Northern organizations. This article is an appraisal of BAI's many and diverse activities that aim to empower people and communities in Africa through access to books and appropriate information. The article also looks at aspects of monitoring and evaluation of BAI's and its partners' work.

1426 Zell, Hans M. **"The Other Famine."** *Libri* 37, no. 4 (December 1987): 294-306.
Summarizes the grave book famine in Africa [as at 1987], presenting the facts in an overview and assessment. Reports on what action is being taken by various organizations in the UK and what measure of success they have attained.

Book fairs

1427 Accone, Darryl **Searching for the Golden Mean.** ZA&Play June 15, 2007
http://www.chico.mweb.co.za/art/2007/2007june/070615-fair.html
[15/03/08]
Looks at the impressive success of the Cape Town Book Fair, but offers a number of reservations and states that the Fair is an event about letters and words, but that, in its official media releases at least, it seems "to be obsessed instead with figures and numbers"; and the Fair's success needs to find the right balance, and will have to be assessed, and ultimately appreciated, in terms of rights transactions and rights sold for South African titles.

1428 Accone, Darryl **Growing Healthily.** ZA&Play June 21 2007
http://www.chico.mweb.co.za/art/2007/2007june/070621-fair.html
[15/03/08]
The author believes the Cape Town Book Fair has achieved much in its second year, and attracted thousands more members of the general public than the inaugural event in 2006. However "what beckons for 2008 is to enlarge the representivity of that public, which remains overwhelmingly white and middle class, and to build on the international network of publishing and rights sales that the first fair set up."

1429 Adeniyi, Dapo **"Tantenda Zimbabwe."** *Glendora Review* 1, no. 4 (1996): 11-16.
A report about the 1996 Zimbabwe International Book Fair, and about some the meetings and special events which coincided with the Fair, including a workshop for

African journal editors, at which the writer (who was Editor of the *Glendora Review. African Quarterly of the Arts*) was one of the participants.

1430 Amanor-Wilks, Dede **"Zimbabwe International Book Fair 2000."** *Bellagio Publishing Network Newsletter*, no. 26-27 (November 2000): 4-6
Online: http://www.bellagiopublishingnetwork.com/newsletter26-27/amanor-wilks.htm [15/03/08]
Originally published in *NewsAfrica* 1, no. 7 (August 28, 2000).
Reports about the 2000 fair – which was held in an environment of political uncertainty in the country – including the supporting 'Indaba' events and a number of workshops. Also looks at the challenges of traditional book publishing in Africa posed by the new information and communication technologies and the Internet.

1431 Badisang, Bobana **"Report on the Zimbabwe International Book Fair, Harare."** *African Research & Documentation*, no. 70 (1996): 69-71.
Reports about the 1996 Zimbabwe Book Fair and about a number of meetings and workshops held during the Fair including one on the acquisitions of African-published materials by African libraries. Argues that some of the suggestions put forward at the workshops which might improve the acquisitions of African books are impractical, and suggests that APNET should have a permanent showroom, and should become a stock-holding operation to process libraries' orders from a central distribution point.

1432 Badroodien, Vanessa **"A Book Affair Continued."** *Bookmark. News Magazine of the South African Booksellers' Association* 11 (April-July 2007): 16.
An interview with Vanessa Badroodien, Director of the Cape Town Book Fair, in which she reflects on the success of the inaugural Fair in 2006, and looks at the challenges in the years ahead.

1433 Bond, Frances **"Experiencing the Zimbabwean Bookfair."** *Writers' World*, no. 13 (1994): 15-16.
The author, a South African literary agent, was part of a group of South African delegates to the 1995 Zimbabwe International Book Fair, and found it an exciting experience.

1434 Bugembe, Mary. H., ed. **Book Fair Magazine. 3rd Pan-African Children's Book Fair. 'Learning Science at an Early Age'. Kenyatta International Conference Centre, 28-31 May 1994.** Nairobi: CHISCI Press, 1994. 56 pp.
The official Book Fair catalogue and guide, containing background material on the Pan African Children's Book Fair and its organizers, profiles of some writers of children's books in Africa, excerpts of seminar papers presented during the Fair, and company profiles of exhibitors.

1435 Bugembe, Mary H. **"The 3rd Pan-African Children's Book Fair."** *The African Book Publishing Record* 20, no. 4 (1994): 249-251.

Another version also published in *Bellagio Publishing Network Newsletter* no. 12 (December 1994): 4-5; and in *Maktaba* 12, no. 1 (March 1995): 7, 12. Report on the 3rd Pan-African Children's Book Fair held in Nairobi in May 1994, organized by the **→ Foundation for the Promotion of Children's Science Publishing in Africa (16).** Sets out the background to the Fair, its aims, achievements, and impact to date.

1436 Cochran, Christopher Lee **"Freedom of Expression at the Zimbabwe Book Fair."** *Information Development* 12, no. 2 (June 1996): 74.
States that the article by Brenda Mitchell-Powell (*see* entry **→ 1453** below) was marred by "a selective oversight by the author" by leaving out some vital reporting of important events that occurred during the Fair, namely the banning of the Gay and Lesbian's organization of Zimbabwe from exhibiting at the Fair, and the vitriolic attack on gays by President Mugabe, which made a mockery of the Fair's theme of 'Human rights and justice'.

1437 de Beer, Johanna **"Zimbabwe Book Fair 1998."** *Cape Librarian* 42, 6 (1998): 12-15.
A South African librarian reports about her visit to the 1998 Zimbabwe Book Fair.

1438 Dekutsey, Woeli **"Ghana's Successes with Rural Book Fairs."** *African Publishing Review* 4, no. 5 (September/October 1995): 10.
A report about a series of successful 'mini book fairs' held in three small towns in Ghana.

1439 Dekutsey, Woeli **"Looking Back, Looking Ahead. Book Fairs in Africa. "** *Glendora Review* 2, no. 1 (1997): 96-98.
A review and assessment of the growth of book fairs in Africa, the significant role they play in book promotion, and examining some of their successes and failures. Looks at some of the factors that make for a successful book fair in an African environment, and how African book fairs might develop in the years ahead.

1440 Dunton, Chris, and Mai Palmberg **Human Rights and Homosexuality in Southern Africa**. Uppsala: Nordiska Afrikainstitutet (Current African Issues, 19), 1996. 41 pp.
At the 1995 Zimbabwe International Book Fair one of the exhibitors, the organization of Gays and Lesbians in Zimbabwe (GALZ), were prevented from taking part on the orders of the Zimbabwean government. This opened up an unprecedented, vigorous, and sometimes agonizing debate in Southern Africa. The debate on these and other issues is conveyed in this report on the book fair drama in Zimbabwe, and the debates that followed in Botswana, Namibia and South Africa.

1441 Epstein, Rheina **"The Cape Town Book Fair: A Personal Perspective."** *Cape Librarian* 50, no. 4 (July/August 2006): 10-12.

Online:
http://www.capegateway.gov.za/Text/2006/11/ja06_book_fair.pdf
[15/03/08]
An enthusiastic endorsement of the success of the 1st Cape Town International Book Fair held in 2006, describing it as "a truly memorable experience for anybody connected with the book."

1442 Jay, Mary **"The 1st Ghana International Book Fair."** *The African Book Publishing Record* 23, no. 1 (1997): 9-11.
A critical assessment of the first (1996) Ghana International Book Fair, examining organization, exhibitor and visitor participation, supporting events held around the fair, and other aspects.

1443 Leishman, A.D.H. **"The First Zimbabwe International Book Fair."** *The African Book Publishing Record* 9, no. 4 (1983): 179-181.
Describes the first Zimbabwe Book Fair as an experiment which, the author believes, holds hope for the future as long as books remain free from government taxation and censorship.

1444 Ling, Margaret **"How Can an International Book Fairs Stimulate African Book Fair Production?"** In *Academic Book Production and Distribution in Africa. Support from Nordic Countries. Report from a Conference at Chr. Michelsen Institute, Bergen, 10-11 April 1997,* edited by Kirsti Hagen Andersen. Fantoft, Norway: Ch. Michelsen Institute 1997, 30-39.
Appraises the contribution the Zimbabwe International Book Fair has made in generating interest in African publishing output, and acting as a catalyst for trade and development, and how it has helped African publishers to break into international markets.

1445 Mbanga, Trish **"The Zimbabwe International Book Fair - Africa's Publishing Showcase."** *The African Book Publishing Record* 19, no. 4 (1993): 223-227.
Reports in some detail about the 8th Zimbabwe International Book Fair (ZIBF) held in August 1993, with a brief review of past fairs, and describing current problems, funding and sponsorship, and choice of venues. Focuses on the role and significance of ZIBF as an African book fair and sets out the considerable achievements to date of the fair.

1446 Mbanga, Trish, and Margaret Ling **"An Aspiring Frankfurt Emerges in Africa."** *Logos. The Journal of the World Book Community* 4, no. 4 (1993): 209-14.
Online:
http://www.atypon-link.com/LOG/doi/pdf/10.2959/logo.1993.4.4.209
Charts the growth of the Zimbabwe International Book Fair (ZIBF), and the remarkable success it has achieved over a short period of time. Reflects on its

growing importance as a trading venue and as a point of access for exhibitors to wider African markets.

1447 Mbanga, Trish **"The Zimbabwe International Book Fair."** *Information Development* 10, no. 1 (March 1994): 13-19.
A profile of the Zimbabwe International Book Fair by Trish Mbanga (who was its Director until 1996.) Recounts the rapid growth of the Fair since it was first held in 1983, and the international success and recognition is has gained to date as "the Frankfurt of Africa", and as an important trading crossroads for the African book industries.

1448 Mbanga, Trish **"The African Book Fairs."** In *Development Directory of Indigenous Publishing 1995*, compiled by Carol Priestley. Harare: African Publishers Network, 1995, 48-51.
Primarily an account of the development and growth of the Zimbabwe International Book Fair.

1449 Mbanga, Trish **"The Zimbabwe International Book Fair, 1994."** *Information Development* 11, no. 2 (June 1995): 102-104.
An account of the 1994 Zimbabwe International Book Fair, which was then [mid-1990s] widely recognized as Africa's premier book trade gathering. However, the fact that the Fair continues to attract new exhibitors from many parts of the world calls for new approaches to meet their needs. The author also restates one of ZIBF's principal aims, namely "to combine the function of a commercially viable trade fair with a public celebration of books and reading."

1450 Mbanga, Trish **"The Zimbabwe International Book Fair: Where to Now?"** *African Publishing Review* 5, no. 2 (March/April 1996): 6-7.
Trish Mbanga, Director of the Zimbabwe International Book Fair until 1996, in conversation with Lesley Humphrey, in which she looks back over the past five years of the Fair and discusses some of its future plans.

1451 Miller, Jonathan **"The South Comes Off the Shelf."** *South* (October 1987): 99-107.
A critical assessment of the role of book fairs in the countries of the South.

1452 Mitchell-Powell, Brenda **"Booksellers, Librarians Celebrate African Literature ZIBF'95."** *American Libraries* 26, no. 9 (October 1995): 880-882.
An American librarian reports about her visit to the 1995 Zimbabwe International Book Fair, and the various special events and activities that coincided with the Fair. Also offers some observations on library services in the region, and finds that "on a continent overwhelmed with subsistence survival, African librarians face awesome challenges."

1453 Mitchell-Powell, Brenda **"The Zimbabwe International Book Fair 1995."** *Information Development* 12, no. 1 (March 1996): 33-37.

A further account about ZIBF 95 by this American librarian, including the pre-Fair meeting on 'Freedom of Expression' which was attended by several prominent African writers. Also provides some information about the ➔ **African Publishers Network (5)** and the collective African Periodicals Exhibit.

1454 Moss, Glenn **"The Frankfurt Book Fair and the 'Third World'. A Personal View."** *Zeitschrift für Kulturaustausch* 41, no. 3 (1991-3): 372-374.
The [former] manager of Ravan Press, South Africa, describes his first visit to the Frankfurt Book Fair and concludes that as well as being an enjoyable event, it was also well worthwhile attending, even for small publishers.

1455 Mugo, Macharia, ed. **5th Pan African Children's Book Fair Magazine (May 27th-31st, 1996).** Nairobi: CHISCI Press, 1996. 44 pp.
The official exhibitor catalogue and companion to the 5th Pan-African Children's Book Fair. In addition to the full programme and exhibitor listings, etc., the magazine contains a number of short contributions on writing and publishing for children and the 'Children's Reading Tent', which is now a well-established feature at the Fair. Enclosed as a loose insert: "The Pan African Children's Bookfair. From Experimentation to Institutionalisation" by Mary Bugembe, which gives the background to the Fair, how it is organized, and describes activities during the Fair; also provides some statistical analysis of exhibitor and visitor participation since the first Fair was held in 1992.

1456 Nwoga, Chinyere **"Nigerian International Book Fair 2002 in Abuja."** *Bellagio Publishing Network Newsletter,* no. 31 (2002): 8-11
Online:
http://www.bellagiopublishingnetwork.com/newsletter31/nwoga.htm [03/02/08]
A report about the Nigeria International Book Fair 2002 – "the first serious international book fair since the demise of the Ife Book Fair 20 years ago" – which was relatively well attended, but suffered from a number of organizational problems, as well as distinct lack of support, moral or financial, by the Nigerian government despite earlier pledges that it would provide assistance for the fair.

1457 Nyika, Tambayi **"The Right to Read."** *West Africa,* no. 4064 (28 August 1995): 1374-1375.
Reports on the 1995 Zimbabwe International Book Fair, the 'Indaba' on Human Rights and Freedom of Expression which preceded the Fair, and the controversy caused by the withdrawal of exhibit facilities for the Gay and Lesbians Group of Zimbabwe by the Fair organizers, acting under a directive issued by the Zimbabwe government.

1458 Olden, Tony **"The 1997 Zimbabwe International Book Fair."** *African Research & Documentation,* no. 75 (1997): 43-47
Reports about the 1997 Zimbabwe International Book Fair, the various satellite events and workshops that coincided with the Fair, and reviews some of the papers presented at the 1997 'Indaba' whose theme was 'Access to Information'.

1459   Ranger, Terence **"Zimbabwe Book Fair: Controversy in 1995."**
Bellagio Publishing Network Newsletter, no. 15 (November 1995): 1-2.
About the widely condemned exclusion of the Gay and Lesbians of Zimbabwe
(GALZ) from exhibiting at the 1995 Zimbabwe International Book Fair. Although the
ZIBF organizers had offered and allocated a booth to GALZ they were compelled at
the last minute to withdraw exhibit facilities under a directive from the Zimbabwe
Government Director of Information. This was followed by a hostile attack on gays
by President Mugabe during his speech at the opening of the Fair.

1460   Reece, Jane **"What's in it for Us?"** *Zimbabwe Review,* no. 1 (December
1994): 10-12.
A critical view of the 1994 Zimbabwe International Book Fair. Questions who
benefits from the Fair – other than book trade professionals – and what it offers for
writers, general book buyers, and the reading public at large. Suggests that the Fair
needs more non-book activities, and more co-ordinated arts and cultural events to
bring it alive.

1461   Rudiak,   Michael D. **"A View from the Frankfurt Book Fair."** *Bellagio
Publishing Network Newsletter,* no. 8 (December 1993): 8-9.
A personal view of the 'Frankfurt experience', and an evaluation of publishers'
benefits exhibiting at Frankfurt's North-South Centre, which consists a number of
collective stands grouping together publishers from Africa, and others from the
developing world, in a composite area.

1462   Salahi, Katherine **"Bellagio in Accra."** *Glendora Books Supplement,* no. 1
(1997): 22-23.
Online:
http://digital.lib.msu.edu/projects/africanjournals/html/itemdetail.cfm?re
cordID=2831 [03/01/08]
Also published, as "Bellagio Group Supports First Ghana International Book
Fair" in *Bellagio Publishing Network Newsletter,* no. 19, (March 1997): 4-5.
An account about the discussions and debates at a Bellagio Group-sponsored
roundtable on the significance of holding and running book fairs, and which
coincided with the first Ghana International Book Fair in November 1996.

Southern African Book Development Education Trust **Africa at the Fair.
How Can Literary Festivals and Book Fairs Promote African Books and
Reading?** *see* ➔ **African books in the international market place** entry
1295

1463   Stringer, Roger **"An African Publisher at Frankfurt."** *African
Publishing Review* 3, no. 1 (January/February 1994): 1-2. [same in French, pp.
2-3].
A critical evaluation of the benefits that the Frankfurt Book Fair offers to African
publishers.

1464 Umbina, Anna **"Time Warp."** *Zimbabwean Review* 2, no. 4 (October-December 1996): 28.
Describes the attempts to silence the Gay and Lesbians of Zimbabwe (GALZ) at the 1996 Zimbabwe International Book Fair, which, for the second year running, was once again overshadowed by issues of human rights and freedom of expression.

Book marketing and promotion

See also
→ **African Books Collective Ltd. (ABC)**
→ **African books in the international market place**
→ **Book fairs**
→ **Bookselling and book distribution**
→ **Intra-African book trade**
→ **Publishing in African languages**
→ **Rights sales, licensing and publishing partnerships**

Note: for articles about marketing African books in the countries of the North, *see* → **African books in the international market place**; for articles about marketing of indigenous language books *see* → **Publishing in African languages**.

1465 Bgoya, Walter **"Taking Books to the Non-Literary Market Place."**
The African Book Publishing Record 10, no. 3 (1984): 141-145.
Also reprinted in *Readings on Publishing in Africa and the Third World*, edited by Philip G. Altbach. Buffalo, NY: Bellagio Publishing Network, Research and Information Center (Bellagio Studies in Publishing 1), 1993, 37-39.
Walter Bgoya, then General Manager of the Tanzania Publishing House (TPH), describes bookselling in Tanzania in 1984 and the role of book fairs and exhibitions. Examines what people want to read, the problems with communication in more remote areas of the country, how to price books, and how to increase sales. Includes interviews with people who visited various exhibitions held by TPH, some at book fairs and some in food markets in various parts of the country, as illustrations of how ordinary people feel about and react to books.

1466 Bgoya, Walter **"Taking Books to the Non-Literary Market Place."**
[Updated version] In *Publishing in Africa: The Crisis and the Challenge. An ASA Roundtable. The African Book Publishing Record* 20, no. 1 (1994): 13-15.
The former General Manager of the Tanzania Publishing House describes (in an update of the preceding entry (*see* → **1465**) their experience of selling books in the main markets in Dar es Salaam's three districts. The author draws attention to the marked decline in literacy in the 1990s, and the weaknesses of local publishing houses. He argues that there is a need for different approaches to library and book development, and calls for more innovative book programmes and strategies to

bring books to the "non-literary marketplace" and into the economic reach of the rural poor and the disadvantaged.

1467   Chakava, Henry **"Book Marketing and Distribution: The Achilles' Heel of African Publishing."** In *Publishing in Africa: One Man's Perspective*, by Henry Chakava. Chestnut Hill, MA: Bellagio Publishing Network, Research and Information Center (Bellagio Studies in Publishing, 6), 1996, 109-133.
Also published in *Development Dialogue*, nos. 1-2 (1997): 59-60; and, as a slightly different and shorter version, **"Selling Books in Africa: A Publisher's Reflection."** *Logos. The Journal of the World Book Community* 8, no. 3 (1997): 159-164.
Online: http://www.atypon-link.com/LOG/doi/pdf/10.2959/logo.1997.8.3.159
A major article that looks at the challenges of book distribution in Africa today. Presents an overview of book promotion and marketing strategies available to the African book industry, and examines "the extent to which these marketing possibilities are being exploited by the African publisher today." Finds that marketing and promotion by many African publishers is frequently feeble; there is lack of advance information about new books, unattractive and ineffective promotion material, and that some African publishers fail to make use of the many opportunities that exist for free publicity and listings of their books in the major bibliographic services. The author is also critical of the sometimes sub-standard production quality of African-published books, sloppy editing and proofreading, poor binding and finishing; or books which lack proper title pages and essential copyright data, have no ISBNs, and which show evidence of "lack of proper quality controls and discipline at all levels of the African book publishing chain." Also considers the role of book development councils and national publishers associations, and makes a number of recommendations how to tackle the problems of book marketing and distribution in Africa. Concludes that although marketing and distribution comes at the end of the publishing process it will determine "success or failure of any publishing house".

1468   Chipidza, Chipo **"Marketing Books in Southern Africa."** In *Indaba 2000. Millennium Marketplace,* edited by the Zimbabwe International Book Fair Trust. Harare: Zimbabwe International Book Fair Trust, 2001, 218-220.
Examines the particular characteristics of marketing books in Southern Africa and suggests a number of strategies for successful promotion books in that part of Africa.

1469   Crabbe, Richard **"Market Trends in the African Book Industry."** In *Indaba 2000. Millennium Marketplace,* edited by the Zimbabwe International Book Fair Trust. Harare: Zimbabwe International Book Fair Trust, 2001, 13-16.
Another version published in *African Publishing Review* 9, no. 4 (2000): 4-5.
A keynote plenary address by the former Chair of the ➜ **African Publishers Network (5)** presented at the Zimbabwe International Book Fair Indaba 2000. It

outlines some of the major market trends and developments in the African book industry, and the changing needs of African readers. Increasing gender awareness, the growing significance of local language publishing, the rising influence of information technology, improved networking, and increasing cross-border trade are among them.

Easterbrook, David L. **"American Libraries, American Markets, African Books"** *see* ➔ **African books in the international market place**, entry **1277**

1470 Hurst, Christopher **"Why African Publishers Must Export."** *The Bookseller*, no. 3993 (3 July 1982): 30-31.
A condensed version of a paper presented to the 1982 Bookweek Africa seminar at the Africa Centre in London. Advocates the printing of Nigerian books in Nigeria and offers a number of suggestions for promoting and marketing of African books in the UK.

1471 Hurst, Christopher **"Letter."** *IASP Newsletter*, no. 5 (September 1983): 5-6.
Response by Hurst to Arthur A. Nwankwo's rebuttal of his article "Why African Publishers Must Export" (*see* entries ➔ **1479** and ➔ **1470**).

1472 Impey, Bridget **"Book Marketing and Distribution in Southern Africa."** In *Book Marketing and Promotion: A Handbook of Good Practice*, edited by Hans M. Zell. Oxford: International Network for the Availability of Scientific Publications (distributed by African Books Collective Ltd), 2001, 197-209.
One in a series of case studies which describe the current [2001] state of book marketing and distribution in various regions of Africa. Provides an overview of distribution infrastructures and major constraints, followed by sections on marketing and distribution to specific markets (booksellers, libraries, schools, and the general public), marketing techniques used and their effectiveness, regional and export marketing and promotion, rights sales, and co-editions.

1473 Jay, Mary **"How Can Publishers Effectively Distribute Books in and out of Africa?"** In *Academic Book Production and Distribution in Africa. Support from Nordic Countries. Report from a conference at Chr. Michelsen Institute, Bergen, 10-11 April 1997*, edited by Kirsti Hagen Andersen. Fantoft, Norway: Ch. Michelsen Institute 1997, 77-82.
Examines the role and contribution of the ➔ **African Books Collective Ltd. (3)** in the promotion and marketing of African books, and providing much needed visibility for African creative writing, culture, and African scholarship. Also offers some suggestions how African publishers could more effectively distribute their books both within Africa and reaching markets overseas.

Jay, Mary **"African Books Collective and Creative Writing and Publishing in Africa"** *see* ➔ **African Books Collective** entry **1280**

1474 Kantey, Mike **"New Approaches to Marketing and Distribution."** In *Book Publishing in South Africa for the 1990s.* Cape Town: South African Library, 1991, 100-117.
Describes the different elements that go into creating a successful marketing package: the right product for the right audience, with the right package at the right price, at the right time, and in the right place. Primarily on the book markets in South Africa.

1475 Kanuya, Albert **"Marketing Books. The Tanzanian Experience."** In *Millennium Marketplace.* [Proceedings of the ZIBF] *Indaba 2000, Harare, Zimbabwe, 31 July – 1 August 2000.* Harare: Zimbabwe International Book Fair Trust, n.d. [2001], 88-92.
A short account of the development of indigenous publishing in Tanzania, and the problems and challenges of marketing books in the country.

1476 Maja-Pearce, Adewale **"Selling Africa."** *The New Gong Magazine* (2006)
http://thenewgong.com/ALAconference.html [03/01/08]
New Gong are a Lagos-based publishing house and writers' cooperative with a small list of titles, including fiction, poetry and essays, and are also the publishers of an online cultural and literary magazine. This article recounts their experience of promoting and selling their books at an exhibit during the 32nd annual meeting and conference of the (US) African Literature Association, which was held in Accra in May 2006. The article includes some rather uninformed comments about the activities, and policies, of the Oxford-based ➜ **African Books Collective (3).**

1477 Milner, Toby **"Publishing and Distribution Problems for African Studies in the United Kingdom: Distribution of Publications from and about Africa; Third World Publications Coop Ltd."** In *African Studies. Papers presented at a colloquium at the British Library 7-9 January 1985.* London: The British Library, 1986, 66-72.
Describes the experiences of Third World Publications a [former] UK distributor of African-published books.

1478 Moutchia, William **"Book Promotion in Africa - Yaoundé."** In *Book Promotion and the Sharing of Resources in Africa,* edited by K. Bonde *et al.* Maseru: Lesotho Library Association, 1980, 74-83.
Describes the structure, mission and activities of the Yaoundé-based Centre Régional de Promotion du Livre en Afrique/Regional Centre for Book Promotion in Africa (CREPLA), and calls for more active cooperation among the book professions in the furtherance of book promotion in Africa. The author was for many years Director of this ➜ **UNESCO (118)**-supported regional centre, but which has been dormant for many years now.

1479 Nwankwo, Arthur A. **"Indigenous Publishing in Africa."** *IASP Newsletter*, no. 4 (July 1983): 2-4.
A rebuttal, by the chairman of Fourth Dimension Publishing Co. Ltd., Nigeria, to Christopher Hurst's address to Bookweek Africa (June 1982) entitled "African Publishers Must Export", *see* entry ➜ **1470**.

1480 Nwankwo, Victor **"Book Marketing and Distribution in West Africa."** In *Book Marketing and Promotion: A Handbook of Good Practice*, edited by Hans M. Zell. Oxford: International Network for the Availability of Scientific Publications (distributed by African Books Collective Ltd), 2001, 211-223.
One in a series of case studies which describe the current [2000] state of book marketing and distribution in various regions of Africa. Provides an overview of distribution infrastructures and major constraints, followed by sections on marketing and distribution to specific markets (booksellers, libraries, schools, the general public, and other distribution channels), marketing techniques used and their effectiveness, regional and export marketing and promotion, rights sales, and co-editions.

1481 Nyeko, Janet A. **"The Experience of the Institute of Southern African Studies, National University of Lesotho, in Publishing, Marketing and Distributing Internationally."** *African Research & Documentation*, no. 73 (1997): 39-42.
A short account of the scholarly publishing activities of the Institute of Southern African Studies at the University of Lesotho, its principal objectives, structure, and marketing and sales strategies to reach overseas markets.

1482 Ofori-Mensah, Akoss **"Modern Marketing Techniques. The Ghanaian Experience."** In *Millennium Marketplace.* [Proceedings of the ZIBF] *Indaba 2000, Harare, Zimbabwe, 31 July – 1 August 2000.* Harare: Zimbabwe International Book Fair Trust, n.d. [2001], 80-87.
Makes some recommendations for more effective marketing and promotion by book publishers in Ghana and elsewhere in Africa, and urges publishers to take advantage of the many marketing opportunities now offered on the Web.

Odaga, Asenath Bole **"Women's Books: Marketing and Distribution"** *see* ➜ **Section 4, Studies by topic: Women in African publishing/Publishing by and for women** entry **2401**

1483 Ogunleye, Bisi **"Marketing Scholarly Works."** *Books* 1, no. 2 (April 1988): 35-38.
Examines the role of marketing in scholarly publishing in Nigeria, highlights its strengths and weaknesses, and suggests distribution strategies for more effective marketing of scholarly publishing output.

1484 Okonkwo, Lawrence **"Marketing African Books. The Nigerian Scenario."** In *Millennium Marketplace.* [Proceedings of the ZIBF] *Indaba 2000, Harare, Zimbabwe, 31 July – 1 August 2000.* Harare: Zimbabwe International Book Fair Trust, n.d. [2001], 51-64.
Aims to shed light on current marketing practices by publishers in Nigeria. Analyzes the different market segments within Nigeria, promotional methods used, and the requirements for successful export marketing.

1485 Owusu-Bour, Yaw **"Marketing in the Book Trade."** *Ghana Book World*, no. 5 (1991): 52-53.
Highlights the marketing aspects which are deemed necessary to develop and promote the book publishing industry in Ghana.

1486 Stebbing, Lyle **"Report on the Bellagio Publishing Network Round Table on Book Marketing and Distribution in Africa."** Supplement to *African Publishing Review* 4, no. 3 (May/June 1995), 8 pp
In November 1994 African publishers met in Dar es Salaam to discuss marketing and distribution in Africa. This is a synthesis of the nine papers presented, which examine some of the key problems that impede the growth of the African book industries within and across African nations. Groups the problems, and proposed solutions/strategies, around three areas: (i) publishing and marketing, (ii) distribution, and (iii) retailing.

1487 Watts-Russell, Pru, ed. **"Marketing and Selling Books in Africa."** London: Southern African Book Development Education Trust, 2000. http://www.zibf.org/LIBFseminar.htm [page not available [15/03/08]
A report on the presentations and discussions held at two seminars held during the London Book Fair in March 2000, and which included participation by publishers and booksellers from several African countries. Seminar 1 was devoted to "Changes in Government Procurement—Policy and Practice", with presentations on textbook procurement policies in Zambia, Tanzania and The Gambia. Seminar 2 was on the topic "Bookselling and Booksellers—Enterprise and Success", with presentations by booksellers from Kenya, Botswana and Ghana.

1488 Wiggans, Rachel **"Marketing and Selling Books in Africa."** *Bellagio Publishing Network Newsletter*, no. 26-27 (November 2000): 12-14.
Online: http://www.bellagiopublishingnetwork.com/newsletter26-27/wiggans2.htm [15/03/08]
Reports about two seminars on marketing and selling books in Africa held during the London Book Fair in March 2000, hosted by the ➔ **Southern African Book Development Education Trust (113)** in association with the Zimbabwe International Book Fair. The first, on "Changes in Government Procurement - Policy and Practice" presented case studies from Zambia, Tanzania and Gambia where state control and centralization of textbook provision is being dismantled. The second seminar, "Bookselling and Booksellers - Enterprise and Success", looked at some of the challenges booksellers face and how they are being met.

1489 World Trade Organization. International Trade Centre. **Etudes de l'offre et de la demande sur les livres scolaires, l'édition et la diffusion.** [2003 surveys for African countries]
http://www.intracen.org/south-south/ [03/02/08] (Select Reference Documents, and then set the search filter for "All years", "Supply/Demand surveys", and for Sectors select "Books" from the pull-down menu.)
As part of the initiatives of the WTO South-South Trade Promotion Programme (ITC/UNCTAD/WTO) seeking to promote cross-border trade within Africa – including intra-African book trade – it has published a series of supply and demand surveys for a number of francophone African countries for the Sector "Printed matter, Periodicals, Stationery, Books". Each country survey has the sub-title *Etude de l'offre et de la demande sur les livres scolaires, l'édition et la diffusion,* and all of them are freely downloadable as pdf files. Surveys for the year 2003 were published for these francophone African countries, although no later surveys are available at this time [February 2008]: Benin, Burkina Faso, Cameroon, Central African Republic, Chad, Côte d'Ivoire, Gabon, Mali, Senegal, and Togo. Each study provides overviews of the structure and activities of the book industries in each country, the nature of their publishing programmes, production capacity and production standards, import/export profiles and volume of books imported/exported, trading conditions, financing of export credit, and other analysis.

Zell, Hans M. **Book Marketing and Promotion: A Handbook of Good Practice** *see* ➔ **Section 5, Book industry training/Self-publishing: Training manuals and resources,** entry **2488**

1490 Zell, Hans M. **"The Production and Marketing of African Books: A Msungu Perspective."** *Logos. The Journal of the World Book Community* 9, no. 2 (1998): 104-108.
Online: http://www.atypon-link.com/LOG/doi/pdf/10.2959/logo.1998.9.2.104
Also published in a French translation **"La production et la distribution de livres Africains: le point de vue d'un Msungu."** *Annales Aequatoria* 20 (1999): 465-473.
A sharp-edged appraisal of African publishers' marketing methods on the one hand, and the sometimes unacceptably poor production standards of African books on the other. The author is critical of African publishers' persistent failure to promote their books adequately, including their failure to take advantage of the many opportunities that exist for free publicity for their books--for example listings in major international bibliographic services, or promoting to journals who give space to notices and reviews. The author states "the African publishing scene is increasingly becoming a field for too much mealy-mouthed commentary and political correctness", and that "publishing is a business. It is about markets and competitions, not a political movement. Confusion between politics and business is often evident in African writers who may have a strong commitment to support and publish with autonomous African publishers, but are not always happy with the quality of the books, or the way they have been marketed at home and abroad."

While conceding that the autonomous African book industries face harsh market realities and many constraints which are real and serious, the author also believes that production quality, for the most part, is simply not good enough, and unless it significantly improves most indigenous African publishers will continue to find it difficult to compete with the multinationals, and there can be no levelling of the playing field.

1491 Zimbabwe International Book Fair Trust **Indaba 2000. Millennium Marketplace.** Harare: Zimbabwe International Book Fair Trust, 2001. 272 pp.
The Zimbabwe International Book Fair annual 'Indaba' in 2000 focused on a major weakness in the African book scene, that of marketing. Forty-three papers reflect the wide mixture of professionals involved from all parts of the book chain and the diverse nature of the theme. Papers from plenary sessions are included and thereafter papers are grouped into four parts: publishing, writing, scholarship and marketing, and policy and access. The sections on publishing include some (mostly very short) papers on book marketing and distribution in individual African countries, on marketing techniques, selling rights, market trends in the African book industry, and promoting cross-border book trade. *Note:* some of the papers in this collection are individually abstracted elsewhere in this bibliography.

1492 Zimbabwe International Book Fair **ZIBF 2000 — Open Forum on Marketing African Scholarship**
Panel One: *The North American Market for Scholarship*
http://www.zibf.org/ZIBF2000/openforum1.htm;
Panel Two: *Co-publishing as a Marketing Strategy*
http://www.zibf.org/ZIBF2000/openforum2.htm;
Panel Three: *The Internet and African Scholarship*
http://www.zibf.org/ZIBF2000/openforum3.htm;
Panel Four: *The South African Market for African Scholarship*
http://www.zibf.org/ZIBF2000/openforum4.htm
[None of the above pages available at 03/02/08]
The panel discussions that took place at an open forum on marketing of African scholarship held during the Zimbabwe International Book Fair in August 2000. Unfortunately the pages at the above URLs don't seem to be accessible any longer, but may still be available in print format from the ➔ **Zimbabwe International Book Fair Trust (1205).**

Bookselling and book distribution

See also
→ **African Books Collective Ltd. (ABC)**
→ **African books in the international market place**
→ **Book marketing and promotion**
→ **Educational and school book publishing**
→ **Intra-African book trade**
→ **Libraries and publishing**

Note: for interviews with prominent booksellers in different African countries *see* under individual countries in → **Section 3, Country studies**.

1493 Adam, Gibrin **"Bookselling in Ghana: the EPP Experience."** *African Publishing Review* 9, no. 2 (2000): 10-11.
Some observations on bookselling in Ghana by the head of EPP Book Services, who believes booksellers in the country will want to attain a higher profile, but in order to do so they will need to adopt a more dynamic, aggressive, and more professional approach to their profession.

1494 Adegbonmire, Wunmi **"The Hazards of Bookselling in Africa."** In *Publishing in Africa in the Seventies,* edited by Edwina Oluwasanmi, Eva McLean, and Hans M. Zell. Ile-Ife: University of Ife Press, 1975, 47-58.
The author uses his own experience [as the former Managing Director of the University of Ife Bookshop, now Obafemi Awolowo University Bookshop] to highlight the fact that although vast sums of money are spent on education in Africa, the level of literacy in the continent does not reflect this. Discusses the problems of bookselling, the role of university booksellers, difficulties in obtaining overseas credit facilities, the publisher-bookseller relationship, and trade within Africa. Concludes with a range of suggestions and recommendations for the retail trade sector in Africa. Now inevitably dated, but this remains a useful account of the challenges of the retail book trade in Africa.

1495 Alemna, A.A. **"Bookselling and the Library: A Partnership for Enhancing the Book Trade in Ghana."** *African Research & Documentation*, no. 82 (2000): 31-37.
Describes the activities of the different types of booksellers in Ghana, the problems they face, and the library's role as a partner with booksellers to enhance the book trade in Ghana. The author suggests a number of ways in which libraries can help in promoting the book trade in the country, and proposes a series of measures that would help to strengthen the retail sector, and booksellers' relations with both libraries and publishers.

L'association internationale des libraires francophones: Nos libraires *see*
→ **Section 1, Serials and reference: Directories of publishers and the book trade** entry **195**

1496 Brickhill, Paul **"Bookselling in Africa. Forgotten, Silent, and Undermined."** *Bellagio Publishing Network Newsletter*, no. 19 (March 1997): 12-15.

The author argues forcefully that, while pinpointing distribution as a major weakness in book provision, in practice, policymakers, donors, and publishers negate the role of booksellers. Brickhill says that bookselling is in crisis all over Africa: "it is disorganized, barely viable, grossly undercapitalized and for the most part an unrewarding commercial undertaking." He points out that booksellers have been excluded in all state-monopoly systems of book supply, and that there is a tendency in commercial textbook systems to exclude booksellers from the educational market. Moreover, alternatives to bookshop distribution "are mooted without considering whether existing bookshops and their distribution systems might not serve the purpose. One hears everything from donkey carts moving books to vegetable sellers selling books, seriously discussed, while bookshops struggle for survival and are ignored. Non-conventional book distribution is required and desirable as a supplement, not an alternative, to the bookshop and its range of extension services." The author also contends that many African publishers fail to have a proper appreciation of the role and services provided by booksellers, and the special problems they face. Publishers who do not work with booksellers do so at their peril: "every limitation of bookselling in Africa is a step towards the impoverishment of African publishers and authors and their further dependency on donor support. Ultimately, the booksellers' problems will come to haunt even the most successful publishers."

1497 Brickhill, Paul **"New Challenges in Book Distribution in Africa."** In *Development Directory of Indigenous Publishing 1995*, compiled by Carol Priestley. Harare: African Publishers Network, 1995, 52-56.

Surveys the state of the retail book trade in African countries (as at 1994), drawing attention to the inadequacies of the distribution network and the weakness of the bookselling sector as an essential component in the "book chain" as a whole. Argues that booksellers' associations need strengthening as the institutional base for development of book distribution.

1498 Cofie, Sam O. **"University Bookselling: Problems and Prospects."** *Ghana Book World*, no. 3 (1982): 16-19.

Describes problems and constraints of academic bookselling in Ghana, such as staffing, range of stocks, and the problem of collecting payment.

1499 Cofie, Sam O. **"Bookselling in Ghana Today."** *Ghana Book World*, no. 4 (1988): 20-24.

The [former] Manager of the University of Ghana Bookshop in Legon provides a brief history of bookselling in Ghana, followed by a description of the role of the Ghana Booksellers Association, and the activities of university bookshops and general booksellers. Discusses the problems and prospects inherent in the book trade, and touches on issues of censorship and pornography.

1500 Czerniewicz, Laura **"Interministerial Collaboration for More Effective Book Distribution."** In *Millennium Marketplace.* [Proceedings of the ZIBF] *Indaba 2000, Harare, Zimbabwe, 31 July – 1 August 2000.* Harare: Zimbabwe International Book Fair Trust, n.d. [2001], 254-60.
A Powerpoint presentation that aimed to demonstrate key issues affecting book provision and distribution in Africa. It shows how book distribution is at the centre of sometimes conflicting government policies, how educational curriculum policies impact on book supply; and offers a number of suggestions how book distribution issues can be put on inter-ministerial agendas.

1501 Dekutsey, Woeli **"Bookselling in Ghana: Is the Informal Sector the Key?"** *The African Book Publishing Record* 21, no. 2 (1995): 109-12.
Provides a history of the retail book trade in Ghana, past government involvement in bookselling and book distribution, and reports about a new trend in bookselling in Ghana initiated by the informal sector. The author finds that traditional or conventional booksellers are a rather sleepy lot and are on their way out, pushed out by a new generation of more enterprising, more aggressive, and truly street-wise pavement booksellers, itinerant book peddlers, and market stall book traders.

1502 Impey, Bridget **"People's Book Centres: A New South African Initative."** *Bellagio Publishing Network Newsletter,* no. 28 (November 2001): 4-5.
Online: http://www.bellagiopublishingnetwork.com/newsletter28/impey.htm [15/03/08]
Reports about a proposal being developed in South Africa to set up a number of 'people's book centres', which will be located within libraries and will work within the communities served by those libraries. They will promote book owning through the concept of book clubs, and will also be encouraged to develop the commercial side of the business by selling textbooks into local schools. The proposal is not aimed at replicating traditional retail bookstores.

1503 Irura, Stanley **"Effective Communication between Publishers and Bookseller in the Promotion of Published Materials."** *The Kenya Bookseller* 4, no. 1 (1992): 8-9.
Calls for more effective collaboration between publishers and booksellers in Kenya.

1504 Isnard, F. Lalande **"Vendre des livres en Afrique? Une expérience."** *The African Book Publishing Record* 6, no.3/4 (1980): 205-207.
The [former] director of the Centre de Diffusion du Livre Camerounais uses her many years of experience to describe what bookselling is really like in West Africa. She cover topics such as how to sell, what to sell, and how much to charge.

1505 Kor, Buma **"A Country Report - Cameroon."** *The Kenya Bookseller* 1, no. 4 (October/December 1988): 28-29.

Discusses bookselling in Cameroon, the nature of the different types of book traders, the state of the retail trade, competition between booksellers, and the relationship of booksellers with the government.

1506 McNaught, Sue and Jennie Bowen **"Bookselling in South Africa: Comments from a Bookseller's Perspective."** *Innovation. Journal of Appropriate Librarianship and Information Work in Southern Africa*, no. 8 (June 1994): 16-23.
Online:
http://www.library.unp.ac.za/Innovation/InnovationPdfs/No8pp16-23McNaught&Bowen.pdf [15/03/08]
Outlines the problems, issues and challenges facing South African booksellers. Includes a general overview of the economics of bookselling, bookshop selection policies for stocks, pricing, and problems of distribution.

Machet, M.P. **"Publishing and Book Selling in South Africa with Specific Reference to the Black Market"** *see* ➜ **Section 3, Country studies: South Africa** entry **1040**

1507 Mosuro, Kolade **"Publishing and Bookselling: A Bookseller's Observations."** *African Publishing Review* 10, no. 1 (2001): 3-5.
Also published in *The Publisher* 7, no. 1 (August 2000)
A hard-hitting examination of publisher-bookseller relationships, especially the situation prevailing in Nigeria. The author is critical of many publishers' failings in several areas: wrong or inadequate assignment of ISBNs; a lack of catalogues and other bibliographic tools from most publishers; lack of quality control in the production process resulting in poor quality or shoddily-produced books which booksellers find difficult to sell both within the country, much less elsewhere; cumbersome or amateurish orders processing and invoicing procedures; and publishers not availing themselves of analytical information such as dues analysis. He is also critical of publishers failing to pass on realistic trade discounts to booksellers (fixed arbitrarily, for the entire retail trade, at a publishers' forum), or publishers bypassing booksellers altogether by selling direct to government ministries. The author states "lack of appreciable returns have stifled the growth of bookselling and served as a disincentive for newcomers", but concludes that despite this situation there is now emerging a second generation of booksellers who "are educated, well-exposed and result-driven. They are applying modern principles of management to bookselling. We need many more of them. They are at par, if not ahead of many of the publishers in their embrace of technology in running the business. The future of bookselling in Nigeria is well paved."

1508 Mosuro, Kolade **"Information Generation and Utilisation in Bookshops and Libraries."** In *Creating a Conducive Environment for Book Publishing*, edited by Chukwuemeka Ike. Awka, Nigeria: Nigerian Book Foundation, 1996, 66-70.

Makes some suggestions for good practice in bookselling, reviews some tools of the trade, and stresses the need for proper management information systems and adequate stock control.

Muhate, Zephanias **"Interministerial Collaboration. More Effective Book Distribution: The Mozambique Experience"** *see* ➔ **Section 3, Country studies: Mozambique** entry **708**

Nfila, Reason Baathuli **"Academic Library-Supplier Relationship: The Experience of Supplier Selection and Evaluation at the University of Botswana Library."** *see* ➔ **Libraries and publishing** entry **1994**

1509 Nyoni, Todd **"The Challenge of General Book Distribution in Africa."** *African Publishing Review* 3, no. 6 (November/December 1994): 11-12.
Deals with the promotion of general books, the challenges of creating readership and finding successful marketing strategies; describes how these challenges are being tackled by the [now defunct] Zimbabwe Book Marketing Trust.

1510 Nyoni, Todd **"Tackling Africa's Book Distribution Problem Headlong."** *Glendora Review* 1, no. 1 (June-August 1995): 51-53.
Online:
http://digital.lib.msu.edu/projects/africanjournals/html/itemdetail.cfm?recordID=2341 [06/01/08]
Looks at the challenges of promoting books for the general reader, and asserts "the engine of book development is the creation of the book market and book consumers of African books." Also reviews an innovative book marketing scheme in Zimbabwe pioneered by Harare bookseller Grassroots Books.

1511 Ogunleye, Bisi **"Who Killed the Bookshop System in Nigeria?"** *Bellagio Publishing Network Newsletter*, no. 10 (June 1994): 8-9.
Deplores the demise of well-stocked bookshops in Nigeria, particularly university bookshops, and examines the factors which have led to the virtual collapse of the retail book trade in Nigeria.

Ogunleye, Bisi **"Establishing a Cost-Effective National Book Distribution Network in Nigeria"** *see* ➔ **Section 3, Country studies: Nigeria** entry **830**

Olude, O.O. **"The National Book Distribution Network: Suggestion for Textbook Distribution to Schools"** *see* ➔ **Section 3, Country studies: Nigeria** entry **841**

1512 Orimalade, Oluronke **"Problems Facing Bookselling in Nigeria."** In *Women Empowerment Through Publishing. Papers Presented at the Second*

Nigeria International Book Fair, 8-12 May, 2003. Lagos: Nigerian Book Fair Trust [c/o Literamed Publications Ltd., PMB 21068, Ikeja, Lagos, Nigeria], 2003, 103-112.

Ronke Orimalade probes into some of the issues "which have more or less paralyzed bookselling in Nigeria", and which includes marginalization of booksellers and the retail sector by the Nigerian government at both Federal and State levels, as well as poor relations between publishers and booksellers, marred by accusations and counter accusations, with each group citing long lists of grievances and lack of collaboration. She reports about the activities of a Joint Action Committee established by both parties, designed to improve publisher-bookseller relations, but whose decisions and action plans are yet to be implemented. Other problems identified are the lack of a strong professional association for booksellers, no code of conduct for business practices, lack of training, and the absence of a national book development council.

1513 Philombe, René **"Le libraire Camerounais! Le cas de Yaoundé (une enquête sectorielle)."** *CREPLA Bulletin d'Informations,* no. 9 (August 1984): 15-18.

Looks at bookshops in Cameroon, focusing on Yaoundé, and aims to provide an inventory of the different types of retail outlets in the country.

Print Industries Cluster Council **Book Retail Industry Survey 2006 Report** *see* **Section 3, Country studies: South Africa** entry ➜ **1074**

1514 Reimer, F.J. **"Ghana: The Function of the Bookseller as a Link Between Author and Reader."** *Literatur Nachrichten* 12, no. 3 (August 1988): 59-62.

Discusses the importance of the link between the author as the begetter of the book and the bookseller as the distributor, with the publisher in between.

1515 Read, Tony; Carmelle Denning, and Vincent Bontoux **Upgrading Book Distribution in Africa.** London: Association for the Development of Education in Africa (ADEA), Working Group on Books and Learning Materials (Perspectives on African Book Development, 12), 2001. 252 pp. (distributed by African Books Collective Ltd., Oxford) Also published in French as **Améliorer les systèmes de distribution du livre en Afrique.**

This study is currently the most comprehensive survey of textbook distribution in sub-Saharan Africa. If offers a detailed survey and analysis of the key policy issues affecting book distribution in Africa today. The study was organized and co-ordinated by International Book Development Ltd. in London, and Danaé-Sciences, a Paris-based consultancy company specialising in editorial support, training and written communication. It draws on a series of major case studies carried out in Ghana, Guinea, Kenya, Malawi, Nigeria and Uganda, together with mini case studies from Botswana, Burkina Faso, Cameroon, Chad, Côte d'Ivoire, Mali, Senegal, Tanzania and Togo, undertaken by book practitioners in these countries, most from the private sector. All of the case studies cover some common elements, including, for example, information on the national education system (including basic education statistics), and a discussion of the main players and mechanisms in the book distribution chain; they also review regional trade in books, and most case studies comment upon the impact of funding, agency investment, and government policies affecting national book development. In addition to the case studies, a useful feature is the inclusion of a fold-out chart "Critical issues on upgrading book distribution in Africa – A decision tree for policy-makers", which shows the key options that policy makers need to consider in developing a national framework for textbook delivery. An extensive glossary of common terms and acronyms used in education, development and the book trade, completes the volume. The survey concludes "there is already a policy change underway among a number of governments and funding agencies in their approaches toward national textbook distribution. This change is more apparent in Anglophone than in Francophone countries and is by no means universal even in Anglophone countries. But the reaction against the inefficiencies, the lack of a service culture and the typically high cost operations of state centralist policies is now almost ten years old." It also notes that times are changing, and that senior government officials in many countries now openly acknowledge and welcome the increasing involvement of the private sector in educational book provision activity.

Reviews:
The African Book Publishing Record vol. 28, no. 1, 2002
Bellagio Publishing Network Newsletter 29, December 2001
Online:
http://www.bellagiopublishingnetwork.com/newsletter29/publications.htm
[23/02/08]

1516 Segbawu, Frank **"Improving Book Distribution. The Ghana Experience ."** In *Millennium Marketplace.* [Proceedings of the ZIBF] *Indaba 2000, Harare, Zimbabwe, 31 July – 1 August 2000.* Harare: Zimbabwe International Book Fair Trust, n.d. [2001], 227-233.
Describes the nature of distribution in Ghana and constraints and problems in textbook school supply, and offers a number of possible suggestions and solutions to improve the situation.

1517 Sheikh, Mohamoud Mohamed **"Book Selling in Kenya."** *Asian/Pacific Book Development*, 27, no. 2 (1997): 11-12.
[Not examined]

Book trade and book development organizations

See also
→ **African Books Collective Ltd**
→ **African Publishers Network**

1518 Ahmed, Medani M. **"Survey of Capacity Building of National Publishers Associations in Africa."** *African Publishing Review* 8, no. 6 (2000): 4-5.
Examines four areas of capacity building by African national book trade associations, covering organizational and institutional capacity building, resource base and material capacity (i.e. ownership of equipment etc.), communications capacity, and financial capacity and sources of funding.

1519 Alemna, A. Anaba **"The Role of Book Development Councils in the Book Industry: The Case of Ghana and Nigeria."** *Ghana Book World*, no. 4 (1988): 29-32.
Reviews the historical development and functions of book development councils in West Africa, with special reference to Ghana and Nigeria. Comparisons are drawn between the two countries including their council's objectives, achievements and problems.

1520 Anderson, Elisabeth **"The Centre for the Book – South Africa."** *The African Book Publishing Record* 26, no. 4 (2000): 255-258.
The [former] Head of the Cape Town-based **Centre for the Book (934)** provides an account of the mission and objectives, governance and funding of this book development organization, one of the most active in Africa. She also describes its programmes and activities, how it works with writers, publishers and libraries, and the information services it offers.

1521 Bamhare, Miriam **"The Zimbabwe Book Development Council."** *Information Development* 10, no. 1 (March 1994): 21-22.
Describes the book supply infrastructure in Zimbabwe and the objectives, structure and work of the → **Zimbabwe Book Development Council (1203).**

1522 Chanin, Clifford **"Reflections on the Bellagio Group."** *Bellagio Publishing Network Newsletter*, no. 11 (September 1994): 12-13.
Reflects on the work of the Bellagio Group of donors and their efforts to support and strengthen the indigenous African book industries through the [currently dormant] → **Bellagio Publishing Network Secretariat (37).**

1523 Drabeck, Anne Gordon **"Future Directions for the Bellagio Donor Group of Africa Publishing."** *Bellagio Publishing Network Newsletter*, no. 8 (December 1993): 1-2.
Charts the possible future directions, and range of support activities, for the Bellagio donors group. Calls for a number of in-depth studies on the economics of the African

publishing industry (including country case studies), and asks whether economic reforms currently being encouraged in Africa are consistent with the needs of the African book industry.

1524 Hasan, Abul **"The Afro-Asian Book Council. Eight Years in Support of Publishing in the South."** *INASP Newsletter*, no. 9 (November 1997): 13-14.
Online: http://www.inasp.info/newslet/nov97.html#7
The [former] Director of the New Delhi-based → **Afro-Asian Book Council (7)** looks back at the achievements of the Council since its establishment in 1990, in terms of its support for books, author development, training programmes, exhibits organized, and its role as a catalyst paving the way for a healthy growth of the Afro-Asian book industry.

1525 Hasan, Abul **"South/South Cooperation: A Five Year-Old Initiative Gathers Strength."** *Logos. The Journal of the World Book Community* 5, no. 3 (1994): 130-32.
Online:
http://www.atypon-link.com/LOG/doi/pdf/10.2959/logo.1994.5.3.130
An account about the objectives, activities and achievements to date [to 1994] of the → **Afro-Asian Book Council (7)**, whose goal is to assist the growth of self-sufficient publishing industries in all the countries of Africa and Asia, and encourages active collaboration between publishers from the two continents.

1526 Hurry, Burford **"Helping Zimbabwe to Read. The Need for a National Book Council of Zimbabwe."** *Zimbabwe Librarian* 15, nos. 3&4 (July/December 1983): 33-35.
Discusses the important role which books and book-related material have in Zimbabwe's cultural and educational development, and the need for a book and journals council.

1527 Ike, Chukwuemeka **"Book Development Organisations in Africa."** In *Development Directory of Indigenous Publishing 1995*, compiled by Carol Priestley. Harare: African Publishers Network, 1995, 16-22.
Reviews the establishment of national book development councils and similar bodies in a number of African countries, with a critical assessment of their impact and success, or lack of success, to date. Suggests that national book development councils as conceived at present are not necessarily the only option for book development.

1528 Kamugisha, Thomas A.R. **"National Publishers' Associations in Africa."** In *Development Directory of Indigenous Publishing 1995*, compiled by Carol Priestley. Harare: African Publishers Network, 1995, 23-31.
Examines some of the factors that have hindered the development of indigenous African publishing, and traces the establishment of national publishers' associations from the late 1980s. Also reviews the principal objectives of African book trade bodies that have been set up to date [to mid-1990s]. However, the author finds that a

"a serious imbalance exists between the objectives and performance of these associations"; he argues that they have a vital role to play and should be seen "to act as the prime movers and accelerators to ensure the development of the indigenous publishing industry."

1529 Kromberg, Steve **"The Case for a National Book Development Council."** In *Publishing for Democratic Education*, edited by Steve Kromberg *et al*. Johannesburg: The Sached Trust, 1993, 163-176.
Sets out the need for a National Book Development Council (NBDC), what its aims and objectives ought to be, whether it should have some sort of policing function, the role which the state should have vis-à-vis an NBDC, and how it should be governed and coordinate with the different players in the book chain.

1530 Mbome, P.H. **"Namibia Book Development Council."** *Namibia Review* 2, no. 2 (1993): 20-22.
[Not examined]

1531 McCallum, Kate **"South African Print Industries Cluster."**
Bellagio *Publishing Network Newsletter*, no. 24 (December 1998): 9-10.
http://www.bellagiopublishingnetwork.com/newsletter24/mccallum.htm
[07/01/08]
Reports about a new initiative in South Africa, launched in 1998, which saw the various links in the print supply chain – publishers, booksellers, printers, paper manufacturers, newspapers and magazines – working together formally and harmoniously to establish a ➔ **Print Industries Cluster Council (943)**. It was brought about by a recognition that there was a great deal to be gained by sharing information, understanding the chain better, and working together more closely on matters of common interest; and "if the various industries were to become internationally competitive, they had to co-operate in order to compete." *Note:* in 2007 the Print Industries Cluster became part of the ➔ **South African Book Development Council (950)**.

1532 Moutchia, William **"Le développement du livre en Afrique au Sud du Sahara."** In *Actes de la Table Ronde sur le Partenariat dans l'Edition Francophone: vers le renforcement des actions de coédition et la création de consortiums*. Abidjan: Ministère de l'Education Nationale de Côte d'Ivoire, 1990, 113-127.
Gives a detailed overview of the [now dormant] Yaoundé-based Centre Régional de Promotion du Livre en Afrique au Sud du Sahara (CREPLA). Although CREPLA did not publish, produce nor distribute books, it was active in many areas of book promotion including book fairs, national book councils, training, and literacy development. The author was its former Director.

1533 Nair, Chandran **"Book Development Council - An Overview."** *The Kenya Bookseller* 4, no. 1 (1992): 22-25.

Argues that book development, and a national book development council, "is a *sine qua non* for national development."

1534 Nigerian Book Foundation **Books Build the Nation. The Nigerian Book Foundation.** Awka, Nigeria: The Nigerian Book Foundation, n.d. [1994]. 7 pp.
A brief history of the ➜ **Nigerian Book Foundation (738)**, established in 1991, describing its structure and objectives.

1535 Pan African Booksellers Association (PABA) **PABA Strategic Plan 2004-2008, July 2004.** Eldoret, Kenya: Pan African Booksellers Association, 2004. 29 pp.
Online:
http://www.panafricanbooksellersassociation.org/PABA_STRATEGICPLA N.pdf [07/01/08]
The ➜ **Pan African Booksellers Association/PABA (21)** is a non-profit making umbrella organization of national booksellers associations from across Africa, with headquarters in Kenya. In this plan it sets out PABA's strategic objectives to achieve its mandate to become a major player in the promotion and strengthening of the book chain throughout Africa and, in particular, to support the bookselling sector and the retail book trade.

1536 Reece, Jane **"Book Development Councils in Africa: Part One."** *African Publishing Review* 4, no. 2 (March/April 1995): 20-21.
Part one of a two-part report that traces the chequered history of book development councils in Africa and evaluates their effectiveness and impact, or lack of impact, to date [to mid-1990s].

1537 Reece, Jane **"Book Development Councils in Africa: Part Two: The Zimbabwean Story."** *African Publishing Review* 4, no. 3 (May/June 1995): 12-14.
Concludes the report in the preceding entry, focusing on Zimbabwe and the activities of the ➜ **Zimbabwe Book Development Council (1203).**

1538 Seeber, Monica **"Publishers Association of South Africa."** *African Publishing Review* 4, no. 4 (July/August 1995): 11-12.
Describes the background that led to the formation of the ➜ **Publishers Association of South Africa/PASA (945),** in November 1992, its aims and objectives, the three different interest groups (Education, Academic, General) it serves, and its activities to date [to mid-1990s].

1539 Seeber, Monica **"The Relevance of National Organisations in South Africa."** (Paper presented under the title of "The Role of Industry Organisations in African Publishing" at the International Conference on the Book, Oxford Brookes University, September 2005)
http://www.sabdet.com/ICB2005seeber.htm [16/03/08]

Examines the activities of book sector related organizations and associations in South Africa, the issues they tackle, the role they have played in demographic change, promoting publishers' and authors' rights, training and skills development, and the opening up of the publishing profession to black South Africans.

Children's book publishing

See also
→ **African books in the international market place**
→ **Publishing in African languages**
→ **Reading culture and reading promotion**
→ **Women in African Publishing/Publishing by and for women**

Note: this section includes primarily articles that deal, in whole or in part, with publishing aspects of producing children's literature, including the important aspect of artwork and illustrations. Studies of children's or young people's reading habits appear in the section → **Reading culture and reading promotion**, while articles on publishing children's books in African languages are listed under → **Publishing in African languages**.

Articles that deal exclusively with *writing* for children are not included, nor are articles that focus on different genres in children's writing, storytelling, oral literature and culture, or those that examine themes and images in African children's literature.

1540 Acholonu, Catherine Obianju **"Writing and Publishing for Children: Nigerian Children's Literature in English: A Critique."** *Journal of African Children's and Youth Literature*, no. 1 (1989): 60-78.
Considers the inherent dangers when publishers produce material for children that is not suitable for an African child. Examines what factors should be considered in creating children's literature: the age, mental and psychological development of children, and the impact and usefulness of the written word. Also looks at what is available in children's literature in Nigeria and concludes that the genre could benefit from more attention.

1541 African Children's Literature
http://www.childlit.org.za/SAChildLit.html (South African Children's Literature pages) [08/01/08]
http://www.childlit.org.za/acl/index.html (African Children's Literature pages) [these pages, currently (08/01/08) *not* accessible, but may become available again later in 2008]
These rich resources are part of the Web site of the → **Children's Literature Research Unit (935)**, which functions as a Unit of the Department of Information Science of the University of South Africa. Its mission is to promote children's literature and reading

through study, research, community programmes and other promotional activities. Established in 1996, the Unit has organized a series of workshops and international conferences and also maintains an archive and a library collection. There are a variety of resources and author portraits on South African children's writers and illustrators, book awards, book reviews, discussions, bibliographies and lists, including pages on children's books in Afrikaans. The pages dedicated to African children's literature and reading by children in Africa other than South Africa, offer short online articles and book reviews for Botswana, Ghana, Lesotho, Malawi, Nigeria, South Africa, Uganda, Zambia, and Zimbabwe, and some pages devoted to children's books submitted (in 2001 and 2002) for the ➜ **Noma Award for Publishing in Africa (98).** There are also author portraits of two prominent African children's writers, Meshack Asare and Sam Aryeetey.

1542 African Publishers Network **APNET Children's Catalogue: 1995/96.** Harare: African Publishers Network, 1995. 45 pp.
Illustrated catalogue containing full details of over 400 children's titles (in English and Swahili) from 61 African publishers. Many of the entries are annotated and some "have the uncensored comments of young reviewers." Includes an index of authors and titles, and a directory giving ordering addresses of publishers. No further editions would appear to have been published to date.

1543 Amabhuku. Illustrations d'Afrique/ Illustrations from Africa. Paris: Les Amis de la Joie par les Livres, 1999. 88 pp.
Each year the Bologna Book Fair, the leading international showcase for children's book publishing, honours a different "guest country" and its illustrators through special exhibits and events. At the 1999 Fair it was the turn of Africa, and this coincided with a competition and exhibition of the work of African illustrators. To mark the occasion, the French book promotion organization that co-ordinated the event, Les Amis de la Joie par les Livres – now ➜ **La Joie par les Livres. Centre National du Livre pour Enfants (86)** – published a most attractive exhibition catalogue entitled *Amabhuku* (which means "books" in Zulu). The handsomely produced catalogue, in addition to containing full colour illustrations of the work of 34 African book illustrators, also includes a useful directory of 176 African illustrators with their full names and contact addresses, together with a directory of African publishers producing children's books, arranged by country. In an introductory section (with text in French and English), three prominent African authors – Francis Bebey, Charles Mungoshi, and Véronique Tadjo – reflect on their experience of, and what it means to them, writing for children, and the six members of the jury also provide their own perspective on the topic of writing and illustrating for children.

1544 Apronti, Jawa **"A Critical Review of Literature for Children."** *Ghana Book World,* no. 5 (1991): 19-24.
Emphasizes the obstacles which stand in the way of a flourishing book culture among children in Ghana. Expresses the need for more books in Ghanaian languages, books for girls, poetry, and books "that treat with ample empathy people of ethnic origins other than the author's own."

1545 Asare, Meshack **"The African Writer in the Child's World."** In *Proceedings, Papers and Summaries of Discussions at the Seminar on Creative Writing and Publishing for Children in Africa Today. 12th-14th January 1983.* Freetown: Central Library, 1983, 13-19.

Ghanaian artist and children's book writer and illustrator Meshack Asare, winner of the 1982 ➔ **Noma Award for Publishing in Africa (98)**, discusses the case of the African writer, the African heritage, the African child and society, and goes on to examine the seriousness of writing, knowledge, creativity and social conditioning as three progressive factors in writing.

1546 Asare, Meshack **"Writing for Children in Africa."** In *A Handbook for African Writers*, edited by James Gibbs. Oxford: Hans Zell Publishers, 1988, 80-85.

Another version, **"An African Writer Writing for Children in Africa"**, published In *Meeting the Educational Needs of our Children. 2nd African Books Festival Brochure, 18-21 November 1987*, edited by Hilary Benton London: Foundation for Afrikan Arts, 1987, 16-17.

The award-winning Ghanaian children's writer argues that children's literature has not enjoyed the boom of other sectors of book publishing in Africa. He relates his own experiences and encourages young writers to continue to write and illustrate for children "as if it is the most important thing to do in Africa."

1547 Ashimole, Elizabeth O. **"Nigerian Children's Literature and the Challenges of Social Change."** In *Children and Literature in Africa,* edited by Chidi Ikonne, Emelia Oko, and Peter Onwudinjo. Ibadan: Heinemann Educational Books, 1992, 70-81.

Looks at the literature available in Nigeria for children and contrasts it with the influence of the mass media, especially television, video and video games. The author stresses that in order to compete with the electronic age, books for children must be of the highest quality.

1548 Bamhare, Miriam **Catch them Young.**

http://www.childlit.org.za/acl/artzimbabwe.htm [07/01/08]

Examines perceptions of picture books in Zimbabwe, and publishing of picture story books by Zimbabwean publishers, The author, who is Director of the ➔ **Zimbabwe Book Development Council (1203),** is critical of local publishers: "Zimbabwe publishers will at anytime tell you that 'picture books are not our field yet'. They are said to be too expensive to produce, making the unit price prohibitive for a resistant market. The effort there is may be full-colour picture books, put on bad paper with shoddy artwork and lack of appreciation of design. There is need for a lot of training in writing and design of picture books." Bamhare offers a range of possible solutions to the problems she describes.

1549 Beau, Nathalie **"Amabhuku, illustrations d'Afrique."** *La Revue des Livres pour Enfants*, no. 187 (June 1999): 59-60.

A report about the ➔ **Amabhuku (1543)** exhibition of African children's books and the work of African children's book illustrators held during the 1999 Bologna Children's Book Fair, which effectively demonstrated the rapid growth of writing and publishing for African children, both in Africa and elsewhere.

1550 Bebye, Kidi **La presse africaine de jeunesse** [with] Diakhaté, Lydie **La literature africaine de jeunesse en Afrique sub-Saharienne.** Varennes-Vauzelles, France: Association l'Ilot-Livres [20 rue de 8 Mai 1945, 58640 Varennes-Vauzelles] 2001. 20 pp.
Two essays (in one booklet) about (i) magazine publishing for children and teenagers in francophone Africa; and (ii) writing and publishing for children in Africa, with short reviews of a number of titles.

1551 Bennett, Rosey **"Criteria for Successful Children's Books in South Africa."** In *Book Publishing in South Africa for the 1990s.* Cape Town: South African Library, 1991, 70-77.
Gives a general background to children's books, followed by an exposition of the criteria that the author believes should be used in publishing for children, together with a brief discussion on picture books with particular reference to South Africa.

1552 Bessière, Audrey, ed. **Livres d'images d'Afrique noire: auteurs-illustrateurs Africains: catalogue des collections des bibliothèques pour enfants de la Ville de Paris.** Paris: Paris-Bibliothèques éditions [10, rue de Clichy, 75009 Paris]. 2001. 116 pp.
An attractive catalogue and bibliography of children's books by African authors, and the work African children's book illustrators, held in library collections in the city of Paris. Includes titles in French and English, with an author index and index of illustrators, and listings of publishers and distributors.

1553 Bgoya, Walter **"Intra-African Trading in Children's Books. Opportunities and Constraints."** In *Book Fair Magazine. 3rd Pan-African Children's Book Fair.* Nairobi: CHISCI Press, 1994, 30-31.
Looks at the opportunities, and some of the constraints, for promoting and selling African children's books across country borders within Africa.

1554 Bookbird: A Journal of International Children's Literature. [Special issues on African children's literature] Basle: International Board on Books for Young People/Toronto: University of Toronto Press.
Bookbird. Special issue: African Children's Literature 36, no. 1 (1998)
http://www.utpjournals.com/bookbird/bookbird361.html (Complete table of contents only)
Bookbird, the journal of the ➔ **International Board on Books for Young People (71)**, devoted most of its Spring 1998 number to contemporary African children's literature, and it is an interesting and varied issue.
Bookbird. Special issue: Children's Literature and Africa 42, no. 3 (2004)

http://www.utpjournals.com/bookbird/bookbird423.html (Complete table of contents only)
Another special issue of *Bookbird* with articles on various aspects of children's literature and writing for children in Africa, some of which are individually abstracted in this section.

1555 Boye, Mary **"A Decade of Ghanaian Children's Literature in English (1968/69-1979)."** *Ghana Book World*, no. 4 (1988): 8-12.
Draws attention to the rich source of material for children in Ghanaian folktales, myths, legends and animal stories, and assesses the transition from oral story telling to books. Discusses a number of authors and their books in detail.

1556 Boye, Mary **"Ghanaian Children's Literature in English. The Second Decade (1979-1989)."** *Ghana Book World*, no. 5 (1991): 9-16.
A follow-up to the preceding entry (*see* ➔ **1555**). Reviews some outstanding Ghanaian books for children, with a range of subjects such as traditional stories, fantasy, picture story books, poetry, drama and non-fiction.

1557 Boye, Mary **"The Developing Field of Ghanaian Children's Literature."** *Journal of African Children's and Youth Literature*, no. 4 (1992-93): 29-43.
[Not examined]

1558 Boye, Mary **"Practices and Variables Affecting the Quality of Ghanaian's Children's Literature."** *African Journal of Library, Archives & Information Science* 3, no. 1 (April 1993): 35-44
Discusses the results of a survey of six publishing houses which produce books for Ghanaian children. Identifies some of the practices and variables which contribute to the unattractive nature of some Ghanaian children's books and makes suggestions for improving the situation.

1559 Bugembe, Mary **"Marketing Children's Books in the Pan-African Context."** *Focus on International & Comparative Librarianship* 29, no. 2 (10 September 1998): 91.93
Reports about the various initiatives and activities of the ➔ **Foundation for the Promotion of Children's Science Publishing in Africa (16)**, who are the organizers of the annual Pan-African Children's Book Fair held in Nairobi.

1560 Cassiau, Christophe; Véronique Botte, and Paul Tete **"L'édition de jeunesse au Kenya et au Congo Démocratique."** *Takam Tikou. Le Bulletin de la Joie par les Livres*, no. 10 (February 2003): 21-23.
Three authors provide an overview of children's book publishing in Kenya and the Democratic Republic of the Congo, looking at aspects of author development, readership, and distribution, with short descriptions of the activities of individual publishers and the nature of their books.

1561 Chakava, Henry **"Children and Books: Kenya. A Decade of African Publishing for Children 1988-1998."** In *Books and Children. Proceedings of the ZIBF Indaba 1998, Harare, Zimbabwe, 1-2 August 1998,* edited by the Zimbabwe International Book Fair Trust. Harare: Zimbabwe International Book Fair Trust, 1998, 42-46.

Slightly shorter version also published as **"A Publisher's Perspective on Children's Books"** in *African Publishing Review* 7, no. 6 (November/December 1998): 4-5.

Henry Chakava recounts his experience of publishing children's books as head of East African Educational Publishers in Nairobi, including publishing of children's books by prominent African writers such as Ngugi wa Thiong'o and Chinua Achebe, and a series of readers both in English and in various Kenyan languages. He explains the reasons why some books in mother tongue languages were not a commercial success, until they were incorporated into to the curriculum to strengthen the teaching of English in primary schools, and were given a series image and a standard design. He also describes the changes in the company's policies and focus for their children's book programmes over the years.

1562 Chitando, Anna **"Children's Literature in Zimbabwe: Considerable Creativity and Innovation."** *Mediaforum,* no. 3-4 (2005): 38-40.

A short account of the historical development of children's literature in Zimbabwe, the achievements of some Zimbabwean children's authors, and the challenges of publishing and distributing children's books.

1563 Cilliers, Isabel, ed. **Towards Understanding: Children's Literature for Southern Africa/ Op Weg na Begrip: Kinderliteratuur vir Suider Afrika.** Cape Town: Maskew Miller Longman, 1988. 314 pp. [Text in English and Afrikaans]

[Not examined]

1564 Cilliers, Isabel, ed. **Towards More Understanding: The Making and Sharing of Children's Literature in Southern Africa.** Cape Town: Juta, 1993. 255 pp.

A useful resource book for teachers, writers, illustrators, educators and academics concerned with children's literature. Includes chapters on the development of indigenous children's literature for a culturally heterogeneous society and offers ideas on how to market children's books, and, at the same time, how to create and sustain a reading culture among young readers.

1565 Cotton, Dulcie **"Publishing for Children in a Changing South Africa (1)."** In *Book Publishing in South Africa for the 1990s.* Cape Town: South African Library, 1991, 78-80.

Examines the publishing needs of the 'new' South Africa as far as children's book publishing is concerned, by considering the role of publishers and the literary needs for a changing society.

1566 Council for the Promotion of Children's Science Publications in Africa **Report on the Establishment of the Council for the Promotion of Children's Science Publications in Africa 1988-1990.** Nairobi: CHISCI, 1991. 14 pp.
A description of the role of the Council, later ➜ **Foundation for the Promotion of Children's Science Publications in Africa (16)**, its governance, the meetings of the governing body of the council, membership, a progress report on implementation of CHISCI's initial projects, and human and financial resources.

1567 Davies, Shirley **Reading Roundabout: A Review of South African Children's Literature.** Pietermaritzburg: Shuter & Shooter, 1992. 200 pp.
[Not examined]

1568 Dekutsey, Woeli **"Publishing for Children - Graphic Presentation."** In *Children's Reading Needs. The Challenges of the Next Century to Parents, Educators, Publishers and Librarians in Africa,* edited by Serah W. Mwanycky. CHISCI: Nairobi, 1993, 7-10.
Discusses the need for attractive presentation, and effective illustration and typography when publishing for children.

1569 Dekutsey, Woeli **"Publishing Comic Books in Africa."** In *Books and Children. Proceedings of the ZIBF Indaba 1998, Harare, Zimbabwe, 1-2 August 1998.* Harare: Zimbabwe International Book Fair Trust, 1998, 175-178.
Finds that, unlike in other parts of the world, the publication of indigenous comic books in English-speaking Africa is still not widespread and explains some of the reasons why this is so. The author believes that the comic genre has a potentially large but as yet largely unexploited market, and that comics can in fact provide effective learning tools for educating the public about serious issues affecting their everyday life.

1570 Dike, Virginia W. **"Children's Literature: The Nigerian Situation: Secondary and Young Adolescents."** *Nigerian Libraries* 21, no. 2 (1985): 61-70.
[Not examined]

1571 Dike, Virginia W. **"Wanted: African Picture Books for Nigerian Children."** *Pan African World* 1, no. 1 (August 1981): 13-18.
Dwells on the need for Nigeria to make use of the rich artistic tradition of the country, as an inspiration for illustrating children's books.

1572 Dike, Virginia W. **"Developing Fiction for Today's Nigerian Youth."** *Sankofa. A Journal of African Children's and Young Adult Literature* 4, (2005): 6-17.
Online: http://www.sacbf.org.za/2004%20papers/Virginia%20Dike.rtf
[07/01/08]

This is a sensitive and comprehensive overview of English-language fiction, written by Nigerian authors for Nigerian youth between the ages of 11 and 19 years, and published over the last twenty-five years by both indigenous Nigerian publishers and multinationals. Virginia Dike documents the body of fiction literature written for Nigerian young people, tracing its history from the beginnings in the 1960s, through its blossoming in the 1980s, to the present day. The article examines the different series, their target audience, and the characteristics of the novels in terms of societal realities and the personal concerns and challenges facing youth. The author finds that "novels for young people address issues in current Nigerian life, but relatively few touch on the immediate concerns of youth in any meaningful way". While a few timely themes are touched on, the treatment is not usually in depth, nor are issues approached from a young person's point of view. "Since developing one's identify and values are primary tasks of adolescence, a little more introspection and facing of immediate hard realities seems called for." The author offers a number of suggestions on the way forward, and the steps that can and should be taken to develop fiction that will more fully meet the varied and complex needs of today's Nigerian youth. She also urges publishers to adopt more aggressive marketing strategies, "rather than to assume no one wants to read fiction in Nigeria."

1573 Dillsworth, Gloria **"Children's Literature in Sierra Leone: A Librarian's View."** In *Children's Book Production and Distribution in Developing Countries,* edited by Doros Theodoulou and Pavlos Ioannides. Nicosia: Cyprus Association on Books for Young People, 1985, 73-90.
Describes public libraries in Sierra Leone and examines what children in Sierra Leone read. Discusses book promotional events and activities, story telling sessions, and film shows, and provides an overview publishing in the country, examining printing facilities, and the contribution of authors, creative writers and artists.

1574 Ekwensi, Cyprian D. **"The Problems of Writing, Illustrating and Publishing Adolescent Teenage Literature for Children."** *The African Book Publishing Record* 14, no. 2 (1988): 95-97.
A paper originally presented to the Workshop on Children's Literature in Africa and the Third World held at the 4th Zimbabwe International Book Fair in Harare in August 1987. The prominent Nigerian novelist discusses why writing for adolescents and teenagers has not been a priority with African writers and goes on to address wider issues of publishing for children in Africa.

1575 Fahari, Gladys **"The Long-Lasting Memory of Storybooks."**
UNESCO Courier, no. 7 (2007)
Online:
http://portal.unesco.org/en/ev.php-
URL_ID=39023&URL_DO=DO_TOPIC&URL_SECTION=201.html
[16/03/08]
An account of the ➜ **Children's Book Project of Tanzania/CBP (1117)** which was awarded the ➜ **UNESCO (118)** King Sejong Literacy Prize in 2007 in recognition for its outstanding work promoting the love of books among children and adults. The project was started in 1991 by ➜ **CODE (48)**, in response to Tanzania's acute

shortage of books for children, and the lack of adequate skills among book sector personnel to produce appropriate reading materials. CBP set out to assist with the production and distribution of relevant reading materials and to encourage and support indigenous authorship. In collaboration with local publishers it has published a wide variety of children's books in Kiswahili, and 3,000 copies of the total print run of 5,000 copies is then distributed free. The project, which is currently supported by several international donor organizations, has also established 99 school libraries in the country.

1576 Fayose, Philomena Osazee **"Picture Books for African Children."** *Sierra Leone Library Journal* 5, no. 1/2 (March 1980): 9-23.
Highlights the lack of books in African languages for children, and the generally unattractive appearance of many African-published children's books.

1577 Fayose, Philomena Osazee **"How to Promote the Reading Habit in the Child."** *The Book - Nigeria* 1, no. 1 (December 1980): 55-63.
Discusses the reading habits of Nigerian children and the factors that can influence and promote reading for children.

1578 Fayose, Philomena Osazee **A Guide to Children's Literature for African Teachers, Librarians and Parents.** Ibadan: AENL Educational Publishers, 1995. 132 pp.
A bibliography of 628 annotated entries (in English and some in French), arranged by type of materials, i.e. picture-story books, fairy tales, poetry, drama, etc. With country and author indexes.

1579 Fayose, Philomena Osazee **Nigerian Children's Literature in English**. Ibadan: AENL Educational Publishers, 1995. 116 pp.
Critical review of Nigerian children's books, arranged by type of books. Also includes short biographical profiles of some of the best known Nigerian children's writers.

1580 Fayose, Philomena Osazee **Nigerian Children's Literature and the Changing Social Scenes.** In *Other Worlds, Other Lives: Children's literature Experiences. Proceedings of the International Conference in Children's Literature, 4-6 April 1995,* vol. 3, edited by Myrna Machet, Sandra Olën and Thomas van der Walt. Pretoria: Unisa Press, 1996, 173-182.
Online: http://www.childlit.org.za/acl/fayose.html [08/01/08]
Reviews the patterns and themes of Nigerian children's literature for the periods of 1960 to 1978 on the one hand, and Nigerian children's fiction since 1979 on the other. The author concludes "Nigerian children's literature has tried to express the changing needs of society. Many of the writers see themselves as social critics. Their main purpose in writing is to make their society a better one."

1581 Fayose, Philomena Osazee **"Not Only Books for Africa But a Reading Culture Too."**
http://www.sacbf.org.za/2004%20papers/Osazee%20Fayose.rtf [16/03/08]

A keynote address presented at the 29th IBBY Congress, Cape Town, 5-9 September 2004. The author asserts that African-published children's books "exist in their own rights exhibiting qualities peculiar to them, though most of the developed world has the erroneous impression that African children suffer from a dearth of good books. This is not so, since the 1970s good quality books written specifically for African children have been published in West, East, South and North Africa." She provides a brief history of children's book publishing in Africa and the different phases it went through, examining the variety and forms of children's books, the genres and themes, the promotion of the reading habit, and calls for more collaboration between authors, illustrators, publishers, librarians and teachers to work more closely together and help to provide a wider variety of children's books.

1582 Fox, Mem **Handbook for Writers of Children's Books.** Paris: UNESCO, Division of Basic Education [7, Place de Fontenoy 75352 Paris Cedex], 2000. Available as print version upon request. Email: j.kjaersgaard@unesco.org
Online: http://www.unesco.org/education/blm/opmIIforeword_en.php [15/03/08]
Also published in French as **Vade-mecum des auteurs de livres pour enfants** http://www.unesco.org/education/blm/blmintro_fr.php [15/03/08]
The idea for this helpful handbook was inspired by two workshops for writers of children's books held in Tanzania and Uganda in January-February 2000. The workshops were organized by the → **National Book Development Council of Tanzania (1119)** and the → **Book Development Council of Uganda (1150),** under the → **UNESCO/DANIDA Basic Learning Materials Initiative (119),** with the aim of assisting the countries to enliven their publishing industries by promoting local writing and the production of attractive children's books. The Handbook draws on some of the lessons learned in the Tanzania and Uganda workshops. It does not pretend to provide a detailed and comprehensive guide, but aims to present some basic principles that should be taken into account when writing for children. There is also a useful checklist of 'dos and don'ts' for writers of picture story books to make sure nothing vitally important has been left out, and some stories that were written during the workshop for writers are also included.

1583 Granqvist, Raoul, and Jürgen Martini, eds. **Preserving the Landscape of Imagination: Children's Literature in Africa.** Special issue, no. 17-18, of *Matatu. Journal of African Culture and Society.* Amsterdam: Editions Rodophi. 1997. 361 pp.
A special issue of *Matatu* on the writing and publishing for children in Africa today. Contains 14 articles on the topic, and one on Caribbean children's literature, by contributors from Africa and from Europe, and some of which – i.e. those dealing with publishing aspects in whole or in part – are individually listed and abstracted in this volume. Some of the papers were first presented at an international conference on African children's literature held in Umeå, Sweden in March 1992.

1584   Granqvist, Raoul **"Staying in Touch with Tradition. Interview with Stephen J. Chifunyise."** *Matatu* no. 17-18 (1997): 243-256.
Stephen Chifunyise is head of the Cultural Division in the Ministry of Education and Culture in Zimbabwe; he is a theatre artist and works with children in children's performing arts. He and his wife Tisa were also the driving force behind the launching, in 1991, of a children's magazine called *Probe. The Magazine for Young People in Southern Africa,* and which is discussed during this interview.

1585   Gray, Stephen **"Véronique Tadjo Speaks with Stephen Gray."** *Research in African Literatures* 34, 3 (Fall 2003): 142-147.
Véronique Tadjo, from the Côte d'Ivoire, is a celebrated writer, artist and author and illustrator of several children's books. In this interview with South African writer Stephen Gray she talks about her writing and projects, feminism, censorship, and her publishers.

1586   Heale, Jay **South African Authors and Illustrators.** Grabouw, South Africa: Bookchat, 1994. 48 pp.
Profiles of 23 authors and illustrators of South African children's books, together with listings of the books published by each of them.

1587   Heale, Jay **Getting your Children Hooked on Books, 1994.** Grabouw, South Africa: Jay Heale/Bookchat, 1994. 48 pp.
A compendium of ideas for parents and librarians which suggests ways in which children can be encouraged to read, and contains information about the production of books as well as a list of recommended titles for children.

1588   Heale, Jay **"Which Way the Wind Blows?"** *Writers World*, no. 13 (1994): 33-34.
Looks at trends in children's book publishing in South Africa, and states that it is not so much a matter of teaching children how to read, but that there will have to be teaching that will make children want to read, and that reading should be fun.

1589   Heale, Jay **"So What do Young Readers Want to Read?"** *African Publishing Review* 4, no. 6 (November/December 1995): 14.
Argues that children's opinions are important and that children (in South Africa) should have a right to decide for themselves what they want to read, rather than having books imposed on them which are officially approved or prescribed by educational bodies. Calls for a well-endowed children's book award, with prize winners selected by panels of children themselves, along the lines of the Smarties Prize in the UK.

1590   Heale, Jay **From the Bushveld to Biko: The Growth of South African Children's Literature in English from 1907 to 1992 Traced Through Over 110 Notable Books.** Grabouw, South Africa: Bookchat, 1996. 48 pp.
[Not examined]

1591 Heale, Jay **"What Publishers are Publishing and What Children Want to Read."** *Bookbird* 36, no. 1 (Spring 1998): 36-38.
A critical examination whether publishers and authors are satisfying the reading needs of children (largely in South Africa), and asks whether there is a conflict between what children want to read and what publishers *think* they should read. The author argues that children do not approve of any books "that have a sniff of being educationally approved."

1592 Heale, Jay **"Children's Book Publishing in South Africa: The Good News and the Bad."** *Focus on International & Comparative Librarianship* 29, no. 2 (10 September 1998): 78-82.
The author reports that the good news is that South African children's literature is alive and well, producing around 200 quality books every year, but that the bad news is that nobody is buying them. "There are young readers ready and waiting. South Africans are becoming steadily more aware of the value of good indigenous children's literature. Some day, soon we hope, the education authorities will find the money to buy the books."

1593 Heale, Jay **"IBBY in Africa."** *Bookbird* 40, no. 3 (2002): 34-38.
Sees the activities of the ➔ **International Board on Books for Young People/IBBY (71)** and the provision and publication of children's books in Africa as interlinked, but not closely enough for their full potential to be realized. Concludes that, if IBBY wants to extend its activities into Africa and offer something of benefit to the continent, then greater awareness of the situation in Africa could bring tangible improvement.

1594 Heale, Jay **Adamastor: A View over the Children's Literature of South Africa.** Kenilworth, South Africa: Jay Heale (Bookchat booklets), 2004. 32 pp.
A short overview of children's book publishing activities, and the promotion of books and reading in South Africa.

Heale, Jay, ed. **SACIP: South African Children's Books in Print** *see* ➔ **Section 3, Country studies: South Africa** entry **963**; and *see also* **Bookchat** ➔ **Section 1, Serials and reference** entry **130**

Hugo, Nadine **Bringing the Story Home. A Guide for Developing and Selecting Materials for Early Childhood Education: The South African Perspective** *see* ➔ **Section 3, Country studies: South Africa** entry **1027**

1595 Ikhigbonoareme, E.B. **"Writing and Publishing Children's Literature: Problems and Prospects."** In *Children and Literature in Africa*, edited by Chidi Ikonne, Emelia Oko, and Peter Onwudinjo. Ibadan: Heinemann Educational Books, 1992, 61-69.
Discusses the nature of children's literature, why we write for children, what children like to read, and what the role the publisher is in this.

1596 Ikonne, Chidi; Emelia Oko, and Peter Onwudinjo, eds. **Children and Literature in Africa.** Ibadan: Heinemann Educational Books, 1992. 219 pp.
Examines the role of children as narrators and creators of literature as well as their place as both potential characters and as audience. This collection of essays also includes contributions on publishing aspects of children's writing.

1597 The Illustrators Portfolio [South Africa]
http://www.illustrators.co.za/childrens.htm [08/01/08]
Part of an extensive listing and portfolios of illustrators in South Africa. These particular pages feature illustrators doing children's book illustrations and cartoons. For each artist there is a short biographical profile, main focus of work, details of past work undertaken, and examples of illustrations and book covers.

1598 International Board on Books for Young People (IBBY). **Books for Africa/Books from Africa**
http://www.ibby.org/index.php?id=552 [16/03/08]
Presented on the occasion of the 29th ➜ **IBBY (71)** Congress held in Cape Town in 2004 – and envisaged as source of information for quality African published children's books for teachers, researchers, parents and for all those interested in children's literature – this is a virtual exhibition of 84 children's books from Africa for Africa. It covers picture books for small children, children's fiction, folktales, and fiction for young adults, and includes books in English, French, Afrikaans, and in several African languages. The virtual exhibition displays the cover of each book, one or two extracts from the book (as small images that can also be viewed in enlarged size) together with a review and commentary about its contents. Additionally, there are informative profiles of African children's book authors, illustrators, and publishing houses whose books are included (the latter with full contact and email addresses, and with links to Websites where available). This is a splendid resource.

1599 Jenkins, Elwyn, comp. **South African Children's and Young Adult Books in English. A Select Bibliography of History, Criticism and Bibliography. August 2002.**
http://www.childlit.org.za/biblenglish.html [08/01/08]
A four page online bibliography (without annotations) listing 53 books and articles on South African children's and adolescent literature. Primarily on aspects of writing for children, and images and themes in South African children's literature (not covered by this bibliography).

1600 Kamani, Wacango **"Gender Analysis in Book Publishing."** In *5th Pan African Children's Book Fair Magazine.* Nairobi: CHISCI Press, 1996, 19-21.
Draws attention to the need of children's books to come under scrutiny and that they must be gender sensitive, gender responsive and gender balanced. For example, in many traditional stories girls are always portrayed as victims – "caught by the ogre only to cry feebly for help" – whereas boys never have such problems! Reports how a number of Kenyan publishers are dealing with this situation and have deliberately incorporated gender screening in their publishing policy. The author argues that

"gender sensitisation and training is necessary for publishers to understand the social order that sets our society's thinking."

1601 Kebiditswe, Kgakgamatso **The Dearth of Children's Books in Botswana.**
http://www.childlit.org.za/acl/artbotswana.htm [08/01/08]
A short overview of the status of children's books in Botswana and local publishing programmes for children's literature.

1602 Keïta, Fatou **Le livre pour enfants: Une nécessité en Afrique?**
http://www.sacbf.org.za/2004%20papers/Fatou%20Keita.rtf [16/03/08]
A paper presented to the 29th IBBY World Congress held in Cape Town 2004, which asks whether despite extreme poverty, poor health, severe economic problems, and the ravages of war in many African countries, there is still a place for reading and the book. The author believes it is precisely because of these harsh conditions that it is more imperative than ever that African children are being exposed to books and the pleasure of reading, and are given access to relevant books that reflect their own environment, realities, and ambitions.

1603 Khorana, Meena **Africa in Literature for Children and Young Adults: An Annotated Bibliography of English-language Books**. Westport, CT: Greenwood Press, 1994. 368 pp.
This bibliography contains entries for nearly 700 books, written in English by both African and Western authors and published between 1873 and 1994. A useful introductory essay provides an analysis of the social, political, cultural, and literary contexts of three phases of the development of African children's literature: colonial, with its heavy Eurocentric bias; postcolonial Western, in which bias took on new forms; and postcolonial Africa. Includes some listings of African-published children's books.

1604 Khorana, Meena **"Children's Publishing in Africa: Can the Colonial Past be Forgotten?"** In *Critical Perspectives on Postcolonial African Children's and Young Adult Literature*, edited by Meena Khorana. Westport, CO & London: Greenwood Press, 1998, 1-13.
A penetrative study which examines some of the key issues that confront the publication of children's books in postcolonial Africa: the question of language – which remains one of the most crucial and most hotly debated issue – the most popular literary genres (for example the retelling of folktales and narrative fiction, myths, legends, heroic sagas, proverbs and riddles, etc.), the question of national identity, and the most dominant themes in African published children's books.

1605 Khorana, Meena, ed. **Critical Perspectives on Postcolonial African Children's and Young Adult Literature.** Westport, CO & London: Greenwood Press (Contributions in Afro-American and African Studies, 187), 1998. 187 pp.

An interesting collection of essays that provide a great deal of insight into the depth, complexity, richness and diversity of African children's books. The contributors examine the major issues relating to African children's literature from several directions and from a variety of angles. The essays take either a postcolonial or revisionist approach to the study of colonial children's literature, or examine the books published since independence in various African countries, and covering North, East, West and Southern Africa. Additionally, three of the essays focus on books written by Western authors for Western readers, and which analyze colonial bias, stereotyping, or blatant racism in some of these books, although one of the articles, by Jean Perrot, is in fact a spirited rebuttal in defence of Jean de Brunhoff's much-maligned Babar books. There are a total of twelve essays in this collection, by both contributors from North America and from Africa, the latter including Osayimwense Osa, Mbara Ngom, and Kenyan author and publisher Asenath Bole Odaga.
Reviews:
The African Book Publishing Record vol. 24, no. 4, 1998

1606 Kola, Pamela **"The Future of African Publishing for Children."** In *Books and Children. Proceedings of the ZIBF Indaba 1998, Harare, Zimbabwe, 1-2 August 1998.* Harare: Zimbabwe International Book Fair Trust, 1998, 55-58.
Pamela Kola, a prominent Kenyan children's writer, sets out the main factors which she believes will determine the future of indigenous African publishing for children, including development of authorship, issues of language and readership, and distribution and marketing.

1607 Kola, Pamela **"A Writer's Perspective on Children's Books."** *African Publishing Review* 7, no. 6 (November/December 1998): 6-7.
Looks back at children's book publishing in Kenya from the late sixties through to the late nineties. Finds that from the early days of euphoria and enthusiasm for locally produced children's books in the 1960s, the publishing situation changed dramatically between 1988 and 1998 and when it went into a period of decline. The author analyzes some of the reasons for this and believes parents, communities, and teachers must play a much greater role to inculcate reading skills and habits in children; that there should be more awards and competitions to motivate manuscript development and creating writing skills; and she also offers some suggestions to publishers how they might gain access to a wider readership and thus in turn achieve a better return for their publishing investment.

1608 Komasi, Mabel Mliwomore **"A Bibliography of Ghanaian Children's Storybooks in English."** *African Research & Documentation*, no. 103 (2007): 45-64.
A bibliography (without annotations) of 264 Ghanaian children's story books in English, spanning a period of 45 years, most of them published by Ghanaian publishers. The bibliography is preceded by an informative introduction that charts the development of Ghanaian children's writing, with short profiles of some of the most prominent and most prolific Ghanaian authors writing for children, including Meshack Asare, J.O. deGraft Hanson, Peggy Appiah, and Akosua Gyamfuaa-Fofie.

1609 Konaté, Sié **La littérature d'enfance et de jeunesse en Afrique Noire Francophone: les cas du Burkina Faso, de la Côte d'Ivoire, et du Sénégal.** Québec: Université Laval, Faculté des Sciences Sociales, Département de Sociologie, 1993. PhD thesis 378 pp.
Another version also published by Banque internationale d'information sur les États francophones, Ottawa [1994?] 248 pp.
Discusses the dangers and effect of "cultural imperialism" in the production and distribution of children's books. Concludes that Africa is capable of producing quality literature for children on its own.

1610 Konaté, Sié **Literature d'enfance et de jeunesse en Côte-d'Ivoire: structures de production et de distribution du livre pour enfants** Paris: L'Harmattan, 1996. 159 pp.
On children's literature and publishing in the Côte d'Ivoire. [Not examined]

1611 Kor, Buma **"Contemporary Changes and Trends in Young Children's Literature in Africa."** In *Proceedings, Papers and Summaries of Discussions at the Seminar on Creative Writing and Publishing for Children in Africa Today. 12th-14th January 1983.* Freetown: Central Library, 1983, 75-80.
Catalogues the problems in the publishing of young children's books in Africa, and draws attention to the urgent need for more relevant books to inform and educate.

1612 Kotei, S.I.A., and Colin Ray **"The Legon Seminar on Writing and Production of Literature for Children, 5-10 April, 1976."** *The African Book Publishing Record* 2, no. 4 (October 1976): 227-229.
Surveys meetings to date in the area of writing and publishing for children in Africa, and reports about the important 1996 Legon seminar, with short précis of some of papers presented.

1613 La Joie par les livres - Centre national du livre pour enfants **L'édition africaine pour la jeunesse 2006.** Paris: La Joie par les livres - Centre national du livre pour enfants, 2006. 36 pp.
Online:
http://www.lajoieparleslivres.com/masc/Integration/JOIE/statique/pages/13_documents/biblio_afrique_2006.pdf [16/03/08]
Published by ➔ **La Joie par les Livres. Centre National du Livre pour Enfants (86)** and organized by country, this is the latest edition an extremely useful directory of publishers, booksellers, public libraries, documentation centres, and professional associations in sub-Saharan Africa with a strong interest in children's books. Gives full address information, telephone and fax numbers, email, and Web sites where available. Additionally, the directory also includes listings for publishers, organizations, and associations outside Africa with an interest in African children's books and promoting readership in Africa.

1614 Laurentin, Marie, and Viviana Quiñones, eds. **Livres Africains pour la jeunesse.** Paris: La Joie par les livres, secteur interculturel, 1994, 59 pp.

An illustrated catalogue containing extensive reviews of African-published books for children and teenagers (in French), as well books on Africa or the African oral tradition, published in France. To some extent this is a cumulation of reviews which have appeared earlier in the journal ➜ **Takam Tikou (166).**

1615 Laurentin, Marie, and Viviana Quiñones **"Les livres Africains pour enfant dans les Grands Salons Européens du Livre: une présence nouvelle et significative."** *Takam Tikou*, no. 6 (January 1997): 10-11.
Reports about two book events that focussed on African publishing in French for children: the 11th Montreuil Youth Book Salon and the Bologna International Children's Book Fair in 1996. Ends on a note of optimism for growth and improvement in children's book publishing in francophone Africa.

1616 Laurentin, Marie **"African Children's Books in France. Distributing, Translating, Publishing."** In *Books and Children. Proceedings of the ZIBF Indaba 1998, Harare, Zimbabwe, 1-2 August 1998.* Harare: Zimbabwe International Book Fair Trust, 1998, 152-155.
Describes the distribution African-published children's books in France, book promotional activities undertaken by a number of organizations, translation projects, and publishers in France with a commitment to publish books by African authors.

1617 Lawal-Solarin, O.M. **"Books and Children."** In *Books and Children. Proceedings of the ZIBF Indaba 1998, Harare, Zimbabwe, 1-2 August 1998.* Harare: Zimbabwe International Book Fair Trust, 1998, 59-63.
A Nigerian publisher's perspective on publishing for children in Africa, discussing the factors that are crucial in developing a children's book list, including matters of design and illustrations, production, and marketing and distribution. The author also makes a number of recommendations to improve the quality and quantity of children's titles on a continent-wide basis.

1618 Lebon, Cécile **"La littérature africaine de jeunesse sort de ses frontières."** *La Revue des livres pour enfants,* no. 185 (February 1999): 123-128.
Notes a dramatic increase in the number of book titles for African children and young adults and the emergence of more African publishers catering for this hitherto neglected market.

1619 Lema, Elieshi **"Building a Book Industry: Start with Children."** *Logos. The Journal of the World Community* 8, no. 2 (1997): 91-95.
Online: http://www.atypon-link.com/LOG/doi/pdf/10.2959/logo.1997.8.2.91
Reports about the ➜ **Children's Book Project (1117)** in Tanzania, an innovative new approach to promote books and developing reading skills, and to encourage indigenous authorship, publishing, printing and bookselling. The project – which includes a training component in the form of courses and workshops that are attended by writers, editors, illustrators, and publishers – was initiated by ➜ **Code Canada (48)** and the author of this article managed the project from 1991 to 1996. She

describes how the project works, its success and achievements to date, and also identifies some of the problems it encountered in terms of marketing and distribution of the books that were produced.

1620 Lewin, Hugh **"Avoiding Crocodiles."** *The Zimbabwean Review* 4, no. 2 (April-June 1998): 8-9.
A talk given at a workshop by Hugh Lewin on the importance of children's books to national development, based partly on a study compiled by the [then] Book Development Council of South Africa for the South African Department of Arts and Culture, and partly informed by the author's experience as a former editor and publisher of children's books at Baobab Books in Harare.

1621 Lucan, Talabi Aisie **"Problems of Creative Writing and Publishing for Children in Sierra Leone."** In *Proceedings, Papers and Summaries of Discussions at the Seminar on Creative Writing and Publishing for Children in Africa Today. 12th-14th January 1983.* Freetown: Central Library, 1983, 49-55.
Describes the problems facing a creative writer for children in Sierra Leone, including motivation and inspiration. Follows up with the practicalities involved in the publishing business, such as capital, training and language.

1622 Machet, Myrna; Sandra Olën, and Thomas van der Walt, eds. **Other Worlds, Other Lives: Children's Literature Experiences. Proceedings of the International Conference on Children's Literature, 4-6 April 1995**. Pretoria: UNISA Press, 1995. 3 vols. 358 pp., 285 pp., 257 pp.
A total of 59 papers are brought together in these three volumes, with articles on children's literature in all parts of the world, including a large number on the topic of children's literature in Africa. Among these are "The Spirit of My Story" (Gcina Mhlophe); "Children's Literature in Cameroon" (Edward O. Ako); "Context and Culture as a Factor in Black Children's Responses to Books" (Thuli Radebe); "Archetypes or Stereotypes: Fantastic Realism in Children's Literature" (Miriam W. Maranga); "Ideological Inscription in Children's Fiction: Strategies of Encodement in Ngugi and Achebe" (Peter T. Simatei); "Creating an Awareness of the Importance of Reading in Schools: The Whole School Approach Used by READ in the Independent Development Trust Project" (Cynthia Hugo); "Literacy in a Multicultural Environment" (Myrna Machet); "The Implications for Humour in Children's Literature, with Particular Reference to the Contemporary South African Situation" (Sandra Braude); "Popular Themes in Children's Literature in Uganda: Some Case Studies" (Evangeline L. Barongo); "A 25 Year Retrospective of South African Children's Reading of other World's Books" (Rosey Bennet); "Children's Books in African Languages: An Overview" (Johan Lenake); "Children's Books in African Languages: Translations, Adaptations or New Materials" (Denise Diamond); "Nigerian Children's Literature and the Changing Social Scenes" (P. Osazee Fayose); and "Discovering One's African Identity: Two Kenyan Voices Speak" (Jenny Janisch).

1623 Martin-Koné, Mary-Lee **"La littérature pour enfants."** *Notre Librairie. Revue du Livre Afrique Noire, Maghreb, Caraïbes, Océan Indien. Littérature de Côte d'Ivoire*: 2. Ecrire aujourd'hui, no. 87 (April-June 1987): 123-124.

Reviews children's literature in Côte d'Ivoire including the efforts of publishers in the promotion of the writing down of oral traditions, new writing, poetry, the use of comic strips, and encouraging the discovery of the country and of the wider world.

1624 Mbure, Sam **"African Children's Literature or Literature for African Children?"** *Matatu*, no. 17-18 (1997): 3-9.
Using the Kenyan background, the author faults language choice (i.e. English) as the reason for the slow development of books for African children, and he critically examines the extent to which colonization promoted the literature of the colonizer at the expense of indigenous literature. Declares "children's literature should basically teach children simple, yet very important things like who they are, about their surroundings, etc. These things should be written and taught in the children's own language."

1625 McDonald, Elsa **"Children's Books for Africa."** *South African Panorama* 34, no. 5 (1989): 1-7.
[Not examined]

1626 Melching, Molly **"Meeting Children on their Own Terms in Senegal."** *Wilson Library Bulletin* 54, no. 2 (October 1979): 109-111.
On the activities of the Dakar-based Démb ak Tey Children's Resource Centre (*see also* entry ➜ **1627** below).

1627 Melching, Molly **"Children's Literature in Senegal."** In *Children's Book Production and Distribution in Developing Countries*, edited by Doros Theodoulou and Pavlos Ioannides. Nicosia: Cyprus Association on Books for Young People, 1985, 91-94.
Describes the work of the inventive Démb ak Tey Children's Resource Centre in Dakar founded in 1976, which Molly Melching established in collaboration with Bollé Mbaye to "satisfy the needs of the approximately 80% of the children who can not adequately read a French text". She explains the parameters for the books and materials produced, and the extensive testing these materials underwent.

1628 Meniru, Teresa E. **"Children's Literature. Progress and Problems."** In *Children and Literature in Africa,* edited by Chidi Ikonne, Emelia Oko, and Peter Onwudinjo. Ibadan: Heinemann Educational Books, 1992, 43-51.
Delineates the problems of authors, publishers, the reading audience, and attitudes by government on the issue of children's literature. Offers a range of possible solutions – above all the need for libraries to carry more extensive collections of African children's literature – but places the responsibility of remedying the situation firmly with the government.

1629 Morolong, Paul Motlatsi **The Lesotho Experience on Picture Books and Children's Books.**
http://www.childlit.org.za/acl/artlesotho.htm [08/01/08]

A short overview of publishing for children in Lesotho, supported by some statistical analysis.

1630 Mpesha, Nyambura **African Children's Literature. A Bibliography.** Bloomington, IN, and Milton Keynes, UK: Author House, 2007. 290 pp. [Available from the author, Nyambura Mphesa, 7659 Honeysuckle Lane NE, Rockford, MI 49341, Email: nm@nyamburampesha.com]

This bibliography, by a Kenyan scholar and children's author, lists 1,759 titles in English and in Kiswahili. In her introduction the author states that a proportion of the books were personally examined by her, while other entries are based on listings in → **Kenya Books in Print (586)**, publishers' catalogues, as well as catalogues issued by → **African Books Collective (3)**. It includes children's books written by both African and non-African authors. The majority of the titles are published in Africa, but there are also listings of African children's books published in the UK and in North America. Material is listed alphabetically by name of author. Each entry gives author name, title, page extents for some titles, ISBN, and name of publisher; names of illustrators are also given for a number of entries. There are no annotations, nor indications of reading levels or age groups. Includes a list of publishers, but which lacks address or distributor details. While this is a fairly comprehensive listing – and some public libraries may find it useful as a starting point for acquiring African children's books – without annotations, evaluations, or analysis of any kind, it is difficult to see how the bibliography can serve much purpose in its present form. However, in her introduction the author promises that a much fuller and improved version, with annotations, age levels, more titles in African languages, as well as including African children's books in French and in Portuguese, will shortly appear on her Web site at http://www.nyamburampesha.com/.[pages not available as at 17/03/08]
Reviews:
The African Book Publishing Record vol. 34, no. 1, 2008

1631 Mwankumi, Dominique, and Jean-Claude Kimona **"Dossier: African Children's Literature."** *The Courier ACP-EU*, (September-October 2002): 57-59

Online:
http://europa.eu.int/comm/development/body/publications/courier/courier194/en/en_057_ni.pdf [17/03/08]

African children's literature, published both in Europe and in Africa, has blossomed in recent years, but there are still inadequate structures and professional organizations for authors and illustrators of African children's books. Moreover, the work of some African illustrators is still often amateurish, primarily due to lack of training. A new professional association, → **Illusafrica. Association Panafricaine d'Illustrateurs (17)**, set up by three African artists in 1999, aims to put this right. The objective of this pan-African illustrators' association is to assist African authors and illustrators to develop a professional career. It is organizing exhibitions, workshops, and training courses, and also hopes to create a children's literature network in Africa.

1632 Mwanycky, Serah W., and Mary H. Bugembe, eds. **Science Culture in Africa from the Beginning: What our Children Read.** Nairobi: CHISCI, 1990. 418 pp.

A descriptive catalogue that lists available scientific materials for children between 2 and 14 years of age in Kenya, discussing opportunities which exist, goals for future development, and methods for achieving those goals. The content is based on a pilot project for the survey of science literature available to children in Africa, which has been ongoing in Kenya since 1988. The catalogue is arranged by subject and gives complete bibliographic details and contents of books listed.

1633 Mwanycky, Serah W., ed. **Children's Reading Needs. The Challenges of the Next Century to Parents, Educators, Publishers and Librarians in Africa.** Nairobi: CHISCI, 1993. 33 pp.

The proceedings of a number of seminars held at the second Pan African Children's Book Fair at the Kenyatta International Conference Centre, Nairobi, May 1993. Deals with writing, publishing and graphic presentation in books for children, as well as the values of a story as an information medium, the contribution of children's literature to personality development in children, how children read at home, and training for the publishing industry.

1634 Nemukula, Albert **"Publishing for Children in Africa: The South African Experience."** *Focus on International & Comparative Librarianship* 29, no. 2 (10 September 1998): 83-86.

Albert Nemukula, head of Vivlia Publishers, looks at the problems of publishing, marketing, and distribution of locally produced children's books in South Africa, including those in African languages. One of the problems is that most of the books published in the country are directed at the formal education markets, and publishers focus their attention on the kind of books that are likely to be prescribed for classroom use. As a result "readers and manuals in all eleven of the official languages abound, but very little is produced locally to cultivate the habit of reading for pleasure or entertainment."

1635 Njoroge, Janet **"The Longhorn Experience. A Decade of African Publishing for Children 1988-1998."** In *Books and Children. Proceedings of the ZIBF Indaba 1998, Harare, Zimbabwe, 1-2 August 1998*, edited by the Zimbabwe International Book Fair Trust. Harare: Zimbabwe International Book Fair Trust, 1998, 47-49.

Chronicles ten years of children's book publishing by Longhorn Ltd., formerly Longman Kenya Ltd.

1636 Nwapa, Flora **"Writing and Publishing for Children in Africa."** *Matatu*, no. 17-18 (1997): 265-275.

Flora Nwapa, one of the foremost Nigerian writers, and its first woman publisher (as head of Tana Press), died in November 1993. This article is an account of her personal experience of writing for children, which also discusses the problems of printing and publishing costs, illustrators, distribution and how to select subjects upon which to write.

1637 Nyariki, Lily K. **"Promotion of Children's Literature in Africa."** *Maktaba* 11, no. 2 (1991): 28-29.
Discusses the role of publishers, booksellers, and librarians in the promotion of children's books in Kenya.

1638 Nyarko, Francis **"The Production and Distribution of Children's Literature in Africa: A Diagnostic Survey."** In *Children's Book Production and Distribution in Developing Countries*, edited by Doros Theodoulou and Pavlos Ioannides. Nicosia: Cyprus Association on Books for Young People, 1985, 53-63.
Contends "in no part of the world, is there such an urgent need to produce and distribute children's books as in Africa today" and asks why this need is failing to be recognized. The author believes that there is more to publishing in Africa than publishing textbooks for children and sees a brighter future in the years ahead.

1639 Nyren, Penny *"Ants Magazine."* *The African Book Publishing Record* 9, nos. 2/3 (1983): 89-90.
Reports on an exciting and innovative children's magazine published by the Zimbabwe Publishing House (sadly, now long defunct), run by an editorial board of ten children in conjunction with the editor. *Ants* magazine appeared twice monthly, was handwritten and illustrated by children. It also had an educational emphasis whilst, at the same time providing entertaining reading. Articles and jokes were published in English, Shona and Ndebele.

1640 Odaga, Asenath Bole **Children's Book Production and Distribution in Kenya."** In *Children's Book Production and Distribution in Developing Countries*, edited by Doros Theodoulou and Pavlos Ioannides. Nicosia: Cyprus Association on Books for Young People, 1985, 95-99.
Describes the "highly competitive but apparently ... lucrative" business of children's book publishing in Kenya.

1641 Odaga, Asenath Bole **Literature for Children and Young People in Kenya.** Nairobi: Kenya Literature Bureau, 1985. 106 pp.
[Not examined]

Odaga, Asenath Bole **"The Excitement and Challenges of Publishing for Kenyan Children: A Writer's Perspective"** *see* ➜ **Women in African Publishing/Publishing by and for women** entry **2400**

1642 Odejide, Abiola **"The Origins, Growth and Future of Nigerian Children's Literature."** *ANA Review* 6, no. 8 (October 1991): 3, 27.
Identifies the traditional forms of children's literature in Nigeria, including poetry, folktales, narratives, songs, chants and recitations. Discusses the central themes in

these forms and the culture change which occurred during Islamicization. Examines policies under the colonial regime and the "Africanization" of texts. Stresses the need for a varied literary output.

1643 Odiase, J.O.U. **African Books for Children and Young Adults: A Select Bibliography and Check List.** Benin City, Nigeria: Nationwide Publications Bureau in collaboration with Unique Bookshop, 1986. 48 pp. [Not examined]

1644 Ofei, Eric **"Children's Book Publishing in Ghana."** *Focus on International & Comparative Librarianship* 29, no. 2 (10 September 1998): 95-96. Reports about the current [1998] situation of publishing for children in Ghana, and the major problems and constraints in this area of publishing.

1645 Okafor, N.R. **"Technical and Economic Problems of Writing and Publishing Children's Literature in Africa with Particular Reference to Nigeria."** In *Children and Literature in Africa*, edited by Chidi Ikonne, Emelia Oko, and Peter Onwudinjo. Ibadan: Heinemann Educational Books, 1992, 52-60.
Describes the limitations placed on the production of good quality literature for children, the state of the printing technology in Nigeria, the high cost of importing materials, the difficulty of distributing Nigerian produced books overseas, and a general lack of financial support for the book industries.

1646 Okanlawon, Tunde **"Nigerian Children's Literature: Problems and Goals."** *Journal of Commonwealth Literature* 15, no. 1 (1980): 30-37.
Seeks the answers to questions such as: who are the authors of Nigerian children's literature? In what languages do they write and for which audience? What do Nigerian children like to read? Also touches on illustrations, the history of children's literature in Nigeria, the sources, and the publishers of these books.

1647 Okediran, Wale **"The Gift of Memory. Interview with Mabel Segun."** *Matatu*, no. 17-18 (1997): 231-241.
Interview with the prominent Nigerian writer and children's books author Mabel Segun, who was also the founder of the Children's Literature Association of Nigeria and the ➔ **Children's Literature Documentation and Research Centre CLIDORC (734),** both based in Ibadan.

1648 Okoye, Ifeoma **"In Search of a Child Reader and a Writer of Children's Books."** In *Creating a Conducive Environment for Book Publishing*, edited by Chukwuemeka Ike. Awka, Nigeria: Nigerian Book Foundation, 1996, 208-217
Laments the fact that "publishing for children is in a very poor state in Nigeria today", with writing for the very young children in their most formative years being the most seriously neglected. Makes a number of suggestions for more effective promotion of the reading habit.

1649 Omotoso, Kole **"Children's Books in an African Context."** In *The Slant of the Pen. Racism in Children's Books,* edited by Roy Preiswerk. Geneva: World Council of Churches, 1980, 46-61.
Emphasizes the importance of language in children's primary experiences. Summarizes the case of Nigeria where children's books are now actively produced and analyzes the prevalent themes in African children's books. Concludes "there is no doubt in my mind that the future of African literature lies in the indigenous languages of Africa."

1650 Omotoso, Kole **"Racist Stereotypes in Nigerian Children's Books."** *Afriscope* 10, no. 1 (1981): 28-30.
A critical examination of Nigerian children's books, and the racist stereotypes that some of them portray.

1651 Omotoso, Kole **"Writing Rights and Wrongs for our Children."** In *Proceedings, Papers and Summaries of Discussions at the Seminar on Creative Writing and Publishing for Children in Africa Today. 12th-14th January 1983.* Freetown: Central Library, 1983, 5-12.
A philosophical view of how, why and what should be written for children. Discusses the "false conflict" in African culture which exists as a result of colonialism, and pleads that writing and publishing for children in Africa should enlist the sympathy of African children.

1652 Omowunmi, Segun **"Children's Magazines in Africa."** *Bookbird* 28, (May 1990): 4-5.
A brief survey of a number of African-published children's magazines.

1653 Onduso, Brown **"Jacaranda Designs: Experiences in Publishing for the Children of Africa."** *Focus on International & Comparative Librarianship* 29, no. 2 (10 September 1998): 88-90.
Reports about the publishing, marketing, and distribution experiences of Jacaranda Designs, a company set up in Kenya in 1991 with a focus on publishing for children. The company is also aiming to sell its book to the North American markets.

1654 Osa, Osayimwense **"The Rise of African Children's Literature."** *Reading Teacher*, no. 38 (1985): 750-754.
Also published in *Journal of African Children's Literature* 1 (1989): 20-29.
Examines the ways in which children's literature in Africa has changed and how new genres of children's writing have gained momentum.

1655 Osa, Osayimwense **"African Children's Literature from the 1976 Legon Seminar to the 1987 Zimbabwe International Book Fair."** *International Review of Children's Literature and Librarianship* 4, no. 1 (1989): 34-41.
Charts the remarkable growth of African children's books since the mid-1970s.

1656 Osa, Osayimwense **African Children's and Youth Literature.** Boston: Gale, 1995. 162 pp.
An analysis of African children's and young adults literature, primarily from West Africa, especially Nigeria. Seeks to shed light on the aspects and genres of the literature and African cultural assumptions – especially those about love and marriage – as well as aspects of social conduct, and traditional values. Focuses chiefly on the writing, rather than on publishing aspects of children's books.

1657 Osaki, Lillian Temu **"African Children's Literature: A Scholar's Guide."** *University of Dar es Salaam Library Journal* 5, no. 1 (2003): 67-79.
The author states that "African children's books remain unparalleled in their ability to nurture the imagination and to provide relevant instruction and delight to the African child." However, she asserts that little research has been carried out on African literature, its nature, forms, and source of materials. The paper offers a selected checklist of the works by African children's authors.

1658 Osaki, Lillian Temu **African Children's Literature**
http://web.uflib.ufl.edu/cm/africana/children.htm [17/03/08]
This useful set of Web pages (last updated May 2004) from the University of Florida Libraries introduces scholars interested in African children's literature to a variety of material that is available for research in this area, and it can serve as a starting point for those interested in studying or doing research in African children's literature. Includes profiles of some prominent African children's writers, links to a number of other Web sites devoted to African children's literature, and a select bibliography.

1659 Oyeoku, Kalu K. **"Producing Reading Material for Children and Adults in Rural Communities.** In *Proceedings, Papers and Summaries of Discussions at the Seminar on Creative Writing and Publishing for Children in Africa Today. 12th-14th January 1983.* Freetown: Central Library, 1983, 75-80.
Looks at the provision of well produced books for the rural community, based on local traditions, folk tales and in a local dialect or a simplified version of the state language. Discusses the collection of material, transfer from sound to word, dissemination of the printed word, translation of material, and examines technical and financial considerations.

1660 Pellowski, Anne **Made to Measure: Children's Books in Developing Countries.** Paris: UNESCO (Books about Books series), 1980. 129 pp.
Discusses the writing, illustrating, designing, editing and publishing of children's books in developing countries. Includes contributions from children's literature experts from Africa that were solicited by means of a questionnaire.

Pick, Martin **"Co-Editions of Children's Books: International But Not (Yet) Global"** *see* ➔ **Rights sales, licensing, and publishing partnerships** entry **2255**

1661 Potgieter, Alida **"Children's Book Publishing in South Africa."** In *How to Get Published in South Africa*, by Basil van Rooyen. Halfway House, South Africa: Southern Book Publishers, 2nd ed. 1996, 29-37.
Looks at the opportunities that exist in South Africa for publication of children's books for the general market. Examines market constraints, language issues, children's book awards, and the type of fiction and non-fiction books published by South African imprints, and how these publishers evaluate manuscript proposals and come to a publishing decision.

1662 Quiñones, Viviana **Livres et bibliothèques pour enfants: l'Afrique et la France, coopération pour l'accès au livre**
http://www.ifla.org/IV/ifla70/papers/034f_trans-Quinones.pdf [17/03/08]
A paper presented to the 70th ➔ **IFLA (74)** General Conference held in Buenos Aires in August 2004, which surveys international collaboration between France and the countries of Africa in the area of children's book publishing and access to books by children in Africa. The article also looks at the development of public library services, reading promotion, training for the book professions, and production and distribution of children's books within Africa. It describes some of the initiatives and activities by some of the French organizations and agencies involved in this area, offers a number of recommendations how future collaboration might be strengthened, and stresses the need for further partnerships to provide access to "Books for All" in Africa. The author is one of the editors of the journal ➔ **Takam Tikou (166).**

1663 Quiñones, Viviana **Les livres et la lecture des enfants en Afrique francophone et le travail de La Joie par les livres.**
http://www.sacbf.org.za/2004 papers/Viviana Quinones.rtf [17/03/08]
A paper presented to 29th ➔ **IBBY (71)** World Congress held in Cape Town in September 2004. Describes children's books and reading in francophone Africa, cultural cooperation between France and the countries of Africa – particularly in the development of public libraries – and the work of the Paris-based organization ➔ **La Joie par les Livres. Centre National du Livre pour Enfants (86)** and its journal ➔ **Takam Tikou (166).** The author notes that much progress has been made in recent years, but that many challenges remain in the promotion of books and reading for children in French-speaking Africa.

1664 Randall, Isobel **"Publishing Children's Books in South Africa: A Courageous Venture in an Apartheid Society."** *Bookbird* 27, (September 1989): 5-6.
Describes the publishing activities in the area of children's books by oppositional publisher Ravan Press during the repressive apartheid days.

1665 Richter, Horst, and Jeffrey Garrett, eds. **Afrikanische Jugendliteratur Heute und Morgen/African Youth Literature Today and Tomorrow.** Bonn:

Deutsche UNESCO-Kommission; Munich: Internationale Jugendbibliothek, 1988. 128 pp. [Text in German and English]
[Not examined]

Schär, Helene "**Children's Books from South to North**" *see* ➜ **African books in the international market place** entry **1290**

1666 Schmidt, Nancy J. **Children's Books on Africa and their Authors. An Annotated Bibliography.** New York: Africana Publishing Co., 1975. 291 pp.
A comprehensive annotated bibliography that lists and critically evaluates 839 children's books published about and in Africa. Nancy Schmidt, formerly Africana Librarian at Indiana University Libraries, played a pioneering role in bringing African-published children's books to the attention of libraries and the international book community in the countries of the North. (For a supplementary listing to this bibliography *see* entry ➜ **1669**.)

1667 Schmidt, Nancy J. **"Legon Seminar on the Writing and Production of Literature for Children."** *Research in African Literatures* 8, no. 3 (Winter 1977): 350-352.
A short report on the 1976 Legon, Ghana, seminar which aimed to assess the state of the art of book production for children in Africa.

1668 Schmidt, Nancy J. **"The Development of Written Literature for Children in Sub-Saharan Africa."** *Zeitschrift für Kulturaustausch* 29, no. 3 (1979): 267-270.
An informative account of children's book publishing in sub-Saharan Africa. Examines the differences between children's books produced by African publishers and European- and US-based publishers, the plots, subjects used most frequently, and the use of folkloric themes. The author also reviews trends in content and authorship of children's literature, which reflect the desire of African political and educational leaders to Africanize curricula and curriculum related materials.

1669 Schmidt, Nancy J. **Supplement to Children's Books on Africa and their Authors: An Annotated Bibliography**. New York: Africana Publishing Co., 1979. 273 pp.
Lists a further 501 titles, many published in Africa; for main volume *see* entry ➜ **1666** above.

1670 Schmidt, Nancy J. **"Children's Books in Sub-Saharan Africa."** *African Studies Outreach* (Spring 1984-85): 1-4.
Reviews the history and content of books for children in Africa, from the nineteenth century to the present day and focuses on the publication of children's books in the 1980s. Forecast, correctly, "there is every reason to expect that the publication of African children's literature will triple again before the end of this century."

1671 Schmidt, Nancy J. **"4th Zimbabwe International Book Fair, 1987: An Overview of Published African Children's Literature."** *The African Book Publishing Record* 13, no. 4 (1987): 237-239.
Text of a paper presented to the Workshop on Children's Literature in Africa and the Third World, at the 4th ZIBF held in Harare in August 1987. Charts the progress of writing and publishing for children in Africa from 1957 to 1987. Reviews established practices and suggests further improvements.

1672 Schmidt, Nancy J. **"The Africanization of Children's Literature in English-speaking Sub-Saharan Africa."** *Journal of African Children's Literature* 1, no. 1 (1989): 7-18 pp.
Published in 1989, this article examined some major trends in the Africanization of children's literature in the post-colonial era, specifically exploring the changes that occurred in the 1980s. Nancy Schmidt predicted that "...Africanization will continue to be more specifically related to the different paths of nation-building..." and that "important innovations in African children's literature are happening", and which has indeed proven to be the case.

Schmidt, Nancy J. **"Award-Winning Children's Books: The Noma Selections 1980-1994"** *see* ➔ **The Noma Award for Publishing in Africa** entry **2060**

1673 Scull-Carvalho, Susan **"Publishing for Children in Africa."** *Maktaba* 12, no. 1 (March 1995): 3-4.
Also published in *African Publishing Review* 4, no. 1 (January/February 1995): 9-10.
A short account of the setting up, in 1991, of a new Kenyan imprint - Jacaranda Designs, which aims to publish quality African story books for children - and the company's development since its launch.

Scull-Carvalho, Susan **"The Jacaranda Experience. Kenyan Children's Books in America"** *see* ➔ **African books in the international market place** entry **1293**

1674 Segun, Mabel D. **"Children's Book Production and Distribution in Nigeria."** In *Children's Book Production and Distribution in Developing Countries*, edited by Doros Theodoulou and Pavlos Ioannides. Nicosia: Cyprus Association on Books for Young People, 1985, 101-105.
Describes children's book publishing in Nigeria discussing production, distribution and some other problems, and offering a range of suggestions towards a viable book industry.

1675 Segun, Mabel D. **"Current Children's Book Publishing in Africa."** *The African Book Publishing Record* 14, no. 3 (1988): 167-172.

Also reprinted in *Readings on Publishing in Africa and the Third World*, edited by Philip G. Altbach. Buffalo, NY: Bellagio Publishing Network, Research and Information Center (Bellagio Studies in Publishing 1), 1993, 31-36.
Concentrates on the positive and often innovative activities which have taken place in Africa between 1982-1987 in the area of children's book publishing, particularly grassroots publishing, the retail trade, library development, literacy and reading promotion campaigns, writing and illustration. Also deals with publishing in African languages, distribution, co-publishing and the role of book fairs in promoting children's books.

1676 Segun, Mabel D. **"The Writer and Her Art."** *Books* 1, no. 3 (1988): 15-19.
Examines some of the most important elements in writing and publishing for children.

1677 Segun, Mabel D. **"Children's Literature in Africa: Problems and Prospects."** In *Children and Literature in Africa*, edited by Chidi Ikonne, Emelia Oko, and Peter Onwudinjo. Ibadan: Heinemann Educational Books, 1992, 24-42.
A detailed discussion of children's literature, defining and describing the subject matter and providing a history of early African writing for children. Examines the importance of illustrations for children's books, the lack of writing for adolescents, and stresses the need to encourage writing in African languages. The author also suggests that more effective efforts must be made in the area of marketing and distribution, as well as documenting African children's literature.

1678 Segun, Mabel D. **"Illustrating for Children."** *Matatu*, no. 17-18 (1997): 77-89.
Examines the children's picture book scene in Africa and finds "it is not an inspiring one". Argues that the paucity of outstanding picture-story books is largely due to a dearth of good authors, very few trained children's book illustrators (and poor remuneration for children's book illustrators where they do exist), the prohibitive costs of publishing in four colours, and that there is "a general lack of awareness of the importance in illustrations in children's books." The author calls for more systematic training of children's book illustrators, and also the setting up of an association to bring together book illustrators in Africa.

1679 Sierra Leone Library Board **Proceedings, Papers and Summaries of Discussions at the Seminar on Creative Writing and Publishing for Children in Africa Today. 12th-14th January 1983.** Freetown: Central Library, 1983. 126 pp.
Contains a series of papers presented by an array of well known African writers and book professionals, and covers subjects such as the constraints associated with publishing for children, editorial considerations, the problems of creative writing for children, and the production of reading materials for children and adults in rural communities.

1680 Smith, Arthur **"The Present Situation for Writing and Publishing Creative Writing for Children in Africa."** *EzineArticles* 26 September 2007
http://ezinearticles.com/?The-Present-Situation-For-Writing-And-Publishing-Creative-Writing-For-Children-In-Africa&id=752256 [12/01/08]
The author believes that, despite some good progress in recent years, there is still a dearth of children's books, especially picture story books for younger children, reflecting an African environment both in textual context and illustration. He offers an overview of the present situation for writing and publishing creative literature for children in various parts of Africa, examines some of the problems militating against a more rapid growth in writing and publishing for children in Africa, and assesses the prospects for the development of that sector.

1681 **South African Children's Book Forum. 29th IBBY World Congress, Cape Town, South Africa – September 2004. Presentations and Papers.**
http://www.sacbf.org.za/ [09/01/08]
A large number of papers can be downloaded at the Web site of the ➔ **South African Children's Book Forum (952)**, the South African section of the International Board on Books for Young People (IBBY), and which hosted the 29th IBBY World Congress in September 2004. Those touching on publishing aspects of children's books are individually listed and abstracted in this section.

1682 Staunton, Irene **"The Zimbabwe Book Publishers Association. Promoting Collective Strategies for Trade in Children's Books."** In *Books and Children. Proceedings of the ZIBF Indaba 1998, Harare, Zimbabwe, 1-2 August 1998*. Harare: Zimbabwe International Book Fair Trust, 1998, 77-81.
An account of collective strategies by book trade associations and book promotional organizations in Zimbabwe in promoting children's books locally, regionally, and internationally, and describes some of the constraints which have made trading within the region problematic.

Stein, Claudia **"Selling African Children's Literature. Some practical experiences in Europe"** *see* ➔ **African books in the international market place** entry **1296**

1683 Swart, Kobie **"Books that Matter to South African Children"**
Innovation, no. 7 (December 1993): 19-21.
Also published in *Artes Natales* 12, no. 2 (1993).
The text of an address presented at a SAILIS workshop on children and their books in Pietermaritzburg, which discusses the challenges of publishing contemporary children's books in South Africa.

1684 Tadjo, Véronique **"Le 'Royaume d'enface' de Véronique Tadjo."**
Takam Tikou, no. 6 (January 1997): 18-21.
An interview with Ivoirian children's author and illustrator Véronique Tadjo, extolling the originality of her work which is based on traditional folk tales. She

recounts how she began to write, and later to illustrate her own books, and explains what she is trying to convey to the children who read her books.

1685 Tadjo, Véronique **"The Challenges of Publishing for Children in French-Speaking Africa: The Example of Côte d'Ivoire."** *Sankofa. A Journal of African Children's and Young Adult Literature* 4, (2005): 18-22.
Provides some background to the emergence of indigenous publishing in francophone Africa – after a long period of domination by French multinationals – and the development of children's literature, and describes the activities of Les Nouvelles Editions Ivoiriennes (NEI), Côte d'Ivoire's main publisher today, and the work a number of Ivoirian children's authors. While the Côte d'Ivoire is a success story in terms of children's book production, unfortunately the political upheavals in recent years have impacted negatively on it. Nonetheless, the author is upbeat about the future production of children's books in French-speaking Africa: children's books from this region are beginning to attract international attention, and there is a wealth of talent. "The diversity of themes makes one confident that children have a literature with which they can identify", and by grounding themselves firmly in the rich culture of the continent, African writers and illustrators have succeeded in giving their books a 'universal' quality that is appealing not only to African children, but also children all over the world.

1686 Theodoulou, Doros, and Pavlos Ioannides, eds. **Children's Book Production and Distribution in Developing Countries.** Nicosia: Cyprus Association on Books for Young People, 1985. 230 pp.
The proceedings of the 19th Congress of the International Board on Books for Young People, 9-14 October 1984, held in Nicosia, Cyprus. Includes contributions from all over the world, including papers on children's book publishing in Africa. *Note:* some of the papers in this collection are individually abstracted elsewhere in this bibliography.

1687 Tötemeyer, Andrée Jeanne **"An Outline of the Development of Black African Children's and Youth Literature."** *A Journal on the Teaching of English* 16, no. 166 (October 1982).
{Not examined]

1688 Tötemeyer, Andrée Jeanne **"Namibian Children's Book Award: Four-year Masterplan for the Promotion of Children' Book Production for a Multi-lingual Nation."** *Innovation*, no. 7 (December 1993): 22-25.
Presents an outline of a four year evaluation programme for Namibian children's books, and examines whether literary awards promote the quality and quantity of children's books.

1689 Tötemeyer, Andrée Jeanne **"Desert Survival and Wilderness Adventures. Juvenile Literature for a Young Namibian Nation."** *Matatu*, no. 17-18 (1997): 119-136.

Provides an overview of Namibian juvenile literature – published for children and youth in Namibia, books with a Namibian theme, or published outside Namibia (mostly in Germany and South Africa) – which has a long history of almost 100 years, dating from the German colonial era to the present post-apartheid period. From a socio-linguistic point of view, the authors finds that the colonial era has had a profound influence on the language reality in present day Namibia, and although the German-speaking community in Namibia today constitutes less than two per cent of the total population, German culture has remained a dominant factor. The author analzses some of the contents of the colonial and Germanocentric literature, and their often stereotype or racist depictions of African life and culture, and then goes on to review the emergence of modern Namibian juvenile literature of today [1997], including material in African languages, and publishing output from local publishing houses.

1690 Travis, Madelyn **"Traditional Modern. Author and Illustrator Véronique Tadjo Talks to Madelyn Travis about the Influences on her Work."**
http://www.booktrusted.co.uk/articles/documents.php4?articleid=38 [09/01/08]
Véronique Tadjo began to write children's books almost by chance. The Ivory Coast-born author, artist and academic had already won an award for her poetry and had produced a novel for adults when a publisher asked her to write a book specifically for African children. In this interview she talks about the influences on her work.

1691 Tumusiime, James **"A Decade of Publishing for Children: Uganda"**
In *Books and Children. Proceedings of the ZIBF Indaba 1998, Harare, Zimbabwe, 1-2 August 1998*. Harare: Zimbabwe International Book Fair Trust, 1998, 50-54.
James Tumusiime, Chairman and Managing Director of Fountain Publishers in Kampala, describes his company's experience in publishing material for children, and looks at the challenges, and prospects, of children's book publishing in Uganda in particular, and Africa in general.

1692 van der Walt, Thomas **"The Depiction of the Zulu Wars in South African Children's Books."** In *The Love of Books. Proceedings of the Seventh South African Conference of Bibliophiles held at The South African Library, Cape Town, 8-10 May 1996*, edited by Pieter E. Westra and Leonie Twentyman Jones. Cape Town: South African Library (Bibliophilia Africana VII, South African Library General Series, 26), 1997, 187-203.
Examines the portrayal of the Zulu wars, and the conflict between the Boers and the Zulus, in South African children's literature, focusing on a selection of books (in English and Afrikaans) to show what and how authors have written about the subject. Notes that the earlier books in Afrikaans and English "were to a large extent a celebration of nationalism and chauvinism and that the wars were regarded as a positive and a justifiable method of colonial expansion."

1693 van Heerden, Marjorie **Books for the Children of Southern Africa. Some Personal Notes Jotted Down and Some Questions Answered.**
http://www.capetownbookfair.com/press-and-media/3/releases-and-news/19/books-for-the-children-of-southern-africa [12/01/08]
Marjorie van Heerden is a well known South African children's author. When approached by the organizers of the 2007 Cape Town Book Fair to write down some thoughts about her experience as a children's book writer and illustrator she decided to use the opportunity also to get some clearer insights for herself. So, after offering some personal notes about her own experience, she put a number of pertinent questions to a couple of her friends who work in the industry (one a prominent South African publisher, the other a colleague from Namibia) the responses to which are reproduced here.

1694 van Vuuren, Kathrine Ruth **A Study of Indigenous Children's Literature in South Africa.** 1994. Cape Town: University of Cape Town, 1995. MA thesis. 195 l.
Since the mid-1970s there has been a marked increase in the local production of children's literature in South Africa. This thesis considers various issues relevant to the field of children's literature in South Africa, through both traditional means of research as well as through a series of interviews with people involved in the field itself. It also examines racial and gender stereotypes in children's literature and the manner in which people's attitudes to and about children's literature are shaped. The author stresses the need to broaden the scope of current publishing methods and the ways in which publishers foresee themselves doing this is considered. The limitations of current methods of distribution are similarly investigated, and some more innovative approaches, a number of which are currently being used in other parts of Southern Africa, are suggested. The gap between the 'black' and the 'white' markets is reviewed, and possible methods of overcoming this divide are considered.

Violet, Jean-Marie **"A 'Good' Children's Book is One Which Arises from the Child's Own Culture. An Interview with Mary Jay"** *see* ➜ **African books in the international market place** entry **1297**

1695 Wabbes, Marie **"La littérature pour la jeunesse en Afrique Noire : enfin des créations originales!"** *Africultures* no. 57 (December 2003): 95-98. Online:
http://www.africultures.com/index.asp?menu=revue_affiche_article&no=3 189&dispo=fr [17/03/08]
Author and illustrator Marie Wabbes looks back at the development of African children's literature since the 1970s, publishing for children, and the training of writers and illustrators. She describes a number of initiatives that have helped to create a book market for children, including the pioneering children's imprints Akomba Mba in Cameroon and Editions Ruisseaux d'Afrique in Benin.

1696 Wade, Emmie **"Children's Science Books. The Kawi Project."** In *Books and Children. Proceedings of the ZIBF Indaba 1998, Harare, Zimbabwe, 1-2 August 1998.* Harare: Zimbabwe International Book Fair Trust, 1998, 228-232.
Describes the 'The Science for Africa (SAP) KAWI Project', a collaborative effort between the ➔ **African Publishers Network (5)** and ➔ **UNESCO (118)**, which has thus far produced the *KAWI Renewable Energy Series,* consisting of six culturally relevant pan-African scientific readers on renewable energy, and targeted for teenagers in Africa. The six titles in the series were published in 1999, and each has extensive illustrations in full colour. Authors were drawn from across the continent to give the series a truly pan-African perspective. Apart from highlighting traditional scientific principles that Africans have used for centuries, the series builds on that knowledge to bring about modern scientific thinking on renewable energy. The books are designed for use as supplementary science readers and are intended to influence the perceptions of teenagers on renewable energy and the environment, as well as cultivating a reading culture. Five themes were addressed in this initial series: solar, hydro, wind, biogas and wood fuel. These themes on renewable energy are introduced and discussed in a typically African cultural context, which include practical and familiar examples, exercises, activities, stories, poetry, songs, and folklore, which has added relevance and appropriateness to the series.

1697 Wafawarowa, Brian **"Publishing and Distributing Children's Books in Africa: Opportunities and Challenges."**
http://www.ibby.org/index.php?id=686 [17/03/08]
A paper presented to the 2006 Congress of the ➔ **International Board of Books for Young People (74)**. It provides a brief but succinct overview of the state of children's book publishing in Africa, highlighting the opportunities and challenges of this sector, including aspects of production capacity, distribution, the editorial skills needed to develop a children's list, competition with international titles, as well as stiff competition from the electronic entertainment industries, the preferred media of most teenagers. The author offers a number of possible solutions how current obstacles might be overcome.

1698 Wagner, Gülten **"Nigerian Children's Books: An Evaluation."** *The African Book Publishing Record* 2, no. 4 (1976): 231-236.
This article is a condensed version of an MLS thesis entitled *An Evaluative Study of Children's Books Published in Nigeria,* (University of Ibadan, Nigeria, 1974). Covers oral literature, early missionary contributions, curriculum developments, Nigerian writers and illustrators, while evaluating the need for further research, and discussing the role of teachers in the development of children's literature.

1699 Walter, Scott **"Children's Book Publishing from an African Perspective."** *The African Book Publishing Record* 19, no. 1 (1993): 13-15.
A critical assessment of funding programmes and publishing assistance for African children's books, first presented at a ➔ **World Bank (124)** seminar entitled "Promoting Independent Reading". Discusses support to indigenous publishing (including subsidies for purchasing books rather than production subsidies), support for training, and for libraries.

1700 Walter, Scott **"Promoting Children's Book Publishing in Anglophone Africa."** *Reading Online. Electronic Journal of the International Reading Association* n.d. [1996?] 10 pp.
http://129.7.160.115/COURSE/Dillner/walter.htm [pages not accessible 09/02/08]
Examines how local publishing capacity is determined and presents some guiding principles to be considered in publishing, and that will facilitate a sustained book supply. The author outlines some programmes and initiatives in several African countries that support these principles and demonstrate how children can gain access to entertaining, exciting and educational books. He concludes by suggesting a range of measures how children's book publishing in Africa might progress successfully in the years ahead.

1701 Wiggans, Rachel **"Amabhuku. African Illustrators at Bologna Children's Book Fair, April 1999."** *Bellagio Publishing Network Newsletter*, no. 25 (July 1999): 9-10.
Online:
http://www.bellagiopublishingnetwork.com/newsletter25/wiggans2.htm
[19/03/08]
A report about the 1999 Bologna Children's Book Fair which focused on Africa in that year, and also featured a major exhibition of the work of sub-Saharan African children's book illustrators. (*See also* entry ➜ **1543**.)

1702 Wiredu, E. Oti **"Promoting Reading Habits among Children."** *The Book Industry* 2, no. 3 (September 1991): 4-5.
Describes a reading club approach designed to encourage Ghanaian children to increase their reading habit.

1703 Zell, Hans M. **"Publishing for Children in Africa Today: An Overview."** In *Proceedings, Papers and Summaries of Discussions at the Seminar on Creative Writing and Publishing for Children in Africa Today. 12th-14th January 1983.* Freetown: Central Library, 1983, 20-32.
Presents an overview of African-published children's books [as at 1983]. Stresses the need for collaboration and cooperation between writers, artists, publishers and printers in order to develop alternative methods of producing relevant books for African children.

1704 Zell, Hans M. **"Writing Rights and Wrongs for African Children."** *The African Book Publishing Record* 9, no. 1 (1983): 13-14.
Also published in a shorter version as **"Writing Wrongs for Children"**, *West Africa*, no. 3421 (7 March 1983): 607-610.
Report of a seminar on creative writing and publishing for children in Africa, held in Freetown, Sierra Leone, in January 1983. The title for this article draws on the topic of Kole Omotoso's keynote address (*see* entry ➜ **1651**), which was followed by a presentation given by Noma Award-winning Ghanaian author Meshack Asare.

There are also reports on contributions to the seminar by those involved in the publishing of children's books.

1705 Zimbabwe International Book Fair Trust **Books and Children. Proceedings of the ZIBF Indaba 1998, Harare, Zimbabwe, 1-2 August 1998.** Harare: Zimbabwe International Book Fair Trust, 1998. 260 pp. (distributed by African Books Collective Ltd., Oxford)
The theme of the 1998 Zimbabwe International Book Fair was 'Books and Children', and children were the main focus in all the deliberations, from policy debates to storytelling. This is a collection of 56 papers, report-backs and discussions that were presented at the Indaba. The papers are grouped in five parts; those from the plenary sessions; Policy; Children's Literature; Scholarship and Research; and Access and Technology. *Note:* A number of the more substantive papers that touch on aspects of publishing for children are included as separate entries in this section.

Christian publishing and mission presses

1706 Alemna, A. Anaba "**Christian Mission Presses in Ghana: A Brief Review.**" *Ghana Book World*, no. 5 (1991): 30-34.
Describes eight mission presses in Ghana and surveys the history of the Christian presses in Ghana. It charts their establishment, achievements, relations with other publishers, and discusses the problems which they face.

1707 Ayee, E.S.A. "**A General Survey of Christian Literature in Kenya.**" In *Christian Literature for Africa*. Potchefstroom, South Africa: Institute for Reformational Studies, 1989, 46-61.
Discusses the readership, publishing and distribution of Christian literature in Kenya.

1708 Amegatcher, Andrew "*The Christian Messenger.*" *West Africa*, (13-19 January 1997): 57-61.
Provides a history of one of the publishing products during British colonial rule: *The Christian Messenger*, a pioneering journal and newspaper (with text in English and in Ghanaian languages) founded by German and Swiss missionaries as a joint venture between the Methodist Church and the Basel Mission. Besides publishing this newspaper, the mission press also produced translations of the bible, published dictionaries, and commissioned textbooks on many subjects.

1709 Benedetto, Robert "**The Presbyterian Mission Press in Central Africa, 1890-1922.**" *American Presbyterians* 68, no. 1 (1990): 55-69.
[Not examined]

1710 Eilers, Franz-Josef, *et al*, eds. **Christian Communication Directory Africa.** Paderborn, Germany: Ferdinand Schöningh (Communicatio Socialis, Beiheft, 8),1980. 544 pp.

A directory and source book providing very full information on Christian media institutions in Africa, including: church communication centres, news and information services, publishing houses, printing presses, periodicals, research and training institutes. Listings are by country and the volume also includes an index of names. No further editions published to date.

Fiedler, Klaus **"A Community of Teaching and Learning, Research and Publishing"** *see* ➜ **Scholarly publishing (General)** entry **2285**

1711 Froise, Margaret **"A General Survey of Christian Literature in South Africa."** In *Christian Literature for Africa*, edited by Claude de Mestral. Potchefstroom, South Africa: Institute for Reformational Studies, 1989, 142-165.
Discusses the readership, publishing and distribution of Christian literature in South Africa.

1712 Gillmore, Alex **Agenda for Development. The Future of Third World Christian Publishing.** London, SPCK Publishing, 1996, and Washington, DC: International Academic Publishers, (US ed.) 2000. 472 pp.
An extensive discussion of the role of Christian publishers in book provision, and Christian publishing and book distribution in the countries of the South. It examines pertinent issues under three major areas of activity: (1) general Christian publishing, covering, for example, the problems of creating and maintaining a 'commercial' publishing house in the Third World, including aspects of training and scholarship programmes; (2) publishing for newly literates and new readers, which includes a case study of the Adult Literacy Organization of Zimbabwe (ALOZ), its achievements, strengths and weaknesses, its funding, and relationship with partners, etc.; and, (3) theological education and the development of theological libraries. The book concludes with some practical proposals on the way ahead and a possible agenda for development.

1713 Henige, David P. **Catholic Missionary Journals Relating to Africa: A Provisional Checklist and Union List for North America.** Waltham, MA: Crossroads Press [African Studies Association] (Archival and Bibliographic Series), 1980. 71 pp.
A bibliography and union list of more than 500 Catholic mission journals containing material related to Africa, identifying their holdings in 85 North American locations, and with an indication of their sponsoring missionary order.

1714 Kumah, D.P. **"A General Survey of Christian Literature in Ghana."** In *Christian Literature for Africa*, edited by Rita Swanepoel. Potchefstroom, South Africa: Institute for Reformational Studies, 1989, 46-61.
Discusses the readership, publishing and distribution of Christian literature in Ghana.

1715 Kuruman Mission Trust **Printing for Africa: The Story of Robert Moffat and the Kuruman Press.** Kuruman, South Africa: Kuruman Moffat Mission Trust, 1987. 36 pp.
Provides a history of the Kuruman Press in South Africa, founded by Lutheran Methodist Society missionary Robert Moffat, together with a list of publications produced there between 1831 and 1870.

1716 Leoli, C.T. **"A General Survey of Christian Literature in Lesotho."** In *Christian Literature for Africa*, edited by Rita Swanepoel. Potchefstroom, South Africa: Institute for Reformational Studies, 1989, 135-141.
Discusses the readership, publishing and distribution of Christian literature in Lesotho.

1717 Munguya, A.W. **"A General Survey of Christian Literature in Zambia."** In *Christian Literature for Africa*, edited by Rita Swanepoel. Potchefstroom: Institute for Reformational Studies, 1989, 113-121.
Discusses the readership, publishing and distribution of Christian literature in Zambia.

1718 Oduyoye, Modupe **"The Role of Christian Publishing Houses in Africa Today."** In *Publishing in Africa in the Seventies*, edited by Edwina Oluwasanmi, Eva McLean, and Hans M. Zell. Ile-Ife: University of Ife Press, 1975, 209-231.
The [former] manager of Daystar Press in Nigeria discusses the activities of Christian publishing houses in Africa [in the mid-1970s]: their substantive publishing output, their significance in the development and the encouragement of authorship with commitment, their capacity in the organization of large-scale distribution outlets, management of efficient printing presses, and the wide range of subjects published. Although now very dated, this remains of the most comprehensive overviews of Christian publishing on the continent.

1719 Oduyoye, Modupe **"The Advocacy Publisher and Costing Strategy."** In *Communication Industry in Nigeria. The Crisis of Publications*, edited by A. Tom Adaba, Ololeka Ajia and Ikechukwu Nwosu. Nairobi, African Council for Communication Education, 1988, 258-262.
A Nigerian Christian publisher explains what advocacy publishing is, how the price of a book is crucial in this kind of publishing, and how to get the costings right.

Peires, Jeffrey **"Lovedale Press: Literature for the Bantu Revisited"** *see* ➔ **Publishing in African languages** entry 2132

1720 Philipparts, Michel **"A Continent in Search of Publishers."** *Catholic Media Council. Information Bulletin,* no. 1 (1996): 1-6.
An overview of the current [mid-1990s] state of publishing in Africa, reviewing the major problems facing the book industries, and the role of the church and church publishers in book development. Includes some statistics of the number of

publishers in Africa: secular, Catholic, and Protestant. Also reports about the establishment of the ➜ **Association of Catholic Publishers in Africa (11)** based in Nairobi.

1721 Reuster-Jahn, Uta. **"The Entertainment Programme of Ndanda Mission Press: Its Contribution to Swahili Literature in Tanzania."** *Matatu,* no. 13/14 (1995): 339-352.
Assesses the "entertainment" programme of this Christian publisher's books in Kiswahili, and its contribution in promoting writing in African languages. Includes a bibliography of the Press's Kiswahili publications.

1722 Rossouw, Fransie **"The Area of Learning is Fast Approaching a Grand Climax."** *Quarterly Bulletin of the South African Library* 48, no. 2 (1993): 57-61.
Describes the activities of the first Wesleyan mission press in South Africa.

1723 Soisvert, Raymond, Bro., and Sr. Teresa Marcazzan **Publishing at the Service of Evangelization. Proceedings of the Seminar of the Catholic Publishers in Africa. Nairobi, 12-20 February 1996.** Nairobi: Paulines Publications, 1996. 192 pp.
The report and papers of a two-week seminar organized by the Daughters of St. Paul which brought together representatives of 17 Catholic publishing houses from 13 African countries. The proceedings of the meeting focused on the role of the Catholic church in publishing in Africa, but there are also chapters on the oral and reading traditions in Africa, the book industry in Africa, book marketing, NGO publishing, professionalism in publishing, and some perspectives on religious publishing. The seminar also led to the establishment of the ➜ **Association of Catholic Publishers in Africa (11)**.

1724 Spencer, B.M. **"Mission Presses in Natal."** In *The Love of Books. Proceedings of the Seventh South African Conference of Bibliophiles held at The South African Library, Cape Town, 8-10 May 1996,* edited by Pieter E. Westra and Leonie Twentyman Jones. Cape Town: South African Library (Bibliophilia Africana VII, South African Library General Series, 26), 1997, 77-84.
A historical account of the development of mission presses in Natal and their prodigious output. Discusses the activities of the American Board of Mission presses, and those of the Anglican, Catholic and Lutheran presses.

1725 Swanepoel, Rita, ed. **Christian Literature for Africa.** Potchefstroom, South Africa: Institute for Reformational Studies, 1989. 249 pp.
Discusses the project 'Christian Literature for Africa' launched by the International Association of Reformed Faith and Action in conjunction with the Institute for Reformational Studies in 1987. Includes various contributions discussing the readership, publishing, and distribution of Christian literature in a number of African countries, some of which are individually abstracted in this section.

1726 Usman, P.S. **"Religious Publishing."** *The Publisher* 1, no. 1 (December 1985): 20-23.
A short overview of religious publishing houses in Nigeria.

1727 van der Merwe, D., and B.H. Groenewald **"A General Survey of Christian Literature in Zimbabwe."** In *Christian Literature for Africa,* edited by Rita Swanepoel. Potchefstroom: Institute for Reformational Studies, 1989, 122-134.
Discusses the readership, publishing and distribution of Christian literature in Zimbabwe.

1728 van der Walt, B.J. **"Christian Literature for Africa. A Survey of Problems and Prospects in Writing, Printing, Publishing and Distribution."** In *Christian Literature for Africa,* edited by Rita Swanepoel. Potchefstroom, South Africa: Institute for Reformational Studies, 1989, 21-29.
Offers an overview Christian publishing in Africa as a whole [in the late 1980s], examining the problems and constraints that are associated with it, especially in the area of distribution.

White, Tim **"The Lovedale Press During the Directorship of R.H.W. Shepherd, 1930-1955"** *see* ➜ **Publishing in African languages** entry **2148**

1729 Zingani, W.T. **"A General Survey of Christian Literature in Malawi."** In *Christian Literature for Africa,* edited by Rita Swanepoel. Potchefstroom, South Africa: Institute for Reformational Studies, 1989, 91-112.
Discusses the readership, publishing and distribution of Christian literature in Malawi.

Community and rural publishing

1730 Bond-Stewart, Kathy **"The Community Publishing Process in Zimbabwe."** *The African Book Publishing Record* 19, no. 2 (1993): 93-96.
An interesting article about a remarkable and innovative publishing enterprise which aims to build up the skills, confidence, and creativity of grassroots development workers and community leaders by involving them in the collective production and distribution of books.

1731 Bond-Stewart, Kathy **"Community Publishing as a Process of Change."** In *Courage and Consequence. Women Publishing in Africa,* edited by Mary Jay and Susan Kelly. Oxford: African Books Collective Ltd., 2002, 61-69.
Describes the activities and publications of the innovative Community Publishing Process in Zimbabwe in order to train 7,000 village community workers, the majority of whom were women. Through a community based, participatory process of

publishing, the project aims to enable marginalized groups to use their creative energies to build dynamic leadership, tackle poverty, take charge of their lives, and make the decisions to shape their future. Representatives of the village readership participated in creating the books and civic education manuals, contributed material orally, and tested and distributed it through local book launches. The project also initiated a series of children's traditional stories and a book about children's rights, produced with 500 children aged from three to seventeen. A local leadership programme for writers provides training in journalism and editing, and the publication of a monthly journal from a village publishing house equipped with a computer, duplicator and stapler. The author concludes by stating "as women radically questioning autocratic institutions and processes, we have been able to shape a tool that can be used by marginalized groups anywhere to claim their voice in the public life."

1732 Cookey, Samuel J. **"Publishing for Rural Areas in Africa."** In *Publishing for Rural Areas in Developing Countries. Proceedings of an International Seminar held on 1,3,4 March 1980, at New Delhi.* New Delhi: National Book Trust, India, 1981, 55-60.
Redefines the meaning of "publishing for rural areas" and argues that the term should include publishing information on health, nutrition and housing. Points out that governments should be aware that the provision of books to rural areas is just as, or even more important than the provision of buildings and furniture.

1733 Djoleto, S.A. Amu **"Production of Books with Reference to the Rural Press, its Location, Type of Machinery and Raw Materials Required, Designing and Illustration."** In *Publishing for Rural Areas in Developing Countries, Proceedings of an International Seminar held on 1, 3, 4 March 1980 at New Delhi.* New Delhi: National Book Trust India, 1981, 89-95.
Also published in *Ghana Book World*, no. 3 (1982): 38-45.
The [former] Chairman of the ➜ **Ghana Book Development Council (536)** discusses production of books by rural presses, requirements in terms of printing equipment, and stresses the vital role of design and illustration in the provision of books for rural areas in Africa.

1734 Etemesi, Horace **"Production of Books with Reference to the Rural Press, its Location, Type of Machinery and Raw Material Required, Illustration and Designing."** In *Publishing for Rural Areas in Developing Countries. Proceedings of and International Seminar held on 1, 3, 4 March 1980 at New Delhi.* New Delhi: National Book Trust India, 1981, 96-100.
Covers the same ground as the preceding entry (*see* ➜ **1733**), but focuses on Kenya.

1735 Ike, Chukwuemeka **Meeting the Book Needs of the Rural Family.** Awka, Nigeria: Nigerian Book Foundation, 1997. 104 pp.
[Not examined]

1736 Ngeze, Pius B. ed. **Seminar on Techniques for Writing, Editing, Publishing and Distributing Reading Materials in Rural Areas.**
Bukoba, Tanzania: Kagera Writers and Publishers Co-operative Society, 1991. 84 pp.
The proceedings of a ➜ **UNESCO (118)** co-sponsored seminar hosted by the ➜ **Kagera Writers and Publishers Co-operative Society (1118)** and held in Tanzania in 1989. The seminar focussed on writing, publishing, and distributing materials for rural communities. Contains contributions in English and in Kiswahili.

1737 Odaga, Asenath Bole **"The Day Rural Talent was Displayed."** *The Kenya Bookseller* 4, no. 1 (1992): 28-29.
The Kenyan woman publisher Asenath Bole Odaga reports about the Kenya Women Literature Groups' short story contest, which involved people in rural areas with all levels of education "from zero to 'A' level."

Copyright and legal deposit/Authors' rights

See also
➜ **Authors and publishers/Publishing of African writers and African literature**
➜ **Rights sales, licensing and publishing partnerships**

Note: this section is primarily confined to articles and papers that deal with copyright of *books*, the rights of authors, book piracy, and African perspectives on copyright. General articles on intellectual property rights, intellectual property legislation in African countries, copyright issues related to access of learning materials and Open Content licensing, or studies on protecting African traditional knowledge, are *not* included here, unless they also contain some discussion on copyright issues as they relate to books, textbook provision, or the rights of African writers and scholars.

1738 **African Copyright Forum Conference. Copyright and Access to Information, 28-30 November 2005, Kampala, Uganda.**
http://www.nlu.go.ug/presentations.htm [18/03/08]
This National Library of Uganda site offers free access to 15 presentations (in pdf and PowerPoint formats) made at the above conference. They address issues of copyright and problems with access to knowledge on the continent, including discussions of publishing industry practises. Topics covered included access to information in higher education in Africa; copyright and libraries in francophone Africa; copyright and open distance e-learning (which recounts the experience of the African Virtual University/AVU); digital rights management in the developing world; the impact of copyright on access to digital resources in libraries; the challenges of current copyright regimes in protecting indigenous knowledge and African traditions; free trade agreements and access to information in Africa, and more. One of the outcomes

of the conference was the establishment of the African Access to Knowledge Alliance, and the launching of ➜ **Access to Knowledge (A2K) Southern Africa (24).**

1739 Adewopo, Adebambo **"Emerging Issues in the Management of Author's Reprographic Rights."** In *National Book Policy, HIV/AIDS and Sustainable Development. Papers Presented at the Fifth Nigeria International Book Fair, 8-13 May, 2006.* Lagos: Nigerian Book Fair Trust [c/o Literamed Publications Ltd., PMB 21068, Ikeja, Lagos, Nigeria], 2007, 127-137.
Examines the challenges of emerging digital technologies and the Internet in the management of authors' reprographic rights in Nigeria, and possible solutions available to authors in meeting these challenges. Reviews legislate reforms in copyright conventions, the provisions of the Nigerian Copyright Act (1990), and current licensing practices.

1740 Aguolu, C.C. et al **"Publishing and Copyright Protection in Nigeria: The Awareness Factor."** *Education Libraries Journal* 43, no. 1 (2000): 25-30.
[Not examined]

1741 Ajidahun, C. **"Book Piracy and Nigerian Copyright Law."** *Library Management* 19, no. 1 (1998): 22–25.
The Nigerian copyright Decree No. 47 of 1988 gives protection to copyright owners with stiff penalties in the event of violations and piracy. This paper considers these provisions of the law in relation to the persistent book famine in the country, and offers suggestions which might help enhance the execution of the law.

1742 Alemna, A.A., and V. Dodoo **"Copyright and Literary Piracy in Ghana."** *African Research &Documentation,* no. 100 (2006): 21-27.
Discusses issues of copyright, especially as it pertains to Ghana, and examines the extent of literary piracy and its impact on authors and on the book industry in Ghana. The author proposes a number of possible remedies how piracy might be curbed, and stresses the need to create more copyright awareness, and more vigorous prosecution of offenders.

1743 Altbach, Philip G., ed. **Copyright and Development: Inequality in the Information Age.** Chestnut Hill, MA: Bellagio Publishing Network, Research and Information Centre (Bellagio Studies in Publishing, 4), 1995. 109 pp. (distributed by African Collective Ltd., Oxford)
Online: (full-text, freely accessible)
http://www.bc.edu/bc_org/avp/soe/cihe/publications/pub_pdf/copyright.pdf [18/03/08]
A collection of six papers that aim to fill a void in the current debate about copyright and, at the same time, to bring some balance to the debate by providing a number of perspectives from the developing world. These include a paper by Henry Chakava "International Copyright and Africa: An Unequal Exchange'" (*see* entry ➜ **1755** below) and one by Urvashi Butalia "The Issues at Stake: An Indian Perspective on Copyright". Lynette Owen, Rights and Contracts Director at Longman's, provides a

perspective on copyright by that of a UK publisher.
Reviews:
The African Book Publishing Record vol. 21, no. 1, 1995
African Research & Documentation no. 78, 2000

1744 Altbach, Philip G. **"The Subtle Inequalities of Copyright."** In
Copyright and Development: Inequality in the Information Age, edited by Philip
G. Altbach. Chestnut Hill, MA: Bellagio Publishing Network, Research and
Information Centre (Bellagio Studies in Publishing, 4), 1995, 1-12.
Also published in *Logos. The Journal of the World Book Community* 3, no. 3
(1992): 144-148;
Online: http://www.atypon-
link.com/LOG/doi/pdf/10.2959/logo.1992.3.3.144
and also reprinted in *Readings on Publishing in Africa and the Third World,*
edited by Philip G. Altbach. Buffalo, NY: Bellagio Publishing Network,
Research and Information Center (Bellagio Studies in Publishing 1), 1993,
152-156.
Argues that those who control knowledge distribution have a responsibility to
ensure that knowledge is available throughout the world at a price that can be
afforded by the Third World. Altbach states that there must be recognition that all
knowledge products are not the same, and that while it may be justified to insist on
commercial terms on, for example, Nintendo games, some flexibility for scientific
materials, textbooks and the like is appropriate. The author believes that the owners
of knowledge ought to modify their purely profit-oriented approach to certain
segments of the knowledge industry.

1745 Altbach, Philip G. **"Haves and Have-nots in the World of
Copyright."** *The Bookseller* (22 January 1993): 19-21.
Examines the dangers inherent in "the inequality between the information-rich and
information-poor as long as the intellectual property system is controlled by the
West."

1746 Amegatcher, A.O. **Ghanaian Law of Copyright.** Accra: Omega Law
Publishers, 1993. 190 pp.
There are very few books on copyright in Africa, and this one provides a good
general overview of the principles of copyright in all its dimensions. It includes
sections on duration of copyright, copyright protection, rights of authors (and those
in the performing arts), and procedures for copyright registration. The author – a
barrister, who was formerly the Acting Copyright Administrator in Ghana – draws
on a number of case histories and examines individual cases of copyright
infringement. There is also a description of the work of the Copyright Society of
Ghana (COGSA), now ➜ **CopyGhana (534).**

1747 Academic and Non-Fiction Authors' Association of South Africa
**Authors' Rights: A Brief Guide. Intellectual Property – The Products of
the Mind.**

http://www.anfasa.org.za/genguide.htm [10/01/08]
A guide to the rights of authors, intellectual property, and the South African
Copyright Act of 1978 that protect the fruits of their labour from unauthorized
exploitation. It also deals with author-publisher relations and author-publisher
contracts, and aims to give authors a sound understanding how their creative works
may realize economic benefits, and to demonstrate to them the advantages of
developing sound relationships with publishers. The pages also contain a useful set
of FAQs.

1748 Athumani S. Samzugi **"An Appraisal of Legal Deposit Laws in
Tanzania."** *University of Dar es Salaam Library Journal* 5, no. 1 (2003): 34-45.
Addresses the issues and problems as they relate to legal deposit laws in Tanzania,
including aspects such as enforcement of legal deposit. Currently, under existing
legislation, two libraries have been accorded a status of legal deposit of the country's
national heritage, but the author questions whether it is reasonable to place all
national heritages in merely two libraries, and makes a series of recommendations on
how to improve the scope of the existing operation.

1749 Balkwill, Richard, and Monica Seeber **The Management of
Intellectual Property in the Book Publishing Industry - A Business-
Oriented Information Booklet.** Geneva: World Intellectual Property
Organisation [PO Box 18, CH-1211 Geneva 20], forthcoming 2008.
[Not examined]

1750 Bankole, S. Bodunde **"Copyright: Another Look?"** *Books* 1, no. 2
(April 1988): 9-12.
Examines assumptions generally made about copyright and its attendant problems:
e.g. ownership of copyright, and whether the state should enforce copyright and
copyright laws that protect the rights of author. The author argues that piracy can be
stopped through firmer laws and enforcement; rampant piracy will lead to the death
of creativity. The author, a lawyer, is the former director of the University of Lagos
Press.

1751 Bankole, S. Bodunde **"Publishers' Rights and the Copyright Decree."**
The Publisher 2, no. 2 (October 1993): 19-21.
Considers the rights and duties which the Nigerian Copyright Decree confers on
publishers.

1752 Bankole, S. Bodunde **"Authors' Rights and Remuneration in
Nigeria."**
Nigerian Libraries. Journal of the Nigerian Library Association 34, no. 1 (2000):
29-36.
Discusses copyright laws in a Nigerian context, including issues such as author'
rights and obligations, implications of copyright laws for both authors and
publishers, the matter of due remuneration for an author's work (and the factors that
influence this aspect), author-publisher relations and the sometimes thorny issue of

publishing contracts, as well as setting out details of the ➜ **Nigerian Publishers Association/NPA (739)** Code of Conduct. Bankole, a former president of the NPA and former Director of the University of Lagos Press, believes there is a great need for better understanding by authors of the publishing process and publishers' work practices.

1753 Barlas, Chris **"The New Gatekeepers?"** In *Access to Information. Indaba 97.* Harare: Zimbabwe International Book Fair Trust, 1997, 64-72.
Looks at issues of copyright in the new electronic environment, the role of libraries as gatekeepers of the digital culture, the concerns and anxieties of rights holders in the age of digital information, technology for rights management, measures taken to protect intellectual property on networks, and electronic copyright management systems. Concludes that "the new digital promised land offers many possibilities, but there will be many confrontations on the way", between rights holders and user, rights holders and telecommunication providers, and between rights holders and the potential new gatekeepers.

1754 Bonde, D. **"Copyright and the Right to Write."** *Moto,* no. 124 (1993): 8-10, 17.
On copyright issues affecting African writers. [Not examined]

1755 Chakava, Henry M. **"International Copyright and Africa: An Unequal Exchange."** In *Copyright and Development: Inequality in the Information Age,* edited by Philip G. Altbach. Chestnut Hill, MA: Bellagio Publishing Network, Research and Information Center (Bellagio Studies in Publishing, 4), 1995, 13-34.
An African perspective to the debate about copyright, its inequalities, and current practice in international rights trading. Contends that many aspects of international copyright reciprocity are illusory, that the main beneficiaries are still the publishers in the North, and that the latter are using copyright as a weapon to maintain the dependency relations that currently exist. Chakava pleads for more equity, honesty, understanding, and fair play to correct the present imbalance in copyright conventions, and which will help to strengthen the indigenous African book industries in the years ahead.

1756 Chakava, Henry **"Partnerships Between Rights Owners and Users. A Prerequisite for an Effective Copyright System."**
http://www.nlu.go.ug/dwnld/Henry_Chakava.ppt [18/03/08]
A PowerPoint presentation to the African Copyright Forum Conference, Copyright and Access to Information, held in November 2005 in Kampala, Uganda. It reviews the prerequisites for effective copyright systems in an African setting, partnerships between rights holders and users – and how such partnerships can be enhanced through public sensitization and public awareness campaigns – the challenges in rights protection posed by new technologies and new media, as well as the vital role played by national reproduction rights organizations.

Chege, John Waruingi **Copyright Law and Publishing in Kenya** *see* ➔ **Section 3, Country studies: Kenya** entry **599**

1757 Chavula, Serman W.D. **Cultural, Social and Economic Aspects of Authors' Rights: Legal and Practical Challenges in a Developing Country.** www.kopinor.no/content/download/2136/15475/file/Legal%20and%20pr actical%20challenges-kopinor.pdf [02/03/08]
Examines the legal and practical challenges in the administration, protection, and enforcement of authors' rights in Malawi, and reviews the experience and activities of the ➔ **Copyright Society of Malawi (657).**

1758 Copeling, A.J.C. **Copyright Law in South Africa.** 2nd ed. Durban: Butterworths, 1983. 420 pp.
[Not examined]

1759 Dean, O.H. **Handbook of South African Copyright Law.** Kenwyn, South Africa: Juta. 1987- Loose-leaf format 650 pp.
First published in 1987, this publication has established itself as the leading authority in its field. Content includes: Synopsis of the law of copyright and ancillary matters; Digest of South African Authorities; Transitional provisions of the Copyright Act, 1978; Compendium of Legislation; and Precedents. Last updated in January 2005 to reflect the latest developments in copyright law.

1760 de Freitas, Denis **The Copyright System. Practice and Problems in Developing Countries.** London: Commonwealth Secretariat, 1983. 87 pp.
A basic guide, still useful but now somewhat dated, to both national and international copyright systems, written for authors, editors and publishers in developing countries. Includes a special section with advice on publishing agreements.

1761 Egonwa, Osa D. **"'Copying Right' in Nigeria's Tertiary Institutions."** In *Publishing in Indigenous Languages. Papers Presented at the Fourth Nigeria International Book Fair, 10-14 May, 2005.* Lagos: Nigerian Book Fair Trust [c/o Literamed Publications Ltd., PMB 21068, Ikeja, Lagos, Nigeria], 2006, 119-37.
Examines the issues surrounding infringement of authors' rights at Nigerian institution of higher education through photocopying and other means, and describes how the ➔ **Reproduction Rights Society of Nigeria (741)** seeks to curb such illegal activities.

1762 Erinle, E.K. **"A Literature Review of Written Materials on Legal Deposit Laws for Nigerian Libraries since 1950."** *African Research and Documentation,* no. 57 (1991): 21-26.
A review of the literature on legal deposit in Nigeria (citing 32 references), preceded by a short account of legal deposit legislation in the country, and a discussion of implications of legal deposit on acquisitions and collection development policies by libraries.

1763 Ekpo, Moses F. "**The Berne Convention: Implications for Book Subsidy Schemes and Availability of Books.**" In *Making Books Available and Affordable*, edited by Ezenwa-Ohaeto. Awka, Nigeria: Nigerian Book Foundation, 1995, 18-24.
Assesses the implications of a number of programmes and subsidy schemes established by the Nigerian government with regard to copyright conventions, the special provisions for developing countries, and the aspect of compulsory licensing. Reviews the work of the Nigerian Copyright Council and how it assists publishers to tackle problems of book scarcity in the country.

1764 Emifene, Andrew "**Practical Strategies for Enforcing the Copyright Law.**" *This Week* 2, no. 2 (October 1993): 37-39.
A paper presented at the International Workshop on Copyright in Lagos in 1991, by a representative from the legal department of the Federal Investigations and Intelligence Bureau of the Nigerian Police Force, exploring the ramifications of copyright protection and enforcement.

1765 Fennessy, Eamon T. "**US Copyright Expert Goes to Nigeria and is Impressed.**" *The Journal of the World Book Community* 4, no. 3 (1993): 159-61. Online:
http://www.atypon-link.com/LOG/doi/pdf/10.2959/logo.1993.4.3.159
The writer, formerly President and Chief Executive Officer of the (US) Copyright Clearance Center, was invited to participate in a Nigerian Copyright Forum in November 1992, and was impressed with the seriousness of efforts to combat piracy and protection of copyright.

1766 Fiofori, Tan "**Young, Gifted and...Exploited.**" *West Africa*, no. 4055 (19-25 June 1995): 974-975.
An interview with Moses Ekpo, Director General of the Nigerian Copyright Council, in which he assesses the impact and achievements of the Council since its inception in 1990.

1767 Gray, Eve "**Proposed Framework for the Collective Management of Copyright and Neighbouring Rights in South Africa.**" *African Publishing Review* 10, no. 3 (2001): 3-4, 6.
Sets out the broad conclusions and recommendations from a workshop held in South Africa in 2000 involving government representatives, publishers, collecting societies, artists and writers, and other rights holders, which aimed to establish a new framework for the collective administration and management of copyright and allied rights.

1768 Gray, Eve, and Monica Seeber, eds. **PICC Report on Intellectual Property Rights in the Print Industries Sector.** Cape Town: Print Industries Cluster Council 2004. 205 pp.
Online:

http://www.publishsa.co.za/docs/Intellectual_Copyright_Report.pdf
[18/03/08]

This report on copyright in the print industries sector was commissioned by the (South African) Department of Arts and Culture, through the ➔ **Print Industries Cluster Council (943)** as part of a broader initiative to identify policy and development needs in the cultural industries. The report deals in particular with copyright as an aspect of Intellectual Property Rights (IPRs) and the impact of these rights on growth and development in the print industries sector. It surveys the state of copyright as it relates to the written word and identifies ways in which copyright laws and practices in South Africa are aiding or inhibiting growth. Finally, it sets out a range of recommendations for further action that could contribute towards growth and development in the book and print industries sector.

Gray, Eve *see also* Horwitz Gray, Eve

1769 Hasan, Abul **"Copyright and Development."** *Copyright Bulletin* 16, no. 1/2 (1982): 10-15.
[Not examined]

1770 Horwitz Gray, Eve **"Copyright – Taking the Debate Into Distance Education. A Publisher's Perspective."** *Meta-info Bulletin* 9, no. 1 (2000), 1-11. Online:
http://colfinder.net/materials/Supporting_Distance_Education_Through_
Policy_Development/resources/nadeosa/conference1999/gray.htm
[31/01/08]

The debate between the ➔ **Dramatic Artistic and Literary Rights Organisation/DALRO (938)**, the ➔ **Publishers' Association of South Africa (945)**, and the higher education institutions in South Africa about a possible change to the Regulations for Fair Dealing in the Copyright Act has generated a lot of heat, as have negotiations with DALRO around the introduction of blanket licences for institutional photocopying. The higher education institutions, and particularly those involved in distance education, are concerned about the fact that many students lack the means to purchase books, and are not able to access sufficient library resources for study purposes. They therefore plead for high limits to fair dealing provisions in the Copyright Regulations. This paper argues that there are constructive ways in which the publishing industry, authors, academics and librarians can approach these problems of tertiary information provision by working in partnership with one another. New developments in information provision, particularly in the electronic domain, are radically changing the nature of academic information provision, and are challenging the traditional roles of author, publisher, librarian and education provider, and the author asserts "we need to find imaginative new ways of working within this environment to position South African higher education and South African academic information delivery for the needs of students in the new millennium."

Horwitz Gray, Eve *see also* Gray, Eve

1771 Ike, V. Chukwuemeka **"Copyright and the Challenges of Indigenous Publishing."** *This Week* 2, no. 2 (October 1993): 23-24.
Reviews the publishing scene in Nigeria, the question of copyright protection for literary works, and concludes that effective protection of copyright in Nigeria is essential to the survival and growth of the indigenous publishing industry.

1772 Irura, Stanley **"Collective Administration of the Rights of Authors and Strengthening of Copyright Organizations Internationally."** *African Publishing Review* 4, no. 2 (March/April 1995): 7-8.
With an African audience in mind, describes the basic rules of copyright, copyright law and its provisions, and the major international protocols which have been formulated by international bodies to enhance worldwide adherence to copyright laws.

1773 Irura, Stanley **"Protection of the Rights of the Author: An Approach."** *African Publishing Review* 4, no. 3 (May/June 1995): 10-11.
Calls for a central body to administer the rights of intellectual property in any country, to protect the rights of authors, enforce copyright legislation, and to fight piracy and massive illegal photocopying of copyright material. Reports about the establishment of ➜ **Kopiken (584)**, a Kenyan reproduction rights organization, which follows the model of Norway's ➜ **Kopinor (89)**.

1774 Jegede, Oluremi **"Publications Laws of Nigeria: Need for a Review."** *African Journal of Library, Archives & Information Science* 6, no. 1 (1996): 11-22.
Critically examines the various legal deposit laws currently in force in Nigeria. Discusses the probable reasons for non-compliance by publishers, and suggests new approaches, and new methods, that might be tried to enforce the law. It also calls for a draft model bill of publication law by the Law Reform Commission, which is necessary to encourage both Federal and state governments to review or enact publication laws, a bill that should reflect new advances in educational, socio-cultural, and technological developments.

1775 Kedem, Kosi A. **"The Impact of Legal Deposit and Copyright Laws on Ghanaian Libraries."** *World Libraries* 1, no. 2 (1992): 50-51.
Online: http://www.worlib.org/vol01no2/kedem_v01n2.shtml [18/03/08]
Ghana's Book and Newspaper Registration Act (1961) and the Copyright Law (1985) have relevance to library development, since both laws are concerned with the collection and preservation of the nation's literature. However, while both acts were thorough in their intent, in practice both pieces of legislation have had disappointing results. The 1961 Act is not being enforced and so publishers have stopped depositing their publications as required. Moreover, those publications that have been deposited are not properly handled; the Registrar–General has not created a professional depository, and deposited materials that are sent to his office are housed casually. In addition to the trifling penalty imposed on publishers who fail to comply, the Act also has a serious flaw: it exempts government publications, the category that still constitutes the bulk of publications in Ghana.

1776 Kigongo-Bukenya, T. Isaac **"The Uganda Copyright and Neighbouring Rights Bill, 2002: Prospects and Challenges to the Information Professionals."** *University of Dar es Salaam Library* Journal 5, no. 2. (2003): 71-81.

Discusses the concept and philosophy of copyright, international provisions as they relate to copyright, and copyright infringement, with special reference to ICT. The paper also identifies gaps in the Uganda Copyright Bill 2002 and examines the role of information professionals in copyright protection. The author makes a number of recommendations for enhancements to the existing Copyright Bill 2002.

1777 Knutsen, Unni **"Survey on the State of National Bibliographies in Africa."**

http://www.ifla.org/VII/s12/pubs/Survey-Africa-report.pdf [18/03/08]

A paper presented to the 73rd ➔ **IFLA (74)** General Conference and Council in 2007, reporting about the state of national bibliographies in Africa, which includes a discussion of the survey results as they relate to legal deposit legislation and enforcement, the type of materials covered by national bibliographies, their formats, and their distribution. Unfortunately only 10 national bibliographic agencies responded to the survey questionnaire, and thus the picture presented here is probably incomplete; or it may well be an indication of the current dismal state of national bibliographies in Africa, with only a small number of countries publishing them on a reasonably regular basis.

1778 Kukubo, R. **Copyright Laws of Botswana, Lesotho, and Swaziland: An Historical view.** Lesotho: Institute of Southern African Studies, University of Lesotho, 1989. 62 pp.

[Not examined]

1779 Lawal-Solarin, O.M. **"Copyright and Education. A Publishers Perspective from a Developing Country."**

http://www.wipo.int/edocs/mdocs/copyright/en/educ_cr_im_05/educ_c r_im_05_www_53637.pdf [10/01/08]

A paper presented at the meeting on Education and Copyright in the Digital Age, November 2005, at the Headquarters of the ➔ **World Intellectual Property Organisation (126)** in Geneva. It offers a perspective, by a Nigerian publisher, on international copyright and copyright issues as they affect developing countries.

1780 Letshela, P.Z, and P.J. Lor **"Implementing Legal Deposit of Electronic Publications in Africa: Progress Report from Africa."**

http://www.ifla.org/IV/ifla68/papers/072-124e.pdf [10/01/08]

A paper presented to the 68th ➔ **IFLA (74)** Council and General Conference, August 18-24, 2002. Provides a progress report from Africa, concentrating on two countries whose legal deposit laws have already been updated to cover electronic publications, namely South Africa and Namibia. The paper describes what has been achieved so far, the problems and challenges encountered in implementing the law, and plans designed to overcome these obstacles. The authors assert that "notwithstanding the fact that electronic publishing in Africa is still in its infancy, the need for African countries to have laws that cover this medium is without question."

1781 Mefe, Guy-Marc Tony **Droit d'auteur et droits voisins : guide d'initiation pour l'Afrique francophone, pour mieux comprendre et avoir l'œil dessus**. Yaoundé: Ed. Scène d'Ebène, 2005. 68 pp.
A short practical guide for writers and authors in French-speaking Africa on matters of authors' rights, royalty payments from publishers, etc. It provides basic information relating to the protection of copyright of creative works, as well as to the general principles of copyright and neighbouring rights and the application of these rights, notably through collective management. It endeavours to make authors (and artists) understand the importance of being informed about the rights they have, so that they can protect them more effectively.

1782 Morolong, Siamisang **"The Botswana Copyright and Neighbouring Rights Act, 2000: An Overview."** *Lesotho Law Journal* 12, no. 1 (1999): 51-66.
The author presents an overview of the new Botswana Copyright Act which came into force in April 2000, in succession to the Copyright Act of 1965, which covered primarily written works. The new law legislates over areas not previously covered, including expressions of folklore, computer programmes and databases, and aims to strengthen the economic and moral rights of copyright owners.

1783 Mosuro, Kolade **"Handling Pirates and Piracy."** *African Publishing Review* 10, no. 4 (2001): 1-2.
A Nigerian bookseller's perspective piracy in Nigeria, and how to deal with it.

1784 Mould-Iddrisu, Betty **"Protection of Writers and Publishers in Africa. A Comparative Study of Copyright Legislation of Four Countries."** *African Publishing Review* 11, no. 2 (2002): 1-4.
Examines some of the aspects of copyright legislation in Nigeria, Namibia, Kenya, and Malawi, and assesses how copyright provisions in these countries have assisted and enhanced the protection of writers and publishers. The author argues that governments in many developing countries fail to appreciate the importance of vibrant intellectual property legislation, and that there is a need to recognize that modern and well-drafted copyright legislation is indispensable in the protection of authors' rights.

1785 Ndiaye, Ndéné **"International Copyright Conventions and the Production of School Textbooks in Developing Countries, with Special Reference to French-speaking Black Africa."** In *Educational Publishing in Developing Countries, Proceedings of an International Seminar held from 12 February to 15 February 1978 at New Delhi*. New Delhi: National Book Trust, India, 1980, 187-200.
A detailed discussion of how copyright conventions affect various African countries in different ways, depending on their indigenous languages, infrastructure, and "cultural standard" of the population.

1786 Ndiaye, Papa Toumané **"The Economic Importance of Copyright and Neighbouring Rights in the Cultural Industries of African Countries Having French as a Common Language."** *Copyright Bulletin* 30, no. 1 (January-March 1996): 3-12.
Discusses the economic dimensions created by the production, use and dissemination of works, and the performance of artists, in the form of earnings and employment in francophone African countries. Looks at copyright legislation in these countries, the various types of the cultural industries (including publishing) and the circulation of their products, the economic influence of cultural industries, and the position of the audio-visual sector. Concludes that cultural industries are capable of contributing a much greater share to the GNP of African countries, just as much as they do on the North American and European continents, but that "surveys and studies are needed to assess these industries' real economic impact and potential, with a view to encouraging investment."

1787 Ngombe, Laurier Yvon **Le droit d'auteur en Afrique**. Paris: L'Harmattan, 2004. 178 pp.
A helpful introductory guide to the rights of authors (and those in the music industry) and the principal aspects of copyright law in Africa. The author provides a comparative analysis of the theoretical and practical aspects of the topic, deals with the matter of remuneration, as well as offering a synthesis from an African point of view. It includes an analysis of Annex VII of the Bangui Agreement – of the ➔ **African Intellectual Property Organization/OAPI (19)** – in the context of international copyright conventions.

1788 Nicholson, Denise Rosemary **"What has Copyright Got to Do with Newspapers? A South African Perspective."** *Cape Librarian* 49, no. 2 (March/April 2005): 6-9.
Online: http://www.capegateway.gov.za/Text/2005/6/mar_apr05_06-09.pdf [20/03/08]
Primarily on the practical implications of copyright for newspaper publishers in South Africa, as well as their implications for consumers and collectors of newspapers such as libraries, and their efforts to preserve archival material through microfilming and digitization projects of newspaper collections. The author believes appropriate provisions for this should be included in either the Legal Deposit Act or in the country's Copyright Act, in order to facilitate, rather than restrict, access to such material and which forms part of the country's heritage.

1789 Nicholson, Denise Rosemary **International Copyright Trends and Access to Knowledge Initiatives in Africa.**
http://www.ifla.org/IV/ifla73/papers/135-Nicholson-en.pdf [20/03/08]
A paper presented to the 73rd ➔ **IFLA (74)** General Conference and Council in 2007. Discusses copyright issues and various 'Access to Knowledge' initiatives in Africa, from a South African perspective. The author argues that creators, publishers, custodians, and consumers of information, as well as libraries and educational institutions, need to be more vocal in international law-making bodies, otherwise, when a treaty is implemented years later it is too late to effect any changes. Their

participation in the national legislative process is also crucial. Nicholson states, "multinationals operating content industries in African countries lock up indigenous knowledge, cultural heritage resources and even public domain material in commercial digital archives. Excessive subscription fees, restrictive licences and copyright laws, including technological protection measures, effectively block access to the majority of Africans." Another concern in South Africa (and most likely in other African countries) is that material that should be in the public domain, e.g. official documents, legislation, court reports, etc. is being outsourced by the government and locked up in commercial works and digital archives, which are fee-based and not easily accessible to the public. Copyright is then held by the publishers or content providers of these resources. As a result of these concerns, the African Copyright and Access to Information Alliance was established at the African Copyright Forum, held in Uganda, in 2005. In 2006, the Alliance was registered as a Chapter in Uganda and its name was changed to African Access to Knowledge Alliance (*see also* ➜ **24**), and it was subsequently registered as a continental body in Botswana in January 2007. The purpose of this Alliance is to assist African countries when reviewing their copyright laws, to encourage them to adopt legal flexibilities and provisions to address the needs of libraries, education and the sensory-disabled, as well as to preserve their cultural heritage. The author concludes "African knowledge and research is conspicuous by its absence in the global arena. Africans, however, have a great deal to offer to global knowledge-sharing. They also deserve to share in the benefits of that knowledge. Proper rights for users of information therefore need to be enshrined in a balanced international framework to preserve and share the world's resources equitably and for future generations. To achieve this, Africans must become more pro-active in the global copyright debate and access to knowledge (A2K) initiatives, so that their important needs will be addressed."

1790   Nwauche, E.S. **Intellectual Property Rights, Copyright and Development Policy in a Developing Country: Options for Sub-Saharan African Countries.**
http://www.kopinor.org/content/download/1777/13422/file/zibf.pdf
[20/03/08]
A thought-provoking paper by the Director General of the Nigerian Copyright Commission presented to a copyright workshop held during the 2003 Zimbabwe International Book Fair. The author contends that intellectual property is a key to technological and economic development, even for developing countries, and therefore "for any developing country it can never be out of fashion to interrogate the relationship between its intellectual property policy and its development." The paper argues that a development oriented strong copyright protection is fundamental to the economic and technological advancement of sub-Saharan African countries and synthesizes such a policy. However, development must come from within to be meaningful. "More often than not, aid of whatever sort including free copyright goods is paternalistic at the least and induces dependence not development. Sub-Saharan Africa must stop believing that they are helpless in the face of an unjust international intellectual property system. They need to confront their problems and come up with imaginative solutions. Each country must encourage a debate amongst a wide spectrum of stakeholders to fashion out policies that ensure that their intellectual property rights are in aid of their development."

1791 Nyadzi, Ben K. **"Licensing Reprographic Reproduction: The Ghana Experience."** In *Publishing in Indigenous Languages. Papers Presented at the Fourth Nigeria International Book Fair, 10-14 May, 2005.* Lagos: Nigerian Book Fair Trust [c/o Literamed Publications Ltd., PMB 21068, Ikeja, Lagos, Nigeria], 2006, 46-52.

The Managing Director of ➜ **CopyGhana (534)**, a Ghanaian reproduction rights organization, sets out their experience in managing and protecting reprographic rights for authors and publishers, and the legal background that led to CopyGhana's establishment. The activities of the organization have now ensured that photocopying of books and articles at tertiary institutions in the country take place in a legally regulated environment.

1792 Oddoye, David E.M. **"Legal Deposit and Copyright in Ghana."** *Ghana Book World*, no. 5 (1991): 41-50.

Traces the history and growth of legal deposit and copyright in Ghana from 1897 to 1985. Examines the extent to which legal deposit succeeded in preserving national output of literature. Criticizes the provisions of The Book and Newspaper Registration Act of 1961 and the PNDC Law 110 of 1985.

1793 Ojiji, C.O. **"Report of the Anti-Piracy and Protection Committee."** *The Publisher* 1, no.1 (December 1985): 8-17.

Reports on piracy in Nigeria and details the legal process and action which should be taken against copyright infringements. The report includes information on copyright laws and gives advice on what to do when pirated books are discovered.

1794 Okiy, Rose B. **"Photocopying and the Awareness of Copyright in Tertiary Institutions in Nigeria."** *Interlending & Document Supply* 33, no. 1 (2005): 49-52.

Investigates photocopying practices in tertiary institutions in Nigeria as they relate to the existing copyright law. The author offers a number of suggestions how to regulate photocopying practices to create greater awareness of the copyright law in tertiary institutions, and that might in turn reduce infringement of copyright laws through photocopying.

Okwilagwe, Andrew Oshiotse **"Book Piracy. Robbery of Intellectual Property"** *see* ➜ **Section 3, Country studies: Nigeria** entry 839

1795 Oladitan, Olalere **"The Role of Collecting Societies in the Collective Administration of Rights."** In *Publishing in Indigenous Languages. Papers Presented at the Fourth Nigeria International Book Fair, 10-14 May, 2005.* Lagos: Nigerian Book Fair Trust [c/o Literamed Publications Ltd., PMB 21068, Ikeja, Lagos, Nigeria], 2006, 119-37.

Examines the components that are required for collective action in securing, protecting, and asserting the rights of authors and other rights owners and makes some suggestions how this might be achieved. Also discusses the role of publishers, the collective administration of rights, and practical aspects of licensing and collection of licensing fees. The author is Executive Secretary of the → **Academic and Non-Fiction Authors' Association of Nigeria (731).**

1796 Oman, Ralph **Copyright – Engine of Development. An Analysis of the Role of Copyright in Economic Development and Cultural Vitality.** Paris: UNESCO Publishing, 2000. 152 pp. E-book (pdf) http://upo.unesco.org/bookdetails.asp?id=3004# (e-book download, cost €10.70) [20/03/08]
Highlights the economic benefits to developing countries from strong copyright legislation and protection, and documents the cultural benefits that spring from the elimination of piracy. Includes chapters devoted to the basic tenets of a modern national copyright regime, multilateral conventions, copyright and new technologies, together with chapters on economic analysis of copyright in developing countries, the future of copyright in developing countries, and a section on "answering the hard question of cost for developing countries."

1797 Ouma, Marisella **The Copyright Act 2001: A New Era for Copyright Protection in Kenya.** *e-Copyright Bulletin* July - September 2004 http://portal.unesco.org/culture/en/ev.php-URL_ID=23854&URL_DO=DO_TOPIC&URL_SECTION=201.html [10/01/08]
A comprehensive review of the new Kenya 2001 Copyright Act, which was passed by the Kenyan Parliament, after several rounds of consultations between the government and the different stakeholders and industry players. It came into force in February 2003 and repealed the 1966 Copyright Act. The most distinctive new features of the new Copyright Act include the introduction of an anti-piracy security device; the registration and supervision of collective management societies in Kenya; the appointment of public prosecutors and inspectors who deal with copyright cases and help the enforcement of the rights protected under the Act; the provision of enhanced criminal sanctions; and the protection of rights management systems and technological protection measures. The author welcomes the 2001 Copyright Act as a step in the right direction, yet "the success of the new law can only be seen if it is effectively enforced; a good law without the proper enforcement is of no use to those it seeks to protect. Along with the new law, Kenya needs to have strong mechanisms to fight piracy, a well educated population on matters of copyright and related rights, strong and efficient collective management societies, and a functional administrative infrastructure."

1798 Owen, Lynette **"Copyright-Benefit or Obstacle?"** In *Copyright and Development: Inequality in the Information Age,* edited by Philip G. Altbach. Chestnut Hill, MA: Bellagio Publishing Network, Research and Information Center (Bellagio Studies on Publishing, 4), 1995, 93-108.
A perspective on copyright from that of "a publisher who has worked for more than twenty-five years in multinational, educational and academic publishing", which stresses that "a keen awareness of the importance of copyright [is] a necessary background to trading in rights worldwide." Examines compulsory licensing, the implications of granting licences, and the nature of licensing terms with publishers in

developing countries. Also reviews the rapid advances in new technologies, and their implications for copyright protection.

1799 Oyediran, O.O. **"The Importance of Copyright as a Crucial Component in the Creative Industries."** *The Publisher* 3, no. 1 (January 1995): 52-55.
A keynote address delivered by the [then] Vice-Chancellor of the University of Ibadan to an international copyright forum held in Nigeria in 1994.

1800 Publishers' Association of South Africa **Copyright: Frequently Asked Questions.**
http://www.publishsa.co.za/index.php?cmd=copy_faq [20/03/08]
Intellectual property lies at the heart of the publishing and printing industries. The → **Publishers' Association of South Africa (945)** believes "instead of seeing themselves merely as book publishers, publishers could see themselves as acquirers, custodians and managers of intellectual property rights in the process of exploiting these rights to the best advantage of themselves, authors and users." In the midst of sometimes complex big-picture copyright issues, authors, publishers and users of intellectual property get confronted with specific and practical questions. This is a useful set of FAQs on some of the questions on copyright most frequently asked of the Publishers' Association of South Africa, and likely to be asked elsewhere in an African context.

1801 Publishers' Association of South Africa **PICC Report on Intellectual Property Rights in the Print Industries Sector, May 2004.**
http://www.publishsa.co.za/index.php?cmd=copy_intprop [20/03/08]
A summary version of a report on copyright in the print industries sector that was commissioned by the South African Department of Arts and Culture, through the → **Print Industries Cluster Council (943)** – now integrated with the → **South African Book Development Council (950)** – as part of a broader initiative to identify policy and development needs in the cultural industries. The Report deals in particular with copyright as an aspect of Intellectual Property Rights (IPRs) and the impact of these rights on growth and development in the print industries sector. It surveys the state of copyright as it relates to the written word and identifies ways in which copyright laws and practices in South Africa are aiding or inhibiting growth. It also makes recommendations for further action that could contribute towards growth and development in the print industries sector.

1802 Rens, Andrew; Achal Prabhala, and Dick Kawooya **Intellectual Property, Education and Access to Knowledge in Southern Africa.**
Stellenbosch: Trade Law Centre for Southern Africa [PO Box 224, Stellenbosch 7599, South Africa], with International Centre for Trade and Sustainable Development (ICTSD), and UNCTAD, 2006. 69 pp.
Online:
http://www.iprsonline.org/unctadictsd/docs/06%2005%2031%20tralac%20amended-pdf.pdf [20/03/08]

There can be little doubt that education is a cornerstone of social and economic development, and that access to learning materials is a crucial factor in the success of any educational system. "In a world which values the production and dissemination of information and knowledge, human capital growth is a serious developmental concern. First, societies of the global south are struggling with everyday challenges of education and literacy, while their institutions and governments perform the inevitable balancing act between scarce resources and vast needs. Second, producers of knowledge goods, heretofore located in the north, are increasingly global in scope; exporting, with their expansion, an intellectual property rights (IPR) regime that poses current and potential deterrents to learning." The first section in this paper defines broad issues to consider and examines the barriers to access to learning materials faced in the Southern African Customs Union (SACU), analyzing the responsibility of intellectual property legislation within the complex structure of systems that are consequential to consumers and learners. In the second section the authors remind us that the informal economy in knowledge goods is an access mechanism, prompting a conceptual consideration of the phenomenon of piracy, and then, through a case study in Uganda, they suggest possible policy lessons. The third section frames the environment described in the first two sections in a survey of intellectual property law in SACU member countries, and audits the limitations or exceptions available within the law, in the light of those that may be made use of, as a consequence of access to learning materials. The authors conclude that currently "neither does copyright legislation in SACU countries make significantly positive provisions for access to learning materials, nor does it take full advantage of the flexibilities provided by TRIPs. Ironically, it is precisely in this disabling legal environment that the SACU countries are being asked – by domestic and international publishing industry lobbies – to strengthen the enforcement of criminal sanctions for certain copyright violations, even as they constitute an access mechanism in a context that offers few alternatives."

1803 Rønning, Helge **"The Rights of Writers."** In *Academic Book Production and Distribution in Africa. Support from Nordic Countries. Report from a Conference at Chr. Michelsen Institute, Bergen, 10-11 April 1997,* edited by Kirsti Hagen Andersen. Fantoft, Norway: Ch. Michelsen Institute 1997, 58-67.
Uses the experience of the Nordic writers' associations and ➔ **Kopinor. The Norwegian Reproduction Rights Organization (89),** as an illustration of some of the principal components relating to the rights of writers internationally, including those in Africa.

1804 Rudolph, John-Willy **"The International Implications of Reproduction Rights: Essence and Limitations."** *The Publisher* 3, no. 1 (January 1995): 45-50.
First presented as a guest lecture during a copyright forum held in Nigeria in 1994, by the [former] Executive Director of ➔ **Kopinor. The Norwegian Reproduction Rights Organization (89),** this paper looks at collective administration of reprographic and similar rights, and urges Nigerian publishers to establish a collective administrative body of their own.

1805 Rudolph, John-Willy **"Why are Intellectual Property Rights Important? What Mechanisms Constrain or Encourage Creation and Proper Utilization of Intellectual Property?"** In *National Book Policies for Africa*, edited by Murray McCartney. Harare: Zimbabwe International Book Fair Trust, 1996, 42-46.
The [former] Executive Director of ➔ **Kopinor. The Norwegian Reproduction Rights Organization (89)** argues the case for the establishment of more collective reproduction rights organizations in Africa, to protect intellectual property and to ensure that writers, artists, photographers, or illustrators receive due remuneration for their creative work. He states that "on whatever level we attempt to develop a book policy, it should be founded on the understanding that respect for copyright encourages creativity."

1806 Savahl, Aneeka **"Is Copyright 'un-African'?"** *Bookmark. News Magazine of the South African Booksellers' Association* 10 (July-September 2006): 19.
Reflects on some of the issues debated at a 'Copyright Lekgotla' during the inaugural Cape Town Book Fair, and the arguments by some participants that copyright is an inherently "un-African" concept in that it promotes private ownership and knowledge; and the concerns, as they relate to indigenous knowledge systems, that indigenous people may be robbed of their traditional knowledge through private ownership.

1807 Savahl, Aneeka **"Responsible Publishing in the Information Age."** *Bookmark. News Magazine of the South African Booksellers' Association* 11 (October 2006-March 2007): 14.
A perspective on copyright in Africa generally and in South Africa in particular. "It seems that copyright laws are considered with much suspicion in Africa—another silent oppressor designed to hold the knowledge within the grasp of the moneyed few." The author believes better awareness and understanding of copyright would help in exposing myths and dispelling negative perceptions of copyright's role in the publishing industry.

1808 Seeber, Monica **"Copyright Infringement and Unauthorized Photocopying."** *African Publishing Review* 7, no. 1 (January/February 1998): 7-10.
Describes how unauthorized photocopying can adversely affect the publishing industries, and discusses some solutions to this ongoing problem.

1809 Seeber, Monica **"Perspective on Copyright."** *African Publishing Review* 7, no. 6 (November/December 1998): 13-14.
Reports about African participation at the ➔ **International Publishers Association (82)** 4th International Copyright Symposium and the problems and challenges facing African publishers in the area of copyright.

1810 Seeber, Monica **"Protecting the Publishing Industry: Reprographic Rights Administration as a Strategy and Tool for National Book Publishing Development."** In *The Politics of Publishing in South Africa,* edited by Nicholas Evans and Monica Seeber. London: Holger Ehling Publishing and Scotsville, South Africa: University of Natal Press, 2000, 279-293.
Examines the role of reproduction rights administration in national book development, and the nature of the threat to the publishing industry in Africa posed by unauthorized reprographic reproduction (i.e. institutional or private photocopying of extracts from published works). Using South Africa as a case study, it points to the importance, for the local publishing industry, of the collective administration of reprographic reproduction rights as a strategy for growth and sustainability. Argues that "if it is maintained that the protection of intellectual property is in the public interest and the debate is no longer around whether or not one portion of society embraces it while the other reject it, that copyright is neither friend to rights holders nor foe to users as long as licensing proffers fair to both, then a major step forward will have been taken."

1811 Seeber, Monica **Reprographic Reproduction Rights Administration as a Strategy and Tool for the Development of the National Publishing Industry.** Geneva: World Intellectual Property Organisation (WIPO/CR/ACC/00/9, March 2000) [PO Box 18, CH-1211 Geneva 20], 2002. [Not examined]

1812 Seeber, Monica **Academic and Non-fiction Writing and Authors' Rights.**
http://www.anfasa.org.za/assets/dac_paper.pdf [09/01/08]
An amended version of a paper presented by Director of the ➔ **Academic and Non-fiction Authors' Association of South Africa/ANFASA (932)** at a (South African) Department of Arts and Culture consultative workshop on copyright and national legislation, held in Pretoria, in July 2006. It sets out the role of ANFASA in raising the status of non-fiction authors as part of encouraging and promoting the development of knowledge production in South Africa, and creating an awareness of, and respect for, authors' rights. The purpose of this particular presentation was to draw special attention to authors' interests, as distinct from the rights of publishers.

1813 Shuaibu-Adamu, B.F. **"Legal Deposit Obligations: Issues, Benefits and Challenges."** In *National Book Policy, HIV/AIDS and Sustainable Development. Papers Presented at the Fifth Nigeria International Book Fair, 8-13 May, 2006.* Lagos: Nigerian Book Fair Trust [c/o Literamed Publications Ltd., PMB 21068, Ikeja, Lagos, Nigeria], 2007, 164-177.
Describes legal deposit legislation in Nigeria, the practicalities of legal deposit requirements, problems encountered in enforcing legal deposit, and the advantages accruing to publishers who systematically deposit copies of their publications with the National Library of Nigeria.

1814 Sonaike, S.E.A. **"Legal Deposit Provision of the National Library Act: Implementation, Preservation and Benefits."** *Lagos Journal of Library and Information Science* 1, no. 1 (2003): 59-66.
A critical examination of the Legal Deposit Act of the National Library of Nigeria as it relates to its components, implementation, and benefits. The author identifies some of the problems militating against the successful implementation of the Act, and offers a range of recommendations how compliance with the Act by publishers might be improved.

1815 Story, Alan; Colin Darch, and Debora Halbert, eds. **The Copy/South Dossier. Issues in the Economics, Politics, and Ideology of Copyright in the Global South.** Canterbury: University of Kent Law School, The Copy/South Research Group, 2006. 210 pp.
Online: http://www.copysouth.org/ (can be freely downloaded, in part or in its entirety, in RTF or PDF formats) [20/03/08]
This unique dossier was assembled by the activist ➜ **Copy South Research Group (53)**, a loosely-affiliated group of researchers based in a number of countries across the South and the North who seek to research the inner workings of the global copyright system and its effects on the global South. The dossier contains more than 50 articles examining many dimensions of the issue of copyright across the global South, such as access, culture, economics, libraries, education, software, the Internet, the public domain, and resistance. The dossier is addressed to readers who want to learn more about the global role of copyright and, in particular, its sometimes negative role in the global South. The articles critically analyze and assess a wide range of copyright-related issues that impact on the daily lives, and future lives, of those who live in the countries of the South. It aims to do so in a manner which the editors hope will bring these questions 'alive', show the direct human stakes of the many debates, "and make the issues accessible to those who want to go beyond the platitudes, half-truths, and serious distortions that often plague discussions of this topic."

1816 Taylor, Ian **"Approaches to Countering Piracy."** *The Publisher* 2, no. 2 (October 1993): 41-42.
In a paper first presented at a Copyright Forum held in Lagos in 1991, the [former] director of the UK Book Development Council explores the question of what measures can be implemented to counteract piracy.

1817 Taylor, Ian **"Some Aspects of Copyright Issues."** In *Educational Publishing in Global Perspective. Capacity Building and Trends,* edited by Shobhana Sosale. Washington, DC: The World Bank, 1998, 155-157.
Ian Taylor, a former Director of the UK Publishers Association, persuasively argues that copyright is a crucial incentive for indigenous publishers and authors alike, that in a copyright environment monopolized by the government there is little incentive for publishers and authors to thrive, and that it is not in the interest of any publisher to see copyright protection set aside for short-term gain.

1818 Thomas, Akin **"Copyright and the Future of Publishing. (Particularly Electronic Publishing)."** *The Publisher* 2, no. 1 (March 1991): 41-44.
Discusses the ramifications of copyright in publishing in general and the specialized problems of copyright in electronic publishing in particular.

1819 Thomas, Akin **"Piracy Activities as a Measure for Sustenance of Creativity - global perspective."** *The Publisher* 2, no. 2 (October 1993): 43-48.
Explores the issue of the copyright system by looking at forms and causes of piracy and the book industry, piracy and the music industry, the national and international scope of copyright, economic, political and cultural benefits and recent improvements in the situation.

1820 United Nations Conference on Trade and Development/UNCAT **The TRIPS Agreement and Developing Countries**. New York and Geneva: United Nations [Sales no. 96.II.D.10], 1996. 64 pp.
The Trade Related Intellectual Property Rights (TRIPS) agreement, signed on 15 April 1994 in the framework of the Uruguay Round negotiations, represents an important change in international standards for protecting intellectual property in developing countries, and covers a wide range of disciplines. Following an introductory section on the main findings and conclusions, this study provides a detailed analysis of the implications of the TRIPS agreement for developing economies, and examines the different areas of copyright protection relevant under TRIPS agreement standards.

1821 Uvieghara, Egerton E. **Essays on Copyright Law and Administration in Nigeria.** Ibadan: Y-Books [for Nigerian Copyright Council], 1992. 243 pp.
Contains the papers of a national seminar on the Nigerian Copyright Law held in Lagos in March, 1988. The papers cover a wide area of issues relating to copyright and intellectual property, and as they affect authors/books, the film industry, broadcasting, and the visual arts. Part 1 presents an introduction to Nigerian copyright law and its relevance to social change; part 2 focuses on the international dimensions of copyright protection and sanctions, while part 3 deals with various aspects of Nigerian copyright law, copyright exceptions, legal action for infringement of copyright, and copyright and licensing. The final part 4 focuses on the administration and practice of copyright, with papers on the need for an effective infrastructure to administer copyright, reprography and intellectual property, intellectual property and book piracy, copyright and emerging trends in technology, and the implications of copyright law for performing artists.

1822 Uvieghara, Egerton E. **"An Evaluation of the Operational Strategies for the Enforcement of Copyright in Nigeria."** *Copyright News* 2, no.7 (April-June 1993): 8, 9, 16.
Paper presented by the chairman of the governing board of the Nigerian Copyright Council at the special seminar on the adjudication of copyright cases organized by the Nigerian Copyright Council Lagos, May 1993.

1823 Uvieghara, Egerton E. **"Copyright Law in Nigeria: Its Role in the Development of Arts and Culture."** *Copyright News* 2, no. 8 (July-September 1993): 7-9.
An address by the chairman of the Nigerian Copyright Council at the 1993 Public Service Lecture.

1824 Wafawarowa, Brian **"Legal Exception to Copyright and the Development of the Developing Countries' Information Sector."** *African Publishing Review* 9, no. 6 (2000): 3-4.
Argues that a "hopeful strategy on access to information in the developing world should seek to create conditions which stimulate creativity and not strategies which stifle it." The author stresses that the developing world does not only need access to information, but "it also needs relevant and appropriate information. It also needs to be an equal participant in the global information system and to be able to do this, it needs to be both a consumer of world information as well as a producer of global content." Calls for ways to subsidize access to information, and thus not place the whole burden on the shoulder of the rights holders. Concludes that "universal access to information is a very plausible proposition for the developing world, but the responsibility to enhance access to information is a responsibility of society, including government and the private sector."

1825 Wafawarowa, Brian **"Legislation, Law Enforcement and Education: Copyright Protection in the Developing Regions."** *Bellagio Publishing Network Newsletter*, no. 30 (May 2002): 13-16.
Online:
http://www.bellagiopublishingnetwork.com/newsletter30/wafawarowa.htm [20/03/08]
First presented at the ➔ **International Publishers Association (82)** Copyright Conference held in Accra in February 2002, this paper examines the copyright situation in South Africa as an example of a developing publishing environment. It evaluates the role of legislation and law enforcement institutions in combating copyright infringements, and argues that "cutting across these two pillars is the need for a third pillar: education and awareness"; and that there is a need for a concerted campaign to make sure that those responsible for illegal copying and other copyright violations are fully aware of the implications and the criminality of their action.

1826 Wafawarowa, Brian **"Development, Education, and Enforcement: Securing the Future of Copyright Protection."** *African Publishing Review* 13, no. 3 (2004): 1-3.
A position paper presented on behalf of the ➔ **African Publishers Network (5),** at the 27th annual congress of the ➔ **International Publishers Association (82)** in Berlin in June 2004. The author notes with concern the current unsatisfactory copyright situation in many countries of Africa, the lack of respect for copyright, rampant piracy, erratic availability of international textbooks, and lack of finance by local publishers who are thus unable to fulfil demand. Sets out a number of proposals how copyright protection might be secured in such a difficult environment, and on the basis of a long term and prudent strategy.

1827 Wafawarowa, Brian **Intellectual Property Rights and Knowledge Production in Africa.**
http://www.iccwbo.org/uploadedFiles/ICC/policy/intellectual_property/pages/BrianWafawarowa.doc [20/03/08]
A policy statement (on the Web site of the International Chamber of Commerce's Commission on Intellectual Property) succinctly setting out the current [2006] situation of publishing and knowledge production in Africa. The author asserts that, despite the considerable gains made by indigenous publishers in the late 1980s and in the 1990s, the 21st century has seen significant erosion of these gains, the worst affected region being French-speaking Africa "where almost all publishing is now done by multinationals." Wafawarowa believes there are a number of reasons why the African publishing sector is in the current unsatisfactory state: "The most important is the failure to establish an ideal and secure environment which encourages authors to create content and publishers to publish. These include an unsupportive business environment, lack of proper national book development policies and overdependence on seasonal donor and World Bank driven programmes. The dire needs of education and the unauthorized copying of education materials hits local publishers hardest, in a sector that they depend on most. The increase in unauthorized copying usually follows declines in the economic fortunes of a country and reductions in education budgets. This suggests quite clearly that lack of access to content in African education is more a budgetary issue than an intellectual property or of overpricing." He concludes that, to allow Africa to become an equal global player in knowledge production and dissemination in the years to come "the continent needs to set itself on a long road towards self-sufficiency in knowledge production. This is possible because already there are indigenous publishing companies in every part of the continent that are capable of producing world class content, if the ideal environment is created for them."

1828 Wafo, Dieubéni **La protection, par le droit d'auteur, du logiciel en Afrique noire: le pénible éveil.** *Penant: Revue de Droit des Pays d'Afrique* 105, no. 818 (1995): 156-171.
An examination of the Togo law on copyright of 1990, and that of Angola of 1990, on the rights of authors, and issues relating to royalty payments. Primarily covers aspects of rights protection and legislation for software.

1829 Zhangazha, Witness Paridzirai **A User's Guide to Copyright Law in Zimbabwe.** Harare: National Arts Council of Zimbabwe, 2005. 48 pp.
[Not examined]

Digital media and electronic publishing/
New printing technology

See also
→ Journals and magazine publishing
→ Open access publishing
→ Scholarly publishing (General)
→ Scientific, technical and medical publishing

1830 Adebowale, Sulaiman **"Disseminating the Electronic Publishing Philosophy in Developing Countries."** *INASP Newsletter*, no. 16 (March 2001): 4-5.
A longer version of this paper published in INASP's *Electronic Journal Publishing. A Reader (Version 2.0)*
http://www.inasp.info/uploaded/documents/8.2-%20Adebowale.html [11/01/08]
The author states that the increasing interest and widespread acceptance of email and use of online discussion lists by scholars from the developing world suggests that a viable market for electronic publishing does exist, and is "waiting to be tapped". However, he cautions "dreams of electronic information will be determined by more complex factors than the level of connectivity." Adebowale concludes that "the acceptance, involvement or rejection of electronic publishing in these [developing] countries will be influenced by how the issues are engaged vis-à-vis the roles. For instance, the need to continue to produce print versions of journals may still be imperative for the developing world, publishers in this part of the world must take this necessity into serious consideration in electronic publishing plans, rather than desist from electronic publishing. Furthermore, electronic publishing will demand new ways of working, bring up new actors into the trade, or reconstruct structures. The onus for journal publishing in the developing world is to engage these changes pro-actively, in order to preserve its meaning for its community and guarantee its relevance at any particular point in time."

1831 Adebowale, Sulaiman **"Is the Future Print-on-Demand? Increasing Revenue for Publishers in the 21st Century."** *Bellagio Publishing Network Newsletter*, no. 30 (May 2002): 3-4.
Online:
http://www.bellagiopublishingnetwork.com/newsletter30/adebowale.htm [20/03/08]
Presents some views about a seminar held at the London Book Fair in March 2002, which explored recent advances in digital printing and the key issues in print-on-demand technology (POD). The articles aims to demystify the technology, reviews the benefits of POD, and encourages publishers in Africa, and in other parts of the developing world, to consider the new technology where it is, or will become available, for example for publication of indigenous language publishing projects which have limited market potential.

1832 Aina, L.O., and Stephen M. Mutula **"Opportunities for Electronic Publishing in Africa."** In *African Scholarly Publishing Essays,* edited by Alois Mlambo. Oxford: African Books Collective Ltd.; Uppsala: Dag Hammarskjöld Foundation; and Oxford: International Network for the Availability of Scientific Publications (INASP), 2006, 193-200.

The authors, of the Department of Library and Information Studies at the University of Botswana, describe the experience of the ➜ **African Journal of Library, Archives and Information Science (128)** and examine the present state of electronic publishing in Africa, the issues that must be addressed to encourage electronic scholarly publishing in Africa, and the obstacles that will have to be overcome. Electronic publishing on the continent, at this time [2006], is still largely confined to journal publishing, but also includes some digitization projects to make theses and dissertations available in electronic formats. The authors believe "it is possible that if attractive electronic business models are developed and Internet infrastructure improved, [book] publishers will be enticed into electronic publishing to capture a potentially lucrative market", albeit without offering offer suggestions what type of products this might, and the kind of projects that might be suitable and could provide significant revenue streams for African publishers.

Davis, Jason **African Books Collective. PDF File Production Manual** *see* ➜ **Section 5, Book industry training/Self-Publishing: Training manuals and resources** entry **2455**

1833 Esseh, Samuel Smith, and John Willinsky **Strengthening Scholarly Publishing in Africa: Assessing the Potential of Online Systems.** http://pkp.sfu.ca/files/AfricanWorkshops.pdf [26/02/08]

Outlines details of a scholarly publishing initiative that will aim to increase access to African research and advance local research capacities, and which is intended to assess the potential contribution of online publishing systems for African scholarly journals. It is part of the Strengthening African Research Culture and Capacities project (*see also* http://pkp.sfu.ca/node/1334), funded by the ➜ **International Development Research Center (72)** the ➜**Open Society Institute (100)**, and the ➜ **Carnegie Corporation (47).** Working in association with the Public Knowledge Project (PKP) http://pkp.sfu.ca/at the University of British Columbia, one of the authors, Samuel Smith Esseh, visited eight universities across sub-Saharan Africa, to meet with and survey journal editors and academic librarians in an effort to assess both the current state of scholarly journal publishing and the potential value of utilizing online journal management and publishing systems that could increase both African research and global access to African research. As a result of this analysis, this study will assess (1) the state of scholarly publishing among journals in 6-8 regions of Africa, with regard to editorial structures, economics, technologies (print and Internet), and incentives; (2) levels of support for online access to scholarly materials, both African and global; and (3) the feasibility of research libraries or other academic centres establishing Online Scholarly Publishing Sites (OSPS) to host and support existing and new academic journals through the use of PKP's Open Journal Systems (OJS), an open source journal management and publishing system. The proposed OSPS model is based on the IBICT SEER program in Brazil, which supports the online management and publishing of 63 Brazilian journals using OJS.

1834 Gedin, Per **"A Real Cultural Revolution."** *Development Dialogue*, nos. 1-2 (1997): 61-67.
Swedish publisher Per Gedin examines the evolution of electronic publishing, and, in particular, the new techniques of digital printing and print-on-demand technology (POD), which are revolutionizing publishing on a global level; a process, he states, that will change publishing in every country, and whose advent means that "African countries can make a great leap forward, catching up on several decades." Arguing that the new techniques seem almost to have been invented for book production in developing countries, since they obviate the need for long print runs, warehouses and transportation, he urges African publishers to take full advantage of digital printing, and calls on the ➔ **African Publishers Network (5)** to undertake a study of this new technology as a matter of priority, and to investigate its full potential for the development of indigenous publishing.

1835 Gray, Eve **"Caxton or the Ethernet? Academic Publishing in an African Context."**
Cape Librarian 44, no. 3 (2000).
Online:
http://home.imaginet.co.za/liasa/Caxton%20or%20the%20Ethernet.htm [30/10/07]
Also at http://www.evegray.co.za/downloads/webcopyCaxton.doc [31/01/08]
A paper delivered at the South African Library and Information Science Association's annual conference in August 2000, at a time when the international book trade press were awash with articles about the advent of e-books and the impact that these will have on the publishing industry. This article charts the state of affairs and explores the potential for digital media, e-books and e-content, in academic publishing in a developing world context, and more particularly in South Africa. The author believes the future of South African academic publishing might well lie in an electronic vision. "South African universities, authors, publishers, booksellers, librarians and printers will have to be bold, innovative and highly professional if they are to seize this opportunity", but adds a caveat: "Is this just a romantic dream – or is it realistic or practical in the environment in which we operate?"

1836 Gray, Eve **Supply Chain Solutions for Transformation in South African Publishing: Print on Demand Digital Content Management for Market Expansion.**
http://www.evegray.co.za/downloads/POD_DCM_for_transformation.pd f [31/01/08]
New technologies such as print on demand (POD) – now extensively used to open new markets, to extend the life of niche publications, and to provide for a reduced-risk approach in publishing short-run titles – are offering major opportunities for a country like South Africa. This paper explores these opportunities and questions

why its publishing industry is still not taking advantage of the potential. The author provides a range of examples how integrated digital printing could help to grow markets in South Africa.

1837 Hussein, Janet **"Science Journals in Zimbabwe. Will Electronic Publishing Improve their Long Term Viability?"** In *Scientific Communication and Publishing in the Information, Oxford Workshop, 10–12 May 1999.*
http://web.archive.org/web/20040502081718/www.inasp.info/psi/scpw/papers/hussein.html [20/03/08]
Discusses some of the problems facing journal editors and publishers in Zimbabwe and highlight some of the benefits that electronic publishing could offer to reduce costs and increase income to publishers. The problems of access to electronic publishing in Zimbabwe is also discussed. The author, who is Editor of *Zimbabwe Science News* and Secretary of the Zimbabwe Scientific Association, states that electronic publishing offers a wonderful opportunity to reduce printing and distribution time/costs and to greatly increase national and international exposure for African-published journals. However, the access by Zimbabwean readers to electronic publishing is currently limited by the high cost and poor availability of email and Internet facilities, especially in rural areas. Thus, for the foreseeable future, journals will continue be distributed both as hard copy and electronically.

1838 Ifaturoti, Adedamola A. **"Implications of the Opening up of the World's 'Information Superhighway' and the Proliferation of 'Electronic Communications' in the Industrialized World for Nigeria and the Developing Countries."** *The Publisher* 5, no. 1 (October 1997): 28-31.
Assesses some of the implications of the electronic revolution and the new information and communication technology for Nigerian publishers. States that "the problem of inadequate infrastructure probably constitutes the single most salient drawback for the growth of electronic publishing in Nigeria", which are unlikely to be remedied in the near future. The present anxieties of some observers in the developing world about the proliferation of electronic publishing in the countries of the North, should "not drive them into blindly pursuing goals which they are ill-equipped to take on successfully at the present time." The book is not about to be replaced by the electronic medium in Nigeria; nevertheless Nigerian publishers should fully exploit the benefits of the new production technology for print origination and production.

1839 International Network for the Availability Scientific Publications (INASP). **Scientific Communication and Publishing in the Information Age.**
http://www.inasp.info/uploaded/documents/8.1%20summary%20of%20oxford%20workshop1999.html (Summary report, and access to archive of full-text papers) [20/03/08]
Summary report also published in *Information Development* 15, no. 3 (1999): 185-188.

The summary report, and full-text papers, of a workshop jointly organized by ➔ **The British Council (43)** and the ➔ **International Network for the Availability of Scientific Publications/INASP (81)** held in Oxford 10-12 May, 1999. The online pages also provide access to the abstracts and full text of the papers that were presented, and which includes papers on electronic journal publishing in Latin America and the Caribbean, Africa, as well as a paper on the INASP-sponsored African Journals Online project.

International Network for the Availability Scientific Publications (INASP) **Electronic Journal Publishing: A Reader Version 2.0** *see* ➔ **Section 5, Book industry training/Self-publishing: Training manuals and resources** entry **2459**

International Network for the Availability Scientific Publications (INASP) **INASP Publishing Workshops/Resource Pack for Journals: Online Publishing Strategy** *see* ➔ **Section 5, Book industry training/Self-publishing: Training manuals and resources** entry **2468**

1840 Jay, Mary **"Print on Demand: The ABC Experience."** In *African Scholarly Publishing Essays*, edited by Alois Mlambo. Oxford: African Books Collective Ltd.; Uppsala: Dag Hammarskjöld Foundation; and Oxford: International Network for the Availability of Scientific Publications (INASP), 2006, 205-211.

The Oxford-based ➔ **African Books Collective/ABC (3)** has successfully pioneered the use of, and access to, new digital printing technology such as print-on-demand (POD), and in this paper Mary Jay describes the ABC experience of using POD for the books of some of its member publishers. She sets out the benefits, and the significant savings achieved (e.g. eliminating shipping costs) by African publishers, as well as the advantages from the point of view of ABC as a distribution and marketing organization, with production-quality of POD-produced books generally of a higher standard than books printed in Africa. She also describes a pilot project pioneered by the late Victor Nwankwo (➔ *see* entry **1850**) in association with ABC and Lightning Source, a leading POD printer.

1841 Kotze, Antoinette **"Publication of the Index to South African Periodicals (ISAP) on CD-ROM."** In *The Love of Books. Proceedings of the Seventh South African Conference of Bibliophiles held at The South African Library, Cape Town, 8-10 May 1996*, edited by Pieter E. Westra and Leonie Twentyman Jones. Cape Town: South African Library (Bibliophilia Africana VII, South African Library General Series, 26), 1997, 59-66.

Discusses the *Index to South African Periodicals* (ISAP) on the South African Studies (SAS) CD-ROM (and published by NISC) as an example of a recent CD-ROM database publishing project in support of comprehensive and cost-effective information services and online access.

1842 Kromberg, Steve **"How Digital Technologies are Transforming Book Publishing."** In *The Politics of Publishing in South Africa,* edited by Nicholas Evans and Monica Seeber. London: Holger Ehling Publishing and Scotsville, South Africa, University of Natal Press, 2000, 257-278.
Examines the far-reaching impact of digitization of text, sound and image on book publishing, notably the book industries in South Africa. The author attempts to define some emerging trends in media ownership, in the convergence and consolidation of different media, and in the place of the print media within an information environment that is now dominated by electronic communication. Also looks at aspects of e-commerce and online publishing, the range of commercial possibilities offered to publishers by the Internet, and the prospects of online marketing and selling in the years ahead. Concludes "the publishing industry cannot afford to ignore developments in the electronic media. And yet many publishers and booksellers are not in a position to take on the challenge alone. Even those who are successfully adopting the 'wait-and-see' approach now need to ensure that they are closely monitoring developments in order to time their eventual, and inevitable, entry into the fray."

Letshela, P.Z, and P.J. Lor **"Implementing Legal Deposit of Electronic Publications in Africa: Progress Report from Africa"** *see* ➔**Copyright and legal deposit/Authors' rights** entry **1780**

Levey, Lisbeth E. **"Slipping Through the Cracks No More. Better Dissemination of African Research Information"** *see* ➔ **Scholarly publishing (General)** entry **2306**

1843 Limb, Peter **"The Digitization of Africa."** *Africa Today* 52, no. 2 (Winter 2005): 3-19.
Globalization and technological change are driving new developments in electronic publishing and learning, developments that are increasingly dominating global educational and scientific trends. African studies in the North are harnessing these developments to enhance the study of Africa. While control of, and profits from, these trends have thus far largely bypassed Africa, there is growing evidence of successful African digital ventures. Meanwhile there is a "new scramble for Africa" for information resources to be digitized – either for open access or for profit – as part of the process of the digitization of Africa. This perceptive article outlines these trends and discusses priorities and principles underlining evolving partnerships in the field and looks at issues such as the complexities of creating, accessing, using digital resources, and maintaining sustainability, and the still huge digital divide— both the North-South divide, as well as within African countries. It also provides an informative overview of some current [as at 2005] African digitization projects, including African e-journals and newspapers, virtual and digital libraries, citation databases, bibliographic and indexing services, digital dissertations, archival sources, and some other digitization initiatives. While the author does not see digitization as the panacea of publishing woes, he asserts that that e-publishing in Africa has the potential to achieve savings, greatly increase speed of delivery to information within Africa, and allows African information products to reach a global audience. At the

same time he notes disturbing trends "toward takeovers of African publishers by transnational publishers interested in absorbing – rather like giant vacuum cleaners – all matter of digital content." The author argues that in view of still weak information infrastructures in Africa, the high cost of online access, and significant connection problems "building more Web sites or digital libraries in African countries, or at least based on their information resources, may be one solution, but continuing scarcities of local resources are likely to make such projects future casualties of the technology gap." Meantime, "the challenge for scholars, librarians, publishers, and others involved in the digitization of African resources is to ensure access, sustainability, and fairness in the sharing of these resources."

1844 Madondo, Mwazvita Patricia **"The On-line Book Trade in Zimbabwe."** In *Indaba 2000. Millennium Marketplace,* edited by the Zimbabwe International Book Fair Trust. Harare: Zimbabwe International Book Fair Trust, 2001, 40-45.
Uses a fictitious scenario of a linguistics student in Cape Town ordering books online and comparing prices from different suppliers, to demonstrate how an online book trade might be developed in neighbouring Zimbabwe. Reviews the constraints of the existing conventional methods of bookselling and book distribution, and sets out the requirements for the way forward to develop an online book trade in Zimbabwe. Concludes "players that make no effort to get involved will the see window of opportunity closing."

1845 McHardy, Francois **"Surf or Sink: Scholarly Publishing and New Technologies."** In *Access to Information. Indaba 97.* Harare: Zimbabwe International Book Fair Trust, 1997, 170-178
Describes the precarious state of scholarly publishing in Africa in general, and South Africa in particular. Examines some of the strategies that will be required by publishers to adapt in an environment of severe budget cuts at academic institutions, and achieving sustainability for operations that historically have always run at a substantial loss in the past. Also urges African scholarly publishers to take advantage of the opportunities offered by the new production technologies and the Internet, and argues that "if we are not able to keep apace with the so-called developed world with regard to access to information, the seemingly insurmountable gap between the North and the South, the 'haves' and the 'have-nots', will grow even bigger and we will only have ourselves to blame."

1846 Mills, Paul **"Rare Books and the Internet."** In *From Papyrus to Print-out: The Book in Africa Yesterday, Today and Tomorrow. Bibliophilia Africana 8 Conference Proceedings. Centre of the Book Cape Town, 11-14 May 2005,* edited by Cora Owens. Pretoria and Cape Town: National Library of South Africa/Centre of the Book, 2005, 254-258.
Paul Mills, of Clarke's Africana and Rare Books, the well-known Cape Town vendor, describes the work of AuctionExplorerBooks.com, a South African Internet book auction Web site, and offers some observations on how the Internet has changed bookselling and book buying.

1847 Monnier, Philippe D. **Cybermarketing. A Guide for Managers in Developing Countries**
Geneva: International Trade Centre UNCTAD/WTO (ITC), (Technical Paper ref. ITC/288/2A/00-I-TP)), 1999. 132 pp.
Published by the ➔ **International Trade Centre UNCTAD/WTO (84)**, this helpful manual (albeit now a little bit dated) is targeted to business managers and executives in developing countries "willing to take advantage of the commercial possibilities of the Internet", and it will also be of interest to publishers in Africa, as indeed those elsewhere. It is intended for "generalists", is jargon free, and contains a great deal of hard-nosed practical advice. Although the manual is not designed to serve as an introduction to the Internet, the first part sets out some of the fundamentals of the Internet, the use of email and electronic mailing lists. Thereafter it provides an outline of the different categories of a "virtual shop", the basics of Web security, and systems for online payments and payment platforms. The subsequent part deals with strategic and commercial aspects of a presence on the Web, how to generate traffic to a site, how to choose a platform, the key ingredients of an effective Web site, legal aspects, the difficulties generated by distance selling, and the challenges of targeting international markets through a Web site. A conclusion summarizes the key success factors of commercial Web sites, the opportunities for developing countries, and it also explodes some die-hard myths about e-commerce that have been generated by the "hype galore".
Reviews:
The African Book Publishing Record, vol. 27, no 1, 2001

1848 Naidoo, Kuma **"Print and the Electronic Media."** In *Publishing for Democratic Education*, edited by Steve Kromberg *et al.* Johannesburg: The Sached Trust, 1993, 131-137.
Argues that linking books to electronic media can serve both the financial interests of publishers and the educational interests of South Africans.

1849 Nwankwo, Victor **"Access to New Technologies for Africa's Publishers."** In *Publishing in Africa: The Crisis and the Challenge. An ASA Roundtable. The African Book Publishing Record* 20, no. 1 (1994): 16-19.
Examines to what extent African publishers have been in a position to take advantage of the new technologies in publishing, and the revolution that the new technology has brought to the production of conventional printed material. The author narrates the experience of his own firm (Fourth Dimension Publishing Co., Enugu, Nigeria) in setting up computerized typesetting – teaching staff to cope with the new technology, problems of maintenance and securing adequate technical support services, etc. – which had been a sometimes painful and costly learning experience. The author sees the new technology "as a kind of liberation for African publishers", and states that electronic publishing is a welcome reality in Africa.

1850 Nwankwo, Victor **"Print-on-Demand for an African Publisher."**
African Publishing Review 10, no. 5 (2001): 1-4.

Another (expanded) version, **"Print-on-Demand: An African Publisher's Experience"**, presented to the Seminar on Strengthening Scholarly in Africa (Arusha IV) Zanzibar, 1-4 July 2002, reprinted in *African Publishing Review* 11, no. 5 (2002): 28-37.

Reports about the experience of Fourth Dimension Publishing Company in Nigeria of reprinting 100 select backlist titles using print-on-demand (POD) technology, as part of a new initiative organized by the Oxford-based ➔ **African Books Collective Ltd. (3)**, and working in partnership with Lighting Source Inc in the US and Lighting Source UK. Also provides cost comparisons for printing costs using conventional offset printing vs. POD, and offers some thoughts about the future potential of this technology for publishers in Africa.

1851 Ross, Alan **"The Impact of Technology on the Publishing Trade."**
African Publishing Review 9, no. 3 ((2000): 2-4.
An assessment how new technologies and the Internet are likely to impact on publishing and the book trade in Africa.

1852 Sherwin, Ros **"ABC's Experience — Selling Books on the Web."**
African Research & Documentation, no. 84 (2000): 3-7.
Based on a paper delivered to the ➔ **SCOLMA (114)** Annual Conference in June 2000, Ros Sherwin describes the experience of ➔ **African Books Collective (3)** in setting up a Web site and promoting it to a worldwide audience; and the new opportunities this has brought to promote and sell books strategically to different and new audiences.

1853 Smart, Pippa **"E-journals: Developing Country Access Survey."**
Learned Publishing 16, no. 2 (April 2003): 143-148.
Online:
http://www.ingentaconnect.com/content/alpsp/lp/2003/00000016/00000 002/art00011 [12/01/08]
Concern over the information gap between developed and developing countries has led to a series of initiatives to promote access to information, but the author believes that the increasing number of such initiatives could well be confusing the recipients, that there is a danger of overlapping and conflicting information being given to them, and that publishers' attitudes towards the supply of their content at greatly reduced prices, or for free, is not always clear. During 2002 the ➔**International Network for the Availability of Scientific Publications (81)** was commissioned to undertake a survey to identify publishers' activities and opinions in this area. The survey found that the majority of respondents were involved in one or more access programmes and there was a willingness from both the commercial and the non-commercial sector to provide their information in this way.

1854 Smart, Pippa **"Two-Way Traffic: Information Exchange Between the Developing and Developed World."** *Serials. The Journal for the Serials Community* 17, no. 2 (2004):183-187.
Online: http://dx.doi.org/10.1629/17183 [12/01/08]

Over the last ten years there has been an increasing recognition of the gap in information provision between the developed and developing world, and online publishing has enabled many initiatives to provide content at low or no cost. Although the current initiatives are to be welcomed, easy access to international information may further weaken national publications, potentially resulting in a loss of indigenous knowledge. To counteract this, several organizations are working with developing-country publishers to give them online visibility and help strengthen their future. This article describes the Programme for the Enhancement of Research Information (PERI), launched by the ➜ **International Network for the Availability of Scientific Publications (81)** and, in particular, the African Journals Online (AJOL) initiative which supports journals published in Africa. In her conclusion the author states: "access to information should not be the definitive goal – the aim should be access to relevant information. The Internet offers unprecedented opportunities to locate content, but it is important that it serves a balanced sharing of information, so that indigenous knowledge is promoted, made available to all and, most importantly, not lost to future generations."

1855 Smart, Pippa; Carole Pearce, and Nyerhovowo J. Tonukari **"E-publishing in Developing Economies."** *Canadian Journal of Communication* 29, no. 3 (2004): 329-341.
Online: http://www.cjc-online.ca/viewarticle.php?id=837 [21/03/08]
Electronic publishing has been heralded as a worldwide solution to information dissemination. This article considers the current problems experienced by traditional journals published in the developing world, with particular reference to those published in sub-Saharan Africa. The opportunities offered by electronic online publishing are discussed to determine how they can resolve the current problems in dissemination and improve quality. Two case studies of different initiatives are presented: an online-only journal, the *African Journal of Biotechnology (AJB)*, and an online journal table of contents and abstracting service, ➜ **African Journals Online AJOL (28)**. The authors conclude that although online publishing is not a quick fix solution for all the problems experienced by journals in developing countries, it offers great potential for increasing the visibility and quality of indigenous knowledge, and thus offers journals the opportunity to take a place in the global publishing community. "It is imperative that African journals and authors embrace this model for research communication to ensure their continued existence and recognition of the importance of indigenous research."

1856 Smith, James **"The Role and Place of Electronic Publishing in Developing Countries."** In *Educational Publishing in Global Perspective. Capacity Building and Trends,* edited by Shobhana Sosale. Washington, DC: The World Bank, 1998, 195-205.
Discusses the place and role of educational content on CD-ROM and on the Internet in developing countries, analyzing the advantages and drawbacks of the new electronic media.

1857 Stringer, Roger **"Desktop Publishing in Zimbabwe: Opportunities Outweigh Problems."** In *Information 90: Proceedings of the Third International*

Conference held at Bournemouth International Centre, England, 17-20 September 1990, edited by J. Rowley. London: Aslib, 1991, 287-291.
[Not examined]

1858 Teferra, Damtew **"The Significance of Information Technology for African Scholarly Journals."** In *Knowledge Dissemination in Africa: The Role of Scholarly Journal*, edited by Philip G. Altbach and Damtew Teferra. Chestnut Hill, MA: Bellagio Publishing Network Research and Information Center (Bellagio Studies in Publishing, 8), 1998, 39-61.
Reviews the state of African scholarly journals and examines the significance of new production technologies and DTP in helping them to dramatically improve the quality of their publications, although achievements in DTP are still marred by poor and underdeveloped printing capabilities on the continent. Some journals also suffer from poor quality editing and design, and one of the main problems is irregular publication. Teferra also probes into the use of email and the Web in the promotion and marketing of African journals. Although it will take a good many years for most African countries to become capable of fully utilizing the recent advances in ICT, "without a deep commitment to benefit from these technologies, the existing gap in information creation and dissemination will grower deeper and more wider, further marginalizing African scientists and their forum of communication."

1859 Teferra, Damtew **"Striving at the Periphery, Craving for the Centre: The Realm of African Scholarly Communication in the Digital Age."**
Journal of Scholarly Publishing 35, no. 3 (April 2004): 159-171.
Explores the state of the knowledge domain and the capacity of scholarly communication on the African continent at the beginning of the twenty-first century. The author examines the challenges and opportunities in the digital age and proposes ways of capitalizing on the vast resources of global knowledge. He believes that the way forward, in as far as the state of universities and institutions (and by extension scholarly publishing output from these institutions) is unlikely to improve in the near future despite recent national and international policies intended to revitalize them, is for Africa to "position itself to explore and tap the vast oceans of knowledge outside its borders."

1860 Wafawarowa, Brian **"Digital Print on Demand for African Publishing."** In *African Scholarly Publishing Essays*, edited by Alois Mlambo. Oxford: African Books Collective Ltd.; Uppsala: Dag Hammarskjöld Foundation; and Oxford: International Network for the Availability of Scientific Publications (INASP), 2006, 201-206.
Earlier (shorter) version also published in *African Publishing Review* 12, no. 2 (2003): 1-3.
Brian Wafawarowa makes a compelling case for increased use of print-on-demand (POD) to boost African publishing, and to enable scholarly publishers to deliver their books more effectively and efficiently to Northern markets. He describes the different categories of books that will be suitable for POD production, and the benefits it brings to publishers by using this technology, for which they do not

require developing and mastering their own POD capabilities, but can rely on service providers and fulfilment companies that can undertake the work.

1861 Zell, Hans M. **"African Journals in a Changing Environment of Scholarly Communication."** In *APEX 96. African Periodicals Exhibit 1996.* Catalogue. Harare: Zimbabwe International Book Fair Trust; and London: Southern African Book Development Education Trust, 1996, 3-6.
Changes of considerable magnitude have been taking place in the academic and library communities, involving changes and advances in electronic technology, and behavioural changes within the academic community in accessing information through online electronic networks and through document delivery. Looks at the implications for African journal publishers, reviews serials acquisitions patterns and selection procedures in libraries, examines the bias by the world's major indexing and abstracting services and online databases in not covering African serials, and offers some suggestions how African journals might survive in the electronic publishing age and prevent becoming marginalized even more.

1862 Zell, Hans M. **"African Journal Publishers in a Digital Environment."** In *Knowledge Dissemination in Africa: The Role of Scholarly Journal*, edited by Philip G. Altbach and Damtew Teferra. Chestnut Hill, MA: Bellagio Publishing Network Research and Information Center (Bellagio Studies in Publishing, 8), 1998, 85-97.
An updated version of the preceding entry (*see* ➔ **1861**), looking at the challenges facing African journal editors and publishers by the new scholarly communications environment, and by digital technologies and the Internet. Argues that "the thinking by African journal publishers, while trying to exploit the opportunities offered by the Internet, should not be dominated by concerns about technology: they should be concentrating on content and quality rather than form." That they should try to anticipate and respond to market needs and aim to focus on definite market niches, have a clear mission, set high standards in order to build for themselves a reputation of excellence, promote their product vigorously and extensively, and at the same time operate with strictly-business like efficiency.

1863 Zell, Hans M. **"Journals Marketing on the Internet."** In *Knowledge Dissemination in Africa: The Role of Scholarly Journal*, edited by Philip G. Altbach and Damtew Teferra. Chestnut Hill, MA: Bellagio Publishing Network Research and Information Center (Bellagio Studies in Publishing, 8), 1998, 127-137.
Slightly re-written and updated extracts from the author's ➔ **A Handbook of Good Practice in Journals Publishing (2489),** presenting a round-up how African journal editors and publishers can take advantage of the many opportunities now offered by the Internet to promote their journals: through electronic discussion groups and mailing lists, online table of contents services, creating their own Web presence, as well as exploiting the Internet as a mailing list and information resource.

1864 Zell, Hans M. **"The Internet, E-commerce, and Africa's Book Professions."** *Bellagio Publishing Network Newsletter*, no. 28 (November 2001): 10-15.
Online:
http://www.bellagiopublishingnetwork.com/newsletter28/zell.htm [21/03/08]
Now somewhat dated, this article examines some of the opportunities and benefits that the Internet, and the World Wide Web more specifically, now offers to publishers in Africa. However, the author cautions that before publishers can make effective use of the Internet as a marketing tool and information resource, or as an aid to research, they will first need to learn the basics of using and searching the Web, get a proper feel of how the Internet works; and understand what makes a good and user-friendly Web site in terms of its design, structure, principles of navigation, download times, currency, and the use of meta tags. The author also looks at developments – and likely opportunities for African publishers in the near future – in the area of online publishing and electronic commerce, but is sceptical about some of the hype and exaggerated claims currently made about the prospects for e-books and e-commerce in Africa.

1865 Zell, Hans M. **Digital Media and African Publishing.** *The Book & the Computer*, November 12, 2003.
http://www.honco.net/os/index_0310.html [*Note*: no longer available at this URL, request copy from the author at hanszell@hanszell.co.uk]
The digital age and innovations in printing and publishing technologies offer many opportunities and challenges for the African book professions. This article examines the problems faced in different aspects of African book culture and how technology might address them. It reports about a number of new ICT initiatives and partnerships, looks at the current [October 2003] use of the Web by the African book sector, the prospects of online publishing in Africa, the promise of print-on-demand and e-books, and the challenges that lie ahead.

Educational and school book publishing

See also
→ **Bookselling and book distribution**
→ **National book policies**
→ **Reading culture and reading promotion**
→ **Section 2: Comparative studies**

Note: for a number of articles and studies on textbook provision and production in developing countries, but not specifically discussing the situation in Africa, *see* → **Section 2, General, comparative, and regional studies: Comparative studies**. For country-specific studies see *see* → **Section 3, Country studies**.

1866 Agence de la Francophonie (ACCT). Direction Générale de l'Education et de la Formation. Ecole International de la Francophonie.
L'édition scolaire dans les pays du Sud. Enjeux et perspectives. Bordeaux: Agence de la Francophonie (ACCT)/Ecole Internationale de la Francophonie (EIF) [15-16 Quai Louis XVIII, 3300 Bordeaux], 1996. 62 pp.
A study sponsored by the Agence de la Francophonie (now → **Organisation Internationale de la Francophonie 101)** that looks at the current state and prospects of educational publishing in the countries of the South. It examines the basic issues as they relate to infrastructural and social factors, surveys the different players involved in the writing and publishing of educational materials and the common problems they face, examines the financial and training aspects of book development, and makes a number of suggestions that might lead to a healthy environment for the development of effective national book policies. A number of short glossaries are interspersed in the various chapters, and a series of appendixes include a range of sample costings for educational books, an outline of the Florence and Nairobi copyright agreements, and the basic rights of authors.

1867 African Publishers Network **"World Bank Bidding Procedures."**
African Publishing Review 8, no. 1 (1999): 8-9.
A report arising from an → **APNET (5)** regional workshop on the → **World Bank's (124)** standard procedures for international competitive bidding, which was convened to sensitize African publishers on current procurement and bidding procedures for World Bank-financed educational book programmes. The report identifies some of the most crucial issues that require the attention of African publishers and national book trade associations, sets out common problems involved in the bidding process, and makes a number of recommendations that should be considered by the World Bank.

1868 Bgoya, Walter, and Eero Syrjänen, *et al*, eds. **The Economics of Publishing Educational Materials in Africa.** London: Association for the Development of Education in Africa (ADEA), Working Group on Books and

Learning Materials (Perspectives on African Book Development, 2), 1997. 147 pp. (distributed by African Books Collective Ltd., Oxford)
Also published in French as **Les aspects économiques de la publication de matériel educatif en Afrique**.
Online: (full-text)
http://www.adeanet.org/publications/docs/Economic%20eng.pdf [21/03/08]
Drawing on research data from 18 African countries, this important study examines the relationship between government policy and decision makers and the educational book industries, concentrating on three main areas concerning textbook publishing in Africa: (1) the business environment, (2) the publishing industry, and (3) the critical success and failure factors related to book provision. Primary data was gathered through a series of questionnaires delivered to various organizations concerned with textbook provision, as well as follow-up through direct interviews with government officials and those representing the book professions in each country. Secondary data for the study was collected through published and unpublished sources. Individual chapters provide essential background information about textbook publishing and thereafter analyze current market structures and publishing systems, demand and supply, the size and ownership of the publishing industry, market research, and patterns in purchasing and funding of textbooks. A final chapter "Looking Ahead: Issues and Priorities" provides an overall picture of the major issues as they relate to textbook publishing, sets out a number of recommendations what the authors perceive to be priority targets for textbook provision, and suggests an outline for implementation strategies according to a division of responsibilities between governments and Ministries of Education on the one hand, and publishers on the other. A conclusion states that "the basic problem of publishing in Africa is financial: lack of assets, low level of equity capital and difficulties in meeting loan conditions. Lending institutions in Africa do not consider publishing bankable. And even if they did, present interest rates, which are as high as 44 per cent in some countries, would prohibit any publisher from making use of the facility." An Appendix provides background facts on all the countries covered by the study, including educational indicators such as literacy rates, government expenditure on education, enrolment ratios, pupil/teacher ratio, and school age population projections.
Reviews:
African Research & Documentation no. 78, 2000
International Journal of Educational Development vol. 19, nos. 4-5, July 1999

Brickhill, Paul; Catherine Odora Hoppers, and Kajsa Pehrsson **Textbooks as an Agent of Change. Gender Aspects of Primary School Textbooks in Mozambique, Zambia and Zimbabwe** *see* ➔ **Women in African publishing/Publishing by and for women** entry 2372

1869 The British Council **Conference on Textbook Provision and Library Development in Africa**. Manchester: The British Council, 1992. 27 pp.
The proceedings of a ➔ **British Council (43)** hosted conference held in Manchester in October 1991, which was the first international conference to examine all the issues

raised by the African book sector studies commissioned by the ➔ **World Bank (124)** and the UK's Overseas Development Administration/ODA. A comprehensive book sector study, it is argued, provides a multifaceted analysis and research which is needed to guide policy makers, book project designers, investors, and both national and donor agencies. Includes discussions of policy issues connected with the book sector studies, covering publishing, printing, distribution, raw materials, regional co-operation and library development, and which were drawn from nine African book sector studies.

1870 Brunswic, Etienne, and Habib Hajjar, eds. **Planning Textbook Development for Primary Education in Africa.** Stockholm: SIDA, and Paris: International Institute for Educational Planning, 1992. 58 pp.
Report of a seminar organized by the ➔ **International Institute for Educational Planning (78)** held in Maputo. Gives an overview of the state of textbook development in several African countries, addresses specific issues, and makes some recommendations for future action.

1871 Buchan, Amanda; Carmelle Denning, and Anthony Read **African Book Sector Studies. Summary Report.** London: International Book Development, 1991. 137 pp.
Also available in French as **Etudes sur le secteur du livre en Afrique. Rapport analytique.**
Provides background documentation to the special conference of Ministers of Education in Africa, "Textbook and Library Development in Africa", held under the auspices of the Overseas Development Administration in Manchester in 1991 (*see* entry ➔ **1869**).

1872 da Cruz, A..J *et al* **Financing Textbooks and Teacher Training Materials.** London: Association for the Development of Education in Africa (ADEA), Working Group on Books and Learning Materials (Perspectives on African Book Development, 10), 2000. 120 pp. (distributed by African Books Collective Ltd., Oxford)
Through four case studies, this book examines some of the key issues in funding provision of textbooks and training materials in Africa. The case studies, contributed by experts in textbook production and distribution, offer individual country perspectives from The Gambia, Lesotho, Mozambique and Côte d'Ivoire. They review the strengths and weaknesses of the different schemes, and represent a number of different strategies that have been developed in order to respond to the urgent need for more teaching and learning materials within an affordable, equitable, and sustainable framework.

1873 Evans, John **Regional Seminar on Textbook Provision for Primary Schools in Africa.** Stockholm: SIDA, 1992. 73 pp.
Report on a seminar jointly produced by ➔ **SIDA (115)** and the Educational Materials Unit of the Ministry of Education, Zambia. Provides an overview of

primary school textbook provision in Africa, containing some country profiles, descriptions of policies, recommendations and future plans.

1874 Favier, Annie "**Afrique Francophone: l'édition scolaire passe au sur mesure."** *Livres Hebdo*, no. 21 (21 May 1984): 66-68.
A short overview and discussion of educational publishing in francophone Africa.

1875 Levis, Mugumya "**Publishing and Education for All (EFA): Key Stakeholders in Materials Provision."** *Focus on International and Comparative Librarianship* 31, no. 1 (2000): 25-29.
Online: http://www.cilip.org.uk/NR/rdonlyres/F0063F4F-1EC5-4819-9A70-F1D628BF399A/0/focus3112000.pdf [15/01/08]
A perspective by a teacher, who examines how a "lack of ideas" in developing countries, especially Africa, is an impediment to EFA, focusing on the lack of published materials in Ugandan schools. She looks at the problems that are linked with the lack of textbooks, the use of books by teachers, and makes a series of recommendations how the situation might be improved.

1876 McGregor, Charles "**Doing it Better."** *Bellagio Publishing Network Newsletter*, no. 18 (November 1996): 12, 14
Asks what proportion of the world's textbook projects funded by international lenders and donors over the past ten years have failed, what caused these failures, and how can the failure rate be reduced. Presents a formula, the 'Epsilon index', by which success or failure of projects can be measured and scored.

1877 Network of Educational Innovation for Development in Africa **Reducing the Cost of School Textbooks in Africa.** Dakar: UNESCO Regional Office for Education in Africa, 1983. 71 pp.
The final report of a regional seminar on reducing the costs of school textbooks in Africa, which took place in Bujumbura, Burundi in 1983, and focussed on raising the awareness of government organizations about textbooks, what measures should be taken regarding the importation of textbooks, the manufacture and distribution of textbooks, training in the book industry, and regional cooperation. There are contributions from several countries including Benin, Botswana, Cameroon, Guinea, Madagascar, Niger, Togo and [former] Zaïre.

1878 Njoroge, Janet "**Textbook Provision in Africa: APNET's Perspective."** *African Publishing Review* 13, no. 1 (2004): 3.
Outlines the views and perspective of the ➜ **African Publishers Network (5)** on the matter of textbook provision in Africa, and the issues that will need to be addressed to support the indigenous African book industries to ensure long term, sustainable textbook provision in the countries of Africa.

1879 Nwankwo, Victor "**Enhancing the Role of Local African Publishers in Book Procurement Schemes."** In *Educational Publishing in Global*

Perspective. Capacity Building and Trends, edited by Shobhana Sosale, Washington, DC: The World Bank, 1998, 139-143.

The late Victor Nwankwo, former chair of the ➔ **African Publishers Network (5),** argues for the need to enhance the role of indigenous publishers in ➔ **World Bank (124)** book provision schemes, using the Nigerian situation as an example. He identifies the key stakeholders in World Bank procurement schemes, the issues involved, and the bidding process. He states that "the time has come to take a definite and definitive decision to put the local African publisher in the equation of book procurement" and cites the reasons for doing so.

1880 Nyambura, Gillian **"Capacity Building Challenges for African Publishers."** *African Publishing Review* 7, no. 1 (January/February 1998): 3-4.

Looks at the opportunities in educational publishing in Africa and how indigenous publishers can seize them, work together to fight marginalization by the multinationals, and establish a capacity building agenda to strengthen the African book sector.

1881 Nyambura, Gillian **"National Textbook Policies in Africa: A Sample of Current Trends from Five Countries."** *African Publishing Review* 7, no. 5 (September/October 1998): 6-9.

An overview of the different textbook policies, and textbook provision and strategies, in five African countries: Ghana, Kenya, Mozambique, Tanzania, and Zimbabwe. The information and analysis provided is based on a number of policy documents issued by the Ministries of Education in these countries.

1882 O'Connor, Brigid **"Donor Support for Textbooks in Africa."** In *Educational Publishing in Global Perspective. Capacity Building and Trends,* edited by Shobhana Sosale,. Washington, DC: The World Bank, 1998, 115–122.

Analyzes the impact of donor support for book purchases on both the education systems and the domestic publishing industry. The author (formerly with the British Council in Lagos) identifies a number of positive impacts of textbook donation programmes, and suggests ways of improving the delivery of such donor provision in future by taking the process down to communities and away from central government.

1883 Priestley, Carol **"Textbook Provision and Feasibility of Cooperation among SADC Countries."** *Bellagio Publishing Network Newsletter,* no. 7 (September 1993): 10-11.

A review of a number of ➔ **UNESCO (118)**/UNDP-supported studies on textbook provision in four Southern African countries, and reports about an interregional consultative meeting held in Harare in August 1993 to consider these studies. Also sets out the recommendations and plans for action put forward at that meeting.

1884 Rosenberg, Diana, ed. **Books for Schools: Improving Access to Supplementary Reading Materials in Africa.** London: Association for the

Development of Education in Africa (ADEA), Working Group on Books and Learning Materials (Perspectives on African Book Development, 9), 2000. 201 pp. (distributed by African Books Collective Ltd., Oxford)
An earlier version published as **Getting Books to School Pupils in Africa**. London: Department for International Development (Education Research, 26), 1998. 134 pp.
Also published in French as **Des livres pour les écoles: améliorer l'accès aux ouvrages de lecture en Afrique**.
The aim of this study was to examine some of the models through which the school population in Africa gain access to supplementary reading material, and to reach some conclusions which methods work best, and in which circumstances, and to recommend strategies that are affordable and sustainable. Given the lack of published data, it was decided that a case study approach was the most feasible and practical. A range of different modalities were examined and evaluated in depth in seven different African countries: school library services (Ghana and Tanzania); school libraries (Mali); NGO-supported classroom libraries (South Africa); book box libraries (Mozambique); teachers resource centres (Kenya); and community resources centres (Botswana). The case studies, carried out by academics and librarians in these countries, highlight various issues which contribute to the effectiveness, or otherwise, of ways of providing access to supplementary education materials to school pupils in Africa. Many of the case studies conclude that a corollary of any strategy to provide supplementary reading materials is local book production, and the way forward is to develop a viable indigenous publishing industry in tandem with improved professional training of teachers, and in teaching with books. The book includes an extensive bibliography.
Reviews:
The African Book Publishing Record, vol. 31, no. 3, 2005 (review of French edition)

1885 Sosale, Shobhana, ed. **Educational Publishing in Global Perspective. Capacity Building and Trends.** Washington, DC: The World Bank, 1998. 229 pp.
This is something of a benchmark volume on the subject of publishing and book development in Africa (and in some other developing countries). It contains the proceedings, and reflects the thinking and the deliberations that emerged from a seminar on "Understanding the Educational Book Industry", which was organized by the ➔ **World Bank (124)** in Washington DC in September 1997. Participants included representatives of publishing houses and book trade associations from both industrial and developing countries, as well as donor representatives with a strong interest in strengthening publishing capacity in Africa and in other parts of the world. The objective of the seminar was to offer World Bank Group staff from education, finance, and private sector development networks with a better understanding of the nature of educational publishing, including the linkages between government textbook policies, the publishing industry, and Bank-financed textbook operations. It also provided an opportunity for some participants to voice their current grievances about the World Bank's textbook procurement procedures and bidding systems. The book contains over 30 papers which are grouped under four major themes: "Policies for the Long-Term Provision of Educational Materials'"

"Finance and Book Trade Issues", "Procurement, Protection, and Copyright", and "The Role of Publishing Partnerships", together with a section on "The Publishing Industry in the Twenty-First Century". Contributions include papers reporting about the publishing industries in various countries of Africa, in Central and South America, the Caribbean, as well as in Eastern Europe. A record of the discussions that took place follows each section. *Note:* several of the papers in this collection are individually abstracted elsewhere in this bibliography.

Reviews:
The African Book Publishing Record, vol. 25, no. 3, 1999
Same review also in *Bellagio Publishing Network Newsletter,* no. 26-27, November 2000
Online:
http://www.bellagiopublishingnetwork.com/newsletter26-27/zell.htm [15/01/08]
Logos. The Journal of the World Book Community vol. 11, no. 2, 2000
Online: http://www.atypon-link.com/LOG/doi/pdf/10.2959/logo.2000.11.2.106

1886 Woodhall, Maureen, ed. **Cost-Effectiveness of Publishing Educational Materials in African Languages**. London: Association for the Development of Education in Africa (ADEA), Working Group on Books and Learning Materials (Perspectives on African Book Development, 1), 1997. 131 pp. (distributed by African Books Collective Ltd., Oxford)
Online:
http://www.adeanet.org/downloadcenter/publications/WGBLM/CostEff ectiveness.pdf [15/01/08]
Also published in French as **Côut-efficacité de la publication de matériel educatif en languages Africaines**.

The ➔**Association for the Development of Education in Africa Working Group on Books and Learning Materials (35)** organized two workshops held in Dakar in 1996 on the cost-effectiveness of publishing educational materials in African languages, and it also commissioned five case studies which are published in this volume. The objective of the workshop, and the case studies, was to gather information about the costs of publishing materials in national and local languages, to try to identify the benefits of these materials, both in schools and in adult literacy programmes and other non-formal education, and to review strategies to promote and encourage publication and use of educational materials from the point-of-view of cost-effectiveness. The five case studies cover The Gambia (Abdoulie Jobe), Madagascar (Louis Lai Seng), Namibia (Laurentius Davids), Senegal (Gaston Pierre Coly), and Zambia (Shadreck Hakalima). Each case study systematically examines the social, economic and educational context in each country: language policy and policies on publishing in national languages, costs of publishing educational materials, strategies for minimizing costs, and perceived benefits and effectiveness. An introductory chapter by the editor summarizes the main features and the methodology used, the problems encountered in the data gathering process, and the main findings and conclusions of the five case studies.

Reviews:
African Research & Documentation, no. 78, 2000

1887 The World Bank, Africa Region **World Bank Support for Provision of Textbooks in Sub-Saharan Africa - 1985-2000.** [Review conducted by Ian Montagnes, publishing consultant, under the supervision of Sakhevar Diop, World Bank textbook specialist]
Washington, DC: The World Bank, Human Development Sector, Africa Regions (Africa Region Human Development Working Paper Series, 27; Report no. 24564), 2002. 103 pp.
Online:
http://siteresources.worldbank.org/AFRICAEXT/Resources/no_27.pdf [22/03/08]
Also published in French as **L'assistance de la Banque Mondiale à la fourniture de manuels scolaires en Afrique Subsaharienne 1985-2000.**
To help countries establish systems that can ensure reliable provision of textbooks has been an important element of the ➜ **World Bank's (124)** support for education development in Africa over the last two decades. Other development agencies, and African governments, have made similar investments. However, despite more than a quarter century of effort and massive investment many African students still lack adequate access to textbooks; or where they have been produced they are not always available in sufficient numbers. The main purpose of this comprehensive report is to explore why this is so, and to identify the challenges that need to be overcome to ensure that every student has adequate access to high quality textbooks. The report is based on a desk review of 89 Bank-financed education projects with textbooks components, and under implementation during the period 1985-2000 in 40 sub-Saharan African countries. It identifies problems and good practices at all stages of textbook provision, from authorship to classroom use, looks at World Bank policies and procedures that were modified during the review period, and examines progress that has been made during the period under review in key areas such as manuscript development, editing, production, distribution, and procurement. The report concludes with a section on the lessons learned for the period, and a series of recommendations how to improve the quality of textbooks, and to improve equity of access for all to good primary education.

UNESCO. Basic Learning Materials Initiative **Guidelines for the Conduct and Organization of National Book Sector Consultations** *see* ➜ **Section 2, General, comparative, and regional studies: Comparative studies** entry **244**

Intra-African book trade

See also
→ **Book marketing and promotion**
→ **Bookselling and book distribution**

1888 African Publishers Network **"Promoting Buying and Selling: ITC-APNET Collaboration."** *African Publishing Review* 7, no. 4 (July-August 1998): 4-7
A report about a buyer/sellers meeting organized by the International Trade Centre (ITC) and the → **African Publishers Network (5)** convened during the 1998 Zimbabwe International Book Fair, which aimed to match partners with complementary business interests. The main objective of the matching exercise was to strengthen ties and encourage partnerships across borders among the book and printing industries in different parts of Africa. The report includes some charts showing intra-African trade in printed matter, African exports of printed matter, imports of printing machinery, intra-African trade in books, main African exporters of books to Africa, and imports of printed matter by different product group.

1889 Alabi, Dayo **"Cross-Border Trade: Options and Challenges"** In *National Book Policy, HIV/AIDS and Sustainable Development. Papers Presented at the Fifth Nigeria International Book Fair, 8-13 May, 2006.* Lagos: Nigerian Book Fair Trust [c/o Literamed Publications Ltd., PMB 21068, Ikeja, Lagos, Nigeria], 2007, 201-209.
Offers some observations on the opportunities, challenges, and constraints of cross-border trade in African books – and getting African books to the international market place – and the various options that are available to publishers: conventional book exporting, co-publishing and licensing, using print-on-demand, or electronic publishing on the Web.

1890 **APNET-ADEA Study Project on Intra-African Book Trade**
Accra: African Publishers Network, London: DFID/ADEA [1 Palace Street, London SW1E 5HE], [no date, print version last updated 2006; online version 2007]. 42 pp.
Online: http://www.apnet.org/documents/adea_apneta_study.pdf [22/03/08]
Also published in French as **Etude APNET-ADEA sur le commerce intra-africain de livre.**
Online: http://www.apnet.org/documents/adea_apneta_study_french.pdf [22/03/08]
Following on an earlier study (*see* entry → **1894**) on the inter-African book trade that was commissioned by the →**Association for the Development of Education in Africa: Working Group on Books and Learning Materials/ADEA (35)** in association with the →**African Publishers Network/APNET (5)**, ADEA recommended that APNET should facilitate the sharing of information between national publishers' associations as it relates to the different procedures that need to be followed when

exporting books from/to a particular African country, and with which all publishers and booksellers need to be familiar when embarking on the export of their books to another African country. Each national book trade association was asked to complete a detailed questionnaire setting out current procedures, and the legal and fiscal regulations in each country. A total of 29 national book trade associations responded and completed questionnaires. Each country response offers useful information not only on aspects of book export/import procedures and financial aspects (e.g. customs tariffs on imports, exemptions, tax systems on inputs, other taxes such as VAT, export regulations, cost of financial transactions such as bank transfers, etc.), but also a variety of information on the "book chain" in each country, for example number and type of publishers, printers, booksellers and book distributors, public libraries, legislation on copyright, book trade associations, national book policy situation, and other information relating to the state of the book in each country. This a valuable and information-rich resource.

Bgoya, Walter **"Intra-African Trading in Children's Books. Opportunities and Constraints"** *see* ➜ **Children's book publishing** entry **1553**

1891 International Trade Centre/UNCTAD/GATT **Promotion of Intra-African Trade. Buyers/Sellers Meeting for the African Publishing and Printing Industry, Grand-Baie, Mauritius, 10-14 May 1993. Report on a** Mission, edited by H.G. Roelofsen and R.J. Kohlmann. Geneva: International Trade Centre, UNCTAD/GATT (ITC/DTC/93/1930; restricted distribution), 1993. 46 pp.
A report about an ➜ **International Trade Centre (84)**/➜ **APNET (5)** co-sponsored buyers/sellers meeting, held in Mauritius in May 1993, which brought together 62 participants from 12 African countries. The meeting was convened to initiate business contacts, to develop trading partnerships between publishers and printers throughout Africa, and to promote intra-African book trade.

1892 International Trade Centre/UNCTAD/WTO **Intra-African Trade Promotion Programme. Report on the 4th Buyers/Sellers Meeting: African Publishing and Printing Industry. Harare, Zimbabwe 30 July – 2 August 2000.** Geneva: International Trade Centre/UNCTAT/WTO (ITC/DTCC/00/2525, Restricted), 2000. 29 pp.
Online: http://www.intracen.org/iatp/surveys/pub2000.pdf [pages not accessible 15/01/08]
As parts of its ongoing efforts to assist in the promotion of intra-African trade, the ➜ **International Trade Centre (84)** has been convening a series of Buyer/Sellers meetings at the Zimbabwe International Book Fair in collaboration with the ➜ **African Publishers Network (5)** and the ➜ **Pan-African Booksellers' Association (21).** Each meeting brought together key players in the African publishing and printing sectors, and was designed to promote cross-border trade and cooperation, and that includes a 'Matchmaker Programme'. This is the report of the meeting held during ZIBF 2000, and includes a "Statistical overview of recent trade patterns in Africa for books and other printed matter". Although this a welcome initiative, some of the figures and statements can provide a somewhat misleading picture, and

sometimes the figures have been a source of bewilderment by some African publishers who see no evidence of, or have not benefited from, any significant cross-border trade within Africa, and the statistical analysis does not seem to distinguish between the intra-African trade in printed books, as opposed to "printed matter" in general, and print and paper for newspapers.

1893 Lawal-Solarin, O.M. **"History and Cultures in Africa: The Movement of Books."** *African Publishing Review* 12, no. 4-6 (2003): 2-4.
Online: http://www.apnet.org/documents/vol_12_4-6_en.doc [22/03/08]
Offers some thoughts on the development of an intra-African book trade and the movement of books between African countries, and the obstacles that are associated with it.

1894 Makotsi, Ruth, with Flora Musonda **Expanding the Book Trade Across Africa: A Study of Current Barriers and Future Potential.** London: Association for the Development of Education in Africa (ADEA), Working Group on Books and Learning Materials (Perspectives on African Book Development, 7), 2000. 116 pp. (distributed by African Books Collective Ltd., Oxford)
Also published in French as **Pour le développement du commerce du livre à travers l'Afrique. Etude des obstacles actuels et du potentiel future**.
A ground-breaking study commissioned by the ➔ **Association for the Development of Education in Africa (ADEA), Working Group on Books and Learning Materials (35)** on the fiscal, legal, communication, and other constraints of intra-African book trade. The study was designed to present information on the potential of the book industry in African countries, their capacity to trade with each other, reviewing the policies that govern the publishing sector, and the opportunities and barriers that promote or hinder such trade. Phase one of the project focused on the book trade in the Southern African region, but also gathered comparative case study material and overviews of national book industries in East and West Africa. It includes a number of recommendations addressed to African governments, African publishers, and national publishers' associations. The second part of the study examines policies on intra-African book trade in books, and makes recommendations on how regional economic policies could be more responsive to the needs of the African book industries.
Reviews:
The African Book Publishing Record, vol. 31, no. 2, 2005

1895 Makotsi, Ruth **"Regional Economic Policies and the Intra-African Book Trade."**
In *Indaba 2000. Millennium Marketplace,* edited by the Zimbabwe International Book Fair Trust. Harare: Zimbabwe International Book Fair Trust, 2001, 234-247.
The author of a major ADEA study on intra-African book trade – *see* ➔ **Expanding the Book Trade Across Africa: A Study of Current Barriers and Future Potential (1894)** – revisits some of the issues raised by the study and examines what the study

established. She summarizes some of the key aspects in favour of a cross-border book trade in Africa (such as trade liberalization, harmonization and reduction of import taxes, reform of exchange rate regimes, and facilitation of movement of goods and people) and then makes a number of recommendations for more effective collaboration between African publishers, and book trade and book development organizations, with regional economic communities. The author concludes "lobbying regional economic communities for favourable policy formation on book trade will result in harmonised national book policies in most African countries and equitably upgrade their levels of book trade."

1896 Mpanga, Egidio **"Regional Economic Policies and the Intra-African Book Trade. The Campaign in Malawi."** In *Indaba 2000. Millennium Marketplace,* edited by the Zimbabwe International Book Fair Trust. Harare: Zimbabwe International Book Fair Trust, 2001, 245-247.
A short account of a campaign in Malawi to persuade the government to remove taxes and duties on books.

1897 Munamwimbu, Ray **"Regional Economic Policies and the Intra-African Book Trade. Lobbying Initiative for Implementing the Recommendations of the Policy Study."** In *Indaba 2000. Millennium Marketplace,* edited by the Zimbabwe International Book Fair Trust. Harare: Zimbabwe International Book Fair Trust, 2001, 252-253.
Deals with the implementation of the Makotsi study (*see* ➜ **1894**) in Zambia.

1898 Nigerian Book Fair Trust **Books Across Boundaries. Papers Presented at the Third Nigeria International Book Fair, 6-10 May, 2004.** Lagos: Nigerian Book Fair Trust [c/o Literamed Publications Ltd., PMB 21068, Ikeja, Lagos, Nigeria], 2005. 85 pp.
One in a series of collections from the ➜ **Nigerian Book Fair Trust (737)** containing the opening addresses, keynote speeches, and papers presented at the Nigeria International Book Fair, held annually since 2002, each fair focusing on a special topic or topics. The third volume is devoted to intra-African book trade and African books in the international market place. [Not examined]

1899 Nyariki, Lily **"The Intra-Africa Book Trade Project."** *BookLinks,* no. 7 (August 2007): 8-9.
Online:
http://www.bookaid.org/resources/downloads/booklinks/BookLinks_7.pdf [22/03/08]
Another version **"Looking Back at the Intra Africa Book Purchase Project supported by Book aid International (BAI), African Publishers Network (APNET) and the Pan Africa Booksellers Association (PABA)"** at http://www.bookaid.org/resources/downloads/where_we_work/PABA-review-book-trade-project.doc [10/03/08]
Reports about the lessons learnt from a recent project to stimulate cross border book purchasing within Africa. The project was funded by the UK's ➜ **Department for**

International Development (57), and operated through grants provided by → **Book Aid International (38)** to national library services to enable them purchase children's books outside their own countries. Three national library services, Malawi, Kenya and Uganda, were selected to participate in the project.

1900 Tumusiime, James **"Cross-Border Book Trade: The East African Experience."** In *Educational Publishing in Global Perspective. Capacity Building and Trends,* edited by Shobhana Sosale. Washington, DC: The World Bank, 1998, 123-125.

James Tumusiime, who heads Fountain Publishers in Kampala, draws attention to some of the requirements which are conducive for active cross-border or intra-African book trade in books, and some the factors which currently impede it. Unlike trade in any other consumer items, special conditions are needed for a flourishing cross-border trade in books to take place, such as a shared language and a shared curriculum.

Journals and magazine publishing

See also
→ **Digital media and electronic publishing/New printing technology**
→ **Open access publishing**
→ **Scholarly publishing (General)**
→ **Scientific, technical and medical publishing**

Note: this section includes a number of articles on specific African journals and magazines (e.g. *Black Orpheus, The Classic, Drum, Okike, Staffrider, Transition,* etc.), but it should be noted that this is restricted to articles that mainly deal with the publishing history and/or distribution aspects of these journals. Although coverage, as elsewhere in the bibliography, is primarily of articles published since 1980, a number of earlier studies that are still of historical interest are also included.

1901 Abrahams, Lionel *"The Purple Renoster: An Adolescence."* English in Africa 7, no. 2 (September 1980): 32-49.

Recollections by the former editor of this lively and influential South African literary magazine, which provided an important outlet for South African writers in the 60s and 70s, both black and white, until it ceased publication in 1977.

1902 Achebe, Chinua **"The *Okike* Story."** *Okike,* no. 21 (July 1982): 1-5.

Reviews the history and vision of the Nigerian literary magazine *Okike,* founded by Chinua Achebe in 1971, and discusses projects undertaken by the magazine, its educational supplement, the Okochi festival organized by *Okike,* and looks at future needs. The journal has been published sporadically over recent years.

1903   Adamu, S.O. **"Quantitative Content of the** *Nigerian Journal of Economic and Social Studies."* *Nigerian Journal of Economic and Social Studies* 21, no. 1-3 (1983): 67-87.
[Not examined]

1904   Adebowale, Sulaiman **"The Scholarly Journal in the Production and Dissemination of Knowledge on Africa. Exploring Some Issues for the Future."** In *Africa and the New Millenium: challenges and prospects*, edited by Eddy Maloka and Elizabeth Le Roux. Pretoria: Africa Institute of South Africa, 2001, 96-113.
Also published in *Journal of Cultural Studies* 3, no. 1 (2001): 26-42.
Examines the problems facing the development of scholarly journals in Africa and, more specifically, seeks to analyze the patterns in scholarly enquiry in the last two decades by assessing the focus of four multidisciplinary journals from the period 1980 to 1999, and what these patterns portend for African scholarly publishing in the new millennium. The analysis draws on some of the work undertaken by Paul Zeleza (*see* e.g. Zeleza, Paul Tiyambe **"Trends and Inequalities in the Production of Africanist Knowledge"** entry ➜ **2332**) and also examines some of the wider issues as they relate to knowledge production and dissemination in Africa. The author recognizes that in view of the dramatic recent changes in scholarly communication, and the rapid growth of the Internet, the gap between the developed world and developing countries is in danger of increasing even more, and "the publishers of scholarly journals in Africa now face a greater challenge in bridging the widening gap with their counterparts in the North." He makes some suggestions how this might be achieved and how African journal publishing might survive, including the active development of technical expertise, training and capacity building, regional cooperation (for which there are successful models in, e.g. Latin America or the Caribbean), and stresses the need that "scholarship in Africa must think of carving and consolidating niches to survive."

1905   Adesokan, Akin **"Retelling a Forgettable Tale.** *Black Orpheus* and *Transition* **Revisited."** *Glendora Review* 1, no. 3 (1996): 49-57.
Online:
http://digital.lib.msu.edu/projects/africanjournals/html/itemdetail.cfm?re
cordID=2193 [22/03/08]
Retells the story of the life and times of two of Africa's most exciting literary and cultural magazines: *Transition*, founded in Uganda by the late Rajat Neogy (and later published from Ghana where it was edited by Wole Soyinka in the mid-1970s), and *Black Orpheus*, founded by Ulli Beier, Janheinz Jahn and Gerald Moore. Provides some insightful information about editorial policies, sources of funding, contributors to the journals, clashes of personality and, in the case of *Transition*, clashes with the Obote government of the day who felt threatened by the journal's outspokenness. Concludes with a look at the 'new' *Transition* which, after a period of dormancy, recommended publication from the USA some years ago. (*See also* Ulli Beier's rejoinder to this article, entry ➜ **1923** below)

1906   Adomi, Esharenana E., and Chinedum Mordi **"Publication in Foreign Journals and Promotion of Academics in Nigeria."** *Learned Publishing* 16, no. 4, (October 2003): 259-263

Examines promotion criteria in Nigerian universities, and the emphasis placed on publishing in foreign journals as a basis for assessment and promotion to senior posts in some universities. The article reviews these policies and the arguments for and against publication in foreign journals, which some academics see as unachieveable because they feel that funding to their universities makes it impossible for them to provide the kind of research facilities and library resources necessary to produce work of the highest international standards. The policy also weakens the status of Nigerian research journals, giving them less of a chance of making the jump to becoming 'international.' However, the authors believe the points for insistence on such a policy far outweigh those against, and academics in Nigeria, rather than protest against such regulations, should "fight for improvement in the quality of the academic environment so that the challenges presented by the various university management may be more easily met."

1907   African Association of Science Editors, comp. **Directory of Scholarly Journals Published in Africa.** Nairobi: Academy Science Publishers and the African Association of Science Editors, 1990. 50 pp.

Lists 150 journals published in 11 African countries arranged by country and subject, and alphabetically by journal. Aims to create a greater awareness of journal publishing within each African country, both among local scientists and by those in other African countries and overseas. Was promised to be revised and reissued every three years, but no further editions have been published.

1908   African e-Journals Project **African Journals Directory.**
http://africa.msu.edu/AEJP/directory.php [22/03/08]

This very useful online directory and database (last updated in 2006) contains information about more than 1,900 journals published in or about Africa in all disciplines. The directory is searchable by journal title, key words, country or language(s) of publication, or by broad subject chosen from a pull-down menu. Searches can be limited to search only periodicals published in Africa. The record for each journal contains information, and links to, tables of contents, indexes, abstracts, and full text of articles for journals (for those freely accessible) and also the Web site of each journal, where one exists. For journals that do not have Web sites, the directory record includes information about the journal publisher, address, ISSN, and whether the journal is active or has ceased publication. However, for several journals this information is incomplete. The directory is part of the African e-Journals Project, a project at Michigan State University that aims to make journals published in Africa and about Africa more widely accessible to scholars worldwide. As part of this project, an archive of back issues of 11 African scholarly journals in the social sciences and the humanities is available online as full-text and is freely accessible.

1909   Aina, L.O. **"The Prospects for Reducing the High Mortality Rate of African Library Science Journals."** In *Survival Under Adverse Conditions:*

Proceedings of the African Library Science Journals Workshop, edited by Michael Wise. The Hague: IFLA (IFLA Professional Reports, 38), 1994. 37-47.
Investigates the factors which contribute to the high rate of failure among science journals in Africa in general, and library science journals in particular. Examines 16 African library science journals to determine whether they meet certain criteria that might ensure their survival, and reviews their editorial management, financial capacity, international recognition, marketing and distribution, and other factors.

1910 Aina, L.O., and I.M. Mabawonku **"Management of a Scholarly Journal in Africa: A Success Story."** *African Journal of Library, Archives and Information Science* 6, no. 2 (1996): 63-84.
An evaluation of the ➔ **African Journal of Library, Archives and Information Science (128)** following five years of publication. Provides some background information about the journal's mission and goals, analyzes the number of papers submitted for publication and their acceptance rate, and provides a detailed analysis of the number and type of subscribers and their country of origin. Also discusses some inhibiting factors affecting the journal's growth and development and day-to-day management, such as unreliable postal systems, high bank charges, foreign exchange constraints, and currency devaluations in Africa. Concludes that "with commitment and determination on the part of all the role players, a sustainable scholarly journal can be produced in Africa", but that its survival will largely depend on whether it will be able to attract a sufficient number of foreign subscriptions and thus generate hard currency earnings.

1911 Aina, L.O. **"***African Journal of Library, Archives and Information Science* **as a Resource Base for Library and Information Science Research in Africa."** *African Journal of Library, Archives and Information Science* 12, no. (2002): 167-176.
Discusses the establishment of the ➔ **African Journal of Library, Archives and Information Science (128)** in 1991 as a medium for African researchers in librarianship, archives, information science and other related information fields to disseminate their research findings. It appraises the journal's success and recognition for the period 1996-2000, as a resource base for library and information science research in Africa, and provides a citation analysis.

1912 Alao, George **"The Development of Lusophone Africa's Literary Magazines"** *Research in African Literatures* 30, no. 1 (1999): 169-183.
A study of literary periodicals and 'little magazines' published in Angola, Cape Verde and Mozambique, from colonial days through to independence and the 1980s, and their role in the development of a national literature.

1913 Alemna, Anaba A. **"African Library Science Journals: The Missing Link."** *Scholarly Publishing* 25, no. 1 (October 1993): 48-52.
Discusses the problems of publication of library and information science journals in Africa, most of which have been very short-lived. Offers some possible solutions as to how the trend might be reversed, especially through better organization and sharing of resources.

1914 Alemna, Anaba A.; Vitalicy Chifwepa, and Diana Rosenberg **African Journals. An Evaluation of the Use Made of African-published Journals in African Universities.** London: Department for International Development (Education Research, 36), 1999. 54 pp.
Other versions published in *African Journal of Library, Archives and Information Science* 10, no. 2 (2000): 93-112; and, as **"The Role of Libraries in the Use of African-published Journals in African Universities",** in *International Information and Library Review* 33, (2001): 3-22.
Summary of report also published as **"African Journals and their Use in African Universities. Some Conclusions"** *The African Book Publishing Record* 26, no. 1 (2000): 9-11; and another shorter version published as **"The Use of African Journals by African Academics"** in *African Publishing Review* 9, no. 2 (2000): 5-6.
Reports about a survey carried out at two African universities (University of Ghana and University of Zambia) over a period of three years (1996-1998) on the use made of African-published scholarly journals by academics and researchers, in order to evaluate the journals' impact on research, and compare the use made of African-published journals with those published elsewhere. The study concluded that, although useful and wanted, journals published in Africa will not be able to attain their full impact on teaching and research in African universities, unless they become more easily accessible and more readily available. "African academics have to know what is being published in their subject areas. What is being published needs to be more regular and of better quality. There need to be reliable and systematic channels for obtaining the required journals and journals articles." Includes a range of recommendations what journal publishers can do to improve their operations, their marketing and promotion, and improve both production and content quality.

1915 Alemna, Anaba A. **"The Periodical Literature of Library and Information Science in Africa: 1996-2000."** *Information Development* 17, no. 4 (December 2001): 257-260.
An analysis of the contents of the first ten volumes of ➔ **African Journal of Library, Archives and Information Science/AJLAIS (128)**, with the aim of providing an insight into the patterns and directions of the library and information professions in Africa, and the extent of the impact of AJLAIS on the continent. It is a follow-up to a previous study that covered the period 1991-1995. 79 papers were analyzed by various factors, including the status of the authors, gender, country of origin, most cited periodicals, and the nature of the research. The study found that the major areas of interest are information technology, publishing, and records management. The author also concludes that "AJLAIS has achieved its aim of becoming a major medium for reporting research findings in the information profession in Africa."

1916 Altbach, Philip G. **"The Role and Nurturing of Journals in the Third World."** *Scholarly Publishing* 16, no. 3 (April 1985): 211-222.
Also published in *Knowledge Dissemination in Africa: The Role of Scholarly Journals* edited by Philip G. Altbach and Damtew Teferra. Chestnut Hill,

MA: Bellagio Publishing Network Research and Information Center
(Bellagio Studies in Publishing, 8), 1998, 1-12.
Also reprinted in *Readings on Publishing in Africa and the Third World*, edited
by Philip G. Altbach. Buffalo, NY: Bellagio Publishing Network, Research
and Information Center (Bellagio Studies in Publishing 1), 1993, 140-151.
A classic albeit now dated article that describes how the industrialized countries of
the world dominate the creation and distribution of knowledge. Suggests that
developing countries must establish and nurture scholarly journal of their own to
deal with issues and approaches relevant to themselves.

1917 Altbach, Philip G., and Damtew Teferra, eds. **Knowledge
Dissemination in Africa: The Role of Scholarly Journals.** Chestnut Hill,
MA: Bellagio Publishing Network Research and Information Center
(Bellagio Studies in Publishing, 8), 1998. 140 pp. (distributed by African
Books Collective Ltd., Oxford)
A collection of papers on academic journal publishing and scholarly communication
in Africa, which aims to provide a better understanding of the nature, role, current
status, and future prospects of journals in the African context. Papers address issues
such as the challenges of editing scholarly journals in Africa, the significance of the
new information technology for African journals, African journals in a digital
environment, and journals marketing on the Internet. There is also a case study of the
"tribulations" and problems encountered by a science journal published in Ethiopia.
A paper on Latin America and the Caribbean rounds off the volume, and provides
both comparisons and contrasts with Africa. *Note:* some of the papers in this
collection are individually abstracted elsewhere in this bibliography.
Reviews:
The African Book Publishing Record, vol. 24, no. 2, 1998
Glendora Books Supplement no. 3 & 4, 1998
Online:
http://digital.lib.msu.edu/projects/africanjournals/html/issue.cfm?colid=312
[15/01/08]

1918 Anon. **"Revues littéraires et culturelles."** *Notre Librairie,* no. 94 (1988):
173-178.
A listing of African-published (primarily francophone) literary and cultural
magazines, including special issues.

1919 Anon. [A.N.N.] **"Ten Years of *Okike*."** *West Africa,* no. 3383 (7 June
1982): 1530.
Reviews a special edition of one of the most influential African-published literary
magazines.

1920 Antwi, I.K. **"Publishing the *Ghana Library Journal*: Trends,
Challenges, and the Way Forward."** *Ghana Library Journal* 18 (2006): 79-90.
Documents and discusses the experience of the Ghana Library Journal, published by
the Ghana Library Association (GLA) since its inception in 1963, including the role of

the GLA as its publisher, its editorial board, editorial direction, and the role of members of the Association in ensuring its sustainability. It also examines the constraints and challenges facing the ongoing publication of the journal, and concludes with a number of recommendations. These include expanding the financial base of the journal, more effectively marketing the journal, and empowering prospective authors through workshops and seminars on writing and research skills.

1921 Banjo, Gboyega "**Measures at Rehabilitating a Library Journal: The Example of *Nigerian Libraries*, 1984-88.**" In *Survival Under Adverse Conditions: Proceedings of the African Library Science Journals Workshop*, edited by Michael Wise. The Hague: IFLA (IFLA Professional Reports, 38), 1994, 49-57.
Sketches the history of *Nigerian Libraries* – established in 1962 as the official bulletin of the Nigerian Library Association, but which ceased publication in 1987 – and attempts made to revive it on several occasions.

1922 Bankole, E.B. "**Organisation of Journal Publishing: A Publisher's Viewpoint.**" In *Survival Under Adverse Conditions: Proceedings of the African Library Science Journals Workshop*, edited by Michael Wise. The Hague: IFLA (IFLA Professional Reports, 38), 1994, 33-36.
Argues that in order for an academic or professional journal to survive it should meet certain conditions, and at the same time maintaining and adhering to certain specific criteria.

1923 Beier, Ulli "**Some Errors in the Article in *Glendora* no. 3.**" *Glendora Review* 1, no. 4 (1996): 8-9.
A rejoinder to the Adesokan article (*see* entry ➔ **1905** above), in which Ulli Beier, former editor of *Black Orpheus* and co-founder of Mbari Club in Ibadan, sets the record straight and points out a number of inaccuracies in the Adesokan piece.

1924 Benson, Peter "**'Border Operators': *Black Orpheus* and the Genesis of Modern African Art and Literature.**" *Research in African Literatures* 14, no. 4 (1983): 431-473.
An in-depth history of *Black Orpheus*, the pioneering cultural journal founded by Ulli Beier in Nigeria in 1957. Describes in detail Beier's editorial goals, including his aim to provide an "inspirational" magazine. Presents Beier's influence on the content of the magazine including the artwork, poetry and fiction and his reporting of the performing arts. Assesses Beier's critical voice, his "discoveries", and charts the reincarnation of the magazine in the latter half of the 1960s and its eventual demise in the late 1970s.

1925 Blake, David "**Periodicals from Africa: The Next Step.**" *African Research and Documentation*, no. 38 (1985): 11-19.
Reports on the ➔ **Standing Conference on Library Materials (114)** ➔ **Periodicals from Africa (172)** publications project.

1926 Bozimo, Doris O. **"Nigerian Scientific Serial Literature."**
International Library Review 15, no. 1 (1983): 49-60.
[Not examined]

1927 Cnockaert, André **"La revue *Zaïre-Afrique*: 30 ans de chronique littéraires."** *Zaïre-Afrique*, no. 260 (1991): 551-562.
[Not examined]

1928 Coetzee, J.M. ***"Staffrider."*** *The African Book Publishing Record* 5, no. 4 (October 1979): 235-236.
J. M. Coetzee – himself a former Ravan Press author and now a celebrated award-winning writer – provides some background about the magazine *Staffrider*, an exciting South African literary and cultural journal published by oppositional publisher Ravan Press. Describes how it is put together, its readership, how it is distributed and the problems it faced [during the apartheid days] vis-à vis the South African government's Publications Control Board.

1929 Cope, Jack **"The World of *Contrast*."** *English in Africa* 7, no. 2 (September 1980): 1-21.
The founder and [former] editor of *Contrast*, one of South Africa's leading 'little magazines' which published its first issue in 1960, here commemorates its 20th anniversary by providing a short history of the journal and describes its struggle for survival over the years.

1930 Crampton, Margaret **"An African Vision for African Journals Online (AJOL)."** *INASP Newsletter*, no. 29 (Summer 2005): 3.
Online: http://wsb-inasp.mantis.esw.zomo.co.uk/uploaded/documents/29-jul-05-INASPNews29.pdf [22/03/08]
In March 2005 NISC South Africa were appointed to take over management of the ➔ **African Journals Online/AJOL (28)** project from the ➔ **International Network for the Availability of Scientific Publications/ INASP (81)**, so that the service henceforth would be fully managed and owned within the African continent. Here the Managing Director of NISC provides her vision for the future development of AJOL.

1931 Cumming, Sioux **"African Journals Online (AJOL)."** *INASP Newsletter*, no. 29 (Summer 2005): 1.
Online: http://wsb-inasp.mantis.esw.zomo.co.uk/uploaded/documents/29-jul-05-INASPNews29.pdf [22/03/08]
A short account of the development of the ➔ **African Journals Online/AJOL (28)** service from its humble beginnings in 1998 to becoming a major showcase for over 200 African-published journals by the end of 2004.

1932 Cumming, Sioux **African Journals Online (AJOL). A Second International Evaluation, 2003-2005**. Oxford: INASP, 2006. 40 pp. Online: http://www.inasp.info/uploaded/documents/AJOL-evaluation-2006-web1.pdf [22/03/08]
A second evaluation of the → **African Journals Online/AJOL (28)** project http://www.ajol.info/, which examines the development and status of the project since the last evaluation in 2002 (*see* entry → **1973**) to the end of 2005, and when it was handed over to African management, NISC South Africa (Pty) Ltd. It aims to provide participating journals with information about the use of their journals within the AJOL service, and offers a variety of analysis, including number of page requests for each journal, registered users of the service, a record and analysis of document delivery requests fulfilled, by country of publication, by journal, and by subject. There is also analysis about the nature of AJOL registered users, collected through a questionnaire mailing, which examines usage information, and areas of special interest of AJOL users. A series of appendices provide tables showing the number of hits per journal for the 2004-2005 period (although these could be somewhat misleading, and number of unique visits to each journal's AJOL Web pages might give a better idea of the interest in any journal), document delivery requests for each journal, and email alerts requested for each.

1933 Drum Publications (EA) Ltd. **The Beat of Drum: The Story of a Magazine that Documented the Rise of Africa**. Nairobi: Drum Publications (EA) Ltd, 1988. 168 pp.
Another edition **The Beat of Drum: The Story of a Magazine that Documented the Rise of Africa, as Told by Drum's Publisher, Editors, Contributors, and Photographers**, Braamfontein, South Africa: Ravan Press, in association with Drum magazine, [1982]-1984. 4 vols.[?]
[Not examined]

Esseh, Samuel Smith, and John Willinsky **Strengthening Scholarly Publishing in Africa: Assessing the Potential of Online Systems** *see* → **Digital media and electronic publishing/New printing technology** entry **1833**

1934 Ezenwa-Ohaeto *"Okike* **and the Evolution of Modern African Literature."** *African Literature Association Bulletin* 17, no. 3 (Summer 1991): 37-40.
The journal *Okike* played a pioneering role in the "introduction of new writers and the presentation of germane issues to African literature". This article celebrates the thirtieth issue of *Okike*.

1935 Fleming, Tyler **"Africa's Media Empire: Drum 's Expansion to Nigeria."** *History in Africa* 32 (2005): 133-164.
Charts the history of *Drum* magazine, a popular magazine written for and by Africans, that was established in South Africa in 1951. It enjoyed a great deal of success and is now widely recognized as having been a driving force in black South

African culture and life throughout the 1950s and 1960s. The magazine's impact on South African journalism, literature, gender configurations, African resistance, and urban South African culture has been documented and often lauded by various scholars. Many former members of the South African edition's payroll, both editors and staff alike, have gone on to become successes in literature, journalism, and photography. While *Drum* greatly influenced South Africa, its satellite projects throughout Africa, for example in Nigeria and as described in this article, were no less important and cemented *Drum's* reputation as the leading magazine newspaper in Africa.

1936 Frederiksen, Bodil Folke *"Joe,* **the Sweetest Reading in Africa: Documentation and Discussion of a Popular Magazine in Kenya."** *African Languages and Cultures* 4, no. 2 (1991): 135-155.
An account of *Joe* magazine, a popular magazine founded and edited by Terry Hirst (*see also* ➜ **1954**).

1937 Gibbs, Wayt W. **"Lost Science in the Third World."** *Scientific American* (August 1995): 76-83.
Discusses the predicament of scientific journals in the developing world, which are trapped in a vicious circle of neglect, and bias: (i) articles are not cited because the journals have low visibility and are not well known, and because they are not included in the major citation databases and indexing/abstracting services. Or, (ii) because the journal's peer review process is not of a sufficiently high standard, because the journal's limited accessibility discourages top scholars to act as referees; and (iii) domestic journals are unable to gain prestige and wide international circulation, because scholars from developing countries publish their best work with journals in the North because they feel domestic journals cannot adequately disseminate their work in the international academic community. The article also critically examines the power the Institute of Scientific Information (ISI) yields through its *Science Citation Index* in deciding what is "worthy" of inclusion in their citation databases, and what criteria must be met for inclusion of African and other journals published in developing countries.

1938 Grah Mel, Frédérick **Expériences coloniales et réactions Africaines à travers trois revues culturelles du monde noir:** *Présence Africaine, Black Orpheus, Transition.* Paris: Université Paris XII, 1985. PhD dissertation. 182 l.
This dissertation on three cultural magazines from black Africa is an attempt to assess the effect of the colonial era on, and African reactions to, colonialism through changes in literature and book development.

1939 Haron, Muhammed **"Periodicals of Islam in South Africa."** *Bulletin on Islam and Christian-Muslim Relations in Africa* 6, no. 2 (1988): 15-26.
[Not examined]

1940 Huannou, Adrien **"Première revue scientifique et littéraire du Bénin."** *Notre Librairie*, no. 124 (October/December 1995): 35-39.

An interesting account of the early, influential scholarly and literary review *La Reconnaissance Africaine*, which started publication in Benin (then Dahomey) in 1925; it later became *Etudes Dahoméennes*, but ceased publication in 1970 because of financial difficulties.

1941 Hussein, Janet, and Pippa Smart **"Journal Publishing in Africa."** In *African Scholarly Publishing Essays*, edited by Alois Mlambo. Oxford: African Books Collective Ltd.; Uppsala: Dag Hammarskjöld Foundation; and Oxford: International Network for the Availability of Scientific Publications (INASP), 2006, 172-183.

Presents a brief overview of the current [2006] status of scholarly journals in Africa, and reports about projects to assist African journals to achieve wider international attention and dissemination, through initiatives such as the ➔ **African Journals Online/AJOL (28)** project http://www.ajol.info/, or made available online through other collaborative national and international projects that have dramatically increased access to journals both within Africa and externally, and has significantly broadened the use of African scholarship. The second part of the essay examines the processes involved in running a journal, including publishing methodology, editorial and peer review processes, production, copyright, distribution and orders fulfilment, and marketing. Journal publishing is also examined from the perspective of the author: how they should choose and what they should write for journals, and what their expectations should be.

1942 Ifidon, Sam E. **"Overview of the State of Nigerian Library Journal Publishing."** In *Survival under Adverse Conditions: Proceedings of the African Library Science Journals Workshop*, edited by Michael Wise. The Hague: IFLA (IFLA Professional Reports, 38), 1994, 19-25.

Identifies 21 past and current Nigerian library science journals; reviews the factors that inhibit Nigerian journal publishing, and offers a number of recommendations for more regular publication and more efficient journals management.

1943 Ifidon, Sam E. **"Publishing of Library Journals in Nigeria."** *Third World Libraries* 3, no. 2 (Spring 1993): 45-49.

Online: http://www.worlib.org/vol03no2/ifidon_v03n2.shtml [26/03/08]

Considers the past and present [as at 1993] status of Nigerian professional library journals, 19 of which are cited. Although it is difficult to gather even basic information about the publications, the author finds that only nine of the periodicals are still being published. The reasons for journal failure are numerous, but some of the major causes are the establishment of journals specifically as research outlets for certain academics; lack of financial security; rising costs of production, due in part to antiquated methods; and the general lack of interest in professional reading by Nigerian librarians. Some recommendations are made that might lead to an improvement of the situation.

1944 Irele, Abiola *"Black Orpheus*: **A Journal of African and Afro-American Literature."** *Journal of Modern African Studies*, no. 3 (1965): 151-154.
Abiola Irele, at one time joint editor of *Black Orpheus*, assesses the significance of this famous African-published magazine as a vehicle for the expression of all forms of African literature and art.

1945 James, Louis **"The Protest Tradition:** *Black Orpheus* **and** *Transition."* In *Protest and Conflict in African Literature*, edited by Cosmo Pieterse and Donald Munro. London: Heinemann Educational Books Ltd.; New York: Africana Publishing Corporation, 1969, 109-124.
Traces the protest tradition of these two distinguished African journals, two periodicals which have been "part of a continuing cultural dialogue, sensitive to all the tensions of African conflict."

1946 Jaygbay, Jacob **"African Scholarly Journals: Slow Decline or Quantum Leap?"** *Logos. The Journal of the World Book Community* 8, no. 2 (1997): 85-89.
Online:
http://www.atypon-link.com/LOG/doi/pdf/10.2959/logo.1997.8.2.85
Jaygbay contends that "many journals are launched in Africa without any-long term vision of editorial policies or adequate financial resources" and that this self-serving approach to journal publishing by African scholars has created a "Volume 1, Number 1" syndrome. The author believes that this, and the frequently sub-standard quality of African-produced journals, together with the difficulties faced by libraries in actually acquiring these publications, makes competition in the international scholarly market unattainable. Examines some of the problems faced by struggling journal publishers operating in Africa, but states that African scholarly publishers, both non-profit making and profit-seeking, "have to face the fact that the only key to increased market share in a limited market is to improve quality and content and/or identify new niches. Fund-strapped libraries are bound to use quality as their criterion." The author also discusses the new digital environment in scholarly communication, electronic networking, and the opportunities now offered by the Internet. He urges African journal publishers, as they acquire new technologies, "they should not lose sight of the fact that the presumed symbiosis of technical innovation and culture change is not automatic, certain or inevitable. Traditional book culture has barely taken root in Africa, and this fact fits well with the expense of accessing electronic information", and goes on to say that "any attempt to create information networks in Africa has to understand both the basic objectives and the constraints."

1947 Jaygbay, Jacob **"The Politics of and Prospects for African Scholarly Journals in the Information Age."** In *Knowledge Dissemination in Africa: The Role of Scholarly Journals*, edited by Philip G. Altbach and Damtew Teferra. Chestnut Hill, MA: Bellagio Publishing Network Research and Information Center (Bellagio Studies in Publishing, 8), 1998, 63-73.

Online:
http://pkp.sfu.ca/ojs/demo/present/index.php/joe/article/view/158/37
[26/03/08]

The aim of this paper is twofold: to scrutinize the current [1998] context in which African scholarly journal publishing operates; and to examine its prospects and challenges in the information age. It discusses some of the major concerns, problems and constraints of journal editors and publishers, and offers a number of suggestions how journals could increase their visibility, particularly in terms of effective marketing strategies and by taking advantage of the opportunities now offered by the Internet and new publishing technology: "African research institutions need not be overwhelmed by technology, but they need some awareness of what is – and what will be – available."

1948 Kahn, Ellison **"The Birth and Life of** *The South African Law Journal.*" *The South African Law Journal* 100, no. 4 (1983): 594-641.
[Not examined]

1949 Kirkwood, Mike **"Remembering** *Staffrider.*" In *Ten Years of Staffrider 1978-1988,* edited by Andries Walter Oliphant and Ivan Vladislavic. Johannesburg: Ravan Press, 1988, 1-9.
Staffrider magazine was an important literary and artistic forum for work from the [then] oppressed communities in South Africa. This article tells the story of the early days of the magazine in a lively anecdotal way and goes on to question whether it fulfilled its potential.

1950 Krieger, Milton **"Building the Republic through Letters:** *Abbia*: *Cameroun Cultural Review,* **1963-82, and its Legacy."** *Research in African Literatures* 27, no. 2 (Summer 1996): 153-177.
Narrates the life of *Abbia*, a leading Cameroonian literary and cultural magazine that was founded by Bernard Fonlon in 1962, flourished in the 1960s, but then faltered in the late 1970s and finally lapsed in 1982 after publishing 40 volumes. It constituted "one of Africa's most prolific and comprehensive efforts to document and shape a national culture through the medium of the scholarly periodical." The article draws on interviews with some the surviving founders of the journal, examines contents, themes, and editorial policies over the years, and *Abbia*'s legacy and future bearings in Cameroon.

1951 Lindfors, Bernth **"A Decade of** *Black Orpheus.*" *Books Abroad*, no. 42 (1968): 509-516.
Assesses the impact of the influential Nigerian literary journal *Black Orpheus* ten years after it was launched.

1952 Lindfors, Bernth **"The New** *Black Orpheus.*" *Books Abroad*, no. 44 (1970): 404-407.
An update to the above entry (*see* ➜ **1951**) about *Black Orpheus*, which began to recommence publication in a 'new series' after being dormant for several years.

1953 Lindfors, Bernth **"Interview: Terry Hirst."** *The African Book Publishing Record* 5, no. 2 (April 1979): 88-91.
Also published in *Mazungumzo: Interviews with East African Writers, Publishers, Editors and Scholars,* Ohio University Press, 1980, 29-37.
Interview with Terry Hirst who was Managing Editor of the popular *Joe* magazine, Nairobi. The interview examines how the magazine was started, the ways in which it changed over the years, its striking graphics, and the organization management of the magazine.

1954 Lindfors, Bernth **"The Ibadan Cluster:** *Black Orpheus."* In *European-Language Writing in Sub-Saharan Africa* vol. 2, edited by Albert S. Gérard. Budapest: Akadémiai Kiado, 1986, 669-679.
Reviews this influential journal of African and Afro-American literature that was first published in Nigeria in September 1957 and which was formed to encourage contemporary African writing. It included creative writing from English-speaking Africa, oral traditions, and articles discussing art from many parts of Africa. Documents the changes in the magazine during the 1960s and the period after founder editor Ulli Beier left Nigeria.

1955 Lindfors, Bernth **"African Little Magazines."** *The African Book Publishing Record* 13, no. 2 (1987): 87-89.
Describes the important role of small magazines in the development of anglophone African writing.

1956 Moser, Gerald M. **"A Daring Initiative: Starting a Literary Periodical in Wartime Mozambique."** *Luso-Brazilian Review* 34, no. 2 (1997): 123-126.
[Not examined]

1957 Murray, Susan, and Margaret Crampton **Access to African Published Research: the Complementary Approaches of NISC SA and African Journals Online.**
http://www.ifla.org/IV/ifla73/papers/137-Crampton_Murray-en.pdf
[26/03/08]
NISC in South Africa is a bibliographic database publishing company whose mission is to promote the publications and research output of Africa and an improved information flow from South to North. NISC compiles licenses and aggregates bibliographic databases, including its *Africa-Wide NiPAD,* a collection of 40 bibliographic databases. Since 2003 NISC has also hosted the → **African Journals Online/AJOL (28)** service originally developed by the → **International Network for the Availability of Scientific Publications/INASP (81)**, whose mandate is to promote access to African research output and support African scholarly journal publishing. NISC and AJOL collaborate to apply different but complementary models to provide integrated and practicable solutions to the challenges of global and sustainable access to African research output. This paper details the current models, the challenges and the potential of these services to the African research, library and publishing communities.

1958 Mwanycky, Serah W. **"Forging Partnerships in Publishing of African Scholarly Journals."** In *African Periodicals Exhibit Catalogue 1999.* Harare: Zimbabwe International Book Fair Trust; London: Southern African Book Development Education Trust: Nairobi: The African Journals Support and Development Centre, African Academy of Sciences, 1999, 3-5.

An overview of African scholarly journal publishing [in the late 1990s], looking at problems and challenges, the new opportunities now offered by electronic publishing, and describing various new initiatives designed to strengthen African journals and provide more international visibility for them, including the (now defunct) African Journals Support and Development Centre.

1959 Odendaal, Welma *"Donga:* **One Angry Voice."** *English in Africa* 7, no. 2 (September 1980): 67-74.

An account of the relatively short-lived *Donga* magazine - "the name was never meant to mean anything and was used because it lay easy on the tongue and we liked it" - which faced several banning orders under the [then] apartheid regime.

1960 Olanlokun, S. Olajine **"Publishing of Learned Journals in Nigeria."** *Libri,* no. 35 (1985): 330-33.

Notes the increase in the number Nigerian scholarly journals [in the mid-1980s], and reviews their periodicity and their chances of survival in the long term. Also includes, as an appendix, a list of scholarly Nigerian journals classified by broad subject groups.

1961 Oliphant, Andries Walter *"Staffrider* **Magazine and Popular History: the Opportunities and Challenges of Personal Testimony."** *Radical History Review,* nos. 46/47 (1990): 357-367.

[Not examined]

1962 Oliphant, Andries Walter **"Forums and Forces: Recent Trends in South African Literary Journals."** *Kunapipi* 13, no. 1/2 (1991): 91-103.

An informative overview of literary journals in South Africa. The author argues that "journals constitute a site in which the forces at work in a given society are reflected, articulated, analyzed, recreated and developed." He urges South Africans to rise to the challenge of developing "a new multi-dimensional literature and democratic culture in which the experiences and visions of all South African are reflected." The author, a poet and fiction writer, has been involved in independent publishing in South Africa as an editor of Ravan Press and *Staffrider* magazine, and later as general editor of the publishing house of the Congress of South African Writers.

1963 Oliphant, Andries Walter **COSAW and Publishing for All.** In *Afrikaans Literature: Recollection, Redefinition, Restitution. Papers held at the 7th Conference on South African Literature at the Protestant Academy, Bad Boll,* edited by Robert Kriger and Ethel Kriger. *Matatu* 15-16 (1996): 166-182.

[Not examined]

1964 Ouma, Symphrose **"Publishing Library Science Journals: The Case of** *Maktaba* **and other Kenya Library Association Publications."** In *Survival under Adverse Conditions: Proceedings of the African Library Science Journals Workshop,* edited by Michael Wise. The Hague: IFLA (IFLA Professional Reports, 38), 1994, 79-84.
Reviews the publication history of the Kenyan library journal *Maktaba* and the problems encountered in its regular publication, including editorial and funding problems.

1965 Oyelola, Pat **"Forty Years of Nigerian Art Journals."** *Glendora Books Supplement,* no. 1, (1997): 23-24.
Online:
http://digital.lib.msu.edu/projects/africanjournals/html/issue.cfm?colid=310 [15/01/08]
Also published as **"Journals of the Arts Published in Nigeria 1957-97",** *Nigerian Field* 62, no. 1&2 (1997): 74-75
A listing, with brief profiles, of a number of Nigerian arts journals both current and defunct, including *Black Orpheus, New Culture, Kurio Africana, The Eye, Uso,* and *Agufon.*

1966 Pearce, Carole **"Editing an African Scholarly Journal."** *Learned Publishing* 16, no. 1 (January 2003): 54-60.
Online:
http://titania.ingentaconnect.com/vl=2633937/cl=42/nw=1/fm=docpdf/rpsv/catchword/alpsp/09531513/v16n1/s9/p54 [26/03/08]
An insightful article that looks at the multiple challenges of African scholarly publishing, a continent where scholars are handicapped by poor library facilities, and often find it difficult in getting published in scholarly journals overseas. The various issues and problems are examined through the practical experience of the [former] editor of the Harare-based *Journal of Social Development.* The author discusses aspects of manuscript submissions, peer reviewing practices, journal production and production costs, promotion, marketing on the Internet, and attempts at networking and collaboration with other journals.

1967 Randriamanantena, Josette **"Un lieu de rencontre entre l'Europe et Madagascar dans la deuxième moitié du XIXe siècle: la revue *Teny Soa* (Bonnes paroles)."** *Revue Française d'Histoire d'Outre-Mer* 73, no. 270 (1986): 27-45.
[Not examined]

1968 Richard, Nadette **"*Ngouvou,* une revue pour les collégiens du Congo."** *Notre Librairie. Revue du Livre Afrique Noire, Maghreb, Caraïbes, Océan Indien. Guide du Bibliothécaire, Special issue* (January 1991): 95-99.
Charts the progress of the children's magazine *Ngouvou,* started in 1988. This magazine was aimed at encouraging children to use written materials as fact finding tools and at enhancing enjoyment of reading and books.

Rosenberg, Diana "**African Journals Distribution Programme: Report on its Co-ordination by the International African Institute, with an Update to 1995**"*see* **Book and journals assistance programmes** entry **1415**

1969   Rosenberg, Diana **"The African Journals Online Pilot Project."**
Bellagio Publishing Network Newsletter, no. 25 (July 1999): 12-15.
Online:
http://www.bellagiopublishingnetwork.com/newsletter25/rosenberg.htm
[26/03/08]
A brief description of the pilot version of the ➜ **African Journals Online/AJOL (28)** project, and its principal objectives. For a fuller description of AJOL *see* entries ➜ **1971** and ➜ **1972** below.

1970   Rosenberg, Diana **"Global Readership for African Journals."**
Tanzania S & T News 9, nos. 1&2 (1999): 6-8.
[Not examined]

1971   Rosenberg, Diana **"African Journals Online: Giving Journals Published in Africa a Presence on the Web."** *The African Book Publishing Record* 25, no. 3 (1999): 225-227.
Also published in *Serials Librarian* 37, no. 3 (2000): 71-82.
Describes the pilot version of the ➜ **African Journals Online/AJOL (28)** project, a project designed to give African published scholarly journals more visibility on the Web. (For a fuller description of AJOL *see* entries ➜ **1972** and ➜ **1973**.)

1972   Rosenberg, Diana"**African Journals Online: Improving Awareness and Access."** *Learned Publishing* 15, no. 1 (January 2002): 51-57.
Online:
http://titania.ingentaconnect.com/vl=3079646/cl=17/nw=1/fm=docpdf/r
psv/catchword/alpsp/09531513/v15n1/s7/p51 [26/03/08]
Describes the scope and development of ➜ **INASP's (81)** ➜ **African Journals Online/AJOL (28)** project http://www.ajol.info/(now administered by NISC-South Africa), a free service that provides online access to the tables of contents and abstracts of scholarly journals published in Africa, backed by a document delivery service. The service has recently been expanded to take in several more journals, and has now become a major showcase for African journal publishing. The article reviews the objectives of the expanded programme, its coverage and components, its management, current usage, and the benefits to participating journal publishers. It also examines aspects of the scheme's long-term sustainability, and draws attention to areas of African journal publishing that require improvement, notably journal management, marketing, and improvements in quality of content. The author concludes that it is equally important that "the profile of the journals and their value to scholarship in their own country must be raised and acknowledged", as a first step towards getting them better used and read.

JOURNALS AND MAGAZINE PUBLISHING 521

1973 Rosenberg, Diana **African Journals Online (AJOL). An Internal Evaluation, 2000-2002.** Oxford: International Network for the Availability of Scientific Publications/INASP, 2003. 15 pp.
Online:
http://www.inasp.info/uploaded/documents/AJOL%202002%20report.pd f [26/03/08]
An internal evaluation of the ➔ **African Journals Online/AJOL (28)** project following the first three years of the full programme, aimed at discovering the overall impact of AJOL and how the service might be improved. The main objectives of the evaluation were to find out (i) whether the results of research published in African journals were becoming more widely known and used, and, (ii) whether the journals had benefited, either through increased income from subscriptions or other ways from exposure in AJOL. (For a subsequent evaluation *see also* entry ➔ **1932**.)

1974 Semajanga, Josias "**Le rôle de revues littéraires et des maisons d'édition dans la spécification de la (des) littérature(s) de l'Afrique Subsahariennes Francophone.**" *Etudes Littéraires* 24, no. 2 (1991).
Examines the role of African literary magazines and publishing houses in the literature area in francophone Africa.

1975 Sepamla, Sipho "**A Note on** *New Classic* **and** *S'ketsh.*" *English in Africa* 7, no. 2 (September 1980): 81-85.
The distinguished South African poet Sipho Sepamla took over "the scattered remains of *The Classic*" in 1975 (*see also* entry ➔ **1976** below) and relaunched the journal as *New Classic* (as well as taking on the editorship of *S'ketsh*, a black theatre magazine). Run on a shoestring, faced by government harassment or censorship, having to rely on person-to-person distribution because the major bookshops did not stock the journal, or having to rely on grocery shops as outlets - "shopkeepers had the dubious reputation of tearing up a slow-moving magazine for wrapping up a loaf or half-loaf of bread" - the magazines did not unfortunately survive beyond 1978.

1976 Simon, Barney "**My Years with** *The Classic*: **A Note.**" *English in Africa* 7, no. 2 (September 1980): 75-80.
Personal recollections by Barney Simon, who took over (from Nat Nakasa) the editorship of this literary and cultural magazine in the early sixties, and which was an important vehicle for many black writers of the 50s and 60s. It ceased publication in 1971.

Smart, Pippa "**E-journals: Developing Country Access Survey**" *see* ➔ **Digital media and electronic publishing/New printing technology** entry **1853**

Smart, Pippa; Carole Pearce, and Nyerhovowo J. Tonukari "**E-publishing in Developing Economies**"*see* ➔ **Digital media and electronic publishing/New printing technology** entry **1855**

1977 Smart, Pippa **"African Journals OnLine."** *Serials Review* 31, no. 4 (December 2005): 261-265
Reports about the ➔ **African Journals Online/AJOL (28)** project, designed to increase awareness of African-published research, and launched in 1998 to index and promote African-published journals using the Web. The service now includes over 220 titles and 18,000 article abstracts. AJOL has been evaluated twice (*see* entries ➔ **1932** and ➔ **1973**) and responds to areas for development and change. In 2005, management of AJOL was moved from the ➔ **International Network for the Availability of Scientific Publications (81)** in the UK to the National Inquiry Services Centre (NISC) in South Africa.

1978 Smart, Pippa **"Increasing the Visibility of Published Research: African Journals Online."** *Africa Today* 52, no. 2 (Winter 2005): 39-53.
Investigates the current visibility of African journals in the international research community and discusses initiatives that have been developed to help researchers gain access to African-published research to provide more visibility for both African journals and African scholarship. The articles focuses on the ➔ **African Journals Online/AJOL (28)** http://www.ajol.info/ project (developed by the ➔ **International Network for the Availability of Scientific Information/INASP (81)**, and now hosted by NSIC in South Africa), launched in 1998 to provide an online catalogue and current awareness service for African journals. AJOL started off with ten science and four medical titles, but which has grown rapidly over the years and now covers over 220 journals from most academic disciplines, with full-text access to articles for some of the journals, and it also offers document delivery and email alerts services. The article looks at some of the lessons learnt in the management of the AJOL project and the many challenges faced by African journal editors and publishers, and examines what support is required to build sustainability.

1979 Smart, Pippa **"Journals - The Wrong Model for Africa?"** *Learned Publishing*, 20, no. 4 (October 2007): 311–313.
An interesting albeit contentious perspective that takes a gloomy view about the future prospects of African journals. It asks whether journals may be the wrong model for communicating African research, and proposes that repositories may be a better solution for Africa. Pippa Smart states that "unfortunately the majority of journals published in Africa do a disservice to the research they contain – they are poorly produced, have low visibility (even within their own communities), and struggle to survive. ... There are also many cases of poor editorial management and non-existent communication." She goes on to say that many of the titles are multidisciplinary, which requires a large editorial board and referee list. The author estimates that approximately 1,200 peer reviewed journals are published in the 52 countries within the African continent; the majority from Nigeria and South Africa (about 400 each). Of these, only 27 titles are listed in the ISI indices – of which 25 are from South Africa. "It is very difficult to see how the low visibility and respect (national as well as international) for the majority of journals from this [the African] continent could be improved." As a secondary problem, "the printing industry in many of the African countries is poorly resourced and combines an expensive service with poor-quality printing, finishing, and paper. As a result, many journals simply do not look professional and authoritative." The author also argues that the focus of

most journals is firmly on the editorial activities, "with scant regard for the subsequent publishing processes; thus the journal is handicapped by limited experience or knowledge of publishing and little or no investment in the publishing function." She is critical of the fact that most journals still look to the Western model and are expected to be self-financing – obtaining money from subscriptions and advertising to pay for publication – which in most cases is considered to be an unrealistic goal. Meantime, local journals are generally held in low esteem within their own library, research, and policy-making communities. The author further asserts that moving journals online, and indeed to an open access publication model, will help visibility, but will not overcome their editorial, production, and financial problems. "In an ideal world these problems would be resolved before increasing visibility, so that what is made more visible is more likely to be well received; I fear that increasing visibility before increasing editorial and production reliability and quality will simply lower the journals' credibility and thus further disadvantage them." She concludes "I believe that it is necessary completely to re-evaluate the methods and models of scholarly communication in these regions, and to find a way of replacing the journal as the only means of accrediting and disseminating research. The entrenched views of the overly conservative establishment need to be challenged to make better use of their investment into education and research."

1980 Soyinka, Wole **"A Time of *Transition*."** *Transition*, no. 51 (1991): 4-5.
Wole Soyinka's thoughts on the second revival of *Transition* magazine, which he edited for a period while the magazine was published from Accra in the early 1990s (now published in the USA).

1981 Stevenson, W.H. **"*The Horn*: What it Was and What it Did."** *Research in African Literatures* 6, no. 1, (Spring 1975): 5-32.
Also published in *Critical Perspectives on Nigerian Literatures*, edited by Bernth Lindfors, Washington, D.C.: Three Continents Press, 1976, 215-241.
Describes the magazine *The Horn*, a Nigerian student poetry magazine, which had an extensive influence on creative writing during the early 1960s. It published authors such as Abiola Irele, Aig Higo, and Wole Soyinka.

1982 Stevenson, W.H. **"The Ibadan Cluster: *The Horn*."** In *European-Language Writing in Sub-Saharan Africa*, vol. 2, edited by Albert S. Gérard. Budapest: Akadémiai Kiado, 1986, 659-668.
Describes the creation and evolution of this Nigerian student poetry magazine, which began in 1958 and ended in about 1961. It encouraged poetry writing from Nigerians at three universities: Ibadan, Zaria and Nsukka and displayed a flowering of talent among students who were at university during the late 1950s.

Switzer, Les, and Donna Switzer **The Black Press in South Africa and Lesotho: A Descriptive Bibliographic Guide to African, Coloured and Indian Newspapers, Newsletters and Magazines 1836-1976** *see* ➜ **Section 3, Country studies: South Africa** entry **1095**

Teferra, Damtew "**The Significance of Information Technology for African Scholarly Journals**" *see* ➜ **Digital media and electronic publishing/New printing technology** entry **1858**

1983 Vaughan, Michael "*Staffrider* **and Directions within Contemporary South African Literature.**" *Literature and Society in South Africa*, no. 3900 [n.d.]: 196-212.
[Not examined]

1984 Vinck, Honoré "**Le Centre Aequatoria de Bamanya: 50 ans de recherches africanistes.**" *Zaïre-Afrique*, no. 212 (1987): 79-102.
Primarily charts the history of the periodical *Aequatoria*, published annually by the Centre Aequatoria de Bamanya in Zaire [now Congo Democratic Republic].

1985 Visser, Nick, and Mike Kirkwood "*Staffrider*: **An Informal Discussion.**" *English in Africa* 7, no. 2 (September 1980): 32-49.
An interview with Mike Kirkwood, [formerly] of Ravan Press, in which he sets out the background which lead to the launch of *Staffrider*, the writers and artists featured in its pages, its readership, its promotion and distribution, and the magazine's future role within the Ravan Press publishing programme.

1986 Wise, Michael, ed. **Survival Under Adverse Conditions: Proceedings of the African Library Science Journals Workshop.** The Hague: IFLA (IFLA Professional Reports, 38), 1994. 193 pp.
The proceedings of a workshop held at Bayero University in Kano, Nigeria, that brought together the editors of several Nigerian library science journals to review the factors that have created difficulties in the publication of professional journals in the field of library and information science on the African continent. *Note:* some of the papers in this collection are individually abstracted elsewhere in this bibliography.

1987 Woodson, Dorothy C. "'**Pathos, Mirth, Murder and Sweet Abandon':** **The Early Life and Times of** *Drum*." In *Africana Resources and Collections: Three Decades of Development and Achievement: A Festschrift in Honor of Hans Panofsky*, edited by Julian Witherell. Metuchen, NJ & London: Scarecrow Press, 1989, 228-246.
Charts the life and times of South Africa's famous *Drum* magazine founded by Jim Bailey.
Note: for a good account of *Drum* magazine, with a bibliography and further literature references and links to some newspaper articles, *see also* the Wikipedia entry at http://en.wikipedia.org/wiki/Drum_(Magazine) [15/01/08]

1988 Yesufu, Abdul R. "*Black Orpheus* **and Mbari Club: Partners in Mid-century African Literary and Artistic Efflorescence.**" *Africana Research Bulletin* 16, nos. 1-2 (1989): 24-51.

Discusses the influence of *Black Orpheus* and the output of Mbari Publications of Ibadan.

Yesufu, Abdul R. **"Mbari Publications: A Pioneer Anglophone African Publishing House"** *see* ➔ **Section 3, Country studies: Nigeria entry 862**

1989 Zeleza, Paul Tiyambe **"The New Frontiers for African Scholarly Journals."** In *African Periodicals Exhibit Catalogue 1997*. Harare: Zimbabwe International Book Fair Trust; London: Southern African Book Development Education Trust: Nairobi: The African Academy of Sciences (AAS) 1997, 3-6.
Analyzes the reasons that have contributed to, and hindered, the publication of scholarly journals in Africa, and the difficulties that the editors of such journals face. The author states that the responsibility on the part of Africa-based scholars and publishers is that "they must export well-produced texts of impeccable scholarship. They are unlikely to attract their compatriots based in the North seeking to ascend the slippery poles of tenure and promotion if their publications are shoddy and reinforce the perceived inferiority and marginality of African scholarship." Zeleza believes African and Africanist scholars and intellectuals in the diaspora, in turn, have a responsibility "to patronize these [African-published] journals by writing for them, and whenever possible subscribing to them, and by ensuring that they are acquired by their libraries and protecting them against possible library cuts and cancellations."

1990 Zeleza, Paul Tiyambe **"The Challenges of Editing Scholarly Journals in Africa."** In *Knowledge Dissemination in Africa: The Role of Scholarly Journals*, edited by Philip G. Altbach and Damtew Teferra. Chestnut Hill, MA: Bellagio Publishing Network Research and Information Center (Bellagio Studies in Publishing, 8), 1998, 13-38.
Seeks to examine the forces that have contributed to, and constrained, the publication of scholarly journals in Africa over the last two decades or more. Specifically, the author examines the challenges of editing journals in the social sciences and the humanities, and the difficulties the editors of such journals face, which are infrastructural, institutional, and intellectual in nature, interwoven with the performance and problems of the wider political economy in Africa, and the changing technologies of information and cultures of education. Zeleza's wide ranging paper is divided into two parts: (i) The Political Economy of Scholarly Knowledge Production, and (ii) The Joys and Tribulations of Being an Editor. He argues that African scholars and intellectuals in the countries of the North should try as much as possible to publish in Africa-based journals and monograph series "not for some misguided nationalist sentiments, but out of a firm conviction that nobody else but ourselves will develop vibrant and valued African scholarly communities." Zeleza maintains that the high premium that African academics place on publishing abroad is a sign of "insecure provincialism". It also leads to a vicious circle: weak African journals attract weak contributions and they are left with work not good enough for acceptance overseas, which in turn will weaken them further.

Zell, Hans M. **"African Journals in a Changing Environment of Scholarly Communication"** *see* ➜ **Digital media and electronic publishing/New printing technology** entry **1861**

Zell, Hans M. **"African Journal Publishers in a Digital Environment"** *see* ➜ **Digital media and electronic publishing/New printing technology** entry **1862**

Zell, Hans M. **A Handbook of Good Practice in Journal Publishing** *see* ➜ **Section 5, Book Industry training/Self-publishing: Training manuals and resources**, entry **2489**

Zell, Hans M. **"Journals Marketing on the Internet"** *see* ➜ **Digital media and electronic publishing/New printing technology** entry **1863**

1991   Zimbabwe International Book Fair Trust/Southern African Book Development Education Trust **African Periodicals Exhibit Catalogue 1999** Harare: Zimbabwe International Book Fair Trust; London: Southern African Book Development Education Trust; Nairobi: African Journals Support and Development Centre, African Academy of Sciences, 1999. 39 pp.
A catalogue of almost 100 African-published serials displayed at a collective exhibit at the 1999 Zimbabwe International Book Fair/ZIBF. It provides full acquisitions data for each journal, including publisher name and address, Email, frequency, ISSN, circulation, names of editors, subscription rates, as well as a descriptive annotation of contents. This was the 7th such catalogue produced for the annual APEX exhibit at ZIBF, which became a well-established feature at each year's Fair. In addition to publicizing African publishing output, the exhibit catalogues have been very valuable as selection and acquisitions tools for African journals. Unfortunately no further APEX exhibits have been held since 1999.

Libraries and publishing

See also ➜ **The Acquisition of African-published material**

1992   Easterbrook, David **"North-South Information Links."** In *Access to Information. Indaba 97*. Harare: Zimbabwe International Book Fair Trust, 1997, 179-186.
The Curator of Africana at Northwestern University Library describes the work and activities of the ➜ **Africana Librarians Council/ALC (26)** of the (US) African Studies Association and sets out the information and institutional links between North America and Africa that exist today. Also reports about a number of projects that aim to strengthen links between the ALC and librarians in Africa; and the links that exist that bring books published in Africa on to the shelves of North American

libraries, and "those that bring information about Africa's expanding publishing industries to those who build our library collections."

1993 Mchombu, Kingo J. **"The Role of Special Libraries and Documentation Centres in the Distribution of Published Products in Africa."** In *Academic Book Production and Distribution in Africa. Support from Nordic Countries. Report from a conference at Chr. Michelsen Institute, Bergen, 10-11 April 1997,* edited by Kirsti Hagen Andersen. Fantoft, Norway: Ch. Michelsen Institute 1997, 68-70.
Laments poor distribution and marketing by African publishers, made worse by the lack of bibliographic tools or acquisitions lists about local publications issued by libraries, weak enforcement of legal deposit laws, and national bibliographies which are only published sporadically, and sometimes with a time lag of several years. The net result usually means totally inadequate bibliographic control over a country's intellectual output. The author believes special libraries and documentation centres in Africa should play a more pro-active role in disseminating local publishing output.

1994 Nfila, Reason Baathuli **"Academic Library-Supplier Relationship: The Experience of Supplier Selection and Evaluation at the University of Botswana Library."** *African Journal of Library, Archives and Information Science* 14, no. 2 (2004): 125-138.
Describes the relationship between the University of Botswana Library and its book suppliers, including the processes of supplier selection and evaluation. The author suggests areas where there is a need for improvement to ensure more effective supplier performance.

1995 Nwafor, B.U. **"Nigerian Librarians and Publishing."** *Nigerian Libraries* 22, nos. 1&2 (1987).
[Not examined]

1996 Nweke, Ken M.C. **"A Librarian Looks at the Reality and the Dream of Book Supply in Nigeria."** *Logos. The Journal of the World Book Community* 6, no. 1 (1995): 33-37.
Online:
http://www.atypon-link.com/LOG/doi/pdf/10.2959/logo.1995.6.1.33
A critical analysis of the shortage of reading materials in Nigeria, and the causes and factors which have led to this unhappy situation. "The book in Nigeria today is the victim of a vicious circle. Readers are waiting for writers; writers for publishers; and publishers for the government." The author suggests a number of measures "in which the Nigerian book community would cooperate if the government would create a positive climate towards the book."

Raseroka, H.K. **"Acquisition of African-published Materials by Libraries in Botswana - and Elsewhere in Africa."** *see* ➔ **The Acquisition of African-published material** entry **1254**

Sturges, Paul, and Richard Neill **The Quiet Struggle. Libraries and Information for Africa** *see* → **Section 2, General, comparative and regional studies, Africa: General studies** entry **317**

1997   Zeleza, Paul Tiyambe **"Manufacturing and Consuming Knowledge. African Libraries and Publishing."** *Development in Practice* 6, no. 4 (November 1996): 293-303.
Examines the problems facing African scholars, publishers, and libraries in the context of rapid developments in information technology, a deepening economic gulf between industrialized and developing countries, and a continuing dependency on Western forms of knowledge and systems to validate all forms of intellectual activity. The author calls on the scholarly community in Africa to reclaim African studies: "importing knowledge from abroad is no panacea. And for Africa to depend on external sources for knowledge about itself is a cultural and an economic travesty of monumental proportions." The real challenge is "not simply to fill empty library shelves and acquire gadgets for faster information retrieval, but to produce the knowledge in the first place." Also examines the challenges, and constraints, of publishing in Africa, and argues that "libraries must do their part" and "having fed for so long on Western imports and donations of information materials and technologies, African libraries have not always ventured with enough appetite to acquire local publications." In his conclusion the author questions the terms 'information-rich' and 'information poor', and stresses the needs for Africans to develop the means to generate, value, and effectively disseminate their own forms of knowledge.

Zeleza, Paul Tiyambe **"The Dynamics of Book and Library Development in Anglophone Africa"** *see* → **Section 2: General, comparative, and regional studies, Africa: General studies** entry **331**

Mass market and popular literature publishing

1998   Alston, Robin C., with Peter Hogg **"Technology and African Studies: Machine-readable Databases for Printed Materials (from Slave-trade Tracts to Onitsha Pamphlets.)"** In *African Studies. Papers Presented at a Colloquium at the British Library 7-9 January 1985*, edited by Ilse Sternberg. London: The British Library, 1985, 278-287.
Describes the compilation of a catalogue of Onitsha market materials and explains the development of software designed to provide a computer database which would eventually produce camera ready-copy for a catalogue of these popular books printed in Eastern Nigeria (*see also* entry → **2005**).

1999   Apronti, E.O. **"David G. Maillu and his Readers - An Unusual Poll of Readers' Evaluation of a Popular Writer's Work."** *The African Book Publishing Record* 6, no. 3/4 (1980): 219-224.

Also reprinted in *Readings on Publishing in Africa and the Third World*, edited by Philip G. Altbach. Buffalo, NY: Bellagio Publishing Network, Research and Information Center (Bellagio Studies in Publishing 1), 1993, 40-45.

This article was written almost 30 years ago, but it remains an insightful and intriguing perspective of popular and mass-market publishing in Africa. It was inspired by "the novelty of the idea of a readership survey conducted among ordinary readers, as opposed to professional critics or teachers of literature." It analyzes the response to questionnaires inserted by David Maillu into his books and returned to him by readers. As well as evaluating the questionnaire itself, it includes a brief biography of David Maillu and discusses the banning of five of his books in Tanzania, concluding "the career of David G. Maillu represents a remarkable phenomenon in the evolution of written literature in Eastern Africa."

2000 Coulon, Virginia **"Onitsha Goes National: Nigerian Writing in Macmillan's Pacesetter Series."** *Research in African Literatures* 18, no. 3 (1987): 304-319.

Draws attention to the similarities between Onitsha market literature and the Macmillan 'Pacesetters' series of popular fiction through a detailed analysis of several titles.

2001 Dodson, Don **"The Role of the Publisher in Onitsha Market Literature."** *Research in African Literatures* 4, no. 2 (1973): 172-188.

Also published in *Readings in African Popular Fiction*, edited by Stephanie Newell. Oxford: James Currey Publishers; Bloomington: Indiana University Press, 2002.

This article, based on the findings of field research on Onitsha pamphlets conducted in 1971, was written almost 40 years ago, but it warrants inclusion here as one of the best analyses of popular fiction publishing from the publisher's point of view. It compares the popular conception of Onitsha market literature with popular art, written by the common man for the common man, and describes the pivotal role of publishers in pamphleteering, the relationship publishers have with one another, and their relations with printers, writers and readers.

2002 Dunton, Chris **"Pulp for the People."** *West Africa* (September 1982): 2348-2351.

A critical review of some of the "pulp" literature widely circulated in Nigeria. Examines the Macmillan's Pacesetters series and compares the style of some of them with that of Onitsha pamphlets. Discusses literacy values and questions the role of popular fiction in the total concept which Nigerian students have of their society. Concludes by asking "Why train children to read, if what they read is mainly anaesthetising, de-sensitising pulp?"

2003 Ekwensi, Cyprian D. **"Why Hadley Chase? An Examination of Compulsive Versus Compulsory Reading."** *Pan African Book World* 2, no. 1 (February 1982): 24-25.

The distinguished Nigerian writer, the late Cyprian Ekwensi argues for more aggressive promotion of African writing aimed at a mass readership.

2004 Furniss, Graham **"Documenting Kano 'Market' Literature."** In *Africa Bibliography 1998*, compiled by T.A. Barringer. London: International African Institute/Edinburgh: Edinburgh University Press, 2000, vii-xxiii.
Republished online as "**Documenting Hausa Popular Literature**" at http://hausa.soas.ac.uk/hausa.pdf [26/03/08]
Documents the growth of Hausa popular literature and publishing through non-conventional publishing outlets—the facilitative mechanism of writers' groups and writers' clubs. The author describes the nature and themes of these books (sometimes also called Kano market literature, or Soyayya Books 'love stories') and how they are produced, sold and distributed. This interesting account also includes some discussion about the mushrooming Hausa video film industry.

2005 Hogg, Peter, and Ilse Sternberg, eds. **Market Literature from Nigeria: A Checklist.** London: British Library, 1990. 160 pp.
Probably the most comprehensive bibliography of Onitsha market literature published to date, listing almost 1,600 titles; also includes a bibliography of writings about the literature (*see also* ➜ **1995**).

2006 Keim, Karen R. **"Popular Fiction Publishing in Cameroon."** *The African Book Publishing Record* 9, no. 1 (1983): 7-11.
An overview of publishing (in English and French) in Cameroon in the early 1980s, focusing on popular fiction publishing. The article also offers a detailed description of the career and books of one of Cameroon's most popular fiction writers, Naha Désiré.

2007 Lindfors, Bernth **"East African Popular Literature in English."** *Journal of Popular Culture*, no. 13 (1979): 106-115.
On East African popular writing and publishing, with particular reference to Kenya. Gives a brief history and discusses certain books in detail including the problems of poor literary quality, pornography and political orientation.

2008 Lindfors, Bernth **"The New David Maillu."** *Kunapipi* 4, no. 1 (1982): 103-143.
On Kenyan popular writer David Maillu, as an author and publisher (of Comb Books) in the 1980's.

2009 Martini, Jürgen **"Sex, Class and Power: The Emergence of a Capitalist Youth Culture in Nigeria."** *Journal of African Children's Literature*, no. 1 (1989): 43-58.
Considers the effects upon culture in Nigeria of the political situation, rapid urbanization and the emergence of capitalism. Examines this factor in relation to school books, literary works, and the effect of mass market novels.

2010 McCarthy, C.M. **"Printing in Onitsha: Some Personal Observations on the Production of Nigerian Market Literature."** *African Research & Documentation,* no. 35 (1985): 22-25.
Examines the phenomenon of Onitsha market pamphlets, and its publishing and distribution infrastructures.

2011 Newell, Stephanie **"From the Brink of Oblivion: The Anxious Masculinism of Nigerian Market Literatures."** *Research in African Literatures* 27, no. 3 (Fall 1996): 50-67.
A perceptive analysis of the content of some of the mass-produced popular literature published in Nigeria (which flourished largely in the 1960s) known as 'Onitsha market literature'. The article examines the themes, protagonists, and preoccupations of Nigerian pamphlet literature and aims to provide a "comment on the contradictory and tension-ridden nature of urban masculine identities at a time when gender roles were in the process of being actively re-negotiated." Titles examined, many written under pseudonyms, include Highbred Maxwell's *Our Modern Ladies Characters Towards Boys,* C.N.O. Moneyhard's *Why Harlots Hate Married Men and Love Bachelors,* Joseph Nnadozie's *Beware of Harlots and Many Friends,* Eric Speedy's *Mabel the Sweet Honey that Poured Away,* or Ogali Agu Ogali's *Veronica My Daughter,* which reportedly sold 100,000 copies between 1956 and 1965.

2012 Obiechina, Emmanuel **An African Popular Literature: A Study of Onitsha Market Pamphlets.** Cambridge: Cambridge University Press, 1973, 246 pp.
Published in 1973, this remains the most comprehensive study of Onitsha market literature, including a detailed examination of publishing and distribution aspects of this popular literature.

2013 Okeke, Chika **"Onitsha. A Commercial City and its Middle Arts."** *Glendora Review* 2, no. 1 (1997): 42-50.
A profile of the colourful city of Onitsha in Nigeria, "a dynamic and regenerative melting pot of peoples and cultures", and its artists and writers. Reviews the literary tradition known as Onitsha market (or pamphlet) literature, which was "spawned by the twin factors of Christianity and commerce."

2014 Russell, Terry, and Steve Murray **Popular Publishing for Environmental and Health Education: Evaluation of** *Action Magazine.* Liverpool: Liverpool University Press, 1993. 242 pp.
Southern African edition: Harare: Action Magazine [PO Box 4696, Harare, Zimbabwe], 1995.
Action Magazine is a non-government donor-funded project based in Harare, which produces a magazine for schools targeted at top primary level using a 'popular publishing' format - with comic book elements, fun and games features, cartoons, etc. - to present health and environmental science material in a manner which is attractive and easily accessible to children. The magazine was distributed to every school in Zimbabwe and, more recently, to some other countries in the Southern African

region. This evaluation assessed the use of the magazine in Zimbabwe and in Botswana. Issues examines included children's visual literacy and appreciation of the health education messages, as well as the broader impact of health and environment science information on schools, children and the wider community, especially the remote and disadvantaged rural communities.

Multinational publishers in Africa

2015 Altbach, Philip G. **"Preparing for Multinationals in African Publishing: The Inevitable Impact."** *Bellagio Publishing Network Newsletter,* no. 22 (July 1998): 13-15.
Online:
http://www.bellagiopublishingnetwork.com/newsletter22/altbach.htm [26/03/08]
Looks at "the invasion of the multinationals" [in the late 1990s] into African publishing, bookselling and the media, and warns that as Africa emerges as a lucrative market, the giants of the international publishing industry will invest in the region, similarly as they have done so elsewhere, e.g. in Singapore. He states that "in a perverse way, African's current economic difficulties may help indigenous publishers in emerging markets, since the multinationals are not poised for market penetration in countries facing severe economic problems." The author offers a number of possible strategies and initiatives that might strengthen emerging local book industries, thus ensuring that they will not be swept away with the tide of the multinationals.

2016 Apeji, Eric Adeche **The Contributions of Multinational Publishers to the Provision of Books in Nigeria.** Ibadan: University of Ibadan, 1995. PhD thesis.
[Not examined]

2017 Chakava, Henry **"Dealing with the British."** *Logos. The Journal of the World Book Community* 10, no. 1 (1999): 52-54.
Online:
http://www.atypon-link.com/LOG/doi/pdf/10.2959/logo.1999.10.1.52
Shorter version also in *Bellagio Publishing Network Newsletter,* no. 25 (July, 1999): 15-17.
Online:
http://www.bellagiopublishingnetwork.com/newsletter25/chakava.htm [23/03/08]
Henry Chakava recounts his experience of working with British publishers – the high points and the low points – since he joined the book business in 1972. "I can call myself a modest expert on African/British relations, but I am not sure I understand them or that they understand me."

2018   Davis, Caroline **"The Politics of Postcolonial Publishing: Oxford University Press's Three Crowns Series 1962-1976."** *Book History* 8 (2005): 227-244.

In 1962, the Rex Collings, then an editor at Oxford University Press "discovered" the early plays of Wole Soyinka, and immediately attempted to persuade his manager that these plays should be included in the 'Three Crowns series', a collection of books about Africa published in London for both the UK and international markets. After encountering initial opposition, Collings wrote an emphatic response arguing that for the publication of original African literature by OUP hinged on its political expedience. He emphasized the importance of embedding "high culture" in the African publishing programme for the purpose of prestige and public relations, and predicted that the 'Three Crowns series' might serve an important function in compensating for the more commercial activities of the press. This argument was evidently persuasive, and he was given permission to begin commissioning African writing for the series, initially with the publication of Soyinka's plays *A Dance in the Forest* and *The Lion and the Jewel*, published in 1963, followed by *Three Short Plays* in 1964, and *The Road* in 1965. (Later Collings, who died in 1996, was to set up his own publishing company, Rex Collings Ltd., and became the publisher of Soyinka's prison notes *The Man Died*, and his autobiographical *Aké. The Years of Childhood*.) This is a very interesting account for those researching aspects of the history of publishing in former colonial countries.

Gedin, Per **"Private Enterprise Publishing in Africa. Why and How it Should be Fostered"** *see* ➔ **Section 2, General, comparative and regional studies, Africa: General studies** entry 282

2019   Graham, Gordon **"Reproaches from the Third World."** *The Bookseller* (20 January 1979): 253-256.

A critical review article of the Philip Altbach and Keith Smith edited special issue of *Library Trends* (vol. 26, no. 4, Spring 1978) devoted to 'Publishing in the Third World'. Graham takes issue with the suggestion that book publishers "have a duty to society over and above that of those in other types of business", and challenges the preconception that European and American publishers are still cultural colonialists who aim resist the growth of indigenous publishers in developing countries.

2020   Graham, Gordon **"Multinationals and Third World Publishing."** In *Publishing and Development in the Third World*, edited by Philip G. Altbach. London: Hans Zell Publishers, 1992, 29-41.
Also published in *Publishing and Development: A Book of Readings*, edited by Philip G. Altbach and Damtew Teffera. Chestnut Hill, MA: Bellagio Publishing Network Research and Information Center (Bellagio Studies in Publishing, 9), 1998, 17-30.

Multinational publishing companies of Western Europe and North America with business interests in the countries of the developing world, are generally regarded by the indigenous publishers with "at best reserve, at least suspicion, and at worst dislike." This paper probes into the "uneasy relationship" between the multinational publishing houses and indigenous publishers. It seeks to redefine publishing along linguistic rather than nationalistic lines, and discusses building publishing industries from virtually nothing, using India as a case study. The author examines the important factors of copyright and language, reviews the changes in publishing structures in the West, and the lessons that can be learnt from the past. He concludes with an analysis of common ground, and how aid agencies can help. Graham argues that there is reciprocity of need: "The key to progress is to see the development of publishing everywhere as a common cause in which all publishers are involved, and from which all will ultimately benefit."

2021 Hill, Alan **In Pursuit of Publishing.** London: John Murray (Publishers) Ltd., 1988. 390 pp.
The autobiography of the late Alan Hill who was associated with Heinemann Educational Books for many years, from its inception to the point where it was one of the two educational publishing giants in the Commonwealth, with branches world-wide, including several in Africa. Alan Hill's work in Africa was particularly valuable in making African writers known throughout the world through the Heinemann 'African Writers Series'. The book contains a foreword by Chinua Achebe, the distinguished Nigerian writer.

2022 Hutchinson, Robert **"Neo-Colonial Tactics."** *Africa, an international business ... monthly,* no. 23 (July 1973): 74-79.
While published over 30 years ago and now very dated, this critical examination of the partnership between the Macmillan Company and the Tanzania Publishing House (TPH) remains of interest as it was widely quoted at the time. Gives details of the agreements and arrangements between TPH and Macmillan and asserts that this "partnership" was "partly in order to create the veneer of a national publishing house." Gives examples of how Macmillan "made easy money", vigorously criticizes the management's poor attempts at publishing of creative writing and the lack of training opportunities offered to Tanzanians. Concludes by observing that TPH faces a "major challenge of building a strong self-reliant publishing house that combines professional efficiency and financial integrity with a comprehensive and creative editorial programme."

2023 Johnstone, Ian **"Supporting National Publishers: Macmillan's Experience."** [and] Muita, David **"Supporting National Publishers: Macmillan Kenya Publishers."** In *Educational Publishing in Global Perspective. Capacity Building and Trends,* edited by Shobhana Sosale. Washington, DC: The World Bank, 1998, 149-151, 152-154.
Ian Johnstone, Special Projects Manager at Macmillan Education in the UK, and David Muita, Managing Director of Macmillan Kenya, provide (i) an overview of Macmillan's role in educational book publishing in Africa and elsewhere, and (ii) set out the perspective of one of its African sister companies in Kenya. Johnstone describes Macmillan's approach to its presence in Africa and in other developing countries, and makes a spirited defence of their contribution to strengthening local publishing industries and helping to develop regional materials. "If international trade refers to multinational publishing companies such as Macmillan, Hachette, and others", he says, "I would like to disagree with this surmise and show why there is

no reason the two cannot be understood and treated in a similar light with a view to strengthening indigenous publishing." He goes on to state "I feel that we should not spend too much time on this issue of what constitutes a national publisher and what does not constitute a national publisher, and that we should focus on the fundamental goals of supporting local writers and making available to students and teachers the best and most appropriate learning materials" — a statement that might beg the question who decides what is "best", and what is "most appropriate"?

2024 Paren, Elizabeth **"The Multinational Publishing Firm in Africa: The Macmillan Perspective."** *The African Book Publishing Record* 4, no. 1 (January 1978): 15-17.
Examines the role and activities of multinational publishing companies operating in Africa, with particular reference to Macmillan. Explains the special role which multinational publishers play in the education of young people in developing countries. Reviews marketing considerations and influences, mother tongue materials, children's books, creative writing, and assesses the future role of multinational firms in Africa.

2025 Postcolonial Publishing
http://www.brookes.ac.uk/schools/apm/publishing/culture/colonial/col cont.html [26/03/08]
An excellent set of Web pages created by Caroline Davis, Senior Lecturer in Publishing at Oxford Brookes University, whose library maintains a special collection about African publishing (*see* entry ➜ **178**). There are pages on 'Cultural Imperialism and Publishing'; 'History of British Publishing in Colonial Countries', with a useful colonial publishing chronology, and a review and analysis of the major British publishers that were actively involved in publishing in colonial Africa, notably Oxford University Press and Heinemann. 'Reviews of Colonial and Postcolonial Publishing', examines how the role of these British publishers has come under scrutiny by a number of cultural critics. Having addressed some of the cultural problems associated with transnational publishers, there is also a brief consideration of 'Postcolonial Publishing', and the 'Cultural Necessity for Indigenous Publishing' looks at some of the obstacles in the development of an independent publishing industry, in particular in Africa.

2026 Smith, Keith **"Who Controls Book Publishing in Anglophone Middle Africa?"** *Annals AAPSS*, no. 4421 (September 1975): 140-150.
Also in: *Perspectives on Publishing*, Lexington. MA: D.C.Heath and Company, 1976, 129-140.
A provocative paper, published in the mid-1970s, that considers various aspects of publishing against a background of illiteracy, an emphasis on achievement reading rather than reading to for pleasure, and the numerous constraints that limit the development of a local publishing industry. Contends that international market forces determine general and non-fiction publishing and that educational publishing is dominated by multinational publishing companies. The author finds that state participation in publishing has not been very successful, and that African

governments have taken only limited action to strengthen their indigenous book industries.

2027 Zell, Hans M. **"Interview: James Currey."** *The African Book Publishing Record* 5, no. 4 (October 1979): 237-239.
Before setting up his own imprint in 1985, James Currey was editorial director of Heinemann Educational Books Ltd., London, in charge of their African studies list and the famous 'African Writers Series.' (AWS). In this interview, conducted in 1979, he reflects the views of one of the major multinational companies active in Africa at the time, and a company that went on to become internationally synonymous with African literature publishing. While now very dated, there are some interesting insights here about author-publisher relations, the financial rewards for authors and, in particular, the role and dominance of the AWS.

2028 Zell, Hans M. **"Multinationals' Role in Publishing."** *West Africa* (3 September 1979): 1601-1602.
A survey of the publishing scene in West Africa [in the late 1970s]. It describes the history of multinational publishing companies in Africa and examines the changes which have taken place over the years in their roles and policies. Also provides a round-up of the activities of small indigenous publishing houses and predicts the rise of small "independent and commercially oriented publishing houses that will become the back-bone of a solid African book industry in the years to come."

National book policies

See also
→ **Book trade and book development organizations**
→ **Educational and school book publishing**

Note: articles and studies on national book policies in individual African countries are listed under the appropriate country in → **Section 3, Country studies**.

2029 Aina, Take Akin **"Book Policy and Information Objectives: Some Reflections on Relationships and Problems."** In *National Book Policies for Africa*, edited by Murray McCartney. Harare: Zimbabwe International Book Fair Trust, 1996, 66-70
Argues that it is necessary to question the notion of book policy and information objectives - and the assumptions and practices they embody - and first ask the broader and troublesome questions: Whose books? Whose policies? Whose information? Whose objectives? "We cannot talk about policies and national objectives without remembering the grim existence of systematic polarization and exclusion, extensive inequality, and in some cases barbaric domination and exploitation."

2030 Garzón, Álvaro **National Book Policy. A Guide for Users in the Field**. Paris: UNESCO Publishing (The Professional Training Library), 1997. 88 pp.
Also published in French as **La politique nationale du livre : Un guide pour le travail sur le terrain.**
A useful practical guide for all those involved in setting up book policy strategies, and the formulation and adoption of national book acts, especially those in the developing world. It sets out the objectives of a national book policy, and then deals with a review of the sub-sectors concerned (i.e. author, publisher, printer, distributor/bookseller, and the reader and libraries), examining policy definitions, the law relating to books, the different components of book development, and providing guidelines for book policy strategies. A separate chapter deals with textbooks for schools, and two appendices cover "Formulating a national book policy" (including aspects of evaluation and development strategies), and "A model book law".
Reviews:
The African Book Publishing Record vol. 24, no.1, 1998

2031 Ike, Chukwuemeka **"The Relationship Between State, Private and NGO Development Sectors in Book Policy Formulation."** In *National Book Policies for Africa*, edited by Murray McCartney. Harare: Zimbabwe International Book Fair Trust, 1996, 21-27.
The Director of the ➜ **Nigerian Book Foundation (738)** examines the role of the three key players in book development and the formation of a national book policy: the state, the private sector, and NGOs. He warns that there will be serious problems in leaving national book policy formation entirely in state hands, and that experience had shown that government concern for book development has been largely limited to textbook development. The private sector tends to be more preoccupied with showing a healthy balance sheet, and their concern for authorship "is confined to organizing workshops for the production of school textbooks, and few of them pay more than lip service to the problems of national or indigenous book development." NGOs, on the other hand, have no monetary interest in the book industry and no shareholders to keep happy, and they are therefore able to take a detached, comprehensive, and holistic view of the problems of national book development.

2032 McCartney, Murray, ed. **National Book Policies for Africa. The Key to Long-Term Development. Proceedings of the Zimbabwe International Book Fair Indaba 1996, Harare, Zimbabwe, 26-27 July 1996.** Harare: Zimbabwe International Book Fair Trust, 1996. 84 pp.
The proceedings of an 'Indaba' on national book policies held immediately before the 1996 Zimbabwe International Book Fair, and which attracted participants and speakers from many parts of Africa and elsewhere, representing the whole spectrum of book sector interests. Conceived in collaboration with the ➜ **Association for the Development of African Education Working Group on Books and Learning Materials (35)**, the 'Indaba' deliberated extensively on the desirability of effective instruments to promote the development of the African book industries. A national book policy "was recognized as constituting the basic framework within which the

legitimate interests of all actors and stakeholders in book-related industries are recognized, and they are empowered to contribute towards the creation of a book reading democratic society."

2033 Momoh, Ansu **"National Book Policy."** *Bellagio Publishing Network Newsletter,* no. 21 (December 1997): 11-12.
Online:
http://www.bellagiopublishingnetwork.com/newsletter21/momoh.htm
[26/03/08]
Looks at the essential requirements for effective national book policies in African countries, and how to turn policy into practice.

2034 Newton, Diana **"National Policies for the Book Sector."** In
Educational Publishing in Global Perspective. Capacity Building and Trends,
edited by Shobhana Sosale. Washington, DC: The World Bank, 1998, 13-18.
Seeks to convince all those involved in designing, supporting, financing or implementing publishing projects and programmes in the developing countries for the need and usefulness of national book sector polices. The author defines the objectives of a national book policy and its prerequisites, the components of a national book policy, the areas of responsibility for policy formulation and policy implementation, and the avenues for the promotion of national book policies.

2035 Omotoso, Kole **"The Literate Environment: Its Relationship to National Development."** In *National Book Policies for Africa,* edited by
Murray McCartney. Harare: Zimbabwe International Book Fair Trust,
1996, 9-12.
A keynote address, by a prominent Nigerian writer, presented at the 'Indaba' on national book policies during the 1996 Zimbabwe International Book Fair. Deplores the lack of vision by African governments, their failure to create a literate environment, and states that there is a need for the creation of a community which cherishes fundamental moral values: "We cannot have national book policies if we do not have personal book policies. We cannot create a national literate environment if such an environment does not exist in our immediate surroundings. There can be no national development if there is no individual development."

2036 Treffgarne, Carew **"Book Policy Priorities: Update since ZIBF 96."** In
Access to Information. Indaba 97. Harare: Zimbabwe International Book Fair
Trust, 1997, 28-34.
An 'Indaba' on national book policies was held in Harare in July 1996 immediately before the Zimbabwe International Book Fair, convened in collaboration with the ➔ **Association for the Development of Education in Africa Working Group on Books and Learning Materials (35)**. Here the ADEA Working Group Leader provides a brief overview of key developments in book policies since the 'Indaba' was held, and which have contributed to the fundamental aim of national book policies in improving access to books, and access to information.

2037 Walter, Scott; Diana Newton, and Paul Osborn **"National Book Sector Outlines."** Paris: UNESCO, Book and Copyright Division, 1996. 22 pp. [restricted circulation]
A discussion paper prepared for the International Meeting of Book Promotion Networks/INTERBOOK, Paris, May 22-24, 1996. Describes a model for the preparation of national book sector outlines, intended to provide a "snapshot" of the current state of the book and the publishing industries in any country, and quick access to relevant and up-to-date information. Sets out the proposed classification system of headings and sub-headings for the outlines, and, in an appendix, gives a sample national book sector outline, using Mali as an example.

UNESCO. Basic Learning Materials Initiative **Guidelines for the Conduct and Organization of National Book Sector Consultations** *see* ➔ **Section 2, General, comparative, and regional studies: Comparative studies** entry **244**

2038 Zeleza, Paul Tiyambe **"National Book Policy: The Key to Long-term Development."** *Southern Africa Political & Economic Monthly* 10, no. 1 (October 1996): 33-36.
[Not examined]

The Noma Award for Publishing in Africa

This section includes articles and reports about the ➔ **Noma Award for Publishing in Africa (98)**, as well as a small number of articles on African book prizes in general.

Founded by Japanese publisher and philanthropist Shoichi Noma in 1979, the Noma Award for Publishing in Africa is now well established as Africa's premier book prize. For more details about the Noma Award, including background information, terms and conditions of entry for the competition, the sponsors of the award, the composition of the jury, and details of past winners (as well as titles selected for 'Special Commendation' or 'Honourable Mention') visit http://www.nomaaward.org/.

There is also a useful Wiki entry about the Noma Award at http://en.wikipedia.org/wiki/Noma_Award, which includes a complete list of past winners, some with links to Wiki entries for Noma Award-winning authors, providing biographical profiles about the authors.

2039 Anon. **"1984 Noma Award Presented During Zimbabwe Book Fair."** *The African Book Publishing Record* 10, no. 3 (1984): 136-138.
Reports about the presentation of the 1984 Noma Award for Publishing in Africa, jointly won by Kenyan Gakaara wa Wanjau for *Mesandiki wa Mau Mau Ithaamirio-ini*

(prison memoirs, in Gikuyu), and by South African Njabulo Simakahle Ndebele for *Fools and Other Stories*. The report includes the complete text of Ndebele's acceptance speech made during the ceremony.

2040 Anon. **"The Noma Award for Publishing in Africa."** *Southern African Review of Books*, no. 41 (January-February 1996): 18-19.
For the first time in the Noma Award's history, the annual Award ceremony took place in South Africa, in February 1996. The winner of the 1995 prize was Marlene van Niekerk for her novel in Afrikaans *Triomf*, and which was also the first time that a book written in Afrikaans had won the Award. This is a selection of the speeches given at the ceremony, including those by Chair of the Noma Award Committee, Walter Bgoya, and the Award winner's speech.

2041 Anon. **"The Noma Award at Twenty."** *Glendora Books Supplement* 1, no. 5 (2002): 32.
Online:
http://digital.lib.msu.edu/projects/africanjournals/html/issue.cfm?col id=313 [16/01/08]
Reports about the 20th Noma Award competition.

2042 Anon. **"The Noma Award 2003 Presentation."** *African Publishing Review* 13, no. 2 (2004): 9-10.
Online: http://www.apnet.org/documents/vol_13_2.doc
The 2003 Noma Award for Publishing in Africa was presented to that year's winner, Elinor Sisulu, in Addis Ababa in June 2004 by the President of the Federal Republic of Ethiopia. This account about the ceremony includes the full text of the acceptance speech by Elinor Sisulu, who won the award for her book *In Our Lifetime*, her biographical account of one family's role in bringing South Africa to democracy.

2043 Coetzer, Diane **LeboLive!** August 2007
http://www.women24.com/Readers_Digest/Display/ReadersDigest_A rticle/0,,938-983_15129,00.html [16/01/08]
Interview with 2006 Noma Award winner Lebogan Mashile, who is also well known in South Africa as a performance poet. These pages include sound clips from her performances.

2044 Dekutsey, W.A. **"A Chat with the Noma Award Winner."** *African Publishing Review* 7, no. 1, (January/February 1998): 1-2.
An informal interview with Ghanaian historian Adu Boahen, who was the winner of the 1997 Noma Award for his study *Mfantsispim and the Making of Ghana*.

2045 Emanuel, Abosede **"The Two Cultures. Acceptance Speech for the 2001 Noma Award."** In *National Book Policy, HIV/AIDS and Sustainable Development. Papers Presented at the Fifth Nigeria International Book Fair, 8-13 May, 2006*. Lagos: Nigerian Book Fair Trust [c/o Literamed Publications Ltd., PMB 21068, Ikeja, Lagos, Nigeria], 2002, 74-82.

The acceptance speech by Nigerian scholar (but gynaecologist by profession) Abosede Emanuel, who was the winner of the 2001 Noma Award for Publishing in Africa for his book *Odun Ifa/Ifa Festival*. The 2001 award was presented, by Nobel laureate Wole Soyinka, during the first Nigeria International Book Fair held in Abuja in 2002.

2046 Gibbs, James **"Africa's Not So Glittering Prizes."** *New African* (January 1985): 36-37.
Surveys prizes awarded to African writers in Africa, and finds that they are rather thin on the ground.

2047 Harrell-Bond, Barbara **"Interview: Mariama Bâ."** *The African Book Publishing Record* 6, no. 3/4 (1980): 209-214.
The late Mariama Bâ was the first recipient of the Noma Award for Publishing in Africa in 1980, for her novel *Une si longue letter* (published by Les Nouvelles Editions Africaines, Dakar, in 1979), which is now considered a classical statement on the female condition in Africa. This is an interview conducted with her in Dakar before she travelled to Germany to receive the prize at a special award ceremony held during the 1980 Frankfurt Book Fair.

2048 Irele, Abiola "**The Noma Award and African Publishing.**" *The African Book Publishing Record* 9, nos. 2/3 (1983): 103-104.
Recounts the first four years of existence of the Noma Award for Publishing in Africa and suggests that the award has become the major book prize in Africa, and one of the most significant in international publishing. Describes the award as a recognition of the effort that has gone into the development of publishing in Africa, and the need to give these efforts encouragement.

2049 Jay, Mary "**Managing the Noma.**" *Glendora Books Supplement*, no. 1 (1997): 20-21.
Online: http://digital.lib.msu.edu/projects/africanjournals/html/issue.cfm?colid=310 [16/01/08]
The current Secretary of the Noma Award for Publishing in Africa describes the work of administering Africa's premier book prize, focusing on the 1996 competition, won by the Côte d'Ivoire writer Kitia Touré for his novel *Destins Paralleles* (Nouvelles Editions Africaines Côte d'Ivoire, 1995), and the presentation of the Award to the winner during the Ghana International Book Fair.

2050 Jay, Mary **"25 Years of the Noma Award for Publishing in Africa: An Historic Overview."** *The African Book Publishing Record* 32, no. 2 (2006): 116-118.
Reports about the 25th Noma Award competition and provides some background about this prestigious book prize, including the jury process and information about the sponsors of the award, Kodansha Publishers in Japan. Also offers some statistical analysis of past Noma Award competitions as they relate to languages of submission,

countries and publishers who have had award winners, categories of winning titles, and gender.

2051 Jones, Eldred "**The Noma Award for Publishing in Africa - Ten Years On.**" *Scholarly Publishing* 21, no. 2 (January 1990): 108-123.
A detailed history of the Noma Award for Publishing in Africa, established in 1979, by the former Chairman of the Noma Award during its first ten years. It describes the contribution of the award to publishing in Africa and shows how it can be a measure of activity and achievement. Points out that as far as scholarly books are concerned, it is not just the subject matter that is considered but that special consideration is also given to books whose methods of investigation are particularly suitable to the subject in an African setting.

2052 Jones, Eldred "**The Noma Award - Africa's Leading Book prize. The First Decade.**" *West Africa* (18-24 May 1992): 842.
The retiring chairman of the Managing Committee of the Noma Award offers an overview of the objectives and achievements of the Award since it was established in 1979.

2053 Makgetla, Tumi **Lebo Mashile's African Voice.** ZA@Play (November 17, 2006)
http://www.chico.mweb.co.za/art/2006/2006nov/061117-lebo.html
[16/01/08]
An interview with South African poet, actress, record producer and TV presenter Lebo Mashile, winner of the 2006 Noma Award for Publishing in Africa, for her poetry anthology *In a Ribbon of Rhythm.*

2054 Noma Award Archives
http://www.ub.bw/subportals/archives/classlists/NOMANoma.doc
[30/03/08]
A descriptive inventory of the Noma Award archives held at the University of Botswana Libraries covering the period 1995 to 2002. Material held includes press releases, entry forms for each year's award, award presentation speeches, acceptance speeches by winners, and jury documentation, i.e. independent readers' reports of submissions for each year. (Restrictions are in place for access to some materials in order to preserve confidentiality of jury discussions and names of readers.)
Note: earlier material, covering the period is 1979 to 1994, is held as part of the Lilly Library Manuscript Collections at Indiana University Libraries, see
http://www.indiana.edu/~liblilly/lilly/mss/html/nomaawar.html. [16/01/08].

2055 Noma Award Managing Committee **The Noma Award for Publishing in Africa. Winners, Special Commendations and Honourable Mentions, 1990-1995**. Oxford: The Noma Award for Publishing in Africa [Noma Award Secretariat, PO Box 128, Witney, OX8 5XU, UK], 1995. 12 pp.

Updated brochure giving details of winners of the Noma Award for Publishing in Africa, special commendations, and honourable mentions for 1990-1995, with jury citations, etc. Also includes a complete list of winners for 1980-1989.

2056 Osundare, Niyi **"The Possibilities of Hope."** *The Kenya Bookseller* 4, no. 1 (1992): 15-16.
Also published in *Echoes of the Sunbird. An Anthology of Contemporary African Poetry*, edited by Don Burness. Athens, OH: Ohio University Press, 1993, 128-131.
The text of the acceptance speech by Nigerian poet Niyi Osundare, who was the recipient of the Noma Award in 1991, for his poetry volume, *Waiting Laughters*. The prize was presented in Harare in August of that year.

2057 Osundare, Niyi **"Of Prizes and Literary Giants."** *Glendora Review* 1, no. 1 (June-August 1995): 54-56.
Online:
http://digital.lib.msu.edu/projects/africanjournals/html/itemdetail.cfm?re cordID=2342 [16/01/08]
Niyi Osundare, one of Africa's foremost poets - and winner of the Commonwealth Poetry Prize in 1986 and the Noma Award for Publishing in Africa in 1991 - bemoans the fact that "apart from the omnibus Noma Award which has come to be through the generosity and vision of a Japanese publisher, there [is] no single continental literary prize of substantial worth in Africa." He goes on to say that "this crucial lack must be laid at the door of a monster other than our perennial poverty", and asserts that "Africa's failure to institute her own literary prizes was due to a monumental lack of vision by African rulers." He concludes that foreign prizes and their attendant recognition "have played a valuable diplomatic role in the lives and struggles of African literary ambassadors", and that there is nothing wrong with foreign prizes as long as the recognition provided is healthy, genuine and unpatronizing.

2058 Perry, Alison **"Portrait of an Artist."** *West Africa* (2 May 1983): 1073-1074.
An interview with Noma Award-winning Ghanaian children's author and artist Meshack Asare, discussing his books and an exhibition of his work held at London's Africa Centre. Asare won the prize in 1982 for his children's picture-story book *The Brassman's Secret*.

2059 Samb, Djibril **Allocution de Djibril Samb lauréat du Prix Noma 1999. Perth, 26 novembre 1999.** *Mot Pluriels*, no 13 (April 2000)
http://motspluriels.arts.uwa.edu.au/MP1300sambspeachfr.html [16/01/08]
Also published in an English version **1999 Noma Award Djibril Samb Acceptance Speech. Perth, 26 November 1999.** [16/01/08]]
http://motspluriels.arts.uwa.edu.au/MP1300sambspeacheng.html
The acceptance speech by the winner of the 1999 Noma Award for Publishing in Africa, the Senegalese scholar Djibril Samb, who received the prize for his study

L'interpretation des reves dans la region Senegambienne. Suivi de la clef des songes de la Senegambie de l'Egypte pharaonique et de la tradition islamique.

2060 Schmidt, Nancy J. **"Award-Winning Children's Books: The Noma Selections 1980-1994."** In *Critical Perspectives on Postcolonial African Children's and Young Adult Literature,* edited by Meena Khorana. Westport, CO & London: Greenwood Press, 1998, 27-44
This essay is based on the author's research using the archival papers of the Noma Award that are housed at the Lilly Library at Indiana University in Bloomington. The archive is the official repository of material related to the founding and history of the Noma Award for Publishing in Africa up to 1994 (the archives from 1995 onwards are housed at the University of Botswana Library, *see* entry ➔ **2054**). The essay sets out the background to the Noma Award and the encouragement this book prize has provided for indigenous African publishers, examines the number of children's books submitted to the Award between 1980-1994, and also provides an analytical overview of the various children's titles which have been singled out for 'Honourable mention' over the years. Thereafter she presents a critical study of the work of two of the authors who have won the Noma Award: Meshack Asare (Ghana, the 1982 Award winner) and Charles Mungoshi (Zimbabwe, the 1992 joint winner).

Violet, Jean-Marie **"A 'Good' Children's Book is One Which Arises from the Child's Own Culture. An Interview with Mary Jay"** *see* ➔ **African books in the international market place** entry **1297**

2061 Zeleza, Paul Tiyambe **Noma Award Acceptance Speech** *Issue: A Journal of Opinion* 23, no. 1, (Winter - Spring, 1995): 7-8
Paul Zeleza's acceptance speech made during the presentation of the 1994 Noma Award for Publishing in Africa, awarded for his scholarly study *A Modern Economic History of Africa. Volume 1: The Nineteenth Century.*

2062 Zell, Hans M. **"The First Noma Award for Publishing in Africa."** *The African Book Publishing Record* 6, nos. 3/4 (1980): 199-201.
A full report on the first Noma Award for Publishing in Africa, presented at a special ceremony during the 1980 Frankfurt Book Fair. Nearly 130 works by African writers and scholars from 17 African countries were submitted for the first Award, established and sponsored by the late Shoichi Noma, Chairman of Kodansha, the Japanese publishing giant. The first award was won by a woman novelist from Senegal, Mariama Bâ, for her book *Une si longue letter* (Such a Long Letter), published by Les Nouvelles Editions Africaines, Dakar in 1979. The book was subsequently translated into 17 languages.

2063 Zell, Hans M. **"A Sixteen-year Japanese Contribution to African Publishing."** *Logos. The Journal of the World Book Community* 7, no. 2 (1996): 162-167 [Appendix 2 & 3 in this article published in *Logos.The Journal of the World Book Community* 7, no. 3 (1996): 245-246.]
Online:

http://www.atypon-link.com/LOG/doi/pdf/10.2959/logo.1996.7.2.162
Slightly shorter version also published in *African Publishing Review* 6, no. 1
(January/February 1997): 5-7.
The former Secretary of the Noma Award for Publishing looks back at the
accomplishments of the Award since its inception in 1979. He sets out the
background that led to the establishment of the Award, the vision of the Award's
sponsor the late Shoichi Noma, the categories in which books may be submitted for
the prize, and the working methods of the Noma Award jury and secretariat, which
is assisted by a pool of a large number assessors and subject authorities from
throughout the world. Also reflects on the Noma Award's relationship with African
books, the exposure that has been given over the years to a wide spectrum of African
writing and scholarship, and the success it has achieved in its main mission to
promote publishing in Africa. Three appendixes include a complete list of winners
from 1980-1995; an analysis of Award winners by nationality, gender, language of
publication, and categories; and a Noma Award publisher's 'League Table'.

Open access publishing

See also
→ **Digital media and electronic publishing/New printing technology**
→ **Journals and magazine publishing**
→ **Scholarly publishing (General)**
→ **Scientific, technical and medial publishing**

Note: this section on open access publishing is restricted to articles and
papers – primarily those available online – that deal, in whole or in part,
with open access, or open access models, for African scholarly book and
journal publishing. More general articles about open content, the open
access movement, or open access for e-learning, etc. are not included, nor are
those that deal with open access publishing in the developing world
generally.

2064 Asamoah-Hassan, Helena **Open Access Publishing and Access to
Development Information in Africa — The Vision.**
campus.iss.nl/~vanhelden/Presentations/AsamoahHelena.ppt [05/02/08]
A PowerPoint presentation delivered at the EADI-IMWG Conference, The Hague,
Netherlands, September 2007. Presents the issues for and against open access.
Discusses current obstacles for access to scholarly publications in Africa, the
significance of open access for researchers in Africa, and outlines the author's vision
for the development of open access in Africa.

2065 Asamoah-Hassan, Helena **Embracing Electronic Scholarly
Publishing in Africa. The Kwame Nkrumah University of Science and
Technology (KNUST) Library, Kumasi, Ghana as a Case Study.**

http://ocs.sfu.ca/pkp2007/papers/Asamoah-Hassan.pdf [05/02/08]
Argues the need for Africa to accept electronic scholarly publishing, as libraries are becoming more and more involved as electronic publishers. The participation of African libraries as publishers of scholarly electronic journals and other scholarly communications is discussed using the KNUST Library as the focus. The author examines the usefulness and suitability of the PKP (Public Knowledge Project) software, Open Journals System (OJS) for scholarly journal publishing, and concludes with recommendations as it relates to the OJS and its use in emerging electronic scholarly journal publishing, as well as for other information access functions by African libraries.

2066 De Beer, Jennifer A. **Open Access Scholarly Communication in South Africa: A Role for National Information Policy in the National System of Innovation.** Stellenbosch: Department of Information Science, University of Stellenbosch, 2005. MPhil thesis. 206 pp.
Online:
http://eprints.rclis.org/archive/00003110/01/DeBeerJenniferThesisMPhil2004.pdf [05/02/08]
South African science, the author argues, shows a decline in its global competitiveness in that its scholarly publication rate has not kept pace with that of other countries, both developed and developing. This, together with a decline in publication rate especially among junior South African scholars, suggests a structural problem in the South African national system of innovation. A declining publication rate indicates a problem of knowledge diffusion for South Africa, and hints at a possible knowledge generation problem. This thesis limits itself to the dynamics of knowledge diffusion with specific reference to Open Access scholarly communication. It is structured around two core sections, a theoretical framework based in the literature, and an empirical study. De Beer aims to assess levels of awareness of and investment in Open Access modes of scholarly communication within defined scholarly communities, and to create a benchmark document of South Africa's involvement to date in various Open Access initiatives. The author argues for the openness of scholarly systems, and believes that the disparate and uncoordinated nature of Open Access in South Africa needs a policy intervention. She recommends an amendment of the current statutory reporting mechanism – used by scholars to report and obtain publication rate subsidies – which would require that scholars make their research available via an Open Access mode of scholarly communication and, moreover, would require scholars to report on having done so.

2067 Dennis, Alasia Datonye **The Impact of the Open Access Movement on Medical Based Scholarly Publishing in Nigeria.** *First Monday* 12, no. 10 (1 October 2007)
http://www.uic.edu/htbin/cgiwrap/bin/ojs/index.php/fm/article/view/1957/1834 [06/02/08]
Open Access initiatives have helped to improve the global dissemination of scholarly research of scholarly publications in the developing world. This study attempts to provide an insight into the current state of medical journal publishing in Nigeria and

assesses the impact of the open access movement and its initiatives on medical publishing in Nigeria. The author aims to demonstrate that open access initiatives have impacted positively on medical scholarly publishing in Nigeria, with the African Journals Online project (AJOL) and the *African Index Medicus* projects being the most significant influences. The paper also examines some of the obstacles to the growth of open access in Nigeria and suggests a number of recommendations to optimize the benefits derivable from open access to medical scholarly publishing in Nigeria. The author believes the prospects for further development of medical scholarly publishing using open access initiatives are enormous, but that in spite of the gains made to date the potentials of open access to medical scholarly publishing are yet to be maximized. Medical scholars in Nigeria need to develop a coordinated plan to overcome many of the current obstacles.

Esseh, Samuel Smith, and John Willinsky **Strengthening Scholarly Publishing in Africa: Assessing the Potential of Online Systems** *see* ➜ **Digital media and electronic publishing/New printing technology** entry **1833**

2068 Fullard, Allison **"South African Responses to Open Access Publishing: A Survey of the Research Community."** *South African Journal of Libraries and Information Science* 73, no. 1 (2007): 40-50.
Online: http://eprints.rclis.org/archive/00010749/01/SAJLIS_73(1)04.pdf [04/02/08]
The author argues that open access publishing offers wide benefits to the scholarly community and may also afford relief to financially embattled academic libraries. However, the progress of the open access model rests upon the acceptance and validation of open access journals, and open archives or institutional repositories by the academic mainstream, particularly by publishing researchers. Fullard investigates to what extent are the key actors in the South African research system aware of the advantages of open access, and reports on the findings of a recent survey undertaken to assess the current awareness, concerns, and depth of support for open access amongst local researchers, research managers and policy makers in South Africa. The study focuses on issues of quality, article or author charges, and the established academic reward system. It concludes that within the prevailing framework, there is little prospect that academics would choose to publish within open access journals. The author concludes with a series of recommendations for proactive direct interventions by the library community to bring about the benefits of open access as soon as possible.

2069 Gray, Eve **Digital Publishing and Open Access for Social Science Research Dissemination: A Case Study.** Cape Town: Eve Gray & Associates [PO Box 16185, Vlaeberg, Cape Town 8018], 2004. 25 pp.
Online: http://www.codesria.org//Links/conferences/el_publ/grey.pdf [11/01/08]
Charts the planning and implementation of a digital publishing programme over a three-year period at the Human Sciences Research Council, a large South African social science research body. The case study is contextualised in the need to

overcome the digital divide to give African scholars a real voice in the global community. It deals with the challenges faced by African scholarly publishers and organizations wanting to use digital media to disseminate their research findings: the importance of strategic choices, finding the right mix of technologies, managing the technical and organizational process of getting a digital publishing programme up and running, and putting effective promotional and distribution strategies in place to ensure the success of a digital publishing programme. The case study also examines how applicable its findings are to other countries in Africa and, in particular, explores the limitations of digital dissemination in a South African context and identifies the ways in which a multi-pronged approach, using digital, print, e-mail and fax, can most effectively reach a wider market. It concludes that such a multi-pronged approach can be an effective way of ensuring the international reach of Africa scholarship.

2070 Gray, Eve **Emerging from the Twilight Zone: Open Content and African Research Dissemination. The Successful Implementation of an Open Access Publishing Programme.**
http://www.evegray.co.za/downloads/webcopyCcreative_commons.ppt [30/01/08]
A PowerPoint presentation arguing the case for open access publishing in South Africa. It sets out the strategy and implementation of a consultancy assignment undertaken by Eve Gray Associates for the Human Science Research Council/HSRC Publishing, the problems and successes of this new strategy, and assessment of the potential for Open Access publishing programmes elsewhere in Africa (and *see also* entry ➔ **2069** above).

2071 Gray, Eve **"At the South-eastern Frontier: The Impact of Higher Education Policy on African Research Publication."**
http://www.ascleiden.nl/Pdf/elecpublconfgray.pdf [22/01/08]
A paper presented at the conference on Bridging the North-South Divide in Scholarly Communication on Africa--Threats and Opportunities in the Digital Era, held at the African Studies Centre, Leiden, The Netherlands, September 6-8, 2006. Digital media, with their capacity to reduce the cost of information dissemination and to effortlessly cross borders, offer new possibilities for overcoming the marginalization of African research publication in the global community. In turn, Open Access publishing models show signs of generating substantially greater research impact and increasing citation levels, particularly for publications from the developing world. This paper tackles a relatively neglected area of study: the policy context in which research publication happens in African universities. In particular, it maps the contradictions and distortions that can occur when national research policy initiatives targeting development goals meet up with policies for publication reward systems that effectively drive publication – even of African studies – out of Africa into the USA and Europe. The context of the paper is a research programme the author is undertaking as part of the Open Information Working Group of the International Policy Fellowship programme of the Open Society Institute in Budapest. It is a qualitative study, exploring research and research dissemination policy and practice in South Africa and comparing this with other African countries.

The author critically examines African policy and practice in the light of global debates challenging the complacencies of traditional publication. Tracking the problems inherent in the traditional 'publish-or-perish' scholarly publishing system to which African universities continue to subscribe, the paper explores the potential offered by Internet publication and Open Access publishing models for African scholarship. She offers a number of recommendations for policy initiatives and publishing models that might help strengthen the voice of African scholarship globally. The author believes "the use of a combination of Open Access publication in Africa and the development of Open Access repositories for work published internationally by African researchers could provide the best of both worlds: local impact plus international dissemination and prestige." Meantime, and most importantly, "the topic of publishing and dissemination needs to be given a much higher profile and be subjected to more rigorous critique, so that awareness of the issues is increased. It has to be accepted that research dissemination is of vital importance and needs support if investment in developmental R&D and Innovation policies is to maximise its effectiveness." This is a cogent and penetrative analysis of the current state of scholarly communication and scholarly publishing in Africa in general, and in South Africa in particular, and how it might be taken forward successfully into the 21st century.

2072 Gray, Eve **ICT and Research Dissemination in African Universities. Policy Issues: Intellectual Property, Open Access and Sustainability.** http://www.foundation-partnership.org/pubs/leaders/assets/papers/GraySession8.ppt [11/01/08] A PowerPoint presentation made at the Frontiers of Knowledge in Science and Technology for Africa conference at the University of Cape Town in November 2006. The conference was convened by the ➜ **Partnership for Higher Education in Africa (102)** and focussed in particular on the immense potential of information and communication technologies to transform the teaching, learning, and research environments in African universities, and the capacity of those technologies to stimulate large changes in Africa's growing economies. This presentation argues that there is a fundamental need to develop policies and strategies that could grow the output and effective dissemination of African-based research in and from Africa, and published in the most appropriate media and formats. It looks at the new opportunities presented by ICT and reviews the ethos and advantages of open access publishing in Africa on the basis of a number of case studies. *Note:* other papers presented at this conference can be found at http://www.foundation-partnership.org/pubs/leaders/assets/toc.html.

Gray, Eve **Achieving Research Impact for Development. A Critique of Research Dissemination Policy in South Africa, with Recommendations for Policy Reform** *see* **Section 3, Country studies: South Africa** entry ➜ **1008**

2073 Möller, Allison Melanie **The Case for Open Access Publishing, with Special Reference to Open Access Journals and their Prospects in South Africa.** Bellville, South Africa: Department of Library and Information

Science, University of the Western Cape 2006. MBibl thesis. 202 pp.
Online:
http://ww3.uwc.ac.za/docs/%20Library/Theses/Theses_2006/Moller_a_
m_2006.pdf [04/02/08]
also online at
http://eprints.rclis.org/archive/00005815/01/MollerThesis.pdf (2.05MB)
[04/02/08]
Presenting the case for open access publishing, this thesis explores the contemporary research environment, changing modes of knowledge production, the problems associated with the existing academic journal system, and the subsequent growth of the open access movement as an intervention to reclaim scientific communication. The author argues that free access to publicly funded scientific research is more democratic and is necessary for knowledge dissemination and production in a knowledge economy, particularly for developing countries such as South Africa. The study also closely interrogates the economic viability of open access journals, and shows how the 'author pays' model represents a reasonable approach, but by no means the only one available to publishers considering the transition to open access. The main research question centres on the feasibility of open access journals becoming widespread within the South African research system, and the study presents the findings of an investigation undertaken to assess the current awareness, concerns and depth of support for open access amongst South African stakeholders. The conclusion recommends proactive engagement by faculty librarians and organized advocacy on the part of Library & Information Association of South Africa (LIASA) to promote the cause of open access within South Africa. It further calls for government to mandate open access to publicly funded research as a more democratic, cost-effective and strategic intervention to promote South African science.

2074 Ouya, Daisy **Open Access Survey of Africa-Published Journals.**
Oxford: International Network for the Availability of Scientific Publications (Infobrief, 7) 2006. 4 pp.
Online: http://www.inasp.info/uploaded/documents/InfoBrief7-OA-web.pdf [15/01/08]
Also published as Ouya, Daisy, and Pippa Smart **"Open Access Survey of Africa-published Journals."**
http://www.ascleiden.nl/Pdf/elecpublconfouyasmart.pdf [15/01/08]
A paper presented at the conference on Bridging the North-South Divide in Scholarly Communication on Africa--Threats and Opportunities in the Digital Era, African Studies Centre, Leiden, The Netherlands, September 6-8, 2006. The author reports about a survey of African journal editors that was undertaken by the ➔ **International Network for the Availability of Scientific Publications (81)** in 2005 to ascertain their awareness and understanding of the Open Access movement, and to discover if their journals would be willing to move to Open Access publication. The survey showed that there was limited awareness and understanding of Open Access and journal editors expressed some reservations regarding its suitability for their journals. There was also level of apprehension about journal sustainability on an Open Access basis. The survey highlighted the need for more information about

emerging publishing models, and the Open Access movement, to be provided to publishers of sub-Saharan African journals.

2075 van der Werf-Davelaar, Titia **"Facilitating Scholarly Communication in African Studies."** D-Lib Magazine 12, no. 2 (February 2006)
http://www.dlib.org/dlib/february06/vanderwerf/02vanderwerf.html
[04/02/08]
Web publishing and its technical possibilities, as well as the Open Access movement that has accompanied it, have resulted in a number of tendencies with mixed implications for scholarly communication. This article examines the impact of these changes in the field of the African studies, where the North-South divide in scholarly publishing poses an additional challenge to the issues at stake. It looks at several initiatives taken by the Africanists community in the Netherlands to bridge the divide, in particular the establishment of a digital platform for African studies. It concludes that these initiatives are all geared towards redressing the balance and establishing open scholarly communication on an equal footing, but that true Open Access can only be achieved if practiced both ways (by North and South) and not at the expense of academic quality standards. In addition "it requires the active commitment of each and every individual scholar. This commitment still needs to grow in Africanist circles".

2076 Winterbottom, Anna, and James North **"Building an Open Access African Studies Repository Using Web 2.0 Principles"** *First Monday,* 12, no. 4 (April 2007)
http://www.firstmonday.org/issues/issue12_4/winterbottom/index.html
[04/02/08]
Describes the aims and design of an open access African Studies Repository (ASR) http://www.africanstudiesrepository.org/ that is currently under development. The ASR is a relational database compatible with the open repository platform DSpace but incorporating the participatory online tools collectively known as 'Web 2.0'. The aim of the ASR is to create a space where everyone who works on Africa, both inside and outside the continent, can store their work, access useful resources, make contacts, and join discussions.

Publishing in African languages

Note: this section lists books and articles that deal with various aspects of publishing in African languages, and marketing and distribution of indigenous language books. Articles that deal exclusively with *writing* in indigenous languages, and issues relating to orthographies, etc., are not included.

See also ➔ **Reading culture and reading promotion**

2077   Adams, Cynthia **"Marketing Indigenous Language Books. The Success Story."** In *Millennium Marketplace.* [Proceedings of the ZIBF] *Indaba 2000, Harare, Zimbabwe, 31 July – 1 August 2000.* Harare: Zimbabwe International Book Fair Trust, n.d. [2001], 93-99.
An earlier version, **Marketing Indigenous Books in Namibia**, also published in *African Publishing Review* 9, no. 4 (2000): 6-8.
Describes marketing approaches for indigenous language publishing in Namibia, language policies in the country, the influence of government policies on publishing in local languages, and the constraints and challenges faced by the Namibian book industries in the new millennium.

 2078   Adeaga, Tomi **Translating and Publishing African Language(s) and Literature(s): Examples from Nigeria, Ghana and Germany**. Frankfurt am Main: IKO Verlag für Interkulturelle Kommunikation, 2006. 303 pp.
Examines the challenges of translating African literatures into European languages and, in particular, the problems of translating African voices into German. Chapter 3 is devoted to publishing African literature in Germany, the reception and the book market for African writing, while Chapter 5 looks back at the Frankfurt Book Fair in 1980 which in that year focused on African and African writing.

2079   Adedeji, 'Remi **"Problems of Writing and Publishing for Children in Nigerian Languages."** *Nigerbiblios* 9, no. 1 (January 1984): 15-18.
Highlights problems of writing and publishing for children, which may be surmountable as long as "the institutions or individuals concerned are prepared to accept the challenge which the nation's new language policy has thrust upon them." Seeks government support for the production of supplementary readers for children, especially in indigenous languages.

 2080   *African Publishing Review* **[Special issue on publishing in African languages]**, volume 9, no. 1 (2000).
This entire issue of APNET's ➔**African Publishing Review (129)** is devoted to language policy, and publishing in African languages, with short case studies from a number of African countries.

2081 Alidou-Ngame, Hassana **Stratégies pour le dévelopment d'un secteur editorial en langues nationales dans les Pays du Sahel—Burkina Faso, Mali, Niger, et Sénégal.** London: Association for the Development of Education in Africa (ADEA), Working Group on Books and Learning Materials (Perspectives on African Book Development, 8), 2000. 116 pp. (distributed by African Books Collective Ltd., Oxford)
A synthesis of policies in several francophone African countries of the development and use of African languages as an essential strategy for the improvement and expansion of education programmes, and the provision of relevant teaching materials.

2082 Alemna, A. Anaba **"Preservation of Indigenous Languages in Africa."** [Paper presented to] 61st IFLA General Conference, 20 26- August 1995, Istanbul, Turkey. The Hague: IFLA, Division of Libraries Serving the General Public, Section on Library Services to Multicultural Populations, 1995, 96-100.
Provides an overview of the oral tradition in Africa, addresses issues in the development of indigenous languages in Africa, and offers possible strategies for the preservation of theses languages. Briefly examines publishing aspects and finds that the vernacular Literature Bureaux in various African countries have been underfunded, "exist in name only", and have therefore not been able to achieve their mission to eradicate illiteracy though mass adult education. Also urges libraries to play a more active role in the acquisition and preservation of indigenous language materials.

2083 Alemna, A. Anaba **"Publishing in Ghanaian Languages: Problems and Prospects."** *International Information, Communication and Education* 8, no. 2 (1989): 179.
Discusses the problems of publishing in Ghanaian languages and suggests ways in which the situation could be improved, including the establishment of a Ghanaian language publications board and sponsorship of publications in native languages.

2084 Altbach, Philip G., and Damtew Teferra, eds. **Publishing in African Languages: Challenges and Prospects.** Chestnut Hill, MA: Bellagio Publishing Network, Research and Information Center (Bellagio Studies in Publishing, 10), 1999. 163 pp. (distributed by African Books Collective Ltd., Oxford)
A collection of essays on an important ongoing debate, the publication of material in indigenous languages. Three African publishers – Dumisani Ntshangase (Juta Publishers, South Africa), Victor Nwankwo (Fourth Dimension Publishing Company, Nigeria), and Mamadou Aliou Sow (Les Editions Ganndal, Conakry, Guinea) – two African writers-editors/academics M. Mulokozi (Tanzania) and Damtew Teferra (Ethiopia); a woman publisher from India, Urvashi Butalia (Kali for Women, New Delhi), and Thomas Clayton, an American academic, look at the situation of indigenous language publishing in Africa, analyzing the problems, and offering possible prescriptions for advancing the cause of publishing in African

languages. The contributors examine the situation in the various countries and regions covered, including issues such as colonial heritage, lack of national publishing policies, ambiguities towards the use of mother tongue in education beyond the first few years of primary school, forbidding economics of minority language publishing, as well as other aspects such as orthography, and technical issues related to management of the publishing and printing industries. The papers provide informative overviews of publishing in indigenous languages in African countries and elsewhere. *Note:* some of the papers in this collection are individually abstracted elsewhere in this bibliography.

Reviews:
The African Book Publishing Record, vol. 26, no. 1, 2000
H-AfrLitCine, H-Net Reviews, July, 2000.
http://www.h-net.org/reviews/showrev.cgi?path=12183964642078 [19/01/08]

2085 Altbach, Philip G. **"Publishing in National Languages. What Africa Could Learn from Other Continents."** *Logos. The Journal of the World Book Community* 10, no. 2 (1999): 75-80.
Online:
http://www.atypon-link.com/LOG/doi/pdf/10.2959/logo.1999.10.2.75
Examines some of the arguments in favour of indigenous language publishing in Africa, and looks at the problems for African-language publishing, such as the multiplicity of languages and linguistic complexities, and the fact that for many languages there is an insufficient number of speakers, and readers, to make the language viable for publishing. The author argues that much of the failure of indigenous language publishing in Africa stems from current economic and political factors, and that developing countries in other continents have faced similar challenges. However, some small developing countries, e.g. Laos and Cambodia, have painstakingly managed to build up indigenous-language publishing, and remain firmly committed to their national languages, despite poor economic conditions and small markets. Altbach concedes that Africa has more unfavourable economic and political circumstances at the present time [1999] than the rest of the world, many African languages simply have too few speakers to support a viable publishing industry, purchasing power is generally limited, and many languages have no standard script or grammatical structure. However, despite these considerable problems, African governments – who thus far have been less committed to the development of indigenous languages than governments in post-colonial Asia – could learn from the experience in other continents.

2086 **"The Asmara Declaration on African Languages and Literatures."**
http://www.outreach.psu.edu/C&I/AllOdds/declaration.html [27/03/08]
Declaration by writers and scholars made at the 'Against All Odds: African Languages and Literatures into the 21st Century' conference, held in Asmara, Eritrea, 11-17 January 2000. Conference delegates examined the state of African languages in literature, scholarship, publishing, education, and administration in Africa and throughout the world.

2087 Bahta, Samuel Ghile, and Stephen M. Mutula **"Indigenous Publishing in Botswana: The Current Situation and the Way Forward."** *Information Development* 18, no. 4 (December 2002): 231-235.
Examines the challenges of publishing in local languages in Botwana, discussing aspects such as readership and the limited market for books, the prospects for developing local language publishing, and the important role indigenous language publishing has in eliminating illiteracy and creating a reading and writing culture.

2088 Bill, Mary C. **"100 Years of Tsonga Publications, 1883-1983."** *African Studies* 43, no. 2 (1984): 67-81.
This is a condensed version of the introduction to the author's *Mbita ya Vutivi; Tsonga Bibliography, 1883-1983* (Johannesburg: Sasavona Publishers, 1983). Tsonga is usually spoken of, disparagingly, as a "minority language", yet the bibliography contains over 550 titles, proof enough of the vitality and viability of this language. Includes an overview of Tsonga publications during the missionary era 1883-1938 and during the later period of 1939 to 1983, as well as Tsonga publications in Mozambique.

2089 Bouquiaux, Luc **"Les problèmes de l'édition en matière de langues à tradition orale."** *Mondes et Cultures* 42, no. 4 (1982): 825-833.
Discusses the problems of publishing in indigenous languages in societies with a strong oral tradition.

Bureau of Ghana Languages **The Bureau of Ghana Languages at a Glance** *see* ➔ **Section 3, Country studies: Ghana** entry **550**

Büttner, Thomas, and Anja Frings **De l'idée au texte: Guide des auteurs** *see* ➔ **Section 5, Book Industry training/Self-publishing: Training manuals and resources** entry **2451**

2090 Châtry-Komarek, Marie **"Des auteurs et des manuels. A propos une programme éducatif pour l'essor de l'édition scolaire en language nationales."** *D+C. Développement et Coopération*, no. 1 (January/February 1997): 18-22.
Underlines the necessity for thriving national textbook industries, and publication of material in African languages, using examples of books produced by the Institut National de Documentation, de Recherche et d'Animation Pédagogique de Niamey (INDRAP) in Niger, and which is supported by the Deutsche Stiftung für Internationale Entwicklung, now part of ➔ **InWEnt/Capacity Building International (85)**. INDRAP has produced books textbooks in Fula, Hausa and Zarma. The author stresses the importance of testing the books, and the need for training of book industry personnel, as well as providing training for authorship and textbook writing skills.

2091 Chitsike, B.C. **"Publishing in Indigenous Languages in Zimbabwe."** *African Publishing Review* 5, no. 4 (July/August 1996): 5-6.

An account of the development of publishing in Zimbabwe's two major national languages, Shona and Ndebele, and the pioneering role played by the Zimbabwe Literature Bureau (a former government department, now defunct, in the Ministry of Education) in producing and distributing this material, and in encouraging authorship in these languages.

2092 Coates, Nick **Publishing in Namibian Languages**. In *African Languages in Basic Education, Proceedings of the 1st Workshop on African Languages in Basic Education*, edited by K. Légère. Windhoek: Gamsberg Macmillan, 1996, 80-89.
One of 31 contributions in a collection of presentations made during a workshop on African languages in elementary education, which examines the challenges and constraints of publishing material in mother tongue languages in independent Namibia.

2093 Dintwe, Motumi, and Bobana E. Badisang **"The Inter-Agency Material Production Committee (IAMPC)."** *African Research & Documentation* no. 73 (1997): 1-7.
Describes the work of the Inter-Agency Material Production Committee (IAMPC) established in Botswana in 1988, whose principal aim is to support education of neo-literates, and to support adult literacy programmes and village reading rooms by producing a variety of simple readers in local languages (mainly Setswana) and in English. It has thus far published 21 titles in the 'Ipalele Series' and 14 'Thoto Boswa' manuscripts are awaiting publication. IAMPC's main thrust is mainly through writers' workshops, where authors are trained at pre-workshop seminars, while the actual writing is done during the workshops. The article, by two librarians at the University of Botswana, examines the evolution of the organization, assesses its achievements to date, and makes a number of recommendations regarding future development and the way forward.

2094 Dirar, Solomon **"Marketing Indigenous Languages. Eritrea's Success."** In *Millennium Marketplace.* [Proceedings of the ZIBF] *Indaba 2000, Harare, Zimbabwe, 31 July – 1 August 2000.* Harare: Zimbabwe International Book Fair Trust, n.d. [2001], 70-79.
Describes the development of national language policies in Eritrea, attitudes towards education in mother tongue languages, the production of textbooks and teachers guides in Eritrean languages, and the marketing of these materials.

2095 Durrani, Shiraz **"The Right to Publish: People's Struggle for Publishing in Nationality Languages, with Particular Reference to Kenya."** *Focus on International & Comparative Librarianship* 24, no. 2 (10 September 1993): 74-86.
Analyzes the main reasons why publishing in national languages has faced neglect; recounts the experience in Kenya, and argues that publishing in African and other national languages plays a crucial role in the development of society as a whole.

2096 Fagerberg-Diallo, Sonja **"Publishing in Pulaar: The Inter-Reactive Role of an NGO."** *Bellagio Publishing Network Newsletter*, no. 13 (April 1995): 8-10.
Describes the publishing activities and the experience of the ➔ **Groupe d'Initiative pour la Promotion du Livre en Langues Nationales/GIPLLN (873)** founded in Dakar, Senegal, in 1989, who have published a wide range of books in Pular, Wolof, Soninke, and Mandkinga. The Group has developed a range of inexpensive books that aim to develop fluent reading skills, and which are books "that encourage people to take an advocacy position on the crucial issues in their lives."

2097 Fagerberg-Diallo, Sonja **"Création d'un Milieu Lettré en Langues Nationales. L'exemple du Pulaar au Sénégal."** *D+C. Développement et Coopération*, no. 1 (January/February 1997): 16-18.
Examines the experience of creating a Pulaar written culture in Senegal, and the innovative publishing programme of ➔ **Associates in Research & Education for Development /ARED (873)** an NGO whose activities are directed towards reaching a growing group of new literates. ARED works in partnership with the Groupe d'Initiative pour la Promotion du Livre en Langues Nationales, a Senegalese organization dedicated to publishing in African languages. The two organizations work together through publishing training and curriculum development for use in non-formal education in national languages. A substantial number of books have been published on a variety of issues, most of them in Pulaar, but also some in other African languages.

2098 Fagerberg-Diallo, Sonja **"Publishing for New Literates: The Role of an African Language Publisher."** In *Courage and Consequence. Women Publishing in Africa,* edited by Mary Jay and Susan Kelly. Oxford: African Books Collective Ltd., 2002, 1-9.
The author is the founder and director of the non-profit publisher ➔ **Associates in Research & Education for Development/(ARED (873)** in Dakar, that works in partnership with the Groupe d'Initiative pour la Promotion du Livre en Langues Nationales. In this paper she describes the background to the creation of these two organizations, their activities, the development of its publishing programme, and its efforts to establish a literate environment in the Pulaar language. Since it was founded in 1990 ARED has produced a very large number of titles, most of them experimental literacy materials in Pulaar, and it has also trained literacy teachers how to use these materials.

2099 Fajemisin, Martins Olusegun **The Experience of Publishing in Indigenous African Languages: A Survey of Nigeria, Ghana, Togo, Zimbabwe, Namibia, Lesotho and Kenya**. Harare: African Publishers Network, 1995. 24 pp.
This is a summary version of an important study commissioned by the ➔ **IFLA (74)**, Section on Library Services to Multicultural Populations and supervised by the ➔ **African Publishers Network (5)**, which reviews the status [in 1995] of indigenous language publishing in seven African countries. Identifies African language material available from each country and its publishers; examines the development of the

orthographies of each language and its implications for language utilization and publishing; and also looks at support structures in various countries, i.e. indigenous language literature bureaux, book development councils, book trade and library associations, authors' groups etc.

Note: the full report was never published, but extracts from it, covering the situation in four African countries, have been published in APNET's ➜ **African Publishing Review (129)** as follows, each reported authored by Martins O. Fajemisin:

2100   "An APNET Survey of Local Language Publishing. Part One: Ghana." *African Publishing Review* 4, no. 5 (September/October 1995): 13.

2101   "An APNET Survey of Local Language Publishing: Part Two: Kenya." *African Publishing Review* 4, no. 6 (November/December 1995): 5.

2102   "An APNET Survey of Local Language Publishing: Part Three: Togo." *African Publishing Review* 5, no. 1 (March/April 1996): 5.

2103   "An APNET Survey of Local Language Publishing: Part Four: Zimbabwe." *African Publishing Review* 5, no. 2 (March/April 1996): 11.

2104   Fredericks, G.H., and Z. Mvunelo **"Publication of Books in Indigenous South African Languages and their Availability and Use in Public Libraries."** *South African Journal of Library and Information Science* 69, no. 2 (2003): 133-139.

Presents the findings of a study conducted to investigate the impact of the adoption of the eleven official languages in South Africa and related new democratic policies on the production of books in indigenous languages, as well as the role of public libraries in promoting the use of books written in indigenous languages. The study reveals that, despite the provisions of the new constitution regarding language, it would appear that publishing houses have not made much effort to reduce the predominant status traditionally enjoyed by Afrikaans and English in the South African publishing industry. The findings also show that most libraries have collections published mainly in English and Afrikaans. In addition, it was found that books in indigenous languages made up less than 1% of the collections of most of the responding libraries. The results of the study portray a poor state of publishing in indigenous South African languages, and the authors make a number of recommendations to promote the use of these languages more widely and enhance the profile of indigenous language publishing.

Furniss, Graham **"Documenting Kano 'Market' Literature"** *see* ➜ **Mass market and popular literature publishing** entry **2004**

2105   Gyr-Ukunda, Agnes **Publishing in African Languages Using Editions Bakame as a Model.**

http://www.ibby.org/index.php?id=723 [17/03/08]

Sets out the prerequisites for successful publishing of children's books in national languages based on the model used by Editions Bakame, the first Rwandan publisher to offer children's and youth's literature in Kinyarwanda, the national language understood by all Rwandan. Founded in 1995, after the genocide in 1994, Editions Bakame aimed to give children reading books in Kinyarwanda to help them overcome the horrors of war, by means of appropriate reading based on their culture. However many obstacles remain: distributing networks are still too weak, books are still a luxury object for many Rwandans and the purchasing power of the population is very low, there is no a reading culture and public and school libraries in the rural areas are few.

2106 Hubert, Souad **"Les langues vernaculaires en Afrique Noire Francophone: édition et enseignement."** [Paper presented at] *61st IFLA General Conference, 20-26 August 1995, Istanbul, Turkey.* The Hague: IFLA, Division of Libraries Serving the General Public, Section on Library Services to Multicultural Populations, 1995, 107-119.
Examines attitudes – both by the former colonial rulers and by Africans themselves – towards local languages in francophone Africa, and provides the historical background necessary to understand the present situation [1995] of vernacular languages as a method of teaching and their role in published form. Analyzes publishing and distribution problems of African language material, and describes some current initiatives in Senegal of organizations promoting African language publishing output.

2107 Jones, Bronwen **"Writing and Publishing in Indigenous Languages."** In *Proceedings of the First Annual National Conference on Women in Writing – Beyond 2000,* edited by Tembeka Mbobo, Joyce Siwani, and Charlotte Witbooi. Kwa-Zuma, South Africa: Centre for Cultural and Artistic Expression [PO Box 908, Kwa-Zuma 1868], 2000, 45-47.
Bronwen Jones, a social activist and founder of Ithemba Publishing, describes the difficulties of publishing in mother tongue languages titles in South Africa, including matters such as translation and orthographies, and trying to get African language titles stocked by the major retail chains.

2108 Jung, Ingrid **"Toward Literate Societies: Publishing in Local Languages."** In *Educational Publishing in Global Perspective. Capacity building and trends,* edited by Sobhana Sosale. Washington, DC: The World Bank, 1999, 24-33.
Shorter version, **"Publishing in African Languages in Francophone Africa"**, also published in *African Publishing Review* 9, no. 2 (2000): 12-14.
An analysis of publishing in African languages in four countries of francophone Africa (Burkina Faso, Mali, Niger, and Senegal), where the Deutsche Stiftung für Internationale Entwicklung/German Foundation for International Development (now ➜ **InWent/Capacity Building International (85)**), in cooperation with other agencies, has been developing training programmes for textbook authors to create local capacity in the writing of textbooks for local language teaching. It reports about the main lessons learnt during the execution of the programme. Ingrid Jung argues that the development of societies depends crucially on the access to and the written processing of information, and discusses what this means for local language publishing. She concludes that the present situation in Africa is characterized by a broad gap between what is necessary to contribute to social change and education, and what local book industries offer in the field of local language publications for educational and other purposes. "To satisfy the demand for books and learning

materials in African languages in the long run, it is necessary to contribute to the development of national and regional publishing houses and to the capacity building of all links of the book chain."

2109 Kamwendo, Gregory H. **"The Use of Vernacular Languages in the Malawi Literary Industry."** *Alternation. Journal of the Centre for the Study of Southern African Literature and Languages* 5, no. 1 (1998): 32-38.
Examines the consequences of post-colonial language policies for the Malawian literary industry, and publishing output in African languages, including aspects such as publishers' lack of interest in Malawian creative writing in indigenous languages, and negative attitudes towards writing in indigenous languages.

2110 Kganela, Lesego D. **"The Risk of Producing Books in Indigenous Languages."** In *Changing Lives. Promoting a Reading Culture in Africa. Indaba 2001. Harare, Zimbabwe 4-5 August, 2001,* edited by the Zimbabwe International Book Fair Trust. Harare: Zimbabwe International Book Fair Trust, n.d. [2002], 75-81.
Describes the factors that influence production of materials in African languages, and the risks publishers face producing such materials. Some of the factors identified include size of population, multiple regional variations that exist in indigenous languages, the level of development of indigenous languages and current state of orthography, low levels of literacy of native speakers of particular languages, and government policies.

2111 Khati, T.E., and T.E. Khalanyane **"Publishing in Indigenous Languages in Lesotho."** *African Publishing Review* 8, no. 2 (March/April 1999): 15-16.
A short account of the problems and constraints of publishing in African languages in Lesotho.

2112 Komarek, Kurt **"Publishing in Africa or African Publishing?"** *African Publishing Review* 6, no. 6 (November/December 1997): 1-2.
Challenges African publishers to produce more books in African languages. States that there is a market for written information in African languages, but "it is no easy, low-risk, demand-led market. It is a supply supply-led market, whose capacity has never even been studied."

2113 Macola, Giacomo. **"Historical and Ethnographical Publications in the Vernaculars of Colonial Zambia: Missionary Contribution to the 'Creation of Tribalism'."** *Journal of Religion in Africa* 33, no. 4 (2003): 343-364.
Examines the chronology and attributes of literate ethno-history in Northern Rhodesia (now Zambia). While the earliest published authors were members of missionary societies whose evangelical policies were predisposed towards the Christianization of local chieftaincies, the expansion and Africanization of vernacular historiography from the late 1930s owed much to the intervention of the colonial government in its publishing activities. A survey of their contents shows that

vernacular histories and ethnographies mirrored preconceptions and preoccupations typical of the times of their composition. By placing these texts in the political and economic context of the colony, and by providing new data on their wide circulation among literate Africans, the article contends that published ethnohistories were one of the principal cultural components of the process of crystallization of ethnic identities in the middle and late colonial era.

2114 Maake, Nhlanhla **"Publishing and Perishing: Books, People and Reading in African Languages in South Africa."** In *The Politics of Publishing in South Africa,* edited by Nicholas Evans and Monica Seeber. London: Holger Ehling Publishing and Scotsville, South Africa: University of Natal Press, 2000, 127-159.

Studies the factors that have influenced the writing, production, dissemination, criticism, and overall development of literature in the nine official languages of South Africa. It reviews some of the conditions under which this literature had to survive, the language debates and the status of these languages in the country, publishing conditions, the development of genres and readership, the distribution of the books and their reception, as well as literary prizes for works in African languages. The author suggests a number of strategies that would help to enhance the profile of African language publishing, support and promote writing in African languages, lead to the prescription of African language books at school level, and at the same time would encourage young and adult readership of literary works in indigenous languages.

2115 Mahommed, Alli Andre **An Evaluation of the Nature and State of Published Children's Literature in Indigenous African Languages.** Belleville, South Africa: University of the Western Cape, Department of Library and Information Science, 2000. MBibl thesis. 96 l.

Offers an overview of publishing in indigenous African languages in South Africa and, at the same time, aims to provide an insight into the current [2000] problems experienced by the South African publishing industry.

2116 Mchombu, Kingo **"Why Do African Readers Want Indigenous Publications?"** In *African Scholarly Publishing Essays,* edited by Alois Mlambo. Oxford: African Books Collective Ltd.; Uppsala: Dag Hammarskjöld Foundation; and Oxford: International Network for the Availability of Scientific Publications (INASP), 2006, 113-119.

Sets out the reasons for the need for locally published products in Africa, highlighting the key factors which make it difficult to translate the potential demand to a wide readership. The author examines the publication of indigenous research and scholarship written from an African perspective, recreational and leisure readers, and functional and literacy reading. In his conclusion Mchombu argues that demand for more indigenous publications "has to be preceded by higher awareness and demand for knowledge and information products in general", and that sustainability of publishing and reading, and the need to build, consolidate and expand an African knowledge base capable of addressing African aspirations, requires innovative solutions in the production of locally published materials.

2117 Motimedi, E.K. "**Relevant Reading Materials: Botswana. The Production of Setswana Language Publications in the National Library Service.**" In *Access to Information. Indaba 97.* Harare: Zimbabwe International Book Fair Trust, 1997, 143-150.

As part of the activities the National Library Service of Botswana, through its Inter-Agency Materials Production Committee, publishes and distributes a range of books and pamphlets for newly literates designed to provide those in the rural communities with a variety of readings materials both in Setswana and in simplified English, for both leisure reading and educational purposes. This paper describes the historical background of this initiative, the factors leading to the establishment of the Agency, its terms of reference and structure, the problems encountered by the Committee and their possible solutions, as well as methods of manuscript development, production, and distribution.

Mpe, Phaswane "**Language Policy and African Language Publishing in South Africa**" *see* → **Section 3, Country studies: South Africa** entry **1053**

2118 Mulokozi, M.M. "**Publishing in Kiswahili: A Writer's Perspective.**" In *Publishing in African Languages: Challenges and Prospects*, edited by Philip G. Altbach and Damtew Teferra. Chestnut Hill, MA: Bellagio Publishing Network, Research and Information Center (Bellagio Studies in Publishing, 10), 1999, 11-41.

Discusses the problems and issues of publishing in Kiswahili from the point of view of a creative writer. It provides a historical review of publishing in Kiswahili in Kenya and Tanzania, together with an analysis of the general socio-political context in which it takes place. A final part analyzes the problems of publishing in Kiswahili in terms of authorship, publishing, book distribution and sales, and readership. The author finds that the situation of Kiswahili writers in East Africa is still highly precarious, made worse by the socio-economic context in which publishing takes place—a context replete with financial, infrastructural, cultural, and political obstacles.

2119 Mulokozi, M.M. "**Scholarly Writing and Publishing in African Languages—With Special Emphasis on Kiswahili: Problems and Challenges.**" In *African Scholarly Publishing Essays*, edited by Alois Mlambo. Oxford: African Books Collective Ltd.; Uppsala: Dag Hammarskjöld Foundation; and Oxford: International Network for the Availability of Scientific Publications (INASP), 2006, 104-111.

Scholarly publishing in most African languages is not flourishing, and the author explains some of the reasons why this is the case, and sets out the major constraints that publishers face, including that of a limited audience and hence lack of demand. The position is somewhat different for Kiswahili, spoken by some 80 million people in Africa, and also the official language, or one of the official languages, in several African countries, and therefore offering much greater potential in terms of audience and readership. However, Mulokozi notes that one of the main problems that hinders greater use of Kiswahili in scholarly writing and publishing is closely related to language policies pursued in the different countries that use Kiswahili, and that in some of them Kiswahili's status as an official language is only symbolic. Meantime very few of the existing academic publishers in Africa publish scholarly work in Kiswahili at this time, apart from one or two notable exceptions, such as the publishing output of the Institute of Kiswahili Research at the University of Dar es Salaam. The author offers some suggestions how the picture might be improved, and how current attitudinal problems might be addressed, thus enhancing the status and use of Kiswahili and at the same time likely to lead to greater demand for scholarly materials written in Kiswahili.

2120 Musi, Joyce **"Re-Thinking African Languages Publishing in South Africa: A Publisher's Experience."** In *Proceedings of the First Annual National Conference on Women in Writing – Beyond 2000*, edited by Tembeka Mbobo, Joyce Siwani, and Charlotte Witbooi. Kwa-Zuma, South Africa: Centre for Cultural and Artistic Expression [PO Box 908, Kwa-Zuma 1868], 2000, 43-44.
Joyce Musi, of Heinemann-South Africa, offers a short account of the constraints and challenges of publishing in the indigenous languages of South Africa.

2121 Ndiaye, A. Raphaël **"Langues locales et élaboration de matériels à la base."** *African Environment* 11, no. 41/42 2000): 103-116.
On publishing in mother tongue languages in Senegal. [Not examined]

2122 Newton, Robert C. **"Writing and Publishing in National Languages Today: The Case of the Bamanankan."** *Matatu* no. 17-18 (1997): 315-325.
Examines the problematics and challenges of writing and publishing in national languages, in this case the Bamana language, by two writers from Mali, Ismaila Samba Traoré and Berehima Wulale. It reviews the publishing activities of a number of small publishing houses such as Editions Jamana, a cultural cooperative that became the first independently owned publishing house and distribution company (following the demise of the previously state-run publishing industry), which is committed to the development of national languages. The Direction Nationale de l'Alphabétisation et de la Lingustique Appliqué (DNAFLA) is the principal publisher in Mali of texts designed for general literacy programmes and for those of specific projects, but has been widely criticised for the dryness of texts produced by them, and which largely fail to engage the reader through their own cultural expressions and genres, or the social contexts and activities of their everyday lives.

2123 Ngandu, Freddie **"Publishing for Small Language Groups in a Bilingual Community."** In *Changing Lives. Promoting a Reading Culture in Africa. Indaba 2001. Harare, Zimbabwe 4-5 August, 2001*, edited by the Zimbabwe International Book Fair Trust. Harare: Zimbabwe International Book Fair Trust, n.d. [2002], 87-91.
Also published in *African Publishing Review* 10, no. 4 (2001): 6-11.
Describes the problems and challenges of publishing for small language groups in Cameroon – a country which has 260 mother tongues – focusing on the publishing activities of the Société Internationale de Linguistique (SIL), and a number of other organizations.

2124 Nigerian Book Fair Trust **Publishing in Indigenous Languages. Papers Presented at the Fourth Nigeria International Book Fair, 10-14 May, 2005**. Lagos: Nigerian Book Fair Trust [c/o Literamed Publications Ltd., PMB 21068, Ikeja, Lagos, Nigeria], 2006. 167 pp.
One in a series of collections from the ➔ **Nigerian Book Fair Trust (737)** containing the opening addresses, keynote speeches, and papers presented at the Nigeria International Book Fair, held annually since 2002, each fair focusing on a special topic or topics. The fourth collection focuses on the topic "Publishing in Indigenous Languages" and indigenous knowledge systems. It contains over 20 contributions, including some of those presented at Eastern and Western zones satellite book fair events. (The papers emanating from the workshops held during the regional book fairs are primarily on issues relating to copyright protection and enforcement in Nigeria, rights administration, and the role of reproduction rights organizations.) *Note:* some of the papers in this collection are individually abstracted elsewhere in this bibliography.
Reviews:
The African Book Publishing Record vol. 34, no. 1, 2008

2125 Ntshangase, Dumisani K. **"Publishing in Southern African Languages: History, Challenges and Opportunities."** In *Publishing in African Languages: Challenges and Prospects*, edited by Philip G. Altbach and Damtew Teferra. Chestnut Hill, MA: Bellagio Publishing Network, Research and Information Center (Bellagio Studies in Publishing, 10), 1999, 43-63.
Looks at the challenges and opportunities of publishing in African languages, and provides an analysis of the language situation in Southern Africa, discussing language issues from a non-political boundary perspective. The author believes a regional approach to language issues is far more important than localized efforts. The paper charts the history of writing in African languages from the advent of Christianity in Africa and early writings that reflected a strong Christian flavour; the period from 1910 to the 1940s which saw the emergence of a whole new wave of original works by Africans; the period of the fifties and sixties when many small indigenous publishers were in involved in publishing material in African languages, through to the 1970 to 1990s when publishing in African languages increased very substantially throughout the region. The author thereafter discusses some issues as they relate to the nature and quantity of publishing output in African languages, the major players involved, and the interaction between governments, the private sector, and NGOs in strengthening a publishing infrastructure for publishing in indigenous languages. Ntshangase notes, however, that a huge divide exists between policy, planning, and implementation, with many issues and obstacles still to be resolved, including matters relating to language policies and orthographies for the various languages spoken in the Southern African region. Nonetheless, the author concludes that publishing in African languages is viable, and that "it will continue to flourish once the regional governments create an enabling environment."

2126 Nwankwo, Victor U. **"Publishing in Local Languages in Nigeria: A Publisher's Perspective."** In *Publishing in African Languages: Challenges and Prospects*, edited by Philip G. Altbach and Damtew Teferra. Chestnut Hill,

MA: Bellagio Publishing Network, Research and Information Center (Bellagio Studies in Publishing, 10), 1999, 111-128.
Examines the status of the implementation of Nigeria's national language policy and discusses its effect on publishing in indigenous languages as an essential and sustainable activity for the achievement of permanent literacy. It also offers a number of suggestions for moving its implementation forward, and how the Nigerian government might facilitate investment by publishers in developing new books in indigenous languages, by way of translation subsidies and development support.

2127 Ogechi, Nathan Oyori **"Publishing in Kiswahili and Indigenous Languages for Enhanced Adult Literacy in Kenya."** *African Research & Documentation*, no. 88 (2002): 19-34.
Argues the case for increased publishing of reading materials in Kiswahili, and other indigenous languages, to support and enhance adult education programmes. The author reviews the current state of adult literacy in Kenya, the nature and viability of publishing for adult education, the role of African languages in adult literacy, and recommends measures to be taken to avoid relapse to illiteracy by newly-literates by providing affordable and relevant materials.

2128 Ogechi, Nathan Oyori, and Emily Bosire-Ogechi **"Educational Publishing in African Languages, with a Focus on Swahili in Kenya."** *Nordic Journal of African Studies* 11, no. 2 (2002): 167-184.
Online: http://www.njas.helsinki.fi/ [27/03/08]
Champions the case for more educational publications in Swahili as an appropriate medium for educational and national development. Educational development cannot be achieved without support services such as books in all fields, and in a language that is readily understood by many people. The authors aim to demonstrate that Swahili, the national and co-official language of Kenya, can play an important role in the production of educational materials, and explore the extent of publishing in Swahili and other African languages for various educational levels in Kenya, including children's books, school textbooks, tertiary level texts, special education, adult education and fiction. The authors argue that Kenya stands to gain a great deal if they assign Swahili publishing a larger role, but at the same time caution against downplaying the international significance of English.

2129 Opland, Jeff **"The Publication of A.C. Jordan's Xhosa Novel,** *Ingqumbo yeMinyanya."* *Research in African Literatures* 21, no. 4 (1990): 135-147.
Describes the publication history of Archibald Campbell (A.C.) Jordan's Xhosa novel *Ingqumbo yeMinyanya* (The Wrath of the Ancestors), his most famous work, published by Lovedale Press in South Africa in 1940, and subsequently also published in English.

2130 Orimalade, Oluronke **"Challenges of Marketing Books in Indigenous Languages."** In *Publishing in Indigenous Languages. Papers Presented at the Fourth Nigeria International Book Fair, 10-14 May, 2005.* Lagos:

Nigerian Book Fair Trust [c/o Literamed Publications Ltd., PMB 21068, Ikeja, Lagos, Nigeria], 2006, 18-22.
Shorter version also published as **"A Lesson in Language"** in *Bookmark. News Magazine of the South African Booksellers' Association* 10 (October 2005-March 2006): 27, 34
Offers some suggestions how Nigerian booksellers can market books in the country's numerous indigenous languages, and reviews some the opportunities, challenges and likely obstacles associated with such activities.

2131   Ouane, Adama **"L'écologie de l'apprentissage dans les languages Africaines."** *D+C. Développement et Coopération,* no. 1 (January/February 1997): 14-15.
Describes the complexities of the linguistic situation in Africa and discusses the practical difficulties experienced in trying to promote the use of African languages. Makes a number of recommendations for measures to be taken to facilitate promotion of African languages, and to create an environment favourable for the growth of publishing in national languages.

2132   Peires, Jeffrey **"Lovedale Press: Literature for the Bantu Revisited."** *English in Africa* 7, no.2 (March 1980): 71-85.
Provides an insight into the early work of Lovedale Press in South Africa from 1823 onwards, when Lovedale was the focal point of the literate Christian culture that emerged among the Xhosa in the Eastern Cape region, and which up until the turn of the century concentrated on evangelical and educational texts. Describes the change in the press and its publication policies after R.H.W. Shepherd took charge of its operations in 1929, until his departure in 1950. Contains five case studies of editorial interference culled from the detailed records of the Lovedale Press. Peires contends that while the Lovedale Press undoubtedly published manuscripts in Xhosa which would otherwise never have been published, "the effective monopoly of the Lovedale Press...stifled the development of a meaningful vernacular historiography."

2133   Pugliese, Cristiana **"Kenyan Publishers in Vernacular Languages: Gikuyu, Kikamba and Dholuo."** *Africa* [Rome] 49, no. 2 (1994): 250-59.
Outlines the history of Kenyan publishing in African languages starting with the work of mission presses in the early 20th century, the role of the East African Literature Bureau founded in 1947, through to developments since independence. Describes the activities of three Kenyan publishers producing books in indigenous languages: Gakaara wa Wanjau, David Maillu of Maillu Publishing House, and Asenath Bole Odaga of Lake Publishers.

2134   Reiner, Peter **"Promise and Pitfalls. A Commercial View of Publishing in African Languages."** Windhoek: Peter Reiner, c/o Gamsberg Macmillan Publishers [Email: gmpubl@iafrica.com.na], 2005. 14 pp.
(*Note:* this interesting paper, first presented at an ➔ **ADEA (34)** Regional Conference on Bilingual Education and the Use of Local Languages, held in Windhoek, Namibia, August 3-5, 2005 *see* http://www.adeanet.org/meetings/en_Aug-locallanguages-

2005.htm, is *not* currently available in published format, but may become available online soon on the ADEA Web site; alternatively contact the author at the above email address.)

The position of African languages has been the subject of much debate over the years, especially within the context of what is often referred to as the African Renaissance. Similarly, many have written and spoken at length about how African languages could and should contribute to the development of individual African countries and the upliftment of the continent as a whole. The purpose of this paper, by the Publishing Manager of Gamsberg Macmillan Publishers in Windhoek, is to contribute to this debate not from an academic or purely theoretical point of view, but to provide inputs of a more practical nature, based on the experiences of a company involved in African-languages publishing for well over 25 years now. The author states that Namibia is probably one of Africa's success stories when it comes to publishing in African languages, and one of a select few countries on the continent in which private-sector publishing of African languages is not only viable, but in fact profitable. In this study he seeks to demonstrate that "publishing in African languages is not only possible, but can be conducted as a viable, profitable and sustainable commercial activity. However, it will not necessarily be an easy task to achieve this objective, and there are certain prerequisites that need to be met before any effort has even a moderate chance of succeeding. Also, publishers venturing into this field will have to overcome obstacles during the establishment phase and be prepared to deal with unfavourable conditions and factors as part of their normal publishing routine, as well as to take risks and accept compromise. Ultimately, publishing in African languages must be seen as a long-term investment, and – like any consumer-oriented industry – publishers need to create a market for their products before they can hope to generate profits."

2135 Salawu, Abiodun, ed. **Indigenous Language Media in Africa.** Lagos: Centre for Black and African Arts and Civilisation & Concept Publications, 2006. 398 pp. (distributed by African Books Collective)

A collection of 22 papers on the indigenous language press (and other media) in Cameroon, Kenya, Malawi, Nigeria, Uganda, and Zimbabwe, primarily devoted to the activities of African language newspapers and periodicals. Some papers examine the significant and pioneering role religious publications – both Christian and Islamic – have played in the development of indigenous languages presses in Africa, while others examine some of the socio-political and economic changes that have greatly affected indigenous language media over the years, and have lead to its demise to some extent. (Also included as an Appendix is a paper in Dutch by Honoré Vinck, "Het belang van de periodieke koloniale pers in Afrikaanse talen", which examines the role of the African language press during colonial days in the Belgian Congo)

2136 Seame, G.B. **"Distributing Setswana Literature."** In *Conference on Producing Setswana Literature, National Museum, Gaborone.* Gaborone: Botswana National Cultural Council, 1979, 14-17.

The [then] Director of Library Services describes the activities of the Botswana National Library Service network, and offers some ideas for publishing children's story books and other books in Setswana.

2137 Segbawu, C. Kwami **"Marketing Indigenous Language Books. The Ghana Experience."** In *Millennium Marketplace.* [Proceedings of the ZIBF] *Indaba 2000, Harare, Zimbabwe, 31 July – 1 August 2000.* Harare: Zimbabwe International Book Fair Trust, n.d. [2001], 65-69.
Discusses marketing and selling of books in local languages in Ghana, "and the environment, philosophies and strategies that surround and guide our selling efforts."

2138 Sow, Mamadou Aliou **"African Publishing and National Languages. The West African Experience."** In *Publishing in African Languages: Challenges and Prospects,* edited by Philip G. Altbach and Damtew Teferra. Chestnut Hill, MA: Bellagio Publishing Network, Research and Information Center (Bellagio Studies in Publishing, 10), 1999, 65-74.
Few African countries give "working language" status to the local languages spoken by the majority of the population, and this restricts the scope and usage of these languages for teaching and scientific research, and due to their poor utilitarian value the written resources have had very limited influence. This article discusses the challenges of publishing in African languages in this context, analyzing constraints in writing, publishing and distribution, and the trends in local language publishing in French-speaking West Africa in general and in Guinea in particular. Mamadou Sow argues that while trying to improve the reading and writing abilities of the majority of its citizens, each country should integrate linguistic policy and the effective use of national languages into mainstream national life, especially as it concerns education and administration. "Maintaining and enriching national cultures should also not be separated from development plans; national languages can provide a base to make this possible." He calls for educational reforms that would promote national language use, at least during the first five years of schooling. "Publishing in African languages will advance only if these prerequisites are fulfilled and only if we stop considering national languages as rural dialects."

2139 Sow, Mamadou Aliou **"Publishing in National Languages: Some Key Issues in Guinea."** *African Publishing Review* 6, no. 6 (November/December 1997): 3-4.
Sets out the literate environment and the education sector in Guinea, and describes current initiatives of publishing in national languages. Also reviews the work and objectives of the Group d'Action pour la Promotion de l'Edition en Langues Africaines (GRAPELA; Action Group for the Promotion of Publication in African Languages).

2140 Teferra, Damtew **"The Politics of Multilingual Education and Publishing in Ethiopia."** In *Publishing in African Languages: Challenges and Prospects,* edited by Philip G. Altbach and Damtew Teferra. Chestnut Hill, MA: Bellagio Publishing Network, Research and Information Center (Bellagio Studies in Publishing, 10), 1999, 75-109.
Analyzes the significance of government policies in Ethiopia on education, language, and publishing. In the late 1990's the [then] new government, as part of wide-ranging

social and political changes, introduced a policy of vernacularization of primary education. This extensive study focuses on the implementation of this policy in Ethiopian schools, its impact on education and textbook production, and assesses the pros and cons of implementing a vernacularization policy within the context of education and publishing. The author offers a number of practical proposals for change, for example that the language policy debate ought to be depoliticized, and that widely spoken regional languages should be used for instruction until such time as the other, smaller languages are able to build an effective infrastructure.

2141 Temu, Canute W. **Feasibility Study on the Joint Production of Kiswahili Reading Matter: Eastern and Central Africa - (Mission).** Paris: UNESCO (Doc. FMR/COM/LPE/85/113; RP/1984-1985/III/1.1/Technical report, 1985. 11 pp.
Online: http://unesdoc.unesco.org/images/0006/000643/064354eo.pdf [27/03/08]
The report of a feasibility study investigating possible joint production of reading materials in mother tongues used by more than one country in the Kiswahili-speaking African nations of Eastern and Central Africa, namely Burundi, Kenya, Mozambique, Rwanda, Tanzania, Uganda and Zaire (now Congo Democratic). For each country it reviewed the different types of printed materials available in Kiswahili, determined the number of Kiswahili-speaking persons having reading and writing abilities in this language, identified national needs as regards printed material and the areas in which each country might eventually produce material in Kiswahili within the framework of a sub-regional project for co-production, and evaluated production capacity of public and private printing and publishing houses, as well as the human resources available for implementing the project.

2142 Turquety, Sarah **"L'édition en langues africaines: regards sur le Sénégal.** *Africultures* no. 57 (December 2003): 113-115.
Online:
http://www.africultures.com/index.asp?menu=revue_affiche_article&no=3198&dispo=fr [27/03/08]
A short report about publishing in African languages in Senegal, through government initiatives, private sector publishers, and a number of NGOs, all of whom are experiencing major difficulties in the distribution of their publishing output.

2143 Udoada, M.P. **"Publishing in Minority Languages: Problems and Prospects."** *Ife Psychologia* 6, no. 1 (1998): 154-164.
Examines the problems and prospects of publishing in hundreds of Nigerian minority languages, while reporting that many minority languages are not only disadvantaged with respect to publishing in them, but are also endangered. The author concludes that "the survival and development of publishing in a minority language almost entirely depend on the commitment of its speakers who alone have the inherent emotional and cultural motivation for the preservation of their language."

2144 Uzochukwu, Sam **"The Challenge of Writing Books in Indigenous Languages: The Igbo Experience."** In *Publishing in Indigenous Languages. Papers Presented at the Fourth Nigeria International Book Fair, 10-14 May, 2005.* Lagos: Nigerian Book Fair Trust [c/o Literamed Publications Ltd., PMB 21068, Ikeja, Lagos, Nigeria], 2006, 23-33.

Looks at the role of indigenous languages in cultural preservation. The author pays tribute to the pioneering role of F.C. Ogbalu of Varsity Printing Press and University Publishing Company in Onitsha who published a large number of Igbo texts during the 1960s and 70s, and thereafter examines some of the attitudes of publishers, reluctant to publish material in indigenous languages in view of its perceived limited market; and when they do publish such material are slow in paying royalties. He also reviews common problems faced by authors of indigenous language texts, including policies of SSC/GCE examination bodies, unsettled orthographies (notably Igbo), and the low public regard for local languages in aiding the learning process and cultural preservation. The author makes a number of recommendations how the profile of indigenous language publishing might be enhanced.

2145 Van Schalkwyk, P.B, ed. **Symposium for Promoting the Publication and Use of Literature in the African Languages.** Pretoria: South African Institute for Librarianship and Information Science, Northern Transvaal Branch, 1982. 10 pp. with 2 microfiche with abstracts in pocket

Papers read at a symposium held in Pretoria in 1982. [Not examined]

2146 Vawda, Ayesha Yaqub, and Harry Anthony Patrinos **"Producing Educational Materials in Local Languages: Costs from Guatemala and Senegal."** *International Journal of Educational Development* 19, nos. 4-5 (July 1999): 287-299

Examines production costs of local language materials, budgetary implications of such programmes and cost-saving strategies that have and can be usefully employed in Guatemala and Senegal. Information from Guatemala indicates that investments in bilingual education programs are time-intensive but not prohibitive. The Senegal case study estimates the impact on the unit cost of local language materials if production is expanded to include all potential students in two neighbouring countries, Senegal and The Gambia, which share a common local language. Results indicate that inter-country cooperation is beneficial, especially when factoring in demand constraints in any single country.

2147 Vink, C.M., and J.H. Frylinck **"The Publication and Use of Literature in the African Languages in Southern Africa."** *South African Journal for Library and Information Sciences* 51, nos. 3&4 (1983): 64-66.

Reports on a symposium held for people committed to promoting the publication and use of literature in the African languages of South Africa.

2148 White, Tim **"The Lovedale Press During the Directorship of R.H.W.Shepherd, 1930-1955."** *English in Africa* 19, no. 2 (1992): 69-84.

A critical appraisal of the history and achievements of the Lovedale Press in South Africa under the directorship of R.H.W. Shepherd. (*See also* entry → **2132**)

Woodhall, Maureen, ed. **Cost-Effectiveness of Publishing Educational Materials in African Languages** *see* → **Educational and school book publishing** entry **1886**

2149 Zell, Hans M. **"Problems of Publishing in African Languages."** *West Africa* (16 June 1980): 1071-1073.
Also published in *Bendel Library Journal* 3, no. 1 (June 1980): 20-22.
That the future of African literature belongs to the literature in the African languages is a view that has been voiced by many writers. However, at this time [1980s] "it would seem that a decision to publish creative writing in one of the indigenous African languages will have to be prompted more by nationalistic rather than commercial considerations", primarily because the intended readers of books in indigenous languages are "largely the poor, non-elitist urban communities" who cannot afford to buy books. The author also believes that "the critical issue of the audience has not anywhere been adequately stated, studied, and investigated—for books of the 'right' kind." The article is based on survey conducted among some of the major African publishers who produce material in African languages.

Reading culture and reading promotion

See also
→ **Children's book publishing**
→ **Educational and school book publishing**
→ **Publishing in African languages**

Note: no attempt has been made to provide comprehensive coverage of the wide-ranging topic of reading in Africa, which is strongly linked with aspects such as literacy, language policies, book distribution and, not least, book affordability. Books and articles on teaching reading in schools, or developing reading and writing skills, are not included.

Only a very small number of items in French are included, but for a comprehensive bibliography on attitudes to books and reading, and promoting a reading culture in (primarily francophone) Africa, *see* → Sophie Gazza's **Les habitudes de lecture en Afrique-Sub-Saharienne et les apprentisages traditionels. Bibliographie analytique**, entry **2172**.

2150 Aduda, David **"How Can the Media Promote Reading in Africa?"**
African Publishing Review 10, no. 2 (2001): 1-2.
A journalist from the Nation Media Group in Kenya looks at avenues how newspapers and other independent media in Africa can help to promote reading and

books in Africa through a variety of book-related programmes, news, and reviews, including pages devoted to books in online newspapers.

2151 Adutola, K., and K. Mosuro, eds. **In a Nutshell. Report of the Workshops on Encouraging Free Speech, and Promoting the Reading Culture.** Lagos: Promote the Reading Culture [PO Box 1322, Surulere, Lagos], 1997. 49 pp.
[Not examined]

2152 Aitchison, Jenny; Fiona Bell, and Dot Proctor, eds. **"The Promotion of Reading in South Africa."** [Special issue of] *Innovation. Journal of Appropriate Librarianship and Information Work in Southern Africa*, no. 26 (June 2003).
This special issue of *Innovation* contains eight articles on various aspects of reading and reading promotion in South Africa, including descriptions and analysis of policies, programmes and literacy campaigns, social book clubs, promoting reading in high schools, and community publishing projects. A number of the articles are individually listed and abstracted in this section.

2153 Anon. **"Conférence de Yaoundé sur la promotion de la lecture en Afrique."** *CREPLA Bulletin,* Numéro special/Special issue, June 1980, 3-23.
Contains the papers and extracts and recommendations put before the Conference on the Promotion of Reading in Africa, Yaoundé, June 17 and 20, 1980.

Apeji, E. Adeche **"Readers without Books. A Nigerian Case Study."** *see* ➜ **Section 3, Country studies: Nigeria**, entry **768**

2154 Appiah-Padi, Stephen K. **"Socio-Cultural Obstacles to Reading in Ghana."** *Ghana Book World*, no. 5 (1991): 36-39.
Seeks to provide social and cultural reasons for unfavourable attitudes of Ghanaians towards reading. Concludes that the solitary activity of reading is not in harmony with traditional communal life.

2155 Arua, Arua E., ed. **Reading for All in Africa: Building Communities Where Literacy Thrives.** Newark, DE: International Reading Association, 2003. 178 pp.
Contains the proceedings of the 2nd Pan-African 'Reading for All' conference held in Abuja, Nigeria, in October 2001, convened as a forum for the interchange of ideas about the development of literacy in Africa. The volume includes 40 papers, (selected from more than 150 conference presentations), which are grouped under seven sections or themes. Among papers included are "Towards a Reading Society" (Pai Obanya); "Destroying the Reading Culture-A Way Backwards: A Beginner's Guide to Millennial Ignorance" (Tony Marinho); "Concept of the Children's Reading Tent as Practised in Chitungwiza, Zimbabwe" (Agrena Mushonga); "Portable Libraries as Vehicles for Literacy Development: A Library Service to Pupils and Prisoners in Nigeria" (Virgina W. Dike); "Mobilising Local Resources for Reading Promotion" (Miriam Bamhare); "What are Students in Botswana's High Schools Reading?" (Arua

E. Arua and Mary Lederer); "Cultivating a Reading Culture in a High School in Swaziland" (Virginia Thontea Dlamini); "Developing and Promoting Lifetime Reading Habits in Kenya: The Reading Tent Project and Njoro Reading Facility" (Margaret Makenzi); "Masifunde Sonke: Building a Nation of Readers in South Africa" (Mandla Maseko and Beulah Thumbadoo); "Multipronged Approach to Promoting a Reading Culture: The East African Experience" (James Tumusiime); and "Promoting a Reading Culture" (Pilli Dumea). This useful collection addresses the varied needs to develop materials on best practices in African literacy education and offers a wide range of perspectives. It will be of interest not only to literacy workers, but also to professionals in Africa working in publishing or other areas of the book chain.

2156 Baatjes, Ivor **"Reading in South Africa: An Overview of Policy, Programmes and Campaigns Since 1994."** *Innovation. Journal of Appropriate Librarianship and Information Work in Southern Africa,* no. 26 (June 2003): 1-10. Focuses on the need for a reading policy in South Africa and the significance of reading as integral to the enrichment of human life and its role in national development. Provides an overview of policy developments in relation to reading and their role in creating an enabling policy and legal frame work to support reading. The author also offers some thoughts why literacy campaigns of the last decade have failed, and argues that a national policy is needed that specifically addresses reading.

2157 Baffour-Awuah, Margaret, and Morwadi Pilane "**Village Reading Rooms: Book Outreach in Botswana.**" *School Libraries Worldwide* 7, no.2 (2001): 65- 70.
Village reading rooms (VRRs) are an extension of Botswana's Public Library Service into rural areas. At its beginning in 1986, the VRR project was closely linked to the adult literacy programme of the Department of Non-Formal Education. The VRRs were intended primarily to serve adult literacy learners and newly literate adults. However, because the VRRs had to be housed at first in existing school buildings, school children have become the most active and most numerous users. The villages have claimed the VRRs as an important part of community life.

2158 Bamberger, Richard **Promoting the Reading Habit**. Paris: UNESCO (Reports and Papers in Mass Communication, 72), 1975. 52 pp.
Online: http://unesdoc.unesco.org/images/0001/000134/013412eo.pdf (3.8MB)
A classic study that presents a summary of the findings of international research concerning the reading habit, drawing on sources from all over the world. Surveys studies of reading habits in many parts of the world, the effective teaching of reading, results of research on motivation for reading, factors which influence reading interests, the promotion of developing reading interests, and suggests some avenues for future research.

2159 Bamhare, Miriam **"ZBDC Strategies. Promoting Books and Developing Reading: A Summary."** In *Books and Children. Proceedings of the*

ZIBF Indaba 1998, Harare, Zimbabwe, 1-2 August 1998. Harare: Zimbabwe International Book Fair Trust, 1998, 97-100.

The Director of the ➜ **Zimbabwe Book Development Council (1203)** summarizes her organization's projects and activities in the children's books area, which include a national book week project, a book fund project, a programme of seminars, and the successful Children's Reading Tent, which has been a prominent feature at each year's Zimbabwe International Book Fair.

2160 Bedaysee, S. **Reading for Pleasure.** Quatre Borne, Mauritius: Editions Capucines, 1996. 91 pp.
[Not examined]

2161 Birhanu, T. **"Leisure Reading and Readership of Books: With Reference to Some Literate Groups in Bahir Dar."** *Ethiopian Journal of Languages and Literature*, no. 9 (1999): 89-123.
[Not examined]

2162 Boniface, Sheila **"Book Clubs in South Africa."** *African Research & Documentation*, no. 83 (2000): 95-105.

Reports about the activities of the large variety of book clubs in South Africa, their policies, objectives, focus and the way they operate, covering both commercial book clubs and those that are much more informal and have social concerns at their centre, or those which supply people living in rural areas with books and reading opportunities. Formal and social book clubs have become an established and important part of South Africa's reading and publishing history. "They attract thousands of readers, of all ages, from across the country and continue to fulfil some very important broad functions: distributing books to rural areas, promoting a culture of reading and book buying, and supporting local artists and authors."

2163 Chakava, Henry **"Reading in Africa - Some Obstacles."** *IFLA Journal* 10, no. 4 (1984): 348-356.

Gives a brief overview of the book situation in Africa but focuses mainly on three main obstacles to the development of reading in Africa, namely: language, literacy, and an underdeveloped readership. The author points out that these problems can best be solved within a broad framework of national development policies, for example, a literacy or book awareness campaign would also benefit writing and the book industries. He urges careful preparation of targets and priorities for each country.

2164 Charlewood, Lucy **"Book Preferences, Conceptions of Books and Reading Practices Among Urban Adults with a Basic Level of Literacy."** *African Research & Documentation*, no. 83 (2000): 61-73.

An article extracted from an Honours dissertation of the same title (Department of African Literature, University of the Witwatersrand) on reading practices, literacy, and conceptions about books among adults in the greater Johannesburg area. The study is based on a series of interviews conducted during 1996, and the case studies of two interviews are presented here: "Case study one—The didactic function of books", and "Case study two—Books and migrancy". The study found that the book market in South Africa is still completely dominated by white, educated, middle-class, English-speaking dwellers, and that the general book publishing sector caters almost exclusively to the tastes and concerns of this section of the population. The author believes that the market for easy readers for those who have been educationally disadvantaged is potentially vast and potentially hugely profitable, even given the lower levels of disposable income which are inherent to it. However, this market is not likely to be successfully tapped "if it is viewed through the lens of white, middle-class assumptions about reading culture, or if insufficient time and effort is taken on the part of the providers of easy readers for adults to thoroughly acquaint themselves with their market, with all its particularities, eccentricities, and special, varied needs."

2165 Coly, Gaston-Pierre **"The Government's Role in Reading Promotion."** *African Publishing Review* 10, no. 6 (2001): 5-6.
Examines some of the aspects of the role of African governments in the development of a culture of reading, the strengths and weaknesses of national book policies, and the need for governments to become more pro-active in the promotion of the reading habit.

2166 Coulibaly, Souleymane **Le livre et la lecture dans les familles Burkinabe. Le cas de la ville de Ouagadougou.** Ecole de Bibliothécaires, Archivistes et Documentalistes, Université Cheikh Anta Diop [BP 3252, Dakar, Senegal], 1989. 103 p.
Discusses the role and status of books and reading in families in Burkina Faso, with a special focus on Ouagadougou. Notes the weak infrastructural facilities for the book trade, and the absence of a national book policy that would aid more effective reading development.

2167 D'Almeida, Francisco **"L'Afrique aussi se mobilise pour la lecture."** *Bibliothèques* 8 (April 2002): 30-33
Reports about the activities and reading projects of the Grenoble-based ➔ **Culture et Développement (54)** Association that has been fostering cultural partnerships between communities/institutions in France and their counterparts in African countries. Recent initiatives by the Association in Togo, the Côte d'Ivoire and Mali have led to concrete projects for reading promotion, mobile libraries and resource centres, and for audio libraries in semi-literate rural areas.

2168 Danset, F. **"Public Reading in French-speaking Africa."** *International Library Review* 21, no. 2 (1989): 245-248.
Examines reading habits in francophone Africa, with an emphasis on the situation in Mali and Côte d'Ivoire.

2169 Djoleto, S.A. Amu **"Conference on the Promotion of Reading in Africa Held at the Regional Centre for Book Promotion in Africa South of**

the Sahara (CREPLA) in Yaoundé, Cameroon, from June 17 to 20, 1980."
Ghana Book World, no. 3 (1982): 33-37.
A report about the above conference, and suggests a range of strategies for the
promotion of reading in Africa.

2170 Ezeigbo, Theodora Akachi **"The Dynamics of Literary Response:
Students as Readers of African Women's Writing."** *African Research &
Documentation*, no. 83 (2000): 37-47.
Discusses some of the factors that militate against the development of a reading
culture in Nigerian society, focusing on the reading and teaching of African women's
writing in order to highlight the multiple and diverse groups of readers whose
sensibilities are polarized and affected by gender, age, class and religion. It is based
on the author's classroom interactions with students at the English Department at the
University of Lagos, and from discussions, essays, questionnaires and assignments
administered to students.

2171 Furlonger, David, ed. **New Chapters: 10 Years of Rally To Read.**
Durban, South Africa, McCarthy Ltd. [203 Northridge Road, Morningside],
and Ormonde, South Africa, Read Educational Trust, 2007. 156 pp.
Rally To Read is a joint venture between the South African newspaper *The Financial
Mail*, McCarthy Motor Holdings, and the ➔ **READ Educational Trust (946).**
Annually, during the weekends in May, convoys of off-road vehicles depart from
main cities across the country to deliver portable libraries and reading materials to
some of the country's most neglected schools. This is an account of 10 years of its
activities.

2172 Gazza, Sophia **Les habitudes de lecture en Afrique-Sub-Saharienne
et les apprentisages traditionels. Bibliographie analytique.** London:
Association for the Development of Education in Africa (ADEA), Working
Group on Books and Learning Materials (Perspectives on African Book
Development, 4), 1997. 64 pp. (distributed by African Books Collective Ltd.,
Oxford)
This study and bibliography addresses African attitudes to the book, the reading
habit, and the politics of promoting a reading culture. The bibliography provides
details of 218 literature references, most of them in French, but also including a good
number of articles and other documents in English. A fairly full descriptive
annotation is provided for each entry.

2173 Gibbe, A.K. **"What Tanzanian Publishers Have Done for Readers."**
In *Changing Lives. Promoting a reading culture in Africa. Indaba 2001. Harare,
Zimbabwe 4-5 August, 2001*, edited by the Zimbabwe International Book Fair
Trust. Harare: Zimbabwe International Book Fair Trust, n.d. [2002], 117-123.
A brief overview of publishing activities in Tanzania, the nature of readership in the
country, and what publishers have done to promote reading.

2174 Greaney, Vincent **Promoting Reading in Developing Countries**. Newark, DE: International Reading Association, 1996. 225 pp.
Describes the many obstacles involved with literacy promotion in the developing nations of Africa, Asia, and South America. The authors of the 10 articles in this collection share their knowledge and experience of literacy promotion in the developing world, including the challenges faced by those who publish, print, and distribute reading materials with limited support and resources. The articles also offer suggestions and possible solutions for increasing the developing world's access to quality indigenous reading materials. Among papers included are: "Reading in Developing Countries: Problems and Issues" (Vincent Greaney); "Developing Local Publishing Capacity for Children's Literature" (Tony Read); "Promoting Children's Book Publishing in Anglophone Africa" (Scott Walter); and "Donated Book Programs: An Interim Measure" (Rosamaria Durand and Suzanne M. Deehy).

Griswold, Wendy **Bearing Witness. Readers, Writers, and the Novel in Nigeria** *see* ➜ **Authors and publishers/Publishing of African writers and African literature**, entry **1339**

2175 Gueye, Seydou **"Qui lit quoi en Côte d'Ivoire."** *Notre Librairie. Revue du Livre Afrique Noire, Maghreb, Caraïbes, Océan Indien. Littérature de Côte d'Ivoire: 2. Ecrire aujourd'hui,* no. 87 (April-June 1987): 113-114.
Discusses who reads what in Côte d'Ivoire, with an examination of oral traditions, the role of school and public libraries, why some schools are without books, and ends with a discussion on the reading habit.

2176 Hanson, Ben J. **"We Need a New Revolution."** *Book Power*, no. 1 (1994): 3-6.
Argues that the promotion of the reading habit in Africa needs some rethinking and radical action.

2177 Hanson, Ben J. **"Encouraging Children to Read."** *Book Power*, no. 2 (1994): 30-31.
Offers some suggestions how to promote the reading habit among children in Zimbabwe.

2178 Ike, Chukwuemeka **"Structures to Promote a Reading Culture: Nigeria."** In *Books and Children. Proceedings of the ZIBF Indaba 1998, Harare, Zimbabwe, 1-2 August 1998.* Harare: Zimbabwe International Book Fair Trust, 1998, 101-107.
Discusses the state of reading development in Nigeria, structures for promoting the reading habit, and the role, activities, and projects of the ➜ **Nigerian Book Foundation (738)** in promoting a reading culture in the country. Deplores the lack of adequate government funding for reading promotion in the country, and which means that the sustainability of most projects is dependent on outside donor support.

2179 Ike, Chukwuemeka **"Reading Promotion in Nigeria."** *African Publishing Review* 7, no. 6 (November/December 1998): 1-3
A spirited rebuttal of the often heard statement – "uttered and accepted as an incontrovertible truth" – that Nigeria does not have a reading culture. Chukwuemeka Ike, a prominent Nigerian writer and the Director of the ➔ **Nigerian Book Foundation (738),** argues that "there is nothing physiological or racial in the low level of book readership in Nigeria today." Instead, the low readership level is attributable to two major factors: the disappointing level of basic literacy throughout the country, and the absence of appropriate and relevant books and other reading materials for the majority of the Nigerian population. "Little conscious effort is made by government, publishers, or authors to ascertain and provide for needs of the children, adolescents, and adults of all ages and both sexes outside the formal education system." The author reviews some initiatives to promote the reading habit, reading promotion programmes, and the activities of the Nigerian Book Foundation.

2180 Irvine, Mark **"A Kind of Vision. The Story of READ Educational Trust."** *Optima* 43, no. 2 (July 1997): 52-58.
Illustrated with colour photographs, this article tells the story of the ➔ **READ Educational Trust (946)** an NGO established in 1979. READ aims to stimulate a culture of learning, and promote reading through the systematic introduction into locals schools of the best books, many developed by READ itself, together with providing encouragement for learner-centred teaching methods. Financially supported by a number of foundations and South African companies both large and small, READ works closely with teachers and communities in 13 different regions in South Africa, on more than 3,000 learning projects and in some 2,000 schools. It operates a Box Library system that consists of large, brightly painted wooden packing cases housing mini-libraries of about 60 books each, which are interchangeable between classes of the same group. Additionally it provides reading packages to colleges of education, libraries and community education programmes.

2181 Jam, Z. **"Promoting Reading Among Children in Nigeria."** *African Journal of Library, Archives & Information Science* 6, no. 2 (October 1996): 107-112.
Suggests what teachers and librarians ought to do to encourage children to read, and that this reading should focus on three principal areas: the child's growth, development and needs; the child's learning processes; and the child's learning situation both at home and at school and in the wider society. Also urges for more effective and more positive government support for the provision of libraries in primary and secondary schools.

2182 Kevane, Michael, and Alain Joseph Sissao **"The Cost of Getting Books Read in Rural Africa: Estimates from a Survey of Library Use in Burkina Faso."** *World Libraries* 14, no. 2 (Fall 2004).
Online: http://www.worlib.org/vol14no2/kevane_v14n2.shtml [21/03/08]
This paper aims to answer a simple question: What is the cost of generating greater reading by establishing small village libraries in rural Africa? The answer, the authors say, is $0.74 per book read. The main body of this paper consists of an

analysis of results from a survey of villages in Burkina Faso, four with libraries and four without. Estimates of the impact of libraries on reading in these eight villages, and the costs of running libraries, enable the authors to suggest that the cost of getting an extra book read a year varies from $0.74 to $1.30, according to the size of the school in the village, and the cost of an extra school year equivalent likewise varies from $43.42 to $75.98 per year. These costs are comparable to the costs of increasing schooling, and suggest the desirability of more careful assessment of the choice between schooling and book availability.

2183 Leach, Athol, and Jennifer Verbeek **"The Reading Habits of Adults in Anglophone Sub-Saharan Africa: A Historical Overview."** *African Journal of Library, Archives & Information Science* 3, no. 2 (October 1993) 95-105.
A historical overview of reading habits in anglophone sub-Saharan Africa, challenging the generalized thesis that 'Africans don't read' from a historical perspective, and finds this thesis to be untrue. Argues that reading has always taken place, albeit under certain constraints.

2184 Leach, Athol; Christine Stilwell, and Jennifer Verbeek **"The Reading of Black South Africans: An Historical Review"**. *African Journal of Library, Archives and Information Science* 4, no. 2 (1994): 1-13.
Examines reading habits of black South Africans from a historical perspective and from the earliest colonial times. Describes the effects of colonial policies of segregation, and Nationalist legislated apartheid, on reading and literacy; discusses publishing of books in African languages, and reports about new initiatives which aim to alleviate the lack of access to reading material through improved library services.

2185 Lebotsa, M.M. **"Readership Situation in Lesotho."** *Lesotho Books and Libraries* 3 (1982-3): 37-49.
[Not examined]

2186 Liyong, Taban Lo **"Pass-Time Reading is a Must for Any Society."** *The Kenya Bookseller* 4, no. 2 (1992): 27-28.
Ugandan writer Taban lo Liying advocates that African writers and publishers should produce a new type of African popular novels, aimed at the mass markets.

2187 Machet, Myrna; Sll Olën, and A. Chamberlain, eds. **Young People's Reading in South Africa: A Pilot Project**. Pretoria: Department of Information Science, Faculty of Arts, University of South Africa [PO Box 392, UNISA 0003], 2001. 165 pp.
This survey and report is the result of a pilot project and survey of the reading interests and information use of South African children and young adults. It was carried out in primary and secondary schools in Pretoria, and provides insight into children and young adult's reading interests and information usage. The project surveyed a representative sample of over two thousand learners in the age group 10 to 16 of South African learners from Grades 5 to 10 by means of a detailed

questionnaire. The survey focuses on identifying why and how young people in South Africa choose books (and other texts such as comics and magazines), as understanding this process may help those involved in writing, publishing and providing texts, from comics to novels and electronic publications. The survey also tried to find ways of identifying what kind of material is most suitable for different types of readers. It was one of the goals of the study to provide a better understanding of the relationship between reading and attitudes to a range of topical social issues such as AIDS and pregnancy; to examine the ways in which children and young adults encounter and choose what to read; to provide information about the reading habits and information usage of children and young adults of different age, sex, class, ethnic background, geographical location and educational sector; and to study the influence and effect on reading of new media such as electronic texts.

2188 Machet, Myrna **"Who Reads What? Fiction Reading by Young People in South Africa."** *Innovation. Journal of Appropriate Librarianship and Information Work in Southern Africa*, no. 26 (June 2003): 20-28.
Reports on the key findings of a survey conducted by the ➔ **Children's Literature Research Unit (935)** at the University of South Africa into young people's fiction interests in an urban area of South Africa (and *see also* entry ➔ **2187** above). The author argues that in fostering the reading habit in children it is essential that they are provided with books that they enjoy reading, and that will meet their needs, and that it is impossible to do so without accurate knowledge of what children and young people want to read; and that more surveys of reading interests are needed in South Africa to establish children's reading interests.

2189 Magara, Elisam, and Charles Batambuze **"Towards a Reading Culture for Uganda"** *African Journal of Library, Archives and Information Science* 15, no. 1 (2005): 35-42.
Discusses the efforts undertaken by the Uganda Library Association in the promotion of a reading culture in Uganda and explores possible strategies to build a culture of reading for life-long learning. Qualitative data were collected through reading camps and consultative meetings with both teachers and librarians. The paper stresses the need for promoting a reading culture in Uganda by providing networking and strategic alliances among the stakeholders, including publishers.

2190 Mammah, Richard **"Encouraging Reading in Nigeria—The Synergy Story."** *Bellagio Publishing Network Newsletter*, no. 26-27 (November 2000): 15-16.
Online: http://www.bellagiopublishingnetwork.com/newsletter26-27/mammah.htm [28/03/08]
The author is the Project Director of the Lagos-based ➔ **Synergy Educational Nigeria (742)**, a Nigerian book promotional body that organizes book fairs, conferences, touring book exhibits, and a variety of reading promotional projects and events. Here he reports about some of their recent activities.

2191 Makenzie, Margaret **Reaching Out to the Less Advantaged: Reading Tents in Kenya.**
http://www.ifla.org/IV/ifla70/papers/081e-Makenzi.pdf [28/03/08]
A paper presented to the 70th ➔ **IFLA (74)** General Conference and Council in 2004. Mobile libraries have been defined as portable libraries that travel from place to place promoting reading and the development of literacy, particularly in the rural and urban poor communities. Their main objective is to promote reading with the aim to develop life long reading skills and culture and to encourage literacy. Apart from the mobile reading tents, other types of mobile libraries that have been used in Kenya include motor vehicles, bicycles, donkeys and camel mobile libraries. This paper discusses the mobile reading tent approach as an effective outreach tool in the promotion and development of literacy and reading skills.

2192 Maseko, Mandla **"The Year of the Reader – The South African Campaign."** In *Changing Lives. Promoting a reading culture in Africa. Indaba 2001. Harare, Zimbabwe 4-5 August, 2001,* edited by the Zimbabwe International Book Fair Trust. Harare: Zimbabwe International Book Fair Trust, n.d. [2002], 109-116.
Reports about an innovative national reading campaign in South Africa, *Masifunde Sonke.*

2193 Mashishi, Thapelo **"The Storage Place of Tradition: The Reading Experiences of Black Adults in African Languages."** *African Research & Documentation,* no. 83 (2000): 75-84.
Tries to debunk some of the often stated, blunt assumptions and generalizations about reading cultures in black communities, for example that blacks inhabit an 'oral' culture while whites live in a 'literate' one, "which overlooks centuries of interaction of oral and written forms in South Africa and the fact that there is no longer anything like a 'pure' oral culture." The author's research is focusing on a group of adults involved in a parent/child reading club in South Africa, who enjoy reading in African languages. By describing the complex detail and nuance of their reading worlds, the article "seeks to problematize the commonsensical and often stereotypical ideas which currently dominate discussion on leisure reading African languages."

2194 Mbae, J.G. **"Kenya, a Reading Nation?"** *Wajibu* 19, no. 1, (April/May 2004): 13-17.
[Not examined]

2195 McCartney, Murray **"First Sell the Idea of Books."** *Book Power,* no. 2 (1994): 20-22.
A response to Hanson (*see* ➔ **2176** above). Suggests that his arguments "hang in a mist of nostalgia and optimism which doesn't serve his cause particularly well." Argues that what needs to be sold more aggressively than the books themselves is the idea of books, and of that of reading.

2196 Milliken, Phoebe **"How to Make Children Sit Quietly for Long Periods of Time: Lessons from the Children's Reading Tent at the Zimbabwe International Book Fair."** *African Publishing Review* 5, no. 6 (November/December 1996): 10-11.

Reports about reactions by children to activities and readings taking place at a reading tent during the Zimbabwe International Book Fair. The author found that most children preferred to read the glossier imported books with plentiful illustrations, rather than locally-produced children's books, the vast majority of which were easy readers with rather narrow appeal. Urges local publishers to become more committed to the children's market by allocating more resources to the production of creative texts and picture-story books that are visually appealing.

2197 Mini, T. **"Reading Habits and Library Use by Blacks in Edendale."** *Innovation*, no. 1 (1990): 18-31.

Presents the results of a study that was designed to discover whether and what type of books black people in the Edenvale Valley (South Africa) read.

2198 Moyana, Rosemary **Reading Literature at Junior Secondary Level in Zimbabwe.** Harare: University of Zimbabwe Publications, 2000. 193 pp.

This book is part of a study undertaken between 1989 and 1992 by the International Association for the Evaluation of Educational Achievement's Reading Literacy Research Study (*see* http://www.iea.nl/reading_literacy.html), which sampled 31 countries worldwide, including three in Africa (Botswana, Nigeria and Zimbabwe.) It seeks to discover what the reading literacy levels, and reading habits, are at junior secondary schools in Zimbabwe, and to analyze the reasons for the success or failure at different schools. The author also studied the qualifications, teaching methods and length of teaching experience of teachers, together with their personal reading habits, thus providing an insightful appraisal of the current [1990s] situation. While – given the poverty levels at individual and national level – the picture looks grim, the author ends on a more positive note by offering a range of detailed recommendations to improving literacy standards, by making more effective use of existing resources rather than requiring huge increases in educational budgets.

2199 Mulindwa, Gertrude Kayaga **Can Reading Research in Africa be Done in Isolation? The Influence of Literacy, Education, Publishing and the Book Industry on Reading in Africa.**

http://www.ifla.org/IV/ifla67/papers/179-113e.pdf [28/03/08]

A paper presented at the 67th ➜ **IFLA (74)** Council and General Conference, August 2001. The author asserts that research on reading is so heavily intertwined with research on literacy, language policy, publishing, book distribution, and book affordability and available, that it is unwise to undertake research without linking it to these related components; and that any research should therefore cover all the different issues that influence and affect reading and the development of a reading culture.

2200 Myambo, Mmashikwane **"'Sometimes Reading Can be Your Friend': Black Professional South African Women Readers."** *African Research & Documentation*, no. 83 (2000): 85-93.
Challenges stereotypical views such as "Black people don't read books" – as expressed, for example, by South African writer Zakes Mda writing in a popular South African newspaper – which the author believes are "replete with generalization and based on unexamined assumption." Instead, the article seeks to move in a different direction, and "rather than assuming that hardly anybody reads, it locates a group of passionate readers and attempts to delineate their views." The group concerned is a small cluster of black professional women (who mainly read romances), and this article strives to give a detailed insight into their reading worlds, obtained through a series of in-depth interviews.

2201 Nuttall, Sarah **"Reading in the Lives and Writing of Black South African Women."** *Journal of Southern African Studies* 20, no. 1 (March 1994): 85-98.
Black South African women writers in South Africa have generally written for foreign audiences and this raises questions about black South African women readers, who are unlikely to be reading many of these texts. Taking this as a starting point, this article discusses interviews the author has conducted with black South African women readers about their reading lives. The interviews "focus as much on reading as an 'act' in women's lives as on the interpretation of texts." Although the main focus of the article is on women readers, texts by black women writers, and specifically the portrayal of readers within them, are also briefly discussed.

Nwankwo, Victor U. **"Readers without Books: A Nigerian Publisher's Response"** *see* ➜ **Section 3, Country studies: Nigeria,** entry **824**

2202 Nweke, Ken M.C. **"Promoting the Reading Habit among the Literate in Nigeria."** *Reading Teacher* 40, no. 7 (March 1987): 632-638.
Describes efforts to promote the desire to read and the availability of materials for Nigerians who have already been introduced to reading.

2203 Nwokolo, Chuma **"From Road Shows to Book Fairs: Reading is Fun."** *African Publishing Review* 10, no. 2 (2001): 3.
Describes the work and activities of ➜ **Synergy International Nigeria (742)** in promoting reading in Nigeria.

2204 Okediran, Wale **"Nigeria Reads."** *BookLinks*, no., 7 (August 2007): 10-11.
Online:
http://www.bookaid.org/resources/downloads/booklinks/BookLinks_7.pdf [28/03/08]
Wale Okediran shares his experiences of working to promote a culture of reading in Nigeria. He sets out the reasons for the poor reading culture in the country and describes the "Nigeria Reads Project", a public-private initiative of the ➜

Association of Nigerian Authors (732), the Abuja Library Society, the Rainbow Book Club, and the Federal Ministry of Education, which aims to resuscitate a reading culture through practical, cost-effective means, and getting Nigerians to read for leisure and self- development.

2205 Okoro, C.C., and N.A. Azubogu **"Bibliotherapy: A Tool for Improving Reading Culture among Nigerian Children."** *The Information Technologist* 4, no. 1 (2007): 81-88.
[Not examined]

2206 Omotoso, Kole **Readership Survey Mainly of Students in Langa, Guguletu and Khayelitsha.** Bellville, South Africa: Department of English, University of the Western Cape. 1993. 32 pp. [+ survey pages]
A survey of the reading habits of black students in South Africa, undertaken by the Nigerian writer Kole Omotoso, now resident in South Africa. Gives details of the survey procedure, an analysis and comments on the findings that identify specific problem areas, together with a series of recommendations resulting from the survey.

2207 Omotoso, Kole **"Why do we Read?"** *West Africa*, no. 4270 (9-15 April 2001): 38-39.
A talk given by the Nigerian writer and academic Kole Omotoso at a seminar held during the London International Book Fair in March 2001. The author examines the motivation for reading in an African context, drawing on his own experience. He believes that "we need to extend the practices of our oral tradition into the practices of our written tradition, and that we need to publish more and more in African languages, both of which are necessary if we are to truly encourage reading in African countries."

2208 Osanyin, Bode **"Cultivating a Reading Public - A Way to Nigerian Identity."** *Nigeria Magazine* 57, no. 3/4 (1989): 68-75.
[Not examined]

2209 Pawlitzky, Christine **High Reputation - Low Priority? Reading Habits in Multilingual Kenya.** Hamburg: Universität Hamburg, 2005. PhD dissertation. 356 pp.
Online: http://deposit.ddb.de/cgi-bin/dokserv?idn=977780600&dok_var=d1&dok_ext=pdf&filename=977780600.pdf [28/03/08]
This substantial thesis – supported by a very extensive range of tables and appendices – explores voluntary reading habits in the multilingual environment of Kenya. Designed as a case study, it focuses on the social image of reading, the functions of reading, the factors impacting on reading habits, and the language use in reading among members of the ethnolinguistic Kikuyu and Luo communities in Nyeri District (Central Kenya) and Kisumu District (Western Kenya). By taking a reader-oriented perspective the study aims to add a new dimension to the discussion

on the status of reading in the Kenyan context, which has thus far been mainly debated from the point of view of publishers.

2210   Popoola, Dimeji; Buki Adesanya, and Lolese Adamolekun **"Nigeria: Not Yet a Reading Public."** *Books* 1, no. 3 (1988): 5-8.
Probes into reading habits and the nature of the reading public in Nigeria, the existence of a reading tradition, and asks whether the acquisition of knowledge through books is fully appreciated.

Print Industries Cluster Council **National Survey into the Reading Book Reading Behaviour of Adult South Africans** *see* ➜ **Section 3, Country studies: South Africa** entry **1077**.

Print Industries Cluster Council **Project Book Worm – Final Report. National Survey into the Reading and Book Reading Behaviour of Adult South Africa** *see* ➜ **Section 3, Country studies: South Africa** entry **1078**

2211   Radebe, Thuli **"Reading Interests of Zulu-speaking Standard Two Children in Pietermaritzburg."** *South African Journal of Library and Information Science* 63, no. 4 (December 1995): 161-172
A study conducted in response to the need, expressed by parents, teachers, information workers, and publishers, for information and guidance regarding the reading interests of black children in South Africa. A sample of children's books was selected and presented to a group of children to test their interests. The study found that children did not necessarily prefer settings and situations which were familiar to their own circumstances; they did not necessarily select books which were written in an African language (i.e. Zulu); reading emerged as an individual matter regardless of ethnicity or race; and children's preferences had no significant relationship to the ethnic origin of the story.

2212   Reece, Jane **"Debate: Zimbabweans do not Read: Whose Fault is It?"** *Book Power*, no. 1 (1994): 13-17.
A report about a debate between publishers, booksellers, writers, and teachers, about the reading habit (or the lack of it) of Zimbabweans, and the need for more effective approaches, and more innovative campaigns, to promote a reading culture.

2213   Rosenberg, Diana, ed. **Reader Development and Reading Promotion: Recent Experiences from Seven Countries in Africa.**
Oxford: International Network for the Availability of Scientific Publications (INASP), 2003. 86 pp.
Online:
http://www.inasp.info/file/359/reader-development-and-reading-promotion-recent-experiences-from-seven-countries-in-africa.html
(download by sections) [30/04/08]

http://www.inasp.info/uploaded/documents/Reader%20Development%2
0for%20website.pdf (download complete document) [30/04/08]
The result of a workshop held during the Standing Conference of Eastern, Central
and Southern Africa Librarians (SCESAL) held in Johannesburg in April 2002, this
volume reviews current reader development activities by public libraries in different
regions of Africa. It includes accounts and case studies by contributors from Ghana,
Kenya, Nigeria, South Africa, Tanzania, Uganda and Zambia, covering
predominantly work with children, but with three papers devoted to adult reader
development. An introduction provides a summary of the papers, and reviews
factors such as availability and accessibility of relevant books, the importance of
building partnerships with other interested sectors, aspects of training, monitoring
and evaluation, and the need for the establishment of reader development policies.

Rosenberg, Diana, ed. **Books for Schools: Improving Access to
Supplementary Reading Materials in Africa** *see* → **Educational and school
book publishing** entry **1884**

2214 Sack, Mathias **"Le Camerounais lit-il?"** *CREPLA Bulletin
d'Informations*, no. 9 (August 1984): 18-20.
Reflects on the reading habits of Cameroonians.

2215 Sagna, R. **"Popular Reading in Francophone Sub-Saharan Africa."** In
*Proceedings of the Seminar on Information Provision to Rural Communities in
Africa, held in Gaborone, Botswana, 22-25 June, 1994,* edited by Eve Johansson.
Gaborone: Botswana National Library Services; and Uppsala: Department of
Non-Formal Education, Uppsala University Library, 1995, 17-20.
Discusses the role and promotion of popular reading in francophone Africa through
the establishment of national networks for reading in urban, semi-rural and rural
communities. Focuses on the role played by the French government's Centre de
Lecture et d'Animation Culturelle (CLAC) – the libraries and cultural centres
established in many francophone African countries – and its schemes and
experiments. (*See also* http://planete.francophonie.org/images/clac.htm). CLAC is
part of the → **Organisation Internationale de la Francophonie/OIF (101).**

2216 Sarjant, Robert **Developing Best Practice in Reading Tents in East
Africa.**
http://www.ifla.org/IV/ifla71/papers/137e-Sarjant.pdf [28/03/08]
A paper presented to the 71st → **IFLA 74)** General Conference and Council in 2005.
The UK book charity → **Book Aid International (38)** and the → **East African Book
Development Association /EABDA (13)** are working in partnership to establish best
practice in running reading tents in East Africa. The aim of the tents, which have been
running since 1997, is to promote reading to school pupils and the wider community.
They are organized by the Book Development Councils of Kenya, Uganda and
Tanzania under the EABDA umbrella. This paper uses the IFLA Reading Section's
Guidelines for Library-based Literacy Programs: Some Practical Suggestions as a framework
to look at the strengths and weaknesses of this important initiative.

2217 Serie, R.T. **"Un exemple de recherche sur les pratiques de lecture des etudiants Abidjanais."** *Africa Media Review* 7, no. 1 (1993): 73-85.
Describes the reading habits of students in Abidjan.

2218 Shaffe, Hyeladzira A.B. **"On Books and Our Reading Culture: Are we Ruined Forever?"** *ANA Review* 6, no. 8 (October 1991): 35, 22.
Comments on various aspects of the Nigerian literary scene and the reading culture in the country, including the calibre of entries for literary prizes, the proliferation of pulp fiction, the quality of writing in English, as well as the allegedly iniquitous behaviour of some Nigerian publishers and the poor quality of print and paper.

2219 Sisulu, Elinor **The Culture of Reading and the Book Chain: How do we Achieve a Quantum Leap?**
http://www.nlsa.ac.za/NLSA/News/publications/culture-of-reading [28/03/08]
An eloquent keynote address presented by Elinor Sisulu – winner of the 2003 ➔ **Noma Award for Publishing in Africa (98)** – at a Symposium on the Cost of a Culture of Reading, held at the National Library of South Africa in September 2004. The absence of a culture of reading is a major concern not only in South African society but for the whole of the Southern African region. The author proposes a vision of building a sustainable culture of reading, and examines the compelling reasons why South Africans should inspire to such a vision. She examines the successes and failures of the Masifunde Sonke Campaign, one of the most ambitious reading promotion campaign undertaken in South Africa in recent years, and what can be learnt from it. Elinor Sisulu pays tribute to the sponsors of the Noma Award and the IBBY-Ashai Award (both Japanese-sponsored awards), and says "I think it is a sad reflection on the literary and publishing communities of this continent, African governments and wealthy individuals, that we are unable to mobilize the resources to establish literary awards, organize literary exhibitions and indeed to do more to build and strengthen the publishing industry in Africa." She bemoans the fact that the potential of the book development and publishing sector in South Africa, despite a favourable policy environment, has largely remained unfulfilled. "Lack of investment, resources and capacity in the sector has meant that many of our wonderful plans to promote a vibrant book industry and library system cannot be realized. I sometimes wonder why it is that in a country in which the president and most members of cabinet are bibliophiles, library budgets in real terms have actually fallen in this decade of our democracy." Cutbacks in library purchases have also had a negative effect on African-language publishing because black communities cannot afford to buy books in volume, and even those who can afford it will not find bookshops willing to stock books in African languages: "it is the libraries that are the biggest purchasers of African language titles. Black communities are doubly deprived if existing libraries cannot stock up on the required volumes of books in African languages and there are not even libraries in the townships." In her conclusion the author suggests that "perhaps in our lobbying and advocacy on reading promotion and book development we have focused entirely on the educational and cultural benefits of reading and not enough on the economic value", and goes to say "we need to develop a bold vision that will convince those who

control the national purse that South Africa has the potential to become a major player in global publishing. Our vision should demonstrate that the development of a flourishing publishing industry is not only good business sense, it is a prerequisite to realizing the dream of an African renaissance."

2220 Southern Africa Book Development Education Trust **The Business of Reading**.
http://www.sabdet.com/seminarseries.htm#top [28/03/08]
Report of a seminar hosted by the➔ **Southern African Book Development Education Trust (113)** held during the London International Book Fair in March 2001. The seminar included presentations under two major topics 'Books and Libraries' and 'Press, Media and the Internet'. The material offered here includes summaries of papers presented, and transcripts of the discussion that ensued after each presentation. The seminar attracted participants from several African countries, including booksellers, publishers, writers, and journalists.

2221 Southern Africa Book Development Education Trust **Reading Africa: Readers, Libraries and African Publishing**
http://www.sabdet.com/RAOxB05.htm#Panel [28/03/08]
Report of a one-day conference hosted by the ➔ **Southern African Book Development Education Trust/SABDET (113)** and the Oxford International Centre for Publishing Studies in October 2004. "Reading Africa" was a nationwide initiative by SABDET to raise awareness in the United Kingdom of African writing and publishing and to promote reading of African books. The conference brought together a number of distinguished African writers and publishers, and representatives of organizations promoting the initiative in the UK. The material offered here includes summaries of papers presented, and transcripts of the discussion that ensued after each presentation. It also includes the keynote address presented at the conference by Véronique Tadjo, the well-known poet, author of children's books, illustrator, and painter from the Côte d'Ivoire.

2222 Staiger, Ralph C. **Roads to Reading.** Paris: UNESCO (Books about Books series), 1979. 141 pp.
This classic study provides information about reading and the promotion of the reading habit in all parts of the world, including developing countries. Includes two valuable bibliographies: "Motivation for reading: an international bibliography", pp. 99-128, and "Select bibliography on reading motivation", pp. 129-141. Reports on a variety of practical methods used in different parts of the world in the promoting of the reading habit.

2223 Staiger, Ralph C., and C. Casey **Planning and Organising Reading Campaigns: A Guide for Developing Countries.** Paris: UNESCO, 1983. 75 pp.
A companion volume to Ralph Staiger's **Roads to Reading** (*see* entry ➔ **2222** above), now inevitably rather dated, but still provides helpful guidelines and strategies for planning successful reading campaigns.

2224   Standing Conference on Library Materials on Africa (SCOLMA) and the African Studies Centre, Cambridge **"Reading Africa"** special issue (no. 83, 2000) of *African Research & Documentation* edited by Stephanie Newell, Terry Barringer, Isabel Hofmeyr and Phaswane Mpe.

This special issue of ➔ **African Research & Documentation (150)** contains eight articles in which contributors (from Africa and the UK) explore the varied groups of readers who respond to African and other texts inside and outside the African continent, and a range of essays analyze the interactions between readers, texts, and the means of production. There are four papers each on reading and readership in West Africa (Nigeria and Ghana more specifically), and four on reading practices and reading experiences in South Africa. *Note:* most of the papers in this issue are individually abstracted elsewhere in this bibliography.

2225   Staunton, Irene **"'Sorry, no Free Reading'."** In *Africa Bibliography 1994*, compiled by Christopher H. Allen. Edinburgh: Edinburgh University Press, 1995, vi-xi.

Also published in *African Research & Documentation*, no. 69 (1995): 17-22.

The former Publishing Director of Baobab Books in Harare (now head of Weaver Press) describes the provision of textbooks and other reading materials to children in Zimbabwe from the period immediately following independence until the current situation today [mid 1990s]. She finds that most school children's experience of books is often a negative one and sets out some of the reasons why this is so. Irene Staunton cites a number of recent [as at 1994] developments and initiatives which might lead to an improvement of the situation in the future, and states that "if people are given access to books that they want to read, and if they are encouraged to see books as providing more than a source of information which must be learned for an examination, the potential for developing a more broadly based reading culture is promising."

2226   Staunton, Irene **"Strategies for Targeting Readers. What Can Publishers do to Promote a Reading Culture?"** In *Changing Lives. Promoting A Reading Culture in Africa. Indaba 2001. Harare, Zimbabwe 4-5 August, 2001*, edited by the Zimbabwe International Book Fair Trust. Harare: Zimbabwe International Book Fair Trust, n.d. [2002], 225-231.

Argues that the challenges to developing a reading society in Africa are huge, but also exciting, and describes some of the many economic and social factors that hinder the development of the reading habit. The author, who was the Managing Editor at Baobab Books in Harare for several years, states that while many publishers may well develop a small subsidiary list of fiction or children's books, the development of these titles is often dependent on the publisher's textbook lists. When cutbacks have to be made it will always be the fiction, non-fiction and children's books that are the first to go, because "the general public have either not created a market for them nor insisted that we want our taxes to go into book purchase." She then describes some of the projects and schemes in which she has been involved, which have enjoyed a measure of success and which might also work in other African countries; one such scheme involves a multiplicity of publishing partners, thus extending print runs and reducing the unit costs for markets that would not otherwise be able to afford them.

Taiwo, Oladele **Reading and Writing for National Development: The Nigerian Experience** *see* → **Section 3, Country studies: Nigeria** entry **856**

2227 Thumbadoo, Beula **Making Reading Matter: Guidelines for Selecting, Developing and Disseminating Easy Readers for Adults**. London & Paris: Association for the Development of Education, ADEA Working Group on Books and Learning Materials (Perspectives on African Book Development, 16), 2006. 52 pp.
This useful guide is targeted primarily at libraries that need to support communities by selecting appropriate materials, and adult literacy facilitators and community workers who are seeking suitable reading materials to maintain learners' interest in keeping up their reading habits. The guide is based on the experiences of a civil society organization, the Easy Reading for Adults (ERA) initiative, which was active in South Africa during the 1990's, but also draws on experience elsewhere in Africa, as well as in Asia and Canada. 'Easy reading' is interpreted to mean "any reading matter in any language that makes concessions to a lack of reading skills or to difficulties with mastering the language of the text." The author sets out the key processes and approaches involved in successfully selecting, developing and disseminating easy reading material for adults, and raises a number of pertinent questions on issues that need to be considered, to ensure that materials required for adults wanting to improve their reading skills are relevant to their needs. The book also contains sections on the production process, dissemination and distribution aspects, monitoring and evaluation of projects, and there is a select bibliography.
Reviews:
The African Book Publishing Record vol. 33, no. 3, 2007

2228 Tötemeyer, Andree-Jeanne **"Speaking from a Book: The Transfer of Re-recorded Information to the Information Starved."** *IFLA Journal* 20, no. 4 (1994): 410-417.
Argues that the considerable writing talent in Africa is being frustrated by a totally depressed publishing industry, and by constantly deteriorating library services. Discusses literacy and its implications for library use, and challenges a number of widely held beliefs and assumptions concerning literacy and reading; calls for "appropriate oralities for information transfer" and for the training of a new kind of "information mediator" at the para-professional level.

2229 Tötemeyer, Andree-Jeanne **"The National Readathon of Namibia 1988-2001."** *School Libraries Worldwide* 7, no.2 (2001): 57-64.
Readathon in Namibia is a weeklong reading and book festival held annually in schools, culminating in the National Readathon Day on the Friday. The aim is primarily to develop a love of reading among learners in an effort to nurture a book culture in the country, and secondarily to help schools raise funds to develop their school libraries. From small beginnings in 1988, Readathon has now developed into a national movement in which all primary and junior secondary schools participate. The article describes the development of Readathon over a 14 year period, the organization of Readathon by the → **Namibian Children's Book Forum (713)**, and the Readathon celebrations of September 2001.

2230 United Nations Educational, Scientific and Cultural Organisation **Towards a Reading Society. Targets for the 80s.** Paris: UNESCO, 1982. 45 pp.
Describes the preparations for and results of the World Congress on Books held in London 7-11 June 1982. Includes extensive recommendations for the promotion of a reading society during the 1980s, such as the formulation of national book strategies, the recognition that the book industry is vital, integration of new technologies, creation of a reading environment throughout society, stimulation of international co-operation. The appendix lists the documents of the World Congress.

2231 Zawua, J. **"Promoting Reading Among Children in Nigeria."** *African Journal of Library, Archives and Information Science* 6, no. 2 (1996), 107-112.
[Not examined]

2232 Zimbabwe International Book Fair Trust, ed. **Changing Lives. Promoting a Reading Culture in Africa. Indaba 2001. Harare, Zimbabwe 4-5 August, 2001.** Harare: Zimbabwe International Book Fair Trust, n.d. [2002]. 310 pp. (distributed by African Books Collective Ltd., Oxford)
Also published in a French edition as **Changer les vies. Promouvoir une culture de la lecture en Afrique. Indaba 2001.**
The theme of the 2001 Indaba at the Zimbabwe International Book Fair was devoted to "Changing People's Lives: Promoting a Reading Culture in Africa", and this volume brings together 34 of the papers that were presented, together with a record of some of the discussions that took place following each presentation, the conclusions from some sessions, and concluding remarks. Papers are presented in five parts: Plenary Sessions, Publishing, Writing, Scholarship, and Policy & Access. The papers – from contributors in anglophone, francophone, lusophone, and North Africa – examine some of the "obstacles and opportunities inherent in the ambiguities of the continent's complex post-colonial linguistic inheritance." What are publishers, writers, booksellers, and governments doing, or not doing, to overcome these obstacles? Is the indigenous linguistic richness of the continent a drawback or a benefit for the publisher? Participants in the Policy & Access sessions also addressed issues such as strategies for targeting readers, strategies for promoting readership, and policy implications for developing a reading culture. *Note*: some of the papers in this collection are individually abstracted elsewhere in this bibliography.

Rights sales, licensing, and publishing partnerships

See also
→ **Copyright and legal deposit/Authors' rights**
→ **Intra-African book trade**

2233   African Publishers Network **APNET Rights Catalogue 1994**. Harare: African Publishers' Network, 1994. 20 pp.
Intended to promote intra-African trading, this was the first in a series of catalogues giving details of titles that are on offer from African publishers. (Two editions only published.)

2234   Bankole, Bodunde **"Buying Rights for Local Production of Books. A Nigerian Experience."** *African Publishing Review* 7, no. 3 (May/June 1998): 9, 12-14.
An interesting account of the experience in rights trading of the University of Lagos Press, and the lessons that were learnt from it, one of which was that in order to trade successfully in rights, an African publisher must be visible, with a reputable imprint, that a great element of trust is involved in any rights transaction, and that books produced in co-editions (or offered for reprints) must of be of a high production quality. And one lesson learnt from trying to negotiate rights deals during the Frankfurt Book Fair – and being rebuffed for the most part – was that, for a small Nigerian university press to acquire or sell rights, it was "often easier to get the ears of a small publisher than those of an octopus publisher."

2235   Bourgueil, Isabelle **"Et si l'Afrique travaillait avec l'Afrique?"** *Africultures* no. 57 (December 2003): 149-152.
http://www.africultures.com/index.asp?no=3212&menu=revue_affiche_art icle [28/03/08]
Offers a number of suggestions about possible approaches, and modalities, for North-South or South-South co-publishing ventures and, with the aid of a chart, demonstrates how co-editions at both levels have rapidly increased in recent years between publishers in the francophone regions of Africa and those in France, Switzerland, Belgium, Canada, and elsewhere.

2236   Chakava, Henry **"Publishing Partnerships between Africa and the North: A Dream or a Possibility?"** *Bellagio Publishing Network Newsletter*, no. 15 (November 1995): 4-6.
Examines the prospects of more equitable partnerships and joint ventures between publishers in Africa and those in the North. Argues that "the best way to end state publishing in Africa and stop its future recurrence is for the Northern publishers to support commercial publishing and thereby help to create credible partners with whom they can trade in the future."

2237 Currey, James **"Co-publishing: A Model."** In *The African Writers' Handbook*, edited by James Gibbs and Jack Mapanje. Oxford: African Books Collective Ltd., 1999, 220-224.

James Currey Publishers is the leading UK publisher of books on African studies. Co-publishing is central to the philosophy of James Currey, and his firm has pioneered a series of co-publication arrangements with publishers in different parts of Africa. The model he has developed with African partners is now widely admired as being an equitable relationship for publishers, as well as for writers and scholars. Here he explains the evolution of this method of working, defining the meaning of co-publishing, and providing some examples of co-publishing agreements with publishers in Ghana, Kenya, Uganda, South Africa, and Tanzania.

Currey, James **"African Scholarly Network Press. A Co-publishing Model"** *see* ➜ **Scholarly publishing (General)** entry **2280**

2238 Frenette, Guy **"Les consortiums d'édition: les conditions de leur réussite."** In *Actes de la Table Ronde sur le Partenariat dans l'Edition Francophone: vers le renforcement des actions de coédition et la création de consortiums.* Abidjan: Ministère de l'Education Nationale de Côte d'Ivoire, 1990, 105-111.

Sets out the problems of establishing a publishing consortium, in particular the difficulties of identifying possible partners, and the requirements for their success.

Hasan, Abul **"South/South Cooperation: A Five Year-Old initiative Gathers Strength"** *see* ➜ **Book trade and book development organizations** entry **1525**

2239 Impey, Bridget **"Books Crossing Borders. Developing Rights and Translations Deals in the South."** In *Millennium Marketplace.* [Proceedings of the ZIBF] *Indaba 2000, Harare, Zimbabwe, 31 July – 1 August 2000.* Harare: Zimbabwe International Book Fair Trust, n.d. [2001], 32-35.

Examines the obstacles that have to be overcome to create more of a two-way traffic in rights and translations deals between publishers in the South and the North, and which books have the ability to travel across national borders in Africa.

2240 International Trade Centre UNCTAD/WTO. **Intra-African Trade Promotion Programme Contractual Agreements in the Publishing and Printing Industry: A Practical Guide.** Geneva: International Trade Centre UNCTAD/WTO, South-South Trade Promotion Unit, Division of Technical Cooperation Coordination, 2000. 117 pp.

This useful practical manual consists of a range of model contracts and users' guides put together by Lynette Owen, Rights Director of Pearson Education Ltd., and well known for her classic text *Selling Rights. A Publisher's Guide to Success.* The contracts draw on a variety of publishing agreements currently in use in the book trade, but have been adapted for use by the African publishing and printing industries, and there are also explanatory notes to cover the relationships between key players in

contractual negotiations. The book is divided into three major sections: Chapter I deals with author contracts and provides a model for an author-publisher contract, together with a model for a contractual letter between an author and a literary agent. Chapter II covers the relationship of publishers with their suppliers and distributors via contractual agreements, including a model for a printer's terms of contract, and one for a contract with an agent or distributor for sales and marketing of a publisher's list. Chapter III covers the aspect of publishers' agreements with licensees covering a variety of rights deals. Models, and accompanying users' guides, are provided for four such rights agreements (i) Same Language Reprint License: Royalty Agreement, (ii) Translation License: Royalty Agreement, (iii) Co-edition Translation Contract, and, (iv) Co-edition Same Language Contract.
Reviews:
The African Book Publishing Record, vol. 28, no. 2, 2002

2241 Jay, Mary **"First African Rights Indaba."** *Bellagio Publishing Network Newsletter*, no 11 (September 1994): 6-7.
A report about the 'First African Rights Indaba' held in August 1994 which coincided with the Zimbabwe International Book Fair. The objectives of the meeting were to look at all aspects of rights, co-publishing, licensing, copyright, etc. in African publishing, and to seek ways to correct the imbalance in South/North relations in this area.

2242 Jay, Mary **"The Role and Experience of African Books Collective in Facilitating Rights Sales and Co-editions of African Books."** *African Publishing Review* 4, no. 4 (July/August 1995): 6-9.
Reviews the role and policies of ➔ **African Books Collective Ltd**. (3) as a facilitator of rights sales for its member publishers and their authors, and its experience in the rights sector to date [to 1995]. Although ABC's chief mission is to promote and distribute African-published books in the countries of the North, it aims to develop a rights facilitation service (covering both sales of rights and buying-in rights for publication in Africa under license), and to act as a clearinghouse for member publishers in rights deals.

2243 Kats, Ivan **"New Project: Encouraging the Printing of Key Books Under License in Asia and Africa for Sale at a Low Price."** *Bellagio Publishing Network Newsletter* 1, no. 4 (December 1992): 7-8.
The [then] director of the Obor Foundation puts forward the case for providing books to African countries at low prices, through licensing agreements.

2244 Konate, Hamidou **"A Publishing Partnership between France and Francophone Africa."** In *Educational Publishing in Global Perspective. Capacity Building and Trends,* edited by Shobhana Sosale. Washington, DC: The World Bank, 1998, 177-179.
Shorter version also published as **"North-South Publishing Partnerships. A Case of Francophone Africa"** *African Publishing Review* 7, no. 2 (March/April 1998): 8-9.

Reports about a successful publishing partnership between Canadian and French publishers and Editions Jamana in Mali, and outlines some of the essential requirements for equitable partnerships between publishers in the North and those in the countries of the South.

2245 Loric, Laurent **"Donor Support for Book Imports."** In *Educational Publishing in Global Perspective. Capacity Building and Trends,* edited by Shobhana Sosale. Washington, DC: The World Bank, 1998, 106-114.
Examines the question of aid for book imports in the francophone region of Africa, and takes a critical look at some current strategies for aid schemes in terms of their effectiveness and cost-efficiency.

2246 Loric, Laurent **"A Global Partnership Experience: EDICEF in Cameroon."** In *Educational Publishing in Global Perspective. Capacity Building and Trends,* edited by Shobhana Sosale. Washington, DC: The World Bank, 1998, 13-18.
The partnership between EDICEF (part of the French Hachette Group) and Edition CLE of Yaoundé in Cameroon is used to draw general conclusions about publishing partnerships between industrial and developing countries, examining which aspects work and those that are rendered difficult by the intrinsic nature of the publishing industry.

2247 McCartney, Murray, ed. **African Rights Indaba. Edited Proceedings of the Conference Held in Harare 1994**. Harare: African Publishers Network (African Publishing Handbooks, 1), 1994. 64 pp.
Contains the edited proceedings of the 'African Rights Indaba' held during the 1994 Zimbabwe International Book Fair. Following two introductory overview contributions, the papers are assembled under two broad themes: (i) the legal and professional environment of rights and rights protection, and (ii) the advice and experiences offered by publishers from their own countries and perspectives. *Note:* some of the papers in this collection are individually abstracted elsewhere in this bibliography.
Reviews:
The African Book Publishing Record, vol. 21, no. 2, 1995

2248 Moingeon, March **"Local and Foreign Partnerships: Attracting Foreign Investment."** In *Educational Publishing in Global Perspective. Capacity Building and Trends,* edited by Shobhana Sosale. Washington, DC: The World Bank, 1998, 103-105.
Reports about a partnership between the French publisher Hachette Livre and local publishers in the Côte d'Ivoire (notably Nouvelles Editions Ivoriennes), how Hachette came to invest in the publishing industry in the country, and the resulting benefits for both partners.

2249 Molteno, Robert **"Co-publishing and Co-production as an Answer to Sustainable Book Production in Africa."** In *Academic Book Production and*

Distribution in Africa. Support from Nordic Countries. Report from a conference at Chr. Michelsen Institute, Bergen, 10-11 April 1997, edited by Kirsti Hagen Andersen. Fantoft, Norway: Ch. Michelsen Institute 1997, 49-57.
Robert Molteno examines the prospects for African publishers finding co-publishing partners in the countries of the North, the essential components for successful co-publishing projects, the obstacles to co-publishing ventures, and the possible role of aid in assisting co-publishing arrangements.

2250 Newton, Diana **"Commercial Publishing Partnerships."** In *Educational Publishing in Global Perspective. Capacity Building and Trends,* edited by Shobhana Sosale. Washington, DC: The World Bank, 1998, 165-168.
Diana Newton succinctly defines the characteristics of genuine and sustainable partnerships, identifies criteria for the success of such partnerships, outlines the benefits to be derived, presents the rationale for their promotion, and proposes avenues and policy measures to encourage their emergence and growth.

2251 Nwankwo, Victor **"Publishing Partnerships Between Africa and the North. A Dream or a Possibility?"** *African Publishing Review* 5, no. 3 (May/June 1996): 6-7.
Also published in *Bellagio Publishing Network Newsletter,* no. 18 (November 1996): 18-19.
Another African perspective on North/South partnerships (*see also* entry ➜ **2236** by Chakava above). Reports about a meeting on North/South publishing cooperation held during the Frankfurt Book Fair in 1995. Outlines the main factors that come into play in publishing partnerships between African publishers and those in the North, and examines the case of one ongoing partnership between New Namibia Books and Heinemann Educational Publishers. Nwankwo concludes that "sufficient experience in ongoing collaborations exist to make it possible to identify characteristics on which to build models for future cooperation."

2252 Owen, Lynette **"To License, or Not to License."** *The Bookseller* (December 1986): 2338-2342.
The [then] subsidiary rights manager at Longman examines ways through which publishers in developed countries can provide low cost books to Third World countries. Considers the political and commercial implications of licensing and stresses the necessity for "publishers in an affluent country" to "be prepared to explore viable alternatives to licensing."

2253 Owen, Lynette **"Licensing: A Look at Developed Country-Third World Relations."** *Rights* 1, no. 2 (Summer 1987): 2-4.
A condensed version of the article in the preceding entry, *see* ➜ **2252**.

Owen, Lynette **"Copyright-Benefit or Obstacle?"** *see* ➜ **Copyright and legal deposit/Authors' rights** entry **1798**

2254 Parry, Rex **"Co-operative Ventures with the Third World: Practical Proposals and the Involvement of International Organizations."** *IASP Newsletter,* no. 4 (September 1990): 5-8.
Another version also published in *Learned Publishing* 3, no. 2 (April 1990).
Discusses the kind of co-operative ventures which might be successful; examining the likely obstacles to success, and the kind of donor organizations who might provide assistance in a co-operative venture. Gives practical ideas, including suggestions on how to formulate a proposal to a partner or a donor. First presented as a paper at the ALPSP seminar on co-operative ventures with the Third World in London, 12 May 1989.

2255 Pick, Martin **"Co-Editions of Children's Books: International But Not (Yet) Global."** *Logos. The Journal of the World Book Community* 3, no. 4 (1992): 186-191.
Online:
http://www.atypon-link.com/LOG/doi/pdf/10.2959/logo.1992.3.4.186
Examines the issues involved in publishing co-editions of children's books, including cross-cultural appeal, financing and cooperation with governments, for the production of well adapted books which can suit the needs of a specific country.

2256 Randle, Ian, and Ciaran MacGlinchey **"The Caribbean Law-Publishing Company Ltd. A Model for South-South Cooperation."** *Bellagio Publishing Network Newsletter,* no. 19 (March 1997): 5-6.
Describes a partnership in legal publishing between Ian Randle Publishers in Kingston, Jamaica, and Juta & Company, South Africa's oldest and largest legal publishers, who agreed to set up a new joint venture company: The Caribbean Law Publishing Company (CLP). CLP will have as its main activity the publishing of primary legal materials, in both conventional printed as well as electronic formats on CD-ROM and publication on the Internet. The first products were released in early 1997. "Mutual respect and trust have formed the basis of the alliance, ingredients that both sides believe are more essential for the success of the venture than formal written agreements."

2257 Read, Anthony **"Trick or Treat? Low Cost Books for Low Income Countries."** *The Bookseller* (7 November 1986): 1904-1908.
Examines two important issues in publishing in and for developing countries: access to low cost books, and the growth of Third World publishing. Urges publishers in the developed world to reconsider their attitudes to their Third World markets. Concludes that "nothing will promote the development of books in the Third World more than the existence of a marketplace which will stimulate publishing growth."

2258 Reboul, Amande **"Editer autrement - du Nord au Sud, qu'est-ce que la coédition?"** *Africultures* no. 57 (December 2003): 134-140.
Online:
http://www.africultures.com/index.asp?no=3207&menu=revue_affiche_article [25/03/08]

Sets out the parameters and practicalities of co-publication ventures between publishers in the North and those in the South, provides some examples of both North-South and South-South collaborative projects and co-editions, and makes some recommendations how to avoid the pitfalls in co-publishing agreements. Also describes the activities of the ➜ **L'Alliance des éditeurs independents (31).**

2259 Reddy, Bangar N. **Publishing Co-operation in the Afro-Asian Region. Papers Presented at the Fourth Annual Conference and Book Exhibition of the Afro-Asian Book Council at the University of Durban-Westville.** New Delhi: Afro-Asian Book Council, 1994. 128 pp.
[Not examined]

2260 Ripken, Peter **"Books Crossing Borders. Translation and Rights Deals in the North."** In *Indaba 2000. Millennium Marketplace,* edited by the Zimbabwe International Book Fair Trust. Harare: Zimbabwe International Book Fair Trust, 2001, 30-31.
A short but helpful overview of the pattern of foreign rights deals and translations of works of African literature into the major European languages, and particularly translations for the German markets.

2261 Seck, Mamadou **"La coédition comme facteur de coopération Nord-Sud et Sud-Nord."** In *Actes de la Table Ronde sur le Partenariat dans l'Edition Francophone: vers le renforcement des actions de coédition et la création de consortiums.* Abidjan: Ministère de l'Education Nationale de Côte d'Ivoire, 1990, 97-104.
A detailed analysis of the area of co-publishing, concluding that co-publishing should not be seen as only being initiated by "richer" countries.

2262 Sulley, Robert **"A Publishing Partnership between the United Kingdom and Namibia."** In *Educational Publishing in Global Perspective. Capacity Building and Trends,* edited by Shobhana Sosale. Washington, DC: The World Bank, 1998, 173-176.
Describes a publishing partnership between Heinemann Educational Publishers UK and New Namibia Books in Windhoek, examines this partnership in the light of the criteria set out by Diana Newton (*see* entry ➜ **2250** above), and reports about some of the lessons that were learned from the experience.

2263 Zell, Hans M. **"Buying and Selling Rights: The Prospects, and the Constraints, for African Publishers."** *African Publishing Review* 3, no. 6 (November/December 1994): 13-17.
Probes into the opportunities and prospects for rights sales of African books, and identifies the type of books that might have the greatest potential for rights deals. Provides advice how African publishers might go about identifying rights buyers for their books, and recommends the best sources of information and reference tools to assist publishers to find the partners for rights sales or co-editions.

Scholarly publishing (General)

See also
→ **African books in the international market place**
→ **Book marketing and promotion**
→ **Digital media and electronic publishing/New printing technology**
→ **Journals and magazine publishing**
→ **Open access publishing**
→ **Scientific, technical and medical publishing**

2264 Afele, Senyo John *et al* **Now and in the Next Millenium, 1990s-3000 CE. Assessing Africa's Scholarly Publishing Needs and Industry.** Kampala: RA-Global Communications & JARP [order from L. Njinya-Mujinya, Box 1604, 75146 Uppsala, Sweden] (2nd and expanded ed.), 2001. 250 pp. (for first ed. *see* entry → **2290** below)
A collection of papers on various aspects of scholarly writing and publishing in Africa, mostly by African academics based in the diaspora. [Not examined.]

2265 Aguolu, C.C., and I.E. Aguolu **"Scholarly Publishing and Nigerian Universities."** *Journal of Scholarly Publishing* 29, no. 2 (January 1998): 118-129. In this wide-ranging article the authors set out the reasons why, in the face of the prevailing scarcity of scholarly publications in Nigeria, universities should play an important role in enhancing the availability of scholarly publications in the country. They argue that university presses have a special obligation to help disseminate the results of the research and the ideas of Nigerian scholars, as some African scholarship may be rejected by international publishers for being too local in orientation; and that they must strive to maintain their independence of editorial judgement and of function, and must not be seen as a merely revenue-yielding service. The authors also believe that, in an African situation, university presses should go beyond publishing research monographs, learned journals and conference proceedings, and "should embrace the publication of tertiary-level textbooks and creative writing that reflect Nigerian culture and creativity." They also challenge other concepts of university press publishing, e.g. "a university press need not have its own printing house. Printing is a separate industry that has become highly technological", and that new approaches will have to be found for the marketing and distribution of scholarly materials. Makes a number of recommendations: fiscal policies and incentives at individual institutions and in government must be changed to support scholarly publishing; presses should more actively explore cooperative publishing ventures; more attention must be given to protecting authors and publishers rights; university presses ought to negotiate licensing rights from publishing partners overseas for titles appropriate for the Nigerian markets; and promotional and marketing strategies must be improved. The authors conclude by stating "the real value of scholarly publications does not lie in the revenues they generate, but in their impact upon the scientific, cultural, and socio-economic development of the society."

2266 Aina, L.O. **"The Problems of Tertiary Publishing in Africa and Implications for the Training and Education of Library and Information Professionals."** *Library Review* 48, no. 8 (1999): 399-402.

Trainees in the library and information profession in Africa depend on textbooks emanating from outside Africa because of a dearth of locally published books. Moreover, even if available, local books are generally patterned along Western lines and they are either descriptive or historical, and Aina argues that none of them can be used as a basic textbook for any of the courses offered in library and information science schools in Africa. This has greatly affected the training of library and information professionals in Africa as trainees are exposed to literature that is largely suited to situations outside their immediate environments. The author identifies several factors that he sees as being responsible for inadequate tertiary publications for the information professions in Africa. He recommends that authors should embark on team authorship, and that international funding agencies and national governments should commission textbooks that are appropriate for an African setting.

2267 Aina, Tade Akin **"Social Science Scholarly Publishing in Africa: The CODESRIA Experience."** *Focus on International and Comparative Librarianship* 26, no. 2 (September 1995): 72-78.

Also published in *African Research & Documentation*, no. 69 (1995): 23-27.

Describes the book and journals publishing programme of the Council for the Development of Social Science Research in Africa (CODESRIA) based in Dakar, Senegal. Examines some of the constraints faced by scholarly publishers in Africa, "hindered by problems of distribution, and linguistic, political, cultural and fiscal barriers", and sets out how CODESRIA has tackled these problems. Also reports about CODESRIA's attempts to provide more visibility for their books in the major academic libraries in the North.

2268 Aina, Tade Akin **"South-South Co-operation in Relation to Publications and Access to Scholarship Materials."** In *Access to Information. Indaba 97.* Harare: Zimbabwe International Book Fair Trust, 1997, 81-90.

Examines the new scholarly communication environment and states that "the so-called information society that we live in today is very much an age of gross and extreme inequality, not only of access to these and other resources but also of benefits and advantages resulting from its control and deployment." Calls for new approaches, and new techniques to foster more South-South co-operation – in research, scholarship, and publications – based on mutual benefits and identity of interests in all their dimensions: economic, cultural, and political. Asserts that "in publishing (both print and electronic publishing) tremendous areas of possible co-operation and exchange not yet sufficiently developed exist." The author goes on to say "apart from Indian publishers, it seems other Southern interests in Latin America and Asia have not seen Africa as possible areas of co-operation and penetration. They are often limited by uncertainties, ignorance, fear, and prejudice." Concludes that an institution must be found that can facilitate and encourage South-South contacts to bring to the fore the range of mutual benefits possible.

2269 Alemna, A. Anaba **"Scholarly Publishing in Ghana."** *Scholarly Publishing* 13, no. 2 (January 1982): 174-178.
Despite lack of materials, economic setbacks, difficulties in marketing and distribution, and other obstacles, the state-supported Ghana Universities Press has reduced its country's dependence on imported books.

2270 Andersen, Kirsti Hagen, ed. **Academic Book Production and Distribution in Africa. Support from Nordic Countries. Report from a conference at Chr. Michelsen Institute, Bergen, 10-11 April 1997.** Fantoft, Norway: Ch. Michelsen Institute [Fantoftvegen 38, N-5036 Fantoft], 1997. 112 pp.
This is a report about, and the papers presented at, a conference jointly sponsored by the Norwegian Library Association, the Norwegian Non-fiction Writers, and the Chr. Michelsen Institute, which focussed on the role and support from Nordic countries to academic book production and distribution in Africa. Invited speakers included academics, government officials, publishers, and booksellers and librarians from Africa as well as some from the USA and Europe. It presents a useful collection of views and perspectives on the current state of the scholarly book in Africa and its distribution and dissemination. *Note:* most of the papers in this collection are individually abstracted elsewhere in this bibliography
Reviews:
The African Book Publishing Record vol. 24, no. 1, 1998

2271 Anon. **"Book Development and Agriculture. Not by Word of Mouth Alone."** *Spore*, no. 99 (June 2002): 4-5.
Looks at the problems and challenges of the promotion of the book and readership in ACP countries; publishing in areas regarded as marginal and unprofitable by publishers; and the absence of a viable market for technical and agricultural publications because most readers simply cannot afford to pay a realistic price.

2272 Bankole, S. Bodunde **"Running Scholarly Presses as a Business: The Nigerian Experience."** In *The Future of Small Presses in Scholarly Publishing, proceedings from the 4th International Conference on Scholarly Publishing, Helsinki, June 1-3, 1988.* Oslo: IASP, 1988, 105-114.
Describes the numerous problems and obstacles faced by scholarly publishers in Nigeria, and contends that forming a limited liability company for a university press "may in fact be more of a liability than an asset in the long run."

2273 Bankole, S. Bodunde **"Scholarly Publishing in Nigeria."** *Scholarly Publishing* 21, no. 2 (January 1990): 92-98.
The [former] Managing Director of the University of Lagos Press reviews the structure and management of Nigerian university presses in the 1980s and 1990s. He examines their shortcomings, and the fallacious thinking by university administrators who view their presses as an opportunity for making money in times of dwindling resources, rather than as an outlet for dissemination of scholarship, This arises "from the general misconception within the system, and indeed outside

the system, that a publisher is essentially a printer and that most printers downtown make quick money for little effort." The author goes on to say "the universities also seem to be oblivious to the fact that the ability of a press to compete in the open market is constrained by the degree to which its management is free and is given the resources to function as a proper business." Also describes the aims and objectives of the Scholarly Publishers Association of Nigeria (SPAN), founded in 1978, but which did not unfortunately last long and petered by the end of the 1980s, largely, in the author's view, because of rapid turnover of staff at university presses in Nigeria which is "still very much an issue today and has consistently bedevilled any attempts to evolve a tradition of cooperation among the presses." Makes some suggestions how university press publishing might be revitalized in the future, and calls for renewed collaborative ventures between Nigeria's scholarly presses.

2274   Bankole, S. Bodunde **"Law Publishing in Nigeria."** *The Publisher* 2, no. 1 (March 1991): 47-51.
Looks at various aspects of law publishing in Nigeria, including law reports, law books and monographs, statute publications, periodicals, and digest and index publications. Examines the particular problems of law publishing, current trends [1991], and concludes that law publishing is a fast growing and possibly lucrative area in Nigeria.

2275   Bankole, S. Bodunde **"Scholarly Publishing in Africa - The Case of Africa and Nigeria."** *Zeitschrift für Kulturaustausch* 41, no. 3 (1991): 355-361.
Discusses the "genre and extent" of scholarly publishing in the context of the lack of contact between professionals involved in this sector. States that the market for scholarly publishing in Africa is largely underdeveloped, but foresees a thriving future for scholarly publishing on the continent.

2276   Bankole, S. Bodunde **"Scholarly Publishing in Nigeria: The Dilemma."** *Bellagio Publishing Network Newsletter*, no. 8 (December 1993): 5-7. Also published in *The Publisher* 3, no. 1 (January 1995): 31-32.
Probes into the crisis in Nigerian scholarly publishing and the enormous problems faced by the country's university presses. Assesses future prospects, and calls for a change in attitudes by university administrators regarding the role and function of Nigerian university presses and the dissemination of scholarly publishing output.

2277   Bgoya, Walter **"Scholarly Publishing in Africa: An Overview."** In *African Scholarly Publishing Essays*, edited by Alois Mlambo. Oxford: African Books Collective Ltd.; Uppsala: Dag Hammarskjöld Foundation; and Oxford: International Network for the Availability of Scientific Publications (INASP), 2006, 1-10.
This is the introductory essay to **African Scholarly Publishing Essays** (*see* entry ➔ **2312**), which takes stock of scholarly publishing in Africa in the early years of the 21st century. It examines the major issues and obstacles, which include, the author believes, the marginalization internationally of African scholarly publishing output, and "the low priority given by African governments to their universities does a great deal of harm to their reputation as centres of higher learning". Bgoya rightly argues

that the state of many African universities is abysmal, with poor facilities for research, and grossly inadequate and sometime totally outdated library resources, which contributes significantly to marginalize Africa-based scholars, and hardly encourages home-grown scholarly productions. High-quality scholarly publishing requires much more than finance, "foremost is editorial capacity and competence, an inescapable resource without which scholarly publishing is not possible", as poorly edited and poorly designed books will stand out and reflect badly on their authors and publishers. The author also acknowledges the benefits now available to African publishers through digital printing and print-on-demand (POD), but that at the moment it is only relevant where small quantities of less than 500 copies are required. In his conclusion Bgoya challenges ➔ **World Bank (124)** education policies for sub-Saharan Africa, which (in 1998) advocated drastic reduction of resources being allocated to higher education in favour of the so-called 'education for all' programme, and that, instead of heeding the World Bank's advice, African countries and their governments ought to increase resources to African universities. While this is a perceptive overview of the current situation of scholarly publishing on the continent, Bgoya also makes a few startling claims in this paper: for example, in asserting that "the international book market place is only marginally interested in African books", he says "the predominant attitude of the European and American book trades from buyers to booksellers to librarians is at best to disregard African intellectuals' input and at worst to deny any place in international knowledge production to Africa and the Africans." This claim seems irreconcilable with, for example, the very considerable success the Oxford-based ➔ **African Books Collective (3)** has enjoyed, for almost two decades now, in getting thousands of African-published books, from a very large number of African publishers, on to the shelves of academic and public libraries in many parts of the world.

2278 Braham, Abdelwahed **Projet des presses universitaires et scolaires d'Afrique (PUSAF): République de Côte d'Ivoire - (mission)**. Paris: UNESCO (Doc. FMR/CC/BAE/86/139; RP/1984-1985/III.3.2/Rapport technique) [Restricted circulation, available on request], 1986. 19 pp.
UNESCO mission report to help establish a university press in the Côte d'Ivoire.

2279 Chakava, Henry **"Scholarly Publishing in Africa: The Perspective of an East African Commercial and Textbook Publisher."** In *African Scholarly Publishing Essays*, edited by Alois Mlambo. Oxford: African Books Collective Ltd.; Uppsala: Dag Hammarskjöld Foundation; and Oxford: International Network for the Availability of Scientific Publications (INASP), 2006, 66-75.
Kenyan publisher Henry Chakava traces the decline of academic publishing in the East African region. Using Kenya as a case study, he explains how the decline has come about, with most university libraries and university bookshops currently in a state of decay, unable to perform their traditional services to students and faculty. He bemoans the fact that very little original research is currently undertaken at Kenya's universities; and that "sadly our lecturers continue to teach from the same books they themselves learnt from, recycling ideas long discarded" and goes on to say "if we cannot generate new knowledge for ourselves, then we should not mourn the influx of imported books into our market." Meantime the performance by

university presses in the East African region has been disappointing. Chakava sees partnerships between university presses at the national or regional levels – possibly also involving partnerships with private sector publishers – as the only viable way forward to strengthen scholarly publishing on the continent.

2280 Currey, James **"African Scholarly Network Press. A Co-publishing Model"** In *African Scholarly Publishing Essays*, edited by Alois Mlambo. Oxford: African Books Collective Ltd.; Uppsala: Dag Hammarskjöld Foundation; and Oxford: International Network for the Availability of Scientific Publications (INASP), 2006, 97-102.

In this interesting paper James Currey, the well-known African studies publisher, sets out a possible model how a network of African academic publishers, and/or a consortium of academic institutions – using the benefits of new technologies such as digital printing, and relying primarily on freelancers for editing, composition and proofreading – might be able to publish and disseminate work not only of the highest standards of scholarship, but also with the highest standards of editing and production. The proposed African Scholarly Network Press, which would only disseminate electronically, would (1) select work by peer group review, (2) find funding for pre-press editorial and typographical origination, (3) distribute by electronic means, and (4) put the books into the public domain. (*See also* ➜ **2237**)

2281 Darko-Ampem, Kwasi **Scholarly Publishing in Africa: A Case Study of African University Presses.** Stirling, Scotland: University of Stirling, 2003. PhD dissertation (Department of English Studies, e-theses). 235 l.

Online: http://dspace.stir.ac.uk/dspace/handle/1893/71 [29/03/08, full-text freely downloadable as 8 pdf files]

This wide-ranging dissertation examines the policies and practices of six sub-Saharan Africa university presses in five African countries (in Ghana, Kenya, South Africa, Zambia and Zimbabwe), to investigate how far the presses have adopted, and/or have adapted, their policies to suit the environment and special needs of Africa. The study examines the extent to which current constraints impede their publishing activities and publishing strategies. The author finds that there is "a serious absence of competition and cooperation between the presses surveyed", lack of aggressive fund raising strategies, together with weak or non-existent policies for commissioning and list building, and without a clearly defined subject focus. The author also examines the various strategies adopted by the presses to adapt to the rapidly changing scholarly communications environment. In his conclusions he recommends the setting-up of a continent-wide consortium of African university presses, with each press "to operate as a Trust in order to enjoy autonomy as a private company, but be registered as a non-profit organization." The author calls for more active collaboration among African scholarly presses (including joint publishing ventures, sharing of resources and expertise, reciprocal distribution, etc.); much stronger emphasis on the use of new technology, particularly print-on-demand; makes some suggestions regarding possible sources of funding for the presses, and recommends further research into the effect of ICTs on university press publishing in Africa.

2282 Darko-Ampem, Kwasi **"A University Press Publishing Consortium for Africa: Lessons from Academic Libraries."** *Journal of Scholarly Publishing* 36, no. 2, (January 2005): 89-114.
This article (based on the author's PhD dissertation, *see* entry ➔ **2281** above) presents the results of a case study of the policies and practices of six African university presses, in Ghana, Kenya, South Africa, Zambia and Zimbabwe. It reviews their press policies, sales figures (annually and over a 15 year period), manuscript acquisitions and editorial boards, the nature of books published and areas of specialization, marketing and distribution, together with an examination of deficiencies in their current operations. Based on the findings, the author proposes the formation of a consortium of African university presses, along the same lines as consortium formation in the library world, which "seems to be a sensible means to reduce the financial burden on each individual press or institution and at the same time provides a sustainable source of funding for each institution's publishing programs." The author believes that hard-pressed African university presses have no option but to merge, form a consortium, or "face total collapse. Unless current pressures for self-sufficiency are removed, press directors have little choice but to forge alliances that will keep them in business."

2283 DeLancey, Mark **"The Nigerian Institute of International Affairs."** *The African Book Publishing Record* 7, no. 2 (1981): 107-108.
Describes the publishing activities Nigerian Institute of international Affairs (NIIA) which "has become the most significant research and publishing centre for the study of international relations in Sub-Saharan Africa."

2284 Diouf, Jean Pierre **"La publication académique en panne: Quelles perspectives pour l'Afrique?"**
http://www.ascleiden.nl/Pdf/elecpublconfdiouf.pdf [22/01/08]
A paper presented at the conference on Bridging the North-South Divide in Scholarly Communication on Africa--Threats and Opportunities in the Digital Era, African Studies Centre, Leiden, The Netherlands, September 6-8, 2006. For many African scholars getting published, despite the huge number of academic journals published in all disciplines throughout the world, remains a challenge and can be a frustrating experience for those seeking publishing outlets – and see their work cited by their peers – particularly for young scholars at the beginning of their professional career. The author describes some of the contributory factors that have led to this situation, which only offer limited publishing opportunities to African scholars, and which persist today despite the changes in the scholarly communications environment and the move from print to electronic formats. He proposes some possible approaches how the current gap between the North and the South in the production of academic publications might be bridged, for them to be "freed from the shackles and orientation of commercial publishing."

2285 Fiedler, Klaus **"A Community of Teaching and Learning, Research and Publishing."** In *African Scholarly Publishing Essays*, edited by Alois Mlambo. Oxford: African Books Collective Ltd.; Uppsala: Dag

Hammarskjöld Foundation; and Oxford: International Network for the Availability of Scientific Publications (INASP), 2006, 83-90.

Klaus Fiedler tells the story of the 'Kachere Books series' http://www.sdnp.org.mw/kachereseries/ [30/03/08] developed at the Department of Theology and Religious Studies at Chancellor College, University of Malawi. Fiedler believes Africa has a lot to offer for academic publishing in Africa, "forget about the handicaps and look at the opportunities", and, despite frequent statements to the contrary, a market for academic books does exist in Africa, "and it is a market in the right place, since books on Africa are needed first of all in Africa." He proves his point by drawing attention to the remarkable success of the Kachere series launched in 1995, supported by some statistical analysis of sales at home, elsewhere in Africa, as well as overseas through ➔ **African Books Collective (3)**. The series started with a remit to publish primarily books on theology and religion in Malawi, but soon expanded to include books with more political content, and titles on Malawian culture and society. Over a hundred titles have been published (of which 33 have been reprinted) with page extents ranging from a slim 28 pages to as much as 607 pages, with initial print runs of 500-700 copies. The author says "what has been possible here may well be possible elsewhere" and urges other publishers to get started: "Complaining, though emotionally satisfying, does not achieve anything... It is better to find practical solutions."

2286   Ganu, K.M. **"Scholarly Publishing in Ghana: The Role of Ghana Universities Press."** *Journal of Scholarly Publishing* 30, no. 3 (April 1999): 111-123.

The Director of the Ghana Universities Press (GUP) discusses the challenges of academic publishing in Ghana, a country in which scholarly publishing is still in an embryonic stage, where funding for publishing ventures is scarce, and where it is difficult to find high-quality printers for scholarly books and journals. Describes the experience of GUP, established in 1962 as the academic publishing outlet of five of Ghana's universities, and its development since that time; the problems and challenges it faces (e.g. dealing with large numbers of manuscripts from five universities and finding suitable and reliable readers to assess publishing proposals), its attempts to increase market share for its products both locally and overseas, and relations with booksellers. It also describes the Press's policy that requires authors to contribute 50% toward printing costs. Although supported by the Government of Ghana by a subvention to cover salaries and a limited range of operational expenses, the Press has to finance book production from its own resources and contributions from sponsors and authors. The author believes the Press has achieved a good measure of success and recognition over the years, and that "a university is best known in the international community not by the number of students it turns out but by the number of published works of scholarship that emanates from it."

2287   Gray, Eve **"Academic Publishing in South Africa."** In *The Politics of Publishing in South Africa,* edited by Nicholas Evans and Monica Seeber. London: Holger Ehling Publishing and Scotsville, South Africa: University of Natal Press, 2000, 163-188.

A penetrating analysis of the challenges and obstacles faced by scholarly publishers in South Africa and elsewhere in Africa, and in an environment of ever decreasing markets for academic writing. The article examines the South African tertiary milieu and its demographics and trends; higher education policies and their influence on academic publishing; the role of distance-education providers in the academic textbook market; changing book buying habits; the current status of the academic textbook publishing sector in South Africa; and publishing in the field of African studies, an area "where the most complex and most difficult of all the problems facing South African and African scholarly presses arises from the dominance of academic discourse by the countries of the North." While the academic monograph in its conventional format is "under siege", the author believes there may well be an electronic future for African scholarly publishing if publishers are prepared to seize the opportunity. Eve Gray suggests that scholarly publishing can only survive by joining the global network and its links with the global academic community, or otherwise be hopelessly left behind. She believes that this is the only way forward to overcome regional isolation, indifferent scholarship and the constraints of a small and regional market for academic publications; and that academic publishers in Africa, as elsewhere, will have to adapt extremely quickly to a completely transformed environment of scholarly communication.

2288 Gray, Eve **A Plan for the Expansion of an African University Press. A Case Study.**
http://www.evegray.co.za/downloads/africanuniversity.pdf [31/01/08]
Eve Gray & Associates were contracted in 2005 to conduct a strategic planning exercise for an African university press (not named in this report). The desired outcome was to be the creation of a strategic plan and a vision for the future growth of the press. It emerged that the best path forward for the university press would be to resist pressure being exerted by its mother institution to become viable, but rather to persuade the institution that subsidizing a professionally managed and actively marketed publishing programme linked to institutional, national and regional priorities, would bring tangible benefits to the institution. Some of these benefits would be difficult to measure – such as increased research impact – but there would also be also concrete and quantifiable benefits, as the prestige generated by such a programme would raise the reputation of the institution, allowing it to attract quality staff and students and placing the institution in a strong position to secure government and donor support.

2289 Gray, Eve **A Terminal Case…Perished, not Perishing. The Malaise in Humanities Publishing in South Africa.**
http://www.evegray.co.za/downloads/webcopyTerminal_case.ppt [31/01/08]
A compelling PowerPoint presentation to the Faculty of Humanities at the University of Cape Town in November 2005, in which the author argues that while the state of scholarly publishing might well be in crisis in the USA, in Africa and the rest of the developing world it is a terminal case. The author contends that traditional publishing models in the humanities have never worked in South Africa. Knowledge resources are dominated by powerful countries in the North; research policies and accreditation systems reinforce this dominance, and the result is marginalization of

African knowledge, with Africa always perceived as a consumer of knowledge. Gray also argues that there are many practical barriers, for example that US and UK libraries are reluctant to buy publications from the South, and that African universities are reluctant to support or fund publishing activities. She believes publishing on the Internet offers lower cost combined with greater reach, and open access could unlock even more doors. She sees the open access model as the only way forward for journal publishing, when the reach of the journal is not limited by subscriptions or library purchase policies.

Gray, Eve *see also* ➜ Horwitz Gray, Eve

2290 Habomugisha, Peace; Asafo, Dziedzorm R; and L. Njinya-Mujinya **Now and in the Next Millennium 1990s-3000 CE. Assessing Africa's Scholarly Publishing Needs and Industry.** Ho, Ghana [PO Box 203], and Mbarara, Uganda [PO Box 16000]: RA-Global Communcations, 1998. 178 pp.
An interesting if somewhat quirky collection of papers by a number of African academics on various aspects of African scholarly publishing, the wider issues relating to the dissemination of African scholarship, and the status of research at African universities. Most papers also address the urgent need to strengthen local capacity-building for research, writing and publishing in Africa. According to the foreword the volume's main objective "is to heighten the awareness of the need to increase the production of books and other reading matter in the continent" and "to convert unprocessed information into tangible and organized knowledge by both Africans and non-Africans, and in the continent rather than outside." Interspersed with the articles there are a series of interviews (conducted by email) with some prominent African scholars in various parts in Africa and in the diaspora. The book also includes a sharp dissection, described as "a critical introduction", of Hans Zell's ➜ **"Publishing in Africa: The Crisis and the Challenge"** (1993, *see* entry ➜ **333**), in which five different contributors challenge some of Zell's views and statements. (*Note:* a new edition was published in 2001, *see* entry ➜ **2264** above.)

2291 Haroon, Mohammed Mahjoub **"Interview: The KUP's New Man Pressing Ahead."** *Sudanow* (October 1983): 52-53.
Interview with Khalid el Moubarak, [former] Director of the Khartoum University Press.

2292 Harris, John **"Printing and Publishing."** In *The West African Intellectual Community*, edited by M. Dowuona and J.T. Saunders. Ibadan: Ibadan University Press, 1962, 289-313.
An interesting account of the early years of scholarly publishing in West Africa by John Harris, who was University Librarian at Ibadan in the 1960s and was also the founder of the Ibadan University Press.

2293 Horwitz Gray, Eve **"Strategies for Survival as an African Academic Publisher."** In *Academic Book Production and Distribution in Africa. Support from Nordic Countries. Report from a conference at Chr. Michelsen Institute, Bergen, 10-11 April 1997,* edited by Kirsti Hagen Andersen. Fantoft, Norway:

Ch. Michelsen Institute 1997, 17-29.
Also published in *IASP Newsletter*, no. 1 (1997): 1-8.
Analyzes the difficult conditions of the scholarly publisher in Africa in general and those in South Africa in particular, regarded by the author as a "threatened species". The author states that "the most complex and the most difficult of all the problems facing African academic publishing arise from the dominance of academic discourse by countries of the North", and that this domination has led to a situation whereby African academic publishing has been largely consigned to the margins of the international market. She argues "we have to lure the best scholars from Africa back to Africa. We have to extend our commissioning beyond the borders of our own countries, to include the best authors we can locate in Africa and beyond"; and African academic publishers ought to publish titles with a broader appeal than those currently being published. The author also proposes a possible survival scenario based, primarily, on electronic communication and increasing use of the Internet for disseminating important African scholarship, rather than relying on the traditional print media of books and journals.

Horwitz Gray, Eve *see also* ➔ Gray, Eve

2294 Hurst, Christopher **"Publishing and Distribution Problems for African Studies in the United Kingdom: Scholarly Publishing and Africa."** In *African Studies. Papers Presented at a Colloquium at the British Library 7-9 January 1985*. London: The British Library, 1986, 61-65.
Presents an account of the processes of scholarly publishing in general, and relates this to the problems of scholarly publishing in Africa in particular.

2295 Hussein, Janet **"Learned Society Publishing."** In *African Scholarly Publishing Essays*, edited by Alois Mlambo. Oxford: African Books Collective Ltd.; Uppsala: Dag Hammarskjöld Foundation; and Oxford: International Network for the Availability of Scientific Publications (INASP), 2006, 76-82.
Describes the nature of learned society publishing in Africa, helping learned societies to raise the standards of research, development and reporting in their particular disciplines, and focusing on the publishing activities of the Zimbabwe Scientific Association. The author makes a number of recommendations to strengthen learned society publishing on the continent, through collaboration, sharing of experiences, and training programmes, improving quality and output, and thus enhancing the role of African scholarship on the world stage.

2296 Irele, Abiola **"The Challenge of University Publishing in Africa, with Special Reference to Nigeria."** *The African Book Publishing Record* 12, no. 3 (1986): 149-152.
Also reprinted in *Readings on Publishing in Africa and the Third World*, edited by Philip G. Altbach. Buffalo, NY: Bellagio Publishing Network, Research and Information Center (Bellagio Studies in Publishing 1), 1993, 74-77.
The text of a talk given by Abiola Irele to a meeting at the Royal Commonwealth Society, London, as part of the supporting programme of the 2nd Bookweek Africa,

held at the Africa Centre in October 1985. Defines the role of the university press in Africa as "having the responsibility of publishing not only scholarly works emanating from the specialized research devoted to the continent, but also of promoting a literate culture upon which the foundation of the university as a national institution must ultimately rest." Discusses the peculiarities of scholarly publishing in Africa and especially in Nigeria, including an examination of textbook and general publishing. Suggests some possible avenues of expansion for African scholarly presses.

Iwerebon, Felix **"Academic Book Development in Nigeria"** *see* ➜ **Section 2, Country studies: Nigeria** entry 805

2297 Jagar, T. **"Scholarly Publishing in Africa."** *Toguna: The African Studies Program Newsletter* 1, no. 3 (Fall 1997): 1-4.
[Not examined]

2298 Jaygbay, Jacob **"Commercialize or Wither: The Dilemma of Non-Commercial Scholarly Publishers in Africa."** *Bellagio Publishing Network Newsletter*, no. 13 (April 1995): 11-12.
Contends that "if African scholarly publishers are to become commercially competitive, professionalization of the respective publishing entities must be pursued as a priority", and states that there is a need for a pan-African distribution network for African-published scholarly books.

2299 Jaygbay, Jacob **"Scholars and Academic Publishers: The African Context."** *Bellagio Publishing Network Newsletter*, no. 14 (August 1995): 14.
Looks at the role of African scholarly publishers in the development of Africa's communication environment, and reports about a survey to establish the views of African scholars "regarding the under-representation of African produced scholarly work in their respective university and what solutions they envisaged to bridge this gap." Calls for more cooperation among African scholarly publishers and for more effective marketing and distribution beyond national boundaries.

2300 Jaygbay, Jacob **"Scholarly Publishing in Francophone Africa."** *The African Book Publishing Record* 22, no. 2, (1996): 99-105.
Focuses on the production and dissemination of scholarly books in Africa, with special emphasis on francophone countries. Particular attention is given to issues relating to the transfer of knowledge from one language to another; the nature of African scholarship and the constraints under which African academics currently work; the reading culture of Africans and stereotype views and assumptions relating to the reading habit; the impact of the new technologies and electronic publishing; the production, distribution, promotion of scholarly publishing output; and the emerging trends in financing scholarly publishing in Africa. Concludes that "publishers, scholars and creative writers who want to reach the African public should go beyond unproven assumptions" regarding the reading habit, and "must become more 'market oriented' by striving to understand the reading needs of the

African readership, how these needs are expressed, and how they can be met by more innovative approaches."

2301 Jaygbay, Jacob **"Self-Censorship in African Scholarship and Scholarly Publishing."** *Journal of Scholarly Publishing* 29, no. 2 (January 1998): 112-117.
For the scholarly publisher the most visible manifestations of freedom of judgement are expressing and publishing opinion, and this freedom cannot be separated from freedom of speech. The author argues, however, that "the writings of many African scholars today bear signs of censorship in the form of non-state intervention, or at least indirect state censorship ... a form of censorship that is part of the African education system." This study questions some of the self-censorial factors affecting African scholarship and how they impinge on the development of a sustainable scholarly publishing trade on the continent.

2302 Jaygbay, Jacob **"Consortia Repositories and Content Management for African Scholarly Publishers."**
http://www.ascleiden.nl/Pdf/elecpublconfjaygbay.pdf [22/01/08]
A paper presented at the conference on Bridging the North-South Divide in Scholarly Communication on Africa – Threats and Opportunities in the Digital Era, African Studies Centre, Leiden, The Netherlands, September 6-8, 2006. The use of consortia repositories – a grouping of individual research institutions based on region, discipline or other interests, with a common research and publishing agenda – is currently one of the emerging solutions that has created a measure of excitement in the scholarly publishing community. These repositories can be databases, closed file systems, or a combination of both. The author argues that the small size of most social science research institutions in Africa makes collaboration at the consortia level more appropriate than at the institutional level, and that collaborative mechanisms could contribute significantly to promote increased visibility for African social science research. The paper primarily focuses on publication content management systems (CMS) of the type used to track and manage the life cycle of publication content such as books, journals, manuals, etc. It examines technical issues such as system integration requirements, and sets out some of the prerequisites for a consortia CMS to succeed, and some of the questions consortia members will need to ask themselves: for example, what do African researchers, or those elsewhere, expect from a African consortia repository? How is content to be archived, and what are the tools and resources required to maintain archives? What will be the main target market? How will its impact be measured? The author warns that, given the intricacies of the African context, such as multiple languages, the varied formats of existing data, not to mention current socio-economic constraints in most African countries, could make the setting up of an African consortia repository a fairly daunting task. However, "the way African scholars acquire and consume scientific knowledge is changing, and African scholarly publishers can change along with it to remain relevant to African scholarship, or simply wither."

2303 July, Richard [sic], i.e. July, Robert W. **"Book Publishing for African Universities."** *Bellagio Publishing Network Newsletter* 1, no. 4 (December 1992): 3-4.

Relates the personal experience of the problems of the publishing industries in Africa by Robert W. July (author of *History of the African People* and *The Origins of Modern African Thought*) during a year spent in Kenya as visiting a professor at Kenyatta University. Describes a survey conducted by the author in Nigeria, Senegal, Ghana and Kenya, concerning book shortages in Africa and suggests ways in which to relieve the situation.

2304 Kasankha, Samuel **"Publishing Returns to the University of Zambia."** *Bellagio Publishing Network Newsletter*, no. 21 (December 1997): 9-10.

Online:

http://www.bellagiopublishingnetwork.com/newsletter21/kasankha.htm [01/02/08]

Publishing activities at the University of Zambia - operated as the university's printing and publishing department UNZA Press - have been "in the doldrums for at least ten years", due to lack of policy direction, and "mismanagement and internal feuding between the printing and publishing sections of the department led to a total collapse of the publishing function, largely due to the fact that the publishing section was by design totally dependent on profits from the printing section." However, the press has now been revived, and the university has recruited two more editors and a typesetter to join the team of publishing manager and four other staff. One of the most important activities of the new team will the resuscitation of six scholarly journals which have been dormant for some time, and which will now recommence publication by virtue of financial support from ➔ **Sida (115)**. However, the author concedes that "the real task ahead for UNZA will be getting customers for their products; sustaining sales such that, even where there is no donor funding, production continues, deadlines are met and subscribers are not frustrated by indefinite waiting for their copies."

2305 Katama, Agnes **"Resource Sharing, Marketing and Self-Sustainability in Africa: ENVIRONET-Towards a Model for Resource Sharing in Africa's Tertiary Readership."** *African Research and Documentation*, no. 69 (1995): 28-29.

Calls for more sharing of resources and expertise among Africa's scholarly publishers to lessen their dependence on donor funding.

2306 Levey, Lisbeth E. **"Slipping Through the Cracks No More. Better Dissemination of African Research Information."** In *Access to Information. Indaba 97*. Harare: Zimbabwe International Book Fair Trust, 1997, 91-97.

Presents an analysis of coverage of African research in the sciences in selected international databases, showing visibility of African scholarship and book and journals output on the Internet, which is still very limited. The author believes "information and communication technology offers African publishers outlets undreamed of a few years ago, but it requires planning and commitment over the long term together with technical proficiency." Cautions that while new technologies hold out much hope they are not a panacea, and that unless information and communication technology is deployed wisely, the result can be the opposite of the one intended. "Inadequate, incorrect, or out-of-date information on a Web site can foster disrespect for the organization that placed it there."

2307 Manji, Firoze **"Publishing through ICTs for Social Justice in Africa."** In *African Scholarly Publishing Essays,* edited by Alois Mlambo. Oxford: African Books Collective Ltd.; Uppsala: Dag Hammarskjöld Foundation; and Oxford: International Network for the Availability of Scientific Publications (INASP), 2006, 212-222.
Describes the publishing experience of Fahamu http://www.fahamu.org/, and asks whether there are lessons for other NGOs and not-for-profit organizations from these experiences. Fahamu has developed a series of innovative interactive electronic course materials on CD-ROM, and they are also the publishers of *Pambazuka News,* an electronic newsletter covering news, commentary, analysis and a range of other resources on human rights and development in Africa, which currently reaches a readership of more than 70,000 people every week, most of them in Africa.

2308 McLean Rathgeber, Eva-Maria **"Nigeria's University Presses: Problems and Prospects."** *The African Book Publishing Record* 5, no. 1 (January 1979): 13-17.
Identifies the problems and prospects for scholarly publishing in Nigeria in the 1970s and early 1980s. It reports about a study undertaken by the author in 1978, which included a series of interviews with a wide range of book professionals and authors of scholarly books, to seek their views and perceptions of the prospects and constraints of the indigenous scholarly book industries. The author assesses the future prospects for Nigerian university presses, who were [at that time] taking a first step away from university involvement by becoming limited liability companies "which can be seen as a promise of a brighter future for indigenous scholarly publishers." Very dated now, but this remains a useful background study, and is partially based on an MA thesis by Rathgeber entitled **A Study of the Role of the University Press in Nigerian Intellectual Life** *see* entry ➔ **2321**.

McLean Rathgeber, Eva-Maria *see also* Rathgeber, Eva-Maria

2309 McMaster, David N. **"Occasional Papers of the Department of Geography, Makerere, Uganda, 1967-."** *African Research and Documentation,* no. 51 (1989): 8-18.
Reports about the prolific publishing output by the Department of Geography at Makerere University [in the 1960s and 70s].

2310 Mlambo, Alois **"Problems of Writing, Publishing and Distribution of Scholarly Materials: Problems of Access."** In *Access to Information. Indaba*

97. Harare: Zimbabwe International Book Fair Trust, 1997, 98-105.
The author is an academic writer and the national chairperson of the ➔ **Zimbabwe Academic and Non-Fiction Authors' Association (1202)**, and in this paper he highlights some of the constraints facing the academic researcher in present-day Zimbabwe, and seeks to show how the problems specific to academic authors contribute to the general national problem of lack of access to information. Identifies some of the major obstacles confronting academics, including poor or non-existent funding for research and writing, the absence of a coherent and viable national book promotion and distribution policy, and "the reluctance of local publishers to publish academic and non-fiction works (for understandable commercial reasons), the unwillingness of overseas publishers to publish materials produced by unknown foreign authors writing on what they regard as unknown, foreign and parochial subjects, and the absence of a national reading culture."

2311 Mlambo, Alois **"The Case for Publishing African Scholarship in Africa."** In *African Scholarly Publishing Essays,* edited by Alois Mlambo. Oxford: African Books Collective Ltd.; Uppsala: Dag Hammarskjöld Foundation; and Oxford: International Network for the Availability of Scientific Publications (INASP), 2006, 11-24.
The Zimbabwean scholar Alois Mlambo aims to provide a synopsis of the current state of the scholarship and publishing in Africa, and seeks to explore the factors and constraints that have contributed to "the underdevelopment of African publishing." The author contends that "over the past two decades, channels for publishing African scholarship in Africa have declined considerably. Consequently, African scholarship either remains unpublished or is published in the North." He believes there is a compelling case for African scholarship to be published *in* Africa: "if African scholarship is to serve the African people well and best, it should be published where it is most easily accessible to the people whose interests and problems it investigates and addresses, preferably in languages that are understood by the majority of people."

2312 Mlambo, Alois, ed. **African Scholarly Publishing Essays.** Oxford: African Books Collective Ltd.; Uppsala: Dag Hammarskjöld Foundation; and Oxford: International Network for the Availability of Scientific Publications (INASP), 2006. 273 pp. (distributed in North America by Michigan State University Press)
This volume grew out of a seminar on scholarly publishing held in Arusha, Tanzania in 2002. It was originally announced for publication as *The African Scholarly Writers and Publishers Handbook,* as a sequel to the much acclaimed ➔ **African Writers' Handbook (2507)** published by African Books Collective in 1999, but was subsequently recast primarily as a collection of essays by book practitioners and a number of African academics. The preface to the volume offers no explanation why the original handbook concept was abandoned, although the essay collection does contain a few more practical papers such as Alois Mlambo's "Choosing a Publisher", Mary Jay's "The Book Publishing Process", and Charles Bewlay's "A Publisher's Expectations of Academic Authors". Also useful, published as an appendix in the book, is a reprint of CODESRIA's *Guide for Authors,* a small booklet published by

them in 2003 that contains a great deal of helpful guidance as well as a glossary. The collection takes stock of the current status of academic publishing on the continent. and contains a total of 25 papers, together with an index. Following two introductory essays, papers are grouped under a number of headings and sub-headings: Part 1, Perspectives: Scholars and Publishers, African-Language Publishing, Librarianship; and Part 2, Writing and Publishing; New Technologies. This essay collection offers a rich resource on many aspects of African scholarly publishing today. *Note:* most of the papers in the collection are individually abstracted elsewhere in this bibliography.
Reviews:
Africana Libraries Newsletter, no. 120, May 2007
Online: http://www.indiana.edu/~libsalc/african/ALN%20120/alnbookrvw.html [01/02/08]
The African Book Publishing Record, vol. 33, no. 2, 2007

2313 Mugo, Micere G. **"Research and Publishing in Africa."** *Southern Africa Political & Economic Monthly* 11, no. 9, (July/August 1998): 19-20. [Not examined]

2314 Mutowo, Maurice K. **"Academic Publishing at the University of Zimbabwe."** *African Publishing Review* 8, no. 5 (September/October 1999): 4-6.
Describes publishing activities at the University of Zimbabwe [as at 1999] and some of the problems that are associated with it, including problems of funding, a sometimes unsatisfactory peer review process in the evaluation of new manuscript proposals, skills shortages, and underfunded marketing. Offers some suggestions on the way forward in terms of marketing and distribution, exploring possibilities for co-publication with publishing partners in the countries of the North, and measures to keep costs down.

2315 Nukpezah, H.M. **"Problems of Scholarly Publishing in Ghana. A Case Study of Ghana Universities Press."** *The Book Industry* 3, no. 1 (January-March 1993): 4-5.
Discusses the problems of finance, marketing, and skilled personnel as they relate to scholarly publishing in Ghana, and more specifically to Ghana Universities Press.

2316 Nwankwo, Victor **"Local Publishing and the Shortage of Tertiary Textbooks in Nigeria."** *The Publisher* 2, no. 1 (March 1991): 27-29.
Examines the combined effects of the economic crisis, and an astronomic rise in the pressure on places at universities in Nigeria, on publishing in the country resulting in an acute shortage of tertiary level textbooks.

2317 Olukoju, Ayodeji **"The Crisis of Research and Academic Publishing in Nigerian Universities: The Twentieth Century and Beyond."**
http://www.codesria.org/Links/conferences/universities/Ayodeji_Olukoj u.pdf [01/02/08]

A paper presented at the 28th annual Spring Symposium, African Universities in the Twenty-First Century, University of Illinois/CODESRIA, Dakar, Senegal, 25-27 April 2002. Academic publishing in Nigeria, especially university press publishing, has been in decline for the last two decades at least. This paper examines the strategies adopted by Nigerian scholars to cope with the collapse, or near-collapse, of academic journals and university presses to publish their scholarly research. The paper traces the beginnings of academic publishing in Nigeria up to the period of the late 1970s, and provides some background of the reasons that led to the crisis in Nigerian higher education and its negative impact on academic research and scholarly publishing. It discusses the survival strategies adopted by Nigerian academics to cope with the situation, their search for alternative publishing outlets, the emergence of self-publishing, and the decline of high standards in scholarship, and the near-abandonment of the peer-review process by (usually short-lived) new Nigerian journals. In his conclusion the author offers a set of recommendations for encouraging research and scholarship, and for the funding and revitalization of publication outlets for scholarly research in Nigeria.

2318 Olukoshi, Adebayo, and Francis B. Nyamnjoh **"CODESRIA: Over 30 Years of Scholarly Publishing."** In *African Scholarly Publishing Essays*, edited by Alois Mlambo. Oxford: African Books Collective Ltd.; Uppsala: Dag Hammarskjöld Foundation; and Oxford: International Network for the Availability of Scientific Publications (INASP), 2006, 57-65.
Created in 1973, the Dakar-based Council for the Development of Social Science Research (CODESRIA) has over the years published a most impressive array of scholarly work – in both book and journals formats, publishing in English, French, Arabic and Portuguese – attracting authors from all over Africa and the diaspora, and promoting greater visibility and competitiveness for African scholarship. This article narrates its major contribution to scholarly publishing on the continent and its vital role in the dissemination of African scholarship. The authors also describe CODESRIA's support for scholars through its various programmes, its publishing list of books and journals, its rigorous peer review process, editorial organization, and editorial advisory boards.

2319 Ondari-Okemwa, Ezra **Scholarly Publishing in Sub-Saharan Africa in the Twenty-first Century: Challenges and Opportunities.**
First Monday 12, no. 10 (1 October 2007)
http://www.uic.edu/htbin/cgiwrap/bin/ojs/index.php/fm/article/view/1966/1842 [01/02/08]
Explores the challenges and opportunities of scholarly publishing in sub-Saharan Africa in the 21st century, although the title of the study is somewhat misleading as it primarily presents an analysis of *journal* publishing and there is no discussion of scholarly book publishing by, for example, African university presses. Information on scholarly publishing in sub-Saharan Africa between 1997 and 2007 was extracted by way of an analysis from the *Science Citation Index* (SCI), the *Social Sciences Citation Index* (SSCI) and the *Arts and Humanities Citation Index* (A&HCI). Publications authored by African scholars residing in the diaspora were excluded. Comparative figures of scholarly publishing output in other regions of the world are also

provided, and the author hopes the study may serve as an indicator of the contribution of the African region to overall world production and generation of knowledge. She examines some of the principal reasons why the African region still compares unfavourably with scholarly publishing output in other parts of the world, which include underfunded African universities, poor library and research facilities, unsatisfactory work conditions and lack of incentives, slow development of ICT, and the author states that "most scholars do not have access to the Internet."

2320 Peterson, Lorna **"Using the Ghanaian Journal *Research Review* as an Example for Demonstrating Access to African Research and Scholarship."** *World Libraries* 12, no. 2 (Fall 2002)
Online: http://www.worlib.org/vol12no2/peterson_v12n2.shtml [01/02/08]
Reports the results of bibliographic searching, indexing and citation analysis of the Ghanaian journal *Research Review* in order to determine barriers to access. Barriers to the dissemination of information are defined as: lack of indexing, lack of abstracting, lack of abstracting in a culturally relevant way, lack of a culturally relevant thesaurus, lack of holdings/purchasing by European and North American libraries, lack of citing indigenous African authors publishing in indigenous journals, and lack of preservation of originals for long term access. The author evaluates citation analysis of selected writers as authors and cited authors, the production quality of the journal, and the efforts to digitize its contents, are also addressed. Peterson argues "the preservation of African research and scholarship should not be an either/or proposition of digital versus paper. There is no reason that both cannot be supported and nurtured." She goes on to say "barriers to the dissemination of African research and scholarship are surmountable. Improved indexing, and inclusion of African published materials by American and European international bibliographic tools can be accomplished and would help to dissolve this knowledge barrier."

2321 Rathgeber, Eva-Maria **A Study of the Role of the University Press in Nigerian Intellectual Life.** Montréal: McGill University, 1978. MA thesis. 128 l.
[Not examined]

Seeber, Monica **Academic and Non-fiction Writing and Authors' Rights** *see* → **Copyright and legal deposit/Authors' rights** entry **1812**

2322 Shaba, Steve **"Flogging a Dead Horse? The State of Tertiary Book Publishing in Nigeria."** *Glendora Review* 1, no. 3 (1996): 39-41.
Online:
http://digital.lib.msu.edu/projects/africanjournals/html/itemdetail.cfm?recordID=2191 [15/01/08]
Takes stock of the tertiary publishing crisis in Nigeria; finds that it is "comatose", and offers a number of strategies and suggestions which the author believes will improve the current situation "with or without a depressed economy".

2323 Shibanda, George Gundu **"Scholarly Publishing in Kenya: A Review of the Past and Present Transformation Eras."** *African Journal of Library, Archives & Information Science* 7, no. 1 (April 1997): 51-62.
Sets out the historical background and then examines the growth of scholarly publishing in Kenya since 1964, including the activities of the (now defunct) East African Literature Bureau. Thereafter looks at current academic and scholarly publishing and the establishment of the Nairobi University Press in 1984 with a grant from the British American Tobacco Company; also reviews scholarly publishing activities elsewhere in Kenya, and current problems encountered in the publication of scholarly books.

2324 Sifuniso, Monde **"Publishing at the University of Zambia."** In *Proceedings from the Third International Conference on Scholarly Publishing, London, October, 20-21 1983.* Oslo: International Association of Scholarly Publishers, 1983, 50-52.
Charts the history of publishing at the University of Zambia, from 1937 to 1983.

Smith, Datus C. jr. **"Scholarly Publishing in the Third World"** *see* ➔ **Section 2, General, comparative and regional studies: Comparative studies** entry **243**

2325 Southern Africa Book Development Education Trust **Open Forum on Scholarly Publishing, 10 August 2001.**
http://www.sabdet.com/openforum2001.htm#sess1 [01/02/08]
This open forum was organised during the 2001 Zimbabwe International Book Fair by the ➔ **Zimbabwe Academic and Non-Fiction Authors Association (1202)**, and the ➔ **Southern African Book Development Education Trust (113)**, with the aim of promoting information exchange, debate and networking. The material offered here includes summaries of the papers presented – on academic writing and publishing, and how to get published – together with transcripts of the discussion that ensued after each presentation.

2326 Udoeyop, N.J. **"Scholarly Publishing in Nigeria."** *Scholarly Publishing* 4, no. 1 (October 1972): 51-60.
A portrayal of scholarly publishing in Nigeria in the 1970s by a former editor of Ibadan University Press, the oldest of Nigeria's indigenous scholarly publishers, which evolved gradually over more than a decade. The article sets out the press's role in education at all levels and in encouraging the study of Nigeria's national heritage, describes how the press operates, examines some problems and constraints, and looks at the challenges for the press in the years ahead.

2327 Udoeyop, N.J. **"The Problems of Publishing for a University Press in Africa."** In *Publishing in Africa in the Seventies,* edited by Edwina Oluwasanmi, Eva McLean, and Hans M. Zell. Ile-Ife: University of Ife Press, 1975, 318-328.

An early account of university press publishing in Africa. Argues that the problems of publishing for an African university press stem, in part, from the history of the press and that of its parent body, together with inexperience and lack of publishing skills, awkward management structures, the slow process of decision-making, and other factors. The author believes university presses should focus on "African humanities", and should be wary of too great a diffusion of subject areas, which will make promotion difficult. While university presses should develop and publish tertiary level textbooks, the author warns that textbook publishing is risky and should be approached with caution and only after a period of consolidation. University press editors and directors should have more autonomy in list development and the decision-making process. The author was formerly Editor and Acting Director of the Ibadan University Press during the 1970s.

2328 Wafawarowa, Brian **"Models of Scholarly Publishing Houses."** In *African Scholarly Publishing Essays*, edited by Alois Mlambo. Oxford: African Books Collective Ltd.; Uppsala: Dag Hammarskjöld Foundation; and Oxford: International Network for the Availability of Scientific Publications (INASP), 2006, 52-56.
A short overview of the different types of scholarly publishing platforms in Africa, (primarily in South Africa) and the nature of their operations. The author explains that the simple need to survive has shaped the traditional institutional models that exist at the moment, and how attempts to enhance the viability of these publishing operations, by taking advantage of new technologies, has led to the development of new and alternative models based on new production, publishing, storage, transmission and transactional methods that can support low economies of scale. "These alternative models are the models of the future and the hope for scholarly publishing in Africa."

2329 Wole, Darge, and Messelech Habte **"The Addis Ababa University Press: Experiences and Reflections."** In *African Scholarly Publishing Essays*, edited by Alois Mlambo. Oxford: African Books Collective Ltd.; Uppsala: Dag Hammarskjöld Foundation; and Oxford: International Network for the Availability of Scientific Publications (INASP), 2006, 91-96.
Describes the experience and activities of the Addis Ababa University Press in Ethiopia (established in 1967), and the constraints and problems it has faced over the years in terms of the recruitment and training of staff, finance, publishing capacity, finding suitable reviewers for manuscript assessments, production, and sales and marketing.

2330 Zegeye, Abebe **"Knowledge Production and Publishing Africa."** *CODESRIA Bulletin*, no. 3 & 4 (2005): 31-34.
Online: http://www.codesria.org/Links/Publications/bulletin3_05/zegeye.pdf [01/02/08]
An attempt to provide an analysis of the relationship between knowledge production and the publishing industry in Africa, which, the author believes, is still dominated

by Western publishers. Examines the publishing activities of a number of institutional and commercial publishers in Ethiopia and in Zimbabwe, and looks at issues such as readership and access to written material.

2331 Zeleza, Paul Tiyambe **"The Challenges of Academic Publishing for African Scholars."** *Bellagio Publishing Network Newsletter*, no. 13 (April 1995): 4-5.

The winner of the 1994 ➔ **Noma Award for Publishing in Africa (98)** examines the publishing opportunities for African scholars in the West, the marginalization of African scholarship by some of the leading Western Africanist journals, and the structural and conjectural constraints of academic publishing and distribution in Africa.

2332 Zeleza, Paul Tiyambe **"Trends and Inequalities in the Production of Africanist Knowledge."** In *Manufacturing African Studies and Crises,* by Paul Tiyambe Zeleza. Dakar: CODESRIA, 1997, 44-69.

This is a much cited article that examines the spatial and institutional locations of the leading Africanist academic productions in English, and the national and gender identities of those who produce, categorize, disseminate, and safeguard this particular form of knowledge. More specifically, it looks at the publishing trends in five leading English-language Africanist journals between 1982 and 1992. While it primarily deals with an analysis of the politics of academic publishing in North America and Western Europe, it also includes a fairly extensive discussion of academic publishing in Africa, and suggests that the publishing crisis of the 1980s has undermined African scholarship and increased African scholars' dependency on Africanist publication outlets elsewhere. The author concludes "it is more than evident that Africans and women are grossly under-represented in most Africanist journal publications [i.e. those published North America and Europe]". In the final analysis, Zeleza states, "the solution lies in Africans developing and sustaining their own publishing outlets, out of which can emerge truly African intellectual communities capable of directing and controlling African studies. When that is done, and current developments seem encouraging, the exclusionary practices of the Africanist academic media will not matter much and the doors will be open for more fruitful and equitable intellectual relations between Africans, both at home and abroad, and the Africanists."

2333 Zell, Hans M. **"African Scholarly Publishing in the Eighties."** *Scholarly Publishing* 18, no. 1 (January 1987): 97-107.

Also reprinted in *Readings on Publishing in Africa and the Third World*, edited by Philip G. Altbach. Buffalo, NY: Bellagio Publishing Network, Research and Information Center (Bellagio Studies in Publishing 1), 1993, 20-30.

A detailed examination of the state of African scholarly publishing in the 1980s. Reviews the decline in publishing output, and the demise of small literary magazines; diminishing markets in Africa, book piracy, and the significance of the impact of the "book famine". Offers an overview of scholarly publishing in Africa and discusses the problems and misconceptions affecting this sector of the industry.

Scientific, technical and medical publishing

See also
→ **Digital media and electronic publishing/New printing technology**
→ **Journals and magazine publishing**
→ **Open access publishing**
→ **Scholarly publishing (General)**

Academy of Science of South Africa **Report on a Strategic Approach to Research Publishing in South Africa** *see* → **Section 3, Country studies: South Africa** entry **970**

2334 African Academy of Sciences. **Proceedings AAS/IAMP Workshop on Scientific Writing for Young Scientists and Clinicians. October 23-26, 2006.** Nairobi. Nairobi: African Academy of Sciences, 2006. 12 pp.
Online: http://www.iamp-online.org/resources/folder.2007-01-15.6568256148/aas_iamp-workshop-proceedings.pdf [01/02/08]
A report about a workshop organized by African Academy of Sciences (AAS) and the Inter-Academy Medical Panel (IAMP) held for young scientists and clinicians from the East African region. Includes some discussion about journal publishing, the editorial processes of journal publishing and submission of articles to scientific journals.

2335 Aziz, Abdoul **"La problématique de l'édition scientifique en Afrique francophone. Bilan et perspectives."** In *L'édition en Afrique francophone*, compiled and edited by Gilles Vilasco and Dominique Hado Zidouemba. Abidjan: Association des Rédacteurs et Editeurs Scientifiques d'Afrique Francophone, 1990, 31-35.
Presents some facts and figures as they relate to science publishing in francophone Africa, and examines matters of government policies in this area.

2336 Bgoya, Walter **The Development of Technical Publishing in Africa.** Wageningen, Netherlands: Centre Technique de Coopération Agricole et Rurale (CTA) (Special Paper; extract from CTA Annual Report 1992), n.d. [1993]. 8 pp.
Reviews the role, relevance and affordability of technical publications in an African situation. The authors puts forward strategies for developing and financing the indigenous publishing industry, and makes a number of suggestions for creating a market for technical publications in Africa.

2337 Burafuta, Jean-Paul **"L'édition scientifique au Burundi."** In *L'édition en Afrique francophone*, compiled and edited by Gilles Vilasco and Dominique Hado Zidouemba. Abidjan: Association des Rédacteurs et Editeurs Scientifiques d'Afrique Francophone, 1990, 119-122.
A short overview of scientific and scholarly publishing in Burundi.

2338   Centre Technique de Coopération Agricole et Rurale ACP-UE
**Promoting Technical Publishing in Africa. Seminar Proceedings. Arnhem,
Netherlands, 3-6 November 1992.** Wageningen: Technical Centre for
Agricultural and Rural Cooperation of ACP-EU (CTA), 1994. 129 pp.
Also published in French as **La promotion du livre technique en Afrique.
Actes de seminaire. Arnhem, Pays-Bays, 3-6 novembre 1992.**
The proceedings of an important seminar sponsored by the ➔ **Technical Centre for
Agricultural and Rural Cooperation of ACP-EU/CTA (116)** held in the Netherlands
in November 1992 that brought together some 60 professionals from the book
industries in 22 countries. The seminar examined the obstacles facing the technical
book in Africa, and how to breathe new life into African publishing. The proceedings
are divided into three sections: (i) 'The Challenge' contains four papers delivered at
the plenary session; (ii) 'Suggestions' is a summary of the joint deliberations of the
seminar participants, presenting the strategic and practical recommendations in three
parts; and (iii) presents profiles of all participant organizations on the basis of
completed questionnaires. *Note:* some of the papers in this collection are individually
abstracted elsewhere in this bibliography.
Reviews:
The African Book Publishing Record vol. 21, no. 2, 1995

2339   Certain, Edith **"FAME: An Initiative to Promote Local Medical
Research Publishing in Africa."** *Saudi Medical Journal* 25, no. 1 (January
2004): [Supplement] S46-S46.
Through a wide range of grants, the UNDP/World Bank/WHO Special programme
for Research and Training in Tropical Diseases (TDR) supports major health research
projects in African countries as well as in other regions, the results of which are
published in well-known biomedical journals. Bibliometric analyses to assess the
impact of TDR grants in published literature have shown that the vast majority of
TDR grant recipients publish in mainstream biomedical journals with a high impact
factor rather than in their national medical journals, and since most of these research
results are cited by scientists outside Africa, the impact of this research on local
researchers, health professionals and policy makers in Africa, all of whom have little
access to major international health journals, is questionable. In 2002, TDR/RCS
(Research and Capacity Strengthening) launched an initiative to strengthen local
publication of health research conducted in or relevant to Africa in order to give
greater visibility to African medical research. A postal survey carried out of 63
African medical journals in July 2002 found that the majority of medical and health
journals were under-funded, did not publish regularly, lacked high quality articles
and standard peer review practice, and were mostly invisible to the rest of the
international medical community. In October 2002, 15 African medical journal
editors, 4 mainstream medical journal editors, and representatives of international
editors' associations and other interested partners were brought together in a
consultative meeting and workshop in Geneva. Setting up the ➔ **Forum of African
Medical Editors/FAME (15)** a professional association and network was the first step
taken by the African editors in reviewing the problems faced by their journals and
trying to find common solutions. Capacity building within existing African medical
journals and collaborative projects with interested parties should lead to greater

journal sustainability and regular publishing, improved quality of the peer review process and contents, as well as higher regional and international visibility of African medical research through indexing in major bibliographic databases.

2340 Chabrol, Didier, and Paul Osborn **"The Study on Technical Publishing in Africa: Findings and Conclusions."** In *Promoting Technical Publishing in Africa. Seminar Proceedings. Arnhem, Netherlands, 3-6 November, 1992.* Wageningen, Netherlands: Technical Centre for Agriculture and Rural Cooperation of ACP-EU (CTA), 1994, 11-24.
A summary of the findings of a major study on technical publishing in Africa, which was used as a point of departure for the CTA workshop in Arnhem, Netherlands, in November 1992 (*see also* ➔ **2338** above).

2341 Chandravanshi, B.S. **"Opportunities and Problems Facing Authors and Publishers in Science Publishing within the African Continent."** In *African Scholarly Publishing Essays*, edited by Alois Mlambo. Oxford: African Books Collective Ltd.; Uppsala: Dag Hammarskjöld Foundation; and Oxford: International Network for the Availability of Scientific Publications (INASP), 2006, 39-44.
Examines the problems related to publishing science research within Africa. The author laments the fact that only a very small percentage of scientific books and journals published in the world originate from Africa and argues that African books and journals are less frequently read and cited. He contends that African scientists prefer to publish in Northern science journals as first choice, and that African libraries prefer to subscribe to science journals published in the North. The author believes that the situation can only change when African scientists start publishing their best work in African-published books and journals, but that this in turn "will happen only when African universities subscribe to African journals and purchase other African publications, and when library users demand that their libraries provide African publications because they perceive African scientific publications to be of good and reliable quality and thus put a high value on them."

2342 Déazon, André, and Gilles Vilasco **"L'édition scientifique à l'Université Nationale de Côte d'Ivoire."** In *L'édition en Afrique francophone*, edited by Gilles Vilasco and Dominique Hado Zidouemba. Abidjan: Association des Rédacteurs et Editeurs Scientifiques d'Afrique Francophone, 1990, 63-74.
Charts the development of scholarly and scientific publishing l'Université Nationale de Côte d'Ivoire, and reviews the publishing activities of its university press.

2343 Diop, Bara, *et al.* **"L'édition scientifique au Sénégal."** In *L'édition en Afrique francophone*, compiled and edited by Gilles Vilasco and Dominique Hado Zidouemba. Abidjan: Association des Rédacteurs et Editeurs Scientifiques d'Afrique Francophone, 1990, 81-92.
Analyzes the main structures that comprise scientific and scholarly publishing in Senegal. Contains information on scientific publishing by the government, the

activities of UNESCO's Regional Bureau for Education in Africa (BREDA), and discusses the role of non-governmental organizations, foundations, and associations.

2344 Doumbia, A.T., and R. Ba Touré **"L'édition scientifique au Mali."** In *L'édition en Afrique francophone*, compiled and edited by Gilles Vilasco and Dominique Hado Zidouemba. Abidjan: Association des Rédacteurs et Editeurs Scientifiques d'Afrique Francophone, 1990, 75-79.
Reviews the state of scholarly and scientific publishing in Mali concluding that, although inseparable from scientific research, it seems to have been left to flounder.

2345 Field-Juma, Alison **"Policy Reform for Commercially Viable Publishing in Africa."** In *Promoting Technical Publishing in Africa. Seminar Proceedings. Arnhem, Netherlands, 3-6 November 1992.* Wageningen, Netherlands: Technical Centre for Agricultural and Rural Cooperation of ACP-EU (CTA), 1994, 25-28.
There are many obstacles to technical publishing in Africa and different ways to remove them. In this brief discussion the policy level is examined with particular reference to Kenya, based on the experiences of a small academic publishing house, Initiatives Ltd.

2346 Groupe de Recherche et d'Echanges Technologiques (GRET) **Promouvoir le livre technique en Afrique.** Paris: GRET, 1991. 87 pp.
Looks at the challenges of promoting technical books in Africa. Finds that some of the books offered for sale are either not suitable or inappropriate, or are far too expensive. Examines some of the problems in book distribution and promotion, including a weak retail trade in most countries. Proposes a number of measures that might help to improve the situation.

2347 Isoun, T.T. **"Publishing and Productivity of Science in Africa: Scientometrics."** *Whydah* 5, no. 1 (March 1996): 1-4.
Looks at funding of scientific research in Africa, criteria for measuring productivity of sciences, and provides a short overview of the current state of science and technology research in Africa. Reviews the activities of Academy Science Publishers in Nairobi, including its journal *Discovery and Innovation*. States that despite the fact that some progress has been made by African publishers, the publication of scientific and scholarly works in Africa is still "beset with a multiplicity of problems and constraints", and calls on African governments and development institutions to provide more encouragement and positive support for science publishing in Africa.

2348 Katjavivi, Jane **"Producing Science Books in Africa."** *African Publishing Review* 7, no. 2 (March/April 1998): 1-2, 7.
Based on her experience as head of New Namibia Books in Windhoek the author describes how they developed a science course for junior secondary school pupils. The books were written by Namibian authors, drawing on local examples, using local available resources, with recognisable images and relevance for the everyday lives of

Namibian school children, and with text and illustrations that were inclusive, non-racist and non-sexist.

2349 Maphasa, Nthunzi; Dominic Nyoro; Daniel M. Brande, and Amerly A. Ollennu **"Issues Affecting Science Publishing in Africa."** *African Publishing Review* 7, no. 2 (March/April 1998): 10-11.
A round-up of the major issues, problems and constraints as it relates to the development and production of science books for primary and secondary schools in three African countries: Ghana, Kenya, and Lesotho.

2350 Miranda, Maria Filomena Ribeiro **"L'édition scientifique en Guinée-Bissau."** In *L'édition en Afrique francophone*, compiled and edited by Gilles Vilasco and Dominique Hado Zidouemba. Abidjan: Association des Rédacteurs et Editeurs Scientifiques d'Afrique Francophone, 1990, 109-113.
Reflects on the lack of dynamism in scientific and scholarly publishing in Guinea-Bissau.

2351 Mouton, Johann; Nelius Boshoff, and Robert Tijssen **"A Comprehensive Analysis of South African Research Journals."** In *Report on a Strategic Approach to Research Publishing in South Africa.* Pretoria: Academy of Science of South Africa, 2006, 29-59.
Online:
http://search.sabinet.co.za/images/ejour/assaf/Report/assaf_chapter3.pdf [30/03/08]
The authors report that there are currently at least 255 South African scientific or scholarly journals recognized by the South African Department of Education as meeting the minimum requirements for a state subsidy under the policy of supply-side support for authors (and their institutions) who publish in these journals. Twenty-three of these journals appear in one of the ISI's (Institute of Scientific Information, now Thomson Scientific) citation indexes, 14 are indexed in the *International Bibliography of the Social Sciences*, while the remaining 220 journals are accredited separately by the Department. Supported by extensive statistical data, the authors provide a comprehensive analysis of these journals, examining the history of journal accreditation in South Africa, reviewing scientific databases and citation indexes, and present profiles of South African research journals in terms of ISI cited and non-cited, and foreign vs. local journals. They also provide an analysis of publication data by main scientific field and over time; institutional patterns in journal publication; basic demographic analyses of South African authors by race, gender, age and by scientific field; and review current practice to assess the impact factors and citation profiles of South African journals.

2352 Negash, Legesse **"*SINET: An Ethiopian Journal of Science* — The Tribulations of an African Journal."** In *Knowledge Dissemination in Africa: The Role of Scholarly Journal*, edited by Philip G. Altbach and Damtew Teferra. Chestnut Hill, MA: Bellagio Publishing Network Research and Information Center (Bellagio Studies in Publishing, 8), 1998, 75-84.

Focuses on a leading Ethiopian scientific journal, published twice yearly since 1978 by the Faculty of Science at Addis Ababa. Over the years the journal went through numerous difficult patches because of lack of financial support, an absence of qualified and dedicated secretarial support or inadequately trained staff, the lack of publishable papers, unreliable referees who sit on papers for over a year, frequent changes of editors, lack of visibility of the journal due to poor circulation, and a troubled academic atmosphere in the university due to political instability. However, during recent years *SINET* has managed to significantly enhance its reputation as a journal of quality and, while some problems remain, it has improved both content and volume and has made it possible for numerous young local scholars to have their work published.

2353 Nomenyo, Adzowavi Dzigbodi **"L'édition scientifique au Togo."** In *L'édition en Afrique francophone*, compiled and edited by Gilles Vilasco and Dominique Hado Zidouemba. Abidjan: Association des Rédacteurs et Editeurs Scientifiques d'Afrique Francophone, 1990, 93-107.
Examines Togo's national policy regarding scholarly and scientific publishing, and presents an inventory of scientific publications, both periodical and other publications.

2354 Nwagwu, Williams **"Mapping the Landscape of Biomedical Research in Nigeria since 1967."** *Learned Publishing* 18, no. 3 (July 2005): 200-211
Online:
http://www.ingentaconnect.com/content/alpsp/lp/2005/00000018/00000 003/art00006 [30/03/08]
Maps the biomedical literature of Nigeria by source/origin of publications and authorships from 1967 to 2002. The mapping exercise – which includes an exmination of local journals, their publications and their authorships – was designed to provide crucial information to both government and others taking funding and related decisions regarding biomedical research in Nigeria. Data was collected from MEDLINE. Scientists publishing on Nigerian biomedicine have written 6,820 articles in 295 journals/sources. Only eight of the 121 local journals that published biomedical research in Nigeria during the period were included in MEDLINE's listing (2.72%), while there were 32 (10.84%) regional and 255 (86.44%) external journals used. Local journals appeared to be more heavily used than regional and external ones. It was also shown that MEDLINE does not adequately represent Nigeria's biomedical literature.

2355 Odhiambo, Thomas R. **"Creating an African Publishing Forum for International Science."** *African Crop Science Journal* 1, no. 2 (1993): 73-74.
A review of the publishing policies of the *African Crop Science Journal*, which aims to publish only "results reflecting quality work, reflection and theories which are both appropriate as well as stimulating for human knowledge".

2356 Pouris, Anastassios **"An Assessment of the Impact and Visibility of South African Journals."** *Scientometrics* 62, no. 2 (January 2005): 213-222.

The assessment of scientific journals is of particular interest to South Africa's higher education institutions as their research is partly funded according to the number of publications of their members of staff. This article has two objectives: (1) to identify the effects of the government's withdrawal of financial support on these journals' impact factors; (2) to provide an assessment of the visibility of the South African journals indexed in *Journal Citation Report* (JCR). The findings indicate that the termination of the government interference in the affairs of the journals generally had a beneficial effect on the impact factors of the journals. South African journals are found to be well represented in JCR, similar or better to that of the scientifically small countries in Europe, and represent approximately 90% of the African continent's journals in the JCR database. The author reviews specific scientific disciplines and the journals are assessed according to their impact factors, the impact factors of journals citing them, and the self-citing and self-cited rates.

2357   Pouris, Anastassios **"A Bibliometric Assessment of South African Research Publications in the International Indexed Database of Thomson ISI."** In *Report on a Strategic Approach to Research Publishing in South Africa.* Pretoria: Academy of Science of South Africa, 2006, 9-28.
Online:
http://search.sabinet.co.za/images/ejour/assaf/Report/assaf_chapter2.pdf [30/03/08]
Supported by an extensive range of tables and statistics, this study offers fresh analytical insights related to South African research publications and journals indexed by Thomson Scientific (previously Institute for Scientific Information/ISI), and is designed to inform the development of appropriate approaches for the promotion of South African research journals. The information provided is made up of three components: the first component presents an analysis of the number of South African publications (i.e. articles where at least one author gives a South African address) captured in the ISI databases according to scientific discipline and sub-discipline for the period 1981 to 2004. These are classified in the ISI set of 106 selected fields and subsequently aggregated into 20 science fields, 4 social sciences fields and 10 fields in the arts and humanities. The second component is related to the citation impacts of indexed South African articles in the various fields and for the period 1981 to 2004. The third component provides information related to all the journals which are included in each field in the *Science Citation Index* and the *Social Sciences Citation Index*, and compares the South African journals listed in the two indices with their peer journals in the field.

2358   Seck, Camara Sarang, and Nabé Mohamed **"L'édition scientifique en Guinée."** In *L'édition en Afrique Francophone*, compiled and edited by Gilles Vilasco and Dominique Hado Zidouemba. Abidjan: Association des Rédacteurs et Editeurs Scientifiques d'Afrique Francophone, 1990, 114-117.
A short overview of scholarly and scientific publishing in Guinea.

2359 Siegfried, N.; K. Busgeeth, and E. Certain **Scope and Geographical Distribution of African Medical Journals Active in 2005**. *South African Medical Journal* 96, no. 6 (June 2006): 533-538
Reports about a project that aimed to identify all African medical journals actively publishing in 2005, and to create a geodatabase of these to evaluate and monitor future journal activity. A search was undertaken for relevant African medical journals on electronic databases, library catalogues and Web sites, and a list was compiled of active journals. The survey was conducted via questionnaire addressed to editors of all listed African medical journals defined as having an editorial base on the continent. 158 African medical journals were identified, published in 33 countries; 153 editors were surveyed via email, post and/or fax, achieving a 39% response rate. Of those which responded, 51 journals were published in English, 7 in French and 1 in Portuguese. Most journals were owned by an association or a society and were funded from a combination of sources. Journals covered general medical and specialist medical interest equally. Most (41 of 59 journals) had a circulation below 1,000, and most (52/59) published 4 or fewer issues a year. Almost all the journals included original research, and articles were peer reviewed. However few were indexed on Medline or EMBASE. Plotting journal location using Geographic Information Systems (GIS) software provided a snapshot view of current journal activity. This study is likely to represent the most comprehensive list of current African medical journals. It confirmed growth in African health care research and journal activity on the continent, but limited inclusion in international databases and accessibility to African researchers remain challenges in achieving publication of high-quality African research in high-quality African journals.

2360 Silver, Keith "**Pressing the 'Send' Key — Preferential Journal Access in Developing Countries.**" *Learned Publishing* 15, no. 2 (April 2002): 91-97. Online:
http://www.ingentaconnect.com/content/alpsp/lp/2002/00000015/00000 002/art00003 [30/03/08]
Arguably the most striking recent departure in online publishing has been the succession of initiatives designed to provide free or reduced-rate journal access to the developing world. This article examines the motives behind some of these campaigns – including those serving African libraries and scholars – and probes the difficulties associated with supplying scientific information equitably, productively, and to an appropriate readership in developing or transitional countries. It considers the strengths and weaknesses of the main solutions currently on offer, while advocating a more unified approach based on the three C's of co-ordination, comprehensiveness, and clarity.

2361 Tahiri-Zagret, C., and R. Traoré-Serie. "**Actualité de l'édition scientifique en Côte d'Ivoire.**" In *L'edition en Afrique francophone*, edited by Gilles Vilasco and Dominique Hado Zidouemba. Abidjan: Association des Rédacteurs et Editeurs Scientifiques d'Afrique Francophone, 1990, 47-55.
A review of the state of scholarly and scientific publishing in Côte d'Ivoire with a detailed analytical methodology and an analysis of the results of a survey of scientific

publications. Concludes that it is essential that scientific results be published in accordance with international norms and suggests a national policy to help with this.

Technical Centre for Agricultural and Rural Cooperation of ACP-EU (CTA), *see* ➜ **Centre Technique de Coopération Agricole et Rurale ACP-UE** entry **2338**

2362 Teferra, Damtew **"The Status and Capacity of Science Publishing in Africa."** *Journal of Scholarly Publishing* 27, no. 1 (October 1995): 28-36.
Reviews the state of scientific publishing and, in particular, attempts to assess the scientific research published by individual countries of Africa on the basis of an analysis of data from the *Scientific Citation Index* (published by the Institute of Scientific Information/ISI) between 1981 and 1993. The author compares the position of and the trends in science publishing in individual African countries, and by region, and finds that most of the publications are in the life sciences, especially agriculture and health, and that publishing output in the physical sciences is still very small. The analysis also showed that output in some of the largest producers, such as Nigeria, has declined; in other countries, such as Kenya and Morocco, it has increased dramatically.

2363 Vilasco, Gilles, and Dominique Hado Zidouemba, eds. **L'édition scientifique en Afrique francophone. Actes de la table ronde.** Abidjan: Association des Rédacteurs et Editeurs Scientifiques d'Afrique Francophone, 1990. 136 pp.
Contains the papers presented during a round table session, the aim of which was to take a critical look at the state and problems of scientific publishing in francophone Africa. *Note:* some of the papers in this collection are individually abstracted elsewhere in this bibliography

Wade, Emmie **"Children's Science Books. The Kawi Project"** *see* ➜ **Children's book publishing** entry **1696**

2364 Yonli, Emile D. **"L'édition scientifique au Burkina Faso."** In *L'édition en Afrique francophone,* compiled and edited by Gilles Vilasco and Dominique Hado Zidouemba. Abidjan: Association des Rédacteurs et Editeurs Scientifiques d'Afrique Francophone, 1990, 39-42.
A general view of scholarly publishing in Burkina Faso, including a discussion of the problems and constraints, possible solutions, and future prospects.

2365 Youdeowei, Anthony **"Writing and Publishing on Agricultural Sciences in Africa."** In *African Scholarly Publishing Essays,* edited by Alois Mlambo. Oxford: African Books Collective Ltd.; Uppsala: Dag Hammarskjöld Foundation; and Oxford: International Network for the Availability of Scientific Publications (INASP), 2006, 45-51.

Attempts to present an overview of some of the key issues associated with writing and publishing in the agricultural sciences in Africa, drawing mainly on the author's personal experience of writing for all levels of the educational system and for rural development. The author looks at the diverse target readership for agricultural science books in Africa, and those on rural development, and its potential for publishing. However, while there are many book publishers in Africa undertaking a wide range of general, educational and scholarly publishing, there are as yet very few that publish primarily in the agricultural science fields, which is due to lack of expertise in a number of areas, among them the lack of scientific illustrators who can produce high-quality and scientifically accurate artwork. This is in turn makes it difficult for African authors in the agricultural sciences to place their work. Youdeowei believes the situation could be markedly improved through capacity-building training programmes and writing workshops for authors, editorial staff in publishing houses, as well as for scientific illustrators in agriculture and biology.

2366 Zidouemba, Dominique Hado; Gilles Vilasco, R. Ba Touré, and S. Nzassi Ibouanga, eds. **Guide de publication scientifique.** Dakar: Association des Rédacteurs et Editeurs Scientifiques d'Afrique Francophone, 1991. 92 pp.
Aims to assist authors to familiarize themselves with common usage and the rules governing the writing and editing of scientific works and journals. Explains the problems which exist in the scientific and scholarly publishing sector in francophone Africa, one of the most serious of which is the absence of a formalized network of trained professionals

Women in African publishing/Publishing by and for women

See also
➔ **Children's book publishing**
➔ **Reading culture and reading promotion**

Note: this section also includes papers that deal with gender sensitivity in publishing, and articles on the issue of gender equity in the preparation of textbooks and other educational materials.

African Books Collective Ltd. Research & Dissemination Unit **Women in Publishing and the Book Trade in Africa. An Annotated Directory** *see* ➔ **Section 1, Serials and reference: Directories of publishers and the book trade** entry **191**

2367 Aboyade, Bimpe **"Academic Publications and Women Empowerment."** In *Women Empowerment Through Publishing. Papers Presented at the Second Nigeria International Book Fair, 8-12 May, 2003.* Lagos: Nigerian

Book Fair Trust [c/o Literamed Publications Ltd., PMB 21068, Ikeja, Lagos, Nigeria], 2003, 39-48.

The author states that although universal free primary education provides for all children, irrespective of gender, to go to school, in practice more girls drop out or are withdrawn from school for a variety of reasons. Aboyade – who heads Nigerian publishing house Fountain Publications Ltd. – argues compellingly that both the government and publishers in Nigeria have neglected producing books for the girl-child, and school drop-outs who can barely read and who suffer from other disadvantages of being female in a male-dominated society. While conceding that such books are unlikely to be commercial successes, she believes that there is nevertheless a growing need for them, and that a case can be made that they should benefit from publication subsidies from the government or donor agencies. Women currently active as publishers, in the news media, or as editors in publishing houses, are best placed to create and develop such books, as they will be more sensitive to a woman's viewpoint on societal problems, and they are in a vantage position to empower other women.

2368 Akachie-Ezeigbo, Adimora **"Heard and Unheard Voices: Empowering Women Through Publishing."** In *Women Empowerment Through Publishing. Papers Presented at the Second Nigeria International Book Fair, 8-12 May, 2003.* Lagos: Nigerian Book Fair Trust [c/o Literamed Publications Ltd., PMB 21068, Ikeja, Lagos, Nigeria], 2003, 80-93.

Examines some of the factors responsible for women's unequal access to writing and publishing in Nigeria, and looks at the publishing experience of some prominent Nigerian writers. The author offers some possible strategies to enhance the profile of women in African publishing, and make African women writers' voices heard more vociferously.

2369 Anderson, Elisabeth **"Women in Publishing and the Wider Book Chain in South Africa, 2001."** In *Courage and Consequence. Women Publishing in Africa,* edited by Mary Jay and Susan Kelly. Oxford: African Books Collective Ltd., 2002, 95-109.

Elisabeth Anderson is the [former] head of the ➜ **Centre for the Book (934)** in South Africa, whose aim is to promote the writing, publishing, reading, marketing and distribution of South African books in order to develop a truly South African literary culture. In this paper Anderson probes into the position of women in the publishing and bookselling industry in the country, drawing on a number of research reports, personal experience, and interviews with people in the industry, especially women. She examines some of the factors which still prevent women reaching the upper echelons in the publishing, and especially the bookselling business; and those who wish start their own publishing or bookselling enterprises face stereotype perceptions of women in business. However, Anderson notes that there have recently been some positive changes regarding women, notably in the publishing field. She also looks at aspects of training for the book professions, the impact and opportunities of new technologies, and the challenges that lie ahead: "Over the next few generations black women could, through improved and earlier access to books and reading, play as powerful a role in the industry as do white women. What is lacking now is a bridging mechanism so that this dearth of black women in the sector can be overcome more quickly."

Anon. **Ghanaian Private Sector Case Story: Ms. Akoss Ofori-Mensah – Sub Saharan Publishers** *see* ➜ **Section 3, Country studies: Ghana** entry **548**

2370 Anon. **"In Memoriam: Flora Nwapa 1931-1993."** *African Literature Association Bulletin* 20, no. 1 (Winter 1994): 6-17.
Tributes to the late Flora Nwapa, Nigeria's first female novelist, who was also the first Nigerian woman publisher. The tributes are by fellow-writers and academics Abena Busia, Marie Umeh, Ernest Emenyonu, Gay Willentz, Molara Ogundipe Leslie, and Phanuel Akubueze Egejuru.

2371 Bamhare, Miriam **"Gender Issues and National Book Policy."** In *Women's Voices. Gender, Books and Development. Proceedings of the ZIBF Indaba 1999, Harare, Zimbabwe, 31 July – 1 August 1999,* edited by the Zimbabwe International Book Fair Trust. Harare: Zimbabwe International Book Fair Trust, 1999, 40-45.
Argues that "despite a sprinkling of women" in indigenous publishing (notably in Zimbabwe), "book content and book provision remain in practice totally devoid of sensitivity to the issue of gender", and that is essential for the book sector to provide equally for the two sexes. The author offers a number of practical suggestions – addressed to the various links in the book chain, such as writers, publishers and booksellers – that will impact positively upon gender issues.

2372 Brickhill, Paul; Catherine Odora Hoppers, and Kajsa Pehrsson **Textbooks as an Agent of Change. Gender Aspects of Primary School Textbooks in Mozambique, Zambia and Zimbabwe.** Stockholm: Sida, Department for Democracy and Social Development - DESO Education Division (Education Division Documents, 3), 1996. 31 pp. [with 7 appendices, var. pp.].
This report is the result of a joint study of gender aspects in textbooks used in primary schools in Mozambique, Zambia and Zimbabwe, which was commissioned by the ➜ **Swedish International Development Co-Operation Agency/Sida (115)** to be used as an input to the development of programmes which address the issue of quality in basic education. The report consists of three separate country-specific studies, supplemented by information gathered through interviews with individuals involved in textbook production, mainly in Zimbabwe. The three case studies examine gender aspects of primary school textbooks, gender policies, stereotyping of gender roles, stereotyping of women's roles in textbooks, and the role of publishers. The authors state that "gender issues have not featured in African publishing debates. The issues are not yet perceived as a component of African publishing development", and that there are two inter-related aspects to gender equity in African publishing, namely (1) the role of African women in publishing, and (2) the content of books and editorial policies of publishers. The report makes a number of recommendations that should be addressed by publishers to produce more gender aware textbooks, to involve women in buying books, reading and writing, and to

facilitate women entering management levels in publishing and textbook procurement.

2373 Butalia, Urvashi, and Rita Menon **Making a Difference: Feminist Publishing in the South.** Chestnut Hill, MA: Bellagio Publishing Network, Research and Information Center (Bellagio Studies in Publishing, 5) 1995. 90 pp.
An attempt "to map a history of feminist or women's publishing in what is known as the Third or Southern World", and a study of the challenges which women publishers face in developing countries. Examines feminist publishing in the North, South and Southeast Asia, Africa, Latin America, and the Pacific. Also discusses the economics of publishing for women's presses, and marketing and distribution. States that women's presses "often find themselves pulled in two quite contrary directions: attempting to be successful in the marketplace, and balancing this with an adherence to feminist politics"; and "trying to strike a balance with publishing for social change in difficult trading conditions, and retaining financial stability at the same time. "
Reviews:
The African Book Publishing Record vol. 21, no. 4, 1995

2374 Clarke, Rebecca **"Women Publishers in Africa and the North."** In *Women in African Studies Scholarly Publishing,* edited by Cassandra Rachel Veney and Paul Tiyambe Zeleza. Trenton, NJ: Africa World Press, 2001, 45-64.
Examines the challenges women publishers face in African studies, and publishing African women's writings, both in Africa and in the countries of the North, including lack of finance, shortages of technical skills, widespread occupational gender discrimination, the problems of stereotyping writings by women, and accessing the mainstream markets. It investigates the strategies that have been, and should be, devised to promote women's publishing and to avoid the ghettoization of women's writing; the sort of publishing practices that would enhance women's publishing, and how the readership of women's writings can be promoted. The author reviews the activities of women's presses in Africa, Black women's presses in the North, publishing by women writers in the mainstream publishing houses in the UK and the US, and current [2001] North-South linkages in terms of co-publication and co-production projects. Clarke concludes that the state of women's publishing in Africa and Northern countries "is firmly tied to the positions of women in their respective societies, as well as the organizational structure of the book publishing industry, and how these two affect, and are affected by, the prevailing educational system and intellectual trends."

2375 Commonwealth Secretariat. Women's and Youth Affairs Division **Gender Bias in School Text Books.** London: Commonwealth Secretariat, 1995. 96 pp.
In response to the lack of information on gender bias in existing textbooks in the countries of the Commonwealth, the ➔ **Commonwealth Secretariat (51)** commissioned three major studies of primary school textbooks: one in the Caribbean, one in Asia, and one in Africa, the latter undertaken by Wanja Thairu (Kenya). The

major findings of these studies are reported in this volume, which also includes further sections on "Inclusive and gender sensitive language", "Guidelines for textbook writers and producers", and "Suggestions for teachers and teacher educators". The final section is an "Evaluation guide", which presents a tool for the evaluation of gender bias in textbooks and other learning materials. Also includes a bibliography.

2376 Frank, Katherine **"Flora Nwapa, Africa's First Woman Publisher."** *Africa Now* (May 1983): 61-62.
An interview with the late Flora Nwapa, the first woman novelist to be published in Africa and founder, Managing Director and guiding spirit of Tana Press Limited and Flora Nwapa & Co.

2377 Friedman, Michelle **"Agenda 'A Labour of Love' – 10 Years of Feminist Publishing in South Africa."** *Agenda*, no. 34 (2002).
An organizational analysis of the South African journal *Agenda*, a feminist publishing project committed to giving women a forum, a voice and skills to articulate their needs and interests towards transforming unequal gender relations in South Africa.

2378 George, Lavona **"The Strength of the Printed Word in Creating a Gender Sensitive Society."** In *Women's Voices. Gender, Books and Development. Proceedings of the ZIBF Indaba 1999, Harare, Zimbabwe, 31 July – 1 August 1999,* edited by the Zimbabwe International Book Fair Trust. Harare: Zimbabwe International Book Fair Trust, 1999, 86-87.
Another version also published as **"The Printed Word and a Gender Sensitive Society: The South African Experience"** *African Publishing Review* 8, no. 4 (July/August 1999): 5-6.
Part one of this paper examines some of the issues of a gender-sensitive society in a South African context, while part two looks at the strength, or potential strength, of the printed word in creating a gender-sensitive society. Part three outlines proposed book or materials development and reading promotion strategies to advance promotion of gender equality, and to ensure that more books are produced that transcend stereotypes based on culture, race or class.

2379 Iloegbunam, Chris **"Flora Nwapa (1931 to 1993)."** *West Africa*, no. 3973 (15-21 November 1993): 2088.
An obituary and appreciation of the pioneering Nigerian woman writer and publisher Florence Nwanzuraha Nwakuche (née Nwapa) who died on 16 October 1993. Flora Nwapa was the Managing Director of the Enugu-based Tana Press.

2380 Jay, Mary, and Susan Kelly, eds. **Courage and Consequence. Women Publishing in Africa.** Oxford: African Books Collective Ltd., 2002. 108 pp.
An insightful collection of papers and personal accounts providing a picture of African women in publishing in Africa today, primarily in English-speaking Africa. The eleven contributors are all women who have made notable achievements and impacts in publishing in Africa, have headed publishing companies, or have set up

their own imprints. The contributors are from Ghana, Kenya, Namibia, Nigeria, Senegal, South Africa, Uganda and Zimbabwe, who came to publishing from different routes, and have been active, or are currently active, in a variety of publishing operations, such state and commercial publishing, activist, non-profit or community publishing, and there is also a contribution by a bookseller. *Note*: most papers in this collection are individually abstracted elsewhere in this bibliography.
Reviews:
The African Book Publishing Record vol. 28, no. 4, 2002
African Publishing Review vol. 11, no. 1, 2002
Spore no. 99, June 2002
West Africa no. 4327 (27 May - 2 June 2002)

2381 Kamani, Wacango **"Gender Analysis in Book Publishing."** In *5th Pan African Children's Book Fair Magazine.* Nairobi: CHISCI Press, 1996, 19-21.
Draws attention to the need for children's books to come under scrutiny and that they must be gender sensitive, gender responsive and gender balanced. For example, the author says, in many traditional stories girls are always portrayed as victims – "caught by the ogre only to cry feebly for help" – whereas boys never have such problems! Reports how a number of Kenyan publishers are dealing with this situation and have deliberately incorporated gender screening in their publishing policy. The author argues "gender sensitization and training is necessary for publishers to understand the social order that sets our society's thinking."

2382 Katjavivi, Jane **"The Publisher's Role in the Future: Perspective from Namibia."** In *Women's Voices. Gender, Books and Development. Proceedings of the ZIBF Indaba 1999, Harare, Zimbabwe, 31 July – 1 August 1999,* edited by the Zimbabwe International Book Fair Trust. Harare: Zimbabwe International Book Fair Trust, 1999, 103-109.
This succinct short paper examines two main issues: (1) what, realistically, can be expected from publishers with regard to materials for the girl child, and, (2) how does the development of materials for the girl child link to other projects for the girl child. The author argues that publishers need training and awareness in the area of gender sensitivity, that they need to learn to be aware of the images of girls in their books, and that they should be encouraged to help develop and publish non-fiction by women.

2383 Katjavivi, Jane **"Women in Publishing and Publishing for Women. A Namibian View."** In *Proceedings of the First Annual National Conference on Women in Writing – Beyond 2000,* edited by Tembeka Mbobo, Joyce Siwani, and Charlotte Witbooi. Kwa-Zuma, South Africa: Centre for Cultural and Artistic Expression [PO Box 908, Kwa-Zuma 1868], 2000, 56-62.
Jane Katjavivi, the [former] Publisher and Managing Director of New Namibia Books in Windhoek, reviews the status of writing and publishing in Namibia "and where women are in that environment." She describes the background to publishing in Namibia and offers an overview of current [2000] publishing activities, including aspects of ownership, capacity of publishers, and training of publishing personnel. She proposes a measure of specific steps that ought to be taken to promote the

development of books by for and by women, and to provide an enabling environment for book development generally.

2384 Katjavivi, Jane **"The Four Cs of Publishing: Capital, Capacity, Courage and Consequence."** In *Courage and Consequence. Women Publishing in Africa,* edited by Mary Jay and Susan Kelly. Oxford: African Books Collective Ltd., 2002, 27-38.

Jane Katavivi narrates her personal experience as founder and head of New Namibia Books in Windhoek, and tells of the many hurdles and setbacks that had to be overcome in the intitial years, until the company achieved some stability and status, primarily as a result of a junior secondary physical science course developed and co-published with Heinemann's in the UK, although co-publishing arrangements created their own problems. New Namibia Books later also published a wide range of general books, including fiction, history, life stories, and children's books. In her section on 'Capacity' she tells of her trials and tribulations as an employer, and seemingly endless staff problems, until she decided "it was time to settle for less flair and more reliability. And definitely no more relatives." However, after ten years of running the business, "when capital and capacity were at rock bottom", and energy reserves at a low level, she decided to sell the publishing side of the business and concentrate on the retail book trade instead. Nonetheless a legacy remains and, under its new owner, many of the New Namibia titles stay alive and in print.

2385 Kyomuhendo, Goretti **"Writing and Publishing in Africa."** In *Courage and Consequence. Women Publishing in Africa,* edited by Mary Jay and Susan Kelly. Oxford: African Books Collective Ltd., 2002, 87-93.

Goretti Kyomuhendo is a Ugandan writer who in 1997, along with other Ugandan women writers, established ➜ **FEMRITE. The Uganda Women' Writers Association (1151)** which she currently runs, establishing it as a publishing house producing fiction, short stories and poetry by women writers in Uganda. Here she describes the background and motivation that led to the launching of FEMRITE, its initial list and manuscript submissions, methods of sales and distribution, the challenges ahead and their vision for the future.

2386 Lalloo, Pushpa Hargovan **"Organising Women's Organisations: The Developmental Work of Zimbabwe Women Writers."** In *Proceedings of the First Annual National Conference on Women in Writing – Beyond 2000,* edited by Tembeka Mbobo, Joyce Siwani, and Charlotte Witbooi. Kwa-Zuma, South Africa: Centre for Cultural and Artistic Expression [PO Box 908, Kwa-Zuma 1868], 2000, 84-87.

Describes the aims and activities of ➜ **Zimbabwe Women Writers (1206)** – who have 65 branches throughout Zimbabwe, both rural and urban – and the development of its publishing programme.

2387 Lema, Elieshi **"Light Beyond the Bend: Experiences of Women in Publishing in Africa."** In *Courage and Consequence. Women Publishing in*

Africa, edited by Mary Jay and Susan Kelly. Oxford: African Books Collective Ltd., 2002, 37-53.

Elieshi Lema tells the story of how she and her partner Demere Kitunga got into publishing and established E&D Limited, a successful publisher in Tanzania, whose principal mission was to bring a more gender balanced view of social development into literature and publishing. She recounts the opportunities, challenges, and obstacles in the setting up of an indigenous publishing company, which is active in two areas of publishing: commercial publishing, and package publishing (e.g. repackaging information to suit the needs of particular readerships). The author also offers her thoughts on aspect of gender and publishing, and provides a survey and analysis of women actively engaged in Tanzania's publishing industry, and the activities of local and international NGOs in the book sector. In her conclusion Elieshi Lema argues that the subject of women's experiences in publishing in Africa "is not really about a comparative analysis of our contribution to publishing as opposed to that of men. It is not even about whether it is more difficult for women to survive in the industry than it is for men, because once a woman has made it into publishing and secured her niche, the playing field is even." Instead, to ensure equitable participation and visibility in publishing by both men and women, "gender mainstreaming is a more effective strategy than integration", and that in any development interventions, at all levels, gender concerns "must be addressed during the project formulation process (not at implementation with token co-option) and with balanced participation of women and men."

2388 Ling, Margaret **"Celebrating African Women in Publishing."** *Wiplash* [Women in Publishing UK], (February 2000): 9-10.

Reports about gender inequality within the African publishing industry, and about the focus theme of the Zimbabwe International Book Fair in 1999, which was devoted to "Women's Voices—Gender, Books and Development".

2389 Madondo, Mwazvita Patricia **"Women in Textbook Publishing Management. The Zimbabwe Experiences."** In *Proceedings of the First Annual National Conference on Women in Writing – Beyond 2000*, edited by Tembeka Mbobo, Joyce Siwani, and Charlotte Witbooi. Kwa-Zuma, South Africa: Centre for Cultural and Artistic Expression [PO Box 908, Kwa-Zuma 1868], 2000, 63-66.

The author, who is Managing Editor at the Zimbabwe Publishing House, examines the role and contribution by women in educational and textbook publishing management in Zimbabwe. She investigates the organizational structure of three leading textbook publishers, how women were promoted into management positions, and the problems and challenges they faced. She finds that although top editorial positions are now held by women in Zimbabwe there is still a dearth of manuscript submissions of textbook material written by women authors.

2390 Maliyamkono, Todo **"Gender Balance in Books: the Publisher's Perception from Tanzania."** In *Women's Voices. Gender, Books and Development. Proceedings of the ZIBF Indaba 1999, Harare, Zimbabwe, 31 July – 1*

August 1999, edited by the Zimbabwe International Book Fair Trust. Harare: Zimbabwe International Book Fair Trust, 1999, 116-122.

Todo Maliyamkono, of Tema Books in Dar es Salaam, provides a short history of the development of publishing in Tanzania, and thereafter describes the challenges publishers face in providing more gender balance and sensitivity in their books, and the difficulties her company encountered in attracting manuscripts by women authors.

2391 Matenjwa, Nish-Muthoni **"NGO Publishing: Setbacks and Successes."** In *Women's Voices. Gender, Books and Development. Proceedings of the ZIBF Indaba 1999, Harare, Zimbabwe, 31 July – 1 August 1999,* edited by the Zimbabwe International Book Fair Trust. Harare: Zimbabwe International Book Fair Trust, 1999, 113-115.

Narrates the publishing experience – both the success stories, and the disappointments – of ABANTU for Development, an NGO with branches in several parts of Africa, founded in 1991 by African women with the aim of providing training, particularly for African women, in the skills necessary for analysis and management in the local economy, the media, the environment, and in the health sector. States that one of the difficulties they face is the lack of experienced women publishers, and the author calls on the ➜ **African Publishers Network (5)** to examine ways of increasing the number of qualified African women publishers, and to assist in the establishment of feminist publishing houses in Africa.

2392 Mbobo, Tembeka; Joyce Siwani, and Charlotte Witbooi **Proceedings of the First Annual National Conference on Women in Writing—Beyond 2000**. Kwa-Zuma, South Africa: Centre for Cultural and Artistic Expression [PO Box 908, Kwa-Zuma 1868], 2000. 105 pp.

The papers from a conference held in August 2000 to examine the position of women in the media and the literary world of South Africa, elsewhere in Africa, and abroad. One of the aims of the conference was to create a network of women in writing and publishing in Southern Africa and to establish a women's press. The conference attracted a number of distinguished women writers from the Southern African region, and the conference proceedings also include several contributions by women in publishing in Southern Africa. *Note:* some of the papers in this collection are individually abstracted elsewhere in this bibliography.

2393 Moshoeshoe-Chadzingwa, Matseliso **"The Convergence of Writing, Publishing, Gender and Development. A View from Lesotho."** In *Proceedings of the First Annual National Conference on Women in Writing – Beyond 2000,* edited by Tembeka Mbobo, Joyce Siwani, and Charlotte Witbooi. Kwa-Zuma, South Africa: Centre for Cultural and Artistic Expression [PO Box 908, Kwa-Zuma 1868], 2000, 67-71.

Presents an overview of the publishing situation in Lesotho and, in particular, attempts "to highlight the interrelatedness and interdependence of writing, publishing, information, knowledge, gender and development."

2394 Mundondo, Tainie **"Reading Materials for the Girl Child: What Publishers have Done."** In *Women's Voices. Gender, Books and Development. Proceedings of the ZIBF Indaba 1999, Harare, Zimbabwe, 31 July – 1 August 1999,* edited by the Zimbabwe International Book Fair Trust. Harare: Zimbabwe International Book Fair Trust, 1999, 101-102.
A brief overview of the contribution by African publishers in producing gender-sensitive reading materials.

2395 Mugo, Micere Githae **"Women and Books in Africa: A Question of Survival?"** *Journal of Humanities* no. 1 (April 1987): 91-100.
The keynote address presented at a Writer's Workshop during the 1985 Zimbabwe International Book Fair. Addresses the problem of discrimination in books against working-class and peasant women. Mugo asserts that these women are seen as having "no business - nay, right - to associate with books", and describes this as "book apartheid". Calls for cooperation in combating this state of affairs, from men and women of the book world together with workers and peasants, to counteract negative attitudes and conditions that alienate women from books and to produce relevant and appropriate literature. Contends that the cause underlying this problem is the social and political conditions which women experience.

2396 Mwangi, Serah **"Vision and Challenges."** In *Courage and Consequence. Women Publishing in Africa,* edited by Mary Jay and Susan Kelly. Oxford: African Books Collective Ltd., 2002, 79-85.
Serah Mwangi is founder and Managing Director of Focus Publications Ltd. in Nairobi. Here she describes the reasons and inspiration for setting up her publishing house, the financial and other constraints that had to be overcome, the nature of the initial list, and the marketing challenges. Focus Publications specializes in books that encourage the integral development of the human person, but have also published primary school science courses, professional books, as well as fiction and children's stories in English and in Kiswahili.

2397 Nigerian Book Fair Trust **Women Empowerment Through Publishing. Papers Presented at the Second Nigeria International Book Fair, 8-12 May, 2003**. Lagos: Nigerian Book Fair Trust [c/o Literamed Publications Ltd., PMB 21068, Ikeja, Lagos, Nigeria], 2003. 130 pp.
One in a series of collections from the ➜ **Nigerian Book Fair Trust (737)** containing the opening addresses, keynote speeches, and papers presented at the Nigeria International Book Fair, held annually since 2002, each fair focusing on a special topic or topics. The proceedings of the 2003 book fair, which had the theme "Women Empowerment Through Publishing", contain the keynote address delivered by the Indian feminist publisher Urvashi Butalia, together with papers on the challenges and obstacles faced by women writers and the experience of African women in publishing, including those by Unni Nielsen of the Norwegian Authors' Association, Akoss Ofori-Mensah of Sub-Saharan African Publishers in Accra, and Nigerian publisher Bimpe Aboyade. *Note:* some of the papers in this collection are individually abstracted elsewhere in this bibliography.
Reviews: The African Book Publishing Record vol. 34, no. 1, 2008

2398 Njoroge, Janet **"A Personal Account."** In *Courage and Consequence. Women Publishing in Africa,* edited by Mary Jay and Susan Kelly. Oxford: African Books Collective Ltd., 2002, 21-25.
Janet Njoroge recounts her personal experience and career of two decades in publishing in Kenya. She joined what was then Longman Kenya, a subsidiary of the Longman UK group, as a Humanities Editor in 1988. In 1993 Longman UK decided to pull out of Kenya and the company became Longhorn Publishers, a company wholly owned by Kenyans, for whom she was appointed Publishing Manager and subsequently General Manager. In 2001 she was elected Chairperson of the ➔ **Kenya Publishers Association (581),** the first woman ever to hold that position.

2399 Nwapa, Flora **"Writing and Publishing for Children in Africa."** *Matatu*, no. 17-18 (1997): 265-275.
Flora Nwapa, one of the foremost Nigerian women writers, and its first woman publisher (as head of Tana Press), died in November 1993. This article is a slightly revised and shortened version of a paper first presented at a seminar in Freetown, Sierra Leone in 1983, and subsequently published in **Proceedings, Papers and Summaries of Discussions at the Seminar on Creative Writing and Publishing for Children in Africa Today, 12th-14th January 1983,** ➔ *see* entry **1679**.

2400 Odaga, Asenath Bole **"The Excitement and Challenges of Publishing for Kenyan Children: A Writer's Perspective"** In *Critical Perspectives on Postcolonial African Children's and Young Adult Literature,* edited by Meena Khorana. Westport, CO & London: Greenwood Press, 1998, 15-25.
Asenath Bole Odaga set up Lake Publishers & Enterprises Ltd. in Kisumu in 1983, but found it to be an uphill struggle initially, and was confronted by male colleagues who suggested that publishing was a complex business best left to men, and that it might be rather more appropriate if she were to set up a restaurant instead of a publishing house! This is an account of her experience, both as a writer of more than 30 children's books, and as a publisher. The article also looks at aspects of co-publication of children's books, children's literature research, and the future of children's literature in Kenya.

2401 Odaga, Asenath Bole **"Women's Books: Marketing and Distribution."** In *Women and Activism. ZIBF Women Writers; Conference 1999,* edited by Zimbabwe Women Writers. Harare: Zimbabwe Women Writers, 2000, 111-118.
Looks at the challenges and problems of marketing books by women writers – including distribution to women who live in the rural areas – and the prejudices women face in getting published; and when they do get into print, the chauvinism they encounter from the book trade establishment. Describes some of the methods used to promote and distribute books published by Osenath Odaga's Lake Publishers in Kenya, and calls for new, innovative, and unconventional marketing methods: "Marketing and distribution must emphasize methods which will have an impact on the communities for which women write. African women will have to write, market and distribute their own works without waiting for outsiders to do it for them. At one level the outsiders may have their own agenda while parading as

experts in African affairs, but with no solid understanding of the people, their culture and their needs."

2402 Ofori-Mensah, Akoss **"Women in Publishing. Profiles from Ghana."** *African Publishing Review* 6, no. 5 (September/October 1997): 4-5.
Akoss Ofori-Mensah, herself a publisher, profiles three women in publishing in Ghana: Senna Tagboto, editor and publisher of the children's magazine *Playpen*; Agnes Ofosua Vandyck, the current executive director of the → **Ghana Book Development Council (536);** and Mary Asirifi, who heads the family business Allgoodbooks, who have thus far published in excess of 200 schoolbook titles. Mary Asirifi also contributes a short piece "Publishing in Ghana Today" to round up the profiles.

2403 Ofori-Mensah, Akoss **"Gender Sensitivity in Publishing."** In *Women's Voices. Gender, Books and Development. Proceedings of the ZIBF Indaba 1999, Harare, Zimbabwe, 31 July – 1 August 1999,* edited by the Zimbabwe International Book Fair Trust. Harare: Zimbabwe International Book Fair Trust, 1999, 71-79.
Slightly shorter version, published as **"Gender-Sensitivity in Publishing: Lessons from Ghana"**, *African Publishing Review* 8, no. 4 (July/August 1999): 1-4.
Discusses some areas of gender bias in textbook production in Africa, and suggests how these books could be improved to reflect gender equity, and thus help children, especially girls, to develop a more positive image of themselves. The author examines the books in terms of their language bias, portrayal of academic activity, participation in travel and use of transport, as well as in terms of recreation and leisure activities, occupations, division of labour, and character roles and location. The analysis is based on some of the primary English, mathematics, and science textbooks used in West Africa. The author is Managing Director of Sub-Saharan Publishers in Accra.

2404 Ofori-Mensah, Akoss "**Getting into Publishing. My Story."** In *Courage and Consequence. Women Publishing in Africa,* edited by Mary Jay and Susan Kelly. Oxford: African Books Collective Ltd., 2002, 11-20.
Personal recollections of Akoss Ofori-Mensah's experience as the head of Sub-Saharan African Publishers in Accra, charting the history of what at first was as a struggling tiny publishing operation, but which despite adverse local conditions rapidly grew into one of Africa's most enterprising indigenous publishers, several of whose children's books of which were the recipients of prestigious international book awards. Here she narrates her experience; the support she enjoyed from the → **Danida (56)** Private Sector Development Programme (PSDP) whose start-up project provided equipment, DTP training, and contacts; her publishing and marketing strategies; co-publishing projects with publishers in other parts of Africa and in the countries of the South, and her more recent experience of venturing into the primary school book markets. She stresses that quality of production was always of paramount importance, and which despite involving considerable initial expense

had always proved to be a worthwhile investment—"the material may be first class, but if the packaging is lousy marketing becomes difficult."

2405 Ofori-Mensah, Akoss **"Women Empowerment Through Publishing."** In *Women Empowerment Through Publishing. Papers Presented at the Second Nigeria International Book Fair, 8-12 May, 2003.* Lagos: Nigerian Book Fair Trust [c/o Literamed Publications Ltd., PMB 21068, Ikeja, Lagos, Nigeria], 2003, 27-38.
Ghanaian publisher Akoss Ofori-Mensah writes about abuse and social exploitation of young girls and African women through traditional practises, thus disempowering them and preventing them to make their full contribution to national development. She examines gender stereotyping in school textbooks published in Ghana and Nigeria, and stresses the need for gender balance and sensitivity in both text and illustrative matter in textbooks. She also profiles a number of successful African publishing houses which are headed by women.

2406 Okurut, Mary Karooro **"Gender Balance in Books: The Publisher's Perception."** In *Women's Voices. Gender, Books and Development. Proceedings of the ZIBF Indaba 1999, Harare, Zimbabwe, 31 July – 1 August 1999,* edited by the Zimbabwe International Book Fair Trust. Harare: Zimbabwe International Book Fair Trust, 1999, 110-112.
Describes the experience of ➜ **FEMWRITE (1151)** the Ugandan women writers association, their publishing activities and their efforts to provide more gender balance in books, and providing an outlet for more and more women writers.

2407 Orford, Margie **"Recounting our View of the World: Women Writing, Women Editing, Women Publishing."** *African Publishing Review* 6, no. 5 (September/October 1997): 6-7.
Margie Orford, joint editor of the anthology *Coming on Strong: Writing by Namibian Women,* published by New Namibia Books in 1996, writes about the process of putting together this collection and seeing it through to successful publication. The collection has reportedly sold well and "what was perceived by many to be a risky area – women's stories, non-standard English, little bits and pieces of writing – has stimulated Namibians to buy, to read and to write."

2408 Orimalade, Oluronke **"My Romance with Books."** In *Courage and Consequence. Women Publishing in Africa,* edited by Mary Jay and Susan Kelly. Oxford: African Books Collective Ltd., 2002, 71-77.
Ronke Orimalade recounts her career and professional experience in the book world in Nigeria, first as a librarian with the National Library of Nigeria, and thereafter as Manager of the University of Lagos Bookshop and Acting Director of the University of Lagos Press respectively. She was also instrumental in the setting up of the ➜ **Pan African Booksellers Association/PABA (21)**, and was elected its first chairperson in July 2000. She has now established her own bookshop, Books and Print Limited in Lagos, which describes itself as a "development bookshop".

2409 Press, Karen **"Women Writers in South Africa Today."** In *Women and Activism. ZIBF Women Writers Conference 1999,* edited by Zimbabwe Women Writers. Harare: Zimbabwe Women Writers, 2000, 23-44.
Offers a brief overview of literary writing and publishing in South Africa, and the publication of works of fiction and poetry published in book form by women writers. This is followed by a more detailed description of the situation of women writers in South Africa and the particular problems they face. Also surveys writers' and politically-orientated organizations, and suggests a number of interventions that could help to raise the profile of women writers.

2410 Read, Alison **"Gender, Books and the African Information Market."** *Focus on International & Comparative Librarianship* 30, no. 2 (1999): 63-87.
Report about a series of seminars organized by the ➜ **Southern African Book Development Education Trust (113)** at the London International Bookfair in March 1999. The report includes summaries of presentations made by several African women publishers and booksellers.

Salahi, Katherine "**Serah Mwangi Interviewed by the Editor**" *see* ➜ Section 3, Country studies: Kenya entry 628

2411 Sifuniso, Monde *et al*, eds. **Gender-Sensitive Editing.** London: Association for Development of Education in Africa. Working Group on Books and Learning Materials (Perspectives on African Book Development, 11), 2000. 108 pp. (+13 loose-leaf, plastic laminated training cards in cover pocket) A4 size wire-bound (distributed by African Books Collective Ltd., Oxford)
This excellent manual is intended as a guide for running training courses or workshops for groups of writers, illustrators, editors and others involved in producing popular reading material. Divided into six chapters, the manual takes the reader through various stages: how to develop a gender perspective; how gender is constructed socially, and how to develop a framework for analyzing gender. Illustrations are looked at for what they show, how they show it, and what they do not show. Developed in a series of workshops, the book is accompanied by a detailed checklist to analyze works for gender-sensitivity, a glossary of terms, and an annotated bibliography for those who wish to read further. The training modules have been designed for use in workshop situations, and are accompanied by a pack of laminated training cards in a cover pocket of the A4 format wire-bound book, which can be used in different combinations by trainers or for self-study purposes.
Reviews:
The African Book Publishing Record vol. 27, no. 3, 2001

2412 Sow, Fatou "**Writing, Publishing and Distributing Feminist Research in Africa: The Senegalese Experience."** In *African Scholarly Publishing Essays,* edited by Alois Mlambo. Oxford: African Books Collective Ltd.; Uppsala: Dag Hammarskjöld Foundation; and Oxford: International Network for the Availability of Scientific Publications (INASP), 2006, 27-38.

Offers "a glimpse behind the veil which is concealing the huge difficulties in the production, publication, and dissemination" which African feminist research is encountering in Africa in general, and in francophone Africa in particular. The author sets out the difficulties of financing appropriate academic research in African universities, or seeking outside donor support for it, and the obstacles to publish works of scholarship or those of more general interest. She addresses the issue of language and audience in feminist writing and discourse, describes publication outlets within Africa and elsewhere, and examines the challenges that lie ahead for more effective dissemination of feminist research.

2413 Staunton, Irene **"Releasing Voices."** In *Courage and Consequence. Women Publishing in Africa,* edited by Mary Jay and Susan Kelly. Oxford: African Books Collective Ltd., 2002, 55-60.

Irene Staunton's personal recollections of her career in publishing, first in the UK, and later in Zimbabwe, where she became instrumental in developing a high quality list for Baobab Books, focusing on literature, culture, history, and children's books. The imprint attracted some of Zimbabwe's best known writers, and several Baobab titles were the recipients of major international book prizes, with rights for many of their titles sold in international markets. However, despite theses successes, the author describes Baobab Books as an anomaly, a small company that had to co-exist within a larger group of companies that pursued a strictly commercial business ethic, and with the inevitable pressures on Baobab to generate more sales and more income for the group. Irene Staunton left Baobab in 1999 to set up her own new imprint Weaver Press, also based in Zimbabwe. She believes, regardless of gender, that honesty, patience, sensitivity, generosity and receptivity are qualities that make a good editor and publisher, and that these are the values to which she aspires. Every title published in unique, "serious publishing is about empowering people with new ideas, new language, new ways of seeing the world and sharing experience."

Tervonen, Taina **"Sur le chemin de l'indépendance. Entretien avec Béatrice Lalinon Gbado, directrice des Editions Ruisseaux d'Afrique (Bénin)"** *see* ➔ **Section 3, Country studies: Benin** entry **429**

Turquety, Sarah **"L'universel est là, pas là-bas. Entretien avec Aminata Sow Fall"** *see* ➔ **Section 3, Country studies: Senegal** entry **909**

2414 van der Merwe, Annari **"Women in Writing: A Publisher's View."** In *Proceedings of the First Annual National Conference on Women in Writing — Beyond 2000,* edited by Tembeka Mbobo, Joyce Siwani, and Charlotte Witbooi. Kwa-Zuma, South Africa: Centre for Cultural and Artistic Expression [PO Box 908, Kwa-Zuma 1868], 2000, 79-83.

Annari van der Merwe [formerly] of Kwela Books, sets out the challenges of publishing creative writing in South Africa in the face of a still very limited demand for leisure and pleasure reading, and describes some of Kwela's experience in publishing, distribution and marketing general books in African languages. She also provides a few practical tips for writers who hope to break into print, and offers a range of recommendations that will help to create and grow a reading culture in the country. The author believes that there has been rather too much concentration of the production of books, the writing and the publishing of the books, rather than the *consumption* of books, and analysis of the reading, the use, and the buying of the books; and argues that there should be much more substantial financial support for libraries in the country: "as money is a real issue for many people, libraries should be where we start."

2415 Veney, Cassandra Rachel, and Paul Tiyambe Zeleza, eds. **Women in African Studies Scholarly Publishing.** Trenton, NJ: Africa World Press, 2001. 171 pp.

Five essays that seek to examine the challenges that women face in African studies scholarly publishing, and which aims to offer insights "into the shifting, intellectual, institutional, and ideological contexts and contests in African studies, as practiced in Africa and the North, by men and women, and among women themselves who are united by their gender as they are separated by the politics of race, resources, and location." The book attempts to do three things: first, analyze the patterns and prospects of women's scholarly publishing in the mainstream media in both Africa and the North; second, outline the development of women's presses and other publishing initiatives; and, third, examine the growth and politics of feminist scholarship in each of, and across, the two regions.

2416 Zimbabwe International Book Fair Trust, ed. **Women's Voices. Gender, Books and Development. Proceedings of the ZIBF Indaba 1999, Harare, Zimbabwe, 31 July – 1 August 1999.** Harare: Zimbabwe International Book Fair Trust, 1999. 296 pp. (distributed by African Books Collective Ltd., Oxford)

A collection of thirty-six papers, report-backs and discussions from the Zimbabwe International Book Fair Indaba 1999. The papers are grouped in four parts: those from the plenary sessions; Publishing; Writing; Research; and Access. *Note:* several of the papers in this collection are individually abstracted elsewhere in this bibliography.

2417 Zimbabwe Women Writers, eds. **Women and Activism. ZIBF Women Writers; Conference 1999.** Harare: Zimbabwe Women Writers, 2000. 160 pp. (distributed by African Books Collective Ltd., Oxford)

A collection of twenty-four papers and discussions from a conference on women writers that took place during the Zimbabwe International Book Fair in 1999. It includes papers by a variety of voices of women from around the world, including major African women writers. A series of country reports included provide useful inventories of publishing output by women writers in several African countries. *Note:* a few of the papers touch on publishing aspects, and the marketing and distribution of women's books (in Africa and elsewhere), are individually abstracted in this bibliography.

5
Book industry training/
Self-publishing

Articles and reports

2418 African Association of Science Editors-Ethiopian Chapter **Proceedings of the Seminar on Managing and Editing Journals, 9-11 March 1993, IAR, Addis Ababa, Ethiopia,** edited by Damtew Teferra. Addis Ababa: African Association of Science Editors, Ethiopian Chapter, 1994. 76 pp.
The fruits of a seminar hosted by the ➔ **African Association of Science Editors (2)** on managing and editing journals. The proceedings of the seminar contain synopses of the different presentations that were made and a record of the discussions that followed each presentation. The topics included aspects such as editorial advisory boards, office management, communicating with authors, copyright, manuscript tracking, ethics in scientific publishing, peer review, scientific and technical editing, and subscription management and distribution.

2419 African Publishers Network **"Special Edition. Proposals for the APNET Training Programme."** *African Publishing Review* 1, no. 3 (August-October 1992).
A condensed version of the comprehensive 96 page ➔ **African Publishers Network (5)** training report on publishing training in Africa, **Towards an African Publishing Institute**, by Laura Czerniewicz, *see* entry ➔ **2426**.

2420 African Publishers Network/African Publishing Institute **African Publishing Institute's Curriculum.** Harare, African Publishers Network, and Nairobi: African Publishing Institute, Regional Office, [PO Box 31191, Nairobi], 1996. 39 pp.
The African Publishing Institute (API) was established by the ➔ **African Publishers Network (5)** to co-ordinate and initiate training for the African publishing industry. In pursuit of its training goals, API prepared a curriculum for training designed to meet the training needs for all professional levels within the industry. This document sets out the structure of the curriculum, with some of the courses split into modules according to the nature of their objects and contents. The duration of courses, which includes a foundation course, range from one to five days.

2421 African Publishers' Network (APNET) **APNET Training 1992-2002. The African Publishing Institute/L'Institut Africain d'Edition/Instituto Africano de Edição.** [in English, French and Portuguese] Harare: African Publishers' Network, 2002. 60 pp.

The African Publishing Institute of the ➜ **African Publishers Network (5),** in collaboration with national book trade associations, operates an integrated pan-African training programme for the African book professions. It conducts short, intensive courses, trains trainers, and places people on periods of attachments with publishers in various parts of the continent. This booklet reviews the nature of the training programmes, the courses and workshops conducted over a period of ten years, and also includes a complete list of participants of all courses run between 1995 and 2001.

2422 Aladji, Weka-Yawo **"Training for Publishers in Africa: Prospects and Problems, the Francophone and West Africa Perspective."** In *Development Directory of Indigenous Publishing 1995,* compiled by Carol Priestley. Harare: African Publishers Network, 1995, 44-47.
Looks at the training opportunities available for publishing personnel in francophone West Africa, and reports about a series of training programmes and workshops to be undertaken under the umbrella of the ➜ **African Publishers Network (5).**

2423 Appiah-Padi, Stephen K. **"Report on a Course in Techniques of Editing for Book Publishing Editors."** *Ghana Book World,* no. 5 (1991): 55-59.
Details of a course organized by the ➜ **Ghana Book Development Council (536)** in August 1990. The course served both as initial training for some participants and as complementary in-service training for editors which also helped in updating their knowledge and skills.

2424 Brickhill, Paul **"Publishing Training in Africa: The Current Situation."** In *Development Directory of Indigenous Publishing 1995,* compiled by Carol Priestley. Harare: African Publishers Network, 1995, 37-43.
An inventory [as at 1995] of training support and training institutions, courses, on-the-job-training, etc. for book industry personnel in English-speaking East, West and Southern Africa.

2425 Centre Africain de Formation à l'Edition et à la Diffusion **Annuaire des stagiaires 1991-2005. 15e anniversaire CAFED.** Paris: Agence intergouvernementale de la Francophonie, and Tunis: CAFED, 2005. 136 pp. Online: http://www.capjc.nat.tn/pdf_doc/928508.PDF [05/01/08]
A commemorative publication to mark 15 years of the Tunis-based ➜ **Centre Africain de Formation à l'Edition et à la Diffusion/CAFED (12).** It includes a history of the Centre, an account of its contribution to training for the book professions in francophone Africa over the years, and information about the nature of its training programmes. This is followed by a complete listing of students who completed courses at the Centre, with indexes by country, and by type of organizations on whose behalf they attended training courses.

2426 Czerniewicz, Laura **Towards an African Publishing Institute.** Harare: African Publishers Network, 1992. 82 pp. [+ unpaged appendices]

A major report – probably the most comprehensive survey of publishing training facilities undertaken to date – prepared for the ➜ **African Publishers Network (5)** and sub-titled "An investigation of existing publishing training, a survey of African publishers' training need and a proposed five-year plan for an African Publishing Institute (API)". The report surveys existing training provision [as at 1992], training needs, proposed API activities, structure and plans for the Institute, course development, and funding.

2427 Czerniewicz, Laura **"Publishing Training for African Publishers."** In *Proceedings of the Info Africa Nova Conference 1993,* vol. 1, edited by A.G. Coetzer. Pretoria: Info Africa Nova CC, 1993, 198-204.
Sets out the different stages of the book publishing process, reviews the professional skills required, and surveys opportunities for training, and the training institutions and courses for book industry personnel, both in Africa and elsewhere.

2428 Czerniewicz, Laura, and Monica Seeber **"Transform, Support, Stimulate: Professional Development in the Book Publishing Industry 1990-2000."** In *The Politics of Publishing in South Africa,* edited by Nicholas Evans and Monica Seeber. London: Holger Ehling Publishing and Scotsville, South Africa: University of Natal Press, 2000, 233-258.
Charts training for publishing in South Africa over the ten year period of 1990-2000, an area of publishing dominated by politics to one dominated by emerging government policy. The first part of the paper focuses on the historical development of a number of training initiatives in the book industry, drawing conclusions about the nature and success of these initiatives. The second part examines the current social and institutional contexts within which training can be located, as well as the impact of multimedia in publishing, and makes the point that "training involves much more than individuals acquiring skills by registering to attend training courses."

2429 Dekutsey, Woeli **"Ten Years of the Book Industry Course in Ghana."** *African Publishing Review* 3, no. 5 (September/October 1994): 10-11.
Provides a short history of the multidisciplinary book industry course at the University of Science and Technology [now Kwame Nkrumah University of Science and Technology] in Kumasi, Ghana, and examines the prospects for the development of a regional training centre in the years ahead.

2430 Dossier: Formation au métiers du livre *Takam Tikou,* no. 13, November 2006. Edited by Nic Diament, Viviana Quiñones, *et al.* Paris: La Joie par les Livres, 2006. 128 pp.
Online:
http://www.lajoieparleslivres.com/masc/Integration/JOIE/statique/pages /06_revues_en_ligne/062_takam_tikou/presentation_tt13.htm (details only, full text will become available online shortly)
An informative special issue of the journal ➜ **Takam Tikou (166)** on the topic of training for the book professions in francophone Africa, and in some other parts of

the developing world. In a series of short articles it looks at training issues and training needs for various players in the book chain, including authors, illustrators, editors, publishers, booksellers, and librarians, particularly those involved in writing and publishing children's books. It also examines the role of library and book trade associations in the training field, and includes interviews with a number of prominent editors, publishers, and booksellers. Additionally, it contains a bibliography of training resources for authors and book professionals (primarily in French), and a directory of training institutions and book promotional bodies in Africa with full address and contact details, as well as a short profile about the activities of each institution or organization.

2431 Fasemore, Akin **"Training for African Publishers."** *African Publishing Review* 7, no. 3 (May/June 1998): 1-2.
Examines training for African publishing personnel in the past and today [as at 1998]. Discusses the type of training that is, or should be, available for both executive and middle-management levels, and the kind of training that should now be considered priority areas in the light of the rapidly changing publishing environment worldwide and recent technological advances in many areas of publishing and book production.

2432 Gidney, Michael **"APNET and VSO Launch a New Programme to Support African Publishing."** *Bellagio Publishing Network Newsletter*, no. 11 (September 1994): 2-3.
Reports about a pilot scheme developed as a joint programme of the ➜ **African Publishers Network (5)** and the UK-based ➜ **Voluntary Service Overseas/VSO. (123)**. The programme will provide training in support of indigenous publishing through a series of placements in various countries of Africa of professionally qualified VSO volunteers working on a range of different jobs at different levels.

2433 Hasan, Abul **Developing Human Resources of the Book Industry in West Africa.** Paris: UNESCO (Serial no. FMR/CC/BCE/81/183), 1981. 56 pp.
Online: http://unesdoc.unesco.org/images/0004/000463/046364eo.pdf [23/02/08]
Report of a ➜ **UNESCO (118)** mission to advise and assist in the establishment of a three-year degree course in book publishing at the University of Science and Technology in Kumasi, Ghana [now Kwame Nkrumah University of Science and Technology], as well as exploring the possibility of creating a "Regional Centre for Training Personnel in Book Publishing" as a future development of the course.

2434 Hasan, Abul **"Promoting Professionalism in African Publishing - The Ghana Project."** *The African Book Publishing Record* 14, no. 2 (1988): 101-104.
Also reprinted in *Readings on Publishing in Africa and the Third World*, edited by Philip G. Altbach. Buffalo, NY: Bellagio Publishing Network, Research and Information Center (Bellagio Studies in Publishing 1), 1993, 83-86.

An account of the BA (Publishing Studies) course established at the Department of Book Industry at the University of Science and Technology [now Kwame Nkrumah University of Science and Technology] in Kumasi in 1984, by the former director of the department. Describes the background and structure of the programme, and deals in some detail with aspects such human resource development and the setting up of appropriate training facilities.

2435 Irura, Stanley **"Training for Book Publishing in East Africa: Some Perspectives and Prospects."** *African Publishing Review* 3, no. 3 (May/June 1994): 8-9.
Identifies training needs and training opportunities for book industry personnel in East Africa.

2436 Karanja, A. Njeri **"Training for the Publishing and Bookselling Industries in Kenya."** *Bellagio Publishing Network Newsletter*, no. 11 (September 1994): 14-15.
The author, who is acting head of the Department of Publishing and Book trade at the Faculty of Information Science at Moi University, describes the nature of the courses offered at that institution to prepare students for a career in publishing or its related industries.

2437 Malhotra, D.N. **"Training for Book Publishing in Developing Countries."** In *International Publishing Today. Problems and Prospects.* Delhi: The Bookman's Club, 1984, 81-86.
Reviews the history of training in the publishing industry in the developing world and the state of training facilities that are currently [mid 1980s] available.

2438 Mate, Fredrick **"Establishment of the B.A. Degree Programme in Book Industry, College of Art, University of Science and Technology, Kumasi, Ghana."** *Ghana Book World*, no. 4 (1988): 16-24.
Gives the history and the aims and objectives of the Kumasi BA programme, with details of other programmes and a list of entry requirements.

2439 Membrey, David **"A Resource Package for African Publishers."** *Bellagio Publishing Network Newsletter*, no. 5 (March 1993): 5-6.
An account of a scheme sponsored by ➔ **Book Aid International (38)** to provide core professional library collections of books and journals on publishing to individual publishers and national publishers' association in Africa. Includes full details of the books and journals selected as most appropriate and most relevant for the scheme. (*See also* ➔ **2450**)

2440 Montagnes, Ian **"Training Editors in the Third World."** *Scholarly Publishing* 20, no. 2 (April 1989):163-172.
Discusses the International Rice Research Institute's pilot project for training editors, where the trainees learned about the importance of clear writing, design, editing,

promotion and distribution, and audio-visual presentation, and demonstrated those skills by producing materials on the spot. Ian Montagnes was the course director.

2441 Montagnes, Ian **"North/South Interdependence: The Part that Book Publishing Plays."** *Logos. The Journal of the World Book Community* 1, no. 4 (1990): 6-13.
Online:
http://www.atypon-link.com/LOG/doi/pdf/10.2959/logo.1990.1.4.6
Surveys the involvement of the countries in the North in the training of publishing professionals in developing countries, and describes the course set up at the International Rice Research Institute (IRRI) in the Philippines in the 1980s with donor assistance from Canada. Provides guidelines for conducting similar training courses such as the one established at IRRI. (*See also* entries ➔ **2475**, ➔ **2476**)

2442 Montagnes, Ian **"The African Publishing Institute and Local Initiative."** *Bellagio Publishing Network Newsletter*, no. 12 (December 1994): 8-9.
Reflects on the plans of the ➔ **African Publishers Network (5)** to set up an African Publishing Institute (API). Suggests that, in the short term, such a training institution might wish to give priority to producing instructional materials, and thereafter to make them available to national book trade associations and other local book promotional bodies.

2443 Montagnes, Ian **"Education for Publishing: The Needs of the Global South."** *Journal of Scholarly Publishing* 28, no. 4 (July 1997): 246-256.
Examines the need for professional education of book industry personnel in the countries in the South, and reviews some of the training initiatives that have been undertaken so far [to 1996], including those supported by governments, NGOs and donors, and mostly involving short-terms workshops. Also looks at some of the publishing courses offered by institutions in the UK and elsewhere. Montagnes argues that special needs include intensive hands-on training in technical procedures and expertise, financial management, marketing, and manuscript development, and that much could be done by local groups exchanging knowledge and experience. He calls for the establishment of an International Centre for Publishing Training in the South which could undertake training of trainers, produce training materials, co-ordinate with other organizations concerned with education for publishing, and thus help to reduce the current duplication of effort and optimize the use of donor funds.

2444 Muriithi, F.K. **"Book Publishing Management: The Challenge in Kenyan Book Publishing."** *Focus on International & Comparative Librarianship* 24, no. 1 (10 May 1993): 7-11.
Describes the impact which the restructuring of the education system has had on the book publishing in Kenya. Discusses the need to develop effective management techniques in the book publishing industry. Outlines the training available at Moi University and reports on a 10 day workshop on book publishing management held at Eldoret in August 1992.

2445 Mwang'ombe, Chrispus **"Training for the Publishing Industry."** In *Children's Reading Needs. The Challenges of the Next Century to Parents, Educators, Publishers and Librarians in Africa,* edited by Serah Mwanycky. CHISCI: Nairobi, 1993, 28-30.
Provides information about the training opportunities offered at the Kenya Polytechnic for potential authors, illustrators, graphic designers, editors, proof-readers and printers.

2446 Okwilagwe, Andrew Oshiotse **"Professionalism in Book Publishing: Current Trends."** *The Publisher* 2, no. 1 (March 1991): 35-39.
Examines the relationship between publishing and society, both historically and in a modern context. Surveys the book "as a medium of mass communication" and analyzes the elements of the publishing profession such as training, ethics and relative autonomy. Also looks at current [early 1990s] trends in promoting professionalism in Nigerian book publishing.

2447 Tettey, Edem **Developing Human Resources of the Book Industry in West Africa. A Decade of Promoting Professionalism in African Publishing: A Review and Evaluation of the Ghana Project.** Kumasi, Ghana: Department of Book Industry, College of Arts, University of Science and Technology [now Kwame Nkrumah University of Science and Technology] 1996. 14 pp.
A review and evaluation of the first ten years of the BA (Publishing Studies) course which has been offered at the Department of Book Industry at the University of Science and Technology [now Kwame Nkrumah University of Science and Technology] in Kumasi since 1984. Sets out the aims and objectives of the programme, the teaching curriculum, staffing, and administration, followed by an analysis of graduates produced for the first decade, the placement of graduates, how they obtained jobs in the book industries, and an assessment of the performance of graduates on the jobs they now do. A final section looks at development plans for the Department until the year 2000.

2448 Vaughan, Keith **"Oxford Polytechnic: A Combined Degree Course Including Publishing."** *The African Book Publishing Record* 9, nos. 2/3 (1983): 95.
The publishing course at the Oxford Polytechnic [now Oxford Brookes University] has attracted a considerable number of African students over the years. The course was subsequently upgraded to Diploma in Publishing degree status. Keith Vaughan, [formerly] senior tutor in publishing at the Oxford Polytechnic, outlines some of the changes in the course structure.

2449 Zell, Hans M. **"A Professional Library for African Publishers."** *The African Book Publishing Record* 13, no. 3 (1987): 161-165.
A checklist of works recommended as a basic library for publishers in Africa, or for use as in-house training materials. Titles include reference works, monographs, and training guides and manuals covering various aspects of the publishing process.

Training manuals and resources

African Publishers' Network/African Publishing Institute **African Publishing Institute's Curriculum** *see* ➜ **Articles and reports** in this section, entry **2420**

2450 Book Aid International **Information and Training Resources for the Book Chain 2004.** Edited by Brian Steenson, Yaso Kunaratnam, and Faith Emmett. London: Book Aid International, 2004. 76 pp.
Online:
http://www.bookaid.org/resources/downloads/ITRcatalogue_2004.pdf
[pages not accessible 30/03/08]
The seventh edition of a very useful and attractively presented catalogue, which contains a collection of resources designed for building the capacity and supporting the training strategies of all stakeholders in the book chain, especially in Africa and the Caribbean. The material was chosen through consultation with partners and professionals in librarianship, publishing and bookselling, and is designed to highlight new subject areas not covered in traditional academic courses, such as monitoring and evaluation, reading promotion and advocacy. Titles are grouped broadly by subject areas including writing, design and production, editorial functions and procedures, librarianship, bookselling, marketing and promotion, management, legal issues, reference, and the catalogue also offers a range of resources on ICT and the Internet.

2451 Büttner, Thomas, and Anja Frings **De l'idée au texte: guide des auteurs.** Niamey: Editions Alpha, [BP 2685, Niamey, Niger], and Bonn: Deutsche Stiftung für Internationale Entwicklung/, Zentralstelle für Erziehung, Wissenschaft und Dokumentation, 2000. 215 pp.
De l'Idée au texte is a co-publication produced by Editions Alpha in Niamey and the Deutsche Stiftung für internationale Entwicklung/DSE [now ➜ **InWEnt. Capacity Building International (85)**]. It is the first in a series planned in the framework of a programme to train the personnel of publishing houses that publish in African languages. This program is supported by DSE, the non-governmental organization ➜ **Associates for Research and Education for Development/ARED (873)** based in Senegal, and the ➜ **African Publishers Network (5)**. The aim of this useful and highly practical book is to encourage people to write and to become published authors. It deals with the process of writing – and identifying the motive for writing, what the reader expects of a book, and the role of the publisher in producing the finished product – and the creation of a text from inception through to publication.
Reviews:
The African Book Publishing Record vol. 27, no. 4, 2001

2452 Châtry-Komarek, Marie **Tailor-Made Textbooks. A Practical Guide for the Authors of Textbooks in Primary Schools in Developing Countries.** Translated from the French. Oxford: CODE Europe, in association with the Deutsche Stiftung für internationale Entwicklung, 1996. 232 pp.

Originally published in French in 1994 as **Des manuels scolaires sur mesure: guide pratique à l'intention des auteurs de manuels scolaires pour le primaire dans les pays en développement.**
A handbook for all those involved in the writing and production of textbooks in developing countries, although primarily intended as a tool and practical guide to assist textbook authors. It includes detailed, step-by-step descriptions of how to produce a textbook, covering all aspects of planning and preliminary research, development, illustrations, design and format, typography, artwork, page make up, as well as reviewing aspects of costs. There is also an appendix of project evaluations, a bibliography, and a helpful glossary of terms.
Reviews:
The African Book Publishing Record vol. 23, no.1, 1997, p. 5

2453 Commonwealth of Learning/The World Bank **Editing Educational Materials. A Course for Editors in Sub-Saharan Africa.** 1 CD + manual in pdf format *Editing Educational Materials: A Manual for Editors in Africa.* 65 pp. Project Manager: Angela Kwan, in association with Paola Scalabrin, The World Bank, Office of the Publisher, Africa Publishing Initiative. Vancouver, Canada: Commonwealth of Learning, and Washington, DC: The World Bank, Office of the Publisher [contact Paola Scalabrin Pscalabrin@worldbank.org], 2007.
Developed by the ➜ **Commonwealth of Learning (50)** in association with the ➜ **World Bank's (125)** Africa Publishing Initiative (API), this is an excellent resource for all those keen to acquire editorial skills. It is part of a series of distance learning tools currently being developed by the World Bank's API in collaboration with the ➜ **African Publishers Network (5)** and partner universities. Each self-learning programme will consist of a CD with examples, exercises, videos, modules for face-to-face training, together with an accompanying manual for self study. This pilot on editorial skills was launched in the summer of 2007 and was trialled in five African countries: Ghana, Kenya, Uganda, Zambia, and Zimbabwe. Attractively designed and very user-friendly, the CD consists of a Course Guide: Getting Started; Module 1: Planning and Organizing Textbooks; Module 2: Language Editing; and Module 3: Copy Editing and Design, plus a manual in pdf format *Editing Educational Materials: A Manual for Editors in Africa.* The manual is designed to provide learners with practical guidance in the work and business of editing, whether they are currently a textbook editor, or are considering working in the field. It provides an overview of the editing processes and a basic understanding of the different roles involved, and offers guidance on the business practices involved in editing and publishing. It is divided into five major sections: (i) Book production in brief: An overview of the publication process; (ii) Organization: Time management, file management, project management; (iii) Development of a publisher's list: Identifying potential publications, working with authors in development; (iv) Communication with authors and others: Letters and contracts; and (v) Manuscript preparation: Quality control in the manuscript preparation process. A series of helpful appendices are included: sample letters – between publishers and prospective authors, publishers and ministry of education officials, correspondence with series editors, etc. – sample contracts, and a model letter of agreement.

Reviews:
The African Book Publishing Record vol. 34, no. 1, 2008

2454 Council for the Development of Social Science Research in Africa. **CODESRIA Guide for Authors.** Dakar: CODESRIA, 2003, reprinted with revisions 2005. 44 pp.
Online: http://www.codesria.org/Links/Publications/guide_authors.pdf [04/02/08]
Also published in *African Scholarly Publishing Essays*, edited by Alois Mambo. Oxford: African Books Collective, 2006, 221-263.
A comprehensive guide for authors – especially students and budding scholars – designed to facilitate communication and understanding between authors and editors at CODESRIA, covering aspects of presentation and organization of manuscripts, notes and reference systems, tables and illustrations, obtaining permissions to reproduce material, preparing text on disk, dealing with copy editing queries and proofs, preparing an index, and more. While principally designed for CODESRIA authors, it will be useful for any author preparing a manuscript for publication.

2455 Davis, Jason **African Books Collective. PDF File Production Manual.** Oxford: African Books Collective, 2006. 9 pp.
Online:
http://www.africanbookscollective.com/stuff/ABC-Manual.pdf [30/03/08]
The Oxford-based ➔ **African Books Collective (5)** has successfully pioneered the use of, and access to, new printing technology such as Print-on-Demand (POD), which has brought considerable benefits to its participating publishers. This useful manual aims to provide the necessary technical know-how needed to make use of Print-on-Demand and Portable Data Format (PDF) technologies, thus enabling African publishers to reach a level of knowledge and technology to become self-reliant in the production of PDF files for Print-on-Demand. The manual sets out the hardware and software requirements for Windows, guidelines for installing Adobe Acrobat/Acrobat Distiller, print-on-demand trim sizes and requirements, settings for Acrobat Distiller for PDF production and the various processes for creation of PDF files, guidelines on print quality and font embedding, through to delivery of PDF files.

Gibbs, James, and Jack Mapanje, eds. **The African Writers' Handbook** ➔ *see* **Handbooks for authors and self-publishing** entry 2507

2456 Hall, John; Etienne Brunswic, and Jean Valérien **Planning the Development of School Textbooks. A Series of Twelve Training Modules for Educational Planners and Administrators**. Paris: International Institute of Educational Planning, 1995. Boxed set with 12 separate modules, separate Introduction/Instructions booklet, and Trainer's guide; var. pp., plus spreadsheets disk for Module 3.

Developed by the ➔ **International Institute of Educational Planning/IIEP (78)** and designed for guided self-instruction, these twelve modules are intended both for planners – especially those working in central units of the Ministry of Education – and for administrators involved in the development of textbooks at its various stages. The modules cover financing strategies, costing/programming, design, production, quality control, distribution and use, as well as management of the publishing process. Module 8 provides an introduction to desktop publishing. The modules "propose a methodology which should enable the participants to analyze a situation at any given time and to identify specific solutions to propose to decision-makers." A Trainer's Guide is included, as is a simulation model (on diskette) for Module 3: Quantifying Needs.

2457   Hughes, Sally **A Primer on Typography & Design, for Users of PageMaker and QuarkXPress.** Oxford: Oxford Centre for Publishing Studies [Oxford Brookes University, Richard Hamilton Building, Headington Hill Campus, Headington OX3 0PB), 1997. 104 pp. [with PC and Mac formatted disks for text and graphics for exercises]
This easy-to-use (albeit now rather dated) manual is primarily geared to people working in community organizations – and especially those in Africa and other developing countries – who are using DTP-generated documents to reach their audience and to get their message across. The book aims to impart skills to format text in a manner that will enhance the message contained in a document, to design a page so that readers can find their way easily through a document, and to further enhance the design with graphics and appropriate and attractive typography. The materials contained in the primer are intended to be used without a course tutor, be self-paced, to work with any version of Adobe PageMaker or QuarkXPress, augment software knowledge but not replace software training, and provide guidance in matters of design and typography.

2458   Impey, Bridget **Marketing and Promoting Agricultural and Rural Development Publications. A Practical Guide.** Oxford: International Network for the Availability of Scientific Publications (INASP); Wageningen, Netherlands: ACP-EU Technical Centre for Agricultural and Rural Co-operation (CTA), 2000. 89 pp.
Also published in French as **Guide pratique de marketing et promotion des publications sur le développement agricole et rural**.
(both editions distributed by African Books Collective Ltd., Oxford)
Produced in landscape format and attractively designed, this is a valuable practical marketing manual that aims to assist small publishers to make sense of the publishing world, particularly NGOs with publishing activities, but where publishing is not the core function. The manual will guide them through the principles and processes of effective marketing, and linking the capabilities of a publishing company to the needs of the customer. The author was formerly Marketing and Managing Director of David Philip Publishers in Cape Town, and is well known for a series of successful marketing workshops she has conducted during each year's Zimbabwe International Book Fair. Those that are struggling with their marketing will find a wealth of practical, hard-nosed advice in this guide, which

covers these topics: (1) Defining your Market, (2) What is Marketing? (3) The Marketing Plan, (4) Sales and Selling, (5) Distribution, Co-operative Publishing and Rights, (6) Publishing, Marketing and Finance, (7) Development Agencies, Donors and Commercial Publishers, and (8) Strategic Planning. Interspersed with the text are a number of practical exercises, and there are also reproductions of flyers and other publicity material as illustrative examples of good practice.

Reviews:
The African Book Publishing Record vol. 27, no. 3, 2001

2459 International Network for the Availability Scientific Publications
Electronic Journal Publishing: A Reader Version 2.0
http://www.inasp.info/file/370/electronic-journal-publishing-a-reader-version-20.html [30/03/08]
A new edition of ➔ **INASP's (81)** useful reader primarily for novices in electronic publishing – and especially those in the developing world – but also of interest to those more experienced in the field. It brings together a wide variety of articles, overviews, and perspectives that have been published in both print and electronic form, together with a number of new and especially commissioned papers for this Reader. This includes contributions on the economics of electronic publishing, copyright and archiving issues, and descriptions of different models of electronic journal publishing used in developing countries.

2460 International Network for the Availability of Scientific Publications
INASP Publishing Workshops/Resource Pack for Journals.
http://www.inasp.info/file/277/inasp-publishing-workshops.html [and see individual files below, 04/02/08]
To assist publishers, editors and all those associated with the publication of science information, the ➔ **International Network for the Availability of Scientific Publications/INASP (81**) has run a series workshops on publishing skills for editors and publishers of scholarly information, in particular journals. These workshops are participatory in nature, and involve group work and discussion with the objective of providing delegates with the knowledge to help make informed decisions about their own publications. Modules have been developed to be two hours in duration (unless indicated otherwise). All of the materials below are freely available to download. The following modules include notes for the facilitator, module presentation, exercises, and reference documents as appropriate.

2461 Copyediting and Proofreading
http://www.inasp.info/downloadDocument.php?documentid=214
2462 Copyright http://www.inasp.info/downloadDocument.php?documentid=215
2463 Dealing with Authors
http://www.inasp.info/downloadDocument.php?documentid=216
2464 Journal Design http://www.inasp.info/downloadDocument.php?documentid=217
2465 Journal Finance http://www.inasp.info/downloadDocument.php?documentid=218
2466 Journal Strategy (full day)
http://www.inasp.info/downloadDocument.php?documentid=219
2467 Managing the Review Process
http://www.inasp.info/downloadDocument.php?documentid=225
2468 Online Publishing Strategy (full day)
http://www.inasp.info/downloadDocument.php?documentid=220

2469   Planning Online Publication (full day)
http://www.inasp.info/downloadDocument.php?documentid=221
2470   Production http://www.inasp.info/downloadDocument.php?documentid=223
2471   Production Quality Control
http://www.inasp.info/downloadDocument.php?documentid=222
2472   Promotion (full day)
http://www.inasp.info/downloadDocument.php?documentid=224

2473   Kitson, Norma **Creative Writing. A Handbook, with Exercises and Examples.** Harare: Baobab Books/Academic Books, 1997.134 pp.
A handbook for aspiring writers in Africa which contains many practical tips and information on the craft of writing, and covers topics such as writer's block, conflict and tension, discipline, flashbacks, plots and themes, character and dialogue, description and imagery. There are also sections on short story writing, the novel and poetry, writing on 'unsafe issues', and advice on how to submit work to publishers. Exercises and examples accompany each chapter – some drawn from workshops organized by the author, as well as extracts from the work of published writers – and aim to introduce the reader to a wide range of different styles and works of literature.

2474   Laguere, Jean-Pierre, and Georges Stern, eds. **Le manuel pratique d'édition pour l'Afrique francophone, suivi du Le libraire en Afrique.** 2nd ed. Tunis: Centre Africain de Formation à l'Edition et à la Diffusion (CAFED), 2002. 324 pp.
A training manual for publishers and booksellers. [Not examined]

2475   Montagnes, Ian **Editing and Publication: A Training Manual.** Manila: International Rice Research Institute and Ottawa: International Development Research Centre, 1991. 445 pp.
Developed at a fourteen-week training course at the International Rice Research Institute, this manual – designed primarily for use in developing countries and which has also been used for training courses in Africa – discusses editorial and publishing procedures with the emphasis on practical matters. The book includes concrete examples, checklists, and questions and exhortations to the students. Although now somewhat dated, this training manual remains one of the best introductory guides to book publishing. (*See also* ➔ **2476**)

2476   Montagnes, Ian **Editing and Publication: A Handbook for Trainers.** Manila: International Rice Research Institute and Ottawa: International Development Research Centre, 1991. 116 pp.
A companion volume to ➔ **Editing and Publication: A Training Manual (2475)** that aims to guide trainers through the best use of the Manual, offering sample exercises and ways in which to stimulate creative thinking.

2477   Montagnes, Ian **An Introduction to Publishing Management.** London: Working Group on Books and Learning Materials/ADEA (Perspectives on Publishing, 5), 1998. 136 pp. (distributed by African Books Collective Ltd., Oxford)

This is an excellent, concise introduction to publishing management, published in a series that focuses on the issues involved in publishing and developing educational materials in Africa. However, the book is equally valuable to the book professions elsewhere in the developing world, and while much of the emphasis is on textbooks, the principles apply to all types of publishing, and to most countries of the world. The book sets out the basics of efficient, economical, and prudent management of time and money in publishing. After some general considerations it deals with strategic planning in publishing textbooks, developing manuscripts (commissioning, appraisal, copy-editing, working with designers, pre-testing, etc.), costs of production, preparing a title budget, as well as the various aspects of financial management: different methods of accounting, records required to track financial progress and aid forecasting, and preparing a cash flow projection. There is also a short chapter on marketing and a glossary.

Reviews:
The African Book Publishing Record vol. 25, no. 2, 1999
African Research & Documentation no. 80. 1999
Bellagio Publishing Network Newsletter no. 26-27, November 2000
Online: http://www.bellagiopublishingnetwork.com/newsletter26-27/ofori-mensah2.htm [04/02/08]
Logos. The Journal of the World Book Community vol. 10, no. 3, 1999
Online: http://www.atypon-link.com/LOG/doi/pdf/10.2959/logo.1999.10.3.180

2478 Morris, Sally **Getting Started in Electronic Publishing,** 5th ed.
Oxford: International Network for the Availability of Scientific Publications 2006. 29 pp.
Online: http://www.inasp.info/file/179/getting-started-in-electronic-publishing.html [30/03/08]
The 5th edition of a popular guide that provides an overview of the potentials and pitfalls of electronic journal publishing. While not specifically written for an African audience, it is an excellent resource for African journal editors and publishers who are contemplating switching to an electronic environment. It introduces all the issues that will need to be considered before taking such a step. This includes a discussion of the benefits and challenges of electronic publishing; the decisions that will have to be made when changing to an online (or print/online) publication; the hosting issues involved; licensing considerations; issues relating to open access; the changes that would be required in editorial procedures, sales and marketing; and the likely costs in terms of both time and money/people, and how these costs might be recouped. It also offers a range of sales models for online journals and step-by-step guidelines how to plan for a switch to online publication.
Reviews:
The African Book Publishing Record vol. 31, no. 4, 2005 (review of 4th ed. 2002)

2479 Moyo, Promise **Editorial Functions and Procedures.** Abidjan: African Publishing Institute, African Publishers' Network, 2002. 60 pp.
One in a series of training manuals developed by the African Publishing Institute (API) of the ➜ **African Publishers Network (5)** to facilitate intra-African training among its members, and which can be used for both formal training or individual study. Arranged under four modules: (1) Commissioning, (2) Copy-editing, (3)

Advanced Copy-editing, and (4) Editorial management, supported by activity suggestions and practical tasks designed to make the modules interactive and participatory.
Reviews:
The African Book Publishing Record vol. 29, no. 3, 2003

2480 Nyeko, Janet **The ABC of Book Publishing. A Training Manual for NGOs in Africa**. Kampala: JANyeko Publishing Centre Ltd. [PO Box 25613, Kampala, Uganda; Email: ayatnyeko@hotmail.com]; Wageningen, ACP-EU Technical Centre for Agricultural and Rural Co-operation (CTA) 1999. 116 pp
This is probably one of the first training manuals for African publishers to come from an African imprint, and this one – co-published with the **Technical Centre for Agricultural and Rural Co-operation ACP-EU (116)** – is targeted primarily at NGOs with publishing activities. It aims to equip users with basic and relevant skills in publishing by first discussing concepts and then providing tips and examples. To reinforce the lessons, a range of exercises follow each chapter. The book contains many useful suggestions, it is attractively designed, has a good range of model forms, and makes effective use of icons to draw attention to new terms, to provide tips and advice, and warn about potential pitfalls. However, one or two chapters are somewhat flawed, particularly the section on electronic publishing.
Reviews:
The African Book Publishing Record vol. 26, no. 2, 2000

2481 Nyeko, Janet **Book Marketing, Sales and Distribution.** Abidjan: African Publishing Institute, African Publishers' Network, 2002. 43 pp.
One in a series of training manuals developed by the African Publishing Institute (API) of the ➜ **African Publishers' Network (5)** to facilitate intra-African training among its members, which can be used for both formal training or individual study. Arranged under four modules: (1) Book Marketing, (2) Book Promotion, (3) Book Sales and Distribution, and (4) The Bookshop as an Outlet, which looks at the different kinds of bookshops and other retail outlets that are common in Africa, and the difficult conditions under which they have to operate. Each module starts off with a statement of objectives and concludes with a practical exercise.
Reviews:
The African Book Publishing Record vol. 29, no. 3, 2003

2482 Orimalade, Oluronke, and Bridget Impey, eds. **A Practical Guide to Bookselling.** Oxford: International Network for the Availability of Scientific Information (INASP) and Wageningen, Netherlands, ACP-EU Technical Centre for Agricultural and Rural Co-operation (CTA), 2005. 108 pp. (distributed by African Books Collective, Oxford)
Also published in French as **Guide pratique de la librairie**.
Although the retail book trade in Africa face problems and obstacles of equal magnitude as their publishing colleagues, bookselling in Africa has perhaps received less attention and support than the more "glamorous" area of publishing, but as is rightly pointed out in the foreword of this guide, booksellers have an important role

to play in book development in Africa, and they have the capacity to nurture a culture of reading within the local community. This excellent guide is edited by two highly experienced African booksellers, and it also contains contributions by several successful booksellers from around the continent. Attractively designed and laid out in landscape format, the guide aims to assist both novice booksellers as well those with established businesses. Two introductory chapters set out bookselling in an African context and the role of the bookseller in the book chain, followed by seven themed chapters. These cover the establishment of a bookshop (and examining what opportunities exist for those new to the book trade), business planning and management, training staff, dealing with customers, and maintaining and expanding a bookselling business. They are supported by a number of case studies presenting real-life examples of successes, or failures. A final chapter deals with non-traditional methods of selling books, such as mobile bookselling, book clubs, street vendors, market book stalls, as well as online bookselling. Each chapter contains a wealth of practical, hard-nosed advice, not only on the day-to-day management of a bookshop, but also on all the finer aspects of running a successful retail operation. Additionally, the book includes a number of model guidelines and forms, and other documentation that provide examples of good practice, and good housekeeping. A series of appendices include resources for booksellers, listings of book trade organizations, associations, journals, and useful Web sites.
Reviews:
The African Book Publishing Record vol. 32, no. 1, 2006

2483 Pieters, Jacqueline. **Techniques et coûts de fabrication du livre : guide du fabricant : le rôle de l'éditeur dans la chaine de production**. Bamako: Deutsche Stiftung für Internationale Entwicklung/DSE (Editer en Afrique), 2001. 153 pp.
[Not examined]

2484 Sakupwanya, Lillian T. **Professional Skills for Publishers.** Abidjan: African Publishing Institute, African Publishers' Network, 2002. 63 pp.
One in a series of training manuals developed by the African Publishing Institute (API) of the ➔ **African Publishers Network (5)** to facilitate intra-African training among its members, which can be used for both formal training or individual study. Arranged under three modules: (1) Communication Skills, (2) Negotiation Skills, and (3) Managing Staff, the course is designed to equip publishing staff with the "fundamental inter-personal skills necessary for professionalism in the publishing industry." A variety of practical exercises and tasks are included to make the manual as interactive as possible.
Reviews:
The African Book Publishing Record vol. 29, no. 3, 2003

Sifuniso, Monde *et al*, eds. **Gender-Sensitive Editing** *see* ➔ **Section 4, Studies by topic: Women in African Publishing/Publishing by and for Women** entry **2411**

2485 Smith, Datus C. Jr. **A Guide to Book Publishing**. 2nd ed. Seattle: University of Washington Press, 1989; Lagos: University of Lagos Press, 1990. 268 pp.

A second revised edition of a classic guide to publishing (though now inevitably very much dated), which describes each part of the process clearly and simply. Covers editorial preparation, production, promotion and distribution, as well as the publisher's relationship with authors, printers, booksellers, librarians and educators. Gives special attention to the problems of publishing in developing countries, and an African edition was published by the University of Lagos Press in 1990.

2486 Stilwell, Christine **"Venturing Into Academic Journal Publishing: Some Issues and Guidelines for New Authors."** *African Journal of Library, Archives and Information Science* 10, no. 2 (2000): 167-175.

Publishing in academic journals is vitally important for African scholars who wish to communicate their ideas and the results of research to their professional communities. For some, however, venturing into publishing in academic journals can still be a daunting task. This paper shares insights derived from the literature and from some recent Southern African initiatives. A helpful checklist to guide new authors – covering the basic items for preparing and submitting an academic paper for publication – is also provided.

2487 Youdeowei, Anthony (with contributions by Maritza Hee Houng, Paul Neate and Paul Stapleton) **A Guidebook on Journal Publishing for Agriculture and Rural Development.** Oxford: International Network for the Availability of Scientific Publications (INASP); Wageningen, Netherlands: ACP-EU Technical Centre for Agricultural and Rural Co-operation (CTA), 2001. 100 pp.

Also published in French as **Guide pratique pour l'édition de revues sur l'agriculture et le développement rural.** (Both editions distributed by African Books Collective Ltd., Oxford)

One in a series of guidebooks and training manuals for journal editors in developing countries that are active in the field of agriculture and rural development. They aim to assist editors to improve their publishing operations, and provide more effective communication of the scholarship and the research results published in their journals. The book is organized under nine chapters "that cover what we consider to be the essential basic elements in successful journal publishing." Interspersed with the text there are a variety of model forms, reproductions of title pages, covers of journals, and other documentation that provide illustrative examples of good practice, together with checklists and listings of address sources.
Reviews:
The African Book Publishing Record vol. 28, no. 2, 2002

2488 Zell, Hans M. **Book Marketing and Promotion: A Handbook of Good Practice.** Oxford: International Network for the Availability of Scientific Publications (INASP), 2001. 384 pp.

This is a compendium of practical 'how-to' advice on all aspects of book marketing and promotion, particularly for publishers in developing and emerging countries. It is also designed to serve as an information and reference resource for research institutions, NGOs, and other non-profit organizations with publishing activities. Organized under seventeen chapters, the book sets out the different types of marketing methods, techniques, and approaches, with each chapter providing guidelines for good practice. A number of model forms, checklists, and other documentation are interspersed with the text to provide illustrative examples of good practice. A special chapter (now a bit dated) "The Internet for the Book Professions" presents an overview of the Internet and the World Wide Web as a tool for the book professions in developing countries. Five case studies, by leading marketing practitioners, provide a broad picture of book promotion and distribution in different regions of Africa, and in India, the Caribbean, and the Pacific region. A sixth case study highlights the experience of African Books Collective in marketing African books worldwide. *Note:* three of the case studies are individually abstracted elsewhere in this bibliography.

Reviews:
Africana Libraries Newsletter no. 105, March/July 2001
Online: http://www.indiana.edu/~libsalc/african/aln/no105.htm [04/02/08]
Logos. The Journal of the World Book Community vol. 12, no. 4, 2001
Online: http://www.atypon-link.com/LOG/doi/pdf/10.2959/logo.2001.12.4.225
Mediaforum no. 3, 2001
PABA [Pan-African Booksellers Association] *Newsletter* no. 2, 2001
PEGboard. Professional Editors' Group Newsletter [South Africa] vol. 9, no. 2, May 2002
Publishing Research Quarterly vol. 18, no. 1, Spring 2002

2489 Zell, Hans M. **A Handbook of Good Practice in Journal Publishing**. London: International African Institute; Oxford: African Books Collective 2nd revised ed., 1998. 248 pp.
Aims to assist journal editors in Africa to improve their publishing operations, and provides guidelines for good practice, and good housekeeping, not only for those coming to journals publishing for the first time, but also for those who already have some experience in academic serials publishing. This second edition has been revised, expanded and updated after being tested during a series of practical workshops held for African journal editors and publishers. Covering most aspects of journals publishing and management, the handbook puts special emphasis on systems management, subscription fulfilment, financial control, and effective marketing and distribution, including a chapter (now somewhat dated) on journals marketing on the Internet. It also includes a series of model guidelines, model forms, and other documentation that provide illustrative examples of good practice. Additionally, there is a resources section, an annotated bibliography, and a glossary. Two specially commissioned contributions cover desk-top publishing for journal production, and computerized subscription invoicing and fulfilment for small journal publishers.

Reviews:
Bellagio Publishing Network Newsletter no. 23 October 1998
Online: http://www.bellagiopublishingnetwork.com/newsletter23/hassan.htm [30/03/08]

Focus on International & Comparative Librarianship vol. 29, no. 2, September 1998
Information Development vol. 14, no. 4, December 1998

2490 Zimbabwe Book Publishers' Association **Making Books. A Handbook for Textbook Evaluators.** Harare: The Zimbabwe Publishers' Association 1992. 36 pp. (distributed by African Books Collective Ltd., Oxford)
A handbook prepared jointly by the Curriculum Development Unit and the ➔ **Zimbabwe Book Publishers Association (1204)** to encourage the development of high quality and relevant textbooks. Asserts that the essence of a good evaluation is to support and promote authorship and publication of much-needed materials. Contains guidelines on how to evaluate a manuscript, together with an overview of the publishing process, sections on artwork, editing, copy-editing, and notes on the issue of copyright.

Handbooks for authors and self-publishing

2491 Anderson, Peter **"Literary Publishing."** In *How to Get Published in South Africa. A Guide for Authors* by Basil van Rooyen. Halfway House, South Africa: Southern Book Publishers, 2nd ed. 1996, 19-28.
Provides guidance and tips how to get published in the field of literature, and surveys publishing outlets in South Africa in the four broad areas of literary writing: poetry, fiction, drama, and belles-lettres.

2492 Centre of the Book, Cape Town **"Pamphlet Series for Writers"** Series editor: Colleen Higgs, Editor: Karen Press. Cape Town: Centre of the Book, 2006. var. pp.
Published by the ➔ **Centre of the Book (934)** in Cape Town, this useful pamphlet series address some of the most frequent questions and concerns writers have, and as they begin to engage with publishing. While primarily targeted at writers in South Africa, they will be useful to writers and writers' groups elsewhere on the continent.

2493 **1: Getting Started as a Writer**, by Rosamund Stanford, 12 pp.
2494 **2: Start a Writing Group and Make it Work**, by Makhosazana Xaba, 16 pp.
2495 **3: Writing Practice: Keeping your Writing Alive**, by Anne Schuster, 16 pp.
2496 **4: Editing your Own Writing**, by Robert Berold, 8 pp.
2497 **5: Advice from an Editor**, by Helen Moffett, 24 pp.
2498 **6: 'The End'. What Now? Turning a First Draft into a Manuscript**, by Chanette Paul
2499 **7: Publishing Opportunities for New Writers**, by Alan Finlay, 24 pp.
2500 **8: Finding your Way around a Publishing Contract**, by Karen Press, 24 pp.
2501 **9. Legal Issues that Concern Writers**, by Karen Press, 16 pp.
2502 **10. ISBN and Places of Legal Deposit: What they do Mean for a Writer**, by Karen Press, 11 pp.

2503 Cross, Michael, and Karin Brodie **Getting Published and Getting Read : A Handbook for Writers of Scholarly Articles.** Kenwyn, South Africa: Juta, 1998. 73 pp.
[Not examined]

2504 du Toit, Thomas **How to Publish and Market your Own Book: The Key for South African Writers.** Somerset West, South Africa: T. Du Toit, 1993. 63 pp.
Offers advice to authors on editing, targeting their readership, dealing with printers and producing promotional material.

2505 Frances, Robert **A Writer's Guide to South African Magazines.** Somerset West, South Africa: Options Publishing, 1996. 117 pp.
A useful, although now dated, reference resource providing practical guidelines for freelance writers who wish to tap into the opportunities for publishing outlets offered by a variety of South African magazines. Each listing contains an analysis of a sample copy of the various magazines (type of features and material accepted for publication, regular columns, payment offered, guidelines for contributors, etc.) together with full name and address, telephone and fax numbers (and Email addresses for some), name of editor, frequency, format, average page extent per issue, and advertising content. No further editions published to date.

2506 Gibbs, James, ed. **A Handbook for African Writers.** Oxford: Hans Zell Publishers, 1988. 218 pp.
A pioneering volume containing a wealth of practical information and advice for African authors. Describes how to present a manuscript, how to find a publisher, dealing with literary agents, and offering advice about contracts, remuneration, copyright, and writing for the media. Illustrated with some amusing cartoons by Ghanaian artist Ato Delaquis. Now largely superseded by **The African Writers' Handbook**, *see* entry ➔ **2507** below.

2507 Gibbs, James, and Jack Mapanje, eds. **The African Writers' Handbook.** Oxford: African Books Collective Ltd. (in association with the Dag Hammarskjöld Foundation, Uppsala, Sweden) 1999. 432 pp.
This handbook is not only a very useful reference tool for writers, but also presents something of a benchmark volume on the sensitive and sometimes hotly debated issue of author-publisher relations. The book aims to provide all the answers African writers will want to know about publishing, how to break into print, publishing agreements, authors' rights, and how to find resources. The book contains contributions by many distinguished African authors writing about their experience in getting published and their relations with publishers, and there are also several articles providing the publisher's perspective. Additionally, the book includes a vast array of practical information on, e.g. book prizes and awards, writers' organizations, magazines, self-publishing, literary agents, book fairs and book launches, together with an annotated directory of publishers with African literature lists, resources for writers on the Internet, an author's bookshelf, and more. The book is the outcome of an African Writers-Publishers seminar jointly organized by the ➔**African Books Collective Ltd. (3)** and the ➔ **Dag Hammarskjöld Foundation (55)** held in Arusha, Tanzania, in February 1998. The seminar concluded with a statement issued by participants "Arusha III. A 'New Deal between African Writers and Publishers", which is included in the handbook. *Note:* several of the papers in this collection are individually abstracted elsewhere in this bibliography.

Reviews:
The African Book Publishing Record vol. 25, no. 2, 2000
Bellagio Publishing Network Newsletter no. 26-27, November 2000
Online:
http://www.bellagiopublishingnetwork.com/newsletter26-27/tadjo.htm [04/02/08]
Glendora Books Supplement vol. 1, no. 5 2000
Online:
http://digital.lib.msu.edu/projects/africanjournals/html/issue.cfm?colid=313
[04/02/08]
Journal of Oriental and African Studies [Athens] vol. 10, 1999
Research in African Literatures vol. 32, no. 1, 2001
Takam Tikou. Le Bulletin de la Joie par les Livres no. 8, 2000
Times Higher Education Supplement 11 February, 2000
Times Literary Supplement 22 October, 1999
Voices. The Wisconsin Review of African Languages and Literature vol. 3, 2000
West Africa 28 February 2000

2508 Higgs, Colleen **"Assisting Writers to Self-Publish."** *Mediaforum*, no. 2 (2004): 9-10.
Earlier version published as **"The Community Publishing Project: Assisting Writers to Self-publish"** in *Innovation. Journal of Appropriate Librarianship and Information Work in Southern Africa*, no. 26 (June 2003): 53-56.
Describes the programmes, activities, and *modus operandi* of the Community Publishing Project (CPP) at the➔ **Centre of the Book (934)** in South Africa, which assists self-publishers to acquire basic skills in book publishing, marketing and distribution, and which also provides small grants to groups of writers and would-be publishers to cover printing costs of small prints runs of books that are of interest to specific readerships, but that would not be of interest to commercial publishers. (*See also* entry ➔ **2509** below)

2509 Higgs, Colleen, ed. **A Rough Guide to Small-Scale and Self-Publishing.** Cape Town: Centre for the Book, 2005. 78 pp.
This guide is one in a series of excellent resources published by the Community Publishing Project of the ➔ **Centre of the Book (934)** in Cape Town. The project provides funding and technical support for small publishers, individual writers, and writers' groups in South Africa and helps them to develop publishing skills. The guide offers practical advice on the main stages of the publishing process, from manuscript preparation, editing, design, printing, through to marketing and distribution, and is intended for both published writers and those who are hoping to break into print. In particular it is aimed to assist individuals and community based organizations, whose books are unlikely to be published by commercial publishers and who wish to pursue the self-publishing route. In addition to guidelines and recommendations for good practice the guide includes stories about publishing "from those who have a great deal of experience and from those who have just begun to learn about it", among them some of the Community Publishing Project grantees.
Reviews:
The African Book Publishing Record vol. 32, no. 3, 2006

2510 Ike, V. Chukwuemeka **How to Become a Published Writer.** Ibadan: Heinemann Educational Books Nigeria plc, 1991. 230 pp.
Written by one of Nigeria's most distinguished and most widely published novelists – and for many years now Director of the ➜ **Nigerian Book Foundation (738)** – Chukwuemeka Ike here shares his wide experience as a writer of both fiction and non-fiction, using an informal and conversational style. The book is designed to lend a helping hand to aspiring writers and to assist them to become published. Part 1 of the book is devoted to writing fiction (creating characters, plots, organizing a story, style, etc.), and part 2 deals with non-fiction (articles, essays, book reviews, biography, textbooks, etc.). The final part provides advice how to find a publisher and how to safeguard the author's interest, and also looks at the prospects for authors contemplating the self-publishing route.

2511 Lewis, Heather Parker **Successful Self-publishing in South Africa.** Cape Town: Ihilihili Press (Self-help series) 2nd rev. ed., 2006. 140 pp.
A practical step-by-step guide for self-publishers how to run a successful publishing operation, from manuscript preparation, design and production, through to distribution and marketing and promotion.

2512 Matthews, Edward H. **Strike it Rich! How to Write and Publish in South Africa and Overseas.** Faerie Glen, South Africa: MCI Publishers [PO Box 37011, Faerie Glen 0043], 1995. 92 pp.
Deals with practical and motivational aspects of publishing, and finding suitable publishing outlets. Includes a list of selected local (and some overseas) publishers, and listings of South African newspapers and magazines that carry book reviews.

2513 Norton, Michael **"How to Publish Your Own Book."** In *The African Writers' Handbook,* edited by James Gibbs and Jack Mapanje. Oxford: African Books Collective Ltd., 1999, 278-294.
Although now a bit dated (e.g. it does not cover online publishing) this essay in ➜ **The African Writers' Handbook (2507)** is arguably one of the best short guides to self-publishing. It is based to large extent on the author's own involvement in self-publishing, as the former Director of the Directory of Social Change (which provides information and training to the UK voluntary sector), and founder of Books for Change, a development publishing initiative based in Bangalore. It examines self-publishing as an option and self-publishing in practice; what is required to embark on the self-publishing route; writing the book, cost-effective design, finding a printer, and marketing and distribution of the book. For each stage in the self-publishing process the author also offers a number of helpful checklists.

2514 Osborne, Helen, and Ginny Porter **Getting Published. Art, Science or Luck?** Kloof, South Africa: Writers' Circle Publishing [Postnet Suite 522, PB X4, Kloof 3640], 2007. 119 pp. + CD
Divided into three sections, the first part of this somewhat quirky guide addresses the art of writing, while part two is devoted to "the Science of Writing", covering aspects of grammar, sentence structure, plots, etc. "and all the boring, but essential,

stuff that you need to know". This section also offers some advice about how to get published and how to avoid the pitfalls, dealing with literary agents, assessing the pro's and con's of self-publishing, and the challenges of marketing and selling a self-published book. The third section entitled "Luck" looks at elements of luck that might be needed and some of the factors that will determine whether or not a book gets published, although the authors express the hope that by following their advice in the first two sections, luck won't play such a large part for novice writers seeking to get published. The guide offers some helpful, practical advice about many aspects of writing, the nuts and bolts of the writer's craft, and how to break into print, but the sections on self-publishing – and taking advantage of the opportunities now offered by new digital print technologies such as Print-on-Demand (POD) – are rather weak, as is the short section offering marketing tips. It would also have been useful if the authors had included a least a short chapter on the Internet, as the Web is now an enormously rich resource for writers of all kind. A novel and useful feature is that the book comes with a CD with interactive modules, worksheets, exercises and tutorials, and a variety of ideas to get the creative juices flowing.
Reviews:
The African Book Publishing Record vol. 34, no. 2, 2008

2515   Peter, C.B. **A Guide to Academic Writing.** Eldoret, Kenya: Zapf Chancery [PO Box 4988, Eldoret], 1994. 283 pp.
A useful companion (albeit now fairly dated) for African academic authors to assist them in the process of preparing research papers. Includes a great deal of sound practical advice on writing for publication, including a chapter entitled "How to publish your work".

2516   van Rooyen, Basil **How to Get Published in South Africa. A Guide for Authors.** Halfway House, South Africa: Southern Book Publishers, 2nd ed., 1996. 254 pp.
A very useful hands-on type of guide for authors, containing many helpful tips and a great deal of practical advice, and also examining the business of publishing from the publisher's point of view. Part 1 of the book consists of a range of overview articles on the book publishing industry in South Africa and the different areas of publishing, including a chapter on publishing in African languages. Part 2 provides advice on how to find the right publisher and describes how a publisher decides what to publish; part 3 sets out how publishing works (including an excellent chapter on publishing contracts and royalty agreements discussing a standard publisher's contract on a clause-by-clause basis); part 4 gives helpful advice on how to prepare a manuscript, and how to structure a book, read proofs, and prepare an index (where required); and part 5 is a fully annotated directory of South African publishers giving details of each publisher's list, and pointing authors directly to the publishing house most suitable for his or her type of book. Although intended primarily for authors and writers in South Africa, this guide provides a valuable companion for authors in other parts of the continent. The first edition (1994) also included overviews of different sectors of the book publishing industry in South Africa, with four contributed chapters on "The Afrikaans Market" (Kerneels Breytenbach), "'Alternative Publishing" (Russell Martin), "Educational Publishing" (Kate McCallum), and "Tertiary-level Publishing" (Mike Jacklin).

Reviews:
The African Book Publishing Record vol. 21, no. 4, 1995 (review of the first edition)

2517 van Rooyen, Basil **Get Your Book Published in 30 (Relatively) Easy Steps: A Hands-on-Guide for South African Authors.** Johannesburg: Penguin Books (South Africa), 2005. 386 pp.
A revised and updated edition of the popular ➜ **How to Get Published in South Africa (2516)**, dealing with all the steps involved in finding the right publisher and breaking into print. The focus is on non-fiction, although there is much practical advice here for writers of all genres.

Author index
(and selected titles)

This index comprises authors and editors (personal and corporate). Names of authors of papers in edited collections are indexed if they have their individual entry, but if they are mentioned as part of the annotations they are not indexed. Author headings have been standardized as far as possible.

Also indexed are selected titles, comprising all serial titles listed as main entries, including African book trade journals and national bibliographies, as well as book trade directories, bibliographies, and some other reference works such as books in print. Serial titles appear in *italic* typeface.

Aboyade, Bimpe 2367
Abraha, Assefaw 503
Abrahams, Lionel 1901
Abrahamsson, Hans 699
Academic and Non-Fiction Authors' Association of South Africa 1747
Accessions List of the Library of Congress Office, Nairobi 167
Accone, Darryl 1427, 1428
Achebe, Chinua 1316, 1317, 1902
Acholonu, Catherine Obianju 1540
Adaba, Tom A. 749
Adam, Gibrin 1493
Adamolekun, Lolese 2210
Adams, Cynthia 2077
Adamu, S.O. 1903
Adeaga, Tomi 2078
Adebowale, Sulaiman 1830, 1831, 1904
Adedeji, 'Remi 2079
Adegbonmire, Wunmi 1494
Adeniyi, Dapo 1318, 1429
Adesanoye, Festus A. 750, 751, 752, 753, 754, 755, 756
Adesanya, Buki 2210
Adesokan, Akin 1905
Adewopo, Adebambo 1739
Adichie, Chimamanda Ngozi 757
Adimorah, E.N.O. 758
Adomi, Esharenana E. 1906
Adresboek van Suid Afrikaanse Uitgewers 968
Aduda, David 2150

Adutola, K. 2151
Afele, Senyo John 2264
Africa Book Centre Book Review 148
Africa in Literature for Children and Young Adults. An Annotated Bibliography 1603
Africa Review of Books (ARB) 152
African Academy of Sciences 2334
African Association of Science Editors 127, 1907
African Association of Science Editors Newsbrief 127
African Association of Science Editors-Ethiopian Chapter 2418
African Book Publishing Record, The 168
African Book World and Press: A Directory, The 192
African Books Collective Ltd 191, 193
African Books in Print 188
African Children's Literature. A Bibliography 1630
African Children's Literature 1541
African Copyright Forum Conference 1738
African e-Journals Project 1908
African Journal of Library, Archives and Information Science 128
African Periodicals Exhibit Catalogue 1991
African Publishers Network 201, 880, 1300, 1542, 1867, 1888, 2233, 2419, 2421
African Publishers Network/African Publishing Institute 2420
African Publishers' Networking Directory 193
African Publishing Companion, The 194
African Publishing Review 129

African Publishing Review 2080
African Research & Documentation 150
African Review of Books (AroB) 151
African Writers' Handbook, The 2507
Africana Libraries Newsletter 149
Africultures 153
Afrilivres. Livres d'Afrique et des Disasporas 185
Agada, Jerry 1274
Agbebi, E.A. 760
Agenau, Robert 202
Agence de Coopération Culturelle et Technique 361
Agence de la Francophonie (ACCT) 362
Agence de la Francophonie (ACCT). Direction Générale de l'Education et de la Formation. Ecole International de la Francophonie 1866
Aguolu, C.C. 1740, 2265
Aguolu, I.E. 2265
Ahmad, Mahmoud 433
Ahmed, Medani M. 1107, 1518
Aime, Albert, 635
Aina, L.O. 128, 1832, 1909, 1910, 1911, 2266
Aina, Tade Akin 2029, 2267, 2268
Aitchison, Jenny 2152
Ajia, Olalekan 749
Ajidahun, C.O. 1231, 1741
Akachie-Ezeigbo, Adimora 2368
Akakpo, Claudine Assiba 1147
Akesson, Gunilla 700, 705, 706
Akindes, Simon Adetona 363
Akinfolarin, O. 761
Akinleye, Michael 203
Akporji, Chii P. 245
Alabi, Dayo 1889
Aladji, Weka-Yawo 2422
Alao, George 1912
Alemna, Anaba A. 169, 545, 546, 1495, 1519, 1706, 1742, 1913, 1914, 1915, 2082, 2083, 2269
Alidou-Ngame, Hassana 2081
Alimole, Nat B. 762
Alman, M. 172
Al-Mubarak, Khalid 1108
Alston, Robin C. 1998
Altbach, Philip G. 155, 170, 171, 204, 205, 206, 207, 208, 209, 210, 211, 212, 213, 214, 215, 216, 246, 247, 248, 1743, 1744, 1745, 1916, 1917, 2015, 2084, 2085
Amabhuku. Illustrations d'Afrique/ Illustrations from Africa 1543
Amanor-Wilks, Dede 1430
Amegatcher, Andrew O. 1708, 1746
Amoikon-Fauquembergue, Marie-Agathe 493

Andersen, Kirsti Hagen 2270
Anderson, Elisabeth 1520, 2369
Anderson, Peter 2491
Andrew, Jeff 547, 589, 971
Andriamalala, E.D. 652
Andrianombana, Alice 653
Annuaire du livre malgache 651
Antwi, I.K. 1920
Anyakoha, Maduha W. 173
Aparaicio, Alexandra 417
Apeji, Eric Adeche 765, 766, 767, 768, 769, 2016
APNET Children's Catalogue 1542
APNET Trade Directory 201
Appiah-Padi, Stephen K. 542, 2154, 2423
Apronti, E.O. 1999
Apronti, Jawa 1544
Arboleda, Amadio A. 206, 207
Armah, Ayi Kwei 1319, 1320
Armstrong, James C. 1232, 1233
Arnold, Anna-Marie 973
Arua, Arua E. 2155
Asafo, Dziedzorm R 2290
Asamoah-Hassan, Helena 2064, 2065
Asare, Meshack 1546
Ashimole, Elizabeth O. 1547
Askerud, Pernille 217
Association Culture et Développement 162, 365
Association des Editeurs du Bénin (ASEDIB) 424
Association des Editeurs Ivoiriens 494
Association for the Development of Education in Africa (ADEA) 436
Association internationale des libraires francophones: Nos libraires 195
Augi, Abdullahi 780
Awolalu, Tosin 1321
Awoniyi, Adedeji 770
Ayalew, Solomon 510
Ayee, E.S.A. 1707
Ayodeji Fatehinse, G. 144
Aziz, Abdoul 2335
Azubogu, N.A. 2205
Azubuike, Abraham A. 831

Ba Touré, R. 2366
Baatjes, Ivor 2156
Badejo, Rotimi 771
Badijo, Auguy 477
Badisang, Bobana E. 249, 434, 1234, 1431, 2093
Badroodien, Vanessa 1432
Baffour-Awuah, Margaret 2157
Bah, Fory 407
Bahah, S.T. 1322

Bahta, Samuel Ghile 435, 2087
Baï, Vréza Christian 366
Bailey, Barbara 974
Baillargeon, Jean-Paul 367
Bailor, M. 927
Bakare, Muhtar 772
Bakouan, Bali Augustin 444
Balarabe, Ahmed Abdu 1372
Balkema, A. A. 975
Balkwill, Richard 1749
Bamberger, Richard 2158
Bamhare, Miriam 1211, 1212, 1213, 1221, 1521, 1548, 2159, 2371
Banjo, Ayo 773
Banjo, Gboyega 1921
Bankole, Chris 774
Bankole, E. Bejide 775, 1922
Bankole, S. Bodunde 776, 777, 778, 779, 1750, 1751, 1752, 2234, 2272, 2273, 2274, 2275, 2276
Banks Henries, Doris 645
Barbier Wiesser, François-G. 340
Baritaud, B. 888
Barker, R.E. 218
Barlas, Chris 1753
Barnett, Stanley A. 1373
Barra, Yacoubou 425
Barringer, Terry 150
Bartlett, Richard 151
Batambuze, Charles 2189
Beau, Nathalie 1549
Bebye, Kidi 1550
Bedaysee, S. 2160
Behrstock, Julian 219
Beier, Ulli 1923
Bekele, Shiferaw 513
Bell, Fiona 2152
Bellagio Publishing Network Newsletter 155
Bello, Sule 780
Benedetto, Robert 1709
Bennett, Rosey 1551
Benoit, Gaëtan 688, 689
Benoit, Marie 688, 689
Benson, Peter 1924
Berger, Guy 976
Berkhout, Joop 781
Berold, Robert 2496
Bessat, Jose 368
Bessat, Colette, 368
Bessière, Audrey 1552
Bgoya, Walter 250, 251, 252, 253, 254, 255, 782, 1126, 1127, 1136, 1465, 1466, 1553, 1868, 2277, 2336
Bibliodiversité 156
Bibliographie de la Côte d'Ivoire 492

Bibliographie du Benin 423
Bibliographie du Burkina Faso 443
Bibliographie du Sénégal 877
Bibliographie nationale [de la République démocratique du Congo] 480
Bibliographie nationale de Guinée 568
Bibliographie nationale de Madagascar 649
Bibliographie nationale de Mauritanie 683
Bibliographie nationale du Cameroun 450
Bibliographie nationale du Gabon 525
Bibliographie nationale du Mali 677
Bibliography on Publishing and Book Development in the Third World 171
Bibliothèque nationale [Madagascar] 650
Bibliothèque Universitaire de la Réunion 865
Bill, Mary C. 2088
Billany, Nigel 1272
Birhanu, T. 2161
Birrell, Natalie 1036
Birungi, Phenny 1157
Bischof, Phyllis B. 256
Bissoondoyal, Surendra 690, 691
Bjornson, Richard 453
Black African Literature in English 176
Blake, David 1925
Blue, Sophie 1374
Bo Sedin Consultants AB 1128
Bohm, Fredric 1275
Bolodeoku, B.O. 783
Bolton, Patricia 349
Bolze, Louis W. 1214
Bond, Frances 1433
Bonde, D. 1754
Bond-Stewart, Kathy 1730, 1731
Boniface, Sheila 2162
Bontoux, Vincent 1515
Book Aid International 257, 258, 1375, 2450
Book and Publishing Assistance Programmes 1413
Book Chain in Anglophone Africa: A Survey and Directory, The 196
Book Industry, The 131
Bookbird: A Journal of International Children's Literature 1554
Bookchat 130
BookLinks 157
Bookman Consultants Ltd 197
Books for Africa 1376
Bortey, Emmanuel 549
Boshoff, Nelius 2351
Bosire-Ogechi, Emily 2128
Botswana. Ministry of Education 436
Botte, Véronique 1560
Bouquiaux, Luc 2089
Bourdin, Florence 882

Bourgueil, Isabelle 369, 370, 371, 372, 1215, 2235
Bowen, Jennie 1506
Boyd, Allen R. 1236
Boye, Mary 1555, 1556, 1557, 1558
Bozimo, Doris O. 1926
Braham, Abdelwahed 2278
Brande, Daniel M. 2349
Breytenbach, Kerneels 977
Brickhill, Paul 259, 260, 261, 262, 350, 1303, 1304, 1305, 1306, 1497, 2372, 2424
British Council, The 1869
Broady, Marie 978
Brodie, Karin 2503
Brunswic, Etienne 1870, 2456
Buchan, Amanda 1377, 1871
Bugembe, Mary H. 1434, 1435, 1559, 1632
Bukku 133
Bullock, Adrian 883
Bundy, Caroline 192, 979
Burafuta, Jean-Paul 2337
Bureau of Ghana Languages 550
Busgeeth, K. 2359
Butalia, Urvashi 2373
Büttner, Thomas 2451

Cabuço, Gabriel 418
Cabutey-Adodoadji, E. 551
Cachalia, Coco 980
Canadian Organisation for Development through Education (CODE) 1176
Candela, A. 379
Cape Town Book Fair. Exhibitor Catalogue 198
Cardorelle, David 478
Carew, F.C. 784
Carlos, Jérôme 495
Carpenter, Julia 1129, 1183
Casey, C. 2223
Cassiau-Haurie, Christophe 481, 482
Catalogue 2005 of French-speaking Publishers 186
Centre Africain de Formation à l'Edition et à la Diffusion 2425
Centre of the Book [South Africa] 2492
Certain, Edith 2339, 2359
Cévaér, Françoise 374, 496, 1323
Chabert, Laurence 373
Chabrol, Didier 2340
Chachage, C.S.L. 1130, 1131
Chahinian, Hasmig 166
Chakava, Henry M. 263, 264, 265, 266, 267, 268, 269, 270, 271, 590, 591, 592, 593, 594, 595, 596, 597, 598, 1307, 1324, 1467, 1561, 1755, 1756, 2017, 2163, 2236, 2279

Chali, Katongo A. 1177
Chamberlain, A. 2187
Chandravanshi, B.S. 2341
Chanin, Clifford 1522
Charles, Kiven 468
Charlewood, Lucy 2164
Châtry-Komarek, Marie 2090, 2452
Chavula, Serman W.D. 1757
Che Tita, Julius 462
Chege, John Waruingi 599
Cheh, M.M. 981
Chifwepa, Vitalicy 1178, 1914
Childs, William M. 1378
Chinweizu 1325
Chipidza, Chipo 1468
Chirwa, Christopher H. 262, 1177, 1179, 1180
Chitando, Anna 1562
Chitsike, B.C. 1216, 2091
Choi, Hyaeweol 171
Christensen, Lars P. 1315
Christian Booksellers Association Southern Africa Members [Directory] 958
Christopher, Nkechi M. 785
Chupty, Shanoo 1061
Cilliers, Isabel 1563, 1564
Clarke, Rebecca 1326, 1327, 2374
Clavea, Katia 720
Cloete, Dick 982
Cnockaert, André 1927
Coates, Nick 2092
Cochran, Christopher Lee 1436
Coelho, Jill Young 1237
Coetzee, J.M. 1928
Coetzer, Diane 2043
Cofie, Sam O. 1498, 1499
Cohen, P. 927
Colimalay, Clifford 692, 693
Coll, Sandrine 1425
Coly, Gaston-Pierre 2165
Combrinck, Nicholas 983
Commonwealth of Learning 2453
Commonwealth Secretariat. Women's and Youth Affairs Division 2375
Cookey, Samuel J. 1732
Cope, Jack 1929
Copeling, A.J.C. 1758
Corder, Hugh 984
Cordor, Henry S. 644
Correa, Antoinette 884
Cotton, Dulcie 1565
Coulibaly, N'Golo 678
Coulibaly, Souleymane 2166
Coulon, Virginia 2000
Council for the Development of Social Science Research in Africa 2454

Council for the Promotion of Children's Science Publications in Africa 1566
Courtney, Dana 1263
Coussy, Denise 985
Crabbe, Richard 272, 273, 543, 1469
Crampton, Margaret 1930, 1957
CREPLA bulletin d'Information 134
CREPLA Bulletin of Information 134
Cromhout, Monica 147, 986
Cross, Michael 2503
Crowder, Michael 1379
Cruise, Wilma 987
Cultures Sud 158
Cumming, Sioux 1931, 1932
Currey, James 1328, 1329, 1330, 1331, 2237, 2280
Curry, Ann 1380
Czerniewicz, Laura 988, 989, 1217, 1500, 2426, 2427, 2428

da Costa, Juliao José 871
da Cruz, A.J. 1872
D'Almeida, Francisco 2167
Danset, F. 2168
Darch, Colin M. 701, 1815
Darko-Ampem, Kwasi 275, 553, 2281, 2282
Date, Lara 1181
Davey, Maggie 983, 990
Davies, Shirley 1567
Davies, Wendy 276
Davis, Caroline 2018
Davis, Geoffrey V. 991
Davis, Jason 2455
Dayeko, Paul 1332
de Beer, Jennifer A. 2066
de Beer, Johanna 1437
de Freitas, Denis 1760
de Kock, Leon 993
de Souza, Oscar 426
de Villiers, G.E. 994
Dean, Elizabeth 1182
Dean, O.H. 1759
Déazon, André 2342
Deffontaines, Marie Therèse 679
Dekutsey, Woeli A. 277, 554, 555, 1308, 1333, 1438, 1439, 1501, 1568, 1569, 2044, 2429,
DeLancey, Mark 2283
Denning, Carmelle 512, 702, 1132, 1183, 1515, 1871
Dennis, Alasia Datonye 2067
Development Directory of Indigenous Publishing 200
Diabate, Dafina Blacksher 1309
Diala, Isidore 786
Diallo, Abdou Karim 885

Diallo, Mariam 886
Diamond, Denise 992
Dieye, Adama Sow 887, 888
Dihang, Jean 454
Dike, Virginia W. 1570, 1571, 1572
Dilevko, Juris 1276
Dillsworth, Gloria 918, 1573
Dingome, Jeanne N. 787
Dintwe, Motumi N. 1234, 2093
Diongue Diop, Mariétou 889
Diop, Bara 2343
Diop, Sakhevar 1887
Diouf, Jean Pierre 2284
Dirar, Solomon 2094
Direction du Livre et de la Lecture, Senegal 878, 879
Directory of Book Donation Programs. 1381
Directory of Book Publishing in South Africa 969
Directory of Libraries ... and Bookshops in Mauritius 686
Directory of Namibian Libraries, Publishers and Booksellers 715
Directory of Nigerian Book Development 743
Directory of South African Publishers 968
Directory of Zimbabwe Publishers 1208
Diso, Lukman Ibraheem 788
Dixon, D. 1132
Djoleto, S.A. Amu 556, 557, 636, 919, 1184, 1733, 2169
Dodoo, V. 1742
Dodson, Don 2001
Dogbé, Yves-Emmanuel 375, 1334
Domatob, Jerry 278
Donker, Ad 995
Doo Bell, Jacques 455
Dorsinville, Roger 890
Doumbia, A.T. 2344
Doyle, Robert P. 1382
Drabeck, Anne Gordon 1523
Drew, Lisa 996
Drum Publications (EA) Ltd 1933
du Toit, Thomas 2504
Dunton, Chris 456, 1440, 2002
Dupper, Marion 997
Durand, Rosamaria 220, 1383
Durrani, Shiraz 600, 2095
Dyck, Robert 1384
East African Bookseller, The 135
Easterbrook, David L. 1238, 1239, 1277, 1992
Ecole de Bibliothécaires, Archivistes et Documentalistes, Université de Dakar 174
Edwards, Karen 157
Egejuru, Phanuel Akubeze 1335
Egonwa, Osa D. 1761

Ehling, Holger G. 991
Ehmeir, Walter 1336
Eilers, Franz-Josef 1710
Eisenberg, Brenda 998
Ekpo, Moses F. 1763
Ekwensi, Cyprian D. 1337, 1574, 2003
Elaturoti, Folorunso 358
Ellerman, Evelyn 339
Emanuel, Abosede 2045
Emifene, Andrew 1764
Enahoro, Peter 279
Enyia, Christian O. 789
Epstein, Rheina 1441
Erinle, E.K. 1762
Escarpit, Robert 218, 221
Escudier, Denis 498
Esseh, Samuel Smith 1833
Essery, Isabel 999, 1000
Estivals, Robert 376
Etemesi, Horace 1734
Ethiope Publishing Corporation 790
Ethiopian Publications 507
Evans, John 1873
Evans, Julie 351
Evans, Nicholas 1001, 1002, 1003
Ezeigbo, Theodora Akachi 2170
Ezenwa-Ohaeto 791, 1934

Fagerberg-Diallo, Sonja 2096, 2097, 2098
Fahari, Gladys 1575
Fajemisin, Martins Olusegun 2099
Fall, Anne-Marie 891
Fallon, Helen 920
Fanoiki, M.F.I. 792
Farrell, Joseph P. 222
Fasemore, Akin 2431
Favier, Annie 1874
Fawcett, Graham 1338
Faye, Djibril 892, 893
Fayose, Philomena Osazee 793, 1576, 1577, 1578, 1579, 1580, 1581
Fennessy, Eamon T. 1765
Ferns, Martin 1185
Ficquet, Eloi 513
Fiedler, Klaus 2285
Field-Juma, Alison 2345
Finlay, Alan 2499
Fiofori, Tan 1766
Fisher, Maire 959
Fleming, Tyler 1935
Fofana, Chérif Moctar 680
Fofana, Ramatoulaye 894
Fofana, Souleymane 377
Fondjo, Bertin 139
Fontaine, Régine 340

Foster, Michael 1264
Fourth Dimension Publishing Company 142
Fox, Mem 1582
Frances, Robert 2505
Frank, Katherine 2376
Fredericks, G.H. 2104
Frederiksen, Bodil Folke 1936
French, Edward 1004
French, Tom 883
Frenette, Guy 2238
Friedman, Michelle 2377
Friends-of-the Book Foundation 1385
Frings, Anja 2451
Froise, Margaret 1711
Frylinck, J.H. 2147
Fullard, Allison 2068
Furlonger, David 2171
Furniss, Graham 2004
Fyle, Clifford M. 958

Galiwango, M.L.C. 1158
Galler, Anne M. 1218
Galliand, Etienne 156
Galloway, Francis 1005, 1006
Gambia National Bibliography 530
Ganu, K.M. 2286
Gardiner, Maggie 1389
Garrett, Jeffrey 1665
Garzón, Álvaro 2030
Gassama, Makhily 895
Gazza, Sophia 2172
Gebhardt, L. 718
Gedin, Per I. 280, 281, 282, 1834
George, Lavona 2378
Gérard, Albert S. 896
Ghana Book Development Council 136
Ghana Book Publishers Association Catalogue 543
Ghana Book Trust 1386
Ghana Book World 136
Ghana National Bibliography 544
Gibbe, A.K. 2173
Gibbs, James 2046, 2506, 2507
Gibbs, Wayt W. 1937
Gidney, Michael 2432
Gillmore, Alex 1712
Glendora Books Supplement 159
Global Knowledge Partnership 1310
Gomez, Michel Robert E. 427, 428
Gopinathan, S. 206, 207, 208
Gordon-Brown, Alfred 1007
Gottlieb, Lisa 1276
Govender, Meneesha 1036
Grah Mel, Frédérick 1938
Graham, Gordon 160, 1265, 2019, 2020

Grahm, Leif 1133
Granqvist, Raoul 1583, 1584
Gray, Eve 1008, 1767, 1768, 1835, 1836, 2069,
    2070, 2071, 2072, 2287, 2288, 2289
    see also Horwitz Gray, Eve
Gray, Stephen 1159, 1585
Greaney, Vincent 2174
Griswold, Wendy 1339
Groenewald, B.H. 1727
Groupe de Recherche et d'Echanges
    Technologiques (GRET) 2346
Groves, T. 1387
Gueye, Seydou 2175
Gulbraar, Kari 1134
Gundu, George S. 601
Gupta, S. 514
Gurnah, Abdulrazak 663
Gyr-Ukunda, Agnes 2105

Habila, Helon 1340
Habomugisha, Peace 2290
Habte, Messelech 2329
Hadao, R. A. 614
Hadley Grave, Jessica 132
Hajjar, Habib 1870
Hakalima, S. 1183
Halbert, Debora 1815
Hall, John 2456
Hall, Jolyon D.S. 1240
Hameso, Seyoum Y. 515
Hamilton-Jones, Ruth 1341
Hamrell, Sven 602
Hanson, Ben J. 2176, 2177
Harding, Oliver 921
Haricombe, Lorraine J. 1009
Harman, Elenanor 161
Haron, Muhammed 1010, 1939, 2291
Harrell-Bond, Barbara 2047
Harris, John 2292
Harrity, Sara 1388, 1389, 1390
Hasan, Abul 1524, 1525, 1769, 2433, 2434
Hategekimana, Grégoire 869, 870
Haut Conseil de la Francophonie 378
Hayatu, Husaini 794
Heale, Jay 130, 1586, 1587, 1588, 1589, 1590,
    1591, 1592, 1593, 1594
Hechter, Rhodé 1011
Heisslier, Nina 379
Hendriksz, Colleen 1012
Hendrikz, Francois 1013
Henige, David P. 1713
Heyneman, Stephen P. 222, 223, 224, 1160
Higgs, Colleen 959, 1014, 1015, 2508, 2509
Higo, Aigboje 795
Hill, Alan 1342, 1343, 2021

Hillebrecht, Werner 719, 725, 726
Himwiinga, Paulsen A. 483
Hobbs, Philippa 987
Hofmeyr, Isabel 283, 352, 1016
Hogarth, David 1241
Hogg, Peter 1998, 2005
Holland, Mel 1017
Hooper, A.S.C. 1018, 1019
Hoppers, Catherine Odora 2372
Horn, Caroline 1020
Horowitz, Irving Louis 1021
Horwitz Gray, Eve 1022, 1023, 1024, 1025,
    1026, 1770, 2293
    see also Gray, Eve
Howard-Reguindin, Pamela 1242
Howe, Adrian 148
Huannou, Adrien 1940
Hubert, Souad 2106
Hughes, Sally 2457
Hugo, Nadine 1027
Human, Koos 1028
Humery, Marie-Eve 720
Humphrey, Lesley 199, 1311
Huppert, Rémi 703
Hurry, Burford 1526
Hurst, Christopher 1470, 1471, 2294
Hussein, Janet 1837, 1941, 2295
Hutchinson, Robert 2022
Hutchison, John P. 380
Hyltenstam, Kenneth 704

IBBY. Books for Africa/Books from Africa
    1598
Ibouanga, S. Nzassi 2366
Ibrahim, Jibrin 853
Ifaturoti, Adedamola A. 1838
Ifidon, B.I. 796
Ifidon, Sam E. 1942, 1943
Ike, V. Chukwuemeka 359, 797, 798, 799,
    1344, 1527, 1735, 1771, 2031, 2178, 2179,
    2510
Ikhigbonoareme, E.B. 1595
Ikoja-Odongo, J.R. 1161, 1162, 1163
Ikonne, Chidi 1596
Illustrators Portfolio, The 1597
Iloegbunam, Chris 2379
Ilomo, C.S. 1137
Impey, Bridget 1472, 1502, 2239, 2482, 2458
INASP Directory 1392
Information and Training Resources for the
    Book Chain 2450
Instituto Caboverdeano do Livro 472
International Board on Books for Young
    People (IBBY) 1598

International Book Bank/Dialogue of Partners 1391
International Book Development Ltd 227
International Federation of Library Associations 227
International ISBN Agency 353
International Network for the Availability of Scientific Publications (INASP) 1392, 1839, 2459, 2460
International Trade Centre/UNCTAD/GATT 1891, 1892, 2240
Ioannides, Pavlos 1686
Irele, Abiola 284, 800, 801, 1944, 2048, 2296
Irele, Bassey 149
Iroh, Eddie 802
Irura, Stanley 135, 1503, 1772, 1773, 2435
Irvine, Mark 2180
Isnard, F. Lalande 1504
Isoun, T.T. 285, 2347
Itatiro, Mello 1135
Iwe, J.I. 803
Iwerebon, Felix A. 804, 805

Jack, Belinda 866
Jacquemin, Jean-Pierre 381
Jacquey, Marie-Clotilde 681
Jagar, T. 2297
Jam, Z. 2181
Jamal, Amir H. 287
James, Louis 1945
Jamison, Dean T. 1160
Janssens, Jean-Claude 382
Jay, Mary 782, 1266, 1267, 1268, 1269, 1270, 1278, 1279, 1280, 1281, 1282, 1442, 1473, 1840, 2049, 2050, 2241, 2242, 2380
Jaygbay, Jacob 897, 1946, 1947, 2298, 2299, 2300, 2301, 2302
Jegede, Oluremi 806, 1774
Jenkins, Elwyn 1599
Jenkins, Ray 558
Joachim, Paulin 457
Johnson, Timothy 149
Johnston, Laurie 225
Johnstone, Ian 2023
Jones, Bronwen 2107
Jones, Eldred 922, 2051, 2052
Jordaan, Amanda 1061
Joubert, Susan Ruth 1029
Journal of African Children's and Youth Literature 137
Journal of Scholarly Publishing 161
Journals Catalogue of Nigeria 744
July, Robert W. 2303
Jung, Ingrid 2108

Kaboré, Armand Joseph 445
Kadima-Nzur, Mukala 484
Kadzamira, Esme 664, 665
Kagan, Alfred 1243
Kahn, Ellison 1948
Kalenga, E.M. 288
Kaligula, C. 1135
Kalugula, Charles 1136
Kamani, Wacango 1600, 2381
Kamm, Anthony 531
Kamugisha, Thomas A.R. 1528
Kamwendo, Gregory H. 2109
Kangafu, Gudumbagana 485
Kantey, Mike 1030, 1031, 1032, 1033, 1063, 1474
Kanuya, Albert 1475
Karanja, A. Njeri 2436
Kargbo, John Abdul 923
Kasankha, Samuel 2304
Kasonde, Christine 1186
Katama, Agnes 1164, 2305
Katjavivi, Jane 721, 722, 723, 726, 1043, 1272, 2348, 2382, 2383, 2384
Kats, Ivan 1393, 2243
Kaungamno, E.E. 1137, 1138
Kawooya, Dick 1802
Keartland, E. 807, 1183
Kebiditswe, Kgakgamatso 1601
Kedem, Kosi A. 1775
Keim, Karen R. 2006
Keïta, Fatou 1602
Kellerman, Barbara C. 1034
Kelley, Lorraine 1380
Kelly, Gail P. 209
Kelly, Susan 2380
Kemp, Ivor 1129
Kenya Books in Print 586
Kenya National Bibliography 587
Kevane, Michael 2182
Kganela, Lesego D. 2110
Kgosidintsi, Thandiwe 437
Khalanyane, T.E. 2111
Khati, T.E. 2111
Khorana, Meena 165, 1603, 1604, 1605
Kibble, Matt 1345
Kigongo-Bukenya, T. Isaac 1165, 1776
Kimani, Peter 338
Kimenye, Barbara 1346
Kimona, Jean-Claude 1631
Kirkpatrick, Roger 286
Kirkwood, Mike 1949, 1985
Kistler, John M. 1244
Kitinya, Ishmael O. 341
Kitson, Norma 2473
Kloeckner, Hélène 383, 458, 499, 898

Klother, Annelie 1219
Knutsen, Unni 1777
Kobia, J.M. 603
Koenig, Mary 175
Kola, Pamela 1606, 1607
Komarek, Kurt 2112
Komasi, Mabel Mliwomore 1608
Konate, Hamidou 2244
Konaté, Sié 384, 385, 1610
Kor, Buma 1505, 1611
Korley, Nii Laryea 1347
Kotei, S.I.A. 289, 290, 438, 1612
Kotze, Antoinette 1841
Kotzé, Arend 1035
KPA News 138
Krieger, Milton 1950
Kriel, Lize 352
Kromberg, Steve 1036, 1037, 1529, 1842
Krut, David 987
Krut, Orenna 1038
Krynauw, Paula 291
Kukubo, R. 1778
Kumah, D.P. 1714
Kumar, Arvind 226
Ku-Mesu, Katalin Egri 1348
Kuruman Mission Trust 1715
Kyomuhendo, Goretti 2385

L'Afrique en livres 189
L'édition africaine pour la jeunesse 1613
La Joie par les livres - Centre national du livre
   pour enfants 1613
Lafarge, Jacques 382
Laguere, Jean-Pierre 2474
Lalloo, Pushpa Hargovan 2386
Lambert, Fernando 459
Larby, Patricia M. 1257
Laroussinie, Claude 386
Larson, Charles R. 1349
Laurentin, Marie 166, 1614, 1615, 1616
Lavy, P. 379
Lawal, L.D. 1245
Lawal-Solarin, O.M. 808, 1350, 1351, 1617,
   1779, 1893
Le Livre Africain 139
Le livre et la presse en Afrique au Sud du
   Sahara 174
Leach, Athol 2183, 2184
Lebon, Cécile 1618
Lebotsa, M.M. 2185
Leguéré, Jean-Pierre 387
Leishman, A.D.H. 1283, 1443
Leka, Wanna 516
Lema, Elieshi 292, 342, 1619, 2387
Leoli, C.T. 1716

Lesothana 634
Letshela, P.Z 1780
Levey, Lisbeth E. 1394, 2306
Levine, Charles M.
Levis, Mugumya 1875
Lewin, Hugh 1620
Lewis, Heather Parker 2511
Liljeson, Lars 705, 706
Lillie, K. 1132
Limb, Peter 1246, 1843
Lindahl, Bengt 262
Lindfors, Bernth 176, 604, 605, 606, 1352, 1395,
   1951, 1952, 1953, 1954, 1955, 2007, 2008
Ling, Margaret 1284, 1444, 1446, 2388
Lionnet, Guy 912
Lisher, T. 609
Liste des éditeurs au Sénégal 878
Liste des librairies au Sénégal 879
Livres africains disponibles 188
Livres d'images d'Afrique noire: auteurs-
   illustrateurs Africains 1552
Liyong, Taban Lo 2186
Ljungman, Cecilia Magnusson 1271
Logos 160
Lomer, Cécile 168, 182, 188
Longe, H.O.D. 809
Lopes, Carlos 574
Lor, P.J. 1780
Loric, Laurent 2245, 2246
Low, Gail 1353
Lucan, Taban Aisie 924, 1621
Lukomo, Bivuatu Nsundi 486
Ly, Oumou Khairy 899

Maack, Mary Niles 388
Maake, Nhlanhla 2114
Maasdorp, Eben 724, 729
Mabawonku, I.M. 1910
MacGlinchey, Ciaran 2256
Machet, Myrna 1039, 1040, 1622, 2187, 2188
MacLam, Helen 293
Macola, Giacomo. 2113
Macpherson, John 229, 1396
Made, S.M. 294
Madolo, Yolisa 1043
Madondo, Mwazvita Patricia 1844, 2389
Mafela, Lily 1312
Magara, Elisam 2189
Mahommed, Alli Andre 2115
Mairot, F. 637
Maiyanga, Alex A. 744
Maja-Pearce, Adewale 1354, 1355, 1476
Makenzie, Margaret 2191
Makgetla, Tumi 2053
Makotsi, Ruth 343, 607, 1272, 1894, 1895

Malanchuk, Peter 1247
Malawi National Bibliography 661
Malhotra, D.N. 2437
Maliyamkono, Todo 2390
Mamari, K. 500
Mammah, Richard 745, 810, 2190
Manji, Firoze 2307
Mapanje, Jack 2507
Maphasa, Nthunzi 2349
Marcazzan, Sr. Teresa 1723
Marchadour, Saara 148
Maree, Jean 1100
Marsaud, Olivia 570, 682
Martin, David 1220
Martin, Lianda 1041
Martini, Jürgen 1583, 2009
Martin-Koné, Mary-Lee 1623
Maseko, Mandla 2192
Mashishi, Thapelo 2193
Masokoane, Glenn Ujabe 1042
Masson, Brigitte 694
Mate, Fredrick 2438
Matenjwa, Nish-Muthoni 2391
Mateso, Emmanuel Locha 389
Matola, Samuel 707
Matovelo, Doris S. 1285
Matthews, Edward H. 2512
Mavuso, Makana 1113
Mbae, J.G. 2194
Mbanga, Trish 1445, 1446, 1447, 1448, 1449,
    1450
Mba-Zue, Nicolas 526
Mbobo, Tembeka 1043, 2392
Mbome, P.H. 1530
Mbonde, J.P. 1139
Mbure, Sam 1624
Mbye, Abdou 532
McCall, James 608
McCallum, Kate 1044, 1531
McCarthy, C.M. 2010
McCartney, Murray 228, 2032, 2195, 2247
McDonald, Elsa 1625
McGregor, Charles 609, 1876
Mcharazo, Alli A.S. 1140, 1397
McHardy, Francois 1845
Mchazime, Hartford 664, 665
Mchombu, Kingo J. 1993, 2116
McIlwaine, John 1248, 1249
McKee, Malcolm D. 1250
McLean, Eva 301
McLean Rathgeber, Eva-Maria 2308
    see also McLean, Eva;
    Rathgeber, Eva-Maria
McMaster, David N. 2309
McNaught, Sue 1506

Medcalfe, P. 1135
Médéhouégnon, Pierre 428
Médianes 162
Medugu, Burbur J. 744
Mefe, Guy-Marc Tony 1781
Melching, Molly 1626, 1627
Meldrum, Andrew 354
Membrey, David J. 1398, 2439
Meniru, Teresa E. 1628
Menon, Rita 2373
Mensah, Ayoko 153
Merrett, Christopher 1045
Michelman, Frederic 390
Milazi, D.B.T. 438
Miller, Jonathan 1451
Milliken, Phoebe 2196
Mills, Paul 1846
Milner, Toby 1477
Mini, T. 2197
Minowa, Shigeo 230
Minzi, L.T.D. 1133
Miranda, Maria Filomena Ribeiro 2350
Mitchell-Powell, Brenda 1452, 1453
Mlambo, Alois 2310, 2311, 2312
Moçambique a Través dos Livros 698
Moen, Jorunn 1134
Moffett, Helen 2497
Mohamed, Nabé 2358
Moingeon, March 2248
Möller, Allison Melanie 2073
Molteno, Robert 2249
Momoh, Ansu 925, 926, 2033
Monkasa-Bitumba 381
Monnier, Philippe D. 1847
Montagnes, Ian 161, 177, 231, 232, 1887, 2440,
    2441, 2442, 2443, 2475, 2476, 2477
Monteith, Mary 1079
Mordi, Chinedum 1906
Morija Press Board 638
Morolong, Paul Motlatsi 639, 1629
Morolong, Siamisang 1782
Morris, Sally 2478
Mortimer, K. 609
Moser, Gerald M. 1956
Moshoeshoe, June 1046
Moshoeshoe-Chadzingwa, Matseliso 2393
Moss, Glenn 1047, 1048, 1049, 1050, 1051,
    1052, 1454
Mosuro, Kolade 140, 812, 1507, 1508, 1783,
    2151
Motimedi, E.K. 2117
Motlhabane, Ratanang 440
Mould-Iddrisu, Betty 1784
Mountain, Penny 811
Moutchia, William 134, 1478, 1532

Mouton, Johann 2351
Moyana, Rosemary 2198
Moyo, Promise 2479
Mpanga, Egidio H. 666, 1896
Mpe, Phaswane 1053, 1054
Mpesha, Nyambura 1630
Mphisa, Simon Q. 1211, 1221
Msiska, Augustine W.C. 667, 668
Mugo, Macharia 1455
Mugo, Micere Githae 2313, 2395
Muhate, Zephanias 708
Muita, David 610
Mukuama, L. 487
Mulindwa, Gertrude Kayaga 441, 2199
Mulokozi, M.M. 2118, 2119
Munamwimbu, Ray 1187, 1188, 1189, 1897
Mundondo, Tainie 129, 2394
Munguya, A.W. 1717
Munoo, Rajeen 1055
Munyiri, Wilfred 611
Muriithi, F.K. 2444
Murray, Steve 2014
Murray, Susan 1957
Musakali, Joseph 626
Musi, Joyce 2120
Musonda, Flora 1894
Mutlaotse, Mothobi 1056
Mutowo, Maurice K. 2314
Mutula, Stephen M. 435, 1166, 1832, 2087
Mwacalimba, Hudwell 1190
Mwangi, David M. 344
Mwangi, Serah 2396
Mwang'ombe, Chrispus 2445
Mwankumi, Dominique 1631
Mwanycky, Serah W. 1632, 1633, 1958
Mwiyeriwa, Steve S. 669, 670, 671
Mvunelo, Z. 2104
Mwoltu, P.P. 813
Mwroroha, Emile 447
Myambo, Mmashikwane 2200

Nabwera, Alice 612
Naidoo, Kuma 1848
Nair, Chandran 1533
Najar, Ridha 404
Nakitto, Mabel M.T. 1166
Nalumango, Mbuyu 1191
Namhila, Ellen 725
Namibia National Bibliography 717
Namibian Books in Print 716
Namponya, C.R. 672
Nancasse, Dillia 900
Nassimbeni, Mary 1057
National Archives of Malawi 662
National Bibliography of Botswana 432

National Bibliography of Ethiopia 508
National Bibliography of Mauritius 687
National Bibliography of Nigeria 746
National Bibliography of the Seychelles 911
National Bibliography of Uganda 1156
National Bibliography of Zambia 1174
National Education Co- ordinating
  Committee (NECC) 1086
National Library of South Africa 968
Navorro, Júlio 709
Ndachi-Tagne, David 451
Ndegwa, John 613
Ndiaye, A. Raphaël 2121
Ndiaye, Ndéné 1356, 1785
Ndiaye, Papa Toumané 1786
Ndwandwe, Elias 1114
Negash, Legesse 2352
Neill, Richard 317
Nemukula, Albert 1634
Network of Educational Innovation for
  Development in Africa 1877
Neumann, Peter H. 233
Newell, Stephanie 2011
Newton, Diana C. 295, 391, 392, 393, 394, 395,
  460, 461, 1400, 2034, 2037, 2250
Newton, Robert C. 2122
Nfila, Reason Baathuli 1994
Ngandu, Freddie 462, 1286, 2123
Ngeze, Pius B. 1736
Ngoma 163
Ngombe, Laurier Yvon 1787
Ngou, Honorine 527
Nguessan, Michael K. 380
Ngwane, Mwalimu George 463
Nicholson, Denise Rosemary 1788, 1789
Nigerian Book Fair Trust 296, 814, 815, 1898,
  2124, 2397
Nigerian Book Foundation 1534
Nigerian Books Directory and Guide 745
Nigerian Books in Print 747, 748
Nigerian Bookseller 140
Nigerian Publishers Association 747, 748
Nilsson, Anders 699
Nimako, Annor 559, 560
N'Jie, S.P.C. 533
Njinya-Mujinya, L. 2290
Njoroge, Janet 138, 1635, 1878, 2398
Nnana-Rejasef, Marie-Claire 396
Noma Award Archives 2054
Noma Award Managing Committee 2055
Nomenyo, Adzowavi Dzigbodi 2353
Nordberg, Olle 602
North, James 2076
Norton, Michael 2513
Nott, Chris 849

Nottingham, John 297, 344
Ntonfo, André 464
Ntshangase, Dumisani K. 2125
Nukpezah, H.M. 2315
Nuttall, Sarah 2201
Nwafor, B.U. 234, 1995
Nwagwu, Williams 2354
Nwakanma, Chukwuemeka Dean 816
Nwali, L.O. 817
Nwankwo, Arthur A. 818, 1479
Nwankwo, B.C. 819
Nwankwo, Victor U. 820, 821, 822, 823, 824,
    1313, 1399, 1480, 1849, 1850, 1879, 2126,
    2251, 2316
Nwapa, Flora 1636, 2399
Nwauche, E.S. 1790
Nweke, Ken M.C. 1996, 2202
Nwodo, C.O. 842
Nwoga, Chinyere 825, 1456
Nwokolo, Chuma 2203
Nwosu, C.B. 826
Nwosu, Ikechukwu E. 749
Nyadzi, Ben K. 1791
Nyambura, Gillian 1314, 1880, 1881
Nyamfukudza, Stanley 1222
Nyamnjoh, Francis B. 298, 299, 1357, 2318
Nyangulu, Juliet N. 356, 664, 665
Nyariki, Lily K. 141, 607, 614, 615, 1637, 1899
Nyarko, Francis 1638
Nyarko, Kwame 561, 562
Nyeko, Janet A. 1481, 2480, 2481
Nyika, Tambayi 1457
Nyoni, Todd 1509, 1510
Nyoro, Dominic 2349
Nyren, Penny 1639

Obasi, John U. 1251, 1252
Obidiegwu, Dan 827, 828
Obiechina, Emmanuel 2012
Obioma, Godswell 829
O'Connor, Brigid 1882
Odaga, Asenath Bole 1640, 1641, 1737, 2400,
    2401
Oddoye, David E.M. 1792
Odejide, Abiola 1642
Odendaal, Welma 1959
Odhiambo, Thomas R. 2355
Odiase, J.O.U. 1643
Odini, Cephas 616
Oduyoye, Modupe 1718, 1719
Ofei, Eric 563, 1644
Ofeimun, Odia 300
Ofori-Mensah, Akoss 564, 1482, 2402, 2403,
    2404, 2405
Ogechi, Nathan Oyori 2127, 2128

Ogunleye, Bisi 830, 1483, 1511
Ojeniyi, Ayo 755
Ojiji, C.O. 1793
Okafor, N.R. 1645
Okanlawon, Tunde 1646
Okediran, Wale 1647, 2204
Okeke, Chika 2013
Okia, Martin 146
Okiy, Rose B. 1794
Oko, Emelia 1596
Okojie, Victoria 831
Okoli, Enukora Joe 832
Okonkwo, Lawrence 1484
Okoro, C.C. 2205
Okoro, Innocent 833
Okoye, Ifeoma 1648
Okurut, Mary Karooro 2406
Okwanya, Fred Ojienda 617
Okwilagwe, Andrew Oshiotse 834, 835, 836,
    837, 838, 839, 2446
Oladitan, Olalere 1795
Olajide, Akin 840
Olanlokun, S. Olajine 1960
Olden, Anthony 235, 345, 346, 1397, 1458
Olën, Sandra 1622
Olën, Sll 2187
Oliphant, Andries Walter 1058, 1059, 1060,
    1961, 1962, 1963
Oliveira, Ruy 710
Ollennu, Amerly A. 2349
Olude, O.O. 841
Olukoju, Ayodeji 2317
Olukoshi, Adebayo 2318
Oluwasanmi, Edwina 301
Oman, Ralph 1796
Omobowale, Emmanuel Babatunde 853
Omotoso, Kole 1649, 1650, 1651, 2035, 2206,
    2207
Omowunmi, Segun 1652
Ondari-Okemwa, Ezra 2319
Ondo, Rose 528
Onduso, Brown 1653
Onibonoje, Gabriel O. 302
Onwudinjo, Peter 1596
Onwueme, Tess 1358
Opland, Jeff 2129
Orford, Margie 2407
Orimalade, Oluronke 1401, 1512, 2130, 2408,
    2482
Osa, Osayimwense 137, 1654, 1655, 1656
Osaki, Lillian Temu 1657, 1658
Osakwe, G.C. 843
Osanyin, Bode 2208
Osborn, Paul 2037, 2340
Osborne, Helen 2514

Osofisan, Femi 1359
Osségué, Nelly 901
Osundare, Niyi 1360, 1361, 2056, 2057
Otiende, James E. 1402
Otike, J.N. 618
Otokunefor, H.C. 842
Ouane, Adama 2131
Ouma, Marisella 1797
Ouma, Symphrose 1964
Ourgay, M. 517
Ouya, Daisy 2074
Overton, John 635
Owen, Lynette 1798, 2252, 2253
Owens, Cora 303
Owusu-Bour, Yaw 1485
Oxford Brookes University Library 178
Oyediran, O.O. 1799
Oyelola, Pat 1965
Oyeoku, Kalu K. 304, 305, 1659

PABA Newsletter 141
Pala, Francis Otieno 619
Palmberg, Mai 1440
Palmeri, Robert J. 501
Pan African Book World 142
Pan African Booksellers Association (PABA)
    1535
Pankhurst, Richard 518
Paren, Elizabeth 2024
Parry Jones, R. 927
Parry, Rex 2254
Parsons, Neil 437
Partners in African Publishing 164
PASA Freelancer's Directory 960
PASA Member's Directory 961
Patrinos, Harry Anthony 2146
Paul, Chanette 2498
Pawlitzky, Christine 2209
Pearce, Carole 1855, 1966
Pearce, Douglas 229, 236, 237
PEGboard 143
Pehrsson, Kajsa 2372
Peires, Jeffrey 2132
Pellowski, Anne 1660
Perera, Santosh 306
Pereson, Kajsa 1133
Periodicals from Africa 172
Perold, Helene 1061
Perry, Alison 2058
Perry-Widstrand, Rede 307
Peter, C.B. 2515
Petersen, Kirsten Holst 1362
Peterson, Lorna 2320
Phikani, Chris 439
Philip, David 1062, 1063

Philipparts, Michel 1720
Philippe, Nathalie 158
Phillips, Howard 1064
Philombe, René 465, 466, 1513
Piault, Fabrice 373, 397
Pick, Martin 2255
Pieters, Jacqueline 2483
Pilane, Morwadi 2157
Pinfold, John 1253
Pinhas, Luc 398, 399
Plangger, A.B. 1223, 1224
Politis, Karen 1065
Pontefract, Caroline 620
Popoola, Dimeji 2210
Porter, Ginny 2514
Postcolonial Publishing [Web portal] 2025
Potenza, Emilia 1066
Potgieter, Alida 1661
Poulsen, A.K. 1225
Pouris, Anastassios 2356, 2357
Poussou, Vincent 400
Prabhala, Achal 1802
Prakash, O. 240
Press, Karen 2409, 2500, 2501, 2502
Priestley, Carol 179, 200, 1403, 1404, 1405,
    1406, 1407, 1408, 1409, 1410, 1411, 1412,
    1413, 1883
Prillaman, Jerry 401
Print Industries Cluster Council 1067, 1074,
    1075, 1076, 1077, 1078
Proctor, André 1079
Proctor, Dot 2152
Publisher, The 144
Publishers Association of Cameroon 467
Publishers' Association of South Africa 962,
    1800, 1801
Publishers' Association of Tanzania 1141
Publishing and Book Development in Africa:
    A Bibliography 181
Publishing and Book Development in Sub-
    Saharan Africa: An Annotated
    Bibliography 182
Publishing in Africa Collection [Oxford
    Brookes University Library] 178
Pugliese, Cristiana 621, 622, 2133

Quarterly Index to African Periodical Literature
    169
Quiñones, Viviana 166, 1614, 1615, 1662, 1663

Radebe, Thuli 2211
Radko, Tom 161
Rakotobe, Mamy Emmanuel 654
Rakotomalala, Voahangy 655

Rall, Pieter 1083
Randall, Isobel 1664
Randall, Peter 1080, 1081
Randle, Ian 2256
Randriamanantena, Josette 1967
Ranger, Terence 1459
Raseroka, H.K. 1254
Rathgeber, Eva-Maria 170, 308, 309, 1255, 2321
  see also McLean, Eva;
  McLean Rathgeber, Eva-Maria
Ray, Colin 1612
Rea, Julian 310
Read, Alison 2410
Read, Anthony 238, 239, 419, 420, 641, 845, 846, 927, 1135, 1414, 1515, 1871, 2257
Reboul, Amande 2258
Reddy, Bangar N. 2259
Redhi, Guru 1084
Reece, Jane 355, 1460, 1536, 1537, 2212
Reimer, F.J. 1514
Reiner, Peter 726, 2134
Remaoun, Hassan 152
Rens, Andrew 1802
Répertoire ... des maisons d'éditions ... et des librairies de Madagascar 650
Reuster-Jahn, Uta 1721
Revista da da Ediçãos Africana 129
Revue de l'Edition Africaine 129
Ricard, Alain 847, 848
Richard, Nadette 1968
Richards, Tony 163
Richter, Horst 1665
Ridge, Stanley G.M. 1082
Ripken, Peter 1287, 1288, 1363, 2260
Roberts, Kern 849
Rocher, Annie 402
Roda, J.C. 867
Rønning, Helge 311, 1803
Rosenberg, Diana 1415, 1884, 1914, 1969, 1970, 1971, 1972, 1973, 2213
Rosi, Mauro 1416
Ross, Alan 1851
Rossouw, Fransie 1722
Rotich, Daniel Chebutuk 623, 624, 625, 626
Rouaud, Alain 519, 520
Roukbah, B.F. 850
Roussow, Fransie 1085
Rudiak, Michael D. 403, 1461
Rudolph, John-Willy 1804, 1805
Ruppert, Sophie 1364
Russell, N. 851
Russell, Terry 2014

SA BookNews Online 145
SACBIP. South African Children's Books in Print 963
Sached Trust 1086
Sack, Mathias 2214
Sadji, Youssoupha 902
Sagna, R. 2215
Saint-Dizier, Jacqueline 474
Sakupwanya, Lillian T. 2484
Salahi, Katherine 627, 628, 852, 1167, 1462
Salawu, Abiodun 2135
Salon Livres d'Afrique 1289
Salzano, Carmela 312
Samb, Djibril 2059
Samuel, John 1087
Samuelson, Jeff 1417
Samzugi, Athumani S. 1748
SANB: South African National Bibliography 964
Sani, Abba Aliyu 853
Sankale, Eva 903
Sankofa 165
Sanon, J. Bernardin 444, 446
SAPnet/BookData 187
Sarjant, Robert 2216
Saro-Wiwa, Ken 854
Sarr, Charles Malick 904
Sarvi, Jouko 1192
Sauvageau, Florian 385
Savahl, Aneeka 1806, 1807
Schär, Helene 1290
Schieffer, Jean Pierre 404
Schifano, Elsa 1365
Schmidt, Nancy J. 313, 1666, 1667, 1668, 1669, 1670, 1671, 1672, 2060
Schramm, Sally 1256
Schulz, Hermann 1291
Schur, Michael 1088
Schuster, Anne 2495
Scull-Carvalho, Susan 1292, 1293, 1673
Seakhoa, Raks 151
Seame, G.B. 2136
Seck, Camara Sarang 2358
Seck, Mamadou 2261
Seeber, Monica 1002, 1054, 1538, 1539, 1749, 1768, 1808, 1809, 1810, 1811, 1812, 2428
Segbawu, C. Kwami 2137
Segbawu, Frank 1516
Segun, Mabel D. 1674, 1675, 1676, 1677, 1678
Semajanga, Josias 1974
Sene, Henri 905, 906
Sene, Mamadou 907
Sepamla, Sipho 1975
Sgwane, Pontso 642
Shaba, Steve 2322
Shafack, Rosemary M. 468

Shaffe, Hyeladzira A.B. 2218
Sharples, Carolyn 1418, 1419
Sheikh, Mohamoud Mohamed 1517
Sherwin, Ros 1281, 1852
Shetler, Jan Bender 1142
Shibanda, G. 629
Shuaibu-Adamu, B.F. 1813
Sibanyoni, Mxolisi 1036
Sida. Department for Democracy and Social
    Development 1271, 1272, 1315
Siegfried, N. 2359
Sierra Leone Library Board 1679
Sierra Leone Publications 917
Sifuniso, Monde 1183, 2324, 2411
Silver, Keith 2360
Simkins, T. 927
Simon, Barney 1976
Simon, Günter 405
Simwinga, Gideon 1193
Singh, Tejeshwar 1271
Sissao, Alain Joseph 2182
Sisulu, Elinor 2219
Sithole, Cynthia 1226
Sivry, Jean Michel 488
Siwani, Joyce 2392
Smart, Pippa 1853, 1854, 1855, 1941, 1977,
    1978, 1979
Smith, Arthur 928, 929, 1680
Smith, Datus C. jr. 241, 242, 243, 2485
Smith, Inese A. 1285
Smith, James 1856
Smith, Keith 314, 347, 2026
Smith, Kelvin 164, 1294
Snyders, André 143
Soisvert, Raymond, Bro. 1723
Sonaike, S.E.A. 1814
Sosale, Shobhana 1885
South Africa. Department of the Arts,
    Culture, Science and Technology 1090
South African Book Development Council
    965
South African Booksellers Association-
    Member List 966
South African Children's Book Forum 1681
South African Library 1091
South African Small Publishers' Catalogue
    959
Southern Africa Book Development
    Education Trust 315, 1295, 1991, 2220, 2221,
    2325
Southern African Books in Print 967
Sow, Fatou 2412
Sow, Mamadou Aliou 133, 316, 406, 571, 572,
    573, 2138, 2139
Soyinka, Wole 1980

Spencer, B.M. 1724
Staiger, Ralph C. 2222, 2223
State Library, Pretoria 968
Stanford, Rosamund 2493
Staunton, Irene 1682, 2225, 2226, 2413
Stebbing, Lyle 1486
Stein, Claudia 1296
Steinhauer, D.R. 1115
Stern, Georges 2474
Sternberg, Ilse 1257, 2005
Stevenson, Michael 987
Stevenson, W.H. 1981, 1982
Stilwell, Christine 2184, 2486
Story, Alan 1815
Stoye, Peter 705, 706
Strauss, A. 727
Stringer, Roger 196, 1227, 1228, 1463, 1857
Stroud, Christopher 704
Struik, Willem 1092, 1093, 1094
Sturges, Paul 317
Suid-Afrikaanse Nasionale Bibliografie 964
Sulley, Robert 2262
Swanepoel, Rita 1725
Swart, Kobie 1683
Swaziland National Bibliography 1111
Sweetman, David 348
Switzer, Donna 1095
Switzer, Les 1095
Sylla, Ibrahima 407
Syndicat national des auteurs, éditeurs et
    libraires de Madagascar (SYNAEL) 651
Syrjänen, Eero 1868

Tadjo, Véronique 1684, 1685
Tahir, Gidado 855
Tahiri-Zagret, C. 2361
Taitz, Laurie 969
Taiwo, Oladele 856
Takam Tikou 166
Tambwe Kitenge Bin Kitoko, Eddie 408
Tamuno, O.G. 857
Tanzania National Bibliography 1124
Taole, Nthabiseng 643
Taubert, Sigfred 318
Taylor, Ian 1816, 1817
Taylor, Sally 357, 1096
Teffera, Damtew 215, 1858, 1859, 1917, 2084,
    2140, 2362
Tejuoso, Olakunle 159
Temu, Canute W. 2141
Tervonen, Taina 429
Tete, Paul 1560
Tettey, Edem 2447
Tewafo, Ferdinand 469
Theodoulou, Doros 1686

Thiessen, Tanya 1380
Thomas, Akin 858, 1818, 1819
Thumbadoo, Beula 2227
Tijssen, Robert 2351
Tlali, Miriam 1366
Tonukari, Nyerhovowo J. 1855
Tötemeyer, Andrée Jeanne 1687, 1688, 1689, 2228, 2229
Touré, R. Ba 2344
Touzard, Philippe 908
Traoré-Serie, R. 2361
Travis, Carole 172
Travis, Madelyn 1690
Treffgarne, Carew 2036
Trudel, Pierre 385
Tumusiime, James 319, 320, 1168, 1169, 1170, 1691, 1900
Turay, Sallieu 930, 931
Turquety, Sarah 909, 2142
Twentyman Jones, Leonie 327

Udoada, M.P. 2143
Udoeyop, N.J. 2326, 2327
Uganda Book News 146
Ulanda, A.E. 673
Umbina, Anna 1464
Umomadu, N.O. 1367
United Nations Conference on Trade and Development/UNCAT 1820
United Nations Educational, Scientific, and Cultural Organisation 321, 322
Unwin, Vicky 1368
Usman, P.S. 1726
Uvieghara, Egerton E. 1821, 1822, 1823
Uwalaka, M.N. 859
Uzochukwu, Sam 2144

Valérien, Jean 2456
van de Werk, Jan Kees 409, 1149, 1229
van der Merwe, Annari 2414
van der Merwe, D. 1727
van der Sandt, Elitha 1097
van der Walt, B.J. 1728
van der Walt, Thomas 1622, 1692
van der Werf-Davelaar, Titia 2075
van Gend, Cecily 1098
van Heerden, Marjorie 1693
van Rooyen, Basil 2516, 2517
van Schaik, J.J. 1099
van Schalkwyk, P.B 2145
van Vuuren, Kathrine Ruth 1694
van Zijl, Carole 1100
Van-Dunem, Domingos 421
Vaughan, Keith 2448
Vaughan, Michael 1983

Vawda, Ayesha Yaqub 2146
Veney, Cassandra Rachel 2415
Venter, Rudi M.R. 1006
Vera, Yvonne 1369
Verbeek, Jennifer 2183, 2184
Vilasco, Gilles 410, 411, 2342, 2363, 2366
Vinck, Honoré 412, 489, 1984
Vink, C.M. 2147
Violet, Jean-Marie 1297
Visser, Nick 1985
Vitabu vya Tanzania 1125

Waal, Pieter 1112
Wabbes, Marie 1695
Wade, Assane 910
Wade, Emmie 1696
Wafawarowa, Brian 323, 324, 1101, 1102, 1697, 1824, 1825, 1826, 1827, 1860, 2328
Wafo, Dieubéni 1828
Wagner, Gülten 1698
Wallace, M.S. 325
Wallace, Marion 1258
Walsh, Gretchen 326, 1259, 1260, 1420, 1421
Walter, Scott 1422, 1699, 1700, 2037
Warricker, Hendri 1083
Waruingi, Gachege 630
Wassie, Antafu 523, 521, 522
Watkins, Christine 1423
Watts-Russell, Pru 1487
Webb Spies, Delani 145
Wedgeworth, Robert 996
Weidhaas, Peter 318, 728
Were, Nereah 620
West, R.C. 729
Westra, Pieter E. 327, 1103
White, Tim 2148
Wiggans, Rachel 1488, 1701
Wilfrid, F. 1009
Williams, Geoffrey J. 1194, 1195
Williams, Jean 1424
Williams, Nelly Temu 1425
Willinsky, John 1833
Wilson, Paul 1261
Winterbottom, Anna 2076
Wiredu, E. Oti 1702
Wise, Michael 1986
Witbooi, Charlotte 2392
Wolcke-Renk, Irmtraud D. 1262
Wole, Darge 2329
Wolters, Stephanie 861
Women in Publishing and the Book Trade in Africa. An Annotated Directory 191
Woodhall, Maureen 1886
Woodson, Dorothy C. 1987

World Bank, The 1887, 2453
    for various World Bank studies and reports
    see under names of individual authors of
    these reports
World Trade Organization. International
    Trade Centre 1489
Wright, Claire 1104
Writers' World 147
Writings in Nine Tongues. A Catalogue of
    Literature and Readers ... 962

Xaba, Makhosazana 2494

Yates, Barbara A. 490
Yesufu, Abdul R. 862, 1988
Yonli, Emile D. 2364
Youdeowei, Anthony 2365, 2487
Yougbare, Elie 444

Zaher, Celia R. 328
Zambia. Ministry of Education 1196, 1197
Zambian Books in Print and ISBN Publishers'
    Directory 1175
Zawua, J. 2231
Zegeye, Abebe 329, 2330

Zeleza, Paul Tiyambe 330, 331, 1989, 1990,
    1997, 2038, 2061, 2331, 2332, 2415
Zell, Hans M. 168, 181, 182, 192, 194, 301,
    332, 333, 334, 335, 336, 360, 863, 864, 1273,
    1298, 1370, 1371, 1426, 1490, 1703, 1704,
    1861, 1862, 1863, 1864, 1865, 2027, 2028,
    2062, 2063, 2149, 2263, 2333, 2449, 2488,
    2489
Zewde, Bahru 152
Zhangazha, Witness Paridzirai 1829
Zidouemba, Dominique Hado 410, 411, 413,
    414, 475, 2363, 2366
Ziduche, S. 1230
Zimbabwe Book Publishers' Association 2490
Zimbabwe Books in Print 1209
Zimbabwe International Book Fair Trust 337,
    1491, 1492, 1705, 1991, 2232, 2416
Zimbabwe National Bibliography 1210
Zimbabwe Women Writers 2417
Zingani, W.T. 1729
Zogo, F. 470
Zulu, R.S. 1183
Zurbrugg, Tony 1299

Subject and geographical index

This subject and geographical index aims to complement the arrangement in the main sequence and the different sections of the bibliography. All references are to item numbers. Alphabetical order is letter-by-letter. In addition to subject and country headings, the following material is indexed:

- Articles about prominent members of the book professions, and particular African publishing houses and imprints.
- Biographical and autobiographical accounts of publishers, as well as profiles and interviews, personal recollections, and tributes and obituaries.
- Articles and studies focussing on the history and activities of particular publishers or imprints, e.g. Mbari Publications in Nigeria, or oppositional publishers in South Africa during the apartheid years such as Ravan Press or David Philip Publishers.
- Studies and histories of famous African-published journals and magazines, such as *Black Orpheus*, *Drum* magazine, *Staffrider*, *Transition*, etc.
- Articles, analysis, and evaluations of special projects, such as African Journals Online (AJOL).
- Publishing in African languages in general, and in specific languages of the continent.
- Articles about book fairs and major book promotional events in Africa.
- Other extra subjects not already covered by the broader main topic headings in Section 4.

Many items have multiple index entries, e.g. are indexed by both country and by subject; or as part of the main sequence of the index as well as under individual countries. For index terms with multiple entries, general studies are listed first, followed by more specific topics and/or countries as subentries.

Book trade and book professional associations, writers' associations, agencies, networks, foundations, and other organizations supporting the book and information sector in Africa are indexed in the ➜ **Index of organizations and associations**. The exceptions are articles or profiles about particular organizations, which are indexed here.

Serial titles, book trade reference resources, and African national bibliographies are indexed as part of the ➜ **Author index** (and selected titles).

ABC *see* African Books Collective Ltd.
Academic publishing *see* Scholarly publishing
Acquisition of African-published material
　1231-1261, 1277
　African literature 1262
　African language materials 1243, 1259
　Africana Librarians Council (ALC) 1238,
　　1992
　African serials acquisition 1246
　Africa, Southern 1253, 1256
　bibliographic control of Africana 1249
　Botswana 1234, 1254, 1994

collections and collection development
　1239, 1257, 1258, 1276, 1285
ephemera 1252
government publications 175
Library of Congress Nairobi Office 1242
Nigeria 1231, 1245, 1251
Standing Conference on Library Materials
　on Africa (SCOLMA) 1240, 1250
vendors 1235, 1236, 1241, 1261, 1262, 1299,
　1283, 1477
AFRICA, general studies 245-337

AFRICA, EAST, regional studies (general) 338-357, 1397
see also individual countries
African languages, publishing in 2118, 2119, 2141
book industry training 2435
East African Literature Bureau 329, 345-347
intra-African book trade 1900
reading culture and reading promotion 2216
Richard, Charles, profiles and interviews 345, 346, 347
scholarly publishing 2279
AFRICA, FRANCOPHONE, regional studies (general) 295, 316, 340, 361-414, 1286, 1289
see also individual countries
African languages, publishing in 2081, 2089, 2090, 2096, 2097, 2106, 2108, 2131, 2138, 2451
authors' rights 1781, 1787, 1828
book industry training 2430
bookselling and book distribution 195, 386
children's book publishing 1609, 1613, 1685
copyright 1785, 1786
educational and school book publishing 382, 383, 387, 396, 1866, 1874
Francophone African books in the international market place 370, 1286, 1289
French development assistance for the book sector 371, 377, 389, 391, 403, 1663
journals and magazine publishing 1974
national book policies 372
reading culture and reading promotion 2153, 2167, 2168, 2172, 2215
scholarly publishing 2284, 2300
AFRICA SOUTHERN, regional studies (general) 349-357, 1468, 1472
see also individual countries
acquisition of African-published material 1253, 1256
African languages, publishing in 2125, 2147
copyright 1802
educational and school book publishing 1881, 1883, 2372
AFRICA, WEST, regional studies (general) 358-360, 1480
see also individual countries
book industry training 2433
scholarly publishing 2292
Afrilivres 370
"Africa's 100 Best Books" 298, 315, 1284
African Bookman, The, South Africa 1082

African Books Collective Ltd 1263-1273, 1275, 1280, 1281
and African literature 1269, 1280
as facilitator of rights sales and co-editions 2242
evaluations 1271, 1272, 1473
Intra-African Book Support Scheme 1397
marketing activities 1281, 1473, 1852
print-on-demand production 1840, 2455
African Books in Print 336
African books in the international market place 728, 1274-1299, 1338
African literature 1280, 1284, 1287, 1291, 1364, 1365
book fairs 1288, 1295
children's books 1290, 1292, 1293, 1296, 1297
France 1364, 1365
Francophone African publishers 370, 1286, 1289
Germany 1291, 1296
marketing and promotion 1281, 1298
North American markets 1275, 1276, 1292, 1293
vendors 1283, 1299
African Journals Online (AJOL) 1930, 1931, 1932, 1957, 1969, 1970, 1971, 1972, 1973, 1977, 1978
African languages, publishing in 435, 590, 1053, 1216, 1243, 2077-2149
acquisition of African language materials 1243, 1259
Africa, East 2118, 2119, 2141
Africa, Francophone 2081, 2089, 2090, 2451, 2096, 2106, 2108, 2131, 2138
Africa, Southern 2125, 2147
Asmara Declaration 2086
Bamana 2133
Botswana 435, 2087, 2093, 2110, 2117, 2136
Cameroon 2123
Congo Democratic Republic 2135
educational materials 550, 1886, 2081, 2090, 2106, 2117, 2128, 2134, 2138, 2140, 2146
Eritrea 2094
Ethiopia 2140
Ghana 550, 2078, 1083, 2100, 2137
Guinea 2138, 2139
Hausa 2004
Igbo 2144
Kenya 590, 2095, 2101, 2127, 2128, 2133
Kiswahili 2118, 2119, 2127, 2128, 2141
Lesotho 2111
Malawi 2109
Mali 2122

marketing of indigenous language books 2077, 2130
Namibia 2077, 2092, 2134
Nigeria 2004, 2078, 2079, 2124, 2126, 2143, 2144
Pulaar 2096, 2097, 2098
Rwanda 2105
Senegal 2096, 2097, 2098, 2121, 2142
Setswana 2093, 2117, 2136
South Africa 1053, 2088, 2104, 2107, 2114, 2115, 2120, 2129, 2132, 2146, 2147, 2148
Tanzania 2118, 2119
Togo 2102
Tsonga 2088
Xhosa 2129, 2132
Zambia 2113
Zimbabwe 1216, 2091, 2103
African literature publishing
see also Authors and publishers
Nigeria 772, 786, 853
Sierra Leone 929
South Africa 1060
Togo 1149
Zimbabwe 1217, 1219, 2386, 2417
African Publishers Network 1300-1315
African publishing consultants 1300
Brickhill, Paul, profiles and interviews 1311
evaluations 1315
International Publishers Association, relations with 1313
Nwankwo, Chief Victor,
profiles and interviews 852
tributes and obituaries 759, 782, 864
training programmes 2419, 2420, 2421, 2426, 2432, 2442
Akoma Ba Publishing House, Cameroon 452
Alternative press and publishing, South Africa 972, 976, 982, 994, 1029, 1045, 1051, 1052, 1062, 1081, 1082
ANGOLA 417-421
APNET *see* African Publishers Network
Art publishing 987
Authors and publishers 1316-1371
see also African literature publishing; Authors' rights; Authors' and writers' handbooks
Achebe, Chinua, on African publishers 1371, 1325
African Writers Series 1319, 1326, 1327, 1328, 1329, 1330, 1331, 1342, 1343, 1355, 1362, 1368
Armah, Ayi Kwei, views on publishers 1319
Cameroon 1323, 1332
Ghana 1333

Heinemann Educational Publishers *see* African Writers Series
Kenya 1324, 1346
L'Harmattan 1364
Maja-Pearce, Adewale, publishing experience 1354
Ngugi wa Thiong'o, publishing of 1324
Nigeria 786, 1321, 1322, 1337, 1339, 1344, 1350, 1351, 1359, 1360, 1361, 1367
Osofisan, Femi, publishing experience 1359
Osundare, Niyi, publishing experience 1360
Per Ankh Publishing Cooperative 1320, 1347
Senegal 1356
South Africa 1336, 1357, 1366
Tlali, Miriam, publishing experience 1366
Togo 1334
Tutuola, Amos, publishing history 1352, 1353
Vera, Yvonne, publishing experience 1369
Authors' and writers' handbooks 2454, 2473, 2507, 2486, 2491, 2492-2502, 2503, 2505, 2506, 2507, 2510, 2515
Authors' rights 1739, 1803
see also Copyright
academic authors 1747, 1812
Africa, Francophone 1781, 1787, 1828
developing countries 1757
Kenya 1773
Nigeria 1752
South Africa 1747, 1813

Bailey, Jim, biography 974
see also Drum magazine
Balkema, A.A., Festschrift 975
Bellagio Donors Group/Bellagio Publishing Network 1462, 1522, 1523
BENIN 363, 424-429
children's book publishing 1695
Editions Ruisseaux d'Afrique 429, 1695
journals and magazine publishing 1940
women in African publishing/publishing by and for women 429
Berthe, Ibrahim, profiles and interviews 681
Bibliographic control of publishing output
Kenya 618
Nigeria 758, 793, 809, 826, 838
Bibliographic standards *see* Bibliographic control of publishing output
Bibliographies and continuing sources 167-182
Black Orpheus 862, 1905, 1923, 1924, 1938, 1944, 1945, 1951, 1952, 1954, 1988
Boirot, François, profiles and interviews

Book Aid International 1374, 1375, 1388, 1389,
    1390, 1419, 1425
Book and journals assistance and donation
    programmes 227, 1372-1426, 1663, 1882,
    2245, 2360
    see also Word Bank
    African Journals Distribution Programme
        1415
    Biblionef SA 1424
    Book Aid International 1374, 1375, 1388,
        1389, 1390, 1419, 1425
    Books for Africa 1376, 1423
    Book subsidy schemes 1401
    children's books 1575, 1619, 1699
    Children's Book Project of Tanzania 1575,
        1619
    CODE 1384
    Commonwealth Book Development
        Programme 1396
    Department for International Development
        1417
    Directories of book aid programmes 1378,
        1381, 1392, 1406, 1413, 1420
    Donors to African Education 1410, 1412
    Franklin Book Programs 1373
    Friends-of-the-Book Foundation 1385, 1402
    Ghana Book Trust 1386
    International Book Bank 1383, 1391
    International Campus Book Link 1404, 1418
    International Network for the Availability
        of Scientific Publications 1387, 1392, 1407
    International Publishing Partnership 1400
    Intra-African Book Support Scheme 1397
    literature review 1380
    Nigeria 1372, 1399, 1476
    North American libraries, role of 1421
    Obor Foundation 1393
    South Africa Books Aid Project 1417
    Sub-Saharan Africa Journal Distribution
        Programme 1394
    USAID 1373
Book boycott, South Africa, during the
    apartheid period 996, 1009, 1019, 1021
Book distribution see Bookselling and book
    distribution
Book fairs 1295, 1427-1464
    Cape Town Book Fair 1427, 1428, 1432,
        1441
    Frankfurt Book Fair 1288, 1454, 1461, 1463
    Ghana International Book Fair 1442, 1462
    Ghana, rural book fairs 1438
    Nigeria International Book Fair 1361, 1456
    Pan-African Children's Book Fair 1434,
        1435, 1455

    Zimbabwe International Book Fair 1429,
        1430, 1431, 1433, 1436, 1437, 1440, 1443
        1444, 1445, 1446, 1447, 1449, 1450, 1452,
        1453, 1457, 1458, 1459, 1460, 1464
Book famine in Africa see Book and journals
    assistance and donation programmes
Book industry training 980, 2418-2490
    Africa, East 2435
    Africa, Francophone 2430
    African languages, training for
        publishing in 2451
    African Publishers Network (APNET)
        training programmes 2419, 2420, 2421,
        2426, 2432, 2442
    Africa, West 2433
    book marketing and promotion 2458, 2481,
        2488
    book publishing training and training
        resources 203, 211, 2422, 2423, 2427, 2431,
        2439, 2445, 2449, 2450, 2453, 2455, 2457,
        2475, 2476, 2477, 2479, 2480, 2483, 2484,
        2488
    bookselling 2482
    Centre Africain de Formation à l'Edition et
        à la Diffusion 2425
    developing countries 2437, 2440, 2441,
        2443, 2485
    digital media 2455, 2459, 2460, 2468, 2469,
        2478
    gender-sensitive editing 2411
    Ghana 2429, 2433, 2434, 2438, 2447
    handbooks and guides for writers and
        academic authors 2454, 2473, 2507, 2486,
        2491, 2492- 2502, 2503, 2505, 2506, 2507,
        2510, 2515
    journals editing and publishing
        management 2418, 2460, 2487, 2489
    Kenya 2436, 2444, 2445
    Nigeria 2510
    Oxford Brookes University, UK 2448
    print-on-demand, training manuals 2455
    self-publishing 2504, 2508, 2511, 2512, 2513,
        2514, 2616, 2517
    South Africa 980, 2428, 2504, 2505, 2508,
        2509, 2511, 2512, 2514, 2516, 2517
    surveys and inventories of training
        institutions 2424, 2426, 2430
    textbook writing and development 2452,
        2456, 2490
Book piracy see Copyright
Book marketing and promotion 272, 547, 589,
    849, 971, 1024, 1031, 1465-1492
    see also African books in the international
    market place

African Books Collective Ltd 1281, 1473, 1852
Africa, Southern 1468, 1472
Africa, West 1480
children's books 1559
export markets 1470, 1471, 1479
Ghana 1482, 1485
Internet marketing 1846, 1847, 1851, 1852, 1863, 1864
intra-African book trade 1489
Lesotho 1481
Nigeria 1476, 1483, 1884
non-literary market place 1465, 1466
scholarly books 1483, 1492
South Africa 1472, 1474
Tanzania 1475
training manuals and resources 2458, 2481, 2488
vendors 1477
women's books 2401
Book policies see National book policies
Book prizes and awards 2046, 2057
see also Noma Award for Publishing in Africa
Book review media for African-published material 148-154, 158, 159, 166, 168
Bookselling and book distribution 499, 500, 528, 693, 708, 760, 812, 830, 841, 1012, 1112, 1128, 1493-1517, 1993
Africa, Francophone 195
Botswana 1994
Cameroon 1504, 1505, 1513
Chad 379
Ghana 1495, 1498, 1499, 1501, 1514, 1616, 1993
Kenya 1503, 1517
library suppliers 1994
Nigeria 1507, 1511, 1512
South Africa 1502, 1506
training manuals and resources 2482
university bookselling 1498
Zimbabwe 1509, 1510
Zimbabwe Book Marketing Trust 1509, 1510
Books in print 188, 189
Ghana 543
Kenya 586
Madagascar 651
Mozambique 698
Namibia 716
Nigeria 747, 748
South Africa 963, 967
Tanzania 1125
Zambia 1175
Zimbabwe 1209

Book trade and book development organizations 636, 756, 930, 1184, 1518-1539
see also African Books Collective Ltd; African Publishers Network
Afro-Asian Book Council 1524, 1525
Centre for the Book, South Africa 1520
Centre Régional de Promotion du Livre en Afrique (CREPLA) 1478, 1532
Foundation for the Promotion of Children's Science Publications in Africa 1566
Ghana 1519
Kenya 1533
Namibia 1530
Namibia Book Development Council 1530
Nigeria 1519, 1534
Nigerian Book Foundation 1534
Pan African Booksellers Association 1535
Print Industries Cluster Council, South Africa 1531
Publishers Association of South Africa 1538
South Africa 1520, 1529, 1531, 1538, 1539
Zimbabwe 1521, 1526, 1537
Zimbabwe Book Development Council 1521, 1526
Book trade and book professional journals 127-147
see also ➔ Author index (and selected titles)
Book trade directories 190-201
see also ➔ Author index (and selected titles)
Cameroon 451
Ghana 542
Kenya 588
Madagascar 650
Mauritius 686
Namibia 715
Nigeria 743
Réunion 865
Senegal 878, 879
South Africa 958, 959, 960, 961, 966, 968, 969
Zimbabwe 1208
BOTSWANA 433-441
acquisition of African-published material 1234, 1254
African languages, publishing in 435, 2087, 2093, 2110, 2117, 2136
bookselling and book distribution 1994
children's book publishing 1601
copyright 1778, 1782
libraries and publishing 434, 1994
national book policy 436, 438
reading culture and reading promotion 2157

BREDA, Senegal 903
Brickhill, Paul, profiles and interviews 1311
Bureau of Ghana Languages, Ghana 550
BURKINA FASO 444-446
  reading culture and reading promotion
    2166, 2182
  scientific, technical and medical publishing
    2364
BURUNDI 447
  scientific, technical and medical publishing
    2337

CAMEROON 366, 452-470
  Akoma Ba Publishing House 452, 1695
  African languages, publishing in 2123
  authors and publishers 1323, 1332
  bookselling and book distribution 1504,
    1505, 1513
  book trade directories 451
  Centre Régional de Promotion du Livre en
    Afrique (CREPLA) 1478, 1532
  children's book publishing 1695
  Dayeko, Paul, profiles and interviews 457,
    1323
  Editions CLE 456, 459
  Editions Semences Africaines 465
  Editions Silex 457, 1332
  journals and magazine publishing 1950
  Kouam, Serge, profiles and interviews 458
  mass market and popular literature
    publishing 2006
  national book policy 467
  Philombe, Réne, profiles and interviews
    466
  Prosper, Komlan, profiles and interviews
    407
  publishing partnerships 2246
  reading culture and reading promotion
    2214
CAPE VERDE 472
CENTRAL AFRICAN REPUBLIC 474-475
CHAD
  bookselling and book distribution 379
  reading culture and reading promotion 379
Chakava, Henry, profiles and interviews 606,
    627
Children's Book Project of Tanzania 1575,
    1619
Children's book publishing 1540-1705
  Africa, Francophone 1609, 1613, 1685
  African children's books in the
    international market place 1290, 1292,
    1293, 1296, 1297
  Akoma Ba Publishing House, Cameroon
    452, 1695

Ants magazine 1639
Benin 1695
bibliographic tools, catalogues, and
    directories 863, 1542, 1543, 1550, 1552,
    1578, 1579, 1580, 1586, 1599, 1603, 1608,
    1613, 1630, 1632, 1643, 1657, 1658, 1666,
    1669
Bookchat 130
Botswana 1601
Children's Book Project of Tanzania 1575,
    1619
comic books 1569
co-editions of children's books 2255
Cameroon 1695
Congo Democratic Republic 1560, 1968
Côte d'Ivoire 1610, 1623, 1685
Editions Ruisseaux d'Afrique, Benin 1695
Foundation for the Promotion of Children's
    Science Publications in Africa 1566
French cultural cooperation for children's
    books 1663
gender issues 1600
Ghana 1544, 1555, 1556, 1557, 1558, 1608,
    1644, 1702
handbooks for children's book writers 1582
IBBY and African children's books 1393,
    1598
illustrators and illustrating 1543, 1549,
    1552, 1597, 1678, 1701
intra-African book trade 1553
Jacaranda Designs, Kenya 1293, 1653, 1673
Journal of African Children's and Youth
    Literature 137
Kenya 1293, 1560, 1561, 1566, 1606, 1607,
    1624, 1632, 1635, 1637, 1640, 1641, 1653,
    1673, 2400
Lesotho 1628
marketing of children's books 1559
Namibia 1688, 1689
Ngouvou 1968
Nigeria 1540, 1547, 1570, 1571, 1572, 1577,
    1642, 1645, 1646, 1647, 1648, 1650, 1675,
    1698
Noma Award-winning children's books
    2060
Probe. The Magazine for Young People in
    Southern Africa
publishing assistance for children's books
    1699
Sankofa. A Journal of African Children's and
    Young Adult Literature 165
Science for Africa KAWI Project 1696
Segun, Mabel, profiles and interviews 1647
Senegal 1626
Sierra Leone 1573, 1621, 1679

South Africa 130, 963, 1027, 1541, 1551,
    1563, 1564, 1565, 1567, 1586, 1587, 1588,
    1589, 1590, 1591, 1592, 1594, 1597, 1599,
    1634, 1661, 1664, 1681, 1683, 1692, 1693,
    1694
  Tadjo, Véronique, profiles and interviews
    1585, 1684, 1690
  Takam Tikou. Le bulletin de la joie par les livres
    166
  Tanzania 1575, 1619
  Uganda 1691
  Zimbabwe 1548, 1562, 1584, 1639, 1682
Christian publishing and mission presses
    1706-1729, 2285
  see also Early printing in Africa
  Central Africa 1709
  Catholic mission journals, bibliography
    1713
  Christian Messenger, The 1708
  directories 1710
  Ghana 1706, 1708, 1714
  Kenya 1707
  Kuruman Press, South Africa 1715
  Lesotho 1716
  Malawi 1729
  Ndanda Mission Press, Tanzania 1721
  Nigeria 1719, 1726
  South Africa 1711, 1715, 1722, 2132, 2148
  Tanzania 1721
  Wesleyan Mission Press, South Africa 1722,
    1724
  Zambia 1717
  Zimbabwe 1727
Classic (New Classic) 1975, 1976
Comb Books, Kenya 604
  see also Maillu, David G., profiles and
  interviews
Community and rural publishing 614, 1659,
    1730-1737
  Community Publishing Process 1730, 1731
  Ghana 1733
  Kenya 1734, 1737
  Nigeria 1735
  Tanzania 1736
  Zimbabwe 1730, 1731
Community Publishing Process, Zimbabwe
    1730, 1731
Comparative studies
  developing countries 203-244, 830, 1854,
    1856
  Europe 202
CONGO (BRAZZAVILLE) 477-478
CONGO DEMOCRATIC REPUBLIC 412,
    481-490
  African languages, publishing in 2135

children's book publishing 1560
early printing 489, 490
journals and magazine publishing 1927,
    1984
Co-publishing *see* Rights sales, licensing, and
  publishing partnerships
Copyright 1738-1829
  see also Authors' rights; Legal deposit
  Access to Knowledge Initiative 1789
  Africa, Francophone 1785, 1786
  Africa, Southern 1802
  book piracy 839, 1783, 1793, 1816, 1819
  Botswana 1778, 1782
  developing countries 1760, 1779, 1785,
    1798, 1815, 1820, 1824, 1825
  digital media 1739, 1780, 1818
  Ghana 1742, 1746, 1775, 1791, 1792
  Kenya 599, 1772, 1773, 1784, 1797
  Lesotho 1778
  Malawi 1784
  Namibia 1784
  Nigeria 1740, 1741, 1751, 1761, 1763, 1764,
    1765, 1766, 1771, 1779, 1783, 1784, 1793,
    1795, 1799, 1804, 1816, 1819, 1821, 1822,
    1823
  South Africa 1747, 1758, 1759, 1767, 1768,
    1770, 1788, 1789, 1800, 1801, 1802, 1806,
    1807, 1810, 1812, 1825
  Swaziland 1778
  Tanzania 1748
  Uganda 1776
  Zimbabwe 1829
COSAW Publishing, South Africa 1059
CÔTE D'IVOIRE 363, 493-501
  bookselling and book distribution 499, 500
  children's book publishing 1610, 1623, 1685
  privatization of the book sector 501
  Kacou, Venance, profiles and interviews
    407
  publishing partnerships 2248
  reading promotion and reading culture
    2175, 2217
  scholarly publishing 2278
  scientific, technical and medical publishing
    2342, 2361
  Tadjo, Véronique, profiles and interviews
    1585, 1684, 1690
Council for the Development of Social
  Science Research (CODESRIA) 2267,
  2318
Cross-border book trade *see* Intra-African
  book trade
Currey, James, profiles and interviews 1000,
    1328, 2027

Dayeko, Paul, profiles and interviews 457, 1323

Digital media and electronic publishing 1830-1865
  see also Print-on-demand (POD)
  African Books Collective Ltd 1840, 1852
  CD-ROM 1841
  copyright issues 1739, 1780, 1818
  developing countries 830, 1854, 1856
  digitization projects 1843
  for journal publishing 1837, 1853, 1855, 1856, 1858, 1862, 1863
  for scholarly publishing and communication 1833, 1835, 1839, 1845, 1859, 2306
  Internet marketing 1846, 1847, 1851, 1852, 1863, 1864
  legal deposit issues 1780
  Nigeria 1849, 1850
  South Africa 1836, 1841, 1842, 1848
  training manuals and resources 2455, 2459, 2460, 2468, 2469, 2478
  Zimbabwe 1837, 1844, 1857

Directories see Book trade directories

Distribution see Bookselling and book distribution

Donation programmes see Book and journals assistance and donation programmes

Drum magazine 974, 1833, 1935, 1987

Early printing in Africa 489, 490, 517, 518, 519, 520, 669, 672, 766, 856, 1007, 1018, 1085, 1161
  see also Christian publishing and mission presses

East African Educational Publishers, Kenya 338, 592, 606, 627

East African Literature Bureau, Kenya 339, 345, 346, 347
  see also Richard, Charles, profiles and interviews

Educational and school book publishing (General)
  208, 209, 213, 217, 222-225, 229, 231, 233, 236-239, 278, 349, 356, 357, 361, 382, 383, 387, 389, 396, 512, 553, 564, 603, 608, 609, 610, 620, 624, 625, 626, 635, 641, 664, 665, 665, 699, 700, 704, 705, 706, 729, 771, 784, 792, 795, 804, 813, 819, 841, 845, 846, 851, 855, 858, 860, 884, 919, 927, 989, 992, 998, 1003, 1023, 1032, 1033, 1036, 1042, 1047, 1048, 1049, 1050, 1066, 1079, 1086, 1087, 1128, 1132, 1133, 1135, 1142, 1160, 1164, 1177, 1185, 1192, 1196, 1197, 1221, 1866-1900

see also World Bank; and individual countries

Africa, Francophone 1866, 1874

Africa, Southern 1881, 1883, 2372

cost and financing of textbooks 1886, 1872, 1877

donor support 1882, 1885, 1887

educational materials in African languages 550, 1886, 2081, 2090, 2106, 2117, 2128, 2134, 2138, 2140, 2146

Education for All (EFA) 1875

textbook writing and development 1870, 1872, 2452, 2456, 2490

Editions de l'Océan Indien, Mauritius 690, 691

Editions Cilex, Cameroon 457

Editions CLE, Cameroon 456, 459

Editions HaHo, Togo 409

Editions-Imprimeries du Mali, Mali 681

Editions Le Figuier, Mali 682

Editions Ruisseaux d'Afrique, Benin 429

Editions Semences Africaines, Cameroon 465

Electronic publishing see Digital media and electronic publishing

ERITREA 503
  African languages, publishing in 2094

Ethiope Publishing Corporation, Nigeria 800

ETHIOPIA 509-523
  African languages, publishing in 2140
  early printing 517, 518, 519, 520
  educational and school book publishing 512
  journal and magazine publishing 2352
  privatization of the book sector 522
  reading culture and reading promotion 2161
  scholarly publishing 2329
  scientific, technical and medical publishing 2352

Faye, Djbril, tributes and obituaries 880

Foundation for the Promotion of Children's Science Publications in Africa 1566

Frankfurt Book Fair 1288, 1454, 1461, 1463

GABON 526-528
  bookselling and book distribution 528
  reading culture and reading promotion 527

Gakaara wa Wanjau, profiles and interviews 621, 622

GAMBIA 531-533

Gaskiya Corporation, Nigeria 794

Gender issues in publishing 1104, 1600, 2371, 2372, 2375, 2378, 2381, 2394, 2406, 2410, 2411, 2418

see also Women in African
publishing/publishing by and for women
GHANA 545-564, 1333, 1386
  African languages, publishing in 550, 2078,
    1083, 2100, 2137
  authors and publishers 1333
  book and journals assistance and donation
    programmes 1386
  book industry training 2429, 2433, 2434,
    2438, 2447
  book marketing and promotion 547, 1482,
    1485
  bookselling and book distribution 1495,
    1498, 1499, 1501, 1514
  books in print 543
  book trade and book development
    organizations 1519
  book trade directories 542
  Bureau of Ghana Languages 550
  children's book publishing 1544, 1555,
    1556, 1557, 1558, 1608, 1644, 1702
  Christian publishing and mission presses
    1706, 1708, 1714
  community and rural publishing 1733
  copyright 1742, 1746, 1775, 1791, 1792
  educational and school book publishing
    553, 564
  Ghana Book Trust 1386
  Ghana International Book Fair 1442, 1462
  legal deposit and legal deposit laws 1775
  Ofori-Mensah, Akoss, profiles and
    interviews 548
  open access publishing 2065
  privatization of the book sector 552
  reading promotion and reading culture
    2154
  rural book fairs 1438
  scholarly publishing 2269, 2286, 2315, 2320
  Sub-Saharan African Publishers 548
  women in African publishing/publishing
    by and for women 548, 2402, 2404
Globalization and African publishing 254,
  286, 299, 829
Goretti, Kyomuhendo, profiles and
  interviews 1159
GUINEA 569-573
  African languages, publishing in 2138, 2139
  scientific, medical and technical publishing
    2358
  Sow, Mamadou Aliou, profiles and
    interviews 569, 570
GUINEA-BISSAU 574
  scientific, medical and technical publishing
    2350

Higo, Chief Aigboje, Festschrift 755
History of the book in Africa 283, 303, 334,
  352, 1161, 1162, 1163, 1214
HIV/AIDS 781, 815
Hond Publishing, South Africa 985
Hove, Chenjerai, profiles and interviews 1215
Human, Koos, autobiography 1028

Ife (1973) conference on publishing and book
  development in Africa 301, 308
Illustrators and illustrating, of African
  children's books 1543, 1549, 1552, 1597,
  1678, 1701
International Network for the Availability of
  Scientific Publications 1387, 1392, 1407
Intra-Africa Book Purchase Project 1899
Intra-African Book Support Scheme 1397
Intra-African book trade 1489, 1888-1900
  children's books 1553
  Africa, East 1900
  Intra-Africa Book Purchase Project 1899
  Intra-African Book Support Scheme 1397
  ITC buyers/sellers meetings 1888, 1891,
    1892
  Malawi 1896
  Zambia 1897
ISBN system, use of 642, 689, 690, 719
Iwerebon, Chief Felix Arimoku, tributes and
  obituaries 763

Jacaranda Designs, Kenya 1293, 1653, 1673
Jay, Mary, profiles and interviews 1297
Journals and magazine publishing 1901-1991
  Abbia 1950
  Action Magazine 2014
  Aequatoria 1984
  Africa, Francophone 1974
  Africa, Lusophone 1912, 1956
  African Crop Science Journal 2355
  African e-Journals Project 1908
  *African Journal of Library, Archives and
    Information Science* 1910, 1911, 1915
  African Journals Online (AJOL) 1930, 1931,
    1932, 1957, 1969, 1970, 1971, 1972, 1973,
    1977, 1978
  Benin 1940
  Black Orpheus 862, 1905, 1923, 1924, 1938,
    1944, 1945, 1951, 1952, 1954, 1988
  Cameroon 1950
  catalogues and directories of African
    literary and scholarly journals 1907,
    1908, 1918, 1925, 1991
  Classic (New Classic) 1975, 1976
  Congo Democratic Republic 1927, 1984
  Contrast 1929

developing countries 1916
digital media 1833, 1837, 1853, 1855, 1856,
1858, 1862, 1863
Donga 1959
Drum magazine 974, 1833, 1935, 1987
Ethiopia 2352
Ghana 1920
Ghana Library Journal 1920
Horn, The 1981
Islamic periodicals 1939
Joe magazine 1936, 1953
Journal of Social Development 1966
journals editing and publishing
management 2418, 2460, 2487, 2489
Kenya 1936, 1953, 1964
library science journals 1909, 1910, 1911,
1913, 1915, 1920, 1921, 1942, 1943, 1964,
1986
Madagascar 1967
Nigeria 1902, 1903, 1905, 1906, 1919, 1921,
1923, 1924, 1926, 1934, 1935, 1938, 1942,
1943, 1944, 1945, 1951, 1952, 1954, 1960,
1965, 1981, 1982, 1986, 1988
*Nigerian Journal of Economic and Social
Studies* 1903
Nigerian Libraries 1921
Okike 1902, 1919, 1934
Présence Africaine 1938
Purple Renoster 1901
Reconnaissance Africaine 1940
Research Review (Ghana) 2320
scholarly journal publishing 1861, 1862,
1904, 1906, 1908, 1907, 1910, 1914, 1916,
1917, 1918, 1925, 1937, 1941, 1943, 1946,
1947, 1957, 1958, 1960, 1966, 1978, 1979,
1989, 1900, 1991, 2356
SINET. An Ethiopian Journal of Science 2352
S'ketsh 1975
South Africa 1095, 1928, 1929, 1933, 1939,
1948, 1949, 1959, 1961, 1962, 1963, 1975,
1976, 1983, 1985, 1987, 2356
South African Law Journal 1948
Staffrider 1928, 1949, 1961, 1983, 1985
Teny Soa 1967
Transition 1905, 1938, 1980
Zaïre-Afrique 1927
Zimbabwe 1966

Kacou, Venance, profiles and interviews 407
KAWI Project *see* Science for Africa KAWI
Project
KENYA 267, 589-630
African languages, publishing in 590, 2095,
2101, 2127, 2128, 2133
authors and publishers 1324, 1346

authors' rights 1773
bibliographic control of publishing output
618
book industry training 2436, 2444, 2445
book marketing and promotion 589
bookselling and book distribution 1503,
1517
books in print 586
book trade and book development
organizations 1533
book trade directories 588
censorship and publications control 598
Chakava, Henry, profiles and interviews
606, 627
children's book publishing 1560, 1561,
1566, 1606, 1607, 1624, 1632, 1635, 1637,
1640, 1641, 1653, 1673, 2400
Christian publishing and mission presses
1707
Comb Books 1999, 2008
Maillu, David G., profiles and interviews
604
community and rural publishing 1734, 1737
copyright 599, 1772, 1773, 1784, 1797
East African Educational Publishers 338,
592, 606, 627
East African Literature Bureau 339, 345,
346, 347
educational and school book publishing
603, 608, 609, 610, 620, 624, 625, 626
Focus Publications 2389
Mwangi, Serah, profiles and interviews
628
Gakaara wa Wanjau, profiles and
interviews 621, 622
gender issues in publishing 2381
journals and magazine publishing 1936,
1953, 1964
libraries and publishing 615
loan-guarantee programme 602
mass market and popular literature
publishing 1999, 2007, 2008
multinational publishers 2023
national book policy 612
Nottingham, John, profiles and interviews
605
Pan-African Children's Book Fair 1434,
1435, 1455
reading culture and reading promotion
591, 2191, 2194, 2209
rural communities, publishing for 614
scientific, technical and medical publishing
2345
women in African publishing/publishing
by and for women 2396, 2398, 2400, 2401

Konate, Moussa, profiles and interviews 682
Kouam, Serge, profiles and interviews 458
Language issues 254, 380
   see also African languages, publishing in
Legal deposit and legal deposit laws 1748,
   1777
   digital media 1780
   Ghana 1775
   Namibia 1780
   Nigeria 1762, 1774, 1813, 1814
   South Africa, 1780
   Tanzania 1748
LESOTHO 635-643
   African languages, publishing in 2111
   book marketing and promotion 1481
   book trade and book development
      organizations 636
   children's book publishing 1628
   Christian publishing and mission presses
      1716
   copyright 1778
   educational and school book publishing
      635, 641
   ISBN system, use of 642
   reading culture and reading promotion
      2185
LIBERIA 644-645
Libraries and publishing 234, 235, 256, 257,
   261, 293, 305, 317, 330, 331, 340, 351, 355,
   388, 434, 615, 688, 765, 806, 1057, 1100, 1134,
   1992-1997, 2221
   Botswana 1994
   Nigeria 1995, 1996
Licensing *see* Rights sales, licensing, and
   publishing partnerships
Loan-guarantee programmes 602

MADAGASCAR 652-655
   books in print 651
   book trade directories 650
   journals and magazine publishing 1967
   reading culture and reading promotion 654
Magazine publishing *see* Journals and
   magazine publishing
Maillu, David G., profiles and interviews 604
MALAWI 663-673
   African languages, publishing in 2109
   Christian publishing and mission presses
      1729
   copyright 1784
   early printing 669
   educational and school book publishing
      664
   intra-African book trade 1896
   Kachere Book Series 2285

Popular Publications 673
   scholarly publishing 2285
MALI 678-682
   Berthe, Ibrahim, profiles and interviews
      681
   Editions-Imprimeries du Mali 681
   Editions Le Figuier 682
   Konate, Moussa, profiles and interviews
      682
   national book policy 678
   reading culture and reading promotion 679
   scientific, medical and technical publishing
      2344
Mambo Press, Zimbabwe 1224
Marketing and promotion *see* Book marketing
   and promotion
Mass market and popular literature
   publishing 833, 1998-2014
   Action Magazine 2014
   Cameroon 2006
   Kano market literature 2004
   Kenya 1999, 2007, 2008
   Maillu, David G. 1999, 2008
   Nigeria 1998, 2000, 2001, 2002, 2003, 2004,
      2005, 2009, 2010, 2011, 2012, 2013
   Onitsha market literature 1998, 2001, 2005,
      2010, 2011, 2012, 2013
   Pacesetters series 2000, 2002
   Zimbabwe 2014
MAURITIUS 689-694
   bookselling and book distribution 693
   book trade directories 686
   Editions de l'Océan Indien 690, 691
   ISBN system, use of 689, 690
   libraries and publishing 688
   reading culture and reading promotion
      2160
Mbari Publications, Nigeria 787, 862
Medical publishing *see* Scientific, technical
   and medical publishing
Meroueh, Ali, profiles and interviews 881, 887
Mission presses *see* Christian publishing and
   mission presses
MOZAMBIQUE 699-710
   bookselling and book distribution 708
   books in print 698
   educational and school book publishing
      699, 700, 702, 704, 705, 706
Multinational publishers in Africa 253, 280,
   282, 287, 291, 310, 403, 2015-2028
   Heinemann Educational Publishers 1319,
      2021, 2025, 2027
   Kenya 2023
   Macmillan Company 2022, 2023, 2024
   Nigeria 2016

Oxford University Press 2018, 2025
Tanzania 2022
NAMIBIA 718-729
  African languages, publishing in 2077, 2092, 2134
  books in print 716
  book trade and book development organizations 1530
  book trade directories 715
  children's book publishing 1688, 1689
  copyright 1784
  educational and school book publishing 729
  gender issues in publishing 2382
  ISBN system, use of 719, 724
  legal deposit and legal deposit laws 1780
  Namibia Book Development Council 1530
  Namibian books in the international market place 728
  national book policy 727
  New Namibia Books 2383, 2384
  publishing partnerships 2262
  reading culture and reading promotion 2229
  women in African publishing/publishing by and for women 2383, 2384
National bibliographies in Africa, status of 1777
  for individual national bibliographies *see* → **Author Index** (with selected titles)
National book policies 244, 312, 322, 2029-2038
  Botswana 436, 438
  Cameroon 467
  Mali 678
  Namibia 726
  Nigeria 779, 823
  Sierra Leone 918
  South Africa 1001, 1037, 1097
  Tanzania 1136
  Uganda 1157
  Zambia 1189
  Zimbabwe 1213, 1227
National Educational Company of Zambia, Zambia (NECZAM) 1179
Ndanda Mission Press, Tanzania 1721
New Gong Publishing House, Nigeria 861
NIGERIA 203, 749-864, 1321, 1322, 1337, 1339, 1344, 1361, 1399
  acquisition of African-published material 1231, 1245, 1251
  African languages, publishing in 2004, 2078, 2079, 2124, 2126, 2143, 2144
  African literature publishing 772, 786, 853

authors and publishers 786, 1321, 1322, 1337, 1339, 1344, 1350, 1351, 1352, 1353, 1359, 1360, 1361, 1367
authors' rights 1752
bibliographic control of publishing output 758, 793, 809, 826, 838
book and journals assistance and donation programmes 1372, 1399
book industry training 2510
book marketing and promotion 849, 1476, 1483, 1484
book piracy 839
bookselling and book distribution 760, 812, 830, 841, 1507, 1511, 1512
books in print 747, 748
book trade and book development organizations 756, 1519, 1534
book trade directories 743
children's book publishing 1540, 1547, 1570, 1571, 1572, 1577, 1642, 1645, 1646, 1647, 1648, 1650, 1675, 1698
Christian publishing and mission presses 1719, 1726
community and rural publishing 1735
copyright 1740, 1741, 1747, 1751, 1761, 1763, 1764, 1765, 1766, 1771, 1779, 1783, 1784, 1793, 1795, 1799, 1804, 1816, 1819, 1821, 1822, 1823
digital media and electronic publishing 1849, 1850
early printing 766, 856
educational and school book publishing 771, 784, 792, 795, 804, 813, 819, 841, 845, 846, 851, 855, 858, 860, 1879
Ethiope Publishing Corporation 800
Gaskiya Corporation 794
Higo, Chief Aigboje, Festschrift 755
HIV/AIDS 781, 815
Iwerebon, Chief Felix Arimoku, tributes and obituaries 763
journals and magazine publishing 1902, 1903, 1905, 1906, 1919, 1921, 1923, 1924, 1926, 1934, 1935, 1938, 1942, 1943, 1944, 1945, 1951, 1952, 1954, 1960, 1965, 1981, 1982, 1986, 1988
Kano market literature 2004
legal deposit and legal deposit laws 1762, 1774, 1813, 1814
library and information science publishing 816
libraries and publishing 765, 806, 1995, 1996
Maja-Pearce, Adewale, profiles and interviews 861

mass market and popular literature
publishing 1998, 2000, 2001, 2003, 2004,
2005, 2009, 2010, 2011, 2012, 2013
Mbari Publications 787, 862
multinational publishers 2016, 2018, 2025
national book policy 779, 823, 829
New Gong Publishing House 861
Nigeria International Book Fair 1361, 1456
Nigerian Book Foundation 1534
Nwankwo, Arthur, profiles and interviews
832
Nwankwo, Chief Victor,
profiles and interviews 852
tributes and obituaries 759, 782, 864
Nwapa, Flora 2376, 2379, 2399
Onitsha market literature 833, 1998, 2001,
2005, 2010, 2011, 2012, 2013
open access publishing 2067
printer-publishers relationship 754
print-on-demand production 1850
publishing partnerships 2234
reading culture and reading promotion
757, 768, 824, 856 1339, 2151, 2170, 2178,
2179, 2181, 2190, 2203, 2204, 2205, 2208,
2210, 2218, 2231
Saros International Publishers 854
Saro-Wiwa, Ken, tributes and obituaries
863
scholarly publishing 773, 776, 805, 2265,
2272, 2273, 2274, 2275, 2276, 2284, 2296,
2308, 2316, 2317, 2321, 2322, 2326, 2327
scientific, technical and medical publishing
2067, 2354
Solaru, Rev. T. Tanimowo, tributes and
obituaries 764
Spectrum Books Ltd 774, 844
Tana Press 2376, 2379
women in African publishing/publishing
by and for women 2367, 2368, 2376, 2379,
2397, 2408
Nigeria International Book Fair 1361, 1456
Noma Award for Publishing in Africa 2039-
2060
acceptance speeches by Noma Award
winners
Njabule Ndebele (1984 joint winner)
2039
Niyi Osundare (1991 winner) 2056
Djibril Samb (1999 winner) 2059
Elinor Sisulu (2003 winner) 2042
Gakaara wa Wanjau (1984 joint winner)
2039
Marlene van Niekerk (1996 winner) 2040
Paul Tiyambe Zeleza (1994 winner) 2061

Noma Award archives 2054, 2060
Noma award-winning children's books
2060
profiles and interviews with Noma Award
winners
Meshack Asare (1982 winner) 2058
Mariama Bâ (1980 winner) 2047
Adu Boahen (1997 winner) 2044
Abosede Emanuel (2001 winner) 2045
Lebogan Mashile (2006 winner) 2043,
2053
Nordic countries, support for African
publishing 311, 2270
Nouvelles Editions Africaines, Senegal 888,
896, 898, 907, 908
Nottingham, John, profiles and interviews
605
Nwankwo, Arthur, profiles and interviews
832
Nwankwo, Chief Victor,
profiles and interviews 852
tributes and obituaries 759, 782, 864
Nwapa, Flora 2376, 2379
personal recollections 2399

Ofori-Mensah, Akoss, profiles and interviews
548
Okike 1902, 1919, 1934
Onitsha market literature 833, 1998, 2001,
2005, 2010, 2011, 2012, 2013
Open access publishing 1833, 2064-2076
African studies 2075
Ghana 2065
medical journals 2067
Nigeria 2067
South Africa 1008, 2066, 2068, 2069, 2070,
2071, 1073
Oppositional publishing, South Africa see
South Africa, Alternative press and
publishing
Oral sources, publication of 1142

Periodicals publishing see Journals and
magazine publishing
Philip, David, Publishers 999, 1000
Philip, David and Marie, profiles and
interviews 991
Philombe, Réne, profiles and interviews 466
Piracy see Copyright
Popular literature publishing see Mass market
and popular literature publishing
Popular Publications, Malawi 673
Printing technology, new see Print-on-
demand (POD)

Print-on-demand (POD) 1831, 1834, 1836, 1860, 2455
see also Digital media and electronic publishing
African Books Collective Ltd 1840
Nigeria 1850
Printing in Africa, early *see* Early printing in Africa
Privatization of the book sector 247, 248, 260, 262, 501, 522, 552, 1180, 1188
Promotion *see* Book marketing and promotion
Prosper, Komlan, profiles and interviews 407
Publishing in Africa Collection, Oxford Brookes University 178
Publishing in African languages *see* African languages, publishing in
Publishing management and training *see* Book industry training
Publishing partnerships *see* Rights sales, licensing, and publishing partnerships

Ravan Press, South Africa 972, 994, 1051, 1052, 1082
Reading culture and reading promotion 290, 345, 438, 527, 591, 654, 679, 757, 856, 1043, 1316, 1663, 1884, 2003, 2150-2232
Africa, East 2216
Africa, Francophone 2153, 2167, 2168, 2172, 2215
bibliographic resources 2172
book clubs 2162
Botswana 2157
Burkina Faso 2166, 2182
Cameroon 2214
Chad 379
Côte d'Ivoire 2175, 2217
developing countries 2174, 2222, 2223, 2230
Ethiopia 2161
Ghana 2154
Kenya 591, 2191, 2194, 2209
Lesotho 2185
Mauritius 2160
Namibia 2229
National Readathon of Namibia 2229
Nigeria 757, 768, 824, 856 1339, 2151, 2170, 2178, 2179, 2181, 2190, 2203, 2204, 2205, 2208, 2210, 2218, 2231
Rally to Read 2171
Read Educational Trust 2171, 2180
reading tents 2159, 2191, 2196, 2216
rural communities 2182
South Africa 1043, 1077, 1078, 2152, 2156, 2162, 2164, 2171, 2184, 2187, 2188, 2192, 2193, 2198, 2199, 2200, 2206, 2211, 2219

Synergy Educational Nigeria 2190, 2203
Tanzania 1126, 2173
Uganda 2189
women readers 2200, 2201
Zimbabwe 2159, 2177, 2196, 2198, 2225, 2226
Reading habit *see* Reading culture and reading promotion
Reading promotion *see* Reading culture and reading promotion
Republican Press, South Africa 1041
RÉUNION 866-867
book trade directories 865
Richard, Charles, profiles and interviews 345, 346, 347
Rights sales, licensing, and publishing partnerships 323, 2233-2263
African Books Collective Ltd, facilitating co-editions 2242
Cameroon 2246
children's books 2255
co-publishing models and contracts 2237, 2238, 2240, 2280
Côte d'Ivoire 2248
developing countries 2252, 2253
Namibia 2262
Nigeria 2234
North-South cooperation 2244, 2245, 2246, 2248, 2262, 2253, 2264, 2255, 2257, 2258, 2261, 2262
South-North cooperation 2249, 2251, 2261
South-South cooperation 1525, 2239, 2243, 2256, 2258, 2259, 2268
translations 2260
Rural communities, publishing for *see* Community and rural publishing
RWANDA 869-870
African languages, publishing in 2105

Samb, Sahite Sarr, profiles and interviews 904
SAO TOMÉ AND PRINCIPE 871
Saros International Publishers, Nigeria 854
Saro-Wiwa, Ken, tributes and obituaries 863
Scholarly publishing 2264-2333
see also Journals and magazine publishing; Open access publishing; Scientific, technical and medial publishing
Africa, East 2279
Africa, Francophone 2284, 2300
Africa, West 2292
agricultural publications 2365
book marketing and promotion 1483, 1492
Council for the Development of Social Science Research (CODESRIA) 2267, 2318

co-operative ventures and resource sharing 2237, 2280, 2281, 2305
consortia 2282, 2302
Côte d'Ivoire 2278
digital media and electronic publishing 1833, 1835, 1839, 1845, 1859, 2306
Ethiopia 2329
Ghana 2269, 2286, 2315, 2320
Kachere Book Series 2285
Kenya 2279, 2323
law publications 2274
learned society publishing 2295
library and information sciences 2266
Malawi 2285
NGO publishing 2305, 2307
Nigeria 773, 776, 805, 2265, 2272, 2273, 2274, 2275, 2276, 2284, 2296, 2308, 2316, 2317, 2321, 2322, 2326, 2327
Nigerian Institute of International Affairs 2284
print-on-demand (POD) 1831, 1834, 1836, 1840, 1850, 1860, 2455
rights of academic authors 1812
Senegal 883
South Africa 970, 1008, 1055, 2287, 2288, 2289, 2293, 2328
Sudan 2291
university presses 2269, 2272, 2273, 2276, 2279, 2281, 2282, 2286, 2288, 2289, 2291, 2296, 2303, 2304, 2308, 2314, 2315, 2317, 2321, 2322, 2324, 2326, 2327, 2329
Uganda 2309
Zambia 2304, 2324
Zimbabwe 2295, 2314
School book publishing see Educational and school book publishing
Science for Africa KAWI Project 1696
Scientific, technical and medical publishing 2334-2366
Africa, Francophone 2363
agricultural sciences 2355, 2365, 2458
Burkina Faso 2364
Burundi 2337
Côte d'Ivoire 2342, 2361
Ethiopia 2352
Guinea 2358
Guinea Bissau 2350
Kenya 2345
Mali 2344
medical publishing 2067, 2339, 2354, 2359
Nigeria 2067, 2354
Senegal 2343
South Africa 2351, 2356, 2357
science books for children 1696, 1248

science publishing 1937, 2341, 2347, 2348, 2349, 2362, 2366
technical publishing 2336, 2338, 2340, 2346
Togo 2353

Self-publishing 2504, 2508, 2511, 2512, 2513, 2514, 2616, 2517
SENEGAL 366, 388, 880-910
African languages, publishing in 2096, 2097, 2098, 2121, 2142
Arab book trade 906
authors and publishers 1356
bookselling and book distribution 379, 886, 900
book trade directories 878, 879
children's book publishing 1626
Council for the Development of Social Science Research (CODESRIA) 2267, 2318
educational and school book publishing 884
Boirot, François, profiles and interviews 898
BREDA 903
Faye, Djbril, tributes and obituaries 880
feminist publishing 2412
Meroueh, Ali, profiles and interviews 881, 887
Nouvelles Editions Africaines 888, 896, 898, 907, 908
Per Ankh Publishing Cooperative 1320, 1347
Samb, Sahite Sarr, profiles and interviews 904
scholarly publishing 883
scientific, technical and medical publishing 2343
Sow Fall, Aminata, profiles and interviews 909
women in African publishing/publishing by and for women 909
Seroke, Jaki, profiles and interviews 979
SEYCHELLES 912
SIERRA LEONE 918-931
African literature publishing 929
book trade and book development organizations 930
children's book publishing 1573, 1621, 1679
educational and school book publishing 919, 927
national book policy 918
Skotaville Publishers, South Africa 979, 1056
Solaru, Rev. T. Tanimowo, tributes and obituaries 764

SOUTH AFRICA 970-1104, 1417, 1424
  adult education publishing 1004
  African Bookman, The 1082
  African languages, publishing in 1053,
    2088, 2104, 2107, 2114, 2115, 2120, 2129,
    2132, 2146, 2147, 2148
  African literature publishing 1060, 1336
  alternative press and publishing 972, 976,
    982, 994, 1029, 1045, 1051, 1052, 1062,
    1081, 1082
  art publishing 987
  authors and publishers 1336, 1357, 1366
  authors' rights 1747, 1813
  Bailey, Jim, biography 974
  Balkema, A.A., Festschrift 975
  black markets 1040
  black press 1095
  book and journals assistance and donation
    programmes 1424
  book boycott, during the apartheid period
    996, 1009, 1019, 1021
  book history 1016
  book industry surveys and reports 1067-
    1973, 1074, 1077, 1078, 1090, 1094
  book industry training and self-publishing
    980, 2428, 2504, 2505, 2508, 2509, 2511,
    2512, 2514, 2516, 2517
  book marketing and promotion 971, 1024,
    1031, 1472, 1474
  bookselling and book distribution 1012,
    1040, 1502, 1506
  books in print 963, 967
  book trade and book development
    organizations 1520, 1529, 1531, 1538,
    1539, 1531
  book trade directories 958,959, 960, 961,
    966, 968, 969
  Cape Town Book Fair 1427, 1428, 1432,
    1441
  censorship and publications control 981,
    1103
  children's book publishing 130, 963, 1027,
    1541, 1551, 1563, 1564, 1565, 1567, 1586,
    1587, 1588, 1589, 1590, 1591, 1592, 1594,
    1597, 1599, 1634, 1661, 1664, 1681, 1683,
    1692, 1693, 1694
  Christian publishing and mission presses
    1711, 1715, 1722, 2132, 2148
  copyright 1747, 1758, 1759, 1767, 1768,
    1770, 1788, 1789, 1800, 1801, 1802, 1806,
    1807, 1810, 1812, 1825
  COSAW Publishing 1059
  cost of books, factors affecting 1076
  digital media and electronic publishing
    1836, 1841, 1842, 1848

  early printing 1007, 1018, 1085
  educational and school book publishing
    989, 992, 998, 1003, 1023, 1027, 1032,
    1033, 1036, 1042, 1047, 1048, 1049, 1050,
    1066, 1079, 1086, 1087
  feminist publishing 2377
  gender issues in publishing 1104, 2378
  Hond Publishing 985
  Human, Koos, autobiography 1028
  journals and magazine publishing 974,
    1095, 1928, 1929, 1933, 1939, 1948, 1949,
    1959, 1961, 1962, 1963, 1975, 1976, 1983,
    1985, 1987, 2356
  legal deposit and legal deposit laws 1780
  libraries and publishing 1057, 1100
  micro-publishing enterprises 1015
  Muslim communities, publishing for 1010,
    1939
  national book policy 1001, 1037, 1075, 1097
  open access publishing 1008, 2066, 2068,
    2069, 2070, 2071, 1073
  oppositional publishing, during the
    apartheid period see alternative press
    and publishing
  Philip, David and Marie, profiles and
    interviews 991
  Philip, David, Publishers 999, 1000
  Print Industries Cluster Council 1531
  Publishers Association of South Africa,
    policies and activities 1538
  Ravan Press 972, 994, 1051, 1052, 1082
  reading culture and reading promotion
    1043, 1077, 1078, 1126, 2152, 2156, 2162,
    2164, 2171, 2184, 2187, 2188, 2192, 2193,
    2198, 2199, 2200, 2206, 2211, 2219
  Republican Press 1041
  scholarly publishing 970, 1008, 1055, 2287,
    2288, 2289, 2293, 2328
  scientific, medical and technical publishing
    2351, 2356, 2357
  Seroke, Jaki, profiles and interviews 979
  Skotaville Publishers 979, 1056
  South African Booksellers Association,
    policies and activities 1084
  state publishing 1044
  Van Rieebeck Society 1064
  women in African publishing/publishing
    by and for women 2369, 2392, 2409, 2414
Sow, Mamadou Aliou, profiles and
  interviews 569, 570
Sow Fall, Aminata, profiles and interviews
  909
Spectrum Books Ltd, Nigeria 774, 844
Staffrider 1928, 1949, 1961, 1983, 1985
Staunton, Irene, profiles and interviews 1219

Sub-Saharan African Publishers, Ghana 548
SUDAN 1107-1108
SWAZILAND 1112-1115
  bookselling and book distribution 1112
  copyright 1778

Tadjo, Véronique, profiles and interviews
  1585, 1684, 1690
Tana Press, Nigeria 2376, 2379
TANZANIA 1126-1142
  African languages, publishing in 2118, 2119
  bookselling and book distribution 1128
  book marketing and promotion 1465, 1466,
  1475
  books in print 1125
  Children's Book Project of Tanzania 1575,
  1619
  children's book publishing 1575, 1619
  Christian publishing and mission presses
  1721
  community and rural publishing 1736
  copyright 1748
  educational and school book publishing
  1128, 1132, 1133, 1135, 1142
  legal deposit and legal deposit laws 1748
  libraries and publishing 1134
  multinational publishers 2022
  national book policy 1136
  Ndanda Mission Press 1721
  oral sources, publication of 1142
  reading culture and reading promotion
  1126, 2173
  women in African publishing/publishing
  by and for women 2371
Technical publishing see Scientific, technical
  and medical publishing
Tertiary level publishing see Scholarly
  publishing
Textbook publishing and textbook provision
  see Educational and school book publishing
TOGO 409, 1147-1149
  African languages, publishing in 2102
  African literature publishing 1149
  authors and publishers 1334
  Editions HaHo 409
  scientific, technical and medical publishing
  2353
Training see Book industry training
Transition 1905, 1938, 1980
Transnational publishers see Multinational
  publishers in Africa
Tumusiime, James, profiles and interview
  1167
UGANDA 1157-1170
  book history 1161-1163

children's book publishing 1691
copyright 1776
early printing 1161
educational and school book publishing
  1160, 1164
FEMRITE 2385
Goretti, Kyomuhendo, profiles and
  interviews 1159
national book policy 1157
reading promotion and reading culture
  2189
scholarly publishing 2309
Tumusiime, James, profiles and interviews
  1167
women in African publishing/publishing
  by and for women 1159, 2385
UNESCO, support for African publishing and
  book development 219, 220, 321, 322, 328
University presses see Scholarly publishing

Van Rieebeck Society, South Africa 1064

Western dominance of African publishing see
  Multinational publishers in Africa
Women in African publishing/publishing by
  and for women 2367-2417
  see also gender issues in publishing
  academic publications 2367
  African studies publishing 2374, 2415
  Baobab Books 2413
  Benin 429
  book marketing and promotion 2401
  children's books publishing 2399, 2400
  developing countries 2373
  E&D Ltd. 2387
  Editions Ruisseaux d'Afrique 429
  feminist publishing 2373, 2377, 2412
  FEMRITE 2385
  Focus Publications Ltd 2396
  Gbado, Béatrice Lalinon 429
  Ghana 548, 2402, 2404
  Katjavivi, Jane, personal recollections 2384
  Kenya 2381, 2396, 2398, 2400, 2401
  Kwela Books 2414
  Lema, Elieshi, personal recollections 2387
  Lesotho 2393
  Madondo, Mwazvita Patricia, personal
    recollections 2389
  Mwangi, Serah,
    personal recollections 2389
    profiles and interviews 628
  Namibia 2382, 2383, 2384, 2407
  New Namibia Books 2384
  NGO publishing 2391
  Nigeria 2367, 2368, 2376, 2379, 2397, 2408

Njoroge, Janet, personal recollections 2398
Nwapa, Flora 2376, 2379
    personal recollections 2399
Odaga, Asenath Bole, personal
    recollections 2400
Ofori-Mensah, Akoss,
    personal recollections 2404
    profiles and interviews 548, 2402
Orimalade, Oluronke, personal
    recollections 2408
Senegal 909, 2412
South Africa 2369, 2377, 2378, 2392, 2409,
    2413
Sow Fall, Aminata, profiles and interviews
    909
Staunton, Irene,
    personal recollections 2413
    profiles and interviews 1219
Sub-Saharan African Publishers 548
Tana Press 2376, 2379
Tanzania 2387
Uganda 2385
van der Merwe, Annnari, personal
    recollections 2414
Zimbabwe 2371, 2386, 2389, 2413, 2417
World Bank 222, 238, 239, 245, 270, 318, 319,
    320, 1305, 1372, 1867, 1869, 1879, 1885, 1887,
    2453
Writers' handbooks *see* Authors' and writers'
    handbooks

ZAMBIA 1176-1197
    African languages, publishing in 2113
    books in print 1175
    book trade and book development
        organizations 1184
    Christian publishing and mission presses
        1717
    educational and school book publishing
        1177, 1185, 1192, 1196, 1197
    intra-African book trade 1897
    national book policy 1189
    National Educational Company of Zambia
        (NECZAM) 1179
    privatization of the book sector 1180, 1188
    scholarly publishing 2304, 2324
    University of Zambia Press (UNZA) 2304,
        2324
    Zambia Educational Materials Project 1192,
        1196, 1197
ZIMBABWE 309, 1304
    African languages, publishing in 1216,
        2091, 2103
    African literature publishing 1217, 1219,
        2386, 2417

authors and publishers 1369
book history 1214
bookselling and book distribution 1509,
    1510
books in print 1209
book trade and book development
    organizations 1521, 1526, 1537
book trade directories 1208
children's book publishing 1548, 1562,
    1584, 1639, 1682
Christian publishing and mission presses
    1727
community and rural publishing 1730, 1731
copyright 1829
digital media and electronic publishing
    1837, 1844, 1857
educational and school book publishing
    1221
gender issues in publishing 2371
Hove, Chenjerai, profiles and interviews
    215
journals and magazine publishing 1966
Mambo Press 1224
national book policy 1213, 1227
reading culture and reading promotion
    2159, 2177, 2196, 2198, 2225, 2226
scholarly publishing 2295, 2314
Staunton, Irene,
    personal recollections
    profiles and interviews 1219
women in African publishing/publishing
    by and for women 2386, 2389, 2413, 2417
Zimbabwe Book Development Council
    1521, 1526
Zimbabwe Book Marketing Trust 1509,
    1510
Zimbabwe International Book Fair 354,
    1429, 1430, 1431, 1433, 1436, 1437, 1440,
    1443, 1444, 1445, 1446, 1447, 1449, 1450,
    1452, 1453, 1457, 1458, 1459, 1460, 1464
Zimbabwe Publishing House 1220
Zimbabwe Publishing House, Zimbabwe
    1220
Zimbabwe International Book Fair 354, 1429,
    1430, 1431, 1433, 1436, 1437, 1440, 1443,
    1444, 1445, 1446, 1447, 1449, 1450, 1452,
    1453, 1457, 1458, 1459, 1460, 1464

Index of
organizations and associations

Academic and Non-Fiction Authors' Association of Nigeria (ANFAAN) 731
Academic and Non-Fiction Authors' Association of South Africa (ANFASA) 932
Access to Knowledge (A2K) Southern Africa 24
ADEA Working Group on Books and Learning Materials 35
Africa Book Development (ABD) 1
Africa Community Publishing & Development Trust 1198
African Academy of Sciences (AAS) 25
Africana Librarians Council (ALC) 26
African Association of Science Editors (AASE) 2
African Books Collective Ltd (ABC) 3
African Council for Communication Education (ACCE) 27
African Journals Online (AJOL) 28
African Intellectual Property Organisation 19
African Network for Book Development 4
African Publishers Network (APNET) 5
African Publishing Initiative. The World Bank. Office of the Publisher 125
African Regional Intellectual Property Organisation (ARIPO) 6
Afrilivres 8, 29
Afrique Livres. Association d'aide à la publication et à la diffusion 872
Afro-Asian Book Council (AABC) 7
Agence Canadienne de Développement International (ACDI) 46
Agence de Médiation Culturelle des Pays du Sahel 30
Alliance des Éditeurs Independents pour une Autre Mondialisation 31
Alliance of Independent Publishers for Another Globalization 31
Alliance Française 32
Associação dos Editores e Livreiros Angolanos (AELA) 415
Associação dos Escritores Moçambicanos (AEMO) 695
Associates in Research & Education for Development (ARED) 873
Association d'Éditeurs Francophones d'Afrique Sub-saharienne 8, 29
Association des Ecrivains du Sénégal (AES) 874
Association des Editeurs du Benin (ASEDIB) 422
Association des Editeurs du Burkina Faso (ASSEDIF) 442
Association des Editeurs du Cameroun (AEC) 448
Association des Editeurs du Guinée 565
Association des Editeurs Ivoiriens (ASSEDI) 491
Association des Editeurs Mauricien (AEM) 684
Association des Editeurs Rwandaise 868
Association for Progressive Communications (APC) 33
Association for the Development of African Education 34, 35
Association Internationale des Libraires Francophones 9
Association Livres d'Afrique/Salon Livres d'Afrique 10
Association Malienne des Libraries Professionelles 674
Association Nationale des Editeurs et des Imprimeurs [Congo, Brazzaville] 476
Association Nationale des Editeurs et Diffuseurs du Livre (ANEDIL) [Congo Democratic
Republic] 479

Association Nigerienne des Professionnels du Livre (ANPL) 730
Association of Catholic Publishers in Africa 11
Association of Gambian Writers 529
Association of Mauritian Publishers 684
Association of Namibian Publishers (ANP) 711
Association of Nigerian Authors (ANA) 732
Association Pan Africaine des Écrivains 22
Association pour la Diffusion de la Pensée Française (ADPF) 36
Association Senegalaise des Editeurs (ASE) 875
Association Togolaise des Auteurs et Illustrateurs de Livres pour Enfants (ATAILE) 1144
Association Togolaise des Editeurs (ATEL) 1145

Baobab Children's Book Fund 88
Baraza la Maendeleo ya Vitabu Tanzania (BAMVITA) 1119
Bellagio Publishing Network Secretariat 37
Biblionef South Africa 933
Book Aid International (BAI) 28
Book Link 39
Book Development Centre. Nigerian Educational Research and Development Council (NERDC) 733
Book Development Council of Uganda (BODECU) 1150
BookPower 40
Book Publishers Association of Malawi (BPAM) 656
Book Publishers Association of Zambia (BPAZ) 1171
Books Abroad 41
Books for Africa 42
Booksellers Association of Tanzania 1116
Booksellers Association of Zambia 1172
Botswana Publishing Industry Association (BOPIA) 430
Botswana Writers' Group 431
British Council 43
Brother's Brother Foundation 44
Bureau International de l'Édition Française (BIEF) 45
Bureau Togolais du Droit d'Auteur (BUTODRA) 1143

Cameroon Publishers Association 448
Canadian International Development Agency (CIDA) 46
Carnegie Corporation of New York 47
Centre Technique de Coopération Agricole et Rurale ACP-UE (CTA) 116
Centre Africain de Formation à l'Edition et à la Diffusion (CAFED) 12
Centre for the Book [South Africa] 934
Centre Malgache de Promotion du Livre et de l'Art (CMPL) 646
Centre National du Livre pour Enfants 86
Children's Book Project of Tanzania (CBP) 1117
Children's Literature Association of Kenya (CLAK) 575
Children's Literature Documentation and Research Centre (CLIDORC) 734
Children's Literature Research Unit [South Africa] 935
Christian Booksellers Association of Nigeria (CBA-Nigeria) 735
Christian Booksellers Association of Southern Africa 936
Christian Booksellers and Publishers of Kenya 576
Commonwealth Foundation 49
Commonwealth of Learning (COL) 50
Commonwealth Secretariat 51
Club des Amis du Livre (CAL) 566

CODE 48
Comité Provisoire sur le Livre [Mali National Book Development Council] 675
Congress of South African Writers 937
Coopération par l'Éducation et la Culture (CEC) 52
CopyGhana 534
Copy South Research Group 53
Copyright Society of Malawi (COSOMA) 657
Culture et Développment (C&D) 54

Dag Hammarskjöld Foundation 55
Danish International Development Assistance (DANIDA) 56
Department for International Development (DIFD) 57
Direction du Livre et de la Lecture [Senegal] 876
Division Livre et Lecture Publique [Guinea] 567
Dramatic Artistic and Literary Rights Organisation (Pty) Limited (DALRO) 938

East African Book Development Association (EABDA) 13
Electronic Information for Libraries/eIFL.net 58
Electronic Publishing Trust for Development 59
Electronic Supply of Academic Publications to and from Developing Regions (ESAP) 60
Eritrea Publishers Association (ERIPA) 502
Espace Afrique. Diffusion et Promotion du Livre Africain Francophone 14
Ethiopian Booksellers Association (EBA) 504
Ethiopian Publishers Association (EPA) 505
Ethiopia Reads 506

Femart-K - Kenya Women Writers' Foundation 577
FEMRITE - Uganda Women Writers' Association 1151
Finnish Ministry of Foreign Affairs 122
Fondation Charles Léopold Mayer 61
Ford Foundation 62
Forum of African Medical Editors (FAME) 15
Foundation for the Promotion of Children's Science Publishing in Africa (CHISCI) 16
Frankfurt Book Fair 64
Friends-of-the-Book Foundation (FBF) 578

Gates Foundation 63
Gesellschaft zur Förderung der Literatur aus Afrika, Asien, und Latinamerika 64
Ghana Association of Writers 535
Ghana Book Development Council (GBDC) 536
Ghana Booksellers Association (GBA) 537
Ghana Book Publishers Association (GBPA) 538
Ghana Book Trust (GBT) 539
Ghana Section of IBBY 540
Goethe Institut 65
Groupe d'Initiative pour la Promotion du Livre en Langues Nationales (GIPLLN) 873

Heinrich Böll Stiftung/Heinrich Böll Foundation 66
Humanistisch Instituut voor Ontwikkelingssamenwerking (HIVOS) 67

IBBY South Africa 939
IFLA Action for Development through Libraries Programme Core Activity (ALP) 75
IFLA Africa Regional Section 76
Illusafrica. Association Panafricaine d'Illustrateurs 17
International African Institute 68

International Association for Digital Publications (IADP)/IADP - South Africa 69
International Book Bank 70
Illustrators' Portfolio/Sparx Media 940
Institute Africain International 68
Instituto da Biblioteca Nacional e do Livro 471
Instituto Nacional do Livro et do Disco (INLD) 696
International African Institute 68
International Board on Books for Young People (IBBY) 71
International Development Research Center (IDRC) 72
International Education Partners 73
International Federation of Library Associations and Institutions (IFLA), 74-76
International Federation of Reproduction Rights Organisations (IFRRO) 77
International Institute for Educational Planning (IIEP) 78
International Law Book Facility 79
International Library and Information Group of the Chartered Institute of Library and
    Information Professionals (CILIP) 80
International Network for the Availability of Scientific Publications (INASP) 81
International Publishers Association (IPA) 82
International Reading Association 83
International Trade Centre (UNCTAD/WTO) 84
InWEnt – Internationale Weiterbildung und Entwicklung GmbH 85

Joie par les Livres. Centre National du Livre pour Enfants 86
Journal Donation Project. The New School for Social Research 87
Jumuia Ya Waandishi Wa Afrika 22

Kagera Writers and Publishers Co-operative Society 1118
Kenya Booksellers and Stationers Association 579
Kenya Non-Fiction Authors Association (KENFAA) 580
Kenya Publishers Association (KPA) 581
Kinderbuch Fonds Baobab 88
Kopinor. The Reproduction Rights Organisation of Norway 89
Kwani Trust 582

Leshotho Booksellers Association 631
Lesotho Publishers Association (LPA) 632
Lesotho Writers Association 633
Librarians Without Borders (LWB) 90
Link. A Network for North-South Library Development 91
LitNet [South Africa] 941

Malawi Booksellers Association 658
Malawi National Book Development Council 659
Malawi Writers' Union 660
Mauritius Society of Authors (MASA) 685
Mellon Foundation 92
Ministère de la Culture et de la Communication. Direction du Livre et de la Lecture 93
Ministère des Affaires Étrangères. Direction Générale de la Coopération Internationale et du
    Développement 94, 95

Namibia Book Development Council (NBDC) 712
Namibia National Writers Union (NANAWU) 714
Namibian Children's Book Forum 713
National Book Development Council of Cameroon (NBDC) 449
National Book Development Council of Kenya (NBDCK) 543

National Book Development Council of Tanzania 1119
National Book League of Nigeria (NBLN) 736
National Book Trust of Uganda (NABOTU) 1152
Netherlands Ministry of Foreign Affairs. Directorate-General for International Cooperation 96
Network for Information and Digital Access (NIDA) 97
Network of Technical Publications in Africa (TEPUSA) 18
Nigerian Book Fair Trust 737
Nigerian Book Foundation (NBF) 738
Nigerian Publishers Association (NPA) 739
Noma Award for Publishing in Africa 98
Norwegian Agency for Development Co-operation (NORAD) 99

Online Publishers Association – South Africa 942
Open Society Institute 100
Organisation des Nations Unies pour l'Education, la Science et La Culture 118-120
Organisation Africaine de la Propriété Intellectuelle (OAPI) 19
Organisation Internationale de la Francophonie (OIF) 101
Organization Maliene des Editeurs (OMEL) 676
Organization of Women Writers of Africa 20

Pan African Booksellers Association (PABA) 21
Pan African Writers' Association (PAWA) 22
Partnership for Higher Education in Africa 102
Partnerships in Health Information 103
Per Ankh African Publishing Cooperative 23
Poets Palace [Nigeria] 740
Prince Claus Fund for Culture and Development 104
Print Industries Cluster Council (PICC) [South Africa] 943
Ptolemy Project 105
Professional Editors' Group [South Africa] 944
Public Knowledge Project (PKP) 106
Publishers' Association of South Africa (PASA) 945
Publishers Association of Tanzania (PATA) 1120
Publishing Training Centre at Book House 107

READ Educational Trust 946
Reading Association of South Africa 947
Reproduction Rights Organization of Zimbabwe (ZimCopy) 1201
Reproduction Rights Society of Kenya (KOPIKEN) 584
Reproduction Rights Society of Nigeria (REPRONIG) 741
Rockefeller Foundation 108
Room to Read 109

Sabre Foundation 110
Secrétariat du Groupe des Etats d'Afrique, des Caraïbes et du Pacifique (Secrétariat ACP) 111
Secretariat of the African, Caribbean and Pacific Group of States (ACP Secretariat) 111
Shuttleworth Foundation 112
Sierra Leone Book Development Council 913
Sierra Leone Book Trust 915
Sierra Leone Booksellers Association 914
Sierra Leone Publishers Association 916
Sociedade Moçambicana de Autores (SOMAS) 607
Society for the Promotion of African, Asian and Latin American Literatures 64
Society of Children's Books Writers and Illustrators, South African Chapter (SCBWI-SA) 948
Soros Foundation 100

South African Association of Industrial Editors (SAAIE) 949
South African Book Development Council 950
South African Booksellers Association (SABA) 951
South African Children's Book Forum 952
South African Writers' Circle (SAWC) 953
South African Writers' Network 954
Southern African Book Development Education Trust (SABDET) 113
Southern African Writers' Council (SAWCO) 955
Standing Conference on Library Materials on Africa (SCOLMA) 114
Swaziland Book Traders Association 1109
Swedish International Development Co-Operation Agency/Sida 115
Syndicat National des Auteurs, Éditeurs et Libraires de Madagascar (SYNAEL) 647
Synergy Educational Nigeria 742

Tanzania Book Support Trust 1121
Tanzania Writers' Association 1122
Technical Centre for Agricultural and Rural Cooperation ACP-EU 116
TrustAfrica 117

Uganda Booksellers Association 1153
Uganda Children's Illustrators and Writers Association (UCIWA) 1154
Uganda Publishers Association 1155
Umdlandla Swaziland Writers and Authors Association 1110
Umoja wa Waandishi wa Vitabu Tanzania (UWAVITA) 1123
UNESCO Bureau Régional de l'Unesco 120
UNESCO/DANIDA Basic Learning Materials Initiative (BML) 119
UNESCO Regional Office for Education in Africa 120
União dos Escritores Angolanos 416
Union des Editeurs Gabonais (UEG) 524
Union des Poètes et Ecrivains Malgache (HAVATSA-UPEM) 648
United Nations Educational, Scientific and Cultural Organization (UNESCO) 118-120
United States Agency for International Development (USAID). Bureau for Africa 121
Utrikesministeriet, Finland 122

Voluntary Service Overseas (VSO) 123

World Bank 124
World Bank-Office of the Publisher 125
World Intellectual Property Organization (WIPO) 126
Write Company [South Africa] 956
Writers Association of Kenya 585
Writers Fund [Ghana] 541
Writers World [South Africa] 957

Zambia Women Writers Association (ZAWWA) 1173
Zimbabwe Academic and Non-Fiction Writers Association (ZANA) 1202
Zimbabwe Book Development Council (ZBDC) 1203
Zimbabwe Book Publishers Association (ZBPA) 1204
Zimbabwe International Book Fair Trust 1205
Zimbabwe Women Writers 1206
Zimbabwe Writers' Union 1207

Publishing, Books & Reading in
Sub-Saharan Africa
A Critical Bibliography

Some other books by Hans Zell

The African Studies Companion: A Guide to Information Sources
4th revised and expanded edition
(Hans Zell Publishing, 2006)

Book Marketing and Promotion: A Handbook of Good Practice
(International Network for the Availability of Scientific
Publications/INASP, 2001)

A Handbook of Good Practice in Journal Publishing
2nd revised edition
(International African Institute & African Books Collective Ltd, 1998)